MW01026774

gem
Collins
Canadian
French
Dictionary

HarperCollins Publishers
2 Bloor Street East
20th Floor
Toronto
Ontario
Canada M4W 1A8

www.harpercollins.ca

Second Edition 2012

10 9 8 7 6 5 4 3

© HarperCollins Publishers
2007, 2012

ISBN 978-0-00-746369-5

Collins Gem® and Bank of
English® are registered
trademarks of HarperCollins
Publishers Limited

A catalogue record for this book
is available upon request

Typeset by Thomas Callan and
Davidson Publishing Solutions,
Glasgow

Supplement typeset by
Wordcraft Ltd, Glasgow

Printed and bound in Italy by
LEGO SpA, Lavis (Trento)

Acknowledgements
We would like to thank those
authors and publishers who
kindly gave permission for
copyright material to be used in
the Collins Corpus. We would
also like to thank Times
Newspapers Ltd for providing
valuable data.

All rights reserved. No part of
this book may be reproduced,
stored in a retrieval system, or
transmitted in any form or by
any means, electronic,
mechanical, photocopying,
recording or otherwise, without
the prior permission in writing
of the Publisher. This book is
sold subject to the conditions
that it shall not, by way of trade
or otherwise, be lent, re-sold,
hired out or otherwise circulated
without the publisher's prior
consent in any form of binding
or cover other than that in which
it is published and without a
similar condition including this
condition being imposed on the
subsequent purchaser.

Entered words that we have
reason to believe constitute
trademarks have been
designated as such. However,
neither the presence nor absence
of such designation should be
regarded as affecting the legal
status of any trademark.

CONTENTS

EDITORIAL STAFF

MANAGING EDITOR
Maree Airlie

EDITORS
Gaëlle Amiot-Cadey
Gerry Breslin
Joyce Littlejohn
Persephone Lock

EDITORIAL DIRECTOR
Elaine Higgleton

USING THIS DICTIONARY

The *Collins Canadian French Dictionary* is designed specifically for anyone starting to learn French, and has been carefully researched with teachers and students. It is very straightforward, with an accessible layout that is easy on the eye, guiding students quickly to the right translation. It also offers essential help on French culture.

This section gives useful tips on how to use the *Collins Canadian French Dictionary* effectively.

▷ **Make sure you look in the right side of the dictionary**

There are two sides in a bilingual dictionary. Here, the **French-English** side comes first, and the second part is **English-French**. The middle pages of the book have a blue border so you can see where one side finishes and the other one starts.

▷ **Finding the word you want**

To help you find a word more quickly, look at the words in blue at the top of pages. They show the first and last words on the two pages where the dictionary is open.

▷ **Make sure you use the right part of speech**

Some entries are split into several parts of speech. For example 'glue' can either be a noun ("Can I borrow your **glue?**") or a verb ("**Glue** this into your exercise book"). Parts of speech within an entry are separated by a black triangle ▶ and are given on a new line. They are given in their abbreviated form (*n* for noun, *adj* for adjective, etc). For the full list of abbreviations, look at page viii.

> **glue** [glu:] *n* colle *f*
> ▶ *vb* coller

▷ **Choosing the right translation**

The main translation of a word is shown after the part of speech. If there is more than one main translation for a word, each one is numbered. You may also sometimes find bracketed words in *italics* which give you some context. They help you to choose the translation you want.

pool [puːl] *n* **❶** *(for swimming)* piscine *f* **❷** *(pond)*
étang *m* **❸** *(puddle)* flaque *f* **❹** *(game)*
billard *m* américain ▷ *let's have a game of pool.*
Jouons au billard américain.

Often you will see phrases in *italics*, preceded by a white triangle ▷.
These are examples of the word being used in context.

numérique [nymeʀik] *adj* digital ▷ *un*
appareil photo numérique a digital camera

Phrases in **bold type** are phrases which are particularly common and
important. Sometimes these phrases have a completely different
translation.

chausson [ʃosɔ̃] *nm* slipper; **un chausson aux**
pommes an apple turnover

Once you have found the right translation, remember that you may
need to adapt the French word you have found. You may need to make
a **noun** plural, or make an **adjective** feminine or plural. Remember
that the feminine form is given for nouns and adjectives, and that
irregular plural forms are given also.

dancer [ˈdɑːnsəʳ] *n* danseur *m*, danseuse *f*

horse [hɔːs] *n* cheval *m* (*pl* chevaux)

active [ˈæktɪv] *adj* actif (*f* active)

You may also need to adapt the **verb**. Verbs are given in the infinitive
form, but you may want to use them in the present, past or future
tense. To do this, use the **verb tables** in the last section of the
dictionary.

▷ **Find out more**

In the *Collins Canadian French Dictionary*, you will find lots of extra information about the French language. These **usage notes** help you understand how the language works, draw your attention to false friends (words which look similar but have a different meaning), and give you some word-for-word translations.

> **te** [t(ə)] *pron* **❶** you ▷ *Je te vois*. I can
> see you.
>
> > **te** changes to **t'** before a vowel
> > and most words beginning
> > with "h".

> **librairie** [libʀeʀi] *nf* bookstore
>
> > Be careful! **librairie** does not
> > mean **library**.

You can also find out more about life in Canada and French-speaking countries by reading the **cultural notes**.

> **lunch** [lʌntʃ] *n* lunch *m* **to have**
> **lunch** dîner ▷ *We have lunch at 12.30.*
> Nous dînons à midi et demie.
>
> > ● In Canada, **le lunch** is the noon
> > ● meal. In France, it refers to a light
> > ● meal consisting of a cold buffet.

▷ **Remember!**

Never take the first translation you see without looking at the others. Always look to see if there is more than one translation, or more than one part of speech.

ABBREVIATIONS USED IN THIS DICTIONARY

abbr	abbreviation
adj	adjective
adv	adverb
art	article
conj	conjunction
excl	exclamation
f	feminine
n	noun
nf	feminine noun
nm	masculine noun
nmf	masculine or feminine noun
nm/f	masculine or feminine noun
npl	plural noun
num	number
prep	preposition
pp	past participle
pt	past tense
pron	pronoun
sg	singular
vb	verb

SYMBOLS

▷	example
▶	new part of speech
❶	new meaning

Note that to help you decide whether to use **le, la** or **l'** in front of a word starting with 'h', the article is given for all the nouns in letter H on the **French-English** side of the dictionary.

PHONETIC TRANSCRIPTION

CONSONNES		CONSONANTS
N.B. **p**, **b**, **t**, **d**, **k**, **g** sont suivis d'une aspiration en anglais		N.B. **p**, **b**, **t**, **d**, **k**, **g** are not aspirated in French.
pou**p**ée	p	**p**uppy
bom**b**e	b	**b**a**b**y
ten**t**e **th**ermal	t	**t**en**t**
din**d**e	d	**d**a**dd**y
co**q** **q**ui **k**épi	k	**c**ork **k**iss **ch**ord
ga**g** bâ**gu**e	g	**g**a**g** **gu**ess
sale **c**e na**t**ion	s	**s**o ri**ce** ki**ss**
zéro ro**s**e	z	cou**s**in bu**zz**
ta**ch**e **ch**at	ʃ	**sh**eep **s**ugar
gilet **j**uge	ʒ	plea**s**ure bei**ge**
	tʃ	**ch**urch
	dʒ	**j**udge **g**eneral
fer **ph**are	f	**f**arm ra**ff**le
ver**v**eine	v	**v**ery re**v**el
	θ	**th**in ma**th**s
	ð	**th**at o**th**er
lent sa**ll**e	l	**l**itt**l**e ba**ll**
rare **r**entrer	R	
	r	**r**at ra**r**e
ma**m**an fe**mm**e	m	**m**u**mm**y co**mb**
non bo**nn**e	n	**n**o ra**n**
a**gn**eau vi**gn**e	ɲ	
	ŋ	si**ng**ing ba**n**k
	h	**h**at re**h**earse
yeux pa**ill**e p**i**ed	j	**y**et
no**u**er o**ui**	w	**w**all be**w**ail
h**ui**le l**u**i	ɥ	
	x	lo**ch**

DIVERS		MISCELLANEOUS
pour l'anglais: le "r" final se prononce en liaison devant une voyelle	r	in English transcription: final "r" can be pronounced before a vowel
pour l'anglais: précède la syllabe accentuée	'	in French wordlist: no liaison before aspirate "h"

PHONETIC TRANSCRIPTION

VOYELLES

NB. La mise en équivalence de certains sons n'indique qu'une ressemblance approximative.

VOWELS

NB. The pairing of some vowel sounds only indicates approximate equivalence.

ici vie lyrique	i iː	heel bead
	ɪ	hit pity
jouer été	e	
lait jouet merci	ɛ	set tent
plat amour	a æ	bat apple
bas pâte	ɑ ɑː	after car calm
	ʌ	fun cousin
le premier	ə	over above
beurre peur	œ	
peu deux	ø əː	urgent fern work
or homme	ɔ	wash pot
mot eau gauche	o ɔː	born cork
genou roue	u	full hook
	uː	boom shoe
rue urne	y	

DIPHTONGUES

DIPHTHONGS

ɪə	beer tier
ɛə	tear fair there
eɪ	date plaice day
aɪ	life buy cry
aʊ	owl foul now
əʊ	low no
ɔɪ	boil boy oily
ʊə	poor tour

NASALES

NASAL VOWELS

matin plein	ɛ̃
brun	œ̃
sang an dans	ɑ̃
non pont	ɔ̃

In general, we give the pronunciation of each entry in square brackets after the word in question. However, on the English-French side, where the entry is composed of two or more unhyphenated words, each of which is given elsewhere in this dictionary, you will find the pronunciation of each word in its alphabetical position.

a

a [a] *vb see* **avoir**

> **a** should not be confused with the preposition **à**.

Elle a beaucoup d'amis. She has a lot of friends.; **Il a mangé des frites.** He had some fries.; **Il a neigé pendant la nuit.** It snowed during the night.; **il y a (1)** there is ▷ *Il y a un bon film à la télé.* There's a good film on TV. **(2)** there are ▷ *Il y a beaucoup de monde.* There are lots of people.

à [a] *prep*

> **à** should not be confused with the verb form **a**. See also **au** (**=à+le**) and **aux** (**=à+les**).

❶ at ▷ *être à la maison* to be at home ▷ *à trois heures* at 3 o'clock ❷ in ▷ *être à Truro* to be in Truro ▷ *habiter au Portugal* to live in Portugal ▷ *habiter à la campagne* to live in the country ▷ *au printemps* in the spring ▷ *au mois de juin* in

June ❸ to ▷ *aller à Regina* to go to Regina ▷ *aller au Portugal* to go to Portugal ▷ *aller à la campagne* to go to the country ▷ *donner quelque chose à quelqu'un* to give something to somebody ▷ *Cette veste appartient à ma sœur.* This jacket belongs to my sister. ▷ *Je n'ai rien à faire.* I have nothing to do.; **Ce livre est à mon père.** This book is my father's.; **Cette voiture est à nous.** This car is ours. ❹ by ▷ *à bicyclette* by bicycle ▷ *être payé à l'heure* to be paid by the hour; **à pied** on foot; **C'est à côté de chez moi.** It's near my house.; **C'est à dix kilomètres d'ici.** It's 10 kilometres from here.; **C'est à dix minutes d'ici.** It's 10 minutes from here.; **cent kilomètres à l'heure** 100 kilometres an hour; **À bientôt!** See you soon! **À demain!** See you tomorrow! **À samedi!** See you on Saturday! ▷ *À tout à l'heure!* See you later!

abandonner [abɑ̃dɔne] *vb*
❶ to abandon ▷ *Elle a abandonné sa voiture à côté de la route.* She abandoned her car at the side of the road. ❷ to quit ▷ *J'ai décidé d'abandonner mes leçons de natation.* I've decided to quit swimming lessons.

abeille [abɛj] *nf* bee

abîmer [abime] *vb* to damage;
s'abîmer to get damaged

aboiteau [abwato] (*pl* **aboiteaux**)
nm aboiteau

- In New Brunswick and Nova Scotia, dikes were built on the Bay of Fundy to reclaim the marshland next to the sea.
- A gate in the dike, called an **aboiteau**, opened as the tide went out so marsh water could run into the ocean. The gate

- closed when the tide came in so seawater would not flow into the marsh. Modern aboiteaux use the same principle.

abolir [abɔliʀ] vb (law, custom) to do away with

abonnement [abɔnmɑ̃] nm ❶ season ticket ❷ (to magazine) subscription

s'**abonner** [abɔne] vb: s'**abonner à une revue** to take out a subscription to a magazine

abord [abɔʀ] nm: d'**abord** first ▷ Je vais rentrer chez moi d'abord. I'll go home first.

aboyer [abwaje] vb to bark

abri [abʀi] nm shelter; **être à l'abri** to be under cover; **se mettre à l'abri** to take shelter

abricot [abʀiko] nm apricot

s'**abriter** [abʀite] vb to take shelter

absence [apsɑ̃s] nf absence; **Il est passé pendant ton absence.** He came while you were away.

absent [apsɑ̃, -ɑ̃t] (f **absente**) adj absent

Acadie [akadi] nf Acadia ▷ Mes ancêtres étaient originaires de l'Acadie. My ancestors were from Acadia.

acadien [akadjɛ̃, -ɛn] (f **acadienne**) adj, n Acadian; **un Acadien** (man) an Acadian; **une Acadienne** (woman) an Acadian; **les Acadiens** the Acadians

accélérateur [akseleʀatœʀ] nm accelerator

accélérer [akseleʀe] vb to accelerate

accent [aksɑ̃] nm accent ▷ Elle a l'accent de Terre-Neuve. She has a Newfoundland accent.; **un accent aigu** an acute accent; **un accent grave** a grave accent; **un accent circonflexe** a circumflex

accentuer [aksɑ̃tɥe] vb to stress

accepter [aksɛpte] vb to accept;

accepter de faire quelque chose to agree to do something

accès [aksɛ] nm access ▷ avoir accès à quelque chose to have access to something; **être d'accès facile** to be approachable

accessoire [akseswaʀ] nm ❶ accessory ▷ les accessoires de mode fashion accessories ❷ prop

accident [aksidɑ̃] nm accident ▷ un accident de la route a road accident ▷ Elle a eu un accident de ski. She had a skiing accident.; **par accident** by chance

accompagner [akɔ̃paɲe] vb to accompany

accomplir [akɔ̃pliʀ] vb to carry out ▷ Il n'a pas réussi à accomplir cette tâche. He didn't manage to carry out this task.

accord [akɔʀ] nm agreement; **être d'accord** to agree ▷ Tu es d'accord avec moi? Do you agree with me?; **se mettre d'accord** to come to an agreement; **D'accord!** OK!

accordéon [akɔʀdeɔ̃] nm accordion ▷ Il joue de l'accordéon. He plays the accordion.

accorder [akɔʀde] vb ❶ to grant ▷ accorder la permission to grant permission ❷ to tune ▷ accorder une guitare to tune a guitar ❸ (grammatically) to make agree ▷ accorder un adjectif avec un nom to make an adjective agree with a noun; **s'accorder** to agree ▷ Ils s'accordent pour dire que le film est ennuyant. They agree that the movie is boring.

accotement [akɔtmɑ̃] nm shoulder ▷ Elle s'est stationnée sur l'accotement. She parked on the shoulder.

accrochage [akʀɔʃaʒ] nm fender-bender

accrocher [akʀɔʃe] vb: **accrocher**

quelque chose à (1) to hang something on ▷ *Il a accroché sa veste au portemanteau.* He hung his jacket on the coat rack. **(2)** to hitch something up to ▷ *Ils ont accroché la remorque à leur voiture.* They hitched the trailer up to their car.; **s'accrocher à quelque chose** to catch on something ▷ *Sa jupe s'est accrochée à une branche.* Her skirt got caught on a branch.

s'**accroupir** [akʀupiʀ] vb to squat down

accueil [akœj] nm welcome ▷ *un accueil chaleureux* a warm welcome.; **Elle s'occupe de l'accueil des visiteurs.** She's in charge of looking after visitors.

accueillant [akœjɑ̃, -ɑ̃t] (f **accueillante**) adj welcoming ▷ *Ses parents ont été très accueillants.* Her parents were very welcoming.

accueillir [akœjiʀ] vb to welcome

accumuler [akymyle] vb to accumulate; **s'accumuler** to pile up

accusé [akyze] nm accused ▷ *L'accusé a déclaré que...* The accused stated that...

accusée [akyze] nf accused

accuser [akyze] vb to accuse ▷ *accuser quelqu'un de quelque chose* to accuse somebody of something

achat [aʃa] nm purchase; **faire des achats** to do some shopping

acheter [aʃte] vb to buy ▷ *J'ai acheté des livres à la librairie.* I bought some books at the bookstore.; **acheter quelque chose à quelqu'un (1)** to buy something for somebody ▷ *Qu'est-ce que tu lui as acheté pour son anniversaire?* What did you buy her for her birthday? **(2)** to buy something from somebody ▷ *J'ai acheté des œufs au fermier.* I bought some eggs from the farmer.

achigan [aʃigã] nm (fish) bass

acide [asid] nm acid

acier [asje] nm steel

acné [akne] nf acne ▷ *Elle a de l'acné.* She has acne.

acquérir [akeʀiʀ] vb to acquire

acquis [aki] vb see **acquérir**

acquitter [akite] vb to acquit ▷ *L'accusé a été acquitté.* The accused was acquitted.

acrobate [akʀɔbat] nmf acrobat

acrobatie [akʀɔbasi] nf acrobatics

acte [akt(ə)] nm act; **un acte de naissance** a birth certificate

acteur [aktœʀ] nm actor ▷ *Il est acteur.* He's an actor. ▷ *un acteur de cinéma* a film actor

actif [aktif, -iv] (f **active**) adj active

action [aksjɔ̃] nf action; **une bonne action** a good deed

Action de grâce nf Thanksgiving

s'**activer** [aktive] vb ❶ to bustle about ▷ *Elle s'activait à préparer le repas.* She bustled about preparing the meal. ❷ to get moving ▷ *Allez! Active-toi!* Come on! Get moving!

activité [aktivite] nf activity

actrice [aktʀis] nf actress ▷ *Elle est actrice.* She's an actress. ▷ *une actrice de cinéma* a film actress

actualité [aktɥalite] nf current events; **un problème d'actualité** a current issue; **les actualités** the news

actuel [aktɥɛl] (f **actuelle**) adj present ▷ *le système actuel* the present system; **à l'heure actuelle** at the present time

  Be careful! **actuel** does not mean **actual**.

actuellement [aktɥɛlmɑ̃] adv at present

  Be careful! **actuellement** does not mean **actually**.

adaptateur [adaptatœʀ] nm adapter

adaptation [adaptasjɔ̃] nf
adaptation ▷ une adaptation
télévisée d'un roman a TV adaptation
of a novel

addition [adisjɔ̃] nf bill ▷ L'addition,
s'il vous plaît! Can we have the bill,
please?

additionner [adisjɔne] vb to
add up

adhésif [adezif, -iv] (**f adhésive**)
adj: **le ruban adhésif** sticky tape

adieu [adjø] excl farewell!

adjectif [adʒɛktif] nm adjective

admettre [admɛtr(ə)] vb **①** to
admit ▷ Il refuse d'admettre qu'il
s'est trompé. He won't admit that
he made a mistake. **②** to allow
▷ Les chiens ne sont pas admis dans le
restaurant. Dogs are not allowed in
the restaurant.

administration [administrasjɔ̃]
nf administration

admirable [admirabl(ə)] adj
wonderful

admirateur [admiratœr] nm
admirer

admiratrice [admiratris] nf
admirer

admirer [admire] vb to admire

admis [admi] vb see **admettre**

adolescence [adɔlesɑ̃s] nf
adolescence

adolescent [adɔlesɑ̃] nm teenager

adolescente [adɔlesɑ̃t] nf
teenager

adopter [adɔpte] vb to adopt

adoptif [adɔptif, -iv] (**f adoptive**)
adj **①** adopted ▷ un enfant adoptif
an adopted child **②** adoptive
▷ les parents adoptifs the adoptive
parents

adorable [adɔrabl(ə)] adj lovely

adorer [adɔre] vb to love ▷ Il adore
le chocolat. He loves chocolate.
▷ J'adore jouer au tennis. I love playing
tennis.

adresse [adrɛs] nf address; **mon
adresse électronique** my email
address

adresser [adrese] vb: **adresser
la parole à quelqu'un** to speak to
someone; **s'adresser à quelqu'un**
(1) to speak to somebody ▷ C'est
à toi que je m'adresse. It's you
I'm speaking to. **(2)** to go and
see somebody ▷ Adressez-vous
à la patronne. Go and see the
boss. ▷ Adressez-vous au bureau
de renseignements. Ask at the
information desk. **(3)** to be aimed
at somebody ▷ Ce film s'adresse
surtout aux enfants. This film is
aimed mainly at children.

adulte [adylt(ə)] nmf adult

adverbe [advɛrb(ə)] nm adverb

adversaire [advɛrsɛr] nmf
opponent

aérien [aerjɛ̃, -ɛn] (**f aérienne**)
adj: **une compagnie aérienne**
an airline

aérobic [aerɔbik] nm aerobics
▷ Elle fait de l'aérobic. She does
aerobics.

aérogare [aerɔgar] nf (airport)
terminal

aéroport [aerɔpɔr] nm airport

affaire [afɛr] nf **①** case ▷ une
affaire de vol a case of theft
② business ▷ Leur affaire marche
bien. Their business is doing well.;
une bonne affaire a real bargain;
Ça fera l'affaire. This will do nicely.;
avoir affaire à quelqu'un to deal
with somebody

affaires [afɛr] nfpl **①** things
▷ Va chercher tes affaires! Go and
get your things! **②** business
▷ Les affaires marchent bien en
ce moment. Business is good at
the moment. ▷ Mêle-toi de tes
affaires. (informal) Mind your own
business.; **une femme d'affaires** a

businesswoman

affection [afɛksjɔ̃] nf affection

affectueux [afɛktɥø, -øz] (f **affectueuse**) adj affectionate

affiche [afiʃ] nf poster

afficher [afiʃe] vb (a notice) to post ▷ Ils ont affiché les résultats dans le couloir. They've posted the results in the hallway.; « Défense d'afficher » "Post no bills"

affilée [afile] nf: **d'affilée** adv at a stretch ▷ Elle a travaillé douze heures d'affilée. She worked 12 hours at a stretch.

affirmation [afirmasjɔ̃] nf assertion

affirmer [afirme] vb to claim ▷ Il a affirmé que c'était la vérité. He claimed it was the truth.; **s'affirmer** to assert oneself ▷ Il est trop timide, il faut qu'il s'affirme. He's too shy, he should assert himself.

affluence [aflyɑ̃s] nf: **les heures d'affluence** rush hour ▷ Durant les heures d'affluence, les autobus passent toutes les sept minutes. During rush hour, buses come every 7 minutes.

s'affoler [afɔle] vb to panic ▷ Ne t'affole pas! Don't panic!

affranchir [afrɑ̃ʃir] vb to stamp ▷ Elle a affranchi mon passeport. She stamped my passport.

affreux [afrø, -øz] (f **affreuse**) adj awful

affronter [afrɔ̃te] vb to face ▷ Vancouver affronte Montréal en finale. Vancouver will face Montréal in the final.

afin de [afɛ̃d(ə)] conj: **afin de faire quelque chose** in order to do something ▷ Je me suis levé très tôt afin d'être prêt à temps. I got up very early in order to be ready on time.

afin que [afɛ̃k(ə)] conj so that
  afin que is followed by a verb in the subjunctive.

▷ Il m'a téléphoné afin que je sois prêt à temps. He phoned me so that I'd be ready on time.

agacer [agase] vb to get on somebody's nerves ▷ Tu m'agaces avec tes questions! You're getting on my nerves with all your questions!

âge [aʒ] nm age; **Quel âge as-tu?** How old are you?

âgé [aʒe] (f**âgée**) adj old ▷ Mon grand-père est âgé. My grandfather's old. ▷ Elle est âgée de dix ans. She's 10 years old.; **les personnes âgées** the elderly

agence [aʒɑ̃s] nf agency ▷ l'agence pour l'emploi the employment agency; **une agence de voyages** a travel agency; **une agence immobilière** a real estate agency

agenda [aʒẽda] nm (daybook) agenda ▷ J'ai perdu mon agenda. I've lost my agenda.

s'agenouiller [aʒnuje] vb to kneel down

agent [aʒɑ̃] nm: **un agent d'infiltration** a secret agent; **un agent de police** a police officer; **un agent de la GRC** a Mountie

agente [aʒɑ̃t] nf: **une agente d'infiltration** a secret agent; **une agente de police** a police officer; **une agente de bord** a flight attendant

agglomération [aglɔmerasjɔ̃] nf urban area; **l'agglomération de Toronto** Greater Toronto

aggraver [agrave] vb to make worse; **s'aggraver** to get worse

agir [aʒir] vb ① to act ▷ Il a agi par vengeance. He acted out of revenge. ② to take effect ▷ Ce médicament agit vite. This medicine takes effect quickly.; **Il s'agit de...** It's about... ▷ Il s'agit du club d'art dramatique. It's about the drama club. ▷ De quoi s'agit-il? What is it about?; **Il**

s'agit de faire attention. We must be careful.

agité [aʒite] (f **agitée**) adj
❶ restless ▷ *Les élèves sont agités.* The students are restless. **❷** rough ▷ *La mer est agitée.* The sea is rough.; **un sommeil agité** troubled sleep

agiter [aʒite] vb to shake ▷ *Agitez la bouteille.* Shake the bottle.

agneau [aɲo] (pl **agneaux**) nm lamb

agrafe [agʁaf] nf (for papers) staple

agrafeuse [agʁaføz] nf stapler

agrandir [agʁɑ̃diʁ] vb **❶** to enlarge ▷ *J'ai fait agrandir mes photos.* I got my photos enlarged. **❷** to extend ▷ *Ils ont agrandi leur jardin.* They've extended their garden.; **s'agrandir** to expand ▷ *Leur magasin s'est agrandi.* Their store has expanded.

agréable [agʁeabl(ə)] adj nice

agréer [agʁee] vb: **Veuillez agréer, Madame, l'expression de mes sentiments distingués. Jane Ormal.** Yours sincerely, Jane Ormal.

agressif [agʁesif, -iv] (f **agressive**) adj aggressive

agressivité [agʁesivite] nf aggression; **faire preuve d'agressivité envers quelqu'un** to be aggressive towards somebody; **l'agressivité au volant** road rage

agricole [agʁikɔl] adj agricultural ▷ *le matériel agricole* agricultural machinery; **une exploitation agricole** a farm

agriculteur [agʁikyltœʁ] nm farmer; **Il est agriculteur.** He's a farmer.

agricultrice [agʁikyltʁis] nf farmer; **Elle est agricultrice.** She's a farmer.

agriculture [agʁikyltyʁ] nf farming

ai [e] vb see **avoir**; **J'ai deux chats.**

I have two cats.; **J'ai bien dormi.** I slept well.

aide [ɛd] nf **❶** help ▷ *J'ai besoin de ton aide.* I need your help. ▷ *appeler quelqu'un à l'aide* to call to somebody for help; **À l'aide!** Help! **❷** aid ▷ *une aide financière* financial aid; **à l'aide de** using ▷ *J'ai réussi à ouvrir la boîte de conserve à l'aide d'un couteau.* I managed to open the can using a knife.

aide-infirmier (pl **aides-infirmiers**) nm nurse's aid; **Il est aide-infirmier.** He's a nurse's aid.

aide-infirmière (pl **aides-infirmières**) nf nurse's aid ▷ *Elle est aide-infirmière.* She is a nurse's aid.

aider [ede] vb to help

aie [ɛ] vb see **avoir**

aïe [aj] excl Ouch!

aigre [ɛgʁ(ə)] adj sour

aigu [egy] (f **aiguë**) adj (pain) sharp ▷ *J'ai ressenti une douleur aiguë dans le bas du dos.* I felt a sharp pain in my lower back.; **e accent aigu** e with an acute accent

aiguille [egɥij] nf needle ▷ *une aiguille à tricoter* a knitting needle; **les aiguilles d'une montre** the hands of a watch

ail [aj] nm garlic

aile [ɛl] nf wing

aille [aj] vb see **aller**

ailleurs [ajœʁ] adv somewhere else; **partout ailleurs** everywhere else; **nulle part ailleurs** nowhere else; **d'ailleurs** besides

aimable [ɛmabl(ə)] adj kind

aimant [emɑ̃] nm magnet

aimer [eme] vb **❶** to love ▷ *Il aime ses enfants.* He loves his children. **❷** to like ▷ *Tu aimes le chocolat?* Do you like chocolate? ▷ *J'aime bien cette fille.* I like this girl. ▷ *J'aime bien jouer au tennis.* I like playing tennis. ▷ *J'aimerais aller en Grèce.* I'd like to go to Greece.; **J'aimerais mieux ne pas y aller.** I'd rather not go.

aîné [ene] (**aînée**) adj elder ▷ *mon frère aîné* my big brother ▶ *nm* oldest child ▷ *Il est l'aîné.* He's the oldest child.

aînée [ene] nf oldest child ▷ *Elle est l'aînée.* She's the oldest child.

ainsi [ɛ̃si] adv in this way ▷ *Il faut faire ainsi.* This is the way to do it.; **C'est ainsi qu'il a réussi.** That's how he succeeded.; **ainsi que** as well as; **et ainsi de suite** and so on

air [ɛʀ] nm ① *air* ▷ *l'air chaud* warm air; **prendre l'air** to get some fresh air ② *tune* ▷ *Elle a joué un air au piano.* She played a tune on the piano.; **Elle a l'air fatiguée.** She looks tired.; **Il a l'air d'un clown.** He looks like a clown.

aire de jeux [ɛʀ-] nf playground

aire de repos [ɛʀ-] nf (on highway) rest area

aise [ɛz] nf: **être à l'aise** to be at ease ▷ *Elle est à l'aise avec tout le monde.* She's at ease with everybody.; **être mal à l'aise** to be ill at ease; **se mettre à l'aise** to make oneself comfortable

ait [ɛ] vb see **avoir**

ajouter [aʒute] vb to add

alarme [alaʀm(ə)] nf alarm ▷ *donner l'alarme* to raise the alarm

Alberta nf Alberta

album [albɔm] nm album

alcool [alkɔl] nm alcohol ▷ *Je ne bois pas d'alcool.* I don't drink alcohol.; **les alcools forts** spirits

alcoolisé [alkɔlize] (**alcoolisée**) adj alcoholic; **une boisson non alcoolisée** a soft drink

alentours [alɑ̃tuʀ] nmpl: **dans les alentours** in the area; **aux alentours** in the area; **aux alentours d'Ottawa** in the Ottawa area; **aux alentours de cinq heures** around 5 o'clock

algèbre [alʒɛbʀ(ə)] nf algebra

algue [alg(ə)] nf seaweed

alibi [alibi] nm alibi

aliment [alimɑ̃] nm food ▷ *Le fromage est un aliment très nutritif.* Cheese is a very nutritious food. ▷ *les aliments solides* solid food; **les aliments naturels** health food ▷ *un magasin d'aliments naturels* a health food store

alimentaire [alimɑ̃tɛʀ] adj ① *food* ▷ *un groupe alimentaire* a food group ▷ *une banque alimentaire* a food bank; **Le guide alimentaire canadien** Canada's Food Guide ② *eating* ▷ *nos habitudes alimentaires* our eating habits

alimentation [alimɑ̃tasjɔ̃] nf diet ▷ *Elle a une alimentation saine.* She has a healthy diet.

allée [ale] nf ① *path* ▷ *les allées du parc* the paths in the park ② (in street names) *drive*; **les allées et venues** comings and goings

allégé [aleʒe] (**allégée**) adj low-fat ▷ *un yogourt allégé* a low-fat yogurt

aller [ale] vb to go ▷ *Elle est allée à Edmonton.* She went to Edmonton. ▷ *Je dois y aller.* I've got to go. ▷ *Elle ira le voir.* She'll go and see him. ▷ *Je vais me fâcher.* I'm going to get angry.; **s'en aller** to go away ▷ *Je m'en vais demain.* I'm leaving tomorrow.; **aller bien à quelqu'un** to suit somebody ▷ *Cette robe te va bien.* This dress suits you.; **Allez! Dépêche-toi!** Come on! Hurry up!; **« Comment allez-vous? » — « Je vais bien. »** "How are you?" — "I'm fine."; **« Comment ça va? » — « Ça va bien. »** "How are you?" — "I'm fine."; **aller mieux** (after an illness) to be better ▶ *nm* ① *outward journey* ▷ *L'aller nous a pris trois heures.* The journey there took us three hours. ② *one-*

way ticket ▷ *Je voudrais un aller pour Halifax.* I'd like a one-way ticket to Halifax.; **un aller simple** a one-way ticket; **un aller et retour (1)** a return ticket ▷ *Je voudrais deux allers et retours pour Montréal.* I'd like two return tickets to Montréal. **(2)** a round trip ▷ *Elle a fait l'aller et retour en dix heures.* She did the round trip in ten hours.

allergie [alɛʀʒi] *nf* allergy ▷ *J'ai des allergies.* I have allergies.; **une allergie alimentaire** a food allergy

allergique [alɛʀʒik] *adj*: **allergique à** allergic to ▷ *Je suis allergique aux poils de chat.* I'm allergic to cat hair.

allô [alo] *excl (on phone)* Hello! ▷ *Allô! Je voudrais parler à la directrice.* Hello! I'd like to speak to the principal.

s'**allonger** [alɔ̃ʒe] *vb* to lie down ▷ *Il s'est allongé sur son lit.* He lay down on his bed.

allophone [alɔfɔn] *adj* allophone

▪ **Allophone** is a word used mostly
▪ in French Canada to refer to
▪ people whose first language is
▪ neither English nor French.

▷ *nmf* allophone

allumer [alyme] *vb* ❶ to turn on ▷ *Tu peux allumer la lumière?* Can you turn the light on? ▷ *Allume la radio.* Switch on the radio. ❷ to light ▷ *Elle a allumé une bougie.* She lit a candle.; **s'allumer** (light) to come on ▷ *La lumière s'est allumée.* The light came on.

allumette [alymɛt] *nf* match ▷ *une boîte d'allumettes* a box of matches

allure [alyʀ] *nf* ❶ speed ▷ *à toute allure* at top speed ❷ look ▷ *avoir une drôle d'allure* to look odd

alors [alɔʀ] *adv* ❶ then ▷ *Tu as fini? Alors je m'en vais.* Are you finished?

I'm going then. ❷ so ▷ *Alors je lui ai dit de partir.* So I told him to leave.; **Et alors?** So what? ❸ at that time ▷ *Elle habitait alors à Vancouver.* She was living in Vancouver at that time.; **alors que (1)** as ▷ *Il est arrivé alors que je partais.* He arrived just as I was leaving. **(2)** while ▷ *Alors que je travaillais dur, lui se reposait.* While I was working hard, he was resting.

alphabet [alfabe] *nm* alphabet

alphabétique [alfabetik] *adj* alphabetical ▷ *par ordre alphabétique* in alphabetical order

aluminium [alyminjɔm] *nm* aluminum

amande [amɑ̃d] *nf* almond; **la pâte d'amandes** marzipan

amant [amɑ̃] *nm* lover

amante [amɑ̃t] *nf* lover

amateur [amatœʀ] (f **amatrice**) *adj* amateur ▷ *Elle est pianiste amateur.* She's an amateur pianist.

▌ For the adjective **amateur**,
▌ the same form is used for
▌ both masculine and feminine,
▌ but for the noun, there is a
▌ feminine form **l'amatrice**.

▷ *nm* ❶ amateur; **en amateur** as a hobby ▷ *Il fait de la photo en amateur.* He takes photos as a hobby. ❷ fan; **C'est un amateur de jazz.** He's a jazz fan.

amatrice [amatʀis] *nf* ❶ amateur; **en amatrice** as a hobby ▷ *Elle joue du violon classique en amatrice.* She plays classical violin as a hobby. ❷ fan; **C'est une amatrice de sport.** She's a sports fan.

ambiance [ɑ̃bjɑ̃s] *nf* atmosphere ▷ *Je n'aime pas l'ambiance ici.* I don't like the atmosphere here. ❷ *Il y a de l'ambiance dans ce café.* This café has a lot of atmosphere.; **la musique d'ambiance** background music

ambitieux [ɑ̃bisjø, -øz] (f **ambitieuse**) adj ambitious

ambition [ɑ̃bisjɔ̃] nf ambition
▷ Elle a l'ambition de devenir première ministre. Her ambition is to become Prime Minister.; **Il a beaucoup d'ambition.** He's very ambitious.

ambulance [ɑ̃bylɑ̃s] nf ambulance

ambulancier [ɑ̃bylɑ̃sje] nm ambulance driver

ambulancière [ɑ̃bylɑ̃sjɛʀ] nf ambulance driver

âme [ɑm] nf soul

amélioration [ameljɔʀasjɔ̃] nf improvement

améliorer [ameljɔʀe] vb to improve; **s'améliorer** to improve ▷ Le temps s'améliore. The weather's improving.

amende [amɑ̃d] nf fine ▷ une amende de cinquante dollars a 50 dollar fine

amener [amne] vb to bring ▷ Qu'est-ce qui t'amène? What brings you here? ▷ Est-ce que je peux amener un ami? Can I bring a friend?

amer [amɛʀ] (f **amère**) adj bitter

ami [ami] nm friend; **C'est son petit ami.** He's her boyfriend.

amical [amikal, -o] (f **amicale**, mpl **amicaux**) adj friendly

amie [ami] nf friend; **C'est sa petite amie.** She's his girlfriend.

amitié [amitje] nf friendship; **Fais mes amitiés à tes parents.** Give my regards to your parents.; **Amitiés** (in letter) Regards

amour [amuʀ] nm love ▷ l'amour paternel paternal love; **faire l'amour** to make love

amoureux [amuʀø, -øz] (f **amoureuse**) adj in love ▷ être amoureux de quelqu'un to be in love with somebody

amour-propre [amuʀpʀɔpʀ(ə)] nm self-esteem

amplement [ɑ̃pləmɑ̃] adv: **Nous avons amplement le temps.** We have plenty of time.

ampoule [ɑ̃pul] nf ❶ light bulb ❷ blister ▷ J'ai une ampoule au pied. I have a blister on my foot.

amusant [amyzɑ̃, -ɑ̃t] (f **amusante**) adj amusing

amuse-gueule [amyzgœl] nmpl snacks

amuser [amyze] vb to amuse; **s'amuser** (1) to play ▷ Les enfants s'amusent dehors. The children are playing outside. (2) to enjoy oneself ▷ On s'est bien amusés à cette soirée. We really enjoyed ourselves at that party.

amygdales [amidal] nfpl tonsils ▷ se faire opérer des amygdales to have one's tonsils removed

amygdalite [amidalit] nf tonsilitis

an [ɑ̃] nm year; **avoir neuf ans** to be nine years old; **le jour de l'An** New Year's Day; **le Nouvel An** New Year's

analyse [analiz] nf ❶ analysis ❷ (medical) test ▷ une analyse de sang a blood test

analyser [analize] vb to analyse

ananas [anana] nm pineapple

ancêtre [ɑ̃sɛtʀ(ə)] nmf ancestor

anchois [ɑ̃ʃwa] nm anchovy

ancien [ɑ̃sjɛ̃, -ɛn] (f **ancienne**) adj ❶ former ▷ C'est une ancienne élève. She's a former student. ❷ old ▷ notre ancienne voiture our old car ❸ antique ▷ un fauteuil ancien an antique chair

ancre [ɑ̃kʀ(ə)] nf anchor

âne [ɑn] nm donkey

ange [ɑ̃ʒ] nm angel; **être aux anges** to be over the moon

anglais [ɑ̃glɛ, -ɛz] (f **anglaise**) adj, n English ▷ la grammaire anglaise English grammar ▷ Est-ce que *vous parlez anglais?* Do you speak English?

angle [ɑ̃gl(ə)] *nm* ❶ angle ▷ *un angle droit* a right angle ❷ corner ▷ *à l'angle de la rue* at the corner of the street

anglophone [ɑ̃glɔfɔn] *adj* Anglophone ▷ *une communauté anglophone* an Anglophone community
▶ *nmf* Anglophone ▷ *Beaucoup d'anglophones habitent à Montréal.* A lot of Anglophones live in Montréal.

angoissé [ɑ̃gwase] (**f angoissée**) *adj* anxious ▷ *Il était angoissé à l'idée de prendre l'avion.* He was anxious about flying.

animal [animal, -o] (*pl* **animaux**) *nm* animal

animal de compagnie *nm* pet; « *les animaux de compagnie ne sont pas acceptés* » "No pets"

animalerie [animalʀi] *nf* pet shop

animateur [animatœʀ] *nm*
❶ host ▷ *Il est animateur à la télé.* He's a TV host. ❷ youth leader ▷ *Il est animateur au centre sportif.* He is a youth leader at the sports centre.

animatrice [animatʀis] *nf*
❶ host ▷ *Elle est animatrice à la télé.* She's a TV host. ❷ youth leader ▷ *Elle est animatrice au centre sportif.* She is a youth leader at the sports centre.

animé [anime] (**f animée**) *adj* lively ▷ *Cette rue est très animée.* This is a very lively street.; **un dessin animé** a cartoon

anneau [ano] (*pl* **anneaux**) *nm* ring

année [ane] *nf* year ▷ *l'année dernière* last year ▷ *l'année prochaine* next year

anniversaire [anivɛʀsɛʀ] *nm*
❶ birthday ▷ *C'est l'anniversaire de ma sœur.* It's my sister's birthday.

❷ anniversary ▷ *un anniversaire de mariage* a wedding anniversary

annonce [anɔ̃s] *nf* ad ▷ *J'ai lu votre annonce dans le journal.* I saw your ad in the paper. ▷ *passer une annonce* to place an ad; **les petites annonces** the classified ads; **une annonce publicitaire** a commercial; **une annonce radiophonique** a radio ad; **une annonce télévisée** a TV commercial

annoncer [anɔ̃se] *vb* to announce ▷ *Ils ont annoncé leurs fiançailles.* They've announced their engagement.

annuaire [anɥɛʀ] *nm* ❶ phone book ❷ yearbook

annuel [anɥɛl] (**f annuelle**) *adj* annual

annuler [anyle] *vb* to cancel

anonyme [anɔnim] *adj* anonymous

anorexie [anɔʀɛksi] *nf* anorexia

antenne [ɑ̃tɛn] *nf* ❶ aerial; **antenne parabolique** satellite dish; **être à l'antenne** to be on the air ❷ antenna

antibiotique [ɑ̃tibjɔtik] *nm* antibiotic

antigel [ɑ̃tiʒɛl] *nm* antifreeze

antimoustiques [ɑ̃timustik] (*f+pl* **antimoustiques**) *adj* insect repellent ▷ *une lotion antimoustiques* insect repellent lotion

antimoustiques [ɑ̃timustik] *nm* insect repellent

antipathique [ɑ̃tipatik] *adj* unpleasant ▷ *Je le trouve plutôt antipathique.* I find him rather unpleasant.

antiquaire [ɑ̃tikɛʀ] *nmf* antique dealer ▷ *Elle est antiquaire.* She's an antique dealer.

antiquité [ɑ̃tikite] *nf* antique ▷ *un magasin d'antiquités* an antique shop; **pendant l'Antiquité** in classical times

antivol [ɑ̃tivɔl] nm (on bike) lock

anxieux [ɑ̃ksjø, -øz] (f **anxieuse**) adj anxious ▷ Il est anxieux de nature. He's a born worrier.

août [u] nm August; **en août** in August

apercevoir [apɛʀsəvwaʀ] vb to see ▷ J'aperçois la côte. I can see the shore.; **s'apercevoir de quelque chose** to notice something; **s'apercevoir que…** to notice that…

apparaître [apaʀɛtʀ(ə)] vb to appear

appareil [apaʀɛj] nm device; **un appareil orthodontique** braces; **les appareils ménagers** domestic appliances; **un appareil photo** a camera; **Qui est à l'appareil?** (on phone) Who's speaking?

apparemment [apaʀamɑ̃] adv apparently

apparence [apaʀɑ̃s] nf appearance

apparition [apaʀisjɔ̃] nf appearance ▷ Il n'a fait qu'une brève apparition. He appeared only briefly.

appartement [apaʀtəmɑ̃] nm apartment

appartenir [apaʀtəniʀ] vb: **appartenir à quelqu'un** to belong to somebody

apparu [apaʀy] vb see **apparaître**

appel [apɛl] nm ❶ cry ▷ un appel au secours a cry for help ❷ phone call; **faire appel à quelqu'un** to appeal to somebody; **formule d'appel** (in letter) salutation

appeler [aple] vb to call ▷ Elle a appelé le médecin. She called the doctor. ▷ J'ai appelé mon cousin à Trois-Rivières. I called my cousin in Trois-Rivières.; **s'appeler** to be called ▷ Comment ça s'appelle? What is it called? ▷ Elle s'appelle Muriel. Her name's Muriel. ▷ Comment tu

t'appelles? What's your name?

appétissant [apetisɑ̃, -ɑ̃t] (f **appétissante**) adj appetizing

appétit [apeti] nm appetite; **Bon appétit!** Enjoy your meal!

applaudir [aplodiʀ] vb (applaud) to clap

applaudissements [aplodismɑ̃] nmpl applause

appli [apli] nf (computer) app

application [aplikasjɔ̃] nf (computer) application ▷ lancer une application to open an application

appliquer [aplike] vb ❶ to apply ❷ to enforce ▷ appliquer la loi to enforce the law; **s'appliquer** to apply oneself ▷ Elle s'est appliquée à étudier. She applied herself to studying.

apporter [apɔʀte] vb to bring

appréhender [apʀeɑ̃de] vb to dread

apprendre [apʀɑ̃dʀ(ə)] vb ❶ to learn ▷ apprendre quelque chose par cœur to learn something by heart; **apprendre à faire quelque chose** to learn to do something ▷ J'apprends à faire la cuisine. I'm learning to cook. ❷ (news) to hear ▷ J'ai appris son départ. I heard that she had left.; **apprendre quelque chose à quelqu'un (1)** to teach somebody something ▷ Ma mère m'a appris l'anglais. My mother taught me English. ▷ Elle lui a appris à conduire. She taught him to drive. **(2)** to tell somebody something ▷ Il m'a appris la nouvelle. He told me the news.

apprentissage [apʀɑ̃tisaʒ] nm learning ▷ On dit que l'apprentissage de l'arabe est très difficile. They say learning Arabic is very difficult.

appris [apʀi] vb see **apprendre**

approbation [apʀɔbasjɔ̃] nf approval ▷ donner son approbation to give one's approval

approcher [apʀɔʃe] vb: **approcher de** to approach ▷ **Nous approchons de Fredericton.** We are approaching Fredericton.; **s'approcher de** to come close to ▷ **N'approche pas, j'ai la grippe!** Don't get too close to me, I've got the flu!

approprié [apʀɔpʀije] (f **appropriée**) adj suitable ▷ **une réponse appropriée** a suitable answer

approuver [apʀuve] vb to approve of ▷ **Je n'approuve pas ses méthodes.** I don't approve of his methods.

approximatif [apʀɔksimatif, -iv] (f **approximative**) adj
① approximate ▷ **un prix approximatif** an approximate price
② rough ▷ **un calcul approximatif** a rough calculation

appui [apɥi] nm support ▷ **J'ai besoin de votre appui.** I need your support.

appuyer [apɥije] vb to lean ▷ **Elle a appuyé son vélo contre la porte.** She leaned her bike against the door.; **appuyer sur** to press ▷ **Appuyez sur le bouton.** Press the button.; **s'appuyer** to lean ▷ **Elle s'est appuyée contre le mur.** She leaned against the wall. ▷ **Il s'est appuyé sur la table.** He leaned on the table.

après [apʀe] prep, adv ① after ▷ **après le déjeuner** after lunch ▷ **après son départ** after he had left ▷ **après qu'il est parti** after he left ▷ **Nous viendrons après avoir fait la vaisselle.** We'll come after we've done the dishes. ② afterwards ▷ **aussitôt après** immediately afterwards; **après coup** afterwards ▷ **J'y ai repensé après coup.** I thought about it again afterwards.; **d'après** according to ▷ **D'après elle, c'est une erreur.** According to her, that's a mistake.; **après tout** after all

après-demain [apʀɛdmɛ̃] adv the day after tomorrow

après-midi [apʀemidi] m or nf afternoon

arachide [aʀaʃid] nf peanut ▷ **le beurre d'arachide** peanut butter

araignée [aʀɛɲe] nf spider

arbitre [aʀbitʀ(ə)] nmf ① referee ② umpire

arbre [aʀbʀ(ə)] nm tree; **un arbre généalogique** a family tree

arbuste [aʀbyst(ə)] nm shrub

arc [aʀk] nm bow ▷ **son arc et ses flèches** his bow and arrows

arc-en-ciel [aʀkɑ̃sjɛl] (pl **arcs-en-ciel**) nm rainbow

architecte [aʀʃitɛkt(ə)] nmf architect ▷ **Elle est architecte.** She's an architect.

architecture [aʀʃitɛktyʀ] nf architecture

aréna [aʀena] nm arena ▷ **On construit un nouvel aréna à Timmins.** They're building a new arena in Timmins.

arène [aʀɛn] nf bullring; **des arènes romaines** a Roman amphitheatre; **l'arène politique** the political arena

arête [aʀɛt] nf fish bone

argent [aʀʒɑ̃] nm ① silver ▷ **une bague en argent** a silver ring ② money ▷ **Je n'ai plus d'argent.** I have no more money.; **l'argent de poche** allowance ▷ **Est-ce que tu reçois de l'argent de poche chaque semaine?** Do you get a weekly allowance?; **l'argent liquide** cash

argile [aʀʒil] nf clay

argot [aʀgo] nm slang

arme [aʀm(ə)] nf weapon; **une arme à feu** a firearm

armée [aʀme] nf army; **l'armée de l'air** the Air Force

armoire [aʀmwaʀ] nf wardrobe

armure [aʀmyʀ] nf armour ▷ **une**

chevalier en armure a knight in armour

arnaquer [aʀnake] vb (*informal*) to con

aromatisé [aʀɔmatize] (f **aromatisée**) adj flavoured

arôme [aʀom] nm ❶ aroma ❷ (added to food) flavouring; *arômes naturels* natural flavours

arpenter [aʀpɑ̃te] vb to pace up and down ▷ *Il arpentait le couloir.* He was pacing up and down the corridor.

arrache-pied [aʀaʃpje]: **d'arrache-pied** adv furiously ▷ *travailler d'arrache-pied* to work furiously

arracher [aʀaʃe] vb ❶ to take out ▷ *La dentiste m'a arraché une dent.* The dentist took one of my teeth out. ❷ to tear out ▷ *Arrachez la page.* Tear the page out. ❸ to pull up ▷ *Il a arraché les mauvaises herbes.* He pulled up the weeds.; *arracher quelque chose à quelqu'un* to snatch something from somebody

arranger [aʀɑ̃ʒe] vb ❶ to arrange ▷ *arranger des fleurs dans un vase* to arrange flowers in a vase ❷ to suit ▷ *Ça t'arrange de partir plus tôt?* Would it suit you to leave earlier?; *s'arranger* to come to an agreement ▷ *Arrangez-vous avec le patron.* You'll have to come to an agreement with the boss.; **Je vais m'arranger pour venir.** I'll organize things so that I can come.; **Ça va s'arranger.** Things will work themselves out.

arrestation [aʀɛstasjɔ̃] nf arrest ▷ *en état d'arrestation* under arrest

arrêt [aʀɛ] nm ❶ stop ▷ *un arrêt d'autobus* a bus stop; **sans arrêt** (1) non-stop ▷ *Elle travaille sans arrêt.* She works non-stop. (2) continually ▷ *Ils se disputent sans*

arrêt. They quarrel continually.

arrêter [aʀete] vb ❶ to stop; **Arrête!** Stop it!; *arrêter de faire quelque chose* to stop doing something ❷ to switch off ▷ *Il a arrêté le moteur.* He switched the engine off. ❸ to arrest ▷ *Ma voisine a été arrêtée.* My neighbour's been arrested.; *s'arrêter* to stop ▷ *Il s'est arrêté devant une vitrine.* He stopped in front of a store window.; *s'arrêter de faire quelque chose* to stop doing something ▷ *s'arrêter de fumer* to stop smoking

arrière [aʀjɛʀ] nm back ▷ *l'arrière de la maison* the back of the house; **à l'arrière** at the back; **en arrière** behind ▷ *Ils sont restés en arrière.* They stayed behind.
▸ adj (f+pl arrière) back ▷ *le siège arrière* the back seat ▷ *les roues arrière* the rear wheels

arrière-grand-mère [aʀjɛʀɡʀɑ̃mɛʀ] (pl arrière-grands-mères) nf great-grandmother

arrière-grand-père [aʀjɛʀɡʀɑ̃pɛʀ] (pl arrière-grands-pères) nm great-grandfather

arrivée [aʀive] nf arrival ▷ *l'arrivée des passagers* the passengers' arrival; **ligne d'arrivée** finish line ▷ *Elle a franchi la ligne d'arrivée.* She crossed the finish line.

arriver [aʀive] vb ❶ to arrive ▷ *J'arrive à l'école à huit heures.* I arrive at school at 8 o'clock. ❷ to happen ▷ *Qu'est-ce qui est arrivé à maman?* What happened to Mom?; *arriver à faire quelque chose* to manage to do something ▷ *J'espère que je vais y arriver.* I hope I can manage it.; **Il m'arrive de dormir jusqu'à midi.** I sometimes sleep till noon.

arrogant [aʀɔɡɑ̃, -ɑ̃t] (f **arrogante**) adj arrogant

arrondissement [aʀɔdismɑ̃]
nm district

arroser [aʀoze] *vb* to water ▷ *Il
arrose ses tomates.* He is watering his
tomatoes.

arrosoir [aʀozwaʀ] *nm* watering
can

art [aʀ] *nm* art

artère [aʀtɛʀ] *nf* **❶** artery
❷ main road ▷ *les grandes artères de
Calgary* the main roads of Calgary

article [aʀtikl(ə)] *nm* **❶** article
▷ *un article de journal* a newspaper
article **❷** item ▷ *les articles en
promotion* items on special; **un
article de forum** (*on a listserv*)
a post

articulation [aʀtikylɑsjɔ̃] *nf*
joint ▷ *l'articulation du genou* the
knee joint

articuler [aʀtikyle] *vb* to
pronounce clearly

artificiel [aʀtifisjɛl] (*f* **artificielle**)
adj artificial ▷ *des plantes artificielles*
artificial plants

artisan [aʀtizɑ̃] *nm* (*self-employed*)
crafter; **être artisan de quelque
chose** to be the architect of
something

artisanat [aʀtizana] *nm* crafts;
boutique d'artisanat craft shop

artisane [aʀtizan] *nf* (*self-
employed*) crafter

artiste [aʀtist(ə)] *nmf* **❶** artist
❷ performer

artistique [aʀtistik] *adj* artistic

arts plastiques *nmpl* fine arts

as [ɑs] *vb see* **avoir**; **Tu as de beaux
cheveux.** You have nice hair.
▸ *nm* ace ▷ *l'as de trèfle* the ace
of clubs

ascenseur [asɑ̃sœʀ] *nm* elevator

aspect [aspɛ] *nm* appearance

asperge [aspɛʀʒ(ə)] *nf* asparagus

aspirateur [aspiʀatœʀ]
nm vacuum cleaner; **passer

l'aspirateur** to vacuum

aspirine [aspiʀin] *nf* aspirin

assaisonner [asezɔne] *vb* to
season

assassin [asasɛ̃] *nm* murderer
▷ *Cette femme est un assassin.* This
woman is a murderer.

assassiner [asasine] *vb* to murder

**Assemblée des Premières
Nations** *nf* Assembly of First
Nations

assembler [asɑ̃ble] *vb* to
assemble; **s'assembler** to gather
▷ *Une foule énorme s'était assemblée.*
A huge crowd had gathered.

s'**asseoir** [aswaʀ] *vb* to sit down
▷ *Asseyez-vous, s'il vous plaît.* Please
sit down. ▷ *Assieds-toi à côté de moi.*
Sit beside me.

assez [ase] *adv* **❶** enough ▷ *Nous
n'avons pas assez de temps.* We don't
have enough time. ▷ *Est-ce qu'il
y a assez de pain?* Is there enough
bread?; **J'en ai assez!** I've had
enough! **❷** quite ▷ *Il faisait assez
beau.* The weather was quite nice.

assiette [asjɛt] *nf* plate ▷ *une
assiette à dessert* a dessert plate;
une assiette de charcuterie
assorted cold cuts

assis [asi, -iz] (*f* **assise**) *vb see*
asseoir
▸ *adj* sitting ▷ *Elle est assise par terre.*
She's sitting on the floor.

assistance [asistɑ̃s] *nf*
❶ audience ▷ *Y a-t-il un médecin
dans l'assistance?* Is there a doctor in
the audience? **❷** aid ▷ *l'assistance
humanitaire* humanitarian aid
❸ assistance ▷ *avec l'assistance de
quelqu'un* with the assistance of
somebody

assistant [asistɑ̃] *nm* assistant

assistante [asistɑ̃t] *nf* assistant

assister [asiste] *vb*: **assister à un
accident** to witness an accident;

assister à un cours to attend a class; **assister à un concert** to be at a concert

association [asɔsjɑsjɔ̃] nf association

associé [asɔsje] nm (in business) partner

associée [asɔsje] nf (in business) partner

associer [asɔsje] vb to connect ▷ J'associe l'été au camping. I connect summer with camping.; **s'associer** to go into partnership

assommer [asɔme] vb to knock out ▷ Un coup fort l'a assommé. A heavy blow knocked him out.

assorti [asɔrti] (f**assortie**) adj
❶ matching ▷ des couleurs assorties matching colours ❷ assorted ▷ des chocolats assortis assorted chocolates; **être assorti à quelque chose** to match something ▷ Son sac à main est assorti à ses chaussures. Her purse matches her shoes.

assortiment [asɔrtimɑ̃] nm assortment

assurance [asyrɑ̃s] nf
❶ insurance ▷ une assurance maladie medical insurance
❷ confidence ▷ parler avec assurance to speak with confidence

assurer [asyre] vb ❶ to insure ▷ La maison est assurée. The house is insured. ❷ être assuré contre quelque chose to be insured against something ❷ to assure ▷ Je t'assure que c'est vrai! I assure you it's true!; **s'assurer de quelque chose** to make sure of something ▷ Il s'est assuré que la porte était fermée. He made sure the door was shut.

asthme [asm(ə)] nm asthma ▷ une crise d'asthme an asthma attack

astronaute [astronot] nmf astronaut

astronome [astronɔm] nmf

astronomer

astronomie [astronɔmi] nf astronomy

astucieux [astysjø, -øz] (f **astucieuse**) adj clever

atelier [atalje] nm ❶ workshop ❷ (artist's) studio

athlète [atlɛt] nmf athlete

athlétisme [atletism(ə)] nm track and field ▷ un championnat d'athlétisme a track and field championship

atlas [atlɑs] nm atlas

atmosphère [atmɔsfɛr] nf atmosphere

atomique [atɔmik] adj atomic ▷ la bombe atomique the atomic bomb

atout [atu] nm ❶ asset ▷ L'atout principal de ce joueur, c'est sa vitesse. This player's main asset is his speed. ❷ trump card ▷ J'avais quatre atouts dans mon jeu. I had four trump cards in my hand.

atroce [atrɔs] adj terrible

attachant [atafɑ̃, -ɑ̃t] (f **attachante**) adj lovable

attacher [atafe] vb to tie up ▷ Elle a attaché ses cheveux avec un élastique. She tied her hair up with an elastic band.; **s'attacher à quelqu'un** to become attached to somebody; **une poêle qui n'attache pas** a non-stick frying pan

attaquer [atake] vb to attack

atteindre [atɛ̃dr(ə)] vb to reach

attendant [atɑ̃dɑ̃]: **en attendant** adv in the meantime

attendre [atɑ̃dr(ə)] vb to wait ▷ attendre quelqu'un to wait for someone ▷ J'attends d'avoir un appartement à moi. I'm waiting until I have an apartment of my own. ▷ Attends qu'il ne pleuve plus. Wait until it stops raining.; **attendre un enfant** to be expecting a baby; **s'attendre à** to expect ▷ *Je m'attends à ce qu'ils soient en retard.* I expect they'll be late.

> Be careful! **attendre** does not mean **to attend**.

attentat [atɑta] *nm*: **un attentat à la bombe** a terrorist attack

attente [atɑ̃t] *nf* wait ▷ *deux heures d'attente* a two-hour wait; **la salle d'attente** the waiting room

attentif [atɑtif, -iv] (*f* **attentive**) *adj* attentive

attention [atɑsjɔ̃] *nf* attention ▷ *à l'attention de* to the attention of; **faire attention (1)** to be careful **(2)** to pay attention ▷ *Ne fais pas attention à cette remarque-là.* Pay no attention to that remark.; **Attention!** Watch out! ▷ *Attention, tu vas te faire écraser!* Watch out, you'll get run over!

attentionné [atɑsjone] (*f* **attentionnée**) *adj* thoughtful

attentivement [atɑtivmɑ̃] *adv*
❶ carefully ▷ *lire attentivement* to read carefully ❷ closely ▷ *observer attentivement* to observe closely

atterrir [ateRiR] *vb* to land

atterrissage [aterisaʒ] *nm* (*of plane*) landing

attirant [atiRɑ̃, -ɑ̃t] (*f* **attirante**) *adj* attractive

attirer [atiRe] *vb* to attract ▷ *attirer l'attention de quelqu'un* to attract somebody's attention; **s'attirer des ennuis** to get into trouble ▷ *Si tu continues, tu vas t'attirer des ennuis.* If you keep that up, you'll get yourself into trouble.

attitude [atityd] *nf* attitude

attraction [atRaksjɔ̃] *nf*: **une attraction touristique** a tourist attraction; **un parc d'attractions** an amusement park

attraper [atRape] *vb* to catch

attrayant [atRejɑ̃, -ɑ̃t] (*f* **attrayante**) *adj* attractive

au [o] *prep see* **à**

> **au** is the contracted form of **à** + **le**.

au printemps in the spring

aube [ob] *nf* dawn ▷ *à l'aube* at dawn

auberge [obeRʒ(ə)] *nf* inn; **auberge de jeunesse** a youth hostel

aucun [okœ̃, -yn] (*f* **aucune**) *adj*, *pron* ❶ no ▷ *Il n'a aucun ami.* He has no friends. ▷ *Aucun enfant ne pourrait le faire.* No child could do that. ❷ none ▷ *Aucun d'entre eux n'est venu.* None of them came. ▷ *Aucune de mes amies n'aime le football.* None of my female friends like football. ▷ *« Tu aimes ses films? »* — *« Je n'en ai vu aucun. »* "Do you like his films?" — "I haven't seen any of them."; **sans aucun doute** without any doubt

au-delà [odla] *adv*: **au-delà de** beyond ▷ *Votre ticket n'est pas valable au-delà de cette limite.* Your ticket is not valid beyond this point.

au-dessous [odsu] *adv*
❶ downstairs ▷ *Ils habitent au-dessous.* They live downstairs.
❷ underneath; **au-dessous de** under ▷ *au-dessous du pont* under the bridge ▷ *dix degrés au-dessous de zéro* ten degrees below zero

au-dessus [odsy] *adv* ❶ upstairs ▷ *J'habite au-dessus.* I live upstairs.
❷ above; **au-dessus de** above ▷ *au-dessus de la table* above the table

audio [odjo] (*f+pl* **audio**) *adj* audio ▷ *des fichiers audio* audio files ▷ *le matériel audio* audio equipment; **un audioclip** an audio clip

audiovisuel [odjovizɥɛl] (*f* **audiovisuelle**) *adj* audiovisual

auditeur [oditœR] *nm* (*to radio*)

listener

audition [odisjɔ̃] nf audition

auditionner [odisjɔne] vb to audition

auditrice [oditʁis] nf (to radio) listener

augmentation [ɔɡmɑ̃tasjɔ̃] nf rise ▷ *une augmentation de prix* a rise in prices: **une augmentation de salaire** a raise

augmenter [ɔɡmɑ̃te] vb to increase

aujourd'hui [oʒuʁdɥi] adv today

auparavant [opaʁavɑ̃] adv first ▷ *Vous pouvez utiliser l'ordinateur, mais auparavant vous devez taper le mot de passe.* You can use the computer but first you have to key in the password.

auquel [okɛl] (mpl **auxquels**, fpl **auxquelles**) pron

auquel is the contracted form of **à** + **lequel**.

▷ *l'homme auquel j'ai parlé* the man I spoke to

aura, aurai, auras, aurez, aurons, auront vb see **avoir**

aurore boréale [ɔʁɔʁbɔʁeal] nf northern lights

aussi [osi] adv ❶ too ▷ « *Dors bien.* » — « *Toi aussi.* » "Sleep well." — "You too." ▷ *Elle aussi parle espagnol.* She too speaks Spanish. ❷ also ▷ *J'aimerais aussi que tu achètes le journal.* I'd also like you to get the paper. ▷ *Je parle anglais et aussi allemand.* I speak English and also German.; **aussi ... que** as ... as ▷ *aussi grand que moi* as big as me

aussitôt [osito] adv right away ▷ *aussitôt après son retour* right after his return; **aussitôt que** as soon as ▷ *aussitôt que tu auras fini* as soon as you're finished

autant [otɑ̃] adv: **autant de** **(1)** so much ▷ *Je ne veux pas autant*

de gâteau. I don't want so much cake. **(2)** so many ▷ *Je n'ai jamais vu autant de monde.* I've never seen so many people.; **autant ... que (1)** as much ... as ▷ *J'ai autant d'argent que toi.* I've got as much money as you have. **(2)** as many ... as ▷ *J'ai autant d'amis que lui.* I've got as many friends as he has.; **d'autant plus que** all the more since ▷ *Elle est d'autant plus déçue qu'ils le lui avaient promis.* She's all the more disappointed since they had promised her.; **d'autant moins que** even less since ▷ *C'est d'autant moins pratique pour nous que nous devons changer deux fois d'autobus.* It's even less convenient for us since we have to change buses twice.

auteur [otœʁ] nm author

auteure [otœʁ] nf author

auto [oto] nf car

autobus [otobys] nm bus ▷ *en autobus* by bus ▷ *l'autobus scolaire* school bus

autochtone [otɔktɔn] adj, nmf Aboriginal; **un autochtone** an Aboriginal man; **une autochtone** an Aboriginal woman; **les autochtones** the Aboriginal peoples

autocollant [otɔkɔlɑ̃, -ɑ̃t] (f **autocollante**) adj self-adhesive ▷ *une étiquette autocollante* a self-adhesive label; **une enveloppe autocollante** a self-seal envelope ▶ nm sticker

auto-école [otoekɔl] (pl les **auto-écoles**) nf driving school

automatique [otɔmatik] adj automatic

automne [otɔn] nm fall; **en automne** in the fall

automobile [otɔmɔbil] adj: **une course automobile** a car race ▶ nf car

automobiliste [ɔtɔmɔbilist(ə)] nmf motorist

autoradio [ɔtɔradjo] nm car radio

autorisation [ɔtɔrizasjɔ̃] nf ❶ permission ▷ Elle m'a donné l'autorisation de sortir ce soir. She's given me permission to go out tonight. ❷ permit ▷ Il faut une autorisation pour camper ici. You need a permit to camp here.

autoriser [ɔtɔrize] vb to give permission for ▷ Il m'a autorisé à en parler. He's given me permission to talk about it.

autoritaire [ɔtɔritɛr] adj authoritarian

autorité [ɔtɔrite] nf authority

autoroute [ɔtɔrut] nf highway

auto-stop [ɔtɔstɔp] nm: **faire de l'auto-stop** to hitchhike

auto-stoppeur [ɔtɔstɔpœr] nm hitchhiker

auto-stoppeuse [ɔtɔstɔpøz] nf hitchhiker

autour [otur] adv around ▷ autour de la maison around the house

autre [otr(ə)] adj, pron other ▷ Je viendrai un autre jour. I'll come some other day. ▷ J'ai d'autres projets. I've got other plans.; **autre chose** something else; **un autre** another ▷ Tu veux un autre morceau de gâteau? Would you like another piece of cake?; **l'autre** the other ▷ Non, pas celui-ci, l'autre. No, not that one, the other one.; **d'autres** others ▷ Je t'en apporterai d'autres. I'll bring you some others.; **les autres** others ▷ Les autres sont arrivés plus tard. The others arrived later.; **ni l'un ni l'autre** neither of them; **entre autres** among other things ▷ Nous avons parlé, entre autres, de nos projets de vacances. We talked about our holiday plans, among other things.

autrefois [otrəfwa] adv in the old days

autrement [otrəmã] adv ❶ differently ▷ Elle l'a fait autrement. She did it differently. ❷ otherwise ▷ Je n'ai pas pu faire autrement. I couldn't do otherwise.; **autrement dit** in other words

autruche [otryʃ] nf ostrich

aux [o] prep see **à**

> **aux** is the contracted form of **à** + **les**.

▷ J'ai dit aux enfants d'aller jouer. I told the children to go and play.

auxquelles [okɛl] pron

> **auxquelles** is the contracted form of **à** + **lesquelles**.

▷ les revues auxquelles il est abonné the magazines to which he subscribes

auxquels [okɛl] pron

> **auxquels** is the contracted form of **à** + **lesquels**.

▷ les enfants auxquels il a parlé the children he spoke to

avaient, avais, avait vb see **avoir; Il y avait beaucoup de monde.** There were a lot of people.

avalanche [avalɑ̃ʃ] nf avalanche

avaler [avale] vb to swallow

avance [avɑ̃s] nf: **être en avance** to be early; **à l'avance** beforehand ▷ réserver une place à l'avance to book a seat beforehand; **d'avance** in advance ▷ payer d'avance to pay in advance; **l'avance rapide** fast forward

avancé [avɑ̃se] (**avancée**) adj advanced ▷ à un niveau avancé at an advanced level; **bien avancé** well under way ▷ Les travaux sont déjà bien avancés. The work is already well under way.

avancer [avɑ̃se] vb ❶ to move forward ▷ Elle avançait prudemment. She was moving forward cautiously. ❷ (date) to move up ▷ *La date de l'examen a été avancée.* The date of the exam has been moved up. ❸ to put ahead ▷ *Il a avancé sa montre d'une heure.* He put his watch ahead an hour. ❹ (*watch*) to be fast ▷ *Ma montre avance d'une heure.* My watch is an hour fast. ▷ *Peux-tu m'avancer dix dollars?* Can you lend me 10 dollars?

avant [avɑ̃] *prep, adj* ❶ before ▷ *avant qu'il ne pleuve* before it rains ▷ *avant de partir* before leaving ❷ front ▷ *la roue avant* the front wheel ▷ *le siège avant* the front seat; **avant tout** above all

▶ *nm* front ▷ *l'avant de la voiture* the front of the car; **à l'avant** in front; **en avant** forward ▷ *Elle a fait un pas en avant.* She took a step forward.

avantage [avɑ̃taʒ] *nm* advantage

avant-dernier [avɑ̃dɛʁnje, -jɛʁ] (*f* **avant-dernière**, *mpl* **avant-derniers**) *adj* second-last ▷ *l'avant-dernière page* the second-last page ▷ *Ils sont arrivés avant-derniers.* They arrived second-last.

avant-hier [avɑ̃tjɛʁ] *adv* the day before yesterday ▷ *Il est arrivé avant-hier.* He arrived the day before yesterday.

avec [avɛk] *prep* with ▷ *avec ma mère* with my mother; **Et avec ça?** (*in store*) Anything else?

avenir [avniʁ] *nm* future; **à l'avenir** in future ▷ *À l'avenir, essayez d'être à l'heure.* Try to be on time in future.; **dans un proche avenir** in the near future

aventure [avɑ̃tyʁ] *nf* adventure

aventureux [avɑ̃tyʁø, -øz] (*f* **aventureuse**) *adj* adventurous

aventurier [avɑ̃tyʁje] *nm* adventurer

aventurière [avɑ̃tyʁjɛʁ] *nf* adventurer

avenue [avny] *nf* avenue

averse [avɛʁs(ə)] *nf* (*of rain*) shower

avertir [avɛʁtiʁ] *vb* to warn; **avertir quelqu'un de quelque chose** to warn somebody about something

avertissement [avɛʁtismɑ̃] *nm* warning

aveugle [avœɡl(ə)] *adj* blind

avion [avjɔ̃] *nm* plane; **aller en avion** to go by plane ▷ *Il est allé en Alberta en avion.* He flew to Alberta.; **par avion** by airmail

aviron [aviʁɔ̃] *nm* (*canoe*) paddle ▷ *un aviron en bois* a wooden paddle

avis [avi] *nm* ❶ opinion ▷ *J'aimerais avoir ton avis.* I'd like to have your opinion. ▷ *à mon avis* in my opinion; **changer d'avis** to change one's mind ▷ *J'ai changé d'avis.* I've changed my mind. ❷ notice ▷ *jusqu'à nouvel avis* until further notice

avocat [avɔka] *nm* ❶ lawyer ▷ *Il est avocat.* He's a lawyer. ❷ avocado

avocate [avɔkat] *nf* lawyer ▷ *Elle est avocate.* She's a lawyer.

avoine [avwan] *nf* oats

avoir [avwaʁ] *vb* ❶ to have ▷ *Ils ont deux enfants.* They have two children. ▷ *Elle a les yeux bleus.* She has blue eyes. ▷ *J'ai déjà mangé.* I've already eaten. ▷ *Est-ce que tu as vu ce film?* Have you seen this film? ▷ *Je leur ai parlé hier.* I spoke to them yesterday.; **On t'a bien eu!** (*informal*) You've been had! ❷ to be ▷ *Elle a trois ans.* She's three. ▷ *J'avais dix ans quand je l'ai rencontré.* I was ten when I met him.; **il y a (1)** there is ▷ *Il y a quelqu'un à la porte.* There's somebody at the door. **(2)** there are ▷ *Il y a des chocolats sur la table.* There are some chocolates on the table. **(3)** ago ▷ *Je l'ai rencontré il y a deux ans.* I met him two years ago.; **Qu'est-ce qu'il y a?** What's the matter?; **Il n'y a qu'à partir plus tôt.** We'll just have to leave earlier.

avortement [avɔrtəmɑ̃] *nm* abortion

avouer [avwe] *vb* to admit

avril [avril] *nm* April; **en avril** in April

ayez, ayons *vb* see **avoir**

b

babillard [babijar] *nm* billboard; **un babillard électronique** (*computer*) a bulletin board

baby-foot [babifut] *nm* foosball ▷ *jouer au baby-foot* to play foosball

bac [bak] *nm* = **baccalauréat**

baccalauréat [bakalɔrea] *nm* B.A. ▷ *un baccalauréat en histoire* a B.A. in history

bâcler [bɑkle] *vb* to botch ▷ *Je déteste le travail bâclé!* I hate work that's not done properly!

bagage [bagaʒ] *nm* luggage; **faire ses bagages** to pack; **les bagages à main** hand luggage ▷ *un bagage à main* a piece of hand luggage

bagarre [bagar] *nf* fight ▷ *Une bagarre a éclaté dans la cour de l'école.* A fight broke out in the schoolyard.

se bagarrer [bagare] *vb* to fight ▷ *Il s'est encore bagarré avec son frère.* He's been fighting with his brother again.

bague [bag] nf ring

baguel [begœl] nm bagel ▷ *un baguel grillé* a toasted bagel

baguette [baget] nf ❶ stick of French bread ❷ chopstick ▷ *manger avec les baguettes* to eat with chopsticks; **une baguette magique** a magic wand

baie [bɛ] nf ❶ hay ❷ berry

baie d'Hudson Hudson Bay

baignade [bɛɲad] nf: **« baignade interdite »** "no swimming"

se baigner [beɲe] vb to go swimming ▷ *Si on allait se baigner?* Shall we go swimming?

baignoire [bɛɲwaʀ] nf bathtub

bâiller [baje] vb to yawn

bain [bɛ̃] nm bath ▷ *prendre un bain* to take a bath ▷ *prendre un bain de soleil* to sunbathe

baiser [beze] nm kiss

baisse [bɛs] nf decrease ▷ *la baisse du taux de chômage* the fall in the unemployment rate; **être en baisse** to be falling

baisser [bese] vb ❶ to turn down ▷ *Tu peux baisser le chauffage.* You can turn down the heat. ❷ to fall ▷ *Le prix des lecteurs MP3 a baissé.* The price of MP3 players has fallen.; **se baisser** to bend down ▷ *Elle s'est baissée pour ramasser son cahier.* She bent down to pick up her notebook.

bal [bal] nm dance ▷ *un bal populaire* a local dance

balade [balad] nf (informal) walk ▷ *faire une balade* to go for a walk

se balader [balade] vb (informal) to wander around ▷ *J'adore me balader dans les rues du Vieux-Québec.* I love to wander around the streets of old Quebec City.

baladeur [baladœʀ] nm personal stereo

balai [balɛ] nm broom ▷ *Je vais donner un coup de balai dans la cuisine.* I'm going to sweep the kitchen.

balance [balɑ̃s] nf (for weighing) scales; **la Balance** Libra ▷ *Elle est Balance.* She's a Libra.

se balancer [balɑ̃se] vb to swing

balançoire [balɑ̃swaʀ] nf swing

balayer [baleje] vb ❶ to sweep ▷ *J'ai balayé la cuisine.* I swept the kitchen. ❷ to sweep up ▷ *Va balayer les feuilles sur le patio.* Go and sweep up the leaves on the patio.

balbutier [balbysje] vb to stammer

balcon [balkɔ̃] nm balcony

baleine [balɛn] nf whale

balle [bal] nf ❶ ball ▷ *une balle de tennis* a tennis ball ❷ bullet

ballerine [balʀin] nf ❶ ballet dancer ❷ ballet shoe ▷ *une paire de ballerines rouges* a pair of red ballet shoes

ballet [balɛ] nm ballet

ballon [balɔ̃] nm ❶ ball ▷ *lancer le ballon* to throw the ball; **un ballon de football** a football; **le ballon chasseur** dodgeball ❷ balloon

balnéaire [balneɛʀ] adj: **une station balnéaire** a seaside resort

banal [banal] (f **banale**, mpl **banaux**) adj ❶ commonplace ▷ *La violence est devenue banale à la télévision.* Violence has become commonplace on television. ❷ clichéd ▷ *L'intrigue du film est très banale.* The plot of the film is very clichéd.

banane [banan] nf banana ▷ *La banane est un fruit.* The banana is a fruit.

banc [bɑ̃] nm bench; **le banc de neige** snowbank

bancaire [bɑ̃kɛʀ] adj: **une carte bancaire** a bank card

bandage [bɑ̃daʒ] nm bandage

bande [bɑ̃d] nf ❶ gang ▷ *une bande de voyous* a gang of thugs ❷ bunch

▷ *C'est une bande d'idiots!* They're a bunch of idiots! ❶ (hockey) boards ▷ *L'autre joueuse m'a poussée dans la bande.* The other player shoved me into the boards.; **une bande dessinée** a comic strip; **une bande magnétique** a tape; **la bande sonore** the sound track; **Elle fait toujours bande à part.** She always keeps to herself.

bandeau [bɑ̃do] (pl **bandeaux**) nm headband

bander [bɑ̃de] vb to bandage ▷ *L'infirmière lui a bandé la jambe.* The nurse bandaged his leg.

bandit [bɑ̃di] nm bandit

banique [banik] nf bannock

banlieue [bɑ̃ljø] nf suburbs ▷ *Elle habite en banlieue.* She lives in the suburbs.; **les trains de banlieue** commuter trains

banque [bɑ̃k] nf bank; **la banque alimentaire** food bank

banquet [bɑ̃kɛ] nm banquet ▷ *le banquet annuel de l'association* the club's annual banquet

banquette [bɑ̃kɛt] nf seat ▷ *la banquette arrière de la voiture* the back seat of the car

baquet [bakɛ] nm (laundry) tub

barachois [baraʃwa] nm barachois

⊙ A **barachois** is a tidal pond partly
⊙ obstructed by a sand bar. In the
⊙ Atlantic provinces and the Gulf of
⊙ St. Lawrence, people often moor
⊙ small boats in barachois. Many
⊙ restaurants and hotels bear
⊙ names such as "Au Barachois" or
⊙ "Auberge Le Barachois."

barbare [baʀbaʀ] adj barbaric

barbe [baʀb(ə)] nf beard ▷ *Il porte la barbe.* He beard.; **la barbe à papa** cotton candy

barbecue [baʀbəkju] nm barbecue ▷ *être invité à un barbecue*

to be invited to a barbecue ▷ *faire griller du saumon au barbecue* to barbecue salmon; **du poulet grillé au barbecue** barbecued chicken

barbouiller [baʀbuje] vb to smear ▷ *Les murs étaient barbouillés de graffitis.* The walls were plastered with graffiti.; **J'ai l'estomac barbouillé.** (informal) I feel queasy.

barbu [baʀby] (f **barbue**) adj bearded ▷ *un grand barbu* a big, bearded man

baromètre [baʀɔmɛtʀ(ə)] nm barometer

barrage [baʀaʒ] nm dam; **un barrage de police** a police roadblock

barre [baʀ] nf (metal) bar ▷ *une barre de fer* an iron bar; **la barre d'outils** (computer) toolbar; **la barre oblique inverse** backslash

barreau [baʀo] (pl **barreaux**) nm (on window) bar ▷ *Il s'est retrouvé derrière les barreaux.* He ended up behind bars.

barrer [baʀe] vb to block ▷ *Il y a un tronc d'arbre qui barre la route.* There's a tree trunk blocking the road.

barrette [baʀɛt] nf barrette

barrière [baʀjɛʀ] nf fence

bas [bɑ, bɑs] nm ❶ bottom ▷ *en bas de la page* at the bottom of the page ▷ *en bas de l'escalier* at the bottom of the stairs ❷ stocking ▷ *une paire de bas* a pair of stockings ▷ adj, adv (f **basse**) low ▷ *parler à voix basse* to speak in a low voice; **en bas (1)** down ▷ *Ça me donne le vertige de regarder en bas.* I get dizzy if I look down. **(2)** at the bottom ▷ *Son nom est tout en bas.* His name is at the bottom. ▷ *Il y a une porte en bas de l'escalier.* There's a door at the bottom of the stairs. **(3)** downstairs ▷ *Elle habite en bas.* She lives downstairs.

Bas-Canada nm Lower Canada

base [baz] nf base ▷ *la base de la pyramide* the base of the pyramid; **de base** basic ▷ *Le pain et le lait sont des aliments de base.* Bread and milk are basic foods.; **à base de** made from ▷ *des produits de beauté à base de plantes* cosmetics made from plants; **une base de données** a database

basket-ball [basketbol] nm basketball ▷ *jouer au basket-ball* to play basketball

basse [bɑs] adj see **bas**

basse-cour [baskur] (pl **basses-cours**) nf barnyard

bassin [basɛ̃] nm ❶ pond ▷ *Il y a un bassin à poissons rouges dans le parc.* There's a goldfish pond in the park. ❷ pelvis ▷ *une fracture du bassin* a fractured pelvis

bassine [basin] nf washbasin

bas-ventre [bavɑ̃tr(ə)] nm stomach ▷ *Elle se plaint de douleurs dans le bas-ventre.* She is complaining of pains in her stomach.

bataille [batɑj] nf battle

bateau [bato] (pl **bateaux**) nm boat

bateau-mouche [batomuʃ] (pl **bateaux-mouches**) nm pleasure boat

bâti [bɑti] (f **bâtie**) adj: **bien bâti** well-built

bâtiment [bɑtimɑ̃] nm building

bâtir [bɑtir] vb to build

bâton [bɑtɔ̃] nm stick ▷ *un coup de bâton* a blow with a stick ▷ *un bâton de hockey* a hockey stick

battement [batmɑ̃] nm: **J'ai dix minutes de battement.** I've got ten minutes free.; **un battement de cœur** heartbeat

batterie [batri] nf ❶ battery ❷ (car) ▷ *La batterie est à plat.* The battery is dead. ❸ drums ▷ *jouer de la batterie* to play the drums; **la batterie de cuisine** the pots and pans

batteur [batœr] nm drummer

battre [batr(ə)] vb to beat ▷ *Quand je la vois, mon cœur bat plus vite.* When I see her, my heart beats faster.; **se battre** to fight ▷ *Je me bats souvent avec mon frère.* I fight a lot with my brother.; **battre les cartes** to shuffle the cards; **battre les blancs en neige** beat the egg whites until stiff; **battre son plein** to be in full swing ▷ *A minuit, la fête battait son plein.* At midnight, the party was in full swing.

bavard [bavar, -ard(ə)] (f **bavarde**) adj talkative

bavardage [bavardaʒ] nm chat

bavarder [bavarde] vb to chat

baveux [bavø, -øz] (f **baveuse**) adj ❶ runny ▷ *une omelette baveuse* a runny omelette ❷ (informal) arrogant ▷ *Il est un peu trop baveux à mon goût.* I find him a bit too arrogant.

bavure [bavyr] nf blunder ▷ *une bavure policière* a police blunder

BD [bede] nf (= bande dessinée) comic strip ▷ *Elle adore les BD.* She loves comic strips.

béant [beɑ̃, -ɑ̃t] (f **béante**) adj gaping ▷ *un trou béant* a gaping hole

beau [bo, bɛl] (f **belle**, mpl **beaux**) adj, adv ❶ lovely ▷ *un beau cadeau* a lovely present ▷ *une belle journée* a lovely day

> **beau** changes to **bel** before a vowel and most words beginning with "h".

▷ *un bel été* a lovely summer ❷ beautiful ▷ *C'est une belle femme.* She is a beautiful woman. ❸ handsome ▷ *C'est un beau garçon.* He is a handsome boy.; **Il fait beau aujourd'hui.** It's a nice day today.; **J'ai beau essayer, je n'y arrive pas.** No matter how hard I try, I just can't do it.

beaucoup [boku] *adv* ❶ a lot
▷ *Il mange beaucoup.* He eats a lot.
❷ much ▷ *Elle n'a pas beaucoup d'argent.* She doesn't have much money. ▷ *Elle est beaucoup plus grande que moi.* She is much taller than me.; **beaucoup de** a lot of
▷ *Il y avait beaucoup de monde au concert.* There were a lot of people at the concert. ▷ *J'ai fait beaucoup de fautes.* I made a lot of mistakes.;
J'ai eu beaucoup de chance. I was very lucky.

beau-fils [bofis] (*pl* **beaux-fils**) *nm*
❶ son-in-law ❷ stepson

beau-frère [bofʀɛʀ] (*pl* **beaux-frères**) *nm* brother-in-law

beau-père [bopɛʀ] (*pl* **beaux-pères**) *nm* ❶ father-in-law
❷ stepfather

beauté [bote] *nf* beauty

beaux-arts [bozaʀ] *nmpl* fine arts

beaux-parents [boparɑ̃] *nmpl* in-laws

bébé [bebe] *nm* baby

bec [bɛk] *nm* ❶ beak ❷ little kiss
▷ *un petit bec sur la joue* a little kiss on the cheek; **le bec sucré** sweet tooth ▷ *Ma petite sœur a le bec sucré.* My little sister has a sweet tooth.

bêche [bɛʃ] *nf* spade

bêcher [beʃe] *vb* to dig ▷ *Il bêchait son jardin.* He was digging the garden.

bégayer [begeje] *vb* to stammer

beige [bɛʒ] *adj* beige

beigne [bɛɲ] *nf* doughnut

bel [bɛl] *adj see* **beau**

bélier [belje] *nm* ram; **le Bélier** Aries ▷ *Elle est Bélier.* She's an Aries.

belle [bɛl] *adj see* **beau**

belle-famille [bɛlfamij] (*pl* **belles-familles**) *nf* in-laws

belle-fille [bɛlfij] (*pl* **belles-filles**) *nf* ❶ daughter-in-law
❷ stepdaughter

belle-mère [bɛlmɛʀ] (*pl* **belles-mères**) *nf* ❶ mother-in-law
❷ stepmother

belle-sœur [bɛlsœʀ] (*pl* **belles-sœurs**) *nf* sister-in-law

bénédiction [benediksjɔ̃] *nf* blessing

bénéfice [benefis] *nm* profit ▷ *On a réalisé un bénéfice de 170 $ sur la vente de chocolats.* We made a profit of 170 $ on the chocolate sales.

bénévole [benevɔl] *adj* volunteer
▷ *du travail bénévole* volunteer work
▶ *n* volunteer

bénir [beniʀ] *vb* to bless

benjamin [bɛ̃ʒamɛ̃] *nm*
The youngest boy in a family is sometimes called **le benjamin**.

benjamine [bɛ̃ʒamin] *nf*
The youngest girl in a family is sometimes called **la benjamine**.

béquille [bekij] *nf* crutch ▷ *Il marche avec des béquilles.* He walks on crutches.

berceau [bɛʀso] (*pl* **berceaux**) *nm* cradle

bercer [bɛʀse] *vb* to rock

berceuse [bɛʀsøz] *nf* lullaby

béret [beʀɛbask(ə)] *nm* beret; **les bérets bleus** peacekeepers

berge [bɛʀʒ(ə)] *nf* (*of river*) bank

bernache du Canada [bɛʀnaʃ-] *nf* Canada goose

besoin [bəzwɛ̃] *nm* need; **avoir besoin de quelque chose** to need something ▷ *J'ai besoin d'argent.* I need some money. ▷ *J'ai besoin d'y réfléchir.* I need to think about it.; **une famille dans le besoin** a needy family

bétail [betaj] *nm* livestock

bête [bɛt] *nf* animal
▶ *adj* stupid

bêtise [betiz] *nf*: **faire une bêtise**
to do something stupid ▷ *Je crois
que j'ai fait une bêtise.* I think I've
done something stupid.; **dire des
bêtises** to talk nonsense ▷ *Tu dis
des bêtises!* You're talking nonsense!

béton [betɔ̃] *nm* concrete: **un alibi
en béton** a cast-iron alibi

betterave [bɛtʀav] *nf* beet

beurre [bœʀ] *nm* butter ▷ *une sauce
au beurre* a sauce made with butter;
beurre d'arachide peanut butter

beurrer [bœʀe] *vb* to butter

biberon [bibʀɔ̃] *nm* baby's bottle

bibliographie [biblijɔgʀafi] *nf*
bibliography

bibliothécaire [biblijɔtekɛʀ] *nmf*
librarian

bibliothèque [biblijɔtɛk] *nf*
❶ library ▷ *emprunter un livre à la
bibliothèque* to borrow a book from
the library ❷ bookcase ▷ *une
bibliothèque en chêne massif* a solid
oak bookcase

bicyclette [bisiklɛt] *nf* bicycle

bidon [bidɔ̃] *nm* can ▷ *un bidon
d'essence* a can of gas

bidonville [bidɔ̃vil] *nm* shanty
town

bidouiller [biduje] *vb* (*computer*)
to hack ▷ *Il passe des heures chaque
soir à bidouiller sur son ordinateur.*
He spends every night hacking on his
computer every night.

bidouilleur [bidujœʀ] *nm*
(*computer*) hacker

bidouilleuse [bidujøz] *nf*
(*computer*) hacker

bien [bjɛ̃] *nm* ❶ good ▷ *le bien et
le mal* good and evil ▷ *Elle m'a dit
beaucoup de bien de toi.* She told
me a lot of good things about
you. ▷ *C'est pour ton bien.* It's for
your own good.; **faire du bien à**

quelqu'un to do somebody good
▷ *Ses vacances lui ont fait beaucoup de
bien.* His holiday has done him a lot
of good. ❷ possession ▷ *son bien
le plus précieux* her most treasured
possession
▶ *adj, adv* ❶ well ▷ *Elle travaille
bien.* She works well. ▷ *Je me sens
bien.* I feel fine. ▷ *Je ne me sens pas
bien.* I don't feel well. ❷ good ▷ *Ce
restaurant est vraiment bien.* This
restaurant is really good. ❸ quite
▷ *bien assez* quite enough; **Je veux
bien le faire.** I'm quite willing to
do it.; **bien mieux** much better;
J'espère bien y aller. I very much
hope to go. ❹ right ▷ *Ce n'est pas
bien de dire du mal des gens.* It's not
right to say nasty things about
people. ▷ *Il croyait bien faire.* He
thought he was doing the right
thing.; **C'est bien fait pour lui!** It
serves him right!

bien-être [bjɛ̃nɛtʀ(ə)] *nm* well-
being ▷ *une sensation de bien-être* a
feeling of well-being

bienfaisance [bjɛ̃fəzɑ̃s]
nf charity; **une œuvre de
bienfaisance** a charity

bien que [bjɛk(ə)] *conj* although
▷ *Il fait assez chaud bien qu'il n'y
ait pas de soleil.* It's quite warm
although there's no sun.

bien sûr [bjɛ̃syʀ] *adv* of course

bientôt [bjɛ̃to] *adv* soon ▷ *À
bientôt!* See you soon!

bienvenu [bjɛ̃vny] *nm*: **Vous
êtes le bienvenu!** (*to visitor*) You
are welcome! ▷ *Vous êtes tous les
bienvenus!* You're all welcome!

bienvenue [bjɛ̃vny] *nf* welcome
▷ *Bienvenue à Calgary!* Welcome to
Calgary! ▷ *Vous êtes la bienvenue!*
You're welcome!

bifteck [biftɛk] *nm* steak

bijou [biʒu] *nm* (*pl* **bijoux**) *nm* jewel

bijouterie [biʒutʀi] nf jewellery store

bijoutier [biʒutje] nm jeweller

bijoutière [biʒutjɛʀ] nf jeweller ▷ *Elle est bijoutière.* She's a jeweller.

bilan [bilɑ̃] nm: **faire le bilan de quelque chose** to assess something ▷ *Il faut faire le bilan de la situation.* We need to assess the situation.

bilingue [bilɛ̃g] adj bilingual

bilinguisme [bilɛ̃gųism(ə)] nm bilingualism

billard [bijaʀ] nm pool

bille [bij] nf (toy) marble

billet [bijɛ] nm ❶ ticket ▷ *un billet d'avion* a plane ticket ❷ (paper money) bill ▷ *un billet de dix dollars* a 10-dollar bill

billion [biljɔ̃] nm trillion

binette [binɛt] nf (emoticon) smiley

biocarburant [bjɔkaʀbyʀɑ̃] nm biofuel

biodégradable [bjɔdegʀadabl(ə)] adj biodegradable

biographie [bjɔgʀafi] nf biography

biologie [bjɔlɔʒi] nf biology

biologique [bjɔlɔʒik] adj ❶ organic ▷ *des légumes biologiques* organic vegetables ❷ biological ▷ *des armes biologiques* biological weapons

biscotte [biskɔt] nf (sold in packets) toasted bread

biscuit [biskųi] nm cookie

bise [biz] nf ❶ kiss ▷ *Grosses bises de Terre-Neuve.* Love and kisses from Newfoundland.; **faire la bise à quelqu'un** (informal) to give somebody a peck on the cheek

bison [bizɔ̃] nm bison

bisou [bizu] nm (informal) kiss ▷ *Viens faire un bisou à maman!* Come and give Mummy a little kiss!

bissextile [bisɛkstil] adj: **une**

année bissextile a leap year

bizarre [bizaʀ] adj strange

blague [blag] nf ❶ (informal) joke ▷ *raconter une blague* to tell a joke; **Sans blague!** No kidding! ❷ trick ▷ *Il nous a encore fait une blague!* He's played a trick on us again!

blaguer [blage] vb (informal) to joke

blâmer [blame] vb to blame

blanc [blɑ̃, blɑ̃ʃ] (f **blanche**) adj ❶ white ▷ *un chemisier blanc* a white blouse ❷ blank ▷ *une page blanche* a blank page ▶ nm white ▷ *Elle était habillée tout en blanc.* She was dressed all in white.; **un blanc d'œuf** an egg white

Blanc [blɑ̃] nm white man

Blanche [blɑ̃ʃ] nf white woman

blanche [blɑ̃ʃ] adj see **blanc**

blé [ble] nm wheat; **le blé d'Inde** corn

blessé [blese] (f **blessée**) adj injured ▶ nm injured person ▷ *L'accident a fait trois blessés.* Three people were injured in the accident.

blessée [blese] nf injured person

blesser [blese] vb ❶ to injure ▷ *Il a été blessé dans un accident de voiture.* He was injured in a car accident. ❷ to hurt ▷ *Elle a fait exprès de le blesser.* She hurt him on purpose.; **se blesser** to hurt oneself ▷ *Je me suis blessé au pied.* I've hurt my foot.

blessure [blesyʀ] nf injury

bleu [blø] (f **bleue**) adj ❶ blue ▷ *une veste bleue* a blue jacket ❷ (steak) very rare ▶ nm ❶ blue ▷ *J'aime le bleu.* I like blue. ❷ bruise ▷ *Il a un bleu au front.* He's got a bruise on his forehead.

bleuet [blœɛ] nm blueberry ▷ *la tarte aux bleuets* blueberry pie

bleu marine (f+pl **bleu marine**)

adj navy blue ▷ *des vêtements bleu marine* navy blue clothes

bloc [blɔk] nm pad ▷ *un bloc de papier à lettres* a pad of writing paper; **un bloc de glace** a block of ice

bloc-notes [blɔknɔt] (pl **blocs-notes**) nm notepad

blogue [blɔg] nm blog

blond [blɔ̃, -ɔ̃d] (f **blonde**) adj blond ▷ *les cheveux blonds* blond hair; **blond cendré** ash blond ▷ *Elle a les cheveux blond cendré.* She has ash blond hair.

blonde [blɔ̃d] nf (informal) girlfriend ▷ *Ma blonde a fait son propre siteWeb.* My girlfriend made her own Web site.

bloquer [blɔke] vb to block ▷ *bloquer le passage* to block the way; **être bloqué dans un embouteillage** to be stuck in a traffic jam

se **blottir** [blɔtir] vb to huddle ▷ *Ils étaient blottis l'un contre l'autre.* They were huddled together.

blouse [bluz] nf blouse

blouson [bluzɔ̃] nm jacket ▷ *un blouson en cuir* a leather jacket

bobettes [bɔbɛt] nfpl underpants

bobine [bɔbin] nf reel ▷ *une bobine de fil* a reel of thread

bocal [bɔkal, -o] (pl **bocaux**) nm jar

bœuf [bœf] nm ① ox ② beef ▷ *un rôti de bœuf* a roast of beef

bof [bɔf] excl (informal), « **Le film t'a plu ?** » — « **Bof! C'était pas terrible!** » "Did you like the film?" — "Well... it wasn't that great!"; « **Comment ça va ?** » — « **Bof! Pas très bien.** » "How is it going?" — "Oh... not too well actually."

boire [bwar] vb to drink

bois [bwa] nm wood; **en bois** wooden ▷ *une table en bois* a wooden table

boisson [bwasɔ̃] nf drink ▷ *une boisson chaude* a hot drink ▷ *une boisson non alcoolisée* a soft drink

boîte [bwat] nf ① box ▷ *une boîte d'allumettes* a box of matches; **une boîte aux lettres** a mailbox ② can ▷ *une boîte de thon* a can of tuna; **une boîte de conserve** (of food) a can; **en boîte** canned ▷ *des petits pois en boîte* canned peas

boiter [bwate] vb to limp

bol [bɔl] nm bowl

bombarder [bɔ̃barde] vb to bomb

bombe [bɔ̃b] nf ① bomb ② spray can ▷ *du déodorant en bombe aérosol* spray deodorant

bon [bɔ̃, bɔn] (f **bonne**) adj, adv ① good ▷ *un bon restaurant* a good restaurant ▷ *Le tabac n'est pas bon pour la santé.* Smoking isn't good for you.; **être bon en maths** to be good at math; **sentir bon** to smell good; **Bon courage!** Good luck!; **Bon voyage!** Have a good trip!; **Bonne fin de semaine!** Have a good weekend!; **Bonne chance!** Good luck!; **Bonne journée!** Good luck!; **Bonne journée!** Have a good day!; **Bonne nuit!** Good night!; **Bon anniversaire!** Happy birthday!; **Bonne Année!** Happy New Year! ② right ▷ *Il est arrivé au bon moment.* He arrived at the right moment. ▷ *Ce n'est pas la bonne réponse.* That's not the right answer.; **bon marché** cheap ▷ *Les fraises ne sont pas aussi bon marché en hiver.* Strawberries aren't cheap in winter.; **Ah bon?** Really? ▷ « *Je pars aux États-Unis la semaine prochaine.* » — « *Ah bon?* » "I'm going to the States next week." — "Really?"; « *J'aimerais vraiment que tu viennes!* » — « **Bon, d'accord.** » "I'd really like you to come!" — "OK then, I will."; **Est-ce que ce yogourt est encore bon?**

Is this yogurt still OK?
▶ *nm* voucher ▷ *un bon d'achat* a
voucher; **le bon de réduction**
coupon; **pour de bon** for good
▷ *Cette fois, c'est pour de bon.* This
time it's for good.

bonbon [bɔ̃bɔ̃] *nm* candy; **les
bonbons haricots** jelly beans
bondé [bɔ̃de] (*f* **bondée**) *adj*
crowded
bondir [bɔ̃diʀ] *vb* to leap
bonheur [bɔnœʀ] *nm* happiness;
porter bonheur to bring luck
bonhomme [bɔnɔm] (*pl*
bonshommes) *nm*:
bonhomme de neige a snowman
  ● Le **Bonhomme Carnaval**, a large
  ● snowman wearing a red tuque
  ● and a woven belt, symbolizes
  ● the Carnaval de Québec and can
  ● be seen at the various activities
  ● throughout its two week
  ● duration. The Carnaval is the
  ● biggest festival in the world.
bonjour [bɔ̃ʒuʀ] *excl* ❶ Hello!
▷ *Donne le bonjour à tes parents de ma
part.* Say hello to your parents for
me. ❷ Good morning! ❸ Good
afternoon!

  ▌ **bonjour** is used in the morning
  ▌ and afternoon; in the evening
  ▌ **bonsoir** is used instead.
  ▌ **C'est simple comme bonjour!** It's
  ▌ easy as pie!

bonne [bɔn] *adj* see **bon**
bonnet [bɔnɛ] *nm* ❶ hat ▷ *un
bonnet de laine* a woolly hat
❷ (*women's*) **un bonnet de bain** a
bathing cap
bonsoir [bɔ̃swaʀ] *excl* Good
evening!
bonté [bɔ̃te] *nf* kindness
bord [bɔʀ] *nm* ❶ edge ▷ *le bord de
la table* the edge of the table ❷ side
▷ *Jane a garé sa voiture au bord de la
route.* Jane parked her car on the

side of the road.; **au bord de la mer**
by the sea; **au bord de l'eau** by the
water; **monter à bord** to go on
board; **être au bord des larmes** to
be on the verge of tears
border [bɔʀde] *vb* ❶ to line ▷ *une
route bordée d'arbres* a tree-lined
street ❷ to trim ▷ *un col bordé de
dentelle* a collar trimmed with lace
❸ to tuck in ▷ *Ma mère borde ma
petite sœur tous les soirs.* My mother
tucks in my little sister every night.
bordure [bɔʀdyʀ] *nf* border; **une
auberge en bordure de mer** an inn
right by the sea
bosse [bɔs] *nf* ❶ bump ▷ *Elle a une
grosse bosse au front.* She has a big
bump on her forehead. ▷ *La route
est pleine de bosses.* The road is very
bumpy.
botanique [bɔtanik] *adj* botanical
▷ *les jardins botaniques* the botanical
gardens
  ▶ *nf* botany
botte [bɔt] *nf* ❶ boot ▷ *une paire
de bottes* a pair of boots; **les bottes
de caoutchouc** rubber boots
❷ bunch ▷ *une botte de radis* a
bunch of radishes
bottin [bɔtɛ̃] *nm* phone book
bouc [buk] *nm* ❶ goatee ❷ billy
goat; **un bouc émissaire** a
scapegoat
bouche [buʃ] *nf* mouth; **une
bouche d'égout** (*in road*) **une**
maintenance hole; **une bouche de
métro** a subway entrance
bouchée [buʃe] *nf* mouthful
boucher [buʃe] *vb* to plug
▷ *boucher un trou* to plug a hole
▷ *L'évier est bouché.* The sink is
clogged. ▷ *J'ai le nez bouché.* My nose
is stuffed up.
  ▶ *nm* butcher ▷ *Il est boucher.* He's
a butcher.
bouchère [buʃɛʀ] *nf* butcher ▷ *Elle*

est bouchère. She's a butcher.

boucherie [buʃʀi] nf butcher shop

bouchon [buʃɔ̃] nm **1** (of plastic bottle) top **2** (of wine bottle) cork **1** traffic jam ▷ *Il y avait beaucoup de bouchons sur l'autoroute.* There were a lot of traffic jams on the motorway.

boucle [bukl(ə)] nf (of hair) curl; **une boucle d'oreille** an earring ▷ *une paire de boucles d'oreilles* a pair of earrings

bouclé [bukle] (f **bouclée**) adj curly

bouclier [buklije] nm shield; **le Bouclier canadien** the Canadian Shield

bouddhiste [budist(ə)] adj Buddhist
▶ n Buddhist

bouder [bude] vb to sulk

boue [bu] nf mud

bouée [bwe] nf buoy; **une bouée de sauvetage** a life buoy

boueux [bwø, -øz] (f **boueuse**) adj muddy

bouffe [buf] nf (informal) food ▷ *La bouffe est infecte à la cafétéria.* The food in the cafeteria is revolting.

bouffée [bufe] nf: **une bouffée d'air frais** a breath of fresh air

bouffe-minute nf fast food

bouffer [bufe] vb (informal) to eat

bouger [buʒe] vb to move

bougie [buʒi] nf candle

bouillabaisse [bujabɛs] nf fish soup

bouillant [bujɑ̃, -ɑ̃t] (f **bouillante**) adj **1** boiling ▷ *Faites cuire les pâtes à l'eau bouillante.* Cook the pasta in boiling water. **2** piping hot ▷ *La soupe est servie bouillante.* The soup should be served piping hot.

bouillir [bujiʀ] vb to boil ▷ *L'eau bout.* The water's boiling.; **Je bous d'impatience.** I'm bursting with impatience.

bouilloire [bujwaʀ] nf kettle

bouillon [bujɔ̃] nm stock ▷ *du bouillon de légumes* vegetable stock

boulanger [bulɑ̃ʒe] nm baker ▷ *Il est boulanger.* He's a baker.

boulangère [bulɑ̃ʒɛʀ] nf baker
▷ *Elle est boulangère.* She's a baker.

boulangerie [bulɑ̃ʒʀi] nf bakery

boule [bul] nf ball ▷ *une boule de cristal* a crystal ball; **une boule de neige** a snowball; **la machine à boules** pinball machine

bouleau [bulo] nm birch

bouleverser [bulvɛʀse] vb **1** to move deeply ▷ *Leur histoire déchirante m'a bouleversée.* I was very moved by their heartbreaking story. **2** to shatter ▷ *La mort de son ami l'a bouleversé.* He was shattered by the death of his friend. **3** to turn upside down ▷ *Cette rencontre a bouleversé sa vie.* This meeting turned her life upside down.

boulimie [bulimi] nf bulimia

boulot [bulo] nm **1** (informal) job ▷ *Elle a trouvé du boulot.* She has found a job. **2** work ▷ *J'ai beaucoup de boulot en ce moment.* I've got a lot of work to do at the moment.

bouquet [bukɛ] nm bunch of flowers ▷ *un bouquet de roses* a bunch of roses

bourdonner [buʀdɔne] vb to buzz

bourgeois [buʀʒwa, -waz] (f **bourgeoise**) adj middle-class ▷ *un quartier bourgeois* a posh area

bourgeon [buʀʒɔ̃] nm bud

bourré [buʀe] (f **bourrée**) adj: **bourré de** stuffed with ▷ *un portefeuille bourré de billets* a wallet stuffed with bills

bourreau [buʀo] (pl **bourreaux**) nm: **C'est un véritable bourreau de travail.** He's a real workaholic.

bourrer [buʀe] vb to stuff ▷ *bourrer une valise de vêtements* to stuff clothes into a suitcase

bourse [buʀs(ə)] *nf* grant; **la Bourse** the Stock Exchange

bous [bu] *vb see* **bouillir**

bousculade [buskylad] *nf* rush
▷ *la bousculade de dernière minute* the last-minute rush

bousculer [buskyle] *vb* ❶ to jostle ▷ *être bousculé par la foule* to be jostled by the crowd ❷ to rush ▷ *Je n'aime pas qu'on me bouscule.* I don't like to be rushed.

boussole [busɔl] *nf* compass

bout [bu] *vb see* **bouillir**

bout [bu] *nm* ❶ end ▷ *Elle habite au bout de la rue.* She lives at the end of the street. ▷ *Il est assis en bout de table.* He is sitting at the end of the table. ❷ tip ▷ *le bout du nez* the tip of the nose ❸ little piece ▷ *un petit bout de fromage* a little piece of cheese; **un bout de papier** a scrap of paper; **au bout de** after ▷ *Au bout d'un moment, il s'est endormi.* After a while he fell asleep.; **au bout du compte** ultimately ▷ *Au bout du compte, c'est à toi de décider.* Ultimately, it's your decision.; **Elle est à bout.** She's at the end of her tether.

bouteille [butɛj] *nf* bottle ▷ *une bouteille d'eau* a bottle of water

boutique [butik] *nf* shop ▷ *une boutique de cadeaux* a giftshop ▷ *une boutique de souvenirs* a souvenir shop

bouton [butɔ̃] *nm* ❶ button ❷ pimple ▷ *J'ai un bouton sur le nez.* I've got a pimple on my nose. ❸ bud ▷ *un bouton de rose* a rosebud; **un bouton d'or** a buttercup

boxe [bɔks(ə)] *nf* boxing

boxeur [bɔksœʀ] *nm* boxer

boycotter [bɔjkɔte] *vb* to boycott

bracelet [bʀaslɛ] *nm* bracelet

bracelet-montre [bʀaslɛmɔ̃tʀ(ə)] (*pl* bracelets-montres) *nm* wristwatch

branche [bʀɑ̃ʃ] *nf* branch

branché [bʀɑ̃ʃe] (f **branchée**) *adj* (*informal*) trendy ▷ *avoir un look branché* to look trendy

brancher [bʀɑ̃ʃe] *vb* ❶ to connect ▷ *Le téléphone est branché?* Is the phone connected? ❷ to plug in ▷ *L'aspirateur n'est pas branché.* The vacuum cleaner isn't plugged in.

bras [bʀa] *nm* arm

brasse [bʀas] *nf* breaststroke ▷ *nager la brasse* to do the breaststroke

brave [bʀav] *adj* ❶ nice ▷ *C'est un brave type.* He's a nice guy. ❷ brave ▷ *Ta mère est une femme très brave.* Your mother is a very brave woman.

> Be careful! The meaning of the French adjective **brave** changes according to its position. Before the noun, it means "nice"; after the noun, it means "brave".

bravo [bʀavo] *excl* Bravo!

bref [bʀɛf, bʀɛv] (f **brève**) *adj, adv* short ▷ *Sa lettre était brève.* Her letter was short.; **en bref** in brief ▷ *l'actualité en bref* the news in brief; **Bref, ça s'est bien terminé.** In short, it turned out all right in the end.; **être bref et précis** to be short and to the point

bretelle [bʀətɛl] *nf* strap ▷ *La bretelle de ton soutien-gorge dépasse.* Her bra strap is showing.; **les bretelles** suspenders ▷ *Il porte des bretelles.* He's wearing suspenders.

brève [bʀɛv] *adj see* **bref**

bricolage [bʀikɔlaʒ] *nm* do-it-yourself ▷ *Il aime le bricolage.* He loves working on do-it-yourself projects. ▷ *un magasin de bricolage* a store selling do-it-yourself supplies

bricoler [brikɔle] vb to work on do-it-yourself projects ▷ Il aime bricoler. He loves working on do-it-yourself projects.

brièvement [brijɛvmɑ̃] adv briefly ▷ Expliquez-moi brièvement ce qui s'est passé. Tell me briefly what happened.

brigade [brigad] nf (of police) squad ▷ la brigade des stups (informal) the drug squad

brillamment [brijamɑ̃] adv brilliantly ▷ Il a réussi brillamment à son examen. He did brilliantly in the exam.

brillant [brijɑ̃, -ɑ̃t] (f **brillante**) adj ❶ brilliant ▷ une brillante carrière a brilliant career ❷ shiny ▷ des cheveux brillants shiny hair

briller [brije] vb to shine

brin [brɛ̃] nm: **un brin d'herbe** a blade of grass; **un brin de muguet** a sprig of lily of the valley

brindille [brɛ̃dij] nf twig

brioche [brijɔʃ] nf bun

brique [brik] nf brick

briquet [brike] nm lighter

brise [briz] nf breeze

brise-glace [brizglas] (pl **brise-glaces**) nm ice-breaker ▷ On utilise des brise-glaces pour naviguer dans l'Arctique. Ice-breakers are used to navigate the Arctic.

se briser [brize] vb to break ▷ Le vase s'est brisé en mille morceaux. The vase broke into a thousand pieces.

brisure [brizyr] nf chocolate chip ▷ un biscuit aux brisures de chocolat a chocolate chip cookie

broche [brɔʃ] nf brooch ▷ une broche en argent a silver brooch; **à la broche** spit-roasted ▷ un poulet à la broche a spit-roasted chicken

brochet [brɔʃe] nm pike

brochette [brɔʃɛt] nf skewer; **les brochettes d'agneau** lamb kebabs

brocheuse [brɔʃøz] nf stapler

brochure [brɔʃyr] nf brochure

broder [brɔde] vb to embroider

broderie [brɔdri] nf embroidery

bronchite [brɔ̃ʃit] nf bronchitis ▷ avoir une bronchite to have bronchitis

bronze [brɔ̃z] nm bronze

bronzer [brɔ̃ze] vb to get a tan ▷ Il est bien bronzé. He's got a good tan.; **se bronzer** to sunbathe

brosse [brɔs] nf brush; **une brosse à cheveux** a hairbrush; **une brosse à dents** a toothbrush

brosser [brɔse] vb to brush; **se brosser les dents** to brush one's teeth ▷ Je me brosse les dents tous les soirs. I brush my teeth every night.

brouette [bruɛt] nf wheelbarrow

brouillard [brujar] nm fog ▷ Il y a du brouillard. It's foggy.

brouillon [brujɔ̃] nm first draft ▷ Ce n'est qu'un brouillon. It's just a first draft.

broussailles [brusaj] nfpl undergrowth

brouter [brute] vb (animals) to graze

broyer [brwaje] vb to crush; **broyer du noir** to be down in the dumps

bruine [bruin] nf drizzle ▷ On prévoit de la bruine aujourd'hui. They're forecasting drizzle today.

bruiner [bruine] vb to drizzle

bruit [brui] nm ❶ noise ▷ J'ai entendu un bruit. I heard a noise. ▷ faire du bruit to make a noise; **sans bruit** without a sound ❷ rumour ▷ Des bruits circulent à son sujet. There are rumours going round about him.

bruitage [bruitaʒ] nm sound effects

bruiteur [bruitœr] nm sound effect specialist

bruiteuse [bʀɥitøz] nf sound effect specialist

brûlant [bʀylɑ̃, -ɑ̃t] (f **brûlante**) adj ❶ blazing ▷ un soleil brûlant a blazing sun ❷ boiling hot ▷ Elle boit son café brûlant. She drinks her coffee boiling hot.

brûlé [bʀyle] nm smell of burning ▷ Ça sent le brûlé. There's a smell of burning.

brûler [bʀyle] vb to burn; **se brûler** to burn oneself

brûlure [bʀylyʀ] nf burn; **des brûlures d'estomac** heartburn

brume [bʀym] nf mist

brumeux [bʀymø, -øz] (f **brumeuse**) adj misty

brun [bʀœ̃, -yn] (f **brune**) adj brown; **Elle est brune.** She has dark hair.

brunch [bʀœntʃ] nm brunch ▷ prendre le brunch to have brunch

brusque [bʀysk(ə)] adj abrupt; **d'un ton brusque** brusquely

brusquer [bʀyske] vb to rush ▷ Il ne faut pas la brusquer. You mustn't rush her.

brut [bʀyt] (f **brute**) adj: **le champagne brut** dry champagne; **le pétrole brut** crude oil; **son salaire brut** his gross salary

brutaliser [bʀytalize] vb to treat roughly ▷ Il a été brutalisé par la police. He was treated roughly by the police.

bruyamment [bʀɥijamɑ̃] adv noisily

bruyant [bʀɥijɑ̃, -ɑ̃t] (f **bruyante**) adj noisy

bu [by] vb see **boire**

buanderie [bɥɑ̃dʀi] nf coin laundry

bûcheron [byʃʀɔ̃] nm woodcutter

budget [bydʒe] nm budget

buffet [byfɛ] nm ❶ sideboard ▷ un buffet en chêne an oak sideboard ❷ buffet ▷ un buffet froid a cold buffet; **un buffet à salades** a salad bar

buisson [bɥisɔ̃] nm bush

bulle [byl] nf bubble ▷ une bulle de savon a soap bubble

bulletin [byltɛ̃] nm ❶ bulletin; **le bulletin d'informations** the news bulletin ❷ report card ▷ Ton bulletin n'est pas fameux. Your report card isn't very good.; **le bulletin de salaire** pay slip; **le bulletin de vote** the ballot; **le bulletin scolaire** report card

bureau [byʀo] (pl **bureaux**) nm ❶ desk ▷ Posez le dossier sur mon bureau. Put the file on my desk. ❷ office ▷ Il vous attend dans son bureau. He's waiting for you in his office.; **le Bureau** (computer) the desktop; **un bureau de change** a foreign exchange; **le bureau de poste** the post office; **le bureau de vote** the polling station

bus [bys] vb see **boire**

bus [bys] nm bus

buste [byst(ə)] nm bust

but [by] vb see **boire**
▶ nm ❶ aim ▷ Ils n'ont pas de but dans la vie. They have no aim in life.; **Quel est le but de votre visite?** What's the reason for your visit?; **dans le but de** with the intention of ▷ Je suis venue dans le but de vous aider. I came to help you. ❷ goal ▷ marquer un but to score a goal

butane [bytan] nm butane

butin [bytɛ̃] nm loot ▷ Les cambrioleurs se sont partagé le butin. The burglars shared the loot.

buvais, buvait vb see **boire**

C

c' [s] *pron see* **ce**

ça [sa] *pron* ❶ this ▷ *Est-ce que vous pouvez m'aider avec ça?* Can you help me with this? ❷ that ▷ *Est-ce que tu peux prendre ça, là-bas dans le coin?* Can you bring that from over there in the corner? ❸ it ▷ *Ça ne fait rien.* It doesn't matter.; **Comment ça va?** How are you?; **Ça alors!** Well, well!; **C'est ça.** That's right.; **Ça y est!** That's it!

çà [sa] *adv:* **çà et là** here and there

cabane [kaban] *nf* hut; **la cabane à sucre** sugar shack; **une cabane dans l'arbre** a treehouse

cabine [kabin] *nf* (on a ship) cabin; **une cabine d'essayage** a fitting room; **une cabine téléphonique** a phone box

cabinet [kabinε] *nm* (of doctor, of dentist) consulting room; **un cabinet d'avocats** a law firm

câble [kɑbl(ə)] *nm* cable; **la**

télévision par câble (television) cable; **les câbles de démarrage** booster cables

cabosser [kabɔse] *vb* to dent

cacao [kakao] *nm* cocoa; **le beurre de cacao** cocoa butter

cache-cache [kaʃkaʃ] *nm*

⬛ No article is ever used with **cache-cache**.

jouer à cache-cache to play hide-and-seek

cacher [kaʃe] *vb* to hide ▷ *J'ai caché les cadeaux sous le lit.* I hid the presents under the bed. ▷ *Tu me caches quelque chose!* You're hiding something!; **se cacher** to hide ▷ *Elle s'est cachée sous la table.* She's hiding under the table.

cachet [kaʃε] *nm* ❶ tablet; **un cachet d'aspirine** an aspirin ❷ (for performer) fee ▷ *Il a touché un gros cachet pour ce concert.* He got a big fee for the concert.; **le cachet de la poste** the postmark

cachette [kaʃεt] *nf* hiding place; **en cachette** on the sly ▷ *Il est sorti en cachette sans réveiller ses parents.* He crept out on the sly without waking his parents.; **jouer à la cachette** to play hide-and-seek

cadavre [kadavʀ(ə)] *nm* corpse

cadeau [kado] (*pl* **cadeaux**) *nm* present ▷ *un cadeau d'anniversaire* a birthday present; **faire un cadeau à quelqu'un** to give somebody a present

cadenas [kadna] *nm* padlock

cadet [kadε, -εt] (*f* **cadette**) *adj* ❶ (brother, sister) younger ▷ *ma sœur cadette* my younger sister ❷ (son, daughter) youngest ▷ *son fils cadet* his youngest son ▶ *nm* youngest ▷ *C'est le cadet de la famille.* He's the youngest in the family.

cadette [kadεt] *nf* youngest

▷ *C'est la cadette de la famille.* She's the youngest in the family.

cadre [kɑdʀ(ə)] *nm* ❶ frame ▷ *un cadre en bois* a wooden frame ❷ surroundings ▷ *L'hôtel est situé dans un très beau cadre.* The hotel is located in beautiful surroundings. ❸ executive ▷ *un cadre supérieur* a senior executive

café [kafe] *nm* ❶ coffee ❷ café

cafétéria [kafeteʀja] *nf* cafeteria

cafetière [kaftjɛʀ] *nf* ❶ coffee maker ❷ coffee pot

cage [kaʒ] *nf* cage; **la cage d'escalier** the stairwell

cagoule [kagul] *nf* balaclava

cahier [kaje] *nm* ❶ workbook ❷ notebook

caillou [kaju] (*pl* **cailloux**) *nm* pebble

caisse [kɛs] *nf* ❶ box ▷ *une caisse à outils* a tool box ❷ cash register; **le ticket de caisse** the sales slip ❸ checkout ▷ *J'ai dû faire la queue à la caisse.* I had to wait in line at the checkout.

caissier [kesje] *nm* cashier

caissière [kesjɛʀ] *nf* cashier

Cajun [caʒɛ̃] (*f* **Cajun**) *adj*, *n* Cajun ▷ *la cuisine cajun* Cajun cuisine; **un Cajun** (*man*) a Cajun; **une Cajun** (*woman*) a Cajun

calcul [kalkyl] *nm* ❶ calculation ▷ *Je me suis trompé dans mes calculs.* I made a mistake in my calculations. ❷ arithmetic ▷ *Je ne suis pas très bon en calcul.* I'm not very good at arithmetic.

calculatrice [kalkylatʀis] *nf* calculator

calculer [kalkyle] *vb* to work out ▷ *J'ai calculé combien ça allait coûter.* I worked out how much it was going to cost.

cale [kal] *nf* wedge

caleçon [kalsɔ̃] *nm* ❶ underpants

▷ *un caleçon* a pair of underpants ❷ (*men's*)

calendrier [kalɑ̃dʀije] *nm* calendar

calepin [kalpɛ̃] *nm* notebook

caler [kale] *vb* to stall ▷ *La voiture a calé dans une côte.* The car stalled on a hill.

câlin [kɑlɛ̃, -in] (*f* **câline**) *adj* cuddly ▶ *nm* cuddle ▷ *faire un câlin à quelqu'un* to give somebody a cuddle

calmant [kalmɑ̃] *nm* tranquillizer

calme [kalm(ə)] *adj* ❶ quiet ▷ *un endroit calme* a quiet place ❷ calm ▷ *Il est resté très calme.* He stayed very calm. ▶ *nm* peace and quiet ▷ *J'ai besoin de calme pour travailler.* I need peace and quiet to work.; **Du calme, s'il vous plaît!** Please stay calm!

calmer [kalme] *vb* to soothe ▷ *Cette pommade calme les démangeaisons.* This ointment soothes itching.; **se calmer** to calm down ▷ *Calme-toi!* Calm down!

calorie [kalɔʀi] *nf* calorie

camarade [kamaʀad] *nmf* friend; **un camarade de classe** a school friend

cambriolage [kɑ̃bʀijolaʒ] *nm* burglary

cambrioler [kɑ̃bʀijole] *vb* to burgle

cambrioleur [kɑ̃bʀijolœʀ] *nm* burglar

cambrioleuse [kɑ̃bʀijoløz] *nf* burglar

camelot [kamlo] *nmf* paper carrier

camelote [kamlɔt] *nf* (*informal*) junk ▷ *C'est vraiment de la camelote.* It's absolute junk.

caméra [kameʀa] *nf* (*movie, TV*) camera; **une caméra numérique** a digital camera

caméscope [kameskɔp] *nm*

camcorder

camion [kamjɔ̃] *nm* truck; **un camion citerne** a tanker truck

camionnette [kamjɔnɛt] *nf* pickup truck

camionneur [kamjɔnœʀ] *nm* truck driver

camionneuse [kamjɔnøz] *nf* truck driver

camisole [kamizɔl] *nf* (men's or women's) undershirt

camomille [kamɔmij] *nf* camomile tea

camp [kɑ̃] *nm* camp ▷ **un camp d'été** a summer camp ▷ **un camp de prisonniers** a prison camp

campagne [kɑ̃paɲ] *nf* ❶ country; **à la campagne** in the country ▷ **Nous passons nos vacances à la campagne.** We spend our holidays in the country. ❷ campaign ▷ **une campagne publicitaire** a marketing campaign

camper [kɑ̃pe] *vb* to camp

campeur [kɑ̃pœʀ] *nm* camper

campeuse [kɑ̃pøz] *nf* camper

camping [kɑ̃piŋ] *nm* camping ▷ **faire du camping** to go camping; **un terrain de camping** a campground; **le camping sauvage** wilderness camping

Canada [kanada] *nm* Canada; **au Canada (1)** in Canada **(2)** to Canada

canadien [kanadjɛ̃, -ɛn] (f **canadienne**) *adj, n* Canadian; **un Canadien** (man) a Canadian; **une Canadienne** (woman) a Canadian

canadien-anglais (f **canadienne-anglaise**) *adj* English Canadian

Canadien anglais (pl **Canadiens anglais**) *nm* (man) English Canadian

Canadienne anglaise (pl **Canadiennes anglaises**) *nf* (woman) English Canadian

canadien-français (f

canadienne-française) *adj* French Canadian

Canadien français (pl **Canadiens français**) *nm* (man) French Canadian

Canadienne française (pl **Canadiennes françaises**) *nf* (woman) French Canadian

canal [kanal, -o] (pl **canaux**) *nm* canal

canapé [kanape] *nm* open-faced sandwich

canard [kanaʀ] *nm* duck

cancer [kɑ̃sɛʀ] *nm* cancer ▷ **le cancer du poumon** lung cancer; **le Cancer** Cancer ▷ **Elle est Cancer.** She's a Cancer.

candidat [kɑ̃dida] *nm* ❶ (in exam, election) candidate ❷ (for job) applicant

candidate [kɑ̃didat] *nf* ❶ (in exam, election) candidate ❷ (for job) applicant

candidature [kɑ̃didatyʀ] *nf*: **poser sa candidature à un poste** to apply for a job ▷ **Il a posé sa candidature à des dizaines de postes.** He has applied for dozens of jobs.

caneton [kantɔ̃] *nm* duckling

canette [kanɛt] *nf*: **une canette de boisson gazeuse** a can of pop

caniche [kaniʃ] *nm* poodle

canicule [kanikyl] *nf* heat wave

canif [kanif] *nm* jackknife

canne [kan] *nf* walking stick; **une canne à pêche** a fishing rod

canneberge [kanbɛʀʒ] *nf* cranberry ▷ **du jus de canneberge** cranberry juice

cannelle [kanɛl] *nf* cinnamon ▷ **une brioche à la cannelle** cinnamon roll

canola [kanɔla] *nm* canola ▷ **de l'huile de canola** canola oil

canon [kanɔ̃] *nm* cannon

canot [kano] *nm* ❶ canoe

❷ dinghy ▷ *un canot pneumatique* a rubber dinghy; **un canot de sauvetage** a lifeboat

canotage [kanɔtaʒ] *nm* canoeing ▷ *faire du canotage* to go canoeing

cantine [kɑ̃tin] *nf* snack bar

caoutchouc [kautʃu] *nm* rubber; **des bottes en caoutchouc** rubber boots

cap [kap] *nm* (*landform*) cape

capable [kapabl(ə)] *adj*: **Elle est capable de marcher pendant des heures.** She can walk for hours.; **Il est capable de changer d'avis au dernier moment.** He's capable of changing his mind at the last minute.

cape [kap] *nf* (*garment*) cape

capitale [kapital] *nf* capital ▷ *la capitale de la Colombie-Britannique* the capital of British Columbia

capot [kapo] *nm* (*of car*) hood

caprice [kapʀis] *nm*: **faire des caprices** to make a fuss ▷ *Il n'aime pas les enfants qui font des caprices.* He doesn't like children who make a fuss.

capricieux [kapʀisjø, -øz] (*f* **capricieuse**) *adj*: **un enfant capricieux** a difficult child

Capricorne [kapʀikɔʀn] *nm* Capricorn ▷ *Elle est Capricorne.* She's a Capricorn.

captivant [kaptivɑ̃, -ɑ̃t] (*f* **captivante**) *adj* fascinating

captivité [kaptivite] *nf* captivity ▷ *en captivité* in captivity

capturer [kaptyʀe] *vb* to capture

capuche [kapyʃ] *nf* hood ▷ *un manteau à capuche* a coat with a hood

capuchon [kapyʃɔ̃] *nm* (*of pen*) cap

car [kaʀ] *conj* because ▷ *Nous sommes inquiets car ils ne sont pas encore rentrés.* We're worried because they're not back yet.

carabine [kaʀabin] *nf* rifle

caractère [kaʀaktɛʀ] *nm* personality ▷ *Elle a le même caractère que son père.* She has the same personality as her father.; **Il a bon caractère.** He's good-natured.; **Elle a mauvais caractère.** She's bad-tempered.; **Il n'a pas un caractère facile.** He isn't easy to get along with.

caractéristique [kaʀakteʀistik] *adj* characteristic
▶ *nf* characteristic

carafe [kaʀaf] *nf* jug ▷ *une carafe d'eau* a jug of water

caramel [kaʀamɛl] *nm* ❶ caramel ▷ *la crème caramel* crème caramel
❷ toffee

caravane [kaʀavan] *nf* RV

carbonique [kaʀbɔnik] *adj*: **le gaz carbonique** carbon dioxide

carburant [kaʀbyʀɑ̃] *nm* fuel

carcajou [kaʀkaʒu] *nm* wolverine

cardiaque [kaʀdjak] *adj*: **une crise cardiaque** a heart attack; **Ma tante est cardiaque.** My aunt has heart trouble.

cardiologue [kaʀdjɔlɔg] *nmf* heart specialist

caresse [kaʀɛs] *nf* stroke ▷ *faire des caresses à un chat* to caress a cat

caresser [kaʀese] *vb* to stroke

caribou [kaʀibu] *nm* caribou; **la peau de caribou** caribou hide

caricature [kaʀikatyʀ] *nf* (*drawing*) cartoon

carie [kaʀi] *nf* tooth decay ▷ *J'ai une carie.* I have a cavity.

caritatif [kaʀitatif, -iv] (*f* **caritative**) *adj*: **une organisation caritative** a charity

carnaval [kaʀnaval] *nm* carnival

carnet [kaʀnɛ] *nm* ❶ notebook
❷ book ▷ *un carnet d'adresses* an address book ▷ *un carnet de chèques* a chequebook ▷ *un carnet de timbres*

a book of stamps

carotte [kaʀɔt] *nf* carrot ▷ *les carottes râpées* grated carrots

carré [kaʀe] (*f* **carrée**) *adj* square; **un mètre carré** a square metre ▶ *nm* square; **le carré au chocolat** brownie

carreau [kaʀo] (*pl* **carreaux**) *nm* ① (*pattern*) check ▷ *une chemise à carreaux* a checked shirt ② (*floor, wall*) tile ▷ *Je viens de laver les carreaux de la cuisine.* I've just washed the kitchen floor. ③ pane ▷ *Elle a cassé un carreau.* She broke a windowpane. ④ (*cards*) diamonds ▷ *l'as de carreau* the ace of diamonds

carrefour [kaʀfuʀ] *nm* intersection

carrelage [kaʀlaʒ] *nm* tiled floor

carrément [kaʀemã] *adv* ① completely ▷ *C'est carrément impossible.* It's completely impossible. ② straight out ▷ *Dis-moi carrément ce que tu penses.* Tell me straight out what you think.

carrière [kaʀjɛʀ] *nf* career; **un militaire de carrière** a professional soldier

carrure [kaʀyʀ] *nf* build ▷ *Il a une carrure d'athlète.* He has an athletic build.

cartable [kaʀtabl(ə)] *nm* binder

carte [kaʀt(ə)] *nf* ① card; **une carte d'anniversaire** a birthday card; **une carte postale** a postcard; **une carte de vœux** a Christmas card; **une carte bancaire** a bank card; **une carte de crédit** a credit card; **une carte de fidélité** a frequent customer card; **une carte d'embarquement** a boarding card; **une carte d'identité** an ID card; **une carte de séjour** a residence permit; **une carte téléphonique** a phonecard; **un jeu de cartes (1)** a pack of cards

(2) a card game ② map ▷ *une carte du Manitoba* a map of Manitoba ▷ *une carte routière* a road map; **manger à la carte** to eat à la carte ▷ *Nous allons manger à la carte.* We'll choose from the à la carte menu.

carton [kaʀtɔ̃] *nm* cardboard ▷ *un morceau de carton* a piece of cardboard; **une boîte de carton** a cardboard box ▷ *un carton à chaussures* a shoe box

cartouche [kaʀtuʃ] *nf* cartridge; **une cartouche d'imprimante** a printer cartridge

cas [kɑ] (*pl* **cas**) *nm* case ▷ *plusieurs cas* several cases; **ne faire aucun cas de** to take no notice of; **en aucun cas** under no circumstances; **en tout cas** at any rate; **au cas où** in case ▷ *Prends un sandwich au cas où la cantine serait fermée.* Take a sandwich in case the snack bar's closed.; **en cas de** in case of ▷ *En cas d'incendie, appelez ce numéro.* In case of fire, call this number.

cascade [kaskad] *nf* waterfall

cascadeur [kaskadœʀ] *nm* stuntman

cascadeuse [kaskadøz] *nf* stuntwoman

case [kɑz] *nf* ① (*in board game*) square ② (*on form*) box; **la case postale** post office box

caserne [kazɛʀn(ə)] *nf* barracks

casier [kazje] *nm* locker

casque [kask(ə)] *nm* helmet; **un casque d'écoute** a pair of headphones

casquette [kaskɛt] *nf* cap

cassant [kasɑ̃, -ɑ̃t] (*f* **cassante**) *adj*: **Il m'a parlé d'un ton cassant.** He spoke to me curtly.

casse-croûte [kɑskʀut] (*pl* **casse-croûte**) *nm* snack

casse-noix [kɑs-] (*pl* **casse-noix**)

nm nutcracker.

casser [kase] *vb* to break ▷ *J'ai cassé un verre.* I've broken a glass.; **se casser** (*bone*) to break ▷ *Il s'est cassé la jambe en faisant du ski.* He broke his leg skiing.; **se casser la tête** (*informal*) to go to a lot of trouble ▷ *Je ne vais pas me casser la tête pour le dîner : je vais ouvrir une boîte de conserve.* I'm not going to go to a whole lot of trouble over dinner: I'll just open a can.

casserole [kasrɔl] *nf* **❶** saucepan **❷** casserole ▷ *une casserole de thon* a tuna casserole

casse-tête [kastɛt] (*pl* **casse-tête**) *nm*: **C'est un vrai casse-tête!** It's a real headache!

cassette [kasɛt] *nf* cassette

cassis [kasis] *nm* black currant

cassonade [kasɔnad] *nf* brown sugar

castor [kastɔr] *nm* beaver

catalogue [katalɔg] *nm* catalogue

catastrophe [katastrɔf] *nf* disaster

catégorie [kategɔri] *nf* category

catégorique [kategɔrik] *adj* firm ▷ *un refus catégorique* a flat refusal

cathédrale [katedral] *nf* cathedral

catholique [katɔlik] *adj* Catholic ▶ *n* Catholic

cauchemar [koʃmar] *nm* nightmare ▷ *faire un cauchemar* to have a nightmare

cause [koz] *nf* cause; **à cause de** because of ▷ *Nous n'avons pas pu sortir à cause du mauvais temps.* We couldn't go out because of the bad weather.

causer [koze] *vb* to cause ▷ *La tempête a causé beaucoup de dégâts.* The storm caused a lot of damage.

cavalier [kavalje] *nm* **❶** rider **❷** (*at dance*) partner

cavalière [kavaljɛr] *nf* rider

cave [kav] *nf* cellar

caverne [kavɛrn(ə)] *nf* cave

CD [sede] (*pl* **CD**) *nm* CD

CD-ROM [sederɔm] (*pl* **CD-ROM**) *nm* CD-ROM

ce [sə, sɛt] (*msg* **cet**, *f* **cette**, *pl* **ces**) *adj*

> ce changes to **cet** before a vowel and most words beginning with "h".

❶ this ▷ *Tu peux prendre ce livre.* You can take this book. ▷ *cet après-midi* this afternoon ▷ *cet hiver* this winter; **ce livre-ci** this book; **cette voiture-ci** this car **❷** that ▷ *Je n'ai pas du tout aimé ce film.* I didn't like that movie at all.; **ce livre-là** that book; **cette voiture-là** that car

▶ *pron*

> ce changes to **c'** before the vowel in **est**, **était** and **étaient**.

it ▷ *Ce n'est pas facile.* It's not easy.; **c'est** (1) it is ▷ *C'est vraiment trop cher.* It's really too expensive. ▷ *Ouvre, c'est moi!* Open the door, it's me! (2) he is ▷ *C'est un peintre du début du siècle.* He's a painter from the turn of the century. (3) she is ▷ *C'est une actrice très célèbre.* She's a very famous actress. (4) this is ▷ *C'est inacceptable!* This is unacceptable! (5) that is ▷ *C'est bien beau, mais...* That's all very fine, but...; **ce sont** they are ▷ *Ce sont des amis à mes parents.* They're friends of my parents.; **Qui est-ce?** Who is it?; **Qu'est-ce que c'est?** What is it?; **ce qui** what ▷ *Ce qui compte.* That's what matters.; **ce qui** what ▷ *C'est ce qui compte.* That's what matters.; **tout ce qui** everything that ▷ *J'ai rangé tout ce qui traînait par terre.* I've tidied up everything that was on the floor.; **ce que** what ▷ *Je vais lui dire ce que je pense.* I'm going to tell him what I think.; **tout ce que** everything ▷ *Tu* *peux avoir tout ce que tu veux.* You can have everything you want.

ceci [səsi] *pron* this ▷ *Prends ceci, tu en auras besoin.* Take this, you'll need it.

céder [sede] *vb* to give in ▷ *Elle a tellement insisté qu'il a fini par céder.* She was so adamant that he finally gave in.; **céder à** to give in to ▷ *Je ne veux pas céder à ses caprices.* I'm not going to give in to his whims.

cédérom [sederɔm] *nm* CD-ROM

cédille [sedij] *nf* cedilla

cèdre [sɛdr(ə)] *nm* cedar; **le bois de cèdre** cedar (wood)

cégep [seʒɛp] *nm* = **collège d'enseignement général et professionnel** *(general and vocational college)* CEGEP
  - In Québec, a **cégep** is an institution offering two- or three-year programs in pre-university and vocational studies.

ceinture [sɛtyr] *nf* belt ▷ *une ceinture en cuir* a leather belt; **une ceinture de sauvetage** a lifebelt; **votre ceinture de sécurité** your seatbelt

cela [səla] *pron* ❶ it ▷ *Cela dépend.* It depends. ❷ that ▷ *Je n'aime pas cela.* I don't like that.; **C'est cela.** That's right.; **à part cela** apart from that

célèbre [selɛbr(ə)] *adj* famous

célébrer [selebre] *vb* to celebrate

céleri [sɛlri] *nm* celery; **des branches de céleri** celery stalks

célibataire [selibatɛr] *adj, n* single; **un célibataire** a bachelor; **une célibataire** a single woman

celle [sɛl] *pron see* **celui**

celles [sɛl] *pron see* **ceux**

cellule [selyl] *nf* cell

Celsius [sɛlsjys] *(f, pl* **Celsius**) *adj* Celsius ▷ *vingt degrés Celsius* 20

degrees Celsius

celui [səlɥi, sɛl] *(f* **celle**, *mpl* **ceux**, *fpl* **celles**) *pron* the one ▷ *Prends celui que tu préfères.* Take the one you like best. ▷ *Je n'ai pas d'appareil photo mais je peux emprunter celui de ma sœur.* I don't have a camera but I can borrow my sister's. ▷ *Je n'ai pas de planche à roulettes mais je peux emprunter celle de mon frère.* I don't have a skateboard but I can borrow my brother's.; **celui-ci** this one; **celle-ci** this one; **celui-là** that one; **celle-là** that one

cendre [sɑ̃dr(ə)] *nf* ash

cendrier [sɑ̃drije] *nm* ashtray

censé [sɑ̃se] *(f* **censée**) *adj* : **être censé faire quelque chose** to be supposed to do something ▷ *Vous êtes censé arriver à l'heure.* You're supposed to get here on time.

cent [sɑ̃] *num* a hundred ▷ *cent dollars* a hundred dollars

> **cent** is spelt with an **-s** when there are two or more hundreds, but not when it is followed by another number, as in "a hundred and two".

▷ *trois cents ans* 300 years ▷ *cent deux kilomètres* 102 kilometres ▷ *trois cent cinquante kilomètres* 350 kilometres ▷ *trois cent mille kilomètres* 300 000 kilometres

cent [sɑ̃] *nm* (currency) cent

centaine [sɑ̃tɛn] *nf* about a hundred ▷ *Il y avait une centaine de personnes dans la salle.* There were about a hundred people in the hall.; **des centaines de** hundreds of ▷ *Des centaines de réfugiés se sont présentés à l'ambassade.* Hundreds of refugees came to the embassy.

centenaire [sɑ̃tnɛr] *nm* centennial

centième [sɑ̃tjɛm] *adj* hundredth

centimètre [sɑ̃timɛtr(ə)] *nm*

centimetre

central [sɑ̃tRal, -o] (f **centrale**, mpl **centraux**) adj central

centrale [sɑ̃tRal] nf power plant ▷ *une centrale nucléaire* a nuclear power plant

centre [sɑ̃tR(ə)] nm centre; **un centre commercial** a shopping centre; **un centre communautaire** a community centre; **un centre d'appels** a call centre; **le centre local de services communautaires** (also **CLSC** in Québec) local community service centre; **le centre de jour** drop-in centre; **le centre de villégiature** resort

centre-ville [sɑ̃tRavil] (pl **centres-villes**) nm town centre

cependant [səpɑ̃dɑ̃] adv however

cercle [sɛRkl(ə)] nm circle ▷ *Entourez d'un cercle la bonne réponse.* Put a circle round the right answer.; **un cercle vicieux** a vicious circle

cercueil [sɛRkœj] nm coffin

cereals [sereal] nfpl cereal ▷ *un bol de céréales* a bowl of cereal; **un pain multicéréales** a multigrain loaf

cérémonie [seremɔni] nf ceremony

cerf [sɛR] nm deer

cerf-volant [sɛRvɔlɑ̃] (pl **cerfs-volants**) nm kite

cerise [səRiz] nf cherry

cerisier [səRizje] nm cherry tree

cerné [sɛRne] (f **cernée**) adj: **avoir les yeux cernés** to have dark circles under one's eyes ▷ *Elle avait les yeux cernés.* She had dark circles under her eyes.

cerner [sɛRne] vb: **J'ai du mal à le cerner.** I can't figure him out.

certain [sɛRtɛ̃, -ɛn] (f **certaine**) adj ❶ certain ▷ *Je suis certain que je l'ai remis en place.* I'm certain

that I put it back. ▷ *Ce n'est pas certain.* It's not certain. ❷ some ▷ *Certaines personnes n'aiment pas la crème.* Some people don't like cream.; **un certain temps** quite some time ▷ *J'ai mis un certain temps à comprendre ce qu'elle disait.* It took me quite some time to understand what she was saying.

certainement [sɛRtɛnmɑ̃] adv ❶ definitely ▷ *C'est certainement le meilleur film que j'ai vu cette année.* It's definitely the best film I've seen this year. ❷ of course ▷ *« Est-ce que je peux t'emprunter ton stylo? » « Mais certainement! »* "Can I borrow your pen?" "Of course!"

certains [sɛRtɛ̃] pron ❶ some ▷ *certains de mes amis* some of his friends ▷ *certains d'entre vous* some of you ❷ some people ▷ *Certains pensent que le film est meilleur que le roman.* Some people think that the film is better than the novel.

certes [sɛRt(ə)] adv certainly ▷ *Nous nous connaissons, certes, mais nous ne sommes pas amis.* We know each other, certainly, but we are not friends.

certificat [sɛRtifika] nm certificate; **le certificat-cadeau** gift certificate

cerveau [sɛRvo] (pl **cerveaux**) nm brain

cervelle [sɛRvɛl] nf brain; **se creuser la cervelle** (informal) to rack one's brains

ces [se] adj ❶ these ▷ *Tu peux prendre ces photos si tu veux.* You can have these photos if you like.; **ces photos-ci** these photos ❷ those ▷ *Ces montagnes sont dangereuses en hiver.* Those mountains are dangerous in winter.; **ces livres-là** those books

cesse [sɛs] vb: **sans cesse** adv

continually; **Elle me dérange sans cesse.** She keeps interrupting me.

cesser [sese] vb to stop ▷ *cesser de faire quelque chose* to stop doing something

cessez-le-feu [seselfø] (pl **cessez-le-feu**) nm ceasefire

c'est-à-dire [setadiʀ] adv that is ▷ *Est-ce que tu peux venir lundi prochain, c'est-à-dire le quinze?* Can you come next Monday, that is, the 15th?

cet [sɛt] (f **cette**) adj

> ce changes to **cet** before a vowel and most words beginning with "h".

❶ this ▷ *cet après-midi* this afternoon ▷ *cet hiver* this winter ▷ *cette année* this year; **cette semaine-ci** this week ❷ that ▷ *Est-ce que tu peux me passer cette assiette?* Could you pass me that plate?; **cet homme-là** that man; **cette nuit (1)** tonight ▷ *On prévoit de l'orage pour cette nuit.* A storm is forecast for tonight. **(2)** last night ▷ *J'ai très mal dormi cette nuit.* I slept very badly last night.

ceux [sø] (fpl **celles**) pron ▷ *Prends ceux que tu préfères.* Take the ones you like best. ▷ *Je n'ai pas de skis mais je peux emprunter ceux de ma sœur.* I don't have any skis but I can borrow my sister's. ▷ *Je n'ai pas de jumelles mais je peux emprunter celles de mon frère.* I don't have any binoculars but I can borrow my brother's.; **ceux-ci** these ones; **celles-ci** these ones; **ceux-là** those ones; **celles-là** those ones

chacun [ʃakœ̃, -yn] pron (f **chacune**) ❶ each ▷ *Il nous a donné un cadeau à chacun.* He gave us each a present. ▷ *Nous avons chacun donné dix dollars.* We each gave 10 dollars. ▷ *Ces verres coûtent cinq dollars chacun.* These glasses cost 5 dollars each. ❷ everyone ▷ *Chacun fait ce qu'il veut.* Everyone does what they like.

chagrin [ʃagʀɛ̃] nm: **avoir du chagrin** to be very upset ▷ *Elle a eu beaucoup de chagrin à la mort de son oncle.* She was terribly upset by the death of her uncle.

chahut [ʃay] nm bedlam ▷ *Il y avait du chahut dans la classe.* There was bedlam in the classroom.

chaîne [ʃɛn] nf ❶ chain ▷ *une chaîne en or* a gold chain ❷ (on TV) channel ▷ *Le film passe sur quelle chaîne?* What channel is the film on?; **la chaîne alimentaire** food chain; **une chaîne de montagnes** a mountain range; **une chaîne stéréo** an audio system; **travailler à la chaîne** to work on an assembly line

chair [ʃɛʀ] nf flesh; **en chair et en os** in the flesh ▷ *Je l'ai vu en chair et en os.* I saw him in the flesh.; **avoir la chair de poule** to have goose pimples

chaise [ʃɛz] nf chair; **une chaise berçante** a rocking chair; **une chaise longue** a lounge chair

chaleur [ʃalœʀ] nf ❶ heat ❷ warmth

chaleureux [ʃalœʀø, -øz] (f **chaleureuse**) adj warm ▷ *un accueil chaleureux* a warm welcome

chaloupe [ʃalup] nf rowboat ▷ *Les enfants sont partis en chaloupe.* The kids left in the rowboat.

se chamailler [ʃamaje] vb (informal) to squabble ▷ *Elle se chamaille sans cesse avec son frère.* She's always squabbling with her brother.

chambre [ʃɑ̃bʀ(ə)] nf ❶ room ▷ *C'est la chambre de ma sœur.* This is my sister's room.; **une chambre à**

coucher a bedroom; **une chambre d'amis** a spare room; **une chambre à un lit** a single room; **une chambre pour une personne** a single room; **une chambre pour deux personnes** a double room; **la Chambre des communes** House of Commons

chameau [ʃamo] (pl **chameaux**) nm camel

champ [ʃɑ̃] nm field

champignon [ʃɑ̃piɲɔ̃] nm mushroom ▷ *une omelette aux champignons* a mushroom omelette

champion [ʃɑ̃pjɔ̃] nm champion

championnat [ʃɑ̃pjɔna] nm championship ▷ *le championnat du monde* the world championship

championne [ʃɑ̃pjɔn] nf champion

chance [ʃɑ̃s] nf ❶ luck; **Bonne chance!** Good luck!; **par chance** luckily; **avoir de la chance** to be lucky ▷ *Tu as de la chance de partir au soleil!* You're lucky, going off to a sunny place! ❷ chance ▷ *Il n'a aucune chance.* He doesn't have a chance. ▷ *Elle a des chances de réussir.* She has a good chance of passing.

chandail [ʃɑ̃daj] nm sweater ▷ *un chandail de laine* a wool sweater

change [ʃɑ̃ʒ] nm exchange ▷ *le taux de change* the exchange rate

changement [ʃɑ̃ʒmɑ̃] nm change ▷ *Elle n'aime pas le changement.* She doesn't like change. ▷ *le changement climatique* climate change

changer [ʃɑ̃ʒe] vb to change ▷ *Elle n'a pas beaucoup changé.* She hasn't changed much. ▷ *J'ai changé les draps ce matin.* I changed the sheets this morning. ▷ *J'ai changé trois cents dollars.* I changed 300 dollars.; **se changer** to get changed ▷ *Je*

vais me changer avant de sortir. I'm going to get changed before I go out.; **changer de** to change ▷ *Je change de chaussures et j'arrive!* I'll change my shoes and then I'll be ready!; **changer d'avis** to change one's mind; **changer de chaîne** to change the channel

chanson [ʃɑ̃sɔ̃] nf song

chant [ʃɑ̃] nm singing ▷ *des cours de chant* singing lessons; **un chant de Noël** a Christmas carol

chantage [ʃɑ̃taʒ] nm blackmail ▷ *faire du chantage à quelqu'un* to blackmail somebody

chanter [ʃɑ̃te] vb to sing

chanteur [ʃɑ̃tœr] nm singer

chanteuse [ʃɑ̃tøz] nf singer

chantier [ʃɑ̃tje] nm building site

Chantilly [ʃɑ̃tiji] nf whipped cream

chantonner [ʃɑ̃tɔne] vb to hum

chapeau [ʃapo] (pl **chapeaux**) nm hat

chapitre [ʃapitr(ə)] nm chapter

chaque [ʃak] adj ❶ every ▷ *chaque année* every year ❷ each ▷ *Donne un livre à chaque élève.* Give a book to each student.

char [ʃar] nm (military) tank

charabia [ʃarabja] nm (informal) gibberish ▷ *Je n'y comprends rien : c'est du charabia.* I don't understand any of it: it's gibberish.

charade [ʃarad] nf ❶ riddle ❷ charade ▷ *jouer aux charades* to play charades

charbon [ʃarbɔ̃] nm coal; **le charbon de bois** charcoal; **être sur des charbons ardents** to be on pins and needles

charcuterie [ʃarkytri] nf ❶ deli ❷ cold cuts

chardon [ʃardɔ̃] nm thistle

charger [ʃarʒe] vb to load; **charger quelqu'un de faire quelque chose**

to tell somebody to do something
▷ *Il m'a chargé de vous dire que la clé est sous le paillasson.* He told me to tell you that the key's under the mat.

chargeur [ʃaʀʒœʀ] nm charger

chariot [ʃaʀjo] nm shopping cart

charmant, -ât [ʃaʀmɑ̃, -ɑ̃t] (f **charmante**) adj charming

charme [ʃaʀm(ə)] nm charm

charmer [ʃaʀme] vb to charm

charrue [ʃaʀy] nf plough

chasse [ʃas] nf hunting ▷ *un chien de chasse* a hunting dog ▷ *la chasse au canard* duck hunting; **tirer la chasse d'eau** to flush the toilet

chasse-neige [ʃasnɛʒ] (pl **chasse-neige**) nm snowplow

chasser [ʃase] vb ❶ to hunt ▷ *Mon père hunts le lapin.* My father hunts rabbits. ❷ to chase away ▷ *Ils ont chassé les cambrioleurs.* They chased away the robbers. ❸ to get rid of ▷ *Ouvre donc la fenêtre pour chasser les odeurs de cuisine.* Open the window to get rid of the cooking smells.

chasseur [ʃasœʀ] nm hunter

chasseuse [ʃasøz] nf hunter

chat [ʃa] nm cat

châtain [ʃatɛ̃] (f+pl **châtain**) adj brown ▷ *J'ai les cheveux châtain.* I've got brown hair.

château [ʃato] (pl **châteaux**) nm ❶ castle ▷ *un château fort* a castle ❷ palace ▷ *le château de Versailles* the palace of Versailles

chaton [ʃatɔ̃] nm kitten

chatouiller [ʃatuje] vb to tickle

chatouilleux, -euse [ʃatujø, -øz] (f **chatouilleuse**) adj ❶ ticklish ❷ touchy ▷ *Il est un peu chatouilleux sur cette question.* He's a bit touchy on that issue.

chatte [ʃat] nf (female) cat

chaud, -ode [ʃo, -od] (f **chaude**) adj ❶ warm ▷ *des vêtements chauds* warm clothes; **avoir chaud** to

be warm or hot ▷ *J'ai assez chaud.* I'm warm enough. ❷ hot ▷ *Il fait chaud aujourd'hui.* It's hot today. ▷ *Attention, c'est chaud!* Careful, it's hot! ▷ *J'ai trop chaud!* It's too hot!

chauffage [ʃofaʒ] nm heating ▷ *Le chauffage est en panne.* The heating isn't working. ▷ *Baisse le chauffage.* Turn down the heat.; **le chauffage central** central heating

chauffe-eau [ʃofo] (pl **chauffe-eau**) nm water heater

chauffer [ʃofe] vb to heat ▷ *Je vais mettre de l'eau à chauffer pour faire du thé.* I'm going to put some water on to make tea.

chauffeur [ʃofœʀ] nm driver ▷ *un chauffeur de taxi* a taxi driver

chauffeuse [ʃoføz] nf driver ▷ *une chauffeuse d'autobus* a bus driver

chaussée [ʃose] nf roadway ▷ *Ne fais pas de la planche à roulettes sur la chaussée.* Don't skateboard on the road.

chausser [ʃose] vb: **Vous chaussez du combien?** What size shoe do you take?

chaussette [ʃosɛt] nf sock

chausson [ʃosɔ̃] nm slipper; **un chausson aux pommes** an apple turnover

chaussure [ʃosyʀ] nf shoe; **les chaussures de ski** ski boots

chauve [ʃov] adj bald

chauve-souris [ʃovsuʀi] (pl **chauves-souris**) nf (animal) bat

chef [ʃɛf] nmf ❶ head ▷ *une chef de famille monoparentale* a single parent; **le chef de l'État** the Head of State; **un chef d'entreprise** the director of a company ❷ chef ▷ *la spécialité de la chef* the chef's specialty; **un chef d'orchestre** a conductor; **le chef de bande** band chief

chef-d'œuvre [ʃɛ-] (pl **chefs-**

d'œuvre nm masterpiece

chemin [ʃəmɛ̃] nm ❶ path ▷ *Je suis descendu à la plage par un petit chemin.* I took a little path down to the beach. ❷ way ▷ *Quel est le chemin le plus court pour aller à l'aéroport?* What's the quickest way to the airport?; **en chemin** on the way ▷ *Je mangerai mon sandwich en chemin.* I'll eat my sandwich on the way.; **le chemin de fer** the railway

cheminée [ʃəmine] nf ❶ chimney ❷ fireplace

chemise [ʃəmiz] nf ❶ shirt ▷ *une chemise à carreaux* a checked shirt; **une chemise de nuit** a nightgown ❷ folder

chemisier [ʃəmizje] nm blouse

chêne [ʃɛn] nm oak ▷ *une armoire en chêne* an oak wardrobe

chenil [ʃənil] nm kennels

chenille [ʃənij] nf caterpillar

chèque [ʃɛk] nm cheque; **les chèques de voyage** traveller's cheques

chéquier [ʃekje] nm chequebook

cher [ʃɛʁ] (f **chère**) adj, adv ❶ dear ▷ *Chère Madame...* Dear Madam... ❷ expensive ▷ *C'est trop cher.* It's too expensive. ▷ *coûter cher* to be expensive

chercher [ʃɛʁʃe] vb ❶ to look for ▷ *Je cherche mes clés.* I'm looking for my keys. ❷ to look up ▷ *chercher un mot dans le dictionnaire* to look up a word in the dictionary; **aller chercher (1)** to go to get ▷ *Il est allé chercher du pain pour ce midi.* He's gone to get some bread for lunch. **(2)** to pick up ▷ *J'irai te chercher à la bibliothèque.* I'll pick you up at the library.

chercheur [ʃɛʁʃœʁ] nm researcher

chercheuse [ʃɛʁʃøz] nf researcher

chère [ʃɛʁ] adj *see* **cher**

chéri [ʃeʁi] (f **chérie**) adj darling

▷ *ma petite fille chérie* my darling daughter
▶ nm darling; **mon chéri** darling

chérie [ʃeʁi] nf darling; **ma chérie** darling

cheval [ʃəval, -o] (pl **chevaux**) nm horse ▷ *un cheval de course* a racehorse; **à cheval** on horseback; **faire du cheval** to go riding

chevalier [ʃəvalje] nm knight

chevaux [ʃəvo] nmpl *see* **cheval**

chevet [ʃəvɛ] nm: **une table de chevet** a bedside table; **une lampe de chevet** a bedside lamp

cheveux [ʃəvø] nmpl hair ▷ *Elle a les cheveux courts.* She has short hair.; **tiré par les cheveux** far-fetched ▷ *Son excuse était complètement tirée par les cheveux.* His excuse was totally far-fetched.

cheville [ʃəvij] nf ankle ▷ *se fouler la cheville* to sprain one's ankle

chèvre [ʃɛvʁ(ə)] nf goat; **le fromage de chèvre** goat cheese

chevreau [ʃəvʁo] (pl **chevreaux**) nm (animal, leather) kid

chevreuil [ʃəvʁœj] nm ❶ deer ❷ venison

chez [ʃe] prep: **chez mon ami (1)** at my friend's house **(2)** to my friend's house ▷ *Je suis resté chez moi cette fin de semaine.* I stayed from this weekend. **(2)** to my house ▷ *Je vais rentrer chez moi.* I'm going home.; **chez le dentiste (1)** at the dentist's ▷ *J'ai rendez-vous chez le dentiste demain matin.* I've got an appointment at the dentist's tomorrow morning. **(2)** to the dentist's ▷ *Je vais chez le dentiste.* I'm going to the dentist's.

chic [ʃik] (f+pl **chic**) adj ❶ smart ▷ *une tenue chic* a smart outfit ❷ nice ▷ *C'est chic de sa part.* (informal) That was nice of her.

chien [ʃjɛ̃] nm dog; « Attention, chien méchant » "Beware of dog"

chienne [ʃjɛn] nf (dog) bitch

chiffon [ʃifɔ̃] nm (cleaning, polishing) cloth

chiffonner [ʃifɔne] vb to crease ▷ Ma robe est toute chiffonnée. My dress is all creased.

chiffre [ʃifr(ə)] nm figure ▷ en chiffres ronds in round figures; **les chiffres romains** Roman numerals

chignon [ʃiɲɔ̃] nm (hair) bun ▷ Elle s'est fait un chignon. She put her hair in a bun.

chimie [ʃimi] nf chemistry ▷ un cours de chimie a chemistry lesson

chimique [ʃimik] adj chemical ▷ une réaction chimique a chemical reaction; **les armes chimiques** chemical weapons; **les produits chimiques** chemicals

Chinook [ʃinuk] nm (warm wind) chinook ▷ Un coup de chinook peut faire fondre trente centimètres de neige en une heure. A chinook can melt 30 centimetres of snow in one hour.

chiot [ʃjo] nm puppy

chirurgical [ʃiryʒikal, -o] (f chirurgicale, mpl chirurgicaux) adj: **une intervention chirurgicale** an operation

chirurgie [ʃiryʒi] nf surgery; **la chirurgie esthétique** plastic surgery

chirurgien [ʃiryʒjɛ̃] nm surgeon

chirurgienne [ʃiryʒjɛn] nf surgeon

choc [ʃɔk] nm shock ▷ Ça m'a fait un choc de le voir comme ça. It gave me a shock to see him in that state.; **Elle est encore sous le choc.** She's still in shock.

chocolat [ʃɔkɔla] nm chocolate; **un chocolat chaud** a hot chocolate; **le chocolat noir** dark chocolate

choisir [ʃwazir] vb to choose

choix [ʃwa] nm ❶ choice; **avoir le choix** to have the choice ❷ selection ▷ Il n'y a pas beaucoup de choix dans ce magasin. There's not a very wide selection in this store.

chômage [ʃomaʒ] nm unemployment; **être au chômage** to be unemployed

chômeur [ʃomœr] nm unemployed person ▷ Il est chômeur. He's unemployed.

chômeuse [ʃomøz] nf unemployed woman ▷ Elle est chômeuse. She's unemployed.

choquer [ʃɔke] vb to shock ▷ Cette remarque m'a choqué. I was shocked by that remark.

chorale [kɔral] nf choir

chose [ʃoz] nf thing ▷ J'ai fait des choses intéressantes pendant les vacances. I did some interesting things during the holidays.; **C'est peu de chose.** It's nothing really.

chou [ʃu] (pl choux) nm cabbage; **les choux de Bruxelles** Brussels sprouts; **un chou à la crème** a cream puff

chouchou [ʃuʃu] nm (informal) teacher's pet

chouchoute [ʃuʃut] nf (informal) teacher's pet

choucroute [ʃukrut] nf (with sausages and ham) sauerkraut

chouette [ʃwɛt] nf ❶ owl ❷ (to young girl) dear ▷ Oui, ma chouette! Yes, my dear!
▶ adj (informal) interesting ▷ un jeu très chouette a very chouette game

chou-fleur [ʃuflœr] (pl choux-fleurs) nm cauliflower

chrétien [kretjɛ̃, -ɛn] (f chrétienne) adj Christian ▷ Il est chrétien. He's a Christian.

chronique [krɔnik] adj chronic

▷ *une toux chronique* a chronic cough

chronique [kʀɔnik] *nf* column ▷ *Il écrit une chronique pour le journal de l'école.* He writes a column for the school newspaper.

chronologique [kʀɔnɔlɔʒik] *adj* chronological

chronomètre [kʀɔnɔmɛtʀ(ə)] *nm* stopwatch

chronométrer [kʀɔnɔmetʀe] *vb* to time

chuchoter [ʃyʃɔte] *vb* to whisper

chut [ʃy] *excl* Shh!

chute [ʃyt] *nf* fall; **faire une chute** to fall; **les chutes Niagara** Niagara Falls; **une chute d'eau** a waterfall

-ci [si] *adv* ▷ *ce livre-ci* this book; *ces bottes-ci* these boots

cible [sibl(ə)] *nf* target

ciboulette [sibulɛt] *nf* chives

cicatrice [sikatʀis] *nf* scar

se **cicatriser** [sikatʀize] *vb* to heal up ▷ *Cette plaie s'est vite cicatrisée.* This wound has healed up quickly.

ci-contre [sikɔ̃tʀ(ə)] *adv* opposite ▷ *la page ci-contre* the opposite page

ci-dessous [sidəsu] *adv* below ▷ *la photo ci-dessous* the picture below

ci-dessus [sidəsy] *adv* above

cidre [sidʀ(ə)] *nm* cider

ciel [sjɛl] *nm* ❶ sky ▷ *un ciel nuageux* a cloudy sky ❷ heaven ▷ *être au ciel* to be in heaven

cierge [sjɛʀʒ(ə)] *nm* (in church) candle

cigale [sigal] *nf* cricket

cigare [sigaʀ] *nm* cigar ▷ *Il ne fume plus le cigare.* He no longer smokes cigars.

cigarette [sigaʀɛt] *nf* cigarette

ci-joint [siʒwɛ̃] *adv* enclosed ▷ *Veuillez trouver ci-joint mon curriculum vitæ.* Please find enclosed my résumé.

cil [sil] *nm* eyelash

ciment [simɑ̃] *nm* cement

cimetière [simtjɛʀ] *nm* cemetery

cinéaste [sineast(ə)] *nmf* filmmaker

cinéma [sinema] *nm* movie theatre

cinq [sɛ̃k] *num* five ▷ *Il est cinq heures du matin.* It's five in the morning. ▷ *Elle a cinq ans.* She's five.; **le cinq février** the fifth of February

cinquantaine [sɛ̃kɑ̃tɛn] *nf* about fifty ▷ *Il y avait une cinquantaine de personnes.* There were about fifty people there.; **Il a la cinquantaine.** He's in his fifties.

cinquante [sɛ̃kɑ̃t] *num* fifty ▷ *Elle a cinquante ans.* She's fifty.; **cinquante et un** fifty-one; **cinquante-deux** fifty-two

cinquième [sɛ̃kjɛm] *adj* fifth ▷ *au cinquième étage* on the fifth floor ▷ *Mon frère est en cinquième année.* My brother is in Grade 5.

cintre [sɛ̃tʀ(ə)] *nm* coat hanger

cirage [siʀaʒ] *nm* shoe polish

circonflexe [siʀkɔ̃flɛks(ə)] *adj*: **un accent circonflexe** a circumflex

circonstance [siʀkɔ̃stɑ̃s] *nf* circumstance ▷ *dans les circonstances actuelles* in the present circumstances

circulation [siʀkylasjɔ̃] *nf* ❶ traffic ▷ *Il y avait beaucoup de circulation.* There was a lot of traffic. ❷ circulation ▷ *Elle a des problèmes de circulation.* She has bad circulation.

circuler [siʀkyle] *vb* to run ▷ *Il n'y a qu'un autobus sur trois qui circule.* Only one bus in three is running.

cire [siʀ] *nf* wax

cirer [siʀe] *vb* (shoes, floor) to polish; **papier ciré** waxed paper

cirque [siʀk(ə)] *nm* circus

ciseaux [sizo] *nmpl*: **une paire de ciseaux** a pair of scissors

citadin [sitadɛ̃] nm city person

citation [sitasjɔ̃] nf quotation

cité [site] nf town ▷ *une cité industrielle* an industrial town

> Be careful not to translate the French word **cité** as **city**.

une cité universitaire a university campus; **la cité parlementaire** Parliament buildings (in Québec city)

citer [site] vb to quote

citoyen [sitwajɛ̃] nm citizen

citoyenne [sitwajɛn] nf citizen

citoyenneté [sitwajɛnte] nf citizenship

citron [sitʁɔ̃] nm lemon

citrouille [sitʁuj] nf pumpkin

civière [sivjɛʁ] nf stretcher

civil [sivil] (f **civile**) adj civilian; **en civil** in civilian clothes

civilisation [sivilizasjɔ̃] nf civilization

civique [sivik] adj ● civic ▷ *son devoir civique* one's civic duty ● civil ▷ *les droits civiques* civil rights; **avoir le sens civique** to be public-spirited

clair [klɛʁ] (f **claire**) adj, adv ● light ▷ *vert clair* light green ▷ *C'est une pièce très claire.* It's a very bright room. ● (water) clear; **voir clair** to see clearly; **le clair de lune** moonlight

clairement [klɛʁmɑ̃] adv clearly

clairière [klɛʁjɛʁ] nf clearing

clandestin [klɑ̃dɛstɛ̃, -in] (f **clandestine**) adj: **un passager clandestin** a stowaway

claque [klak] nf slap

claquer [klake] vb ● to bang ▷ *On entend des volets qui claquent.* You can hear shutters banging. ● to slam ▷ *Elle est partie en claquant la porte.* She left, slamming the door.

claquette [klakɛt] nf: **danser la claquette** to tap-dance

clarinette [klaʁinɛt] nf clarinet

classe [klas] nf ● class ▷ *C'est le meilleur élève de la classe.* He's the best student in the class. ▷ *voyager en première classe* to travel first class ● classroom

classer [klase] vb to arrange ▷ *Les livres sont classés par ordre alphabétique.* The books are arranged in alphabetical order.

classeur [klasœʁ] nm filing cabinet

classique [klasik] adj ● classical ▷ *de la musique classique* classical music ● classic ▷ *un style classique* a classic style

clavardage [klavaʁdaʒ] nm (online) chat

clavarder [klavaʁde] vb (online) to chat

clavardoir [klavaʁdwaʁ] nm chat room

clavier [klavje] nm (computer, typewriter) keyboard; **le clavier numérique** keypad

clé [kle] nf ● key ▷ *une clé de voiture* a car key ● clef ▷ *la clé de sol* the treble clef ▷ *la clé de fa* the bass clef; **une clé anglaise** a wrench; **une clé électronique** a dongle

clef [kle] nf = **clé**

clic [klik] nm (computer mouse) click

client [klijɑ̃] nm customer

cliente [klijɑ̃t] nf customer

clientèle [klijɑ̃tɛl] nf customers

cligner [kliɲe] vb: **cligner des yeux** to blink

clignotant [kliɲɔtɑ̃] nm turn signal ▷ *Il a mis son clignotant gauche.* He's signalling left.

climat [klima] nm climate

climatisation [klimatizasjɔ̃] nf air conditioning

climatisé [klimatize] (f **climatisée**) adj air-conditioned ▷ *L'hôtel est climatisé.* The hotel is air-conditioned.

clin d'œil [klɛ̃-] (pl **clins d'œil**) nm wink; **en un clin d'œil** in a flash

clinique [klinik] nf clinic

clipart [klipart] nm clip-art

cliquer [klike] vb to click ▷ **cliquer sur une icône** to click on an icon

clochard [klɔʃar] nm tramp

cloche [klɔʃ] nf bell

clone [klon] nm clone

cloner [klone] vb to clone

clou [klu] nm nail; **un clou de girofle** a clove

clown [klun] nmf clown

CLSC nm = **Centre local de services communautaires**

- The **CLSC**, known as a **local community service centre** in English, is a public institution found in Québec communities. It provides social and health services.

club [klœb] nm club

cobaye [kɔbaj] nm guinea pig

cocaïne [kɔkain] nf cocaine

coccinelle [kɔksinɛl] nf ladybug

cocher [kɔʃe] vb to mark with a check ▷ **Cochez la bonne réponse.** Put a check beside the right answer.

cochon [kɔʃɔ̃] nm pig; **un cochon d'Inde** a guinea pig

coco [kɔko] nm: **une noix de coco** a coconut

cocotte [kɔkɔt] nf (pan) casserole

code [kɔd] nm code; **le code à barres** barcode; **le code postal** the postal code

cœur [kœr] nm ❶ heart; **avoir bon cœur** to be kind-hearted; **la dame de cœur** the queen of hearts; **avoir mal au cœur** to feel sick; **par cœur** by heart ▷ **apprendre quelque chose par cœur** to learn something by heart

coffre [kɔfr(ə)] nm ❶ (of car) trunk ❷ (furniture) chest

coffre-fort [kɔfrəfɔr] nm (pl **coffres-**

forts) nm safe

coffret [kɔfrɛ] nm: **un coffret à bijoux** a jewellery box

se **cogner** [kɔɲe] vb: **se cogner à quelque chose** to bump into something ▷ **Je me suis cogné à la table.** I bumped into the table. ▷ **Je me suis cogné la tête contre la porte du placard.** I bumped my head on the cupboard door.

coiffé [kwafe] (f **coiffée**) adj: **Tu es bien coiffée.** Your hair looks nice.

coiffer [kwafe] vb: **se coiffer** to do one's hair

coiffeur [kwafœr] nm hairdresser

coiffeuse [kwaføz] nf hairdresser

coiffure [kwafyr] nf hairstyle ▷ **Cette coiffure te va bien.** That hairstyle suits you.; **un salon de coiffure** a hair salon

coin [kwɛ̃] nm ❶ corner; **au coin de la rue** on the corner of the street; **Tu habites dans le coin?** Do you live around here?; **le dépanneur du coin** the local convenience store

coincé [kwɛ̃se] (f **coincée**) adj ❶ stuck ▷ **La clé est coincée dans la serrure.** The key is stuck in the lock. ❷ stuffy ▷ **Il est un peu coincé.** (informal) He's a bit stuffy.

coincer [kwɛ̃se] vb to jam ▷ **La porte est coincée.** The door's jammed.

coïncidence [kɔɛ̃sidɑ̃s] nf coincidence

col [kɔl] nm ❶ collar; **un col roulé** a turtleneck ❷ (mountain) pass

colère [kɔlɛr] nf anger; **Je suis en colère.** I'm angry.; **se mettre en colère** to get angry

colique [kɔlik] nf stomach pain

colis [kɔli] nm parcel

collaborer [kɔlabɔre] vb to collaborate

collant [kɔlɑ̃, -ɑ̃t] (f **collante**) adj ❶ sticky ❷ clingy; **Je la trouve**

un peu collante. (informal) She's always hanging around me.
▶ nm tights ▷ un collant en laine woollen tights

collation [kɔlasjɔ̃] nf snack

colle [kɔl] nf glue ▷ un tube de colle a tube of glue; **Je m'en sais rien : tu me poses une colle.** (informal) I don't know: you've got me there.

collecte [kɔlɛkt(ə)] nf (of money) collection ▷ On a fait une collecte au profit des victimes. There was a collection for the victims.; **une collecte de bouteilles vides** a bottle drive

collection [kɔlɛksjɔ̃] nf collection ▷ une collection de timbres a stamp collection

collectionner [kɔlɛksjɔne] vb to collect

collège [kɔlɛʒ] nm college; **collège communautaire** community college

collégien [kɔleʒjɛ̃] nm student

collégienne [kɔleʒjɛn] nf student

collègue [kɔlɛg] nmf colleague

coller [kɔle] vb ① to stick ▷ Il y a de la gomme à mâcher collée sous la chaise. There's a wad of chewing gum stuck under the chair. ② to be sticky ▷ Ce ruban ne colle plus. This tape is no longer sticky. ③ to press ▷ J'ai collé mon oreille au mur pour écouter. I pressed my ear against the wall to listen.

collier [kɔlje] nm ① necklace ▷ un collier de perles a pearl necklace ② (of dog, cat) collar

colline [kɔlin] nf hill; **la Colline du Parlement** Parliament Hill (in Ottawa)

collision [kɔlizjɔ̃] nf crash

colombe [kɔlɔ̃b] nf dove

Colombie-Britannique nf British Columbia

colonie [kɔlɔni] nf colony ▷ la colonie de la Nouvelle France the colony of New France

colonne [kɔlɔn] nf pillar; **la colonne vertébrale** the spinal column

colorant [kɔlɔrɑ̃] nm ① colouring ② dye

coma [kɔma] nm coma ▷ être dans le coma to be in a coma

combat [kɔ̃ba] nm fighting ▷ Les combats ont repris ce matin. Fighting started again this morning.; **un combat de boxe** a boxing match

combattant [kɔ̃batɑ̃] nm ① un ancien combattant a war veteran

combattre [kɔ̃batr(ə)] vb to fight

combien [kɔ̃bjɛ̃] adv ① how much ▷ Vous en voulez combien? Un kilo? How much do you want? One kilo?; **C'est combien?** How much is that? ▷ Combien est-ce que ça coûte? How much does it cost? ▷ Combien ça fait? How much does it come to? ▷ Tu en veux combien? Deux? How many do you want? Two?; **combien de (1)** how much ▷ Combien de purée de pomme de terre est-ce que je vous sers? How much mashed potato shall I give you? **(2)** how many ▷ Combien de personnes as-tu invitées? How many people have you invited?; **combien de temps** how long ▷ Combien de temps est-ce que tu seras absente? How long will you be away?; **Il y a combien de temps?** How long ago? ▷ Il est parti il y a combien de temps? How long ago did he leave?; **« On est le combien aujourd'hui? » — « On est le vingt. »** "What's the date today?" — "It's the 20th."

combinaison [kɔ̃binɛzɔ̃] nf combination ▷ J'ai changé la combinaison de mon antivol. I've changed the combination on my bike lock.; **une combinaison**

de plongée a wetsuit; **une combinaison de ski** a ski suit

comédie [kɔmedi] *nf* comedy; **une comédie musicale** a musical

comédien [kɔmedjɛ̃] *nm* actor

comédienne [kɔmedjɛn] *nf* actress

comestible [kɔmɛstibl(ə)] *adj* edible

comique [kɔmik] *adj* comical
▸ *n* comedian

comité [kɔmite] *nm* committee

commandant [kɔmɑ̃dɑ̃] *nm* (ship, plane) captain

commandante [kɔmɑ̃dɑ̃t] *nf* (ship, plane) captain

commande [kɔmɑ̃d] *nf* order ▸ *un bon de commande* an order form; **être aux commandes** to be at the controls

commander [kɔmɑ̃de] *vb* ❶ to order ▸ *J'ai commandé une robe par catalogue.* I've ordered a dress from the catalogue. ❷ to give orders ▸ *C'est moi qui commande ici, pas vous!* I give the orders here, not you!; **Elle commande le respect.** She commands respect.

comme [kɔm] *conj, adv* ❶ like ▸ *Elle est comme son père.* She's like her father. ▸ *Je voudrais un manteau comme celui de la photo.* I'd like a coat like the one in the picture. ❷ for ▸ *Qu'est-ce que tu veux comme dessert?* What would you like for dessert? ❸ as ▸ *J'ai travaillé comme serveuse cet été.* I worked as a waitress this summer. ▸ *Faites comme bon vous semble.* Do as you like.; **comme ça** like this ▸ *Ça se plie comme ça.* You fold it like this. ▸ *C'était un poisson grand comme ça.* The fish was this big.; **comme il faut** properly ▸ *Mets le couvert comme il faut!* Set the table properly!; **Comme tu as grandi!**

How you've grown!; **Regarde comme c'est beau!** Look, isn't it lovely!; **comme ci comme ça** so-so ▸ « *Comment est-ce que tu as trouvé le film?* » « *Comme ci comme ça.* » "What did you think of the film?" "So-so."

commencement [kɔmɑ̃smɑ̃] *nm* beginning

commencer [kɔmɑ̃se] *vb* to start ▸ *Les cours commencent à huit heures.* Classes start at 8 o'clock. ▸ *Il a commencé à pleuvoir.* It started raining. ▸ *J'ai commencé à réviser pour les examens.* I've started studying for the exams.

comment [kɔmɑ̃] *adv* how ▸ *Comment arrives-tu à travailler dans ce bruit?* How can you possibly work with this noise?; **Comment allez-vous?** How are you?; **Comment dit-on « pomme » en anglais?** How do you say "pomme" in English?; **Comment s'appelle-t-elle?** What's her name?; **Comment?** What did you say?

commentaire [kɔmɑ̃tɛr] *nm* comment

commérages [kɔmeraʒ] *nmpl* gossip

commerçant [kɔmɛrsɑ̃] *nm* storekeeper

commerçante [kɔmɛrsɑ̃t] *nf* storekeeper

commerce [kɔmɛrs(ə)] *nm* ❶ trade ▸ *le commerce extérieur* foreign trade; **le commerce électronique** e-commerce ❷ business ▸ *Il fait des études de commerce.* He's studying business. ▸ *tenir un commerce* to have a business

commercial [kɔmɛrsjal, -o] (*f* **commerciale**, *mpl* **commerciaux**) *adj*: **un centre commercial** a shopping centre

commettre [kɔmɛtr(ə)] *vb* to

commit ▷ *Elle a commis un crime grave.* She has committed a serious crime.

commissions [kɔmisjɔ̃] *nfpl* errands ▷ *J'ai quelques commissions à faire.* I've got some errands to run.

commode [kɔmɔd] *adj* handy ▷ *Ce sac est très commode pour les voyages.* This bag is very handy for travelling.; *Son père n'est pas commode.* His father is a difficult character.
▶ *nf* dresser

commun [kɔmœ̃, -yn] (f **commune**) *adj* shared ▷ *une salle de bain commune* a shared bathroom ▷ *Nous avons des intérêts communs.* We have interests in common.; **en commun** in common ▷ *Ils n'ont rien en commun.* They have nothing in common.; **les transports en commun** public transport; **mettre quelque chose en commun** to share something ▷ *Nous mettons tous nos livres en commun.* We share all our books.

communauté [kɔmynote] *nf* community

communication [kɔmynikasjɔ̃] *nf* communication; **une communication scientifique** a scientific conference

communiquer [kɔmynike] *vb* to communicate

communiste [kɔmynist(ə)] *adj* communist ▷ *le Parti communiste* the Communist Party

compact [kɔ̃pakt] (f **compacte**) *adj* compact; **un disque compact** a compact disc

compagne [kɔ̃paɲ] *nf* ❶ companion ❷ (*living together*) partner

compagnie [kɔ̃paɲi] *nf* company ▷ *J'aime avoir de la compagnie.* I like to have company. ▷ *Je viendrai te tenir compagnie.* I'll come and keep you company.; **une compagnie d'assurances** an insurance company; **une compagnie aérienne** an airline

compagnon [kɔ̃paɲɔ̃] *nm* ❶ companion ❷ (*living together*) partner

comparaison [kɔ̃parɛzɔ̃] *nf* comparison ▷ *en comparaison de* in comparison with

comparer [kɔ̃pare] *vb* to compare

compartiment [kɔ̃partimɑ̃] *nm* compartment

compas [kɔ̃pa] *nm* (*for drawing circles*) compass

compatible [kɔ̃patibl(ə)] *adj* compatible

compétence [kɔ̃petɑ̃s] *nf* ❶ skill ▷ *compétences de vie* life skills ❷ competence

compétent [kɔ̃petɑ̃, -ɑ̃t] (f **compétente**) *adj* competent

compétitif [kɔ̃petitif, -iv] (f **compétitive**) *adj* competitive

compétition [kɔ̃petisjɔ̃] *nf* competition; **avoir l'esprit de compétition** to be competitive

complet [kɔ̃plɛ, -ɛt] (f **complète**) *adj* ❶ complete ▷ *les œuvres complètes de Shakespeare* the complete works of Shakespeare ❷ full ▷ *L'hôtel est complet.* The hotel is full.; « complet » "no vacancies"
▶ *nm* (*men's*) suit

complètement [kɔ̃plɛtmɑ̃] *adv* completely ▷ *J'avais complètement oublié que tu venais.* I'd completely forgotten that you were coming.

compléter [kɔ̃plete] *vb* to complete ▷ *Complétez les phrases suivantes.* Complete the following sentences.

complexe [kɔ̃plɛks(ə)] *adj* complex

complication [kɔ̃plikasjɔ̃] nf
complication

complice [kɔ̃plis] nmf accomplice

compliments [kɔ̃plimɑ̃]
nmpl compliment; **faire des
compliments** to compliment ▷ Il
m'a fait des compliments sur ma robe.
He complimented me on my dress.

compliqué [kɔ̃plike] (f
compliquée) adj complicated
▷ C'est une histoire compliquée. It's a
complicated story.

complot [kɔ̃plo] nm (conspiracy)
plot

comportement [kɔ̃pɔʁtəmɑ̃] nm
behaviour

comporter [kɔ̃pɔʁte] vb ❶ to
consist of ▷ Le château comporte
trois parties. The castle consists
of three parts. ❷ (as a part) to
have ▷ Ce modèle comporte un écran
couleur. This model has a colour
screen.; **se comporter** to behave
▷ Elle s'est comportée de façon odieuse.
She behaved atrociously.

composer [kɔ̃poze] vb (music,
text) to compose; **composer
un numéro** to dial a number;
se composer de to consist of
▷ L'uniforme se compose d'une veste,
d'un pantalon et d'une cravate. The
uniform consists of a jacket, pants,
and a tie.

compositeur [kɔ̃pozitœʁ] nm
composer

composition [kɔ̃pozisjɔ̃] nf
(music, writing) composition

compositrice [kɔ̃pozitʁis] nf
composer

compostage [kɔ̃pɔstaʒ] nm
composting

composter [kɔ̃pɔste] vb to
compost

compote [kɔ̃pɔt] nf stewed fruit;
la compote de prunes stewed
plums

compréhensible [kɔ̃pʁeɑ̃sibl(ə)]
adj understandable

compréhensif [kɔ̃pʁeɑ̃sif,
-iv] (f **compréhensive**) adj
understanding

> Be careful! **compréhensif** does
not mean **comprehensive**.

compréhension [kɔ̃pʁeɑ̃sjɔ̃]
nf ❶ comprehension ▷ la
compréhension orale listening
comprehension ❷ sympathy;
**Elle a fait preuve de beaucoup
de compréhension.** She was very
sympathetic.

comprendre [kɔ̃pʁɑ̃dʁ(ə)]
vb ❶ to understand ▷ Je ne
comprends pas ce que vous dites. I
don't understand what you're
saying. ❷ to include ▷ Le forfait ne
comprend pas la location des skis. The
package doesn't include ski rental.

compris [kɔ̃pʁi, -iz] (f **comprise**)
adj included ▷ Le service n'est pas
compris. Service is not included.;
y compris including ▷ Ils ont tout
vendu, y compris leur voiture. They
sold everything, including their
car.; **non compris** excluding
▷ vingt dollars, frais de livraison
non compris 20 dollars, excluding
delivery charges; **cent dollars tout
compris** 100 dollars all-inclusive

compromettre [kɔ̃pʁɔmetʁ(ə)]
vb to compromise

compromis [kɔ̃pʁɔmi] nm
compromise ▷ Ils sont parvenus
à un compromis. They came to a
compromise.

comptabilité [kɔ̃tabilite]
nf accounting ▷ un cours de
comptabilité a course in accounting

comptable [kɔ̃tabl(ə)] nmf
accountant ▷ Elle est comptable.
She's an accountant.

comptant [kɔ̃tɑ̃] adv: **payer
comptant** to pay cash

compte [kɔ̃t] nm ❶ account ▷ *J'ai déposé le chèque dans mon compte.* I've deposited the cheque into my account. ❷ bill ▷ *le compte d'électricité* electricity bill ▷ *le compte de téléphone* telephone bill; **Le compte est bon.** That's the right amount.; **tenir compte de (1)** to take into account ▷ *Ils ont tenu compte de mon expérience.* They took my experience into account. **(2)** to pay attention to ▷ *Il n'a pas tenu compte de mes conseils.* He paid no attention to my advice.; **travailler à son compte** to be self-employed; **en fin de compte** all things considered ▷ *Le voyage ne s'est pas mal passé, en fin de compte.* The trip wasn't bad, all things considered.

compter [kɔ̃te] vb to count

compte rendu [-ʀɑ̃dy] (pl **comptes rendus**) nm report

compteur [kɔ̃tœʀ] nm meter

comptoir [kɔ̃twaʀ] nm counter ▷ *au comptoir* at the counter

se concentrer [kɔ̃sɑ̃tʀe] vb to concentrate ▷ *J'ai du mal à me concentrer.* I'm having trouble concentrating.

conception [kɔ̃sepsjɔ̃] nf design

concernant [kɔ̃sɛʀnɑ̃] prep regarding ▷ *Concernant notre nouveau projet, je voudrais ajouter que...* Regarding our new project, I would like to add that...

concerner [kɔ̃sɛʀne] vb to concern ▷ *en ce qui me concerne* as far as I'm concerned; **Je ne me sens pas concerné.** I figure it has nothing to do with me.

concert [kɔ̃sɛʀ] nm concert

concierge [kɔ̃sjɛʀʒ(ə)] nmf caretaker

conclure [kɔ̃klyʀ] vb to conclude

conclusion [kɔ̃klyzjɔ̃] nf conclusion

concombre [kɔ̃kɔ̃bʀ(ə)] nm cucumber

concorder [kɔ̃kɔʀde] vb *(agree)* to match ▷ *Les dates concordent.* The dates match.

concours [kɔ̃kuʀ] nm ❶ competition ▷ *un concours de chant* a singing competition ❷ contest

concret [kɔ̃kʀɛ, -ɛt] (f **concrète**) adj concrete

conçu [kɔ̃sy] vb designed ▷ *Ces appartements sont très mal conçus.* These apartments are very badly designed.

concurrence [kɔ̃kyʀɑ̃s] nf competition ▷ *La concurrence est vive sur ce marché.* There's a lot of competition in this market.

concurrent [kɔ̃kyʀɑ̃] nm competitor

concurrente [kɔ̃kyʀɑ̃t] nf competitor

condamner [kɔ̃dane] vb ❶ to sentence ▷ *Il a été condamné à deux ans de prison.* He was sentenced to two years in prison. ▷ *condamner à mort* to sentence to death ❷ to condemn ▷ *Le gouvernement a condamné cette décision.* The government condemned this decision.

condition [kɔ̃disjɔ̃] nf condition ▷ *Je le ferai à une condition...* I'll do it, on one condition...; **à condition que** provided that ▷ *Je viendrai à condition qu'elle me le demande.* I'll come provided she asks me to.; **les conditions de vie** living conditions

conditionnel [kɔ̃disjɔnɛl] nm conditional tense

condoléances [kɔ̃dɔleɑ̃s] nfpl sympathy ▷ *Veuillez accepter mes plus sincères condoléances.* Please accept my sincere sympathy.

condom [kɔ̃dɔm] nm condom

conducteur [kɔ̃dyktœʀ] nm driver

conductrice [kɔ̃dyktʀis] nf driver

conduire [kɔ̃dɥiʀ] vb to drive
▷ *Est-ce que tu sais conduire?* Can you drive? ▷ *Je te conduirai chez le docteur.* I'll drive you to the doctor.; **se conduire** to behave ▷ *Il s'est mal conduit.* He behaved badly.

conduite [kɔ̃dɥit] nf behaviour; **la conduite en état d'ivresse** impaired driving

confédération [kɔ̃federasjɔ̃] nf confederation ▷ *Le Canada est une confédération.* Canada is a confederation.; **la Confédération** Confederation

conférence [kɔ̃feʀɑ̃s] nf
❶ lecture ▷ *donner une conférence* to give a lecture ❷ conference ▷ *une conférence internationale* an international conference

confetti [kɔ̃feti] nm confetti

confiance [kɔ̃fjɑ̃s] nf ❶ trust; **avoir confiance en quelqu'un** to trust somebody ▷ *Je n'ai pas confiance en lui.* I don't trust him. ❷ confidence; **Tu peux avoir confiance. Il sera à l'heure.** You don't need to worry. He'll be on time.; **confiance en soi** self-confidence ▷ *Elle manque de confiance en elle.* She lacks self-confidence.

confiant [kɔ̃fjɑ̃, -ɑ̃t] (f **confiante**) adj confident

confidences [kɔ̃fidɑ̃s] nfpl: **faire des confidences à quelqu'un** to confide in someone ▷ *Elle me fait quelquefois des confidences.* She sometimes confides in me.

confidentiel [kɔ̃fidɑ̃sjɛl] (f **confidentielle**) adj confidential

confier [kɔ̃fje] vb: **se confier à quelqu'un** to confide in somebody ▷ *Il s'est confié à son meilleur ami.* He confided in his best friend.

confirmer [kɔ̃fiʀme] vb to confirm

confiserie [kɔ̃fizʀi] nf candy store

confisquer [kɔ̃fiske] vb to confiscate

confiture [kɔ̃fityʀ] nf jam ▷ *la confiture de fraises* strawberry jam

conflit [kɔ̃fli] nm conflict

confondre [kɔ̃fɔ̃dʀ(ə)] vb to mix up ▷ *On la confond souvent avec sa sœur.* People often get her mixed up with her sister.

confort [kɔ̃fɔʀ] nm comfort; **tout confort** luxurious ▷ *un appartement tout confort* a luxurious apartment

confortable [kɔ̃fɔʀtabl(ə)] adj comfortable ▷ *des chaussures confortables* comfortable shoes

confus [kɔ̃fy, -yz] (f **confuse**) adj ❶ unclear ▷ *J'ai trouvé ses explications confuses.* I thought his explanation was unclear. ❷ embarrassed ▷ *Il avait l'air confus.* He looked embarrassed.

confusion [kɔ̃fyzjɔ̃] nf ❶ confusion ❷ embarrassment ▷ *rougir de confusion* to blush with embarrassment

congé [kɔ̃ʒe] nm ❶ holiday ▷ *une semaine de congé* a week off; **en congé** on holiday ▷ *Je serai en congé la semaine prochaine.* I'll be on holiday next week. ❷ leave ▷ *être en congé de maladie* to be on sick leave ▷ *congé de maternité* maternity leave

congélateur [kɔ̃ʒelatœʀ] nm freezer

congeler [kɔ̃ʒle] vb to freeze

conjonction [kɔ̃ʒɔ̃ksjɔ̃] nf conjunction

conjugaison [kɔ̃ʒygɛzɔ̃] nf conjugation

connaissance [kɔnɛsɑ̃s] nf ❶ knowledge ▷ *pour approfondir vos connaissances* to increase your knowledge ❷ acquaintance ▷ *Ce* *n'est pas vraiment une amie, juste une connaissance.* She's not really a friend, just an acquaintance.; **perdre connaissance** to lose consciousness; **faire la connaissance de quelqu'un** to meet somebody ▷ *J'ai fait la connaissance de sa mère.* I met her mother.

connaître [kɔnɛtʀ(ə)] *vb* to know ▷ *Je ne connais pas du tout cette région.* I don't know this area at all. ▷ *Je le connais de vue.* I know him by sight.; **Ils se sont connus à Sudbury.** They first met in Sudbury.; **s'y connaître en quelque chose** to know about something ▷ *Je ne m'y connais pas beaucoup en musique classique.* I don't know much about classical music.

se **connecter** [kɔnɛkte] *vb* to log on ▷ *Je me suis connecté sur Internet il y a dix minutes.* I logged onto the Internet ten minutes ago.; **être connecté à un serveur** to be connected to a server

connu [kɔny] (*f* **connue**) *adj* well-known ▷ *C'est un acteur connu.* He's a well-known actor.

conquérir [kɔ̃keʀiʀ] *vb* to conquer

consacrer [kɔ̃sakʀe] *vb* to devote ▷ *Il consacre beaucoup de temps à ses enfants.* He devotes a lot of time to his children. ▷ *Je suis désolé, je n'ai pas beaucoup de temps à y consacrer.* I'm afraid I can't spare much time for it.

conscience [kɔ̃sjɑ̃s] *nf* conscience ▷ *avoir mauvaise conscience* to have a guilty conscience; **prendre conscience de** to become aware of ▷ *Ils ont fini par prendre conscience de la gravité de la situation.* They eventually became aware of the seriousness of the situation.

consciencieux [kɔ̃sjɑ̃sjø, -øz] (*f* **consciencieuse**) *adj*
conscientious

conscient [kɔ̃sjɑ̃, -ɑ̃t] (*f* **consciente**) *adj* conscious

consécutif [kɔ̃sekytif, -iv] (*f* **consécutive**) *adj* consecutive

conseil [kɔ̃sɛj] *nm* advice ▷ *Est-ce que je peux te demander conseil?* Can I ask you for some advice?; **un conseil** a piece of advice; **un conseil de bande** a band council; **le conseil étudiant** student council; **le conseil municipal** city council

conseiller [kɔ̃seje] *vb* ❶ to advise ▷ *Je te conseille de ne pas y aller.* I advise you not to go there. ❷ to recommend ▷ *Il m'a conseillé ce livre.* He recommended this book to me.
▶ *nm* ❶ (*political*) councillor ▷ *un conseiller municipal* a town councillor ❷ adviser ❸ counsellor; **un conseiller en orientation** a guidance counsellor

conseillère [kɔ̃sejɛʀ] *nf* ❶ (*political*) councillor ▷ *une conseillère municipale* a town councillor ❷ adviser ❸ counsellor; ▷ *une conseillère familiale* a family counsellor; **une conseillère en orientation** a guidance counsellor

consentement [kɔ̃sɑ̃tmɑ̃] *nm* consent ▷ *le consentement de tes parents* your parents' consent

consentir [kɔ̃sɑ̃tiʀ] *vb* to agree ▷ *consentir à quelque chose* to agree to something

conséquence [kɔ̃sekɑ̃s] *nf* consequence; **en conséquence** consequently

conséquent [kɔ̃sekɑ̃, -ɑ̃t] (*f* **conséquente**) *adj* ❶ rational ▷ *un comportement conséquent* rational behaviour ❷ consistent ▷ *de manière conséquente* in a consistent manner; **par conséquent** consequently

conservatoire [kɔ̃sɛʀvatwaʀ] *nm*

school of music ▷ **Elle fait du piano au conservatoire.** She's taking piano at the school of music.

conserve [kɔ̃sɛʀv(ə)] nf can ▷ **Je vais ouvrir une conserve.** I'll open a can.; **une boîte de conserve** a can; **les conserves** canned food ▷ **Il n'est pas bon de manger des conserves tous les jours.** It's not healthy to eat canned food every day.; **en conserve** canned ▷ **des petits pois en conserve** canned peas

conserver [kɔ̃sɛʀve] vb to keep ▷ **J'ai conservé toutes ses lettres.** I've kept all her letters.; **se conserver** to keep ▷ **Ce pain se conserve plus d'une semaine.** This bread will keep for more than a week.

considérable [kɔ̃sideʀabl(ə)] adj considerable ▷ **Il a fait des progrès considérables.** He's made considerable progress.

considération [kɔ̃sideʀasjɔ̃] nf: **prendre quelque chose en considération** to take something into consideration

considérer [kɔ̃sideʀe] vb to consider ▷ **Je la considère compétente.** I consider her to be competent.; **considérer que** to believe that ▷ **Elle considère que la décision du directeur était juste.** She believes that the principal's decision was fair.

consistant [kɔ̃sistɑ̃, -ɑ̃t] (f **consistante**) adj substantial ▷ **un petit déjeuner consistant** a substantial breakfast

▮ Be careful! **consistant** does not mean **consistent**.

consister [kɔ̃siste] vb: **consister à** to consist of ▷ **Mon travail consiste à répondre au téléphone et à recevoir les clients.** My job consists of answering the phone and welcoming customers. ▷ **En quoi consiste votre travail?** What does your job involve?

console de jeu [kɔ̃sɔl-] nf game console

consoler [kɔ̃sɔle] vb to comfort

consommateur [kɔ̃sɔmatœʀ] nm ❶ consumer ❷ (in café) customer

consommation [kɔ̃sɔmasjɔ̃] nf consumption ▷ **la consommation d'électricité** hydro consumption

consommatrice [kɔ̃sɔmatʀis] nf ❶ consumer ❷ (in café) customer

consommer [kɔ̃sɔme] vb to use ▷ **Ces grosses voitures consomment beaucoup d'essence.** These big cars use a lot of gas.

consonne [kɔ̃sɔn] nf consonant

constamment [kɔ̃stamɑ̃] adv constantly ▷ **Elle se plaint constamment.** She's constantly complaining.

constant [kɔ̃stɑ̃, -ɑ̃t] (f **constante**) adj constant

constater [kɔ̃state] vb to notice

constitué [kɔ̃stitɥe] (f **constituée**) adj: **être constitué de** to consist of

constituer [kɔ̃stitɥe] vb to make up ▷ **les dix provinces et les trois territoires qui constituent le Canada** the ten provinces and three territories that make up Canada

constitution [kɔ̃stitysjɔ̃] nf constitution ▷ **la Constitution canadienne** the Canadian Constitution

construction [kɔ̃stʀyksjɔ̃] nf building ▷ **des matériaux de construction** building materials; **une maison en construction** a house being built

construire [kɔ̃stʀɥiʀ] vb to build ▷ **Ils font construire une maison neuve.** They're having a new house built.

consultation [kɔ̃syltasjɔ̃] nf consultation

consulter [kɔ̃sylte] vb ❶ to consult ▷ *Tu devrais consulter un médecin.* You should see a doctor. ❷ to see patients ▷ *La docteure ne consulte pas le samedi.* The doctor doesn't see patients on Saturdays.

contact [kɔ̃takt] nm contact ▷ *les contacts humains* human contact; **garder le contact avec quelqu'un** to keep in touch with somebody

contacter [kɔ̃takte] vb to get in touch with ▷ *Je te contacterai dès que j'aurai des nouvelles.* I'll get in touch with you as soon as I have some news.

contagieux [kɔ̃taʒjø, -øz] (f **contagieuse**) adj ❶ infectious ▷ *une maladie contagieuse* an infectious disease ❷ contagious ▷ *Restez chez vous si vous êtes contagieux.* Stay at home if you're contagious.

contaminer [kɔ̃tamine] vb to contaminate ▷ *de l'eau contaminée* contaminated water

conte [kɔ̃t] nm story ▷ *un livre de contes* a storybook; **un conte de fées** a fairy tale

contempler [kɔ̃tɑ̃ple] vb to gaze at

contemporain [kɔ̃tɑ̃pɔʀɛ̃, -ɛn] (f **contemporaine**) adj contemporary; **un auteur contemporain** a modern writer

contenant [kɔ̃tnɑ̃] nm container ▷ *un contenant en plastique* a plastic container

contenir [kɔ̃tniʀ] vb to contain ▷ *un portefeuille contenant de l'argent* a wallet containing money

content [kɔ̃tɑ̃, -ɑ̃t] (f **contente**) adj glad ▷ *Je suis content que tu sois venu.* I'm glad you came.; **content de** pleased with ▷ *Elle m'a dit qu'elle était contente de mon travail.* She told me she was pleased with my work.

contenter [kɔ̃tɑ̃te] vb to please ▷ *Il est difficile à contenter.* He's hard to please.; **Je me contente de peu.** I can make do with very little.

contesté [kɔ̃teste] (f **contestée**) adj controversial ▷ *Cette décision est très contestée.* This is a very controversial decision.

conteur [kɔ̃tœʀ] nm storyteller

conteuse [kɔ̃tøz] nf storyteller

continent [kɔ̃tinɑ̃] nm mainland

continu [kɔ̃tiny] (f **continue**) adj continuous

continuellement [kɔ̃tinɥɛlmɑ̃] adv constantly

continuer [kɔ̃tinɥe] vb to continue ▷ *Continuez sans moi!* Go on without me! ▷ *Il ne veut pas continuer ses études.* He doesn't want to continue his studies.; **continuer à faire quelque chose** to go on doing something ▷ *Ils ont continué à regarder la télé sans me dire bonjour.* They went on watching TV without saying hello to me.; **continuer de faire quelque chose** to go on doing something ▷ *Elle continue de fumer malgré son asthme.* She continues to smoke despite her asthma.

contourner [kɔ̃turne] vb to go around ▷ *La route contourne la ville.* The road goes around the town.

contraceptif [kɔ̃trasɛptif] nm contraceptive

contraception [kɔ̃trasɛpsjɔ̃] nf contraception

contradiction [kɔ̃tradiksjɔ̃] nf contradiction; **par esprit de contradiction** just to be difficult ▷ *Il a refusé de venir par esprit de contradiction.* He refused to come, just to be difficult.

contraire [kɔ̃trɛr] nm opposite ▷ *C'est exactement le contraire.* It's just the opposite.; **au contraire** on the contrary

contrarier [kɔ̃traʀje] vb ❶ to annoy ▷ Il avait l'air contrarié. He looked annoyed. ❷ to upset ▷ Est-ce que tu serais contrarié si je ne venais pas? Would you be upset if I didn't come?

contraste [kɔ̃trast(ə)] nm contrast

contrat [kɔ̃tra] nm contract

contravention [kɔ̃travɑ̃sjɔ̃] nf parking ticket

contre [kɔ̃tr(ə)] prep ❶ against ▷ Ne mets pas ton vélo contre le mur. Don't put your bike against the wall. ❷ You are pour ou contre ce projet? Are you for or against this plan? ❷ for ▷ échanger quelque chose contre quelque chose to trade something for something; **par contre** on the other hand

contrebande [kɔ̃trəbɑ̃d] nf smuggling; **des produits de contrebande** smuggled goods

contrebasse [kɔ̃trəbas] nf double bass

contrecœur [kɔ̃trəkœr]: **à contrecœur** adv reluctantly ▷ Elle est venue à contrecœur. She came reluctantly.

contredire [kɔ̃trədir] vb to contradict ▷ Il ne supporte pas d'être contredit. He can't stand being contradicted.

contretemps [kɔ̃trətɑ̃] nm: Désolé d'être en retard; j'ai eu un contretemps. Sorry I'm late; I was held up.

contribuer [kɔ̃tribɥe] vb to contribute ▷ contribuer au succès d'un projet to contribute to the success of a project

contrôle [kɔ̃trol] nm ❶ control ▷ le contrôle des passeports passport control ❷ check; **un contrôle d'identité** an identity check;

le contrôle des billets ticket inspection ❸ test ▷ un contrôle antidopage a drug test

contrôler [kɔ̃trole] vb to check ▷ Personne n'a contrôlé mon billet. Nobody checked my ticket.

controversé [kɔ̃trɔvɛrse] (f **controversée**) adj controversial

convaincre [kɔ̃vɛ̃kr(ə)] vb ❶ to persuade ▷ Il a essayé de me convaincre de rester. He tried to persuade me to stay. ❷ to convince ▷ Tu n'as pas l'air convaincu. You don't look convinced.

convenable [kɔ̃vnabl(ə)] adj ❶ decent ▷ un hôtel convenable a decent hotel; **Ce n'est pas convenable.** It's bad manners.

convenir [kɔ̃vnir] vb: **convenir à** to suit ▷ Est-ce que cette date te convient? Does this date suit you? ▷ J'espère que cela vous conviendra. I hope this will suit you.; **convenir de** to agree on ▷ Nous avons convenu d'une date. We've agreed on a date.

convenu [kɔ̃vny] (f **convenue**) adj agreed ▷ au moment convenu at the agreed time

conversation [kɔ̃vɛrsasjɔ̃] nf conversation

convivial [kɔ̃vivjal] adj user-friendly ▷ Ce logiciel est très convivial. This program is very user-friendly.

cool [kul] adj (informal) cool

coopératif, -iv] [kɔɔperatif, -iv] (f **coopérative**) adj co-operative ▷ Elle s'est montrée très coopérative. She was very co-operative.

coopération [kɔɔperasjɔ̃] nf co-operation

coopérative [kɔɔperativ] nf co-op ▷ une coopérative d'habitation a housing co-op

coopérer [kɔɔpere] vb to co-operate

coordonnées [kɔɔrdɔne] nfpl

contact information ▷ *As-tu ses coordonnées?* Do you have his contact information?

copain [kɔpɛ̃] nm ❶ (informal) friend ▷ *C'est un bon copain.* He's a good friend. ❷ boyfriend ▷ *Je l'ai vue avec son copain.* I saw her with her boyfriend.

copie [kɔpi] nf copy ▷ *Ce tableau n'est qu'une copie.* This picture is only a copy.

copier [kɔpje] vb to copy; **copier-coller** to copy and paste

copieux [kɔpjø, -øz] (f **copieuse**) adj hearty ▷ *un repas copieux* a hearty meal

copine [kɔpin] nf ❶ (informal) friend ▷ *Je sors avec une copine ce soir.* I'm going out with a friend tonight. ❷ girlfriend ▷ *Je ne savais pas qu'il avait une copine.* I didn't know he had a girlfriend.

copropriété [kɔpʁɔpʁijete] nf condominium

coq [kɔk] nm rooster

coque [kɔk] nf (of boat) hull; **un œuf à la coque** a soft-boiled egg

coquelicot [kɔkliko] nm poppy

coquerelle [kɔkʁɛl] nf cockroach

coquillage [kɔkijaʒ] nm shell ▷ *Nous avons ramassé des coquillages sur la plage.* We picked up some shells on the beach.

coquille [kɔkij] nf shell; **une coquille d'œuf** an eggshell; **une coquille Saint-Jacques** a scallop

cor [kɔʁ] nm (instrument) horn ▷ *Je joue du cor.* I play the horn.

corbeau [kɔʁbo] (pl **corbeaux**) nm crow

corbeille [kɔʁbɛj] nf basket ▷ *une corbeille de fruits* a basket of fruit; **une corbeille à papier** a wastepaper basket

corde [kɔʁd(ə)] nf ❶ rope ❷ (guitar, tennis racquet) string;

une corde à linge a clothes line; **une corde élastique** a bungee cord

cordonnerie [kɔʁdɔnʁi] nf shoe repair shop

corne [kɔʁn(ə)] nf (on animal) horn

cornemuse [kɔʁnəmyz] nf bagpipes ▷ *jouer de la cornemuse* to play the bagpipes

cornet [kɔʁnɛ] nm: **un cornet de crème glacée** an ice cream cone

cornichon [kɔʁniʃɔ̃] nm pickle

corps [kɔʁ] nm body

correct [kɔʁɛkt] (f **correcte**) adj ❶ correct ▷ *Ce n'est pas tout à fait correct.* That's not quite correct. ❷ acceptable ▷ *C'est correct de faire des erreurs quand on apprend.* It's OK to make mistakes when you're learning. ▷ *Le repas était tout à fait correct.* The meal was quite acceptable.

correction [kɔʁɛksjɔ̃] nf correction

correspondance [kɔʁɛspɔ̃dɑ̃s] nf ❶ correspondence ▷ *La secrétaire s'occupe de toute la correspondance.* The secretary takes care of all the correspondence. ❷ (train, plane) connection ▷ *Il y a une correspondance pour Montréal à dix heures.* There's a connection for Montréal at ten o'clock.

correspondant [kɔʁɛspɔ̃dɑ̃] nm penpal

correspondante [kɔʁɛspɔ̃dɑ̃t] nf penpal

correspondre [kɔʁɛspɔ̃dʁ(ə)] vb to correspond ▷ *Écrivez le numéro qui correspond à votre réponse.* Write down the number that corresponds to your answer. ▷ *Elle correspond avec sa grand-mère en Inde.* She corresponds with her grandmother in India.

corridor [kɔʁidɔʁ] nm hallway

corriger [kɔʁiʒe] vb to mark ▷ *Vous*

pouvez corriger mon test? Can you mark my test?

corvée [kɔʀve] *nf* chore ▷ *Quelle corvée!* What a drag!

costaud [kɔsto, -od] (*f* **costaude**) *adj* well-built

costume [kɔstym] *nm* ❶ (man's) suit ▷ *Tu devrais mettre un costume et une cravate pour l'entrevue.* You should wear a suit and tie for the interview. ❷ (theatre) costume ▷ *Nous avons fait nous-mêmes tous les costumes pour la pièce.* We made all the costumes for the play ourselves.

côte [kot] *nf* ❶ coastline ▷ *La route longe la côte.* The road follows the coastline.; **la côte Ouest** the West Coast ❷ hill ▷ *J'ai grimpé la côte.* I went up the hill. ❸ rib ▷ *Il s'est cassé une côte en tombant.* He broke a rib when he fell.; **côte à côte** side by side; **les côtes levées** spareribs

côté [kote] *nm* side; **à côté de** (1) next to ▷ *Le café est à côté du sucre.* The coffee's next to the sugar. (2) next door to ▷ *Elle habite à côté de chez moi.* She lives next door to me.; **de l'autre côté** on the other side ▷ *La pharmacie est de l'autre côté de la rue.* The drugstore is on the other side of the street.; **De quel côté sont-ils partis?** Which way did they go?; **mettre quelque chose de côté** to save some money ▷ *J'ai mis de l'argent de côté.* I've saved some money.

côtelette [kotlɛt] *nf* chop ▷ *une côtelette d'agneau* a lamb chop

coton [kɔtɔ̃] *nm* cotton ▷ *une chemise en coton* a cotton shirt; **le coton hydrophile** cotton wool

cou [ku] *nm* neck

couchant [kuʃɑ̃] *adj:* **le soleil couchant** the setting sun

couche [kuʃ] *nf* ❶ layer ▷ *la couche*

d'ozone the ozone layer ❷ (of paint, varnish) coat ❸ diaper

couché [kuʃe] (*f* **couchée**) *adj* ❶ lying down ▷ *Il était couché sur le tapis.* He was lying on the carpet. ❷ in bed ▷ *Il est déjà couché.* He's already in bed.

coucher [kuʃe] *nm:* **un coucher de soleil** a sunset
▶ *vb* ❶ to go to bed ▷ *Je me suis couché tard hier soir.* I went to bed late last night. ❷ (sun) to set

couchette [kuʃɛt] *nf* crib

coude [kud] *nm* elbow; **donner un coup de coude à quelqu'un** to nudge somebody

coudre [kudʀ(ə)] *vb* ❶ to sew ▷ *J'aime coudre.* I like sewing. ❷ to sew on ▷ *Je ne sais même pas coudre un bouton.* I can't even sew a button on.

couette [kwɛt] *nf* duvet

couettes [kwɛt] *nfpl* pigtails ▷ *Quand j'étais petite, ma mère me faisait des couettes.* When I was little, my mother put my hair in pigtails.

couler [kule] *vb* ❶ to run ▷ *Ne laissez pas couler les robinets.* Don't leave the taps running. ▷ *J'ai le nez qui coule.* My nose is running. ❷ to flow ▷ *La rivière coulait lentement.* The river was flowing slowly. ❸ to leak ▷ *Mon stylo coule.* My pen's leaking. ❹ to sink ▷ *Le bateau a coulé.* The boat sank.

couleur [kulœʀ] *nf* colour ▷ *De quelle couleur est leur voiture?* What colour is their car? ▷ *un film couleur* a colour film; **Tu as pris des couleurs.** You've got a tan.

couleuvre [kulœvʀ(ə)] *nf* garter snake

coulisses [kulis] *nfpl* (in theatre) wings; **dans les coulisses** behind the scenes

couloir [kulwaʀ] *nm* hallway

coup [ku] nm ❶ knock ▷ *donner un coup à quelque chose* to give something a knock ❷ blow; **Il m'a donné un coup!** He hit me!; **un coup de coude** a nudge; **un coup de pied** a kick; **un coup de poing** a punch ❸ shock ▷ *Ça m'a fait un coup de le voir comme ça!* (informal) It gave me a shock to see him like that!; **un coup de feu** a shot; **un coup de téléphone** (informal) a call ▷ *Je te donnerai un coup de téléphone demain.* I'll give you a call tomorrow.; **donner un coup de main à quelqu'un** to give somebody a hand ▷ *Je viendrai te donner un coup de main.* I'll come and give you a hand.; **un coup d'œil** a quick look ▷ *jeter un coup d'œil sur quelque chose* to take a quick look at something; **attraper un coup de soleil** to get sunburned; **un coup de tonnerre** a clap of thunder; **après coup** afterwards ▷ *Après coup j'ai regretté de m'être mis en colère.* Afterwards I was sorry I'd got angry.; **à tous les coups** (informal) every time ▷ *Je me trompe de rue à tous les coups.* I get the street wrong every time.; **du premier coup** on the first try ▷ *Elle a été reçue au permis du premier coup.* She passed her driving test on the first try.; **sur le coup** right away ▷ *Sur le coup je ne l'ai pas reconnu.* I didn't recognize him right away.

coupable [kupabl(ə)] adj guilty
▷ n culprit

coupe [kup] nf (sport) cup ▷ *la coupe du monde* the World Cup; **une coupe de cheveux** a haircut; **la coupe glacée** sundae

coupe-ongle [kup-] nm nail clippers

couper [kupe] vb ❶ to cut ❷ to turn off ▷ *couper le courant* to

turn off the power ❸ to take a shortcut ▷ *On peut couper par la forêt.* There's a shortcut through the woods.; **couper l'appétit** to spoil one's appetite; **se couper** to cut oneself ▷ *Je me suis coupé le doigt.* I cut my finger.; **couper la parole à quelqu'un** to interrupt somebody; **couper les cheveux en quatre** to split hairs

couper-coller vb to cut and paste

coupe-vent [kup-] (pl **coupe-vent**) nm (jacket) windbreaker

couple [kupl(ə)] nm couple

coupure [kupyʀ] nf cut; **une coupure de courant** a power outage

cour [kuʀ] nf ❶ yard ▷ *la cour de l'école* the school yard ❷ court ▷ *la cour provinciale* the provincial court

courage [kuʀaʒ] nm courage

courageux [kuʀaʒø, -øz] (f **courageuse**) adj brave

couramment [kuʀamɑ̃] adv ❶ fluently ▷ *Elle parle couramment japonais.* She speaks Japanese fluently. ❷ commonly ▷ *C'est une expression que l'on emploie couramment.* It's a commonly used phrase.

courant [kuʀɑ̃, -ɑ̃t] (f **courante**) adj ❶ common ▷ *C'est une erreur courante.* It's a common mistake. ❷ standard ▷ *C'est un modèle courant.* It's a standard model.
▷ nm ❶ (of river) current; **un courant d'air** a draft ❷ power ▷ *une panne de courant* a power failure; **Je le ferai dans le courant de la semaine.** I'll do it some time during the week.; **être au courant de quelque chose** to know about something ▷ *Je ne suis pas au courant de ses projets pour l'été.* I don't know about her plans for the summer.; **mettre quelqu'un au courant de**

quelque chose to tell somebody about something; **Tu es au courant?** Have you heard?; **se tenir au courant de quelque chose** to keep up with something ▷ *J'essaie de me tenir au courant de l'actualité.* I try to keep up with the news.

courbe [kuʁb(ə)] adj curved ▷ *une surface courbe* a curved surface

courbé [kuʁbe] adj bent ▷ *des branches courbées sous le poids de la neige* branches bent by the weight of the snow

courbe [kuʁb(ə)] nf ❶ curve ❷ bend

coureur [kuʁœʁ] nm runner; **un coureur à pied** a runner; **un coureur cycliste** a racing cyclist; **un coureur automobile** race car driver; **coureur des bois** trapper

coureuse [kuʁøz] nf runner

courgette [kuʁʒɛt] nf zucchini

courir [kuʁiʁ] vb to run ▷ *Il a traversé la rue en courant.* He ran across the street.; **courir un risque** to run a risk

couronne [kuʁɔn] nf crown

courons, courez vb see **courir**

courriel [kuʁjɛl] nm email ▷ *Envoie-moi un courriel.* Send me an email.

courrier [kuʁje] nm mail ▷ *Est-ce qu'il y avait du courrier ce matin?* Was there any mail this morning?; **N'oublie pas de poster le courrier.** Don't forget to mail the letters.; **le courrier électronique** email

▌ Be careful! The French word **courrier** does not mean **courier**.

cours [kuʁ] nm ❶ lesson ▷ *un cours de danse* a dance lesson ▷ *des cours particuliers* private lessons ❷ course ▷ *un cours intensif* a crash course ❸ rate ▷ *le cours du change* the exchange rate; **au cours de**

during ▷ *Il a été réveillé trois fois au cours de la nuit.* He was woken up three times during the night.

course [kuʁs(ə)] nf ❶ running ▷ *la course de fond* long-distance running ❷ race ▷ *une course hippique* a horse race ❸ errand ▷ *J'ai juste une course à faire.* I've just got one errand to do.

court [kuʁ, kuʁt(ə)] (f **courte**) adj short

court de tennis [kuʁ-] nm tennis court

couru [kuʁy] vb see **courir**

couscous [kuskus] nm couscous

cousin [kuzɛ̃] nm cousin

cousine [kuzin] nf cousin

coussin [kusɛ̃] nm cushion

coût [ku] nm cost ▷ *le coût de la vie* the cost of living; **réduire les coûts** to cut costs

couteau [kuto] (pl **couteaux**) nm knife

coûter [kute] vb to cost ▷ *Est-ce que ça coûte cher?* Does it cost a lot?; **Combien ça coûte?** How much is it?

coûteux [kutø, -øz] (f **coûteuse**) adj expensive

coutume [kutym] nf custom

couture [kutyʁ] nf ❶ sewing ▷ *Je n'aime pas la couture.* I don't like sewing.; **faire de la couture** to sew ❷ seam ▷ *La couture de mon pantalon s'est défaite.* The seam of my pants has come apart.

couturier [kutyʁje] nm fashion designer ▷ *un grand couturier* a top designer

couturière [kutyʁjɛʁ] nf dressmaker

couvercle [kuvɛʁkl(ə)] nm ❶ (pot, jar, box, garbage can) lid ❷ (tube, bottle, spray can) cap

couvert [kuvɛʁ] vb see **couvrir**

couvert [kuvɛʁ, -ɛʁt(ə)] (f **couverte**) adj (sky) overcast;

couvert de covered with ▷ *Cet arbre est couvert de fleurs au printemps.* This tree is covered with blossoms in spring.

couverts [kuvɛʀ] nmpl cutlery ▷ *Les couverts sont dans le tiroir de gauche.* The cutlery is in the left-hand drawer.

couverture [kuvɛʀtyʀ] nf ❶ blanket ❷ cover ▷ *la couverture arrière du livre* the back cover of the book; **une page couverture** a cover page ❸ coverage ▷ *la couverture médiatique de l'événement* media coverage of the event

couvre-lit [kuvʀəli] nm bedspread

couvrir [kuvʀiʀ] vb to cover ▷ *Le chien est revenu couvert de boue.* The dog came back covered with mud.; **se couvrir (1)** to dress warmly ▷ *Couvre-toi bien : il fait très froid dehors.* Dress warmly: it's very cold outside. **(2)** to cloud over ▷ *Le ciel se couvre.* The sky's clouding over.

crabe [kʀab] nm crab

cracher [kʀaʃe] vb to spit

crachin [kʀaʃɛ̃] nm drizzle

craie [kʀɛ] nf chalk

craindre [kʀɛ̃dʀ(ə)] vb to fear ▷ *Tu n'as rien à craindre.* You have nothing to fear.

crainte [kʀɛ̃t] nf fear; **de crainte de** for fear of ▷ *Il n'ose rien dire de crainte de la vexer.* He doesn't dare say anything for fear of upsetting her.

craintif [kʀɛ̃tif, -iv] (f **craintive**) adj timid

crampe [kʀɑ̃p] nf cramp ▷ *J'ai une crampe au mollet.* I've got a cramp in my calf.

cran [kʀɑ̃] nm (*in belt*) hole; **avoir du cran** (*informal*) to have guts

crâne [kʀɑn] nm skull

crapaud [kʀapo] nm toad

craquelin [kʀaklɛ̃] nm cracker

craquer [kʀake] vb ❶ to creak ▷ *Le plancher craque.* The floor creaks. ❷ to break ▷ *Les coutures ont craqué sous l'effort.* The seams broke under the strain. ❸ to have a nervous breakdown ▷ *Je vais finir par craquer!* (*informal*) I'll have a nervous breakdown at this rate!; **Quand j'ai vu cette robe, j'ai craqué** (*informal*) When I saw that dress, I couldn't resist it!

crasse [kʀas] nf filth

crasseux [kʀasø, øz] (f **crasseuse**) adj filthy

cravate [kʀavat] nf tie

crawl [kʀol] nm crawl ▷ *nager le crawl* to do the crawl

crayon [kʀejɔ̃] nm pencil ▷ *un crayon de couleur* a pencil crayon; **un crayon feutre** a felt pen

création [kʀeasjɔ̃] nf creation

crédit [kʀedi] nm credit

créer [kʀee] vb to create

crème [kʀɛm] nf cream; **la crème anglaise** custard; **la crème Chantilly** whipped cream; **la crème fouettée** whipped cream; **la crème glacée** ice cream ▷ *un cornet de crème glacée* an ice cream cone; **une crème caramel** a crème caramel; **une crème au chocolat** a chocolate mousse

crémeux [kʀemø, -øz] (f **crémeuse**) adj creamy

crêpe [kʀɛp] nf crêpe

● A crêpe is like a pancake, but
● very thin and not as sweet. It
● can be eaten with syrup or other
● toppings – sweet ones like fruit
● and whipped cream, or savoury
● ones like seafood or vegetables
● in a cream or cheese sauce.
● Often the crêpe is rolled up with
● these inside.

crêperie [kʀɛpʀi] nf restaurant serving crêpes

crépuscule [krepyskyl] *nm* dusk

creuser [krøze] *vb* (*a hole*) to dig; **creuser l'appétit** to give an appetite; **se creuser la cervelle** (*informal*) to rack one's brains

creux [krø, -øz] (*f* **creuse**) *adj* hollow

crevaison [krɛvɛzɔ̃] *nf* flat tire

crevé [krəve] (*f* **crevée**) *adj* ❶ (*tire*) flat ❷ bagged ▷ *Je suis complètement crevé* (*informal*) I'm bagged!

crever [krəve] *vb* ❶ (*balloon*) to burst ❷ (*motorist*) to have a flat tire ▷ *J'ai crevé sur l'autoroute.* I had a flat tire on the highway.; **Je crève de faim!** (*informal*) I'm starving!; **Je crève de froid!** (*informal*) I'm freezing!

crevette [krəvɛt] *nf* shrimp

cri [kri] *nm* ❶ scream ▷ *J'ai entendu un cri.* I heard a scream. ▷ *pousser des cris de douleur* to scream with pain ❷ shout ▷ *des cris de colère* angry shouts ❸ call ▷ *Il sait reconnaître les cris des oiseaux.* He can identify bird calls.; **C'est le dernier cri.** It's the latest style. ▷ *Ce haut est du dernier cri.* This top is the latest style.

criard [krijar, -ard(ə)] (*f* **criarde**) *adj* (*colours*) garish

cric [krik] *nm* (*for car*) jack

crier [krije] *vb* to shout; **crier de douleur** to scream with pain

crime [krim] *nm* crime ▷ *un crime de guerre* a war crime

criminel [kriminɛl] *nm* criminal ▷ *un criminel de guerre* a war criminal

criminelle [kriminɛl] *nf* criminal

crinière [krinjɛr] *nf* mane

crique [krik] *nf* creek

criquet [krikɛ] *nm* grasshopper

crise [kriz] *nf* ❶ crisis; **la crise économique** the recession ❷ attack ▷ *une crise d'asthme* an

asthma attack ▷ *une crise cardiaque* a heart attack; **une crise de foie** an upset stomach; **piquer une crise de nerfs** to go hysterical; **avoir une crise de fou rire** to have the giggles

cristal [kristal, -o] (*pl* **cristaux**) *nm* crystal ▷ *un verre en cristal* a crystal glass

critère [kritɛr] *nm* criterion

critique [kritik] *adj* critical
▶ *nm* critic ▷ *un critique de cinéma* a film critic
▶ *nf* ❶ criticism ▷ *Elle ne supporte pas les critiques.* She can't stand being criticized. ❷ review ▷ *Le film a reçu de bonnes critiques.* The film got good reviews.

critiquer [kritike] *vb* to criticize

crochet [krɔʃɛ] *nm* ❶ hook ❷ detour ▷ *faire un crochet* to make a detour ❸ crochet ▷ *un chandail au crochet* a crocheted sweater ❹ square bracket

crocodile [krɔkɔdil] *nm* crocodile

croire [krwar] *vb* to believe ▷ *Il croit tout ce qu'on lui raconte.* He believes everything he's told.; **croire que** to think that ▷ *Tu crois qu'il fera meilleur demain?* Do you think the weather will be better tomorrow?; **croire à quelque chose** to believe in something; **croire en Dieu** to believe in God

crois [krwa] *vb see* **croire**

croîs [krwa] *vb see* **croître**

croisement [krwazmɑ̃] *nm* intersection ▷ *Tournez à gauche au croisement.* Turn left at the intersection.

croiser [krwaze] *vb*: **J'ai croisé ta sœur dans la rue.** I bumped into your sister in the street.; **croiser les bras** to fold one's arms; **croiser les jambes** to cross one's legs; **se croiser** to pass each other ▷ *Nous nous croisons dans l'escalier tous les* *matins*. We pass each other on the stairs every morning.

croisière [kʀwazjɛʀ] *nf* cruise

croissance [kʀwasɑ̃s] *nf* growth

croissant [kʀwasɑ̃] *nm* croissant ▷ *un croissant au beurre* a butter croissant; **le Croissant-Rouge** the Red Crescent

croit [kʀwa] *vb see* **croire**

croître [kʀwatʀ(ə)] *vb* to grow

croix [kʀwa] *nf* cross; **la Croix-Rouge** the Red Cross

croque-madame [kʀɔkmadam] *nm*

- A **croque-madame** is a toasted
- ham and cheese sandwich with
- a fried egg on top. The same
- thing without the fried egg is a
- **croque-monsieur**. The plural
- form of each is the same as the
- singular.

croquer [kʀɔke] *vb* to munch ▷ *croquer une pomme* to munch an apple

croquis [kʀɔki] *nm* sketch

crosse [kʀɔs] *nf* lacrosse

crotte [kʀɔt] *nf:* **une crotte de chien** dog dirt

crottin [kʀɔtɛ̃] *nm* ❶ manure ▷ *du crottin de cheval* horse manure ❷ small block of goat cheese

croustillant [kʀustijɑ̃, -ɑ̃t] (*f* **croustillante**) *adj* ❶ crisp; **un croustillant aux pommes** an apple crisp ❷ crusty

croustille [kʀustij] *nf* potato chip ▷ *un sac de croustilles* a bag of chips; **des croustilles de maïs** corn chips

croûte [kʀut] *nf* ❶ (*of bread*) crust; **en croûte** in pastry ❷ (*of cheese*) rind ❸ (*on skin*) scab

croûton [kʀutɔ̃] *nm* ❶ (*end of loaf*) crust ❷ crouton ▷ *des croûtons frottés d'ail* garlic croutons

croyons, croyez [kʀwajɔ̃, kʀwaje] *vb see* **croire**

cru [kʀy] (*f* **crue**) *vb see* **croire**

crû [kʀy] *vb see* **croître**

cruauté [kʀyote] *nf* cruelty

cruche [kʀyʃ] *nf* jug

crudités [kʀydite] *nfpl* (*cut up as hors d'œuvre*) raw vegetables

cruel [kʀyɛl] (*f* **cruelle**) *adj* cruel

crustacés [kʀystase] *nmpl* shellfish

cube [kyb] *nm* cube; **un mètre cube** a cubic metre

cueillette [kœjɛt] *nf* picking ▷ *la cueillette de fraises* strawberry picking

cueillir [kœjiʀ] *vb* (*flowers, fruit*) to pick

cuiller [kɥijɛʀ] *nf* spoon; **une cuiller à café** a teaspoon; **une cuiller à soupe** a soup spoon

cuillère [kɥijɛʀ] *nf* spoon; **une cuillère à café** a teaspoon; **une cuillère à soupe** a soup spoon

cuillerée [kɥijʀe] *nf* spoonful

cuir [kɥiʀ] *nm* leather ▷ *un sac en cuir* a leather bag; **le cuir chevelu** the scalp

cuire [kɥiʀ] *vb* to cook ▷ *cuire quelque chose à feu vif* to cook something on high heat; **cuire quelque chose au four** to bake something; **cuire quelque chose à la vapeur** to steam something; **faire cuire** to cook ▷ « *Faire cuire pendant une heure* » "Cook for one hour"; **bien cuit** well done; **trop cuit** overdone

cuisine [kɥizin] *nf* ❶ kitchen ❷ cooking ▷ *la cuisine française* French cooking; **faire la cuisine** to cook

cuisiné [kɥizine] (*f* **cuisinée**) *adj:* **un plat cuisiné** a ready-made meal

cuisiner [kɥizine] *vb* to cook ▷ *J'aime beaucoup cuisiner.* I love cooking.

cuisinier [kɥizinje] *nm* cook

cuisinière [kɥizinjɛʀ] *nf* ❶ cook

❷ stove ▷ *une cuisinière à gaz* a
gas stove

cuisse [kɥis] *nf* thigh; **une cuisse
de poulet** a chicken leg

cuisson [kɥisɔ̃] *nf* cooking ▷ *« une
heure de cuisson »* "cooking time:
one hour"

cuit [kɥi] *vb* see **cuire**

cuivre [kɥivʀ(ə)] *nm* copper

culot [kylo] *nm* (informal:
brazenness) nerve ▷ *Quel culot!*
What nerve!

culotte [kylɔt] *nf* (women's)
underpants

cultivateur [kyltivatœʀ] *nm*
farmer

cultivatrice [kyltivatʀis] *nf*
farmer

cultivé [kyltive] (f **cultivée**) *adj*
cultured ▷ *Elle est très cultivée.* She's
very cultured.

cultiver [kyltive] *vb* to grow ▷ *Ils
cultivent la vigne.* They grow grapes.;
cultiver la terre to farm the land

culture [kyltyʀ] *nf* ❶ culture ▷ *la
culture québécoise* Québecois culture
❷ education ▷ *Pour cet emploi, on
demande une bonne culture générale.*
For this job, a good general
education is needed.; **la culture
physique** physical education
❸ farming ▷ *les cultures intensives*
intensive farming

culturisme [kyltyʀism(ə)] *nm*
bodybuilding

cure-dent [kyʀdɑ̃] (*pl* **cure-dents**)
nm toothpick

curieux [kyʀjø, -øz] (f **curieuse**)
adj curious

curiosité [kyʀjozite] *nf* curiosity

curling [kœʀliŋ] *nm* curling

curriculum vitæ [kyʀikylɔmvite]
nm résumé

curseur [kyʀsœʀ] *nm* cursor

cuvette [kyvɛt] *nf* bowl ▷ *une
cuvette en plastique* a plastic bowl

CV [seve] *nm* (= *curriculum vitæ*)
résumé

cybercafé [sibɛʀkafe] *nm* Internet
café

cyclable [siklabl(ə)] *adj*: **une piste
cyclable** a bike path

cycle [sikl(ə)] *nm* cycle

cyclisme [siklism(ə)] *nm* cycling

cycliste [siklist(ə)] *nmf* cyclist

cyclone [siklon] *nm* cyclone

cygne [siɲ] *nm* swan

cynique [sinik] *adj* cynical

d

d' [d] *prep, art see* de

dactylo [daktilo] *nf* ❶ typist ▷ *Elle est dactylo.* She's a typist. ❷ typing ▷ *Je prends des cours de dactylo.* I'm doing typing lessons.

daim [dɛ̃] *nm* suede ▷ *une veste en daim* a suede jacket

dame [dam] *nf* ❶ lady ❷ (*in cards, chess*) queen

dames [dam] *nfpl* checkers

danger [dɑ̃ʒe] *nm* danger; **être en danger** to be in danger; **« Danger de mort »** "Extremely dangerous"

dangereux [dɑ̃ʒʀø, -øz] (*f* **dangereuse**) *adj* dangerous

danoise [danwaz] *nf* (*pastry*) danish

dans [dɑ̃] *prep* ❶ in ▷ *Je suis dans la cuisine.* I'm in the kitchen. ▷ *dans deux mois* two months from now ❷ into ▷ *Il est entré dans mon bureau.* He came into my office. ❸ out of ▷ *On a bu dans des verres*

en plastique. We drank out of plastic glasses.

danse [dɑ̃s] *nf* ❶ dance ▷ *la danse moderne* modern dance ▷ *des danses folkloriques* folk dances; **la danse classique** ballet ❷ dancing ▷ *des cours de danse* dancing lessons

danser [dɑ̃se] *vb* to dance

danseur [dɑ̃sœʀ] *nm* dancer

danseuse [dɑ̃søz] *nf* dancer

date [dat] *nf* date ▷ *votre date de naissance* your date of birth ▷ *la date limite de vente* the best-before date; **un ami de longue date** an old friend

dater [date] *vb*: **dater de** to date from ▷ *Cette coutume date du moyen âge.* This custom dates from the Middle Ages.

datte [dat] *nf* (*fruit*) date

dauphin [dofɛ̃] *nm* dolphin

davantage [davɑ̃taʒ] *adv* more ▷ *Le gouvernement doit aider les pauvres davantage.* The government must help poor people more.; **davantage de** more ▷ *Il faudrait davantage de stages de formation.* There should be more training courses.

DC [dese] *nm* (= *disque compact*) CD

de [d(ə)] *prep, art*

> See also **du** (= **de** + **le**) and **des** (= **de** + **les**). **de** changes to **d'** before a vowel and most words beginning with "h".

❶ of ▷ *le toit de la maison* the roof of the house ▷ *la capitale de Terre-Neuve* the capital of Newfoundland ▷ *la voiture de mes parents* my parents' car ▷ *la population de l'Alberta* the population of Alberta ▷ *deux bouteilles de vin* two bottles of wine ▷ *un litre d'essence* a litre of gas; **un bébé d'un an** a one-year-old baby; **un billet de cinquante dollars** a 50-dollar bill ❷ from

▷ *de Prince George à Whitehorse* from Prince George to Whitehorse ▷ *Je viens de Kingston.* I come from Kingston. ▷ *une lettre de ma sœur* a letter from my sister ❸ by ▷ *augmenter de dix dollars* to increase by ten dollars

> You use **de** to form expressions with the meaning of **some** and **any**.

Je voudrais de l'eau. I'd like some water. ▷ *du pain et de la confiture* bread and jam; **Il n'a pas de famille.** He hasn't got any family.; **Il n'y a plus de biscuits.** There aren't any more cookies.

dé [de] *nm* (one of a pair of dice) die; **un dé à coudre** a thimble

débâcle [debakl(ə)] *nf* (ice) break-up ▷ *La débâcle printanière cause souvent des inondations.* The spring break-up often creates floods.

déballer [debale] *vb* to unpack

débarbouillette [debaʀbujɛt] *nf* washcloth

débardeur [debaʀdœʀ] *nm* tank top

débarquer [debaʀke] *vb* ❶ (plane, ship) to disembark ▷ *Nous avons dû débarquer à Halifax.* We had to disembark at Halifax. ❷ (bus, train) to get off ▷ *débarquer de l'autobus* to get off the bus; **débarquer chez quelqu'un** (informal) to descend on somebody ▷ *Ils ont débarqué chez nous à dix heures du soir.* They descended on us at ten o'clock at night.

débarras [debaʀa] *nm* junk room; **Bon débarras!** Good riddance!

débarrasser [debaʀase] *vb* to clear ▷ *Tu peux débarrasser la table, s'il te plaît?* Can you clear the table please?; **se débarrasser de quelque chose** to get rid of something ▷ *Je me suis débarrassé*

de mon vieux frigo. I got rid of my old fridge.

débat [deba] *nm* debate

se débattre [debatʀ(ə)] *vb* to struggle

débile [debil] *adj* crazy ▷ *C'est complètement débile! (informal)* That's totally crazy!

débordé [debɔʀde] (*f* **débordée**) *adj*: **être débordé** to be snowed under

déborder [debɔʀde] *vb* (river) to overflow; **déborder d'énergie** to be full of energy

débouché [debuʃe] *nm* job prospect ▷ *Quels débouchés y a-t-il après ces études?* What sort of job does this course qualify you for?

déboucher [debuʃe] *vb* ❶ (sink, pipe) to unblock ❷ (bottle) to open; **déboucher sur** to lead into ▷ *La rue débouche sur une place.* The street leads into a square.

debout [dabu] *adv* ❶ standing up ▷ *Il a mangé ses céréales debout.* He ate his cereal standing up. ❷ upright ▷ *Mets les livres debout sur l'étagère.* Put the books upright on the shelf. ❸ up ▷ *Tu es déjà debout?* Are you up already?; **Debout!** Get up!

déboutonner [debutɔne] *vb* to unbutton

débrancher [debʀɑ̃ʃe] *vb* to unplug

débris [debʀi] *nm*: **des débris de verre** bits of glass

débrouillard [debʀujaʀ, -aʀd(ə)] (*f* **débrouillarde**) *adj* resourceful

se débrouiller [debʀuje] *vb* to manage ▷ *C'était difficile, mais je ne me suis pas trop mal débrouillé.* It was difficult, but I managed OK.; **Débrouille-toi tout seul.** Work things out for yourself.

début [deby] *nm* beginning ▷ *au*

début at the beginning; **début mai** in early May

débutant [debytã] *nm* beginner

débutante [debytãt] *nf* beginner

débuter [debyte] *vb* to start ▷ *Le président a débuté comme concierge.* The president started as a janitor. ▷ *La réunion a débuté par un discours.* The meeting started with a speech.

décaféiné [dekafeine] (f **décaféinée**) *adj* decaffeinated

décalage horaire [dekalaʒ-] *nm* (between time zones) time difference ▷ *Il y a une heure de décalage horaire entre le Nouveau-Brunswick et l'Ontario.* There's an hour's time difference between New Brunswick and Ontario.

décalquer [dekalke] *vb* to trace

décapotable [dekapɔtabl(ə)] *adj* convertible

décéder [desede] *vb* to die ▷ *Son père est décédé il y a trois ans.* Her father died three years ago.

décembre [desãbʀ(ə)] *nm* December; **en décembre** in December

décemment [desamã] *adv* decently

décent [desã, -ãt] (f **décente**) *adj* decent

déception [desɛpsjõ] *nf* disappointment

décerner [deseʀne] *vb* to award

décès [desɛ] *nm* death

décevant [desvã, -ãt] (f **décevante**) *adj* disappointing ▷ *Ses résultats sont plutôt décevants.* His results are rather disappointing.

décevoir [desvwaʀ] *vb* to disappoint

décharger [deʃaʀʒe] *vb* to unload

se déchausser [deʃose] *vb* to take off one's shoes

déchets [deʃɛ] *nmpl* waste ▷ *les*

déchets nucléaires nuclear waste ▷ *les déchets toxiques* toxic waste ▷ *les déchets dangereux* hazardous waste

déchiffrer [deʃifʀe] *vb* to decipher

déchirant [deʃiʀã, -ãt] (f **déchirante**) *adj* heart-rending

déchirer [deʃiʀe] *vb* ❶ (clothes) to tear ❷ to tear up ▷ *déchirer une lettre* to tear up a letter ❸ to tear out ▷ *déchirer une page d'un livre* to tear a page out of a book; **se déchirer un muscle** to tear a muscle

déchirure [deʃiʀyʀ] *nf* (rip) tear; **une déchirure musculaire** a torn muscle

décidé [deside] (f **décidée**) *adj* determined; **C'est décidé.** It's decided.

décidément [desidemã] *adv* certainly ▷ *Décidément, je n'ai pas de chance aujourd'hui.* I'm certainly not having much luck today.

décider [deside] *vb* to decide; **décider de faire quelque chose** to decide to do something ▷ *Ils ont décidé de passer leurs vacances en Alberta.* They decided to go to Alberta for their holiday.; **se décider** to make up one's mind ▷ *Elle n'arrive pas à se décider.* She can't make up her mind.

décisif [desizif, -iv] (f **décisive**) *adj* decisive

décision [desizjõ] *nf* decision

déclaration [deklaʀasjõ] *nf* statement ▷ *Je n'ai aucune déclaration à faire.* I have no statement to make.; **faire une déclaration de vol** to report something as stolen

déclarer [deklaʀe] *vb* to declare ▷ *déclarer la guerre à un pays* to declare war on a country; **se déclarer** to break out ▷ *Un feu s'est* *déclaré dans le gymnase.* A fire broke out in the gymnasium.

déclencher [deklɑ̃ʃe] vb (alarm, explosion) to set off; **se déclencher** to go off

déclic [deklik] nm click

décoiffé [dekwafe] (f **décoiffée**) adj: **Elle était toute décoiffée.** Her hair was in a real mess.

décollage [dekɔlaʒ] nm (of plane) takeoff

décoller [dekɔle] vb ● (sticker) to remove ▷ *décoller une étiquette* to remove a label; **se décoller** to come unstuck ● to take off ▷ *L'avion a décollé avec dix minutes de retard.* The plane took off ten minutes late.

décolleté [dekɔlte] (f **décolletée**) adj low-cut
▶ nm: **un décolleté plongeant** a plunging neckline

se décolorer [dekɔlɔʀe] vb to fade ▷ *Ce T-shirt s'est décoloré au lavage.* This T-shirt faded in the wash.; **se faire décolorer les cheveux** to get one's hair bleached

décombres [dekɔ̃bʀ(ə)] nmpl rubble

se décommander [dekɔmɑ̃de] vb to back out ▷ *Il devait venir mais il s'est décommandé à la dernière minute.* He was supposed to come, but he backed out at the last minute.

déconcerté [dekɔ̃sɛʀte] (f **déconcertée**) adj disconcerted

décongeler [dekɔ̃ʒle] vb to thaw

se déconnecter [dekɔnɛkte] vb to log out

déconseiller [dekɔ̃seje] vb: **déconseiller à quelqu'un de faire quelque chose** to advise somebody not to do something ▷ *Je lui ai déconseillé d'y aller.* I advised her not to go.; **C'est déconseillé.** It's not recommended.

décontenancé [dekɔ̃tnɑ̃se] (f

décontenancée) adj disconcerted

décontracté [dekɔ̃tʀakte] (f **décontractée**) adj relaxed; **des vêtements décontractés** casual clothes

se décontracter [dekɔ̃tʀakte] vb to relax ▷ *Il est allé faire du jogging pour se décontracter.* He went jogging to relax.

décor [dekɔʀ] nm ● décor ● scenery ▷ *un décor de montagnes* mountain scenery ● (for movie, play) set ▷ *un décor de cinéma* the set of a film ▷ *un superbe décor de théâtre* a superb stage set; **faire partie du décor** to be part of the furniture

décorateur [dekɔʀatœʀ] nm interior decorator

décoration [dekɔʀasjɔ̃] nf decoration

décoratrice [dekɔʀatʀis] nf interior decorator

décorer [dekɔʀe] vb to decorate

décortiquer [dekɔʀtike] vb to shell; **des crevettes décortiquées** peeled shrimp

découdre [dekudʀ(ə)] vb: **se découdre** to come unstitched

découper [dekupe] vb to cut out ▷ *J'ai découpé cet article dans le journal.* I cut this article out of the paper.

décourageant [dekuʀaʒɑ̃, ɑ̃t] (f **décourageante**) adj discouraging

décourager [dekuʀaʒe] vb to discourage; **se décourager** to get discouraged ▷ *Ne te décourage pas!* Don't give up!

décousu [dekuzy] (f **décousue**) adj unstitched ▷ *L'ourlet est décousu.* The hem's come unstitched.

découvert [dekuvɛʀ] nm overdraft

découverte [dekuvɛʀt(ə)] nf discovery

découvrir [dekuvʀiʀ] vb to

discover

décriminaliser [dekʀiminalize]
vb to decriminalize

décrire [dekʀiʀ] vb to describe

décrocher [dekʀɔʃe] vb ❶ to take
down ▷ Tu peux m'aider à décrocher
les rideaux? ❷ to pick
up the phone ▷ Il a décroché et a
composé le numéro. He picked up
the phone and dialled the number.
❸ (school) to drop out ▷ Il a décroché
avant de terminer son secondaire cinq.
He dropped out before finishing
Grade 12.; **décrocher le téléphone**
to take the phone off the hook

décrocheur [dekʀɔʃœʀ] nm
dropout

décrocheuse [dekʀɔʃøz] nf
dropout

déçu [desy] vb disappointed

dédaigneux [dedɛɲø, -øz] (f
dédaigneuse) adj disdainful ▷ d'un
air dédaigneux disdainfully

dédain [dedɛ̃] nm disdain ▷ avec
dédain with disdain

dedans [dədɑ̃] adv inside ▷ C'est
une jolie boîte : qu'est-ce qu'il y a
dedans? That's a nice box: what's
in it?; **là-dedans** (1) in there ▷ J'ai
trouvé les clés là-dedans. I found the
keys in there. **(2)** in that ▷ Il y a du
vrai là-dedans. There's some truth
in that.

dédicacé [dedikase] (f **dédicacée**)
adj : **un exemplaire dédicacé** a
signed copy

dédier [dedje] vb to dedicate

déduire [dedɥiʀ] vb ❶ to deduct
▷ Tu as déduit les vingt dollars que je te
devais? Did you deduct the twenty
dollars I owed you?; **déduire que** to
deduce that ▷ J'en déduis qu'elle m'a
menti. That means she must have
been lying.

déesse [deɛs] nf goddess

défaire [defɛʀ] vb to undo; **défaire
sa valise** to unpack; **se défaire** to
come undone

défaite [defɛt] nf defeat

défaut [defo] nm fault

défavorable [defavɔʀabl(ə)] adj
unfavourable

défavorisé [defavɔʀize] (f
défavorisée) adj underprivileged

défectueux [defɛktɥø, øz] (f
défectueuse) adj faulty

défendre [defɑ̃dʀ(ə)] vb ❶ to
forbid; **défendre à quelqu'un
de faire quelque chose** to forbid
somebody to do something ▷ Sa
mère lui a défendu de le revoir. Her
mother forbade her to see him
again. ❷ to defend ▷ défendre
ses idées to defend one's ideas
▷ défendre quelqu'un to defend
somebody

défendu [defɑ̃dy] (f **défendue**) adj
forbidden ▷ C'est défendu. It's not
allowed.

défense [defɑ̃s] nf ❶ defence
▷ prendre la défense de quelqu'un to
take somebody's side; **« défense
de fumer »** "no smoking" ❷ (of
elephant) tusk

défi [defi] nm challenge; **d'un air
de défi** defiantly; **sur un ton de
défi** defiantly

défier [defje] vb ❶ to challenge
▷ Je te défie de trouver un meilleur
exemple. I challenge you to find a
better example. ❷ to dare ▷ Il
m'a défié d'aller à l'école en pyjama.
He dared me to go to school in my
pyjamas.

défigurer [defigyʀe] vb to
disfigure

défilé [defile] nm ❶ parade; **un
défilé de mode** a fashion show
❷ march

défiler [defile] vb to march

définir [definiʀ] vb to define

définitif [definitif, -iv] (f
définitive) adj final; **en définitive**
in the end ▷ En définitive, ils ont
décidé de rester. In the end, they
decided to stay.

définitivement [definitivmã]
adv for good ▷ Elle s'est
définitivement installée en Nouvelle-
Écosse en 1980. She moved to Nova
Scotia for good in 1980.

déformer [defɔRme] vb to stretch
▷ Ne tire pas sur ton chandail, tu vas
le déformer. Don't pull down on
your sweater, you'll stretch it.; **se
déformer** to stretch ▷ Ce T-shirt
s'est déformé au lavage. This T-shirt
got stretched in the wash.

se défouler [defule] vb (relax) to
unwind ▷ Je fais de l'aérobic pour me
défouler. I do aerobics to unwind.

dégagé [degaʒe] (f **dégagée**) adj:
d'un air dégagé casually; **sur un
ton dégagé** casually

dégager [degaʒe] vb ❶ to free
▷ Ils ont mis une heure à dégager
les victimes. They took an hour to
free the victims. ❷ to clear ▷ des
gouttes qui dégagent le nez drops to
clear your nose; **Ça se dégage.**
(weather) It's clearing up.

se dégarnir [degaRniR] vb to
go bald

dégâts [dega] nmpl damage

dégel [deʒɛl] nm thaw

dégeler [deʒle] vb to thaw ▷ faire
dégeler un poulet congelé to thaw out
a frozen chicken

dégivrer [deʒivre] vb ❶ to defrost
❷ to de-ice

dégonfler [degɔfle] vb to let the
air out of ▷ Quelqu'un a dégonflé mes
pneus. Somebody let the air out of
my tires.; **se dégonfler** (informal) to
chicken out

dégouliner [deguline] vb to
trickle

dégourdi [deguRdi] (f **dégourdie**)
adj smart ▷ Il est assez dégourdi. He's
on the ball.

dégourdir [deguRdiR] vb: **se
dégourdir les jambes** to stretch
one's legs

dégoût [degu] nm disgust ▷ une
expression de dégoût a disgusted
expression; **avec dégoût**
disgustedly

dégoûtant [degutã, -ãt] (f
dégoûtante) adj disgusting

dégoûté [degute] (f **dégoûtée**) adj
disgusted; **être dégoûté de tout**
to be sick of everything

dégoûter [degute] vb to disgust
▷ Ce genre de comportement me
dégoûte. That kind of behaviour
makes me sick.; **dégoûter
quelqu'un de quelque chose** to
put somebody off something ▷ Ça
m'a dégoûté de la viande. That put
me off meat.

se dégrader [degRade] vb to
deteriorate

degré [dagRe] nm degree; **dix
degrés Celsius** 10°C

dégringoler [degRɛ̃gɔle] vb ❶ to
rush down ▷ Il a dégringolé l'escalier.
He rushed down the stairs. ❷ to
collapse ▷ Elle a fait dégringoler la
pile de livres. She knocked over the
stack of books.

dégueulasse [degœlas] adj (rude)
disgusting

déguisement [degizmã] nm
disguise

déguiser [degize] vb: **se déguiser
en quelque chose** to dress up
as something ▷ Elle s'est déguisée
en vampire. She dressed up as a
vampire.

déguster [degyste] vb ❶ (sample)
to taste ❷ to enjoy

dehors [dəɔR] adv outside ▷ Je
t'attends dehors. I'll wait for you

outside.; **jeter quelqu'un dehors** to throw somebody out; **en dehors de** apart from ▷ *En dehors de lui, tout le monde était content.* Apart from him, everybody was happy.

déjà [deʒa] *adv* **❶** already ▷ *J'ai déjà fini.* I'm already finished. **❷** before ▷ *Tu es déjà venu au Canada?* Have you been to Canada before?

déjeuner [deʒœne] *vb* to have breakfast
▸ *nm* breakfast
● In Canada, Belgium, Switzerland, and some areas of France, **le déjeuner** is the morning meal. Elsewhere in the francophone world, it refers to the noon meal.

délai [dele] *nm* **❶** extension ▷ *J'ai demandé un délai d'une semaine.* I asked for a week's extension. **❷** time limit ▷ *être dans les délais* to be within the time limit
▨ Be careful! **délai** does not mean **delay**.

délasser [delase] *vb* to relax ▷ *La lecture délasse.* Reading is relaxing.; **se délasser** to relax ▷ *J'ai pris un bain pour me délasser.* I had a bath to relax.

délavé [delave] (*f* **délavée**) *adj* faded ▷ *un jean délavé* a pair of faded jeans

délégué [delege] *nm* representative ▷ *les délégués de classe* the class representatives

déléguée [delege] *nf* representative

déléguer [delege] *vb* to delegate

délibéré [delibere] (*f* **délibérée**) *adj* deliberate

délicat [delika, -at] (*f* **délicate**) *adj* **❶** delicate ▷ *avoir la peau délicate* to have delicate skin ▷ *une situation délicate* a tricky situation **❸** tactful ▷ *Il est toujours très*

délicat. He's always very tactful. **❹** thoughtful ▷ *C'est une attention délicate de sa part.* That was a kind thought on her part.

délicatement [delikatmã] *adv* **❶** gently **❷** tactfully

délice [delis] *nm* delight ▷ *Vivre ici est un vrai délice.* Living here is a real delight. ▷ *Ce gâteau est un vrai délice.* This cake is a real treat.

délicieux [delisjø, -øz] (*f* **délicieuse**) *adj* delicious

délinquance [delẽkãs] *nf* crime ▷ *de nouvelles mesures pour combattre la délinquance juvénile* new measures to fight juvenile delinquency

délinquant [delẽkã] *nm* criminal

délinquante [delẽkãt] *nf* criminal

délirer [deline] *vb*: **Mais tu délires!** (*informal*) You're crazy!

délivrer [delivre] *vb* (*prisoner*) to set free

deltaplane [deltaplan] *nm* hang-glider; **faire du deltaplane** to go hang-gliding

demain [dəmẽ] *adv* tomorrow; **À demain!** See you tomorrow!

demande [dəmãd] *nf* request; **une demande en mariage** an offer of marriage; **faire une demande d'emploi** to apply for a job; **« demandes d'emploi »** "employment wanted"

demandé [dəmãde] (*f* **demandée**) *adj*: **très demandé** very much in demand

demander [dəmãde] *vb* **❶** to ask for ▷ *J'ai demandé la permission.* I've asked for permission. ▷ *On a demandé notre chemin à un chauffeur de taxi.* We asked a taxi driver the way. ▷ *Je lui ai demandé de m'aider.* I asked him to help me. **❷** to require ▷ *un travail qui demande beaucoup de temps* a job that requires a lot of time; **se demander** to wonder

▷ *Je me demande à quelle heure elle va venir.* I wonder what time she'll be coming.

Be careful! **demander** does not mean **to demand**.

demandeur d'emploi
[dəmãdœr-] *nm* job applicant

demandeuse d'emploi
[dəmãdøz-] *nf* job applicant

démangeaison [demãʒɛzɔ̃] *nf* itching

démanger [demãʒe] *vb* to itch ▷ *Ça me démange.* It itches.

démaquillant [demakijã] *nm* make-up remover

démaquiller [demakije] *vb*: **se démaquiller** to remove one's make-up

démarche [demarʃ(ə)] *nf* **①** way of walking ▷ *une drôle de démarche* a funny way of walking **②** step ▷ *faire les démarches nécessaires* to take the necessary steps

démarrer [demare] *vb* **①** (car) to start **②** to boot up

démêler [demele] *vb* to untangle

déménagement [demenaʒmã] *nm* (house) move ▷ *C'était le jour de notre déménagement.* It was the day we moved.; **un camion de déménagement** a moving van

déménager [demenaʒe] *vb* (house) to move

dément [demã, -ãt] (*f* **démente**) *adj* crazy

démentiel [demãsjɛl] (*f* **démentielle**) *adj* insane

demeurer [dəmœre] *vb* to live

demi [dəmi] (*f* **demie**) *adj, adv* half ▷ *Il a trois ans et demi.* He's three and a half.; **Il est trois heures et demie.** It's half past three.; **Il est midi et demi.** It's half past twelve.; **à demi endormi** half-asleep

demi-cercle [dəmisɛrkl(ə)] *nm* semicircle

demi-douzaine [dəmiduzɛn] *nf* half-dozen ▷ *une demi-douzaine d'œufs* half a dozen eggs

demie [dəmi] *nf* half-hour ▷ *L'autobus passe à la demie.* The bus comes by on the half-hour.

demi-finale [dəmifinal] *nf* semifinal

demi-frère [dəmifrɛr] *nm* half-brother

demi-heure [dəmijœr] *nf* half an hour ▷ *dans une demi-heure* in half an hour ▷ *toutes les demi-heures* every half-hour

demi-litre [dəmilitr(ə)] *nm* half litre ▷ *un demi-litre de lait* half a litre of milk

demi-sœur *nf* half-sister

démission [demisjɔ̃] *nf* resignation; **donner sa démission** to hand in one's resignation

démissionner [demisjɔne] *vb* to resign

demi-tarif [dəmitarif] *nm* **①** half-price ▷ *un billet à demi-tarif* a half-price ticket **②** half-fare ▷ *voyager à demi-tarif* to travel half-fare

demi-tour [dəmitur] *nm*: **faire demi-tour** to turn back ▷ *La nuit commence à tomber; il est temps de faire demi-tour.* It's getting dark; it's time we turned back.

démocratie [demɔkrasi] *nf* democracy

démocratique [demɔkratik] *adj* democratic

démodé [demɔde] (*f* **démodée**) *adj* old-fashioned

demoiselle [dəmwazɛl] *nf* young lady; **une demoiselle d'honneur** a bridesmaid

démolir [demɔlir] *vb* to demolish

démon [demɔ̃] *nm* devil

démonter [demɔ̃te] *vb* **①** (tent) to take down **②** (machine) to take apart

démontrer [demɔ̃tre] vb to show

déneiger [deneʒe] vb to clear of snow ▷ déneiger l'entrée to shovel the driveway ▷ déneiger les rues to plow the streets

déneigeuse [deneʒøz] nf ❶ snowplow ❷ snowblower

denim [dɛnim] nm denim ▷ une veste en denim a denim jacket

dénoncer [denɔ̃se] vb to denounce; **se dénoncer** to give oneself up ▷ Elle s'est dénoncée à la police. She gave herself up to the police.

dénouement [denumɑ̃] nm outcome

dent [dɑ̃] nf tooth ▷ une dent de lait a baby tooth ▷ une dent de sagesse a wisdom tooth

dentaire [dɑ̃tɛʀ] adj dental

dentelle [dɑ̃tɛl] nf lace ▷ un chemisier en dentelle a lacy blouse

dentier [dɑ̃tje] nm denture

dentifrice [dɑ̃tifʀis] nm toothpaste

dentiste [dɑ̃tist(ə)] nmf dentist

déodorant [deɔdɔʀɑ̃] nm deodorant

dépannage [depanaʒ] nm: **un service de dépannage** roadside assistance

dépanner [depane] vb ❶ to fix ▷ Elle a dépanné la voiture en cinq minutes. She fixed the car in five minutes. ❷ to help out ▷ Il m'a prêté dix dollars pour me dépanner. (informal) He lent me ten dollars to help me out.

dépanneur [depanœʀ] nm convenience store

dépanneuse [depanøz] nf tow truck

départ [depaʀ] nm departure ▷ Le départ est à onze heures. The departure is at 11.; **Je lui**

téléphonerai la veille de son départ. I'll phone him the day before he leaves.

département [depaʀtəmɑ̃] nm ❶ department ▷ le département d'anglais à l'université the English department at the university ▷ le département des articles ménagers the appliances department ❷ (in store)

dépasser [depase] vb ❶ to pass ▷ Nous avons dépassé Windsor. We've passed Windsor. ❷ Il y a une voiture qui essaie de nous dépasser. There's a car trying to overtake us. ❸ (sum, limit) to exceed

dépaysé [depeize] (f **dépaysée**) adj disoriented

se dépêcher [depeʃe] vb to hurry ▷ Dépêche-toi! Hurry up!

dépendre [depɑ̃dʀ(ə)] vb: **dépendre de** to depend on ▷ Ça dépend du temps. It depends on the weather.; **dépendre de quelqu'un** to be dependent on somebody; **Ça dépend.** It depends.

dépenser [depɑ̃se] vb (money) to spend

dépensier [depɑ̃sje, -jɛʀ] (f **dépensière**) adj: **Il est dépensier.** He's a big spender.; **Elle n'est pas dépensière.** She's not exactly extravagant.

dépilatoire [depilatwaʀ] adj: **une crème dépilatoire** a depilatory cream

dépit [depi] nm: **en dépit de** in spite of ▷ Il y est allé en dépit de mes conseils. He went in spite of my advice.

déplacé [deplase] (f **déplacée**) adj uncalled-for ▷ C'était une remarque déplacée. That remark was uncalled-for.

déplacement [deplasmɑ̃] nm trip ▷ Ça vaut le déplacement. It's worth the trip.

déplacer [deplase] vb ❶ to move
▷ *Tu peux m'aider à déplacer la table?*
Can you help me move the table?
❷ to put off ▷ *déplacer un rendez-vous* to put off an appointment; **se
déplacer (1)** to travel around ▷ *Elle
se déplace beaucoup pour son travail.*
She travels around a lot for her
work. **(2)** to get around ▷ *Elle a du
mal à se déplacer.* She has difficulty
getting around.; **se déplacer une
vertèbre** to slip a disc

déplaire [deplɛʀ] vb: **Cela me
déplaît.** I dislike this.

déplaisant [deplezɑ̃, -ɑ̃t] (f
déplaisante) adj unpleasant

dépliant [deplijɑ̃] nm brochure
▷ *un dépliant touristique* a tourist
brochure; **un dépliant publicitaire**
a flyer

déplier [deplije] vb to unfold

déposer [depoze] vb ❶ to
leave ▷ *J'ai déposé mon manteau
dans le vestiaire.* I left my coat in
the cloakroom. ❷ to put down
▷ *Déposez le paquet sur la table.* Put
the parcel down on the table. ❸ to
deposit ▷ *J'ai déposé cent dollars
dans mon compte.* I deposited 100
dollars into my account.; **déposer
quelqu'un** to drop somebody off

dépotoir [depotwaʀ] nm dump

dépourvu [depuʀvy] (f
dépourvue) adj destitute ▷ *des
gens dépourvus* destitute people;
être dépourvu de quelque chose
to lack something ▷ *Elle n'est pas
dépourvue de talent.* She has no lack
of talent.; **prendre quelqu'un au
dépourvu** to take somebody by
surprise ▷ *Sa question m'a pris au
dépourvu.* His question took me by
surprise.

dépression [depʀesjɔ̃] nf
depression; **faire de la dépression**
to be suffering from depression;

faire une dépression to have a
nervous breakdown

déprimant [depʀimɑ̃, -ɑ̃t] (f
déprimante) adj depressing

déprimer [depʀime] vb to get
depressed ▷ *Il déprime tout le temps.*
He gets depressed all the time.;
Ce genre de temps me déprime.
This kind of weather makes me
depressed.

depuis [dapɥi] prep, adv ❶ since
▷ *Elle habite Saskatoon depuis 1993.*
She's been living in Saskatoon since
1993. ▷ *Je ne lui ai pas parlé depuis.*
I haven't spoken to her since.;
depuis que since ▷ *Il a plu tous les
jours depuis qu'elle est arrivée.* It's
rained every day since she arrived.
❷ for ▷ *Il habite St. Catharines depuis
cinq ans.* He's been living in St.
Catharines for five years.; **Depuis
combien de temps?** How long?
▷ *Depuis combien de temps est-ce que
vous la connaissez?* How long have
you known her?; **Depuis quand?**
How long? ▷ *Depuis quand est-ce que
vous le connaissez?* How long have
you known him?

député [depyte] nm Member
of Parliament; **un député à
l'Assemblée législative** a Member
of the Legislative Assembly; **un
député à l'Assemblée nationale** a
Member of the National Assembly;
un député provincial a Member of
Provincial Parliament

députée [depyte] nf Member
of Parliament; **une députée à
l'Assemblée législative** a Member
of the Legislative Assembly;
**une députée à l'Assemblée
nationale** a Member of the
National Assembly; **une députée
provinciale** a Member of Provincial
Parliament

déraciner [deʀasine] vb to uproot

dérangement [deʁɑ̃ʒmɑ̃] nm: **en dérangement** out of order ▷ *Le téléphone est en dérangement.* The phone's out of order.

● **Le Grand Dérangement**, or **Great Deportation**, refers to the mass expulsion of Acadians by the British military between 1755 and 1762. The exiles were scattered throughout the Maritimes and several American colonies, including Louisiana.

déranger [deʁɑ̃ʒe] vb ❶ to bother ▷ *Excusez-moi de vous déranger.* I'm sorry to bother you.; **Ne vous dérangez pas, je vais répondre au téléphone.** You stay there, I'll answer the phone. ❷ to disorganize ▷ *Ne dérange pas mes livres, s'il te plaît.* Don't disorganize my books, please.

déraper [deʁape] vb to skid

dermatologue [dɛʁmatɔlɔɡ] nmf dermatologist ▷ *Elle est dermatologue.* She's a dermatologist.

dernier [dɛʁnje, -jɛʁ] (f **dernière**) adj ❶ last ▷ *Il est arrivé dernier.* He arrived last. ▷ *la dernière fois* the last time ❷ latest ▷ *leur dernier film* their latest film; **en dernier** last ▷ *Ajoutez le lait en dernier.* Put the milk in last.

dernièrement [dɛʁnjɛʁmɑ̃] adv recently

dérouler [deʁule] vb ❶ to unroll ❷ to unwind; **se dérouler** to take place ▷ *L'action se déroule dans les années vingt.* The action takes place in the 1920s.; **Tout s'est déroulé comme prévu.** Everything went as planned.

derrière [dɛʁjɛʁ] adv, prep behind ▶ nm ❶ back ▷ *la porte de derrière* the back door ❷ backside ▷ *un coup de pied dans le derrière* a kick in the backside

DES [deøɛs] nm (= *diplôme d'études secondaires*) secondary school diploma

des [de] art
 ● **des** is the contracted form of **de** + **les**.
 ❶ some ▷ *Tu veux des croustilles?* Would you like some chips?
 ● **des** is sometimes not translated.
 ▷ *J'ai des cousins en France.* I have cousins in France. ▷ *pendant des mois* for months ▷ *Tu as des frères?* Do you have any brothers? ▷ *la fin des vacances* the end of the holidays ▷ *la voiture des Durand* the Durands' car; **Ils arrivent des États-Unis.** They're arriving from the United States.

dès [dɛ] prep as early as ▷ *dès le mois de novembre* from November; **dès le début** right from the start; **Elle vous appellera dès son retour.** She'll call you as soon as she gets back.; **dès que** as soon as ▷ *Il m'a reconnu dès qu'il m'a vu.* He recognized me as soon as he saw me.

désabusé [dezabyze] (f **désabusée**) adj disillusioned

désaccord [dezakɔʁ] nm disagreement

désagréable [dezaɡʁeabl(ə)] adj unpleasant

désaltérer [dezaltere] vb: **L'eau gazeuse désaltère bien.** Sparkling water is very thirst-quenching.; **se désaltérer** to quench one's thirst ▷ *Nous sommes allés dans un café pour nous désaltérer.* We went into a café to have a drink.

désapprobateur [dezapʁɔbatœʁ, -tʁis] (f **désapprobatrice**) adj disapproving ▷ *un regard désapprobateur* a disapproving look

désastre [dezastʀ(ə)] nm disaster

désavantage [dezavɑ̃taʒ] nm disadvantage

désavantager [dezavɑ̃taʒe] vb: **désavantager quelqu'un** to put somebody at a disadvantage ▷ *Cette nouvelle loi va désavantager les femmes.* The new law will put women at a disadvantage.

descendre [desɑ̃dʀ(ə)] vb ❶ to go down ▷ *Je suis tombé en descendant l'escalier.* I fell as I was going down the stairs. ❷ to come down ▷ *Attends en bas; je descends!* Wait downstairs; I'm coming down! ❸ to get down ▷ *Vous pouvez descendre ma valise, s'il vous plaît?* Can you get my suitcase down, please? ❹ to get off ▷ *Nous descendons à la prochaine station.* We're getting off at the next station.

descente [desɑ̃t] nf way down ▷ *Je t'attendrai au bas de la descente.* I'll wait for you at the bottom of the hill.; **une descente de police** a police raid

description [deskʀipsjɔ̃] nf description

déséquilibré [dezekilibʀe] (f **déséquilibrée**) adj unbalanced

déséquilibrer [dezekilibʀe] vb: **déséquilibrer quelqu'un** to throw somebody off balance ▷ *Le coup de poing l'a déséquilibré.* The punch threw him off balance.

désert [dezɛʀ, -ɛʀt(ə)] (f **déserte**) adj deserted ▷ *Le dimanche, l'école est déserte.* On Sundays, the school is deserted.; **une île déserte** a desert island ▶ nm desert

déserter [dezɛʀte] vb to desert

désertique [dezɛʀtik] adj desert ▷ *une région désertique* a desert region

désespéré [dezespeʀe] (f **désespérée**) adj desperate

désespérer [dezespeʀe] vb to despair ▷ *Il ne faut pas désespérer.* Don't despair.

désespoir [dezɛspwaʀ] nm despair

déshabiller [dezabije] vb to undress; **se déshabiller** to get undressed

déshériter [dezeʀite] vb to disinherit; **les déshérités** the underprivileged

déshydraté [dezidʀate] (f **déshydratée**) adj dehydrated

désigner [dezijne] vb to choose ▷ *On l'a désignée pour remettre le prix.* She was chosen to present the prize.; **désigner quelque chose du doigt** to point at something

désinfectant [dezɛ̃fɛktɑ̃] nm disinfectant

désinfecter [dezɛ̃fɛkte] vb to disinfect

désintéressé [dezɛ̃teʀese] (f **désintéressée**) adj ❶ unselfish ▷ *un acte désintéressé* an unselfish action ❷ impartial ▷ *un conseil désintéressé* impartial advice

désintéresser [dezɛ̃teʀese] vb: **se désintéresser de quelque chose** to lose interest in something

désir [deziʀ] nm ❶ wish ▷ *Vos désirs sont des ordres.* Your wish is my command. ❷ will ▷ *le désir de réussir* the will to succeed ❸ desire ▷ *Ses yeux brillaient de désir.* Her eyes were shining with desire.

désirer [deziʀe] vb to want ▷ *Vous désirez?* (in store) What would you like?

désobéir [dezɔbeiʀ] vb: **désobéir à quelqu'un** to disobey somebody

désobéissant [dezɔbeisɑ̃, -ɑ̃t] (f **désobéissante**) adj disobedient

désobligeant [dezɔbliʒɑ̃, -ɑ̃t] (f

désobligeante adj unpleasant
▷ faire une remarque désobligeante to
make an unpleasant remark
désodorisant [dezɔdɔriză] nm
air freshener
désolé [dezole] (f **désolée**) adj
sorry ▷ Je suis vraiment désolé. I'm
very sorry.; **Désolé!** Sorry!
désopilant [dezɔpilã -ãt] (f
désopilante) adj hilarious
désordonné [dezɔrdɔne] (f
désordonnée) adj untidy
désordre [dezɔrdr(ə)] nm
messiness; **Quel désordre!** What
a mess!; **en désordre** messy ▷ Sa
chambre est toujours en désordre. His
bedroom is always messy.
désorganisé [dezɔrganize] adj
disorganized
désormais [dezɔrmɛ] adv from
now on ▷ Désormais, je travaillerai
plus fort. From now on I'll work
harder.
desquelles [dekɛl] pron
▎ **desquelles** is the contracted
form of **de + lesquelles**.
▷ des négociations au cours desquelles
les patrons ont fait des concessions
negotiations during which the
employers made concessions
desquels [dekɛl] pron
▎ **desquels** is the contracted
form of **de + lesquels**.
▷ les lacs au bord desquels nous avons
campé the lakes on the banks of
which we camped
dessécher [desefe] vb to dry out
▷ Le soleil dessèche la peau. The sun
dries your skin out.
desserrer [desere] vb to loosen
dessert [desɛr] nm dessert
▷ Qu'est-ce que vous désirez comme
dessert? What would you like for
dessert?
dessin [desɛ̃] nm drawing ▷ C'est
un dessin de ma petite sœur. It's a

drawing my little sister did.; **un
dessin animé** (film) a cartoon; **un
dessin humoristique** (drawing)
a cartoon
dessiner [desine] vb to draw
dessous [dəsu] adv underneath;
en dessous underneath ▷ Soulève
le pot de fleurs; la clé est en dessous.
Lift the flowerpot; the key's
underneath.; **par-dessous**
underneath ▷ Le grillage ne sert à
rien; les lapins passent par-dessous.
The fence is useless; the rabbits
get in underneath.; **là-dessous**
under there ▷ Elle s'est cachée
là-dessous. She hid under there.;
ci-dessous below ▷ Complétez les
phrases ci-dessous. Complete the
sentences below.; **au-dessous de**
below ▷ au-dessous de la moyenne
below average
▸ nm underneath; **les voisins
du dessous** the downstairs
neighbours; **les dessous**
underwear ▷ des dessous en soie silk
underwear
dessus [dəsy] adv on top ▷ un
gâteau avec des bougies dessus a cake
with candles on top; **par-dessus**
over ▷ Nous avons sauté par-dessus la
barrière. We jumped over the gate.;
au-dessus above ▷ la taille au-
dessus the size above ▷ au-dessus du
lit above the bed; **là-dessus (1)** on
there ▷ Tu peux écrire là-dessus. You
can write on there. **(2)** with that
▷ « Je démissionne! » Là-dessus, il
est parti. "I resign!" With that, he
left.; **ci-dessus** above ▷ l'exemple
ci-dessus the example above
▸ nm top; **les voisins du dessus**
the upstairs neighbours; **avoir le
dessus** to have the upper hand
destinataire [dɛstinatɛr] nmf
addressee
destination [dɛstinasjɔ̃] nf

destination; **les passagers à destination de Calgary** passengers travelling to Calgary

destine [dɛstine] adj intended for ▷ *Ce livre est destiné aux enfants.* This book is intended for children.; **Elle était destinée à faire ce métier.** She was destined to go into that job.

destruction [dɛstryksjɔ̃] nf destruction

détachant [detaʃɑ̃] nm stain remover

détacher [detaʃe] vb to undo; **se détacher de quelque chose** to come off something ▷ *La poignée de la porte s'est détachée.* The doorknob came off. ▷ *Un wagon s'est détaché du reste du train.* One car broke away from the rest of the train.

détail [detaj] nm detail; **en détail** in detail

détective [detektiv] nmf detective ▷ *un détective privé* a private detective

déteindre [detɛ̃dʀ(ə)] vb (in wash) to fade

détendre [detɑ̃dʀ(ə)] vb to relax ▷ *La lecture, ça me détend.* I find reading relaxing.; **se détendre** to relax ▷ *prendre un bain pour se détendre* to take a bath in order to relax

détente [detɑ̃t] nf relaxation

détenu [detny] nm prisoner

détenue [detny] nf prisoner

se détériorer [deterjɔre] vb to deteriorate

déterminé [detɛrmine] (f **déterminée**) adj ❶ determined ▷ *C'est un homme déterminé.* He's a determined man. ❷ specific ▷ *un but déterminé* a specific aim

détestable [detɛstabl(ə)] adj horrible

détester [detɛste] vb to hate

détonation [detɔnasjɔ̃] nf bang ▷ *J'ai entendu une détonation.* I heard a bang.

détour [detur] nm detour; **Ça vaut le détour.** It's worth the trip.; **sans détour** to someone's face ▷ *Elle me l'a dit sans détour.* She said it right to my face.

détournement [deturnəmɑ̃] nm: **un détournement d'avion** a hijacking

détrempé [detʀɑ̃pe] (f **détrempée**) adj waterlogged

détritus [detʀitys] nmpl litter

détruire [detʀɥir] vb to destroy

dette [dɛt] nf debt

deuil [dœj] nm: **être en deuil** to be in mourning

deux [dø] num two ▷ *Il était deux heures.* It was two o'clock. ▷ *Elle a deux ans.* She's two.; **deux fois** twice; **le deux-points** colon; **tous les deux** both ▷ *Nous y sommes allées toutes les deux.* We both went.; **le deux février** the second of February

deuxième [døzjɛm] adj second ▷ *au deuxième étage* on the second floor

deuxièmement [døzjɛmmɑ̃] adv secondly

devais, devait, devaient vb see **devoir**

dévaliser [devalize] vb to rob

devant [dəvɑ̃] adv, prep ❶ in front ▷ *Il marchait devant.* He was walking in front. ❷ in front of ▷ *Il était assis devant moi.* He was sitting in front of me.; **passer devant** to go past ▷ *Nous sommes passés devant chez toi.* We went past your house.
▶ nm front ▷ *le devant de la maison* the front of the house; **les pattes de devant** the front legs

développement [devlɔpmɑ̃] nm development; **les pays en voie**

de développement developing countries ▷ *le développement durable* sustainable development

développer [devlɔpe] vb to develop ▷ *donner un film à développer* to take a film to be developed; **se développer** to develop

devenir [dəvniʀ] vb to become

devez [dəve] vb see **devoir**

deviez [dəvje] vb see **devoir**

deviner [dəvine] vb to guess

devinette [dəvinɛt] nf riddle ▷ *poser une devinette à quelqu'un* to ask somebody a riddle

devions [dəvjɔ̃] vb see **devoir**

dévisager [devizaʒe] vb: **dévisager quelqu'un** to stare at somebody

devise [dəviz] nf currency ▷ *les devises étrangères* foreign currency

dévisser [devise] vb to unscrew

dévoiler [devwale] vb to unveil

devoir [dəvwaʀ] vb to have to ▷ *Je dois partir.* I've got to go. ❷ must ▷ *Tu dois être fatigué.* You must be tired. ❸ to be due to ▷ *Le nouveau centre commercial doit ouvrir en mai.* The new shopping centre is due to open in May.; **devoir quelque chose à quelqu'un** to owe somebody something ▷ *Combien est-ce que je vous dois?* How much do I owe you?
▶ nm ❶ exercise; **les devoirs** homework ❷ duty ▷ *Aller voter fait partie des devoirs du citoyen.* Voting is part of one's duty as a citizen.

devons [dəvɔ̃] vb see **devoir**

dévorer [devɔʀe] vb to devour

dévoué [devwe] (f **dévouée**) adj devoted

devra, devrai, devras, devrez, devrons, devront vb see **devoir**

diabète [djabɛt] nm diabetes

diabétique [djabetik] adj diabetic ▷ *Je suis diabétique.* I'm diabetic.

diable [djɑbl(ə)] nm devil

diagonal [djagɔnal, -o] (f **diagonale**, mpl **diagonaux**) adj diagonal

diagonale [djagɔnal] nf diagonal; **en diagonale** diagonally

diagramme [djagʀam] nm diagram

dialecte [djalɛkt(ə)] nm dialect

dialogue [djalɔg] nm dialogue

diamant [djamɑ̃] nm diamond

diamètre [djamɛtʀ(ə)] nm diameter

diapo [djapo] nf (informal) slide

diapositive [djapozitiv] nf slide ▷ *projeter des diapositives* to show some slides

diarrhée [djaʀe] nf diarrhoea ▷ *avoir la diarrhée* to have diarrhoea

dictateur [diktatœʀ] nm dictator

dictatrice [diktatʀis] nf dictator

dictature [diktatyʀ] nf dictatorship

dictée [dikte] nf dictation

dicter [dikte] vb to dictate

dictionnaire [diksjɔnɛʀ] nm dictionary

diététiste [djetetist] nmf dietitian

dieu [djø] (pl **dieux**) nm god ▷ *Dieu* God ▷ *Mon Dieu!* Oh my God!

différé [difeʀe] nm: **une émission en différé** a recording

différence [difeʀɑ̃s] nf difference; **la différence d'âge** the age difference; **à la différence de** unlike ▷ *À la différence de certains élèves, j'aime étudier.* Unlike some students, I like to study.

différent [difeʀɑ̃, -ɑ̃t] (f **différente**) adj ❶ different ▷ *pour des raisons différentes* for different reasons ❷ various ▷ *pour différentes raisons* for various reasons; **différent de** different from ▷ *Son point de vue est différent du mien.* Her point of view is different from mine.

difficile [difisil] *adj* difficult ▷ *C'est difficile à comprendre.* It's difficult to understand.

difficilement [difisilmɑ̃] *adv*: **faire quelque chose difficilement** to have trouble doing something ▷ *Ma grand-mère se déplace difficilement.* My grandmother has trouble getting around.; **Je pouvais difficilement refuser.** It was difficult for me to refuse.

difficulté [difikylte] *nf* difficulty ▷ *avec difficulté* with difficulty; **être en difficulté** to be in difficulties

digérer [diʒere] *vb* to digest

digne [diɲ] *adj*: **digne de** worthy of ▷ *digne de confiance* trustworthy

dignité [diɲite] *nf* dignity

dilemme [dilem] *nm* dilemma ▷ *être devant un dilemme* to be faced with a dilemma

diluer [dilɥe] *vb* to dilute

dimanche [dimɑ̃ʃ] *nm* ❶ Sunday ▷ *Aujourd'hui, on est dimanche.* It's Sunday today. ❷ on Sunday ▷ *Dimanche, nous allons déjeuner chez mes grands-parents.* On Sunday we're having lunch at my grandparents'.; **le dimanche** on Sundays ▷ *Le dimanche, je fais la grasse matinée.* I sleep in on Sundays.; **tous les dimanches** every Sunday; **dimanche dernier** last Sunday; **dimanche prochain** next Sunday

dimension [dimɑ̃sjɔ̃] *nf* ❶ size ▷ *avoir la même dimension* to be the same size ❷ measurement ▷ *Quelles sont les dimensions de cette pièce?* What are the measurements of this room? ❸ scope ▷ *la dimension du projet* the scope of the project

diminuer [diminɥe] *vb* to decrease ▷ *Est-ce que tu peux*

diminuer le son? Could you turn down the sound?

diminution [diminysjɔ̃] *nf* ❶ reduction ❷ decrease

dinde [dɛ̃d] *nf* turkey ▷ *la dinde de Noël* the Christmas turkey

dindon [dɛ̃dɔ̃] *nm* turkey

▌ **le dindon** refers to a live turkey, whereas **la dinde** refers most often to the meat; **la dinde** can, however, refer to the live female bird as well.

dîner [dine] *nm* lunch
● In Canada, Belgium, Switzerland, and some areas of France, **le dîner** is the noon meal.
● Elsewhere in the francophone world, it refers to the evening meal.
▶ *vb* to have lunch

dingue [dɛ̃g] *adj* (*informal*) crazy

diplomate [diplɔmat] *adj* diplomatic
▶ *n* diplomat

diplomatie [diplɔmasi] *nf* diplomacy

diplôme [diplom] *nm* diploma

dire [dir] *vb* ❶ to say ▷ *Il a dit qu'il ne viendrait pas.* He said he wouldn't come.; **on dit que…** they say that… ▷ *On dit que la nourriture est excellente là-bas.* They say that the food is excellent there. ❷ to tell; **dire quelque chose à quelqu'un** to tell somebody something ▷ *Elle m'a dit la vérité.* She told me the truth. ▷ *Elle nous a dit de regarder cette émission.* She told us to watch this program.; **On dirait qu'il va pleuvoir.** It looks as if it's going to rain.; **se dire quelque chose** ▷ *Quand je l'ai vu, je me suis dit qu'il avait vieilli.* When I saw him, I thought to myself that he'd aged.; **Est-ce que ça se dit?** Can you say that?; **Ça ne me dit rien.** That doesn't appeal to me.

direct [diʀɛkt] (f **directe**) adj
direct; **en direct** live ▷ *une émission
en direct* a live broadcast

directement [diʀɛktəmã] adv
straight ▷ *Elle est rentrée directement
chez elle.* She went straight home.

directeur [diʀɛktœʀ] nm
❶ principal ▷ *Il est directeur* He's
a principal. ❷ manager ▷ *Il
est directeur du personnel.* He's a
personnel manager.

direction [diʀɛksjɔ̃] nf
❶ management ▷ *la direction
et les ouvriers* management and
labour ❷ direction ▷ *dans toutes les
directions* in all directions

directrice [diʀɛktʀis] nf
❶ principal ▷ *Elle est directrice.*
She's a principal. ❷ manager ▷ *Elle
est directrice commerciale.* She's a
sales manager.

dirent [diʀ] vb see **dire**

dirigeant [diʀiʒã] nm leader

dirigeante [diʀiʒãt] nf leader

diriger [diʀiʒe] vb to manage
▷ *Il dirige une petite entreprise.* He
manages a small company.; **se
diriger vers** to head for ▷ *Il se
dirigeait vers la gare.* He was heading
for the station.

dis [dize] vb see **dire**; **Dis-moi la
vérité!** Tell me the truth!; **dis donc**
hey ▷ *Elle a drôlement changé, dis
donc!* Hey, she's really changed!
▷ *Dis donc, tu te souviens de cette
chanson?* Hey, do you remember
this song?

disaient, disais, disait vb see **dire**

discours [diskuʀ] nm speech

discret [diskʀe, -ɛt] (f **discrète**)
adj discreet

discrimination [diskʀiminasjɔ̃]
nf discrimination ▷ *la discrimination
raciale* racial discrimination
▷ *la discrimination sexuelle* sex

discrimination

discussion [diskysjɔ̃] nf
discussion

discutable [diskytabl(ə)] adj
debatable

discuter [diskyte] vb ❶ to talk
▷ *Nous avons discuté pendant des
heures.* We talked for hours. ❷ to
argue ▷ *C'est ce que j'ai décidé, alors
ne discutez pas!* That's what I've
decided, so don't argue!

disent, disiez, disions vb see **dire**

disons [dizɔ̃] vb see **dire** let's say
▷ *C'est à, disons, une demi-heure à
pied.* It's half an hour's walk, say.

disparaître [dispaʀɛtʀ(ə)] vb
to disappear; **faire disparaître
quelque chose (1)** to make
something disappear ▷ *Il a fait
disparaître le lapin dans son chapeau.*
He made the rabbit disappear in his
hat. **(2)** to get rid of something ▷ *Ils
ont fait disparaître tous les documents
compromettants.* They got rid of all
the incriminating documents.

disparition [dispaʀisjɔ̃] nf
disappearance; **une espèce en
voie de disparition** an endangered
species

disparu [dispaʀy] (f **disparue**) adj:
être porté disparu to be reported
missing

dispendieux [dispãdjø, -øz] (f
dispendieuse) adj expensive

dispense [dispãse] adj: **être
dispensé de quelque chose** to be
excused from something ▷ *Elle
est dispensée de gymnastique.* She's
excused from gym.

disperser [dispɛʀse] vb to
break up ▷ *La police a dispersé les
manifestants.* The police broke up
the demonstrators.; **se disperser**
to break up ▷ *Une fois l'ambulance
partie, la foule s'est dispersée.* Once
the ambulance had left, the crowd

broke up.

disponible [disponibl(ə)] *adj*
❶ available ▷ *Il y a encore des billets disponibles pour le concert.* Tickets are still available for the concert. ▷ *Ce livre est disponible en librairie.* This book is available in bookstores. ❷ free ▷ *Elle est toujours disponible le vendredi après-midi.* She's always free on Friday afternoons.

disposé [dispoze] (*f* **disposée**) *adj:* **être disposé à faire quelque chose** to be willing to do something ▷ *Il était disposé à m'aider.* He was willing to help me.

disposer [dispoze] *vb:* **disposer de quelque chose** to have access to something ▷ *Je dispose d'un ordinateur.* I have access to a computer.

disposition [dispozisjɔ̃] *nf:* **prendre ses dispositions** to make arrangements ▷ *Est-ce que vous avez pris vos dispositions pour partir en voyage?* Have you made arrangements for your trip?; **avoir quelque chose à sa disposition** to have something at one's disposal ▷ *J'ai un graveur de DC à ma disposition pour la semaine.* I have a CD burner at my disposal for the week.; **Je suis à votre disposition.** I am at your service.; **Je tiens les livres à votre disposition.** The books are at your disposal.

dispute [dispyt] *nf* argument
se disputer [dispyte] *vb* to argue
disque [disk(ə)] *nm* record; **un disque compact** a compact disc; **le disque dur** hard disk

disquette [disket] *nf* floppy disk
disséminé [disemine] (*f* **disséminée**) *adj* scattered
disséquer [diseke] *vb* to dissect
dissertation [disɛʀtasjɔ̃] *nf* essay
dissimuler [disimyle] *vb* to

conceal

se dissiper [disipe] *vb* to lift ▷ *Le brouillard va se dissiper dans l'après-midi.* The fog will lift during the afternoon.

dissolvant [disolvɑ̃, -ɑ̃t] *nm*
❶ solvent ❷ nail polish remover
dissoudre [disudʀ(ə)] *vb* to dissolve; **se dissoudre** to dissolve
dissuader [disɥade] *vb:* **dissuader quelqu'un de faire quelque chose** to dissuade somebody from doing something ▷ *Elle m'a dissuadé d'aller voir ce film.* She dissuaded me from going to see the movie.

distance [distɑ̃s] *nf* distance
distingué [distɛ̃ge] (*f* **distinguée**) *adj* distinguished
distinguer [distɛ̃ge] *vb* to distinguish

distraction [distʀaksjɔ̃] *nf* entertainment ▷ *Il lit beaucoup: c'est sa seule distraction.* He reads a lot: it's his only form of entertainment.

distraire [distʀɛʀ] *vb:* **Va voir un film, ça te distraira.** Go see a movie, it'll take your mind off things.

distrait [distʀɛ, -ɛt] (*f* **distraite**) *adj* absent-minded
distribuer [distʀibɥe] *vb* ❶ to give out ▷ *Distribue les livres, s'il te plaît.* Give out the books, please. ❷ (*cards*) to deal

distributrice [distʀibytʀis] *nf* vending machine

dit [di, dit] *vb see* **dire**
dit [di, dit] (*f* **dite**) *adj* known as ▷ *Toronto, dite Hogtown* Toronto, known as Hogtown

dites [dit] *vb see* **dire**; **Dites-moi ce que vous pensez.** Tell me what you think.; **dites donc** hey ▷ *Dites donc, vous, là-bas!* Hey, you there!

divan [divɑ̃] *nm* sofa; **le divan-lit**

sofa bed

divers [divɛʀ, -ɛʀs(ə)] (f **diverse**)
adj diverse; **pour diverses raisons**
for various reasons

se divertir [divɛʀtiʀ] vb to enjoy
oneself

divertissant [divɛʀtisɑ̃, -ɑ̃t] (f
divertissante) adj entertaining

divertissements [divɛʀtismɑ̃]
nmpl entertainment ▷ *Le centre
touristique offre des sports de plein
air, des soirées vidéo et d'autres
divertissements.* The resort offers
outdoor sports, video nights, and
other entertainment.

divin [divɛ̃, -in] (f **divine**) adj divine

diviser [divize] vb to divide
▷ *Quatre divisé par deux égalent deux.*
4 divided by 2 equals 2.

divorcé [divɔʀse] nm divorcee

divorcée [divɔʀse] nf divorcee

divorcer [divɔʀse] vb to get
divorced

dix [di, dis, diz] num ten ▷ *Elle a dix
ans.* She's ten. ▷ *À dix heures* at ten
o'clock; **le dix février** the tenth of
February

dix-huit [dizɥit] num: ▷ *Il a dix-huit
ans.* He's eighteen. ▷ *à dix-huit
heures* at 6 p.m.

dixième [dizjɛm] adj tenth ▷ *au
dixième étage* on the tenth floor

dix-neuf [diznœf] num: ▷ *Elle a dix-
neuf ans.* She's nineteen. ▷ *à dix-
neuf heures* at 7 p.m.

dix-sept [disɛt] num: ▷ *Il a dix-sept
ans.* He's seventeen. ▷ *à dix-sept
heures* at 5 p.m.

dizaine [dizɛn] nf about ten ▷ *une
dizaine de jours* about ten days

do [do] nm ❶ C ▷ *en do majeur* in
C major ❷ do ▷ *do, ré, mi... do,
re, mi...*

docteur [dɔktœʀ] nm doctor

docteure [dɔktœʀ] nf doctor

document [dɔkymɑ̃] nm

document

documentaire [dɔkymɑ̃tɛʀ] nm
documentary

documentation [dɔkymɑ̃tasjɔ̃]
nf documentation

documenter [dɔkymɑ̃te] vb: **se
documenter sur quelque chose** to
gather information on something

dodu [dody] (f **dodue**) adj plump

doigt [dwa] nm finger; **les doigts
de pied** the toes

dois, doit, doivent vb see **devoir**

domaine [dɔmɛn] nm ❶ estate
▷ *Il possède un immense domaine en
Colombie-Britannique.* He owns a
huge estate in British Columbia.
❷ field ▷ *La chimie n'est pas son
domaine.* Chemistry's not her field.

domestique [dɔmɛstik]
adj domestic; **les animaux
domestiques** pets

domicile [dɔmisil] nm place of
residence; **à domicile** at home
▷ *Il travaille à domicile.* He works
at home.

dominer [dɔmine] vb to
dominate; **se dominer** to control
oneself

dominos [dɔmino] nmpl
dominoes ▷ *jouer aux dominos* to
play dominoes

dommage [dɔmaʒ] nm damage
▷ *La tempête a causé d'importants
dommages.* The storm caused a
lot of damage.; **C'est dommage.**
Too bad. ▷ *C'est dommage que tu
ne puisses pas venir.* Too bad you
can't come.

dompter [dɔ̃te] vb to tame

dompteur [dɔ̃tœʀ] nm animal
tamer

dompteuse [dɔ̃tøz] nf animal
tamer

don [dɔ̃] nm ❶ donation ❷ gift
▷ *avoir un don pour quelque chose* to
have a gift for something; **Elle a le**

don de mettre les gens à l'aise. She's got the knack of putting people at ease.

donc [dɔ̃k] *conj* so

donjon [dɔ̃ʒɔ̃] *nm* (of castle) keep

données [dɔne] *nfpl* data

donner [dɔne] *vb* ❶ to give; **donner quelque chose à quelqu'un** to give somebody something ▷ *Elle m'a donné son adresse.* She gave me her address.; *Ça m'a donné faim.* That made me feel hungry. ❷ to give away ▷ *« Tu as toujours ta veste en daim? »* *« Non, je l'ai donnée. »* "Do you still have your suede jacket?" "No, I gave it away."; **donner sur quelque chose** to overlook something ▷ *une fenêtre qui donne sur la mer a window overlooking the sea*

dont [dɔ̃] *pron* ❶ of which ▷ *deux livres, dont l'un est en anglais* two books, one of which is in English ▷ *le prix dont il est si fier* the prize he's so proud of ❷ of whom ▷ *dix blessés, dont deux grièvement* ten people injured, two of them seriously ▷ *la fille dont je t'ai parlé* the girl I told you about

doré [dɔʀe] (*f* **dorée**) *adj* golden ▷ *une étoile dorée* a golden star; **le pain doré** French toast
▶ *nm* (fish) walleye

dorénavant [dɔʀenavɑ̃] *adv* from now on ▷ *Dorénavant, tu feras attention.* From now on, you'll be careful.

dorloter [dɔʀlɔte] *vb* to pamper

dormir [dɔʀmiʀ] *vb* ❶ to sleep ▷ *Tu as bien dormi?* Did you sleep well? ❷ to be asleep ▷ *Ne faites pas de bruit, il dort.* Don't make any noise, he's asleep.

dortoir [dɔʀtwaʀ] *nm* dormitory

dos [do] *nm* back ▷ *dos à dos* back to back; **faire quelque chose dans le dos de quelqu'un** to do something behind somebody's back ▷ *Elle me critique dans mon dos.* She criticizes me behind my back.; **de dos** from behind; **nager le dos crawlé** to swim the backstroke; **« voir au dos »** "see other side"

dose [doz] *nf* dose ▷ *Ne pas dépasser la dose prescrite.* Do not exceed the stated dose.

dossier [dosje] *nm* ❶ file ▷ *une pile de dossiers* a stack of files ❷ record ▷ *un bon dossier scolaire* a good academic record ❸ (computer) folder ❹ (in magazine) feature ❺ (of chair) back

douane [dwan] *nf* customs

douanier [dwanje] *nm* customs officer

douanière [dwanjɛʀ] *nf* customs officer

double [dubl(ə)] *adj* double; **à double interligne** double-spaced; **le double échec** cross-checking ▷ *faire double échec à un adversaire* to cross-check an opponent
▶ *nm*: **le double** twice as much ▷ *Il gagne le double.* He earns twice as much. ▷ *le double du prix normal* twice the normal price; **en double** in duplicate ▷ *Garde cette photo, je l'ai en double.* Keep this photo, I've got a copy of it.; **le double messieurs** (tennis) the men's doubles

double-cliquer [dubl(ə)klike] *vb* to double-click ▷ *double-cliquer sur une icône* to double-click on an icon

doubler [duble] *vb* ❶ to double ▷ *Le prix a doublé en dix ans.* The price has doubled in 10 years. ❷ (in car) to pass ▷ *Il est dangereux de doubler sur cette route.* It's dangerous to pass on this road.; **un film doublé** a dubbed film

douce [dus] *adj see* **doux**

doucement [dusmɑ̃] adv
① gently ▷ *Elle a frappé doucement à la porte.* She knocked gently at the door. **②** slowly ▷ *Roulez doucement!* Drive slowly! ▷ *Je ne comprends pas; parle plus doucement.* I don't understand; speak more slowly.

douceur [dusœʀ] nf **①** softness ▷ *Cette crème maintient la douceur de votre peau.* This cream keeps your skin soft. **②** gentleness ▷ *parler avec douceur* to speak gently; **L'avion a atterri en douceur.** The plane made a smooth landing.

douche [duʃ] nf shower; **les douches** the shower room; **prendre une douche** to have a shower

se doucher [duʃe] vb to take a shower

doué [dwe] (f **douée**) adj talented; **être doué en quelque chose** to be good at something ▷ *Elle est douée en maths.* She's good at math.

douillet [duje, -ɛt] (f **douillette**) adj **①** cozy ▷ *un chandail douillet* a cozy sweater **②** soft ▷ *Je ne supporte pas la douleur; je suis très douillette.* I can't stand pain; I'm a real softie.

douillette [dujɛt] nf comforter

douleur [dulœʀ] nf pain

douloureux [duluʀø, -øz] (f **douloureuse**) adj painful

doute [dut] nm doubt; **sans doute** probably

douter [dute] vb to doubt; **douter de quelque chose** to doubt something ▷ *Je doute de sa sincérité.* I have my doubts about his sincerity.; **se douter de quelque chose** to suspect something ▷ *Je ne me doutais de rien.* I didn't suspect anything.; **Je m'en doutais.** I thought as much.

douteux [dutø, -øz] (f **douteuse**)

adj **①** dubious ▷ *une plaisanterie d'un goût douteux* a joke in dubious taste **②** suspicious-looking ▷ *un individu douteux* a suspicious-looking person

doux [du, dus] (f **douce**, mpl **doux**) adj **①** soft ▷ *un tissu doux* soft fabric ▷ *les drogues douces* soft drugs **②** sweet ▷ *du cidre doux* sweet cider **③** mild ▷ *Il fait doux aujourd'hui.* It's mild out today. **④** gentle ▷ *C'est quelqu'un de très doux.* He's a very gentle person.; **en douce** on the quiet ▷ *Elle m'a donné cinq dollars en douce.* She slipped me 5 dollars on the quiet.

douzaine [duzɛn] nf dozen ▷ *une douzaine d'œufs* a dozen eggs; **une douzaine de personnes** about twelve people

douze [duz] num twelve ▷ *Il a douze ans.* He's twelve.; **le douze février** the twelfth of February

douzième [duzjɛm] adj twelfth ▷ *au douzième étage* on the twelfth floor

dramatique [dʀamatik] adj tragic ▷ *une situation dramatique* a tragic situation; **l'art dramatique** drama

drame [dʀam] nm **①** (incident) drama; **Ça n'est pas un drame si tu ne viens pas.** It's not the end of the world if you don't come.

drap [dʀa] nm (for bed) sheet

drapeau [dʀapo] (pl **drapeaux**) nm flag ▷ *le drapeau canadien* the Canadian flag

dressé [dʀese] (f **dressée**) adj trained ▷ *un chien bien dressé* a well-trained dog

dresser [dʀese] vb **①** to draw up ▷ *dresser une liste* to draw up a list **②** to train ▷ *dresser un chien* to train a dog; **dresser l'oreille** to perk up one's ears ▷ *Quand elle a dit ça, il a* *dressé l'oreille.* When she said that, he perked up his ears.

drogue [dʀɔg] *nf* drug ▷ *le problème de la drogue* the drug problem ▷ *la lutte contre la drogue* the war against drugs; **les drogues douces** soft drugs; **les drogues dures** hard drugs

drogué [dʀɔge] *nm* drug addict

droguée [dʀɔge] *nf* drug addict

droguer [dʀɔge] *vb*: **droguer quelqu'un** to drug somebody; **se droguer** to take drugs

droit [dʀwa, dʀwat] (*f* **droite**) *adj, adv* ❶ right ▷ *le bras droit* the right arm ▷ *le côté droit* the right-hand side* ❷ straight ▷ *une ligne droite* a straight line ▷ *Tiens-toi droite!* Stand up straight!; **tout droit** straight ahead

▶ *nm* ❶ right ▷ *les droits de la personne* human rights; **avoir le droit de faire quelque chose** to be allowed to do something ▷ *On n'a pas le droit de fumer à l'école.* We're not allowed to smoke at school. ❷ (*profession*) law ▷ *faire son droit* to study law ▷ *un étudiant en droit* a law student ▷ *pratiquer le droit* to practise law

droite [dʀwat] *nf* right ▷ *sur votre droite* on your right; **à droite (1)** on the right ▷ *la troisième rue à droite* the third street on the right **(2)** to the right ▷ *à droite de la fenêtre* to the right of the window ▷ *Tournez à droite.* Turn right.; **la voie de droite** the right-hand lane; **la droite** (*in politics*) the right ▷ *Il est très à droite.* He's very right-wing.; **une droite** (*math*) a straight line

droitier [dʀwatje, -jɛʀ] (*f* **droitière**) *adj* right-handed ▷ *Elle est droitière.* She's right-handed.

drôle [dʀol] *adj* funny ▷ *Ça n'est pas drôle.* It's not funny.; **un drôle de**

temps funny weather

du [dy] *art*

■ **du** is the contracted form of **de + le**.

❶ some ▷ *Tu veux du fromage?* Would you like some cheese? ❷ any ▷ *Tu as du chocolat?* Do you have any chocolate? ▷ *la porte du garage* the door of the garage ▷ *le bureau du directeur* the principal's office

dû [dy] *vb* see **devoir**; **Nous avons dû nous arrêter.** We had to stop.

▶ *adj* (*f* **due**, *mpl* **dus**): **dû à** due to ▷ *un retard dû au mauvais temps* a delay due to bad weather

dualité [dɥalite] *nf* duality ▷ *la dualité linguistique du Canada* Canada's linguistic duality

dupe [dyp] *adj*: **Elle me ment mais je ne suis pas dupe.** She lies to me but I'm not taken in.

duplex [dyplɛks] (*pl* **les duplex**) *nm* duplex

dur [dyʀ] (*f* **dure**) *adj, adv* hard ▷ *travailler dur* to work hard ▷ *être dur avec quelqu'un* to be hard on somebody

durant [dyʀɑ̃] *prep* ❶ during ▷ *durant la nuit* during the night ❷ for ▷ *durant des années* for years ▷ *des mois durant* for months

durée [dyʀe] *nf* (*time*) length ▷ *Quelle est la durée des études d'ingénieur?* How long does it take to train as an engineer?; **pour une durée de deux semaines** for a period of two weeks; **de courte durée** short ▷ *un séjour de courte durée* a short stay; **de longue durée** long ▷ *une absence de longue durée* a long absence

durement [dyʀmɑ̃] *adv* harshly

durer [dyʀe] *vb* to last

dureté [dyʀte] *nf* harshness ▷ *traiter quelqu'un avec dureté* to treat

somebody harshly

DVD [devede] *nm* DVD

dynamique [dinamik] *adj* dynamic

dyslexique [dislɛksik] *adj* dyslexic

eau [o] (*pl* **eaux**) *nf* water; **l'eau minérale** mineral water; **l'eau plate** still water; **tomber à l'eau** to fall through ▷ *Nos projets sont tombés à l'eau.* Our plans have fallen through.

ébahi [ebai] (*f* **ébahie**) *adj* amazed

éblouir [ebluiʀ] *vb* to dazzle

ébouillanter [ebujɑ̃te] *vb* to scald

écaille [ekaj] *nf* (*of fish*) scale

s'**écailler** [ekaje] *vb* (*paint*) to peel

écart [ekaʀ] *nm* gap; **à l'écart de** away from ▷ *Ils se sont assis à l'écart des autres.* They sat down away from the others.

écarté [ekaʀte] (*f* **écartée**) *adj* remote; **les bras écartés** arms outstretched; **les jambes écartées** legs apart

écarter [ekaʀte] *vb* to spread apart; **écarter les bras** to open one's arms wide; s'**écarter** to move ▷ *Ils se sont écartés pour le laisser* *passer.* They moved to let her pass.

échafaudage [eʃafodaʒ] *nm*
scaffolding

échalote [eʃalɔt] *nf* shallot

échange [eʃɑ̃ʒ] *nm* exchange
▷ **en échange de** in exchange for;
un échange étudiant a student
exchange

échanger [eʃɑ̃ʒe] *vb* to trade ▷ *Je
t'échange cette carte de hockey contre
celle-là.* I'll trade you this hockey
card for that one.

échantillon [eʃɑ̃tijɔ̃] *nm* sample

échapper [eʃape] *vb*: **échapper
à** to escape from ▷ *Le prisonnier
a réussi à échapper à la police.* The
prisoner managed to escape from
the police.; **s'échapper** to escape
▷ *Il s'est échappé de prison.* He
escaped from prison.; **l'échapper
belle** to have a narrow escape
▷ *Nous l'avons échappé belle.* We had
a narrow escape.

écharde [eʃard(ə)] *nf* splinter

s'**échauffer** [eʃofe] *vb* (before
exercise) to warm up ▷ *Les joueurs
se sont échauffés avant le match.*
The players warmed up before
the game.

échec [eʃɛk] *nm* failure; **subir un
échec** to suffer a setback; **voué à
l'échec** bound to fail

échecs [eʃɛk] *nmpl* chess ▷ *jouer
aux échecs* to play chess

échelle [eʃɛl] *nf* ❶ ladder ❷ (of
map) scale

écho [eko] *nm* echo

échouer [eʃwe] *vb*: **échouer à un
examen** to fail an exam

éclabousser [eklabuse] *vb* to
splash

éclair [eklɛʀ] *nm* flash of lightning;
un éclair au chocolat a chocolate
éclair; **à la vitesse de l'éclair** with
lightning speed; **un éclair de génie**
a brainwave

éclairage [eklɛʀaʒ] *nm* lighting

éclaircie [eklɛʀsi] *nf* sunny period

éclairer [eklɛʀe] *vb*: **Cette lampe
éclaire bien.** This lamp gives
good light.

éclat [ekla] *nm* ❶ (of glass)
fragment ▷ *Le vase a volé en éclats.*
The vase smashed into pieces.
❷ (of sun, colour) brightness; **des
éclats de rire** roars of laughter

éclatant [eklatɑ̃, -ɑ̃t] (f **éclatante**)
adj brilliant ▷ *un jaune éclatant*
a brilliant yellow ▷ *une lumière
éclatante* a brilliant light

éclater [eklate] *vb* ❶ (tire, balloon)
to burst; **éclater de rire** to burst
out laughing; **éclater en sanglots**
to burst into tears ❷ to break
out ▷ *La Seconde Guerre mondiale a
éclaté en 1939.* The Second World War
broke out in 1939.

éclipse [eklips(ə)] *nf* eclipse

écœurant [ekœrɑ̃] *adj* sickening

écœurer [ekœre] *vb*: **Tous ces
mensonges m'écœurent.** All these
lies make me sick.

école [ekɔl] *nf* school ▷ *aller à l'école*
to go to school ▷ *une école privée* a
private school ▷ *une école publique* a
public school

écolier [ekɔlje] *nm* schoolboy

écolière [ekɔljɛʀ] *nf* schoolgirl

écologie [ekɔlɔʒi] *nf* ecology

écologique [ekɔlɔʒik] *adj*
ecological ▷ *un détergent écologique*
an environmentally-friendly
detergent

économe [ekɔnɔm] *adj*
energy-efficient

économie [ekɔnɔmi] *nf*
❶ economy ▷ *l'économie du
Canada* the Canadian economy
❷ economics ▷ *un cours d'économie*
an economics class

économies [ekɔnɔmi] *nfpl*
savings; **faire des économies** to

économique [ekɔnɔmik] adj
❶ economic ▷ *une crise économique* an economic crisis ❷ economical ▷ *Il est plus économique d'acheter une grande boîte de détergent.* It's more economical to buy a big box of detergent. ▷ *Cette petite voiture est économique.* This little car is cheap to run.

économiser [ekɔnɔmize] vb
to save

économiseur d'écran
[ekɔnɔmizœr-] nm screen saver

écorce [ekɔrs(ə)] nf ❶ (of tree) bark; **l'écorce de bouleau** birch bark ❷ (of orange, lemon) peel

s' **écorcher** [ekɔrʃe] vb: **Je me suis écorché le genou.** I've grazed my knee.

écosystème [ekɔsistɛm] nm ecosystem

s' **écouler** [ekule] vb ❶ (water) to flow out ❷ to pass ▷ *Le temps s'écoule trop vite.* Time passes too quickly.

écouter [ekute] vb to listen to ▷ *J'aime écouter de la musique.* I like listening to music.; **Écoute-moi!** Listen!

écouteur [ekutœr] nm (of phone) earpiece

écran [ekrɑ̃] nm screen; **le petit écran** television; **l'écran solaire** sunblock; **l'écran tactile** touchscreen

écraser [ekraze] vb ❶ to crush ▷ *Écrasez une gousse d'ail.* Crush a clove of garlic. ❷ to run over ▷ *Regarde bien avant de traverser, sinon tu vas te faire écraser.* Look carefully before you cross or you'll get run over.; **s'écraser** to crash ▷ *L'avion s'est écrasé dans le désert.* The plane crashed in the desert.

écrémé [ekreme] (f **écrémée**) adj: **le lait écrémé** skim milk

écrevisse [ekrəvis] nf crayfish

écrire [ekrir] vb to write ▷ *Nous nous écrivons régulièrement.* We write to each other regularly.; **Ça s'écrit comment?** How do you spell that?

écrit [ekri] nm piece of writing ▷ *les écrits de Gabrielle Roy* the writings of Gabrielle Roy; **par écrit** in writing

écriture [ekrityr] nf writing ▷ *J'ai du mal à lire son écriture.* I can't read her writing.

écrivain [ekrivɛ̃] nm writer ▷ *Il est écrivain.* He's a writer.

écrivaine [ekrivɛn] nf writer ▷ *Elle est écrivaine.* She's a writer.

écrou [ekru] nm (metal) nut

s' **écrouler** [ekrule] vb to collapse

écru [ekry] (f **écrue**) adj off-white

écureuil [ekyrœj] nm squirrel

écurie [ekyri] nf stable

éditer [edite] vb ❶ to publish ▷ *On vient d'éditer un nouveau dictionnaire.* A new dictionary has just been published. ❷ (computer file) to edit

éditeur [editœr] nm publisher

édition [edisjɔ̃] nf ❶ edition ▷ *une édition de poche* a paperback edition ❷ publishing ▷ *Elle travaille dans l'édition.* She works in publishing.

éducateur [edykatœr] nm (of people with special needs) teacher

éducatif [edykatif, -iv] (f **éducative**) adj educational ▷ *un jeu éducatif* an educational game

éducation [edykasjɔ̃] nf
❶ education; **le cours d'éducation civique** Civics course ▷ *l'éducation physique* physical education ▷ *Il n'a pas beaucoup d'éducation.* He's not very well educated. ❷ upbringing ▷ *Elle a reçu une éducation très stricte.* She had a very strict upbringing.

éducatrice [edykatʀis] nf (of people with special needs) teacher

éduquer [edyke] vb to educate

effacer [efase] vb to erase

effarant [efaʀɑ̃, -ɑ̃t] (**effarante**) adj amazing ▷ Il a mangé une quantité effarante de pain. He ate an amazing amount of bread.

effectivement [efɛktivmɑ̃] adv indeed ▷ Il est effectivement plus rapide de passer par là. It is indeed quicker to go this way. ▷ Oui, effectivement. Yes, indeed.

> Be careful! **effectivement** does not mean **effectively**.

effectuer [efɛktɥe] vb ❶ to make ▷ Ils ont effectué de nombreux changements. They have made a lot of changes. ❷ to do ▷ On vient d'effectuer des travaux dans le bâtiment. They have just done some work in the building.

effet [efɛ] nm effect; **faire de l'effet** to take effect ▷ Ce médicament fait rapidement de l'effet. This medicine takes effect quickly.; **Ça m'a fait un drôle d'effet de le revoir.** It gave me a strange feeling to see him again.; **en effet** yes indeed ▷ « Je ne me sens pas très bien. » « En effet, tu as l'air pâle. » "I don't feel very well." "Yes, you do look pale."

efficace [efikas] adj ❶ efficient ▷ C'est une travailleuse efficace. She's an efficient worker. ❷ effective ▷ un médicament efficace an effective medicine

s'effondrer [efɔ̃dʀe] vb to collapse

s'efforcer [efɔʀse] vb: **s'efforcer de faire quelque chose** to try hard to do something ▷ Il s'efforce d'être aimable avec la clientèle. He tries hard to be polite to the customers.

effort [efɔʀ] nm effort ▷ faire un effort to make an effort

effrayant [efʀejɑ̃, -ɑ̃t] (f

effrayante) adj frightening

effrayer [efʀeje] vb to frighten

effronté [efʀɔ̃te] (**effrontée**) adj mouthy ▷ Cet enfant est vraiment effronté. That kid is really mouthy.

effroyable [efʀwajabl(ə)] adj horrifying

égal [egal, -o] (f **égale**, mpl **égaux**) adj equal ▷ une quantité égale de farine et de sucre equal quantities of flour and sugar; **Ça m'est égal. (1)** I have no preference. ▷ « Tu préfères du riz ou des pâtes? » — « Ça m'est égal. » "Would you rather have rice or pasta?" — "Either is fine with me. (2)** I don't care. ▷ Fais ce que tu veux, ça m'est égal. Do what you like, I don't care.

également [egalmɑ̃] adv also

égaler [egale] vb to equal

égalité [egalite] nf equality; **être à égalité** to be tied ▷ Maintenant les deux joueurs sont à égalité. The two players are now tied.

égard [egaʀ] nm: **à cet égard** in this respect

égarer [egaʀe] vb to mislay ▷ J'ai égaré mes clés. I've mislaid my keys.; **s'égarer** to get lost ▷ Ils se sont égarés dans la forêt. They got lost in the forest.

église [egliz] nf church ▷ aller à l'église to go to church

égoïsme [egɔism(ə)] nm selfishness

égoïste [egɔist(ə)] adj selfish

égout [egu] nm sewer

égratignure [egʀatiɲyʀ] nf scratch

eh [e] excl hey!; **eh bien** well

élan [elɑ̃] nm: **prendre de l'élan** to gather speed

s'élancer [elɑ̃se] vb to rush ▷ Il s'est élancé vers moi. He rushed towards me.

élargir [elaʀʒiʀ] vb ❶ to widen

❷ to expand; **élargir ses horizons** to broaden one's horizons

élastique [elastik] *nm* rubber band

électeur [elɛktœʀ] *nm* voter

élection [elɛksjɔ̃] *nf* election ▷ *une élection provinciale* a provincial election

électrice [elɛktʀis] *nf* (woman) voter

électricien [elɛktʀisjɛ̃] *nm* electrician

électricienne [elɛktʀisjɛn] *nf* electrician

électricité [elɛktʀisite] *nf* ❶ electricity ❷ hydro ▷ *une facture d'électricité* a hydro bill; **allumer l'électricité** to turn on the light; **éteindre l'électricité** to turn off the light

électrique [elɛktʀik] *adj* electric ▷ *le courant électrique* electric current

électronique [elɛktʀɔnik] *nf* electronics

élégant [elegɑ̃, -ɑ̃t] (f **élégante**) *adj* elegant

élémentaire [elemɑ̃tɛʀ] *adj* elementary

éléphant [elefɑ̃] *nm* elephant

élevage [elvaʒ] *nm* cattle farming ▷ *faire de l'élevage* to raise cattle; **un élevage de porcs** a pig farm; **un élevage de poulets** a chicken farm; **le saumon d'élevage** farmed salmon

élevé [elve] (f **élevée**) *adj* high ▷ *Le prix est trop élevé.* The price is too high.; **être bien élevé** to be well brought up; **être mal élevé** to be not very well brought up

élève [elɛv] *nmf* (elementary school) student

élever [elve] *vb* ❶ to bring up ▷ *Il a été élevé par sa grand-mère.* He was brought up by his grandmother.

❷ to breed ▷ *Son oncle élève des chevaux.* Her uncle breeds horses.; **élever la voix** to raise one's voice; **s'élever à** to come to ▷ *À combien s'élèvent les dégâts?* How much does the damage come to?

éleveur [elvœʀ] *nm* ❶ (dogs, horses) breeder ❷ (cattle, pigs, chickens) farmer

éliminatoire [eliminatwaʀ] *adj.* **une note éliminatoire** a failing mark; **une épreuve éliminatoire** (sport) a qualifying round

éliminatoires [eliminatwaʀ] *nfpl* playoffs ▷ *regarder les éliminatoires de hockey à la télévision* to watch the hockey playoffs on TV

éliminer [elimine] *vb* to eliminate

élire [eliʀ] *vb* to elect

elle [ɛl] *pron* ❶ she ▷ *Elle est institutrice.* She is a primary school teacher. ❷ her ▷ *Vous pouvez avoir confiance en elle.* You can trust her. ❶ it ▷ *Prends cette chaise : elle est plus confortable.* Take this chair: it's more comfortable.

    elle is also used for emphasis.
▷ *Elle, elle est toujours en retard!* Oh, SHE's always late!; **elle-même** herself ▷ *Elle l'a choisi elle-même.* She chose it herself.

elles [ɛl] *pron* they ▷ *«Où sont les filles?»* — *«Elles sont allées au cinéma.»* "Where are the girls?" — "They've gone to the movies.";
elles-mêmes themselves

élogieux [elɔʒjø, -øz] (f **élogieuse**) *adj* complimentary ▷ *Ton professeur a été très élogieux à propos de ton travail.* Your teacher was very complimentary about your work.

éloigné [elwaɲe] (f **éloignée**) *adj* distant

s' **éloigner** [elwaɲe] *vb* to go far away ▷ *Ne vous éloignez pas : le dîner est bientôt prêt!* Don't go far away:

dinner will soon be ready!; **Vous vous éloignez du sujet.** You are getting off the point.

emballage [ãbalaʒ] nm: **le papier d'emballage** wrapping paper

emballer [ãbale] vb to wrap; **s'emballer** (informal) to get excited ▷ Elle s'est emballée pour ce projet. She got really excited about this plan.

embarquement [ãbaʀkəmã] nm boarding ▷ embarquement immédiat " "now boarding" ▷ L'embarquement des passagers n'a pas encore été annoncé. Passenger boarding has not been announced yet.

embarras [ãbaʀa] nm embarrassment ▷ Votre question me met dans l'embarras. Your question is an awkward one.; **Vous n'avez que l'embarras du choix.** The only problem is choosing.

embarrassant [ãbaʀasã, -ãt] (f **embarrassante**) adj embarrassing

embarrasser [ãbaʀase] vb to embarrass ▷ Cela m'embarrasse de vous demander encore un service. I'm embarrassed to ask another favour from you.

embaucher [ãboʃe] vb to hire ▷ L'entreprise vient d'embaucher cinquante ouvriers. The firm has just hired fifty workers.

embêtant [ãbetã, -ãt] (f **embêtante**) adj annoying

embêtement [ãbetmã] nm trouble ▷ J'ai eu un embêtement : la voiture est tombée en panne. I had some trouble: the car broke down.

embêter [ãbete] vb to bother ▷ Tu m'embêtes avec tes questions. You're bothering me with your questions.

embouteillage [ãbutejaʒ] nm traffic jam

embrasser [ãbʀase] vb to kiss

▷ Elle m'a embrassé. She kissed me.
▷ Ils se sont embrassés. They kissed.

s' **embrouiller** [ãbʀuje] vb to get confused ▷ Il s'embrouille dans ses explications. He gets confused when he explains things.

émerveiller [emɛʀveje] vb to amaze

émeute [emøt] nf riot

émigrer [emigʀe] vb to emigrate

émission [emisjɔ̃] nf ❶ (radio, TV) show ▷ une émission de télévision a TV show ❷ emission ▷ les émissions de gaz toxique toxic gas emissions

emmêler [ãmele] vb ❶ to tangle up ▷ Mes cheveux sont tout emmêlés. My hair is all tangled up. ❷ to confuse ▷ Elle emmêle tout. She confuses everything.; **s'emmêler** to get tangled up ▷ Sa ligne de pêche s'est emmêlée dans la mienne. His fishing line got tangled up with mine.

emménager [ãmenaʒe] vb to move in ▷ Nous venons d'emménager dans une nouvelle maison. We've just moved into a new house.

emmener [ãmne] vb to take ▷ Ils m'ont emmené au cinéma pour mon anniversaire. They took me to the movies for my birthday.

émotif [emɔtif, -iv] (f **émotive**) adj emotional ▷ Il est très émotif. He's very emotional.

émotion [emosjɔ̃] nf emotion

émotionnel [emosjɔnɛl] (f **émotionnelle**) adj emotional ▷ un choc émotionnel an emotional shock

émouvoir [emuvwaʀ] vb to move ▷ Ta lettre l'a beaucoup émue. She was deeply moved by your letter.

s' **emparer** [ãpaʀe] vb: **s'emparer de** to grab ▷ Elle s'est emparée de ma valise. She grabbed my suitcase.

empêchement [ãpɛʃmã] nm:

Nous avons eu un empêchement de dernière minute. We were held up at the last minute.

empêcher [ɑ̃peʃe] vb to prevent ▷ *Le café le soir m'empêche de dormir.* Coffee at night keeps me awake.; **Il n'a pas pu s'empêcher de rire.** He couldn't help laughing.

empiler [ɑ̃pile] vb to pile up

empirer [ɑ̃pire] vb to worsen ▷ *La situation a encore empiré.* The situation got even worse.

emplacement [ɑ̃plasmɑ̃] nm site ▷ *Un panneau indique l'ancien emplacement du château.* A sign shows the former site of the castle.; **un emplacement de camping** a campsite

emploi [ɑ̃plwa] nm ① job ▷ *trouver un emploi* to find a job ② use ▷ *prêt à l'emploi* ready for use; **un emploi du temps** a timetable; **le mode d'emploi** directions for use

employé [ɑ̃plwaje] nm employee; **un employé de bureau** an office worker

employée [ɑ̃plwaje] nf employee; **une employée de banque** a bank clerk

employer [ɑ̃plwaje] vb ① to use ▷ *Quelle méthode employez-vous?* What method do you use? ② to employ ▷ *L'entreprise emploie dix ingénieurs.* The firm employs ten engineers.

employeur [ɑ̃plwajœʀ] nm employer

empoisonner [ɑ̃pwazɔne] vb to poison

emporter [ɑ̃pɔʀte] vb to take ▷ *N'emportez que le strict nécessaire.* Take only the bare minimum.; **mets à emporter** takeout food; **s'emporter** to lose one's temper ▷ *Je m'emporte facilement.* I'm quick to lose my temper.

empreinte [ɑ̃pʀɛt] nf: **une empreinte digitale** a fingerprint

s'empresser [ɑ̃pʀese] vb: **s'empresser de faire quelque chose** to be quick to do something ▷ *Ils se sont empressés de nous annoncer la nouvelle.* They were quick to tell us the news.

emprisonner [ɑ̃pʀizɔne] vb to imprison

emprunt [ɑ̃pʀœ̃] nm loan

emprunter [ɑ̃pʀœ̃te] vb to borrow; **emprunter quelque chose à quelqu'un** to borrow something from somebody ▷ *Je peux t'emprunter dix dollars?* Can I borrow ten dollars from you?

ému [emy] (**fémue**) adj touched ▷ *J'ai été très ému par sa gentillesse.* I was very touched by her kindness.

en [ɑ̃] prep, pron ① in ▷ *Il habite en Terre-Neuve.* He lives in Newfoundland. ▷ *La mariée est en blanc.* The bride is in white. ▷ *Je le verrai en mai.* I'll see him in May. ② to ▷ *Je vais en Saskatchewan cet été.* I'm going to Saskatchewan this summer. ③ by ▷ *C'est plus rapide en voiture.* It's faster by car. ▷ *On peut apprendre beaucoup en lisant.* You can learn a lot by reading. ④ made of ▷ *C'est en verre.* It's made of glass. ▷ *un collier en argent* a silver necklace ⑤ while ▷ *Il s'est coupé le doigt en ouvrant une boîte de conserve.* He cut his finger while opening a tin.; **Elle est sortie en courant.** She ran out.

> When **en** is used with **avoir** and **il y a**, it is not translated in English.

▷ *« Est-ce que tu as un dictionnaire? »* — *« Oui, j'en ai un. »* "Have you got a dictionary?" — "Yes, I've got one." ▷ *« Combien d'élèves y a-t-il dans ta classe? »* — *« Il y en a trente. »* "How many pupils are there in your class?"

— "There are 30."

en is also used with verbs and expressions normally followed by **de** to avoid repeating the same word.

▷ *Si tu as un problème, tu peux m'en parler.* If you have a problem, you can talk to me about it. ▷ *Est-ce que tu peux me rendre ce livre? J'en ai besoin.* Can you give me back that book? I need it. ▷ *Il a un beau jardin et il en est très fier.* He's got a beautiful garden and is very proud of it.; **j'en ai assez.** I've had enough.

encaisser [ãkese] vb (*chèque*) to cash

enceinte [ãsɛ̃t] adj pregnant ▷ *Elle est enceinte de six mois.* She's 6 months pregnant.

encercler [ãsɛrkle] vb to circle ▷ *Encerclez la bonne réponse.* Circle the right answer.

enchanté [ãʃãte] (f **enchantée**) adj delighted ▷ *Ma mère est enchantée de sa nouvelle voiture.* My mother's delighted with her new car.; **Enchanté!** Pleased to meet you!

encombrant [ãkɔ̃brã, -ãt] (f **encombrante**) adj bulky

encombrer [ãkɔ̃bre] vb to clutter

encore [ãkɔr] adv ❶ again ▷ *Il m'a encore demandé de l'argent.* He asked me for money again. ❷ more ▷ *Mange encore un peu.* Have some more to eat. ❸ still ▷ *Il est encore au travail.* He's still at work. ▷ *Il reste encore deux morceaux de gâteau.* There are two pieces of cake left. ❹ even ▷ *C'est encore mieux.* That's even better.; **encore une fois** once again; **pas encore** not yet ▷ *Je n'ai pas encore fini.* I'm not finished yet.

encourageant [ãkuraʒã, -ãt] (f **encourageante**) adj encouraging

encourager [ãkuraʒe] vb to encourage

encre [ãkr(ə)] nf ink

encyclopédie [ãsiklɔpedi] nf encyclopedia

endommager [ãdɔmaʒe] vb to damage

endormi [ãdɔrmi] (f **endormie**) adj asleep

endormir [ãdɔrmir] vb ❶ to put to sleep ▷ *Il a endormi le bébé en lui chantant une berceuse.* He put the baby to sleep by singing a lullaby. ▷ *Son long discours m'a endormi.* His long speech put me to sleep. ❷ (*with anesthetic*) to put under ▷ *On l'a endormie pour son opération.* They put her under for the operation.; **s'endormir** to go to sleep

endroit [ãdrwa] nm place ▷ *C'est un endroit très tranquille.* It's a very quiet place.; **à l'endroit** (1) right side out ▷ *Remets ton T-shirt à l'endroit.* Put your T-shirt on again right side out. (2) the right way up ▷ *Ce tableau est de travers. Il faut le remettre à l'endroit.* This picture is sideways. It must be put the right way up.

endurant [ãdyrã, -ãt] (f **endurante**) adj (*person*) tough

endurcir [ãdyrsir] vb to toughen up ▷ *Ces exercices servent à vous endurcir.* These exercises are to toughen you up.; **s'endurcir** to become hardened

endurer [ãdyre] vb to endure

énergie [enɛrʒi] nf ❶ energy ▷ *Je n'ai pas beaucoup d'énergie ce matin.* I don't have much energy this morning. ❷ power ▷ **l'énergie nucléaire** nuclear power; **avec énergie** vigorously ▷ *Il a protesté avec énergie.* He protested vigorously.

énergique [enɛrʒik] adj energetic; **des mesures énergiques** strong measures

énerver [enɛʀve] vb: **Il m'énerve!** He gets on my nerves!; **Ce bruit m'énerve.** This noise gets on my nerves.; **s'énerver** to get worked up; **Ne t'énerve pas!** Take it easy!

enfance [ɑ̃fɑ̃s] nf childhood; **Je la connais depuis l'enfance.** I've known her since I was a child.

enfant [ɑ̃fɑ̃] nmf child

enfer [ɑ̃fɛʀ] nm hell

enfermer [ɑ̃fɛʀme] vb ❶ (in a place) to lock ▷ garder son sac à main enfermé dans son tiroir to keep one's purse locked in a drawer ❷ to shut in ▷ Ne restons pas enfermés par ce beau temps. Let's not stay inside in this lovely weather.; **Il s'est enfermé dans sa chambre.** He shut himself up in his bedroom.

enfiler [ɑ̃file] vb ❶ to put on ▷ J'ai rapidement enfilé un chandail avant de sortir. I quickly put on a sweater before going out. ❷ to thread ▷ J'ai du mal à enfiler cette aiguille. I am having a hard time threading this needle.

enfin [ɑ̃fɛ̃] adv finally ▷ J'ai enfin réussi à le joindre. I have finally managed to contact her.

enfler [ɑ̃fle] vb to swell

enfoncer [ɑ̃fɔ̃se] vb: **Elle marchait, les mains enfoncées dans les poches.** She was walking with her hands thrust into her pockets.; **s'enfoncer** to sink ▷ Les roues de la voiture s'enfonçaient dans la boue. The wheels of the car were sinking into the mud.

s'enfuir [ɑ̃fɥiʀ] vb to run off

engagement [ɑ̃gaʒmɑ̃] nm commitment

engager [ɑ̃gaʒe] vb to hire

s'engager [ɑ̃gaʒe] vb to commit oneself ▷ Le premier ministre s'est engagé à combattre le chômage. The Prime Minister has committed himself to fighting unemployment.; **Elle a décidé de ne pas s'engager dans l'armée.** She decided not to join the army.

engin [ɑ̃ʒɛ̃] nm device

> Be careful! The French word **engin** does not mean **engine**.

engouement [ɑ̃gumɑ̃] nm fad

engueuler [ɑ̃gœle] vb (informal); **engueuler quelqu'un** to tell somebody off ▷ Tu vas te faire engueuler! You're going to get told off!

énigme [enigm(ə)] nf riddle

s'enivrer [ɑ̃nivʀe] vb to get drunk

enjambée [ɑ̃ʒɑ̃be] nf stride ▷ monter l'escalier en trois enjambées to go up the stairs in three strides

enjamber [ɑ̃ʒɑ̃be] vb ❶ (by swinging one leg over at a time) to climb over ▷ enjamber une barrière to climb over a fence ❷ to step over ▷ enjamber un fossé to step over a ditch ❸ to straddle

enlèvement [ɑ̃lɛvmɑ̃] nm kidnapping

enlever [ɑ̃lve] vb ❶ to take off ▷ Enlève donc ton manteau! Take off your coat! ❷ to kidnap ▷ Un groupe terroriste a enlevé la femme du ministre. A terrorist group has kidnapped the minister's wife.

enneigé [ɑ̃neʒe] (**f enneigée**) adj snow-covered ▷ Les routes sont encore enneigées. The roads are still covered with snow.

ennemi [ɛnmi] nm enemy

ennemie [ɛnmi] nf enemy

ennui [ɑ̃nɥi] nm ❶ boredom ▷ C'est à mourir d'ennui. It's enough to bore you to death. ❷ problem ▷ avoir des ennuis to have problems

ennuyer [ɑ̃nɥije] vb ❶ to inconvenience ▷ J'espère que cela ne vous ennuie pas trop. I hope it doesn't inconvenience you too much. ❷ to bother ▷ *Arrête de m'ennuyer avec tes questions.* Stop bothering me with your questions.; **s'ennuyer** to be bored

ennuyeux [ãnɥijø, -øz] (f **ennuyeuse**) adj ❶ boring ❷ inconvenient ▷ *Tu ne peux pas venir plus tôt? C'est bien ennuyeux.* You can't come any earlier? That's rather inconvenient.

énorme [enɔʀm(ə)] adj huge

énormément [enɔʀmemã] adv: **Il a énormément maigri.** He's gotten terribly thin.; **Il y a énormément de neige.** There's an enormous amount of snow.

enquête [ãket] nf ❶ investigation ▷ *La police a ouvert une enquête.* The police have launched an investigation. ❷ survey ▷ *une enquête parmi les étudiants a montré que...* a survey of students has shown that...

enquêter [ãkete] vb to investigate ▷ *La police enquête actuellement sur le crime.* The police are currently investigating the crime.

enrageant [ãʀaʒã, -ãt] (f **enrageante**) adj infuriating

enrager [ãʀaʒe] vb to be furious ▷ *J'enrage de n'avoir pas eu le droit de vous accompagner.* I'm furious that I wasn't allowed to go with you.

enregistrement [ãʀʒistʀəmã] nm recording; **l'enregistrement des bagages** baggage check-in

enregistrer [ãʀʒistʀe] vb ❶ to record ▷ *Ils viennent d'enregistrer un nouvel album.* They've just recorded a new album. ▷ *J'ai enregistré l'émission sur vidéocassette.* I taped the TV show. ❷ (*baggage*) to check ▷ *Vous pouvez enregistrer plusieurs valises.* You can check more than one suitcase.

s' enrhumer [ãʀyme] vb to catch a cold ▷ *Elle s'est enrhumée.* She caught a cold.

s' enrichir [ãʀiʃiʀ] vb to get rich

enrouler [ãʀule] vb to wind ▷ *Enroulez le fil autour de la bobine.* Wind the thread around the bobbin.

enseignant [ãsɛɲã] nm teacher

enseignante [ãsɛɲãt] nf teacher

enseignement [ãsɛɲmã] nm ❶ education ▷ *les réformes de l'enseignement* reforms in education ❷ teaching ▷ *l'enseignement des langues étrangères* the teaching of foreign languages

enseigner [ãsɛɲe] vb to teach ▷ *Mon père enseigne les maths dans une école secondaire.* My father teaches math in a secondary school.

ensemble [ãsãbl(ə)] adv together ▷ *tous ensemble* all together ▶ nm ❶ outfit ▷ *Elle portait un ensemble vert.* She was wearing a green outfit. ❷ set ▷ *un ensemble de couteaux* a set of knives; **l'ensemble de** the whole of ▷ *L'ensemble du personnel est en grève.* The whole staff is on strike.; **aller ensemble** to go together ▷ *Le tapis et les meubles ne vont pas ensemble.* The carpet and furniture don't go together.; **dans l'ensemble** on the whole

ensoleillé [ãsɔleje] (f **ensoleillée**) adj sunny

ensuite [ãsɥit] adv then ▷ *Nous sommes allés au cinéma et ensuite au restaurant.* We went to a movie and then to a restaurant.

entamer [ãtame] vb to start ▷ *Qui a entamé le gâteau?* Who started on the cake? ▷ *entamer des négociations* to begin negotiations

entasser [ãtase] vb to cram ▷ *J'ai*

tout entassé dans un tiroir. I crammed everything into a drawer.; **Ils se sont tous entassés dans ma voiture.** They all crammed into my car.

entendre [ãtãdʀ(ə)] *vb* ❶ to hear ▷ *Je ne t'entends pas.* I can't hear you.; **J'ai entendu dire qu'il est dangereux de nager ici.** I've heard that it's dangerous to swim here. ❷ to mean ▷ *Qu'est-ce que tu entends par là?* What do you mean by that?; **s'entendre** to get along ▷ *Il s'entend bien avec sa sœur.* He gets along well with his sister.

entendu [ãtãdy] (*f* **entendue**) *adj*: **C'est entendu.** Agreed! ▷ *Je passerai te prendre à sept heures, c'est entendu.* That's agreed then, I'll pick you up at 7 o'clock.; **bien entendu** of course ▷ *Il est bien entendu que je n'en parlerai à personne.* I won't tell anybody about it, of course.

enterrement [ãtɛʀmã] *nm* (*with burial*) funeral; **avoir une mine d'enterrement** to look gloomy

enterrer [ãteʀe] *vb* to bury

entêté [ãtete] (*f* **entêtée**) *adj* stubborn

s'entêter [ãtete] *vb* to persist ▷ *Il s'entête à refuser de voir le médecin.* He persists in refusing to go to the doctor.

enthousiasme [ãtuzjasm(ə)] *nm* enthusiasm

s'enthousiasmer [ãtuzjasme] *vb* to get enthusiastic ▷ *Elle s'enthousiasme facilement.* She gets very enthusiastic about things.

entier [ãtje, -jɛʀ] (*f* **entière**) *adj* whole ▷ *Il a mangé une quiche entière.* He ate a whole quiche. ▷ *Je n'ai pas lu le livre en entier.* I haven't read the whole book.; **le lait entier** whole milk

entièrement [ãtjɛʀmã] *adv*

completely

entorse [ãtɔʀs(ə)] *nf* sprain ▷ *Elle s'est fait une entorse à la cheville.* She sprained her ankle.

entourer [ãtuʀe] *vb* to surround ▷ *Le jardin est entouré d'un mur de pierres.* The garden is surrounded by a stone wall.

entracte [ãtʀakt(ə)] *nm* intermission

entraînement [ãtʀɛnmã] *nm* training

entraîner [ãtʀene] *vb* ❶ to lead ▷ *Il se laisse facilement entraîner par les autres.* He's easily led. ❷ to coach ▷ *Il entraîne l'équipe de soccer depuis cinq ans.* He's been training the soccer team for five years. ❸ to involve ▷ *Un mariage entraîne beaucoup de dépenses.* A wedding involves a lot of expense.; **s'entraîner** to train ▷ *Elle s'entraîne au hockey tous les samedis matins.* She has hockey practice every Saturday morning.

entraîneur [ãtʀenœʀ] *nm* coach

entraîneure [ãtʀenœʀ] *nf* coach

entre [ãtʀ(ə)] *prep* between ▷ *Il est assis entre son père et sa tante.* He's sitting between his father and his aunt.; **entre eux** among themselves; **l'un d'entre eux** one of them

entrée [ãtʀe] *nf* ❶ entrance ❷ driveway ❸ (*of meal*) appetizer ▷ *Qu'est ce que vous prenez comme entrée?* What would you like for an appetizer?

> Be careful! The French word **entrée** does not mean **entree**.
> **la touche Entrée** the Enter key

entreposage [ãtʀəpozaʒ] *nm* storage

entreprendre [ãtʀəpʀãdʀ(ə)] *vb* (*a process*) to start ▷ *Elle a entrepris des travaux de rénovation.* She has started renovations.

entrepreneur [ɑ̃trəprənœr] nm
small business owner

entrepreneure [ɑ̃trəprənœr] nf
small business owner

entreprise [ɑ̃trəpriz] nf (company)
business

entrer [ɑ̃tre] vb ❶ to come in
▷ *Entrez donc!* Come on in! ❷ to
go in ▷ *Ils sont tous entrés dans la
maison.* They all went into the
house.; **entrer à l'hôpital** to go
into the hospital; **entrer des
données** to enter data ▷ *J'ai entré
toutes les adresses de mes amis sur
mon ordinateur.* I've entered the
addresses of all my friends into my
computer.

entre-temps [ɑ̃trətɑ̃] adv
meanwhile

entretien [ɑ̃trətjɛ̃] nm
❶ maintenance ▷ *un contrat
d'entretien* a maintenance
contract ❷ conversation ▷ *un
entretien téléphonique* a telephone
conversation

entrevue [ɑ̃trəvy] nf ❶ interview
▷ *une entrevue avec le ministre* an
interview with the minister ❷ job
interview ▷ *mon frère a passé une
entrevue pour travailler dans un
restaurant.* My brother had a job
interview to work in a restaurant.

entrouvert [ɑ̃truvɛr, -ɛrt(ə)] (f
entrouverte) adj half open ▷ *La
porte était entrouverte.* The door was
half open.

envahir [ɑ̃vair] vb to invade

envahissement [ɑ̃vaismɑ̃] nm
invasion

enveloppe [ɑ̃vlɔp] nf envelope

envelopper [ɑ̃vlɔpe] vb to wrap

envers [ɑ̃vɛr] prep towards ▷ *Il
est très respectueux envers elle.* He's
very respectful towards her. ▷ *son
attitude envers moi* his attitude

to me
▶ nm: **à l'envers (1)** inside out ▷ *Je
dois repasser ce chemisier à l'envers.* I
have to iron this blouse inside out.
(2) messy ▷ *Ta chambre est à l'envers.*
Your room is messy.

envie [ɑ̃vi] nf: **avoir envie de faire
quelque chose** to feel like doing
something ▷ *J'avais envie de pleurer.*
I felt like crying.; **Ce gâteau me
fait envie.** I wouldn't mind some
of that cake.

envier [ɑ̃vje] vb to envy ▷ *C'est à
soixante kilomètres environ.* It's about
60 kilometres away.

environ [ɑ̃virɔ̃] adv about ▷ *C'est à
soixante kilomètres environ.* It's about
60 kilometres away.

environnement [ɑ̃virɔnmɑ̃] nm
environment

environnementaliste
[ɑ̃virɔnmɑ̃talist(ə)] nmf
environmentalist

environs [ɑ̃virɔ̃] nmpl area ▷ *les
environs d'Ottawa* the Ottawa
area ▷ *Il y a beaucoup de choses
intéressantes à voir dans les environs.*
There are a lot of interesting things
to see in the area.; **aux environs de
dix-neuf heures** around 7 p.m.

envisager [ɑ̃vizaʒe] vb to consider
▷ *Est-ce que vous envisagez de
changer d'école?* Are you considering
changing schools?

s'**envoler** [ɑ̃vɔle] vb ❶ to fly
away ▷ *Le papillon s'est envolé.* The
butterfly flew away. ❷ to blow
away ▷ *Toutes mes notes de cours
se sont envolées.* All my class notes
blew away.

envoyer [ɑ̃vwaje] vb to send ▷ *Ma
tante m'a envoyé une carte pour mon
anniversaire.* My aunt sent me a
card for my birthday.; **envoyer
quelqu'un chercher quelque
chose** to send somebody to get
something ▷ *Sa mère l'a envoyé
chercher du pain.* His mother sent

him to get some bread.; **envoyer un courriel à quelqu'un** to send somebody an email

éolien [eɔljɛ̃, -ɛn] (f **éolienne**) adj wind

éolienne [eɔljɛn] nf wind turbine

épais [epɛ, -ɛs] (f **épaisse**) adj thick

épaisseur [epɛsœʀ] nf thickness

épargner [epaʀɲe] vb (money, energy) to save

épatant [epatɑ̃, -ɑ̃t] (f **épatante**) adj (informal) great ▷ C'est un type épatant. He's a great guy.

épaulard [epolaʀ] nm killer whale

épaule [epol] nf shoulder

épée [epe] nf sword

épeler [eple] vb to spell ▷ Est-ce que vous pouvez épeler votre nom s'il vous plaît? Could you spell your name please?

épice [epis] nf spice

épicé [epise] (f **épicée**) adj spicy ▷ Ce n'est pas assez épicé pour moi. It's not spicy enough for me.

épicerie [episʀi] nf grocery store; **faire l'épicerie** to go grocery shopping

épi de maïs [epi-] nm corn on the cob

épidémie [epidemi] nf epidemic

épinards [epinaʀ] nmpl spinach

épine [epin] nf thorn

épinette [epinɛt] nf spruce; **la bière d'épinette** root beer

épingle [epɛ̃ɡl(ə)] nf pin; **une épingle de sûreté** a safety pin

épisode [epizɔd] nm episode

éplucher [eplyʃe] vb to peel

épluchette [eplyʃɛt] nf

> In French Canada, **l'épluchette** is an end-of-summer celebration where people gather to eat corn on the cob.

éponge [epɔ̃ʒ] nf sponge

époque [epɔk] nf time ▷ à cette époque de l'année at this time of year;

à l'époque at that time ▷ À l'époque, beaucoup de gens n'avaient pas l'eau courante. At that time a lot of people didn't have running water.

épouse [epuz] nf wife

épouser [epuze] vb to marry

épouvantable [epuvɑ̃tabl(ə)] adj terrible

épouvante [epuvɑ̃t] nf terror; **un film d'épouvante** a horror film

épouvanter [epuvɑ̃te] vb to terrify

époux [epu] nm husband; **les nouveaux époux** the newlyweds

épreuve [epʀœv] nf ❶ test ▷ une épreuve orale an oral test ▷ une épreuve écrite a written test ❷ (sports) event

éprouver [epʀuve] vb to feel ▷ Qu'est-ce que vous avez éprouvé à ce moment-là? What did you feel at that moment?

épuisé [epɥize] (f **épuisée**) adj exhausted

épuiser [epɥize] vb to wear out ▷ Ce travail m'a complètement épuisé. This job has completely worn me out.; **s'épuiser** to wear oneself out ▷ Il s'épuise à garder un jardin impeccable. He wears himself out keeping his garden immaculate.

équateur [ekwatœʀ] nm equator

équation [ekwasjɔ̃] nf equation

équerre [ekɛʀ] nf set square

équilibre [ekilibʀ(ə)] nm balance ▷ J'ai failli perdre l'équilibre. I nearly lost my balance.

équilibré [ekilibʀe] (f **équilibrée**) adj well-balanced

équipage [ekipaʒ] nm crew

équipe [ekip] nf team

équipé [ekipe] (f **équipée**) adj: **bien équipé** well-equipped

équipement [ekipmɑ̃] nm equipment

équipements [ekipmɑ̃] nmpl facilities ▷ les équipements sportifs sports facilities

équitation [ekitasjɔ̃] nf riding
▷ faire de l'équitation to go riding

équivalent [ekivalɑ̃] nm
equivalent

érable [eʀabl(ə)] nm maple; **le sirop d'érable** maple syrup

érablière [eʀablijɛʀ] nf sugar bush ▷ Nous irons à une partie de sucre à l'érablière. We're going to a sugaring-off party in the sugar bush.

erreur [ɛʀœʀ] nf mistake; **faire erreur** to be mistaken

es [ɛ] vb see **être**; **Tu es très gentille.** You're very kind.

escabeau [ɛskabo] (pl **escabeaux**) nm stepladder

escalade [ɛskalad] nf rock climbing ▷ faire de l'escalade to go rock climbing

escalader [ɛskalade] vb to climb

escale [ɛskal] nf: **faire escale** to stop off

escalier [ɛskalje] nm stairs ▷ un escalier roulant an escalator

escargot [ɛskaʀɡo] nm snail

escarpement [ɛskaʀpəmɑ̃] nm escarpment ▷ l'escarpement de Niagara the Niagara escarpment

esclavage [ɛsklavaʒ] nm slavery

esclave [ɛsklav] nmf slave

escrime [ɛskʀim] nf fencing

escroc [ɛskʀo] nm crook ▷ Cette femme est un escroc. That woman is a crook.

espace [ɛspas] nm space; **espace de travail** workspace

s'**espacer** [ɛspase] vb to become less frequent ▷ Ses visites se sont peu à peu espacées. His visits became less and less frequent.

espadrille [ɛspadʀij] nf running shoe

espèce [ɛspɛs] nf ❶ sort ▷ Elle portait une espèce de cape en velours.

She was wearing a sort of velvet cloak. ❷ species ▷ une espèce en voie de disparition, an endangered species

espèces [ɛspɛs] nfpl cash ▷ payer en espèces to pay cash

espérer [ɛspeʀe] vb to hope; **j'espère bien.** I hope so. ▷ « Tu penses avoir réussi? » « Oui, j'espère bien. » "Do you think you passed?" "Yes, I hope so."

espiègle [ɛspjɛgl(ə)] adj mischievous

espion [ɛspjɔ̃] nm spy

espionnage [ɛspjɔnaʒ] nm spying; **un roman d'espionnage** a spy novel

espionne [ɛspjɔn] nf spy

espoir [ɛspwaʀ] nm hope

esprit [ɛspʀi] nm mind ▷ Ça ne m'est pas venu à l'esprit. It didn't cross my mind.; **avoir de l'esprit** to be witty ▷ Il a beaucoup d'esprit. He's very witty.

essai [ese] nm attempt ▷ Ce n'est pas mal pour un coup d'essai. It's not bad for a first attempt.; **prendre quelqu'un à l'essai** to hire somebody for a trial period

essayer [eseje] vb ❶ to try ▷ Essaie de rentrer de bonne heure. Try to come home early. ❷ to try on ▷ Essaie ce chandail : il devrait bien t'aller. Try this sweater on: it ought to look good on you.

essence [esɑ̃s] nf (for car) gas

essentiel [esɑ̃sjɛl] (f **essentielle**) adj essential; **Tu es là : c'est l'essentiel.** You're here: that's the main thing.

s'**essouffler** [esufle] vb to get out of breath

essuie-glace [esɥiglas] nm windshield wiper

essuyer [esɥije] vb to wipe; **essuyer la vaisselle** to dry the dishes; **essuyer un échec** to suffer a setback; **s'essuyer** to dry oneself ▷ *Vous pouvez vous essuyer les mains avec cette serviette.* You can dry your hands on this towel.

est [ɛst] *vb see* **être**; **Elle est merveilleuse.** She's marvellous.
▶ *adj* ❶ east ▷ *la côte est du Canada* the east coast of Canada ❷ eastern ▷ *dans la partie est du pays* in the eastern part of the country
▶ *nm* east ▷ *Je vis dans l'est.* I live in the East.; **vers l'est** eastward; **à l'est de Rainy River** east of Rainy River; **l'Europe de l'Est** Eastern Europe; **le vent d'est** the east wind

est-ce que [ɛskə] *adv*: **Est-ce que c'est cher?** Is it expensive?; **Quand est-ce qu'il part?** When is he leaving?

esthéticienne [ɛstetisjɛn] *nf* beautician

estimation [ɛstimasjɔ̃] *nf* estimate ▷ *Nous avons demandé une estimation avant de faire réparer la voiture.* We asked for an estimate before getting the car repaired.

estime [ɛstim] *nf*: **J'ai beaucoup d'estime pour elle.** I have a lot of respect for her.

estimer [ɛstime] *vb*: **estimer quelqu'un** to have great respect for somebody ▷ *Mon père les estime beaucoup.* My father has a lot of respect for them.; **estimer que** to be of the opinion that ▷ *J'estime que c'est de sa faute.* My opinion is that it's her fault.

estomac [ɛstɔma] *nm* stomach

estrade [ɛstʀad] *nf* platform ▷ *La ministre a prononcé son discours sur l'estrade.* The minister gave her speech from the platform.

et [e] *conj* and

établir [etabliʀ] *vb* to establish;

s'établir à son compte to set up a business

établissement [etablismɑ̃] *nm* establishment; **un établissement scolaire** a school

étage [etaʒ] *nm* floor ▷ *au premier étage* on the first floor; **à l'étage** upstairs

étagère [etaʒɛʀ] *nf* shelf

étaient [etɛ] *vb see* **être**

étais, était *vb see* **être**; **Il était très jeune.** He was very young.

étalage [etalaʒ] *nm* display

étaler [etale] *vb* to spread out ▷ *Il a étalé la carte sur la table.* He spread the map out on the table.

étanche [etɑ̃ʃ] *adj* ❶ watertight ▷ *Le toit n'est pas étanche.* The roof isn't watertight. ❷ (*watch*) waterproof

étang [etɑ̃] *nm* pond

étant [etɑ̃] *vb see* **être**; **Mes revenus étant limités...** My income being limited...

étape [etap] *nf* stage ▷ *une étape importante de la vie* an important stage in life; **faire étape** to stop off

État [eta] *nm* (*nation*) state ▷ *un chef d'État* a head of state

état [eta] *nm* ❶ state ▷ *dans votre état de santé* in your state of health ▷ *le chef d'État* the head of state ❷ condition ▷ *en bon état* in good condition ▷ *en mauvais état* in poor condition; **remettre quelque chose en état** to repair something; **un état d'âme** a frame of mind; **être dans tous ses états** to be beside oneself with anxiety

été [ete] *vb see* **être**; **Elle a été licenciée.** She's been laid off.
▶ *nm* summer; **en été** in the summer; **l'été indien** Indian summer

éteindre [etɛ̃dʀ(ə)] *vb* ❶ (*light, TV*) to turn off ▷ *N'oubliez pas* d'éteindre la lumière en sortant. Don't forget to turn off the light when you leave. ❷ (computer) to shut down ▷ Quitte l'application avant d'éteindre l'ordinateur. Exit the application before shutting down the computer. ❸ (cigarette) to put out

étendre [etɑ̃dʀ(ə)] vb to spread ▷ Il a étendu une nappe propre sur la table. He spread a clean cloth on the table.; **étendre le linge** to hang out the wash; **s'étendre** to lie down ▷ Je vais m'étendre cinq minutes. I'm going to lie down for five minutes.

éternité [etɛʀnite] nf: **J'ai attendu une éternité chez le médecin.** I waited for ages at the doctor's.

éternuer [etɛʀnɥe] vb to sneeze

êtes [ɛt] vb see **être**; **Vous êtes en retard.** You're late.

étiez [etje] vb see **être**

étinceler [etɛ̃sle] vb to sparkle

étions [etjɔ̃] vb see **être**

étiquette [etikɛt] nf label ▷ L'étiquette du pot de confiture s'est décollée. The label has come off the jam jar.

s'étirer [etiʀe] vb to stretch ▷ Elle s'est étirée paresseusement. She stretched lazily.

étoile [etwal] nf star; **une étoile de mer** a starfish; **une étoile filante** a shooting star; **dormir à la belle étoile** to sleep under the stars; **le match des étoiles** the all-star game

étonnant [etɔnɑ̃, -ɑ̃t] (f **étonnante**) adj amazing

étonner [etɔne] vb to surprise ▷ Cela m'étonnerait de le voir ici. I'd be surprised to see them here.

étouffer [etufe] vb: **On étouffe ici; ouvre donc les fenêtres.** It's stifling in here; open the windows.; **étouffer un cri** to muffle a cry;

étouffer un incendie to put out a fire; **s'étouffer** to choke ▷ Ne mange pas si vite : tu vas t'étouffer! Don't eat so fast: you'll choke!

étourderie [etuʀdəʀi] nf absent-mindedness; **une erreur d'étourderie** a careless error

étourdi [etuʀdi] (f **étourdie**) adj scatterbrained

étourdissement [etuʀdismɑ̃] nm: **avoir des étourdissements** to feel dizzy

étrange [etʀɑ̃ʒ] adj strange

étranger [etʀɑ̃ʒe, -ɛʀ] (f **étrangère**) adj foreign ▷ un pays étranger a foreign country; **une personne étrangère** a stranger ▶ nm ❶ foreigner ❷ stranger; **à l'étranger** abroad

étrangère [etʀɑ̃ʒɛʀ] nf ❶ foreigner ❷ stranger

étrangler [etʀɑ̃gle] vb to strangle; **s'étrangler** to choke ▷ s'étrangler avec quelque chose to choke on something

être [ɛtʀ(ə)] nm: **un être humain** a human being ▶ vb ❶ to be ▷ Je suis heureux. I'm happy. ▷ Mon père est journaliste. My father's a journalist. ▷ Il est dix heures. It's 10 o'clock. ❷ to have ▷ Il n'est pas encore arrivé. He hasn't arrived yet.

étroit [etʀwa, -wat] (f **étroite**) adj narrow; **être à l'étroit** to be cramped ▷ Nous sommes un peu à l'étroit dans cet appartement. We're a bit cramped in this apartment.

étude [etyd] nf study ▷ une étude de cas a case study; **faire des études** to be studying ▷ Elle fait des études de droit. She's studying law.

étudiant [etydjɑ̃] nm (college and university) student

étudiante [etydjɑ̃t] nf (college and university) student

étudier [etydje] vb to study
▷ *étudier pour un examen* to study for an exam ▷ *étudier une question sous toutes ses coutures* to study a question from every angle

étui [etɥi] nm case ▷ *un étui à lunettes* a glasses case

eu [y] vb see **avoir**; *J'ai eu une bonne note.* I got a good mark.

euh [ø] excl uh ▷ *Euh...je ne m'en souviens pas.* Uh...I can't remember.

euro [øʀo] nm (currency) euro

eux [ø] pron them ▷ *Je pense souvent à eux.* I often think of them.
   ∎ **eux** is also used for emphasis. ▷ *Elle a accepté l'invitation, mais eux ont refusé.* She accepted the invitation, but THEY refused.

évacuer [evakɥe] vb to evacuate

s' **évader** [evade] vb to escape

s' **évanouir** [evanwiʀ] vb to faint

s' **évaporer** [evapɔʀe] vb to evaporate

évasif [evazif, -iv] (f **évasive**) adj evasive

évasion [evazjɔ̃] nf escape ▷ *Ils ont préparé leur évasion pendant des mois.* They spent months planning their escape.

éveillé [eveje] (f **éveillée**) adj
① awake ▷ *Elle est restée éveillée toute la nuit.* She stayed awake all night. **②** bright ▷ *C'est un enfant très éveillé.* He's very bright.

s' **éveiller** [eveje] vb to awaken

événement [evɛnmɑ̃] nm event

éventail [evɑ̃taj] nm (handheld) fan; *un large éventail de prix* a wide range of prices

éventualité [evɑ̃tɥalite] nf: *dans l'éventualité d'un retard* in the event of a delay

éventuel [evɑ̃tɥɛl] (f **éventuelle**) adj possible ▷ *une solution éventuelle* a possible solution ▷ *les conséquences éventuelles* the possible consequences
   ∎ Be careful! **éventuel** does not mean **eventual**.

éventuellement [evɑ̃tɥɛlmɑ̃] adv possibly ▷ *Nous pourrions éventuellement avoir besoin de vous.* It's possible we may need you.
   ∎ Be careful! **éventuellement** does not mean **eventually**.

évidemment [evidamɑ̃] adv
① obviously ▷ *Les tomates sont évidemment chères en cette saison.* Tomatoes are obviously expensive at this time of year. **②** of course ▷ *« Est-ce que je peux utiliser ton téléphone? » « Évidemment, tu n'as pas besoin de demander. »* "Can I use your phone?" "Of course, you don't need to ask."

évidence [evidɑ̃s] nf: *C'est une évidence.* It's quite obvious.; *de toute évidence* obviously ▷ *De toute évidence, elle ne veut pas nous voir.* Obviously she doesn't want to see us.; *être en évidence* to be clearly visible ▷ *La lettre était en évidence sur la table.* The letter was clearly visible on the table.; *mettre en évidence* to reveal

évident [evidɑ̃, -ɑ̃t] (f **évidente**) adj obvious

évier [evje] nm sink

éviter [evite] vb to avoid

évolué [evɔlɥe] (f **évoluée**) adj advanced ▷ *une technologie très évoluée* very advanced technology

évoluer [evɔlɥe] vb to progress
▷ *La chirurgie esthétique a beaucoup évolué.* Plastic surgery has progressed a great deal.; *Il a beaucoup évolué.* He has come a long way.

évolution [evɔlysjɔ̃] nf
① development ▷ *une évolution rapide* rapid development
② evolution ▷ *la théorie de*

l'évolution the theory of evolution

évoquer [evɔke] vb to mention
▷ *Elle a évoqué divers problèmes dans son discours.* She mentioned various problems in her speech.

exact [ɛgzakt] (f **exacte**) adj
❶ right ▷ *Avez-vous l'heure exacte? Have you got the right time?* ▷ *« Tu es en secondaire trois, n'est-ce pas? »* — *« C'est exact. »* "You're in grade nine, right?" — "Right." ❷ exact ▷ *le prix exact, taxes comprises* the exact price including tax

exactement [ɛgzaktəmã] adv exactly ▷ *C'est exactement ce que je cherchais.* That's exactly what I was looking for.

ex æquo [ɛgzeko] adj: **Ils sont arrivés ex æquo.** They finished neck and neck.

exagérer [ɛgzaʒere] vb ❶ to exaggerate ▷ *Vous exagérez!* You're exaggerating! ❷ to go too far ▷ *Ça fait trois fois que tu arrives en retard : tu exagères!* That's three times you've been late: you've gone too far!

examen [ɛgzamɛ̃] nm exam ▷ *Nous allons passer l'examen d'anglais vendredi matin.* We're doing our English exam on Friday morning. ▷ *un examen de français* a French exam; **un examen médical** a medical

examiner [ɛgzamine] vb to examine

exaspérant [ɛgzaspɛrã, -ãt] (f **exaspérante**) adj infuriating

exaspérer [ɛgzaspere] vb to infuriate

excédent [ɛksedã] nm: **l'excédent de bagages** excess baggage

excéder [ɛksede] vb to exceed ▷ *excéder la limite de vitesse* to exceed the speed limit; **excéder quelqu'un** to drive somebody crazy

▷ *Les cris des enfants l'excédaient.* The noise of the children was driving her crazy.

excellent [ɛksɛlã, -ãt] (f **excellente**) adj excellent

excentrique [ɛksãtrik] adj eccentric

excepté [ɛksɛpte] prep except ▷ *Toutes les chaussures excepté les sandales* sont en solde. All the shoes except sandals are reduced.

exception [ɛksɛpsjɔ̃] nf exception; **à l'exception de** except

exceptionnel [ɛksɛpsjɔnɛl] (f **exceptionnelle**) adj exceptional

excès [ɛksɛ] nm: **faire des excès** to overindulge ▷ *On fait souvent des excès aux environs de l'Action de grâce.* People often overindulge around Thanksgiving.; **les excès de vitesse** speeding

excessif [ɛksesif, -iv] (f **excessive**) adj excessive

excitant [ɛksitã, -ãt] (f **excitante**) adj exciting
▶ nm stimulant ▷ *Le thé et le café sont des excitants.* Tea and coffee are stimulants.

excitation [ɛksitasjɔ̃] nf excitement

exciter [ɛksite] vb to excite ▷ *Il était tout excité à l'idée de revoir ses cousins.* He was all excited about seeing his cousins again.; **s'exciter** (*informal*) to get excited ▷ *Ne t'excite pas trop vite : ça ne va peut-être pas marcher!* Don't get excited too soon: it may not work!

exclamation [ɛksklamasjɔ̃] nf exclamation

exclu [ɛkskly] (f **exclue**) adj excluded ▷ *Elle se sentait exclue du groupe.* She felt excluded from the group.; **Il n'est pas exclu que...** It's not impossible that...

exclusif [ɛksklyzif, -iv] (f

exclusive) adj exclusive

excursion [ɛkskyʁsjɔ̃] nf ❶ trip ▷ *faire une excursion* to go on a trip ❷ hike ▷ *une excursion dans la montagne* a hike in the hills

excuse [ɛkskyz] nf ❶ excuse ▷ *Tu trouves toujours une bonne excuse pour ne pas faire la vaisselle.* You always find a good excuse for not doing the dishes. ❷ apology ▷ *présenter ses excuses* to offer one's apologies; **un mot d'excuse** (of explanation) a note ▷ *Vous devez apporter un mot d'excuse signé par vos parents.* You have to bring a note signed by your parents.

excuser [ɛkskyze] vb to excuse ▷ *Son retard a été excusé.* His lateness was excused.; **Excusez-moi.** **(1)** Sorry! ▷ *Excusez-moi, je ne vous avais pas vu.* Sorry, I didn't see you. **(2)** Excuse me. ▷ *Excusez-moi, est-ce que vous avez l'heure?* Excuse me, have you got the time?; **s'excuser** to apologize ▷ *Elle s'est excusée de son retard.* She apologized for being late.

exécuter [ɛgzekyte] vb ❶ to execute ▷ *Le prisonnier a été exécuté à l'aube.* The prisoner was executed at dawn. ❷ to perform ▷ *La pianiste va maintenant exécuter une valse de Chopin.* The pianist will now perform a waltz by Chopin.

exemplaire [ɛgzɑ̃plɛʁ] nm copy

exemple [ɛgzɑ̃pl(ə)] nm example ▷ *donner l'exemple* to set an example; **par exemple** for example

s'**exercer** [ɛgzɛʁse] vb to practise ▷ *Pour jouer bien, tu devras t'exercer davantage.* To play well, you'll have to practise more. ▷ *s'exercer à parler français* to practise speaking French

exercice [ɛgzɛʁsis] nm exercise; **un exercice d'incendie** a fire drill

exhiber [ɛgzibe] vb to show off ▷ *Il aime bien exhiber ses décorations.*

He likes showing off his medals.; **s'exhiber** to expose oneself

exigeant [ɛgziʒɑ̃, -ɑ̃t] (f **exigeante**) adj ❶ hard to please ▷ *Elle est vraiment exigeante.* She's really hard to please. ❷ demanding ▷ *un cours très exigeant* a very demanding course

exiger [ɛgziʒe] vb ❶ to demand ▷ *Le propriétaire exige d'être payé immédiatement.* The landlord is demanding to be paid immediately. ❷ to require ▷ *Ce travail exige beaucoup de patience.* This job requires a lot of patience.

exil [ɛgzil] nm exile

exister [ɛgziste] vb to exist ▷ *Ça n'existe pas.* It doesn't exist. ▷ *Ce manteau existe également en rose.* This coat is also available in pink.

exotique [ɛgzɔtik] adj exotic ▷ *une plante exotique* an exotic plant ▷ *un yogourt aux fruits exotiques* a tropical fruit yogurt

expédier [ɛkspedje] vb to send ▷ *expédier un colis* to send a parcel

expéditeur [ɛkspeditœʁ] nm sender

expédition [ɛkspedisjɔ̃] nf expedition

expéditrice [ɛkspeditʁis] nf sender

expérience [ɛkspeʁjɑ̃s] nf ❶ experience ▷ *Elle a plusieurs années d'expérience.* She's got several years of experience. ❷ experiment ▷ *une expérience de chimie* a chemistry experiment

expérimenter [ɛkspeʁimɑ̃te] vb to test ▷ *Ces produits de beauté n'ont pas été expérimentés sur des animaux.* These cosmetics have not been tested on animals.

expert [ɛkspɛʁ] nm expert

experte [ɛkspɛʁt(ə)] nf expert

expirer [ɛkspiʁe] vb ❶ (document,

passport) to expire ❷ (time allowed) to run out ❸ (person) to breathe out

explication [ɛksplikasjɔ̃] nf explanation

expliquer [ɛksplike] vb to explain ▷ Elle m'a expliqué comment faire. She explained to me how to do it.; **s'expliquer** to explain oneself

exploit [ɛksplwa] nm achievement

exploitation [ɛksplwatasjɔ̃] nf exploitation ▷ Cet organisme lutte contre l'exploitation des femmes. This organization fights against the exploitation of women.; **une exploitation agricole** a farm

exploiter [ɛksplwate] vb to exploit ▷ Il s'est fait exploiter par le patron du restaurant. He was exploited by the owner of the restaurant.

explorer [ɛksplɔʀe] vb to explore

exploser [ɛksploze] vb to explode ▷ La bombe a explosé en pleine rue. The bomb exploded in the middle of the street.

explosif [ɛksplozif] nm explosive

explosion [ɛksplozjɔ̃] nf explosion

exportation [ɛkspɔrtasjɔ̃] nf export

exporter [ɛkspɔrte] vb to export

exposé [ɛkspoze] nm presentation ▷ un exposé sur l'environnement a presentation on the environment; **un exposé écrit** an essay

exposer [ɛkspoze] vb ❶ to show ▷ Il expose ses peintures dans une galerie d'art. He shows his paintings in a private art gallery. ❷ to expose ▷ N'exposez pas le film à la lumière. Do not expose the film to light. ❸ (explain) to lay out ▷ Elle nous a exposé les raisons de son départ. She laid out the reasons for her departure.; **s'exposer au soleil** to stay out in the sun ▷ Ne vous exposez pas trop longtemps au soleil. Don't

stay out in the sun too long.

exposition [ɛkspozisjɔ̃] nf exhibition ▷ une exposition de peinture an exhibition of paintings

exprès [ɛkspʀɛ] adv ❶ on purpose ▷ Je suis sûr qu'il l'a fait exprès. I'm sure he did it on purpose. ❷ specially ▷ J'ai fait ce gâteau exprès pour toi. I made this cake specially for you.

express [ɛkspʀɛs] nm (bus, train) express ▷ Elle a décidé de prendre l'express de dix heures. She decided to catch the express at 10 o'clock.

expression [ɛkspʀesjɔ̃] nf ❶ expression ❷ phrase

exprimer [ɛkspʀime] vb to express; **s'exprimer** to express oneself ▷ Il s'exprime très bien pour un enfant de huit ans. For a child of 8, he expresses himself very well.

exquis [ɛkski, -iz] (f **exquise**) adj exquisite

extérieur [ɛksteʀjœʀ] (f **extérieure**) adj outside ▶ nm outside; **à l'extérieur** outside ▷ Prenons le déjeuner à l'extérieur. Let's eat lunch outside.

extincteur [ɛkstɛ̃ktœʀ] nm fire extinguisher

extra [ɛkstʀa] (f+pl **extra**) adj excellent ▷ Ce fromage est extra! This cheese is excellent!

extraire [ɛkstʀɛʀ] vb to extract

extrait [ɛkstʀɛ] nm extract

extraordinaire [ɛkstʀaɔʀdinɛʀ] adj extraordinary

extra-terrestre [ɛkstʀateʀɛstʀ(ə)] nmf alien

extravagant [ɛkstʀavagɑ̃, -ɑ̃t] (f **extravagante**) adj extravagant

extrême [ɛkstʀɛm] adj extreme ▷ l'extrême droite et l'extrême gauche the far right and the far left ▶ nm extreme; **pousser les choses à l'extrême** to go to extremes

extrêmement [ɛkstʀɛmmɑ̃] *adv*
extremely

Extrême-Orient [ɛkstʀɛmɔʀjɑ̃]
nm the Far East

extrémité [ɛkstʀemite] *nf* end
▷ *La gare est à l'autre extrémité de la ville.* The station is at the other end of the town.

fa [fɑ] *nm (music)* F

fabrication [fabʀikasjɔ̃] *nf*
manufacture

fabriquer [fabʀike] *vb* to make
▷ *fabriqué au Canada* made in Canada

face [fas] *nf*: **face à face** face to face; **en face de** opposite
▷ *L'autobus s'arrête en face de chez moi.* The bus stops opposite my house.; **faire face à quelque chose** to face something; **perdre la face** to lose face; **« Pile ou face? » — « Face. »** "Heads or tails?" — "Heads."

fâché [fɑʃe] (f**fâchée**) *adj* angry; **être fâché contre quelqu'un** to be angry with somebody ▷ *Elle est fâchée contre moi.* She's angry with me.; **être fâché avec quelqu'un** to be on bad terms with somebody ▷ *Elle est fâchée avec sa sœur.* She's on bad terms with her sister.

se fâcher [fɑʃe] *vb*: **se fâcher**

contre quelqu'un to lose one's temper with somebody; **se fâcher avec quelqu'un** to fall out with somebody ▷ Il s'est fâché avec son frère. He had a fight with his brother.

facile [fasil] *adj* easy; **facile à faire** easy to do

facilement [fasilmɑ̃] *adv* easily

facilité [fasilite] *nf*: **un logiciel d'une grande facilité d'utilisation** a very user-friendly piece of software; **Il a de la facilité en langues.** He has a gift for languages.

▌ Be careful! **facilité** does not mean **facility**.

façon [fasɔ̃] *nf* way ▷ De quelle façon? In what way? ▷ **de toute façon** anyway

facteur [faktœʀ] *nm* letter carrier

factrice [faktʀis] *nf* letter carrier

facture [faktyʀ] *nf* bill ▷ une facture de gaz a gas bill

facultatif [fakyltatif, -iv] (*f* **facultative**) *adj* optional

faculté [fakylte] *nf* faculty; **avoir une grande faculté de concentration** to have great powers of concentration

fade [fad] *adj* tasteless ▷ La soupe est un peu fade. The soup is a bit tasteless.

faible [fɛbl(ə)] *adj* weak ▷ Je me sens encore faible. I still feel a bit weak.; **Il est faible en maths.** He's not very good at math.

faiblesse [fɛblɛs] *nf* weakness

faillir [fajiʀ] *vb*: **J'ai failli tomber.** I nearly fell down.

faillite [fajit] *nf* bankruptcy; **une entreprise en faillite** a bankrupt business; **faire faillite** to go bankrupt

faim [fɛ̃] *nf* hunger; **avoir faim** to be hungry

fainéant [feneɑ̃, -ɑ̃t] (*f* **fainéante**) *adj* lazy

faire [fɛʀ] *vb* ❶ to make ▷ Je vais faire un gâteau pour ce soir. I'm going to make a cake for tonight. ▷ Ils font trop de bruit. They're making too much noise. ▷ Je voudrais me faire de nouveaux amis. I'd like to make new friends. ❷ to do ▷ Qu'est-ce que tu fais? What are you doing? ▷ Elle fait de l'italien. She's doing Italian. ▷ Qui veut faire la vaisselle? Who'll do the dishes? ❸ to be ▷ Qu'est-ce qu'il fait chaud! Is it ever hot! ▷ Espérons qu'il fera beau demain. Let's hope it'll be nice weather tomorrow.; **Ça ne fait rien.** It doesn't matter.; **Ça fait cinquante-trois dollars en tout.** That makes fifty-three dollars in all.; **Ça fait trois ans qu'elle habite à Peterborough.** She's lived in Peterborough for three years.; **faire tomber** to knock over ▷ Le chat a fait tomber le vase. The cat knocked over the vase.; **faire faire quelque chose** to get something done ▷ Je dois faire réparer ma voiture. I've got to get my car repaired.; **Je vais me faire couper les cheveux.** I'm going to get my hair cut.; **Ne t'en fais pas!** Don't worry!; **se faire des idées** to imagine things

fais, faisaient, faisais, faisait, faisiez, faisions, faisons, fait *vb* see **faire**

fait [fɛ] *nm* fact ▷ Le fait que… The fact that…; **un fait divers** a news item; **au fait** by the way ▷ Au fait, tu as aimé le film d'hier? By the way, did you enjoy the movie yesterday?; **en fait** actually ▷ En fait, je n'ai pas beaucoup de temps. I haven't got much time actually.; **aller au fait** to get to the point

faites [fɛt] *vb* see **faire**

falaise [falɛz] *nf* cliff

falloir [falwaʀ] vb see **faut**, **faudra**, **faudrait**

famé [fame] (f **famée**) adj: **un quartier mal famé** a rough area

fameux [famø, -øz] (f **fameuse**) adj famous ▷ La Colombie-Britannique est fameuse pour ses montagnes. British Columbia is famous for its mountains.; **Ce n'est pas fameux.** It's not great.

familial [familjal, -o] (f **familiale**, mpl **familiaux**) adj family ▷ une atmosphère familiale a family atmosphere; **les allocations familiales** child benefit

familier [familje, -jeʀ] (f **familière**) adj familiar

famille [famij] nf family ▷ une famille nombreuse a big family ▷ Nous fêtons les anniversaires en famille. We have family birthday celebrations.; **une famille monoparentale** a single-parent family; **une famille nucléaire** a nuclear family; **une famille reconstituée** a blended family ❷ relatives ▷ J'ai de la famille à Windsor. I've got relatives in Windsor.

famine [famin] nf famine

fanatique [fanatik] adj fanatical ▶ n fanatic

fanfare [fɑ̃faʀ] nf brass band

fanion [fanjɔ̃] nm pennant

fantaisie [fɑ̃tezi] nf ❶ imagination ▷ un roman plein de fantaisie a novel full of imagination ❷ whim ▷ Ils lui passent toutes ses fantaisies. They give in to all his whims.; **des bijoux de fantaisie** costume jewellery

fantastique [fɑ̃tastik] adj fantastic

fantôme [fɑ̃tom] nm ghost

faon [fɑ̃] nm fawn

farce [faʀs(ə)] nf ❶ (for chicken, turkey) stuffing ❷ practical joke ▷ Elle aime faire des farces. She likes to play practical jokes.

farci [faʀsi] (f **farcie**) adj stuffed ▷ des poivrons verts farcis stuffed green peppers

farine [faʀin] nf flour

fascinant [fasinɑ̃, -ɑ̃t] (f **fascinante**) adj fascinating

fasciner [fasine] vb to fascinate

fascisme [faʃism(ə)] nm fascism

fasse, fassent, fasses, fassiez, fassions vb see **faire**; **Pourvu qu'il fasse beau demain!** Let's hope it'll be nice out tomorrow!

fatal [fatal] (f **fatale**) adj fatal; **C'était fatal.** It was bound to happen.

fatalité [fatalite] nf fate

> Be careful! **fatalité** does not mean **fatality**.

fatigant [fatigɑ̃, -ɑ̃t] (f **fatigante**) adj tiring

fatigue [fatig] nf tiredness

fatigué [fatige] (f **fatiguée**) adj tired

se fatiguer [fatige] vb to get tired

fauché [foʃe] (f **fauchée**) adj (informal) hard up

faucon [fokɔ̃] nm hawk

faudra [fodʀa] vb

> **faudra** is the future tense of **falloir**.

Il faudra qu'on soit plus rapide. We'll have to be quicker.

faudrait [fodʀɛ] vb

> **faudrait** is the conditional tense of **falloir**.

Il faudrait qu'on fasse attention. We ought to be careful.

se faufiler [fofile] vb: **Il s'est faufilé à travers la foule.** He made his way through the crowd.

faune [fon] nf wildlife

faunique [fonik] adj: **une réserve faunique** a wildlife reserve

fausse [fos] adj see **faux**

faut [fo] vb

  faut is the present tense of **falloir**.

Il faut faire attention. You have to be careful.; **Nous n'avons pas le choix, il faut y aller.** We have no choice, we've got to go.; **Il faut que je parte.** I have to go.; **Il faut du courage pour faire ce métier.** It takes courage to do that job.; **Il me faut de l'argent.** I need money.; **s'il le faut** if need be

faute [fot] nf ❶ mistake ▷ *faire une faute* to make a mistake ❷ fault ▷ *Ce n'est pas de ma faute.* It's not my fault.; **sans faute** without fail ▷ *Je t'appellerai sans faute.* I'll phone you without fail.

fauteuil [fotœj] nm armchair; **un fauteuil roulant** a wheelchair

faux [fo, fos] (f**fausse**) adj, adv ❶ untrue ▷ *C'est entièrement faux.* It's totally untrue. ❷ forged ▷ *un faux passeport* a forged passport; **faire un faux pas** to trip; **Elle chante faux.** She sings out of tune.; **un faux ami** a false friend ▶ nm fake ▷ *Ce tableau est un faux.* This painting is a fake.

faveur [favœʀ] nf favour

favori [favɔʀi, -it] (f**favorite**) adj favourite ▷ *Ce système d'examen favorise ceux qui ont de la mémoire.* This exam system favours people with good memories.

favoriser [favɔʀize] vb to favour ▷ *Ce système d'examen favorise ceux qui ont de la mémoire.* This exam system favours people with good memories.

fédéral [federal] adj federal ▷ *le gouvernement fédéral* the federal government

fée [fe] nf fairy

félicitations [felisitasjɔ̃] nfpl congratulations

féliciter [felisite] vb to congratulate

femelle [fəmɛl] nf (animal) female

féminin [feminɛ̃, -in] (f**féminine**) adj ❶ female ▷ *les personnages féminins du roman* the female characters in the novel ❷ feminine ▷ *Elle est très féminine.* She's very feminine. ❸ women's ▷ *Elle joue dans l'équipe féminine du Canada.* She plays in the Canadian women's team.

féministe [feminist(ə)] adj feminist

femme [fam] nf ❶ woman ❷ wife ▷ *la femme du directeur* the principal's wife; **une femme au foyer** a housewife; **une femme d'affaires** a businesswoman; **une femme d'État** a stateswoman; **une femme de tête** a strong-minded intelligent woman

se fendre [fɑ̃dʀ(ə)] vb to crack

fenêtre [fənɛtʀ(ə)] nf window

fente [fɑ̃t] nf slot

fer [fɛʀ] nm iron; **un fer à cheval** a horseshoe; **un fer à friser** a curling iron; **un fer à repasser** an iron

fera, ferai, feras, ferez vb see **faire**

férié [feʀje] (f**fériée**) adj: **un jour férié** a public holiday

feriez, ferions vb see **faire**

ferme [fɛʀm(ə)] adj firm ▷ *Il s'est montré très ferme à mon égard.* He was very firm with me.
▶ nf farm

fermé [fɛʀme] (f**fermée**) adj ❶ closed ▷ *La pharmacie est fermée.* The drugstore is closed. ❷ off ▷ *Est-ce que le gaz est fermé? Is the gas off?*

fermer [fɛʀme] vb ❶ to close ▷ *N'oublie pas de fermer la fenêtre.* Don't forget to close the window. ❷ to turn off ▷ *As-tu bien fermé le robinet?* Did you turn the tap off?; **fermer à clef** to lock ▷ *N'oublie pas* *de fermer la porte à clef!* Don't forget to lock the door!

fermeture [fɛʀmətyʀ] *nf*: **les heures de fermeture** closing times

fermeture éclair® (*pl* **fermetures éclair**) *nf* zipper

fermier [fɛʀmje] *nm* farmer

fermière [fɛʀmjɛʀ] *nf* ❶ (woman) farmer ❷ farmer's wife

féroce [feʀɔs] *adj* fierce

ferons, feront *vb see* **faire**

fesses [fɛs] *nfpl* buttocks

festival [fɛstival] *nm* festival

fête [fɛt] *nf* ❶ party ▷ *On organise une petite fête pour son départ.* We're having a little farewell party for him.; **faire la fête** to party ❷ birthday ▷ *C'est sa fête aujourd'hui.* It's his birthday today.; **une fête foraine** a funfair; **la fête du Canada** Canada Day; **la fête de Dollard** Dollard Day; **la fête du Travail** Labour Day; **la fête de la Reine** Victoria Day; **les fêtes de fin d'année** the festive season

- In Québec, **la fête de Dollard** is the same day as Victoria Day.
- It commemorates the death of Adam Dollard des Ormeaux and his 16 companions in 1660 in a hopeless battle to avert an Iroquois siege of Ville Marie (now Montréal). In 2002, this holiday was officially replaced by **la Journée nationale des patriotes**.

fêter [fete] *vb* to celebrate

feu [fø] (*pl* **feux**) *nm* ❶ fire ▷ *prendre feu* to catch fire ▷ *faire du feu* to make a fire; **Au feu!** Fire!; **un feu de camp** a campfire; **un feu de joie** a bonfire ▷ *un feu rouge* a red light ▷ *le feu vert* the green light ▷ *Tournez à gauche aux feux.* Turn left at the lights.; **Avez-vous du feu?** Have you got a

light? ❸ heat ▷ *…mijoter à feu doux* …simmer over low heat; **un feu d'artifice** a firework display; **un feu sauvage** a cold sore

feuillage [fœjaʒ] *nm* leaves

feuille [fœj] *nf* ❶ leaf ▷ *des feuilles mortes* fallen leaves; **la feuille d'érable** (to mean "Canada") the maple leaf ❷ sheet ▷ *une feuille de papier* a sheet of paper; **une feuille de présence** attendance sheet; **une feuille de calcul** (*file*) a spreadsheet

feuilleté [fœjte] (*f* **feuilletée**) *adj*: **de la pâte feuilletée** flaky pastry

feuilleter [fœjte] *vb* to leaf through

feuilleton [fœjtɔ̃] *nm* serial

feutre [føtʀ(ə)] *nm* felt; **un stylo-feutre** a felt pen

fève [fɛv] *nf* bean ▷ *les fèves vertes* green beans ▷ *les fèves jaunes* wax beans; **les fèves au lard** baked beans ▷ *Il aime ajouter de la mélasse à ses fèves au lard.* He likes to add molasses to his baked beans.

février [fevʀije] *nm* February; **en février** in February

fiable [fjabl(ə)] *adj* reliable

fiançailles [fjɑ̃saj] *nfpl* engagement; **rompre ses fiançailles** to break off one's engagement

fiancé [fjɑ̃se] (*f* **fiancée**) *adj*: **être fiancé à quelqu'un** to be engaged to somebody

se fiancer [fjɑ̃se] *vb* to get engaged

ficelle [fisɛl] *nf* ❶ string ▷ *Passe-moi un bout de ficelle.* Give me a piece of string. ❷ (*bread*) thin baguette

fiche [fiʃ] *nf* form ▷ *Remplissez cette fiche s'il vous plaît.* Fill in this form, please.

se ficher [fiʃe] *vb* (*informal*); **Je m'en fiche!** I don't care!; **Fiche-moi la paix!** Leave me alone!; **Quoi, tu n'as fait que ça?** Tu te fiches de

moi! You've only done that much? You can't be serious!

fichier [fiʃje] *nm* file; **un fichier joint** (email) an attachment

fichu [fiʃy] (f **fichue**) *adj* (informal); **Ce parapluie est fichu.** This umbrella's had it.

fidèle [fidɛl] *adj* faithful

fier [fjɛʀ] (f **fière**) *adj* proud

fierté [fjɛʀte] *nf* pride

fièvre [fjɛvʀ(ə)] *nf* fever ▷ *J'ai de la fièvre.* I have a temperature. ▷ *Elle a trente-neuf de fièvre.* She has a temperature of 39°C.

fiévreux [fjevʀø, -øz] (f **fiévreuse**) *adj* feverish

figue [fig] *nf* fig

figure [figyʀ] *nf* ❶ face ▷ *Il a reçu le ballon en pleine figure.* The ball hit him smack in the face. ❷ (illustration) figure ▷ *Voir figure 2.1, page 32.* See figure 2.1, page 32.

fil [fil] *nm* ❶ thread ▷ *le fil à coudre* sewing thread ❷ cord ▷ *une souris sans fil* a cordless mouse; **le fil de fer** wire

file [fil] *nf* (of people, objects) line; **une file d'attente** a lineup ▷ *se mettre à la file* to go stand in line; **à la file** one after the other

filer [file] *vb* to speed along ▷ *Les voitures filent sur l'autoroute.* The cars are speeding along the highway. ; **File dans ta chambre!** Off to your room with you!

filet [filɛ] *nm* net

fille [fij] *nf* ❶ girl ▷ *C'est une école de filles.* It's a girls' school. ❷ daughter ▷ *C'est leur fille aînée.* She's their oldest daughter.

fillette [fijɛt] *nf* little girl

film [film] *nm* ❶ movie; **un film policier** a thriller; **un film d'aventures** an action movie; **un film d'épouvante** a horror movie ❷ film ▷ *Avec une caméra numérique,*

on n'a pas besoin de film. With a digital camera, you don't need film.

fils [fis] *nm* son

fin [fɛ̃] *nf* end ▷ *Elle n'a pas regardé la fin du film.* She didn't watch the end of the film.; **« Fin »** "The End"; **À la fin, il a réussi à se décider.** In the end he managed to make up his mind.; **Elle sera en vacances fin juin.** She'll be on holiday at the end of June.; **en fin de journée** at the end of the day; **en fin de compte** ultimately; **sans fin** endless ▷ *adj* ❶ fine; **des fines herbes** mixed herbs ❷ (informal) nice ▷ *Elle est vraiment fine!* She is so nice!

finale [final] *nf* (sports) final ▷ *les quarts de finale* the quarter finals

finalement [finalmɑ̃] *adv* ❶ at last ▷ *Nous sommes finalement arrivés.* At last we arrived. ❷ after all ▷ *Finalement, tu avais raison.* You were right after all.

fin de semaine *nf* weekend ▷ *Nous avons passé la fin de semaine au chalet.* We spent the weekend at the cottage.

fini [fini] (f **finie**) *adj* finished

finir [finiʀ] *vb* to finish ▷ *Le cours finit à onze heures.* The class finishes at 11 o'clock. ▷ *Je viens de finir ce livre.* I've just finished this book.; **Elle a fini par se décider.** She made up her mind in the end.

finissant [finisɑ̃] *nm* graduating student; **le bal des finissants** graduation party

finissante [finisɑ̃t] *nf* graduating student

firme [fiʀm(ə)] *nf* firm

fis [fi] *vb* see **faire**

fissure [fisyʀ] *nf* crack

fit [fi] *vb* see **faire**

fixe [fiks] *adj* ❶ steady ▷ *Il n'a pas d'emploi fixe.* He doesn't have a steady job. ❷ set ▷ *Elle mange* *toujours à heures fixes.* She always eats at set times.; **un menu à prix fixe** a set menu; **une idée fixe** an obsession

fixer [fikse] *vb* ➊ to hold in place ▷ *Les volets sont fixés avec des crochets.* The shutters are held in place with hooks. ➋ (*time*) to set ▷ *Nous avons fixé une heure pour nous retrouver.* We set a time to meet. ➊ to stare at ▷ *Ne fixe pas les gens comme ça!* Don't stare at people like that!

flacon [flakɔ̃] *nm* bottle ▷ *un flacon de parfum* a bottle of perfume

flambé [flɑ̃be] (*f* **flambée**) *adj*: **des bananes flambées** flambéed bananas

flamme [flam] *nf* flame; **en flammes** on fire

flan [flɑ̃] *nm* baked custard

flâner [flɑne] *vb* to stroll

flaque [flak] *nf* (*of water*) puddle

flash [flaʃ] (*pl* **flashes**) *nm* (*of camera*) flash

flatter [flate] *vb* to flatter

flèche [flɛʃ] *nf* arrow

fléchettes [fleʃɛt] *nfpl* darts ▷ *jouer aux fléchettes* to play darts

flétan [fletɑ̃] *nm* halibut

fleur [flœʀ] *nf* flower

fleur de lis [-lis] *nf* fleur-de-lis
● The **fleur-de-lis** is the provincial
● emblem of Québec and is on the
● provincial flag. It is a legacy of
● New France, as it was also the
● emblem of French royalty.

fleurdelisé [flœʀdəlize] *nm* the Québec flag

fleuri [flœʀi] (*f* **fleurie**) *adj* ➊ full of flowers ▷ *Son jardin était très fleuri.* Her garden was full of flowers. ➋ flowery ▷ *un papier peint fleuri* flowery wallpaper

fleurir [flœʀiʀ] *vb* to flower ▷ *Cette plante fleurit en automne.* This plant

flowers in the fall.

fleuriste [flœʀist(ə)] *nmf* florist

fleuve [flœv] *nm* river

flirter [flœʀte] *vb* to flirt

flocon [flɔkɔ̃] *nm* flake

flotter [flɔte] *vb* to float

flou [flu] (*f* **floue**) *adj* blurry

fluorure [flyɔʀyʀ] *nm*: **le dentifrice au fluorure** fluoride toothpaste

flûte [flyt] *nf* flute ▷ *Je joue de la flûte.* I play the flute.; **une flûte à bec** a recorder

foi [fwa] *nf* faith

foie [fwa] *nm* liver; **une crise de foie** a stomach upset

foin [fwɛ̃] *nm* hay; **un rhume des foins** hay fever

foire [fwaʀ] *nf* fair; **la foire du livre** book fair

fois [fwa] *nf* time ▷ *la première fois* the first time ▷ *à chaque fois* each time ▷ *À chaque fois que je vais à la bibliothèque, j'oublie ma carte.* Every time I go to the library, I forget my card. ▷ *deux fois deux font quatre* 2 times 2 is 4; **une fois** once; **deux fois** twice ▷ *deux fois plus de gens* twice as many people ▷ *Je vais nager deux fois par semaine.* I go swimming twice a week.; **une fois que** once ▷ *Tu te sentiras mieux une fois que tu auras mangé.* You'll feel better once you've had something to eat.; **à la fois** at once ▷ *Je ne peux pas faire deux choses à la fois.* I can't do two things at once.

folie [fɔli] *nf* madness ▷ *C'est de la folie pure!* It's absolute madness!; **faire une folie** to be extravagant

folklorique [fɔlklɔʀik] *adj* folk ▷ *de la musique folklorique* folk music

folle [fɔl] *adj* see **fou**

foncé [fɔ̃se] (*f* **foncée**) *adj* dark ▷ *bleu foncé* dark blue

foncer [fɔ̃se] *vb* (*informal*); **je vais**

foncer à la boulangerie. I'm just going to whip over to the bakery.

fonction [fɔksjɔ̃] nf function; **une voiture de fonction** a company car

fonctionnaire [fɔ̃ksjɔnɛʀ] nmf civil servant

fonctionner [fɔ̃ksjɔne] vb to work

fond [fɔ̃] nm ❶ bottom ▷ *Mon porte-monnaie est au fond de mon sac.* My wallet is at the bottom of my purse. ❷ end ▷ *Les toilettes sont au fond du couloir.* The washrooms are at the end of the hall.; **dans le fond** all things considered ▷ *Dans le fond, ce n'est pas si grave.* All things considered, it's not that bad.

fonder [fɔ̃de] vb to found ▷ *Charles Camsell a fondé la Société géographique royale du Canada.* Charles Camsell founded the Royal Geographical Society of Canada.

fondre [fɔ̃dʀ(ə)] vb to melt ▷ *La tablette de chocolat a fondu dans ma poche.* The bar of chocolate melted in my pocket.; **fondre en larmes** to burst into tears

fondu [fɔ̃dy] (f **fondue**) adj: **du beurre fondu** melted butter

font [fɔ̃] vb see **faire**

fontaine [fɔ̃tɛn] nf fountain

foot [fut] nm (informal) football

football [futbɔl] nm football ▷ *jouer au football* to play football

force [fɔʀs(ə)] nf strength ▷ *Je n'ai pas beaucoup de force dans les bras.* I haven't got much strength in my arms.; **à force de** by ▷ *Il a grossi à force de manger autant.* He got fat by eating so much.; **de force** by force ▷ *Ils lui ont enlevé son pistolet de force.* They took the gun from her by force.; **les forces armées** the armed forces

forcé [fɔʀse] (f **forcée**) adj forced ▷ *un sourire forcé* a forced smile; **C'est forcé.** (informal) It's

inevitable.

forcément [fɔʀsemɑ̃] adv: **Ça devait forcément arriver.** That was bound to happen.; **pas forcément** not necessarily

foresterie [fɔʀɛstəʀi] nf forestry ▷ *Elle veut étudier en foresterie.* She wants to study forestry.

forêt [fɔʀɛ] nf forest

forfait [fɔʀfɛ] nm package deal; **C'est compris dans le forfait.** It's included in the package.

formalité [fɔʀmalite] nf formality ▷ *Ce n'est qu'une simple formalité.* It's just a formality.

format [fɔʀma] nm size

formatage [fɔʀmataʒ] nm formatting

formater [fɔʀmate] vb to format ▷ *formater un document* to format a document

formation [fɔʀmasjɔ̃] nf training ▷ *la formation professionnelle* vocational training; **Il a une formation d'ingénieur.** He is a trained engineer.

forme [fɔʀm(ə)] nf shape; **être en forme** to be in good shape; **Je ne suis pas en forme aujourd'hui.** I'm not feeling too good today.; **Tu as l'air en forme.** You're looking well.

formellement [fɔʀmɛlmɑ̃] adv strictly ▷ *Il est formellement interdit de fumer dans les couloirs.* It is strictly forbidden to smoke in the corridors.

former [fɔʀme] vb to form

formidable [fɔʀmidabl(ə)] adj great

formulaire [fɔʀmylɛʀ] nm (to fill out) form

fort [fɔʀ, fɔʀt(ə)] (f **forte**) adj, adv ❶ strong ▷ *Le café est trop fort.* The coffee's too strong. ❷ good ▷ *Elle est très forte en espagnol.* She's very good at Spanish. ❸ loud ▷ *Est-ce que vous pouvez parler plus fort?* Can you speak louder? ❹ hard ▷ frapper fort to hit hard ▷ travailler fort to work hard

fortune [fɔʀtyn] nf fortune; **de fortune** makeshift ▷ Nous avons traversé la rivière sur un radeau de fortune. We crossed the river on a makeshift raft.

forum de discussion [fɔʀɔm-] nm (Internet) discussion group

fossé [fose] nm ditch

fou [fu, fɔl] (f **folle**) adj mad; **Il y a un monde fou sur la plage!** (informal) There are tons of people on the beach!; **attraper le fou rire** to get the giggles

foudre [fudʀ(ə)] nf lightning ▷ Il a été frappé par la foudre. He was struck by lightning.

foudroyant [fudʀwajɑ̃, -ɑ̃t] (f **foudroyante**) adj instant ▷ un succès foudroyant an instant hit

fouet [fwɛ] nm whisk

fouetter [fwete] vb to whip ▷ la crème à fouetter whipping cream

fougère [fuʒɛʀ] nf fern

fouiller [fuje] vb to rummage

fouillis [fuji] nm mess ▷ Sa chambre est un vrai fouillis. Her bedroom is a mess.

foulard [fulaʀ] nm scarf ▷ un foulard en soie a silk scarf

foule [ful] nf crowd; **une foule de** tons of ▷ J'ai une foule de choses à faire en fin de semaine. I have tons of things to do this weekend.

se fouler [fule] vb: **se fouler la cheville** to sprain one's ankle

foulure [fulyʀ] nf sprain

four [fuʀ] nm oven ▷ un four à micro-ondes a microwave oven; **un four à céramique** a kiln

fourchette [fuʀʃɛt] nf fork

fourmi [fuʀmi] nf ant; **avoir des fourmis dans les jambes** to have pins and needles

fourneau [fuʀno] (pl **fourneaux**) nm stove

fourni [fuʀni] (f **fournie**) adj (beard, hair) thick

fournir [fuʀniʀ] vb to supply

fournisseur [fuʀnisœʀ] nm supplier; **un fournisseur de services Internet** an Internet service provider

fournitures [fuʀnityʀ] nfpl: **les fournitures scolaires** school supplies

fourré [fuʀe] (f **fourrée**) adj filled ▷ un gâteau fourré à la confiture a cake with a jam filling

fourrer [fuʀe] vb (informal) to put ▷ Où as-tu fourré mon sac? Where have you put my bag?

fourre-tout [fuʀtu] (pl **fourre-tout**) nm tote bag

fourrure [fuʀyʀ] nf fur ▷ un manteau de fourrure a fur coat

foyer [fwaje] nm home ▷ dans la plupart des foyers canadiens-français in most French-Canadian homes; **un foyer de jeunes** a youth club

fracture [fʀaktyʀ] nf fracture

fragile [fʀaʒil] adj fragile ▷ Attention, c'est fragile! Be careful, it's fragile!

fraîche [fʀɛʃ] adj see **frais**

fraîcheur [fʀɛʃœʀ] nf ❶ cool ▷ la fraîcheur du soir the cool of the evening ❷ freshness ▷ Je ne suis pas sûre de la fraîcheur de ce poisson. I'm not sure about the freshness of this fish.

frais [fʀɛ, fʀɛʃ] (f **fraîche**) adj ❶ fresh ▷ des œufs frais fresh eggs ▷ Cette salade n'est pas très fraîche. This lettuce isn't very fresh. ❷ chilly ▷ Il fait un peu frais ce soir. It's a bit chilly this evening. ❸ cold ▷ des boissons fraîches cold drinks; **« servir frais »** "serve chilled"; **garder au frais** to store in a cool

place
▶ *nmpl* expenses

fraise [frɛz] *nf* strawberry ▷ *une fraise des bois* a wild strawberry

framboise [frãbwaz] *nf* raspberry

franc [frɑ̃, frɑ̃ʃ] **(franche)** *adj* frank

français [frɑ̃sɛ, -ez] **(française)** *adj, n* French ▷ *la grammaire française* French grammar ▷ *Il parle français couramment.* He speaks French fluently.

franche [frɑ̃ʃ] *adj* see **franc**

franchement [frɑ̃ʃmɑ̃] *adv*
❶ frankly ▷ *Elle m'a parlé franchement.* She spoke to me frankly. ❷ really ▷ *C'est franchement mauvais.* It's really bad.

franchir [frɑ̃ʃir] *vb* to get over ▷ *franchir une clôture* to get over a fence ▷ *Un sourire franchit toutes les barrières linguistiques.* A smile crosses all language barriers.

franchise [frɑ̃ʃiz] *nf* frankness

francophone [frɑ̃kɔfɔn] *adj* French-speaking
▶ *n* Francophone ▷ *C'est un francophone.* He's a Francophone.

francophonie [frɑ̃kɔfɔni] *nf* the Francophone world
● **La francophonie** refers to the
● more than 50 French-speaking
● countries and regions of the
● world collectively.

frange [frɑ̃ʒ] *nf* ❶ fringe ❷ bangs

frangipane [frɑ̃ʒipan] *nf* almond cream

frapper [frape] *vb* to strike ▷ *Il n'a jamais frappée ses enfants.* He has never struck his children. ▷ *Son air fatigué m'a frappé.* I was struck by how tired she looked.

fredonner [frədɔne] *vb* to hum

frein [frɛ̃] *nm* brake; **le frein à main** handbrake

freiner [frene] *vb* to brake

frêle [frɛl] *adj* frail

frelon [frəlɔ̃] *nm* hornet

frémir [fremir] *vb* to shudder ▷ *Cette idée me fait frémir.* The idea makes me shudder.

fréquemment [frekamɑ̃] *adv* frequently

fréquent [frekɑ̃, -ɑ̃t] **(fréquente)** *adj* frequent

fréquentée [frekɑ̃te] **(fréquentée)** *adj* busy ▷ *une rue très fréquentée* a very busy street

fréquenter [frekɑ̃te] *vb*
❶ (person) to see ▷ *Je ne le fréquente pas beaucoup.* I don't see him often.
❷ (place) to go to ▷ *Tu fréquentes les vendes-débarras?* Do you go to garage sales?

frère [frɛr] *nm* brother

friand [frijɑ̃] *nm* sausage roll

friandises [frijɑ̃diz] *nfpl* sweets

fric [frik] *nm* (informal) cash

frigidaire [friʒidɛr] *nm* refrigerator

frigo [frigo] *nm* (informal) fridge

frileux [frilø, -øz] **(frileuse)** *adj*:
être frileux to feel the cold ▷ *Je suis très frileuse.* I really feel the cold.

fripé [fripe] **(fripée)** *adj* crumpled

frire [frir] *vb*: **faire frire** to fry ▷ *Faites frire les boulettes de viande dans de l'huile très chaude.* Fry the meatballs in very hot oil.

frisé [frize] **(frisée)** *adj* curly ▷ *Elle est très frisée.* She has very curly hair.

frisson [frisɔ̃] *nm* shiver

frissonner [frisɔne] *vb* to shiver

frit [fri, frit] **(frite)** *adj* fried ▷ *du poisson frit* fried fish

frites [frit] *nfpl* fries; **poisson et frites** fish and chips

friture [frityr] *nf* ❶ fried food ▷ *On lui a conseillé d'éviter les fritures.* He's been advised to avoid fried food. ❷ fried fish ▷ *Nous allons faire une friture ce soir.* We're going

to have fried fish tonight. ❶ static
▷ *Il y a de la friture sur la ligne.* There's
static on the line.

froid [fʀwa, fʀwad] (f **froide**) adj
cold ▷ *Ça me laisse froid.* It leaves me
cold. ▷ *de la viande froide* cold meat
▶ nm cold; **Il fait froid.** It's cold.;
avoir froid to be cold ▷ *Est-ce que tu
as froid?* Are you cold?

se **froisser** [fʀwase] vb ❶ to
crease ▷ *Ce tissu se froisse très
facilement.* This material creases
very easily. ❷ to take offence ▷ *Il se
froisse très facilement.* He's very quick
to take offence.; **se froisser un
muscle** to strain a muscle

frôler [fʀole] vb ❶ to brush
against ▷ *Le chat m'a frôlé au
passage.* The cat brushed against
me as it went past. ❷ to narrowly
avoid ▷ *Nous avons frôlé la
catastrophe.* We narrowly avoided
disaster.

fromage [fʀɔmaʒ] nm cheese; **le
fromage à la crème** cream cheese;
le fromage en grains cheese curds

fromagerie [fʀɔmaʒʀi] nf cheese
shop

froment [fʀɔmɑ̃] nm wheat

froncer [fʀɔ̃se] vb: **froncer les
sourcils** to frown

front [fʀɔ̃] nm forehead

frontière [fʀɔ̃tjɛʀ] nf border

frotter [fʀɔte] vb to rub ▷ *se frotter
les yeux* to rub one's eyes; **frotter
une allumette** to strike a match

fruit [fʀɥi] nm fruit; **un fruit** a
piece of fruit ▷ *Est-ce que vous
voulez manger un fruit?* Would you
like some fruit?; **les fruits de mer**
seafood

fruité [fʀɥite] (f **fruitée**) adj fruity

frustrer [fʀystʀe] vb to frustrate

fugue [fyg] nf: **faire une fugue** to
run away

fuir [fɥiʀ] vb ❶ to flee ▷ *fuir devant
un danger* to flee from danger ❷ to
leak ▷ *Le robinet fuit.* The tap is
leaking.

fuite [fɥit] nf ❶ leak ▷ *Il y a une
fuite de gaz.* There is a gas leak.
❷ (escape) flight; **être en fuite** to
be on the run

fumé [fyme] (f **fumée**) adj smoked
▷ *du saumon fumé* smoked salmon

fumée [fyme] nf smoke

fumer [fyme] vb to smoke

fumeur [fymœʀ] nm smoker

fumeuse [fymøz] nf smoker

funérailles [fyneʀaj] nfpl funeral
▷ *Les funérailles auront lieu demain.*
The funeral is tomorrow.

fur [fyʀ]: **au fur et à mesure** adv as
you go along ▷ *Je vérifie mon travail
au fur et à mesure.* I check my work as
I go along.; **au fur et à mesure que**
as ▷ *Je réponds à mon courrier au fur et
à mesure que je le reçois.* I answer my
mail as I receive it.

furet [fyʀɛ] nm ferret

fureur [fyʀœʀ] nf fury; **faire
fureur** to be all the rage ▷ *Ce genre
de sac à dos fait fureur actuellement.*
This sort of backpack is all the rage
at the moment.

furieux [fyʀjø, -øz] (f **furieuse**)
adj furious

furoncle [fyʀɔ̃kl(ə)] nm (on
skin) boil

fus [fy] vb see **être**

fusée [fyze] nf rocket

fusil [fyzi] nm gun

fut [fy] vb see **être**

futé [fyte] (f **futée**) adj crafty

futur [fytyʀ] nm future

futuriste [fytyʀist(ə)] adj
futuristic

g

gâcher [gɑʃe] vb to waste ▷ Je n'aime pas gâcher la nourriture. I don't like to waste food.

gâchis [gɑʃi] nm mess ▷ Le chien a fait un beau gâchis sur le tapis. The dog made a real mess on the carpet.

gaffe [gaf] nf: **faire une gaffe** to do something stupid

gageure [gaʒyʀ] nf challenge ▷ J'ai fait la gageure d'apprendre l'espagnol. I took the challenge of learning Spanish. ▷ Réussir ce projet tient de la gageure. To succeed in this project will be a challenge.

gagnant [gaɲɑ̃] nm winner

gagnante [gaɲɑ̃t] nf winner

gagner [gaɲe] vb to win ▷ Qui a gagné? Who won?; **gagner du temps** to gain time; **Il gagne bien sa vie.** He makes a good living.

gai [ge] (f **gaie**) adj cheerful ▷ Elle est très gaie. She's very cheerful.

gaieté [gete] nf cheerfulness

galerie [galʀi] nf gallery ▷ une galerie d'art an art gallery; **une galerie marchande** a shopping arcade

galet [galɛ] nm pebble

galette [galɛt] nf round flat cake ▷ une galette de blé noir a buckwheat pancake

galvaude [galvod] nf
● **La galvaude** is a kind of **poutine**.
● It consists of French fries topped
● with bits of chicken, green peas,
● cheese curds, and gravy.

gamin [gamɛ̃] nm (informal) kid

gamine [gamin] nf (informal) kid

gamme [gam] nf (in music) scale ▷ Je dois faire des gammes tous les soirs. I have to do my scales every night.; **une gamme de produits** a range of products; **haut de gamme** top-of-the-line

gammée [game] adj: **la croix gammée** the swastika

gant [gɑ̃] nm glove ▷ des gants en laine woollen gloves

garage [gaʀaʒ] nm garage

garagiste [gaʀaʒist(ə)] nmf
❶ garage owner ❷ mechanic

garantie [gaʀɑ̃ti] nf guarantee

garantir [gaʀɑ̃tiʀ] vb to guarantee

garçon [gaʀsɔ̃] nm boy; **un vieux garçon** a bachelor

garde [gaʀd(ə)] nmf: **un garde de sécurité** a security guard; **un garde du corps** a bodyguard; **un garde forestier** a ranger
▶ nf ❶ guarding ▷ Elle est chargée de la garde des prisonniers. She's responsible for guarding the prisoners. ❷ guard ▷ la relève de la garde the changing of the guard; **être de garde** to be on duty ▷ Mon père est de garde ce soir. My father is on duty tonight.; **la garde des enfants** (in divorce) child

custody ▷ *Le père a eu la garde des enfants.* Child custody was given to the father. ; **mettre en garde** to warn ▷ *Elle m'a mis en garde contre les voleurs à la tire.* She warned me about pickpockets.

garde-côte [gaʀdəkot] (pl **garde-côtes**) nm (boat) coast guard

garder [gaʀde] vb ❶ to keep ▷ *Tu as gardé toutes ses lettres?* Did you keep all his letters? ❷ to look after ▷ *Je garde mon petit cousin samedi après-midi.* I'm looking after my little cousin on Saturday afternoon. ❸ to guard ▷ *Ils ont pris un gros chien pour garder la maison.* They got a big dog to guard the house.; **garder le lit** to stay in bed; **se garder** to keep ▷ *Ces crêpes se gardent bien.* These pancakes keep well.

garderie [gaʀdəʀi] nf daycare

garde-robe [gaʀdəʀob] nf ❶ (clothes) wardrobe ▷ *Elle a une garde-robe bien fournie.* She's got an extensive wardrobe. ❷ closet ▷ *Son garde-robe est bourré de vêtements de sport.* His closet is filled with sportswear.

> In Canadian French, when **garde-robe** is used to mean **closet**, it can be either masculine or feminine.

gardien [gaʀdjɛ̃] nm: **un gardien de but** a goalkeeper; **un gardien de la paix** a peacekeeper; **un gardien d'enfants** a babysitter; **un gardien de prison** a prison guard

gardienne [gaʀdjɛn] nf: **une gardienne de but** a goalkeeper; **une gardienne de la paix** a peacekeeper; **une gardienne d'enfants** a babysitter; **une gardienne de prison** a prison guard

gare [gaʀ] nf station ▷ *la gare d'autobus* the bus station

▶ excl: **Gare aux serpents!** Watch out for snakes!

garer [gaʀe] vb to park; **se garer** to park ▷ *Où t'es-tu garé?* Where are you parked?

garni [gaʀni] (f **garnie**) adj: **un plat garni** (vegetables, fries, rice, etc.) a dish served with something on the side; **une pizza garnie** a pizza with everything on it

gars [ga] nm (informal) guy

gaspillage [gaspijaʒ] nm waste ▷ *Quel gaspillage!* What a waste!

gaspiller [gaspije] vb to waste ▷ *Je n'aime pas gaspiller de la nourriture.* I don't like to waste food.

gâteau [gato] (pl **gâteaux**) nm cake; **le gâteau des anges** angel food cake

gâter [gate] vb to spoil ▷ *Il aime gâter ses petits enfants.* He likes to spoil his grandchildren.; **se gâter** (1) to go bad ▷ *Ces bananes se gâtent.* These bananas are going bad. (2) to change for the worse ▷ *Le temps va se gâter.* The weather's going to change for the worse.

gauche [goʃ] adj left ▷ *le bras gauche* the left arm ▷ *le côté gauche* the left-hand side

▶ nf left ▷ *sur votre gauche* on your left; **à gauche** (1) on the left ▷ *la deuxième rue à gauche* the second street on the left (2) to the left ▷ *à gauche de l'armoire* to the left of the cupboard ▷ *Tournez à gauche.* Turn left.; **la voie de gauche** the left-hand lane; **la gauche** (in politics) the left ▷ *Elle est de gauche.* She's left-wing.

gaucher [goʃe, -ɛʀ] (f **gauchère**) adj left-handed

gaufre [gofʀ(ə)] nf waffle

gaufrette [gofʀɛt] nf wafer

gaz [gaz] nm gas

gazeux [gazø, -øz] (f **gazeuse**) adj:

une boisson gazeuse a soft drink;
de l'eau gazeuse sparkling water

gazon [gazɔ̃] nm lawn

geai bleu [ʒɛ-] nm blue jay

géant [ʒeɑ̃] nm giant

gel [ʒɛl] nm ❶ frost ❷ freeze-up
▷ *Nous devons aller fermer le chalet
avant la saison du gel.* We have to go
close the cottage before freeze-up.

gelée [ʒəle] nf jelly

geler [ʒəle] vb to freeze ▷ *Il a gelé
cette nuit.* There was a frost last
night.

gélule [ʒelyl] nf (*containing
medicine*) capsule

Gémeaux [ʒemo] nmpl Gemini ▷ *Je
suis Gémeaux.* I'm a Gemini.

gémir [ʒemiʀ] vb to moan

gênant [ʒenɑ̃, -ɑ̃t] (f **gênante**)
adj embarrassing ▷ *des questions
gênantes* embarrassing questions
▷ *un silence gênant* an awkward
silence

gencive [ʒɑ̃siv] nf (*in mouth*) gum

**Gendarmerie royale du
Canada** nf Royal Canadian
Mounted Police

gendre [ʒɑ̃dʀ(ə)] nm son-in-law

gêné [ʒene] (f **gênée**) adj
embarrassed

gêner [ʒene] vb ❶ to bother ▷ *Je ne
voudrais pas vous gêner.* I don't want
to bother you. ❷ to embarrass
▷ *Son regard la gênait.* The way he
was looking at her made her feel
embarrassed. ❸ to make nervous
▷ *Faire un exposé oral me gêne.* Giving
oral presentations makes me
nervous.

général [ʒeneʀal, -o] (f **générale**,
mpl **généraux**) adj general; **en
général** usually

généralement [ʒeneʀalmɑ̃] adv
generally

généraliste [ʒeneʀalist(ə)] nmf
family doctor

génération [ʒeneʀasjɔ̃] nf
generation

généreux [ʒeneʀø, -øz] (f
généreuse) adj generous

générosité [ʒeneʀozite] nf
generosity

génétique [ʒenetik] nf genetics

génétiquement [ʒenetikmɑ̃] adv
genetically ▷ *génétiquement modifié*
genetically-modified ▷ *les aliments
génétiquement modifiés* GM foods
▷ *un organisme génétiquement modifié*
a genetically-modified organism

génial [ʒenjal, -o] (f **géniale**, mpl
géniaux) adj (*informal*) great ▷ *Le
film d'hier soir était génial.* The film
last night was great.

genou [ʒnu] (pl **genoux**) nm knee
▷ *Je me suis cogné le genou contre
la table.* I banged my knee on the
table.; **à genoux** on one's knees; **se
mettre à genoux** to kneel down

genre [ʒɑ̃ʀ] nm kind ▷ *C'est un genre
de gâteau.* It's a kind of cake.

gens [ʒɑ̃] nmpl people

gentil [ʒɑ̃ti] (f **gentille**) adj
❶ nice ▷ *Nos voisins sont très gentils.*
Our neighbours are very nice.
❷ kind ▷ *C'était très gentil de votre
part.* It was very kind of you.

gentillesse [ʒɑ̃tijɛs] nf kindness
▷ *Je l'ai remerciée de sa gentillesse.*
I thanked her for her kindness.
▷ *C'est un homme d'une grande
gentillesse.* He is a very nice man.

gentiment [ʒɑ̃timɑ̃] adv ❶ nicely
▷ *Demande-le lui gentiment.* Ask
him nicely. ❷ kindly ▷ *Ils nous ont
gentiment proposé de rester dîner.*
They kindly invited us to stay for
dinner.

géographie [ʒeɔgʀafi] nf
geography

géométrie [ʒeɔmetʀi] nf
geometry

gérant [ʒeʀɑ̃] nm (*bank, store*)

manager

gérante [ʒerɑ̃t] nf (bank, store) manager

gercé [ʒɛrse] adj chapped ▷ *les lèvres gercées* chapped lips

gérer [ʒere] vb to manage ▷ *Qui gère cette entreprise?* Who's managing this outfit?

germain [ʒɛrmɛ̃, -ɛn] (f **germaine**) adj: **un cousin germain** a first cousin

geste [ʒɛst(ə)] nm gesture ▷ *s'exprimer par des gestes* to express oneself using one's hands ▷ *un geste de bonne volonté* a gesture of goodwill; **Ne faites pas un geste!** Don't move!

gestion [ʒɛstjɔ̃] nf management

gifle [ʒifl(ə)] nf slap on the face

gifler [ʒifle] vb to slap on the face

gigantesque [ʒigɑ̃tɛsk(ə)] adj gigantic

gigaoctet [ʒigaɔkte] nm gigabyte ▷ *un disque dur de cent vingt gigaoctets* a 120-gigabyte hard disk

gilet [ʒile] nm cardigan ▷ *un gilet tricoté à la main* a hand-knitted cardigan; **un gilet de sauvetage** a life jacket

gingembre [ʒɛ̃ʒɑ̃br(ə)] nm ginger

girafe [ʒiraf] nf giraffe

gîte [ʒit] nm: **un gîte du passant** a bed-and-breakfast

glace [glas] nf ice ▷ *L'étang est recouvert de glace.* The pond is covered with ice.; **la glace noire** (roads) black ice; **rompre la glace** to break the ice

glacé [glase] (f **glacée**) adj ① icy ▷ *Il soufflait un vent glacé.* An icy wind was blowing. ② iced ▷ *un thé glacé* an iced tea; **la crème glacée** ice cream

glacial [glasjal] (f **glaciale**, mpl **glaciaux**) adj icy

glaçon [glasɔ̃] nm ① ice cube

② icicle

glissade [glisad] nf ice slide ▷ *L'hiver, la ville construit une glissade dans le parc.* In winter the city builds an ice slide in the park.

glissant [glisɑ̃, -ɑ̃t] (f **glissante**) adj slippery

glissement de terrain [glismɑ̃-] nm landslide

glisser [glise] vb ① to slip ▷ *J'ai glissé sur une peau de banane.* I slipped on a banana skin. ② to be slippery ▷ *Attention, ça glisse!* Watch out, it's slippery! ③ to slide ▷ *descendre la colline en glissant* to slide down the hill ④ to glide ▷ *glisser sur la neige* to glide over the snow; **glisser-déposer** drag and drop

global [glɔbal, -o] (f **globale**, mpl **globaux**) adj total ▷ *la somme globale* the total amount

gloire [glwar] nf glory

glucide [glysid] nm carbohydrate ▷ *Les pâtes contiennent beaucoup de glucides.* Pasta is high in carbohydrates.

goéland [gɔelɑ̃] nm seagull

golf [gɔlf] nm golf ▷ *Elle joue au golf.* She plays golf.

golfe [gɔlf(ə)] nm gulf ▷ *le golfe du Saint-Laurent* the Gulf of St. Lawrence

gomme [gɔm] nf (for pencil) eraser

gomme à mâcher nf chewing gum ▷ *de la gomme à mâcher à saveur de cannelle* cinnamon-flavoured chewing gum

gommer [gɔme] vb (pencil) to erase

gonflé [gɔ̃fle] (f **gonflée**) adj ① swollen ▷ *Elle a les pieds gonflés.* Her feet are swollen. ② inflated ▷ *Le ballon de soccer était mal gonflé.* The soccer ball wasn't properly inflated.

gonfler [gɔ̃fle] vb ① to blow up

▷ *gonfler un ballon* to blow up a balloon ❷ to pump up ▷ *Tu devrais gonfler ton pneu arrière.* You should pump up your back tire.

Google® [guɡl(ə)] nm Google® ▷ *faire une recherche Google* to google

gorge [ɡɔʀʒə] nf ❶ throat ▷ *J'ai mal à la gorge.* I've got a sore throat. ❷ gorge ▷ *la gorge Elora* the Elora Gorge

gorgée [ɡɔʀʒe] nf sip ▷ *une gorgée d'eau* a sip of water

gorille [ɡɔʀij] nm gorilla

goudron [ɡudʀɔ̃] nm tar

gouffre [ɡufʀ(ə)] nm chasm; **Cette voiture est un vrai gouffre!** This car is a money pit!

gourmand [ɡuʀmɑ̃, -ɑ̃d] (f **gourmande**) adj greedy

gourmandise [ɡuʀmɑ̃diz] nf greed

gourou [ɡuʀu] nm guru

gousse [ɡus] nf: **une gousse d'ail** a clove of garlic

goût [ɡu] nm taste ▷ *Ça n'a pas de goût.* It has no taste. **avoir le goût de** (doing something) to feel like ▷ *J'ai le goût d'aller au cinéma.* I feel like going to the movies.; **de bon goût** in good taste; **de mauvais goût** in bad taste ▷ *Sa blague était de mauvais goût.* His joke was in bad taste.

goûter [ɡute] vb to taste ▷ *Goûte donc ce fromage.* Have a taste of this cheese.

goutte [ɡut] nf drop; **C'est la goutte d'eau qui a fait déborder le vase!** That was the last straw!; **C'est une goutte d'eau dans l'océan.** It's a drop in the bucket.

gouvernement [ɡuvɛʀnəmɑ̃] nm government

gouverner [ɡuvɛʀne] vb to govern

gouverneur général [ɡuvɛʀnœʀ-] nm Governor General

gouverneure générale [ɡuvɛʀnœʀ-] nf Governor General

grâce [ɡʀɑs] nf: **grâce à** thanks to ▷ *Je suis arrivé à l'heure grâce à toi.* I arrived on time thanks to you.

gracieux [ɡʀasjø, -øz] (f **gracieuse**) adj graceful

gradins [ɡʀadɛ̃] nmpl ❶ (indoor) stands ❷ (outdoor) bleachers

graduel [ɡʀadɥɛl] (f **graduelle**) adj gradual

grain [ɡʀɛ̃] nm grain ▷ *un grain de sable* a grain of sand; **un grain de café** a coffee bean; **un grain de poivre** a peppercorn; **un grain de raisin** a grape

graine [ɡʀɛn] nf seed

graisse [ɡʀɛs] nf fat

grammaire [ɡʀamɛʀ] nf grammar

gramme [ɡʀam] nm gram

grand [ɡʀɑ̃, ɡʀɑ̃d] (f **grande**) adj, adv ❶ tall ▷ *Il est grand pour son âge.* He's tall for his age. ❷ big ▷ *une grande valise* a big suitcase ▷ *ma grande sœur* my big sister; **une grande personne** a grown-up ❸ long ▷ *un grand voyage* a long journey ❹ great ▷ *C'est un grand ami à moi.* He's a great friend of mine.; **un grand magasin** a department store; **au grand air** out in the open air ▷ *Ça te fera beaucoup de bien d'être au grand air.* It'll be very good for you to be out in the open air.; **grand ouvert** wide open ❺ important ▷ *Le centenaire de la ville a été un grand événement.* The city's 100th anniversary was an important event. ▷ *Je porte cette chemise durant les grandes occasions.* I wear this shirt on important occasions.

grand-chose [ɡʀɑ̃ʃoz] n: **pas grand-chose** not much ▷ *Je n'ai pas acheté grand-chose au marché.* I didn't buy much at the market. ▷ Voici un petit cadeau : ce n'est pas grand-chose. Here's a little present : it's nothing much.

grandeur [gʀɑ̃dœʀ] nf size

grandir [gʀɑ̃diʀ] vb to grow ▷ Elle a beaucoup grandi. She's grown a lot.

grand-mère [gʀɑ̃mɛʀ] (pl **grands-mères**) nf grandmother

grand-peine [gʀɑ̃pɛn]: **à grand-peine** adv with great difficulty

grand-père [gʀɑ̃pɛʀ] (pl **grands-pères**) nm grandfather

Grands Lacs nmpl Great Lakes

grands-parents [gʀɑ̃paʀɑ̃] nmpl grandparents

grange [gʀɑ̃ʒ] nf barn

graphique [gʀafik] nm ❶ graph ▷ un graphique à barres a bar graph ❷ chart ▷ un graphique circulaire a pie chart

grappe [gʀap] nf: **une grappe de raisin** a bunch of grapes

gras [gʀa, gʀas] (f **grasse**) adj ❶ (food) fatty ▷ Évitez les aliments gras. Avoid fatty foods. ❷ greasy ▷ des cheveux gras greasy hair ❸ oily ▷ une peau grasse oily skin; **faire la grasse matinée** to sleep in ❹ (type) bold ▷ Mets le titre en caractères gras. Put the title in bold type.

gratte-ciel [gʀatsjɛl] (pl **gratte-ciel**) nm skyscraper

gratter [gʀate] vb ❶ to scratch ▷ Ne gratte pas tes piqûres de moustiques. Don't scratch your mosquito bites. ❷ to be itchy ▷ C'est épouvantable comme ça gratte! It's terribly itchy!

gratuit [gʀatɥi, -ɥit] (f **gratuite**) adj free ❶ free ▷ entrée gratuite entrance free ▷ J'ai deux places gratuites pour le concert. I've got two complimentary tickets for the concert.

grave [gʀav] adj ❶ serious ▷ une

maladie grave a serious illness ▷ Elle avait l'air grave. She was looking serious. ❷ deep ▷ Il a une voix grave. He's got a deep voice.; **Ce n'est pas grave.** It doesn't matter. ▷ « J'ai oublié ma clé. » — « Ce n'est pas grave, j'ai la mienne. » "I forgot my key." — "It doesn't matter, I've got mine."

gravement [gʀavmɑ̃] adv seriously ▷ Il a été gravement blessé. He was seriously injured.

graver [gʀave] vb ❶ (CDs) to burn ❷ to engrave ▷ Son nom était gravé sur la bague. Her name was engraved on the ring.

graveur [gʀavœʀ] nm: **un graveur de DC** a CD burner

grêle [gʀɛl] nf hail

grêler [gʀele] vb: **Il grêle.** It's hailing.

grelotter [gʀəlɔte] vb to shiver

grenade [gʀənad] nf ❶ pomegranate ❷ grenade

grenier [gʀənje] nm attic

grenouille [gʀənuj] nf frog

grève [gʀɛv] nf ❶ strike; **en grève** on strike ▷ Ils sont en grève depuis dix jours. They have been on strike for ten days.; **être en grève** to be on strike; **se mettre en grève** to go on strike; **un piquet de grève** a picket line ❷ shore ▷ Nous nous sommes promenés le long de la grève. We went for a walk along the shore.

gréviste [gʀevist(ə)] nmf striker

grièvement [gʀijɛvmɑ̃] adv: **grièvement blessé** seriously injured

griffe [gʀif] nf ❶ claw ▷ Le chat m'a donné un coup de griffe. The cat scratched me. ❷ label ▷ la griffe d'un grand couturier the label of a top designer

griffer [gʀife] vb to scratch ▷ Le chat m'a griffé. The cat scratched me.

grignoter [gʀiɲɔte] vb to nibble

grillade [gʀijad] nf grilled food
▷ *une grillade de légumes* grilled vegetables

grille [gʀij] nf ❶ (chain-link) fence ▷ *L'usine est entourée d'une haute grille.* The factory is surrounded by a high fence. ❷ (metal) gate ▷ *la grille du jardin* the garden gate

grille-pain [gʀijpɛ̃] (pl **grille-pain**) nm toaster

griller [gʀije] vb ❶ to toast; **du pain grillé** toast ❷ to grill ▷ *des saucisses grillées* grilled sausages

grimace [gʀimas] nf: **faire des grimaces** to make faces

grimper [gʀɛ̃pe] vb to climb

grincer [gʀɛ̃se] vb to creak

grincheux [gʀɛ̃ʃø, -øz] (f **grincheuse**) adj grumpy

grippe [gʀip] nf flu; **avoir la grippe** to have the flu ▷ *J'ai eu une mauvaise grippe l'hiver dernier.* I had a bad attack of the flu last winter ▷ *la grippe H1N1* H1N1 flu

grippé [gʀipe] (f **grippée**) adj: **être grippé** to have the flu

gris [gʀi, gʀiz] (f **grise**) adj grey

grizzly [gʀizli] nm grizzly bear

grogner [gʀɔɲe] vb to growl ▷ *Le chien a grogné quand je me suis approché de lui.* The dog growled when I went near it.

gronder [gʀɔ̃de] vb ❶ to rumble ▷ *J'entends le tonnerre gronder au loin.* I hear thunder rumbling in the distance. ❷ (animal) to roar; **se faire gronder** to get told off ▷ *Tu vas te faire gronder par ton père!* You're going to get bawled out by your father!

gros [gʀo, gʀos] (f **grosse**) adj ❶ big ▷ *une grosse pomme* a big apple ❷ fat; **le gros plan** close-up ▷ *Voici un gros plan de mon petit ami.* Here's a close-up of my boyfriend.

groseille [gʀozɛj] nf: **la groseille**

rouge redcurrant; **la groseille à maquereau** gooseberry

grossesse [gʀoses] nf pregnancy

grossier [gʀosje, -jɛʀ] (f **grossière**) adj rude ▷ *Ne sois pas si grossier!* Don't be so rude!; **une erreur grossière** a serious mistake

grossir [gʀosiʀ] vb to put on weight ▷ *Il a beaucoup grossi.* He's put on a lot of weight.

grosso modo [gʀosomɔdo] adv roughly ▷ *Dis-moi grosso modo ce que tu en penses.* Give me a rough idea what you think of it.

grotte [gʀɔt] nf cave

groupe [gʀup] nm group ▷ *votre groupe sanguin* your blood group

grouper [gʀupe] vb to group ▷ *On nous a groupé dans différentes classes.* We were grouped in different classes.; **se grouper** to gather ▷ *Nous nous sommes groupés autour du feu.* We gathered round the fire.

gruau [gʀyo] nm porridge

guêpe [gɛp] nf wasp

guérir [geʀiʀ] vb to recover ▷ *Elle est maintenant complètement guérie.* She's now completely recovered.

guérison [geʀizɔ̃] nf recovery; **la guérison spirituelle** spiritual healing

guerre [gɛʀ] nf war ▷ *en guerre* at war ▷ *une guerre civile* a civil war ▷ *la Deuxième Guerre mondiale* the Second World War

guetter [gete] vb to watch for ▷ *Elle guette l'arrivée du facteur tous les matins.* She watches for the letter carrier every morning.

gueule [gœl] nf (rude when used for people) mouth ▷ *Le chat a ramené une souris dans sa gueule.* The cat brought a mouse in its mouth.

gueuler [gœle] vb (informal) to bawl

guichet [giʃe] nm (in bank, airport)

counter; **le guichet automatique**
bank machine
guide [gid] nm guide
guider [gide] vb to guide
guidon [gidɔ̃] nm handlebars
guillemets [gijmɛ] nmpl
quotation marks ▷ *entre guillemets*
in quotes

> In French, be careful to use
> angled quotation marks and
> leave a space between the text
> and each mark, e.g. **« Fin »** for
> "The End".

guimauve [gimov] nf
marshmallow; **à la guimauve**
(sentimental) sappy ▷ *C'est vraiment
un film à la guimauve.* This is a really
sappy movie.
guirlande [girlɑ̃d] nf: **des
guirlandes** tinsel; **des guirlandes
en papier** paper chains
guitare [gitar] nf guitar ▷ *Sais-tu
jouer de la guitare?* Can you play
the guitar?
gymnase [ʒimnɑz] nm gym
▷ *L'école a un nouveau gymnase.* The
school has a new gym.
gymnastique [ʒimnastik] nf
gymnastics ▷ *faire de la gymnastique*
to do gymnastics

h

habile [abil] adj skilful ▷ *Elle est très
habile de ses mains.* She's very skilled
with her hands.
habillé [abije] (f **habillée**) adj
❶ dressed ▷ *Il n'est pas encore
habillé.* He's not dressed yet.
❷ smart ▷ *Cette robe fait très habillé.*
This dress looks very smart.
s'**habiller** [abije] vb ❶ to get
dressed ▷ *Je me suis rapidement
habillé.* I got dressed quickly. ❷ to
dress up ▷ *Est-ce qu'il faut s'habiller
pour la réception?* Do you have to
dress up to go to the party?
l'**habitant** [abitɑ̃] nm inhabitant
▷ *Les habitants du quartier sont
contre ce projet.* The local people are
against this plan.
l'**habitante** [abitɑ̃t] nf inhabitant
l'**habitat** [abita] nm habitat
▷ *l'habitat naturel du castor* the
natural habitat of the beaver
▷ *un habitat menacé* a threatened

habitat; **la conservation de l'habitat** habitat conservation

habiter [abite] vb to live ▷ *Il habite à Kitimat.* He lives in Kitimat.

les **habits** [abi] nmpl clothes
  Be sure to make the liaison in the phrase **les habits.**

l' **habitude** [abityd] nf habit ▷ *une mauvaise habitude* a bad habit; **avoir l'habitude de quelque chose** to be used to something ▷ *Elle a l'habitude des enfants.* She's used to children. ▷ *Je n'ai pas l'habitude de parler en public.* I'm not used to speaking in public.; **d'habitude** usually; **comme d'habitude** as usual

habituel [abityɛl] (f **habituelle**) adj usual

s' **habituer** [abitye] vb: **s'habituer à quelque chose** to get used to something ▷ *Il faudra que tu t'habitues à te lever tôt.* You'll have to get used to getting up early.

la **hache** [aʃ] nf axe; **mettre la hache dans les frais** to cut expenses drastically

hacher [aʃe] vb (meat) to grind; **du bœuf haché** ground beef

la **haie** [ɛ] nf hedge

la **haine** [ɛn] nf hatred

haïr [aiʁ] vb to hate ▷ *Je hais les piqûres de moustique.* I hate mosquito bites.

l' **haleine** [alɛn] nf breath ▷ *avoir mauvaise haleine* to have bad breath ▷ *être hors d'haleine* to be out of breath

le **hall** [ol] nm (hotel) lobby; **le hall d'exposition** exhibition hall

la **halte** [alt(ə)] nf stop ▷ *faire halte* to make a stop; **Halte!** Stop!; **une halte routière** a rest stop

l' **haltérophilie** [alteʁofili] nf weightlifting

le **hamburger** [ãbuʁgœʁ] nm hamburger

l' **hameçon** [amsõ] nm fish hook

le **hamster** ['amstɛʁ] nm hamster

la **hanche** [ãʃ] nf hip

le **handball** ['ãdbal] nm handball ▷ *jouer au handball* to play handball

le **handicapé** ['ãdikape] nm disabled man

la **handicapée** ['ãdikape] nf disabled woman

le **harcèlement** ['aʁsɛlmã] nm harassment ▷ *le harcèlement sexuel* sexual harassment

le **hareng** ['aʁã] nm herring

la **harfang** ['aʁfã] nm snowy owl

le **haricot** ['aʁiko] nm bean; **les haricots au lard** baked beans; **les haricots verts** green beans

le **harpon** ['aʁpõ] nm harpoon

le **hasard** ['azaʁ] nm coincidence ▷ *C'était un pur hasard.* It was pure coincidence.; **au hasard** at random ▷ *Choisis un numéro au hasard.* Choose a number at random.; **par hasard** by chance ▷ *Je l'ai rencontrée tout à fait par hasard au supermarché.* I ran into her completely by chance at the supermarket.; **à tout hasard (1)** just in case ▷ *Prends un parapluie à tout hasard.* Take an umbrella just in case. **(2)** on the off chance ▷ *Je ne sais pas s'il est chez lui, mais je vais l'appeler à tout hasard.* I don't know if he's at home, but I'll phone on the off chance.

la **hâte** ['at] nf: **à la hâte** hurriedly ▷ *Elle s'est habillée à la hâte.* She got dressed hurriedly.; **J'ai hâte de te voir.** I can't wait to see you.

la **hausse** ['os] nf ❶ increase ▷ *la hausse des prix* price increase ❷ rise ▷ *On annonce une légère hausse de température.* They're forecasting a slight rise in temperature.

hausser ['ose] vb: **hausser les épaules** to shrug one's shoulders

haut ['o, 'ot] (f **haute**) adj, adv

❶ high ▷ *une haute montagne* a high mountain ❷ aloud ▷ *penser tout haut* to think aloud
▶ *nm* top; **un mur de trois mètres de haut** a wall 3 metres high; **en haut (1)** upstairs ▷ *La salle de bain est en haut.* The bathroom is upstairs. **(2)** at the top ▷ *Le nid est tout en haut de l'arbre.* The nest is right at the top of the tree.

le **Haut-Canada** *nm* Upper Canada

la **hauteur** [otœʀ] *nf* height

le **haut-parleur** [oparlœʀ] *(pl* **haut-parleurs)** *nm* (stereo, computer) speaker

l' **hebdomadaire** [ɛbdɔmadɛʀ] *nm* (magazine) weekly

l' **hébergement** [ebɛʀʒəmã] *nm* accommodation

héberger [ebɛʀʒe] *vb* (guest) to put up ▷ *Mon cousin a dit qu'il nous hébergerait.* My cousin said he would put us up.

hein? [ɛ̃] *excl* eh?; **C'était tout un match, hein?** That was quite a game, eh?; **Tu as pris le dernier morceau de tarte, hein?** You took the last piece of pie, eh?; **Hein? Qu'est-ce que tu dis?** Eh? What did you say?

hélas [elɑs] *adv* unfortunately ▷ *Hélas, il ne restait plus de billets.* Unfortunately there were no tickets left.

l' **hélicoptère** [elikɔptɛʀ] *nm* helicopter

l' **herbe** [ɛʀb(ə)] *nf* grass; **les fines herbes** herbs; **l'herbe à poux** ragweed; **l'herbe à puce** poison ivy

hériter [eʀite] *vb* to inherit

hermétique [ɛʀmetik] *adj* airtight

l' **héroïne** [eʀɔin] *nf* heroine ▷ *l'héroïne du roman* the heroine of the novel

le **héros** ['eʀo] *nm* hero

l' **hésitation** [ezitasjɔ̃] *nf* hesitation

hésiter [ezite] *vb* to hesitate ▷ *Il n'a pas hésité à nous aider.* He didn't hesitate to help us. ▷ *J'ai hésité entre le chandail vert et la chemise jaune.* I couldn't decide between the green pullover and the yellow shirt. ▷ *« Est-ce que tu viens ce soir? » — « J'hésite... »* "Are you coming tonight?" — "I'm not sure..."; **sans hésiter** without hesitating

l' **heure** [œʀ] *nf* ❶ hour ▷ *Le trajet dure six heures.* The trip takes six hours. ❷ time ▷ *Vous avez l'heure?* Have you got the time?; **Quelle heure est-il?** What time is it?; **À quelle heure?** What time? ▷ *À quelle heure arrivons-nous?* What time do we arrive?; **deux heures du matin** 2 o'clock in the morning; **être à l'heure** to be on time; **l'heure avancée** daylight-saving time; **l'heure normale** standard time

heureusement [œʀøzmã] *adv* luckily ▷ *Heureusement qu'elle n'a pas été blessée.* Luckily she wasn't hurt.

heureux [œʀø, -øz] *(f* **heureuse)** *adj* happy

heurter ['œʀte] *vb* to hit ▷ *Je me suis heurté la tête contre la porte.* I hit my head on the door.

hiberner [ibɛʀne] *vb* to hibernate

le **hibou** ['ibu] *(pl* **hiboux)** *nm* owl

hier [jɛʀ] *adv* yesterday; **avant-hier** the day before yesterday

hindou [ɛ̃du] *adj* Hindu
▶ *nm* Hindu

l' **hindoue** [ɛ̃du] *nf* Hindu

l' **hippopotame** [ipɔpɔtam] *nm* hippopotamus

l' **histoire** [istwaʀ] *nf* ❶ history ▷ *un cours d'histoire* a history lesson ❷ story ▷ *Ce roman raconte l'histoire de deux enfants.* This novel tells the story of two children.; **Ne fais pas d'histoires!** Don't make a fuss!;

une histoire à succès a success
story

historique [istɔʀik] *adj* ❶ historic
▷ *un monument historique* a historic
monument ❷ historical ▷ *un
musée historique* a historical
museum

l' **hiver** [ivɛʀ] *nm* winter; **en hiver**
in winter

le **hockey** ['ɔkɛ] *nm* hockey ▷ *une
joueuse de hockey* a hockey player
▷ *un bâton de hockey* a hockey stick;
le hockey sur glace ice hockey

le **homard** ['ɔmaʀ] *nm* lobster

l' **hommage** [ɔmaʒ] *nm* tribute

l' **homme** [ɔm] *nm* man; **un
homme d'affaires** a businessman

homosexuel [ɔmɔsɛksɥɛl] (*f*
homosexuelle) *adj* homosexual

honnête [ɔnɛt] *adj* honest; **bien
honnête** (person) decent

l' **honnêteté** [ɔnɛtte] *nf* honesty

l' **honneur** [ɔnœʀ] *nm* honour ▷ *en
l'honneur de nos grands-parents* in
honour of our grandparents

la **honte** ['ɔ̃t] *nf* shame ▷ *avoir honte
de quelque chose* to be ashamed of
something

l' **hôpital** [ɔpital, -o] (*pl* **hôpitaux**)
nm hospital

le **hoquet** ['ɔkɛ] *nm*: **avoir le
hoquet** to have hiccups

l' **horaire** [ɔʀɛʀ] *nm* ❶ timetable
❷ schedule; **l' horaire d'autobus**
the bus schedule

l' **horizon** [ɔʀizɔ̃] *nm* horizon

horizontal [ɔʀizɔ̃tal, -o] (*f*
horizontale, *mpl* **horizontaux**)
adj horizontal

l' **horloge** [ɔʀlɔʒ] *nf* clock

l' **horreur** [ɔʀœʀ] *nf* horror ▷ *un
film d'horreur* a horror movie; **avoir
horreur de** to hate ▷ *J'ai horreur du
chou.* I hate cabbage.

horrible [ɔʀibl(ə)] *adj* horrible

hors ['ɔʀ] *prep*: **hors de** out of ▷ *Elle
est hors de danger maintenant.* She's
out of danger now.; **hors taxes**
duty-free

le **hors-d'œuvre** (*pl* **hors-
d'œuvre**) *nm* appetizer

hospitalier [ɔspitalje, -jɛʀ] (*f*
hospitalière) *adj* hospitable
▷ *Ils sont très hospitaliers.* They're
very hospitable.; **les services
hospitaliers** hospital services

l' **hospitalité** [ɔspitalite] *nf*
hospitality

hostile [ɔstil] *adj* hostile

le **hot-dog** ['ɔtdɔg] *nm* hot dog
▷ *des hot-dogs relish-moutarde* hot
dogs with relish and mustard

l' **hôte** [ot] *nmf* ❶ host ▷ *N'oubliez
pas de remercier vos hôtes.* Don't
forget to thank your hosts.
❷ guest ▷ *des hôtes payants* paying
guests

l' **hôtel** [otɛl] *nm* hotel; **l'hôtel de
ville** the town hall

l' **hôtesse** [otɛs] *nf* hostess

la **housse** ['us] *nf* cover ▷ *une
housse de couette* a quilt cover ▷ *une
housse de siège* a seat cover

le **houx** ['u] *nm* holly

le **huard** ['ɥaʀ] *nm* ❶ loon
❷ loonie

l' **huile** [ɥil] *nf* oil; **l'huile solaire**
suntan oil

huit ['ɥi(t)] *num* eight ▷ *Il est
huit heures du matin.* It's eight in
the morning. ▷ *Il a huit ans.* He's
eight.; **le huit février** the eighth
of February; **dans huit jours** in a
week's time

la **huitaine** ['ɥitɛn] *nf*: **une
huitaine de jours** about a week
▷ *Nous serons de retour dans une
huitaine de jours.* We'll be back in
about a week.

huitième ['ɥitjɛm] *adj* eighth ▷ *au
huitième étage* on the eighth floor

l' **huître** [ɥitʀ(ə)] *nf* oyster

humain [ymɛ̃, -ɛn] (f **humaine**)
adj human
▶ nm human being

l' **humeur** [ymœʁ] nf mood ▷ Il
est de bonne humeur. He's in a good
mood. ▷ Elle était de mauvaise
humeur. She was in a bad mood.

humide [ymid] adj ❶ damp
▷ L'herbe est humide. The grass is
damp. ▷ un climat humide a damp
climate ❷ moist ❸ humid

l' **humidex** [ymidɛks] n humidex

humilier [ymilje] vb to humiliate

humoristique [ymɔʁistik]
adj humorous; **des dessins
humoristiques** cartoons

l' **humour** [ymuʁ] nm humour
▷ Il n'a pas beaucoup d'humour.
He doesn't have much sense of
humour.

hurler ['yʁle] vb to howl

la **hutte** ['yt] nf hut

hydratant [idʁatɑ̃, -ɑ̃t] (f
hydratante) adj. une crème
hydratante a moisturizing cream

l' **hygiène** [iʒjɛn] nf hygiene

hygiénique [iʒenik] adj hygienic;
une serviette hygiénique
a sanitary napkin; **le papier
hygiénique** toilet paper

l' **hymne** [imn(ə)] nm: **l'hymne
national** the national anthem
▷ Notre hymne national est Ô
Canada. Our national anthem is
O Canada.

l' **hyperlien** [ipeʁljɛ̃] nm hyperlink

hypermétrope [ipeʁmetʁɔp] adj
long-sighted

l' **hypothèse** [ipotɛz] nf
hypothesis

iceberg [isbɛʁg] nm iceberg; **la
pointe de l'iceberg** the tip of the
iceberg

ici [isi] adv here ▷ Les assiettes sont
ici. The plates are here.; **La mer
monte parfois jusqu'ici.** The tide
sometimes comes in as far as this.;
jusqu'ici so far

l' **icône** [ikon] nf icon

idéal [ideal, -o] (f (**idéale**, mpl
idéaux) adj ideal ▷ C'est l'endroit
idéal pour faire un pique-nique. It's an
ideal place to have a picnic.

l' **idée** [ide] nf idea ▷ C'est une bonne
idée. It's a good idea.

identifier [idɑ̃tifje] vb to identify
▷ La police a identifié le voleur. The
police have identified the thief.

identique [idɑ̃tik] adj identical
▷ Ils ont obtenu des résultats
identiques. They obtained identical
results.

l' **identité** [idɑ̃tite] nf identity;

une pièce d'identité a piece of identification ▷ *Avez-vous une pièce d'identité?* Do you have any identification?

idiot [idjo, idjɔt] (f **idiote**) adj ❶ stupid ▷ *une plaisanterie idiote* a stupid joke ❷ silly ▷ *Ne sois pas idiot!* Don't be silly!

iglou [iglu] nm igloo

ignoble [iɲɔbl(ə)] adj horrible ▷ *Il a été ignoble avec elle.* He was horrible to her.

ignorant [iɲɔʀɑ̃, -ɑ̃t] (f **ignorante**) adj ignorant

ignorer [iɲɔʀe] vb ❶ not to know ▷ *J'ignore son nom.* I don't know his name. ❷ to ignore ▷ *Il m'a complètement ignoré.* He completely ignored me.

il [il] pron ❶ he ▷ *Il est parti ce matin de bonne heure.* He left early this morning. ❷ it ▷ *Méfie-toi de ce chien : il mord.* Be careful of that dog: it bites. ▷ *Il pleut.* It's raining.

île [il] nf island; **l'île du Cap-Breton** Cape Breton Island; **l'île de Vancouver** Vancouver Island

illégal [ilegal, -o] (f **illégale**, mpl **illégaux**) adj illegal

illimité [ilimite] (f **illimitée**) adj unlimited

illisible [ilizibl(ə)] adj illegible ▷ *une écriture illisible* illegible handwriting

illuminer [ilymine] vb to floodlight ▷ *Les chutes sont illuminées tous les soirs pendant l'été.* The falls are floodlit every night in the summer.

illusion [ilyzjɔ̃] nf illusion; **Tu te fais des illusions!** Don't kid yourself!

illustration [ilystʀasjɔ̃] nf illustration

illustré [ilystʀe] (f **illustrée**) adj illustrated

▶ nm comic

illustrer [ilystʀe] vb to illustrate ▷ *Vous pouvez illustrer votre rédaction avec des exemples.* You may illustrate your essay with examples.

ils [il] pron they ▷ *Ils nous ont appelés hier soir.* They phoned us last night.

image [imaʒ] nf picture ▷ *Les films donnent une fausse image de l'Amérique.* Movies give a false picture of America.

imagination [imaʒinasjɔ̃] nf imagination ▷ *Elle a beaucoup d'imagination.* She has a vivid imagination.

imaginer [imaʒine] vb to imagine

imam [imam] nm imam

imbécile [ɛ̃besil] nmf idiot

imitation [imitasjɔ̃] nf imitation

imiter [imite] vb to imitate

immatriculation [imatʀikylasjɔ̃] nf: **une plaque d'immatriculation** (of car) a licence plate

immédiat [imedja] adj: **dans l'immédiat** for the moment ▷ *Je n'ai pas besoin de ce livre dans l'immédiat.* I don't need this book for the moment.

immédiatement [imedjatmɑ̃] adv immediately

immense [imɑ̃s] adj ❶ huge ▷ *une immense fortune* a huge fortune ❷ tremendous ▷ *un immense soulagement* a tremendous relief

immeuble [imœbl(ə)] nm building ▷ *un immeuble résidentiel* an apartment building ▷ *un immeuble de bureaux* an office building

immigration [imigʀasjɔ̃] nf immigration

immigré [imigʀe] nm immigrant

immigrée [imigʀe] nf immigrant

immobile [imɔbil] adj motionless

immobilier [imɔbilje, -jɛʀ] (f **immobilière**) adj: **une agence immobilière** a real estate agency

▶ *nm* real estate

immobiliser [imɔbilize] *vb* to immobilize

immunisé [im(m)ynize] (*f* **immunisée**) *adj* immunized

impact [ɛ̃pakt] *nm* impact

impair [ɛ̃pɛʀ] *adj* odd ▷ *un nombre impair* an odd number

impardonnable [ɛ̃paʀdɔnabl(ə)] *adj* unforgivable

impasse [ɛ̃pɑs] *nf* dead end

impatience [ɛ̃pasjɑ̃s] *nf* impatience

impatient [ɛ̃pasjɑ̃, -ɑ̃t] (*f* **impatiente**) *adj* impatient

impeccable [ɛ̃pekabl(ə)] *adj* ❶ immaculate ▷ *Sa cuisine est toujours impeccable.* Her kitchen is always immaculate. ❷ perfect ▷ *Il a fait un travail impeccable.* He's done a perfect job. ▷ *C'est impeccable!* That's perfect!

impératif [ɛ̃peʀatif] *nm* imperative

imperméable [ɛ̃pɛʀmeabl(ə)] *nm* raincoat

impertinent [ɛ̃pɛʀtinɑ̃, -ɑ̃t] (*f* **impertinente**) *adj* mouthy ▷ *Ne sois pas impertinent!* Don't be mouthy!

impitoyable [ɛ̃pitwajabl(ə)] *adj* merciless

impliquer [ɛ̃plike] *vb* to mean ▷ *Si tu vas à l'université, ça implique que tu vas devoir nous quitter.* If you go to university, that means you'll have to leave us.; **être impliqué dans** to be involved in ▷ *Il est impliqué dans un scandale financier.* He's involved in a financial scandal.

impoli [ɛ̃pɔli] (*f* **impolie**) *adj* rude

importance [ɛ̃pɔʀtɑ̃s] *nf* importance ▷ *C'est sans importance.* It doesn't matter.

important [ɛ̃pɔʀtɑ̃, -ɑ̃t] (*f* **importante**) *adj* ❶ important

▷ *un rôle important* an important role ❷ considerable ▷ *une somme importante* a considerable sum

importation [ɛ̃pɔʀtasjɔ̃] *nf* import ▷ *Les importations de pétrole ont baissé.* Oil imports have fallen.

importer [ɛ̃pɔʀte] *vb* ❶ (*goods*) to import ❷ to matter ▷ *Peu importe.* It doesn't matter.

imposant [ɛ̃pozɑ̃, -ɑ̃t] (*f* **imposante**) *adj* imposing

imposer [ɛ̃poze] *vb* to impose; **imposer quelque chose à quelqu'un** to make somebody do something

impossible [ɛ̃pɔsibl(ə)] *adj* impossible

▶ *nm*: **Nous ferons l'impossible pour finir à temps.** We'll do our utmost to finish on time.

imposteur [ɛ̃pɔstœʀ] *nm* fake ▷ *Cette femme est un imposteur.* This woman is a fake.

impôt [ɛ̃po] *nm* tax; **une déclaration d'impôts** an income tax return

imprécis [ɛ̃pʀesi, -iz] (*f* **imprécise**) *adj* imprecise

impression [ɛ̃pʀesjɔ̃] *nf* impression ▷ *Il a fait bonne impression à ma mère.* He made a good impression on my mother.

impressionnant [ɛ̃pʀesjɔnɑ̃, -ɑ̃t] (*f* **impressionnante**) *adj* impressive

impressionner [ɛ̃pʀesjɔne] *vb* to impress

imprévisible [ɛ̃pʀevizibl(ə)] *adj* unpredictable

imprévu [ɛ̃pʀevy] (*f* **imprévue**) *adj* unexpected

imprimante [ɛ̃pʀimɑ̃t] *nf* (*for computer*) printer

imprimé [ɛ̃pʀime] (*f* **imprimée**) *adj* printed ▷ *un tissu imprimé* a printed fabric ▷ *C'est imprimé en* *grandes lettres.* It's printed in large letters.

imprimer [ɛ̃prime] *vb* to print

improvisation [ɛ̃prɔvizasjɔ̃] *nf* (theatre) improv ▷ *Nous avons fondé une ligue d'improvisation à l'école.* We started an improv club at our school.

improviser [ɛ̃prɔvize] *vb* to improvise

improviste [ɛ̃prɔvist(ə)] *adv*: **arriver à l'improviste** to arrive unexpectedly

imprudence [ɛ̃prydɑ̃s] *nf* carelessness; **Ne fais pas d'imprudences!** Don't do anything stupid!

imprudent [ɛ̃prydɑ̃, -ɑ̃t] (f **imprudente**) *adj* ❶ unwise ▷ *Il serait imprudent de prendre la voiture aujourd'hui.* It would be unwise to take the car today. ❷ careless ▷ *un conducteur imprudent* a careless driver

impuissant [ɛ̃pɥisɑ̃, -ɑ̃t] (f **impuissante**) *adj* helpless ▷ *Elle se sentait complètement impuissante.* She felt completely helpless.

impulsif [ɛ̃pylsif, -iv] (f **impulsive**) *adj* impulsive

inabordable [inabɔrdabl(ə)] *adj* unaffordable ▷ *des prix inabordables* unaffordable prices

inaccessible [inaksesibl(ə)] *adj* inaccessible ▷ *Cette plage est inaccessible par la route.* This beach is inaccessible by road.

inachevé [inaʃve] (f **inachevée**) *adj* unfinished

inadmissible [inadmisibl(ə)] *adj* unacceptable ▷ *Ce type de comportement est inadmissible!* This sort of behaviour is unacceptable!

inanimé [inanime] (f **inanimée**) *adj* unconscious ▷ *On l'a retrouvé inanimé sur la route.* He was found

unconscious on the road.

inaperçu [inapɛrsy] (f **inaperçue**) *adj*: **passer inaperçu** to go unnoticed

inattendu [inatɑ̃dy] (f **inattendue**) *adj* unexpected

inattention [inatɑ̃sjɔ̃] *nf*: **une faute d'inattention** a careless mistake

inaugurer [inɔgyre] *vb* (an *exhibition*) to open

incapable [ɛ̃kapabl(ə)] *adj* incapable ▷ *être incapable de faire quelque chose* to be incapable of doing something

incassable [ɛ̃kasabl(ə)] *adj* unbreakable

incendie [ɛ̃sɑ̃di] *nm* fire ▷ *un incendie de forêt* a forest fire

incertain [ɛ̃sɛrtɛ̃, -ɛn] (f **incertaine**) *adj* ❶ uncertain ▷ *Son avenir est encore incertain.* Her future is still uncertain. ❷ unsettled ▷ *Le temps est incertain.* The weather is unsettled.

inciter [ɛ̃site] *vb*: **inciter quelqu'un à faire quelque chose** to encourage somebody to do something ▷ *J'ai incité mes parents à partir en voyage.* I encouraged my parents to go on a trip.

inclure [ɛ̃klyr] *vb* to enclose ▷ *Veuillez inclure une enveloppe timbrée libellée à votre adresse.* Please enclose a stamped self-addressed envelope.; **Les piles sont incluses.** Batteries are included.

incohérent [ɛ̃kɔerɑ̃, -ɑ̃t] (f **incohérente**) *adj* incoherent

incolore [ɛ̃kɔlɔr] *adj* colourless

incompétent [ɛ̃kɔ̃petɑ̃, -ɑ̃t] (f **incompétente**) *adj* incompetent

incompris [ɛ̃kɔ̃pri, -iz] (f **incomprise**) *adj* misunderstood

inconnu [ɛ̃kɔny] *nm* stranger ▷ *Ne parle pas à des inconnus.* Don't speak to strangers.; **l'inconnu** the unknown ▷ *la peur de l'inconnu* the fear of the unknown

inconnue [ɛ̃kɔny] *nf* stranger

inconsciemment [ɛ̃kɔ̃sjamɑ̃] *adv* unconsciously

inconscient [ɛ̃kɔ̃sjã, -ãt] *adv* (f **inconsciente**) *adj* unconscious ▷ *Il est resté inconscient quelques minutes.* He was unconscious for several minutes.

incontestable [ɛ̃kɔ̃tɛstabl(ə)] *adj* indisputable

incontournable [ɛ̃kɔ̃turnabl(ə)] *adj* essential ▷ *Ce livre est incontournable.* This book is essential reading.

inconvénient [ɛ̃kɔ̃venjã] *nm* disadvantage; **si vous n'y voyez pas d'inconvénient** if you have no objection

incorrect [ɛ̃kɔrɛkt] (f **incorrecte**) *adj* ❶ incorrect ▷ *une réponse incorrecte* an incorrect answer ❷ rude ▷ *Il a été incorrect avec la voisine.* He was rude to the woman next door.

incroyable [ɛ̃krwajabl(ə)] *adj* incredible

inculper [ɛ̃kylpe] *vb*: **inculper de** to charge with ▷ *Elle a été inculpée de fraude.* She was charged with fraud.

indécis [ɛ̃desi, -iz] (f **indécise**) *adj* ❶ indecisive ▷ *Il est constamment indécis.* He's always indecisive. ❷ undecided ▷ *Je suis encore indécis.* I'm still undecided.

indéfiniment [ɛ̃definimã] *adv* indefinitely

indélicat [ɛ̃delika, -at] (f **indélicate**) *adj* tactless

indemne [ɛ̃dɛmn(ə)] *adj* unharmed ▷ *Elle s'en est sortie indemne.* She escaped unharmed.

indemniser [ɛ̃dɛmnize] *vb* to compensate ▷ *Les victimes*

demandent maintenant à être indemnisées. The victims are now demanding compensation.

indépendamment [ɛ̃depãdamã] *adv* independently; **indépendamment de** irrespective of ▷ *Les allocations familiales devraient être versées indépendamment des revenus.* The child tax credit should be given irrespective of income.

indépendance [ɛ̃depãdãs] *nf* independence

indépendant [ɛ̃depãdã, -ãt] (f **indépendante**) *adj* independent

index [ɛ̃dɛks] *nm* ❶ index finger ❷ (in book) index

indicatif [ɛ̃dikatif, -iv] (f **indicative**) *adj*: **à titre indicatif** for your information
▶ *nm* ❶ (of verb) indicative ❷ (of TV show) theme song; **l'indicatif régional** area code

indications [ɛ̃dikasjɔ̃] *nfpl* instructions ▷ *Il suffit de suivre les indications.* You just have to follow the instructions.

indice [ɛ̃dis] *nm* clue ▷ *La police cherche des indices.* The police are looking for clues.

indifférence [ɛ̃diferãs] *nf* indifference

indifférent [ɛ̃diferã, -ãt] (f **indifférente**) *adj* indifferent

indigène [ɛ̃diʒɛn] *adj* native ▷ *les peuples indigènes du Canada* the native peoples of Canada ▷ *Cette espèce n'est pas indigène au Canada.* This species is not native to Canada.

indigeste [ɛ̃diʒɛst(ə)] *adj* indigestible

indigestion [ɛ̃diʒɛstjɔ̃] *nf* indigestion

indigne [ɛ̃diɲ] *adj* unworthy

indigner [ɛ̃diɲe] *vb* to outrage

▷ *Ses propos ont indigné toute l'équipe.* Her remarks outraged the whole team ; **s'indigner de quelque chose** to be outraged by something

indiqué [ɛ̃dike] (f**indiquée**) adj advisable ▷ *Ce n'est pas très indiqué.* It's not really advisable.

indiquer [ɛ̃dike] vb to point out ▷ *Il m'a indiqué la mairie.* He pointed out the town hall to me.

indirect [ɛ̃dirɛkt] (f**indirecte**) adj indirect

indiscipliné [ɛ̃disipline] (f **indisciplinée**) adj unruly

indiscret [ɛ̃diskrɛ, -ɛt] (f **indiscrète**) adj indiscreet

indispensable [ɛ̃dispɑ̃sabl(ə)] adj indispensable

individu [ɛ̃dividy] nm individual

individuel [ɛ̃dividɥɛl] (f **individuelle**) adj individual ▷ *servi en portions individuelles* served in individual portions; **Vous aurez une chambre individuelle.** You'll have a room to yourself.

indolore [ɛ̃dɔlɔr] adj painless

indulgent [ɛ̃dylɡɑ̃, -ɑ̃t] (f **indulgente**) adj indulgent; **Elle est trop indulgente avec son fils.** She's not firm enough with her son.

industrie [ɛ̃dystri] nf industry

industriel [ɛ̃dystrijɛl] (f **industrielle**) adj industrial

inédit [inedi, -it] (f**inédite**) adj unpublished

inefficace [inefikas] adj
❶ (treatment) ineffective
❷ inefficient ▷ *un service de transports publics inefficace* an inefficient public transit system

inégal [inegal, -o] (f**inégale**, mpl **inégaux**) adj ❶ unequal ▷ *un combat inégal* an unequal struggle
❷ uneven ▷ *La qualité est inégale.* The quality is uneven.

inévitable [inevitabl(ə)] adj

unavoidable; **C'était inévitable!** That was bound to happen!

inexact [inɛɡzakt] (f**inexacte**) adj inaccurate

infaillible [ɛ̃fajibl(ə)] adj foolproof

infarctus [ɛ̃farktys] nm coronary

infatigable [ɛ̃fatiɡabl(ə)] adj tireless ▷ *Il est infatigable.* He's a tireless worker.

infect [ɛ̃fɛkt] (f**infecte**) adj (meal) revolting

s'**infecter** [ɛ̃fɛkte] vb to get infected ▷ *La plaie s'est infectée.* The wound has become infected.

infection [ɛ̃fɛksjɔ̃] nf infection

inférieur [ɛ̃ferjœr] (f**inférieure**) adj lower ▷ *les membres inférieurs* the lower limbs ▷ *C'est moins cher, mais de qualité inférieure.* It's cheaper but of lower quality.

infernal [ɛ̃fɛrnal, -o] (f**infernale**, mpl**infernaux**) adj terrible ▷ *Ils faisaient un bruit infernal.* They were making a terrible noise.

infini [ɛ̃fini] nm infinite; **à l'infini** indefinitely ▷ *On pourrait en parler à l'infini.* We could discuss this indefinitely.

infinitif [ɛ̃finitif] nm infinitive

infirmerie [ɛ̃firmœri] nf sick room ▷ *Elle est à l'infirmerie.* She's in the sick room.

infirmier [ɛ̃firmje] nm nurse

infirmière [ɛ̃firmjɛr] nf nurse

inflammable [ɛ̃flamabl(ə)] adj flammable

influence [ɛ̃flyɑ̃s] nf influence

influencer [ɛ̃flyɑ̃se] vb to influence

infopublicité [ɛ̃fopyblisite] nf (TV, radio) infomercial

informaticien [ɛ̃fɔrmatisjɛ̃] nm computer scientist

informaticienne [ɛ̃fɔrmatisjɛn] nf computer scientist

information [ɛ̃fɔrmasjɔ̃] nf

information ▷ *Je voudrais de l'information de l'information, s'il vous plaît.* I'd like some information about Saskatchewan, please.; **une information** a piece of information; **les informations** (TV, radio) the news

informatique [ɛ̃fɔrmatik] *nf* computer technology

informer [ɛ̃fɔrme] *vb* to inform; **s'informer** to find out ▷ *Je ne connais pas les heures de fermeture, mais je vais m'informer.* I don't know when they close, but I'm going to find out.

infuser [ɛ̃fyze] *vb* (tea) to steep

infusion [ɛ̃fyzjɔ̃] *nf* herbal tea

ingénieur [ɛ̃ʒenjœr] *nm* engineer

ingénieure [ɛ̃ʒenjœr] *nf* engineer

ingénieux [ɛ̃ʒenjø, -øz] (*f* **ingénieuse**) *adj* clever ▷ *Quelle solution ingénieuse!* What a clever solution!

ingrat [ɛ̃gra, -at] (*f* **ingrate**) *adj* ungrateful

ingrédient [ɛ̃gredjɑ̃] *nm* ingredient

inhabituel [inabituɛl] (*f* **inhabituelle**) *adj* unusual

inhumain [inymɛ̃, -ɛn] (*f* **inhumaine**) *adj* inhuman

ininflammable [inɛ̃flamabl(ə)] *adj* nonflammable

initial [inisjal, -o] (*f* **initiale**, *mpl* **initiaux**) *adj* initial

initiale [inisjal] *nf* initial

initiation [inisjasjɔ̃] *nf* introduction ▷ *un stage d'initiation à la planche à voile* an introductory course in windsurfing

initiative [inisjativ] *nf* initiative ▷ *avoir de l'initiative* to have initiative

injecter [ɛ̃ʒɛkte] *vb* to inject

injection [ɛ̃ʒɛksjɔ̃] *nf* injection

injure [ɛ̃ʒyr] *nf* ❶ insult ▷ *Il a pris ça comme une injure.* He took it as

an insult. ❷ abuse ▷ *lancer des injures à quelqu'un* to hurl abuse at somebody

injurier [ɛ̃ʒyrje] *vb* to insult

injurieux [ɛ̃ʒyrjø, -øz] (*f* **injurieuse**) *adj* (language) abusive

injuste [ɛ̃ʒyst(ə)] *adj* unfair

innocent [inɔsɑ̃, -ɑ̃t] (*f* **innocente**) *adj* innocent

innombrable [inɔ̃brabl(ə)] *adj* countless

innover [inɔve] *vb* to break new ground

inoccupé [inɔkype] (*f* **inoccupée**) *adj* empty ▷ *un appartement inoccupé* an empty apartment

inoffensif [inɔfɑ̃sif, -iv] (*f* **inoffensive**) *adj* harmless

inondation [inɔ̃dasjɔ̃] *nf* flood

inoubliable [inublijabl(ə)] *adj* unforgettable

inoxydable [inɔksidabl(ə)] *adj*: **l'acier inoxydable** stainless steel

inquiet [ɛ̃kjɛ, -ɛt] (*f* **inquiète**) *adj* worried

inquiétant [ɛ̃kjetɑ̃, -ɑ̃t] (*f* **inquiétante**) *adj* worrying

inquiéter [ɛ̃kjete] *vb* to worry ▷ *La santé de ma grand-mère inquiète mes parents.* My grandmother's health worries my parents.; **s'inquiéter** (be worried) to worry ▷ *Ne t'inquiète pas!* Don't worry!

inquiétude [ɛ̃kjetyd] *nf* anxiety

insatisfait [ɛ̃satisfɛ, -ɛt] (*f* **insatisfaite**) *adj* dissatisfied

inscription [ɛ̃skripsjɔ̃] *nf* (for school, course) registration

s' inscrire [ɛ̃skrir] *vb*: **s'inscrire à** (**1**) to join ▷ *Je me suis inscrit au club de tennis.* I've joined the tennis club. (**2**) to register ▷ *N'attends pas trop pour t'inscrire à des cours de natation.* Don't leave it too long to register for swimming lessons.

insecte [ɛ̃sɛkt(ə)] *nm* insect

insensible [ɛ̃sɑ̃sibl(ə)] adj
insensitive ▷ Il la trouve insensible.
He thinks she's insensitive.

insérer [ɛ̃seʀe] vb insert ▷ Insère
le CD dans le lecteur. Insert the CD
in the drive. ▷ Tu devrais insérer un
paragraphe ici pour expliquer. You
should insert a paragraph here,
explaining your point.

insigne [ɛ̃siɲ] nm badge

insignifiant [ɛ̃siɲifjɑ̃, -ɑ̃t] (f
insignifiante) adj insignificant

insister [ɛ̃siste] vb to insist;
N'insiste pas! Don't keep harping
on it!

insolation [ɛ̃solasjɔ̃] nf sunstroke

insolent [ɛ̃solɑ̃, -ɑ̃t] (f **insolente**)
adj cheeky

insouciant [ɛ̃susjɑ̃, -ɑ̃t] (f
insouciante) adj carefree

insoutenable [ɛ̃sutnabl(ə)]
adj unbearable ▷ une douleur
insoutenable an unbearable pain

inspecter [ɛ̃spɛkte] vb to inspect

inspecteur [ɛ̃spɛktœʀ] nm
inspector

inspection [ɛ̃spɛksjɔ̃] nf
inspection

inspectrice [ɛ̃spɛktʀis] nf
inspector

inspirer [ɛ̃spiʀe] vb **1** to
inspire; **s'inspirer de** to take one's
inspiration from ▷ Le peintre s'est
inspiré d'un poème. The painter
took his inspiration from a poem.
2 to breathe in ▷ Inspirez! Expirez!
Breathe in! Breathe out!

instable [ɛ̃stabl(ə)] adj **1** (piece
of furniture) wobbly **2** (person)
unstable

installations [ɛ̃stalasjɔ̃] nfpl
facilities ▷ Cet appartement est
pourvu de toutes les installations
modernes. This apartment has all
modern facilities.

installer [ɛ̃stale] vb to install

▷ installer un logiciel to install a
computer program ▷ installer des
étagères to put up some shelves;
s'installer to settle in ▷ Nous nous
sommes installés dans notre nouvel
appartement. We've settled into our
new apartment.; **Installez-vous,
je vous en prie.** Have a seat, please.

instant [ɛ̃stɑ̃] nm moment ▷ dans
un instant in a moment ▷ Le dîner
sera prêt dans un instant. Dinner
will be ready in a moment. ▷ pour
l'instant for the moment

instantané [ɛ̃stɑ̃tane] (f
instantanée) adj instant ▷ du café
instantané instant coffee

instinct [ɛ̃stɛ̃] nm instinct

institut [ɛ̃stity] nm institute

institution [ɛ̃stitysjɔ̃] nf
institution

instruction [ɛ̃stʀyksjɔ̃] nf
1 instruction ▷ J'ai suivi ses
instructions. I followed her
instructions. **2** education ▷ Il n'a
pas beaucoup d'instruction. He's not
very well-educated.

s'instruire [ɛ̃stʀɥiʀ] vb to educate
oneself

instruit [ɛ̃stʀɥi, -it] (f **instruite**)
adj educated

instrument [ɛ̃stʀymɑ̃] nm
instrument ▷ un instrument de
musique a musical instrument

insuffisant [ɛ̃syfizɑ̃, -ɑ̃t] (f
insuffisante) adj insufficient;
«travail insuffisant» (on report
card) "must make more effort"

insuline [ɛ̃sylin] nf insulin

insultant [ɛ̃syltɑ̃, -ɑ̃t] (f
insultante) adj insulting ▷ Il s'est
montré insultant avec elle. He was
insulting towards her.

insulte [ɛ̃sylt(ə)] nf insult

insulter [ɛ̃sylte] vb to insult

insupportable [ɛ̃sypɔʀtabl(ə)]
adj unbearable

intact [ɛ̃takt] (f **intacte**) *adj* intact

intégral [ɛ̃tegʀal, -o] (f **intégrale**, *mpl* **intégraux**) *adj*: **le texte intégral** unabridged version; **un remboursement intégral** a full refund

intelligence [ɛ̃teliʒɑ̃s] *nf* intelligence

intelligent [ɛ̃teliʒɑ̃, -ɑ̃t] (f **intelligente**) *adj* intelligent

intense [ɛ̃tɑ̃s] *adj* intense

intensif [ɛ̃tɑ̃sif, -iv] (f **intensive**) *adj* intensive; **un cours intensif** a crash course

intention [ɛ̃tɑ̃sjɔ̃] *nf* intention; **avoir l'intention de faire quelque chose** to intend to do something ▷ *J'ai l'intention de lui en parler.* I intend to speak to her about it.

interdiction [ɛ̃tɛʀdiksjɔ̃] *nf*: « interdiction de stationner » "no parking"; « interdiction de fumer » "no smoking"

interdire [ɛ̃tɛʀdiʀ] *vb* to forbid ▷ *Ses parents lui ont interdit de sortir.* His parents have forbidden him to go out.

interdit [ɛ̃tɛʀdi, -it] (f **interdite**) *adj* **①** forbidden ▷ *Il est interdit de fumer dans les couloirs.* Smoking in the halls is forbidden. **②** off-limits ▷ *Cette salle est interdite aux élèves.* This room is off-limits for students.

intéressant [ɛ̃teʀesɑ̃, -ɑ̃t] (f **intéressante**) *adj* interesting ▷ *un livre intéressant* an interesting book; **On lui a fait une offre intéressante.** They made her an attractive offer.; **On trouve des CD à des prix très intéressants dans ce magasin.** You can get CDs really cheap in this store.

intéresser [ɛ̃teʀese] *vb* to interest ▷ *Est-ce que cela t'intéresse?* Does that interest you?; **s'intéresser à** to be interested in ▷ *Est-ce que vous*

vous intéressez à la politique? Are you interested in politics?

intérêt [ɛ̃teʀɛ] *nm* interest; **avoir intérêt à faire quelque chose** had better do something ▷ *Tu as intérêt à te dépêcher si tu veux prendre le prochain autobus.* You'd better hurry up if you want to catch the next bus.

intérieur [ɛ̃teʀjœʀ] *nm* inside ▷ *Il fait plus frais à l'intérieur de la maison.* It's cooler inside the house.

interligne [ɛ̃tɛʀliɲ] *nm*: **à double interligne** double-spaced

interlocuteur [ɛ̃tɛʀlɔkytœʀ] *nm*: **son interlocuteur** the man he's speaking to

interlocutrice [ɛ̃tɛʀlɔkytris] *nf*: **son interlocutrice** the woman he's speaking to

intermédiaire [ɛ̃tɛʀmedjɛʀ] *nm* intermediary; **par l'intermédiaire de** through ▷ *Je l'ai rencontrée par l'intermédiaire de sa sœur.* I met her through his sister.

international [ɛ̃tɛʀnasjɔnal, -o] (f **internationale**, *mpl* **internationaux**) *adj* international

internaute [ɛ̃tɛʀnot] *nmf* Internet user

Internet [ɛ̃tɛʀnet] *nm* Internet ▷ *sur Internet* on the Internet

interphone [ɛ̃tɛʀfɔn] *nm* intercom

interprète [ɛ̃tɛʀpʀɛt] *nmf* interpreter

interpréter [ɛ̃tɛʀpʀete] *vb* to interpret

interrogatif [ɛ̃teʀɔgatif, -iv] (f **interrogative**) *adj* interrogative

interrogation [ɛ̃teʀɔgasjɔ̃] *nf* **①** question **②** test ▷ *une interrogation écrite* a written test

interrogatoire [ɛ̃teʀɔgatwaʀ] *nm* questioning; **C'est un interrogatoire ou quoi?** What are you doing, cross-examining me?

interroger [ɛ̃tɛʁɔʒe] vb to question

interrompre [ɛ̃tɛʁɔ̃pʁ(ə)] vb to interrupt

interrupteur [ɛ̃tɛʁyptœʀ] nm switch

interruption [ɛ̃tɛʁypsjɔ̃] nf interruption; **sans interruption** without stopping ▷ Il a parlé pendant deux heures sans interruption. He spoke for two hours without stopping.

interurbain [ɛ̃tɛʁyʁbɛ̃] adj long-distance call ▷ **faire un interurbain** to make a long-distance call

intervalle [ɛ̃tɛʁval] nm interval; **dans l'intervalle** in the meantime

intervenir [ɛ̃tɛʁvəniʁ] vb ❶ to intervene ❷ to take action ▷ La police est intervenue. The police took action.

intervention [ɛ̃tɛʁvɑ̃sjɔ̃] nf intervention ▷ **une intervention militaire** a military intervention; **une intervention chirurgicale** a surgical operation; **une intervention d'urgence** emergency response

interview [ɛ̃tɛʁvju] nf (on radio, TV) interview

intestin [ɛ̃tɛstɛ̃] nm intestine

intime [ɛ̃tim] adj intimate; **un journal intime** a diary

intimider [ɛ̃timide] vb to intimidate

intimité [ɛ̃timite] nf: **dans l'intimité** in private ▷ Dans l'intimité, il est moins guindé. He's less formal in private.; **Le mariage a eu lieu dans l'intimité.** The wedding ceremony was private.

intitulé [ɛ̃tityle] (f **intitulée**) adj entitled ▷ **un article intitulé** « Les jeunes du Canada » an article entitled "Canada's Youth"

intolérable [ɛ̃tɔleʁabl(ə)] adj intolerable

intolérance [ɛ̃tɔleʁɑ̃s] nf intolerance ▷ **une intolérance aux antibiotiques** an antibiotic intolerance ▷ **une attitude d'intolérance envers les autres** an attitude of intolerance towards others

intoxication [ɛ̃tɔksikasjɔ̃] nf: **une intoxication alimentaire** food poisoning

Intranet nm intranet

intransigeant [ɛ̃tʁɑ̃ziʒɑ̃, -ɑ̃t] (f **intransigeante**) adj uncompromising

intrigue [ɛ̃tʁig] nf (of book, film) plot

introduction [ɛ̃tʁɔdyksjɔ̃] nf introduction

introduire [ɛ̃tʁɔdɥiʁ] vb to introduce

intuition [ɛ̃tɥisjɔ̃] nf intuition

inuit [inɥit] adj, n Inuit; **un Inuit** (man) an Inuk; **une Inuite** (woman) an Inuk; **les Inuits** the Inuits

inusable [inyzabl(ə)] adj durable

inutile [inytil] adj useless

invalide [ɛ̃valid] nmf disabled person

invasion [ɛ̃vazjɔ̃] nf invasion

inventer [ɛ̃vɑ̃te] vb ❶ to invent ❷ to make up ▷ **inventer une excuse** to make up an excuse

inventeur [ɛ̃vɑ̃tœʀ] nm inventor

invention [ɛ̃vɑ̃sjɔ̃] nf invention

inventrice [ɛ̃vɑ̃tʁis] nf inventor

inverse [ɛ̃vɛʁs(ə)] adj: **dans l'ordre inverse** in reverse order; **en sens inverse** in the opposite direction ▷ nm reverse; **Tu t'es trompé, c'est l'inverse.** You've got it wrong, it's the other way round.

investissement [ɛ̃vɛstismɑ̃] nm investment

invisible [ɛ̃vizibl(ə)] adj invisible

invitation [ɛ̃vitasjɔ̃] nf invitation
invité [ɛ̃vite] nm guest
invitée [ɛ̃vite] nf guest
inviter [ɛ̃vite] vb to invite
involontaire [ɛ̃vɔlɔ̃tɛʀ] adj
  unintentional ▷ C'était tout à
  fait involontaire. It was quite
  unintentional.
invraisemblable [ɛ̃vʀɛsɑ̃blabl(ə)]
  adj unlikely ▷ une histoire
  invraisemblable an unlikely story
iPad® [aɪpæd] nm iPad®
iPhone® [aɪfɔn] nm iPhone®
ira, irai, iraient, irais vb see **aller**;
  J'irai demain au supermarché. I'll
  go to the supermarket tomorrow.
iras, irez vb see **aller**
ironie [iʀɔni] nf irony
ironique [iʀɔnik] adj ironic
irons, iront vb see **aller**; Nous
  irons à la plage cet après-
  midi. We'll go to the beach this
  afternoon.
irrationnel [iʀasjɔnɛl] (f
  irrationnelle) adj irrational
irréel [iʀeɛl] (f **irréelle**) adj unreal
irrégulier [iʀegylje, -jɛʀ] (f
  irrégulière) adj irregular
irrésistible [iʀezistibl(ə)] adj
  irresistible
irritable [iʀitabl(ə)] adj irritable
irriter [iʀite] vb to irritate
islamique [islamik] adj Islamic
isolé [izɔle] (f **isolée**) adj isolated
  ▷ une ferme isolée an isolated farm
issue [isy] nf: une voie sans issue
  a dead end; l'issue de secours
  emergency exit
italique [italik] nf italics ▷ mettre
  un mot en italique to put a word
  in italics
itinéraire [itineʀɛʀ] nm route
itinérance [itineʀɑ̃s] nf
  homelessness ▷ Le problème de
  l'itinérance doit être résolu. The
  issue of homelessness needs to be
  resolved.
itinérant [itineʀɑ̃] nm homeless
  man
itinérante [itineʀɑ̃t] nf homeless
  woman
ivre [ivʀ(ə)] adj drunk
ivresse [ivʀɛs] nf drunkenness;
  l'ivresse au volant drunk driving
ivrogne [ivʀɔɲ] nmf drunk

j

j' [ʒ] *pron see* **je**

jalousie [ʒaluzi] *nf* jealousy

jaloux [ʒalu, -uz] (**f jalouse**) *adj* jealous

jamais [ʒamɛ] *adv* ❶ never ▷ «Tu vas souvent au cinéma?» — «Non, jamais.» "Do you go to the movies often?" — "No, never." ▷ *Il n'écoute jamais la radio.* He never listens to the radio. ❷ ever

  When you use a superlative with **jamais** meaning **ever**, remember to put the verb in the subjunctive.

  ▷ *C'est la plus belle chose que j'aie jamais vue.* It's the most beautiful thing I've ever seen.

jambe [ʒɑ̃b] *nf* leg

jambette [ʒɑ̃bɛt] *nf*: **donner une jambette à quelqu'un** to trip somebody up

jambon [ʒɑ̃bɔ̃] *nm* ham

janvier [ʒɑ̃vje] *nm* January; **en**

janvier in January

japper [ʒape] *vb* to bark ▷ *Le chien des voisins jappe constamment.* The neighbours' dog is constantly barking.

jardin [ʒaʀdɛ̃] *nm* garden ▷ *un jardin potager* a vegetable garden

jardinage [ʒaʀdinaʒ] *nm* gardening

jardinier [ʒaʀdinje] *nm* gardener

jardinière [ʒaʀdinjɛʀ] *nf*
  ❶ gardener ❷ flowerpot

jaser [ʒaze] *vb* to chat ▷ *Ton père jase avec le voisin.* Your father is chatting with the neighbour.; **faire jaser** (gossip) to make people talk ▷ *Cela va faire jaser tout le quartier.* That'll set the whole neighbourhood gossiping.

jaune [ʒon] *adj* yellow
  ▶ *nm* yellow; **un jaune d'œuf** an egg yolk

jaunir [ʒoniʀ] *vb* to turn yellow

Javel [ʒavɛl] *n*: **l'eau de Javel** bleach

jazz [dʒaz] *nm* jazz

J.-C. *abbr* = **Jésus-Christ**; **44 avant J.-C.** 44 BCE; **115 après J.-C.** 115 CE

je [ʒ(ə)] *pron*
  je changes to **j'** before a vowel and most words beginning with 'h'.
  ⒈ ▷ *Je t'appellerai ce soir.* I'll phone you this evening. ▷ *J'arrive!* I'm coming! ▷ *J'hésite.* I'm not sure.

jeans [dʒin] *nmpl* jeans

jet [dʒɛt] *nm* (of water) jet; **un jet d'eau** a fountain

jetable [ʒətabl(ə)] *adj* disposable

jetée [ʒəte] *nf* pier

jeter [ʒəte] *vb* ❶ to throw ▷ *Elle a jeté son sac sur le lit.* She threw her bag onto the bed. ❷ to throw away ▷ *Ils ne jettent jamais rien.* They never throw anything away.; **jeter un coup d'œil sur** to have a look at

jeton [ʒətɔ̃] nm (in board game)
counter

jeu [ʒø] (pl **jeux**) nm game ▷ J'aime
les jeux d'adresse. I like games of
skill.; **un jeu d'arcade** a video
game; **un jeu de cartes (1)** a pack
of cards **(2)** a card game; **un jeu
de hasard** a game of chance;
un jeu de mots a pun; **un jeu
électronique** an electronic game;
un jeu interactif an interactive
game; **les Jeux Olympiques** the
Olympic games; **le jeu de rôle
(1)** role-play ▷ Nous avons fait un
jeu de rôle sur les restaurants dans
le cours de français. In French class
we did a role-play about going to
a restaurant. ▷ Le jeu de rôle est une
bonne stratégie d'apprentissage. Role-
play is a good learning strategy.
(2) (computer) role-playing game;
un jeu de société (1) a board game
(2) a party game; **les jeux vidéo**
video games; **en jeu** at stake ▷ Des
vies humaines sont en jeu. Human
lives are at stake.; **hors jeu** (sports)
offside

jeudi [ʒødi] nm ❶ Thursday
▷ Aujourd'hui, nous sommes jeudi. It's
Thursday today. ❷ on Thursday
▷ Il arrivera jeudi matin. He's arriving
on Thursday morning.; **le jeudi**
on Thursdays ▷ Le musée est fermé
le jeudi. The museum is closed on
Thursdays.; **tous les jeudis** every
Thursday; **jeudi dernier** last
Thursday; **jeudi prochain** next
Thursday

jeun [ʒœ̃]: **à jeun** adv on an empty
stomach ▷ Mange quelque chose.
Il est difficile d'étudier à jeun! Eat
something. It's hard to study on an
empty stomach!

jeune [ʒœn] adj young ▷ un jeune
homme a young man ▷ une jeune
femme a young woman; **une jeune**

fille a girl
▶ n young person ▷ un concours pour
les jeunes a contest for young people

jeunesse [ʒœnɛs] nf youth

job [dʒɔb] nf (informal) job

joie [ʒwa] nf joy

joindre [ʒwɛ̃dʀ(ə)] vb ❶ to put
together ▷ On va joindre les deux
tables. We're going to put the two
tables together. ❷ to contact
▷ Vous pouvez le joindre chez lui. You
can contact him at home.

joint [ʒwɛ̃, -ɛt] (f **jointe**) adj: **une
pièce jointe** (in letter) an enclosure

joli [ʒɔli] (f **jolie**) adj pretty

jonc [ʒɔ̃] nm cattail

jonquille [ʒɔ̃kij] nf daffodil

joue [ʒu] nf cheek

jouer [ʒwe] vb ❶ to play ▷ Il est allé
jouer avec les petits voisins. He's gone
to play with the children next door.;
jouer de (instrument) to play ▷ Il
joue de la guitare et du piano. He plays
the guitar and the piano.; **jouer à**
(sport, game) to play ▷ Elle joue au
hockey. She plays hockey. ❷ to act ▷ Je
trouve qu'il joue très bien dans ce film. I
think his acting is very good in this
film.; **On joue Hamlet au Théâtre
de la Ville.** Hamlet is on at the
Théâtre de la Ville.

jouet [ʒwɛ] nm toy

joueur [ʒwœʀ] nm player; **être
mauvais joueur** to be a bad loser

joueuse [ʒwøz] nf player

jour [ʒuʀ] nm ❶ ▷ J'ai passé trois
jours chez mes cousins. I stayed
with my cousins for three days.;
Il fait jour. It's light out.; **mettre
quelque chose à jour** to update
something; **le jour de l'An** New
Year's Day; **un jour de congé** a
day off; **le jour de la marmotte**
Groundhog Day; **un jour férié**
a public holiday; **dans quinze**

jours in two weeks; **de nos jours** nowadays

journal [ʒuʀnal, -o] (pl journaux) nm ❶ newspaper; **le journal télévisé** the news on TV ❷ diary ▷ Elle tient un depuis l'âge de douze ans. She has been keeping a diary since she was 12. ❸ journal

journalier [ʒuʀnalje, -jɛʀ] (f **journalière**) adj daily

journalisme [ʒuʀnalism(ə)] nm journalism

journaliste [ʒuʀnalist(ə)] nmf journalist ▷ Elle est journaliste. She's a journalist.

journée [ʒuʀne] nf day
- In Québec, **la Journée nationale des patriotes** is a holiday that falls on the same day as Victoria Day. It has replaced **la fête de Dollard**.

joyeux [ʒwajø, -øz] (f **joyeuse**) adj happy; **Joyeux anniversaire!** Happy birthday!; **Joyeux Noël!** Merry Christmas!

judo [ʒydo] nm judo

juge [ʒyʒ] nmf judge

juger [ʒyʒe] vb to judge

juif [ʒɥif, -iv] (f **juive**) adj Jewish ▷ la cuisine juive Jewish cooking; **un juif** (man) a Jew; **une juive** (woman) a Jew

juillet [ʒɥijɛ] nm July; **en juillet** in July

juin [ʒɥɛ̃] nm June; **en juin** in June

jumeau [ʒymo] (pl jumeaux) nm twin

jumeler [ʒymle] vb to twin ▷ Thunder Bay est jumelée avec Siderno en Italie. Thunder Bay is twinned with Siderno, Italy.

jumelle [ʒymɛl] nf twin

jumelles [ʒymɛl] nfpl binoculars

jument [ʒymɑ̃] nf mare

jungle [ʒõgl(ə)] nf jungle

jupe [ʒyp] nf skirt

jurer [ʒyʀe] vb to swear ▷ Je jure que c'est vrai! I swear it's true!

juridique [ʒyʀidik] adj (to do with law) legal

jury [ʒyʀi] nm jury

jus [ʒy] nm juice; **un jus de fruit** a fruit juice

jusqu'à [ʒyska] prep ❶ as far as ▷ Nous avons marché jusqu'au village. We walked as far as the village. ❷ until ▷ Il fait généralement chaud jusqu'à la mi-août. It's usually hot until mid-August.; **jusqu'à ce que** until ▷ Tu peux rester ici jusqu'à ce qu'il cesse de pleuvoir. You can stay here until it stops raining.; **jusqu'à présent** so far

jusque [ʒysk(ə)] prep as far as ▷ Je l'ai raccompagnée jusque chez elle. I went with her as far as her house. ▷ Jusqu'ici nous n'avons pas eu de problèmes. Up to now we've had no problems. ▷ Jusqu'où es-tu allé? How far did you go?

juste [ʒyst(ə)] adj, adv ❶ fair ▷ Elle est sévère, mais juste. She's strict but fair. ❷ tight ▷ Ce veston est un peu juste. This jacket is a bit tight.; **juste assez** just enough; **chanter juste** to sing in tune

justement [ʒystəmɑ̃] adv just ▷ C'est justement pour cela qu'il est parti! That's just the reason he left!

justesse [ʒystɛs] nf: **de justesse** just barely ▷ Il a eu son permis de justesse. He just barely passed his driving test.

justice [ʒystis] nf justice

justifier [ʒystifje] vb to justify

juteux [ʒytø, -øz] (f **juteuse**) adj juicy

juvénile [ʒyvenil] adj youthful

k

kilogram

kilomètre [kilɔmɛtʀ(ə)] *nm*
kilometre

kiosque [kjɔsk(ə)] *nm* kiosk; **un
kiosque à journaux** a newsstand

kit [kit] *nm*: **en kit** ready to
assemble ▷ *Nous avons acheté
une étagère en kit.* We bought a
bookshelf that you put together
yourself.

Be careful! **le kit** does not
always mean **kit**.

klaxon [klaksɔn] *nm* (*of car*) horn

klaxonner [klaksɔne] *vb* to blow
the horn

km *abbr* = **kilomètre**; **km/h** kph
(= kilometres per hour)

kaki [kaki] *adj* khaki

kangourou [kɑ̃guʀu] *nm*
kangaroo

karaté [kaʀate] *nm* karate

kayak [kajak] *nm* kayak ▷ *Ils ont
fait une expédition de kayak aux îles de
la Reine-Charlotte.* They went on a
kayak trip to the Queen Charlotte
Islands.; **faire du kayak** to go
kayaking

kayakiste [kajakist] *nmf* kayaker

kétaine [ketɛn] *adj* tacky ▷ *un bijou
kétaine* a tacky piece of jewellery
▷ *des meubles kétaines* tacky
furniture

ketchup [kɛtʃœp] *nm* ketchup

kidnapper [kidnape] *vb* to kidnap

kidnappeur [kidnapœʀ] *nm*
kidnapper

kidnappeuse [kidnapøz] *nf*
kidnapper

kilo [kilo] *nm* kilo

kilogramme [kilɔgʀam] *nm*

I

l' [l] *art, pron* see **la, le**

la [la] *art, pron*

la changes to **l'** before a vowel and most words beginning with "h".

❶ the ▷ *la maison* the house ▷ *l'actrice* the actress ▷ *l'herbe* the grass **❷** her ▷ *Je la connais depuis longtemps.* I've known her for a long time. ▷ *C'est une femme intelligente: je l'admire beaucoup.* She's an intelligent woman: I admire her very much. **❸** it ▷ *C'est une bonne émission: je la regarde tous les jours.* It's a good program: I watch it every day. **❹** one's; **se mordre la langue** to bite one's tongue ▷ *Je me suis mordu la langue.* I bit my tongue.; **deux dollars la douzaine** two dollars a dozen

▶ *nm* **❶** A ▷ *en la bémol* in A flat **❷** la ▷ *sol, la, si, do* so, la, ti, do

là [la] *adv* **❶** there ▷ *Ton livre est là,* *sur la table.* Your book's there, on the table. **❷** here ▷ *Elle n'est pas là.* She isn't here.; **C'est là que...** **(1)** That's where... ▷ *C'est là que je suis né.* That's where I was born. **(2)** That's when... ▷ *C'est là que j'ai réalisé que je m'étais trompé.* That's when I realized I had made a mistake.

là-bas [lɑba] *adv* over there

laboratoire [labɔratwar] *nm* laboratory

labourer [labure] *vb* (fields, soil) to plough

Labrador [labradɔr] *nm* Labrador

labyrinthe [labirɛt] *nm* maze

lac [lak] *nm* lake

lacer [lase] *vb* (shoes) to do up

lacet [lase] *nm* lace; **des chaussures à lacets** lace-up shoes

lâche [laʃ] *adj* **❶** loose ▷ *Le nœud est trop lâche.* The knot's too loose. **❷** cowardly; **Il est lâche.** He's a coward.

▶ *nm* coward

lâcher [lɑʃe] *vb* **❶** to let go of ▷ *Elle n'a pas lâché ma main de tout le film.* She didn't let go of my hand through the whole movie. **❷** to drop ▷ *Il a été tellement surpris qu'il a lâché son verre.* He was so surprised that he dropped his glass. **❸** to fail ▷ *Les freins ont lâché.* The brakes failed.

lâcheté [lɑʃte] *nf* cowardice

lacrymogène [lakrimɔʒɛn] *adj*: **le gaz lacrymogène** tear gas

lacune [lakyn] *nf* gap

là-dedans [ladədɑ̃] *adv* in there ▷ *Qu'est-ce qu'il y a là-dedans?* What's in there?

là-dessous [ladsu] *adv* **❶** under there ▷ *Mon carnet d'adresses est quelque part là-dessous.* My address book is under there somewhere. **❷** behind it ▷ *Il y a quelque chose de* *louche là-dessous.* There's something fishy behind it.

là-dessus [ladsy] *adv* on there

là-haut [lao] *adv* up there

laid [lɛ, lɛd] (**laide**) *adj* ugly

laideur [lɛdœʀ] *nf* ugliness

laine [lɛn] *nf* wool ▷ *un chandail en laine* a wool sweater; **la laine polaire** (*fabric*) fleece ▷ *une veste en laine polaire* a fleece vest

laïque [laik] *adj*: **une école laïque** a state school

laisse [lɛs] *nf* leash ▷ *Tenez votre chien en laisse.* Keep your dog on a leash.

laisser [lese] *vb* ❶ to leave ▷ *J'ai laissé mon parapluie à la maison.* I've left my umbrella at home. ❷ to let ▷ *Laisse-le parler.* Let him speak.; **Elle se laisse aller.** She's letting herself go.; **laisser entendre** to imply ▷ *Elle a laissé entendre qu'elle ne venait pas.* She implied that she wasn't coming.; **laisser tomber quelqu'un** to break up with somebody ▷ *Il a laissé tomber sa copine.* He broke up with his girlfriend.

laisser-aller [leseale] *nm* carelessness

lait [lɛ] *nm* milk; **un lait fouetté** a milk shake; **du lait concentré** condensed milk

laitier [letje, -jɛʀ] (**laitière**) *adj* dairy ▷ *une vache laitière* a dairy cow; **les produits laitiers** dairy products

laitue [lety] *nf* lettuce

lambeaux [lɑ̃bo] *nmpl*: **en lambeaux** tattered

lame [lam] *nf* blade ▷ *une lame de rasoir* a razor blade

lamelle [lamɛl] *nf* thin strip

lamentable [lamɑ̃tabl(ə)] *adj* appalling

se lamenter [lamɑ̃te] *vb* to moan

lampadaire [lɑ̃padɛʀ] *nm* ❶ floor lamp ❷ street light

lampe [lɑ̃p(ə)] *nf* lamp; **une lampe de poche** a flashlight

lance [lɑ̃s] *nf* spear

lancement [lɑ̃smɑ̃] *nm* launch

lancer [lɑ̃se] *vb* ❶ to throw ▷ *Lance-moi le ballon!* Throw me the ball! ❷ to launch ▷ *Ils viennent de lancer un nouveau modèle.* They've just launched a new model.; **se lancer** to embark on ▷ *Il s'est lancé là-dedans sans bien réfléchir.* He embarked on it without thinking it through.
▶ *nm*: **le lancer de poids** the shot put; **le lancer frappé** slapshot

lanceur [lɑ̃sœʀ] *nm* (*baseball*) pitcher

lanceuse [lɑ̃søz] *nf* (*baseball*) pitcher

lancinant [lɑ̃sinɑ̃, -ɑ̃t] (*f* **lancinante**) *adj*: **une douleur lancinante** a shooting pain

langage [lɑ̃gaʒ] *nm* (*other than a specific language*) language ▷ *l'origine du langage* the origin of language ▷ *le langage corporel* body language ▷ *Surveille ton langage!* Watch your language!

langouste [lɑ̃gust(ə)] *nf* crayfish

langue [lɑ̃g] *nf* ❶ tongue ▷ *Un petit garçon m'a tiré la langue.* A little boy stuck his tongue at me.; **sa langue maternelle** her mother tongue ❷ language ▷ *une langue étrangère* a foreign language ▷ *une langue vivante* a modern language ▷ *les langues officielles du Canada* the official languages of Canada; **la langue non sexiste** inclusive language

lanière [lanjɛʀ] *nf* strap

lanterne [lɑ̃tɛʀn(ə)] *nf* lantern

lapin [lapɛ̃] *nm* rabbit

laps [laps] *nm*: **un laps de temps** a

space of time

laque [lak] *nf* hair spray

laquelle [lakɛl] (*pl* **lesquelles**) *pron*
❶ which ▷ *Laquelle de ces photos préfères-tu?* Which of these photos do you prefer? ▷ *À laquelle de tes sœurs ressembles-tu?* Which of your sisters do you look like? ❷ whom ▷ *la personne à laquelle vous faites référence* the person to whom you are referring

> **laquelle** is often not translated in English.

▷ *la personne à laquelle je pense* the person I'm thinking of

lard [laʁ] *nm* fatty pork

large [laʁʒ(ə)] *adj, adv* wide; **voir large** to allow a bit extra ▷ *Achète un autre pain : il vaut mieux voir large.* Buy another loaf of bread: it's better to have a bit extra.
▶ *nm*: **cinq mètres de large** 5 m wide; **le large** the open sea; **au large de** off the coast of ▷ *Le bateau est actuellement au large du Labrador.* The boat is off the coast of Labrador at the moment.

largement [laʁʒəmɑ̃] *adv*: **Vous avez largement le temps.** You have plenty of time.; **C'est largement suffisant.** That's plenty.

largeur [laʁʒœʁ] *nf* width

larme [laʁm(ə)] *nf* tear ▷ *être en larmes* to be in tears

laryngite [laʁɛ̃ʒit] *nf* laryngitis

lasagne [lazaɲ] *nf* lasagna

laser [lazɛʁ] *nm* laser; **une imprimante laser** a laser printer

lasser [lase] *vb*: **se lasser de** to get tired of ▷ *Il s'est lassé de la tapisserie à fleurs du salon.* He got tired of the flowery wallpaper in the living room.

Laurentides [loʁɑ̃tid] *nfpl* the Laurentians ▷ *Nous avons fait du camping dans les Laurentides.* We went camping in

the Laurentians.

lavable [lavabl(ə)] *adj* washable

lavabo [lavabo] *nm* (*bathroom*) sink

lavage [lavaʒ] *nm* wash ▷ *Ce chandail a rétréci au lavage.* This sweater shrank in the wash.
▷ *Avez-vous quelque chose à mettre au lavage?* Do you have anything to put in the wash?; **faire le lavage** to do laundry; **le lavage de cerveau** brainwashing

lave-auto [lav-] (*pl* **lave-autos**) *nm* car wash

laver [lave] *vb* to wash; **se laver** to wash ▷ *se laver les mains* to wash one's hands

lavette [lavɛt] *nf* dishcloth

laveuse [lavøz] *nf* washing machine

lave-vaisselle [lavvɛsɛl] (*pl* **lave-vaisselle**) *nm* dishwasher

lavoir [lavwaʁ] *nm* coin laundry

le [l(ə)] *art, pron*

> **le** changes to **l'** before a vowel and most words beginning with "h".

❶ the ▷ *le livre* the book ▷ *l'arbre* the tree ▷ *l'hélicoptère* the helicopter ❷ him ▷ *C'est un vieil ami : je le connais depuis plus de vingt ans.* He's an old friend: I've known him for over 20 years. ❸ it ▷ *Où est mon stylo? Je ne le trouve plus.* Where's my pen? I can't find it. ▷ *« Où est le fromage? » « Je l'ai mis au frigo. »* "Where's the cheese?" "I put it in the fridge." ❹ one's; **se laver le visage** to wash one's face ▷ *Évitez de vous laver le visage avec du savon.* Avoid washing your face with soap.; **trois dollars le kilo** 3 dollars a kilo; **Il est arrivé le douze mai.** He arrived on 12 May.

lécher [leʃe] *vb* to lick

leçon [ləsɔ̃] *nf* lesson

lecteur [lɛktœʀ] nm ❶ reader ❷ (computer) (disk) drive ▷ *Insérer la disquette dans le lecteur A.* Insert the disk in drive A.; **un lecteur de cassettes** a cassette player; **un lecteur de CD** a CD player; **un lecteur de DVD** a DVD player; **un lecteur de MP3** an MP3 player

lectrice [lɛktʀis] nf reader

lecture [lɛktyʀ] nf reading

> Be careful! The French word **lecture** does not mean **lecture**.

légal [legal, -o] (f**légale**, mpl **légaux**) adj legal

légende [leʒɑ̃d] nf ❶ legend ❷ (of map) key ❸ (of picture) caption

léger [leʒe, -ɛʀ] (f**légère**) adj ❶ light ❷ slight ▷ *un léger retard* a slight delay; **à la légère** thoughtlessly ▷ *Elle a agi à la légère.* She acted thoughtlessly.

légèrement [leʒɛʀmɑ̃] adv ❶ lightly ▷ *Habille-toi légèrement : il va faire chaud.* Wear light clothes: it's going to be hot. ❷ slightly ▷ *Il est légèrement plus grand que sa sœur.* He's slightly taller than his sister.

légume [legym] nm vegetable

lendemain [lɑ̃dmɛ̃] nm next day ▷ *le lendemain de son arrivée* the day after she arrived; **le lendemain matin** the next morning; **le lendemain de Noël** Boxing Day

lent [lɑ̃, lɑ̃t] (f**lente**) adj slow

lentement [lɑ̃tmɑ̃] adv slowly

lenteur [lɑ̃tœʀ] nf slowness

lentille [lɑ̃tij] nf lentil ▷ *un rôti de porc aux lentilles* roast pork with lentils; **des lentilles cornéennes** contact lenses

léopard [leɔpaʀ] nm leopard

lequel [lɛkɛl, lakɛl] (f**laquelle**, mpl **lesquels**, fpl **lesquelles**) pron ❶ which ▷ *Lequel de ces deux films as-tu préféré?* Which of these two movies did you prefer? ❷ whom

▷ *l'homme avec lequel elle a été vue pour la dernière fois* the man with whom she was last seen

> **lequel** is often not translated in English.

▷ *le garçon avec lequel elle est sortie* the boy she went out with

les [le] art, pron ❶ the ▷ *les arbres* the trees ▷ *Elle les a invités à dîner.* She invited them to dinner. ❷ one's; **se brosser les dents** to brush one's teeth ▷ *Elle s'est brossé les dents.* She brushed her teeth.

lesbienne [lɛsbjɛn] nf lesbian

lesquels [lɛkɛl] (f**lesquelles**) pron ❶ which ▷ *Lesquelles de ces photos préfères-tu?* Which of these photos do you prefer? ❷ whom ▷ *les personnes avec lesquelles il joue au hockey* the people with whom he plays hockey

> **lesquels** is often not translated in English.

▷ *les gens chez lesquels nous avons dîné* the people we had dinner with

lessive [lesiv] nf (laundry) wash; **faire la lessive** to do the washing

leste [lɛst(ə)] adj nimble

lettre [lɛtʀ(ə)] nf letter ▷ *écrire une lettre* to write a letter

leur [lœʀ] adj, pron ❶ their ▷ *leur ami* their friend ❷ them ▷ *Je leur ai dit la vérité.* I told them the truth.; **le leur** theirs ▷ *mon camion et le leur* my truck and theirs ▷ *Ma voiture est rouge, la leur est bleue.* My car's red, theirs is blue.

leurs [lœʀ] adj, pron their ▷ *leurs amis* their friends; **les leurs** theirs ▷ *tes livres et les leurs* your books and theirs

levé [lave] (f**levée**) adj: **être levé** to be up ▷ *Est-ce qu'elles sont levées?* Are they up?

levée [lave] nf (of mail) collection ▷ *Prochaine levée : 17 heures* Next collection: 5 p.m.; **la levée de fonds** fund-raising

lever [ləve] vb to raise ▷ *Levez la main si vous connaissez la réponse.* Raise your hand if you know the answer.; **lever le nez sur quelque chose** to turn something down ▷ *Ils ont levé le nez sur notre offre.* They turned down our offer.; **lever les yeux** to look up; **se lever (1)** to get up ▷ *Elle se lève tous les jours à six heures.* She gets up at 6 o'clock every day. ▷ *Lève-toi!* Get up! **(2)** to rise ▷ *Le soleil se lève plus tard en hiver.* The sun rises later in winter. **(3)** to stand up ▷ *Levez-vous!* Stand up!
▷ nm: **le lever du soleil** sunrise

levier [ləvje] nm lever

lèvre [lɛvʀ(ə)] nf lip

levure [ləvyʀ] nf yeast; **la levure chimique** baking powder

lexique [lɛksik] nm word list

lézard [lezaʀ] nm lizard

liaison [ljezɔ̃] nf ❶ affair ▷ *Ils ont eu une liaison dans leur jeunesse.* They had an affair when they were younger. ❷ (in pronunciation) liaison ▷ *Il faut faire la liaison dans l'expression « les amis ».* You have to make a liaison in the phrase "les amis".

libellule [libelyl] nf dragonfly

libérer [libere] vb to free ▷ *Les otages ont été libérés hier soir.* The hostages were freed last night.; **se libérer** to find time ▷ *J'essaierai de me libérer cet après-midi.* I'll try to find time this afternoon.

liberté [libɛʀte] nf freedom ▷ *la liberté d'expression* freedom of speech; **mettre en liberté** to release ▷ *Il a été mis en liberté au bout d'un an de prison.* He was released after a year in prison.; **en liberté surveillée** on probation

libraire [libʀɛʀ] nmf bookseller

librairie [libʀɛʀi] nf bookstore
    Be careful! **librairie** does not mean **library**.

libre [libʀ(ə)] adj ❶ free ▷ *Tu es libre de faire ce que tu veux.* You are free to do as you wish. ▷ *Est-ce que cette place est libre?* Is this seat free?; **Avez-vous une chambre de libre?** Have you got a free room? ❷ clear ▷ *La route est libre : vous pouvez traverser.* The road is clear: you can cross.

libre-échange [libʀeʃɑ̃ʒ] nm free trade ▷ *un accord de libre-échange* a free-trade agreement

libre-service [libʀəsɛʀvis] nm (pl **libres-services**) nm self-serve ▷ *Cette station-service est un libre-service.* This gas station is a self-serve.

licence [lisɑ̃s] nf licence ▷ *une licence d'exportation* an export licence ▷ *la licence de logiciel* software licence

licenciement [lisɑ̃simɑ̃] nm layoff

licencier [lisɑ̃sje] vb to lay off ▷ *Ils viennent de licencier sept employés.* They've just laid off 7 employees.

liège [ljɛʒ] nm cork ▷ *des sous-verres en liège* cork coasters; **un bouchon en liège** (for bottle) a cork

lien [ljɛ̃] nm ❶ connection ▷ *Il n'y aucun lien entre ces deux événements.* There's no connection between these two events.; **un lien de parenté** a family tie ❷ (in computing) link

lier [lje] vb: **lier conversation avec quelqu'un** to get into conversation with somebody; **se lier avec quelqu'un** to make friends with somebody ▷ *Je ne me lie pas facilement.* I don't make friends easily.

lierre [ljɛʀ] nm ivy

lieu [ljø] nm (pl **lieux**) nm place ▷ *votre*

lieu de travail your place of work; **avoir lieu** to take place ▷ *La cérémonie a eu lieu dans la salle des fêtes.* The ceremony took place in the community hall.; **au lieu de** instead of ▷ *J'aimerais une pomme au lieu de la crème glacée.* I'd like an apple instead of ice cream.

lieutenant-gouverneur [ljøtnãguvɛʀnœʀ] *nm* lieutenant-governor

lieutenante-gouverneure [ljøtnãtguvɛʀnœʀ] *nf* lieutenant-governor

lièvre [ljɛvʀ(ə)] *nm* hare

ligne [liɲ] *nf* ❶ line ▷ *La ligne est occupée.* The line is busy. ▷ *des lignes d'autobus* bus lines ▷ *les lignes électriques* power lines; **en ligne** (*computing*) online; **la ligne d'écoute téléphonique** helpline; **une ligne fixe** a landline ❷ figure ▷ *C'est mauvais pour la ligne.* It's bad for your figure.

ligoter [ligɔte] *vb* to tie up

ligue [lig] *nf* league

lilas [lila] *nm* lilac

limace [limas] *nf* slug

lime [lim] *nf*: **une lime à ongles** a nail file

limitation [limitasjɔ̃] *nf*: **la limitation de vitesse** the speed limit

limite [limit] *nf* ❶ (*of property, sports field*) boundary ❷ limit ▷ *Est-ce qu'il y a une limite d'âge?* Is there an age limit?; **À la limite, on pourrait prendre l'autobus.** At a pinch we could go by bus.; **la date limite** the deadline; **la date limite d'utilisation** the best-before date

limiter [limite] *vb* to limit ▷ *Le nombre de billets est limité à deux par personne.* The number of tickets is limited to two per person.

limonade [limɔnad] *nf* lemonade

lin [lɛ̃] *nm* linen

linge [lɛ̃ʒ] *nm* ❶ linen ▷ *le linge sale* dirty linen ▷ *le linge de maison* household linens ❷ washing ▷ *laver le linge* to do the washing; **le linge à vaisselle** tea towel

lion [ljɔ̃] *nm* lion; **le Lion** Leo ▷ *Il est Lion.* He is a Leo.

lionne [ljɔn] *nf* lioness

liqueur [likœʀ] *nf* (*beverage*) pop

liquide [likid] *adj* liquid
▶ *nm* liquid; **payer quelque chose en liquide** to pay cash for something

lire [liʀ] *vb* to read ▷ *Tu as lu des contes de Roch Carrier?* Have you read any stories by Roch Carrier?

lis, lisent, lisez *vb* *see* **lire**; **Je lis beaucoup.** I read a lot.

lisible [lizibl(ə)] *adj* legible

lisse [lis] *adj* smooth

lisseur [lisœʀ] *nm* hair straightener

liste [list(ə)] *nf* list; **faire la liste de** to make a list of

lit [li] *vb* *see* **lire**
▶ *nm* bed ▷ *un grand lit* a double bed ▷ *aller au lit* to go to bed; **faire son lit** to make one's bed ▷ *Je n'ai pas eu le temps de faire mon lit ce matin.* I didn't have time to make my bed this morning.; **un lit de camp** a cot; **un lit d'enfant** a crib

literie [litʀi] *nf* bedding

litière [litjɛʀ] *nf* ❶ (*for cat*) litter ❷ (*of caged pet*) bedding

litre [litʀ(ə)] *nm* litre

littéraire [liteʀɛʀ] *adj* literary; **une œuvre littéraire** a work of literature

littérature [liteʀatyʀ] *nf* literature

littoral [litɔʀal, -o] (*pl* **littoraux**) *nm* coast

livraison [livʀɛzɔ̃] *nf* delivery

livre [livʀ(ə)] *nm* book; **un livre**

de poche a paperback; **un livre numérique** an e-book
▶ nf pound
   The **pound** is a nonmetric unit of mass equal to 454 g.
   ▷ *une livre de beurre* a pound of butter

livrer [livʀe] vb to deliver

livret [livʀɛ] nm booklet

livreur [livʀœʀ] nm delivery person

livreuse [livʀøz] nf delivery person

local [lɔkal, -o] (f **locale**, mpl **locaux**) adj local
▶ nm (pl **locaux**) venue ▷ *Nous cherchons un local pour les répétitions.* We are looking for a venue to rehearse in.

locataire [lɔkatɛʀ] nmf tenant

location [lɔkasjɔ̃] nf: **location de voitures** car rental; **location de skis** ski rental
   Be careful! The French word **location** does not mean **location**.

locaux [lɔko] adj, n see **local**

locomotive [lɔkɔmɔtiv] nf locomotive

loge [lɔʒ] nf dressing room

logement [lɔʒmɑ̃] nm ❶ housing ❷ accommodation

loger [lɔʒe] vb to stay ▷ *Elle loge chez sa cousine.* She's staying with her cousin.; **trouver à se loger** to find somewhere to live ▷ *Ils ont eu du mal à trouver à se loger.* They had difficulty finding somewhere to live.

logiciel [lɔʒisjɛl] nm (computer) program ▷ *un logiciel de traitement de texte* a word-processing program; **un logiciel antivirus** a piece of antivirus software; **le coût des logiciels pour les écoles** the cost of software for schools

logique [lɔʒik] adj logical
▶ nf logic

loi [lwa] nf law

loin [lwɛ̃] adv ❶ far ▷ *Le restaurant n'est pas très loin d'ici.* The restaurant is not very far from here. ❷ far off ▷ *La semaine de relâche n'est plus tellement loin.* March break isn't far off now. ❸ a long time ago ▷ *Les vacances paraissent déjà tellement loin!* The holidays already seem such a long time ago!; **au loin** in the distance ▷ *On aperçoit la mer au loin.* You can see the ocean in the distance.; **de loin (1)** from a long way away ▷ *On voit l'église de loin.* You can see the church from a long way away. **(2)** by far ▷ *C'est de loin l'élève le plus brillant.* He is by far the brightest student.; **C'est plus loin que le théâtre.** It's past the theatre.

lointain [lwɛ̃tɛ̃, -ɛn] (f **lointaine**) adj distant ▷ *un pays lointain* a distant country ▷ *C'est un parent lointain de ma mère.* He's a distant relation of my mother.
▶ nm: **dans le lointain** in the distance

loir [lwaʀ] nm: **dormir comme un loir** to sleep like a log

loisirs [lwaziʀ] nmpl ❶ free time ▷ *Qu'est-ce que vous faites pendant vos loisirs?* What do you do in your free time? ❷ hobby ▷ *Le ski et l'équitation sont des loisirs coûteux.* Skiing and riding are expensive hobbies.

long [lɔ̃, lɔ̃g] (f **longue**) adj long; **à l'année longue** all year round
▶ nm: **un bateau de trois mètres de long** a boat 3 m long; **tout le long de** all along ▷ *Il y a des sentiers de randonnée tout le long de la côte.* There are hiking trails all along the coast.; **marcher de long en large** to walk up and down

longer [lɔ̃ʒe] vb: **La route longe la forêt.** The road runs along the edge of the forest.; **Nous avons longé la**

rivière Rideau à pied. We walked along the Rideau.

longtemps [lɔ̃tɑ̃] adv a long time ▷ J'ai attendu longtemps chez le dentiste. I waited a long time at the dentist's.; **pendant longtemps** for a long time ▷ On a cru pendant longtemps que la Terre était plate. For a long time people thought the Earth was flat.; **mettre longtemps à faire quelque chose** to take a long time to do something ▷ Il a mis longtemps à répondre à ma lettre. He took a long time to answer my letter.

longue [lɔ̃g] adj see **long**

longue [lɔ̃g] nf: **à la longue** (1) in the end ▷ Elle a fini par convaincre tout le monde à la longue. In the end she won everybody over. (2) over the long term ▷ À la longue, la malbouffe est mauvaise pour la santé. Over the long term, junk food is bad for your health.

longuement [lɔ̃gmɑ̃] adv at length ▷ Il m'a longuement parlé de ses projets d'avenir. He talked to me at length about his future plans.

longueur [lɔ̃gœʀ] nf length; **à longueur de journée** all day long ▷ Elle mâche de la gomme à longueur de journée. She chews gum all day long.; **dans le sens de la longueur** lengthwise

loques [lɔk] nfpl: **être en loques** to be torn to shreds ▷ Sa chemise était en loques. His shirt was torn to shreds.

lors [lɔʀd(ə)] prep during ▷ Je l'ai rencontrée lors de ma visite à Prince George. I met her during my stay in Prince George.

lorsque [lɔʀsk(ə)] conj when ▷ J'allais composer ton numéro lorsque tu as appelé. I was about to dial your number when you called.

lot [lo] nm (in draw) prize; **le gros lot** the jackpot

loterie [lɔtʀi] nf ❶ lottery ▷ une loterie nationale a national lottery ❷ raffle ▷ J'ai gagné ce baladeur dans une loterie. I won this personal CD player in a raffle.

lotion [losjɔ̃] nf lotion ▷ une bouteille de lotion solaire a bottle of suntan lotion; **une lotion après rasage** an aftershave; **une lotion démaquillante** facial cleanser

loto [lɔto] nm lottery; **un loto sportif** a sports pool

louche [luʃ] adj fishy ▷ une histoire louche a fishy story
▶ nf ladle

loucher [luʃe] vb to squint

louer [lwe] vb ❶ to rent out ▷ Ils louent des chambres à des étudiants. They rent out rooms to students.; **« à louer »** "for rent" ❷ to rent ▷ Ma sœur loue un petit appartement au centre-ville. My sister rents a little apartment in the centre of town. ▷ Nous allons louer une voiture pour le week-end. We're going to rent a car for the weekend. ❸ to praise ▷ Les journaux ont loué le courage des pompiers. The newspapers praised the courage of the firefighters.

loup [lu] nm wolf

loupe [lup] nf magnifying glass

lourd [luʀ, luʀd(ə)] (f **lourde**) adj ❶ heavy ▷ Mon sac à dos est très lourd. My backpack is very heavy. ❷ (weather) muggy ▷ Le temps est lourd aujourd'hui. It's muggy out today.

loutre [lutʀ(ə)] nf otter

louveteau [luvto] nm wolf cub

loyal [lwajal, -o] (mpl **loyaux**) adj loyal

loyauté [lwajote] nf loyalty

loyer [lwaje] nm rent

lu [ly] vb see **lire**

lucarne [lykarn(ə)] *nf* skylight

luge [lyʒ] *nf* sled

lugubre [lygybr(ə)] *adj* gloomy

lui [lɥi] *pron* ❶ him ▷ *Il a été très content du cadeau que je lui ai offert.* He was very pleased with the present I gave him. ▷ *C'est bien lui!* It's definitely him! ▷ *J'ai pensé à lui toute la journée.* I thought about him all day long. ❷ to him ▷ *Mon père est d'accord : je lui ai parlé ce matin.* My father said yes: I spoke to him this morning. ❸ her ▷ *Elle a été très contente du cadeau que je lui ai offert.* She was very pleased with the present I gave her. ❹ to her ▷ *Ma mère est d'accord : je lui ai parlé ce matin.* My mother said yes: I spoke to her this morning. ❺ it ▷ *« Qu'est-ce que tu donnes à ton chat ? » « Je lui donne de la nourriture sèche. »* "What do you give your cat?" "I give it dry food."

lui is also used for emphasis. ▷ *Lui, il est toujours en retard!* Oh him, he's always late! ▷ *Il a construit ce bateau lui-même.* He built this boat himself.

lumière [lymjɛr] *nf* light; **la lumière du jour** daylight

lumineux [lyminø, -øz] *(f* **lumineuse**) *adj*: **une enseigne lumineuse** a neon sign

lunatique [lynatik] *adj* ❶ absent-minded ▷ *Ma sœur est très lunatique.* My sister is very absent-minded. ❷ temperamental ▷ *Il est plutôt lunatique.* He's rather temperamental.

lunch [lœntʃ] *nm (midday meal)* lunch ▷ *Habituellement, j'apporte mon lunch à l'école.* I usually bring my lunch to school.

In Canada, **le lunch** is the noon meal. In France, it refers to a light meal consisting of a cold buffet.

lundi [lœdi] *nm* ❶ Monday ▷ *Aujourd'hui, nous sommes lundi.* It's Monday today. ❷ on Monday ▷ *Ils sont arrivés lundi.* They arrived on Monday.; **le lundi** on Mondays ▷ *Le lundi, je vais à la piscine.* I go swimming on Mondays.; **tous les lundis** every Monday; **lundi dernier** last Monday; **lundi prochain** next Monday; **le lundi de Pâques** Easter Monday

lune [lyn] *nf* moon; **la lune de miel** honeymoon; **être dans la lune** to daydream ▷ *Elle n'entend pas ; elle est dans la lune.* She doesn't hear you; she's daydreaming.

lunettes [lynɛt] *nfpl* glasses; **des lunettes de soleil** sunglasses; **des lunettes de natation** swimming goggles

lutte [lyt] *nf* ❶ fight ▷ *la lutte contre le racisme* the fight against racism ❷ wrestling ▷ *une épreuve de lutte* a wrestling bout

lutter [lyte] *vb* to fight

luxe [lyks(ə)] *nm* luxury; **de luxe** luxury ▷ *un hôtel de luxe* a luxury hotel

luxueux [lyksɥø, -øz] *(fluxueuse)* *adj* luxurious

lynx [lɛ̃ks] *nm* lynx

m' [m] *pron see* **me**

ma [ma] *adj* my ▷ *ma mère* my mother ▷ *ma montre* my watch

macaron [makaʁɔ̃] *nm* (*with slogan, image*) button ▷ *Elle portait un macaron qui disait : « J'aime le français! »* She was wearing a button that said, "I like French!"

macaronis [makaʁɔni] *nmpl* macaroni

macédoine [masedwan] *nf*: **la macédoine de fruits** fruit salad; **la macédoine de légumes** mixed vegetables

mâcher [mɑʃe] *vb* to chew

machin [maʃɛ̃] *nm* (*informal*) thingy ▷ *Passe-moi le machin pour râper les carottes.* Pass me the thingy for grating carrots. ▷ *Qu'est-ce que c'est que ce vieux machin?* What's this old thing?

machinalement [maʃinalmɑ̃] *adv*: **Elle a regardé sa montre machinalement.** She looked at her watch without thinking.

machine [maʃin] *nf* machine; **une machine à laver** a washing machine; **une machine à écrire** a typewriter; **une machine à coudre** a sewing machine; **une machine à boules** a pinball machine

machiste [matʃist] *nm* male chauvinist

mâchoire [mɑʃwaʁ] *nf* jaw

mâchonner [mɑʃɔne] *vb* to chew

Madame [madam] (*pl* **Mesdames**) *nf* ❶ Mrs ▷ *Madame Legall* Mrs Legall ❷ lady ▷ *Occupez-vous de Madame.* Could you look after this lady? ❸ Madam ▷ *Madame,...* Dear Madam,... ❹ (*in letter*) **Madame! Vous avez oublié votre parapluie!** Ma'am, you forgot your umbrella!

Mademoiselle [madmwazɛl] (*pl* **Mesdemoiselles**) *nf* Miss ▷ *Mademoiselle Martin* Miss Martin
  Mademoiselle is rarely used for single women any more, except in reference to a girl. It is better to use **Madame**, the French equivalent of **Ms**, in person or in a letter.

maganer [magane] *vb* (*informal*) to wreck ▷ *La pluie a magané la récolte de fraises.* The rain wrecked the strawberry crop. ▷ *J'ai magané mon baladeur MP3.* I wrecked my portable MP3 player.

magasin [magazɛ̃] *nm* store ▷ *Les magasins ouvrent à huit heures.* The stores open at 8 o'clock.; **faire les magasins** to go shopping

magasinage [magazinaʒ] *nm* shopping ▷ *J'ai du magasinage à faire.* I have some shopping to do.; **faire du magasinage** to go shopping

magasiner [magazine] *vb* to shop

magasineur [magazinœʀ] nm
shopper

magasineuse [magazinøz] nf
shopper

magazine [magazin] nm
magazine

magicien [maʒisjɛ̃] nm magician

magicienne [maʒisjɛn] nf
magician

magie [maʒi] nf magic ▷ un tour de
magie a magic trick

magique [maʒik] adj magic ▷ une
baguette magique a magic wand

magnétique [maɲetik] adj
magnetic

magnétophone [maɲetɔfɔn] nm
tape recorder; **un magnétophone
à cassettes** a cassette recorder

magnétoscope [maɲetɔskɔp]
nm VCR

magnifique [maɲifik] adj superb

mai [me] nm May; **en mai** in May

maigre [mɛgʀ(ə)] adj ❶ skinny
▷ Mon père me trouve trop maigre.
My father says I'm too skinny.
❷ (meat) lean ❸ (cheese, yogurt)
low-fat

maigrir [megʀiʀ] vb to lose weight
▷ Il fait un régime pour essayer de
maigrir. He's on a diet to try to lose
weight. ▷ Elle a maigri de deux kilos
en un mois. She's lost 2 kilos in a
month.

maillot de bain [majo-] nm
swimsuit

main [mɛ̃] nf hand ▷ Donne-moi la
main! Give me your hand!; **serrer
la main à quelqu'un** to shake
hands with somebody; **se serrer
la main** to shake hands ▷ Les deux
présidents se sont serré la main. The
two presidents shook hands.; **sous
la main** handy ▷ Est-ce que tu as son
adresse sous la main? Have you got
his address handy?

main-d'œuvre [mɛ̃dœvʀ(ə)]
nf workforce ▷ la main-d'œuvre
canadienne the Canadian workforce
▷ la main-d'œuvre de l'usine the
factory workers; **les frais de main-
d'œuvre** labour costs

maintenant [mɛ̃tnɑ̃] adv
❶ now ▷ Qu'est-ce que tu veux faire
maintenant? What do you want
to do now? ▷ C'est maintenant
ou jamais. It's now or never.
❷ nowadays ▷ Maintenant la
plupart des gens font leurs courses
au supermarché. Nowadays most
people do their shopping at the
supermarket.

maintenir [mɛ̃tniʀ] vb to
maintain ▷ Il maintient qu'il n'était
pas là le jour du crime. He maintains
he wasn't there on the day of the
crime.; **se maintenir** to hold
▷ Espérons que le beau temps va se
maintenir pour la fin de semaine! Let's
hope the good weather will hold
over the weekend!

maintien de la paix [mɛ̃tjɛ̃-]
nm peacekeeping ▷ les opérations
du maintien de la paix au Rwanda
peacekeeping operations in
Rwanda

maire [mɛʀ] nmf mayor

mairie [meʀi] nf town hall

mais [me] conj but ▷ C'est cher mais
de très bonne qualité. It's expensive,
but very good quality.

maïs [mais] nm corn; **du maïs
soufflé** popcorn

maison [mezɔ̃] nf house ▷ Ils
habitent dans la maison qui est au bout
de la rue. They live in the house at
the end of the street.; **une maison
de jeunes** a youth club; **une
maison de transition** a halfway
house; **des maisons jumelées**
semi-detached houses; **des
maisons en rangée** townhouses; **à
la maison (1)** at home ▷ Je serai à la

maison cet après-midi. I'll be at home this afternoon. **(2)** *home* ▷ *Elle est rentrée à la maison.* She's gone home.

▶ *adj* (f+pl **maison**) *homemade* ▷ *Je préfère les tartes maison à celles qui sont achetées.* I prefer homemade pies to store-bought ones.

maître [mɛtr(ə)] *nmf* ❶ (*in primary school*) *teacher* ❷ (*of dog*) *master*; **un maître d'hôtel** (*in restaurant*) a head waiter; **un maître nageur** a lifeguard; **une maître nageuse** a lifeguard

maîtresse [mɛtrɛs] *nf* (*in primary school*) *teacher*; **la maîtresse de la maison** the lady of the house

maîtrise [mɛtriz] *nf* master's degree ▷ *Elle a une maîtrise d'anglais.* She's got a master's degree in English.; **la maîtrise de soi** self-control

maîtriser [mɛtrize] *vb*: **se maîtriser** to control oneself ▷ *Il se met facilement en colère et a du mal à se maîtriser.* He loses his temper easily and finds it hard to control himself.

majestueux [maʒɛstɥø, -øz] (f **majestueuse**) *adj* majestic

majeur [maʒœr] (f **majeure**) *adj*: **être majeur** to be of age ▷ *Tu feras ce que tu voudras quand tu seras majeure.* You can do what you like once you're of age. ▷ *Elle sera majeure en août.* She comes of age in August.; **la majeure partie** most ▷ *la majeure partie de mon salaire* most of my salary

majorité [maʒɔrite] *nf* majority ▷ *dans la majorité des cas* in the majority of cases; **la majorité et l'opposition** the government and the opposition

majuscule [maʒyskyl] *nf* upper-case letter ▷ *un M majuscule* an upper-case M

mal [mal] (f+pl **mal**) *adv, adj*
❶ *badly* ▷ *Ce travail a été mal fait.* The work was badly done. ▷ *Il a mal compris.* He misunderstood.
❷ *wrong* ▷ *C'est mal de mentir.* It's wrong to tell lies.; **aller mal** to be ill ▷ *Son grand-père va très mal.* Her grandfather is very ill.; **pas mal** quite good ▷ *Je te trouve pas mal sur cette photo.* I think you look quite good in this photo.

▶ *nm* (*pl* **maux**) ❶ *ache* ▷ *j'ai mal à la tête.* I have a headache. ▷ *J'ai mal aux dents.* I have a toothache. ▷ *J'ai mal au dos.* My back hurts. ▷ *Est-ce que vous avez mal à la gorge?* Do you have a sore throat?; **le mal des transports** motion sickness; **Ça fait mal.** It hurts.; **Où est-ce que tu as mal?** Where does it hurt?; **faire mal à quelqu'un** to hurt somebody ▷ *Attention, tu me fais mal!* Be careful, you're hurting me!; **se faire mal** to hurt oneself ▷ *Je me suis fait mal au bras.* I hurt my arm.; **se donner du mal pour faire quelque chose** to go to a lot of trouble to do something ▷ *Il s'est donné beaucoup de mal pour que cette soirée soit réussie.* He went to a lot of trouble to make the party a success.; **avoir le mal de mer** to be seasick; **avoir le mal du pays** to be homesick; **avoir mal au cœur** to feel nauseous ❷ *evil* ▷ *le bien et le mal* good and evil; **dire du mal de quelqu'un** to speak ill of somebody

malade [malad] *adj* ill; **tomber malade** to fall ill
▶ *n* patient

maladie [maladi] *nf* ❶ illness ❷ disease; **la maladie de la vache folle** mad cow disease

maladif [maladif, -iv] (f **maladive**) *adj* sickly ▷ *C'est un enfant maladif.*

He's a sickly child.

maladresse [maladʀɛs] nf clumsiness

maladroit [maladʀwa, -wat] (f **maladroite**) adj clumsy

malaise [malɛz] nm: **avoir un malaise** to feel faint ▷ Elle a eu un malaise après le déjeuner. She felt faint after lunch.; **Son arrivée a créé un malaise parmi les invités.** Her arrival made the guests uncomfortable.

malbouffe [malbuf] nf junk food ▷ Mes parents sont contre la malbouffe. My parents are against junk food. ▷ La malbouffe est devenue un problème dans notre société. Junk food has become a problem in our society.

malchance [malʃɑ̃s] nf bad luck

mâle [mɑl] adj male

malédiction [malediksjɔ̃] nf curse

mal en point (f+pl **mal en point**) adj: **Il avait l'air mal en point quand je l'ai vu hier soir.** He didn't look too good when I saw him last night.

malentendu [malɑ̃tɑ̃dy] nm misunderstanding

malfaiteur [malfɛtœʀ] nm criminal

malfaitrice [malfɛtʀis] nf criminal

mal famé (f mal famée, f mal famée, mpl mal famés) adj: **un quartier mal famé** a rough neighbourhood

malgré [malgʀe] prep in spite of ▷ Il est toujours généreux malgré ses problèmes d'argent. He's always generous in spite of his financial problems.; **malgré tout** (nevertheless) anyway ▷ Il faisait mauvais mais nous sommes sortis malgré tout. The weather was bad but we went out anyway.

malheur [malœʀ] nm tragedy ▷ Elle a eu beaucoup de malheurs dans sa vie. She's had a lot of tragedy in her life.; **faire un malheur** (informal) to be a smash hit ▷ Leur dernier album a fait un malheur. Their latest album was a smash hit.

malheureusement [malœʀøzmɑ̃] adv unfortunately

malheureux [malœʀø, -øz] (f **malheureuse**) adj miserable ▷ Qu'est-ce que tu as? Tu as l'air malheureux. What's wrong with you? You look miserable.

malhonnête [malɔnɛt] adj dishonest

malice [malis] nf mischief ▷ Son regard était plein de malice. Her eyes were full of mischief.

malicieux [malisjø, -øz] (f **malicieuse**) adj mischievous

Be careful! **malicieux** does not mean **malicious**.

malin [malɛ̃, -iɲ] (f **maligne**) adj **①** crafty; **C'est malin!** (informal) That's clever! ▷ Ah c'est malin! Nous voilà enfermés à cause de toi! That's clever! You've gone and locked us in! **②** malignant ▷ une tumeur maligne a malignant tumor

malodorant [malɔdɔʀɑ̃, -ɑ̃t] (f **malodorante**) adj smelly

malpropre [malpʀɔpʀ(ə)] adj dirty

malsain [malsɛ̃, -ɛn] (f **malsaine**) adj unhealthy

maltraiter [maltʀete] vb to abuse ▷ Il maltraite son chien. He abuses his dog. ▷ des enfants maltraités abused children

malveillant [malvejɑ̃, -ɑ̃t] (f **malveillante**) adj malicious ▷ des rumeurs malveillantes malicious rumours

maman [mamɑ̃] nf mom

mammifère [mamifɛʀ] nm
mammal

manche [mɑ̃ʃ] nf ❶ (of clothes)
sleeve ❷ (of game) round ▷ Ils ont
gagné la première manche du match.
They won the first round of the
match.

> The word **manche** can be
> translated as **set, inning, heat**
> or **round**, depending on what
> kind of sport or game is being
> played.

▸ nm (of pot, pan) handle

manchette [mɑ̃ʃɛt] nf headline;
faire la manchette to make
headlines

mandarine [mɑ̃daʀin] nf
mandarin orange

manège [manɛʒ] nm amusement
park ride; **Nous avons deviné
son manège.** We've seen through
his game.

manette [manɛt] nf ❶ lever
❷ joystick

mangeable [mɑ̃ʒabl(ə)] adj
edible ▷ C'est à peine mangeable! It's
practically inedible!

manger [mɑ̃ʒe] vb to eat

mangue [mɑ̃g] nf mango

maniaque [manjak] adj fussy

manie [mani] nf ❶ obsession;
avoir la manie de to be obsessive
about ▷ Il a la manie du rangement.
He's obsessive about tidying up.
❷ habit ▷ J'essaie de respecter ses
petites manies. I try to go along with
her little ways.

manier [manje] vb to handle

manière [manjɛʀ] nf way; **de
manière à** so as to ▷ Nous sommes
partis tôt de manière à éviter la
circulation. We left early so as
to avoid the traffic.; **de toute
manière** in any case ▷ Je n'aurais pas
pu venir de toute manière. I couldn't
have come in any case.

manières [manjɛʀ] nfpl
❶ manners ▷ apprendre les bonnes
manières to learn good manners
❷ fuss ▷ Ne fais pas de manières :
mange ta soupe! Don't make a fuss:
eat your soup!

manifestant [manifɛstɑ̃] nm
demonstrator

manifestante [manifɛstɑ̃t] nf
demonstrator

manifestation [manifɛstasjɔ̃] nf
demonstration ▷ une manifestation
pour la paix a peace demonstration

manifester [manifɛste] vb to
demonstrate

manipuler [manipyle] vb ❶ to
handle ▷ Ce vase doit être manipulé
avec soin. This vase must be handled
with care. ❷ to manipulate ▷ Tous
les partis essaient de manipuler
l'opinion publique. All the parties
are trying to manipulate public
opinion. ❸ to rig ▷ L'élection a été
manipulée. The election was rigged.

Manitoba nm Manitoba

mannequin [mankɛ̃] nm model
▷ Elle est mannequin. She's a model.

manœuvrer [manœvʀe] vb to
manœuvre

manque [mɑ̃k] nm ❶ lack ▷ Le
manque de sommeil peut provoquer
toutes sortes de troubles. Lack
of sleep can cause all sorts of
problems. ❷ withdrawal ▷ un
drogué en état de manque a drug
addict suffering withdrawal
symptoms

manqué [mɑ̃ke] (f **manquée**) adj:
un garçon manqué a tomboy

manquer [mɑ̃ke] vb to miss ▷ Tu
n'as rien manqué : le film n'était pas
très bon. You didn't miss anything:
the movie wasn't very good. ▷ Il
manque des pages à ce livre. There
are some pages missing from
this book.; **Mes parents me**

manquent. I miss my parents.; **Ma sœur me manque**. I miss my sister.; **Il manque encore dix dollars**. We are still 10 dollars short.; **manquer de** to lack ▷ *La quiche manque de sel*. The quiche doesn't have enough salt. ▷ *Je trouve qu'il a manqué de tact.* I don't think he was very tactful.; **Il a manqué se tuer**. He nearly got killed.

manteau [mɑ̃to] (*pl* **manteaux**) *nm* coat

manuel [manɥɛl] (*f* **manuelle**) *adj* manual
▶ *nm* ❶ textbook ❷ handbook

maquereau [makro] (*pl* **maquereaux**) *nm* mackerel

maquette [makɛt] *nf* model ▷ *une maquette de bateau* a model boat

maquillage [makijaʒ] *nm* make-up

se maquiller [makije] *vb* to put on one's make-up ▷ *Je vais me maquiller en vitesse*. I'll just quickly put on my make-up.

marabout [marabu] (*f* **marabout**) *adj* grumpy ▷ *Elles sont marabouts ce matin.* They're grumpy this morning.

marais [marɛ] *nm* marsh

marbre [marbr(ə)] *nm* marble ▷ *une statue en marbre* a marble statue

marchand [marʃɑ̃] *nm*
❶ storekeeper ❷ merchant

marchande [marʃɑ̃d] *nf*
❶ storekeeper; **une marchande de fruits et de légumes** a fruit and vegetable seller ❷ merchant

marchander [marʃɑ̃de] *vb* to haggle

marchandise [marʃɑ̃diz] *nf* goods

marche [marʃ(ə)] *nf* ❶ step ▷ *Fais attention à la marche!* Mind

the step! ❷ walking ▷ *La marche me fait du bien.* Walking does me good.; **être en état de marche** to be in working order ▷ *Cette voiture est en parfait état de marche.* This car is in perfect running order.; **Ne montez jamais dans un train en marche**. Never try to get into a moving train.; **mettre en marche** to start ▷ *Comment est-ce qu'on met la machine à laver en marche?* How do you start the washing machine?; **la marche arrière** reverse gear; **faire marche arrière** (*vehicle*) to back up ❸ march ▷ *une marche militaire* a military march

marché [marʃe] *nm* market; **un marché aux puces** a flea market; **le marché noir** the black market; **un marché de producteurs** a farmers' market; **le marché du travail** the labour market

marcher [marʃe] *vb* ❶ to walk ▷ *Elle marche cinq kilomètres par jour.* She walks 5 kilometres every day. ❷ to run ▷ *Le métro marche normalement aujourd'hui.* The subway is running normally today. ❸ to work ▷ *Est-ce que l'ascenseur marche?* Is the elevator working? ❹ to go well ▷ *Est-ce que les affaires marchent actuellement?* Is business going well right now?; **Alors les études, ça marche?** (*informal*) How are you doing at school?; **faire marcher quelqu'un** to pull somebody's leg ▷ *Il essaie de te faire marcher.* He's pulling your leg.

marchette [marʃɛt] *nf* (*for babies, elderly*) walker

marcheur [marʃœr] *nm* walker

marcheuse [marʃøz] *nf* walker

mardi [mardi] *nm* ❶ Tuesday ▷ *Aujourd'hui, nous sommes mardi.* It's Tuesday today. ❷ on Tuesday ▷ *Ils reviennent mardi.* They're coming back on Tuesday.; **le mardi** on Tuesdays ▷ *Le mardi, j'ai mes cours de piano.* I have piano lessons on Tuesdays.; **tous les mardis** every Tuesday; **mardi dernier** last Tuesday; **mardi prochain** next Tuesday

mare [mar] *nf* pond

marécage [mareka3] *nm* marsh

marée [mare] *nf* tide ▷ *la marée haute* high tide ▷ *la marée basse* low tide ▷ *La marée monte.* The tide is coming in. ▷ *La marée descend.* The tide is going out.; **une marée noire** an oil slick

margarine [margarin] *nf* margarine

marge [mar3(ə)] *nf* margin

mari [mari] *nm* husband ▷ *son mari* her husband

mariage [marja3] *nm* ❶ marriage ❷ wedding ▷ *un mariage civil* a civil ceremony ▷ *un mariage religieux* a church wedding

marié [marje] (*f* **mariée**) *adj* married
▶ *nm* bridegroom; **les mariés** the bride and groom

mariée [marje] *nf* bride

se marier [marje] *vb* to marry ▷ *Elle s'est mariée avec un ami d'enfance.* She married a childhood friend.

marin [marɛ̃, -in] (*f* **marine**) *adj* sea ▷ *l'air marin* the sea air
▶ *nm* sailor

marinade [marinad] *nf* marinade; **les marinades** pickles

marine [marin] (*f*+*pl* **marine**) *adj*: **bleu marine** navy-blue ▷ *un chandail bleu marine* a navy-blue sweater
▶ *nf* navy ▷ *la marine canadienne* the Canadian navy

maringouin [marɛ̃gwɛ̃] *nm* mosquito ▷ *une piqûre de maringouin*

a mosquito bite

marionnette [marjɔnɛt] *nf* puppet

maritime [maritim] *adj* maritime ▷ *les provinces maritimes* the Maritime provinces; **les Maritimes** the Maritimes; **un chantier maritime** a shipyard

marmelade [marməlad] *nf*: **la marmelade de pommes** applesauce; **la marmelade d'oranges** marmalade

marmite [marmit] *nf* large cooking pot

marmonner [marmɔne] *vb* to mumble

marmotte [marmɔt] *nf* groundhog; **le jour de la marmotte** Groundhog Day

maroquinerie [marɔkinri] *nf* leather goods store

marquant [markã, -ãt] (*f* **marquante**) *adj* significant ▷ *un événement marquant* a significant event

marque [mark(ə)] *nf* ❶ mark ▷ *des marques de doigts* fingermarks ❷ make ▷ *De quelle marque est ta voiture?* What make is your car? ❸ brand ▷ *une grande marque de beurre d'arachide* a well-known brand of peanut butter; **l'image de marque** the public image ▷ *La ministre tient à son image de marque.* The minister cares about her public image.; **une marque déposée** a registered trademark; **À vos marques! prêts! partez!** Ready, set, go!

marquer [marke] *vb* ❶ to mark ▷ *Peux-tu marquer sur la carte où se trouve le village?* Can you mark where the village is on the map? ❷ to score ▷ *L'équipe canadienne a marqué dix points.* The Canadian team scored ten points. ❸ to have a lasting effect on ▷ *La guerre a marqué ces enfants.* War has had a lasting effect on these kids. ▷ *Cette peintre a marqué son époque.* This painter had a lasting effect on her time.

marrant [marɑ̃, -ɑ̃t] (f **marrante**) adj (informal) funny

marre [mar] adv (informal); **en avoir marre de quelque chose** to be fed up with something ▷ *J'en ai marre de faire la vaisselle.* I'm fed up with doing the dishes.

marron [marɔ̃] nm chestnut ▷ *les marrons grillés* roasted chestnuts ▶ adj (f+pl **marron**) brown ▷ *des chaussures marron* brown shoes

marronnier [marɔnje] nm chestnut tree

mars [mars] nm March; **en mars** in March

marteau [marto] (pl **marteaux**) nm hammer

martyriser [martirize] vb to batter ▷ *des enfants martyrisés* battered children

mascotte [maskɔt] nf mascot ▷ *La mascotte de notre équipe est le carcajou.* Our team's mascot is a wolverine.

masculin [maskylɛ̃, -in] (f **masculine**) adj ❶ men's ▷ *la mode masculine* men's fashion ❷ masculine ▷ *« Chat » est un nom masculin.* "Chat" is a masculine noun. ▷ *Elle a une allure assez masculine.* She looks rather masculine.

masque [mask(ə)] nm mask

massacre [masakr(ə)] nm massacre

massacrer [masakre] vb to massacre

massage [masaʒ] nm massage

masse [mas] nf ❶ (volume, weight) mass ▷ *la masse musculaire* muscular mass ❷ majority ▷ *la grande masse des jeunes* the vast majority of young people; **produire en masse** to mass-produce ▷ *Ces jouets sont produits en masse en Chine.* These toys are mass-produced in China.; **venir en masse** to come en masse ▷ *Les gens sont venus en masse pour accueillir Nelson Mandela.* People came en masse to welcome Nelson Mandela.

masser [mase] vb to massage; **se masser** to gather ▷ *Les manifestants se sont massés devant l'ambassade.* The demonstrators gathered in front of the embassy.

massif [masif, -iv] (f **massive**) adj ❶ (gold, silver, wood) solid ▷ *un bracelet en or massif* a solid gold bracelet ❷ massive ▷ *une dose massive d'antibiotiques* a massive dose of antibiotics ❸ mass ▷ *des départs massifs* a mass exodus

mat [mat] (f **mate**) adj matte ▷ *blanc mat* matte white ▷ *Je voudrais mes photos en fini mat.* I would like my photos matte.; **être mat** (chess) to be checkmated

match [matʃ] nm game ▷ *un match de hockey* a hockey game; **faire match nul** to be tied

matelas [matla] nm mattress ▷ *un matelas gonflable* an air mattress

matelot [matlo] nm sailor

matériaux [materjo] nmpl materials

matériel [materjɛl] nm ❶ equipment ▷ *du matériel de laboratoire* laboratory equipment ❷ (computer) hardware ▷ *C'est un problème de matériel ou de logiciel?* Is the problem with the hardware or the software? ❸ gear ▷ *Il a pris tout son matériel de pêche avec lui.* He took all his fishing gear with him.

maternel [matɛʀnɛl] (f **maternelle**) adj motherly ▷ Elle est très maternelle. She's very motherly.; **ma grand-mère maternelle** my mother's mother; **mon oncle maternel** my mother's brother

maternelle [matɛʀnɛl] nf kindergarten

maternité [matɛʀnite] nf: **le congé de maternité** maternity leave ▷ Notre professeur de musique est en congé de maternité. Our music teacher is on maternity leave.

mathématiques [matematik] nfpl mathematics

maths [mat] nfpl (informal) math

matière [matjɛʀ] nf subject ▷ Ma matière préférée, c'est le français. My favourite subject is French.; **sans matières grasses** fat-free; **les matières premières** raw materials

matin [matɛ̃] nm morning ▷ à trois heures du matin at 3 o'clock in the morning; **du matin au soir** from morning till night; **de bon matin** early in the morning

matinal [matinal, -o] (f **matinale**, mpl **matinaux**) adj morning ▷ Je fais mes étirements matinaux avant de déjeuner. I do my morning stretches before breakfast.; **être matinal** to be up early ▷ Tu es bien matinal aujourd'hui! You're up early today!

matinée [matine] nf morning ▷ Je t'appellerai demain dans la matinée. I'll call you sometime tomorrow morning. ▷ en début de matinée early in the morning

matou [matu] nm tomcat

maudire [modiʀ] vb to curse

maudit [modi, -it] (f **maudite**) adj (informal) darned ▷ Où est passé ce maudit parapluie? Where's that darned umbrella got to?

maussade [mosad] adj sulky

mauvais [mɔvɛ, -ɛz] (f **mauvaise**)

adj, adv ❶ bad ▷ une mauvaise note a bad mark ▷ Tu arrives au mauvais moment. You've come at a bad time.; **Il fait mauvais.** The weather's bad.; **être mauvais en** to be bad at ▷ Je suis mauvais en orthographe. I'm bad at spelling. ❷ poor ▷ de mauvaise qualité of poor quality ▷ Il est en mauvaise santé. His health is poor.; **Tu as mauvaise mine.** You don't look well. ❸ wrong ▷ Vous avez fait le mauvais numéro. You've dialled the wrong number.; **des mauvaises herbes** weeds; **sentir mauvais** to smell

maux [mo] (sg **le mal**) nmpl: **des maux de dents** toothache; **des maux de ventre** stomachache; **des maux de tête** headache

maximal [maksimal, -o] (f **maximale**, mpl **maximaux**) adj maximum

maximum [maksimɔm] nm maximum; **au maximum (1)** as much as one can ▷ Remplis le seau au maximum. Fill the pail as full as you can. **(2)** at the very most ▷ Ça va vous coûter deux cents dollars au maximum. It'll cost you 200 dollars at the very most.

mayonnaise [majɔnɛz] nf mayonnaise

mazout [mazut] nm (for furnace) oil

me [m(ə)] pron

> me changes to m' before a vowel and most words beginning with "h".

❶ me ▷ Elle me téléphone tous les jours. She phones me every day. ▷ Il m'attend depuis une heure. He's been waiting for me for an hour. ❷ to me ▷ Il me parle en français. He talks to me in French. ▷ Elle m'a expliqué la situation. She explained the situation to me. ❸ myself

▷ *Je vais me préparer quelque chose à manger.* I'm going to make myself something to eat.

With reflexive verbs, **me** is often not translated.

▷ *Je me lève à sept heures tous les matins.* I get up at 7 every morning.

mécanicien [mekanisjɛ̃] nm
mechanic

mécanicienne [mekanisjɛn] nf
mechanic

mécanique [mekanik] nf
❶ mechanics ❷ (of watch, clock)
mechanism

mécanisme [mekanism(ə)] nm
mechanism

méchamment [meʃamɑ̃]
adv nastily ▷ *Elle lui a répondu méchamment.* She answered her nastily.

méchanceté [meʃɑ̃ste] nf
meanness

méchant [meʃɑ̃, -ɑ̃t] (f **méchante**)
adj nasty ▷ *C'est un homme méchant.*
He's a nasty man.; **Ne sois pas méchant avec ton petit frère.**
Don't be mean to your little brother.; **« Attention, chien méchant »** "Beware of the dog"

mèche [mɛʃ] nf (of hair) lock

mécontent [mekɔ̃tɑ̃, -ɑ̃t] (f **mécontente**) adj: **mécontent de**
unhappy with ▷ *Elle est mécontente de sa coupe de cheveux.* She's unhappy with her haircut.

mécontentement [mekɔ̃tɑ̃tmɑ̃]
nm displeasure ▷ *Il a exprimé son mécontentement.* He expressed his displeasure.

médaille [medaj] nf medal

médecin [medsɛ̃] nmf doctor
▷ *aller chez le médecin* to go to the doctor

médecine [medsin] nf (subject)
medicine ▷ *Elle étudie la médecine.*
She's studying medicine.

médias [medja] nmpl media

médical [medikal, -o] (f **médicale**,
mpl **médicaux**) adj medical ▷ *la recherche médicale* medical research;
passer une visite médicale to have
a medical

médicament [medikamɑ̃] nm
(drug) medicine

médiéval [medjeval, -o] (f
médiévale, mpl **médiévaux**) adj
medieval

médiocre [medjɔkR(ə)] adj poor
▷ *des notes médiocres* poor marks

méduse [medyz] nf jellyfish

méfiance [mefjɑ̃s] nf mistrust

méfiant [mefjɑ̃, -ɑ̃t] (f **méfiante**)
adj mistrustful

se méfier [mefje] vb: **se méfier de
quelqu'un** to distrust somebody
▷ *Si j'étais toi, je me méfierais de lui.* I
wouldn't trust him if I were you.

mégaoctet [megaɔktɛ] nm
megabyte

mégarde [megaRd(ə)] nf: **par
mégarde** by mistake ▷ *J'ai emporté
ton livre par mégarde.* I took your
book by mistake.

meilleur [mɛjœR] (f **meilleure**) adj,
adv, n better ▷ *Ce serait meilleur avec
du fromage râpé.* It would be better
with grated cheese. ▷ *Il paraît que
le film est meilleur que le livre.* They
say that the film is better than the
book.; **le meilleur** the best ▷ *C'est
elle qui est la meilleure en sport.* She's
the best at sports. ▷ *Je préfère
garder le meilleur pour la fin.* I like to
keep the best for last.; **le meilleur
des deux** the better of the two;
meilleur marché cheaper ▷ *Les
vêtements sont meilleur marché dans
ce magasin.* Clothes are cheaper in
this store.

mélancolique [melɑ̃kɔlik] adj
gloomy

mélange [melɑ̃ʒ] nm mixture

mélanger [melãʒe] vb ❶ to mix ▷ *Mélange le tout.* Mix everything together. ❷ to muddle up ▷ *Tu mélanges tout!* You're muddling everything up!

mélangeur [melãʒœr] nm blender

mêlée [mele] nf scuffle

mêler [mele] vb. **se mêler** to mix ▷ *Elle ne cherche pas à se mêler aux autres.* She doesn't try to mix with the others.; **Mêle-toi de tes affaires!** (informal) Mind your own business!

mélodie [melɔdi] nf melody

melon [məlɔ̃] nm melon; **le melon d'eau** watermelon

membre [mãbʀ(ə)] nm ❶ limb ❷ member ▷ *un membre de la famille* a member of the family ▷ *les pays membres de l'OTAN* the member countries of NATO

même [mɛm] adj, adv, pron ❶ same ▷ *J'ai le même manteau.* I've got the same coat. ▷ *Tiens, c'est curieux, j'ai le même!* That's strange, I've got the same one!; **en même temps** at the same time; **moi-même** myself ▷ *Je l'ai fait moi-même.* I did it myself.; **toi-même** yourself ▷ *Est-ce que tu vas faire les travaux toi-même?* Are you going to do the work yourself?; **eux-mêmes** themselves ❷ even ▷ *Il n'a même pas pleuré.* He didn't even cry.

mémoire [memwaʀ] nf memory

menace [mənas] nf threat

menacer [mənase] vb to threaten

ménage [menaʒ] nm housework ▷ *faire le ménage* to do the housework; **une femme de ménage** a cleaning woman

ménager [menaʒe, -ɛʀ] (f **ménagère**) adj: **les travaux**

ménagers housework

mendiant [mãdjã] nm beggar

mendiante [mãdjãt] nf beggar

mendier [mãdje] vb to beg

mener [məne] vb to lead ▷ *Cette rue mène directement au parc.* This street leads straight to the park.; **Cela ne vous mènera à rien!** That will get you nowhere!

menottes [mənɔt] nfpl handcuffs

mensonge [mãsɔ̃ʒ] nm lie

mensuel [mãsɥɛl] (f **mensuelle**) adj monthly

mensurations [mãsyʀasjɔ̃] nfpl measurements

menteur [mãtœʀ] nm liar

menteuse [mãtøz] nf liar

menthe [mãt] nf mint

mentionner [mãsjɔne] vb to mention

mentir [mãtiʀ] vb to lie ▷ *Tu mens!* You're lying!

menton [mãtɔ̃] nm chin

menu [məny] (f **menue**) adj, adv ❶ slim ▷ *Elle est menue.* She's slim. ❷ very fine ▷ *Les oignons doivent être coupés menu.* The onions have to be cut up very fine.
▶ nm menu ▷ *le menu du jour* today's menu ▷ *le menu d'aide* the help menu

menuiserie [mənɥizʀi] nf woodwork

menuisier [mənɥizje] nm carpenter

menuisière [mənɥizjɛʀ] nf carpenter

mépris [mepʀi] nm contempt ▷ *Il nous a traités avec mépris.* He treated us with contempt.

méprisant [mepʀizã, -ãt] (f **méprisante**) adj contemptuous

mépriser [mepʀize] vb to despise

mer [mɛʀ] nf ❶ sea ▷ *en mer* at sea; **au bord de la mer** at the seaside ❷ tide ▷ *La mer est basse.* The tide is

out. ▷ *La mer sera haute à sept heures.*
It'll be high tide at 7 o'clock.

merci [mɛrsi] *excl* thank you
▷ *Merci de m'avoir raccompagné.*
Thank you for taking me home.;
merci beaucoup thank you very
much

mercredi [mɛrkrədi] *nm*
❶ Wednesday ▷ *Aujourd'hui, nous
sommes mercredi.* It's Wednesday
today. ❷ on Wednesday ▷ *Nous
comptons partir mercredi.* We plan to
leave on Wednesday.; **le mercredi**
on Wednesdays ▷ *Le musée est fermé
le mercredi.* The museum is shut on
Wednesdays.; **tous les mercredis**
every Wednesday; **mercredi
dernier** last Wednesday; **mercredi
prochain** next Wednesday

mère [mɛr] *nf* mother; **la fête des
Mères** Mother's Day

méridional [meridjɔnal, -o] (*f*
méridionale, *mpl* **méridionaux**)
adj southern ▷ *la partie méridionale
du Québec* the southern part of
Québec

meringue [mərɛ̃g] *nf* meringue

mériter [merite] *vb* to deserve; **se
mériter** to win ▷ *Vous pourriez vous
mériter un voyage pour deux aux chutes
Niagara!* You could win a trip for two
to Niagara Falls!

merle [mɛrl(ə)] *nm* blackbird

merveille [mɛrvɛj] *nf*: **Cet
ordinateur est une vraie
merveille!** This computer's
really wonderful!; **à merveille**
wonderfully ▷ *Elle joue du violon
à merveille.* She plays the violin
wonderfully.; **les sept merveilles
du monde** the seven wonders of
the world

merveilleux [mɛrvejø, -øz] (*f*
merveilleuse) *adj* extraordinary
▷ *Elle a un don merveilleux pour
l'écriture.* She has an extraordinary

gift for writing.

⬛ Be careful! **merveilleux** does
not mean **marvellous**.

mes [me] *adj* my ▷ *mes parents* my
parents

Mesdames [medam] *nf* ladies
▷ *Bonjour, Mesdames.* Good
morning, ladies.

Mesdemoiselles [medmwazɛl]
nf ladies ▷ *Bonjour, Mesdemoiselles.*
Good morning, ladies.

mesquin [mɛskɛ̃, -in] (*f*
mesquine) *adj* mean

message [mesaʒ] *nm* message

messagerie [mesaʒri] *nf*: **une
messagerie vocale** voice mail; **la
messagerie électronique** email;
la messagerie instantanée
instant messaging

messe [mɛs] *nf* mass ▷ *aller à la
messe* to go to mass

Messieurs [mesjø] *nm* gentlemen
▷ *Que puis-je faire pour vous,
Messieurs?* What can I do for you,
gentlemen?; **Messieurs,...** (*in
letter*) Dear Sirs,...

mesure [məzyr] *nf*
❶ measurement ▷ *J'ai pris les
mesures de la fenêtre.* I took the
measurements of the window.;
sur mesure tailor-made ▷ *un
costume sur mesure* a tailor-made
suit ❷ measure ▷ *L'école a pris
des mesures pour lutter contre le
vandalisme.* The school has taken
measures to combat vandalism.;
au fur et à mesure as one goes
along ▷ *Quand je cuisine, je préfère
faire la vaisselle au fur et à mesure.*
When I'm cooking, I prefer to wash
up as I go along.; **être en mesure
de faire quelque chose** to be in a
position to do something ▷ *Nous
ne sommes pas en mesure de vous
renseigner.* We are not in a position
to give you any information.

mesurer [məzyʁe] vb to measure
  ▷ *Mesurez la longueur et la largeur.*
  Measure the length and the width.;
  **Il mesure un mètre quatre-
  vingts.** He's 1 m 80 tall.
met [mɛ] vb see **mettre**
métal [metal, -o] (pl **métaux**)
  nm metal
métallique [metalik] adj metallic
météo [meteo] nf weather forecast
  ▷ *Qu'est-ce que dit la météo pour cet
  après-midi?* What's the weather
  forecast for this afternoon?
méthode [metɔd] nf method ▷ *des
  méthodes d'enseignement modernes*
  modern teaching methods; **une
  méthode de guitare** a teach-
  yourself-guitar book
métier [metje] nm job ▷ *Tu aimerais
  faire quel métier plus tard?* What job
  would you like to do when you're
  older?
métis [metis] (f **métisse**) adj, n
  Métis ▷ *Les communautés métisses
  datent de 1690.* Métis communities
  date back to 1690.; **un Métis** (man)
  a Métis; **une Métisse** (woman)
  a Métis
mètre [mɛtʁ(ə)] nm metre; **un
  mètre à ruban** a tape measure
métro [metʁo] nm subway
  ▷ *prendre le métro* to take the
  subway
mets [mɛ] vb see **mettre**
metteur en scène [metœʁ-] (pl
  metteurs en scène) nm ❶ (of
  play) producer ❷ (of film) director
metteuse en scène [metøz-]
  (pl **metteuses en scène**) nf ❶ (of
  play) producer ❷ (of film) director
mettre [mɛtʁ(ə)] vb ❶ to put ▷ *Où
  est-ce que tu as mis les clés?* Where
  did you put the keys? ❷ to put
  on ▷ *Je mets mon manteau et j'arrive.*
  I'll put on my coat and then I'll be
  ready. ▷ *Il fait froid. Je vais mettre le*

chauffage. It's cold. I'm going to put
the heating on. ❸ to wear ▷ *Elle ne
met pas souvent de jupe.* She doesn't
often wear a skirt. ▷ *Je n'ai rien à me
mettre!* I've got nothing to wear!
❹ to take ▷ *Combien de temps as-tu
mis pour aller à Chapleau?* How long
did it take you to get to Chapleau?
▷ *Il met des heures à se préparer.*
He takes hours to get ready.;
mettre à pied to lay off; **mettre
quelqu'un en échec** to bodycheck
somebody; **mettre en marche** to
start ▷ *Comment met-on la machine
à laver en marche?* How do you start
the washing machine?; **mettre
les points sur les i** (make clear) to
spell something out; **Vous pouvez
vous mettre là.** You can sit there.;
se mettre au lit to get into bed; **se
mettre en maillot de bain** to put
on one's swimsuit; **se mettre à**
to start ▷ *Il s'est mis à la peinture à
cinquante ans.* He started painting
when he was 50. ▷ *Il est temps de se
mettre au travail.* It's time to start
work. ▷ *Elle s'est mise à pleurer.* She
started crying.
meuble [mœbl(ə)] nm piece of
furniture ▷ *Je me suis cogné contre
un meuble.* I bumped into a piece
of furniture. ▷ *Ce magasin vend de
beaux meubles.* This store sells nice
furniture.
meublé [mœble] nm furnished
apartment
meubler [mœble] vb to furnish
meurtre [mœʁtʁ(ə)] nm murder
meurtrier [mœʁtʁije] nm
murderer
meurtrière [mœʁtʁijɛʁ] nf
murderess
mi [mi] nm ❶ E ▷ *mi bémol* E flat
❷ mi ▷ *do, mi...* do, re, mi...
mi- [mi] pref ❶ half- ▷ *mi-clos*
half-shut ❷ mid- ▷ *à la mi-janvier* in

mid-January

miauler [mjole] *vb* to meow

mi-chemin [miʃmɛ̃]: **à mi-chemin**
adv halfway

micro [mikʁo] *nm* microphone

microbe [mikʁɔb] *nm* germ

micro-ondes *nm* microwave oven

microscope [mikʁɔskɔp] *nm*
microscope

midi [midi] *nm* ❶ noon ▷ *à midi*
at noon; **midi et demi** 12:30
❷ lunchtime ▷ *On a bien mangé
à midi.* We had a good meal at
lunchtime.

mie [mi] *nf* breadcrumbs

miel [mjɛl] *nm* honey

mien [mjɛ̃] *pron:* **le mien** mine
▷ *Ce vélo-là, c'est le mien.* That bike
is mine.

mienne [mjɛn] *pron:* **la mienne**
mine ▷ *Cette valise-là, c'est la mienne.*
That suitcase is mine.

miennes [mjɛn] *pron:* **les miennes**
mine ▷ *Heureusement que tu as tes
clés : j'ai oublié les miennes.* It's lucky
you've got your keys: I forgot mine.

miens [mjɛ̃] *pron:* **les miens** mine
▷ *Ces CD-là, ce sont les miens.* Those
CDs are mine.

miette [mjɛt] *nf (of bread, cake)*
crumb

mieux [mjø] *adv, adj, n* better ▷ *Je
la connais mieux que son frère.* I know
her better than her brother. ▷ *Elle
va mieux.* She's better. ▷ *Les cheveux
courts lui vont mieux.* She looks
better with short hair.; **Il vaut
mieux que tu appelles ta mère.**
You'd better phone your mother.;
le mieux the best ▷ *C'est la région
que je connais le mieux.* It's the area
I know best.; **faire de son mieux**
to do one's best ▷ *Essaie de faire de
ton mieux.* Try to do your best.; **de
mieux en mieux** better and better;
au mieux at best

mignon [miɲɔ̃, -ɔn] *(f* **mignonne**)
adj cute ▷ *Qu'est-ce qu'il est mignon!*
Isn't he cute!

migraine [migʁɛn] *nf* migraine
▷ *J'ai la migraine.* I have a migraine.

mijoter [miʒɔte] *vb* to simmer

milieu [miljø] *(pl* **milieux**) *nm*
❶ middle; **au milieu de** in the
middle of ▷ *Place le vase au milieu de
la table.* Put the vase in the middle
of the table.; **au beau milieu
de** in the middle of ▷ *Quelqu'un
a sonné à la porte au beau milieu
de la nuit.* Somebody rang the
doorbell in the middle of the
night. ❷ background ▷ *le milieu
familial* the family background
▷ *Il vient d'un milieu modeste.* He
comes from a modest background.
❸ environment ▷ *le milieu marin*
the marine environment

militaire [militɛʁ] *adj* military
▷ *faire son service militaire* to do one's
military service
▶ *n* serviceman, servicewoman;
Son père est militaire. Her father
is in the armed forces.; **un militaire
de carrière** a professional soldier

mille [mil] *num* a thousand ▷ *mille
dollars* a thousand dollars ▷ *deux
mille personnes* two thousand
people

millefeuille [milfœj] *nm*
A **millefeuille** is a rectangular
dessert consisting of several
layers of flaky puff pastry with a
mixture of fruit jelly and cream
between them.

millénaire [milenɛʁ] *nm*
millennium ▷ *le troisième millénaire*
the third millennium

millénium [milenjɔm] *nm*
millennium

milliard [miljaʁ] *nm* billion ▷ *cinq
milliards de dollars* five billion dollars

milliardaire [miljaʁdɛʁ] *nmf*

billionaire

millier [milje] nm thousand ▷ *des milliers de personnes* thousands of people; **par milliers** by the thousand

milligramme [miligram] nm milligram

millimètre [milimetʀ(ə)] nm millimetre

million [miljɔ̃] nm million ▷ *deux millions de personnes* two million people

millionnaire [miljɔnɛʀ] nmf millionaire

mime [mim] nmf mime artist

mimer [mime] vb to mimic

mince [mɛ̃s] adj ❶ thin ▷ *une mince tranche de jambon* a thin slice of ham ❷ slim ▷ *Il est grand et mince.* He's tall and slim.

minceur [mɛ̃sœʀ] nf ❶ thinness ▷ *la minceur des murs* the thinness of the walls ❷ (*of person*) slimness

mine [min] nf ❶ (*facial*) expression; **avoir bonne mine** to look well; **Il a mauvaise mine.** He doesn't look well.; **avoir une mine fatiguée** to look tired ❷ appearance ▷ *Il ne faut pas juger les gens d'après leur mine.* You shouldn't judge people by their appearance. ❸ (*of pencil*) lead ❹ mine ▷ *une mine de charbon* a coal mine; **faire mine de faire quelque chose** to pretend to do something ▷ *Elle a fait mine de le croire.* She pretended to believe him.; **mine de rien** somehow or other ▷ *Elle a réussi mine de rien à y entrer.* Somehow or other she got in.

minéral [mineʀal, -o] (f **minérale**, mpl **minéraux**) adj mineral ▷ *l'eau minérale* mineral water

mineur [minœʀ] (f **mineure**) adj minor

▶ nm ❶ (*underage boy*) minor; **les**

mineurs minors ▷ *Il est illégal de vendre des cigarettes aux mineurs.* It's illegal to sell cigarettes to minors. ❷ miner ▷ *Mon grand-père était mineur.* My grandfather was a miner.

mineure [minœʀ] nf (*underage girl*) minor

minijupe [miniʒyp] nf miniskirt

minimal [minimal, -o] (f **minimale**, mpl **minimaux**) adj minimum

minimum [minimɔm] nm minimum ▷ *Elle en fait le minimum.* She does the absolute minimum.; **au minimum** at the very least

ministère [ministɛʀ] nm ministry ▷ *le ministère de l'Environnement* the Ministry of the Environment

ministre [ministʀ(ə)] nmf minister ▷ *la ministre de la Santé* the Minister of Health

minorité [minɔʀite] nf minority

minuit [minɥi] nm midnight ▷ *à minuit et quart* at a quarter past midnight

minuscule [minyskyl] adj tiny
▶ nf lower-case letter

minute [minyt] nf minute; **à la minute** just this minute ▷ *Je viens de l'appeler à la minute.* I just called him this minute.

minutieux [minysjø, -øz] (f **minutieuse**) adj meticulous; **C'est un travail minutieux.** It's a fiddly job.

miracle [miʀakl(ə)] nm miracle

miroir [miʀwaʀ] nm mirror

mis [mi] vb see **mettre**

mis [mi, miz] (f **mise**) adj: **bien mis** well-dressed ▷ *Elle est toujours bien mise.* She's always well-dressed.

mise [miz] nf: **être de mise** to be appropriate ▷ *Ces paroles blessantes ne sont pas de mise.* These hurtful remarks are not appropriate.;

une mise à jour an update; **la mise à pied** layoff; **la mise au jeu** (hockey) face-off; **la mise en page** (document) layout

miser [mize] vb (informal) to count on ▷ On ne peut pas miser là-dessus. We can't count on it.

misérable [mizerabl(ə)] adj
❶ destitute ▷ une famille misérable a destitute family; **d'aspect misérable** shabby-looking
❷ pitiful ▷ des conditions de vie misérable pitiful living conditions

misère [mizer] nf extreme poverty; **un salaire de misère** starvation wages

missionnaire [misjɔner] nmf missionary

mitaine [miten] nf mitten; **la mitaine à four** oven mitt

mi-temps [mitɑ̃] nf ❶ (of game) half ▷ la première mi-temps the first half ▷ la deuxième mi-temps the second half ❷ half-time ▷ Je lui parlerai à la mi-temps. I'll speak to her at half-time.; **travailler à mi-temps** to work part-time

miteux [mitø, -øz] (f **miteuse**) adj
❶ shabby ▷ un imperméable miteux a shabby raincoat ❷ pathetic

mixte [mikst(ə)] adj: **un mariage mixte** a mixed marriage; **une peau mixte** combination skin

Mlle (pl **Mlles**) abbr (= Mademoiselle) Miss ▷ Mlle Renoir Miss Renoir
○ Mlle is rarely used for single women any more, except in reference to a girl. It is better to use Mme, the French equivalent of Ms, in person or in a letter.

Mme (pl **Mmes**) abbr (= Madame) Mrs ▷ Mme Leroy Mrs Leroy

mobile [mɔbil] nm motive ▷ Quel était le mobile du crime? What was the motive for the crime?

mobilier [mɔbilje] nm furniture

mocassin [mɔkasɛ̃] nm moccasin

moche [mɔʃ] adj (informal) awful
▷ Cette couleur est vraiment moche. That colour is really awful.; **Il a la grippe. C'est moche pour lui.** He's got the flu. That's a drag for him.

mode [mɔd] nf fashion ▷ être à la mode to be fashionable
▶ nm: **le mode d'emploi** directions for use; **le mode de vie** the way of life

modèle [mɔdɛl] nm ❶ model ▷ Le nouveau modèle sort en septembre. The new model is coming out in September. ❷ (of clothes) style ▷ Est-ce que vous avez le même modèle en plus grand? Have you got the same style in a bigger size?

modéré [mɔdere] (f **modérée**) adj moderate

moderne [mɔdɛrn(ə)] adj modern

moderniser [mɔdɛrnize] vb to modernize

modeste [mɔdɛst(ə)] adj modest
▷ Ne sois pas si modeste! Don't be so modest!

modestie [mɔdɛsti] nf modesty

moelleux [mwalø, -øz] (f **moelleuse**) adj soft ▷ un coussin moelleux a soft cushion

mœurs [mœr] nfpl social attitudes; **l'évolution des mœurs** changing attitudes

moi [mwa] pron me ▷ Coucou, c'est moi! Hello, it's me!; **Moi, je pense que tu as tort.** I personally think you're wrong.; **à moi** mine ▷ Ce livre n'est pas à moi. This book isn't mine. ▷ un ami à moi a friend of mine

moi-même [mwamɛm] pron myself ▷ J'ai tricoté ce chandail moi-même. I knitted this sweater myself.

moindre [mwɛ̃dr(ə)] adj: **le moindre** the slightest ▷ Il ne fait pas le moindre effort. He doesn't make the slightest effort. ▷ Je n'en ai pas la moindre idée. I haven't the slightest idea.

moine [mwan] *nm* monk

moineau [mwano] (*pl* moineaux) *nm* sparrow

moins [mwɛ̃] *adv, prep* **❶** less ▷ *Ça coûte moins de deux cents dollars.* It costs less than 200 dollars. **❷** fewer ▷ *Il y a moins de gens aujourd'hui.* There are fewer people today.; **il est cinq heures moins dix.** It's 10 to 5. **❸** minus ▷ *quatre moins trois* 4 minus 3 ▷ *Il a fait moins cinq la nuit dernière.* It was minus 5 last night.; **le moins** the least ▷ *C'est le modèle le moins cher.* It's the least expensive model. ▷ *Ce sont les plages qui sont les moins polluées.* These are the least polluted beaches. ▷ *C'est l'album que j'aime le moins.* This is the album I like least.; **de moins en moins** less and less ▷ *Elle vient nous voir de moins en moins.* She comes to see us less and less often.; **Tu as trois ans de moins que moi.** You're three years younger than me.; **au moins** at least ▷ *Ne te plains pas : au moins il ne pleut pas!* Don't complain: at least it's not raining!; **à moins que** unless

> à moins que is followed by a verb in the subjunctive.

▷ *Je te retrouverai à dix heures à moins que le train n'ait du retard.* I'll meet you at 10 o'clock unless the train is late.

mois [mwa] *nm* month

moisi [mwazi] *nm* mould ▷ *Il y a du moisi sur le fromage.* There is mould on the cheese.; **Ça sent le moisi.** It smells musty.

moisir [mwazir] *vb* to go mouldy ▷ *Le pain a moisi.* The bread has gone mouldy.

moisson [mwasɔ̃] *nf* harvest

moite [mwat] *adj* sweaty ▷ *J'ai toujours les mains moites.* My hands are always sweaty.

moitié [mwatje] *nf* half ▷ *Il a mangé la moitié du gâteau à lui seul.* He ate half the cake all by himself.; **la moitié du temps** half the time; **à la moitié de** halfway through ▷ *Elle est partie à la moitié du film.* She left halfway through the movie.; **à moitié** half ▷ *Ton verre est encore à moitié plein.* Your glass is still half-full. ▷ *Ce manteau était à moitié prix.* This coat was half-price.; **partager moitié moitié** to split fifty-fifty ▷ *On partage moitié moitié, d'accord?* We'll split it fifty-fifty, OK?

molaire [mɔlɛr] *nf* back tooth

molle [mɔl] *adj* lethargic ▷ *Je la trouve un peu molle.* I find her a bit lethargic.; *see* **mou**

mollet [mɔlɛ] *nm* (*of leg*) calf
▶ *adj:* **un œuf mollet** a soft-boiled egg

moment [mɔmɑ̃] *nm* moment; **en ce moment** at the moment ▷ *Nous avons beaucoup de travail en ce moment.* We have a lot of work at the moment.; **pour le moment** for the moment ▷ *Nous restons ici pour le moment.* We're staying here for the moment.; **au moment où** just as ▷ *Il est arrivé au moment où j'allais partir.* He turned up just as I was leaving.; **à ce moment-là (1)** at that point ▷ *À ce moment-là, on a vu arriver la police.* At that point, we saw the police coming. **(2)** in that case ▷ *À ce moment-là, je devrai partir plus tôt.* In that case I'll have to leave earlier.; **à tout moment (1)** at any moment ▷ *Elle peut arriver à tout moment.* She could arrive at any moment. **(2)** constantly ▷ *Il nous dérange à tout moment pour des riens.* He's constantly bothering us about nothing.; **sur le moment** at the time ▷ *Sur le moment je n'ai rien dit.* At the time I didn't say anything.; **par moments** at times ▷ *Elle se sent seule par moments.* She feels lonely at times.

momentané [mɔmɑ̃tane] (f **momentanée**) *adj* momentary

momie [mɔmi] *nf* (Egyptian) mummy

mon [mɔ̃] (f **ma**, pl **mes**) *adj* my ▷ *mon frère* my brother ▷ *mon ami* my friend

monarchie [mɔnaʀʃi] *nf* monarchy

monastère [mɔnastɛʀ] *nm* monastery

monde [mɔ̃d] *nm* ❶ world ▷ *faire le tour du monde* to go around the world ❷ people ▷ *Il y avait beaucoup de monde au concert.* There were a lot of people at the concert. ▷ *peu de monde* not many people; **Il y a du monde.** There are a lot of people.

mondial [mɔ̃djal, -o] (f **mondiale**, mpl **mondiaux**) *adj* ❶ world ▷ *la population mondiale* the world population ❷ world-wide ▷ *une crise mondiale* a world-wide crisis

moniteur [mɔnitœʀ] *nm* ❶ instructor ▷ *un moniteur de voile* a sailing instructor ❷ monitor ▷ *le moniteur de mon ordinateur* my computer monitor

monitrice [mɔnitʀis] *nf* instructor ▷ *une monitrice de ski* a ski instructor

monnaie [mɔnɛ] *nf*: **une pièce de monnaie** a coin; **avoir de la monnaie** to have change ▷ *Est-ce que tu as de la monnaie?* Do you have any change? ▷ *Est-ce que vous avez la monnaie de dix dollars?* Do you have change for 10 dollars?; **rendre la monnaie à quelqu'un** to give

somebody their change

monopoliser [mɔnɔpɔlize] *vb* to monopolize ▷ *monopoliser la conversation* to monopolize the conversation ▷ *Tu monopolises le téléphone!* You're monopolizing the phone!

monotone [mɔnɔtɔn] *adj* monotonous

Monsieur [məsjø] (pl **Messieurs**) *nm* ❶ Mr ▷ *Monsieur Dupont* Mr Dupont ❷ man ▷ *Il y a un monsieur qui veut te voir.* There's a man to see you. ❸ Sir ▷ *Monsieur,...* Dear Sir,... ❹ (in letter) ▷ *Monsieur! Vous avez oublié votre parapluie!* Sir! You forgot your umbrella!

monstre [mɔ̃stʀ(ə)] *nm* monster ▶ *adj*: **Nous avons un travail monstre.** We have a terrific amount of work.

mont [mɔ̃] *nm* mount; **le mont Logan** Mount Logan

montagne [mɔ̃taɲ] *nf* mountain ▷ *de hautes montagnes* high mountains ▷ *Nous passons nos vacances à la montagne.* We spend our holidays in the mountains.; **les montagnes russes** roller coaster; **se faire une montagne de quelque chose** to blow something out of proportion ▷ *Ils s'en font une montagne.* They're blowing it out of proportion.; **Tu te fais une montagne d'un petit incident de rien.** You're making a mountain out of a molehill.

montagneux [mɔ̃taɲø, -øz] (f **montagneuse**) *adj* mountainous ▷ *une région montagneuse* a mountainous area

montant [mɔ̃tɑ̃, -ɑ̃t] (f **montante**) *adj* ❶ rising ▷ *la marée montante* the rising tide ▷ *une étoile montante* a rising star ❷ high ▷ *un manteau à col montant* a high-necked coat

monter [mɔ̃te] vb ❶ to go up
▷ Elle a du mal à monter les escaliers. She has difficulty going up stairs. ▷ Les prix ont encore monté. Prices have gone up again. ❷ to assemble ▷ Est-ce que ces étagères sont difficiles à monter? Are these shelves difficult to assemble?; **monter dans** to board ▷ Il est temps de monter dans l'avion. It's time to board the plane.; **monter sur** to climb on ▷ Tu vas devoir monter sur une chaise pour changer l'ampoule. You'll have to climb on a chair to change the light bulb.; **monter à cheval** to ride; **se monter à** (total) to amount to ▷ Ses achats se montaient à quinze dollars. His purchases amounted to 15 dollars.; **se monter la tête** to get worked up ▷ Elle s'est montée la tête pour rien. She got worked up over nothing.

montre [mɔ̃tʀ(ə)] nf watch

montrer [mɔ̃tʀe] vb to show
▷ Est-ce que vous pouvez me montrer le musée sur le plan? Can you show me the museum on the map?

monture [mɔ̃tyʀ] nf (of glasses) frames

monument [mɔnymɑ̃] nm monument

se moquer [mɔke] vb: **se moquer de (1)** to make fun of ▷ Ils se sont moqués de mes chaussures jaunes. They made fun of my yellow shoes. **(2)** (informal) not to care about ▷ Il se moque complètement de la mode. He couldn't care less about fashion.

moquette [mɔket] nf broadloom

moqueur [mɔkœʀ, -øz] (f **moqueuse**) adj mocking

moral [mɔʀal, -o] (mpl **moraux**) adj moral ▷ une obligation morale a moral obligation
▸ nm: **Elle a le moral.** She's in good spirits.; **J'ai le moral à zéro.** I'm feeling really down.

morale [mɔʀal] nf ❶ moral ▷ La morale de cette histoire est... The moral of the story is...; **faire la morale à quelqu'un** to lecture somebody ❷ morality ▷ la morale traditionnelle traditional morality

morceau [mɔʀso] (pl **morceaux**) nm piece ▷ un morceau de pain a piece of bread

mordiller [mɔʀdije] vb to nibble
▷ Ne mordille pas ton crayon. Don't nibble on your pencil.

mordre [mɔʀd(ʀ)] vb to bite

mordu [mɔʀdy] (f **mordue**) adj: **Il est mordu de jazz.** (informal) He's crazy about jazz.

morne [mɔʀn(ə)] adj ❶ drab ▷ un décor morne a drab décor ❷ (person, weather) gloomy ▷ Pourquoi as-tu l'air tellement morne? Why are you looking so gloomy? ▷ un temps morne gloomy weather

morse [mɔʀs(ə)] nm walrus

morsure [mɔʀsyʀ] nf bite

mort [mɔʀ] (f **morte**) adj dead
▸ adj dead ▷ Nous avons trouvé un oiseau mort. We found a dead bird. ▷ Anne Hébert, écrivaine canadienne, est morte en 2000. Canadian writer Anne Hébert died in 2000.; **Il était mort de peur.** He was scared to death.; **Je suis morte de fatigue.** I'm dead tired.

mortel [mɔʀtel] (f **mortelle**) adj ❶ deadly ▷ un poison mortel a deadly poison ▷ Ces réunions de famille sont mortelles! (informal) These family gatherings are deadly! ❷ fatal ▷ une chute mortelle a fatal fall

morue [mɔʀy] nf cod

mosquée [mɔske] nf mosque

mot [mo] nm ❶ word ▷ mot à mot word for word; **des mots croisés** a crossword; **le mot de passe**

the password ❷ note ▷ *Je vais lui écrire un mot pour lui dire qu'on arrive.* I'll write her a note to say we're coming.

motard [mɔtaʀ] nm motorcyclist

motarde [mɔtaʀd(ə)] nf motorcyclist

mot-clé nm keyword ▷ *Entrez le mot-clé dans le moteur de recherche.* Enter the keyword in the search engine.

moteur [mɔtœʀ] nm engine; **un bateau à moteur** a motor boat; **un moteur de recherche** a search engine

motif [mɔtif] nm pattern ▷ *des rideaux avec un motif d'oiseaux* curtains with a bird pattern; **sans motif** for no reason ▷ *Il s'est fâché sans motif.* He got angry for no reason.

motivé [mɔtive] (f **motivée**) adj motivated

moto [mɔto] nf motorbike; **la moto tout-terrain** trail bike

motocycliste [mɔtɔsiklist(ə)] nmf motorcyclist

motoneige [mɔtɔnɛʒ] nf snowmobile

motoneigiste [mɔtɔnɛʒist] nmf snowmobiler

mou [mu, mɔl] (f **molle**) adj ❶ soft ▷ *Mon matelas est trop mou.* My mattress is too soft. ❷ lethargic ▷ *Je le trouve un peu mou.* I find him a bit lethargic. ❸ limp ▷ **devenir mou** to go limp

mouche [muʃ] nf (insect) fly; **la mouche noire** black fly; **prendre la mouche** to get bent out of shape

se moucher [muʃe] vb to blow one's nose

mouchoir [muʃwaʀ] nm handkerchief; **un mouchoir en papier** a tissue

moudre [mudʀ(ə)] vb to grind

moue [mu] nf pout; **faire la moue** to pout

mouette [mwɛt] nf seagull

moufette [mufɛt] nf skunk

mouillé [muje] (f **mouillée**) adj wet

mouiller [muje] vb to get wet ▷ *J'ai mouillé les manches de mon chandail.* I got the sleeves of my sweater wet.; **se mouiller** to get wet ▷ *Attention, tu vas te mouiller!* Careful, you'll get wet!

moulant [mulɑ̃, -ɑ̃t] (f **moulante**) adj slinky ▷ *une robe moulante* a slinky dress

moule [mul] nf mussel
 ▶ nm: **un moule à gâteaux** a cake tin

moulin [mulɛ̃] nm mill

moulu [muly] vb see **moudre**

mourir [muʀiʀ] vb to die; **mourir de faim** to starve ▷ *Des centaines de personnes sont mortes de faim.* Hundreds of people starved to death.; **Je meurs de faim!** I'm starving!; **mourir de froid** to die of exposure; **Je meurs de froid!** I'm freezing!; **mourir d'envie de faire quelque chose** to be dying to do something ▷ *Je meurs d'envie d'aller me baigner.* I'm dying to have a swim.

mousse [mus] nf ❶ moss ▷ *un rocher recouvert de mousse* a rock covered with moss ❷ (on soft drink) froth ❸ (of soap, shampoo) lather ❹ mousse ▷ *une mousse au chocolat* a chocolate mousse ▷ *une mousse au saumon* a salmon mousse; **la mousse à raser** shaving foam

moustache [mustaʃ] nf moustache; **les moustaches** whiskers

moustiquaire [mustikɛʀ] nmf ❶ (on window) screen ❷ mosquito net

In Canada, **moustiquaire** is often masculine. It is usually feminine in other French-speaking countries.

moustique [mustik] *nm* mosquito

moutarde [mutaʀd(ə)] *nf* mustard

mouton [mutɔ̃] *nm* ❶ sheep ▷ *une peau de mouton* a sheepskin ❷ mutton ▷ *un gigot de mouton* a leg of mutton

mouvement [muvmɑ̃] *nm* movement

mouvementé [muvmɑ̃te] (*f* **mouvementée**) *adj* eventful ▷ *une époque mouvementée de l'histoire du Canada* an eventful period in Canada's history

moyen [mwajɛ̃, -ɛn] (*f* **moyenne**) *adj* ❶ average ▷ *Je suis plutôt moyenne en langues.* I'm just average at languages. ❷ medium ▷ *Elle est de taille moyenne.* She's of medium height.; **le Moyen Âge** the Middle Ages; **le Moyen Orient** the Middle East
▶ *nm* way ▷ *Quel est le meilleur moyen de le convaincre?* What's the best way to convince him?; **Je n'en ai pas les moyens.** I can't afford it.; **Ils n'ont pas les moyens de s'acheter une voiture.** They can't afford to buy a car.; **un moyen de transport** a means of transport; **par tous les moyens** by every possible means

moyenne [mwajɛn] *nf*: **avoir la moyenne** to get a passing grade ▷ *J'espère avoir la moyenne en maths.* I hope to get a passing grade in math.; **en moyenne** on average; **la moyenne d'âge** the average age

muet [mɥɛ, -ɛt] (*f* **muette**) *adj* mute; **un film muet** a silent film

multiculturel [myltikyltyʀɛl] (*f* **multiculturelle**) *adj* multicultural

multiple [myltipl(ə)] *adj* numerous ▷ *en de multiples occasions* on numerous occasions

multiplier [myltiplije] *vb* to multiply

municipal [mynisipal, -o] (*f* **municipale**, *mpl* **municipaux**) *adj*: **une élection municipale** a municipal election; **les règlements municipaux** city by-laws; **la bibliothèque municipale** the public library

municipalité [mynisipalite] *nf* town council

munir [myniʀ] *vb*: **munir quelqu'un de** to equip someone with; **se munir de** to equip oneself with

munitions [mynisjɔ̃] *nfpl* ammunition

mur [myʀ] *nm* wall

mûr [myʀ] (*f* **mûre**) *adj* ❶ (*fruit*) ripe ❷ (*person*) mature

mûre [myʀ] *nf* blackberry

mûrir [myʀiʀ] *vb* ❶ to ripen ▷ *Les fraises ont mis du temps à mûrir.* The strawberries took a while to ripen. ❷ to make mature ▷ *Cette expérience l'a beaucoup mûrie.* That experience has made her much more mature.

murmurer [myʀmyʀe] *vb* to whisper ▷ *Il m'a murmuré à l'oreille qu'il allait partir.* He whispered in my ear that he was going to go.

muscade [myskad] *nf* nutmeg

muscle [myskl(ə)] *nm* muscle

musclé [myskle] (*f* **musclée**) *adj* muscular

museau [myzo] (*pl* **museaux**) *nm* muzzle

musée [myze] *nm* museum

musical [myzikal, -o] (*f* **musicale**, *mpl* **musicaux**) *adj* musical; **avoir l'oreille musicale** to be musical

music-hall [myzikol] (pl **les music-halls**) nm variety ▷ *une chanteuse de music-hall* a variety singer

musicien [myzisjɛ̃] nm musician ▷ *Il est musicien de jazz.* He's a jazz musician.

musicienne [myzisjɛn] nf musician ▷ *Elle est musicienne de rue.* She's a street musician.

musique [myzik] nf music

musulman [myzylmã, -an] (f **musulmane**) adj, n Muslim; **un musulman** (man) a Muslim; **une musulmane** (woman) a Muslim

mutation [mytasjɔ̃] nf (job) transfer ▷ *Il a demandé sa mutation à Winnipeg.* He asked for a transfer to Winnipeg.

mye [mi] nf clam ▷ *une chaudrée de myes* clam chowder

myope [mjɔp] adj short-sighted

mystère [mistɛʀ] nm mystery

mystérieux [misteʀjø, -øz] (f **mystérieuse**) adj mysterious

mythe [mit] nm myth

n

n' [n] pron see **ne**

nage [naʒ] nf: **traverser une rivière à la nage** to swim across a river; **être en nage** to be sweating profusely

nageoire [naʒwaʀ] nf fin

nager [naʒe] vb to swim

nageur [naʒœʀ] nm swimmer

nageuse [naʒøz] nf swimmer

naïf [naif, naiv] (f **naïve**) adj naïve

nain [nɛ̃] nm dwarf

naine [nɛn] nf dwarf

naissance [nɛsɑ̃s] nf birth; **votre date de naissance** your date of birth; **de naissance** from birth ▷ *Il est sourd de naissance.* He was born deaf.

naître [nɛtʀ(ə)] vb to be born; **Il est né en 1982.** He was born in 1982.

nappe [nap] nf tablecloth

napperon [napʀɔ̃] nm placemat

narine [naʀin] nf nostril

natal [natal] (f **natale**, mpl **natals**)

adj native ▷ *mon pays natal* my native country

natation [natasjɔ̃] *nf* swimming ▷ *La natation est mon sport favori.* Swimming is my favourite sport.; **faire de la natation** to go swimming

nation [nasjɔ̃] *nf* nation ▷ *les Nations unies* the United Nations

national [nasjɔnal, -o] (*f* **nationale**, *mpl* **nationaux**) *adj* national; **la fête nationale espagnole** the national day of Spain

nationalité [nasjɔnalite] *nf* nationality

nature [natyʀ] *nf* nature (*pl* **nature**)
▶ *adj* plain ▷ *un yogourt nature* a plain yogurt ▷ *des framboises nature* plain strawberries

naturel [natyʀɛl] (*f* **naturelle**) *adj* natural

naturellement [natyʀɛlmɑ̃] *adv* of course ▷ «*Vous viendrez à notre fête?* » « *Naturellement!* » "Are you coming to our party?" "Of course!" ▷ *Naturellement, elle est encore en retard.* Of course, she's late again.

naufrage [nofʀaʒ] *nm* shipwreck

nausée [noze] *nf* nausea; **avoir la nausée** to feel nauseous; **Cela m'a donné la nausée.** It made me nauseous.

nautique [notik] *adj*: **la sécurité nautique** water safety; **les sports nautiques** water sports; **le ski nautique** water-skiing; **une carte nautique** a nautical chart

navet [navɛ] *nm* turnip

navette [navɛt] *nf* shuttle ▷ *la navette entre l'hôtel et l'aéroport* the shuttle between the hotel and the airport; **faire la navette** to commute ▷ *Je fais la navette entre Guelph et Burlington.* I commute

between Guelph and Burlington.

navetteur [navetœʀ] *nm* commuter

navetteuse [navetøz] *nf* commuter

navigateur [navigatœʀ] *nm* (*on computer*) browser ▷ *un navigateur Web* Web browser

navigation [navigasjɔ̃] *nf*
❶ boat traffic ▷ *Il y a beaucoup de navigation sur les Grands Lacs.* There is considerable boat traffic on the Great Lakes.; **La navigation est interdite ici.** Boating is not allowed here. ❷ navigation ▷ *Les récifs rendent la navigation difficile.* Reefs make navigation difficult.; **un système de navigation par écluses** a canal and locks system

naviguer [navige] *vb* ❶ to sail ❷ (*Internet*) to surf ▷ *naviguer sur Internet* to surf the Net

navire [naviʀ] *nm* ship

ne [n(ə)] *adv*

▌ ne is combined with words such as pas, personne, plus, and jamais to form negative phrases.

▷ *Je ne peux pas venir.* I can't come. ▷ *Ils ne regardent jamais la télé.* They never watch TV. ▷ *Je ne connais personne ici.* I don't know anyone here.

▌ ne changes to n' before a vowel and most words beginning with "h".

▷ *Je n'ai pas d'argent.* I don't have any money. ▷ *Il n'habite plus à Labrador City.* He doesn't live in Labrador City any more.

▌ ne is sometimes not translated.

▷ *C'est plus loin que je ne le croyais.* It's further than I thought.

né [ne] *vb see* **naître** born ▷ *Elle est née en 1980.* She was born in 1980.

néanmoins [neɑ̃mwɛ̃] adv
nevertheless

nécessaire [neseser] adj
necessary ▷ *Il est nécessaire de
réserver.* It's necessary to make
reservations.

négatif [negatif, iv] (f **négative**)
adj negative
▶ nm (of photo) negative

négligé [negliʒe] (f **négligée**) adj
scruffy ▷ *une tenue négligée* scruffy
clothes

négliger [negliʒe] vb to neglect
▷ *Ces derniers temps il a négligé son
travail.* He's been neglecting his
work recently.

négocier [negɔsje] vb to negotiate

neige [nɛʒ] nf snow; **la neige
fondante** slush; **un bonhomme de
neige** a snowman

neiger [neʒe] vb to snow

nénuphar [nenyfar] nm water lily

néon [neɔ̃] nm neon ▷ *une lampe
au néon* a neon light ▷ *La cuisine est
éclairée au néon.* The kitchen has a
neon light.

nerf [nɛr] nm nerve; **taper sur
les nerfs de quelqu'un** to get on
somebody's nerves ▷ *Il me tape sur
les nerfs.* He's getting on my nerves.

nerveux [nɛrvø, -øz] (f **nerveuse**)
adj nervous

nervosité [nɛrvozite] nf
nervousness

n'est-ce pas [nɛspa] adv ▶
n'est-ce pas is used to check
that something is true.
▷ *Nous sommes le douze aujourd'hui,
n'est-ce pas?* It's the 12th today,
isn't it? ▷ *Ils sont venus l'an dernier,
n'est-ce pas?* They came last year,
didn't they? ▷ *Elle aura dix-huit ans
en octobre, n'est-ce pas?* She'll be 18 in
October, won't she?

net [nɛt] (f **nette**) adj, adv ❶ clear
▷ *L'image n'est pas nette.* The picture

isn't very clear. ❷ net ▷ *Poids net :
500 g.* Net weight: 500 g. ❸ flatly
▷ *Il a refusé net de nous aider.* He flatly
refused to help us.; **s'arrêter net**
to stop dead

nettement [nɛtmɑ̃] adv much
▷ *Ce magasin est nettement plus cher.*
This store is much more expensive.

nettoyage [nɛtwajaʒ] nm
cleaning; **le nettoyage à sec** dry
cleaning

nettoyer [nɛtwaje] vb to clean

nettoyeur [nɛtwajœr] nm dry-
cleaner ▷ *Je vais porter ce manteau
chez le nettoyeur.* I'm going to take
this coat to the dry-cleaner's.

neuf [nœf, nœv] num nine ▷ *Elle
a neuf ans.* She's nine. ▷ *Il est neuf
heures du matin.* It's nine in the
morning.; **le neuf février** the ninth
of February
▶ adj (f **neuve**) new ▷ *des chaussures
neuves* new shoes

neutre [nøtr(ə)] adj neutral

neuve [nœv] adj see **neuf**

neuvième [nœvjɛm] adj ninth
▷ *au neuvième étage* on the ninth
floor

neveu [nəvø] (pl **neveux**) nm
nephew

nez [ne] nm nose; **se trouver nez
à nez avec quelqu'un** to come face
to face with somebody; **C'était
juste sous mon nez.** It was right
under my nose.; **mettre le nez
dehors** to go outside; **ne pas voir
plus loin que le bout de son nez** to
lack foresight

ni [ni] conj: **ni...ni...** neither...
nor... ▷ *Je n'aime ni les lentilles ni
les épinards.* I like neither lentils
nor spinach. ▷ *Elles ne sont venues
ni l'une ni l'autre.* Neither of them
came.

niaiser [njeze] vb ❶ (informal:
someone) to kid ▷ *Arrête de nous*

niaiser, avec tes histoires incroyables. Stop kidding us with your unbelievable stories. ❷ *(waste time)* to fool around ▷ *Au bout du compte, on a niaisé tout l'après-midi.* We ended up just fooling around the whole afternoon.

niaiserie [njɛzʀi] *nf (informal)* nonsense ▷ *Elle t'a raconté des niaiseries.* What she told you was nonsense. ▷ *Tu dis des niaiseries!* You're talking nonsense!; **faire des niaiseries** to get into trouble ▷ *Il faut surveiller ce petit garçon, sinon il fait des niaiseries.* This little boy needs to be supervised, otherwise he gets into trouble.

niaiseux [njɛzø, -øz] *(f* **niaiseuse)** *adj (informal)* stupid ▷ *J'ai trouvé ce film complètement niaiseux.* I thought that movie was utterly stupid. ▷ *Ne sois pas niaiseuse, fais tes devoirs.* Don't be stupid; do your homework.

niche [niʃ] *nf* kennel

nid [ni] *nm* nest

nièce [njɛs] *nf* niece

nier [nje] *vb* to deny

n'importe [nɛ̃pɔʀt(ə)] *adv:* **n'importe quel** any ▷ *N'importe quel stylo fera l'affaire.* Any pen will do.; **n'importe qui** anybody ▷ *N'ouvre pas la porte à n'importe qui.* Don't open the door to just anybody.; **n'importe quoi** anything ▷ *Je ferais n'importe quoi pour lui.* I'd do anything for him.; **Tu dis n'importe quoi.** You're talking nonsense.; **n'importe où** anywhere ▷ *On trouve ces fleurs n'importe où.* You can find these flowers anywhere.; **Ne laisse pas tes affaires n'importe où.** Don't leave your things lying everywhere.; **n'importe quand** any time ▷ *Tu peux venir n'importe*

quand. You can come any time.; **n'importe comment** any old way ▷ *Ces livres sont rangés n'importe comment.* These books are not put away any old way.

NIP *abbr* (= *le numéro d'identification personnel)* PIN number

niveau [nivo] *(pl* **niveaux)** *nm* level ▷ *le niveau de l'eau* the water level ▷ *Ces deux enfants n'ont pas le même niveau.* These two children aren't at the same level.; **le niveau de vie** the standard of living

noble [nɔbl(ə)] *adj* noble

noblesse [nɔblɛs] *nf* nobility

noce [nɔs] *nf* wedding; **un repas de noce** a wedding reception; **leurs noces d'or** their golden wedding anniversary

nocif [nɔsif, -iv] *(f* **nocive)** *adj* harmful ▷ *une substance nocive* a harmful substance

Noël [nɔel] *nm* Christmas; **Joyeux Noël!** Merry Christmas!

nœud *nm* ❶ knot ▷ *Il a fait un nœud à la corde.* He tied a knot in the rope. ❷ bow ▷ *La petite fille avait un nœud dans les cheveux.* The little girl had a bow in her hair.; **un nœud papillon** a bow tie; **frapper un nœud** *(problem)* to hit a snag

noir [nwaʀ] *(f* **noire)** *adj* ❶ black ▷ *Elle porte une robe noire.* She's wearing a black dress. ▷ *Il est noir.* He's black. ❷ dark ▷ *Il fait noir dehors.* It's dark outside. ▶ *nm* dark ▷ *J'ai peur du noir.* I'm afraid of the dark.; **le travail au noir** moonlighting

Noir *nm* (man) black; **les Noirs** black people

noirceur [nwaʀsœʀ] *nf* darkness ▷ *Nous avons perdu notre chemin dans la noirceur.* We lost our way in the darkness.

Noire *nf* (woman) black

noisette [nwazet] nf hazelnut

noix [nwa] (pl **noix**) nf walnut; **une noix de coco** a coconut; **les noix de cajou** cashews; **une noix de beurre** a dab of butter

nolisé [nɔlize] adj charter ▷ le vol nolisé charter flight

nom [nɔ̃] nm ❶ name ▷ votre nom your name; **mon nom de famille** my surname; **son nom de jeune fille** her maiden name ❷ (in grammar) noun ▷ un nom commun a common noun; **un nom propre** a proper noun; **le nom d'utilisateur** username

nombre [nɔ̃bʀ(ə)] nm number ▷ Treize est un nombre impair. Thirteen is an odd number. ▷ un grand nombre d'amis a large number of friends

nombreux [nɔ̃bʀø, -øz] (f **nombreuse**) adj ❶ many ▷ Il a gagné de nombreux matchs. He's won many games. ❷ large ▷ une famille nombreuse a large family; **être plus nombreux que** to outnumber; **peu nombreux** few ▷ Nous étions peu nombreux à la réunion. There were few of us at the meeting.

nombril [nɔ̃bʀi] nm navel

nommer [nɔme] vb ❶ to name ▷ Elle n'a voulu nommer personne. She didn't want to name anybody. ❷ to appoint ▷ Elle a été nommée directrice. She was appointed director.

non [nɔ̃] adv no ▷ « Tu as vu mon frère ? » « Non. » "Have you seen my brother?" "No."; **non seulement** not only ▷ Il est non seulement intelligent, mais aussi très gentil. Not only is he intelligent, he's also very nice.; **moi non plus** Neither do I. ▷ « Je n'aime pas les hamburgers. » « Moi non plus. » "I don't like hamburgers." "Neither do I." ▷ Elle n'y est pas allée et moi non

plus. She didn't go and neither did I.

non alcoolisé [nɔnalkɔlize] (f **non alcoolisée**) adj non-alcoholic ▷ les boissons non alcoolisées non-alcoholic drinks

non-fumeur [nɔ̃fymœʀ] nm non-smoker ▷ Je suis un non-fumeur. I'm a non-smoker.; **la section non-fumeurs** the non-smoking section

non-fumeuse [nɔ̃fymøz] nf non-smoker ▷ Ma sœur est une non-fumeuse. My sister is a non-smoker.

nord [nɔʀ] nm north ❶ Ils vivent dans le nord de l'île. They live in the north of the island.; **vers le nord** northwards; **au nord de Jonquière** north of Jonquière; **l'Amérique du Nord** North America; **le vent du nord** the north wind
▶ adj ❶ north ▷ la face nord de la montagne the north face of the mountain; **le pôle Nord** the North Pole ❷ northern ▷ Nous avons visité la partie nord de la province. We visited the northern part of the province.

nord-est [nɔʀɛst] nm northeast ▷ les régions du nord-est northeastern regions

nord-ouest [nɔʀwɛst] nm northwest; **le Passage du Nord-Ouest** The Northwest Passage

normal [nɔʀmal, -o] (f **normale**, mpl **normaux**) adj ❶ normal ▷ un bébé normal a normal baby ❷ natural ▷ C'est tout à fait normal. It's perfectly natural.; **Vous trouvez que c'est normal?** Does that seem right to you?

normalement [nɔʀmalmɑ̃] adv normally ▷ Les aéroports fonctionnent tous normalement. The airports are all operating normally.; **Normalement, elle doit arriver à huit heures.** She's supposed to arrive at 8 o'clock.; **« Tu es**

libre en fin de semaine? » « Oui,
normalement. » "Are you free this
weekend?" "Yes, I should be."

nos [no] *adj* our ▷ *Où sont nos
affaires?* Where's our stuff?

notaire [nɔtɛʀ] *nmf* lawyer ▷ *Sa
mère est notaire.* His mother's a
lawyer.

note [nɔt] *nf* ❶ note ▷ *J'ai pris des
notes pendant la classe.* I took notes
in class. ▷ *Il a joué quelques notes au
piano.* He played a few notes on the
piano. ❷ mark ▷ *Elle a de bonnes
notes en maths.* She gets good marks
in math.

noter [nɔte] *vb* to make a note
of ▷ *Tu as noté leur adresse?* Did you
make a note of their address?

notions [nɔsjɔ̃] *nfpl* basics ▷ *Il
faut avoir des notions d'anglais.* You
have to have some basic English.
▷ *Elle a des notions de traitement de
texte.* She knows the basics of word
processing.

notoire [nɔtwaʀ] *adj* notorious
▷ *un criminel notoire* a notorious
criminal

notre [nɔtʀ(ə), no] (*pl* **nos**) *adj*
our ▷ *Voici notre maison.* Here's
our house.

nôtre [notʀ(ə)] *pron*: **le nôtre** ours
▷ *« À qui est ce chien? » — « C'est le
nôtre. »* "Whose dog is this?" — "It's
ours." ▷ *Leur voiture est rouge; la
nôtre est bleue.* Their car is red; ours
is blue.

nôtres [notʀ] *pron*: **les nôtres** ours
▷ *Ces places-là sont les nôtres.* Those
seats are ours.

nouer [nwe] *vb* to tie

nouilles [nuj] *nfpl* noodles

nounours [nunuʀs] *nm* teddy bear

nourrir [nuʀiʀ] *vb* to feed

nourriture [nuʀityʀ] *nf* food;
**la nourriture pour animaux
de compagnie** pet food; **une**

nourriture saine a healthy diet

nous [nu] *pron* ❶ we ▷ *Nous avons
deux enfants.* We have two children.
❷ us ▷ *Viens avec nous.* Come with
us.; **nous-mêmes** ourselves

nouveau [nuvo, -ɛl] (*f* **nouvelle**,
mpl **nouveaux**) *adj* new ▷ *Il me faut
un nouveau pantalon.* I need some
new pants. ▷ *Ils ont une nouvelle
voiture.* They've a new car.

> **nouveau** changes to **nouvel**
> before a vowel and most words
> beginning with "h".

▷ *le nouvel élève dans ma classe* The
new boy in my class; **le Nouvel An**
New Year's; **le nouvel âge** New
Age ▷ *la musique nouvel âge* New
Age music

▶ *nm* (*pl* **nouveaux**) new person
▷ *Il y a plusieurs nouveaux dans la
classe.* There are several new people
in the class.; **de nouveau** again ▷ *Il
pleut de nouveau.* It's raining again.

Nouveau-Brunswick *nm* New
Brunswick

nouveau-né [nuvone] (*mpl* **les
nouveau-nés**, *f* **la nouveau-
née**, *fpl* **les nouveau-nées**) *nm*
newborn

nouveauté [nuvote] *nf* novelty

nouvel [nuvɛl] *adj see* **nouveau**

nouvelle [nuvɛl] *adj see* **nouveau**

▶ *nf* ❶ (*single item*) news ▷ *Tu
connais la nouvelle? Ma grand-mère a
gagné à la loto.* Have you heard the
news? My grandmother won the
lottery. ▷ *C'est une bonne nouvelle.*
That's good news. ❷ short story
▷ *une nouvelle de Janet Lunn* a short
story by Janet Lunn; **les nouvelles**
the news ▷ *J'ai écouté les nouvelles
à la radio.* I listened to the news on
the radio.; **avoir des nouvelles de
quelqu'un** to hear from somebody
▷ *Je n'ai pas eu de nouvelles de lui.* I
haven't heard from him.

Nouvelle-Écosse [nuvɛlekɔs] nf
Nova Scotia

novembre [nɔvɑ̃br(ə)] nm
November; **en novembre** in
November

noyau [nwajo] (pl **noyaux**) nm (of
fruit) stone ▷ *un noyau d'abricot* an
apricot stone

se noyer [nwaje] vb to drown ▷ *Il
s'est noyé dans la rivière.* He drowned
in the river.

nu [ny] (f **nue**) adj ❶ naked ▷ *Ils
se sont baignés nus.* They went
swimming naked. ▷ *tout nus* stark
naked ❷ bare ▷ *Elle avait les bras
nus.* Her arms were bare. ▷ *Les murs
étaient nus.* The walls were bare.

nuage [nɥaʒ] nm cloud; **être dans
les nuages** to daydream

nuageux [nɥaʒø, -øz] (f
nuageuse) adj cloudy

nucléaire [nykleɛr] adj nuclear
▷ *l'énergie nucléaire* nuclear power
▷ *la famille nucléaire* the nuclear
family

nudiste [nydist(ə)] nmf nudist

nuit [nɥi] nf ❶ night ▷ *Ils ont fait
du bruit toute la nuit.* They were noisy
all night. ❷ at night ▷ *se promener
la nuit* to go for a walk at night; **Il
fait nuit.** It's dark out.; **cette nuit**
tonight ▷ *Il va rentrer cette nuit.*
He'll be back tonight.; **Bonne nuit!**
Good night!; **de nuit (1)** by night
▷ *voyager de nuit* to travel by night
(2) nights ▷ *Il travaille de nuit.* He
works nights.; **une nuit blanche**
a sleepless night ▷ *J'ai encore passé
une nuit blanche.* I had yet another
sleepless night.

nul [nyl] (f **nulle**) adj (informal)
no good; **être nul** to be no good
▷ *Je suis nul en éducation physique.*
I'm no good at phys ed. ▷ *Ce film
est nul.* This movie's no good.; **un
match nul** (sports) a tie ▷ *Ils ont fait*

match nul. It was a tie.; **nulle part**
nowhere ▷ *Je ne le vois nulle part.* I
can't see it anywhere.

numérique [nymerik] adj digital
▷ *un appareil photo numérique* a
digital camera

numéro [nymero] nm number
▷ *J'habite au numéro trois.* I live
at number 3.; **mon numéro de
téléphone** my phone number;
le numéro de compte the
account number; **le numéro
d'identification personnel** PIN
number; **le numéro confidentiel**
unlisted number

Nunavut nm Nunavut

nu-pieds [nypje] adj, adv barefoot
▷ *Il se promenait nu-pieds.* He was
walking barefoot.

nuque [nyk] nf nape of the neck

nutriment [nytrimɑ̃] nm nutrient

nutritif [nytritif, -iv] (f **nutritive**)
adj ❶ nutritious ▷ *une collation
nutritive* a nutritious snack
❷ nutritional ▷ *La malbouffe n'a
presque aucune valeur nutritive.* Junk
food has almost no nutritional
value.

nutrition [nytrisjɔ̃] nf nutrition

nutritionniste [nytrisjɔnist(ə)]
nmf nutritionist

nylon [nilɔ̃] nm nylon

O

obéir [ɔbeiʀ] vb to obey; **obéir à quelqu'un** to obey somebody ▷ *Elle refuse d'obéir à ses parents.* She refuses to obey her parents.

obéissant [ɔbeisɑ̃, -ɑ̃t] (f **obéissante**) adj obedient

objet [ɔbʒɛ] nm object; **les objets de valeur** valuables; **les objets perdus** the lost-and-found

obligatoire [ɔbligatwaʀ] adj compulsory

obliger [ɔbliʒe] vb to oblige; **obliger quelqu'un à faire quelque chose** to force somebody to do something; **Je suis bien obligé d'accepter.** I can't really refuse.

obscur [ɔpskyʀ] (f **obscure**) adj dark

obscurité [ɔpskyʀite] nf darkness ▷ *dans l'obscurité* in the dark

obséder [ɔpsede] vb to obsess ▷ *Il est obsédé par le travail.* He's obsessed by work.

observation [ɔpsɛʀvasjɔ̃] nf comment ▷ *J'ai une ou deux observations à faire.* I've got one or two comments to make.

observer [ɔpsɛʀve] vb ❶ to watch ▷ *Nous observions les canards sur le lac.* We watched the ducks on the lake. ❷ *(respect, keep)* to observe ▷ *Ils observent le règlement.* They observe the rules. ▷ *Observer une minute de silence pour le jour du Souvenir* to observe a minute of silence on Remembrance Day

obstacle [ɔpstakl(ə)] nm obstacle ▷ *surmonter un obstacle* to overcome an obstacle; **une course d'obstacles** an obstacle race

obstiné [ɔpstine] (f **obstinée**) adj stubborn

obtenir [ɔptəniʀ] vb ❶ to get ▷ *Ils ont obtenu cinquante pour cent des voix.* They got 50% of the votes. ❷ to achieve ▷ *Nous avons obtenu de bons résultats.* We achieved good results.

occasion [ɔkazjɔ̃] nf ❶ opportunity ▷ *C'est une occasion à ne pas manquer.* It's an opportunity not to be missed. ❷ occasion ▷ *à l'occasion de sa fête* on the occasion of his birthday ▷ *à plusieurs occasions* on several occasions ❸ bargain ▷ *Cet ordinateur est une bonne occasion.* This computer's a real bargain.; **d'occasion** second-hand ▷ *une voiture d'occasion* a second-hand car

Occident nm *(western world)* West; **en Occident** in the West

occidental [ɔksidɑ̃tal, -o] (f **occidentale**, mpl **occidentaux**) adj western; **les pays occidentaux** the West

occupation [ɔkypasjɔ̃] nf *(by troops)* occupation ▷ *la France sous l'Occupation* France during the

Occupation

occupé [ɔkype] (f **occupée**) adj
❶ busy ▷ *Le directeur est très occupé.* The director's very busy. ▷ *La ligne est occupée.* The line is busy. ❷ taken ▷ *Est-ce que cette place est occupée?* Is this seat taken? ❸ occupied ▷ *Les toilettes sont occupées.* The washroom is occupied.

occuper [ɔkype] vb to occupy ▷ *Les enfants ne sont pas faciles à occuper quand il pleut.* Children aren't easy to keep occupied when it rains.; **s'occuper de quelque chose (1)** to be in charge of something ▷ *Elle s'occupe d'un club de sport.* She's in charge of a sports club. **(2)** to deal with something ▷ *Je vais m'occuper de ce problème tout de suite.* I'm going to deal with this problem right away.

océan [ɔseã] nm ocean ▷ *l'océan Indien* the Indian Ocean

octobre [ɔktɔbʀ(ə)] nm October; **en octobre** in October

odeur [ɔdœʀ] nf smell ▷ *Il y a une drôle d'odeur ici.* There's a funny smell here.

œil [œj, jø] (pl **yeux**) nm eye ▷ *J'ai quelque chose dans l'œil.* I've got something in my eye.; **à l'œil nu** with the naked eye; **un coup d'œil** a glance ▷ *Pourrais-tu jeter un coup d'œil sur ce que j'ai écrit, s'il te plaît?* Could you have a glance at what I've written, please?

œillet [œjɛ] nm carnation

œuf [œf] nm egg; **un œuf à la coque** a soft-boiled egg; **un œuf dur** a hard-boiled egg; **un œuf au plat** a fried egg; **un œuf au miroir** an egg fried sunny side up; **un œuf tourné** an egg fried over easy; **les œufs brouillés** scrambled eggs; **un œuf de Pâques** an Easter egg

œuvre [œvʀ] nf work ▷ *les œuvres complètes de Shakespeare* the complete works of Shakespeare; **une œuvre d'art** a work of art

œuvrer [œvʀe] vb to work ▷ *Elle œuvre auprès des jeunes sans-abri.* She works with homeless youth. ▷ *Toute sa vie, il a œuvré pour la cause de la paix.* He has worked all his life for peace.

offenser [ɔfãse] vb to offend ▷ *Est-ce que ma plaisanterie t'a offensé?* Did my joke offend you?; **s'offenser de quelque chose** to be offended by something

offert [ɔfɛʀ] vb see **offrir**

office [ɔfis] nm (government agency) office; **un office du tourisme** a tourist office

- Created in 1977, the **Office québécois de la langue française** has the general mission to promote French and enforce the application of the Charter of French language in Québec. It offers numerous free French language resources, especially on the Web.

officiel [ɔfisjɛl] (f **officielle**) adj official

offre [ɔfʀ(ə)] nf offer ▷ *une offre spéciale* a special offer; **« offres d'emploi »** "Employment Opportunities"

offrir [ɔfʀiʀ] vb: **offrir quelque chose (1)** to offer something ▷ *On lui a offert un poste de secrétaire.* They offered him a secretarial post. ▷ *Elle m'a offert à boire.* She offered me a drink. **(2)** to present something ▷ *Il lui a offert des roses.* He presented her with roses.; **s'offrir quelque chose** to treat oneself to something ▷ *Je me suis offert un sous-marin de 12 pouces.* I treated myself to a twelve-inch sub.

oie [wa] nf goose

oignon [ɔɲɔ̃] nm onion

oiseau [wazo] (pl **oiseaux**) nm bird

olive [ɔliv] nf olive ▷ *l'huile d'olive* olive oil

olympique [ɔlɛ̃pik] adj: **les Jeux olympiques** the Olympic Games

ombre [ɔ̃bʀ(ə)] nf ❶ shade ▷ *Je vais me mettre à l'ombre.* I'm going to sit in the shade. ❷ shadow; **l'ombre à paupières** eye shadow

omnipraticien [ɔmnipʀatisjɛ̃] nm general practitioner ▷ *Il est omnipraticien.* He's a general practitioner.

omnipraticienne [ɔmnipʀatisjɛn] nf general practitioner ▷ *Elle est omnipraticienne.* She's a general practitioner.

on [ɔ̃] pron ❶ we ▷ *On va à la plage demain.* We're going to the beach tomorrow. ▷ *On a pensé que ça te ferait plaisir.* We thought you'd be pleased. ❷ someone ▷ *On m'a volé mon sac à main.* Someone has stolen my purse.; **On m'a dit d'attendre.** I was told to wait.; **On vous demande au téléphone.** There's a phone call for you. ❸ you ▷ *On peut visiter le château en été.* You can visit the castle in the summer. ▷ *D'ici on peut voir la tour CN.* From here you can see the CN Tower.

oncle [ɔ̃kl(ə)] nm uncle

onde [ɔ̃d] nf (on radio) wave ▷ *sur les ondes courtes* on shortwave

ongle [ɔ̃gl(ə)] nm nail; **se couper les ongles** to cut one's nails ▷ *Elle s'est coupé les ongles.* She cut her nails.

ont [ɔ̃] vb see **avoir**; **Ils ont beaucoup d'argent.** They have lots of money.; **Elles ont passé de bonnes vacances.** They had a good holiday.

Ontario nm Ontario

ONU [ɔny] nf (= Organisation des Nations unies) UN (= United Nations)

onze [ɔ̃z] num eleven ▷ *Il a onze ans.* He's eleven. ▷ *à onze heures* at eleven o'clock; **le onze février** the eleventh of February

onzième [ɔ̃zjɛm] adj eleventh ▷ *au onzième étage* on the eleventh floor

opéra [ɔpeʀa] nm opera

opération [ɔpeʀasjɔ̃] nf operation

opérer [ɔpeʀe] vb to operate on ▷ *Elle a été opérée de l'appendicite.* She was operated on for appendicitis.; **se faire opérer** to have an operation ▷ *Il s'est fait opérer.* He had an operation.

opinion [ɔpinjɔ̃] nf opinion

opposé [ɔpoze] (f **opposée**) adj opposite ▷ *Elle est partie dans la direction opposée.* She went off in the opposite direction.; **être opposé à quelque chose** to be opposed to something
▶ nm the opposite

opposer [ɔpoze] vb: **opposer quelqu'un à quelqu'un** to pit somebody against somebody ▷ *Ce match oppose Edmonton à Toronto.* This match pits Edmonton against Toronto.; **s'opposer** to conflict ▷ *Ces deux points de vue s'opposent.* These two points of view conflict.; **s'opposer à quelque chose** to oppose something ▷ *Son père s'oppose à son mariage.* Her father's against her marriage.

opposition [ɔpozisjɔ̃] nf opposition; **par opposition à** as opposed to ▷ *la littérature contemporaine par opposition à la littérature classique* modern literature, as opposed to classics

opticien [ɔptisjɛ̃] nm optician ▷ *Il est opticien.* He's an optician.

opticienne [ɔptisjɛn] nf optician

▷ *Elle est opticienne.* She's an optician.

optimiste [ɔptimist(ə)] *adj*
optimistic

option [ɔpsjɔ̃] *nf* option; **une
matière à option** an optional
subject

or [ɔʀ] *nm* gold ▷ *un bracelet en or* a
gold bracelet
▶ *conj* and yet ▷ *Il était sûr de gagner,
or il a perdu.* He was sure he would
win, and yet he lost.

orage [ɔʀaʒ] *nm* thunderstorm

orageux [ɔʀaʒø, -øz] (f **orageuse**)
adj stormy

oral [ɔʀal, -o] (f **orale**, mpl **oraux**)
adj oral; **une présentation orale**
an oral presentation; **une épreuve
orale** an oral test; **à prendre par
voie orale** to be taken orally

orange [ɔʀɑ̃ʒ] *nf* (fruit) orange
▶ *adj* (f+pl **orange**) (in colour)
orange ▷ *des fleurs orange* orange
flowers

orchestre [ɔʀkɛstʀ(ə)] *nm*
❶ orchestra ▷ *un orchestre
symphonique* a symphony orchestra
❷ band ▷ *un orchestre de jazz* a
jazz band

ordinaire [ɔʀdinɛʀ] *adj* ordinary
▷ *des gens ordinaires* ordinary people
▶ *nm*: **sortir de l'ordinaire** to be
out of the ordinary

ordinateur [ɔʀdinatœʀ] *nm*
computer; **un ordinateur portatif**
a laptop

ordonnance [ɔʀdɔnɑ̃s] *nf*
prescription

ordonné [ɔʀdɔne] (f **ordonnée**)
adj tidy

ordonner [ɔʀdɔne] *vb* to order
▷ *La prof nous a ordonné de nous taire.*
The teacher ordered us to stop
talking. ▷ *On a ordonné aux grévistes
de retourner au travail.* The strikers
were ordered to go back to work.

ordre [ɔʀdʀ(ə)] *nm* order ▷ *en ordre*

alphabétique in alphabetical order;
dans l'ordre in order ▷ *dans le bon
ordre* in the right order; **mettre en
ordre** to tidy up; **jusqu'à nouvel
ordre** until further notice; **l'ordre
publique** law and order

ordures [ɔʀdyʀ] *nfpl* garbage

oreille [ɔʀɛj] *nf* ear; **avoir de
l'oreille** (for music) to have a good
ear; **écouter de toutes ses oreilles**
to be all ears; **Je n'écoutais que
d'une oreille.** I was only half
listening.; **Les oreilles ont dû lui
siffler.** Her ears must have been
burning.

oreiller [ɔʀeje] *nm* pillow

oreillons [ɔʀɛjɔ̃] *nmpl* mumps

organe [ɔʀgan] *nm* (in body) organ

organisateur [ɔʀganizatœʀ]
nm organizer; **l'organisateur
graphique** graphic organizer

organisation [ɔʀganizasjɔ̃] *nf*
organization

organisatrice [ɔʀganizatʀis] *nf*
organizer

organiser [ɔʀganize] *vb* to
organize; **s'organiser** to get
organized ▷ *Elle ne sait pas
s'organiser.* She can't get organized.

organisme [ɔʀganism(ə)] *nm*
(organization) body

orgue [ɔʀg(ə)] *nm* organ ▷ *Il joue de
l'orgue.* He plays the organ.

orgueilleux [ɔʀgœjø, -øz] (f
orgueilleuse) *adj* proud

Orient [ɔʀjɑ̃] *nm* (eastern world)
East; **en Orient** in the East

oriental [ɔʀjɑ̃tal, -o] (f **orientale**,
mpl **orientaux**) *adj* ❶ oriental
▷ *un palais oriental* an oriental
palace ❷ eastern ▷ *la frontière
orientale de la Saskatchewan* the
eastern border of Saskatchewan

orientation [ɔʀjɑ̃tasjɔ̃] *nf*
orientation; **avoir le sens de
l'orientation** to have a good

sense of direction; **l'orientation professionnelle** career counselling

originaire [ɔʀiʒinɛʀ] *adj*: **Elle est originaire de Halifax.** She's from Halifax.

original [ɔʀiʒinal, -o] (**originale**, *mpl* **originaux**) *adj* original ▷ *un film en version originale* a film in the original language
▶ *nm* (*pl* **originaux**) original ▷ *L'original est au Musée des beaux-arts de l'Ontario.* The original is in the Art Gallery of Ontario.; **un vieil original** an old eccentric

origine [ɔʀiʒin] *nf* origin; **à l'origine** originally

orignal [ɔʀiɲal, -o] *nm* moose

orphelin [ɔʀfəlɛ̃] *nm* orphan

orpheline [ɔʀfəlin] *nf* orphan

orteil [ɔʀtɛj] *nm* toe ▷ *mon gros orteil* my big toe

orthographe [ɔʀtɔɡʀaf] *nf* spelling

os [ɔs] *nm* bone

oser [oze] *vb* to dare; **oser faire quelque chose** to dare to do something

otage [ɔtaʒ] *nm* hostage

ôter [ote] *vb* ❶ to take off ▷ *Elle a ôté son manteau.* She took off her coat. ❷ to take away

ou [u] *conj* or; **ou...ou...** either... or... ▷ *Je prendrai ou du lait ou du jus.* I'll have either milk or juice.; **ou bien** or else ▷ *On pourrait aller au cinéma ou bien rentrer directement.* We could go to a movie or else go straight home.

où [u] *pron, adv* ❶ where ▷ *Où est ton frère?* Where's your brother? ▷ *Où allez-vous?* Where are you going? ▷ *Je sais où il est.* I know where he is. ▷ *C'est la maison où je suis né.* That's the house where I was born. ▷ *la ville d'où je viens* the town I come from ❷ that ▷ *Le jour*

où il est parti, tout le monde a pleuré. The day that he left, everyone cried.; **Par où allons-nous passer?** Which way are we going to go?

ouate [wat] *nf* cotton wool

oublier [ublije] *vb* ❶ to forget ▷ *N'oublie pas de fermer la porte.* Don't forget to shut the door. ❷ (*behind*) to leave ▷ *J'ai oublié mon sac à dos dans l'autobus.* I left my backpack on the bus.

ouest [wɛst] *nm* west ▷ *Elle vit dans l'ouest du Québec.* She lives in the western part of Québec.; **à l'ouest de Saint-Boniface** west of St. Boniface; **vers l'ouest** westwards; **les provinces de l'Ouest** the Western provinces; **le vent d'ouest** the west wind
▶ *adj* (*f+pl* **ouest**) ❶ west ▷ *la côte ouest du Canada* the west coast of Canada ❷ western ▷ *la partie ouest du pays* the western part of the country

ouf [uf] *excl* phew!

oui [wi] *adv* yes

ouragan [uʀaɡɑ̃] *nm* hurricane

ourlet [uʀlɛ] *nm* seam

ours [uʀs] *nm* bear; **un ours en peluche** a teddy bear

ourson [uʀsɔ̃] *nm* bear cub

outarde [utaʀd] *nf* Canada goose

outil [uti] *nm* tool

outré [utʀe] (*f* **outrée**) *adj* outraged ▷ *Il a été outré de son insolence.* He was outraged at her lack of respect.

ouvert [uvɛʀ, -ɛʀt(ə)] (*f* **ouverte**) *adj* ❶ open ▷ *Le magasin est ouvert.* The store is open. ❷ on ▷ *Tu as laissé le robinet ouvert.* You left the tap on.; **avoir l'esprit ouvert** to be open-minded

ouverture [uvɛʀtyʀ] *nf* opening ▷ *les heures d'ouverture* hours of operation

ouvre-boîte [uvʀəbwat] *nm* can opener

ouvre-bouteille [uvʀəbutɛj] (*pl* **les ouvre-bouteilles**) *nm* bottle-opener

ouvrier [uvʀije] *nm* worker ▷ *Mon père est ouvrier dans une usine.* My dad is a factory worker.

ouvrière [uvʀijɛʀ] *nf* worker

ouvrir [uvʀiʀ] *vb* to open ▷ *Ouvrez!* Open up! ▷ *Elle a ouvert la porte.* She opened the door.; **s'ouvrir** to open ▷ *La porte s'est ouverte.* The door opened.

ovale [ɔval] *adj* oval

ovni [ɔvni] *nm* (= objet volant non identifié) UFO

oxygène [ɔksiʒɛn] *nm* oxygen

ozone [ozɔn] *nm* ozone ▷ *la couche d'ozone* the ozone layer

p

pacane [pakan] *nf* pecan ▷ *la tarte aux pacanes* pecan pie

pacifiste [pasifist(ə)] *nmf* pacifist

pagaie [pagɛ] *nf* (chiefly kayak) paddle

pagaille [pagaj] *nf* mess ▷ *Quelle pagaille!* What a mess!

page [paʒ] *nf* page ▷ *Tournez la page.* Turn the page.; **la page d'accueil** the home page

paie [pɛ] *nf* wages

paiement [pɛmɑ̃] *nm* payment

paillasson [pajasɔ̃] *nm* doormat

paille [paj] *nf* straw

pain [pɛ̃] *nm* ❶ bread ▷ *un morceau de pain* a piece of bread ▷ *une tranche de pain* a slice of bread ❷ loaf ▷ *J'ai acheté un pain.* I bought a loaf of bread.; **le pain de blé entier** whole grain bread; **le pain d'épice** gingerbread; **le pain aux raisins** raisin bread; **le pain doré** French toast

pair [pɛʀ] (f **paire**) adj even ▷ *un nombre pair* an even number

paire [pɛʀ] nf pair

paisible [pezibl(ə)] adj peaceful ▷ *un village paisible* a peaceful village

paix [pɛ] nf peace; **faire la paix (1)** to make peace ▷ *Les deux pays ont fait la paix.* The two countries have made peace with each other. **(2)** (after quarrel) to make up ▷ *Elle a fait la paix avec son frère.* She made up with her brother.; **avoir la paix** to have peace and quiet ▷ *J'aimerais bien avoir la paix.* I'd like to have a bit of peace and quiet.; **Fiche-lui la paix!** (informal) Leave him alone!

palais [palɛ] nm ❶ palace ▷ *le palais Montcalm* Montcalm Palace; **le palais de justice** court house; **le palais de congrès** convention centre; **le palais des expositions** exhibition hall; **le palais des sports** sports complex ❷ (in mouth) palate

pâle [pɑl] adj pale ▷ *bleu pâle* pale blue

pâleur [pɑlœʀ] nf paleness

palier [palje] nm (on stairway) landing ▷ *Elle m'attendait sur le palier.* She was waiting for me on the landing.

pâlir [pɑliʀ] vb to go pale

palme [palm(ə)] nf (on animal) flipper

palmé [palme] (f **palmée**) adj webbed ▷ *Les canards ont les pieds palmés.* Ducks have webbed feet.

palmier [palmje] nm palm tree

palourde [paluʀd(ə)] nf clam

palpitant [palpitɑ̃, -ɑ̃t] (f **palpitante**) adj thrilling ▷ *un roman palpitant* a thrilling novel

pamplemousse [pɑ̃pləmus] nm grapefruit

pancanadien [pɑ̃kanadjɛ̃, -ɛn] (f **pancanadienne**) adj Canada-wide

▷ *une campagne pancanadienne contre le tabac* a Canada-wide campaign against tobacco

pancarte [pɑ̃kaʀt(ə)] nf sign ▷ *Il y a une pancarte dans la vitrine.* There's a sign in the window.

pandémie [pɑ̃demi] nf pandemic

pané [pane] (f **panée**) adj breaded ▷ *du poisson pané* breaded fish

panier [panje] nm basket

panique [panik] nf panic

paniquer [panike] vb to panic

panne [pan] nf breakdown; **être en panne** to have broken down ▷ *L'ascenseur est en panne.* The elevator's not working.; **tomber en panne** to break down ▷ *Nous sommes tombés en panne sur l'autoroute.* We broke down on the highway. ▷ *Nous sommes tombés en panne d'essence.* We've run out of gas.; **une panne de courant** a power cut

panneau [pano] (pl **panneaux**) nm sign ▷ *Ce panneau dit que la maison est à vendre.* This sign says that the house is for sale.; **panneau d'affichage** billboard

panorama [panɔʀama] nm panorama

pansement [pɑ̃smɑ̃] nm ❶ bandage ❷ bandaid

pantalon [pɑ̃talɔ̃] nm pants ▷ *Son pantalon est trop court.* His pants are too short.; **un pantalon de ski** a pair of ski pants

panthère [pɑ̃tɛʀ] nf panther

pantoufle [pɑ̃tufl(ə)] nf slipper

paon [pɑ̃] nm peacock

papa [papa] nm dad

pape [pap] nm pope

papeterie [papɛtʀi] nf stationery

papier [papje] nm paper ▷ *une feuille de papier* a sheet of paper; **Vos papiers, s'il vous plaît.** Your papers, please.; **les**

papiers d'identité (documents) identification; **le papier à lettres** writing paper; **le papier hygiénique** toilet paper; **le papier peint** wallpaper

papillon [papijɔ̃] nm butterfly

pâquerette [pakʀɛt] nf daisy

Pâques [pak] nm Easter ▷ *Je viendrai te voir à Pâques.* I'll come and see you at Easter.

paquet [pake] nm ❶ pack ▷ *Je voudrais un paquet de gomme à mâcher.* I'd like a pack of gum. ❷ parcel ▷ *Sa mère lui a envoyé un paquet.* His mother sent him a parcel.; **un paquet de** (informal) a ton of ▷ *J'ai un paquet de choses à faire.* I've got a ton of things to do. ▷ *Il est tombé un paquet de neige.* A ton of snow has fallen.

paquet-cadeau [pakekado] (pl **paquets-cadeaux**) nm giftwrapped parcel ▷ *La vendeuse m'a fait un paquet-cadeau.* The salesperson gift-wrapped it for me.

par [paʀ] prep ❶ by ▷ *La lettre a été écrite par son fils.* The letter was written by his son.; **deux par deux** two by two ▷ *Les élèves sont entrés deux par deux.* The pupils went in two by two. ❷ with ▷ *Son nom commence par un H.* His name begins with H. ❸ out of ▷ *Elle regardait par la fenêtre.* She was looking out of the window. ▷ *par habitude* out of habit ❹ via ▷ *Nous sommes passés par Windsor pour aller aux États-Unis.* We went via Windsor to the US. ❺ through ▷ *Il faut passer par la douane avant de prendre l'avion.* You have to go through customs before boarding the plane. ❻ per ▷ *Prenez trois cachets par jour.* Take three tablets per day. ▷ *Le voyage coûte deux mille dollars par personne.* The trip costs two thousand dollars

per person.; **par ici (1)** this way ▷ *Il faut passer par ici pour y arriver.* You have to go this way to get there. **(2)** around here ▷ *Il y a beaucoup de touristes par ici.* There are lots of tourists around here.; **par-ci, par-là** here and there

parachute [paʀaʃyt] nm parachute

parachutiste [paʀaʃytist(ə)] nmf parachutist

paradis [paʀadi] nm heaven

parages [paʀaʒ] nmpl: **dans les parages** in the area ▷ *Il n'y a pas d'hôtel dans les parages.* There are no hotels in the area.

paragraphe [paʀagʀaf] nm paragraph

paraître [paʀɛtʀ(ə)] vb ❶ to seem ▷ *Ça paraît incroyable.* It seems unbelievable. ❷ to look ▷ *Elle paraît plus jeune que son frère.* She looks younger than her brother.; **il paraît que** it seems that ▷ *Il paraît que c'est la faute de la direction.* It seems that it's the fault of the management.

parallèle [paʀalɛl] adj parallel ▷ *les barres parallèles* parallel bars ▷ nm parallel ▷ *Il a fait un parallèle entre ces deux événements.* He drew a parallel between the two events. ▷ nf parallel line

paralysé [paʀalize] (f **paralysée**) adj paralysed

parapluie [paʀaplɥi] nm umbrella

parascolaire [paʀaskɔlɛʀ] adj extracurricular ▷ *L'école offre plusieurs activités parascolaires.* The school offers several extracurricular activities.

parasol [paʀasɔl] nm parasol

parc [paʀk] nm ❶ park ▷ *Le dimanche, elle va se promener au parc.* On Sundays she goes for a walk in the park.; **un parc d'attractions** an amusement park ❷ grounds ▷ *Le château est situé au milieu d'un grand parc.* The castle is surrounded by extensive grounds.; **le parc éolien** wind farm; **le parc industriel** industrial park

parce que [paʁskə] *conj* because ▷ *Il n'est pas venu parce qu'il n'avait pas de voiture.* He didn't come because he didn't have a car.

parcomètre [paʁkɔmɛtʁ] *nm* parking meter

parcourir [paʁkuʁiʁ] *vb* ❶ to cover ▷ *Elle a parcouru cinquante kilomètres à vélo.* She covered 50 kilometres on her bike. ❷ to glance through ▷ *J'ai parcouru le journal d'aujourd'hui.* I glanced through today's newspaper.

parcours [paʁkuʁ] *nm* journey

par-dessous [paʁdəsu] *adv* underneath ▷ *Il portait un chandail et une chemise par-dessous.* He was wearing a sweater with a shirt underneath.

pardessus [paʁdəsy] *nm* overcoat

par-dessus [paʁdəsy] *adv, prep* ❶ on top ▷ *Elle porte un chemisier et un chandail rouge par-dessus.* She's wearing a blouse with a red sweater on top. ❷ over ▷ *Elle a sauté par-dessus le mur.* She jumped over the wall.; **en avoir par-dessus la tête** to have had enough ▷ *J'en ai par-dessus la tête de tous ces problèmes.* I've had enough of all these problems.

pardon [paʁdɔ̃] *nm* forgiveness ▶ *excl* ❶ sorry! ▷ *Oh, pardon! J'espère que je ne vous ai pas fait mal.* Oh, sorry! I hope I didn't hurt you.; **demander pardon à quelqu'un** to apologize to somebody ▷ *Il leur a demandé pardon.* He apologized to them.; **Je vous demande pardon.** I'm sorry. ❷ excuse me! ▷ *Pardon,*

madame! Pouvez-vous me dire où se trouve le théâtre? Excuse me! Could you tell me where the theatre is? ❸ pardon? ▷ *Pardon? Je n'ai pas compris ce que vous avez dit.* Pardon? I didn't understand what you said.

pardonner [paʁdɔne] *vb* to forgive ▷ *Nous lui avons pardonné de nous avoir menti.* We forgave him for lying to us.

pare-brise [paʁbʁiz] (*pl* **pare-brise**) *nm* windshield

pare-chocs [paʁʃɔk] *nm* bumper

pareil [paʁɛj] (*f* **pareille**) *adj* ❶ the same ▷ *Ces deux photos ne sont pas pareilles.* These two photos aren't the same. ❷ like that ▷ *J'aime bien sa montre. J'en veux une pareille.* I like her watch. I want one like that. ❸ such ▷ *Je refuse d'écouter des bêtises pareilles.* I won't listen to such nonsense.; **sans pareil** unequalled ▷ *un talent sans pareil* unequalled talent

parenthèse [paʁɑ̃tɛz] *nf* bracket ▷ *entre parenthèses* in brackets

parents [paʁɑ̃] *nmpl* ❶ (*mother and father*) parents ❷ relatives ▷ *parents et amis* friends and relatives

paresse [paʁɛs] *nf* laziness

paresseux [paʁesø, -øz] (*f* **paresseuse**) *adj* lazy

parfait [paʁfɛ, -ɛt] (*f* **parfaite**) *adj* perfect

parfaitement [paʁfɛtmɑ̃] *adv* perfectly ▷ *Il parle parfaitement l'arabe.* He speaks perfect Arabic.

parfois [paʁfwa] *adv* sometimes

parfum [paʁfœ̃] *nm* ❶ perfume ❷ flavour ▷ *« Je voudrais une crème glacée. » — « Quel parfum veux-tu? »* "I'd like an ice cream." — "What flavour would you like?"

parfumé [paʁfyme] (*f* **parfumée**) *adj* ❶ fragrant ▷ *une rose très*

parfumée a very fragrant rose
❷ flavoured ▷ *des biscuits parfumés au café* coffee-flavoured cookies

pari [paʀi] *nm* bet

parier [paʀje] *vb* to bet

parlement [paʀləmɑ̃] *nm* parliament; **le Parlement du Canada** the Canadian Parliament

parlementaire [paʀləmɑ̃tɛʀ] *adj* parliamentary ▷ *un débat parlementaire* a parliamentary debate; **la Colline parlementaire** Parliament Hill

parler [paʀle] *vb* ❶ to speak ▷ *Vous parlez français?* Do you speak French? ❷ to talk ▷ *Nous étions en train de parler quand la directrice est entrée.* We were talking when the principal came in.; **parler de quelque chose à quelqu'un** to tell somebody about something ▷ *Il m'a parlé de son nouveau vélo.* He told me about his new bike.

parmi [paʀmi] *prep* among ▷ *Ils étaient parmi les meilleurs de la classe.* They were among the best in the class.

paroi [paʀwa] *nf* wall; **une paroi rocheuse** a rock face

paroisse [paʀwas] *nf* parish

parole [paʀɔl] *nf* ❶ speech ▷ *l'usage de la parole* the power of speech ❷ word ▷ *Il m'a donné sa parole.* He gave me his word. ▷ *Elle a tenu parole.* She kept her word.; **les paroles** lyrics ▷ *J'aime les paroles de cette chanson.* I like the lyrics of this song.

parquet [paʀkɛ] *nm* (wooden) floor

parrainer [paʀene] *vb* to sponsor ▷ *Cette entreprise parraine notre équipe de hockey.* This company is sponsoring our hockey team.

pars [paʀ] *vb* see **partir**

part [paʀ] *nf* share ▷ *Vous n'avez pas eu votre part.* You haven't had

your share. ❷ piece ▷ *une part de gâteau* a piece of cake; **prendre part à quelque chose** to take part in something ▷ *Elle va prendre part à la réunion.* She's going to take part in the meeting.; **de la part de (1)** on behalf of ▷ *Je dois vous remercier de la part de mon frère.* I must thank you on behalf of my brother. **(2)** from ▷ *C'est un cadeau pour toi, de la part de ma sœur.* It's a present for you, from my sister.; **à part** except ▷ *Ils sont tous venus à part lui.* They all came except him.

partager [paʀtaʒe] *vb* ❶ to share ▷ *Ils partagent un appartement.* They share a flat. ❷ to divide ▷ *Nous avons partagé le gâteau en quatre.* We divided the cake into four.

partenaire [paʀtənɛʀ] *nmf* partner

parti [paʀti] *nm* party ▷ *le Parti vert* the Green Party

participant [paʀtisipɑ̃] *nm* participant

participante [paʀtisipɑ̃t] *nf* participant

participation [paʀtisipasjɔ̃] *nf* participation

participe [paʀtisip] *nm* participle; **le participe passé** the past participle; **le participe présent** the present participle

participer [paʀtisipe] *vb*: **participer à quelque chose (1)** to take part in something ▷ *Mon frère va participer à la course.* My brother is going to take part in the race. **(2)** to contribute to something ▷ *Je voudrais participer aux frais.* I would like to contribute to the cost.

particularité [paʀtikylaʀite] *nf* characteristic

particulier [paʀtikylje, -jɛʀ] (*f* **particulière**) *adj* ❶ private ▷ *une maison particulière* a private house

❷ distinctive ▷ *Ce fromage a un arôme particulier.* This cheese has a distinctive flavour. ❸ particular ▷ *Dans ce cas particulier, la procédure est différente.* In this particular case, the procedure is different.; **en particulier** (1) particularly ▷ *J'aime les fruits, en particulier les fraises.* I like fruit, particularly strawberries. (2) in private ▷ *Est-ce que je peux vous parler en particulier?* Can I speak to you in private?

particulièrement [partikyljɛrmɑ̃] *adv* particularly

partie [parti] *nf* ❶ part ▷ *Une partie du groupe restera à la ferme.* Part of the group will stay at the farm. ❷ game ▷ *Nous avons fait une partie de badminton.* We played a game of badminton. ▷ *une partie de cartes* a game of cards; **en partie** partly ▷ *Cela explique en partie le problème.* That partly explains the problem.; **en grande partie** largely ▷ *Son histoire est en grande partie vraie.* Her story is largely true.; **faire partie de** to be part of ▷ *Ce tableau fait partie de la collection familiale.* This picture is part of the family collection.

partiel [parsjɛl] (*f* **partielle**) *adj* partial

partir [partir] *vb* to go ▷ *Je t'ai téléphoné mais tu étais déjà parti.* I phoned you but you were already gone.; **partir en vacances** to go on holiday; **partir de** to leave ▷ *Il est parti de Regina à sept heures.* He left Regina at 7.; **à partir de** from ▷ *Je serai chez moi à partir de huit heures.* I'll be at home from eight o'clock onwards.

partition [partisjɔ̃] *nf* (in music) score ▷ *une partition de piano* a piano score

partout [partu] *adv* everywhere

party [parti] *nm* party ▷ *un party d'Halloween* a Halloween party

paru [pary] *vb see* **paraître**

parution [parysjɔ̃] *nf* publication ▷ *la parution de son nouveau livre* the publication of her new book; **Ce roman a eu beaucoup de succès dès sa parution.** This novel was a hit from the moment it came out.

parvenir [parvənir] *vb*: **parvenir à faire quelque chose** to manage to do something ▷ *Elle est finalement parvenue à ouvrir la porte.* She finally managed to open the door.; **faire parvenir quelque chose à quelqu'un** to send something to somebody ▷ *Je vous ferai parvenir le colis avant lundi.* I'll send you the parcel before Monday.

pas [pɑ] *adv*: **ne...pas** not ▷ *Il ne pleut pas.* It's not raining. ▷ *Elle n'est pas venue.* She didn't come. ▷ *Ils n'ont pas de voiture.* They don't have a car.; **Vous viendrez à notre soirée, n'est-ce pas?** You're coming to our party, aren't you?; **C'est lui qui a gagné, n'est-ce pas?** He won, didn't he?; **pas moi** not me ▷ *Elle veut aller au cinéma, pas moi.* She wants to go to a movie, but I don't.; **pas du tout** not at all ▷ *Je n'aime pas du tout ça.* I don't like that at all.; **pas mal** not bad ▷ *Ce n'est pas mal pour un début.* That's not bad for a first attempt. ▷ *« Comment allez-vous? » « Pas mal. »* "How are you?" "Not bad."; **pas mal de** quite a lot of ▷ *Il y avait pas mal de monde au concert.* There were quite a lot of people at the concert.
▷ *nm* ❶ pace ▷ *Il marchait d'un pas rapide.* He walked at a fast pace. ❷ step ▷ *Faites trois pas en avant.* Take three steps forward. ▷ *un pas en arrière* a step backwards ❸ footstep ▷ *J'entends des pas dans*

l'escalier. I can hear footsteps on the stairs.; **au pas** at a walk ▷ *Le cheval est parti au pas.* The horse set off at a walk.; **faire les cent pas** to pace up and down ▷ *Il faisait les cent pas dans le corridor.* He was pacing up and down the corridor.

passage [pɑsaʒ] *nm* passage ▷ *J'ai traduit un passage de ce livre.* I translated a passage from this book.; **J'ai été éclaboussé au passage de la voiture.** I was splashed by a passing car.; **de passage** passing through ▷ *Nous sommes de passage en Cornwall.* We're just passing through Cornwall.; **un passage à niveau** a railway crossing; **un passage à piétons** a pedestrian crossing; **un passage souterrain** an underground walkway

passager [pɑsaʒe, -ɛʀ] (*f* **passagère**) *adj* temporary
▶ *nm* passenger; **un passager clandestin** a stowaway

passagère [pɑsaʒɛʀ] *nf* passenger

passant [pɑsɑ̃] *nm* passer-by

passante [pɑsɑ̃t] *nf* passer-by

passé [pɑse] (*f* **passée**) *adj* ❶ last ▷ *Je l'ai vu la semaine passée.* I saw her last week. ❷ past ▷ *Il est minuit passé.* It's past midnight.
▶ *nm* ❶ past ▷ *dans le passé* in the past ❷ past tense ▷ *Mettez ce verbe au passé.* Put this verb into the past tense.; **le passé composé** the perfect tense

passeport [pɑspɔʀ] *nm* passport

passer [pɑse] *vb* ❶ to cross ▷ *Nous avons passé la frontière ontarienne.* We crossed the Ontario border. ❷ to go through ▷ *Il faut passer la douane en sortant.* You have to go through customs on the way out. ❸ to take ▷ *Mon frère a passé ses examens la semaine dernière.* My

brother took his exams last week.

> Be careful! **passer un examen** does not mean **to pass an exam**.

❹ to spend ▷ *Elle a passé la journée à ne rien faire.* She spent the day doing nothing. ▷ *Ils passent toujours leurs vacances au Québec.* They always spend their holidays in Quebec. ❺ to pass ▷ *Passe-moi le sel, s'il te plaît.* Pass me the salt, please. ❻ to show ▷ *On passe un nouveau film d'animation au cinéma cette semaine.* They're showing a new animated film at the movie theatre this week. ❼ to drop by ▷ *Je passerai chez vous ce soir.* I'll drop by this evening.; **passer à la radio** to be on the radio ▷ *Mon père passe à la radio demain soir.* My father's going to be on the radio tomorrow night.; **passer à la télévision** to be on TV ▷ *Mon film préféré passe à la télé ce soir.* My favourite movie is on TV tonight.; **Ne quittez pas, je vous passe la gérante.** Hold on please, I'm putting you through to the manager.; **passer par** to go through ▷ *Ils sont passés par Brandon pour aller à Winnipeg.* They went through Brandon to get to Winnipeg.; **en passant** in passing ▷ *Je lui ai dit en passant que j'allais me marier.* I told her in passing that I was getting married.; **laisser passer** to let through ▷ *Il m'a laissé passer.* He let me through.; **se passer (1)** to take place ▷ *Cette histoire se passe au Moyen Âge.* This story takes place in the Middle Ages. **(2)** to go ▷ *Comment s'est passé le match?* How did the game go? **(3)** to happen ▷ *Que s'est-il passé?* Un accident? What happened? Was there an accident?; **Qu'est-ce qui se passe? Pourquoi est-ce que**

tu pleures? What's the matter? Why are you crying?; **se passer de** to do without ▷ *Je me passerai de confiture ce matin.* I'll do without jam this morning.

passerelle [pasʀɛl] nf ❶ (over river) footbridge ❷ (onto plane, boat) gangway

passe-temps [pustɑ̃] nm pastime

passif [pasif, -iv] (f **passive**) adj passive
▶ nm passive ▷ *Mettez ce verbe au passif.* Put this verb into the passive.

passion [pasjɔ̃] nf passion

passionnant [pasjɔnɑ̃, -ɑ̃t] (f **passionnante**) adj fascinating

passionné [pasjɔne] (f **passionnée**) adj avid ▷ *Il est un lecteur passionné.* He's an avid reader.; **Elle est passionnée de voile.** She's a sailing fanatic.

passionner [pasjɔne] vb: **Son travail le passionne.** He's passionate about his work.; **se passionner pour quelque chose** to have a passion for something ▷ *Elle se passionne pour la photographie.* She has a passion for photography.

passoire [paswaʀ] nf strainer

pastèque [pastɛk] nf watermelon

pastille [pastij] nf cough drop

patate [patat] nf (informal) potato; **les patates pilées** mashed potatoes; **une patate douce** a sweet potato

pâte [pat] nf ❶ pastry ❷ dough ❸ cake batter; **la pâte à crêpes** pancake batter; **la pâte à modeler** Plasticine®; **la pâte d'amandes** marzipan; **la pâte dentifrice** toothpaste

pâté [pate] nm pâté ▷ *Nous avons mangé du pâté en entrée.* We had pâté as an appetizer.; **le pâté chinois** shepherd's pie; **un pâté de maisons** (of houses) a block

patente [patɑ̃t] nf (imprecise) thing ▷ *Pourrais-tu me passer la patente en arrière de la chaise, là?* Could you pass me that thing behind the chair?; **les patentes** stuff ▷ *Ma mère a laissé tes patentes sur la table.* My mom left your stuff on the table. ▷ *J'ai plein de patentes à faire en fin de semaine.* I have a ton of stuff to do this weekend.

paternel [patɛʀnɛl] (f **paternelle**) adj: **ma grand-mère paternelle** my grandmother on my father's side; **mon oncle paternel** my uncle on my father's side

pâtes [pat] nfpl pasta

patience [pasjɑ̃s] nf patience

patient [pasjɑ̃, -ɑ̃t] (f **patiente**) adj patient
▶ nm patient

patiente [pasjɑ̃t] nf patient

patienter [pasjɑ̃te] vb to wait ▷ *Veuillez patienter un instant, s'il vous plaît.* Please wait a moment.

patin [patɛ̃] nm ❶ skate ▷ *Il a enfilé ses patins.* He put his skates on. ❷ skating ▷ *Ils font du patin tous les mercredis.* They go skating every Wednesday.; **accrocher ses patins** to retire; **être vite sur ses patins** to act very fast; **les patins à glace** ice skates; **les patins à roues alignées** inline skates; **les patins à roulettes** roller skates

patinage [patinaʒ] nm skating; **le patinage artistique** figure skating; **le patinage de vitesse** speed skating

patiner [patine] vb to skate

patineur [patinœʀ] nm skater

patineuse [patinøz] nf skater

patinoire [patinwaʀ] nf skating rink

pâtisserie [pɑtisʀi] nf cake shop; **faire de la pâtisserie** to bake ▷ *J'adore faire de la pâtisserie.* I love baking.; **les pâtisseries** cakes

patrie [patʀi] *nf* homeland

patron [patʀɔ̃] *nm* ❶ boss ❷ (*for dressmaking*) pattern

patronne [patʀɔn] *nf* boss; **Elle est patronne de café.** She runs a café.

patrouille [patʀuj] *nf* patrol

patte [pat] *nf* ❶ (*of dog, cat*) paw ❷ (*of bird, animal*) leg

paupière [popjɛʀ] *nf* eyelid

pause [poz] *nf* ❶ break ▷ *Ils font une pause.* They're having a break. ▷ *une pause de midi* a lunch break ❷ pause ▷ *Il y a eu une pause dans la conversation.* There was a pause in the conversation.

pauvre [povʀ(ə)] *adj* poor ▷ *Sa famille est pauvre.* Her family is poor. ▷ *Pauvre lui! Il n'a pas eu de chance!* Poor him! He was unlucky!

> Be careful! The meaning of
> **pauvre** changes according to
> its position. After the noun,
> it means **not rich**; before the
> noun, it means **pitiable**.

pauvreté [povʀəte] *nf* poverty

pavé [pave] (*f* **pavée**) *adj* cobbled ▷ *Les rues étaient pavées.* The streets were cobbled.

pavé numérique *nm* keypad

payant [pejɑ̃, -ɑ̃t] (*f* **payante**) *adj* ❶ paying ▷ *Ce sont des hôtes payants.* They're paying guests. ❷ profitable; **C'est une profession payante.** It's a highly-paid profession.; **C'est payant.** You have to pay. ▷ *L'entrée de la foire est payante.* You have to pay to get into the fair.

paye [pɛj] *nf* wages

payer [peje] *vb* ❶ to pay for ▷ *Combien as-tu payé ta planche à roulettes?* How much did you pay for your skateboard? **J'ai payé ce T-shirt vingt dollars.** I paid 20

dollars for this T-shirt. ❷ to pay ▷ *Elle a été payée aujourd'hui.* She got paid today. ▷ *Son métier paye bien.* His job pays well. ▷ *Elle est mal payée.* She is underpaid.; **faire payer quelque chose à quelqu'un** to charge somebody for something ▷ *Il me l'a fait payer dix dollars.* He charged me 10 dollars for it.; **payer quelque chose à quelqu'un** to buy somebody something ▷ *Allez, je vous paye un café.* Come on, I'll buy you a coffee.

pays [pei] *nm* country

paysage [peizaʒ] *nm* landscape

paysan [peizɑ̃] *nm* farmer

paysanne [peizan] *nf* farmer

PC [pese] *nm* PC (= *personal computer*) ▷ *Il a tapé le rapport sur son PC.* He typed the report on his PC.

péage [peaʒ] *nm* toll ▷ *Nous avons payé cinq dollars de péage.* We paid a toll of 5 dollars.

peau [po] (*pl* **peaux**) *nf* skin ▷ *Tu as la peau douce.* You have soft skin.

pêche [pɛʃ] *nf* ❶ peach ❷ fishing; **aller à la pêche** to go fishing; **la pêche à la ligne** rod fishing; **la pêche sous la glace** ice fishing

péché [peʃe] *nm* sin

pêcher [peʃe] *vb* ❶ to fish for ▷ *Ils sont partis pêcher la truite.* They've gone fishing for trout. ❷ to catch ▷ *On a pêché deux saumons.* We caught two salmon.

pêcheur [peʃœʀ] *nm* fisherman ▷ *Son père est pêcheur.* Her father's a fisherman.

pêcheuse [peʃøz] *nf* (woman) fisherman ▷ *Elle est pêcheuse.* She's a fisherman.

pédagogique [pedagɔʒik] *adj* educational

pédale [pedal] *nf* pedal

pédestre [pedɛstʀ(ə)] *adj*: **une randonnée pédestre** a hike

peigne [pɛɲ] nm comb

peigner [peɲe] vb to comb ▷ *Elle peigne le bébé*. She's combing the baby's hair.; **se peigner** to comb one's hair ▷ *Il faut que je me peigne.* I must comb my hair.

peignoir [peɲwaʀ] nm dressing gown; **un peignoir de bain** a bathrobe

peindre [pɛ̃dʀ(ə)] vb to paint

peine [pɛn] nf trouble; **avoir de la peine à faire quelque chose** to have a hard time doing something ▷ *J'ai eu beaucoup de peine à la convaincre.* I had a really hard time convincing her.; **se donner de la peine** to go to a lot of trouble ▷ *Il s'est donné beaucoup de peine pour obtenir ces renseignements.* He went to a lot of trouble to get this information.; **prendre la peine de faire quelque chose** to go to the trouble of doing something ▷ *Il a pris la peine de me rapporter ma valise.* He went to the trouble of returning my suitcase to me.; **faire de la peine à quelqu'un** to upset somebody ▷ *Ça me fait de la peine de te voir pleurer.* It upsets me to see you crying.; **ce n'est pas la peine** there's no point ▷ *Ce n'est pas la peine de téléphoner.* There's no point in phoning.; **à peine** (1) hardly ▷ *J'ai à peine eu le temps de me changer.* I hardly had time to get changed. (2) only just ▷ *Elle vient à peine de se lever.* She only just got up.

peintre [pɛ̃tʀ(ə)] nmf painter

peinture [pɛ̃tyʀ] nf ❶ painting ▷ *On expose des peintures d'Emily Carr au musée.* There's an exhibition of Emily Carr's paintings at the museum. ❷ paint ▷ *J'ai acheté de la peinture verte.* I bought some green paint.; **« peinture fraîche »** "wet paint"

pêle-mêle [pɛlmɛl] adv higgledy-piggledy

peler [pəle] vb to peel

pelle [pɛl] nf ❶ shovel ▷ *une pelle à neige* a snow shovel ❷ spade

pellicule de plastique nf plastic wrap

pellicules [pelikyl] nfpl dandruff

pelote [pəlɔt] nf ball ▷ *une pelote de laine* a ball of wool

pelouse [pəluz] nf lawn

peluche [pəlyʃ] nf: **un animal en peluche** a stuffed animal

pemmican [pemikã] nm pemmican

penchant [pãʃã] nm: **avoir un penchant pour quelque chose** to have a liking for something

pencher [pãʃe] vb to tilt ▷ *Ce tableau penche vers la droite.* The picture is tilted to the right.; **se pencher** (1) to lean over ▷ *Elle s'est penchée sur la table.* She leaned over the table. (2) to bend down ▷ *Il s'est penché pour ramasser sa casquette.* He bent down to pick up his cap. (3) to lean out ▷ *Ne te penche pas par la fenêtre.* Don't lean out of the window.

pendant [pãdã] prep during ▷ *Ça s'est passé pendant l'été.* It happened during the summer.; **pendant que** while ▷ *Il a téléphoné pendant que sa sœur prenait son bain.* He phoned while his sister was having a bath.

pendentif [pãdãtif] nm pendant

pendre [pãdʀ(ə)] vb to hang ▷ *Il a pendu son manteau dans la garde-robe.* He hung his coat in the closet.

pendule [pãdyl] nf clock

pénétrer [penetʀe] vb ❶ to enter ▷ *Ils ont pénétré dans la maison en passant par le jardin.* They entered the house through the garden. ❷ to penetrate ▷ *Le soleil ne pénètre pas ce feuillage dense.* The sun cannot penetrate this thick foliage.

pénible [penibl(ə)] *adj* difficult
▷ *une tâche pénible* a difficult task;
Il est vraiment pénible. He's a
real pain.

péniblement [peniblemã] *adv*
with difficulty

pénis [penis] *nm* penis

pénombre [penɔ̃br(ə)] *nf*
half-light

pensée [pãse] *nf* thought ▷ *Il était
perdu dans ses pensées.* He was lost
in thought.

penser [pãse] *vb* to think ▷ *Je
pense qu'elle a eu raison de partir.*
I think she was right to leave.;
penser à quelque chose to think
about something ▷ *Je pense à mes
vacances.* I'm thinking about my
holidays.; **Pensez-y.** Think about
it.; **faire penser quelqu'un à
quelque chose** to remind someone
of something ▷ *Cette photo me fait
penser à notre voyage.* This photo
reminds me of our trip.; **faire
penser quelqu'un à faire quelque
chose** to remind someone to do
something ▷ *Fais-moi penser à
téléphoner à mes parents.* Remind
me to phone my parents.; **penser
faire quelque chose** to be planning
to do something ▷ *Ils pensent partir
en Colombie-Britannique en juillet.*
They're planning to go to British
Columbia in July.

pension [pãsjɔ̃] *nf* pension ▷ *Ma
grand-mère reçoit sa pension tous les
mois.* My grandmother gets her
pension every month.

pensionnat [pãsjɔna] *nm*
boarding school

pente [pãt] *nf* slope ▷ *une pente
raide* a steep slope; **en pente** sloping
▷ *Le toit de cette maison est en pente.*
This house has a sloping roof.

pépin [pepɛ̃] *nm* (in fruit) seed

▷ *Cette orange est pleine de pépins.*
This orange is full of seeds.

perçant [pɛrsã, -ãt] (*f* **perçante**)
adj ❶ sharp ▷ *Il a une vue perçante.*
He has very sharp eyes. ❷ piercing
▷ *un cri perçant* a piercing cry

percer [pɛrse] *vb* to pierce ▷ *Elle
s'est fait percer les oreilles.* She got her
ears pierced.

percuter [pɛrkyte] *vb* to smash
into

perdant [pɛrdã] *nm* loser

perdante [pɛrdãt] *nf* loser

perdre [pɛrdr(ə)] *vb* to lose ▷ *Il a
perdu ses clés.* He lost his keys.; **J'ai
perdu mon chemin.** I've lost my
way.; **perdre un match** to lose a
game; **perdre du temps** to waste
time ▷ *J'ai perdu beaucoup de temps ce
matin.* I've wasted a lot of time this
morning. ▷ *Nous avons perdu notre
temps à cette réunion.* That meeting
was a waste of time.; **se perdre** to
get lost ▷ *Je me suis perdu en route.* I
got lost on the way here.

perdu [pɛrdy] *vb see* **perdre**

père [pɛr] *nm* father

perfectionné [pɛrfɛksjɔne] (*f
perfectionnée*) *adj* sophisticated

perfectionner [pɛrfɛksjɔne]
vb to improve ▷ *Elle a besoin de
perfectionner son anglais.* She needs
to improve her English.

pergélisol [pɛrʒelisɔl] *nm*
permafrost

périmé [perime] (*f périmée*) *adj*
out-of-date ▷ *Mon passeport est
périmé.* My passport is out of date.;
Ces yogourts sont périmés. These
yogurts are past their best-before
date.

période [perjɔd] *nf* period

périodiquement [perjɔdikmã]
adv periodically

périphérique [periferik] *adj*
outlying ▷ *un quartier périphérique*

an outlying district

perle [pɛʀl(ə)] nf pearl

permanence [pɛʀmanɑ̃s] nf:
assurer une permanence to offer a basic service ▷ Ma banque assure une permanence le samedi matin. My bank offers a basic service on Saturday mornings.; **être de permanence** to be on duty ▷ Elle ne peut pas venir, elle est de permanence ce soir. She can't come, she's on duty tonight.; **en permanence** permanently ▷ Il se plaint en permanence. He's always complaining.

permanent [pɛʀmanɑ̃, -ɑ̃t] (f **permanente**) adj ① permanent ▷ Il a un poste permanent. He has a permanent job. ② continuous ▷ J'en ai assez de tes critiques permanentes. I've had enough of your constant criticism.

permanente [pɛʀmanɑ̃t] nf perm

permettre [pɛʀmɛtʀ(ə)] vb to allow; **permettre à quelqu'un de faire quelque chose** to allow somebody to do something ▷ Ses parents lui permettent de sortir le soir. His parents allow him to go out at night.

permis [pɛʀmi] nm permit ▷ Il vous faut un permis pour camper ici. You need a permit to camp here.; **le permis de conduire** driver's licence; **un permis de pêche** a fishing licence; **un permis de travail** a work permit

permission [pɛʀmisjɔ̃] nf permission ▷ Qui t'a donné la permission d'entrer? Who gave you permission to come in?; **avoir la permission de faire quelque chose** to have permission to do something ▷ J'ai la permission d'utiliser son baladeur. I've got the permission to use his personal stereo.; **être en permission** (from

the army) to be on leave

perpétuel [pɛʀpetɥɛl] (f **perpétuelle**) adj perpetual

perplexe [pɛʀplɛks(ə)] adj puzzled ▷ Ma question l'a laissé perplexe. She was puzzled by my question.

perroquet [pɛʀɔkɛ] nm parrot

perruche [pɛʀyʃ] nf budgie

perruque [pɛʀyk] nf wig

persil [pɛʀsij] nm parsley

personnage [pɛʀsɔnaʒ] nm ① figure ▷ des personnages historiques historical figures ② character ▷ le personnage principal du film the main character in the film

personnalité [pɛʀsɔnalite] nf ① personality ▷ Il a une personnalité forte. He has a strong personality. ② prominent figure ▷ Il y avait beaucoup de personnalités politiques à ce dîner. There were lots of prominent political figures at the dinner.

personne [pɛʀsɔn] nf person ▷ Il y avait une trentaine de personnes dans la pièce. There were about 30 people in the room. ▷ une personne âgée an elderly person; **en personne** in person
▶ pron ① nobody ▷ Il n'y a personne à la maison. There's nobody at home. ▷ Personne n'est venu me chercher. Nobody came to fetch me. ② anybody ▷ Elle ne veut voir personne. She doesn't want to see anybody.

personnel [pɛʀsɔnɛl] (f **personnelle**) adj personal
▶ nm staff ▷ Il nous faut plus de personnel. We need more staff.; **le service du personnel** the personnel department

personnellement [pɛʀsɔnɛlmɑ̃] adv personally ▷ Personnellement, je ne suis pas d'accord. Personally, I don't agree.

persuader [pɛʀsɥade] *vb* to persuade; **persuader quelqu'un de faire quelque chose** to persuade somebody to do something ▷ *Elle m'a persuadé de l'accompagner au cinéma.* She persuaded me to go to the movie theatre with her.

perte [pɛʀt(ə)] *nf* ❶ loss ▷ *la perte de poids* weight loss ▷ *Ça fait huit victoires et deux pertes pour notre équipe.* That's 8 wins and 2 losses for our team. ❷ waste ▷ *Cette réunion a été une perte de temps.* That meeting was a waste of time.

perturber [pɛʀtyʀbe] *vb* to disrupt ▷ *Le bruit dans le couloir perturbait la classe.* The noise in the hallway was disrupting the class.

pèse-personne [pɛzpɛʀsɔn] *nm* bathroom scales

peser [pəze] *vb* to weigh ▷ *Il pèse cinquante kilos.* He weighs 50 kilos.; **peser lourd** to be heavy ▷ *Cette valise pèse lourd.* This suitcase is heavy.

pessimiste [pesimist(ə)] *adj* pessimistic

pétale [petal] *nm* petal

pétard [petaʀ] *nm* firecracker

pétillant [petijã, -ɑ̃t] (*f* **pétillante**) *adj* sparkling

petit [pəti, -it] (*f* **petite**) *adj* ❶ small ▷ *Nous habitons une petite ville.* We live in a small town. ❷ little ▷ *Elle a une jolie petite maison.* She has a nice little house.; **petit à petit** bit by bit; **un petit ami** a boyfriend; **une petite amie** a girlfriend; **un petit pain** a bread roll; **des petits pois** peas; **les petits** (*of animal*) young ▷ *la lionne et ses petits* the lioness and her young

petite-fille [pətitfij] (*pl* **petites-**

filles) *nf* granddaughter

petit-fils [pətifis] (*pl* **petits-fils**) *nm* grandson

petits-enfants [pətizɑ̃fɑ̃] *nmpl* grandchildren

pétoncle [petɔ̃kl] *nm* scallop

pétrole [petʀɔl] *nm* oil ▷ *un puits de pétrole* an oil well

peu [pø] *adv*, *n* not much ▷ *J'ai peu mangé à midi.* I didn't eat much for lunch. ▷ *Il voyage peu.* He doesn't travel much.; **un peu** a bit ▷ *Elle est un peu timide.* She's a bit shy. ▷ *un peu de gâteau* a bit of cake; **un petit peu** a little bit ▷ *un petit peu de crème* a little bit of cream; **peu de** (1) not many ▷ *Il y a peu de bons films au cinéma.* There aren't many good movies playing at the theatre. ▷ *Elle a peu d'amis.* She doesn't have many friends. (2) not much ▷ *Il a peu d'espoir de réussir.* He doesn't have much hope of succeeding. ▷ *Il lui reste peu d'argent.* He doesn't have much money left.; **à peu près** (1) more or less ▷ *J'ai à peu près fini.* I've more or less finished. (2) about ▷ *Le voyage prend à peu près deux heures.* The journey takes about two hours.; **peu à peu** little by little; **peu avant** shortly before; **peu après** shortly afterwards; **de peu** (*by a narrow margin*) just ▷ *Elle a manqué son train de peu.* She just missed her train.

peuple [pœpl(ə)] *nm* people ▷ *le peuple canadien* the Canadian people

peur [pœʀ] *nf* fear; **avoir peur de** to be afraid of ▷ *Je n'ai pas peur du noir.* I'm not afraid of the dark.; **avoir peur de faire quelque chose** to be afraid to do something ▷ *Elle a peur d'y aller toute seule.* She's afraid to go on her own.; **faire peur à quelqu'un** to scare somebody ▷ *Cet* *homme-là me fait peur.* That man scares me.

peureux [pœʀø, -øz] (*f* peureuse) *adj* fearful

peut [pø] *vb see* **pouvoir**; **Il ne peut pas venir.** He can't come.

peut-être [pøtɛtʀ(ə)] *adv* maybe
▶ *Je l'ai peut-être oublié à la maison.* Maybe I left it at home.; **peut-être que** it could be that ▶ *Peut-être qu'elles n'ont pas pu téléphoner.* It could be that they weren't able to phone.

peuvent, peux *vb see* **pouvoir**; **Je ne peux pas le faire.** I can't do it.

p. ex. *abbr* (= par exemple) e.g.

phare [faʀ] *nm* ❶ lighthouse ▶ *On voit le phare depuis le pont du bateau.* You can see the lighthouse from the ship's deck. ❷ headlight ▶ *Il a laissé les phares de sa voiture allumés.* He left his headlights on.

pharmacie [faʀmasi] *nf* drugstore

pharmacien [faʀmasjɛ̃] *nm* pharmacist

pharmacienne [faʀmasjɛn] *nf* pharmacist

phénomène [fenomɛn] *nm* phenomenon

philosophie [filozofi] *nf* philosophy

phoque [fɔk] *nm* (animal) seal

photo [foto] *nf* photo ▶ *Elle a fait développer ses photos.* She got her photos developed.; **en photo** in pictures ▶ *Je n'ai vu les montagnes qu'en photo.* I've only ever seen the mountains in pictures.; **prendre quelqu'un en photo** to take a picture of somebody ▶ *Maman nous a pris en photo.* Mom took a picture of us.; **une photo d'identité** a passport photo

photocopie [fotokopi] *nf* photocopy

photocopier [fotokopje] *vb* to photocopy

photocopieuse [fotokopjøz] *nf* photocopier

photographe [fotograf] *nmf* photographer

photographie [fotografi] *nf* ❶ photography ❷ photograph

photographier [fotografje] *vb* to photograph

phrase [fʀaz] *nf* sentence

physique [fizik] *adj* physical
▶ *nm:* **Il a un physique agréable.** He's quite good-looking.
▶ *nf* physics ▶ *Il est professeur de physique.* He's a physics teacher.

pianiste [pjanist(ə)] *nmf* pianist
▶ *Elle est pianiste.* She's a pianist.

piano [pjano] *nm* piano

pic [pik] *nm* peak ▶ *les pics enneigés des Rocheuses* the snowy peaks of the Rockies; **à pic** (1) straight down ▶ *La falaise tombe à pic dans la mer.* The cliff drops straight down into the sea. (2) just at the right time ▶ *Tu es arrivé à pic.* You arrived just at the right time.

pic-bois *nm* woodpecker

pièce [pjɛs] *nf* ❶ room ▶ *Mon lit est au centre de la pièce.* My bed is in the middle of the room. ❷ play ▶ *On joue une pièce de Robert Lepage au théâtre.* There's a play by Robert Lepage on at the theatre. ❸ part ▶ *Il faut changer une pièce du moteur.* There's an engine part that needs changing.; **coin** ▶ *des pièces de un dollar* some one-dollar coins; **cinquante dollars pièce** 50 dollars each ▶ *J'ai acheté ces T-shirts dix dollars pièce.* I bought these T-shirts for ten dollars each.; **un maillot une pièce** a one-piece swimsuit; **un maillot deux-pièces** a two-piece swimsuit; **Avez-vous une pièce d'identité?** Do you have any identification?; **une pièce jointe** an email attachment

pied [pje] nm foot ▷ *J'ai mal aux pieds.* My feet are hurting.; **à pied** on foot; **avoir pied** to be able to touch bottom ▷ *Elle n'aime pas nager là où elle n'a pas pied.* She doesn't like swimming where she can't touch bottom.; **avoir les deux pieds dans la même bottine** to be clumsy; **des pieds à la tête** from head to foot; **le pied d'athlète** athlete's foot; **le pied de page** in document) footer

piège [pjɛʒ] nm trap; **prendre quelqu'un au piège** to trap somebody

piéger [pjeʒe] vb to trap; **un colis piégé** a parcel bomb; **une voiture piégée** a car bomb

pierre [pjɛʀ] nf stone; **une pierre précieuse** a precious stone; **faire d'une pierre deux coups** to kill two birds with one stone

piéton [pjetɔ̃] nm pedestrian

piétonne [pjetɔn] nf pedestrian

piétonnier [pjetɔnje, -jɛʀ] adj: une rue **piétonnière** a traffic-free street; **un quartier piétonnier** a pedestrian zone

pieuvre [pjœvʀ(ə)] nf octopus

pigeon [piʒɔ̃] nm pigeon

piger [piʒe] vb (informal) to understand

pile [pil] nf ❶ pile ▷ *Il y a une pile de disques sur la table.* There's a pile of records on the table. ❷ battery ▷ *La pile de ma montre est usée.* The battery in my watch is dead.
▸ adv: **à deux heures pile** at two on the dot; **jouer à pile ou face** to flip a coin; **Pile ou face?** Heads or tails?

pilote [pilɔt] nmf pilot; **un pilote de course** a race car driver; **un pilote de ligne** an airline pilot

piloter [pilɔte] vb (a plane) to fly

pilule [pilyl] nf pill; **prendre la pilule** to be on the Pill

piment [pimɑ̃] nm chili pepper

pin [pɛ̃] nm pine

pince [pɛ̃s] nf ❶ (tool) pliers ❷ (of crab) pincer; **une pince à épiler** tweezers; **une pince à linge** a clothespin

pinceau [pɛ̃so] (pl pinceaux) nm paintbrush

pincée [pɛ̃se] nf: une pincée de sel a pinch of salt

pincer [pɛ̃se] vb to pinch ▷ *Il m'a pincé le bras.* He pinched my arm.

pingouin [pɛ̃gwɛ̃] nm penguin

ping-pong [piŋpɔ̃g] nm table tennis ▷ *jouer au ping-pong* to play table tennis

pion [pjɔ̃] nm ❶ (chess) pawn ❷ (in checkers) piece

pionnier [pjɔnje] nm pioneer

pionnière [pjɔnjɛʀ] nf pioneer

pipe [pip] nf (for smoking) pipe

piquant [pikɑ̃, -ɑ̃t] (f piquante) adj ❶ prickly ❷ spicy

pique [pik] nm spades ▷ *l'as de pique* the ace of spades

pique-nique [piknik] nm picnic

piquer [pike] vb ❶ to bite ▷ *Nous avons été piqués par les maringouins.* We were bitten by mosquitoes. ❷ to burn ▷ *Cette sauce me pique la langue.* This sauce is burning my tongue. ❸ to steal ▷ *On m'a piqué mon porte-monnaie.* (informal) My wallet was stolen.; **se piquer** to prick oneself ▷ *Il s'est piqué avec une aiguille.* He pricked himself with a needle.

piquet [pikɛ] nm ❶ stake ▷ *Le chien est attaché à un piquet.* The dog is tied to a stake. ❷ peg ▷ *Il nous manque un des piquets de la tente.* One of our tent pegs is missing.; **le piquet de grève** the picket line

piqûre [pikyʀ] nf ❶ injection
▷ *Le médecin m'a fait une piqûre.*
The doctor gave me an injection.
❷ bite ▷ *une piqûre de maringouin* a
mosquito bite ❸ sting ▷ *une piqûre
d'abeille* a bee sting

pirate [piʀat] nmf pirate; **un
pirate informatique** a hacker

pire [piʀ] adj, n worse ▷ *C'est encore
pire qu'avant.* It's even worse than
before.; **le pire** the worst ▷ *C'est
la pire journée que j'aie jamais passée.*
That's the worst day I've ever had.
▷ *Ce gamin est le pire de la bande.*
That boy is the worst in the group.;
le pire de the worst of ▷ *Le pire de
tout, c'est qu'on s'ennuie tout le temps.*
The worst of it is that we're always
bored.

piscine [pisin] nf swimming pool

pistache [pistaʃ] nf pistachio ▷ *une
crème glacée à la pistache* a pistachio
ice cream

piste [pist(ə)] nf ❶ trail ▷ *La
police est sur la piste du criminel.* The
police are on the criminal's trail.
❷ runway ▷ *L'avion s'est posé sur
la piste.* The plane landed on the
runway. ❸ ski run ▷ *La skieuse a
descendu la piste.* The skier came
down the ski run.; **la piste de
danse** the dance floor; **une piste
cyclable** a bike path

pistolet [pistɔlɛ] nm pistol

pitié [pitje] nf pity; **Elle me fait
pitié.** I feel sorry for her.; **avoir
pitié de quelqu'un** to feel sorry for
somebody

pitonner [pitɔne] vb ❶ (TV) to zap
❷ (computer) to key in

pittoresque [pitɔʀɛsk(ə)] adj
picturesque

pizza [pidza] nf pizza

placard [plakaʀ] nm cupboard

place [plas] nf ❶ place ▷ *Elle a eu
la troisième place au concours.* She

got third place in the competition.
▷ *remettre quelque chose en place* to
put something back in its place
❷ square ▷ *la place du marché* the
market square ❸ (space) room ▷ *Il
ne reste plus de place pour se garer.*
There's no more room to park. ▷ *Ça
prend de la place.* It takes up a lot of
room. ❹ seat ▷ *Toutes les places
ont été vendues.* All the seats have
been sold.; **sur place** on the spot;
à la place instead ▷ *Il ne reste plus
de tarte; désirez-vous quelque chose
d'autre à la place?* There's no pie left;
would you like something else
instead?; **à la place de** instead of

placer [plase] vb ❶ to seat ▷ *Nous
étions placés près de la porte.* We were
seated near the door. ❷ to invest
▷ *Il a placé ses économies à la Bourse.*
He invested his money on the Stock
Exchange.

plafond [plafɔ̃] nm ceiling

plage [plaʒ] nf beach

plagiat [plaʒja] nm plagiarism

plaie [plɛ] nf wound

plaindre [plɛ̃dʀ(ə)] vb: **plaindre
quelqu'un** to feel sorry for
somebody ▷ *Je te plains.* I feel sorry
for you.; **se plaindre** to complain
▷ *Il n'arrête pas de se plaindre.* He
never stops complaining.; **se
plaindre à quelqu'un** to complain
to somebody ▷ *Ils se sont plaints
à la gérente.* They complained to
the manager.; **se plaindre de
quelque chose** to complain about
something ▷ *Elle s'est plainte du
bruit.* She complained about the
noise.

plaine [plɛn] nf (level area) plain

plainte [plɛ̃t] nf complaint; **porter
plainte** to lodge a complaint

plaire [plɛʀ] vb: **Ce cadeau me
plaît beaucoup.** I like this present
a lot.; **Ce film plaît beaucoup aux**

jeunes. The film is very popular with young people.; **Ça t'a plu d'aller en Nouvelle-Écosse?** Did you enjoy going to Nova Scotia?; **Elle lui plaît.** He likes her.; **s'il te plaît** please; **s'il vous plaît** please

plaisanter [plɛzɑ̃te] vb to joke

plaisanterie [plɛzɑ̃tʀi] nf joke

plaisir [plezir] nm pleasure; **faire plaisir à quelqu'un** to please somebody ▷ *J'y suis allé pour lui faire plaisir.* I went there to please her. ▷ *Ce cadeau me fait très plaisir.* I'm very happy with this present.

plaît [plɛ] vb see **plaire**

plan [plɑ̃] nm ❶ plan ❷ map ▷ *un plan du centre commercial* a map of the mall; **un plan de la ville** a street map; **au premier plan** in the foreground

planche [plɑ̃ʃ] nf plank; **une planche à neige** a snowboard; **une planche à repasser** an ironing board; **une planche à roulettes** a skateboard; **une planche à voile** a sailboard; **une planche de surf** a surfboard

plancher [plɑ̃ʃe] nm floor

planchiste [plɑ̃ʃist(ə)] nmf (skateboarder, snowboarder) boarder

planer [plane] vb to glide ▷ *Un oiseau planait dans l'air.* A bird glided through the air.

planète [planɛt] nf planet

plante [plɑ̃t] nf plant

planter [plɑ̃te] vb ❶ to plant ▷ *Mon père a planté des tomates.* My dad planted some tomatoes. ❷ to hammer in ▷ *Elle a planté un clou dans le mur.* She hammered a nail into the wall. ❸ to pitch ▷ *Les filles ont planté leur tente au bord du lac.* The girls pitched their tent beside the lake. ❹ (computer) to crash ▷ *Mon ordinateur a encore planté.* My computer crashed again.; **Ne**

reste pas planté là! Don't just stand there!; **se planter** (informal) to fail ▷ *Je me suis planté en maths.* I failed math.

plaque [plak] nf (metal) plate; **une plaque de verglas** a patch of ice

plaqué [plake] (f **plaquée**) adj: **plaqué or** gold-plated; **plaqué argent** silver-plated

plastique [plastik] nm plastic

plat [pla, -at] (f **plate**) adj flat; **être à plat ventre** to be lying face down; **l'eau plate** still water
▶ nm ❶ dish ❷ course ▷ *le plat principal* the main course; **un plat cuisiné** a pre-cooked meal; **le plat du jour** the daily special

plateau [plato] (pl **plateaux**) nm ❶ tray; **un plateau de fromages** a selection of cheeses ❷ plateau

platine [platin] nm platinum
▶ nf (of record player) turntable; **une platine laser** a CD player

plâtre [plɑtʀ(ə)] nm plaster ▷ *une statue en plâtre* a plaster statue; **avoir un bras dans le plâtre** to have one's arm in a cast

plein [plɛ̃, -ɛn] (f **pleine**) adj full; **à plein temps** full-time ▷ *Elle travaille à plein temps.* She works full-time.; **plein de** (informal) lots of ▷ *un gâteau avec plein de crème* a cake with lots of cream; **Il y a plein de gens dans la rue.** The street is full of people.; **en plein air** in the open air; **en pleine nuit** in the middle of the night; **en plein jour** in broad daylight
▶ nm: **faire le plein** (gas) to fill it up ▷ *Faites le plein, s'il vous plaît.* Fill it up, please.

pleurer [plœʀe] vb to cry

pleut [plø] vb see **pleuvoir**

pleuvoir [pløvwaʀ] vb to rain ▷ *Il pleut.* It's raining.; **pleuvoir à boire debout** to rain cats and dogs

pli [pli] *nm* ❶ fold ❷ pleat ▷ *une jupe à plis* a pleated skirt ❸ crease ▷ *Il y a un pli sur la manche de la chemise.* There's a crease in the sleeve of your shirt.

pliant [plijɑ̃, -ɑ̃t] (*f* **pliante**) *adj* folding ▷ *un lit pliant* a folding bed ▷ *nm* folding bed

plier [plije] *vb* ❶ to fold ▷ *plier une serviette* to fold a towel ❷ to bend ▷ *Il a plié le bras.* He bent his arm.

plomb [plɔ̃] *nm* lead ▷ *un tuyau en plomb* a lead pipe; **l'essence sans plomb** unleaded gas

plombier [plɔ̃bje] *nm* plumber; **Il est plombier.** He's a plumber.

plombière [plɔ̃bjɛr] *nf* plumber; **Elle est plombière.** She's a plumber.

plongée [plɔ̃ʒe] *nf* diving ▷ *faire de la plongée* to go diving

plongeoir [plɔ̃ʒwar] *nm* diving board

plongeon [plɔ̃ʒɔ̃] *nm* dive

plonger [plɔ̃ʒe] *vb* to dive ▷ *Il a plongé dans la piscine.* He dived into the swimming pool.; **J'ai plongé ma main dans l'eau.** I plunged my hand into the water.; **être plongé dans son travail** to be absorbed in one's work; **se plonger dans un livre** to get absorbed in a book

plu [ply] *vb see* **plaire, pleuvoir**

pluie [plɥi] *nf* rain ▷ *sous la pluie* in the rain

plume [plym] *nf* feather ▷ *une plume d'oiseau* a bird's feather; **un stylo à plume** a fountain pen

plupart [plypar]: **la plupart** *pron* most (of them) ▷ *La plupart ont moins de quinze ans.* Most of them are under 15.; **la plupart de** most of ▷ *La plupart de mes amis sont allés au concert.* Most of my friends went to the concert. ▷ *La plupart des élèves ont fait les devoirs.* Most of the students did the homework.; **la**

plupart des most ▷ *La plupart des gens ont déjà vu ce film.* Most people have already seen this film.; **la plupart du temps** most of the time

pluriel [plyrjɛl] *nm* plural; **au pluriel** in the plural

plus [plys] *adv, prep:* **ne...plus** not...anymore ▷ *Il ne travaille plus ici.* He doesn't work here anymore.; **Je n'ai plus de pain.** I have no more bread.; **plus...que** more... than ▷ *Il est plus extraverti que son frère.* He's more outgoing than his brother. ▷ *Elle travaille plus que moi.* She works more than me. ▷ *Elle est plus grande que moi.* She's bigger than me.; **C'est le plus grand de la famille.** He's the tallest in his family.; **plus...plus...** the more... the more... ▷ *Plus elle gagne d'argent, plus elle en veut.* The more money she earns, the more she wants.; **plus de** (1) more ▷ *Il nous faut plus de pain.* We need more bread. (2) more than ▷ *Il y avait plus de dix personnes.* There were more than 10 people.; **de plus** more ▷ *Il nous faut un joueur de plus.* We need one more player. ▷ *Le voyage a pris trois heures de plus que prévu.* The journey took 3 more hours than planned.; **en plus** more ▷ *J'ai apporté quelques couvertures en plus.* I brought a few more blankets.; **de plus en plus** more and more ▷ *Il y a de plus en plus de touristes par ici.* There are getting to be more and more tourists around here. ▷ *Il fait de plus en plus chaud.* It's getting hotter and hotter out.; **un peu plus difficile** a bit more difficult ▷ *Il fait un peu plus froid qu'hier.* It's a bit colder than yesterday.; **plus ou moins** more or less; **Quatre plus deux égalent six.** 4 plus 2 is 6.

plusieurs [plyzjœr] *pron* several

▷ *Elle a acheté plusieurs chemises.* She bought several shirts. ▷ *Il y en a plusieurs.* There are several of them.

plus-que-parfait [plyskəparfɛ] nm pluperfect

plutôt [plyto] adv ❶ quite ▷ *Elle est plutôt forte.* She's quite strong. ❷ rather ▷ *La nourriture ici est plutôt chère.* The food here is rather expensive ❸ instead ▷ *Demande-leur plutôt de venir avec toi.* Ask them to come with you instead.; **plutôt que** rather than ▷ *Je prendrai la salade plutôt que les frites avec ça.* I'll have the salad rather than the fries with that.

pluvieux [plyvjø, -øz] (f **pluvieuse**) adj rainy

pneu [pnø] nm tire

pneumonie [pnømɔni] nf pneumonia

poche [pɔʃ] nf pocket; **l'argent de poche** pocket money; **un livre de poche** a paperback; **un ordinateur de poche** a handheld computer

poêle [pwal] nf frying pan; **une poêle à frire** a frying pan

poème [pɔɛm] nm poem

poésie [pɔezi] nf ❶ poetry ❷ poem

poète [pɔɛt] nmf poet

poids [pwa] nm weight ▷ *vendre quelque chose au poids* to sell something by weight; **prendre du poids** to put on weight ▷ *Il a pris du poids.* He's put on weight.; **perdre du poids** to lose weight ▷ *Il a perdu du poids.* He's lost weight.; **un poids lourd** a truck

poignée [pwaɲe] nf ❶ handful ▷ *une poignée de riz* a handful of rice ❷ handle ▷ *la poignée de la porte* the door handle; **une poignée de main** a handshake

poignet [pwaɲe] nm ❶ wrist ▷ *Je me suis fait mal au poignet.* I hurt my

wrist. ❷ (*of shirt*) cuff

poil [pwal] nm ❶ hair ▷ *Il y a des poils de chat partout sur la moquette.* There are cat hairs all over the carpet. ❷ fur ▷ *Ton chien a un beau poil.* Your dog has beautiful fur.; **à poil** (*informal*) stark naked

poilu [pwaly] (f **poilue**) adj hairy

poinçonner [pwɛ̃sɔne] vb to punch ▷ *Le contrôleur a poinçonné les billets.* The conductor punched the tickets.

poing [pwɛ̃] nm fist; **un coup de poing** a punch

point [pwɛ̃] nm ❶ point ▷ *Je ne suis pas d'accord sur ce point.* I don't agree with this point. ▷ *Son point faible, c'est qu'elle est un peu paresseuse.* Her weak point is that she's a bit lazy.; **le point de départ** (*in a race*) the starting line; **point de vue** point of view ❷ (*punctuation*) period ❸ dot ▷ *mettre un point sur un « i »* to dot an "i"; **être sur le point de faire quelque chose** to be just about to do something ▷ *J'étais sur le point de téléphoner.* I was just about to phone you.; **mettre au point** to finalize; **Ce n'est pas encore au point.** It's not finalized yet.; **à point** medium ▷ *« Comment voulez-vous votre steak ? »* — *« À point. »* "How would you like your steak?" — "Medium."; **un point d'exclamation** an exclamation mark; **un point d'interrogation** a question mark; **un point noir** a blackhead

pointage [pwɛ̃taʒ] nm (*sports*) score

pointe [pwɛ̃t] nf point ▷ *la pointe d'un couteau* the point of a knife; **être à la pointe du progrès** to be in the forefront of progress; **sur la pointe des pieds** on tiptoe; **les heures de pointe** peak hours

pointillé [pwɛ̃tije] nm dotted line
pointilleux [pwɛ̃tijø, -øz] (f
  pointilleuse) adj picky ▷ Notre prof
  est pointilleuse sur la grammaire. Our
  teacher is picky about grammar.
pointu [pwɛ̃ty] (f **pointue**) adj
  pointed ▷ un chapeau pointu a
  pointed hat
pointure [pwɛ̃tyʀ] nf size (of shoes)
  ▷ Quelle est votre pointure? What size
  shoes do you take?
point-virgule [pwɛ̃viʀgyl] (pl
  points-virgules) nm semicolon
poire [pwaʀ] nf pear
poireau [pwaʀo] (pl **poireaux**)
  nm leek ▷ la soupe aux poireaux
  leek soup
pois [pwa] nm pea; **les petits pois**
  peas; **les pois chiches** chickpeas; **à
  pois** polka-dotted ▷ une robe à pois a
  polka-dotted dress
poison [pwazɔ̃] nm poison
poisson [pwasɔ̃] nm fish ▷ Je n'aime
  pas le poisson. I don't like fish. ▷ Elle
  a attrapé deux poissons. She caught
  two fish.; **les Poissons** Pisces ▷ Elle
  est Poissons. She's a Pisces.; **Poisson
  d'avril!** April fool!; **un poisson
  rouge** a goldfish
poitrine [pwatʀin] nf **①** chest
  ▷ J'ai mal à la poitrine. I'm having
  chest pains. **②** bust ▷ Quel est votre
  tour de poitrine? What's your bust
  size? **③** breast ▷ une poitrine de
  poulet a chicken breast
poivre [pwavʀ(ə)] nm (spice)
  pepper
poivron [pwavʀɔ̃] nm (vegetable)
  pepper
pôle [pol] nm pole; **le pôle Nord**
  the North Pole; **le pôle Sud** the
  South Pole
poli [pɔli] (f **polie**) adj polite
police [pɔlis] nf police **①** police ▷ La police
  recherche le voleur. The police are
  looking for the thief.; **la police**

de caractères font; **une police
  d'assurance** an insurance policy
policier [pɔlisje, -jɛʀ] (f **policière**)
  adj: **un roman policier** a detective
  novel
  ▶ nm police officer ▷ Il est policier.
  He's a police officer.
policière [pɔlisjɛʀ] nf police officer
  ▷ Elle est policière. She's a police
  officer.
politesse [pɔlites] nf politeness
politique [pɔlitik] nf **①** politics
  ▷ La politique ne l'intéresse pas du
  tout. He's not at all interested in
  politics.; **pratiquer la politique de
  l'autruche** to bury one's head in the
  sand **②** policy ▷ la politique sociale
  du gouvernement the government's
  social policy
  ▶ adj political ▷ une question
  politique a political issue
politiquement correct
  [pɔlitikmã-] adj politically correct
polluer [pɔlɥe] vb to pollute ▷ Les
  lacs ont été pollués. The lakes have
  been polluted.
pollupostage [pɔlypɔstaʒ] nm
  spam
polluriel [pɔlyʀjɛl] nm spam
  message
pollution [pɔlysjɔ̃] nf pollution
polyvalente [pɔlivalãt] nf
  ● In Québec, **la polyvalente** is
  ● a high school that provides
  ● both academic and vocational
  ● programs.
pommade [pɔmad] nf ointment
pomme [pɔm] nf apple; **les
  pommes de terre** potatoes
pompe [pɔ̃p] nf pump; **une pompe
  à essence** a gas pump
pompier [pɔ̃pje] nm firefighter
pompière [pɔ̃pjɛʀ] nf firefighter
ponctuel [pɔ̃ktɥɛl] (f **ponctuelle**)
  adj **①** punctual ▷ Elle est toujours
  très ponctuelle. She's always very

punctual. ❷ occasional; **On a rencontré quelques problèmes ponctuels.** We've had the occasional problem.

pondre [pɔ̃dʀ(ə)] vb (eggs) to lay

poney [pɔnɛ] nm pony

pont [pɔ̃] nm ❶ bridge ❷ (of ship) deck

pop [pɔp] adj (music) pop ▷ **des groupes pop** pop bands

populaire [pɔpylɛʀ] adj ❶ popular ▷ **Ce chanteur est très populaire au Québec.** This singer's very popular in Québec. ❷ working-class ▷ **un quartier populaire de la ville** a working-class area of town

population [pɔpylɑsjɔ̃] nf population; **la population active** the workforce

porc [pɔʀ] nm ❶ pig ▷ **Ils élèvent des porcs.** They breed pigs. ❷ pork ▷ **du rôti de porc** roast pork

porcelaine [pɔʀsəlɛn] nf china ▷ **une tasse en porcelaine** a china cup

porc-épic [pɔʀkepik] (pl **porcs-épics**) nm porcupine

port [pɔʀ] nm ❶ harbour ❷ port

portage [pɔʀtaʒ] nm portage ▷ **Cette rivière comporte huit portages.** This river has 8 portages.; **faire du portage** to portage

portager [pɔʀtaʒe] vb to portage

portail [pɔʀtaj] nm (Web) portal

portatif [pɔʀtatif, -iv] (f **portative**) adj portable

porte [pɔʀt(ə)] nf ❶ door ▷ **Ferme la porte, s'il te plaît.** Close the door, please.; **la porte d'entrée** the front door ❷ gate ▷ **Vol 432 à destination de Calgary : porte numéro trois.** Flight 432 to Calgary: gate 3.; **mettre quelqu'un à la porte** to fire somebody

porte-bagages [pɔʀtbagaʒ] nm luggage rack; **le porte-bagages de**

toit roof rack

porte-clés [pɔʀtəkle] nm keychain

portée [pɔʀte] nf: **à portée de la main** within arm's reach; **hors de portée** out of reach

portefeuille [pɔʀtəfœj] nm wallet

portemanteau [pɔʀtmɑ̃to] (pl **portemanteaux**) nm coat rack

porte-monnaie [pɔʀtmɔnɛ] (pl **porte-monnaie**) nm wallet

porte-parole [pɔʀtpaʀɔl] nmf spokesperson ▷ **Elle est la porte-parole de notre conseil étudiant.** She's the spokesperson for our student council.

porter [pɔʀte] vb ❶ to carry ▷ **Il portait une valise.** He was carrying a suitcase. ❷ to wear ▷ **Elle porte une robe bleue.** She's wearing a blue dress.; **se porter bien** to be well; **se porter mal** to be unwell

porteur [pɔʀtœʀ] nm porter

portion [pɔʀsjɔ̃] nf portion

portrait [pɔʀtʀɛ] nm portrait

poser [poze] vb ❶ to put down ▷ **J'ai posé la cafetière sur la table.** I put the coffee pot down on the table. ❷ to pose ▷ **Cela pose un problème.** That poses a problem.; **poser une question à quelqu'un** to ask somebody a question; **poser des rideaux** to put up curtains; **poser sa candidature** to apply for a job; **se poser** to land ▷ **L'avion s'est posé à huit heures.** The plane landed at 8 o'clock.

positif [pozitif, -iv] (f **positive**) adj positive

position [pozisjɔ̃] nf position

posséder [posede] vb to own ▷ **Ils possèdent une jolie maison.** They own a lovely home.

possibilité [posibilite] nf possibility

possible [posibl(ə)] *adj* possible
▷ *Nous leur avons dit que ce n'était pas possible.* We told them that it wasn't possible.; **le plus de gens possible** as many people as possible; **le plus tôt possible** as early as possible; **le moins d'argent possible** as little money as possible; **Il travaille le moins possible.** He works as little as possible.; **dès que possible** as soon as possible; **faire son possible** to do all one can ▷ *Je ferai tout mon possible.* I'll do all I can.

poste [post(ə)] *nf* mail ▷ *Je vais l'envoyer par la poste.* I'm going to send it by mail.; **le bureau de poste** the post office; **mettre une lettre à la poste** to mail a letter
▶ *nm* ❶ job ▷ *Elle a trouvé un poste de professeure.* She has found a teaching job. ❷ (*phone*) extension ▷ *Pouvez-vous me passer le poste de M. Salzedo?* Can you put me through to Mr Salzedo's extension? ❸ set ▷ *un poste de radio* a radio set; **le poste de péage** tollbooth; **un poste de police** a police station

poster [poste] *vb* to mail ▷ *Je vais poster ce colis.* I'm going to mail this parcel.
▶ *nm* poster

pot [po] *nm* jar ▷ *J'ai fait trois pots de confiture.* I've made three jars of jam.; **un pot de fleurs** a flowerpot

potable [potabl(ə)] *adj*: **eau potable** drinking water; **« eau non potable »** "not drinking water"

pot-de-vin [podvẽ] (*pl* **pots-de-vin**) *nm* bribe

poteau [poto] (*pl* **poteaux**) *nm* post ▷ *Elle s'est appuyée contre un poteau.* She leaned against a post.; **un poteau indicateur** a signpost

potentiel [potɑ̃sjεl] (*f* **potentielle**) *adj* potential

poterie [potʀi] *nf* ❶ pottery

▷ *Nous avons fait de la poterie à l'école.* We did pottery at school. ❷ piece of pottery ▷ *J'ai acheté deux poteries.* I bought two pieces of pottery.

potlatch [potlatʃ] *nm* potlatch

pou [pu] (*pl* **poux**) *nm* louse

poubelle [pubɛl] *nf* garbage can

pouce [pus] *nm* ❶ thumb ▷ *Je me suis coincé le pouce dans la porte.* I trapped my thumb in the door.; **donner un coup de pouce à quelqu'un** to help out someone; **faire du pouce** to hitchhike ❷ inch
● An **inch** is a nonmetric unit of
● length equal to about 2.5 cm.

pouding-chômeur [pudiŋʃomœʀ] *nm*
● Le **pouding-chômeur** is a
● dessert consisting of a thickened
● mixture of brown sugar, water,
● and butter, sometimes mixed
● with maple syrup, under a layer
● of cake.

poudre [pudʀ(ə)] *nf* ❶ powder
❷ face powder; **le lait en poudre** powdered milk; **le café en poudre** instant coffee

poudrerie [pudʀəʀi] *nf* blizzard ▷ *Les écoles sont fermées à cause de la poudrerie.* The schools are closed because of the blizzard.

poulain [pulɛ̃] *nm* foal

poule [pul] *nf* hen

poulet [pulε] *nm* chicken ▷ *J'adore le poulet.* I love chicken. ▷ *un poulet rôti* a roast chicken

pouls [pu] *nm* pulse ▷ *Il m'a pris le pouls.* He took my pulse.

poumon [pumɔ̃] *nm* lung

poupée [pupe] *nf* doll

pour [puʀ] *prep* for ▷ *C'est un cadeau pour toi.* It's a present for you. ▷ *Qu'est-ce que tu veux pour ton déjeuner?* What would you like for breakfast?; **pour faire quelque chose** in order to do something

▷ *Je lui ai téléphoné pour l'inviter.* I phoned him in order to invite him.; **Pour aller à Kamloops, s'il vous plaît?** Which way is it to Kamloops, please?; **pour que** is followed by a verb in the subjunctive. ▷ *Je lui ai prêté mon chandail pour qu'elle n'ait pas froid.* I lent her my sweater so that she wouldn't be cold.; **pour cent** per cent

pourboire [puʀbwaʀ] *nm* tip ▷ *Elle a donné un pourboire au garçon.* She gave the waiter a tip.

pourcentage [puʀsɑ̃taʒ] *nm* percentage

pourquoi [puʀkwa] *adv, conj* why ▷ *Pourquoi est-ce qu'il ne vient pas avec nous?* Why isn't he coming with us? ▷ *Elle ne m'a pas dit pourquoi.* She didn't tell me why.

pourra, pourrai, pourras, pourrez *vb see* **pouvoir**

pourri [puʀi] (*f* **pourrie**) *adj* rotten

pourrir [puʀiʀ] *vb* to go bad ▷ *Ces poires ont pourri.* These pears have gone bad.

pourrons, pourront *vb see* **pouvoir**

poursuite [puʀsɥit] *nf* chase ▷ *se lancer à la poursuite de quelqu'un* to chase after somebody

poursuivre [puʀsɥivʀ(ə)] *vb* to carry on with ▷ *Ils ont poursuivi leur travail.* They carried on with their work.; **se poursuivre** to go on ▷ *Le concert s'est poursuivi très tard.* The concert went on very late.

pourtant [puʀtɑ̃] *adv* however ▷ *Il a raté son examen. Pourtant, il n'est pas bête.* He failed his exam. However, he's not stupid.; **C'est pourtant facile!** But it's easy!

pourvu [puʀvy] *adj*
  pourvu que is followed by a verb in the subjunctive.

pourvu que... (1) let's hope that... ▷ *Pourvu qu'il ne pleuve pas!* Let's hope it doesn't rain! **(2)** (*on condition that*) as long as... ▷ *Tu peux y aller, pourvu que tu fasses tes devoirs avant le souper.* You can go, as long as you do your homework before supper.

pousser [puse] *vb* ❶ to push ▷ *Elle a pu pousser la voiture.* She was able to push the car. ❷ to grow ▷ *Mes cheveux poussent vite.* My hair grows quickly.; **pousser un cri** to give a cry; **se pousser** to move over ▷ *Pousse-toi, je ne vois rien.* Move over, I can't see a thing.

poussette [puset] *nf* stroller

poussière [pusjɛʀ] *nf* dust ▷ *La table est couverte de poussière.* The table's covered with dust.

poussiéreux [pusjeʀø, -øz] (*f* **poussiéreuse**) *adj* dusty

poussin [pusɛ̃] *nm* chick

poutine [putin] *nf*
  ● **La poutine**, a Québécois fast
  ● food staple, consists of French
  ● fries topped with cheese curds
  ● and gravy. In one famous version
  ● (**la poutine italienne**), the gravy
  ● is replaced with a meat spaghetti
  ● sauce. **La poutine râpée** is
  ● a traditional Acadian dish
  ● consisting of dumplings made of
  ● grated potato, salted and filled
  ● with pork.

pouvoir [puvwaʀ] *nm* power ▷ *Le premier ministre a beaucoup de pouvoir.* The prime minister has a lot of power.
  ▶ *vb* can ▷ *Je peux lui téléphoner si tu veux.* I can phone her if you want. ▷ *Puis-je venir vous voir samedi?* May I come and see you on Saturday? ▷ *Je ne pourrai pas venir samedi.* I can't come on Saturday. ▷ *J'ai fait tout ce que j'ai pu.* I did all I could.; **je n'en peux plus.** I'm exhausted.; **Il se**

peut que… It's possible that…

il se peut que is followed by a verb in the subjunctive.

▷ *Il se peut qu'elle ait déménagé.* It's possible that she's moved. ▷ *Il se peut que j'y aille.* I might go.

prairie [pʀɛʀi] *nf* prairie; **les provinces des Prairies** the Prairie provinces

pratique [pʀatik] *nf* practice ▷ *Je manque de pratique.* I'm out of practice.

▶ *adj* practical ▷ *Ce sac à main est très pratique.* This purse is very practical.

pratiquement [pʀatikmɑ̃] *adv* practically ▷ *J'ai pratiquement fini.* I've practically finished.

pratiquer [pʀatike] *vb* to practise ▷ *Je dois pratiquer mon anglais.* I need to practise my English.; **Pratiquez-vous un sport?** Do you play any sports?

pré [pʀe] *nm* meadow

précaution [pʀekosjɔ̃] *nf* precaution ▷ *prendre ses précautions* to take precautions; **par précaution** as a precaution ▷ *Il a pris une assurance par précaution.* He took out insurance as a precaution.; **avec précaution** cautiously; « **à manipuler avec précaution** » "handle with care"

précédemment [pʀesedamɑ̃] *adv* previously

précédent [pʀesedɑ̃, -ɑ̃t] (*f* **précédente**) *adj* previous

précieux [pʀesjø, -øz] (*f* **précieuse**) *adj* precious; **une pierre précieuse** a precious stone; **de précieux conseils** invaluable advice

précipice [pʀesipis] *nm* ravine ▷ *Leur voiture est tombée dans un précipice.* Their car fell into a ravine.

précipitamment [pʀesipitamɑ̃]

adv hurriedly ▷ *Elle est partie précipitamment.* She left hurriedly.

précipitation [pʀesipitasjɔ̃] *nf* haste ▷ *Il a agi avec précipitation.* He acted hastily.

se précipiter [pʀesipite] *vb* to rush

précis [pʀesi, -iz] (*f* **précise**) *adj* precise; **à huit heures précises** at exactly eight o'clock

précisément [pʀesizemɑ̃] *adv* precisely

préciser [pʀesize] *vb* ❶ to be more specific about ▷ *Pouvez-vous préciser ce que vous voulez dire?* Can you be more specific about what you're trying to say? ❷ to specify ▷ *Pouvez-vous préciser les raisons de ce changement?* Can you specify the reasons for this change?

précision [pʀesizjɔ̃] *nf* ❶ precision ❷ detail ▷ *Peux-tu me donner quelques précisions?* Can you give me some details?

prédire [pʀediʀ] *vb* ❶ to predict ▷ *Les climatologues n'ont pas prédit ce tsunami.* Climatologists did not predict this tsunami. ❷ to foretell ▷ *Personne ne peut prédire l'avenir.* No one can foretell the future.

préférable [pʀefeʀabl(ə)] *adj* preferable

préféré [pʀefeʀe] (*f* **préférée**) *adj* favourite

préférence [pʀefeʀɑ̃s] *nf* preference ▷ *Je n'ai pas de préférence.* I have no preference.; **de préférence** preferably

préférer [pʀefeʀe] *vb* to prefer ▷ *Je préfère la cuisine de mon père.* I prefer my dad's cooking. ▷ *Je préfère manger à la cafétéria.* I prefer to eat in the cafeteria.; **Je préférerais du thé.** I'd rather have tea.; **préférer quelque chose à quelque chose** to prefer something to something ▷ *Je* *préfère celui-ci à celui-là.* I prefer this one to that one.

préhistorique [preistɔrik] *adj* prehistoric

préjugé [preʒyʒe] *nm* prejudice ▷ *avoir des préjugés contre quelqu'un* to be prejudiced against somebody

prématernelle [prematernel] *nf* junior kindergarten

premier [prəmje, -jɛr] (*f* **première**) *adj* first ▷ *au premier étage* on the first floor ▷ *C'est notre premier jour de vacances.* It's the first day of our holidays. ▷ *C'est la première fois que je viens ici.* It's the first time I've been here. ▷ *le premier mai* the first of May ▷ *Elle est arrivée première.* She came first.; **le premier ministre** (**1**) the prime minister (**2**) (*of province*) the premier

première [prəmjɛr] *nf* ❶ first class ▷ *Nous avons voyagé en première.* We travelled first class. ❷ first gear ▷ *Passe en première pour prendre ce virage.* Change into first to go around this bend.

premièrement [prəmjɛrmɑ̃] *adv* firstly

Premières Nations *nfpl* First Nations ▷ *l'Assemblée des Premières Nations* the Assembly of First Nations

prendre [prɑ̃dr(ə)] *vb* to take ▷ *Prends tes affaires et viens avec moi.* Take your things and come with me.; **prendre quelque chose à quelqu'un** to take something from somebody ▷ *Elle m'a pris mon stylo!* She took my pen!; **Nous avons pris le vol de huit heures.** We took the eight o'clock flight.; **Je prends toujours l'autobus pour aller à l'école.** I always go to school by bus; **passer prendre** to pick up ▷ *Nous devons passer prendre sa sœur.* We have to pick up his

sister.; **prendre à gauche** to turn left ▷ *Prenez à gauche en arrivant à la prochaine intersection.* Turn left at the next intersection.; **Il se prend pour un génie.** He thinks he's a genius.; **s'en prendre à quelqu'un** (*verbally*) to take it out on somebody ▷ *Il s'en est pris à moi.* He took it out on me.; **s'y prendre** to go about it ▷ *Tu t'y prends mal!* You're going about it the wrong way!; **prendre une décision** to make a decision

prénom [prenɔ̃] *nm* first name ▷ *Quel est votre prénom?* What's your first name?

préoccupé [preɔkype] (*f* **préoccupée**) *adj* worried

préparation [preparɑsjɔ̃] *nf* preparation

préparer [prepare] *vb* ❶ to prepare ▷ *Il prépare le dîner.* He's preparing dinner. ❷ to make ▷ *Je vais préparer le café.* I'm going to make the coffee. ❸ to prepare for ▷ *Ma sœur prépare son examen d'économie.* My sister's preparing for her economics exam.; **se préparer** to get ready ▷ *Ils se préparent à partir.* They're getting ready to go.

préposition [prepozisjɔ̃] *nf* preposition

près [prɛ] *adv*: **tout près** nearby ▷ *J'habite tout près.* I live nearby.; **près de** (**1**) near (to) ▷ *Est-ce que c'est près d'ici?* Is it near here? (**2**) next to ▷ *Assieds-toi près de moi.* Sit down next to me. (**3**) nearly ▷ *Il y avait près de cinq cents spectateurs.* There were nearly 500 spectators.; **de près** closely ▷ *Elle a regardé la photo de près.* She looked closely at the photo.; **à peu de chose près** more or less

prescription [prɛskripsjɔ̃] *nf* (*medical*) prescription

présence [pʁezɑ̃s] nf ❶ presence
▷ Sa présence est rassurante.
Her presence is reassuring.
❷ attendance ▷ La présence aux
cours est obligatoire. Attendance at
classes is compulsory.

présent [pʁezɑ̃, -ɑ̃t] (f présente)
adj present
▶ nm present tense; **à présent** now

présentation [pʁezɑ̃tasjɔ̃]
nf presentation; **faire les
présentations** to do the
introductions

présenter [pʁezɑ̃te] vb to present
▷ Il a présenté son rapport à la classe.
He presented his report to the
class.; **présenter quelqu'un à
quelqu'un** to introduce somebody
to somebody ▷ Il m'a présenté
à sa sœur. He introduced me to
his sister.; **Marc, je te présente
Anaïs.** Marc, this is Anaïs.; **se
présenter (1)** to introduce
oneself ▷ Elle s'est présentée à ses
collègues. She introduced herself
to her colleagues. **(2)** to arise ▷ Si
l'occasion se présente, nous irons au
Yukon. If the chance arises, we'll go
to the Yukon. **(3)** to stand ▷ Elle se
présente encore aux élections. She's
standing for election again.

préservatif [pʁezɛʁvatif] nm
condom

préserver [pʁezɛʁve] vb to
protect ▷ préserver du froid to
protect from the cold

président [pʁezidɑ̃] nm
❶ president ▷ le président des
États-Unis the president of the
United States ❷ (person) chair ▷ le
président du conseil d'administration
the chair of the board of directors

présidente [pʁezidɑ̃t] nf
❶ president ❷ (person) chair
▷ Elle est présidente du conseil
d'administration. She's the chair of

the board of directors.

présider [pʁeside] vb ❶ to chair
▷ Elle a présidé la réunion. She chaired
the meeting. ❷ to be the guest of
honour ▷ Il présidait à table. He was
the guest of honour at the table.

presque [pʁɛsk(ə)] adv nearly ❶ Il
est presque six heures. It's nearly 6
o'clock. ▷ Nous sommes presque
arrivés. We're nearly there.;
presque rien hardly anything ▷ Elle
n'a presque rien mangé. She's hardly
eaten anything.; **presque pas**
hardly at all ▷ Il ne dort presque pas.
He hardly sleeps at all.; **presque
pas de** hardly any ▷ Il n'y a presque
pas de place. There's hardly any
room.

presqu'île [pʁɛskil] nf peninsula

presse [pʁɛs] nf press ▷ les
représentants de la presse
representatives of the press

pressé [pʁese] (f pressée) adj ❶ in
a hurry ▷ Je ne peux pas rester, je suis
pressé. I can't stay, I'm in a hurry.
❷ urgent ▷ Ce n'est pas très pressé.
It's not very urgent.

presser [pʁese] vb ❶ to squeeze
▷ presser un citron to squeeze a
lemon ❷ to be urgent ▷ Est-ce que
ça presse? Is it urgent?; **se presser**
to hurry up ▷ Allez, presse-toi, on va être
en retard! Come on, hurry up, we're
going to be late!; **Rien ne presse.**
There's no hurry.

pression [pʁesjɔ̃] nf pressure;
faire pression sur quelqu'un to
put pressure on somebody; **la
pression des pairs** peer pressure

prêt [pʁɛ, pʁɛt] (f prête) adj ready
▷ Le déjeuner est prêt. Breakfast is
ready. ▷ Tu es prête? Are you ready?
▶ nm loan

prêt-à-porter [pʁɛtapɔʁte] nm
off-the-rack clothing

prétendre [pʁetɑ̃dʁ(ə)] vb to

claim ▷ *Il prétend qu'on lui a volé son sac à dos.* He claims his knapsack was stolen. ▷ *Elle prétend ne pas le connaître.* She claims she doesn't know him.

Be careful! **prétendre** does not mean **to pretend**.

prétendu [pretɑ̃dy] (f **prétendue**) *adj* so-called ▷ *un prétendu expert* a so-called expert

prétentieux [pretɑ̃sjø, -øz] (f **prétentieuse**) *adj* pretentious

prêter [prete] *vb*: **prêter quelque chose à quelqu'un** to lend something to someone ▷ *Elle m'a prêté sa calculatrice.* She lent me her calculator.; **prêter attention à quelque chose** to pay attention to something

prétexte [pretɛkst(ə)] *nm* excuse ▷ *Il avait un prétexte pour ne pas venir.* He had an excuse for not coming.; **sous aucun prétexte** under no circumstances ▷ *Il ne faut la déranger sous aucun prétexte.* She is not to be disturbed under any circumstances.

prétexter [pretɛkste] *vb* to give as an excuse ▷ *Elle a prétexté une réunion.* She gave a meeting as her excuse. ▷ *Il a prétexté qu'il avait un rendez-vous.* He gave the excuse that he had an appointment.

prêtre [prɛtr(ə)] *nm* priest

preuve [prœv] *nf* ➊ evidence ▷ *Il y a des preuves contre lui.* There's evidence against him. ➋ proof ▷ *Vous n'avez aucune preuve.* You have no proof.; **faire preuve de courage** to show courage; **faire ses preuves** to prove oneself ▷ *Pour être embauché ici, il faut faire ses preuves.* To be employed here, you need to prove yourself.

prévenir [prevnir] *vb*: **prévenir quelqu'un** to warn somebody

▷ *Je te préviens, elle est de mauvaise humeur.* I'm warning you, she's in a bad mood.

prévention [prevɑ̃sjɔ̃] *nf* prevention; **des mesures de prévention** preventive measures; **la prévention des incendies** fire prevention; **la prévention routière** road safety

prévision [previzjɔ̃] *nf*: **les prévisions météorologiques** the weather forecast; **en prévision de quelque chose** in anticipation of something

prévoir [prevwar] *vb* ➊ to plan ▷ *Nous prévoyons un pique-nique pour dimanche.* We're planning to have a picnic on Sunday.; **Le départ est prévu pour dix heures.** The departure's scheduled for 10 o'clock. ➋ to allow ▷ *J'ai prévu assez à manger pour quatre.* I allowed enough food for four. ➌ to foresee ▷ *J'avais prévu ce problème dès le début.* I had foreseen this problem from the start.; **Je prévois qu'il me faudra une heure de plus.** I figure it'll take me another hour.

prier [prije] *vb* ➊ to pray ▷ *Les Grecs de l'Antiquité priaient Dionysos.* The Ancient Greeks prayed to Dionysos.; **prier quelqu'un de faire quelque chose** to ask somebody to do something ▷ *Elle l'a prié de sortir.* She asked him to leave.; **je vous en prie (1)** please do ▷ *« Je peux m'asseoir ? » « Je vous en prie. »* "May I sit down?" "Please do." **(2)** please ▷ *Je vous en prie, ne me laissez pas seule.* Please, don't leave me alone. **(3)** don't mention it ▷ *« Merci pour votre aide. » – « Je vous en prie. »* "Thanks for your help." — "Don't mention it."

prière [prijɛr] *nf* prayer ▷ *faire ses prières* to say one's prayers; **« prière**

de ne pas fumer » "no smoking please"

primaire [pʀimɛʀ] nm elementary school ▷ *Ses enfants sont encore au primaire.* His children are still in elementary school.; **une école primaire** an elementary school

prime [pʀim] nf ❶ bonus ▷ *Il a eu une prime de son employeur.* He got a bonus from his employer. ❷ free gift ▷ *J'ai eu ce stylo en prime avec l'agenda.* I got this pen as a free gift with the diary. ❸ premium ▷ *une prime d'assurance* an insurance premium

prince [pʀɛ̃s] nm prince ▷ *le prince de Galles* the Prince of Wales

princesse [pʀɛ̃sɛs] nf princess ▷ *la princesse de Galles* the Princess of Wales

principal, -e [pʀɛ̃sipal, -o] (f **principale**, mpl **principaux**) adj main ▷ *le rôle principal* the main role ▶ nm (pl **principaux**) main thing ▷ *Personne n'a été blessé; c'est le principal.* Nobody was injured; that's the main thing.

principe [pʀɛ̃sip] nm principle; **pour le principe** on principle; **en principe** (1) as a rule ▷ *Elle prend son lunch en principe à midi et demi.* As a rule she has lunch at 12.30. (2) in theory ▷ *En principe le travail doit être assez facile.* In theory, the work should be fairly easy.

printemps [pʀɛ̃tɑ̃] nm spring; **au printemps** in spring

priorité [pʀijɔʀite] nf ❶ priority ▷ *C'est à faire en priorité.* This needs to be a priority. ❷ right of way ▷ *Tu n'as pas la priorité.* You don't have the right of way.

pris [pʀi, pʀiz] (f **prise**) vb see **prendre**

pris [pʀi] adj ❶ taken ▷ *Est-ce que cette place est prise?* Is this seat

taken? ❷ busy ▷ *Je serai très pris la semaine prochaine.* I'll be very busy next week.; **être pris de panique** to be panic-stricken

prise [pʀiz] nf ❶ plug ❷ socket; **une prise de courant** an electrical outlet; **une prise de sang** a blood test

prison [pʀizɔ̃] nf prison ▷ *aller en prison* to go to prison ▷ *être en prison* to be in prison

prisonnier [pʀizɔnje] nm prisoner ▶ nm prisoner

prisonnière [pʀizɔnjɛʀ] nf prisoner

privé [pʀive] (f **privée**) adj private ▷ *la propriété privée* private property ▷ *ma vie privée* my private life; **en privé** in private

priver [pʀive] vb: **priver quelqu'un de quelque chose** to deprive somebody of something ▷ *Le prisonnier a été privé de nourriture.* The prisoner was deprived of food.; **Tu seras privé de dessert!** You won't get any dessert!

prix [pʀi] nm ❶ price ▷ *Je n'arrive pas à lire le prix de ce livre.* I can't see the price of this book. ❷ prize ▷ *Elle a eu le prix de la meilleure actrice.* She got the prize for best actress.; **hors de prix** exorbitantly priced ▷ *Les repas sont hors de prix ici!* Meal prices here are exorbitant!; **à aucun prix** not at any price ▷ *Je n'irai là-bas à aucun prix.* I'm not going there, not at any price.; **à tout prix** at all costs ▷ *Je veux à tout prix voir ce film.* I want to see this movie at all costs.

probable [pʀɔbabl(ə)] adj likely ▷ *Il est probable qu'elle viendra.* It's likely she'll come.; **C'est peu probable.** That's unlikely.

probablement [pʀɔbabləmɑ̃] adv probably

problème [prɔblɛm] nm problem

procédé [prɔsede] nm process

procès [prɔsɛ] nm trial ▷ *Le procès du meurtrier commence mardi.* The murder trial starts on Tuesday.; **Il est en procès avec son employeur.** He's involved in a lawsuit with his employer.

prochain [prɔʃɛ̃, -ɛn] (f**prochaine**) adj next ▷ *Nous descendons au prochain arrêt.* We're getting off at the next stop.; **la prochaine fois** next time; **la semaine prochaine** next week; **À la prochaine!** See you!

prochainement [prɔʃɛnmɑ̃] adv soon

proche [prɔʃ] adj ❶ near ▷ *Les magasins les plus proches étaient à trois kilomètres.* The nearest stores were 3 kilometres away. ▷ *dans un proche avenir* in the near future ❷ close ▷ *un ami proche* a close friend; **proche de** near ▷ *La cathédrale est proche du château.* The cathedral is near the castle.

proches [prɔʃ] nmpl close relatives

proclamer [prɔklame] vb to proclaim

procurer [prɔkyre] vb: **procurer quelque chose à quelqu'un** to get something for somebody ▷ *C'est elle qui m'a procuré ce travail.* She got me this job.; **se procurer quelque chose** to get something ▷ *Je me suis procuré leur dernier catalogue.* I got their latest catalogue.

producteur [prɔdyktœr] nm producer

production [prɔdyksjɔ̃] nf production

productrice [prɔdyktris] nf producer

produire [prɔdɥir] vb to produce; **se produire** to take place ▷ *Ces changements se sont produits l'an*

dernier. The changes took place last year.

produit [prɔdɥi] nm product ▷ *les produits de beauté* beauty products

prof [prɔf] nmf (*informal*) teacher ▷ *Elle est prof de maths.* She's a math teacher.

professeur [prɔfesœr] nm ❶ teacher ▷ *Il est professeur d'histoire.* He's a history teacher. ❷ professor

professeure [prɔfesœr] nf ❶ teacher ▷ *Elle est professeure de physique.* She's a physics teacher. ❷ professor ▷ *Elle est professeure agrégée.* She's a full professor.

profession [prɔfesjɔ̃] nf profession ▷ *Quelle est votre profession?* What's your profession?

professionnel [prɔfesjɔnɛl] (f **professionnelle**) adj professional

profil [prɔfil] nm ❶ (*of person*) profile ▷ *de profil* in profile ❷ (*of object*) contours

profit [prɔfi] nm profit ▷ *La société a fait des profits importants.* The company made significant profits.; **tirer profit de quelque chose** to profit from something; **au profit de** in aid of ▷ *un spectacle au profit d'un organisme de charité local* a show in aid of a local charity

profiter [prɔfite] vb: **profiter de quelque chose** to take advantage of something ▷ *Profitez du beau temps pour aller faire du vélo.* Take advantage of the good weather to go biking.; **Profitez-en bien!** Make the most of it!

profond [prɔfɔ̃, -ɔ̃d] (f**profonde**) adj deep; **peu profond** shallow

profondeur [prɔfɔ̃dœr] nf depth

programme [prɔgram] nm ❶ program ▷ *le programme du festival* the festival program ❷ curriculum ▷ *le programme*

de maths the math curriculum
❶ program ▷ *un programme informatique* a computer program
programmer [pʀɔgʀame] *vb* to program ▷ *Mon ordinateur n'est pas programmé pour ça.* My computer isn't programmed to do that.; **être programmé** to be showing ▷ *Ce film est programmé dimanche soir* That movie is showing Sunday night.

programmeur [pʀɔgʀamœʀ] *nm* programmer ▷ *Il est programmeur.* He's a programmer.

programmeuse [pʀɔgʀamøz] *nf* programmer ▷ *Elle est programmeuse.* She's a programmer.

progrès [pʀɔgʀɛ] *nm* progress ▷ *faire des progrès* to make progress

progresser [pʀɔgʀese] *vb* to progress

progressif [pʀɔgʀesif, -iv] (*f* **progressive**) *adj* progressive

projecteur [pʀɔʒɛktœʀ] *nm*
❶ projector ▷ *un vieux projecteur de diapositives* an old slide projector
❷ spotlight ▷ *sous les projecteurs* in the spotlight

projet [pʀɔʒɛ] *nm* plan ▷ *des projets de vacances* holiday plans; **le projet de construction** building plans ▷ *le projet de construction d'un musée* the building plans for a museum; **un projet de loi** (*in parliament*) a bill

projeter [pʀɔʒte] *vb* ❶ to plan ▷ *Ils projettent d'acheter une maison.* They're planning to buy a house.
❷ to cast ▷ *L'arbre projetait une ombre sur le mur.* The tree cast a shadow on the wall.; **Elle a été projetée hors de la voiture.** She was thrown out of the car.

prolongation [pʀɔlɔ̃gasjɔ̃] *nf* (*sports*) overtime

prolonger [pʀɔlɔ̃ʒe] *vb* ❶ to prolong ▷ *Ne prolonge pas tes*

souffrances; va chez le médecin! Don't prolong the agony; go to the doctor! ❷ to extend ▷ *Je vais prolonger mon abonnement.* I'm going to extend my subscription.; **se prolonger** to go on ▷ *La réunion s'est prolongée tard.* The meeting went on late.

promenade [pʀɔmnad] *nf* walk ▷ *Il y a de belles promenades par ici.* There are some nice walks around here.; **faire une promenade** to go for a walk; **faire une promenade en voiture** to go for a drive; **faire une promenade à vélo** to go for a bike ride

promener [pʀɔmne] *vb* to take for a walk ▷ *Il promène son chien tous les jours.* He takes his dog for a walk every day.; **se promener** to go for a walk ▷ *Elle est partie se promener.* She has gone for a walk.

promesse [pʀɔmɛs] *nf* promise ▷ *faire une promesse* to make a promise ▷ *tenir sa promesse* to keep one's promise

promettre [pʀɔmɛtʀ(ə)] *vb* to promise ▷ *On m'a promis un billet gratuit.* They promised me a free ticket. ▷ *Elle m'a promis de me téléphoner.* She promised to phone me.

promotion [pʀɔmɔsjɔ̃] *nf* promotion ▷ *Il espère avoir bientôt une promotion.* He's hoping to get promotion soon.; **être en promotion** to be on special ▷ *Les côtelettes de porc sont en promotion.* Pork chops are on special.

pronom [pʀɔnɔ̃] *nm* pronoun

prononcer [pʀɔnɔ̃se] *vb* ❶ to pronounce ▷ *Ce mot est difficile à prononcer.* That word is difficult to pronounce. ❷ to deliver ▷ *prononcer un discours* to deliver a speech; **se prononcer** to be pronounced ▷ *Le « e » final ne se prononce pas.* The final "e" isn't pronounced.

prononciation [prɔnɔ̃sjɑsjɔ̃] nf
pronunciation

propagande [prɔpagɑ̃d] nf
propaganda

se **propager** [prɔpaʒe] vb to spread ▷ *Le feu s'est propagé rapidement.* The fire spread quickly.

proportion [prɔpɔrsjɔ̃] nf
proportion

propos [prɔpo] nm: **à propos** by the way ▷ *À propos, quand est-ce que tu viens?* By the way, when are you coming?; **à propos de quelque chose** about something ▷ *C'est à propos de la soirée de vendredi.* It's about the party on Friday.

proposer [prɔpoze] vb: **proposer quelque chose à quelqu'un (1)** to suggest something to somebody ▷ *Nous lui avons proposé une promenade en bateau.* We suggested a boat ride to him. **(2)** to offer somebody something ▷ *Ils m'ont proposé des chocolats.* They offered me some chocolates.

proposition [prɔpozisjɔ̃] nf offer ▷ *J'accepte ta proposition avec plaisir.* I accept your offer with pleasure.

propre [prɔpr(ə)] adj ❶ clean ▷ *Ce mouchoir n'est pas propre.* This handkerchief isn't clean.; **recopier quelque chose au propre** to make a clean copy of something ❷ own ▷ *Elle l'a fabriqué de ses propres mains.* She made it with her own hands.; **propre à** a characteristic of ▷ *C'est une coutume propre à la Gaspésie.* It's a custom you find in the Gaspé region.

proprement [prɔprəmɑ̃] adv properly ▷ *Mange proprement!* Eat properly!; **le village proprement dit** the village itself; **à proprement**

parler strictly speaking

propreté [prɔprəte] nf cleanliness

propriétaire [prɔprijeter] nmf
❶ owner ❷ landlord, landlady

propriété [prɔprijete] nf property ▷ *la propriété privée* private property

prospectus [prɔspɛktys] nm
brochure

prospère [prɔspɛr] adj
prosperous

protecteur [prɔtɛktœr, -tris] (f **protectrice**) adj ❶ protective ▷ *un vernis protecteur* a protective varnish ❷ patronizing ▷ *un ton protecteur* a patronizing tone

protection [prɔtɛksjɔ̃] nf
protection

protéger [prɔteʒe] vb to protect

protéine [prɔtein] nf protein

protestant [prɔtɛstɑ̃, -ɑ̃t] (f **protestante**, f **protestants**) adj Protestant ▷ *une église protestante* a Protestant church

protestation [prɔtɛstasjɔ̃] nf
protest

protester [prɔteste] vb to protest ▷ *Ils protestent contre leurs mauvaises conditions de travail.* They're protesting their poor working conditions.

prouver [pruve] vb to prove

provenance [prɔvnɑ̃s] nf origin; **un avion en provenance de Winnipeg** a plane arriving from Winnipeg

provenir [prɔvnir] vb: **provenir de (1)** to come from ▷ *Ces pêches proviennent de la région du Niagara.* These peaches come from the Niagara region. **(2)** to be the result of ▷ *Cela provient d'un manque d'organisation.* This is the result of a lack of organization.

proverbe [prɔvɛrb(ə)] nm proverb

province [prɔvɛ̃s] nf province

provincial [prɔvɛ̃sjal, -o] (mpl

provinciaux) adj provincial
▷ *le gouvernement provincial* the provincial government

provision [pʀɔvizjɔ̃] nf supply
▷ *une provision de pommes de terre* a supply of potatoes

provisions [pʀɔvizjɔ̃] nfpl food
▷ *Nous n'avons plus beaucoup de provisions.* We don't have much food left.; **faire les provisions** to go grocery shopping

provisoire [pʀɔvizwaʀ] adj temporary ▷ *un emploi provisoire* a temporary job

provoquer [pʀɔvɔke] vb ❶ to provoke ▷ *Il l'a provoquée en la traitant d'imbécile.* He provoked her by calling her stupid. ❷ to cause ▷ *Cet accident a provoqué la mort de quarante personnes.* The accident caused the death of 40 people.

proximité [pʀɔksimite] nf proximity; **à proximité** nearby ▷ *Elle habite à proximité.* She lives nearby.

prudemment [pʀydamɑ̃] adv ❶ carefully ▷ *Conduisez prudemment!* Drive carefully! ❷ wisely ▷ *Prudemment, il a fait des économies.* He wisely saved some money. ❸ cautiously ▷ *Le gouvernement a réagi prudemment.* The government reacted cautiously.

prudence [pʀydɑ̃s] nf caution; **avec prudence** carefully ▷ *Ils ont conduit avec prudence.* They drove carefully.

prudent [pʀydɑ̃, -ɑ̃t] (f **prudente**) adj ❶ careful ▷ *Soyez prudents!* Be careful! ❷ wise ▷ *Laisse ton passeport à la maison, c'est plus prudent.* It would be wiser to leave your passport at home.

prune [pʀyn] nf plum

pruneau [pʀyno] (pl **pruneaux**) nm prune

psychiatre [psikjatʀ(ə)] nmf psychiatrist

psychologie [psikɔlɔʒi] nf psychology

psychologique [psikɔlɔʒik] adj psychological

psychologue [psikɔlɔg] nmf psychologist

pu [py] vb see **pouvoir**; *Je n'ai pas pu venir.* I couldn't come.

pub [pyb] nf ❶ (*informal*) advertising ▷ *C'est de l'excellente pub.* That's excellent advertising. ❷ ad ▷ *des pub percutantes* powerful ads

public [pyblik] (f **publique**) adj ❶ public ▷ *le transport public* public transport ▷ *une école publique* a public school
▶ nm ❶ public ▷ *Ce parc est ouvert au public.* This park is open to the public. ❷ audience ▷ *Le public a applaudi le chanteur.* The audience applauded the singer.; **en public** in public ▷ *Je déteste parler en public.* I hate speaking in public.

publicitaire [pyblisiteʀ] adj: **une agence publicitaire** an advertising agency; **une campagne publicitaire** a publicity campaign

publicité [pyblisite] nf ❶ advertising ▷ *Elle travaille dans la publicité.* She works in advertising. ❷ ad ▷ *Il y a trop de publicités dans ce journal.* There are too many ads in this newspaper.; **faire de la publicité pour quelque chose** to publicize something

publier [pyblije] vb to publish ▷ *Il vient de publier son nouveau roman.* He has just published his new novel.

publique [pyblik] adj see **public**

puce [pys] nf ❶ flea ▷ *Ce chien a des puces.* This dog has fleas.; **un marché aux puces** a flea market

❷ chip ▷ *une puce électronique* a microchip; **une carte à puce** a smart card

puer [pɥe] *vb* to stink ▷ *Ça pue le tabac ici!* It stinks of tobacco here!

puis [pɥi] *vb see* **pouvoir**; **Puis-je venir vous voir samedi?** May I come and see you on Saturday? ▶ *adv* then ▷ *Faites dorer le poulet, puis ajoutez la sauce au miel et à l'ail.* Fry the chicken till golden, then add the honey garlic sauce.

puisque [pɥisk(ə)] *conj* since ▷ *Puisque c'est si cher, nous irons manger ailleurs.* Since it's so expensive, we'll eat elsewhere.

puissance [pɥisɑ̃s] *nf* power ▷ *la puissance de l'imagination* the power of imagination ▷ *Ce pays est une puissance nucléaire.* This country is a nuclear power.

puissant [pɥisɑ̃, -ɑ̃t] (*f* **puissante**) *adj* powerful

puits [pɥi] *nm* well ▷ *Il a un puits dans son jardin.* He has a well in his garden.; **un puits de pétrole** an oil well

pulvérisateur [pylveʀizatœʀ] *nm* spray ▷ *un pulvérisateur de parfum* a perfume spray

pulvériser [pylveʀize] *vb* ❶ to pulverize ▷ *L'explosion a pulvérisé le bâtiment.* The explosion pulverized the building. ❷ to spray ▷ *Elle ne pulvérise jamais d'insecticide sur ses plantes.* She never sprays insecticide on her plants.

punaise [pynez] *nf* thumbtack

punir [pyniʀ] *vb* to punish ▷ *Il a été puni pour avoir menti.* He was punished for lying.

punition [pynisjɔ̃] *nf* ❶ punishment ❷ (*sports*) penalty; **le banc de punition** the penalty box

pupitre [pypitʀ(ə)] *nm* (*for student*) desk

pur [pyʀ] (*f* **pure**) *adj* pure ▷ *L'eau de cette source est très pure.* The water from this spring is very pure.; **c'est de la folie pure** it's sheer madness

purée [pyʀe] *nf* purée; **la purée de pommes de terre** mashed potatoes

puzzle [pœzl(ə)] *nm* jigsaw puzzle

pyjama [piʒama] *nm* pyjamas

pyramide [piʀamid] *nf* pyramid

q

QI [kyi] nm (= quotient intellectuel) IQ

quai [ke] nm **①** dock; **Le navire est à quai.** The ship has docked. **②** platform ▷ *Le train partira du quai numéro quatre.* The train will leave from platform 4.

qualifié [kalifje] (f **qualifiée**) adj qualified

qualifier [kalifje] vb: **se qualifier** to qualify ▷ *Il s'est qualifié pour la demi-finale.* He has qualified for the semifinal.

qualité [kalite] nf quality ▷ *Ces outils sont de très bonne qualité.* These are very good quality tools.

quand [kɑ̃] conj, adv when ▷ *Quand est-ce que tu pars en vacances?* When are you going on vacation? ▷ *Quand je serai riche, j'achèterai une belle maison.* When I'm rich, I'll buy a nice house.; **quand même** anyway ▷ *Je ne voulais pas finir mes devoirs, mais je les ai faits quand même.* I didn't want

to finish my homework, but I did it anyway.

quant à prep regarding ▷ *Quant au problème de chauffage...* Regarding the heating problem... ▷ *Quant à moi, je n'arriverai qu'à dix heures.* As for me, I won't be arriving till 10 o'clock.

quantité [kɑ̃tite] nf amount; **des quantités de** a great deal of

quarantaine [karɑ̃tɛn] nf about forty ▷ *une quarantaine de personnes* about forty people; **Elle a la quarantaine.** She's in her forties.

quarante [karɑ̃t] num forty ▷ *Elle a quarante ans.* She's forty.; **quarante et un** forty-one; **quarante-deux** forty-two

quart [kaʀ] nm quarter; **le quart de** a quarter of ▷ *Il a mangé le quart du gâteau.* He ate a quarter of the cake.; **trois quarts** three quarters; **un quart d'heure** a quarter of an hour; **deux heures et quart** a quarter after two; **dix heures moins le quart** a quarter to ten

quartier [kaʀtje] nm (of town) area ▷ *un quartier tranquille* a quiet area; **un cinéma de quartier** a local movie theatre

quartz [kwaʀts] nm: **une montre à quartz** a quartz watch

quasi [kazi] adv nearly ▷ *La quasi-totalité des récoltes a été détruite.* Nearly all of the crop was destroyed.

quasiment [kazimɑ̃] adv nearly ▷ *Le film est quasiment fini.* The movie's nearly over.; **quasiment jamais** hardly ever ▷ *Ils ne vont quasiment jamais au cinéma.* They hardly ever go to the movies.

quatorze [katɔʀz(ə)] num fourteen ▷ *Mon frère a quatorze ans.* My brother's fourteen. ▷ *à quatorze heures* at 2 p.m.; **le quatorze**

février the fourteenth of February

quatre [katʁ(ə)] num four ▷ Il est quatre heures du matin. It's four in the morning. ▷ Elle a quatre ans. She's four.; **le quatre février** the fourth of February

quatre-vingts [katʁəvɛ̃] num eighty

> **quatre-vingts** is spelled with an **-s** when it is followed by a noun, but not when it is followed by another number.
>
> ▷ quatre-vingts élèves eighty students ▷ Elle a quatre-vingt-deux ans. She's eighty-two.;
> **quatre-vingt-dix** ninety;
> **quatre-vingt-onze** ninety-one;
> **quatre-vingt-quinze** ninety-five;
> **quatre-vingt-dix-huit** ninety-eight

quatrième [katʁijɛm] adj fourth ▷ au quatrième étage on the fourth floor ▷ Il est en quatrième année. He's in Grade 4.

que [kə] conj, pron, adv ❶ that ▷ Il sait que tu es là. He knows that you're here.

> **que** is sometimes not translated.
>
> ▷ la dame que j'ai rencontrée hier the lady I met yesterday ▷ Le gâteau qu'elle a fait est délicieux. The cake she made is delicious.; **Je veux que tu viennes.** I want you to come. ❷ what ▷ Que fais-tu? What are you doing? ▷ Que vas-tu lui dire? What are you going to tell her?; **Qu'est-ce que...?** What...? ▷ Qu'est-ce que tu fais? What are you doing? ▷ Qu'est-ce que c'est? What's that?; **plus...que** more...than ▷ C'est plus difficile que je ne le pensais. It's more difficult than I thought. ▷ Il est plus grand que moi. He's bigger than me.; **aussi...que** as...as ▷ Elle est aussi intelligente que toi. She's

as smart as you are. ▷ Le train est aussi cher que l'avion. The train is as expensive as the plane.; **ne ...que** only ▷ Il ne boit que de l'eau. He only drinks water. ▷ Je ne l'ai vu qu'une fois. I've only seen him once.; **Que tu es bête!** You're so silly!

Québec [kebɛk] nm Québec

québécois [kebekwa, -waz] adj, n Québec ▷ la culture québécoise Québec culture; **un Québécois** (man) a Quebecker; **une Québécoise** (woman) a Quebecker

quel [kɛl] (f **quelle**) adj ❶ what ▷ Quelle est ta couleur préférée? What's your favourite colour? ❷ which ▷ Quel groupe préfères-tu? Which band do you like best? ❸ who ▷ Quel est ton chanteur préféré? Who's your favourite singer? ▷ Quelle heure est-il? What time is it? ▷ Quelle bonne surprise! What a surprise!; **quel que soit** (1) whatever ▷ quel que soit votre avis whatever your opinion (2) whoever ▷ quel que soit le coupable whoever the guilty one

quelle [kɛl] adj see **quel**

quelque [kɛlkə] adj, adv ❶ some ▷ Il a quelques amis à Victoria. He has some friends in Victoria. ▷ J'ai acheté quelques disques. I bought some records. ❷ a few ▷ Il reste quelques pointes de pizza. There are a few pizza slices left. ❸ few ▷ Ils ont fini les quelques sandwichs qui restaient. They finished the few sandwiches that were left.; **quelque chose** (1) something ▷ J'ai quelque chose pour toi. I've got something for you. ▷ Je voudrais quelque chose de moins cher. I'd like something cheaper. (2) anything ▷ Avez-vous quelque chose à déclarer? Have you got anything to declare? ▷ Tu as pensé à quelque chose d'autre? Did you think of anything else?; **quelque part (1)** somewhere ▷ *J'ai oublié mes lunettes quelque part.* I've left my glasses somewhere. **(2)** anywhere ▷ *Vous allez quelque part en fin de semaine?* Are you going anywhere this weekend?

quelquefois [kɛlkəfwa] *adv* sometimes

quelques-uns [kɛlkəzœ̃, -yn] (*f* **quelques-unes**) *pron some* ▷ *As-tu vu ses films? j'en ai vu quelques-uns.* Have you seen her films? I've seen some of them.

quelqu'un [kɛlkœ̃] *pron* ❶ somebody ▷ *Quelqu'un t'a appelé.* Somebody phoned you. ▷ *Il y a quelqu'un à la porte.* There's somebody at the door. ❷ anybody ▷ *Est-ce que quelqu'un a vu mon parapluie?* Has anybody seen my umbrella? ▷ *Il y a quelqu'un?* Is there anybody there?

quenouille [kənuj] *nf* cattail

qu'est-ce que [kɛskə]: *see* **que**

qu'est-ce qui [kɛski]: *see* **qui**

question [kɛstjɔ̃] *nf* ❶ question ▷ *Je t'ai posé une question.* I asked you a question. ❷ matter ▷ *Ils se sont disputés pour des questions d'argent.* They argued over money matters. ❸ issue ▷ *une importante question politique* an important political issue; **Il n'en est pas question.** There's no question about it. ▷ *Il n'est pas question que je paye.* There's no question of me paying.; **De quoi est-il question?** What's it about?; **Il est question de l'organisation du concert.** It's about organizing the concert.; **hors de question** out of the question ▷ *Il est hors de question que nous restions ici.* It's out of the question that we stay here.

questionnaire [kɛstjɔnɛʀ] *nm* questionnaire

questionner [kɛstjɔne] *vb* to question

quétaine [keten] *adj* tacky ▷ *des meubles quétaines* tacky furniture ▷ *un bijou quétaine* a tacky piece of jewellery

queue [kø] *nf* ❶ tail ▷ *Le chien a agité la queue.* The dog wagged its tail.; **faire la queue** to line up; **une queue de cheval** a ponytail ❷ rear ▷ *en queue du train* at the rear of the train ❸ bottom ▷ *en queue de liste* at the bottom of the list ❹ (*of fruit, leaf*) stem ▷ *la queue d'une cerise* a cherry stem

qui [ki] *pron* ❶ who ▷ *Qui a téléphoné?* Who phoned? ❷ whom ▷ *C'est la personne à qui j'ai parlé hier.* It's the person to whom I spoke yesterday. ❸ that ▷ *Donne-moi le manteau qui est sur la chaise.* Give me the jacket that's on the chair.; **Qui est-ce qui...?** Who...? ▷ *Qui est-ce qui t'emmène au spectacle?* Who's taking you to the show?; **Qui est-ce que...?** Whom...? ▷ *Qui est-ce que tu as vu à cette soirée?* Whom did you see at the party?; **Qu'est-ce qui...?** What...? ▷ *Qu'est-ce qui est sur la table?* What's on the table? ▷ *Qu'est-ce qui te prend?* What's the matter with you?; **À qui est ce sac à dos?** Whose knapsack is this?; **À qui parlais-tu?** Who were you talking to?

quille [kij] *nf* bowling pin; **jouer aux quilles** to go bowling

quincaillerie [kɛ̃kajʀi] *nf* hardware store

quinzaine [kɛ̃zɛn] *nf* about fifteen ▷ *Il y avait une quinzaine de personnes.* There were about fifteen people there.; **une quinzaine de jours** two weeks

quinze [kɛ̃z] *num* fifteen ▷ *Elle a quinze ans.* She's fifteen. ▷ *à quinze* *heures* at 3 p.m.; **le quinze février** the fifteenth of February; **dans quinze jours** two weeks from now

quitter [kite] *vb* to leave ▷ *J'ai quitté la maison à huit heures.* I left the house at 8 o'clock.; **se quitter** to part ▷ *Les deux amis se sont quittés devant le café.* The two friends parted in front of the café.; **Ne quittez pas.** (on telephone) Hold the line. ▷ *Ne quittez pas, je vous passe la directrice.* Hold on please, I'll put you through to the director.

quoi [kwa] *pron* what? ▷ *À quoi penses-tu?* What are you thinking about? ▷ *C'est quoi, ce truc?* What's this thing?; **Quoi de neuf?** What's new?; **As-tu de quoi écrire?** Have you got anything to write with?; **Quoi qu'il arrive.** Whatever happens.; **Il n'y a pas de quoi.** Don't mention it.; **Il n'y a pas de quoi s'énerver.** There's no reason to get worked up.; **En quoi puis-je vous aider?** How may I help you?

quoique [kwak(ə)] *conj* even though ▷ *Il va l'acheter quoique ce soit cher.* He's going to buy it even though it's expensive.

quotidien [kɔtidjɛ̃, -ɛn] (f **quotidienne**) *adj* daily ▷ *Il est parti faire sa promenade quotidienne.* He's gone for his daily walk.; **la vie quotidienne** everyday life
▶ *nm* daily paper ▷ *Le Globe and Mail est un quotidien.* The Globe and Mail is a daily paper.

r

rabais [Rabɛ] *nm* (in price) reduction ▷ *25 pour cent de rabais* 25 percent off; **au rabais** at a discount

rabbin [Rabɛ̃] *nm* rabbi

raccompagner [Rakɔ̃paɲe] *vb* to take home ▷ *Peux-tu me raccompagner?* Can you take me home?

raccourci [Rakursi] *nm* (also computer) shortcut

raccrocher [Rakʀɔʃe] *vb* to hang up (telephone)

race [Ras] *nf* ❶ race ▷ *la race humaine* the human race ❷ breed ▷ *De quelle race est ton chat?* What breed is your cat?

racheter [Raʃte] *vb* ❶ to buy another ▷ *J'ai racheté un portefeuille.* I bought another wallet. ▷ *racheter du lait* to buy more milk ❷ to buy ▷ *Il m'a racheté mon vélo.* He bought my bike from me.

racine [Rasin] *nf* root

racinette [Rasinɛt] nf root beer
racisme [Rasism(ə)] nm racism
raciste [Rasist(ə)] adj racist
raconter [Rakɔ̃te] vb to tell
▷ *Raconte-moi ce qui s'est passé.* Tell
me what happened. ▷ *Raconte-moi
une histoire.* Tell me a story. ▷ **Qu'est-
ce que tu racontes?** What are you
talking about?
radar [RadaR] nm radar
radiateur [RadjatœR] nm
radiator; **un radiateur électrique**
an electric heater
radio [Radjo] nf ① radio ▷ *à la radio*
on the radio ② X-ray; **passer une
radio** to have an X-ray ▷ *Elle a passé
une radio des poumons.* She had a
chest X-ray.
radio-réveil [RadjɔRevej] (pl
radios-réveils) nm clock radio
radis [Radi] nm radish
raffoler [Rafɔle] vb: **raffoler de**
to be crazy about ▷ *Elle raffole de la
tarte aux pommes.* She really loves
apple pie.
rafraîchir [RafReʃiR] vb to cool
down; **se rafraîchir (1)** to get
cooler ▷ *Le temps se rafraîchit.* The
weather's getting cooler. **(2)** to
freshen up ▷ *Il a pris une douche pour
se rafraîchir.* He had a shower to
freshen up.
rafraîchissant [RafReʃisɑ̃, -ɑ̃t] (f
rafraîchissante) adj refreshing
rage [Raʒ] nf rabies; **une rage de
dents** a raging toothache; **la rage
au volant** road rage
ragoût [Ragu] nm stew
raide [Rɛd] adj ① steep ▷ *Cette
pente est raide.* This is a steep slope.
② straight ▷ *Elle a les cheveux
raides.* She has straight hair. ③ stiff
▷ *Son bras est encore raide.* His arm's
still stiff.
raie [Rɛ] nf ① (in hair) parting
② (fish) ray

rail [Raj] nm rail ▷ *par rail* by rail
raisin [Rɛzɛ̃] nm grapes ▷ *le raisin
blanc* green grapes ▷ *J'ai mangé du
raisin.* I ate some grapes.; **un grain
de raisin** a grape; **des raisins secs**
raisins
raison [Rɛzɔ̃] nf reason ▷ *sans
raison* for no reason ▷ *Raison de plus
pour y aller.* All the more reason for
going.; **Ce n'est pas une raison.**
That's no excuse.; **avoir raison** to
be right ▷ *Tu as raison.* You're right.;
en raison de because of ▷ *en raison
d'une grève* because of a strike
raisonnable [Rɛzɔnabl(ə)] adj
sensible ▷ *Elle est très raisonnable
pour son âge.* She's very sensible
for her age.
raisonnement [Rɛzɔnmɑ̃] nm
reasoning ▷ *J'ai du mal à suivre son
raisonnement.* I have a hard time
following his reasoning.
rajouter [Raʒute] vb (more) to add
▷ *Ne rajoute pas de sel, j'en ai déjà
mis.* Don't add more salt, I already
put some in.; **en rajouter** to
exaggerate ▷ *Elle en rajoute toujours.*
She always exaggerates.
ralentir [Ralɑ̃tiR] vb to slow down
ramassage [Ramasaʒ] nm: **le
ramassage scolaire** the school
bus service
ramasser [Ramase] vb ① to pick
up ▷ *Il a ramassé son crayon.* He
picked up his pencil. ② to collect
▷ *Il a ramassé les copies.* He collected
the exam papers.
rame [Ram] nf ① (of boat) oar
② subway train
rameau [Ramo] (pl **rameaux**)
nm branch
ramener [Ramne] vb ① to bring
back ▷ *Je t'ai ramené un souvenir
de Jonquière.* I brought you back a
souvenir from Jonquière. ② to
take home ▷ *Peux-tu me ramener à la*

maison? Will you take me home?

ramer [Rame] vb to row ▷ *C'est ma sœur qui ramait.* My sister was rowing.

rampe [Rɑ̃p] nf banister

ramper [Rɑ̃pe] vb to crawl

rancune [Rɑ̃kyn] nf: **garder rancune à quelqu'un** to hold a grudge against somebody ; **Sans rancune!** No hard feelings!

rancunier [Rɑ̃kynje, -jɛR] (f **rancunière**) adj: **Elle est un peu rancunière.** She tends to hold grudges.

randonnée [Rɑ̃dɔne] nf: **une randonnée à vélo** a bike ride; **une randonnée pédestre** a hike; **faire de la randonnée** to go hiking

randonneur [Rɑ̃dɔnœR] nm hiker

randonneuse [Rɑ̃dɔnøz] nf hiker

rang [Rɑ̃] nm (line) row ▷ *au premier rang* in the front row ▷ *se mettre en rangs* to form rows

rangée [Rɑ̃ʒe] nf (line) row ▷ *une rangée de chaises* a row of chairs

ranger [Rɑ̃ʒe] vb ❶ to put away ▷ *J'ai rangé tes affaires.* I put your things away. ❷ to tidy up ▷ *Va ranger ta chambre.* Go and tidy up your room.

rap [Rap] nm rap ▷ *un chanteur de rap* a rap singer

râpe à fromage [Rɑp-] nf cheese grater

râper [Rɑpe] vb to grate ▷ *le fromage râpé* grated cheese

rapide [Rapid] adj ❶ fast ▷ *Cette voiture est très rapide.* This is a very fast car. ❷ quick ▷ *J'ai jeté un coup d'œil rapide sur ton travail.* I had a quick glance at your work.
▶ nm rapids ▷ *Ils ont descendu les rapides en canot.* They went down the rapids in a canoe. ▷ *Ce rapide est très difficile à naviguer.* This set of rapids is very difficult to navigate.

rapidement [Rapidmɑ̃] adv quickly

rappel [Rapɛl] nm ❶ (vaccination) booster ❷ curtain call

rappeler [Raple] vb to call back ▷ *Je te rappelle dans cinq minutes.* I'll call you back in 5 minutes.; **rappeler quelque chose à quelqu'un** to remind somebody of something ▷ *Cette odeur me rappelle mon enfance.* This smell reminds me of my childhood.; **rappeler à quelqu'un de faire quelque chose** to remind somebody to do something ▷ *Rappelle-moi d'acheter des billets.* Remind me to get tickets.; **se rappeler** to remember ▷ *Il s'est rappelé qu'il avait une course à faire.* He remembered he had an errand to run.

rapport [RapɔR] nm ❶ report ▷ *Elle a écrit un rapport.* She wrote a report. ❷ connection ▷ *Je ne vois pas le rapport.* I can't see the connection.; **par rapport à** in comparison with

rapporter [RapɔRte] vb ❶ to bring back ▷ *Je leur ai rapporté un cadeau.* I brought them back a present.

rapporteur [RapɔRtœR] nm tattletale

rapporteuse [RapɔRtøz] nf tattletale

rapports [RapɔR] nmpl relations ▷ *Leurs rapports avec leurs voisins se sont améliorés.* Their relations with their neighbours have improved.; **les rapports sexuels** sexual intercourse

rapprocher [RapRɔʃe] vb ❶ to bring together ▷ *Cet accident a rapproché les deux frères.* The accident brought the two brothers together. ❷ to bring closer ▷ *Elle a rapproché le fauteuil de la télé.* She brought the armchair closer to the

TV.; **se rapprocher** to come closer ▷ *Rapproche-toi, tu verras mieux.* Come closer, you'll see better.

raquette [ʀakɛt] *nf* ❶ (tennis) racquet ❷ (table tennis) paddle ▷ *a crew-neck sweater*

rare [ʀaʀ] *adj* rare ▷ *une plante rare* a rare plant

rarement [ʀaʀmɑ̃] *adv* rarely

ras [ʀa, ʀɑz] (*f* **rase**) *adj, adv* short ▷ *un chien à poil ras* a short-haired dog; **à ras bords** to the brim ▷ *Elle a rempli son verre à ras bords.* She filled her glass to the brim.; **un chandail ras du cou** a crew-neck sweater

raser [ʀɑze] *vb* to shave off ▷ *Mon père a rasé sa barbe.* My dad has shaved off his beard.; **se raser** to shave

rasoir [ʀɑzwaʀ] *nm* razor

rassembler [ʀasɑ̃ble] *vb* to gather together ▷ *Il a rassemblé les enfants dans la cour.* He gathered the children together in the playground.; **se rassembler** to gather ▷ *Les passagers se sont rassemblés près de l'autobus.* The passengers gathered near the bus.

rassurer [ʀasyʀe] *vb* to reassure; **Je suis rassuré.** I don't need to worry any more.; **se rassurer** to be reassured ▷ *Rassure-toi!* Don't worry!

rat [ʀa] *nm* rat

raté [ʀate] (*f* **ratée**) *adj* unsuccessful; **Le gâteau est raté.** The cake didn't turn out.

râteau [ʀɑto] (*pl* **râteaux**) *nm* rake

rater [ʀate] *vb* ❶ to miss ▷ *Elle a raté son train.* She missed her train. ❷ to fail ▷ *J'ai raté mon examen de maths.* I failed my math exam. ▷ *Elle a raté sa pizza.* Her pizza didn't turn out right.

raton laveur [ʀatɔ̃lavœʀ] *nm* raccoon

rattacher [ʀataʃe] *vb* to tie again ▷ *rattacher ses lacets* to tie one's laces

rattrapage [ʀatʀapaʒ] *nm* catching up ▷ *À cause de mon absence, j'ai beaucoup de rattrapage scolaire.* I have a lot of catching up to do at school because I was away.; **le cours de rattrapage** remedial class

rattraper [ʀatʀape] *vb* ❶ to recapture ▷ *La police a rattrapé le voleur.* The police recaptured the thief. ❷ to catch up with ▷ *Je vais la rattraper.* I'll catch up with her. ▷ *Je dois rattraper mon retard à l'école.* I have to catch up at school. ❸ to make up for ▷ *Il faut rattraper le temps perdu.* We must make up for lost time. ▷ *J'ai des heures à rattraper.* I have some hours to make up.; **se rattraper** to make up for it ▷ *Je n'ai pas le temps de sortir, mais je me rattraperai après les examens.* I don't have time to go out, but I'll make up for it after the exams.

rature [ʀatyʀ] *nf* correction ▷ *un texte sans ratures* a text with no corrections

ravi [ʀavi] (*f* **ravie**) *adj*: **être ravi** to be delighted ▷ *Ils étaient ravis de nous voir.* They were delighted to see us. ▷ *Je suis ravi que vous puissiez venir.* I'm delighted that you can come.

se raviser [ʀavize] *vb* to change your mind ▷ *Il allait accepter, mais il s'est ravisé.* He was going to accept, but he changed his mind.

ravissant [ʀavisɑ̃, -ɑ̃t] (*f* **ravissante**) *adj* lovely

rayé [ʀeje] (*f* **rayée**) *adj* striped ▷ *une chemise rayée* a striped shirt

rayer [ʀeje] *vb* ❶ to scratch ▷ *Il a rayé la peinture de sa voiture.* He scratched the paint on his car. ❷ to cross off ▷ *Son nom a été rayé de* *la liste.* Her name has been crossed off the list.

rayon [rɛjɔ̃] *nm* ❶ ray ▷ *un rayon de soleil* a ray of sunshine ❷ radius ▷ *le rayon d'un cercle* the radius of a circle ❸ shelf ▷ *les rayons d'une bibliothèque* the shelves of a bookcase ❹ department ▷ *le rayon des chaussures* the shoe department; **les rayons X** X-rays

rayure [rɛjyʀ] *nf* stripe

ré [ʀe] *nm* ❶ D ▷ *en ré majeur* in D major ❷ re ▷ *do, ré, mi…* do, re, mi…

réaction [ʀeaksjɔ̃] *nf* reaction

réagir [ʀeaʒiʀ] *vb* to react

réalisateur [ʀealizatœʀ] *nm* director (*of film*) ▷ *Egoyan est réalisateur.* Egoyan is a film director.

réalisation [ʀealizasjɔ̃] *nf* ❶ achievement ▷ *Elle compte de nombreuses réalisations à son actif.* She has several achievements to her credit. ❷ fulfillment ▷ *la réalisation d'un grand rêve* the fulfillment of a great dream

  Be careful! **la réalisation** does not mean **realization**.

réalisatrice [ʀealizatʀis] *nf* director (*of film*) ▷ *Patricia Rozema est réalisatrice.* Patricia Rozema is a film director.

réaliser [ʀealize] *vb* ❶ to carry out ▷ *Ils ont réalisé leur projet.* They carried out their plan. ❷ to fulfill ▷ *Il a réalisé son rêve.* He has fulfilled his dream. ❸ to realize ▷ *Réalises-tu ce que tu dis?* Do you realize what you're saying? ❹ to make ▷ *réaliser un film* to make a movie; **se réaliser** to come true

réaliste [ʀealist(ə)] *adj* realistic

réalité [ʀealite] *nf* reality; **en réalité** in fact

rebelle [ʀəbɛl] *nmf* rebel

rebondir [ʀəbɔ̃diʀ] *vb* to bounce

rebord [ʀəbɔʀ] *nm* edge ▷ *le rebord du lavabo* the edge of the sink; **le rebord de la fenêtre** the window ledge

récemment [ʀesamã] *adv* recently

récent [ʀesã, -ãt] (*frécente*) *adj* recent

récepteur [ʀesɛptœʀ] *nm* receiver

réception [ʀesɛpsjɔ̃] *nf* (*in office*) reception

réceptionniste [ʀesɛpsjɔnist(ə)] *nmf* receptionist ▷ *Il est réceptionniste.* He's a receptionist.

recette [ʀəsɛt] *nf* recipe

recevoir [ʀəsvwaʀ] *vb* ❶ to receive ▷ *J'ai reçu une lettre.* I received a letter. ❷ to see ▷ *Elle a déjà reçu trois clients.* She's already seen three clients. ❸ to have over ▷ *Je reçois des amis à dîner.* I'm having friends over for dinner.

rechange [ʀəʃɑ̃ʒ] *nm*: **de rechange** (*battery, bulb*) spare ▷ *des vêtements de rechange* a change of clothes

recharge [ʀəʃaʀʒ(ə)] *nf* refill

réchaud [ʀeʃo] *nm* (*portable*) stove

réchauffement [ʀeʃofmã] *nm* warming (up) ▷ *le réchauffement planétaire* global warming

réchauffer [ʀeʃofe] *vb* ❶ to reheat ▷ *Je vais réchauffer les légumes.* I'll reheat the vegetables. ❷ to warm up ▷ *Un bon chocolat chaud va te réchauffer.* A nice cup of hot chocolate will warm you up.; **se réchauffer** to warm oneself ▷ *Je vais me réchauffer près du feu.* I'm going to warm up by the fire.

recherche [ʀəʃɛʀʃ(ə)] *nf* research ▷ *Je voudrais faire de la recherche.* I'd like to do some research.; **être à la recherche de quelque chose** to be looking for something ▷ *Je suis à la recherche d'un emploi.* I'm looking for a job.; **les recherches** search ▷ *La police a interrompu les recherches.* The police called off the search.

recherché [ʀəʃɛʀʃe] (f **recherchée**) adj ❶ (book, painting, speaker) much sought-after ❷ (criminal) wanted

rechercher [ʀəʃɛʀʃe] vb to look for ▷ La police recherche l'assassin. The police are looking for the killer.

rechute [ʀəʃyt] nf relapse

récipient [ʀesipjɑ̃] nm container

récit [ʀesi] nm story

réciter [ʀesite] vb to recite

réclamation [ʀeklamasjɔ̃] nf complaint ▷ J'ai une réclamation à faire. I want to make a complaint.; **les réclamations** the complaints department

réclamer [ʀeklame] vb ❶ to demand ▷ Nous réclamons la semaine de trente heures. We demand a 30-hour week. ❷ to complain ▷ Elles sont toujours en train de réclamer. They're always complaining about something.

reçois [ʀəswa] vb see **recevoir**

récolte [ʀekɔlt(ə)] nf harvest

récolter [ʀekɔlte] vb ❶ to harvest ▷ Ils ont récolté le blé. They harvested the wheat. ❷ to collect ▷ Ils ont récolté deux cents dollars. They collected 200 dollars. ❸ to get ▷ Elle a récolté une amende. (informal) She got a fine.

recommandé [ʀəkɔmɑ̃de] nm: **en recommandé** by registered mail ▷ Je voudrais envoyer ce paquet en recommandé. I'd like to register this parcel.

recommander [ʀəkɔmɑ̃de] vb to recommend ▷ Je vous recommande ce restaurant. I recommend this restaurant.

recommencer [ʀəkɔmɑ̃se] vb ❶ to start again ▷ Il a recommencé à pleuvoir. It's started raining again. ❷ to do again ▷ S'il n'est pas puni, il va recommencer. If he's not punished,

he'll do it again.

récompense [ʀekɔ̃pɑ̃s] nf reward

récompenser [ʀekɔ̃pɑ̃se] vb to reward ▷ Il m'a récompensée de mes efforts. He rewarded me for my efforts.

réconcilier [ʀekɔ̃silje] vb: **se réconcilier avec quelqu'un** to make up with somebody ▷ Il s'est réconcilié avec sa sœur. He's made up with his sister.

reconnaissant [ʀəkɔnɛsɑ̃, -ɑ̃t] (f **reconnaissante**) adj grateful

reconnaître [ʀəkɔnɛtʀ(ə)] vb ❶ to recognize ▷ Je ne l'ai pas reconnu. I didn't recognize him. ❷ to admit ▷ Je reconnais que j'ai eu tort. I admit I was wrong.

reconstruire [ʀəkɔ̃stʀɥiʀ] vb to rebuild

record [ʀəkɔʀ] nm record ▷ battre un record to break a record

recouvrir [ʀəkuvʀiʀ] vb to cover ▷ La neige recouvre le sol. Snow covers the ground.

récréation [ʀekʀeasjɔ̃] nf recess ▷ Les élèves sont en récréation. The students are having recess.; **la cour de récréation** the playground (of school)

rectangle [ʀɛktɑ̃gl(ə)] nm rectangle

rectangulaire [ʀɛktɑ̃gylɛʀ] adj rectangular

rectifier [ʀɛktifje] vb to correct

rectitude politique [ʀɛktityd-] nf political correctness

reçu [ʀəsy] nm receipt ▶ vb see **recevoir**; **J'ai reçu un colis ce matin.** I received a parcel this morning.

reculer [ʀəkyle] vb ❶ to step back ▷ Il a reculé pour la laisser entrer. He stepped back to let her in. ❷ (vehicle) to back up ▷ J'ai reculé pour laisser passer le camion.

I backed up to let the truck past.
❸ to postpone ▷ Ils ont reculé la
date du spectacle. They postponed
the show.

reculons [ʀəkylɔ̃]: **à reculons**
adv backwards ▷ Elle est entrée à
reculons. She came in backwards.

récupérer [ʀekypeʀe] vb ❶ to
get back ▷ Je vais essayer de récupérer
mon argent. I'm going to try to get
my money back. ❷ to recover ▷ J'ai
besoin de récupérer. I need to recover.
❸ (data, files) to retrieve

recycler [ʀəsikle] vb to recycle;
se recycler to retrain ▷ Il a décidé
de se recycler en informatique. He
decided to retrain as a computer
programmer.

rédaction [ʀedaksjɔ̃] nf ❶ writing
▷ Voici des exercices pour améliorer
vos aptitudes en rédaction. Here are
some exercises to improve your
writing skills. ❷ essay ▷ Il faut
remettre la rédaction sur notre future
carrière demain. We have to hand
in the essay on our future career
tomorrow.

redemander [ʀədmɑ̃de] vb ❶ to
ask again for ▷ Je vais lui redemander
son adresse. I'll ask her for her
address again. ❷ to ask for more
▷ Je vais redemander des carottes. I'm
going to ask for more carrots.

redémarrer [ʀedemaʀe] vb ❶ to
reboot ▷ J'ai redémarré l'ordinateur. I
rebooted the computer. ❷ to start
up again ▷ La voiture a redémarré.
The car started up again.

redescendre [ʀədesɑ̃dʀ(ə)] vb to
go back down ▷ Il est redescendu au
premier étage. He went back down
to the first floor. ▷ Elle a redescendu
l'escalier. She went back down
the stairs.

rediffusion [ʀədifyzjɔ̃] nf rerun;
en rediffusion ▷ Le téléjournal sera

en rediffusion à onze heures. The news
will be rebroadcast at 11.

redoubler [ʀəduble] vb to repeat
a year ▷ Il a raté son examen et doit
redoubler. He failed his exam and
will have to repeat the year.

réduction [ʀedyksjɔ̃] nf
❶ reduction ▷ une réduction du
nombre des touristes a reduction in
the number of tourists ❷ discount
▷ une réduction de vingt dollars a 20
dollar discount

réduire [ʀedɥiʀ] vb to cut ▷ Ils ont
réduit leurs prix. They've cut their
prices. ▷ Elle a réduit de moitié ses
dépenses. She has cut her spending
by half.; **Réduire, réutiliser,
recycler.** Reduce, reuse, recycle.

réel [ʀeɛl] (**réelle**) adj real

réellement [ʀeɛlmɑ̃] adv really

refaire [ʀəfɛʀ] vb ❶ to do again
▷ Je dois refaire ce rapport. I've got to
do this report again. ❷ to take up
again ▷ Je voudrais refaire du ski. I'd
like to take up skiing again.

référence [ʀefeʀɑ̃s] nf reference;
faire référence à quelque chose
to refer to something; **Ce n'est
pas une référence!** That's no
recommendation!

réfléchi [ʀefleʃi] (**réfléchie**) adj
(verb) reflexive; **C'est tout réfléchi.**
My mind's made up.

réfléchir [ʀefleʃiʀ] vb to think ▷ Il
est en train de réfléchir. He's thinking.;
réfléchir à quelque chose to think
about something ▷ Je vais réfléchir
à ta proposition. I'll think about your
suggestion.

reflet [ʀəflɛ] nm reflection ▷ les
reflets du soleil sur la mer the
reflection of the sun on the sea

refléter [ʀəflete] vb to reflect

réflexe [ʀeflɛks(ə)] nm reflex
▷ avoir de bons réflexes to have good
reflexes

réflexion [Refleksjɔ̃] nf ❶ thought ▷ *Elle est en pleine réflexion.* She's deep in thought. ❷ remark ▷ *faire des réflexions désagréables* to make nasty remarks; **réflexion faite** on reflection

refrain [R(ə)fRɛ̃] nm chorus (*of song*)

réfrigérateur [RefRiʒeRatœR] nm refrigerator

refroidir [RəfRwadiR] vb to cool ▷ *Laissez le gâteau refroidir.* Leave the cake to cool.; **se refroidir** to get colder ▷ *Le temps se refroidit.* It's getting colder out.

refroidissement éolien [RəfRwadismɑ̃eɔljɛ̃] nm wind chill ▷ *Le facteur de refroidissement éolien est de moins dix degrés aujourd'hui.* The wind chill factor is -10 today.

se réfugier [Refyʒje] vb to take shelter ▷ *Je me suis réfugié sous un arbre.* I took shelter under a tree.

refus [Rəfy] nm refusal; **Ce n'est pas de refus.** I wouldn't say no. ▷ *«Voulez-vous du thé glacé?»* — *«Ce n'est pas de refus.»* "Would you like some iced tea?" — "I wouldn't say no."

refuser [Rəfyze] vb to refuse ▷ *Il a refusé de payer sa part.* He refused to pay his share. ▷ *On lui a refusé la permission.* She was refused permission.; **Je refuse qu'on me parle ainsi!** I won't let anybody talk to me like that!

se régaler [Regale] vb **Merci beaucoup : je me suis régalé!** Thank you very much: it was absolutely delicious!

regard [RəgaR] nm look ▷ *Il nous a jeté un regard méfiant.* He gave us a mistrustful look. ▷ *On voyait à son regard qu'elle était contrariée.* You could tell from the look in her eyes that she was upset.; **Tous les**

regards se sont tournés vers lui. All eyes turned towards him.

regarder [RəgaRde] vb ❶ to look at ▷ *Il regardait ses photos de vacances.* He was looking at his vacation photos. ▷ *Regarde! J'ai presque fini.* Look! I'm almost finished. ❷ to watch ▷ *Je regarde la télévision.* I'm watching television. ▷ *Regarde où tu mets les pieds!* Watch where you put your feet! ❸ to concern ▷ *Ça ne nous regarde pas.* It doesn't concern us.; **ne pas regarder à la dépense** to spare no expense

régime [Reʒim] nm ❶ régime (*of a country*) ❷ diet ▷ *un régime sans sel* a salt-free diet ▷ *se mettre au régime* to go on a diet ▷ *suivre un régime* to be on a diet; **un régime de bananes** a bunch of bananas

région [Reʒjɔ̃] nf region; **la région des Barrens** the Barrens

régional [Reʒjɔnal, -o] (*f* **régionale**, *mpl* **régionaux**) adj regional

registre [RəʒistR(ə)] nm (*record book*) register ▷ *Veuillez signer le registre.* Please sign the register.

règle [Rɛgl(ə)] nf ❶ ruler ▷ *Elle a souligné son nom avec une règle.* She underlined her name with a ruler. ❷ rule ▷ *C'est la règle.* That's the rule. ▷ *en règle générale* as a general rule; **être en règle** to be in order ▷ *Est-ce que tout est en règle pour votre voyage?* Is everything in order for your trip?; **les règles** (*menstruation*) period

règlement [Rɛgləmɑ̃] nm rules ▷ *Le règlement est affiché à l'entrée.* The rules are posted by the entrance.

régler [Regle] vb ❶ to adjust ▷ *Il faut que je règle mon rétroviseur.* I have to adjust my rearview mirror. ❷ to set ▷ *J'ai réglé le thermostat à vingt* *degrés.* I've set the thermostat to 20 degrees. ❸ to solve ▷ *Le problème est réglé.* The problem is solved. ❹ *(pay up)* to settle ▷ *Elle a réglé sa facture.* She settled her bill.

réglisse [ʀeɡlis] *nf* licorice

règne [ʀɛɲ] *nm* reign ▷ *sous le règne de Henri IV* in the reign of Henry IV

régner [ʀeɲe] *vb* to reign

regret [ʀəɡʀɛ] *nm* regret; **à regret** reluctantly

regretter [ʀəɡʀete] *vb* ❶ to regret ▷ *Elle regrette ce qu'elle a dit.* She regrets what she said.; **Je regrette.** I'm sorry. ▷ *Je regrette, je ne peux pas vous aider.* I'm sorry, I can't help you. ❷ to miss ▷ *Je regrette mon ancienne école.* I miss my old school.

regrouper [ʀəɡʀupe] *vb* to group together ▷ *Nous avons regroupé les enfants selon leur âge.* We grouped the children together according to age.; **se regrouper** to join together ▷ *Les agriculteurs se sont regroupés pour constituer un syndicat.* The farmers joined together to form a union.

régulier [ʀeɡylje, -jɛʀ] *(f* **régulière)** *adj* ❶ regular ▷ *des livraisons régulières* regular deliveries ▷ *des autobus réguliers* a regular bus service ❷ steady ▷ *à un rythme régulier* at a steady rate ❸ scheduled ▷ *des vols réguliers pour Whitehorse* scheduled flights to Whitehorse

régulièrement [ʀeɡyljɛʀmɑ̃] *adv* regularly

rein [ʀɛ̃] *nm* kidney; **les reins** *(of body)* back ▷ *J'ai mal aux reins.* My back hurts

reine [ʀɛn] *nf* queen

rejoindre [ʀəʒwɛ̃dʀ(ə)] *vb* to go back to ▷ *J'ai rejoint mes amis.* I went back to my friends.; **Je te rejoins au café.** I'll see you at the café.; **se**

rejoindre to meet up ▷ *Elles se sont rejointes une heure après.* They met up an hour later.

relâcher [ʀəlɑʃe] *vb (prisoner, animal)* to release; **se relâcher** to get slack ▷ *Il se relâche dans son travail.* He's slacking off in his work.

relais [ʀəlɛ] *nm* relay race ▷ *le relais quatre fois cent mètres* the 4 x 100 metre relay; **prendre le relais** to take over; **le relais routier** truck stop

relation [ʀəlasjɔ̃] *nf* relationship; **les relations entre le Canada et les États-Unis** Canada-US relations; **les relations publiques** public relations

se relaxer [ʀəlakse] *vb* to relax

se relayer [ʀəleje] *vb*: **se relayer pour faire quelque chose** to take turns doing something

relevé [ʀəlve] *nm*: **un relevé de compte** a bank statement

relever [ʀəlve] *vb* ❶ to find ▷ *J'ai relevé six erreurs dans ton devoir.* I found six mistakes in your homework. ❷ to react to ▷ *Je n'ai pas relevé sa réflexion.* I didn't react to his remark.; **relever la tête** to look up; **se relever** to get up ▷ *Il est tombé mais s'est relevé aussitôt.* He fell, but got up immediately.

religieuse [ʀəliʒjœz] *nf* nun

religieux [ʀəliʒjø, -øz] *(f* **religieuse)** *adj* religious

religion [ʀəliʒjɔ̃] *nf* religion

relire [ʀəliʀ] *vb* ❶ to read over ▷ *Elle a relu son examen avant de le rendre.* She read her exam paper over before handing it in. ❷ to read again ▷ *Je voudrais relire ce roman.* I'd like to read this novel again.

remarquable [ʀəmaʀkabl(ə)] *adj* remarkable

remarque [ʀəmaʀk(ə)] *nf*

❶ remark ▷ *une remarque désagréable* a nasty remark ❷ comment ▷ *Avez-vous des remarques à faire?* Do you have any comments?

remarquer [RəmaRke] vb ❶ to notice ▷ *J'ai remarqué qu'elle avait l'air triste.* I noticed she was looking sad.; **faire remarquer quelque chose à quelqu'un** to point something out to somebody ▷ *Je lui ai fait remarquer que c'était un peu cher.* I pointed out to him that it was a bit expensive.; **Remarquez, elle n'est pas si bête que ça.** Mind you, she's not as stupid as all that.; **se remarquer** to be noticeable ▷ *Il ne s'est pas rasé ce matin. Ça se remarque.* It's obvious he didn't shave this morning.; **se faire remarquer** to call attention to oneself

remboursement [Rãbursəmã] nm refund

rembourser [Rãburse] vb ❶ to pay back ▷ *Il m'a remboursé l'argent qu'il me devait.* He paid me back the money he owed me. ❷ to refund ▷ *Le vol a été annulé et on m'a remboursé mon billet.* The flight was cancelled and they refunded my ticket.

remède [Rəmɛd] nm ❶ medicine ❷ cure

remercier [Rəmɛrsje] vb to thank ▷ *Je te remercie pour ton cadeau.* Thank you for your present.; **remercier quelqu'un d'avoir fait quelque chose** to thank somebody for doing something ▷ *Je vous remercie de m'avoir invité.* Thank you for inviting me.

remettre [Rəmɛtr(ə)] vb ❶ to put back on ▷ *Elle a remis son chandail.* She put her sweater back on. ❷ to put back ▷ *Il a remis son manteau dans le garde-robe.* He put his coat

back in the closet. ❸ to put off ▷ *J'ai dû remettre mon rendez-vous.* I had to put off my appointment.; **se remettre** (from illness) to recover ▷ *Ma tante s'est bien remise de son opération.* My aunt has fully recovered from her operation.; **« Satisfaction garantie ou argent remis »** "Satisfaction guaranteed or your money back"

remonte-pente [Rəmɔ̃tpɑ̃t] nm ski lift

remonter [Rəmɔ̃te] vb ❶ to go back up ▷ *Il est remonté à sa chambre.* He's gone back up to his room. ❷ to go up ▷ *Ils ont remonté la pente.* They went up the hill. ❸ to comfort ▷ *Cette nouvelle m'a un peu remonté.* The news comforted me a bit.; **remonter le moral à quelqu'un** to lift somebody's spirits

remords [Rəmɔr] nm: **avoir des remords** to feel remorse

remorque [Rəmɔrk(ə)] nf (of car) trailer

remparts [Rãpar] nmpl city walls

remplaçant [Rãplasã] nm supply teacher

remplaçante [Rãplasãt] nf supply teacher

remplacer [Rãplase] vb to replace ▷ *Il faut remplacer cette ampoule.* We need to replace this bulb. ▷ *Il remplace le prof de maths.* He's replacing the maths teacher.; **remplacer par** to replace with

rempli [Rãpli] (fremplie) adj full ▷ *une journée bien remplie* a very full day; **rempli de** full of ▷ *La salle était remplie de monde.* The room was full of people.

remplir [Rãplir] vb ❶ to fill up ▷ *Elle a rempli son verre d'eau.* She filled her glass with water. ❷ to fill out ▷ *Tu as rempli ton formulaire?* Have you filled out your form?;

se remplir to fill up ▷ *La salle s'est remplie de monde.* The room filled up with people.

remue-méninges [ʀəmymenɛʒ] (pl **remue-méninges**) nm brainstorming ▷ *une séance de remue-méninges* a brainstorming session

remuer [ʀəmɥe] vb **❶** to move ▷ *Elle a remué le bras.* She moved her arm. **❷** to stir ▷ *Remuez la sauce pendant deux minutes.* Stir the sauce for two minutes.

renard [ʀənaʀ] nm fox

renardeau [ʀənaʀdo] (pl **renardeaux**) nm fox cub

rencontre [ʀɑ̃kɔ̃tʀ(ə)] nf: **faire la rencontre de quelqu'un** to meet somebody ▷ *J'ai fait la rencontre de personnes intéressantes ce soir.* I met some interesting people this evening.; **aller à la rencontre de quelqu'un** to go and meet somebody ▷ *Je viendrai à ta rencontre.* I'll come and meet you.

rencontrer [ʀɑ̃kɔ̃tʀe] vb to meet; **se rencontrer** to meet ▷ *Ils se sont rencontrés il y a deux ans.* They met two years ago.

rendez-vous [ʀɑ̃devu] nm **❶** appointment ▷ *J'ai rendez-vous chez le coiffeur.* I've got an appointment at the hairdresser's. ▷ *prendre rendez-vous avec quelqu'un* to make an appointment with somebody **❷** date ▷ *« Tu sors ce soir? » « Oui, j'ai un rendez-vous. »* "Are you going out tonight?" "Yes, I've got a date.".; **donner rendez-vous à quelqu'un** to arrange to meet somebody

rendre [ʀɑ̃dʀ(ə)] vb **❶** to give back ▷ *J'ai rendu ses disques à ta sœur.* I've given your sister her records back. **❷** to take back ▷ *J'ai rendu mes livres à la bibliothèque.* I've taken

my books back to the library.; **rendre quelqu'un célèbre** to make somebody famous; **se rendre** to give oneself up ▷ *Le voleur s'est rendu à la police.* The robber gave himself up to the police.; **se rendre compte de quelque chose** to realize something

renfermé [ʀɑ̃fɛʀme] nm: **sentir le renfermé** to smell stuffy

renifler [ʀənifle] vb to sniff

renne [ʀɛn] nm reindeer

renommé [ʀ(ə)nɔme] (f **renommée**) adj renowned ▷ *La baie de Fundy est renommée pour ses marées.* The Bay of Fundy is renowned for its tides.

renoncer [ʀənɔ̃se] vb: **renoncer à** to give up ▷ *Ils ont renoncé à leur projet.* They've given up their plan.; **renoncer à faire quelque chose** to give up the idea of doing something

renouvelable [ʀ(ə)nuvlabl(ə)] adj renewable; **les ressources non renouvelables** non-renewable resources

renouveler [ʀənuvle] vb (passport, contract) to renew; **se renouveler** to happen again ▷ *J'espère que ça ne se renouvellera pas.* I hope that won't happen again.

renseignement [ʀɑ̃sɛɲmɑ̃] nm piece of information ▷ *Il me manque un renseignement.* There's one piece of information I still need.; **les renseignements (1)** information ▷ *Il m'a donné des renseignements.* He gave me some information. **(2)** information desk

renseigner [ʀɑ̃seɲe] vb: **renseigner quelqu'un sur quelque chose** to give somebody information about something; **se renseigner** to inquire ▷ *Nous nous sommes renseignés sur l'horaire.* We inquired about the schedule.

rentable [Rɑ̃tabl(ə)] *adj* profitable

rentrée [Rɑ̃tʀe] *nf*: **la rentrée (des classes)** the start of the new school year; **la vente de la rentrée** back-to-school sale

rentrer [Rɑ̃tʀe] *vb* ❶ to come in ▷ *Rentre, tu vas prendre froid.* Come in, you'll catch cold. ❷ to go in ▷ *Elle est rentrée dans le magasin.* She went into the store. ❸ to get home ▷ *Je suis rentrée à sept heures hier soir.* I got home at 7 o'clock last night. ❹ to bring in ▷ *As-tu rentré ton vélo?* Did you bring your bike in?; **rentrer dans** to crash into ▷ *Sa voiture est rentrée dans un arbre.* She crashed into a tree.; **rentrer dans l'ordre** to get back to normal

renverse [Rɑ̃vɛʀs(ə)] *nf*: **tomber à la renverse** to fall backwards

renverser [Rɑ̃vɛʀse] *vb* ❶ to knock over ▷ *J'ai renversé mon verre.* I knocked over my glass. ❷ to run over ▷ *Elle a été renversée par une voiture.* She was run over by a car. ❸ to spill ▷ *Il a renversé de l'eau partout.* He has spilled water everywhere.; **se renverser** (*glass, vase*) to fall over

renvoyer [Rɑ̃vwaje] *vb* ❶ to send back ▷ *Il a renvoyé les documents.* He sent back the documents. ❷ to fire ▷ *On a renvoyé deux employés.* Two employees have been fired.

répandu [Repɑ̃dy] (*f* **répandue**) *adj* widespread ▷ *C'est une croyance très répandue.* It's a very widespread belief.; **du jus répandu sur la table** juice spilled on the table; **des papiers répandus sur le sol** papers scattered over the floor

réparateur [Reparatœr] *nm* repairman

réparation [Reparasjɔ̃] *nf* repair

réparatrice [Reparatris] *nf* repairwoman

réparer [Repare] *vb* to repair

repartir [Rəpartir] *vb* to set off again ▷ *Il s'est arrêté pour manger avant de repartir.* He stopped to eat before setting off again. ▷ *Il était là tout à l'heure, mais il est reparti.* He was here a moment ago, but he's gone again.; **repartir à zéro** to start from scratch again

repas [Rəpɑ] *nm* meal; **le repas de midi** lunch; **le repas du soir** supper

repassage [Rəpɑsaʒ] *nm* ironing ▷ *Je déteste le repassage.* I hate ironing.

repasser [Rəpɑse] *vb* ❶ to come back ▷ *Je repasserai demain.* I'll come back tomorrow. ❷ to go back ▷ *Je dois repasser au magasin.* I've got to go back to the store. ❸ to iron ▷ *J'ai repassé ma chemise.* I ironed my shirt. ❹ to resit ▷ *Elle doit repasser son examen.* She has to rewrite her exam.

repérer [Rəpere] *vb* ❶ to spot ▷ *J'ai repéré deux fautes.* I spotted two mistakes.; **se repérer** to find one's way around ▷ *J'ai du mal à me repérer de nuit.* I have a hard time finding my way at night.

répertoire [Repɛrtwar] *nm* directory

répéter [Repete] *vb* ❶ to repeat ▷ *Elle répète toujours la même chose.* She keeps repeating the same thing. ❷ to rehearse ▷ *Les acteurs répètent une scène.* The actors are rehearsing a scene.; **répéter** to happen again ▷ *J'espère que cela ne se répétera pas!* I hope this won't happen again!

répétition [Repetisjɔ̃] *nf* ❶ repetition ▷ *Il y a beaucoup de répétitions dans ce texte.* There's a lot of repetition in this text.; **des grèves à répétition** repeated strikes ❷ rehearsal ▷ *Ils ont une* *répétition cet après-midi.* They have a rehearsal this afternoon.; **la répétition générale** the dress rehearsal

répondeur [Repɔ̃dœr] *nm* answering machine

répondre [Repɔ̃dr(ə)] *vb* to answer ▷ *répondre à quelqu'un* to answer somebody

réponse [Repɔ̃s] *nf* answer ▷ *C'est la bonne réponse.* That's the right answer.

reportage [Rəpɔrtaʒ] *nm*
❶ report ▷ *J'ai vu ce reportage aux informations.* I saw that report on the news. ❷ story ▷ *J'ai lu ce reportage dans La Gazette.* I read that story in the *Gazette.*

repos [Rəpo] *nm* rest

reposer [Rəpoze] *vb* to put back down ▷ *Elle a reposé son verre sur la table.* She put her glass back down on the table.; **se reposer** to rest ▷ *Tu pourras te reposer demain.* You'll be able to rest tomorrow.; **se reposer sur quelqu'un** to rely on somebody

repousser [Rəpuse] *vb* ❶ to grow again ▷ *Ses cheveux ont repoussé.* Her hair has grown again. ❷ to postpone ▷ *Le voyage est repoussé.* The trip's been postponed.

reprendre [Rəprɑ̃dr(ə)] *vb* ❶ to take back ▷ *Il a repris son livre.* He took back his book. ❷ to go back to ▷ *Elle a repris le travail.* She went back to work. ❸ to start again ▷ *La réunion reprendra à deux heures.* The meeting will start again at 2 o'clock.; **reprendre du pain** to take more bread; **reprendre la route** to set off again; **reprendre son souffle** to catch one's breath

représentant [Rəprezɑ̃tɑ̃] *nm* rep ▷ *Il est représentant chez une grande maison d'édition.* He's a rep for a major publisher.

représentante [Rəprezɑ̃tɑ̃t] *nf* rep ▷ *Elle est représentante pour une grande société d'informatique.* She's a sales rep for a big software company.

représentation [Rəprezɑ̃tasjɔ̃] *nf* performance ▷ *la dernière représentation d'une pièce* the final performance of a play

représenter [Rəprezɑ̃te] *vb* ❶ to show ▷ *Le tableau représente un enfant et un chat.* The picture shows a child with a cat. ❷ to represent; **se représenter** to come up again ▷ *Cette occasion ne se représentera pas.* This opportunity won't come up again.

reprise [Rəpriz] *nf* ❶ rerun ▷ *La série Le Canada : une histoire populaire est en reprise ce soir à la télé.* There is a rerun of the series *Canada: A People's History* on TV tonight. ❷ recovery ▷ *la reprise économique* economic recovery; **à plusieurs reprises** repeatedly

reproche [Rəprɔʃ] *nm*: **faire des reproches à quelqu'un** to reproach somebody

reprocher [Rəprɔʃe] *vb*: **reprocher quelque chose à quelqu'un** to reproach somebody for something ▷ *Il m'a reproché mon retard.* He reproached me for being late.; **Qu'est-ce que tu lui reproches?** What have you got against her?

reproduction [Rəprɔdyksjɔ̃] *nf* reproduction

reproduire [Rəprɔdyir] *vb* to reproduce; **se reproduire** to happen again ▷ *Je te promets que ça ne se reproduira pas!* I promise it won't happen again!

république [Repyblik] *nf* republic ▷ *Le Canada n'est pas une république, c'est une confédération.* Canada is not a republic, it's a confederation.

répugnant [Repɥɲɑ̃, -ɑ̃t] (f **répugnante**) adj repulsive

réputation [Repɥtasjɔ̃] nf reputation

requin [Rəkɛ̃] nm shark

réseau [Rezo] (pl **réseaux**) nm network ▷ le réseau social social network

réseautage [Rezotaʒ] nm networking ▷ de bonnes techniques de réseautage good networking techniques ▷ Il est spécialiste du réseautage. He's a networking specialist.

réservation [RezeRvasjɔ̃] nf reservation ▷ J'ai fait des réservations pour un groupe de six personnes. I made reservations for a group of six.

réserve [RezeRv(ə)] nf supply ▷ une réserve énorme d'énergie an enormous supply of energy; **avoir quelque chose en réserve** to have something in stock; **mettre quelque chose en réserve** to put something aside; **la réserve indienne** First Nations reserve

réserver [RezeRve] vb ❶ to reserve ▷ Cette table est réservée. This table is reserved. ❷ to book ▷ Nous avons réservé une chambre. We've booked a room.

réservoir [RezeRvwaR] nm gas tank

résidence [Rezidɑ̃s] nf residence ▷ une résidence pour personnes âgées a seniors' residence; **en résidence surveillée** under house arrest; **le lieu de résidence** place of residence; **une résidence secondaire** a second home

résistant [Rezistɑ̃, -ɑ̃t] (f **résistante**) adj ❶ durable ▷ Ce tissu est résistant. This fabric is durable. ❷ (strong) tough ▷ Il faut

être résistant pour faire ce travail. You have to be tough to do this work. ▷ Elle est rarement malade; elle est très résistante. She's hardly ever sick; she's very tough.

résister [Reziste] vb to resist

résolu [Rezɔly] adj: **Le problème est résolu.** The problem's solved.

résoudre [Rezudʀ(ə)] vb to solve

respect [Rɛspɛ] nm respect; **manquer de respect** to be disrespectful

respecter [Rɛspɛkte] vb to respect

respiration [RɛspiRasjɔ̃] nf breathing

respirer [RɛspiRe] vb to breathe

responsabilité [Rɛspɔ̃sabilite] nf responsibility

responsable [Rɛspɔ̃sabl(ə)] adj responsible ▷ être responsable de quelque chose to be responsible for something

▸ n ❶ person in charge ▷ Je voudrais parler au responsable. I'd like to speak to the person in charge. ❷ person responsible ▷ Il faut punir les responsables. Those responsible must be punished.

ressembler [Rəsɑ̃ble] vb: **ressembler à** (1) to look like ▷ Elle ne ressemble pas à sa sœur. She doesn't look like her sister. (2) to be like ▷ Ça ressemble à un conte de fées. It's like a fairy tale.; **se ressembler** (1) to look alike ▷ Les deux frères ne se ressemblent pas. The two brothers don't look alike. (2) to be very similar ▷ Ces deux jeux vidéo se ressemblent. These two video games are quite similar.

ressort [RəsɔR] nm spring ▷ Le ressort est cassé. The spring is broken.

ressortir [RəsɔRtiR] vb to go out again

restaurant [RɛstɔRɑ̃] nm restaurant

restauroute [RɛstɔRut] nm
roadside restaurant ▷ Nous avons
mangé au restauroute. We ate at the
roadside restaurant.

reste [Rɛst(ə)] nm rest; **un reste de
poulet** some leftover chicken; **les
restes** the leftovers

rester [Rɛste] vb ❶ to stay ▷ Je
reste à la maison en fin de semaine.
I'm staying home this weekend.
❷ to be left ▷ Il reste du pain. There's
some bread left. ▷ Il me reste assez de
temps. I still have enough time.; **Il
ne me reste plus qu'à…** I just have
to… ▷ Il ne me reste plus qu'à ranger
mes affaires. I just have to put my
things away.; **Restons-en là.** Let's
leave it at that.

résultat [Rezylta] nm result ▷ le
résultat des examens the exam
results

résumé [Rezyme] nm summary

▌Be careful! **le résumé** does not
▌mean the same as **résumé** in
▌English.

résumer [Rezyme] vb to
summarize

▌Be careful! **résumer** does not
▌mean **to resume**.

se rétablir [Retablir] vb to get well

retard [RataR] nm delay ▷ un retard
de livraison a delay in delivery;
avoir du retard to be late; **être en
retard de deux heures** to be two
hours late; **prendre du retard** to
be delayed

retarder [RataRde] vb ❶ to be
slow ▷ Ma montre retarde. My watch
is slow. ❷ to put back ▷ Je dois
retarder l'horloge d'une heure. I have
to put the clock back an hour.;
être retardé to be delayed ▷ J'ai été
retardé par un coup de téléphone. I was
held up by a phone call.

retenir [Ratnir] vb ❶ to
remember ▷ Tu as retenu leur

adresse? Do you remember their
address? ❷ to book ▷ J'ai retenu une
chambre à l'hôtel. I've booked a room
at the hotel.; **retenir son souffle** to
hold one's breath

retenu [Ratny] (f **retenue**) adj
❶ reserved ▷ Cette place est retenue.
This seat is reserved. ❷ held
up ▷ J'ai été retenu par un coup
de téléphone. I was held up by a
phone call.

retenue [Ratny] nf detention ▷ Il
est en retenue. He has a detention.

retirer [Ratire] vb ❶ to withdraw
▷ Elle a retiré de l'argent. She
withdrew some money. ❷ to take
off ▷ Il a retiré son chandail. He took
off his sweater.

retour [RatuR] nm return; **être de
retour** to be back ▷ Je serai de retour
la semaine prochaine. I'll be back
next week.

retourner [RatuRne] vb ❶ to go
back ▷ Est-ce que tu es retourné à
Whitehorse? Have you been back
to Whitehorse? ❷ to turn over
▷ Elle a retourné la crêpe. She flipped
the pancake over. ▷ Il a retourné la
poubelle. He turned the garbage can
upside down.; **se retourner (1)** to
turn around ▷ Elle s'est retournée.
She turned around. **(2)** to turn over
▷ La voiture s'est retournée. The car
turned over.

retraite [RatRɛt] nf: **être à la
retraite** to be retired; **prendre sa
retraite** to retire

retraité [RatRete] (f **retraitée**) adj
retired ▷ Mon oncle est maintenant
retraité. My uncle is now retired.
▶ nm retiree

retraitée [RatRete] nf retiree

rétrécir [RetResir] vb to shrink
▷ Mon chandail a rétréci au lavage. My
sweater shrank in the wash.; **se
rétrécir** to get narrower ▷ La rue se

rétrécit. The street gets narrower.

retrouver [ʀətʀuve] vb
❶ (something lost) to find ▷ J'ai retrouvé mon portefeuille. I found my wallet. ❷ to meet up with ▷ Je te retrouve au café à trois heures. I'll meet you at the coffee shop at 3 o'clock ; **se retrouver (1)** to meet up ▷ Ils se sont retrouvés devant le cinéma. They met up in front of the movie theatre. **(2)** to find one's way around ▷ Je n'arrive pas à me retrouver. I can't find my way around.

rétroviseur [ʀetʀɔvizœʀ] nm
rearview mirror

réunion [ʀeynjɔ̃] nf meeting

se réunir [ʀeyniʀ] vb to meet ▷ Ils se sont réunis à cinq heures. They met at 5 o'clock.

réussi [ʀeysi] (f **réussie**) adj successful ▷ une soirée très réussie a very successful party ; **être réussi** to be a success ▷ Le repas était très réussi. The meal was a hit.

réussir [ʀeysiʀ] vb to be successful ▷ Tous ses enfants ont très bien réussi. All her children are very successful. ; **réussir à faire quelque chose** to succeed in doing something; **réussir à un examen** to pass an exam

réussite [ʀeysit] nf success

réutiliser [ʀeytilize] vb to reuse ▷ Les trois R sont « réduire, réutiliser et recycler ». The 3 Rs are "reduce, reuse, recycle".

revanche [ʀəvɑ̃ʃ] nf ❶ revenge ❷ return game; **prendre sa revanche** to get even ▷ Il a pris sa revanche en refusant de lui prêter son vélo. He got even by refusing to lend him his bike. ; **en revanche** on the other hand ▷ C'est cher mais en revanche c'est de la bonne qualité. It's expensive but on the other hand it's

good quality.

rêve [ʀɛv] nm dream; **des vacances de rêve** a dream vacation

réveil [ʀevɛj] nm alarm clock; **mettre le réveil à huit heures** to set the alarm for eight o'clock

réveille-matin [ʀevɛjmatɛ̃] (pl **réveille-matin**) nm alarm clock

réveiller [ʀeveje] vb to wake up ▷ réveiller quelqu'un to wake somebody up; **se réveiller** to wake up

réveillon [ʀevɛjɔ̃] nm: **le réveillon du Jour de l'An** New Year's Eve celebrations; **le réveillon de Noël** Christmas Eve celebrations

réveillonner [ʀevɛjɔne] vb ❶ to celebrate New Year's Eve ❷ to celebrate Christmas Eve

revenir [ʀəvniʀ] vb to come back ▷ Reviens vite! Come back soon! ▷ Son nom m'est revenu cinq minutes après. His name came back to me five minutes later. ; **Ça revient au même.** It comes to the same thing.; **Ça revient cher.** It costs a lot.; **Je n'en reviens pas!** I can't get over it!; **revenir sur ses pas** to retrace one's steps

revenu [ʀəvny] nm income

rêver [ʀeve] vb to dream; **rêver de quelque chose** to dream of something ▷ J'ai rêvé de mes vacances cette nuit. I dreamed about my holidays last night.

réverbère [ʀevɛʀbɛʀ] nm streetlight

revers [ʀəvɛʀ] nm ❶ backhand ▷ Tu as un excellent revers. You have an excellent backhand. ❷ (of jacket) lapel; **le revers de la médaille** the other side of the coin

revient [ʀəvjɛ̃] vb see **revenir**

réviser [ʀevize] vb ❶ to study ▷ Je dois réviser mon français. I have to study my French. ❷ to review

▷ *La prof a révisé l'unité avec nous.* The teacher reviewed the unit with us. **❸** to revise ▷ *l'édition révisée* the revised edition **❹** to service ▷ *Je dois faire réviser ma voiture.* I must get my car serviced.

révision [Reviziʒ̃ɔ] *nf* **❶** studying ▷ *Malgré deux heures de révision, il a raté l'examen.* Despite two hours of studying, he failed the exam. **❷** review ▷ *une révision complète* a thorough review

revoir [RǝvwaR] *vb* **❶** to see again ▷ *Je l'ai revue hier soir.* I saw her again last night. **❷** to study ▷ *Il est en train de revoir sa géographie.* He's studying his geography.; **au revoir** goodbye

révolution [Revɔlysjɔ̃] *nf* revolution ▷ *la révolution tranquille* the Quiet Revolution

• **La révolution tranquille** is
• the name given to the rapid
• political, social, and economic
• modernization of Québec in
• the 1960s. The government
• took on a more prominent role
• in all spheres of power, quickly
• displacing the Roman Catholic
• Church.

revue [Rǝvy] *nf* magazine
rez-de-chaussée [Redʃose] (*pl* **rez-de-chaussée**) *nm* ground floor ▷ *au rez-de-chaussée* on the ground floor

rhinocéros [RinɔseRɔs] *nm* rhinoceros

rhubarbe [RybaRb(ǝ)] *nf* rhubarb
rhume [Rym] *nm* cold ▷ *J'ai attrapé un rhume.* I've caught a cold.; **un rhume de cerveau** a head cold; **le rhume des foins** hay fever

ri [Ri] *vb see* **rire**; **Nous avons bien ri.** We had a good laugh.
riche [Riʃ] *adj* rich ▷ *Sa famille est très riche.* His family's very rich.

▷ *riche en vitamines* rich in vitamins
rideau [Rido] (*pl* **rideaux**) *nm* curtain ▷ *tirer les rideaux* to draw the curtains; **grimper dans les rideaux** to climb the walls ▷ *Cela la fait grimper dans les rideaux quand je suis en retard.* It drives her up the wall when I'm late.

ridicule [Ridikyl] *adj* ridiculous ▷ *Je trouve ça complètement ridicule.* I think that's absolutely ridiculous.

rien [Rjɛ̃] *pron* **❶**
▷ *« Qu'est-ce que tu as acheté? »* — *« Rien. »* "What have you bought?" — "Nothing." ▷ *Il a fait tout ce travail pour rien.* He did all this work for nothing.; **Ça n'a rien à voir.** It has nothing to do with it.; **rien d'intéressant** nothing interesting; **rien d'autre** nothing else; **rien du tout** nothing at all ▷ *Il n'a rien dit.* He didn't say anything.; **rien que (1)** just ▷ *rien que pour lui faire plaisir* just to please her ▷ *Rien que la voiture coûte soixante mille dollars.* The car alone costs sixty thousand dollars. **(2)** nothing but ▷ *rien que la vérité* nothing but the truth; **De rien!** You're welcome! ▷ *« Merci beaucoup! »* — *« De rien! »* "Thank you very much!" — "You're welcome!"

▶ *nm*: **pour un rien** at the slightest thing ▷ *Elle se met en colère pour un rien.* She loses her temper over the slightest thing.; **en un rien de temps** in no time at all

rigoler [Rigɔle] *vb* **❶** (*informal*) to laugh ▷ *Elle a rigolé durant tout le film.* She laughed all the way through the movie. **❷** to have fun ▷ *On a bien rigolé hier soir.* We had a lot of fun last night. **❸** to be joking ▷ *Ne te fâche pas, je rigolais.* Don't get upset, I was only joking.; **pour rigoler** for a laugh

rigolo [ʀigɔlo, -ɔt] (f **rigolote**) adj (informal) funny

rincer [ʀɛ̃se] vb to rinse

rire [ʀiʀ] vb to laugh ▷ *Ce film m'a vraiment fait rire.* That movie really made me laugh. ▷ *Nous avons bien ri.* We had a good laugh.; **pour rire** for a laugh; **Oups, c'était juste pour rire.** Oups, that was just a joke.

▶ nm laughter ▷ *Il a un rire bruyant.* He has a loud laugh.

risque [ʀisk(ə)] nm ❶ risk ▷ *prendre des risques* to take risks ▷ *à tes risques et périls* at your own risk ❷ danger ▷ *Il n'y a pas de risque qu'il l'apprenne.* There's no danger of him finding out.

risqué [ʀiske] (f **risquée**) adj risky

risquer [ʀiske] vb to risk; **Ça ne risque rien.** It's quite safe.; **Elle risque de se tuer.** She could get herself killed.; **C'est ce qui risque de se passer.** That's what might well happen.

rivage [ʀivaʒ] nm shore

rivière [ʀivjɛʀ] nf river

riz [ʀi] nm rice

robe [ʀɔb] nf dress; **une robe de soirée** an evening gown; **une robe de mariée** a wedding dress; **une robe de chambre** a dressing gown

robinet [ʀɔbinɛ] nm tap

robot [ʀɔbo] nm robot; **le robot culinaire** food processor

roche [ʀɔʃ] nf (stone) rock

rocher [ʀɔʃe] nm rock

rock [ʀɔkɛnʀɔl] nm (music) rock ▷ *un chanteur de rock* a rock singer

rôder [ʀode] vb to lurk

rognons [ʀɔɲɔ̃] nmpl (in cooking) kidneys

roi [ʀwa] nm king

rôle [ʀol] nm role

romain [ʀɔmɛ̃, -ɛn] (f **romaine**) adj Roman ▷ *des ruines romaines* Roman ruins

roman [ʀɔmɑ̃] nm novel; **un roman policier** a detective novel; **un roman d'espionnage** a spy novel

romancier [ʀɔmɑ̃sje] nm novelist

romancière [ʀɔmɑ̃sjɛʀ] nf novelist

romantique [ʀɔmɑ̃tik] adj romantic

rompre [ʀɔ̃pʀ(ə)] vb ❶ to split up ▷ *Mon frère et sa petite amie ont rompu.* My brother and his girlfriend have split up. ❷ to break off ▷ *Ils ont rompu leurs fiançailles.* They've broken off their engagement.; **rompre la glace** to break the ice

ronces [ʀɔ̃s] nfpl thornbushes

ronchonner [ʀɔ̃ʃɔne] vb (informal) to gripe

rond [ʀɔ̃, ʀɔd] (f **ronde**) adj ❶ round ▷ *La Terre est ronde.* The earth is round.; **ouvrir des yeux ronds** to stare in amazement ❷ chubby ▷ *Il a les joues rondes.* He has chubby cheeks.

▶ nm circle ▷ *Elle a dessiné un rond sur le sable.* She drew a circle in the sand.; **en rond** in a circle ▷ *Ils se sont assis en rond.* They sat down in a circle.; **tourner en rond** to go around in circles

rondelle [ʀɔ̃dɛl] nf ❶ puck ❷ (of something round) slice ▷ *une rondelle de citron* a slice of lemon

ronfler [ʀɔ̃fle] vb to snore

ronronner [ʀɔ̃ʀɔne] vb to purr

rosbif [ʀɔsbif] nm roast beef

rose [ʀoz] nf rose

▶ adj pink

rosier [ʀozje] nm rosebush

rôti [ʀoti] nm roast meat; **un rôti de bœuf** a roast of beef

rôtir [ʀotiʀ] vb to roast ▷ *faire rôtir quelque chose* to roast something

roue [ʀu] nf wheel ▷ *les roues arrière*

d'une voiture the rear wheels of a
vehicle

rouge [ʁuʒ] *adj* red; **brûler un feu
rouge** to go through a red light
▷ *Il a brûlé un feu rouge.* He went
through a red light.
▶ *nm* red ▷ *Le rouge est ma couleur
préférée.* Red is my favourite colour.;
passer au rouge to change to red
▷ *Le feu est passé au rouge.* The light
changed to red.; **le rouge à lèvres**
lipstick

rougeole [ʁuʒɔl] *nf* measles

rougir [ʁuʒiʁ] *vb* ① *Il
a rougi en me voyant.* He blushed
when he saw me. ② to turn red
▷ *Elle a rougi de colère.* She turned red
with anger.

rouille [ʁuj] *nf* rust

rouillé [ʁuje] (*f* **rouillée**) *adj* rusty

rouiller [ʁuje] *vb* to rust

roulant [ʁulɑ̃, -ɑ̃t] (*f* **roulante**) *adj*:
un fauteuil roulant a wheelchair;
une table roulante a serving cart;
un tapis roulant (1) a treadmill
(2) a moving sidewalk

rouleau [ʁulo] (*pl* **rouleaux**)
nm roll ▷ *un rouleau de tapisserie*
a roll of wallpaper; **un rouleau
du printemps** a spring roll; **un
rouleau à pâtisserie** a rolling pin

rouler [ʁule] *vb* ① to go ▷ *Le train
roulait à 250 km/h.* The train was
going at 250 km an hour. ② to
drive ▷ *Il a roulé sans s'arrêter.* He
drove without stopping. ③ to roll
▷ *Elle a roulé le ballon vers moi.* She
rolled the ball towards me. ④ to
roll up ▷ *Il a roulé le tapis.* He rolled
up the carpet. ⑤ to con ▷ *Ils se
sont fait rouler.* (*informal*) They were
conned.

rousse [ʁus] *adj* see **roux**

rousse [ʁus] *nf* see **roux**

route [ʁut] *nf* ① road ▷ *au bord
de la route* at the roadside ② way

▷ *Je ne connais pas la route.* I don't
know the way.; **Il y a trois heures
de route.** It's a 3-hour journey.; **en
route** on the way ▷ *Ils se sont arrêtés
en route.* They stopped on the way.;
mettre en route to start up ▷ *Elle
a mis le moteur en route.* She started
up the engine.; **se mettre en route**
to set off ▷ *Nous nous sommes mis
en route à cinq heures.* We set off at
5 o'clock.

routier [ʁutje] *nm* truck driver
▷ *Mon père est routier.* My father's a
truck driver.

routière [ʁutjɛʁ] *nf* truck driver

routine [ʁutin] *nf* routine

roux [ʁu, ʁus] (*f* **rousse**) *adj* ① red
▷ *Il a les cheveux roux.* He has red hair.
② red-haired ▷ *la petite fille rousse*
the little red-haired girl
▶ *nm* redhead

royal [ʁwajal, -o] (*f* **royale**, *mpl*
royaux) *adj* royal

royaume [ʁwajom] *nm* kingdom

ruban [ʁybɑ̃] *nm* ribbon; **le ruban
adhésif** adhesive tape

ruban-cache [-kaʃ] *nm* masking
tape

rubéole [ʁybeɔl] *nf* German
measles

ruche [ʁyʃ] *nf* hive

rue [ʁy] *nf* street

ruelle [ʁɥɛl] *nf* alley

rugueux [ʁygø, -øz] (*f* **rugueuse**)
adj rough

ruine [ʁɥin] *nf* ruin ▷ *les ruines de
la cathédrale* the ruins of the
cathedral

ruiner [ʁɥine] *vb* to ruin

ruisseau [ʁɥiso] (*pl* **ruisseaux**)
nm stream

rumeur [ʁymœʁ] *nf* rumour

rupture [ʁyptyʁ] *nf* break-up

ruse [ʁyz] *nf* trickery ▷ *une ruse*
a trick

rusé [ʁyze] (*f* **rusée**) *adj* cunning

rythme [ʀitm(ə)] *nm* ❶ rhythm
▷ *J'aime le rythme de cette musique.* I
like the beat of this music. ❷ pace
▷ *Elle marche à un bon rythme.* She
walks at a good pace.

S

s' [s] *pron see* **se**
sa [sa] *adj* ❶ his ▷ *Il est allé voir
sa grand-mère.* He's gone to see
his grandmother. ❷ her ▷ *Elle a
embrassé sa mère.* She kissed her
mother.
sable [sabl(ə)] *nm* sand; **les sables
bitumineux** tar sands; **des sables
mouvants** quicksand
sablé [sable] *nm* shortbread cookie
sabot [sabo] *nm* ❶ clog ❷ (*of
horse*) hoof
sac [sak] *nm* bag; **un sac de
voyage** a travel bag; **un sac de
couchage** a sleeping bag; **un sac
à main** a purse; **un sac à dos** a
knapsack; **un sac gonflable** an
airbag; **voyager avec son sac au
dos** to go backpacking
sachet [saʃɛ] *nm* (*of sugar, coffee*)
packet; **du potage en sachet**
instant soup
sacoche [sakɔʃ] *nf* ❶ (*for mail,*

newspapers) bag ❷ (bicycle)
pannier; **une sacoche de
bicyclette** (for bike) a seat pack

sacre [sakʁ(ə)] nm swearword

sacré [sakʁe] (f **sacrée**) adj sacred

sacrer [sakʁe] vb to swear

sage [saʒ] adj ❶ (well-behaved)
good ▷ Sois sage. Be good.
❷ (sensible) wise ▷ Il serait plus sage
d'attendre. It would be wiser to wait.

sagesse [saʒes] nf wisdom ▷ Il a eu
la sagesse de ne pas y aller. He wisely
didn't go.; **une dent de sagesse** a
wisdom tooth

Sagittaire [saʒitɛʁ] nm
Sagittarius ▷ Il est Sagittaire. He's a
Sagittarius.

saignant [seɲɑ̃, -ɑ̃t] (f **saignante**)
adj (meat) rare

saigner [seɲe] vb to bleed; **saigner
du nez** to have a nosebleed

sain [sɛ̃, sɛn] adj healthy;
sain et sauf safe and sound

saint [sɛ̃, sɛ̃t] (f **sainte**) adj holy; **la
Saint-Jean-Baptiste** Saint-Jean-
Baptiste Day

- **la Saint-Jean-Baptiste**
- is celebrated on June 24
- throughout French Canada. It
- combines a celebration of the
- summer solstice and of Saint
- Jean-Baptiste, the patron saint
- of French Canadians by official
- proclamation in 1908.

▶ nm saint

sainte [sɛ̃t] nf saint

sais [se] vb see **savoir**; **Je ne sais
pas.** I don't know.

saisir [seziʁ] vb to take hold of;
**saisir l'occasion de faire quelque
chose** to seize the opportunity to
do something

saison [sezɔ̃] nf season ▷ Ce n'est
pas la saison des fraises. Strawberries
are out of season.; **la belle saison**
summer

sait [se] vb see **savoir**; **Il sait que...**
He knows that...; **On ne sait
jamais!** You never know!

salade [salad] nf ❶ lettuce
❷ salad ▷ une salade composée a
mixed salad ▷ une salade de fruits
a fruit salad ▷ une salade César a
Caesar salad; **la salade de chou**
cole slaw

saladier [saladje] nm salad bowl

salaire [salɛʁ] nm salary

salami [salami] nm salami

sale [sal] adj dirty

salé [sale] (f **salée**) adj salty ▷ La
soupe est trop salée. The soup is
too salty.

saler [sale] vb to put salt in ▷ J'ai
oublié de saler la soupe. I forgot to put
salt in the soup.

saleté [salte] nf dirt ▷ J'ai horreur de
la saleté. I hate dirt.; **Il y a une saleté
sur ta chemise.** There's some dirt on
your shirt.

salir [saliʁ] vb: **salir quelque chose**
to get something dirty; **se salir** to
get oneself dirty ▷ Mets un tablier,
sinon tu vas te salir. Put on an apron
or you'll get yourself dirty.

salle [sal] nf ❶ room ❷ audience
▷ Toute la salle l'a applaudi. The
whole audience applauded him.
❸ (in hospital) ward ▷ Elle est à la
salle douze. She's in Ward 12.; **la salle
à manger** the dining room; **la salle
de lavage** the laundry room; **la
salle de bains** the bathroom; **la
salle d'attente** the waiting room;
une salle de classe a classroom;
une salle de concert a concert hall

salon [salɔ̃] nm living room; **le
salon des professeurs** (in school)
staff room; **le salon funéraire**
funeral parlour; **un salon de
coiffure** a hair salon; **un salon de
beauté** a beauty salon

salopette [salɔpɛt] nf overalls

saluer [salɥe] vb: **saluer quelqu'un (1)** to say hello to somebody ▷ *Je l'ai croisé dans la rue et il m'a salué.* I met him in the street and he said hello. **(2)** to say goodbye to somebody ▷ *Elle nous a salués et elle est partie.* She said goodbye and left.

salut [salɥ] excl (informal) Hi!

salutation [salytasjɔ̃] nf greeting

samedi [samdi] nm ❶ Saturday ▷ *Aujourd'hui, nous sommes samedi.* It's Saturday today. ❷ on Saturday ▷ *Nous sommes allés au cinéma samedi.* We went to the movies on Saturday.; **le samedi** on Saturdays ▷ *Le magasin ferme à dix-huit heures le samedi.* The store closes at 6 p.m. on Saturdays.; **tous les samedis** every Saturday; **samedi dernier** last Saturday; **samedi prochain** next Saturday

sandale [sɑ̃dal] nf sandal

sandwich [sɑ̃dwitʃ] nm sandwich; **un sandwich au smoked meat** a smoked meat sandwich

sang [sɑ̃] nm blood; **en sang** covered with blood

sang-froid [sɑ̃fʀwa] nm: **garder son sang-froid** to keep calm; **perdre son sang-froid** to lose one's cool; **faire quelque chose de sang-froid** to do something in cold blood

sangle [sɑ̃gl(ə)] nf (on sandal, backpack) strap

sanglot [sɑ̃glo] nm: **éclater en sanglots** to burst into tears

sans [sɑ̃] prep without ▷ *Elle est venue sans son frère.* She came without her brother.; **un haut sans manches** a sleeveless top

sans-abri [sɑ̃zabʀi] (pl **sans-abri**) nmf homeless person ▷ *les sans-abri* the homeless

sans-gêne [sɑ̃ʒɛn] adj inconsiderate

santé [sɑ̃te] nf health ▷ *en bonne santé* in good health

sapin [sapɛ̃] nm fir tree; **un sapin de Noël** a Christmas tree

sardine [saʀdin] nf sardine

Saskatchewan [...] nf Saskatchewan

satellite [satelit] nm satellite ▷ *la télévision par satellite* satellite TV

satisfaire [satisfɛʀ] vb to satisfy

satisfaisant [satisfəzɑ̃, -ɑ̃t] (f **satisfaisante**) adj satisfactory

satisfait [satisfɛ, -ɛt] (f **satisfaite**) adj satisfied ▷ *être satisfait de quelque chose* to be satisfied with something

sauce [sos] nf ❶ sauce ❷ gravy

saucisse [sosis] nf sausage

saucisson [sosisɔ̃] nm (eaten sliced, cold) sausage

sauf [sof] prep except ▷ *Tout le monde est venu sauf elle.* Everyone came except her.; **sauf si** unless ▷ *On ira se promener, sauf s'il fait mauvais.* We'll go for a walk, unless the weather's bad.; **sauf que** except that ▷ *Tout s'est bien passé, sauf que nous sommes arrivés en retard.* Everything went OK, except that we arrived late.

saule à chaton [sol-] nm pussy willow

saumon [somɔ̃] nm salmon; **le saumon atlantique** Atlantic salmon; **le saumon quinnat** Chinook salmon; **le saumon rouge** Sockeye salmon

saut [so] nm jump; **le saut en longueur** the long jump; **le saut en hauteur** the high jump; **le saut à la perche** the pole vault; **le saut à l'élastique** bungee jumping; **un saut périlleux** a somersault

sauter [sote] vb to jump ▷ *Nous avons sauté par-dessus la barrière.* We jumped over the gate.; **sauter à**

la corde to skip (with a rope); **faire sauter quelque chose** to blow something up ▷ *On a fait sauter le poste de police la nuit dernière.* The police station was blown up last night.; **faire sauter** (food) to stir-fry ▷ *J'ai fait sauter les légumes.* I stir-fried the vegetables.

sauterelle [sotʀɛl] nf grasshopper

sauvage [sovaʒ] adj ❶ wild ▷ *les animaux sauvages* wild animals ▷ *le camping sauvage* wilderness camping; **une région sauvage** a wilderness area ❷ shy ▷ *Il est sauvage.* He's shy.

sauvegarder [sovgaʀde] vb (file on computer) to save

sauver [sove] vb to save; **se sauver (1)** to run away ▷ *Elle s'est sauvée à toutes jambes.* She ran away as fast as she could. **(2)** (informal) to be off ▷ *Allez, je me sauve!* Right, I'm off.

sauvetage [sovtaʒ] nm rescue

sauveteur [sovtœʀ] nm ❶ rescuer ❷ lifeguard

sauveteure [sovtœʀ] nf ❶ rescuer ❷ lifeguard

savais, savait vb *see* **savoir**; **Je ne savais pas qu'il devait venir.** I didn't know he was going to come.

savent vb *see* **savoir**; **Ils ne savent pas ce qu'ils veulent.** They don't know what they want.

saveur [savœʀ] nf flavour

savez vb *see* **savoir**; **Est-ce que vous savez où elle habite?** Do you know where she lives?

savoir [savwaʀ] vb to know ▷ *Je ne sais pas où elle est allée.* I don't know where she's gone. ▷ *Nous ne savons pas s'il est bien arrivé.* We don't know if he's arrived safely. ▷ *Savais-tu que Winnipeg était la capitale du Manitoba?* Did you know Winnipeg was the capital of Manitoba? ▷ *Il ne sait pas ce qu'il va faire ce week-end.*

He doesn't know what he's going to do this weekend.; **Tu sais nager?** Can you swim?

savon [savɔ̃] nm ❶ soap ❷ bar of soap

savons [savɔ̃] vb *see* **savoir**

savoureux [savuʀø, -øz] (f **savoureuse**) adj tasty

saxophone [saksofɔn] nm sax

saxophoniste [saksofɔnist(ə)] nmf sax player

scandale [skɑ̃dal] nm scandal; **faire scandale** to cause a scandal ▷ *Ce film a fait scandale.* The film caused a scandal.

scandaleux [skɑ̃dalø, -øz] (f **scandaleuse**) adj outrageous

scarabée [skaʀabe] nm beetle

scène [sɛn] nf ❶ scene ▷ *une scène d'amour* a love scene ▷ *la scène du crime* the scene of the crime ▷ *Il m'a fait une scène.* He made a scene.; **une scène de ménage** a domestic quarrel ❷ stage ▷ *Elle fait ses débuts sur la scène.* It is her stage debut.; **les arts de la scène** performing arts

sceptique [sɛptik] adj sceptical

schéma [ʃema] nm diagram

schématique [ʃematik] adj oversimplified ▷ *Cette interprétation est un peu trop schématique.* This interpretation is a bit oversimplified.

scie [si] nf saw

science [sjɑ̃s] nf science; **Elle est forte en sciences.** She is good at science.; **les sciences physiques** the physical sciences; **les sciences naturelles** the natural sciences; **les sciences économiques** economics; **les sciences politiques** political science ▷ *Il a un diplôme de sciences politiques.* He has a degree in political science.

science-fiction [sjɑ̃sfiksjɔ̃] nf

science fiction

scientifique [sjɑ̃tifik] *adj*
scientific
▶ *n* scientist

scier [sje] *vb* to saw

scolaire [skɔlɛʀ] *adj* school
▷ *l'année scolaire* the school year
▷ *les vacances scolaires* the school
holidays ▷ *le transport scolaire*
school transportation; **l'abandon
scolaire** dropping out of school

Scorpion [skɔʀpjɔ̃] *nm* Scorpio
▷ *Elle est Scorpion.* She's a Scorpio.

scrupule [skʀypyl] *nm* scruple

sculpter [skylte] *vb* to sculpt

sculpteur [skyltœʀ] *nm* sculptor

sculpteure [skyltœʀ] *nf* sculptor

sculpture [skyltyʀ] *nf* sculpture

se [s(ə)] *pron*

se forms part of reflexive
constructions.

❶ himself ▷ *Il se regarde dans le
miroir.* He's looking at himself in
the mirror. ❷ herself ▷ *Elle se
regarde dans le miroir.* She's looking
at herself in the mirror. ❸ itself
▷ *Le chien s'est fait mal.* The dog
hurt itself. ❹ oneself ▷ *se regarder
dans un miroir* to look at oneself in a
mirror ❺ themselves ▷ *Ils se sont
regardés dans le miroir.* They looked
at themselves in the mirror.

se changes to **s'** before a vowel
and most words beginning
with "h".

▷ *Elle s'admire dans sa nouvelle robe.*
She's admiring herself in her new
dress. ❻ each other ▷ *Ils s'aiment.*
They love each other.

séance [seɑ̃s] *nf* session ▷ *une
séance de physiothérapie* a
physiotherapy session

seau [so] (*pl* **seaux**) *nm* bucket

sec [sɛk, sɛʃ] (*f* **sèche**) *adj* ❶ dry
▷ *un shampooing pour les cheveux
secs* shampoo for dry hair ▷ *Mes*

mitaines sont sèches. My mitts are
dry. ❷ dried ▷ *des figues sèches*
dried figs

séchage [seʃaʒ] *nm* drying
▷ *Voulez-vous un séchage à la
brosse?* Would you like a blow-
dry? ▷ *Le séchage à la machine
n'est pas recommandé pour ce
chandail.* Machine drying is not
recommended for this sweater.

sèche-cheveux [sɛʃʃəvø] (*pl*
sèche-cheveux) *nm* hair dryer

sécher [seʃe] *vb* to dry; **Faire
sécher à plat.** Lay flat to dry.;
sécher à la brosse to blow-dry; **se
sécher** to dry oneself ▷ *Sèche-toi
avec cette serviette.* Dry yourself with
this towel.

sécheresse [seʃʀɛs] *nf* drought
▷ *une terrible sécheresse* a terrible
drought

sécheuse [seʃøz] *nf* dryer

séchoir [seʃwaʀ] *nm* dryer

second [sag̃ɔ̃, -ɔ̃d] (*f* **seconde**)
adj second ▷ *Il est arrivé second.* He
came second.

secondaire [sag̃ɔ̃dɛʀ] *adj*
secondary ▷ *l'école secondaire*
secondary school; **des effets
secondaires** side effects
▶ *nm* (*level*) high school ▷ *les
enseignants et les élèves du secondaire*
high school teachers and students
▷ *Elle est en secondaire cinq.* She's in
Grade 12.

○ Québec high schools have
○ five grades: **le secondaire un**,
○ **deux**, **trois**, **quatre** and **cinq**,
○ corresponding to Grades 8 to
○ 12. Grades are written in Roman
○ numerals: you say **le secondaire
trois**, but write **le secondaire III**.

seconde [sag̃ɔ̃d] *nf* second
▷ *Attends une seconde!* Wait a
second!

secouer [səkwe] *vb* to shake

▷ *secouer la tête* to shake one's head
▷ *L'accident l'a beaucoup secouée.* The accident has really shaken her.

secourir [səkurir] *vb* to rescue

secourisme [səkurism(ə)] *nm* first aid ▷ *J'ai un brevet de secourisme.* I have a first aid certificate.

secours [səkur] *nm* help ▷ *Elle est allée chercher du secours.* She went to get help. ▷ *Au secours!* Help!; **les premiers secours** first aid; **une sortie de secours** an emergency exit; **le pneu de secours** the spare tire

secret [səkrɛ, -ɛt] *nm* secret
▶ *adj* (*f* **secrète**) secret

secrétaire [səkretɛr] *nmf* secretary

secrétariat [s(ə)kretarja] *nm* secretary's office

secteur [sɛktœr] *nm* sector ▷ *le secteur public* the public sector ▷ *le secteur privé* the private sector

section [sɛksjɔ̃] *nf* (*of school*) section

sécuritaire [sekyritɛr] *adj* safe ▷ *un milieu de travail sécuritaire* a safe working environment

sécurité [sekyrite] *nf* ❶ safety; **être en sécurité** to be safe ▷ *On ne se sent pas en sécurité dans ce quartier.* You don't feel safe in this neighbourhood.; **la sécurité routière** road safety; **une ceinture de sécurité** a seatbelt ❷ security ▷ *par mesure de sécurité* as a security measure; **la sécurité de l'emploi** job security

séduisant [sedyizɑ̃, -ɑ̃t] (*f* **séduisante**) *adj* attractive

seigle [sɛgl(ə)] *nm* rye ▷ *un pain de seigle* a loaf of rye bread

Seigneur [sɛɲœr] *nm* (*God*) the Lord

sein [sɛ̃] *nm* breast; **au sein de** within ▷ *le statut des autochtones au sein du Canada* the status of Aboriginals within Canada

seize [sɛz] *num* sixteen ▷ *Elle a seize ans.* She's sixteen. ▷ *à seize heures* at 4 p.m.; **le seize février** the sixteenth of February

seizième [sɛzjɛm] *adj* sixteenth

séjour [seʒur] *nm* stay ▷ *J'ai fait un séjour d'une semaine en Alberta.* I stayed in Alberta for a week.

sel [sɛl] *nm* salt

sélectionner [selɛksjɔne] *vb* to select

selle [sɛl] *nf* saddle

selon [səlɔ̃] *prep* according to ▷ *selon lui* according to him ▷ *selon mon humeur* according to what mood I'm in ▷ *Ils sont répartis selon leur âge.* They're divided up according to age.

semaine [səmɛn] *nf* week; **en semaine** on weekdays; **la semaine de relâche** March Break; **la fin de semaine** the weekend

semblable [sɑ̃blabl(ə)] *adj* similar

semblant [sɑ̃blɑ̃] *nm*: **faire semblant de faire quelque chose** to pretend to do something ▷ *Elle fait semblant de dormir.* She's pretending to be asleep.

sembler [sɑ̃ble] *vb* to seem ▷ *Le temps semble s'améliorer.* The weather seems to be improving. ▷ *Il me semble inutile de s'inquiéter.* It seems pointless to me to worry about it.

semelle [səmɛl] *nf* ❶ sole ❷ insole

Sénat [sena] *nm* Senate

sens [sɑ̃s] *nm* ❶ sense ▷ *avoir le sens de l'humour* to have a sense of humour ▷ *Je n'ai pas le sens de l'orientation.* I have no sense of direction. ▷ *avoir le sens du rythme* to have a sense of rhythm ▷ *Ça n'a* *pas de sens.* It doesn't make sense.; **le bon sens** common sense; **sans bon sens** unreasonably ▷ *Elle conduit vite sans bons sens.* She drives unreasonably fast. ❷ direction ▷ *Tu tournes la poignée dans le mauvais sens.* You're turning the handle in the wrong direction.; **sens dessus dessous** upside down; **un sens interdit** a one-way street ▷ *J'ai failli prendre un sens interdit.* I nearly went the wrong way down a one-way street.; **un sens unique** a one-way street

sensation [sɑ̃sasjɔ̃] *nf* feeling
sensationnel [sɑ̃sasjɔnɛl] (*f* **sensationnelle**) *adj* sensational
sensé [sɑ̃se] (*f* **sensée**) *adj* sensible
sensible [sɑ̃sibl(ə)] *adj* ❶ sensitive ▷ *Elle est très sensible.* She's very sensitive. ▷ *Ce film est déconseillé aux personnes sensibles.* This film contains scenes which some viewers may find disturbing. ❷ noticeable ▷ *une amélioration sensible* a noticeable improvement

Be careful! The French word **sensible** does not mean **sensible**.

sensiblement [sɑ̃siblǝmɑ̃] *adv* ❶ noticeably ▷ *Elle a sensiblement progressé.* She has noticeably progressed. ❷ approximately ▷ *Elles sont sensiblement de la même taille.* They are approximately the same height.
sentence [sɑ̃tɑ̃s] *nf* (judgement) sentence
sentier [sɑ̃tje] *nm* path
sentiment [sɑ̃timɑ̃] *nm* feeling
sentimental [sɑ̃timɑtal, -o] (*f* **sentimentale**, *mpl* **sentimentaux**) *adj* sentimental
sentir [sɑ̃tir] *vb* ❶ to smell ▷ *Ça sent bon.* That smells good. ▷ *Ça sent mauvais.* It smells bad. ❷ to smell

of ▷ *Ça sent les frites ici.* It smells like fries in here. ❸ to taste ▷ *Tu sens l'ail dans le rôti?* Can you taste the garlic in the roast? ❹ to feel ▷ *« Ça t'a fait mal? » « Non, je n'ai rien senti. »* "Did it hurt?" "No, I didn't feel a thing." ▷ *Je ne me sens pas bien.* I don't feel well.; **Il ne peut pas la sentir.** (informal) He can't stand her.
séparation [separasjɔ̃] *nf* separation
séparatisme [separatism(ə)] *nm* separatism
séparé [separe] (*f* **séparée**) *adj* separated ▷ *Mes parents sont séparés.* My parents are separated.
séparément [separemɑ̃] *adv* separately
séparer [separe] *vb* to separate ▷ *Séparez le blanc du jaune.* Separate the yolk from the white.; **se séparer** to separate ▷ *Mes parents se sont séparés l'année dernière.* My parents separated last year.
sept [sɛt] *num* seven ▷ *Il est arrivé à sept heures.* He arrived at seven o'clock. ▷ *Il a sept ans.* He's seven.; **le sept février** the seventh of February; **ouvert sept jours sur sept** open 7 days a week
septembre [sɛptɑ̃br(ə)] *nm* September; **en septembre** in September
septième [sɛtjɛm] *adj* seventh ▷ *au septième étage* on the seventh floor
sera, serai, seras, serez *vb* see **être**; **Je serai de retour à dix heures.** I'll be back at 10 o'clock.
série [seri] *nf* series
sérieusement [serjøzmɑ̃] *adv* seriously
sérieux [serjø, -øz] (*f* **sérieuse**) *adj* ❶ serious ▷ *« Il plaisantait? » « Non, il était sérieux. »* "Was he joking?" "No, he was serious." ❷ responsible

▷ *C'est une employée très sérieuse.*
She's a very responsible employee.
▶ *nm*: **garder son sérieux** to keep
a straight face ▷ *J'ai eu du mal à
garder mon sérieux.* I had trouble
keeping a straight face.; **prendre
quelque chose au sérieux** to take
something seriously; **prendre
quelqu'un au sérieux** to take
somebody seriously; **Il manque
un peu de sérieux.** He's not very
responsible.

seringue [səʀɛ̃g] *nf* syringe
séronégatif [seronegatif, -iv] (*f*
séronégative) *adj* HIV-negative
serons, seront *vb see* **être**
séropositif [seropozitif, -iv] (*f*
séropositive) *adj* HIV-positive
serpent [sɛʀpɑ̃] *nm* snake
serre [sɛʀ] *nf* greenhouse; **l'effet
de serre** the greenhouse effect
serré [seʀe] (*f* **serrée**) *adj*
❶ tight ▷ *Mon pantalon est trop
serré.* My pants are too tight.
❷ (competition) close ▷ *Ça a été un
match serré.* It was a close game.
serrer [seʀe] *vb*: **Ce pantalon me
serre trop.** These pants are too
tight for me.; **serrer la main à
quelqu'un** to shake hands with
somebody; **se serrer** to make
yourself compact ▷ *Serrez-vous
un peu pour que je puisse m'asseoir.*
Squeeze over a bit so I can sit
down.; **serrer quelqu'un dans ses
bras** to hug somebody
serrure [seʀyʀ] *nf* lock
sers, sert *vb see* **servir**
serveur [sɛʀvœʀ] *nm* ❶ (in a café)
waiter ❷ (computer) server
serveuse [sɛʀvøz] *nf* waitress
serviable [sɛʀvjab(ə)l] *adj* helpful
service [sɛʀvis] *nm* ❶ (in
restaurant) service ▷ *Le service
est compris.* Service is included.;
être de service to be on duty;

hors service out of order; **faire
le service** (at table) to serve ▷ *Tu
peux faire le service s'il te plaît?* Could
you serve, please?; **le service
d'assistance téléphonique**
directory assistance ❷ favour
▷ *rendre service à quelqu'un* to do
somebody a favour ▷ *Est-ce que je
peux te demander un service?* Can I
ask you a favour? ❸ (sports) service
▷ *Il a un bon service.* He has a good
serve.; **un service commémoratif**
a memorial service; **le service
militaire** military service; **les
services sociaux** social services;
les services secrets the secret
service
serviette [sɛʀvjɛt] *nf* ❶ towel
▷ *une serviette de bain* a bath
towel; **une serviette hygiénique**
a sanitary napkin ❷ (napkin)
serviette ❸ briefcase
servir [sɛʀviʀ] *vb* to serve ▷ *Est-ce
qu'on vous a servi?* Have you been
served?; **À toi de servir.** (tennis)
It's your serve.; **se servir** to
help oneself ▷ *Servez-vous.* Help
yourself.; **se servir de** to use
▷ *Te sers-tu souvent de ton vélo?* Do
you use your bike a lot?; **servir
à quelqu'un** to be of use to
somebody ▷ *Ça m'a beaucoup servi.*
It was very useful.; **À quoi ça sert?**
What's it for?; **Ça ne sert à rien.** It's
no use.; **Ça ne sert à rien d'insister.**
It's no use insisting.
ses [se] *adj* ❶ his ▷ *Il est parti voir ses
grands-parents.* He's gone to see his
grandparents. ❷ her ▷ *Elle a oublié
ses livres.* She forgot her books.
❸ its ▷ *la ville et ses alentours* the
town and its surroundings
seuil [sœj] *nm* doorstep
seul [sœl] (*f* **seule**) *adj, adv* ❶ alone
▷ *vivre seul* to live alone ❷ by
oneself ▷ *Elle est venue seule.* She

came by herself.; **faire quelque chose tout seul** to do something by oneself ▷ *Elle a fait ça toute seule?* Did she do it by herself?; **se sentir seul** to feel lonely; **un seul livre** one book only ▷ *Vous avez droit à un seul livre.* You're entitled to one book only.; **Il reste une seule nectarine.** There's only one nectarine left.; **le seul livre que...** the only book that... ▷ *C'est le seul Troon Harrison que je n'aie pas lu.* That's the only Troon Harrison I haven't read.; **le seul** the only one ▷ *C'est le seul que je ne connaisse pas.* He's the only one I don't know.

seulement [sœlmɑ̃] *adv* only; **non seulement...mais** not only...but ▷ *Non seulement il a plu, mais en plus il a fait froid.* Not only did it rain, but it was cold as well.

sévère [sevɛʀ] *adj* strict ▷ *Mon prof de maths est très sévère.* My math teacher is very strict.

sexe [sɛks(ə)] *nm* sex

sexuel [sɛksɥɛl] (*f* **sexuelle**) *adj* sexual ▷ *l'éducation sexuelle* sex education ▷ *l'orientation sexuelle* sexual orientation

shampooing [ʃɑ̃pwɛ̃] *nm* shampoo; **se faire un shampooing** to wash one's hair

short [ʃɔʀt] *nm* shorts ▷ *Il était en short.* He was wearing shorts.

si [si] *nm* ❶ B ▷ *en si bémol* in B flat ❷ ti ▷ *la, si, do* la, ti, do
▶ *conj, adv* ❶ if ▷ *si tu veux* if you like ▷ *Je me demande si elle va venir.* I wonder if she'll come. ▷ *si seulement* if only ❷ so ▷ *Elle est si gentille.* She's so kind. ▷ *Tout s'est passé si vite.* Everything happened so fast.

sida [sida] *nm* AIDS ▷ *Il a le sida.* He has AIDS.

siècle [sjɛkl(ə)] *nm* century ▷ *le vingtième siècle* the twentieth century

siège [sjɛʒ] *nm* (*in vehicle*) seat; **un siège pliant** a folding chair; **le siège social** head office

sien [sjɛ̃] *pron:* **le sien (1)** his ▷ *« Est-ce que c'est le vélo de ton frère? »* — *« Oui, c'est le sien. »* "Is this your brother's bike?" — "Yes, it's his." **(2)** hers ▷ *« Est-ce que c'est le vélo de ta sœur? »* — *« Oui, c'est le sien. »* "Is this your sister's bike?" — "Yes, it's hers."

sienne [sjɛn] *pron:* **la sienne (1)** his ▷ *« Est-ce que c'est la montre de ton père? »* — *« Oui, c'est la sienne. »* "Is this your father's watch?" — "Yes, it's his." **(2)** hers ▷ *« Est-ce que c'est la montre de ta mère? »* — *« Oui, c'est la sienne. »* "Is this your mother's watch?" — "Yes, it's hers."

siennes [sjɛn] *pron:* **les siennes (1)** his ▷ *« Est-ce que ce sont les bottes de ton frère? »* — *« Oui, ce sont les siennes. »* "Are these your brother's boots?" — "Yes, they're his." **(2)** hers ▷ *« Est-ce que ce sont les lunettes de ta tante? »* — *« Oui, ce sont les siennes. »* "Are these your aunt's glasses?" — "Yes, they're hers."

siens [sjɛ̃] *pron:* **les siens (1)** his ▷ *« Est-ce que ce sont les sandwichs de ton frère? »* — *« Oui, ce sont les siens. »* "Are these your brother's sandwiches?" — "Yes, they're his." **(2)** hers ▷ *« Est-ce que ce sont les sandwichs de ta sœur? »* — *« Oui, ce sont les siens. »* "Are these your sister's sandwiches?" — "Yes, they're hers."

sieste [sjɛst(ə)] *nf* nap ▷ *faire la sieste* to have a nap

siffler [sifle] *vb* to whistle

sifflet [siflɛ] *nm* whistle

siffleux [siflø] *nm* marmot

sigle [sigl(ə)] *nm* acronym

signal [sinal, -o] (*pl* **signaux**) *nm* signal

signature [sinatyʀ] *nf* signature

signe [siɲ] nm sign; **faire un signe de la main** to wave; **faire signe à quelqu'un d'entrer** to motion to somebody to come in; **les signes du zodiaque** the signs of the zodiac

signer [siɲe] vb to sign

signet [siɲɛ] nm bookmark; **mettre un signet à un site Web** to bookmark a website

signification [siɲifikasjɔ̃] nf meaning

signifier [siɲifje] vb to mean ▷ *Que signifie ce mot?* What does this word mean?

silence [silɑ̃s] nm silence; **Silence!** Be quiet!

silencieux [silɑ̃sjø, -øz] (f **silencieuse**) adj ❶ silent ▷ *Elle est restée silencieuse.* She remained silent. ❷ quiet ▷ *C'est très silencieux ici.* It's very quiet here.

silhouette [silwɛt] nf figure ▷ *J'ai vu une silhouette dans le brouillard.* I saw a figure in the mist.

similaire [similɛʀ] adj similar

simple [sɛ̃pl(ə)] nm (tennis) singles ▷ *le simple messieurs* the men's singles ▷ *le simple dames* the women's singles
▶ adj simple

simplement [sɛ̃pləmɑ̃] adv simply ▷ *C'est tout simplement inadmissible.* It's simply unacceptable.

simuler [simyle] vb to simulate

simultané [simyltane] (f **simultanée**) adj simultaneous

sincère [sɛ̃sɛʀ] adj sincere

sincèrement [sɛ̃sɛʀmɑ̃] adv sincerely

sincérité [sɛ̃seʀite] nf sincerity

singe [sɛ̃ʒ] nm monkey

singulier [sɛ̃gylje] nm singular ▷ *au féminin singulier* in the feminine singular

sinistre [sinistʀ(ə)] adj sinister

sinon [sinɔ̃] conj otherwise

▷ *Dépêche-toi, sinon je pars sans toi.* Hurry up, otherwise I'll leave without you.

sinusite [sinyzit] nf sinusitis ▷ *avoir de la sinusite* to have sinusitis

sirène [siʀɛn] nf mermaid; **la sirène d'alarme** the fire alarm

sirop [siʀo] nm syrup; **le sirop contre la toux** cough syrup; **le sirop d'érable** maple syrup

site [sit] nm setting ▷ *un site très sauvage* a wilderness setting ▷ *un site d'enfouissement* a landfill site; **un site pittoresque** a scenic attraction; **un site touristique** a tourist attraction; **un site archéologique** an archaeological site; **un site Web** a website

sitôt [sito] adv: **sitôt dit, sitôt fait** no sooner said than done; **pas de sitôt** not for a long time ▷ *On ne le reverra pas de sitôt.* We won't see him again for a long time.

situation [situasjɔ̃] nf ❶ situation; **la situation de famille** marital status ❷ job ▷ *Il a une belle situation.* He's got a good job.; **la situation économique** economic conditions

se situer [situe] vb to be situated ▷ *Sudbury se situe à l'ouest de North Bay.* Sudbury is situated to the west of North Bay.; **bien situé** well situated

six [sis] num six ▷ *Elle est rentrée à six heures.* She got back at six o'clock. ▷ *Il a six ans.* He's six.; **le six février** the sixth of February

sixième [sizjɛm] adj sixth ▷ *au sixième étage* on the sixth floor

ski [ski] nm ❶ ski ▷ *J'ai loué des skis.* I rented skis. ❷ skiing ▷ *J'adore le ski.* I love skiing. ▷ *faire du ski* to go skiing; **le ski de fond** cross-country skiing; **le ski nautique** water-skiing; **le ski alpin** downhill skiing;

le ski de randonnée cross-country skiing

skier [skje] vb to ski

skieur [skjœr] nm skier

skieuse [skjøz] nf skier

sloche [slɔʃ] nf slush

snob [snɔb] (f **snob**) adj snobbish

snorkel [snɔrkɛl] nm snorkel; **faire du snorkel** to go snorkelling

sobre [sɔbr(ə)] adj ① sober ② plain ▷ *C'est une veste très sobre.* It's a very plain jacket.

sociable [sɔsjabl(ə)] adj sociable

social [sɔsjal, -o] (f **sociale**, mpl **sociaux**) adj social

socialiste [sɔsjalist(ə)] nmf socialist

société [sɔsjete] nf ① society; **la société distincte** distinct society ② company ▷ *une société financière* a finance company

sociologie [sɔsjɔlɔʒi] nf sociology

sœur [sœr] nf sister; **une bonne sœur** (informal) a nun

soi [swa] pron oneself ▷ *avoir confiance en soi* to have confidence in oneself; **rester chez soi** to stay at home; **Ça va de soi.** It goes without saying.

soi-disant [swadizã] adv, adj supposedly ▷ *Il était soi-disant parti à Moncton.* He had supposedly left for Moncton.; **un soi-disant poète** a so-called poet

soie [swa] nf silk

soif [swaf] nf thirst; **avoir soif** to be thirsty

soigner [swaɲe] vb (ill person, animal) to look after ▷ *Soigne-toi bien en fin de semaine!* Take care of yourself this weekend!

soigneux [swaɲø, -øz] (f **soigneuse**) adj careful ▷ *Tu devrais être plus soigneux avec tes livres.* You should be more careful with your books.

soi-même [swamɛm] pron oneself ▷ *Il vaut mieux le faire soi-même.* It's better to do it oneself.

soin [swɛ̃] nm care; **prendre soin de quelque chose** to take care of something ▷ *Prends bien soin de ce livre.* Take good care of this book.

soins [swɛ̃] nmpl treatment; **les premiers soins** first aid

soir [swar] nm evening ▷ *ce soir* this evening; **à sept heures du soir** at 7 p.m.; **demain soir** tomorrow night; **hier soir** last night

soirée [sware] nf evening ▷ *en tenue de soirée* in evening dress

sois vb see **être**; **Sois tranquille!** Be quiet!

soit [swa] conj: **soit…, soit…** (1) either…or… ▷ *soit lundi, soit mardi* either Monday or Tuesday (2) whether…or… ▷ *Je les ferai, mes devoirs, soit aujourd'hui, soit demain.* I'll do my homework eventually, whether today or tomorrow

soixantaine [swasãtɛn] nf about sixty ▷ *une soixantaine de personnes* about sixty people; **Elle a la soixantaine.** She's in her sixties.

soixante [swasãt] num sixty ▷ *Il a soixante ans.* He's sixty. ▷ *soixante et un* sixty-one ▷ *soixante-deux* sixty-two; **soixante et onze** seventy-one; **soixante-quinze** seventy-five

soixante-dix [swasãtdis] num seventy ▷ *Il a soixante-dix ans.* He's seventy.

sol [sɔl] nm ① floor ▷ *un sol carrelé* a tiled floor; **à même le sol** on the floor ② soil ▷ *sur le sol canadien* on Canadian soil ③ G ④ sol dièse G sharp ④ so ▷ *do, ré, mi, fa, sol…* do, re, mi, fa, so…

solaire [sɔlɛr] adj solar ▷ *le système solaire* the solar system; **la crème solaire** sun cream

soldat [sɔlda] nm soldier

soldate [sɔldat] nf soldier

solde [sɔld(ə)] nm: **être en solde**
to be on sale ▷ *Les chemisiers sont
en solde.* The blouses are on sale.;
les soldes the sales ▷ *les soldes de
janvier* the January sales

soldé [sɔlde] (f **soldée**) adj: **être
soldé** to be on sale ▷ *un article
soldé à dix dollars* an item on sale for
10 dollars

sole [sɔl] nf (fish) sole

soleil [sɔlɛj] nm sun ▷ *au soleil* in
the sun; **Il fait soleil.** It's sunny
out.; **le coup de soleil** sunburn; **le
coucher de soleil** sunset

solfège [sɔlfɛʒ] nm musical theory
▷ *Elle joue du violon sans connaître le
solfège.* She plays the violin but she
can't read music.

solidaire [sɔlidɛʀ] adj: **être
solidaire de quelqu'un** to back
somebody up

solide [sɔlid] adj ❶ (person) strong
❷ (object) solid

solitaire [sɔlitɛʀ] adj solitary
▶ n loner

solitude [sɔlityd] nf loneliness

solution [sɔlysjɔ̃] nf solution;
une solution de facilité an easy
way out

sombre [sɔ̃bʀ(ə)] adj dark

sommaire [sɔmɛʀ] nm summary

somme [sɔm] nf sum
▶ nm nap ▷ *faire un somme* to take
a nap

sommeil [sɔmɛj] nm sleep; **avoir
sommeil** to be sleepy

sommes [sɔm] vb see **être**; **Nous
sommes en vacances.** We're on
vacation.

sommet [sɔmɛ] nm summit

somnifère [sɔmnifɛʀ] nm
sleeping pill

somptueux [sɔ̃ptɥø, -øz] (f
somptueuse) adj sumptuous

son [sɔ̃] (f **sa**, pl **ses**) adj ❶ his
▷ *son père* his father ▷ *Il a perdu
son portefeuille.* He lost his wallet.
❷ her ▷ *son père* her father ▷ *Elle a
perdu son manteau.* She lost her coat.
▶ nm ❶ sound ▷ *Le son n'est pas très
bon.* The sound is not very good.
▷ *baisser le son* to turn down the
sound ❷ bran; **le pain de son**
bran bread

sondage [sɔ̃daʒ] nm survey; **un
sondage d'opinion** an opinion poll

sonder [sɔ̃de] vb to poll ▷ *Nous
avons sondé l'opinion des élèves pour
savoir quelle station de radio est la plus
populaire.* We polled the students
to find out which radio station was
most popular.

sonner [sɔne] vb to ring ▷ *On a
sonné.* Somebody rang the doorbell.
▷ *Le téléphone a sonné.* The phone
rang.

sonnerie [sɔnʀi] nf (electric) bell
▷ *La sonnerie du téléphone l'a réveillée.*
She was woken by the phone
ringing.

sonnette [sɔnɛt] nf bell ▷ *la
sonnette d'alarme* the alarm bell

sont [sɔ̃] vb see **être**; **Ils sont en
vacances.** They're on holiday.

sophistiqué [sɔfistike] (f
sophistiquée) adj sophisticated

sorcier [sɔʀsje] nm wizard

sorcière [sɔʀsjɛʀ] nf witch

sort [sɔʀ] nm ❶ spell ▷ *jeter un
sort à quelqu'un* to cast a spell on
somebody; **un mauvais sort** a
curse; **jeter un sort à quelque
chose** to put a jinx on something
❷ fate ▷ *abandonner quelqu'un à
son triste sort* to leave somebody to
their fate; **tirer au sort** to draw lots

sorte [sɔʀt(ə)] nf sort ▷ *C'est une
sorte de gâteau.* It's a sort of cake.
▷ *toutes sortes de choses* all sorts
of things

sortie [sɔʀti] nf way out ▷ Où est
la sortie? Where's the way out?; **la
sortie de secours** the emergency
exit; **une sortie éducative** a
field trip

sortir [sɔʀtiʀ] vb ① to go out ▷ Elle
est sortie sans rien dire. She went
out without saying a word. ▷ Il est
sorti acheter un journal. He's gone
out to buy a newspaper. ▷ J'aime
sortir. I like going out. ② to come
out ▷ Elle sort de l'hôpital demain.
She's coming out of the hospital
tomorrow. ▷ Je l'ai rencontré en
sortant de la pharmacie. I met him
coming out of the drugstore.
▷ Ce modèle vient juste de sortir.
This model has just come out.
③ to take out ▷ Elle a sorti son
porte-monnaie de son sac. She took
her wallet out of her purse. ▷ Je
vais sortir la voiture du garage. I'll get
the car out of the garage.; **sortir
avec quelqu'un** to be going out
with somebody ▷ Tu sors avec lui?
Are you going out with him?; **s'en
sortir** to manage ▷ Ne t'en fais pas,
tu t'en sortiras. Don't worry, you'll
manage OK.

sottise [sɔtiz] nf: **Ne fais pas de
sottises.** Don't do anything silly.;
Ne dis pas de sottises. Don't talk
nonsense.

sou [su] nm (informal) cent ▷ Les
tranches de pizza ne coûtent que
quatre-vingt-neuf sous aujourd'hui.
Pizza slices are only 89 cents
today.; **Je n'ai pas un sou sur moi.**
I haven't got a penny on me.; **être
près de ses sous** (informal) to be
tight-fisted

souci [susi] nm worry; **se faire du
souci** to worry

soucieux [susjø, -øz] (f **soucieuse**)
adj worried ▷ Tu as l'air soucieux. You
look worried.

soucoupe [sukup] nf saucer; **une
soucoupe volante** a flying saucer

soudain [sudɛ̃, -ɛn] (f **soudaine**)
adj, adv ① sudden ▷ une douleur
soudaine a sudden pain ② suddenly
▷ Soudain, il s'est fâché. Suddenly he
got angry.

souffle [sufl(ə)] nm breath; **à bout
de souffle** out of breath

soufflé [sufle] nm soufflé ▷ un
soufflé au fromage a cheese soufflé

souffler [sufle] vb ① to blow ▷ Le
vent soufflait fort. The wind was
blowing hard. ② to blow out
▷ Souffle les bougies! Blow out the
candles!

souffleuse [sufløz] nf snowblower
▷ Mon père a passé la souffleuse pour
déneiger l'entrée. My father used the
snowblower to clear the driveway.

souffrance [sufʀɑ̃s] nf suffering

souffrant [sufʀɑ̃, -ɑ̃t] (f
souffrante) adj unwell

souffrir [sufʀiʀ] vb to be in pain
▷ Elle souffre beaucoup. She's in a
lot of pain.

souhait [swe] nm wish ▷ faire un
souhait to make a wish ▷ Tous nos
souhaits de réussite. All our best
wishes for your success. ▷ les
souhaits de bonne année New Year's
wishes; **« Atchoum! » « À tes
souhaits! »** "Atchoo!" "Bless you!"

souhaiter [swete] vb to wish ▷ Je
souhaite aller à l'université. I wish
to go to university. ▷ Nous vous
souhaitons une bonne année. We wish
you a happy New Year.

soûl [su, sul] (f **soûle**) adj (informal)
drunk

soulager [sulaʒe] vb to relieve

soulever [sulve] vb ① to lift ▷ Je
n'arrive pas à soulever cette valise. I
can't lift this suitcase. ② to raise
▷ Il faudra soulever la question lors de
la réunion. We'll have to raise the

matter at the meeting.; **soulever un bon point** to make a good point

soulier [sulje] *nm* shoe

souligner [suliɲe] *vb* to underline

soupçon [supsɔ̃] *nm* suspicion; **un soupçon de** a dash of ▷ *Ajoutez un soupçon de crème.* Add a dash of cream.

soupçonner [supsɔne] *vb* to suspect

soupe [sup] *nf* soup ▷ *la soupe au poulet et aux nouilles* chicken noodle soup

souper [supe] *nm* supper ▷ *Qu'est-ce qu'il y a pour souper?* What's for supper?
▶ *vb* to have supper

soupir [supir] *nm* sigh

soupirer [supire] *vb* to sigh

souple [supl(ə)] *adj* flexible

source [surs(ə)] *nf* spring ▷ *l'eau de source* spring water

sourcil [sursij] *nm* eyebrow

sourd [sur, surd(ə)] (*f* **sourde**) *adj* deaf

souriant [surjɑ̃, -ɑ̃t] (*f* **souriante**) *adj* cheerful

sourire [surir] *nm* smile; **avoir le sourire fendu jusqu'aux oreilles** to grin from ear to ear
▶ *vb* to smile ▷ *sourire à quelqu'un* to smile at somebody

souris [suri] *nf* (*also computer*) mouse

sournois [surnwa, -waz] (*f* **sournoise**) *adj* sly

sous [su] *prep* under; **sous terre** underground; **sous la pluie** in the rain

sous-entendu [suzɑ̃tɑ̃dy] (*f* **sous-entendue**) *adj* implied
▶ *nm* insinuation

sous-marin [sumarɛ̃, -in] (*f* **sous-marine**) *adj* underwater
▶ *nm* ❶ submarine ▷ *un sous-marin nucléaire* a nuclear submarine

❷ (*sandwich*) sub ▷ *un sous-marin bacon, laitue et tomates* a BLT sub

sous-produit [suprɔdɥi] *nm* by-product

sous-sol [susɔl] *nm* basement

sous-titre [sutitr(ə)] *nm* subtitle

sous-titré [sutitre] (*f* **sous-titrée**) *adj* with subtitles

soustraction [sustraksjɔ̃] *nf* subtraction

soustraire [sustrɛr] *vb* to subtract

sous-vêtements [suvɛtmɑ̃] *nmpl* underwear

soutenir [sutnir] *vb* to support ▷ *Il m'a toujours soutenu.* He's always supported me.; **soutenir que** to maintain that ▷ *Elle soutenait que c'était impossible.* She maintained that it was impossible.; **soutenir l'allure** to keep up ▷ *Elle marchait trop vite et je n'arrivais pas à soutenir l'allure.* She was walking too fast and I couldn't keep up.

souterrain [suterɛ̃, -ɛn] (*f* **souterraine**) *adj* underground
▶ *nm* underground passage

soutien [sutjɛ̃] *nm* support

soutien-gorge [sutjɛ̃gɔrʒ(ə)] (*pl* **soutiens-gorge**) *nm* bra

souvenir [suvnir] *nm* ❶ memory ▷ *garder un bon souvenir de quelque chose* to have happy memories of something ❷ souvenir; **Garde ce livre en souvenir de moi.** Keep this book to remember me by.; **le jour du Souvenir** Remembrance Day
▶ *vb*: **se souvenir de quelque chose** to remember something ▷ *Je ne me souviens pas de son adresse.* I can't remember his address.; **se souvenir que** to remember that ▷ *Je me souviens qu'il neigeait.* I remember it was snowing.

souvent [suvɑ̃] *adv* often

souveraineté [suvrɛnte] *nf*

sovereignty ▷ Êtes-vous en faveur de la souveraineté du Québec? Are you in favour of Québec sovereignty?

souverainiste [suvʀɛnist] nmf
sovereigntist

soya [soja] nm soya; **des germes de soya** bean sprouts; **du lait de soya** soy milk

soyez, soyons vb see **être**

spacieux [spasjø, -øz] (f **spacieuse**) adj spacious

spaghettis [spageti] nmpl
spaghetti

spécial [spesjal, -o] (f **spéciale**, mpl **spéciaux**) adj ① special ▷ « Qu'est-ce que tu fais en fin de semaine? » « Rien de spécial. » "What are you doing this weekend?" "Nothing special."; **les effets spéciaux** special effects ② peculiar ▷ Elle a des goûts un peu spéciaux. She has rather peculiar tastes.

spécialement [spesjalmɑ̃] adv ① specially ▷ Il est venu spécialement pour te parler. He came specially to speak to you. ② particularly ▷ Ce n'est pas spécialement difficile. It's not particularly difficult.

se **spécialiser** [spesjalize] vb: se **spécialiser dans quelque chose** to specialize in something ▷ Je vais me spécialiser dans biologie marine. I'm going to specialize in marine biology.

spécialiste [spesjalist(ə)] nmf
specialist

spécialité [spesjalite] nf specialty

spécifier [spesifje] vb to specify

spectacle [spɛktakl(ə)] nm show

spectaculaire [spɛktakylɛʀ] adj
spectacular

spectateur [spɛktatœʀ] nm
① member of the audience
② spectator

spectatrice [spɛktatʀis] nf

① member of the audience
② spectator

spermophile [spɛʀmɔfil] nm
gopher

spirituel [spiʀituɛl] (f **spirituelle**) adj ① spiritual ② witty

splendide [splɑ̃did] adj
magnificent

spontané [spɔ̃tane] (f **spontanée**) adj spontaneous

sport [spɔʀ] nm sport ▷ faire du sport to do sports; **les sports d'hiver** winter sports; **le sport extrême** extreme sport
▶ adj (f+pl **sport**) casual ▷ une veste sport a casual jacket

sportif [spɔʀtif, -iv] (f **sportive**) adj ① athletic ▷ Elle est très sportive. She's very athletic. ② sports ▷ un club sportif a sports club
▶ nm sportsman

sportive [spɔʀtiv] nf
sportswoman

squelette [skəlɛt] nm skeleton

SRAS [sʀas] nm = **syndrome respiratoire aigu sévère** SARS

stable [stabl(ə)] adj stable; **un emploi stable** a steady job

stade [stad] nm stadium

stage [staʒ] nm ① training course ▷ faire un stage de formation professionnelle to take a vocational training course ② co-op placement ▷ Il a fait un stage dans une bibliothèque. He did a co-op placement in a library.; **faire un stage en entreprise** to do a work placement

Be careful! The French word **stage** does not mean **stage**.

stagiaire [staʒjɛʀ] nmf trainee

stampede [stampid] nm: **le Stampede de Calgary** Calgary Stampede

stand [stɑ̃d] nm ① (at exhibition) booth ② (at fair) stall

standardiste [stɑ̃daʁdist(ə)] nmf
operator

station [stasjɔ̃] nf: **une station
de métro** a subway station; **une
station de taxis** a taxi stand; **une
station de ski** a ski resort

stationnement [stasjɔnmɑ̃] nm
❶ parking ▷ parking lot;
« **stationnement interdit** » "no
parking"

stationner [stasjɔne] vb to park
▷ *J'ai stationné la voiture dans la rue.* I
parked the car on the street.

> Use **se stationner** if there is no
> object after the verb.

se stationner to park ▷ *Elle s'est
stationnée dans la rue.* She's parked
on the street.

station-service [stasjɔ̃sɛʁvis]
(pl **stations-service**) nf service
station

statistique [statistik] nf
❶ statistic ▷ *Voici des statistiques
sur les exportations canadiennes.* Here
are some statistics on Canadian
exports. ❷ (the science) statistics

steak [stɛk] nm steak; **un steak
haché** a hamburger patty; **le steak
haché** hamburger meat ▷ *J'ai
acheté du steak haché.* I bought some
hamburger meat.

stérile [steʁil] adj sterile

stimulant [stimylɑ̃, -ɑ̃t] (f
stimulante) adj stimulating

stimuler [stimyle] vb to stimulate

stopper [stɔpe] vb to stop

store [stɔʁ] nm (on window) blind
▷ *un store horizontal* horizontal
blinds ▷ *Toutes les fenêtres ont des
stores verticaux.* All the windows
have vertical blinds.

stratégie [stʁateʒi] nf strategy

stratégique [stʁateʒik] adj
strategic

stressant [stʁesɑ̃, -ɑ̃t] (f
stressante) adj stressful

stressé [stʁese] (f **stressée**) adj
stressed out

strict [stʁikt(ə)] (f **stricte**) adj
❶ (person) strict ▷ *Mon prof de
français est très strict.* My French
teacher's very strict. ❷ (clothes)
plain ▷ *une tenue très stricte* a very
plain outfit; **le strict minimum** the
bare minimum

strophe [stʁɔf] nf stanza

studieux [stydjø, -øz] (f
studieuse) adj studious

studio [stydjo] nm ❶ studio
apartment ❷ studio ▷ *un studio
de télévision* a television studio ▷ *un
studio de peintre* a painter's studio

stupéfait [stypefɛ, -ɛt] (f
stupéfaite) adj astonished

stupéfiants [stypefjɑ̃] nmpl
narcotics

stupéfier [stypefje] vb to astonish
▷ *Sa réponse m'a stupéfié.* I was
astonished by his answer.

stupide [stypid] adj stupid

style [stil] nm style

styliste [stilist(ə)] nmf designer

stylo [stilo] nm pen; **un stylo
plume** a fountain pen; **un stylo
à bille** a ballpoint pen; **un stylo-
feutre** a felt pen

su [sy] vb see **savoir**; **Si j'avais su...**
If I'd known...

subir [sybiʁ] vb (defeat) to suffer;
subir une opération to have an
operation

subit [sybi, -it] (f **subite**) adj
sudden

subitement [sybitmɑ̃] adv
suddenly

subjectif [sybʒɛktif, -iv] (f
subjective) adj subjective

subjonctif [sybʒɔ̃ktif] nm
subjunctive

substituer [sypstitɥe] vb to
substitute ▷ *substituer un mot à un
autre* to substitute one word for

another

subtil [syptil] (f **subtile**) adj subtle

subvention [sybvãsjõ] nf subsidy

subventionner [sybvãsjɔne] vb to subsidize

succès [syksɛ] nm success ▷ avoir du succès to be successful

successeur [syksesœʀ] nm successor

successeure [syksesœʀ] nf successor

succursale [sykyʀsal] nf (of company) branch

sucer [syse] vb to suck

suçon [sysõ] nm lollipop

sucre [sykʀ(ə)] nm sugar ▷ « Combien de sucre dans votre café? » — « Deux sucres, s'il vous plaît. » "How many sugars do you take in your coffee?" — "Two, please."; **le sucre brun** brown sugar; **le sucre d'érable** maple sugar; **du sucre en cubes** sugar cubes; **un sucre d'orge** a barley sugar; **du sucre à glacer** icing sugar

sucré [sykʀe] (f **sucrée**) adj ❶ sweet ▷ Ce gâteau est un peu trop sucré. This cake is a bit too sweet. ❷ sweetened ▷ du lait concentré sucré sweetened condensed milk

sucrer [sykʀe] vb to add sugar ▷ J'ai sucré mon café. I added sugar to my coffee.; **se sucrer le bec** to eat sweets ▷ Elle adore se sucrer le bec. She loves sweets.

sucreries [sykʀəʀi] nfpl sweets

sucrier [sykʀije] nm sugar bowl

sud [syd] nm south ▷ Ils vivent dans le sud de la Colombie-Britannique. They live in the south of British Columbia.; **vers le sud** southwards; **au sud d'Edmonton** south of Edmonton; **l'Amérique du Sud** South America; **le vent du Sud** the south wind

▶ adj ❶ south ▷ la côte sud de

Terre-Neuve the south coast of Newfoundland; **le pôle sud** the South Pole ❷ southern ▷ Nous avons visité la partie sud du pays. We visited the southern part of the country.

sud-est [sydɛst] nm southeast ▷ au sud-est in the southeast

sud-ouest [sydwɛst] nm southwest ▷ au sud-ouest in the southwest

suer [sɥe] vb to sweat

sueur [sɥœʀ] nf sweat; **en sueur** sweating

suffire [syfiʀ] vb to be enough ▷ Tiens, voilà dix dollars. Ça te suffit? Here's 10 dollars. Is that enough for you?; **Ça suffit!** That's enough!

suffisamment [syfizamã] adv enough ▷ Ça n'est pas suffisamment grand. It's not big enough. ▷ Il n'y a pas suffisamment de chaises. There aren't enough chairs.

suffisant [syfizã, -ãt] (f **suffisante**) adj ❶ good enough ▷ Ça n'est pas une raison suffisante. That's not a good enough reason. ❷ smug ▷ Il est un peu trop suffisant. He's a bit too smug.

suffoquer [syfɔke] vb to suffocate

suggérer [sygʒeʀe] vb to suggest

se suicider [sɥiside] vb to commit suicide

suis [sɥi] vb see **être**; **suivre**; Je suis rapide. I'm fast.; Suis-moi. Follow me.

suisse [sɥis] nm chipmunk

suite [sɥit] nf ❶ rest ▷ Je vous raconterai la suite de l'histoire demain. I'll tell you the rest of the story tomorrow. ❷ (to book, film) sequel; **tout de suite** right away ▷ J'y vais tout de suite. I'll go right away.; **de suite** in a row ▷ Il a commis la même erreur trois fois de suite. He made the same mistake three times in a row.;

par la suite later ▷ *Elle s'est avérée par la suite qu'elle était coupable.* She later turned out to be guilty.

suivant [sɥivã, -ãt] (f **suivante**) *adj* following ▷ *le jour suivant* the following day ▷ *l'exercice suivant* the following exercise; **Au suivant!** Next!

suivre [sɥivʀ(ə)] *vb* ❶ to follow ▷ *Il m'a suivie jusque chez moi.* He followed me home. ▷ *Vous me suivez ou est-ce que je parle trop vite?* Are you following me, or am I talking too fast? ❷ *(course)* to take ▷ *Elle suit un cours d'anglais au collège.* She's taking an English course at college. ❸ to keep up ▷ *Il n'arrive pas à suivre en maths.* He can't keep up in math. ▷ *J'aime suivre l'actualité.* I like to keep up with the news.; **« à suivre »** "to be continued"; **suivre un régime** to be on a diet

sujet [syʒɛ, -ɛt] (f **sujette**) *adj*: **être sujet à** to be prone to ▷ *Il est sujet au vertige.* He suffers from fear of heights.
▶ *nm* subject; **au sujet de** about ▷ *« C'est à quel sujet? » « C'est au sujet de l'annonce parue dans le Globe and Mail d'aujourd'hui. »* "What's it about?" "It's about the advertisement in today's *Globe and Mail*."; **un sujet de conversation** a topic of conversation; **un sujet d'examen** an examination question; **un sujet de plaisanterie** something to joke about

super [sypɛʀ] *adj* great ▷ *C'est super que tu puisses venir avec nous!* It's great that you can come with us!

superficiel [sypɛʀfisjɛl] (f **superficielle**) *adj* superficial

superflu [sypɛʀfly] (f **superflue**) *adj* superfluous

supérieur [sypeʀjœʀ] (f **supérieure**) *adj* ❶ upper ▷ *la lèvre supérieure* the upper lip ❷ superior ▷ *qualité supérieure* superior quality ▷ *Ne me parle pas sur ce ton supérieur.* Don't talk to me in that superior tone of voice.; **supérieur à** greater than ▷ *Choisissez un nombre supérieur à cent.* Choose a number greater than 100.

supermarché [sypɛʀmaʀʃe] *nm* supermarket

superposé [sypɛʀpoze] (f **superposée**) *adj*: **des lits superposés** bunk beds

superstitieux [sypɛʀstisjø, -øz] (f **superstitieuse**) *adj* superstitious

suppléant [sypleã] *nm* substitute teacher

suppléante [sypleãt] *nf* substitute teacher

supplément [syplemã] *nm*: **payer un supplément** to pay an additional charge; **Le toit ouvrant est en supplément.** The sunroof is extra.; **un supplément de travail** extra work

supplémentaire [syplemãtɛʀ] *adj* additional ▷ *Voici quelques exercices supplémentaires.* Here are some additional exercises.; **faire des heures supplémentaires** to do overtime

supplice [syplis] *nm* torture ▷ *C'était un supplice.* It was torture.

supplier [syplije] *vb*: **supplier quelqu'un de faire quelque chose** to beg somebody to do something ▷ *Je t'en supplie!* I'm begging you!

supportable [sypɔʀtabl(ə)] *adj* bearable

supporter [sypɔʀte] *vb (tolerate)* to stand ▷ *Je ne supporte pas l'hypocrisie.* I can't stand hypocrisy. ▷ *Elle ne supporte pas qu'on la critique.* She can't stand being criticized. ▷ *Je ne peux pas la supporter.* I can't stand her. ▷ *Je supporte mal la chaleur.* I

can't stand hot weather.
Be careful! **supporter** does not
mean **to support**.

supposer [sypoze] vb to suppose

supprimer [syprime] vb ❶ to
cut ▷ *Deux mille emplois ont été
supprimés.* Two thousand jobs have
been cut. ❷ to cancel ▷ *L'autobus
de Nelson a été supprimé.* The bus to
Nelson has been cancelled. ❸ to
get rid of ▷ *Ils ont supprimé les
témoins de l'enlèvement.* They got rid
of the witnesses to the kidnapping.
❹ to delete ▷ *Elle a supprimé
quelques vieux fichiers.* She deleted
some old files.

suprême [syprɛm] adj supreme
▷ *la Cour suprême* the Supreme
Court

sur [syr] prep ❶ on ▷ *Pose-le sur
la table.* Put it on the table. ▷ *Vous
verrez l'hôpital sur votre droite.* You'll
see the hospital on your right. ▷ *une
conférence sur l'écologie* a lecture on
ecology ❷ in ▷ *une personne sur dix*
1 person in 10 ❸ out of ▷ *J'ai eu neuf
sur dix en maths.* I got 9 out of 10 in
math. ❹ by ▷ *quatre mètres sur deux*
4 metres by 2

sûr [syr] (f **sûre**) adj ❶ sure ▷ *Tu es
sûr?* Are you sure?; **sûr et certain**
absolutely certain ❷ reliable
▷ *C'est quelqu'un de très sûr.* He's a
very reliable person. ❸ safe ▷ *Ce
quartier n'est pas très sûr la nuit.* This
neighbourhood isn't very safe at
night.; **sûr de soi** self-confident
▷ *Elle est très sûre d'elle.* She's very
self-confident.

surdose [syrdoz] nf overdose

sûrement [syrmã] adv certainly
▷ *Sûrement pas!* Certainly not! ▷ *Il
est sûrement déjà parti.* He's sure to
have already left.

sûreté [syrte] nf: **mettre quelque
chose en sûreté** to put something

in a safe place

surf [sœrf] nm surfing; **le surf des
neiges** snow surfing

surface [syrfas] nf surface;
les grandes surfaces the
supermarkets

surfaceuse [syrfasøz] nf
Zamboni®

surfer [sœrfe] vb to go surfing;
surfer sur Internet to surf the Net

surgelé [syrʒəle] (f **surgelée**)
adj frozen ▷ *des frites surgelées*
frozen fries

surgelés [syrʒəle] nmpl frozen
foods

surhumain [syrymɛ̃, -ɛn] (f
surhumaine) adj superhuman

surintendant [syrɛ̃tɑ̃dɑ̃] nm
superintendent ▷ *Son père est
surintendant de police.* Her father is a
police superintendent.

surintendante [syrɛ̃tɑ̃dɑ̃t]
nf superintendent ▷ *Sa mère est
surintendante scolaire.* His mother is
a school superintendent.

sur-le-champ [syrləʃɑ̃] adv
immediately

surlendemain [syrlɑ̃dmɛ̃] nm:
le surlendemain de son arrivée
two days after she arrived; **le
surlendemain dans la matinée**
two days later, in the morning

se surmener [syrməne] vb to
work too hard ▷ *Ne te surmène pas
trop pendant la fin de semaine.* Don't
work too hard over the weekend.

surmonter [syrmɔ̃te] vb to
overcome ▷ *Il nous reste de nombreux
obstacles à surmonter.* We still have
many obstacles to overcome.

surnaturel [syrnatyrɛl] (f
surnaturelle) adj supernatural

surnom [syrnɔ̃] nm nickname

surnommer [syrnɔme] n to
nickname ▷ *On l'a surnommé «la
bolle des maths».* We nicknamed him

"the math whiz".

surpeuplé [syʀpœple] (f **surpeuplée**) adj overpopulated

surprenant [syʀpʀənɑ̃, -ɑ̃t] (f **surprenante**) adj surprising

surprendre [syʀpʀɑ̃dʀ(ə)] vb to surprise ▷ *Ça me surprendrait beaucoup qu'elle arrive à l'heure.* I'd be very surprised if she arrived on time.; **surprendre quelqu'un en train de faire quelque chose** to catch somebody doing something ▷ *Je l'ai surpris en train de fouiller dans mon casier.* I caught him rummaging in my locker.

surpris [syʀpʀi, -iz] (f **surprise**) adj surprised ▷ *Elle était surprise de me voir.* She was surprised to see me.

surprise [syʀpʀiz] nf surprise ▷ *faire une surprise à quelqu'un* to give somebody a surprise

sursauter [syʀsote] vb to jump ▷ *J'ai sursauté en entendant mon nom.* I jumped when I heard my name.

surtout [syʀtu] adv ❶ especially ▷ *Il est assez timide, surtout avec les filles.* He's rather shy, especially with girls. ❷ above all ▷ *Ce manteau est bon marché, pratique et, surtout, paraît bien.* This coat is reasonably priced, practical, and above all great-looking. ▷ *Surtout, ne répète pas ce que je t'ai dit!* Whatever you do, don't repeat what I told you!

surveiller [syʀveje] vb ❶ to keep an eye on ▷ *Tu peux surveiller mes bagages?* Can you keep an eye on my luggage? ❷ to keep a watch on ▷ *La police a surveillé la maison pendant une semaine.* The police kept the house under surveillance for a week. ❸ to supervise ▷ *Nous sommes toujours surveillés pendant la récréation.* We're always supervised during recess.; **surveiller sa ligne** to watch one's figure

survêtement [syʀvɛtmɑ̃] nm track suit ▷ *un haut de survêtement* a track top ▷ *un pantalon de survêtement* track pants

survie [syʀvi] nf survival

survivant [syʀvivɑ̃] nm survivor

survivante [syʀvivɑ̃t] nf survivor

survivre [syʀvivʀ(ə)] vb to survive ▷ *survivre à un accident* to survive an accident

survoler [syʀvole] vb to fly over

sus [sy] adv: **en sus** in addition

susceptible [syseptibl(ə)] adj touchy

suspect [syspɛ(kt), -ɛkt(ə)] (f **suspecte**) adj suspicious ▷ *dans des circonstances suspectes* under suspicious circumstances

suspecter [syspɛkte] vb to suspect

suspense [syspɑ̃s] nm suspense; **un film à suspense** a thriller

suture [sytyʀ] nf: **un point de suture** a stitch

svelte [svɛlt(ə)] adj slender

SVP abbr (= s'il vous plaît) please

syllabe [silab] nf syllable

symbole [sɛ̃bɔl] nm symbol

symbolique [sɛ̃bɔlik] adj symbolic

symboliser [sɛ̃bɔlize] vb to symbolize

symétrique [simetʀik] adj symmetrical

sympathie [sɛ̃pati] nf: **J'ai beaucoup de sympathie pour lui.** I like him a lot.

sympathique [sɛ̃patik] adj nice ▷ *Ce sont des gens très sympathiques.* They're very nice people.

   Be careful! **sympathique** does not mean **sympathetic**.

sympathiser [sɛ̃patize] vb to get along well ▷ *Nous avons immédiatement sympathisé avec nos voisins.* We hit it off with our neighbours right away.

▌ Be careful! **sympathiser** does not mean **sympathize**.

symptôme [sɛ̃ptom] *nm* symptom

synagogue [sinagɔg] *nf* synagogue

syndicat [sɛ̃dika] *nm* trade union

syndrome [sɛ̃drom] *nm* syndrome; **le syndrome de Down** Down syndrome; **le syndrome respiratoire aigu sévère** Severe Acute Respiratory Syndrome

synonyme [sinɔnim] *adj* synonymous ▷ *être synonyme de* to be synonymous with
▶ *nm* synonym

synthétique [sɛ̃tetik] *adj* synthetic

syntoniser [sɛ̃tɔnize] *vb (radio)* to tune ▷ *J'ai syntonisé la radio sur Radio-Canada.* I tuned the radio to CBC.

systématique [sistematik] *adj* systematic

système [sistɛm] *nm* system; **le système d'exploitation** DOS (disk operating system)

t' [t(ə)] *pron see* **te**

ta [ta] *adj* your ▷ *J'ai vu ta sœur hier.* I saw your sister yesterday.

tabac [taba] *nm* ❶ tobacco ▷ *Le tabac est originaire d'Amérique.* Tobacco is native to America. ❷ smoking ▷ *Le tabac est mauvais pour la santé.* Smoking is bad for you.

table [tabl(ə)] *nf* table; **mettre la table** to set the table; **se mettre à table** to sit down to eat; **À table!** Dinner's ready!; **une table de jeu** card table; **une table de nuit** a night table; **table des matières** table of contents

tableau [tablo] *(pl* **tableaux**) *nm* ❶ painting ▷ *un tableau de Monet* a painting by Monet; **le tableau d'affichage** the notice board; **le tableau noir** the chalkboard ❷ chart

tablette [tablɛt] *nf:* **une tablette**

de chocolat a bar of chocolate; **une tablette tactile** (computer) a tablet

tableur [tablœʀ] nm spreadsheet

tablier [tablije] nm apron

tabloïd [tablɔid] nm tabloid

tabouret [tabuʀɛ] nm stool

tache [taʃ] nf (stain) mark; **des taches de rousseur** freckles

tâche [taʃ] nf task

tacher [taʃe] vb to leave a stain

tâcher [taʃe] vb: **tâcher de faire quelque chose** to try to do something

tactique [taktik] nf tactics; **changer de tactique** to try something different

taie [tɛ] nf: **une taie d'oreiller** a pillowcase

taille [taj] nf ❶ waist ▷ avoir la taille fine to have a slim waist ❷ height ▷ Ils sont de la même taille. They are the same height. ❸ size ▷ Avez-vous ma taille? Have you got my size?

taille-crayon [tajkʀɛjɔ̃] nm pencil sharpener

tailleur [tajœʀ] nm ❶ tailor ❷ (women's) suit; **Il est assis en tailleur.** He's sitting cross-legged.

se taire [tɛʀ] vb to stop talking; **Taisez-vous!** Be quiet!

talent [talɑ̃] nm ▷ Elle a le talent de mettre les gens à l'aise. She has a talent for putting people at ease.; **avoir du talent** to have talent

talentueux [talɑ̃tyø, -øz] (f **talentueuse**) adj talented

talle [tal] nf patch of shrubs or berries

talon [talɔ̃] nm heel; **les talons hauts** high heels

tambour [tɑ̃buʀ] nm drum

tampon [tɑ̃pɔ̃] nm ❶ pad ▷ un tampon à récurer a scouring pad; **un**

tampon hygiénique a tampon

tandis que [tɑ̃di-] conj while ▷ Elle a toujours de bonnes notes, tandis que les miennes sont mauvaises. She always gets good marks, while mine are poor.

tant [tɑ̃] adv so much ▷ Je l'aime tant! I love him so much!; **tant de** (1) so much ▷ tant de nourriture so much food (2) so many ▷ tant de livres so many books; **tant pis** (1) never mind (2) too bad; **tant que** (1) until ▷ Tu ne sortiras pas tant que tu n'auras pas fini tes devoirs. You're not going out until you've finished your homework. (2) while ▷ Profites-en tant que tu peux. Make the most of it while you can.; **tant mieux** so much the better; **tant pis** never mind

tante [tɑ̃t] nf aunt

tantôt [tɑ̃to] adv sometimes ▷ Nous venons tantôt à pied, tantôt en autobus. Sometimes we walk, sometimes we come by bus.

tapage [tapaʒ] nm ❶ racket ▷ Ils ont fait du tapage toute la nuit. They made a racket all night long. ❷ fuss ▷ On a fait beaucoup de tapage autour de cette affaire. There was a lot of fuss about that business.

taper [tape] vb ❶ to beat down ▷ Le soleil tape. The sun's really beating down.; **taper quelqu'un** to hit somebody ▷ Maman, elle m'a tapé dessus! Mom, she hit me!; **taper sur quelque chose** to bang on something; **taper des pieds** to stamp one's feet; **taper des mains** to clap one's hands ❷ to type ▷ Tapez votre mot de passe. Type your password.

tapis [tapi] nm carpet; **le tapis roulant** (1) the moving sidewalk (2) (in factory) the conveyor belt; **un**

tapis de souris a mouse pad

tapisser [tapise] vb to paper

tapisserie [tapisʀi] nf
❶ wallpaper ▷ Tu aimes la tapisserie de ma chambre? Do you like the wallpaper in my bedroom?
❷ tapestry

tapoter [tapɔte] vb ❶ to pat ▷ Elle lui a tapoté l'épaule affectueusement. She patted his shoulder affectionately. ❷ to tap ▷ Il tapotait impatiemment sur la table. He was tapping impatiently on the table.

taquiner [takine] vb to tease

tard [taʀ] adv late ▷ Il est tard. It's late.; **plus tard** later on; **au plus tard** at the latest

tardif [taʀdif, -iv] (f **tardive**) adj late ▷ un petit lunch tardif a late breakfast

tarif [taʀif] nm: **payer plein tarif** to pay full price; **payer le tarif étudiant** to pay the student rate; **le tarif horaire** hourly rate

tarte [taʀt(ə)] nf pie; **tarte au sucre** sugar pie

tartelette [taʀtəlɛt] nf tart ▷ une tartelette aux raisins secs butter tart

tartine [taʀtin] nf slice of bread ▷ une tartine de confiture a slice of bread and jam

tartiner [taʀtine] vb to spread; **le fromage à tartiner** cheese spread

tas [tɑ] nm heap ▷ un tas de sable a heap of sand; **un tas de** (informal) a ton of ▷ J'ai lu un tas de livres pendant les vacances. I read a ton of books on the holidays.

tasse [tɑs] nf cup

taureau [tɔʀo] (pl **taureaux**) nm bull; **le Taureau** Taurus ▷ Ils sont tous les deux Taureau. They are both Tauruses.

taux [to] nm rate ▷ le taux de change the exchange rate

taxe [taks(ə)] nf tax

taxi [taksi] nm taxi; **la station de taxi** taxi stand

te [t(ə)] pron
te changes to **t'** before a vowel and most words beginning with "h".
❶ you ▷ Je te vois. I can see you. ▷ Elle t'a vu? Did she see you? ❷ to you ▷ Est-ce qu'il te parle en français? Does he talk to you in French? ▷ Elle t'a parlé? Did she speak to you? ❸ yourself ▷ Tu vas te rendre malade. You'll make yourself sick.
With reflexive verbs, **te** is often not translated.
▷ Comment tu t'appelles? What's your name?

technicien [tɛknisjɛ̃] nm technician

technicienne [tɛknisjɛn] nf technician

technique [tɛknik] adj technical ▶ nf technique

techno [tɛkno] nf techno music

technologie [tɛknɔlɔʒi] nf technology

teindre [tɛ̃dʀ(ə)] vb to dye; **se teindre les cheveux** to dye one's hair

teint [tɛ̃] nm complexion ▷ avoir le teint clair to have a clear complexion

teinte [tɛ̃t] nf (colour) shade

teinté [tɛ̃te] adj tinted ▷ des lunettes teintées tinted glasses

tel [tɛl] adj (f **telle**): **Il a un tel enthousiasme!** He's got such enthusiasm!; **rien de tel** nothing like ▷ Il n'y a rien de tel qu'une bonne nuit de sommeil. There's nothing like a good night's sleep.; **j'ai tout laissé tel quel.** I left everything as it was.; **tel que** such as

télé [tele] nf TV ▷ à la télé on TV

téléavertisseur [teleavɛʀtisœʀ] nm pager

télécarte [telekart(ə)] nf
phonecard

téléchargement [teleʃaʁʒəmɑ̃]
nm download/downloading; **un
téléchargement vers le serveur**
an upload

télécharger [teleʃaʁʒe] vb to
download; **télécharger vers le
serveur** to upload

télécommande [telekɔmɑ̃d] nf
remote control

téléconférence [telekɔ̃feʁɑ̃s] nf
video conference

télécopie [telekɔpi] nf fax

télécopier [telekɔpje] vb to fax

télécopieur [telekɔpjœʁ] nm fax
machine

téléphérique [teleferik] nm
cable car

téléphone [telefɔn] nm telephone
▷ Elle est au téléphone. She's on the
phone.; **un téléphone cellulaire**
cellphone

téléphoner [telefɔne] vb to phone
▷ Je vais lui téléphoner. I'll phone her.
▷ Je peux téléphoner? Can I make a
phone call?

téléphonique [telefɔnik] adj:
une carte téléphonique prépayée
a prepaid phone card; **un appel
téléphonique** a phone call

téléphoniste [telefɔnist(ə)] nmf
(telephone) operator

téléroman [teleʁɔmɑ̃] nm soap
opera

télésiège [telesjɛʒ] nm chairlift

téléski [teleski] nm ski lift

téléspectateur [telespektatœʁ]
nm (TV) viewer

téléspectatrice [telespektatʁis]
nf (TV) viewer

téléviseur [televizœʁ] nm
television set

télévision [televizjɔ̃] nf television
▷ à la télévision on television; **la
télévision à haute définition**

HDTV (high-definition TV); **la
télévision numérique** digital TV

telle [tɛl] adj: **Je n'ai jamais eu
une telle peur.** I've never been so
scared.; **telle que** such as

tellement [tɛlmɑ̃] adv ❶ so ▷ Il
est tellement gentil. He's so nice. ▷ Il
travaille tellement. He works so hard.
❷ so much ▷ J'ai tellement mangé
que... I ate so much that... ❸ so
many ▷ Il y avait tellement de monde.
There were so many people.

telles [tɛl] adj such ▷ Je n'ai jamais
entendu de telles niaiseries! I've never
heard such nonsense!

tels [tɛl] adj such ▷ Nous n'avons
pas de tels orages chez nous. We don't
have such storms back home.

témoignage [temwaɲaʒ] nm
testimony

témoigner [temwaɲe] vb to
testify

témoin [temwɛ̃] nmf witness

température [tɑ̃peʁatyʁ]
nf temperature ▷ avoir de la
température to have a temperature

tempête [tɑ̃pɛt] nf storm

temple [tɑ̃pl(ə)] nm ❶ (Protestant)
church ❷ (Hindu, Sikh, Buddhist)
temple

temporaire [tɑ̃pɔʁɛʁ] adj
temporary

temps [tɑ̃] nm ❶ weather ▷ Quel
temps fait-il? What's the weather
like? ❷ time ▷ Je n'ai pas le temps.
I don't have time. ▷ Prends ton
temps. Take your time. ▷ Il est temps
de partir. It's time to go.; **juste
à temps** just in time; **de temps
en temps** from time to time; **en
même temps** at the same time;
à temps in time ▷ Nous sommes
arrivés à temps pour le match. We
arrived in time for the game.; **à
plein temps** full time ▷ Elle travaille
à plein temps. She works full time.; **à**

temps complet full time; **à temps partiel** part time ▷ *le travail à temps partiel* part-time work; **dans le temps** at one time ▷ *Dans le temps, on pouvait circuler en vélo sans danger.* At one time, it was safe to go around by bike. **❸** *(of verb)* tense

tenais, tenait *vb see* **tenir**

tendance [tɑ̃dɑ̃s] *nf* **avoir tendance à faire quelque chose** to tend to do something ▷ *Elle a tendance à exagérer.* She tends to exaggerate.

tendre [tɑ̃dr(ə)] *adj* tender
▶ *vb* to stretch out ▷ *Ils ont tendu une corde entre deux arbres.* They stretched a rope between two trees.; **tendre quelque chose à quelqu'un** to hold something out to somebody ▷ *Il lui a tendu les clés.* He held out the keys to her.; **tendre la main** to hold out one's hand; **tendre le bras** to reach out; **tendre un piège à quelqu'un** to set a trap for someone

tendresse [tɑ̃drɛs] *nf* tenderness

tendu [tɑ̃dy] *(f* **tendue)** *adj* tense ▷ *Il était très tendu aujourd'hui.* He was very tense today.

tenir [tənir] *vb* to hold ▷ *Tu peux tenir la lampe de poche, s'il te plaît?* Can you hold the flashlight, please? ▷ *Elle tenait un enfant par la main.* She was holding a child by the hand.; **Tenez votre chien en laisse.** Keep your dog on the leash.; **tenir à quelqu'un** to be attached to somebody ▷ *Il tient beaucoup à elle.* He's very attached to her.; **tenir à faire quelque chose** to be determined to do something ▷ *Il tient à y aller.* He's determined to go.; **tenir de quelqu'un** to take after somebody ▷ *Il tient de son père.* He takes after his father.; **Tiens, voilà un stylo.** Here's a pen.; **Tiens,**

c'est ta sœur là-bas! Look, that's your sister over there!; **Tiens?** Really?; **se tenir (1)** to stand ▷ *Elle se tenait près de la porte.* She was standing by the door. **(2)** to be held ▷ *Le festival va se tenir au centre communautaire.* The festival will be held at the community centre.; **se tenir droit (1)** to stand up straight ▷ *Tiens-toi droit!* Stand up straight! **(2)** to sit up straight ▷ *Arrête de manger le nez dans ton assiette, tiens-toi droit.* Don't slouch while you're eating, sit up straight.; **se tenir mal** to have bad posture; **Tiens-toi bien!** Behave yourself!

tennis [tenis] *nm* **❶** tennis ▷ *Elle joue au tennis.* She plays tennis.; **le tennis de table** table tennis **❷** tennis court ▷ *Il est au tennis.* He's at the tennis court.

tentant [tɑ̃tɑ̃, -ɑ̃t] *(f* **tentante)** *adj* tempting

tentation [tɑ̃tasjɔ̃] *nf* temptation

tentative [tɑ̃tativ] *nf* attempt

tente [tɑ̃t] *nf* tent

tenter [tɑ̃te] *vb* to tempt ▷ *J'ai été tenté de tout abandonner.* I was tempted to give up. ▷ *Ça ne me tente vraiment pas d'aller à la piscine.* I don't really feel like going to the swimming pool.; **tenter de faire quelque chose** to try to do something ▷ *Il a tenté plusieurs fois de s'évader.* He tried several times to escape.

tenu [təny] *vb see* **tenir**

tenue [təny] *nf* clothes

terme [tɛrm(ə)] *nm*: **à court terme** short-term; **à long terme** long-term

terminaison [tɛrminɛzɔ̃] *nf (on a word)* ending ▷ *une terminaison féminine* a feminine ending

terminer [tɛrmine] *vb* to finish; **se terminer** to end ▷ *Les vacances se* *terminent demain.* The holidays end tomorrow.

terrain [tɛʀɛ̃] nm land ▷ *Elle veut acheter un terrain en Ontario.* She wants to buy some land in Ontario.; **un terrain de camping** a campground; **un terrain de football** a football field; **un terrain de golf** a golf course; **un terrain de jeu** a playground

terrasse [tɛʀas] nf terrace; *Si on s'asseyait à la terrasse?* (at café) Shall we sit outside?

terre [tɛʀ] nf earth; **la Terre** the Earth; *Elle s'est assise par terre.* She sat on the floor.; *Il est tombé par terre.* He fell down.; **la terre cuite** terracotta ▷ *un pot en terre cuite* a terracotta pot; **la terre glaise** clay

Terre-Neuve [tɛʀnœv] nf Newfoundland ▷ *un voyage à Terre-Neuve* a trip to Newfoundland ▷ *La capitale de Terre-Neuve est St. John's.* The capital of Newfoundland is St. John's.

terreur [tɛʀœʀ] nf terror ▷ *un régime de terreur* a reign of terror

terrible [tɛʀibl(ə)] adj terrible ▷ *Quelque chose de terrible est arrivé.* Something terrible has happened.

territoire [tɛʀitwaʀ] nm territory

Territoires du Nord-Ouest [tɛʀitwaʀdynɔʀwɛst] nmpl Northwest Territories ▷ *J'habite aux Territoires du Nord-Ouest.* I live in the Northwest Territories.

terrorisé [tɛʀɔʀize] (f **terrorisée**) adj terrified

terrorisme [tɛʀɔʀism(ə)] nm terrorism

terroriste [tɛʀɔʀist(ə)] nmf terrorist

tes [te] adj your ▷ *J'aime bien tes chaussures de course.* I like your running shoes.

test [tɛst] nm test

testament [tɛstamɑ̃] nm will ▷ *Il est mort sans testament.* He died without leaving a will.

tester [tɛste] vb to test

tétanos [tetanos] nm tetanus

têtard [tɛtaʀ] nm tadpole

tête [tɛt] nf head ▷ *de la tête aux pieds* from head to foot; **se laver la tête** to wash one's hair; **la tête la première** headfirst; **tenir tête à quelqu'un** to stand up to somebody; **en avoir par-dessus la tête** to be fed up; **avoir la tête sur les épaules** to be level-headed; **avoir mal à la tête** to have a headache; **prendre la tête** to take the lead

têtu [tety] (f **têtue**) adj stubborn ▷ *Elle est trop têtue pour changer d'opinion.* She is too stubborn to change her opinion.

texte [tɛkst(ə)] nm text

thé [te] nm tea ▷ *Je vous offre un thé?* Would you like a cup of tea?

théâtre [teatʀ(ə)] nm theatre; **faire du théâtre** to act ▷ *Est-ce que tu as déjà fait du théâtre?* Have you ever acted?

théière [tejɛʀ] nf teapot

thème [tɛm] nm subject ▷ *Quel est le thème de l'émission?* What's the program about?

théorie [teɔʀi] nf theory

thermomètre [tɛʀmɔmɛtʀ(ə)] nm thermometer

thon [tɔ̃] nm tuna; **la salade de thon** tuna salad

tibia [tibja] nm ❶ shinbone ▷ *une fracture du tibia* a broken shinbone ❷ shin ▷ *Elle m'a donné un coup de pied dans le tibia.* She kicked me in the shin.

tic [tik] nm nervous twitch

ticket [tikɛ] nm ticket ▷ *un ticket de métro* a subway ticket; **le ticket de caisse** the cash register receipt

tiède [tjɛd] adj ❶ (water, air) warm ❷ (food, drink) lukewarm

tien [tjɛ̃] pron: **le tien** ▷ J'ai oublié mon stylo. Tu peux me prêter le tien? I forgot my pen. Can you lend me yours?

tienne [tjɛn] pron: **la tienne** yours ▷ Ce n'est pas ma raquette, c'est la tienne. It's not my racquet, it's yours.

tiennes [tjɛn] pron: **les tiennes** yours ▷ J'ai pris mes lunettes de soleil, mais j'ai oublié les tiennes. I brought my sunglasses, but I forgot yours.

tiens [tjɛ̃] pron: **les tiens** yours ▷ Je ne trouve pas mes feutres. Je peux utiliser les tiens? I can't find my markers. Can I use yours?

tiens, tient vb see **tenir**

tiers [tjɛr] nm third ▷ Un tiers de la classe était pour. A third of the class were in favour.

tige [tiʒ] nf stem

tigre [tigr(ə)] nm tiger

timbre [tɛ̃br(ə)] nm stamp

timide [timid] adj shy

timidement [timidmɑ̃] adv shyly

timidité [timidite] nf shyness

tirage [tiraʒ] nm: **par tirage au sort** by drawing lots ▷ Les prix seront attribués par tirage au sort. The prizes will be awarded by drawing lots.

tire [tir] nf taffy; **la tire d'érable** maple taffy

tire-bouchon [tirbuʃɔ̃] nm corkscrew

tirer [tire] vb ❶ to pull ▷ Elle a tiré un mouchoir de son sac à main. She pulled a handkerchief out of her purse. ▷ Il m'a tiré les cheveux. He pulled my hair. ▷ "Tirer" "Pull" ❷ to draw ▷ tirer les rideaux to draw the curtains ▷ tirer un trait to draw a line ▷ tirer des conclusions to draw conclusions; **tirer au sort** to draw lots ❸ to fire ▷ Il a tiré plusieurs

coups de feu. He fired several shots. ▷ Elle a tiré sur les policiers. She fired at the police.

tiret [tirɛ] nm (hyphen) dash

tiroir [tirwar] nm drawer

tisane [tizan] nf herbal tea

tisser [tise] vb to weave

tissu [tisy] nm material

titre [titr(ə)] nm title; **les gros titres** the headlines

tituber [titybe] vb to stagger

toast [tost] nm piece of toast

toi [twa] pron you ▷ «Ça va?» «Oui, et toi?» "How are you?" "Fine, and you?" ▷ J'ai faim, pas toi? I'm hungry, aren't you?; **Assieds-toi.** Sit down.; **C'est à toi de jouer.** It's your turn to play.; **Est-ce que ce stylo est à toi?** Is this pen yours?

toile [twal] nf: **un pantalon de toile** cotton pants; **un sac de toile** a canvas bag; **une toile d'araignée** a spiderweb

toilette [twalɛt] nf: **faire sa toilette** to wash oneself; **une toilette élégante** an elegant outfit

toilettes [twalɛt] nfpl washroom; **les toilettes extérieures** outhouse

toi-même [twamɛm] pron yourself ▷ Tu as fait ça toi-même? Did you do it yourself?

toit [twa] nm roof; **un toit ouvrant** a sunroof

tolérant [tolerɑ̃, -ɑ̃t] (f **tolérante**) adj tolerant

tolérer [tolere] vb to tolerate

tomate [tɔmat] nf tomato; **être rouge comme une tomate** to be beet red

tombe [tɔ̃b] nf grave

tombeau [tɔ̃bo] (pl **tombeaux**) nm tomb

tombée [tɔ̃be] nf: **à la tombée de la nuit** at nightfall

tomber [tɔ̃be] vb to fall ▷ Attention, tu vas tomber! Be careful, you'll fall!;

laisser tomber (1) to drop ▷ *Elle a laissé tomber son stylo.* She dropped her pen. **(2)** to give up ▷ *Elle a laissé tomber le piano.* She quit piano. **(3)** to let down ▷ *Il ne laisse jamais tomber ses amis.* He never lets his friends down.; **tomber sur quelqu'un** to bump into someone ▷ *Je suis tombé sur lui en sortant du restaurant.* I bumped into him coming out of the restaurant.; **Ça tombe bien.** That's lucky.; **Il tombe de sommeil.** He's asleep on his feet.

ton [tɔ̃] (f **ta**, pl **tes**) adj your ▷ *C'est ton stylo?* Is this your pen?
▶ nm ❶ tone of voice ▷ *Ne me parle pas sur ce ton.* Don't speak to me in that tone of voice. ❷ colour ▷ *J'adore les tons pastel.* I love pastel colours.

tonalité [tɔnalite] nf dial tone

tondeuse [tɔ̃døz] nf lawnmower

tondre [tɔ̃dʀ(ə)] vb to mow

tonique [tɔnik] adj energizing

tonne [tɔn] nf tonne

tonneau [tɔno] (pl **tonneaux**) nm barrel

tonnerre [tɔnɛʀ] nm thunder

tonus [tɔnys] nm: **avoir du tonus** to be energetic

torchon [tɔʀʃɔ̃] nm tea towel

tordre [tɔʀdʀ(ə)] vb: **se tordre la cheville** to twist one's ankle

tordu [tɔʀdy] (f **tordue**) adj
❶ bent ▷ *Ce clou est un peu tordu.* This nail's a bit bent. ❷ crazy ▷ *une histoire complètement tordue* a crazy story

tornade [tɔʀnad] nf tornado

torrent [tɔʀɑ̃] nm mountain stream

torse [tɔʀs(ə)] nm chest ▷ *Il était torse nu.* He was bare-chested.

tort [tɔʀ] nm: **avoir tort** to be wrong; **donner tort à quelqu'un** to lay the blame on somebody

torticolis [tɔʀtikɔli] nm stiff neck
▷ *J'ai le torticolis.* I've got a stiff neck.

tortue [tɔʀty] nf tortoise

torture [tɔʀtyʀ] nf torture

torturer [tɔʀtyʀe] vb to torture

tôt [to] adv early; **au plus tôt** at the earliest; **tôt ou tard** sooner or later

total [tɔtal, -o] (f **totale**, mpl **totaux**) adj total
▶ nm (pl **totaux**) total ▷ *faire le total* to add up the total; **au total** in total

totalement [tɔtalmɑ̃] adv totally

totaliser [tɔtalize] n to add up ▷ *Totalise ces chiffres.* Add up these numbers.

totalité [tɔtalite] nf: **la totalité des profs** all the teachers; **la totalité du personnel** the entire staff

touchant [tuʃɑ̃, -ɑ̃t] (f **touchante**) adj touching

toucher [tuʃe] vb ❶ to touch ▷ *Ne touche pas à mes livres!* Don't touch my books!; **Nos deux jardins se touchent.** Our gardens are next to each other. ❷ to feel ▷ *Ce chandail a l'air doux. Je peux toucher?* That sweater looks soft. Can I feel it? ❸ to hit ▷ *La rondelle l'a touché en pleine poitrine.* The puck hit him right in the chest. ❹ to affect ▷ *Ces nouvelles réformes ne nous touchent pas.* The new reforms don't affect us. ❺ to receive ▷ *Elle a touché une grosse somme d'argent.* She received a large sum of money.

toujours [tuʒuʀ] adv ❶ always ▷ *Il est toujours très gentil.* He's always very nice.; **pour toujours** forever ❷ still ▷ *Quand on est revenus, maman était toujours là.* When we got back Mom was still there.

toundra [tundʀa] nf tundra

toupet [tupɛ] nm (informal): **avoir**

du toupet to have a nerve
tour [tuʀ] nf ❶ tower ▷ *la Tour CN* the CN Tower ❷ high-rise; **une tour à bureaux** an office tower; **une tour d'habitation** an apartment high-rise
▶ nm turn ▷ *C'est ton tour de jouer.* It's your turn to play.; **faire un tour** to go for a walk ▷ *Allons faire un tour dans le parc.* Let's go for a walk in the park.; **faire un tour en voiture** to go for a drive; **faire un tour à vélo** to go for a ride ▷ *Tu veux aller faire un tour à vélo?* Do you want to go for a bike ride?; **faire le tour du monde** to travel around the world; **à tour de rôle** alternately; **un tour de magie** magic trick ▷ *faire des tours de magie* to do magic tricks; **le tour du chapeau** (sports) hat trick
tourbillon [tuʀbijɔ̃] nm whirlpool
tourisme [tuʀism(ə)] nm tourism
touriste [tuʀist(ə)] nmf tourist
touristique [tuʀistik] adj tourist
se **tourmenter** [tuʀmɑ̃te] vb to fret ▷ *Ne te tourmente pas, ça s'arrangera.* Don't fret about it, it'll be all right.
tournant [tuʀnɑ̃] nm ❶ bend ▷ *Il y a beaucoup de tournants dangereux sur cette route.* There are a lot of dangerous bends in this road. ❷ turning point ▷ *Ça a été un tournant dans sa vie.* It was a turning point in his life.
tournée [tuʀne] nf ❶ round ▷ *Le facteur commence sa tournée à sept heures du matin.* The letter carrier starts his round at 7 o'clock in the morning. ❷ tour ▷ *Elle est en tournée aux T.N.-O.* She's on tour in the NWT.
tourner [tuʀne] vb ❶ to turn ▷ *Tournez à droite au prochain feu.* Turn right at the next lights. ▷ *Tourne-toi un peu plus vers moi, et*

souris! Turn towards me a bit more, and smile! ❷ to go sour ▷ *Le lait a tourné.* The milk has gone sour.; **mal tourner** to go wrong ▷ *Ça a mal tourné.* It all went wrong.; **tourner le dos à quelqu'un** to have one's back to somebody; **tourner un film** to shoot a movie
tournesol [tuʀnəsɔl] nm sunflower
tournevis [tuʀnəvis] nm screwdriver
tournoi [tuʀnwa] nm tournament
tourtière [tuʀtjɛʀ] nf
  In Canada, **la tourtière** is a pie made with various combinations of ground meat (beef, lamb, veal, and primarily pork) and served at Christmastime. The **tourtière du Lac-Saint-Jean** is a variation using cubed game, chicken, pork, potatoes, and onions, baked for several hours.
tous [tus] adj, pron see **tout**
tousser [tuse] vb to cough
tout [tu, tut] (mpl **tous**, fpl **toutes**) adj, adv, pron ❶ all ▷ *tout le lait* all the milk ▷ *toute la nuit* all night ▷ *tous les livres* all the books ▷ *toutes les filles* all the girls ▷ *toute la journée* all day ▷ *tout le temps* all the time ▷ *C'est tout.* That's all. ▷ *Je les connais tous.* I know them all. ▷ *Nous y sommes toutes allées.* We all went. ▷ *Ça fait combien en tout?* How much is that all together?; **Elle est toute seule.** She's all alone.; **pas du tout** not at all; **tout de même** all the same ❷ every ▷ *tous les jours* every day ▷ *tous les deux jours* every two days; **tout le monde** everybody; **tous les deux** both ▷ *Nous y sommes allés tous les deux.* We both went.; **tous les trois** all three ▷ *Je les ai invités tous les trois.* I invited all three of them. ❸ everything ▷ *Il a tout*

organisé. He organized everything.
❹ very ▷ *J'habite tout près.* I live
very close by.; **tout en haut** right
at the top; **tout droit** straight
ahead; **tout d'abord** first of all;
tout à coup suddenly; **tout à fait**
absolutely ❺ quite; **tout à l'heure**
(1) just now ▷ *Je l'ai vu tout à l'heure.* I
saw him just now. (2) in a moment
▷ *Je finirai ça tout à l'heure.* I'll finish
it in a moment.; **À tout à l'heure!**
See you later!; **tout de suite** right
away; **Nous avons fait notre
travail tout en chantant.** We sang
as we worked.
tout-aller *adj* casual ▷ *des
chaussures tout-aller* casual shoes
▷ *un manteau tout-aller* casual coat
toutefois [tutfwa] *adv* however
toutes [tut] *adj, pron see* **tout**
toux [tu] *nf* cough
toxicomane [tɔksikɔman] *nmf*
drug addict
toxicomanie [tɔksikɔmani] *nf*
drug addiction
toxique [tɔksik] *adj* toxic; **les
déchets toxiques** toxic waste
TPS [tepeɛs] *nf* GST ▷ *Est-ce qu'il
faut payer la TPS sur les livres?* Do you
have to pay GST on books?
trac [trak] *nm:* **avoir le trac** to be
feeling nervous
tracasser [trakase] *vb* to worry
▷ *La santé de ma mère me tracasse.*
My mom's health worries me.; **se
tracasser** to worry ▷ *Arrête de te
tracasser pour rien!* Stop worrying
about nothing!
trace [tras] *nf* ❶ trace ▷ *Le voleur
n'a pas laissé de traces.* The thief left
no traces. ❷ mark ▷ *des traces de
doigts* finger marks; **des traces de
pas** footprints
tracer [trase] *vb* to draw ▷ *tracer
un trait* to draw a line
tracteur [traktœr] *nm* tractor

tradition [tradisjɔ̃] *nf* tradition
traditionnel [tradisjɔnɛl] (*f*
traditionnelle) *adj* traditional
traducteur [tradyktœr] *nm*
translator
traduction [tradyksjɔ̃] *nf*
translation
traductrice [tradyktris] *nf*
translator
traduire [traduir] *vb* to translate
trafic [trafik] *nm* traffic ▷ *le trafic
aérien* air traffic; **le trafic de drogue**
drug trafficking
trafiquant [trafikɑ̃] *nm:* **un
trafiquant de drogue** a drug
trafficker
tragique [traʒik] *adj* tragic
trahir [trair] *vb* to betray
trahison [traizɔ̃] *nf* betrayal
train [trɛ̃] *nm* train; **un train
électrique** a train set; **Elle est en
train de manger.** She's eating.; **le
train de banlieue** commuter train
traîneau [trɛno] (*pl* **traîneaux**)
nm sled
traîner [trɛne] *vb* ❶ to wander
around ▷ *J'ai vu des jeunes qui
traînaient en ville.* I saw some young
people wandering around town.
❷ to dawdle ▷ *Dépêche-toi, ne
traîne pas!* Hurry up, don't dawdle!
❸ to drag on ▷ *La réunion a traîné
jusqu'à midi.* The meeting dragged
on till 12 o'clock.; **traîner des pieds**
to drag one's feet; **laisser traîner
qch** to leave sth lying around ▷ *Ne
laisse pas traîner tes affaires.* Don't
leave your things lying around.
traîne sauvage [trɛn-] *nf*
toboggan; **faire de la traîne
sauvage** to go tobogganing
train-train [trɛ̃trɛ̃] *nm* daily
routine
traire [trɛr] *vb* to milk
trait [trɛ] *nm* ❶ line ▷ *Tracez un
trait.* Draw a line. ❷ feature ▷ *avoir*

les traits réguliers to have regular features ❸ characteristic ▷ *un de tes plus beaux traits* one of the nicest things about you; **un trait de personnalité** personality trait; **boire quelque chose d'un trait** to drink something down in one gulp; **un trait d'union** a hyphen

traité [tʀete] nm treaty

traitement [tʀetmɑ̃] nm treatment; **le traitement de texte** word processing; **le traitement de données** data processing

traiter [tʀete] vb to treat ▷ *Elle le traite bien.* She treats him well.; **Il m'a traité d'imbécile.** He called me an idiot.; **traiter de** to be about ▷ *Cet article traite des sans-abri.* This article is about the homeless.

traiteur [tʀetœʀ] nm caterer

trajet [tʀaʒe] nm ❶ journey ▷ *Ils n'ont pas arrêté de parler pendant tout le trajet.* They talked for the whole journey. ▷ *J'ai une heure de trajet pour aller au travail.* My journey to work takes an hour. ❷ route ▷ *C'est le trajet le plus court.* It's the shortest route.

tramway [tʀamwe] nm streetcar

tranchant [tʀɑ̃ʃɑ̃, -ɑ̃t] (f **tranchante**) adj (knife) sharp

tranche [tʀɑ̃ʃ] nf slice

tranquille [tʀɑ̃kil] adj quiet ▷ *Cette rue est très tranquille.* This is a very quiet street.; **Sois tranquille, il ne va rien lui arriver.** Don't worry, nothing will happen to him.; **Tiens-toi tranquille!** Be quiet!; **Laisse-moi tranquille.** Leave me alone.; **Laisse ça tranquille.** Leave it alone.

tranquillement [tʀɑ̃kilmɑ̃] adv quietly ▷ *Nous étions tranquillement installés dans le salon.* We were just sitting quietly in the living room.; **Je peux travailler tranquillement**

cinq minutes? Can I have five minutes to work in peace?

tranquillité [tʀɑ̃kilite] nf peace and quiet

Transcanadienne [tʀɑ̃skanadjɛn] nf Trans-Canada Highway

transférer [tʀɑ̃sfeʀe] vb to transfer

transformer [tʀɑ̃sfɔʀme] vb ❶ to transform ▷ *Son séjour en Saskatchewan l'a transformé.* His stay in Saskatchewan has transformed him. ❷ to convert ▷ *Ils ont transformé la grange en garage.* They've converted the barn into a garage.; **se transformer en** to turn into ▷ *La chenille se transforme en papillon.* The caterpillar turns into a butterfly.

transfusion [tʀɑ̃sfyzjɔ̃] nf: **une transfusion sanguine** a blood transfusion

transiger [tʀɑ̃ziʒe] vb to compromise

transmettre [tʀɑ̃smetʀ(ə)] vb to broadcast ▷ *On a transmis le discours du premier ministre à la radio.* They broadcast the prime minister's speech on the radio.; **transmettre quelque chose à quelqu'un** to pass something to somebody

transparent [tʀɑ̃spaʀɑ̃] nm transparency ▷ *Mets le transparent dans le rétroprojecteur.* Put the transparency on the overhead projector.

transpercer [tʀɑ̃speʀse] vb to go through ▷ *La pluie a transpercé mes vêtements.* The rain went through my clothes.

transpiration [tʀɑ̃spiʀasjɔ̃] nf perspiration

transpirer [tʀɑ̃spiʀe] vb to perspire

transport [tʀɑ̃spɔʀ] nm

transport; **les transports en commun** public transport

transporter [tʀɑ̃spɔʀte] *vb* **①** to carry ▷ *Le train transportait des marchandises.* The train was carrying freight. **②** to move ▷ *Je ne sais pas comment je vais transporter mes affaires.* I don't know how I'm going to move my stuff.

traumatiser [tʀomatize] *vb* to traumatize

travail [tʀavaj, -o] (*pl* **travaux**) *nm* **①** work ▷ *J'ai beaucoup de travail.* I've got a lot of work. **②** job ▷ *Il a un travail intéressant.* He's got an interesting job.; **Il est sans travail depuis un an.** He has been out of work for a year.; **le travail au noir** moonlighting

travailler [tʀavaje] *vb* to work

travailleur [tʀavajœʀ, -øz] (*f* **travailleuse**) *adj* hard-working ▶ *nm* worker

travailleuse [tʀavajøz] *nf* worker

travaillistes [tʀavajist] *nmpl* the Labour Party

travaux [tʀavo] *nmpl* **①** work ▷ *des travaux de construction* building work **②** roadworks ▷ *Il y a beaucoup de bruit à cause des travaux dans la rue.* There's a lot of noise from the roadworks.; **être en travaux** to be undergoing alterations; **les travaux dirigés** supervised practical work; **les travaux manuels** handicrafts; **les travaux ménagers** housework; **les travaux pratiques** practical work

travers [tʀavɛʀ] *nm*: **en travers de** across ▷ *Il y avait un arbre en travers de la route.* There was a tree lying across the road.; **de travers** crooked ▷ *Son chapeau était de travers.* His hat was crooked.; **comprendre de travers** to misunderstand ▷ *Elle comprend*

toujours tout de travers. She always gets the wrong idea.; **J'ai avalé de travers.** Something went down the wrong way.; **à travers** through ▷ *Cette vitre est tellement sale qu'on ne voit rien à travers.* This window is so dirty that you can't see anything through it.

traversée [tʀavɛʀse] *nf* crossing

traverser [tʀavɛʀse] *vb* **①** to cross ▷ *Traversez la rue.* Cross the street. **②** to go through ▷ *Nous avons traversé l'Alberta pour aller en Colombie-Britannique.* We went through Alberta on the way to British Columbia. ▷ *La pluie a traversé mon manteau.* The rain went through my coat.

traversier [tʀavɛʀsje] *nm* ferry

trébucher [tʀebyʃe] *vb* (trip) to stumble

trèfle [tʀɛfl(ə)] *nm* **①** clover **②** clubs **③** (*at cards*) ▷ *le roi de trèfle* the king of clubs

treize [tʀɛz] *num* thirteen ▷ *Il a treize ans.* He's thirteen. ▷ *à treize heures* at 1 p.m.; **le treize février** the thirteenth of February

treizième [tʀɛzjɛm] *adj* thirteenth

tremblement de terre [tʀɑ̃bləmɑ̃-] *nm* earthquake

trembler [tʀɑ̃ble] *vb* to tremble ▷ *trembler de peur* to tremble with fear; **trembler de froid** to shiver

trempé [tʀɑ̃pe] (*f* **trempée**) *adj* soaking wet; **trempé jusqu'aux os** soaked to the skin

tremper [tʀɑ̃pe] *vb* to soak; **tremper sa main dans l'eau** to dip one's hand in the water

trempette [tʀɑ̃pɛt] *nf* dip ▷ *une trempette à l'ail* a garlic dip

tremplin [tʀɑ̃plɛ̃] *nm* **①** diving board **②** ski jump

trentaine [tʀɑ̃tɛn] *nf* about thirty ▷ *une trentaine de personnes* about thirty people; **Il a la trentaine.** He's in his thirties.

trente [trɑ̃t] *num* thirty ▷ *Elle a trente ans.* She's thirty.; **le trente janvier** the thirtieth of January; **trente et un** thirty-one; **trente-deux** thirty-two

trentième [trɑ̃tjɛm] *adj* thirtieth

très [trɛ] *adv* very

trésor [trezɔr] *nm* treasure

tresse [trɛs] *nf* braid; **les tresses rasta** dreadlocks

tresser [trese] *vb* to braid

triangle [trijɑ̃gl(ə)] *nm* triangle

tribunal [tribynal, -o] *(pl tribunaux)* *nm* court

tribune téléphonique [tribyn-] *nf* (phone-in show) hotline

tricher [triʃe] *vb* to cheat

tricot [triko] *nm* knitting ▷ *Ma grand-mère aime faire du tricot.* My grandmother enjoys knitting.

tricoter [trikɔte] *vb* to knit

trier [trije] *vb* to sort out ▷ *Je vais trier mes papiers avant de partir en vacances.* I'm going to sort out my papers before I go on holiday.

trimestre [trimɛstr(ə)] *nm* term

triomphe [trijɔ̃f] *nm* triumph

triompher [trijɔ̃fe] *vb* to triumph

triple [tripl(ə)] *nm*: **Ça m'a coûté le triple.** It cost me three times as much.; **Il gagne le triple de mon salaire.** He earns three times my salary.

triplées [triple] *nfpl* triplets

tripler [triple] *vb* to treble

triplés [triple] *nmpl* triplets

triste [trist(ə)] *adj* sad

tristesse [tristɛs] *nf* sadness

trognon [trɔɲɔ̃] *nm* core ▷ *un trognon de pomme* an apple core

trois [trwa] *num* three ▷ *à trois heures du matin* at three in the morning ▷ *Elle a trois ans.* She's three. ▷ *trois fois* three times; **le**

trois février the third of February

troisième [trwazjɛm] *adj* third ▷ *au troisième étage* on the third floor

trois-quarts *nmpl* three-quarters ▷ *les trois-quarts de la classe* three-quarters of the class

trombone [trɔ̃bɔn] *nm* ❶ trombone ▷ *Il joue du trombone.* He plays the trombone. ❷ paper clip

trompe [trɔ̃p] *nf* trunk ▷ *la trompe d'un éléphant* an elephant's trunk

tromper [trɔ̃pe] *vb* to deceive; **se tromper** to make a mistake ▷ *Tout le monde peut se tromper.* Anyone can make a mistake.; **se tromper de jour** to get the wrong day; **Vous vous êtes trompé de numéro.** You've got the wrong number.

trompette [trɔ̃pɛt] *nf* trumpet ▷ *Elle joue de la trompette.* She plays the trumpet.; **Elle a le nez en trompette.** She has a turned-up nose.

tronc [trɔ̃] *nm* trunk ▷ *un tronc d'arbre* a tree trunk

trop [tro] *adv* ❶ too ▷ *Il conduit trop vite.* He drives too fast. ❷ too much ▷ *J'ai trop mangé.* I've eaten too much.; **trop de (1)** too much ▷ *J'ai acheté trop de pain.* I bought too much bread. ▷ *trois dollars de trop* 3 dollars too much **(2)** too many ▷ *Nous avons apporté trop de vêtements.* We brought too many clothes.; **trois personnes de trop** 3 people too many

tropique [trɔpik] *nm* tropic

trottoir [trɔtwar] *nm* sidewalk

trou [tru] *nm* hole; **J'ai eu un trou de mémoire.** My mind went blank.; **le trou noir** black hole

trouble [trubl(ə)] *adj, adv* cloudy ▷ *L'eau est trouble.* The water's cloudy.

trouble [trubl(ə)] *nm*: **une période**

de **troubles politiques** a period of political instability; **le trouble alimentaire** eating disorder

trouer [tʀue] vb to make a hole in

trouille [tʀuj] nf: **avoir la trouille** (informal) to be scared to death

troupe [tʀup] nf troop; **une troupe de théâtre** a theatre company

troupeau [tʀupo] (pl troupeaux) nm: **un troupeau de moutons** a flock of sheep; **un troupeau de vaches** a herd of cows

trousse [tʀus] nf kit ▷ *une trousse de secours* a first-aid kit; **une trousse de maquillage** a make-up bag

trouver [tʀuve] vb ❶ to find ▷ *Je ne trouve pas mes lunettes.* I can't find my glasses. ❷ to think ▷ *Je trouve que c'est bête.* I think it's stupid.; **se trouver** to be ▷ *Où se trouve le bureau de poste?* Where is the post office? ▷ *Hull se trouve au Québec. Hull is in Québec.*; **se trouver mal** to pass out

truc [tʀyk] nm ❶ (informal) thing ▷ *un truc en plastique* a plastic thing ❷ trick ▷ *Je vais te montrer un truc qui réussit à tous les coups.* I'll show you a trick that never fails.

truite [tʀɥit] nf trout

T-shirt [tiʃœʀt] nm T-shirt

tu [ty] pron you ▷ *Est-ce que tu as un animal domestique?* Have you got a pet?

tuba [tyba] nm ❶ tuba ▷ *Je joue du tuba.* I play the tuba. ❷ snorkel

tube [tyb] nm tube ▷ *un tube de dentifrice* a tube of toothpaste; **un tube de rouge à lèvres** a lipstick

tuer [tɥe] vb to kill; **se tuer** to get killed ▷ *Elle s'est tuée dans un accident de voiture.* She got killed in a car accident.

tuile [tɥil] nf tile

tunique [tynik] nf tunic

tunnel [tynɛl] nm tunnel
▷ *Empruntez le tunnel qui passe sous le fleuve Fraser.* Take the tunnel under the Fraser River.

turbulent [tyʀbylɑ̃, -ɑ̃t] (f **turbulente**) adj boisterous

tutoyer [tytwaje] vb: **tutoyer quelqu'un** to address somebody as "tu"

● **tutoyer quelqu'un** means to use
● **tu** when speaking to someone,
● rather than **vous**. Use **tu** only
● when talking to one person and
● when that person is someone
● of your own age or whom you
● know well; use **vous** to everyone
● else. If in doubt use **vous**.
On se tutoie? Shall we use "tu" to each other?

tuyau [tɥijo] (pl **tuyaux**) nm pipe; **un tuyau d'arrosage** a hose

tweet [tyit] nm (on Twitter) tweet

tweeter [tyite] vb (on Twitter) to tweet

Twitter® [tyiteʀ] nm Twitter®

tympan [tɛ̃pɑ̃] nm eardrum

type [tip] nm (kind) type ▷ *Il y a plusieurs types de vélo de montagne.* There are many types of mountain bike.

typique [tipik] adj typical

tyran [tiʀɑ̃] nm tyrant ▷ *C'est un vrai tyran.* He's a real tyrant.

u

un [œ̃] art, pron, adj ❶ a ▷ *un garçon* a boy, an ▷ *un œuf* an egg ❷ one ▷ *l'un des meilleurs* one of the best ▷ *un citron et deux oranges* one lemon and two oranges ▷ *« Combien de timbres ? »* — *« Un. »* "How many stamps?" — "One." ▷ *Elle a un an.* She's one year old.; **l'un..., l'autre...** one..., the other... ▷ *L'un est grand, l'autre est petit.* One is tall, the other is short.; **les uns..., les autres...** some..., others... ▷ *Les uns marchaient, les autres couraient.* Some were walking, others were running.; **l'un ou l'autre** either of them ▷ *Prends l'un ou l'autre, ça m'est égal.* Take either of them, I don't mind.; **un par un** one by one ▷ *Ils entraient un par un.* They went in one by one.

unanime [ynanim] *adj* unanimous

unanimité [ynanimite] *nf*: **à**

l'unanimité unanimously

une [yn] *art, pron, adj* ❶ a ▷ *une fille* a girl, an ▷ *une pomme* an apple ❷ one ▷ *une pomme et deux bananes* one apple and two bananas ▷ *« Combien de cartes postales ? »* — *« Une. »* "How many postcards?" — "One." ▷ *à une heure du matin* at one in the morning ▷ *l'une des meilleures* one of the best; **l'une..., l'autre...** one..., the other... ▷ *L'une est grande, l'autre est petite.* One is tall, the other is short.; **les unes..., les autres...** some..., others... ▷ *Les unes marchaient, les autres couraient.* Some were walking, others were running.; **l'une ou l'autre** either of them ▷ *Prends l'une ou l'autre, ça m'est égal.* Take either of them, I don't mind.; **une par une** one by one ▷ *Elles entraient une par une.* They went in one by one.

uni [yni] (*f* **unie**) *adj* ❶ plain ▷ *un tissu uni* a plain fabric ❷ close-knit ▷ *une famille unie* a close-knit family

unifolié [ynifɔlje] *nm* the Canadian flag

uniforme [ynifɔʀm(ə)] *nm* uniform

unilingue [ynilɛ̃g] *adj* unilingual

union [ynjɔ̃] *nf* union

unique [ynik] *adj* unique ▷ *Tout individu a des empreintes uniques.* Everyone's fingerprints are unique. ▷ *C'est une occasion unique.* It's a unique opportunity.; **Il est fils unique.** He's an only child.; **Elle est fille unique.** She's an only child.

uniquement [ynikmɑ̃] *adv* only

unité [ynite] *nf* ❶ unity ▷ *l'unité nationale* national unity ❷ unit ▷ *une unité de mesure* a unit of measurement

univers [ynivɛʀ] *nm* universe

universitaire [ynivɛʀsitɛʀ] *adj* university ▷ *un diplôme universitaire* a university degree ▷ *le campus universitaire* university campus; **faire des études universitaires** to study at university

université [ynivεʁsite] *nf* university ▷ *aller à l'université* to go to university

urgence [yʁʒɑ̃s] *nf*: **C'est une urgence.** It's urgent.; **Il n'y a pas urgence.** It's not urgent.; **le service des urgences** the emergency department; **Il a été transporté d'urgence à l'hôpital.** He was rushed to hospital.; **Téléphonez d'urgence.** Phone as soon as possible.

urgent [yʁʒɑ̃, -ɑ̃t] (**urgente**) *adj* urgent

urine [yʁin] *nf* urine

usage [yzaʒ] *nm* use ▷ *à usage interne* for internal use ▷ *à usage externe* for external use only; **hors d'usage** out of service ▷ *Cet appareil est hors d'usage.* That machine's out of service.

usagé [yzaʒe] (**usagée**) *adj* ❶ old ▷ *un manteau usagé* an old coat ❷ used ▷ *une seringue usagée* a used syringe

usager [yzaʒe] *nm* user ▷ *les usagers de la route* road users

usagère [yzaʒɛʁ] *nf* user ▷ *une usagère des transports publics* a public transit user

usé [yze] (**usée**) *adj* worn ▷ *Mes jeans sont un peu usés.* My jeans are a bit worn.

s'user [yze] *vb* to wear out ▷ *Mes pantoufles se sont usées en quinze jours.* My slippers wore out in two weeks.

usine [yzin] *nf* factory ▷ *une usine de meubles* a furniture factory

ustensile [ystɑ̃sil] *nm*: **un ustensile de cuisine** a kitchen utensil; **les ustensiles** cutlery

usuel [yzɥεl] (**fusuelle**) *adj* everyday ▷ *la langue usuelle* everyday language

utile [ytil] *adj* useful

utilisateur [ytilizatœʁ] *nm* (technology) user ▷ *un utilisateur d'Internet* an Internet user

utilisation [ytilizasjɔ̃] *nf* use ▷ *L'utilisation des calculatrices est interdite.* It is forbidden to use calculators.

utilisatrice [ytilizatʁis] *nf* (technology) user ▷ *une utilisatrice d'Internet* an Internet user

utiliser [ytilize] *vb* to use

utilité [ytilite] *nf* (usefulness) use ▷ *Cet objet n'est pas d'une grande utilité.* This object isn't much use.

V

va [va] *vb see* **aller**

vacances [vakɑ̃s] *nfpl* ❶ vacation ▷ *aller en vacances* to go on vacation ▷ *être en vacances* to be on vacation ❷ holidays ▷ *les vacances de Noël* the Christmas holidays ▷ *les vacances de Pâques* the Easter holidays ▷ *les vacances d'été* the summer holidays

vacarme [vakaʀm(ə)] *nm* racket ▷ *Qu'est-ce que c'est que ce vacarme?* What's all this racket?

vaccin [vaksɛ̃] *nm* vaccination

vaccination [vaksinasjɔ̃] *nf* vaccination ▷ *La vaccination est obligatoire.* Vaccination is compulsory.

vacciner [vaksine] *vb* to vaccinate ▷ *se faire vacciner contre la rubéole* to be vaccinated against German measles

vache [vaʃ] *nf* cow
▶ *adj* (informal) mean ▷ *C'est*

vraiment vache, ce qu'il a dit. What he said was really mean.

vadrouille [vadʀuj] *nf* mop ▷ *J'ai passé la vadrouille sur le plancher.* I mopped the floor.

vagabond [vagabɔ̃] *nm* transient

vagabonde [vagabɔ̃d] *nf* transient

vagin [vaʒɛ̃] *nm* vagina

vague [vag] *nf* (*in sea*) wave; **une vague de chaleur** a heat wave
▶ *adj* vague ▷ *J'ai un vague souvenir d'elle.* I vaguely remember her.

vain [vɛ̃, vɛn] (*f* **vaine**) *adj*: **en vain** in vain

vaincre [vɛ̃kʀ(ə)] *vb* ❶ to defeat ▷ *L'armée a été vaincue.* The army was defeated. ❷ to overcome ▷ *Il a réussi à vaincre sa timidité.* He managed to overcome his shyness.

vainqueur [vɛ̃kœʀ] *nm* winner

vais [vɛ] *vb see* **aller**; **Je vais écrire à mes cousins.** I'm going to write to my cousins.

vaisseau [veso] (*pl* **vaisseaux**) *nm*: **un vaisseau spatial** a spaceship; **un vaisseau sanguin** a blood vessel

vaisselle [vesɛl] *nf* dishes ▷ *Je vais faire la vaisselle.* I'll do the dishes. ▷ *Peux-tu ranger la vaisselle s'il te plaît?* Can you put the dishes away please?

valable [valabl(ə)] *adj* valid ▷ *Ce billet d'avion est valable un an.* This plane ticket is valid for one year.

valentin [valɑ̃tɛ̃] *nm* (*person*) valentine ▷ *Seras-tu mon valentin?* Will you be my valentine?

valentine [valɑ̃tin] *nf* (*person*) valentine ▷ *Seras-tu ma valentine?* Will you be my valentine?

valet [valɛ] *nm* (*in card games*) jack ▷ *le valet de carreau* the jack of diamonds

valeur [valœʀ] *nf* value ▷ *sans*

valeur of no value; **des objets de valeur** valuables ▷ *Ne laissez pas d'objets de valeur dans votre chambre.* Don't leave any valuables in your room.

valider [valide] *vb* to stamp ▷ *Vous devez faire valider votre billet avant votre départ.* You must get your ticket stamped before you leave.

valise [valiz] *nf* suitcase; **faire sa valise** to pack

vallée [vale] *nf* valley; **la vallée du Bas-Fraser** the Lower Mainland

valoir [valwar] *vb* to be worth ▷ *Ça vaut combien?* How much is it worth? ▷ *Cette voiture vaut très cher.* This car's worth a lot of money.; **Ça vaut mieux.** That would be better. ▷ *Il vaut mieux ne rien dire.* It would be better to say nothing.; **valoir la peine** to be worth it ▷ *Ça vaudrait la peine d'essayer.* It would be worth a try.

vampire [vɑ̃pir] *nmf* vampire

vandale [vɑ̃dal] *nmf* vandal

vandaliser [vɑ̃dalize] *vb* to vandalize

vandalisme [vɑ̃dalism(ə)] *nm* vandalism

vanille [vanij] *nf* vanilla ▷ *une crème glacée à la vanille* a vanilla ice cream

vanité [vanite] *nf* vanity

vaniteux [vanitø, -øz] (*f* **vaniteuse**) *adj* conceited

se vanter [vɑ̃te] *vb* to brag

vapeur [vapœr] *nf* steam ▷ *des légumes cuits à la vapeur* steamed vegetables

variable [varjabl(ə)] *adj* (*weather*) changeable

varicelle [varisɛl] *nf* chickenpox ▷ *Elle a la varicelle.* She has chickenpox.

varié [varje] (*f* **variée**) *adj* varied ▷ *Son travail est très varié.* His job is

very varied.

varier [varje] *vb* to vary; **Le menu varie tous les jours.** The menu changes every day.

variété [varjete] *nf* variety ▷ *Il n'y a pas beaucoup de variété.* There isn't much variety.; **une émission de variétés** (*television*) a variety show

vas [va] *vb see* **aller**

vase [vaz] *nm* vase
▷ *nf* mud

vaste [vast(ə)] *adj* vast

vaudrait, vaut *vb see* **valoir**

vautour [votur] *nm* vulture

veau [vo] (*pl* **veaux**) *nm* ❶ (*animal*) calf ❷ (*meat*) veal

vécu [veky] *vb see* **vivre**; **Elle a vécu à Laval pendant dix ans.** She lived in Laval for ten years.

vedette [vədɛt] *nf* ❶ star ▷ *une vedette de cinéma* a movie star ❷ motorboat

végétal [veʒetal, -o] (*f* **végétale**, *mpl* **végétaux**) *adj* vegetable ▷ *l'huile végétale* vegetable oil

végétalien [veʒetaljɛ̃, -ɛn] (*f* **végétalienne**) *adj* vegan

végétarien [veʒetaʁjɛ̃, -ɛn] (*f* **végétarienne**) *adj* vegetarian ▷ *Je suis végétarien.* I'm a vegetarian.

végétation [veʒetasjɔ̃] *nf* vegetation

véhicule [veikyl] *nm* vehicle ▷ *le véhicule utilitaire sport* sport utility vehicle

veille [vɛj] *nf* the day before ▷ *la veille de son départ* the day before he left ▷ *La veille au soir* the previous evening; **la veille de Noël** Christmas Eve; **la veille du jour de l'An** New Year's Eve; **la mode Veille** (*computing*) standby mode

veiller [veje] *vb* to stay up; **veiller sur quelqu'un** to watch over somebody

veine [vɛn] *nf* vein; **avoir de la**

veine (informal) to be lucky

véliplanchiste [veliplɑ̃ʃist(ə)] nmf windsurfer

vélo [velo] nm bike ▷ *faire du vélo* to go biking; **un vélo de montagne** a mountain bike; **un vélo d'exercice** an exercise bike

vélomoteur [velomotœʀ] nm moped

velours [vəluʀ] nm velvet ▷ *une robe en velours* a velvet dress; **le velours côtelé** corduroy ▷ *un pantalon en velours côtelé* corduroy pants

vendeur [vɑ̃dœʀ] nm (in store) salesperson

vendeuse [vɑ̃døz] nf (in store) salesperson

vendre [vɑ̃dʀ(ə)] vb to sell; **vendre quelque chose à quelqu'un** to sell somebody something ▷ *Elle m'a vendu son vélo.* She sold me her bike.; **« à vendre »** "for sale"

vendredi [vɑ̃dʀədi] nm ❶ Friday ▷ *Aujourd'hui, nous sommes vendredi.* It's Friday today. ❷ on Friday ▷ *Il est venu vendredi.* He came on Friday.; **le vendredi** on Fridays ▷ *Je joue au hockey le vendredi.* I play hockey on Fridays.; **tous les vendredis** every Friday; **vendredi dernier** last Friday; **vendredi prochain** next Friday; **le Vendredi saint** Good Friday

vénéneux [venenø, -øz] (f **vénéneuse**) adj (plant) poisonous ▷ *un champignon vénéneux* a poisonous mushroom

vengeance [vɑ̃ʒɑ̃s] nf revenge

se venger [vɑ̃ʒe] vb to get revenge

venimeux [vənimø, -øz] (f **venimeuse**) adj (animal) poisonous ▷ *un serpent venimeux* a poisonous snake

venin [vənɛ̃] nm poison

venir [vəniʀ] vb to come ▷ *Il viendra*

demain. He'll come tomorrow. ▷ *Elle est venue nous voir.* She came to see us.; **venir de** to have just ▷ *Je viens de la voir.* I've just seen her. ▷ *Je viens de lui téléphoner.* I've just phoned her.; **faire venir quelqu'un** to send for somebody ▷ *faire venir le plombier* to send for the plumber

vent [vɑ̃] nm wind ▷ *Il y a du vent.* It's windy.

vente [vɑ̃t] nf sale; **en vente** on sale ▷ *Ce modèle est en vente dans les grands magasins.* This model is on sale in department stores.; **la vente par téléphone** telemarketing; **une vente aux enchères** an auction; **une vente de garage** a garage sale

ventilateur [vɑ̃tilatœʀ] nm (for cooling) fan

ventre [vɑ̃tʀ(ə)] nm stomach ▷ *avoir mal au ventre* to have a stomachache

venu [vəny] vb see **venir**

ver [vɛʀ] nm worm; **un ver de terre** an earthworm

verbe [vɛʀb(ə)] nm verb

verbomoteur [vɛʀbomotœʀ] nm talkative person

verbomotrice [vɛʀbomotʀis] nf talkative person ▷ *Cette politicienne est plutôt verbomotrice.* This politician is quite a talkative person.

verger [vɛʀʒe] nm orchard

verglacé [vɛʀɡlase] (f **verglacée**) adj icy ▷ *La route était verglacée.* The road was icy.

verglas [vɛʀɡla] nm black ice; **la tempête de verglas** ice storm

véridique [veʀidik] adj truthful

vérification [veʀifikasjɔ̃] nf check ▷ *une vérification d'identité* an identity check

vérifier [veʀifje] vb to check

véritable [veʀitabl(ə)] adj real

▷ C'était un véritable cauchemar. It was a real nightmare.; **en cuir véritable** made of real leather

vérité [veʀite] nf truth ▷ *dire la vérité* to tell the truth

verni [vɛʀni] (f **vernie**) adj varnished

vernir [vɛʀniʀ] vb to varnish

vernis [vɛʀni] nm varnish; **le vernis à ongles** nail polish

verra, verrai, verras vb see **voir**; **on verra...** we'll see...

verre [vɛʀ] nm ❶ glass ▷ *un bibelot en verre* a glass ornament ▷ *un verre d'eau* a glass of water ❷ (*of spectacles*) lens ▷ *des verres de contact* contact lenses

verrez, verrons, verront vb see **voir**

verrou [veʀu] nm (*on door*) bolt

verrouiller [veʀuje] vb to bolt ▷ *N'oublie pas de verrouiller la porte du garage.* Don't forget to bolt the garage door.

verrue [veʀy] nf wart

vers [vɛʀ] nm (*of poetry*) line ▷ *au troisième vers* in the third line ▶ prep ❶ towards ▷ *Il allait vers l'école.* He was going towards the school. ❷ about ▷ *Nous sommes rentrés chez nous vers cinq heures.* We went home at about 5 o'clock.

verse [vɛʀs(ə)]: **à verse** adv ▷ *Il pleut à verse.* It's pouring rain.

Verseau [vɛʀso] nm Aquarius ▷ *Il est Verseau.* He's an Aquarius.

versement [vɛʀsəmɑ̃] nm instalment ▷ *en cinq versements* in 5 instalments

verser [vɛʀse] vb to pour ▷ *Est-ce que tu peux me verser un verre d'eau?* Could you pour me a glass of water?

version [vɛʀsjɔ̃] nf ❶ version ❷ (*from the foreign language*) translation; **un film en version originale** a film in the original language

verso [vɛʀso] nm (*of sheet of paper*) back; **voir au verso** see other side

vert [vɛʀ, vɛʀt(ə)] (f **verte**) adj green

vertèbre [vɛʀtɛbʀ(ə)] nf vertebra

vertical [vɛʀtikal, -o] (f **verticale**, mpl **verticaux**) adj vertical

vertige [vɛʀtiʒ] nm fear of heights ▷ *avoir le vertige* to be afraid of heights

veste [vɛst(ə)] nf ❶ jacket ❷ (*sleeveless*) vest ▷ *une veste en polaire* a polar fleece vest

vestiaire [vɛstjɛʀ] nm ❶ (*in theatre, museum*) cloakroom ❷ (*at school, sports complex*) changing room

vestibule [vɛstibyl] nm hall

vêtement [vɛtmɑ̃] nm article of clothing; **les vêtements** clothes

vétérinaire [veteʀinɛʀ] nmf vet ▷ *Elle est vétérinaire.* She's a vet.

veuf [vœf] nm widower ▷ *Il est veuf.* He's a widower.

veuille, veuillez, veuillons, veulent, veut vb see **vouloir**; **Veuillez fermer la porte en sortant.** Please shut the door when you go out.

veuve [vœv] nf widow ▷ *Elle est veuve.* She's a widow.

veux [vø] vb see **vouloir**

vexer [vɛkse] vb: **vexer quelqu'un** to hurt somebody's feelings; **se vexer** to be offended

viande [vjɑ̃d] nf meat; **la viande hachée** hamburger meat

vibrer [vibʀe] vb to vibrate

vice [vis] nm vise

victime [viktim] nf victim

victoire [viktwaʀ] nf victory

vidanges [vidɑ̃ʒ] nfpl garbage ▷ *As-tu sorti les vidanges dehors?* Did you put the garbage out?; **le camion de vidanges** garbage truck;

le sac de vidanges garbage bag
vide [vid] *adj* empty
  ▶ *nm* vacuum ▷ **emballé sous vide**
  vacuum-packed; **avoir peur du
  vide** to be afraid of heights
vidéo [video] *nf* video
  ▶ *adj* (f+pl **vidéo**) video ▷ **des jeux
  vidéo** video games ▷ **une caméra
  vidéo** a video camera
vidéocassette [videokasɛt] *nf*
  videocassette
vidéoclip [videoklip] *nm* music
  video
vidéoclub [videoklœb] *nm* video
  rental store
vidéoconférence [videokɔ̃] *nf*
  videoconference
vider [vide] *vb* to empty
vie [vi] *nf* life; **être en vie** to be alive
vieil [vjɛj] *adj see* **vieux**
vieillard [vjɛjaʀ] *nm* old man
vieille [vjɛj] *adj see* **vieux**
  ▶ *nf* old woman; **Eh bien, ma
  vieille...** (*informal*) Well, my dear...
vieillesse [vjɛjɛs] *nf* old age
vieillir [vjejiʀ] *vb* to age ▷ *Il a
  beaucoup vieilli depuis la dernière fois
  que je l'ai vu.* He's aged a lot since I
  last saw him.
viendrai, vienne, viens *vb
  see* **venir**; **Je viendrai dès que
  possible.** I'll come as soon as
  possible.; **J'aimerais que tu
  viennes.** I'd like you to come.;
  Viens ici! Come here!
Vierge [vjɛʀʒ(ə)] *nf* Virgo ▷ *Elle est
  Vierge.* She's a Virgo.
vierge [vjɛʀʒ(ə)] *adj* ❶ virgin ▷ *Il
  est vierge.* He's a virgin. ❷ blank
  ▷ *une cassette vierge* a blank cassette
vieux [vjø, vjɛj] *adj* (f+pl **vieille**) old
  ▷ *un vieux livre* an old book ▷ *une
  vieille dame* an old lady

> **vieux** changes to **vieil** before
> a vowel and most words
> beginning with "h".

▷ *un vieil arbre* an old tree ▷ *Il fait
plus vieux que son âge.* He looks older
than he is.
  ▶ *nm* old man ▷ *Eh bien, mon vieux...*
  (*informal*) Well, old friend...
vieux jeu (f+pl **vieux jeu**) *adj* old-
  fashioned ▷ *Elle est un peu vieux jeu.*
  She's a bit old-fashioned.
vif [vif, viv] *adj* ❶ (*mentally*)
  sharp ▷ *Elle est très vive.* She's very
  sharp.; **avoir l'esprit vif** to be
  quick-witted ❷ crisp ▷ *L'air est plus
  vif à la campagne qu'en ville.* The air
  is crisper in the country than in the
  city. ❸ (*colour*) bright ▷ *un bleu vif*
  a bright blue
vigne [viɲ] *nf* vine
vignoble [viɲɔbl(ə)] *nm* vineyard
vilain, -e [vilɛ̃, -ɛn] (f **vilaine**) *adj*
  naughty ▷ *C'est très vilain de dire
  des mensonges.* It's very naughty to
  tell lies.
village [vilaʒ] *nm* village
villageois [vilaʒwa] *nm* villager
villageoise [vilaʒwaz] *nf* villager
ville [vil] *nf* town ▷ *Je vais en ville.*
  I'm going into town.; **une grande
  ville** a city
vinaigre [vinɛgʀ(ə)] *nm* vinegar
vinaigrette [vinɛgʀɛt] *nf* salad
  dressing
vingt [vɛ̃] *num* twenty ▷ *Elle a
  vingt ans.* She's twenty. ▷ *à vingt
  heures* at 8 p.m.; **le vingt février**
  the twentieth of February; **vingt
  et un** twenty-one; **vingt-deux**
  twenty-two
vingtaine [vɛ̃tɛn] *nf* about twenty
  ▷ *une vingtaine de personnes* about
  twenty people; **Il a une vingtaine
  d'années.** He's about twenty.
vingtième [vɛ̃tjɛm] *adj* twentieth
viol [vjɔl] *nm* rape
violemment [vjɔlamɑ̃] *adv*
  violently
violence [vjɔlɑ̃s] *nf* violence; **la**

violence familiale family violence

violent [vjɔlɑ̃, -ɑ̃t] (f **violente**) adj violent

violer [vjɔle] vb to rape

violet [vjɔlɛ, -ɛt] (f **violette**) adj purple

violon [vjɔlɔ̃] nm violin ▷ Je joue du violon. I play the violin.

violoncelle [vjɔlɔ̃sɛl] nm cello ▷ Elle joue du violoncelle. She plays the cello.

violoniste [vjɔlɔnist(ə)] nmf violinist

vipère [vipɛʁ] nf viper

virage [viʁaʒ] nm bend ▷ une route pleine de virages dangereux a road full of dangerous turns

virgule [viʁgyl] nf ① comma ② decimal point ▷ trois virgule cinq three point five

virus [viʁys] nm (also computing) virus

vis [vis] vb see **vivre** ▶ nf screw

visa [viza] nm visa

visage [vizaʒ] nm face ▷ Elle a le visage rond. She's got a round face.

vis-à-vis de [vizavi-] prep (informal) with regard to ▷ Ce n'est pas très juste vis-à-vis de lui. It's not very fair to him.

viser [vize] vb to aim at ▷ Il faut viser la cible. You have to aim at the target.

visibilité [vizibilite] nf visibility

visible [vizibl(ə)] adj visible

visière [vizjɛʁ] nf (of cap) visor

visite [vizit] nf visit; **rendre visite à quelqu'un** to visit somebody ▷ Je vais rendre visite à mon grand-père. I'm going to visit my grandfather.; **avoir de la visite** to have visitors ▷ Nous avons de la visite aujourd'hui. We have visitors today.; **une visite guidée** a guided tour; **une visite médicale** a medical examination

visiter [vizite] vb to visit

visiteur [vizitœʁ] nm visitor

visiteuse [vizitøz] nf visitor

visou [vizu] nm (skill at aiming) aim ▷ Ça craque du visou pour jouer au billard. You have to have good aim to play pool.

vit [vi] vb see **vivre**; **Il vit chez ses parents.** He lives with his parents.

vital [vital, -o] (f **vitale**, mpl **vitaux**) adj vital ▷ C'est une question vitale. It's of vital importance.; **les signes vitaux** vital signs

vitamine [vitamin] nf vitamin

vite [vit] adv ① quick ▷ Vite, ils arrivent! Quick, they're coming! ▷ Je peux aller dire au revoir à ma mère? » — « Oui, mais fais ça vite! » "Can I go and say goodbye to my mom?" — "Yes, but be quick!" ▷ Prenons la voiture, ça va aller plus vite. Let's take the car, it'll be quicker.; **Le temps passe vite.** Time flies. ② fast ▷ Elle roule trop vite. She drives too fast. ③ soon ▷ Il va vite oublier. He'll soon forget.

vitesse [vites] nf ① speed ▷ à toute vitesse at top speed ▷ Nous sommes rentrés à toute vitesse. We rushed back home. ② gear ▷ en première vitesse in first gear

vitrail [vitʁaj, -o] (pl **vitraux**) nm stained-glass window

vitre [vitʁ(ə)] nf window ▷ Il a cassé une vitre. He broke a window.

vitrine [vitʁin] nf store window

vivant [vivɑ̃, -ɑ̃t] (f **vivante**) adj ① living ▷ les êtres vivants living creatures ▷ les expériences sur les animaux vivants experiments on live animals ② lively ▷ Elle est très vivante. She's very lively.

vive [viv] (msg vif) adj ① (mentally) sharp ▷ Elle est très vive. She's very sharp. ② (colour) bright ▷ Lavez les couleurs vives à l'eau froide. Wash bright colours in cold water.; **à vive allure** at a brisk pace; **de vive voix** in person ▷ *Je te le dirai de vive voix.* I'll tell you about it when I see you.

▶ *excl:* **Vive la reine!** Long live the queen!

vivement [vivmɑ̃] *adv* ❶ quickly ▷ *Elle a réagi vivement.* She reacted quickly. ❷ brightly ▷ *des tissus vivement colorés* brightly coloured fabrics

vivre [vivʀ(ə)] *vb* to live ▷ *J'aimerais vivre à l'étranger.* I'd like to live abroad. ▷ *Et ta grand-mère? Elle vit encore en bonne santé?* What about your grandmother? Is she still in good health?

vocabulaire [vɔkabylɛʀ] *nm* vocabulary

vocation [vɔkasjɔ̃] *nf* vocation

vœu [vø] *nm* (pl **vœux**) *nm* wish ▷ *faire un vœu* to make a wish ▷ *Meilleurs vœux de bonne année!* Best wishes for the New Year!

vogue [vɔg] *nf* fashion ▷ *C'est très en vogue en ce moment.* It's very fashionable at the moment.

voici [vwasi] *prep* ❶ this is ▷ *Voici mon frère et voilà ma sœur.* This is my brother and that's my sister. ❷ here is ▷ *Tu as perdu ton stylo? Tiens, en voici un autre.* Have you lost your pen? Here's another one.; **Le voici!** Here he is! ▷ *Tu veux tes clés? Tiens, les voici!* You want your keys? Here you are!

voie [vwa] *nf* lane ▷ *une route à trois voies* a 3-lane road; **par voie buccale** orally ▷ *à prendre par voie buccale* to be taken orally; **la voie ferrée** the railway track; **la voie maritime du Saint-Laurent** the Saint Lawrence Seaway

voilà [vwala] *prep* ❶ there is ▷ *Tiens! Voilà ton frère.* Look! There's your brother. ▷ *Tu as perdu ton stylo?*

Tiens, en voilà un autre. Have you lost your pen? There's another one.; **Les voilà!** There they are! ❷ that is ▷ *Voilà ma sœur.* That's my sister.; **Et voilà!** That's it!

voile [vwal] *nm* veil ▷ *un voile de mariée* a wedding veil; **un voile blanc** a whiteout

▶ *nf* ❶ sail ❷ sailing ▷ *faire de la voile* to go sailing; **un bateau à voiles** a sailboat

voilier [vwalje] *nm* sailboat

voir [vwaʀ] *vb* to see ▷ *Venez me voir quand vous serez à Edmonton.* Come and see me when you're in Edmonton. ▷ *Je ne vois pas pourquoi il a fait ça.* I can't see why he did that.; **faire voir quelque chose à quelqu'un** to show somebody something ▷ *Il m'a fait voir sa collection de timbres.* He showed me his stamp collection.; **se voir** to be obvious ▷ *Est-ce que cette tache se voit?* Does that stain show? ▷ « *Ça fait des années qu'elle n'a pas joué au soccer* » « *Oui, ça se voit!* » "She hasn't played soccer for years" "Yes, you can tell"; **avoir quelque chose à voir avec** to have something to do with ▷ *Ça n'a rien à voir avec lui, c'est entre toi et moi.* It's nothing to do with him, it's between you and me.

voisin [vwazɛ̃] *nm* neighbour

voisinage [vwazinaʒ] *nm:* **dans le voisinage** in the neighbourhood

voisine [vwazin] *nf* neighbour

voiture [vwatyʀ] *nf* car ▷ *une voiture de sport* a sports car

voix [vwa] (pl **voix**) *nf* ❶ voice ▷ *à voix basse* in a low voice; **à haute voix** aloud ❷ vote ▷ *Il a obtenu cinquante pour cent des voix.* He got 50% of the votes.

vol [vɔl] *nm* ❶ flight; **à vol d'oiseau** as the crow flies ❷ theft ▷ *un vol à main armée* an armed robbery

volaille [vɔlaj] nf poultry

volant [vɔlɑ̃] nm **1** steering wheel
2 (badminton) birdie

volcan [vɔlkɑ̃] nm volcano

volée [vole] nf (in tennis) volley;
rattraper une balle à la volée to
catch a ball in mid-air

voler [vole] vb **1** to fly ▷ J'aimerais
savoir voler. I'd like to be able to fly.
2 to steal ▷ On a volé mon appareil
photo. My camera's been stolen.;
voler quelque chose à quelqu'un
to steal something from somebody
▷ Ça n'est pas son stylo, il me l'a
volé. That's not his pen, he stole it
from me.; **voler quelqu'un** to rob
somebody

volet [vole] nm shutter

voleur [vɔlœʀ] nm thief; **Au
voleur!** Stop thief!

voleuse [vɔløz] nf thief

volley-ball [vɔlebol] nm volleyball
▷ jouer au volley-ball to play
volleyball

volontaire [vɔlɔ̃tɛʀ] nmf
volunteer

volonté [vɔlɔ̃te] nf willpower ▷ Elle
a beaucoup de volonté. She has a lot
of willpower.; **la bonne volonté**
goodwill; **la mauvaise volonté**
lack of goodwill

volontiers [vɔlɔ̃tje] adv gladly
▷ Je l'aiderais volontiers si elle me le
demandais. I'd gladly help her if she
asked me.

volume [vɔlym] nm volume ▷ un
dictionnaire en deux volumes a two-
volume dictionary

volumineux [vɔlyminø, -øz] (f
volumineuse) adj bulky

vomir [vɔmiʀ] vb to vomit ▷ Il a
vomi toute la nuit. He was vomiting
all night.

vont [vɔ̃] vb see **aller**

vos [vo] adj your ▷ Rangez vos jouets,
les enfants! Children, put your toys
away! ▷ Merci pour vos fleurs. Thanks
for your flowers.

vote [vɔt] nm vote

voter [vɔte] vb to vote

votre [vo] (pl **vos**) adj your ▷ C'est
votre manteau? Is this your coat?

vôtre [votʀ(ə)] pron: **le vôtre** yours
▷ J'aime bien notre prof de maths,
mais la vôtre est plus patiente. I like
our math teacher, but yours is
more patient. ▷ À qui est ce foulard?
C'est le vôtre? Whose scarf is this?
Is it yours?

vôtres [votʀ(ə)] pron: **les vôtres**
yours ▷ J'ai oublié mes lunettes de
soleil. Vous avez apporté les vôtres?
I forgot my sunglasses. Did you
bring yours?

**voudra, voudrai, voudrais,
voudras, voudrez, voudrons,
voudront** vb see **vouloir**; **Je
voudrais...** I'd like... ▷ Je voudrais
deux litres de lait, s'il vous plaît. I'd like
two litres of milk, please.

vouloir [vulwaʀ] vb to want ▷ Elle
veut un vélo pour sa fête. She wants
a bike for her birthday. ▷ Je ne veux
pas de dessert. I don't want any
dessert. ▷ Il ne veut pas venir. He
doesn't want to come. ▷ « On va au
cinéma? » « Si tu veux. » "Shall we go
to the movies?" "If you like."; **Je veux
bien.** I'll be happy to. ▷ Je veux bien
le faire à ta place si ça t'arrange. I don't
mind doing it for you if you prefer.;
sans le vouloir without meaning
to ▷ Je l'ai vexé sans le vouloir. I upset
him without meaning to.; **en
vouloir à quelqu'un** to be angry
at somebody ▷ Il m'en veut de ne pas
l'avoir invité à ma fête. He's angry
at me for not inviting him to my
birthday party.; **vouloir dire** to
mean ▷ Qu'est-ce que ça veut dire?
What does that mean?

voulu [vuly] vb see **vouloir**
vous [vu] pron ❶ you ▷ Vous aimez
la pizza? Do you like pizza? ❷ to
you ▷ Je vous écrirai bientôt. I'll write
to you soon. ❸ yourself ▷ Vous
vous êtes fait mal? Have you hurt
yourself?; **vous-même** yourself
▷ Vous l'avez fait vous-même? Did you
do it yourself?
vouvoyer [vuvwaje] vb: **vouvoyer
quelqu'un** to address somebody
as "vous"

- **vouvoyer quelqu'un** means
- to use **vous** when speaking to
- someone, rather than **tu**. Use
- **tu** only when talking to one
- person and when that person
- is someone of your own age or
- whom you know well; use **vous**
- to everyone else. If in doubt
- use **vous**.

**Est-ce que je dois vouvoyer ta
sœur?** Should I use "vous" to your
sister?
voyage [vwajaʒ] nm journey
▷ Avez-vous fait bon voyage? Did you
have a good journey?; **Bon voyage!**
Have a good trip!
voyager [vwajaʒe] vb to travel
voyageur [vwajaʒœʀ] nm
passenger

- A **voyageur** was also a man
- employed by a fur company as a
- guide or to transport goods to
- and from remote stations in the
- North West, mostly by boat.

voyageuse [vwajaʒøz] nf
passenger
voyaient, voyais, voyait vb
see **voir**
voyelle [vwajɛl] nf vowel
voyez, voyiez, voyions vb
see **voir**
voyons [vwajɔ̃] vb see **voir** ❶ let's
see ▷ Voyons ce qu'on peut faire. Let's
see what we can do. ❷ come on

▷ Voyons, sois raisonnable! Come on,
be reasonable!

voyou [vwaju] nmf thug
vrac [vʀak]: **en vrac** adv loose ▷ du
thé en vrac loose tea ▷ des épices en
vrac loose spices
vrai [vʀɛ] (f **vraie**) adj true ▷ une
histoire vraie a true story ▷ C'est
vrai? Is that true?; **à vrai dire** to tell
the truth
vraiment [vʀɛmɑ̃] adv really
vraisemblable [vʀɛsɑ̃blabl(ə)]
adj likely ▷ C'est peu vraisemblable.
That's not very likely. ▷ Il va falloir
trouver une excuse vraisemblable. We'll
have to find a convincing excuse.
vu [vy] prep given ▷ vu la situation
given the circumstances; **vu que**
in view of the fact that ▷ vu qu'il est
toujours en retard in view of the fact
that he's always late
vue [vy] nf ❶ eyesight ▷ J'ai une
mauvaise vue. I've got bad eyesight.
❷ view ▷ Il y a une belle vue d'ici.
There's a lovely view from here.;
à vue d'œil visibly ▷ Elle grandit à
vue d'œil. Every time you see her,
she's taller.
vulgaire [vylgɛʀ] adj vulgar ▷ Ne
dit pas ça, c'est très vulgaire. Don't say
that, it's very vulgar.

W X

wagon [vagɔ̃] *nm* railway car
wagon-lit [vagɔ̃li] (*pl* **wagons-lits**) *nm* (*on train*) sleeping car
wagon-restaurant [vagɔ̃ʀɛstɔʀɑ̃] (*pl* **wagons-restaurants**) *nm* dining car
wapiti [wapiti] *nm* elk
Web [wɛb] *nm* Web; **naviguer sur le Web** to browse the Web
webmestre [wɛbmɛstʀ] *nmf* webmaster
webographie [wɛbɔgʀafi] *nf* webography
webzine [wɛbzin] *nm* webzine
western [wɛstɛʀn] *nm* (*film*) western
wok [wɔk] *nm* wok

xénophobe [gzenɔfɔb] *adj* prejudiced against foreigners
xénophobie [gzenɔfɔbi] *nf* prejudice against foreigners
xylophone [ksilɔfɔn] *nm* xylophone ▷ *Elle joue du xylophone.* She plays the xylophone.

y [i] *pron* there ▷ *Nous y sommes allés l'été dernier.* We went there last summer. ▷ *Regarde dans le tiroir : je pense que les clés y sont.* Look in the drawer: I think the keys are in there.

> y replaces phrases with **à** in constructions like the ones below:

« Je pensais à l'examen. »
— **« Mais arrête d'y penser! »** "I was thinking about the exam."
— "Well, stop thinking about it!";
« Je ne m'attendais pas à ça. »
— **« Moi, je m'y attendais. »** "I wasn't expecting that." — "I was expecting it."

yeux [jø] (*sg* œil) *nmpl* eyes ▷ *Elle a les yeux bleus.* She has blue eyes.;
regarder quelqu'un dans les yeux to look someone in the eye

yoga [jɔga] *nm* yoga

yogourt [jogurt] *nm* yogurt ▷ *un yogourt nature* a plain yogurt ▷ *un*

yogourt aux bleuets a blueberry yogurt

youpi [jupi] *excl* Yippee!

yoyo [jojo] (*pl* **yoyo**) *nm* yo-yo

Yukon *nm* Yukon

Z

zoological ▷ *un jardin zoologique* zoological gardens
zut [zyt] *excl* Oh heck!

zapper [zape] *vb* to channel hop
zappette [zapεt] *nf (for TV)* remote control
zappeur [zapœʀ] *nm (for TV)* remote control
zèbre [zεbʀ(ə)] *nm* zebra
zéro [zeʀo] *nm* zero; **Ils ont gagné trois à zéro.** They won three-nothing.
zézayer [zezeje] *vb* to lisp ▷ *Il zézaie.* He's got a lisp.
zigonner [zigɔne] *vb* to fiddle ▷ *Comme la serrure était gelée, j'ai zigonné avec la clef.* Since the lock was frozen, I tried fiddling with the key.
zigzag [zigzag] *nm*: **faire des zigzags** to zigzag
zone [zon] *nf* zone; **la zone de but** *(sports)* crease; **une zone piétonne** a pedestrian zone
zoo [zoo] *nm* zoo
zoologique [zɔɔlɔʒik] *adj*

a

a [eɪ, ə] *art*

▌Use **un** for masculine nouns, **une** for feminine nouns.

un *m*, une *f* ▷ *a book* un livre ▷ *a year ago* il y a un an ▷ *an apple* une pomme ▷ *a car* une auto

▌You do not translate **a** when you want to describe somebody's job in French.

▷ *He's a butcher.* Il est boucher. ▷ *She's a doctor.* Elle est médecin.; **once a week** une fois par semaine; **10 km an hour** dix kilomètres à l'heure; **3 dollars a kilo** trois dollars le kilo; **a hundred times** cent fois

abandon [ə'bændən] *vb* abandonner

abbreviation [əbriːvɪ'eɪʃən] *n* abréviation *f*

ability [ə'bɪlɪtɪ] *n*: **to have the ability to do something** être capable de faire quelque chose

able ['eɪbl] *adj*: **to be able to do**

something être capable de faire quelque chose

aboiteau ['æbətəʊ] *n* aboiteau *m* (*pl* aboiteaux) ▷ *Aboiteaus open as the tide comes in and close as it goes out.* Les aboiteaux ouvrent à marée montante et ferment à marée descendante.

abolish [ə'bɒlɪʃ] *vb* abolir

Aboriginal [æbə'rɪdʒɪnəl] *adj* autochtone ▷ *Aboriginal languages* les langues autochtones ▷ *Aboriginal rights* les droits des autochtones ▷ *the Aboriginal peoples of Canada* les autochtones du Canada

abortion [ə'bɔːʃən] *n* avortement *m*

about [ə'baʊt] *prep, adv* ❶ (*concerning*) à propos de ▷ *I'm phoning you about tomorrow's meeting.* Je vous appelle à propos de la réunion de demain. ❷ (*approximately*) environ ▷ *It takes about 10 hours.* Ça prend dix heures environ.; **about a hundred pages** une centaine de pages; **at about 11 o'clock** vers onze heures ❸ (*around*) dans ▷ *to walk around town* se promener dans la ville ❹ sur ▷ *a book about Manitoba* un livre sur Manitoba; **to be about to do something** être sur le point de faire quelque chose ▷ *I was about to go out.* J'étais sur le point de sortir.; **to talk about something** parler de quelque chose; **What's it about?** De quoi s'agit-il?; **How about going to the movies?** Et si nous allions au cinéma?

above [ə'bʌv] *prep, adv* ❶ (*higher than*) au-dessus de ▷ *He put his hands above his head.* Il a mis ses mains au-dessus de sa tête.; **the floor above** l'étage du dessus; **mentioned above** mentionné ci-

dessus; **above all** par-dessus tout
❷ *(more than)* plus de ▷ *above 40 degrees* plus de quarante degrés

abroad [əˈbrɔːd] *adv* à l'étranger
▷ *to go abroad* partir à l'étranger

abrupt [əˈbrʌpt] *adj* brusque ▷ *He was a bit abrupt with me.* Il s'est montré un peu brusque avec moi.

absence [ˈæbsəns] *n* absence *f*

absent [ˈæbsənt] *adj* absent

absent-minded
[ˈæbsəntˈmaɪndɪd] *adj* distrait
▷ *She's a bit absent-minded.* Elle est un peu distraite.

absolutely [ˌæbsəˈluːtlɪ] *adv*
❶ *(completely)* tout à fait ▷ *You're absolutely right.* Tu as tout à fait raison. ❷ absolument ▷ *"Do you think it's a good idea?" — "Absolutely!"* «Tu trouves que c'est une bonne idée?» — «Absolument!»

absorbed [əbˈsɔːbd] *adj*: **to be absorbed in something** être absorbé par quelque chose; **to be absorbed in a book** être plongé dans un livre

absurd [əbˈsɜːd] *adj* absurde
▷ *That's absurd!* C'est absurde!

abuse [əˈbjuːz] *n (misuse)* abus *m*; **to shout abuse at somebody** insulter quelqu'un; **the issue of child abuse** la question des enfants maltraités; **the problem of drug abuse** le problème de la drogue
▶ *vb* ❶ maltraiter ▷ *abused children* les enfants maltraités; **to be abused** *(child, woman)* être maltraité ❷ *(insult)* injurier; **to abuse drugs** se droguer ❸ abuser de ▷ *to abuse a privilege* abuser d'un privilège

abusive [əˈbjuːsɪv] *adj (insulting)* insultant ▷ *abusive behaviour* un comportement insultant; **When I refused, he became abusive.** Quand j'ai refusé, il s'est mis à

m'injurier.; **children with abusive parents** les enfants maltraités par leurs parents

academic [ˌækəˈdɛmɪk] *adj* scolaire ▷ *the academic year* l'année scolaire

academy [əˈkædəmɪ] *n* collège *m* ▷ *a military academy* un collège militaire

Acadia [əˈkeɪdɪə] *n* Acadie *f* ▷ *My ancestors were from Acadia.* Mes ancêtres étaient originaires de l'Acadie.

> Acadia was the part of New France that stretched from south of the St. Lawrence eastward to the sea. It took in the area now covered by part of Québec and the Maritimes, as well as part of what is now the US, and was disputed by the French and British for many years. Many descendants of the original Acadians, who were deported by the British in the mid-1700s, still consider this their homeland.

Acadian [əˈkeɪdɪən] *adj* acadien *m* (facadienne) ▷ *the Acadian flag* le drapeau acadien ▷ *Acadian poutine* la poutine acadienne
▶ *n* Acadien *m*, Acadienne *f* ▷ *He's an Acadian.* C'est un Acadien. ▷ *She's an Acadian.* C'est une Acadienne.

accelerate [ækˈsɛləreɪt] *vb* accélérer

accelerator [ækˈsɛləreɪtəʳ] *n* accélérateur *m*

accent [ˈæksɛnt] *n* accent *m* ▷ *She's got a French accent.* Elle a l'accent français.

accept [əkˈsɛpt] *vb* accepter

acceptable [əkˈsɛptəbl] *adj* acceptable

access [ˈæksɛs] *n* ❶ accès *m* ▷ *He has access to confidential information.* Il a accès à des renseignements confidentiels. ❷ droit de visite *m* ▷ *Her ex-husband has access to the children.* Son ex-mari a le droit de visite.

accessible [æk'sɛsəbl] *adj* accessible

accessory [æk'sɛsərɪ] *n* accessoire *m* ▷ *fashion accessories* les accessoires de mode

accident ['æksɪdənt] *n* accident *m* ▷ *to have an accident* avoir un accident; **by accident (1)** (*by mistake*) accidentellement ▷ *I hit her with my elbow by accident.* Je l'ai heurtée accidentellement du coude. **(2)** (*by chance*) par hasard ▷ *She met him by accident.* Elle l'a rencontré par hasard.

accidental [æksɪ'dɛntl] *adj* accidentel (*f* accidentelle)

accommodate [ə'kɒmədeɪt] *vb* recevoir ▷ *The hotel can accommodate 50 people.* L'hôtel peut recevoir cinquante personnes.

accommodation [əkɒmə'deɪʃən] *n* logement *m*

accompany [ə'kʌmpənɪ] *vb* accompagner

accord [ə'kɔːd] *n*: **of one's own accord** de son plein gré ▷ *She left of her own accord.* Elle est partie de son plein gré.

accordingly [ə'kɔːdɪŋlɪ] *adv* en conséquence

according to [ə'kɔːdɪŋtu] *prep* selon ▷ *according to him* selon lui

accordion [ə'kɔːdɪən] *n* accordéon *m*

account [ə'kaʊnt] *n* ❶ compte *m* ▷ *a bank account* un compte en banque; **to do the accounts** tenir la comptabilité ❷ (*report*) compte rendu *m* (*pl* comptes rendus) ▷ *He gave a detailed account of what happened.* Il a donné un compte rendu détaillé des événements.;

to take something into account tenir compte de quelque chose; **on account of** à cause de ▷ *We couldn't go out on account of the bad weather.* Nous n'avons pas pu sortir à cause du mauvais temps.

account for *vb* expliquer ▷ *If she was ill, that would account for her poor results.* Si elle était malade, cela expliquerait ses résultats médiocres.

accountable [ə'kaʊntəbl] *adj*: **to be accountable to someone for something** être responsable de quelque chose devant quelqu'un

accountancy [ə'kaʊntənsɪ] *n* comptabilité *f*

accountant [ə'kaʊntənt] *n* comptable *m* ▷ *She's an accountant.* Elle est comptable.

accuracy ['ækjʊrəsɪ] *n* exactitude *f*

accurate ['ækjʊrɪt] *adj* précis ▷ *accurate information* des renseignements précis *m*

accurately ['ækjʊrɪtlɪ] *adv* avec précision

accusation [ækjuˈzeɪʃən] *n* accusation *f*

accuse [ə'kjuːz] *vb*: **to accuse somebody of something** accuser quelqu'un de quelque chose ▷ *Her parents accused her of being lazy.* Ses parents l'ont accusée d'être paresseuse.

ace [eɪs] *n* as *m* ▷ *the ace of hearts* l'as de cœur

ache [eɪk] *n* douleur *f* ▶ *vb*: **My leg aches.** J'ai mal à la jambe.

achieve [ə'tʃiːv] *vb* ❶ (*an aim*) atteindre ❷ (*victory*) remporter

achievement [ə'tʃiːvmənt] *n* exploit *m* ▷ *That was quite an achievement.* C'était un véritable exploit.

acid [ˈæsɪd] n acide m

acid rain n pluies fpl acides

acne [ˈækni] n acné f

acre [ˈeɪkər] n demi-hectare m
- In France, land is measured in hectares. One acre is about 0.4 hectares.

acrobat [ˈækrəbæt] n acrobate mf ▷ He's an acrobat. Il est acrobate.

acrobatics [ˌækrəˈbætɪks] n acrobatie f

across [əˈkrɒs] prep, adv de l'autre côté de ▷ The house across the road la maison de l'autre côté de la rue; **to walk across the road** traverser la rue; **to run across the road** traverser la rue en courant; **across from** (opposite) en face de ▷ He sat down across from us. Il s'est assis en face de nous.

act [ækt] vb ❶ (in play, film) jouer ▷ He acts really well. Il joue vraiment bien. ▷ She's acting the part of Juliet. Elle joue le rôle de Juliette. ❷ (take action) agir ▷ The police acted quickly. La police a agi rapidement.; **She acts as his interpreter.** Elle lui sert d'interprète.; **to act like an idiot** se comporter comme un imbécile ▶ n (in play) acte m ▷ in the first act au premier acte

action [ˈækʃən] n action f ▷ The film was full of action. Il y avait beaucoup d'action dans le film.; **to take firm action against** prendre des mesures énergiques contre

active [ˈæktɪv] adj actif (f active) ▷ He's very active. Il est très actif.; **an active volcano** un volcan en activité

activity [ækˈtɪvɪti] n activité f ▷ outdoor activities les activités de plein air

actor [ˈæktər] n acteur m

actress [ˈæktrɪs] n actrice f

actual [ˈæktjuəl] adj réel (f réelle)

▷ The film is based on actual events. Le film repose sur des faits réels.; **What's the actual amount?** Quel est le montant exact?

■ Be careful not to translate **actual** by actuel.

actually [ˈæktjuəli] adv ❶ (really) vraiment ▷ Did it actually happen? Est-ce que c'est vraiment arrivé? ❷ (in fact) en fait ▷ Actually, I don't know her at all. En fait, je ne la connais pas du tout.

■ Be careful not to translate **actually** by actuellement.

acupuncture [ˈækjupʌŋktʃər] n acupuncture f

AD [æd] n ❶ (in paper) annonce f ❷ (on TV, radio) pub f

AD abbr [eɪˈdiː] ap J.-C. (= Jésus-Christ) ▷ in 800 AD en huit cents ap après Jésus-Christ

adapt [əˈdæpt] vb adapter ▷ Her novel was adapted for television. Son roman a été adapté pour la télévision.; **to adapt to something** (get used to) s'adapter à quelque chose ▷ He adapted to his new school very quickly. Il s'est adapté très vite à sa nouvelle école.

adaptation [ˌædæpˈteɪʃən] n adaptation f ▷ a TV adaptation of a novel une adaptation télévisée d'un roman

adapter [əˈdæptər] n adaptateur m

add [æd] vb ajouter ▷ Add two eggs to the mixture. Ajoutez deux œufs au mélange.; **to add up** additionner ▷ Add up the figures. Additionnez les chiffres.

addict [ˈædɪkt] n (drug addict) drogué m, droguée f; **She's a football addict.** C'est une mordue de football.

addicted [əˈdɪktɪd] adj: **to be addicted to** (drug) s'adonner à; **He's addicted to soap operas.**

C'est un mordu des téléromans.; **I'm addicted to chocolate.** Je ne peux résister au chocolat.

addition [əˈdɪʃən] n: **in addition** en plus ▷ He's broken his leg and, in addition, he's caught a cold. Il s'est cassé la jambe et en plus, il a attrapé un rhume.; **in addition to** en plus de ▷ In addition to the price of the cassette, there's a charge for postage. En plus du prix de la cassette, il y a des frais de port.

address [əˈdrɛs] n adresse f ▷ What's your address? Quelle est votre adresse?

adjective [ˈædʒɪktɪv] n adjectif m

adjust [əˈdʒʌst] vb régler ▷ You can adjust the height of the chair. Tu peux régler la hauteur de la chaise.; **to adjust to something** (get used to) s'adapter à quelque chose ▷ He adjusted to his new school very quickly. Il s'est adapté très vite à sa nouvelle école.

adjustable [əˈdʒʌstəbl] adj réglable

administration [ədmɪnɪsˈtreɪʃən] n administration f

admire [ədˈmaɪə] vb admirer

admission [ədˈmɪʃən] n entrée f ▷ "free admission" « entrée gratuite »

admit [ədˈmɪt] vb ❶ (agree) admettre ▷ I must admit that... Je dois admettre que... ❷ (confess) reconnaître ▷ She admitted that she'd done it. Elle a reconnu qu'elle l'avait fait.

admittance [ədˈmɪtəns] n: **"no admittance"** « accès interdit »

adolescence [ædəʊˈlɛsns] n adolescence f

adolescent [ædəʊˈlɛsnt] n adolescent m, adolescente f

adopt [əˈdɒpt] vb adopter ▷ I was adopted. J'ai été adopté.

adopted [əˈdɒptɪd] adj adoptif

(f adoptive) ▷ an adopted son un fils adoptif

adoption [əˈdɒpʃən] n adoption f

adore [əˈdɔː] vb adorer

adult [ˈædʌlt] n adulte mf; **adult education** l'éducation m des adultes

advance [ədˈvɑːns] vb ❶ (move forward) avancer ▷ The troops are advancing. Les troupes avancent. ❷ (progress) progresser ▷ Technology has advanced a lot. La technologie a beaucoup progressé. ▶ n: **in advance** à l'avance ▷ They bought the tickets in advance. Ils ont acheté les billets à l'avance.

advanced [ədˈvɑːnst] adj avancé

advantage [ədˈvɑːntɪdʒ] n avantage m ▷ Going to university has many advantages. Aller à l'université présente de nombreux avantages.; **to take advantage of something** profiter de quelque chose ▷ He took advantage of the good weather to go for a walk. Il a profité du beau temps pour faire une promenade.; **to take advantage of somebody** exploiter quelqu'un ▷ The company was taking advantage of its employees. La société exploitait ses employés.

adventure [ədˈvɛntʃə] n aventure f

adventurer [ədˈvɛntʃərə] n aventurier m, aventurière f

adventurous [ədˈvɛntʃərəs] adj aventureux (f aventureuse)

adverb [ˈædvɜːb] n adverbe m

advertise [ˈædvətaɪz] vb faire de la publicité pour ▷ They're advertising the new model. Ils font de la publicité pour leur nouveau modèle.; **Jobs are advertised in the paper.** Le journal publie des annonces d'emplois.

advertisement [ədˈvɜːtɪsmənt] n ❶ (on TV) publicité f ❷ (in newspaper) annonce f

advertising [ˈædvətaɪzɪŋ] n
publicité f

advice [ədˈvaɪs] n conseils mpl ▷ to
give somebody advice donner des
conseils à quelqu'un; **a piece of
advice** un conseil ▷ She gave me a
good piece of advice. Elle m'a donné
un bon conseil.

advise [ədˈvaɪz] vb conseiller
▷ They advised me to wait. Il m'ont
conseillé d'attendre. ▷ I advise you
not to go there. Je te conseille de ne
pas y aller.

aerial [ˈɛərɪəl] n antenne f

aerobics [ɛəˈrəʊbɪks] npl aérobic f
▷ I'm going to aerobics tonight. Je vais
au cours d'aérobic ce soir.

affair [əˈfɛəˀ] n ❶ (romantic)
aventure f ▷ to have an affair with
somebody avoir une aventure avec
quelqu'un ❷ (event) affaire f

affect [əˈfɛkt] vb ❶ concerner ▷ It
affects all of us. Cela nous concerne
tous. ❷ avoir des conséquences
pour ▷ If you smoke, it will affect the
people around you. Si tu fumes, cela
aura des conséquences pour les
gens autour de toi. ❸ décourager
▷ We mustn't let it affect us. Nous ne
devons pas nous laisser décourager
par cela.

> Be careful not to translate
> **affect** by the French verb
> **affecter**.

affectionate [əˈfɛkʃənɪt] adj
affectueux (f affectueuse)

afford [əˈfɔːd] vb avoir les moyens
d'acheter ▷ I can't afford a new pair
of jeans. Je n'ai pas les moyens
d'acheter un nouveau jean. ; **We
can't afford to go on a holiday.**
Nous n'avons pas les moyens de
partir en vacances.

afraid [əˈfreɪd] adj; **to be afraid of
something** avoir peur de quelque

chose ▷ I'm afraid of spiders. J'ai
peur des araignées.; **I'm afraid
I can't come.** Je crains de ne pouvoir
venir.; **I'm afraid so.** Hélas oui.; **I'm
afraid not.** Hélas non.

after [ˈɑːftəˀ] prep, adv, conj après
▷ after dinner après le dîner ▷ He
ran after me. Il a couru après moi.;
soon after peu après; **after I've
had a rest** après m'être reposé;
after having asked après avoir
demandé; **after that** après tout

afternoon [ˈɑːftəˈnuːn] n après-
midi m ▷ 3 o'clock in the afternoon
trois heures de l'après-midi
▷ this afternoon cet après-midi
▷ on Saturday afternoon samedi
après-midi

afterwards [ˈɑːftəwədz] adv après
▷ She left not long afterwards. Elle est
partie peu de temps après.

again [əˈɡɛn] adv ❶ (one more time)
encore une fois ▷ Can you tell me
again? Tu peux me le dire encore
une fois? ❷ (once more) de nouveau
▷ They're friends again. Ils sont
de nouveau amis.; **not... again**
ne... plus ▷ I won't go there again. Je
n'y retournerai plus.; **Do it again!**
Refais-le!; **again and again** à
plusieurs reprises

against [əˈɡɛnst] prep contre
▷ He leaned against the wall. Il s'est
appuyé contre le mur. ▷ I'm against
nuclear testing. Je suis contre les
essais nucléaires.

age [eɪdʒ] n âge m ▷ at the age of 16
à l'âge de seize ans ▷ an age limit
une limite d'âge; **I haven't been
to the movies in ages.** Ça fait une
éternité que je ne suis pas allé au
cinéma.

aged [ˈeɪdʒɪd] adj; **aged 10** âgé de
dix ans; **their aged parents** leurs
parents âgés

agency [ˈeɪdʒənsɪ] n agence f ▷ a

travel agency une agence de voyages ▷ *a real estate agency* une agence immobilière

agenda [ə'dʒendə] n ❶ ordre m du jour ▷ *on the agenda* à l'ordre du jour ▷ *the agenda for today's meeting* l'ordre du jour de la réunion d'aujourd'hui ❷ agenda *(daybook)* m ▷ *I wrote it in my agenda.* Je l'ai écrit dans mon agenda.

agent ['eɪdʒənt] n agent m, agente f; **a real estate agent** un agent immobilier; **She's a travel agent.** Elle est agente de voyages.

aggressive [ə'ɡresɪv] adj agressif (f agressive)

ago [ə'ɡəʊ] adv: **two days ago** il y a deux jours; **two years ago** il y a deux ans; **not long ago** il n'y a pas longtemps; **How long ago did it happen?** Il y a combien de temps que c'est arrivé?

agony ['æɡənɪ] n: **to be in agony** souffrir le martyre ▷ *I was in agony.* Je souffrais le martyre.

agree [ə'ɡriː] vb: **to agree with** être d'accord avec ▷ *I agree with her.* Je suis d'accord avec elle.; **to agree to do something** accepter de faire quelque chose ▷ *He agreed to go and pick her up.* Il a accepté d'aller la chercher.; **to agree that…** admettre que… ▷ *I agree that it's difficult.* J'admets que c'est difficile.; **Garlic doesn't agree with me.** Je ne supporte pas l'ail.

agreed [ə'ɡriːd] adj convenu ▷ *at the agreed time* au moment convenu

agreement [ə'ɡriːmənt] n accord m; **to be in agreement** être d'accord ▷ *Everybody was in agreement with me.* Tout le monde était d'accord avec moi.

agricultural [æɡrɪ'kʌltʃərəl] adj agricole

agriculture ['æɡrɪkʌltʃə^r] n

agriculture f

ahead [ə'hed] adv devant ▷ *She looked straight ahead.* Elle regardait droit devant elle.; **ahead of time** en avance; **to plan ahead** organiser à l'avance; **Our team is 5 points ahead.** Notre équipe a cinq points d'avance.; **Go ahead!** Allez-y!

aid [eɪd] n: **in aid of charity** au profit d'associations caritatives

AIDS [eɪdz] n sida m

aim [eɪm] vb ❶ pointer ▷ *He aimed his flashlight at me.* Il a pointé sa lampe de poche sur moi. ❷ viser ▷ *Aim at the target.* Vise la cible. ❸ avoir l'intention de ▷ *We aim to leave at 5 o'clock.* Nous avons l'intention de partir à cinq heures.; **The film is aimed at children.** Le film est destiné aux enfants.
  ▶ n objectif m ▷ *The aim of the festival is to raise money.* L'objectif du festival est de collecter des fonds.; **My aim is bad.** Je vise mal.

air [eə^r] n air m ▷ *to get some fresh air* prendre l'air; **by air** en avion ▷ *I prefer to travel by air.* Je préfère voyager en avion.

air bag n sac gonflable m

air-conditioned ['eəkən'dɪʃənd] adj climatisé

air conditioning [-kən'dɪʃnɪŋ] n climatisation f

Air Force n armée f de l'air

airline ['eəlaɪn] n compagnie aérienne f

airmail ['eəmeɪl] n: **by airmail** par avion

airplane ['eəpleɪn] n avion m

airport ['eəpɔːt] n aéroport m

aisle [aɪl] n ❶ (theatre, supermarket) allée f ❷ (airplane) couloir m

alarm [ə'lɑːm] n (warning) alarme f; **a fire alarm** un avertisseur d'incendie

alarm clock n réveil m

Alberta [æl'bəːtə] Alberta f

album ['ælbəm] n album m

alcohol ['ælkəhɒl] n alcool m

alcoholic [ælkə'hɒlɪk] n
alcoolique mf ▷ a clinic for alcoholics
une clinique pour les alcooliques
▶ adj alcoolisé ▷ alcoholic drinks des
boissons alcoolisées

alert [ə'ləːt] adj ❶ (bright) vif (f
vive) ▷ a very alert baby un bébé très
vif ❷ (paying attention) vigilant
▷ We must stay alert. Nous devons
rester vigilants.

alibi ['ælɪbaɪ] n alibi m

alien ['eɪlɪən] n (from outer space)
extra-terrestre mf

alike [ə'laɪk] adv: **to look alike**
se ressembler ▷ The two sisters
look alike. Les deux sœurs se
ressemblent.

alive [ə'laɪv] adj vivant

all [ɔːl] adj, pron, adv tout (mpl tous)
▷ all the time tout le temps ▷ I ate all
of it. J'ai tout mangé. ▷ all day toute
la journée ▷ all the books tous les
livres ▷ all the girls toutes les filles;
All of us went. Nous y sommes
tous allés.; **after all** après tout
▷ After all, nobody can make us go.
Après tout, personne ne peut nous
obliger à y aller.; **all alone** tout seul
▷ She's all alone. Elle est toute seule.;
not at all pas du tout ▷ I'm not tired
at all. Je ne suis pas du tout fatigué.;
The score is 5 all. Le score est de
cinq partout.

allergic [ə'ləːdʒɪk] adj allergique;
to be allergic to something être
allergique à quelque chose ▷ I'm
allergic to cat hair. Je suis allergique
aux poils de chat.

allergy ['ælədʒɪ] n allergie f ▷ I have
allergies. J'ai des allergies.; **a food
allergy** une allergie alimentaire

alley ['ælɪ] n ruelle f

allophone ['æləfəʊn] adj
allophone mf
▶ n allophone mf ▷ Allophones speak
neither French nor English as their
first language. La langue maternelle
des allophones n'est ni le français
ni l'anglais.

allow [ə'laʊ] vb: **to be allowed to
do something** être autorisé à faire
quelque chose ▷ He's not allowed to
go out at night. Il n'est pas autorisé à
sortir le soir.; **to allow somebody
to do something** permettre à
quelqu'un de faire quelque chose
▷ His mom allowed him to go out. Sa
mère lui a permis de sortir.

allowance [ə'laʊəns] n argent
m de poche ▷ Do you get a weekly
allowance? Est-ce que tu reçois de
l'argent de poche chaque semaine?

all right adv ❶ (okay) bien
▷ Everything turned out all right.
Tout s'est bien terminé.; **Are you
all right?** Ça va? ❷ (not bad) pas
mal ▷ The film was all right. Le film
n'était pas mal. ❸ (when agreeing)
d'accord ▷ "We'll talk about it later."
— "All right." « On en reparlera plus
tard. » — « D'accord. »; **Is that all
right with you?** Tu es d'accord?

almond ['ɑːmənd] n amande f

almost ['ɔːlməʊst] adv presque
▷ I'm almost finished. J'ai presque fini.

alone [ə'ləʊn] adj, adv seul ▷ He
lives alone. Il habite seul.; **to leave
somebody alone** laisser quelqu'un
tranquille ▷ Leave me alone!
Laisse-moi tranquille!; **to leave
something alone** ne pas toucher
à quelque chose ▷ Leave my things
alone! Ne touche pas à mes affaires!

along [ə'lɒŋ] prep, adv le long de
▷ I was walking along the beach. Je
me promenais le long de la plage.;
all along depuis le début ▷ He was
lying to me all along. Il m'a menti

depuis le début.

aloud [ə'laʊd] *adv* à haute voix
▷ He read the poem aloud. Il a lu le poème à haute voix.

alphabet ['ælfəbɛt] *n* alphabet *m*

alphabetical [ælfə'bɛtɪkl] *adj* alphabétique ▷ *in alphabetical order* en ordre alphabétique

already [ɔːl'rɛdɪ] *adv* déjà ▷ She had already gone. Elle était déjà partie.

also ['ɔːlsəʊ] *adv* aussi

altar ['ɔːltə'] *n* autel *m*

alter ['ɔːltə'] *vb* changer

alternate ['ɔːltəneɪt] *adj*: **on alternate days** tous les deux jours

alternative [ɔːl'tɜːnətɪv] *n* choix *m* ▷ You have no alternative. Tu n'as pas le choix.; **Fruit is a healthy alternative to chocolate.** Les fruits sont plus sains que le chocolat.; **There are several alternatives.** Il y a plusieurs possibilités.
▶ *adj* autre ▷ They made alternative plans. Ils ont pris d'autres dispositions.; **an alternative solution** une solution de rechange; **alternative medicine** la médecine douce

alternatively [ɔːl'tɜːnətɪvlɪ] *adv*: **Alternatively, we could just stay at home.** On pourrait aussi rester à la maison.

although [ɔːl'ðəʊ] *conj* bien que
▐ **bien que** has to be followed by a verb in the subjunctive.
▷ Although she was tired, she stayed up late. Bien qu'elle soit fatiguée, elle s'est couchée tard.

altogether [ɔːltə'gɛðə'] *adv* ❶ (in total) en tout ▷ You owe me $20 altogether. Tu me dois vingt dollars en tout. ❷ (completely) tout à fait ▷ I'm not altogether happy with your work. Je ne suis pas tout à fait satisfait de votre travail.

aluminum [ə'luːmɪnəm] *n* aluminium *m*

always ['ɔːlweɪz] *adv* toujours
▷ He's always grumbling. Il est toujours en train de ronchonner.

am [æm] *vb see* **be**

a.m. [eɪ'ɛm] *abbr* du matin ▷ at 4 a.m. à quatre heures du matin

amateur ['æmətə'] *n* amateur *m*;
amateur sports le sport amateur

amazed [ə'meɪzd] *adj* stupéfait
▷ their amazed parents leurs parents stupéfaits ▷ I was amazed that I managed to do it. J'étais stupéfait d'avoir réussi.

amazing [ə'meɪzɪŋ] *adj*
❶ (surprising) stupéfait ▷ That's amazing news! C'est une nouvelle stupéfiante! ❷ (excellent) exceptionnel (f exceptionnelle) ▷ My dad's an amazing cook. Mon père est un cuisinier exceptionnel.

ambassador [æm'bæsədə'] *n* ambassadeur *m*, ambassadrice *f*

ambition [æm'bɪʃən] *n* ambition *f*

ambitious [æm'bɪʃəs] *adj* ambitieux (f ambitieuse) ▷ She's very ambitious. Elle est très ambitieuse.

ambulance ['æmbjʊləns] *n* ambulance *f*

amenities [ə'miːnɪtɪz] *npl* aménagements *mpl*; **The hotel has very good amenities.** L'hôtel est très bien aménagé.

among [ə'mʌŋ] *prep* parmi
▷ There were six children among them. Il y avait six enfants parmi eux.; **We were among friends.** Nous étions entre amis.; **among other things** entre autres

amount [ə'maʊnt] *n* ❶ somme *f*
▷ a large amount of money une grosse somme d'argent ❷ quantité *f*; **a huge amount of rice** une énorme quantité de riz

amp [ˈæmpeəʳ] n ❶ (of electricity)
ampère m ❷ (amplifier)
amplificateur m

amplifier [ˈæmplɪfaɪəʳ] n (for hi-fi)
amplificateur m

amuse [əˈmjuːz] vb amuser ▷ She
was not amused by their rude jokes.
Leurs blagues grossières ne l'ont
pas amusée.

amusement arcade [əˈmjuːz-
məntsːˈkeɪd] n salle de jeux
électroniques f

an [æn, ən, n] art see a

analysis [əˈnæləsɪs] n analyse f

analyze [ˈænəlaɪz] vb analyser

ancestor [ˈænsɪstəʳ] n ancêtre mf

anchor [ˈæŋkəʳ] n ancre f

ancient [ˈeɪnʃənt] adj
❶ (civilization) antique ▷ ancient
Greece la Grèce antique ❷ (custom,
building) ancien (f ancienne) ▷ an
ancient monument un monument
ancien

and [ænd] conj et ▷ you and me toi
et moi ▷ 2 and 2 are 4 deux et deux
font quatre; **Please try and come!**
Essaie de venir!; **He talked and
talked.** Il n'a pas arrêté de parler.;
better and better de mieux en
mieux

angel [ˈeɪndʒəl] n ange m

anger [ˈæŋɡəʳ] n colère f

angle [ˈæŋɡl] n angle m

Anglophone [ˈæŋɡləfəʊn]
n anglophone mf ▷ A lot of
Anglophones live in Montréal.
Beaucoup d'anglophones habitent
à Montréal.
▶ adj anglophone ▷ an Anglophone
community une communauté
anglophone

angry [ˈæŋɡrɪ] adj en colère
▷ Dad looks very angry. Papa a l'air
très en colère.; **to be angry with
somebody** être furieux contre
quelqu'un ▷ Mom's really angry with

you. Maman est vraiment furieuse
contre toi.; **to get angry** se fâcher

animal [ˈænɪməl] n animal m (pl
animaux)

animation [ˌænɪˈmeɪʃən] n
❶ film d'animation m ▷ We went
to see the new 3D animation. Nous
sommes allés voir le nouveau film
d'animation 3D. ❷ animation
f ▷ She's studying animation. Elle
étudie l'animation.; **computer
animation** l'animatique f

ankle [ˈæŋkl] n cheville f

anniversary [ˌænɪˈvɜːsərɪ]
n anniversaire m ▷ a wedding
anniversary un anniversaire de
mariage

announce [əˈnaʊns] vb annoncer

announcement [əˈnaʊnsmənt]
n annonce f

annoy [əˈnɔɪ] vb agacer ▷ He's really
annoying me. Il m'agace vraiment.;
to get annoyed se fâcher ▷ Don't
get so annoyed! Ne vous fâchez pas!

annoying [əˈnɔɪɪŋ] adj agaçant
▷ It's really annoying. C'est vraiment
agaçant.

annual [ˈænjʊəl] adj annuel (f
annuelle) ▷ an annual meeting une
réunion annuelle

anorexia [ˌænəˈrɛksɪə] n anorexie f

another [əˈnʌðəʳ] adj un autre, une
autre ▷ Would you like another piece
of cake? Tu veux un autre morceau
de gâteau? ▷ Have you got another
skirt? Tu as une autre jupe?

answer [ˈɑːnsəʳ] vb répondre
à ▷ Can you answer my question?
Peux-tu répondre à ma question?
▷ to answer the phone répondre au
téléphone; **to answer the door**
aller ouvrir ▷ Can you answer the
door please? Tu peux aller ouvrir s'il
te plaît?
▶ n ❶ (to question) réponse f ❷ (to
problem) solution f

answering machine [ˈɑːnsərɪŋ-] n répondeur m

ant [ænt] n fourmi f

antagonize [ænˈtægənaɪz] vb contrarier ▷ *He didn't want to antagonize her.* Il ne voulait pas la contrarier.

Antarctic [æntˈɑːktɪk] n Antarctique f

anthem [ˈænθəm] n: **the national anthem** l'hymne m national ▷ *Our national anthem is "O Canada".* Notre hymne national est « Ô Canada ».

antibiotic [æntɪbaɪˈɒtɪk] n antibiotique m

antifreeze [ˈæntɪfriːz] n antigel m

antique [ænˈtiːk] n antiquité f; **an antique dealer** un marchand d'antiquités

antique shop n magasin d'antiquités m

antivirus software [ˈæntɪˈvaɪərəsˈsɒftweəʳ] n logiciel antivirus m ▷ *to download free antivirus software* télécharger un logiciel antivirus gratuit

antlers [ˈæntləz] npl bois mpl ▷ *The moose sheds its antlers every year.* Les bois de l'orignal tombent chaque année.

anxious [ˈæŋkʃəs] adj anxieux (f anxieuse) ▷ *He's a little anxious about the test.* Il est un peu anxieux à propos du test.; **to be anxious to do something** avoir hâte de faire quelque chose

any [ˈenɪ] adj, pron, adv

> Use **du**, **de la** or **des** to translate **any** according to the gender of the French noun that follows it. **du** and **de la** become **de l'** when they're followed by a noun starting with a vowel.

❶ du ▷ *Do you have any bread?* Tu veux du pain? **❷** de la ▷ *Is there any ice cream?* Est-ce qu'il y a de la crème

glacée? **❸** de l' ▷ *Have you got any mineral water?* Avez-vous de l'eau minérale? **❹** des ▷ *Do you have any CDs?* Avez-vous des DC?

> If you want to say you don't have any of something, use **de** whatever the gender of the following noun is. **de** becomes **d'** when it comes before a noun starting with a vowel.

❺ de, d' ▷ *I don't have any books.* Je n'ai pas de livres. ▷ *I don't have any money.* Je n'ai pas d'argent.

> Use **en** where there is no noun after **any**.

❻ en ▷ *Sorry, I don't have any.* Désolé, je n'en ai pas.; **any more (1)** (additional) encore de ▷ *Would you like any more coffee?* Est-ce que tu veux encore du café? **(2)** (no longer) ne... plus ▷ *I don't see her any more.* Je ne la vois plus.

anybody [ˈenɪbɒdɪ] pron **❶** (in question) quelqu'un ▷ *Does anybody have a pen?* Est-ce que quelqu'un a un stylo? **❷** (no matter who) n'importe qui ▷ *Anybody can learn to swim.* N'importe qui peut apprendre à nager.

> Use **ne... personne** in a negative sentence. **ne** comes before the verb, **personne** after it.

❸ ne... personne ▷ *I can't see anybody.* Je ne vois personne.

anyone [ˈenɪwʌn] pron **❶** (in question) quelqu'un ▷ *Has anyone got a pen?* Est-ce que quelqu'un a un stylo? **❷** (no matter who) n'importe qui ▷ *Anyone can learn to swim.* N'importe qui peut apprendre à nager.

> Use **ne... personne** in a negative sentence. **ne** comes before the verb, **personne** after it.

❸ ne... personne ▷ I can't see anyone. Je ne vois personne.

anything ['ɛnɪθɪŋ] pron ❶ (in question) quelque chose ▷ Would you like anything to eat? Tu veux manger quelque chose? ❷ (no matter what) n'importe quoi ▷ Anything could happen. Il pourrait arriver n'importe quoi.

> Use **ne... rien** in a negative sentence. **ne** comes before the verb, **rien** after it.

❸ ne... rien ▷ I can't hear anything. Je n'entends rien.

anyway ['ɛnɪweɪ] adv de toute façon ▷ He doesn't want to go out, and anyway he's not allowed. Il ne veut pas sortir et de toute façon il n'y est pas autorisé.

anywhere ['ɛnɪwɛə'] adv ❶ (in question) quelque part ▷ Have you seen my coat anywhere? Est-ce que tu as vu mon manteau quelque part? ❷ n'importe où ▷ You can buy stamps anywhere. On peut acheter des timbres presque n'importe où.

> Use **ne... nulle part** in a negative sentence. **ne** comes before the verb, **nulle part** after it.

❸ ne... nulle part ▷ I can't find it anywhere. Je ne le trouve nulle part.

apart [ə'pɑːt] adv: The two towns are 10 kilometres apart. Les deux villes sont à dix kilomètres l'une de l'autre.; **apart from** à part ▷ Apart from that, everything's fine. À part ça, tout va bien.

apartment [ə'pɑːtmənt] n appartement m

apologize [ə'pɒlədʒaɪz] vb s'excuser ▷ He apologized for being late. Il s'est excusé de son retard.; **I apologize!** Je m'excuse.

apology [ə'pɒlədʒɪ] n excuses fpl

apostrophe [ə'pɒstrəfɪ] n

apostrophe f

app [æp] abbr (= application) appli m

apparatus [æpə'reɪtəs] n ❶ (in lab) matériel m ❷ (in gym) agrès mpl

apparent [ə'pærənt] adj apparent

apparently [ə'pærəntlɪ] adv apparemment

appeal [ə'piːl] vb lancer un appel ▷ They appealed for help. Ils ont lancé un appel au secours.; **Greece doesn't appeal to me.** Ça ne me tente pas d'aller en Grèce.; **Does that appeal to you?** Ça te tente? ▶ n appel m ▷ They have launched an appeal. Ils ont lancé un appel.

appear [ə'pɪə'] vb ❶ (come into view) apparaître ▷ The bus appeared around the corner. L'autobus est apparu au coin de la rue.; **to appear on TV** passer à la télé ❷ (seem) paraître ▷ She appeared to be asleep. Elle paraissait dormir.

appearance [ə'pɪərəns] n (looks) apparence f ▷ He takes great care over his appearance. Il prend grand soin de son apparence.

appendicitis [əpɛndɪ'saɪtɪs] n appendicite f

appetite ['æpɪtaɪt] n appétit m

applaud [ə'plɔːd] vb applaudir

applause [ə'plɔːz] n applaudissements mpl

apple ['æpl] n pomme f; **an apple tree** un pommier

applicant ['æplɪkənt] n candidat m, candidate f ▷ There were a hundred applicants for the job. Il y avait cent candidats pour ce poste.

application [æplɪ'keɪʃən] n application (computer) f ▷ to open an application lancer une application; **a job application** une demande d'emploi

application form n ❶ (for job) dossier de candidature m

❷ *(college or university)* demande d'admission *f*

apply [ə'plaɪ] *vb*: **to apply for a job** poser sa candidature à un poste; **to apply to** *(be relevant)* s'appliquer à ▷ *This rule doesn't apply to us.* Ce règlement ne s'applique pas à nous.

appointment [ə'pɔɪntmənt] *n* rendez-vous *m* ▷ *I have a dental appointment.* J'ai rendez-vous chez le dentiste.

appreciate [ə'priːʃɪeɪt] *vb* être reconnaissant de ▷ *I really appreciate your help.* Je vous suis extrêmement reconnaissant de votre aide.

apprentice [ə'prɛntɪs] *n* apprenti *m*, apprentie *f*

approach [ə'prəʊtʃ] *vb* ❶ *(get nearer to)* s'approcher de ▷ *She approached the house.* Elle s'est approchée de la maison. ❷ *(tackle)* aborder ▷ *to approach a problem* aborder un problème

appropriate [ə'prəʊprɪət] *adj* approprié ▷ *That dress isn't very appropriate for an interview.* Cette robe n'est pas très appropriée pour une entrevue.

approval [ə'pruːvəl] *n* approbation *f*

approve [ə'pruːv] *vb*: **to approve of** approuver ▷ *I don't approve of your choice.* Je n'approuve pas ton choix.; **They didn't approve of his girlfriend.** Sa copine ne leur a pas plu.

approximate [ə'prɒksɪmeɪt] *adj* approximatif *(f* approximative)

apricot ['eɪprɪkɒt] *n* abricot *m*

April ['eɪprəl] *n* avril *m*; **in April** en avril; **April Fool's Day** le premier avril

apron ['eɪprən] *n* tablier *m*

Aquarius [ə'kwɛərɪəs] *n* Verseau *m* ▷ *I'm Aquarius.* Je suis Verseau.

Arabic ['ærəbɪk] *n* arabe *m*

arch [ɑːtʃ] *n* arc *m*

archaeologist [ɑːkɪ'ɒlədʒɪst] *n* archéologue *mf* ▷ *He's an archaeologist.* Il est archéologue.

archaeology [ɑːkɪ'ɒlədʒɪ] *n* archéologie *f*

architect ['ɑːkɪtɛkt] *n* architecte *mf* ▷ *She's an architect.* Elle est architecte.

architecture ['ɑːkɪtɛktʃər] *n* architecture *f*

Arctic ['ɑːktɪk] *n* Arctique *m*

are [ɑː] *vb* see **be**

area ['ɛərɪə] *n* ❶ région *f* ▷ *I live in the Kingston area.* J'habite dans la région de Kingston. ❷ quartier *m* ▷ *This is my favourite area of Montréal.* C'est le quartier de Montréal que je préfère. ❸ superficie *f* ▷ *The field has an area of 1500 m².* Le champ a une superficie de mille cinq cent mètres carrés.

area code *n* indicatif *m* régional

arena [ə'riːnə] *n* aréna *m* ▷ *They're building a new arena in Timmins.* On construit un nouvel aréna à Timmins.

argue ['ɑːgjuː] *vb* se disputer ▷ *They never stop arguing.* Ils n'arrêtent pas de se disputer.

argument ['ɑːgjʊmənt] *n*: **to have an argument** se disputer ▷ *They had an argument.* Ils se sont disputés.

Aries ['ɛərɪz] *n* Bélier *m* ▷ *I'm Aries.* Je suis Bélier.

arm [ɑːm] *n* bras *m*

armchair [ɑːm'tʃɛər] *n* fauteuil *m*

armour ['ɑːmər] *n* armure *f*

army ['ɑːmɪ] *n* armée *f*

around [ə'raʊnd] *prep, adv* ❶ autour de ▷ *She wore a scarf around her neck.* Elle portait une écharpe autour du cou. ❷ *(approximately)* environ ▷ *It*

costs around $100. Cela coûte
environ cent dollars. **❸** (date,
time) vers ▷ Let's meet at around 8
p.m. Retrouvons-nous vers vingt
heures.; **around here (1)** (nearby)
près d'ici ▷ Is there a drugstore around
here? Est-ce qu'il y a une pharmacie
près d'ici? **(2)** (in this area) dans les
parages ▷ He lives around here. Il
habite dans les parages.

arrange [əˈreɪndʒ] vb: **to arrange
to do something** prévoir de faire
quelque chose ▷ They arranged to go
out together on Friday. Ils ont prévu
de sortir ensemble vendredi.; **to
arrange a meeting** convenir d'un
rendez-vous ▷ Can we arrange a
meeting? Pouvons-nous convenir
d'un rendez-vous?; **to arrange a
party** organiser une fête

arrangement [əˈreɪndʒmənt] n
(plan) arrangement m; **They made
arrangements to go out on Friday
night.** Ils ont organisé une sortie
vendredi soir.

arrest [əˈrest] vb arrêter ▷ The
police have arrested 5 people. La police
a arrêté cinq personnes.
▷ n arrestation f ▷ You're
under arrest! Vous êtes en état
d'arrestation!

arrival [əˈraɪvl] n arrivée f; **to
welcome the new arrivals**
accueillir les nouveaux venus

arrive [əˈraɪv] vb arriver ▷ I arrived
at 5 o'clock. Je suis arrivé à cinq
heures.

arrogant [ˈærəɡənt] adj arrogant

arrow [ˈærəʊ] n flèche f

art [ɑːt] n art m

artery [ˈɑːtərɪ] n artère f

art gallery n galerie d'art f

article [ˈɑːtɪkl] n article m ▷ a
newspaper article un article de
journal

artificial [ˌɑːtɪˈfɪʃl] adj artificiel (f
artificielle)

artist [ˈɑːtɪst] n artiste mf ▷ She's an
artist. C'est une artiste.

artistic [ɑːˈtɪstɪk] adj artistique

as [æz] conj, adv **❶** (while) au
moment où ▷ He came in as I was
leaving. Il est arrivé au moment où
je partais. **❷** (since) puisque ▷ As
it's a holiday, you can sleep in. Tu peux
faire la grasse matinée, puisque
c'est un jour de congé.; **as...as**
aussi... que ▷ I'm as tall as he is. Je
suis aussi grand que lui.; **twice
as... as** deux fois plus... que ▷ Her
coat cost twice as much as mine. Son
manteau a coûté deux fois plus
cher que le mien.; **as much... as**
autant... que ▷ I don't have as much
money as you. Je n'ai pas autant
d'argent que toi.; **as soon as
possible** dès que possible ▷ I'll do it
as soon as possible. Je le ferai dès que
possible.; **as of tomorrow** à partir
de demain ▷ As of tomorrow, the store
will stay open until 10 p.m. À partir
de demain, le magasin restera
ouvert jusqu'à vingt-deux heures.;
as though comme si ▷ She acted as
though she hadn't seen me. Elle a fait
comme si elle ne m'avait pas vu.; **as
if** comme si; **He works as a waiter.**
Il travaille comme serveur.

ASAP [ˌeɪeɪ esˈiː piː] abbr (= as soon as
possible) dès que possible

ashamed [əˈʃeɪmd] adj: **to be
ashamed** avoir honte ▷ I was
ashamed of my rude behaviour. J'avais
honte d'avoir été si impoli.

ashtray [ˈæʃtreɪ] n cendrier m

ask [ɑːsk] vb **❶** (inquire, request)
demander ▷ 'Are you finished?'
she asked. «Tu as fini?» a-t-elle
demandé.; **to ask somebody
something** demander quelque
chose à quelqu'un ▷ He asked her
how old she was. Il lui a demandé

quel âge elle avait.; **to ask for something** demander quelque chose ▷ *He asked for a cup of tea.* Il a demandé une tasse de thé.; **to ask somebody to do something** demander à quelqu'un de faire quelque chose ▷ *She asked him to do the shopping.* Elle lui a demandé de faire les courses.; **to ask about something** se renseigner sur quelque chose ▷ *I asked about tourist attractions.* Je me suis renseigné sur les attractions touristiques.; **to ask somebody a question** poser une question à quelqu'un ❷ inviter ▷ *Have you asked him to the party?* Est-ce que tu l'as invité à la fête?; **He asked her out.** (*on a date*) Il lui a demandé de sortir avec lui.

asleep [əˈsliːp] *adj*; **to be asleep** dormir ▷ *She's asleep.* Elle dort.; **to fall asleep** s'endormir ▷ *I fell asleep in front of the TV.* Je me suis endormi devant la télé.

asparagus [əsˈpærəɡəs] *n* asperges *fpl*

aspect [ˈæspɛkt] *n* aspect *m*

aspirin [ˈæsprɪn] *n* aspirine *f*

assemble [əˈsɛmbl] *vb* ❶ assembler ▷ *You have to assemble the bookshelf yourself.* Tu dois assembler l'étagère toi-même. ❷ se réunir ▷ *The students assembled in the gym.* Les élèves se sont réunis dans le gymnase.

assembly [əˈsɛmblɪ] *n* réunion d'école *f* (*school*) ▷ *The winner was announced in the assembly on Friday.* Le nom du gagnant a été annoncé durant la réunion d'école vendredi.

Assembly of First Nations *n* Assemblée *f* des Premières Nations

asset [ˈæsɛt] *n* atout *m* ▷ *Her experience will be an asset to the firm.* Son expérience sera un atout pour l'entreprise.

assignment [əˈsaɪnmənt] *n* (*in school*) devoir *m*

assistance [əˈsɪstəns] *n* aide *f*

▪ Be careful not to translate **assistance** by **l'assistance**.

assistant [əˈsɪstənt] *n* ❶ (*in store*) vendeur *m*, vendeuse *f* ❷ (*helper*) assistant *m*, assistante *f*

association [əsəusɪˈeɪʃən] *n* association *f*

assorted [əˈsɔːtɪd] *adj* assorti ▷ *assorted chocolates* des chocolats assortis

assortment [əˈsɔːtmənt] *n* assortiment *m*

assume [əˈsjuːm] *vb* supposer ▷ *I assume you won't be coming.* Je suppose que tu ne viendras pas.

assure [əˈʃuəʳ] *vb* assurer ▷ *He assured me he was coming.* Il m'a assuré qu'il viendrait.

asthma [ˈæsmə] *n* asthme *m* ▷ *I have asthma.* J'ai de l'asthme.

astonish [əˈstɒnɪʃ] *vb* étonner

astonishing [əˈstɒnɪʃɪŋ] *adj* étonnant

astrology [əsˈtrɒlədʒɪ] *n* astrologie *f*

astronaut [ˈæstrənɔːt] *n* astronaute *mf*

astronomer [əsˈtrɒnəməʳ] *n* astronome *mf*

astronomy [əsˈtrɒnəmɪ] *n* astronomie *f*

asylum seeker [-siːkəʳ] *n* demandeur d'asile *m*, demandeuse d'asile *f*

at [æt] *prep*

▪ **à** + **le** becomes **au**, **à** + **les** becomes **aux**.

▷ *at 4 o'clock* à quatre heures ▷ *at Christmas* à Noël ▷ *at 50 km/h* à cinquante km/h ▷ *at home* à la maison ▷ *two at a time* deux à la fois ▷ *at school* à l'école, au ▷ *at the office* au bureau, aux ▷ *at the races* aux courses; **at night** la nuit

ate [eɪt] *vb see* **eat**

athlete [ˈæθliːt] *n* athlète *mf*; **athlete's foot** pied d'athlète

athletic [æθˈletɪk] *adj* athlétique

Atlantic Provinces [ətˈlæntɪkˈprovɪnsəz] *npl* provinces *fpl* atlantiques

atlas [ˈætləs] *n* atlas *m*

atmosphere [ˈætməsfɪəʳ] *n*
❶ atmosphère *f* ❷ ambiance *f*
▷ *J'aime l'ambiance de ce café.* I like the atmosphere in this café.

atom [ˈætəm] *n* atome *m*

atomic [əˈtomɪk] *adj* atomique

attach [əˈtætʃ] *vb* fixer ▷ *He attached a rope to the car.* Il a fixé une corde à la voiture.; **Please find attached.** Veuillez trouver ci-joint...

attached [əˈtætʃt] *adj*: **to be attached to** être attaché à ▷ *He's very attached to his family.* Il est très attaché à sa famille.

attachment [əˈtætʃmənt] *n* (email) pièce jointe *f*

attack [əˈtæk] *vb* attaquer ▷ *The dog attacked her.* Le chien l'a attaquée.
▶ *n* attaque *f*

attempt [əˈtempt] *n* tentative *f*
▷ *She gave up after several attempts.* Elle a renoncé après plusieurs tentatives.
▶ *vb*: **to attempt to do something** essayer de faire quelque chose ▷ *I attempted to write a song.* J'ai essayé d'écrire une chanson.

attend [əˈtend] *vb* assister à ▷ *to attend a meeting* assister à une réunion

Be careful not to translate **to attend** by **attendre**.

attendance [əˈtendəns] *n*: **to take attendance** prendre les présences

attention [əˈtenʃən] *n* attention *f*; **to pay attention to** faire attention à ▷ *He didn't pay attention to what I was saying.* Il ne faisait pas attention à ce que je disais.

attic [ˈætɪk] *n* grenier *m*

attitude [ˈætɪtjuːd] *n* (way of thinking) attitude *f* ▷ *I really don't like your attitude!* Je n'aime pas du tout ton attitude!

attract [əˈtrækt] *vb* attirer ▷ *Niagara Falls attracts lots of tourists.* Les chutes Niagara attirent de nombreux touristes.

attraction [əˈtrækʃən] *n* attraction *f* ▷ *a tourist attraction* une attraction touristique

attractive [əˈtræktɪv] *adj* séduisant ▷ *She's very attractive.* Elle est très séduisante.

auction [ˈɔːkʃən] *n* vente aux enchères *f*

audience [ˈɔːdɪəns] *n* (in theatre) spectateurs *mpl*

audio [ˈɔːdɪəu] *adj* audio (*f+pl* audio) ▷ *audio files* des fichiers audio ▷ *an audio clip* un audioclip ▷ *audio equipment* le matériel audio

audition [ɔːˈdɪʃən] *n* audition *f*
▶ *vb* auditionner

August [ˈɔːgəst] *n* août *m*; **in August** en août

aunt, aunty [ɑːnt, ˈɑːntɪ] *n* tante *f* ▷ *my aunt* ma tante

author [ˈɔːθəʳ] *n* auteur *m*, auteure *f*

autobiography [ɔːtəbaɪˈɒgrəfɪ] *n* autobiographie *f*

autograph [ˈɔːtəgrɑːf] *n* autographe *m*

automatic [ɔːtəˈmætɪk] *adj* automatique ▷ *an automatic door* une porte automatique

autumn [ˈɔːtəm] *n* automne *m*; **in autumn** en automne

available [əˈveɪləbl] *adj* disponible

▷ *Free brochures are available on request.* Des brochures gratuites sont disponibles sur demande. ▷ *Is he available today?* Est-ce qu'il est disponible aujourd'hui?

avalanche [ˈævəlɑːnʃ] n avalanche f

avenue [ˈævənjuː] n avenue f

average [ˈævərɪdʒ] n moyenne f ▷ *on average* en moyenne ▶ adj moyen (f moyenne) ▷ *the average price* le prix moyen

avocado [ævəˈkɑːdəʊ] n avocat m

avoid [əˈvɔɪd] vb éviter ▷ *We avoid him when he's in a bad mood.* Nous l'évitons lorsqu'il est de mauvaise humeur.; **to avoid doing something** éviter de faire quelque chose ▷ *Avoid going out on your own at night.* Évite de sortir seul le soir.

awake [əˈweɪk] adj: **to be awake** être réveillé ▷ *Is she awake?* Elle est réveillée?; **He was still awake.** Il ne dormait pas encore.

award [əˈwɔːd] n prix m ▷ *She won an award.* Elle a remporté un prix. ▷ *the award for the best actor* le prix du meilleur acteur

aware [əˈwɛə] adj: **to be aware of something** être conscient de quelque chose

away adj, adv (not here) absent ▷ *She's away today.* Elle est absente aujourd'hui.; **He's away for a week.** Il est parti pour une semaine.; **The town's 2 kilometres away.** La ville est à deux kilomètres d'ici.; **The coast is 2 hours away by car.** La côte est à deux heures de route.; **Go away!** Va-t'en!; **to put something away** ranger quelque chose ▷ *He put the dishes away in the cupboard.* Il a rangé la vaisselle dans le placard.

away game n match à l'extérieur m (pl matchs à l'extérieur)

awful [ˈɔːfəl] adj affreux (f affreuse) ▷ *That's awful!* C'est affreux!; **an awful lot of...** énormément de...

awkward [ˈɔːkwəd] adj ❶ (difficult to deal with) délicat ▷ *an awkward situation* une situation délicate ❷ (embarrassing) gênant ▷ *an awkward question* une question gênante; **It's a bit awkward for me to come today.** Ce n'est pas très pratique pour moi de venir aujourd'hui.

awoke, awoken [əˈwəʊk, əˈwəʊkn] vb see **awake**

axe [æks] n hache f

b

BA [biː'eɪ] *n* baccalauréat *m*; **a BA in French** un baccalauréat en français

baby ['beɪbɪ] *n* bébé *m*

babysit ['beɪbɪsɪt] *vb* garder des enfants

babysitter ['beɪbɪsɪtər] *n* gardien d'enfants *m*, gardienne d'enfants *f*

babysitting ['beɪbɪsɪtɪŋ] *n* garde d'enfants *f*

bachelor ['bætʃələr] *n* célibataire *m* ▷ *He's a bachelor.* Il est célibataire.

back [bæk] *n* ❶ (of person, horse, book) dos *m* ❷ (of car, house) arrière *m* ▷ *in the back* à l'arrière ❸ (of page) verso *m* ▷ *on the back* au verso ❹ (of room, garden) fond *m* ▷ *at the back* au fond
▶ *adj, adv* arrière (f+pl arrière) ▷ *the back seat* le siège arrière ▷ *The back wheel of my bike* la roue arrière de mon vélo.; **the back door** la porte de derrière; **to get back**

rentrer ▷ *What time did you get back?* À quelle heure est-ce que tu es rentré?; **We went there by bus and walked back.** Nous y sommes allés en autobus et nous sommes rentrés à pied.; **She's not back yet.** Elle n'est pas encore rentrée.; **to call somebody back** rappeler quelqu'un ▷ *I'll call back later.* Je rappellerai plus tard.
▶ *vb* (support) soutenir ▷ *I'm backing the other candidate.* Je soutiens l'autre candidat.; **to back out** se désister ▷ *They promised to help and then backed out.* Ils avaient promis de nous aider et ils se sont désistés.; **to back somebody up** soutenir quelqu'un

backache ['bækeɪk] *n* mal du dos *m* ▷ *to have backache* avoir mal au dos

backfire [bæk'faɪər] *vb* avoir l'effet inverse ▷ *Her tactics could backfire on her.* Sa stratégie pourrait avoir l'effet inverse.

background ['bækgraund] *n* ❶ (of picture) arrière-plan *m* ▷ *a house in the background* une maison à l'arrière-plan; **background noise** les *m* bruits de fond ❷ milieu *m* (pl milieux) ▷ *his family background* son milieu familial

backhand ['bækhænd] *n* revers *m*

backing ['bækɪŋ] *n* (support) soutien *m*

backpack ['bækpæk] *n* sac à dos *m*

backpacker ['bækpækər] *n* ❶ (globetrotter) routard *m*, routarde *f* ❷ (hiker) randonneur *m*, randonneuse *f*

backpacking ['bækpækɪŋ] *n*: **to go backpacking** voyager sac au dos

back pain *n* mal au dos *m* ▷ *to have back pain* avoir mal au dos

backside ['bæksaɪd] *n* derrière *m*

backslash ['bækslæʃ] *n* barre

oblique inverse f

backstroke ['bækstrəuk] n dos crawlé m

backup ['bækʌp] n (support) soutien m; **a backup file** une sauvegarde

backwards ['bækwədz] adv en arrière ▷ **to take a step backwards** faire un pas en arrière; **to fall backwards** tomber à la renverse

backyard [bæk'jɑːd] n cour f

bacon ['beɪkən] n ❶ (British type) bacon m ▷ **bacon and eggs** des œufs au bacon ❷ (French type) lard m

bad [bæd] adj ❶ mauvais ▷ a bad film un mauvais film ▷ the bad weather le mauvais temps ▷ to be in a bad mood être de mauvaise humeur; **to be bad at something** être mauvais en quelque chose ▷ I'm really bad at math. Je suis vraiment mauvais en maths. ❷ (serious) grave ▷ a bad accident un accident grave ❸ (naughty) vilain ▷ bad words vilains mots; **to go bad** (food) se gâter; **I feel bad about it.** Ça m'ennuie.; **not bad** pas mal ▷ That's not bad at all. Ce n'est pas mal du tout.

badge [bædʒ] n badge m

badly ['bædlɪ] adv mal ▷ badly paid mal payé; **badly wounded** grièvement blessé; **He badly needs a rest.** Il a sérieusement besoin de se reposer.

badminton ['bædmɪntən] n badminton m ▷ **to play badminton** jouer au badminton

bad-tempered [bæd'tempəd] adj: **to be bad-tempered** (1) (by nature) avoir mauvais caractère ▷ She's a really bad-tempered person. Elle a vraiment mauvais caractère. (2) (temporarily) être de mauvaise humeur ▷ He was really bad-tempered yesterday. Il était vraiment

de mauvaise humeur hier.

Baffin Island ['bæfɪn'aɪlənd] n île f de Baffin

baffled ['bæfld] adj déconcerté

bag [bæg] n sac m

bagel ['beɪgl] n baguel m ▷ a toasted bagel un baguel grillé

baggage ['bægɪdʒ] n bagages mpl

baggy ['hægɪ] adj ample

bagpipes ['bægpaɪps] npl cornemuse f ▷ She plays the bagpipes. Elle joue de la cornemuse.

bake [beɪk] vb: **to bake a cake** faire un gâteau

baked [beɪkt] adj cuit au four ▷ baked potatoes les pommes de terre cuites au four f; **baked beans** les haricots mpl au lard

baker ['beɪkə'] n boulanger m, boulangère f ▷ She's a baker. Elle est boulangère.

bakery ['beɪkərɪ] n boulangerie f

baking ['beɪkɪŋ] adj: **It's baking in here!** Il fait une chaleur torride ici!

balance ['bæləns] n équilibre m ▷ to lose one's balance perdre l'équilibre

balanced ['bælənst] adj équilibré

balcony ['bælkənɪ] n balcon m

bald [bɔːld] adj chauve

ball [bɔːl] n ❶ (tennis, golf, baseball) balle f ❷ (football, soccer) ballon m

ballet ['bæleɪ] n ballet m ▷ We went to a ballet. Nous sommes allés voir un ballet.; **ballet lessons** les cours de danse classique

ballet dancer n danseur classique m, danseuse classique f

ballet shoes npl chaussons mpl de danse

balloon [bə'luːn] n (for parties) ballon m, ▷ **a hot-air balloon** une montgolfière

ballpoint pen ['bɔːlpɔɪnt'pen] n stylo à bille m

ban [bæn] n interdiction f; **a ban**

on video games une interdiction de jeux vidéo
▶ vb interdire

banana [bəˈnɑːnə] n banane f
▷ a banana peel une peau de banane

band [bænd] n ❶ (rock band) groupe m ❷ (brass band) fanfare f ❸ (First Nations) bande f; **a band chief** un chef de bande

bandage [ˈbændɪdʒ] n bandage m
▶ vb mettre un bandage à ▷ The nurse bandaged my arm. L'infirmière m'a mis un bandage au bras.

bandaid [ˈbændeɪd] n pansement adhésif m

band council n conseil de bande m

bandit [ˈbændɪt] n bandit m

bang [bæŋ] n ❶ détonation f ▷ I heard a loud bang. J'ai entendu une forte détonation. ❷ coup m ▷ a bang on the head un coup sur la tête; **Bang!** Pan!
▶ vb (part of body) se cogner ▷ I banged my head. Je me suis cogné la tête.; **to bang the door** claquer la porte; **to bang on the door** cogner à la porte

bangs [bæŋz] npl frange f ▷ short bangs une frange courte

bank [bæŋk] n ❶ (financial) banque f ❷ (of river, lake) bord m

bank account n compte en banque m

banker [ˈbæŋkəʳ] n banquier m

banned [bænd] adj interdit

bannock [ˈbænək] n banique f

banquet [ˈbæŋkwɪt] n banquet m ▷ the graduation banquet le banquet des finissants

bar [bɑːʳ] n (metal) barre f; **a chocolate bar** une tablette de chocolat; **a bar of soap** une savonnette

barbaric [bɑːˈbærɪk] adj barbare

barbecue [ˈbɑːbɪkjuː] n barbecue

m; **barbecue sauce** la sauce barbecue
▶ vb griller au barbecue ▷ to barbecue chicken griller du poulet au barbecue; **barbecued pork chops** des côtelettes de porc grillées au barbecue

barber [ˈbɑːbəʳ] n coiffeur pour hommes m

bare [bɛəʳ] adj nu

barefoot [ˈbɛəfut] adj, adv nu-pieds (f+pl nu-pieds) ▷ The children go around barefoot. Les enfants se promènent nu-pieds.; **to be barefoot** avoir les pieds nus ▷ She was barefoot. Elle avait les pieds nus.

barely [ˈbɛəlɪ] adv à peine ▷ I could barely hear what they were saying. J'entendais à peine ce qu'ils disaient.

bargain [ˈbɑːgɪn] n affaire f ▷ It was a bargain! C'était une affaire!

bark [bɑːk] n (tree) écorce f
▶ vb aboyer

barn [bɑːn] n grange f

barrel [ˈbærəl] n tonneau m (pl tonneaux)

Barrens [ˈbærənz] npl région des Barrens f

barrier [ˈbærɪəʳ] n barrière f

base [beɪs] n base f

baseball [ˈbeɪsbɔːl] n baseball m; **a baseball cap** une casquette de baseball

based [beɪst] adj: **based on** fondé sur

basement [ˈbeɪsmənt] n sous-sol m

basic [ˈbeɪsɪk] adj ❶ de base ▷ It's a basic model. C'est un modèle de base. ❷ rudimentaire ▷ The accommodation is pretty basic. Le logement est plutôt rudimentaire.

basically [ˈbeɪsɪklɪ] adv tout simplement ▷ Basically, I just don't like him. Tout simplement, je ne l'aime pas.

basics ['beɪsɪks] npl rudiments mpl

basin ['beɪsn] n (washbasin) lavabo m

basis ['beɪsɪs] n: **on a daily basis** quotidiennement; **on a regular basis** régulièrement

basket ['bɑːskɪt] n panier m

basketball ['bɑːskɪtbɔːl] n basket m

bass [beɪs] n ❶ (guitar, singer) basse f ▷ She plays the bass. Elle joue de la basse. ▷ He's a bass. Il est basse.; **a bass guitar** une guitare basse; **a double bass** une contrebasse ❷ (on stereo) graves mpl ❸ (fish) achigan

bass drum n grosse caisse f

bassoon [bə'suːn] n basson m ▷ I play the bassoon. Je joue du basson.

bat [bæt] n ❶ (for baseball) batte f; **Who's up to bat?** Qui est à la batte? ❷ (for table tennis) raquette f ❸ (animal) chauve-souris f (pl chauves-souris)

bath [bɑːθ] n ❶ bain m ▷ to have a bath prendre un bain; **a hot bath** un bain chaud ❷ (bathtub) baignoire f ▷ There's a spider in the bath. Il y a une araignée dans la baignoire.

bathe [beɪð] vb se baigner

bathing suit ['beɪðɪŋ suːt] n maillot de bain m

bathroom ['bɑːθrʊm] n salle de bains f

batter ['bætər] n ❶ pâte f cake batter la pâte à gâteau ❷ (baseball) batteur m

battery ['bætərɪ] n ❶ (for flashlight, toy) pile f ❷ (of car) batterie f

battle ['bætl] n bataille f ▷ the Battle of the Plains of Abraham la bataille des Plaines d'Abraham; **It was a battle, but we succeeded in**

the end. Il a fallu se battre, mais on a fini par y arriver.

bay [beɪ] n baie f

bazaar [bə'zɑː] n bazar m ▷ Our school holds a bazaar every spring. Notre école tient un bazar tous les printemps.

BC [biː'siː] abbr (= before Christ) av. J.-C. (= avant Jésus Christ) ▷ in 200 BC en deux cents avant Jésus-Christ

BCE [biːiː'iː] abbr (= before the Common Era) av. J.-C. (= avant Jésus-Christ) ▷ in 200 BCE en deux cents avant Jésus-Christ

be [biː] vb être ▷ I'm tired. Je suis fatigué. ▷ You're late. Tu es en retard. ▷ She's English. Elle est anglaise. ▷ Iqaluit is in Nunavut. Iqaluit est au Nunavut. ▷ It's 4 o'clock. Il est quatre heures. ▷ We are all happy. Nous sommes tous heureux. ▷ They are in Moncton at the moment. Ils sont à Moncton en ce moment. ▷ I've been ill. J'ai été malade.; **It's the 28th of October today.** Nous sommes le vingt-huit octobre.; **Have you been to Greece before?** Est-ce que tu es déjà allé en Grèce?; **I've never been to Chicoutimi.** Je ne suis jamais allé à Chicoutimi.; **to be killed** être tué

> When you are saying what somebody's occupation is, you leave out the "a" in French.

▷ She's a doctor. Elle est médecin.
▷ He's a student. Il est étudiant.

> With certain adjectives, such as "cold", "hot", "hungry" and "thirsty", use avoir instead of être.

I'm cold. J'ai froid.; **I'm hungry.** J'ai faim.

> When saying how old somebody is, use avoir not être.

I'm fourteen. J'ai quatorze ans.;

How old are you? Quel âge as-tu?
▶ When referring to the weather, use **faire**.
It's cold. Il fait froid.; **It's too hot.** Il fait trop chaud.; **It's a nice day.** Il fait beau.

beach [biːtʃ] n plage f

bead [biːd] n perle f

beak [biːk] n bec m

beam [biːm] n ❶ (of light) rayon m ❷ (wooden) poutre f

beans [biːnz] n ❶ haricots mpl ❷ (baked beans) haricots mpl au lard ▷ I had beans on toast. J'ai mangé des haricots au lard sur du pain grillé.; **green beans** les m haricots verts; **kidney beans** les m haricots rouges

bear [bɛəʳ] n ours m; **a bear cub** un ourson
▶ vb supporter; **I can't bear it!** C'est insupportable!; **to bear up** tenir le coup; **Bear up!** Tiens bon!

beard [bɪəd] n barbe f; **He has a beard.** Il est barbu.; **a man with a beard** un barbu

bearded [ˈbɪədɪd] adj barbu

beat [biːt] n rythme m
▶ vb battre ▷ We beat them 3-0. On les a battus trois à zéro.

beautiful [ˈbjuːtɪfʊl] adj beau (f belle, mpl beaux) ▷ a beautiful smile un beau sourire

The form **beau** changes to **bel** before a vowel and most words beginning with h.
▷ a beautiful afternoon un bel après-midi

beautifully [ˈbjuːtɪflɪ] adv admirablement

beauty [ˈbjuːtɪ] n beauté f

beaver [ˈbiːvəʳ] n castor m

became [bɪˈkeɪm] vb see **become**

because [bɪˈkɒz] conj parce que ▷ I did it because... Je l'ai fait parce que...; **because of** à cause de ▷ because of the weather à cause

du temps

become [bɪˈkʌm] vb devenir ▷ She became a famous writer. Elle est devenue un grand écrivain.

bed [bɛd] n lit m ▷ in bed au lit; **to go to bed** aller se coucher

bed and breakfast n chambre d'hôte f ▷ We stayed in a bed and breakfast. Nous avons logé dans une chambre d'hôte.; **How much is it for bed and breakfast?** C'est combien pour la chambre et le petit déjeuner?

bedding [ˈbɛdɪŋ] n literie f

bedroom [ˈbɛdrʊm] n chambre f

bedspread [ˈbɛdsprɛd] n dessus-de-lit m (pl dessus-de-lit)

bedtime [ˈbɛdtaɪm] n: **Ten o'clock is my usual bedtime.** Je me couche généralement à dix heures.; **Bedtime!** Au lit!

bee [biː] n abeille f

beef [biːf] n bœuf m; **roast beef** (1) (served rare) le rosbif (2) (served well done) le rôti de bœuf

been [biːn] vb see **be**

beep [biːp] n bip m ▷ Leave your message after the beep. Laissez votre message après le bip.

beet [biːt] n betterave rouge f

beetle [ˈbiːtl] n scarabée m

before [bɪˈfɔːʳ] prep, conj, adv ❶ avant ▷ before Tuesday avant mardi ❷ avant de ▷ before going avant de partir ▷ Before opening the box, read the instructions. Avant d'ouvrir la boîte, lisez le mode d'emploi. ▷ I'll phone before I leave. J'appellerai avant de partir. ❸ (already) déjà ▷ I've seen this film before. J'ai déjà vu ce film. ▷ Have you been to Alberta before?; **the day before** la veille; **the week before** la semaine précédente

beforehand [bɪˈfɔːhænd] adv à l'

l'avance

beg [beg] vb ❶ (for money) mendier ❷ supplier ▷ I beg you to stop. Je te supplie d'arrêter.

began [bɪˈgæn] vb see **begin**

beggar [ˈbegər] n mendiant m, mendiante f

begin [bɪˈgɪn] vb commencer; **to begin doing something** commencer à faire quelque chose

beginner [bɪˈgɪnər] n débutant m, débutante f ▷ I'm just a beginner. Je ne suis qu'un débutant.

beginning [bɪˈgɪnɪŋ] n début m ▷ in the beginning au début

begun [bɪˈgʌn] vb see **begin**

behalf [bɪˈhɑːf] n: **on behalf of somebody** pour quelqu'un

behave [bɪˈheɪv] vb se comporter ▷ He behaved like an idiot. Il s'est comporté comme un idiot. ▷ She behaved very badly. Elle s'est très mal comportée.; **to behave oneself** être sage ▷ Did the children behave themselves? Est-ce que les enfants ont été sages?; **Behave!** Sois sage!

behaviour [bɪˈheɪvjər] n comportement m

behind [bɪˈhaɪnd] prep, adv derrière m ▷ behind the television derrière la télévision; **to be behind** (late) avoir du retard ▷ I'm behind with my homework. J'ai du retard dans mes devoirs.
▶ n derrière m

beige [beɪʒ] adj beige

believe [bɪˈliːv] vb croire ▷ I don't believe you. Je ne te crois pas.; **to believe in something** croire à quelque chose ▷ Do you believe in ghosts? Tu crois aux fantômes?; **to believe in God** croire en Dieu

bell [bel] n ❶ (doorbell) sonnette f; **to ring the bell** sonner à la porte ❷ (in church) cloche f ❸ (in school) sonnerie f ❹ clochette f ▷ Our cat

has a bell around its neck. Notre chat a une clochette sur son collier.

belly [ˈbeli] n ventre m

belong [bɪˈlɒŋ] vb: **to belong to somebody** être à quelqu'un ▷ Who does it belong to? C'est à qui? ▷ That belongs to me. C'est à moi.; **Do you belong to any clubs?** Est-ce que tu es membre d'un club?; **Where does this belong?** Où est-ce que ça va?

belongings [bɪˈlɒŋɪŋz] npl affaires fpl

below [bɪˈləʊ] prep, adv ❶ au-dessous de ▷ below sea level au-dessous du niveau de la mer ❷ en dessous ▷ on the floor below à l'étage en dessous; **10 degrees below freezing** moins dix

belt [belt] n ceinture f

bench [bentʃ] n ❶ (seat) banc m ❷ (workbench) établi m

bend [bend] n ❶ (in road) virage m ❷ (in river) coude m
▶ vb ❶ (one's back) courber ❷ (leg, arm) plier ▷ I can't bend my arm. Je n'arrive pas à plier le bras.; **"do not bend"** « ne pas plier » ❸ (road) tourner ▷ The road bends to the right. La route tourne vers la droite. ❹ (object) tordre ▷ You've bent it. Tu l'as tordu.; **to bend** ▷ It bends easily. Ça se tord facilement.; **to bend down** se baisser; **to bend over** se pencher

beneath [bɪˈniːθ] prep sous

benefit [ˈbenɪfɪt] n ❶ (advantage) avantage m ❷ **unemployment benefit** les allocations de chômage
▶ vb: **He'll benefit from the change.** Le changement lui fera du bien.

bent [bent] vb see **bend**
▶ adj tordu ▷ a bent fork une fourchette tordue

beret [ˈbeɪreɪ] n béret m

berry [ˈberi] n baie f

berserk [bə'sə:k] adj : **to go
berserk** devenir fou furieux ▷ *She
went berserk.* Elle est devenue folle
furieuse.

beside [bɪ'saɪd] prep à côté de
▷ *beside the television* à côté de la
télévision; **He was beside himself.**
Il était hors de lui.; **That's beside
the point.** Cela n'a rien à voir.

besides [bɪ'saɪdz] adv en plus
▷ *Besides, it's too expensive.* En plus,
c'est trop cher.

best [best] adj, adv ❶ meilleur
▷ *He's the best player on the team.* Il
est le meilleur joueur de l'équipe.
▷ *She's the best at math.* Elle est la
meilleure en maths. ❷ le mieux
▷ *She sings best.* C'est elle qui chante
le mieux. ▷ *That's the best I can do.*
Je ne peux pas faire mieux.; **to do
one's best** faire de son mieux ▷ *It's
not perfect, but I did my best.* Ça n'est
pas parfait, mais j'ai fait de mon
mieux.; **to make the best of it**
s'en contenter ▷ *We'll have to make
the best of it.* Il va falloir nous en
contenter.

best man n garçon d'honneur m

bet [bet] n pari m ▷ *to make a bet*
faire un pari
▸ vb parier ▷ *I bet you he won't come.*
Je te parie qu'il ne viendra pas.
▷ *I bet she forgot.* Je parie qu'elle
a oublié.

betray [bɪ'treɪ] vb trahir

betrayal [bɪ'treɪəl] n trahison f

better [bɛtə'] adj, adv ❶ meilleur
▷ *This one's better than that one.*
Celui-ci est meilleur que celui-là.
▷ *a better way to do it* une meilleure
façon de le faire ❷ mieux ▷ *That's
better!* C'est mieux comme ça.
▷ *This pen writes better.* Ce stylo-ci
écrit mieux.; **better still** encore
mieux ▷ *Go and see her tomorrow, or
better still, go today.* Va la voir

demain, ou encore mieux,
vas-y aujourd'hui ; **to get better**
(1) (*improve*) s'améliorer ▷ *I hope the
weather gets better soon.* J'espère que
le temps va s'améliorer bientôt.
▷ *My French is getting better.* Mon
français s'améliore. (2) (*from illness*)
se remettre ▷ *I hope you get better
soon.* J'espère que tu vas vite te
remettre.; **to feel better** se sentir
mieux ▷ *Are you feeling better now?*
Tu te sens mieux maintenant? ▷
You'd better do it right away.
Vous feriez mieux de le faire
immédiatement. ; **I'd better go
home.** Je ferais mieux de rentrer.

between [bɪ'twi:n] prep entre
▷ *Moose Jaw is between Swift Current
and Regina.* Moose Jaw est entre
Swift Current et Regina. ▷ *between
15 and 20 minutes* entre quinze et
vingt minutes

beware [bɪ'weə'] vb se méfier
▷ *Beware of strangers.* Méfie-toi des
inconnus.; **"Beware of dog"**
«Attention, chien méchant»

bewildered [bɪ'wɪldəd] adj : **He
looked bewildered.** Il avait l'air
perplexe.

beyond [bɪ'jɔnd] prep au-delà
de ▷ *There was a lake beyond the
mountain.* Il y avait un lac au-delà
de la montagne.; **beyond belief**
incroyable; **beyond repair**
irréparable

biased ['baɪəst] adj partial

bibliography [bɪblɪ'ɒɡrəfɪ] n
bibliographie f

bicycle ['baɪsɪkl] n vélo m

big [bɪg] adj ❶ grand ▷ *a big house*
une grande maison ▷ *her big sister*
sa grande sœur ▷ *He's a big guy.*
C'est un grand gaillard. ❷ (*car,
animal, book, package*) gros (f gross)
▷ *a big car* une grosse voiture

bike [baɪk] n vélo m ▷ *by bike* en vélo

bikini [bɪˈkiːnɪ] n bikini m
bilingual [baɪˈlɪŋgwəl] adj bilingue
bilingualism [baɪˈlɪŋgwəlɪzəm] n bilinguisme m
bill [bɪl] n ❶ (in restaurant) addition f ▷ Can we have the bill, please? L'addition, s'il vous plaît. ❷ (for gas, electricity) facture f ❸ billet m ▷ a five-dollar bill un billet de cinq dollars
billion [ˈbɪljən] n milliard m ▷ two billion people deux milliards de gens
binder [ˈbaɪndə*] n reliure f
bingo [ˈbɪŋgəʊ] n bingo m
binoculars [bɪˈnɒkjʊləz] npl jumelles fpl; **a pair of binoculars** des jumelles
biochemistry [baɪəˈkemɪstrɪ] n biochimie f
biodegradable
[ˈbaɪəʊdɪˈgreɪdəbl] adj biodégradable
biofuel [ˈbaɪəʊfjʊəl] n biocarburant m
biography [baɪˈɒgrəfɪ] n biographie f
biology [baɪˈɒlədʒɪ] n biologie f
birch [bəːtʃ] n bouleau m (pl bouleaux); **birch bark** l'écorce f de bouleau
bird [bəːd] n oiseau m (pl oiseaux)
birth [bəːθ] n naissance f ▷ date of birth la date de naissance
birth certificate n acte m de naissance
birth control n contraception f
birthday [ˈbəːθdeɪ] n anniversaire m ▷ When's your birthday? Quelle est la date de ton anniversaire?; **a birthday cake** un gâteau d'anniversaire; **a birthday card** une carte d'anniversaire; **I had a birthday party.** J'ai fait une fête pour mon anniversaire.
bison [ˈbaɪsən] n bison m
bit [bɪt] vb see **bite**
▶ n: **a bit** un peu ▷ I'm a bit tired.

Je suis un peu fatigué. ▷ a bit too hot un peu trop chaud ▷ Stay a bit longer. Reste un peu plus longtemps. ▷ "Do you play soccer?" — "A bit." «Tu joues au soccer?» — «Un peu.»; **a bit of** un peu de ▷ a bit of music un peu de musique; **It's a bit of a nuisance.** C'est ennuyeux.; **bit by bit** petit à petit
bite [baɪt] vb ❶ (person, dog) mordre ❷ (insect) piquer ▷ I got bitten by mosquitoes. Je me suis fait piquer par des moustiques.; **to bite one's nails** se ronger les ongles
▶ n ❶ (insect bite) piqûre f ❷ (animal bite) morsure f; **to have a bite to eat** manger un morceau
bitten [ˈbɪtn] vb see **bite**
bitter [ˈbɪtə*] adj ❶ amer (f amère) ❷ (weather, wind) glacial (mpl glaciaux) ▷ It's bitter out today. Il fait un froid glacial aujourd'hui.
bizarre [bɪˈzɑː*] adj bizarre
black [blæk] adj noir ▷ a black jacket une veste noire ▷ She's black. Elle est noire.
blackberry [ˈblækbərɪ] n mûre f
black currant [ˈblækˈkʌrnt] n cassis m
black fly n mouche noire f
black hole n trou noir m
blackmail [ˈblækmeɪl] n chantage m ▷ That's blackmail! C'est du chantage!
▶ vb: **to blackmail somebody** faire chanter quelqu'un ▷ He blackmailed them. Il les a fait chanter.
blackout [ˈblækaʊt] n (power cut) panne d'électricité f
blade [bleɪd] n lame f
blame [bleɪm] vb: **Don't blame me!** Ça n'est pas ma faute!; **I blame the police.** À mon avis, c'est la faute de la police.; **He blamed it on my sister.** Il a dit que c'était la faute de ma sœur.

blank [blæŋk] adj ❶ (paper) blanc m (f blanche) ❷ (cassette, video, page) vierge; **My mind went blank.** J'ai eu un trou.

▶ n blanc m ▷ *Fill in the blanks.* Remplissez les blancs.

blank cheque n chèque en blanc m

blanket ['blæŋkɪt] n couverture f

blast [blɑːst] n: **a bomb blast** une explosion

blatant ['bleɪtənt] adj flagrant

blaze [bleɪz] n incendie m

blazer ['bleɪzəʳ] n blazer m

bleach [bliːtʃ] n eau f de Javel

▶ vb décolorer ▷ *She bleached her hair.* Elle a décoloré ses cheveux.; **bleached jeans** jeans délavés

bleachers ['bliːtʃəz] npl gradins mpl

bleak [bliːk] adj (place) désolé; **The future looks bleak.** L'avenir semble peu prometteur.

bleed [bliːd] vb saigner ▷ *My nose is bleeding.* Je saigne du nez.

blender ['blɛndəʳ] n mélangeur m

bless [blɛs] vb (religiously) bénir; **Bless you!** (after sneezing) À tes souhaits!

blew [bluː] vb see **blow**

blind [blaɪnd] adj aveugle

▶ n (for window) store m

blindfold ['blaɪndfəʊld] n bandeau m (pl bandeaux)

▶ vb: **to blindfold somebody** bander les yeux à quelqu'un

blink [blɪŋk] vb cligner des yeux

bliss [blɪs] n: **It was bliss!** C'était merveilleux!

blister ['blɪstəʳ] n ampoule f

blizzard ['blɪzəd] n tempête de neige f

blob [blɒb] n goutte f

block [blɒk] n ❶ (wood) bille f ❷ (stone) bloc m; **They live on our block.** Ils habitent notre quartier.; **It's two blocks away.** C'est à

deux coins de rue.; **to go around the block** faire le tour du pâté de maisons

▶ vb bloquer

blockage ['blɒkɪdʒ] n obstruction f

blog [blɒg] n blogue m

blogger ['blɒgəʳ] n blogueur m, blogueuse f

blond [blɒnd] adj blond ▷ *She has blond hair.* Elle a les cheveux blonds.

blood [blʌd] n sang m

blood pressure n: **to have high blood pressure** faire de la tension

blood test n prise de sang f

blouse [blaʊz] n chemisier m

blow [bləʊ] n coup m

▶ vb (wind, person) souffler; **to blow one's nose** se moucher; **to blow a whistle** siffler; **to blow out a candle** éteindre une bougie; **to blow up** ❶ faire sauter ▷ *They blew up the old bridge and built a new one.* Ils ont fait sauter le vieux pont et en ont bâti un nouveau. ❷ gonfler ▷ *to blow up a balloon* gonfler un ballon; **The house blew up.** La maison a sauté.

blow-dry ['bləʊdraɪ] n séchage à la brosse m; **A cut and blow-dry, please.** Une coupe et un séchage à la brosse, s'il vous plaît.

▶ vb sécher à la brosse ▷ *I blow-dry my hair.* Je me sèche les cheveux à la brosse.

blown [bləʊn] vb see **blow**

blue [bluː] adj bleu ▷ *A blue dress* une robe bleue; **It came out of the blue.** C'était complètement inattendu.

blueberry ['bluːbəri] n bleuet m ▷ *blueberry pie* la tarte aux bleuets

blue jay [bluː-] n geai bleu m

blues [bluːz] npl blues m ▷ *I like blues (music).* J'aime le blues.; **to have the blues** avoir le cafard

bluff [blʌf] vb bluffer

▶ n bluff m ▷ *It's just a bluff.* C'est du bluff.

blunder ['blʌndə[r]] n gaffe f

blunt [blʌnt] adj ❶ (person) brusque ❷ (knife) émoussé

blurry ['blɜːrɪ] adj flou

blush [blʌʃ] vb rougir

board [bɔːd] n ❶ (wooden) planche f ❷ (skateboard) planche à roulettes f ❸ (snowboard) planche à neige f ❹ (chalkboard) tableau m (pl tableaux) ▷ *on the board* au tableau ❺ (notice board) panneau m (pl panneaux) ❻ (for board games) jeu m (pl jeux) ❼ (for chess) échiquier m; **on board** à bord

boarder ['bɔːdə[r]] n interne mf

board game n jeu de société m (pl jeux de société)

boarding ['bɔːdɪŋ] n ❶ (skateboarding) planche à roulettes f ▷ *He loves boarding.* Il adore la planche à roulettes. ❷ (snowboarding) planche à neige f ▷ *She's great at boarding.* Elle est formidable à la planche à neige. ▷ *Want to go boarding?* Si on faisait de la planche à neige?

boarding card ['bɔːdɪŋ-] n carte d'embarquement f

boarding school ['bɔːdɪŋ-] n pensionnat m; **I go to boarding school.** Je suis pensionnaire.

boards [bɔːdz] npl (hockey) bande f ▷ *The other player shoved me into the boards.* L'autre joueur m'a poussé dans la bande.

boat [bəʊt] n bateau m (pl bateaux)

body ['bɒdɪ] n corps m

bodybuilding ['bɒdɪbɪldɪŋ] n culturisme m

bodycheck ['bɒdɪtʃek] vb mettre en échec ▷ *You bodychecked him.* Tu l'as mis en échec.

bodyguard ['bɒdɪɡɑːd] n garde du corps m

bog [bɒɡ] n (marsh) tourbière f

boil [bɔɪl] n furoncle m
▶ vb ❶ faire bouillir ▷ *to boil some water* faire bouillir de l'eau; **to boil an egg** faire cuire un œuf ❷ bouillir ▷ *The water's boiling.* L'eau bout. ▷ *The water's boiled.* L'eau a bouilli.; **to boil over** déborder

boiled [bɔɪld] adj ❶ à l'eau ▷ *boiled potatoes* des pommes de terre à l'eau ❷ bouilli ▷ *boiled water* eau bouillie; **a boiled egg** un œuf à la coque

boiling ['bɔɪlɪŋ] adj: **It's boiling in here!** Il fait une chaleur torride ici!; **boiling hot** torride ▷ *a boiling hot day* une journée torride

bolt [bəʊlt] n ❶ (on door) verrou m ❷ (with nut) boulon m

bomb [bɒm] n bombe f
▶ vb bombarder

bomber ['bɒmə[r]] n bombardier m

bombing ['bɒmɪŋ] n attentat m à la bombe

bond [bɒnd] n lien m

bone [bəʊn] n ❶ (of human, animal) os m ❷ (of fish) arête f

bone dry adj complètement sec (f complètement sèche)

bonfire ['bɒnfaɪə[r]] n feu de joie m (pl feux de joie)

bonus ['bəʊnəs] n ❶ (extra payment) prime f ❷ (added advantage) plus m

book [bʊk] n livre m
▶ vb réserver ▷ *We haven't booked.* Nous n'avons pas réservé.

bookcase ['bʊkkeɪs] n bibliothèque f

booklet ['bʊklɪt] n brochure f

bookmark ['bʊkmɑːk] n (also computing) signet m
▶ vb mettre un signet à ▷ *I'm going to bookmark this Web site.* Je mets un signet à ce site Web.

bookshelf ['bʊkʃelf] n étagère f

f à livres

bookstore ['bʊkstɔːʳ] n librairie f

boost [buːst] vb stimuler ▷ to boost the economy stimuler l'économie; **The win boosted the team's morale.** La victoire a remonté le moral de l'équipe.

boot [buːt] n ❶ (fashion boot) botte f ❷ (for hiking) chaussure f de marche f

boot up vb démarrer

border ['bɔːdəʳ] n frontière f

bore [bɔːʳ] vb see **bear**

bored [bɔːd] adj: **to be bored** s'ennuyer ▷ I was bored. Je m'ennuyais.; **to get bored** s'ennuyer

boredom ['bɔːdəm] n ennui m

boring ['bɔːrɪŋ] adj ennuyeux (f ennuyeuse)

born [bɔːn] adj: **to be born** naître ▷ I was born in 1994. Je suis né en mille neuf cent quatre-vingt-quatorze.

borrow ['bɒrəʊ] vb emprunter ▷ Can I borrow your pen? Je peux emprunter ton stylo?; **to borrow something from somebody** emprunter quelque chose à quelqu'un ▷ I borrowed some money from a friend. J'ai emprunté de l'argent à un ami.

boss [bɒs] n patron m, patronne f

boss around vb: **to boss somebody around** donner des ordres à quelqu'un

bossy ['bɒsɪ] adj autoritaire

both [bəʊθ] adj, pron tous m les deux, toutes f les deux ▷ We both went. Nous y sommes allés tous les deux. ▷ Emma and Jane both went. Emma et Jane y sont allées toutes les deux. ▷ Both of your answers are wrong. Vos réponses sont toutes les deux mauvaises. ▷ Both of them have left. Ils sont partis tous les deux.

▷ Both of us went. Nous y sommes allés tous les deux. ▷ Both Maggie and John are against it. Maggie et John sont tous les deux contre.; **He speaks both German and Italian.** Il parle allemand et italien.

bother ['bɒðəʳ] vb ❶ (worry) tracasser ▷ What's bothering you? Qu'est-ce qui te tracasse? ❷ (disturb) déranger ▷ I'm sorry to bother you. Je suis désolé de vous déranger.; **no bother** aucun problème; **Don't bother!** Ça n'est pas la peine!; **to bother to do something** prendre la peine de faire quelque chose ▷ He didn't bother to tell me about it. Il n'a pas pris la peine de m'en parler.

bottle ['bɒtl] n bouteille f

bottle-opener ['bɒtləʊpnəʳ] n ouvre-bouteille m

bottom ['bɒtəm] n ❶ (of container, bag, sea) fond m ❷ (of page, list) bas m
▶ adj inférieur ▷ the bottom shelf l'étagère inférieure; **the bottom sheet** le drap de dessous

bought [bɔːt] vb see **buy**

bounce [baʊns] vb rebondir

bouncer ['baʊnsəʳ] n videur m

bound [baʊnd] adj: **He's bound to win.** Il va sûrement gagner.

boundary ['baʊndrɪ] n frontière f

bounds [baʊndz] npl: **out of bounds** interdit ▷ The creek is out of bounds for students. Le ruisseau est interdit aux élèves. (2) à l'extérieur du terrain ▷ The ball landed out of bounds. Le ballon est tombé à l'extérieur du terrain.

bow [n baʊ, vb baʊ] n ❶ (knot) nœud m ▷ to tie a bow faire un nœud ❷ arc m ▷ a bow and arrows un arc et des flèches
▶ vb faire une révérence

bowl [bəʊl] n (for soup, cereal) bol m

bowling ['bəʊlɪŋ] n jeu de quilles
m; **to go bowling** jouer aux quilles;
a bowling alley une salle de quilles

bow tie [bəʊ-] n nœud papillon m

box [bɒks] n boîte f ▶ **a box of
matches** une boîte d'allumettes; **a
cardboard box** un carton

boxer ['bɒksə'] n boxeur m

boxer shorts ['bɒksəʃɔːts] npl
caleçon m ▶ **a pair of boxer shorts**
un caleçon

boxing ['bɒksɪŋ] n boxe f

Boxing Day n lendemain de Noël
m ▷ on Boxing Day le lendemain
de Noël

boy [bɔɪ] n garçon m

boycott ['bɔɪkɒt] vb boycotter

boyfriend ['bɔɪfrɛnd] n copain m
▷ Do you have a boyfriend? Est-ce que
tu as un copain?

bra [brɑː] n soutien-gorge m (pl
soutiens-gorge)

brace [breɪs] n appareil m
orthopédique ▷ He wears a leg brace.
Il porte un appareil orthopédique
pour sa jambe.

bracelet ['breɪslɪt] n bracelet m

braces ['breɪsɪz] n (on teeth)
appareil m orthodontique ▷ She
wears braces. Elle a un appareil
orthodontique.

brackets ['brækɪts] npl: **in
brackets** entre parenthèses

brag [bræg] vb se vanter ▷ Stop
bragging! Arrête de te vanter!; **to
brag about something** se vanter
de quelque chose

braid [breɪd] n (hair) tresse f
▶ vb tresser ▷ to braid one's hair
tresser les cheveux

brain [breɪn] n cerveau m (pl
cerveaux)

brainstorm ['breɪnstɔːm] vb
faire un remue-méninges; **a
brainstorming session** une
session de remue-méninges

brainteaser ['breɪntiːzə'] n
casse-tête m

brake [breɪk] n frein m
▶ vb freiner

branch [brɑːntʃ] n ❶ (of tree)
branche f ❷ (of bank) succursale f

brand [brænd] n marque f ▷ a well-
known brand of cereal une marque de
céréales bien connue

brand name n marque f

brand-new ['bænd'njuː] adj tout
neuf (f toute neuve)

brass [brɑːs] n cuivre m; **the brass
section** les cuivres

brass band n fanfare f

brave [breɪv] adj courageux (f
courageuse)

bread [brɛd] n pain m ▷ brown bread
le pain de blé entier ▷ white bread le
pain blanc; **bread and butter** les f
tartines de pain beurrées

break [breɪk] n ❶ (rest) pause
f ▷ to take a break faire une pause
❷ (at school) récréation f ▷ during
morning break pendant la récréation
du matin; **the Christmas break**
les vacances de Noël; **Give me a
break!** Laisse-moi tranquille!; **to
give somebody a break** donner sa
chance à quelqu'un
▶ vb ❶ casser ▷ Careful, you'll
break something! Attention, tu vas
casser quelque chose! ❷ (get
broken) se casser ▷ Careful, it'll break!
Attention, ça va se casser!; **to
break one's leg** se casser la jambe
▷ I broke my leg. Je me suis cassé la
jambe.; **She broke her arm.** Elle
s'est cassé le bras.; **to break a
promise** rompre une promesse; **to
break a record** battre un record; **to
break the law** violer la loi

break down vb tomber en panne
▷ The car broke down. La voiture est
tombée en panne.

break in vb entrer par effraction

break off vb **❶** casser ▷ *He broke off a piece of chocolate.* Il a cassé un bout de chocolat. **❷** se casser ▷ *The branch broke off.* La branche s'est cassée.; **She broke off the engagement.** Elle a rompu ses fiançailles.

break open vb **❶** (door, cupboard) forcer

break out vb **❶** (fire) se déclarer **❷** (war) éclater **❸** (prisoner) s'évader; **to break out in a rash** être couvert de boutons

break up vb **❶** (couple) se séparer; **He broke up with his girlfriend.** Il a rompu avec sa petite amie. **❷** (crowd) se disperser **❸** (meeting, party) se terminer **❹** (divide) répartir ▷ *Break up into groups.* Répartissez-vous en groupes.; **to break up a fight** mettre fin à une bagarre

breakdown ['breɪkdaʊn] n **❶** (in vehicle) panne f ▷ *to have a breakdown* tomber en panne **❷** (mental) dépression f ▷ *to have a breakdown* faire une dépression

breakfast ['brekfəst] n déjeuner m ▷ *What would you like for breakfast?* Qu'est-ce vous voulez pour le déjeuner?

break-in ['breɪkɪn] n cambriolage m

break-up ['breɪkʌp] n **❶** (friendship) rupture f **❷** (ice) débâcle f ▷ *After spring break-up you often get floods.* Après la débâcle printanière, on a souvent des inondations.

breast [brest] n (of woman) sein m; **chicken breast** la poitrine de poulet

breath [breθ] n haleine f ▷ *to have bad breath* avoir mauvaise haleine; **to be out of breath** être essoufflé; **to catch one's breath** reprendre son souffle

breathe ['briːð] vb respirer

breathe in vb inspirer

breathe out vb expirer

breed [briːd] vb (reproduce) se reproduire; **to breed dogs** faire de l'élevage de chiens
▶ n race f

breeze [briːz] n brise f

bribe [braɪb] vb soudoyer

brick [brɪk] n brique f; **a brick wall** un mur en brique

bricklayer ['brɪkleɪə'] n maçon m

bride [braɪd] n mariée f

bridegroom ['braɪdgruːm] n marié m

bridesmaid ['braɪdzmeɪd] n demoiselle d'honneur f

bridge [brɪdʒ] n **❶** pont m ▷ *a suspension bridge* un pont suspendu **❷** (game) bridge m ▷ *to play bridge* jouer au bridge

brief [briːf] adj bref f brève

briefcase ['briːfkeɪs] n serviette f

briefly ['briːflɪ] adv brièvement

briefs [briːfs] npl **❶** (women's) culotte f **❷** (men's) caleçon m

bright [braɪt] adj **❶** (colour, light) vif f vive ▷ *a bright colour* une couleur vive; **bright blue** bleu vif ▷ *a bright blue car* une voiture bleu vif **❷** intelligent ▷ *He's very bright.* Il est très intelligent.

brilliant ['brɪljənt] adj **❶** (clever) brillant ▷ *a brilliant scientist* un savant brillant **❷** (colour, light) éclatant

bring [brɪŋ] vb **❶** apporter ▷ *Bring warm clothes.* Apportez des vêtements chauds. ▷ *Could you bring me my mitts?* Tu peux m'apporter mes mitaines? **❷** (person) amener ▷ *Can I bring a friend?* Est-ce que je peux amener un ami?

bring about vb provoquer ▷ *The*

war brought about a change in people's attitudes. La guerre a provoqué un changement dans l'attitude des gens.

bring back vb rapporter

bring up vb ❶ mentionner ▷ You've brought up an interesting point. Tu as mentionné un fait intéressant. ❷ **élever** ▷ She brought up the children on her own. Elle a élevé les enfants toute seule.

British Columbia ['brɪtɪʃkə'lʌmbɪə] n Colombie-Britannique f

broad [brɔːd] adj (wide) large; **in broad daylight** en plein jour

broadcast ['brɔːdkɑːst] n émission f
▷ vb diffuser ▷ The interview was broadcast all over the world. L'entrevue a été diffusée dans le monde entier.; **to broadcast live** retransmettre en direct

broad-minded [brɔːd'maɪndɪd] adj large d'esprit

broccoli ['brɒkəlɪ] n brocoli m

brochure ['brəʊʃʊəʳ] n brochure f

broil [brɔɪl] vb faire griller; **broiled fish** le poisson grillé

broke [brəʊk] vb see **break**
▷ adj: **to be broke** (without money) être fauché

broken ['brəʊkən] adj cassé ▷ It's broken. C'est cassé. ▷ a broken leg une jambe cassée ▷ She's got a broken arm. Elle a le bras cassé.

bronchitis [brɒŋ'kaɪtɪs] n bronchite f

bronze [brɒnz] n bronze m ▷ the bronze medal la médaille de bronze

brooch [brəʊtʃ] n broche f

broom [brum] n balai m

brother ['brʌðəʳ] n frère m ▷ my brother mon frère ▷ my big brother mon grand frère

brother-in-law ['brʌðərɪn'lɔː] n

beau-frère m (pl beaux-frères)

brought [brɔːt] vb see **bring**

brown [braʊn] adj ❶ (clothes) marron (f+pl marron) ❷ (hair) brun ❸ (tanned) bronzé; **brown bread** le pain de blé entier; **brown sugar** la cassonade

brownie ['braʊnɪ] n carré au chocolat m

browse [braʊz] vb ❶ naviguer sur Internet; **Browse button** bouton Naviguer ❷ (magazine, book) feuilleter ❸ (store) regarder

browser [braʊzəʳ] n (for internet) navigateur m

bruise [bruːz] n bleu m

brunch [brʌntʃ] n brunch m ▷ to have brunch prendre le brunch

brush [brʌʃ] n ❶ brosse f ❷ (paintbrush) pinceau m (pl pinceaux)
▷ vb brosser; **to brush one's hair** se brosser les cheveux ▷ I brushed my hair. Je me suis brossé les cheveux.; **to brush one's teeth** se brosser les dents ▷ I brush my teeth every night. Je me brosse les dents tous les soirs.

Brussels sprout [-spraʊt] n chou m de Bruxelles (pl choux de Bruxelles)

brutal ['bruːtl] adj brutal (mpl brutaux)

BSc [biːsɛsˈsiː] n (= Bachelor of Science) baccalauréat ès sciences m; **a BSc in biology** un baccalauréat en biologie

bubble ['bʌbl] n bulle f

bubble bath n bain moussant m

bubble gum n gomme à mâcher f

bucket ['bʌkɪt] n seau m (pl seaux)

buckle ['bʌkl] n (on belt, watch, shoe) boucle f

Buddhist ['bʊdɪst] adj bouddhiste
▷ n bouddhiste

buddy ['bʌdɪ] n copain m, copine f

budget ['bʌdʒɪt] n budget m

budgie ['bʌdʒɪ] n perruche f

buffet ['bʌfɪt] n buffet m

bug [bʌg] n ❶ (insect) insecte m ❷ (infection) microbe m ▷ There's a bug going round. Il y a un microbe qui traîne. ❸ (in computer) bogue m

bugged [bʌgd] adj sur écoute ▷ The room was bugged. La pièce était sur écoute.

build [bɪld] vb construire ▷ We're building a garage. Nous construisons un garage.; **to build up** (increase) s'accumuler

builder ['bɪldər] n ❶ (owner of firm) entrepreneur m ❷ (worker) maçon m

building ['bɪldɪŋ] n bâtiment m

built [bɪlt] vb see **build**

bulb [bʌlb] n (electric) ampoule f

bulimia [bə'lɪmɪə] n boulimie f

bull [bul] n taureau m (pl taureaux)

bullet ['bulɪt] n balle f

bulletin board ['bulatinbɔːd] n tableau d'affichage

bully ['bulɪ] n intimidateur m ▷ He's a bully. C'est un intimidateur. ▷ She's a bully. Elle fait de l'intimidation.
▶ vb intimider

bullying ['bulɪŋ] n intimidation f ▷ a workshop about bullying un atelier sur l'intimidation ▷ The school has a policy on bullying. L'école a adopté une politique sur l'intimidation.

bum [bʌm] n (bottom) derrière m

bump [bʌmp] n (lump) bosse f
▶ vb: **to bump into something** rentrer dans quelque chose ▷ We bumped into her car. Nous sommes rentrés dans sa voiture.; **to bump into somebody (1)** (literally) rentrer dans quelqu'un ▷ He stopped suddenly and I bumped into him. Il s'est arrêté subitement et je lui suis rentré dedans. **(2)** (meet by chance) rencontrer par hasard ▷ I bumped into your sister in the supermarket. J'ai rencontré ta sœur par hasard au supermarché.

bumper ['bʌmpər] n pare-chocs m (pl pare-chocs)

bumpy ['bʌmpɪ] adj cahoteux (f cahoteuse)

bun [bʌn] n petit pain

bunch [bʌntʃ] n: **a bunch of flowers** un bouquet de fleurs; **a bunch of grapes** une grappe de raisin; **a bunch of keys** un trousseau de clés; **A bunch of students are going.** Un groupe d'élèves y vont.

bungalow ['bʌŋgələu] n bungalow m

bungee cord ['bʌndʒi:kɔːd] n corde élastique f

bungee jumping ['bʌndʒi:'dʒʌmpɪŋ] n saut à l'élastique m

bunk [bʌŋk] n couchette f; **bunk beds** les lits superposés

buoy [bɔɪ] n (swimming) bouée f

burger ['bɜːgər] n hamburger m

burglar ['bɜːglər] n cambrioleur m, cambrioleuse f

burglarize ['bɜːglaraɪz] vb cambrioler

burglary ['bɜːglərɪ] n cambriolage m

burn [bɜːn] n ❶ brûlure f ❷ (sunburn) coup de soleil m
▶ vb ❶ brûler ❷ (food) faire brûler ▷ I burned the cake. J'ai fait brûler le gâteau.; **to burn oneself** se brûler ▷ I burned myself on the oven door. Je me suis brûlé sur la porte du four.; **I've burned my hand.** Je me suis brûlé la main.; **to burn down** brûler ▷ The factory burned down. L'usine a brûlé. ❸ (CD) graver

burst [bɜːst] vb éclater ▷ The balloon burst. Le ballon a éclaté.; **to burst a balloon** faire éclater un ballon; **to burst out laughing** éclater de rire; **to burst into flames** prendre feu; **to burst into tears** fondre en larmes

bury ['berɪ] vb enterrer

bus [bʌs] n autobus m ▷ *a bus stop* un arrêt d'autobus; **the school bus** l'autobus scolaire; **a bus station** une gare routière; **a bus ticket** un ticket de bus

bush [buʃ] n ❶ (shrub) buisson m ❷ (forest) bois mpl; **a sugar bush** une érablière

business ['bɪznɪs] n ❶ (firm) entreprise f ▷ *He's got his own business.* Il a sa propre entreprise. ❷ (commerce) affaires f ▷ *She's away on business.* Elle est en voyage d'affaires.; **a business trip** un voyage d'affaires; **It's none of my business.** Ça ne me regarde pas.

businessman ['bɪznɪsmæn] n homme m d'affaires

businesswoman ['bɪznɪswʊmən] n femme f d'affaires

bust [bʌst] n (chest) poitrine f

busy ['bɪzɪ] adj ❶ (person, phone line) occupé ❷ (day, schedule) chargé ❸ (store, street) très fréquenté

busy signal n tonalité « occupé »

but [bʌt] conj mais ▷ *I'd like to come, but I'm busy.* J'aimerais venir mais je suis occupé.

butcher ['butʃə'] n boucher m ▷ *He's a butcher.* Il est boucher.

butcher shop n boucherie f

butter ['bʌtə'] n beurre m

butterfly ['bʌtəflaɪ] n papillon m

buttocks ['bʌtəks] npl fesses fpl

button ['bʌtn] n bouton m

buy [baɪ] vb acheter ▷ *She bought me an ice cream.* Elle m'a acheté une crème glacée. ▷ *I bought her an ice cream.* Je lui ai acheté une crème glacée.; **to buy something from**

somebody acheter quelque chose à quelqu'un ▷ *I bought a watch from him.* Je lui ai acheté une montre.
▶ n: **It was a good buy.** C'était une bonne affaire.

buzz [bʌz] vb ❶ (insect) bourdonner ❷ (intercom) appeler par interphone

buzzer ['bʌzə'] n sonnerie f

by [baɪ] prep ❶ par ▷ *The thieves were caught by the police.* Les voleurs ont été arrêtés par la police. ❷ de ▷ *a painting by Emily Carr* un tableau d'Emily Carr ▷ *a book by Kenneth Oppel* un livre de Kenneth Oppel ❸ en ▷ *by car* en voiture ▷ *by train* en train ▷ *by bus* en autobus ❹ (close to) à côté de ▷ *"Where's the bank?" — "It's by the post office."* « Où est la banque ? » — « Elle est à côté de la poste. » ❺ (not later than) avant ▷ *We have to be there by 4 o'clock.* Nous devons y être avant quatre heures.; **by the time...** quand... ▷ *By the time I got there it was too late.* Quand je suis arrivé il était déjà trop tard. ▷ *It'll be ready by the time you get back.* Ça sera prêt quand vous reviendrez.; **That's fine by me.** Ça me va.; **all by himself** tout seul; **all by herself** toute seule; **I did it all by myself.** Je l'ai fait tout seul.; **by the way** au fait

bye ['baɪbaɪ] excl salut !

by-product ['baɪprɒdʌkt] n sous-produit m

C

cab [kæb] n taxi m

cabbage ['kæbɪdʒ] n chou m (pl choux)

cabin ['kæbɪn] n (cottage) chalet m; **a log cabin** un chalet en bois rond

cabinet ['kæbɪnɪt] n: **a medicine cabinet** une armoire de salle de bain

cable ['keɪbl] n câble m

cable car ['keɪblkɑːr] n téléphérique m

cable television n télévision par câble f

cactus ['kæktəs] n cactus m

café ['kæfeɪ] n café m

cafeteria [kæfɪ'tɪərɪə] n cafétéria f

cage [keɪdʒ] n cage f

Cajun ['keɪdʒən] adj cajun (f+pl cajun) ▷ Cajun cuisine la cuisine cajun
▶ n Cajun

cake [keɪk] n gâteau m (pl gâteaux)

calculate ['kælkjuleɪt] vb calculer

calculation [kælkju'leɪʃən] n calcul m

calculator ['kælkjuleɪtər] n calculatrice f

calendar ['kæləndər] n calendrier m

calf [kɑːf] n ❶ (of cow) veau m (pl veaux) ❷ (of leg) mollet m

call [kɔːl] n (by phone) appel m ▷ Thanks for your call. Merci de votre appel.; **a phone call** un coup de téléphone; **to be on call** (doctor) être de permanence ▷ She's on call this evening. Elle est de permanence ce soir.
▶ vb appeler ▷ I'll tell him you called. Je lui dirai que vous avez appelé. ▷ This is the number to call. C'est le numéro à appeler. ▷ We called the police. Nous avons appelé la police. ▷ Everyone calls her Marie. Tout le monde l'appelle Marie.; **to be called** s'appeler ▷ The game is called Drago. Le jeu s'appelle Drago. ▷ What's this dish called? Comment s'appelle ce plat?; **to call somebody names** insulter quelqu'un; **He called me an idiot.** Il m'a traité d'imbécile.

call back vb (phone again) rappeler ▷ I'll call back at 6 o'clock. Je rappellerai à six heures.

call for vb (pick up) passer prendre ▷ I'll call for you at 2:30. Je passerai te prendre à deux heures et demie.; **This calls for a celebration!** Il faut fêter ça!

call off vb annuler ▷ The game was called off. Le match a été annulé.

calm [kɑːm] adj calme

calm down vb se calmer ▷ Calm down! Calme-toi!

calorie ['kælərɪ] n calorie f

calves [kɑːvz] npl see **calf**

camcorder ['kæmkɔːdər] n caméscope m

came [keɪm] *vb see* **come**

camel ['kæməl] *n* chameau *m* (*pl* chameaux)

camera ['kæmərə] *n* ❶ (*for photos*) appareil *m* photo (*pl* appareils photo) ❷ (*movie, TV*) caméra *f*

cameraman ['kæmərəmæn] *n* cadreur *m*, cadreuse *f*

camp [kæmp] *vb* camper
▶ *n* camp *m*; **a camp stove** un réchaud de camping; **to break camp** lever le camp; **to set up camp** installer son camp ▷ *We set up camp by the river.* Nous avons installé notre camp à côté de la rivière.

campaign [kæm'peɪn] *n* campagne *f*

camper ['kæmpər] *n* ❶ (*person*) campeur *m*, campeuse *f* ❷ (*van*) caravane *f*

campfire ['kæmpfaɪər] *n* feu de camp *m*

campground ['kæmpgraʊnd] *n* terrain de camping *m*

camping ['kæmpɪŋ] *n* camping *m*; **to go camping** faire du camping ▷ *We went camping in the Yukon.* Nous avons fait du camping au Yukon.

campsite ['kæmpsaɪt] *n* emplacement *m* (de camping)

campus ['kæmpəs] *n* campus *m*

can [kæn] *n* ❶ (*food*) boîte *f* ▷ *a can of corn* une boîte de maïs ❷ (*drink*) canette *f* ▷ *a can of pop* une canette de boisson gazeuse
▶ *vb* ❶ (*be able to, be allowed to*) pouvoir ▷ *I can't come.* Je ne peux pas venir. ▷ *Can I help you?* Est-ce que je peux vous aider? ▷ *Can I use your phone?* Est-ce que je peux me servir de votre téléphone? ▷ *You could rent a bike.* Tu pourrais louer un vélo. ▷ *I couldn't sleep because of the noise.* Je ne pouvais pas dormir à

cause du bruit.

■ **can** is sometimes not translated.

▷ *I can't hear you.* Je ne t'entends pas. ▷ *I can't remember.* Je ne m'en souviens pas. ▷ *Can you speak French?* Parlez-vous français? ❷ (*know how to*) savoir ▷ *I can swim.* Je sais nager. ▷ *He can't drive.* Il ne sait pas conduire.; **That can't be true!** Ce n'est pas possible!; **You could be right.** Vous avez peut-être raison.

Canada ['kænədə] *n* Canada *m*; **in Canada** au Canada; **to Canada** au Canada

Canada Day *n* Fête du Canada *f*

Canada goose *n* outarde *f*

Canadian [kə'neɪdɪən] *adj* canadien (*f* canadienne)
▶ *n* Canadien *m*, Canadienne *f*

Canadian Shield *n* Bouclier canadien *m*

canal [kə'næl] *n* canal *m* (*pl* canaux)

canary [kə'nɛərɪ] *n* canari *m*

cancel ['kænsəl] *vb* annuler ▷ *The game was cancelled.* Le match a été annulé.

cancellation [kænsə'leɪʃən] *n* annulation *f*

cancer ['kænsər] *n* ❶ cancer *m* ▷ *She's got cancer.* Elle a le cancer. ❷ Cancer *m* ▷ *I'm a Cancer.* Je suis Cancer.

candidate ['kændɪdeɪt] *n* candidat *m*, candidate *f*

candle ['kændl] *n* bougie *f*

candy ['kændɪ] *n* bonbons *mpl*; **a candy** un bonbon

canned ['kænd] *adj* (*food*) en conserve

cannot ['kænɒt] *vb see* **can**

canoe [kə'nuː] *n* canot *m*

canoeing [kə'nuːɪŋ] *n* canotage *m*; **to go canoeing** faire du canotage

▷ *We went canoeing.* Nous avons fait du canotage.

canola [kə'nəʊlə] n canola m
▷ *canola oil* l'huile de canola f

can opener [-əʊpnər] n ouvre-boîte m

can't [kɑːnt] vb see **can**

canvas ['kænvəs] n toile f

cap [kæp] n ❶ (hat) casquette f ❷ (of bottle, tube) bouchon m

capable ['keɪpəbl] adj capable

capital ['kæpɪtl] n ❶ capitale f ▷ *Toronto is the capital of Ontario.* Toronto est la capitale de l'Ontario. ❷ (letter) majuscule f ▷ *Write your address in capitals.* Écris ton adresse en majuscules.

capital punishment n peine capitale f

Capricorn ['kæprɪkɔːn] n Capricorne m ▷ *I'm a Capricorn.* Je suis Capricorne.

capsize [kæp'saɪz] vb ❶ chavirer ▷ *The boat capsized.* Le bateau a chaviré. ❷ faire chavirer ▷ *Careful, you'll capsize the boat.* Attention, tu vas faire chavirer le bateau.

captain ['kæptɪn] n capitaine m ▷ *She's captain of the hockey team.* Elle est capitaine de l'équipe de hockey.

caption ['kæpʃən] n légende f

capture ['kæptʃər] vb capturer

car [kɑːr] n voiture f; *to go by car* aller en voiture ▷ *We went by car.* Nous y sommes allés en voiture.; **a car accident** un accident de voiture

caramel ['kærəməl] n caramel m

carbohydrate [kɑːbəʊ'haɪdreɪt] n glucide m ▷ *Pasta is high in carbohydrates.* Les pâtes contiennent beaucoup de glucides.

card [kɑːd] n carte f; **a card game** un jeu de cartes

cardboard ['kɑːdbɔːd] n carton m

cardigan ['kɑːdɪɡən] n cardigan m

care [keər] n ❶ soin m ▷ *with care* avec

soin; **to take care of** s'occuper de ▷ *I take care of the children on Saturdays.* Le samedi, je m'occupe des enfants.; **Take care!** (1) (Be careful!) Fais attention! (2) (Look after yourself!) Prends bien soin de toi!

▶ vb: **to care about** se soucier de ▷ *They don't care about their image.* Ils se soucient peu de leur image.; **I don't care!** Ça m'est égal! ▷ *He doesn't care.* Ça lui est égal.; **to care for somebody** (patients, elderly people) s'occuper de quelqu'un

career [kə'rɪər] n carrière f; **Career day** la journée d'orientation; **Career Studies** (course) Choix de carrières

careful ['keəful] adj: **Be careful!** Fais attention!

carefully ['keəfəlɪ] adv ❶ soigneusement ▷ *He carefully avoided talking about it.* Il évitait soigneusement d'en parler. ❷ (safely) prudemment ▷ *Drive carefully!* Conduisez prudemment!; **Think carefully!** Réfléchis bien!

caregiver ['keəɡɪvər] n ❶ (for children) gardien m, gardienne f ❷ (for sick person) soignant m, soignante f

careless ['keəlɪs] adj ❶ (work) peu soigné; **a careless mistake** une faute d'inattention ❷ (person) peu soigneux (f peu soigneuse) ▷ *She's very careless.* Elle est bien peu soigneuse. ❸ imprudent ▷ *a careless driver* un conducteur imprudent

caribou ['kærɪbuː] n caribou m; **caribou hide** la peau de caribou

caring ['keərɪŋ] adj: **She's a very caring teacher.** C'est un professeur qui se préoccupe du bien-être de ses élèves.; **She has very caring parents.** Ses parents sont très affectueux.

carnation [kɑːˈneɪʃən] n œillet m

carnival [ˈkɑːnɪvl] n carnaval m

carol [ˈkærəl] n: **a Christmas carol** une cantique de Noël

carpenter [ˈkɑːpɪntəʳ] n menuisier m, menuisière f ▷ *He's a carpenter.* Il est menuisier.

carpentry [ˈkɑːpɪntrɪ] n menuiserie f

carpet [ˈkɑːpɪt] n **①** tapis m ▷ *a Persian carpet* un tapis persan **②** (broadloom) moquette f

car rental n location de voitures f

carrot [ˈkærət] n carotte f

carry [ˈkærɪ] vb **①** porter ▷ *I'll carry your bag.* Je vais porter ton sac. **②** transporter ▷ *a plane carrying 100 passengers* un avion transportant cent passagers

carry on vb **①** soutenir ▷ *How can you carry on a conversation with all this noise?* Comment peut-on soutenir une conversation avec tout ce bruit? **②** continuer ▷ *Carry on!* Continue! ▷ *She carried on with her life as before.* Elle a continué sa vie comme auparavant.

carry out vb (orders) exécuter

cart [kɑːt] n charrette f

carton [ˈkɑːtən] n (milk, cream) carton m

cartoon [kɑːˈtuːn] n **①** (film) dessin animé m **②** (in newspaper) caricature f

cartridge [ˈkɑːtrɪdʒ] n cartouche f; **printer cartridge** une cartouche d'imprimante

carve [kɑːv] vb **①** sculpter ▷ *He carved a little boat out of wood.* Il a sculpté un petit bateau en bois. **②** graver ▷ *We carved our initials into the bench.* Nous avons gravé nos initiales sur le banc.

car wash n lave-auto m (pl lave-autos)

case [keɪs] n **①** étui m ▷ *a violin case* un étui de violon **②** cas m (pl cas) ▷ *in some cases* dans certains cas; **in that case** dans ce cas ▷ *"I don't want it." — "In that case, I'll take it."* « Je n'en veux pas. » — « Dans ce cas, je le prends. »; **in case** au cas où ▷ *in case it rains* au cas où il pleuvrait; **just in case** à tout hasard ▷ *Take some money, just in case.* Prends de l'argent à tout hasard.

cash [kæʃ] n argent m ▷ *I'm a bit short of cash.* Je suis un peu à court d'argent.; **in cash** en liquide ▷ *$200 in cash* deux cent dollars en liquide; **to pay cash** payer comptant; **a cash card** une carte de retrait; **the cash desk** la caisse; **a cash dispenser** un guichet automatique; **a cash register** une caisse

cashew [ˈkæʃuː] n noix de cajou f

cashier [kæˈʃɪəʳ] n caissier m, caissière f

cashmere [ˈkæʃmɪəʳ] n cachemire m ▷ *a cashmere sweater* un chandail en cachemire

casino [kəˈsiːnəʊ] n casino m

casserole [ˈkæsərəʊl] n casserole f ▷ *a tuna casserole* une casserole de thon; **a casserole dish** une cocotte

cassette [kæˈsɛt] n cassette f; **a cassette player** un lecteur de cassettes; **a cassette recorder** un magnétophone

cast [kɑːst] n **①** acteurs mpl ▷ *After the play, we met the cast.* Après la représentation, nous avons rencontré les acteurs. **②** (for broken bone) plâtre m

castle [ˈkɑːsl] n château m (pl châteaux)

casual [ˈkæʒjul] adj **①** décontracté ▷ *casual clothes* les vêtements décontractés **②** désinvolte ▷ *a casual attitude* une

attitude désinvolte ❸ en passant
▷ It was just a casual remark. C'était
juste une remarque en passant.

casually ['kæʒjulɪ] adv: **to dress
casually** s'habiller de façon
décontractée

cat [kæt] n chat m, chatte f

catalogue ['kætəlɒg] n
catalogue m

catastrophe [kə'tæstrəfɪ] n
catastrophe f

catch [kætʃ] vb ❶ attraper ▷ to
catch a thief attraper un voleur ▷ My
cat catches birds. Mon chat attrape
des oiseaux.; **to catch somebody
doing something** attraper
quelqu'un en train de faire quelque
chose ▷ If they catch you cheating
s'ils t'attrapent en train de tricher;
to catch a cold attraper un rhume
❷ (bus, train) prendre ▷ We caught
the last bus. On a pris le dernier
autobus. ❸ (hear) saisir ▷ I didn't
catch his name. Je n'ai pas saisi son
nom.; **to catch up** rattraper son
retard ▷ I have to catch up: I was away
last week. Je dois rattraper mon
retard: j'étais absent la semaine
dernière.; **to catch up with
somebody** rattraper quelqu'un; **to
get caught up in something** être
pris dans quelque chose

category ['kætɪgərɪ] n catégorie f

cathedral [kə'θiːdrəl] n
cathédrale f

Catholic ['kæθəlɪk] adj catholique
▶ n catholique ▷ I'm a Catholic. Je
suis catholique.

cattle ['kætl] npl bétail m

caught [kɔːt] vb see **catch**

cauliflower ['kɒlɪflauə'] n chou-
fleur m (pl choux-fleurs)

cause [kɔːz] n cause f
▶ vb provoquer ▷ to cause an
accident provoquer un accident

caution ['kɔːʃən] interjection

Attention!

cautious ['kɔːʃəs] adj prudent

cautiously ['kɔːʃəslɪ] adv avec
précaution ▷ She cautiously opened
the door. Elle a ouvert la porte
avec précaution.; **He reacted
cautiously.** Il a réagi prudemment.

cave [keɪv] n grotte f

cavity ['kævɪtɪ] n (in tooth) carie f
▷ I have cavities. J'ai des caries.

CCTV = **closed-circuit television** n
télévision en circuit fermé f

CD n (abbreviation for disque compact)
CD m (pl CD)

CD burner [-bɜːnə'] n graveur
de CD m

CD player n lecteur de CD m

CD-ROM [siːdiːˈrɒm] n CD-ROM m
(pl CD-ROM)

> **CD-ROM** can also be written
> **cédérom** (pl **cédéroms**) in
> French.

CE abbr (= Common Era) ap. J.-C.
(= après Jésus-Christ) ▷ in 800 CE en
huit cents après Jésus-Christ

ceasefire ['siːsfaɪə'] n cessez-le-
feu m (pl cessez-le-feu)

cedar ['siːdə'] n cèdre m

ceiling ['siːlɪŋ] n plafond m

celebrate ['sɛlɪbreɪt] vb fêter

celebrity [sɪ'lɛbrɪtɪ] n célébrité f

celery ['sɛlərɪ] n céleri m

cell [sɛl] n cellule f

cellar ['sɛlə'] n cave f

cello ['tʃɛləu] n violoncelle m ▷ I
play the cello. Je joue du violoncelle.

cellphone ['sɛlfəun] n téléphone
cellulaire f

Celsius ['sɛlsɪəs] adj Celsius ▷ 20
degrees Celsius vingt degrés Celsius

cement [sə'mɛnt] n ciment m

cemetery ['sɛmɪtrɪ] n cimetière m

cent [sɛnt] n cent m ▷ twenty cents
vingt cents

centennial [sɛn'tɛnɪəl] n
centenaire m

centimetre ['sɛntɪmiːtəʳ] n
centimètre m

central ['sɛntrəl] adj central (mpl
centraux)

central heating n chauffage
central m

centre ['sɛntəʳ] n centre m ▷ a
sports centre un centre sportif

century ['sɛntjʊrɪ] n siècle m
▷ the 20th century le vingtième
siècle ▷ the 21st century le vingt et
unième siècle

cereal ['sɪːrɪəl] n céréales fpl ▷ I
have cereal for breakfast. Je prends
des céréales au petit déjeuner.

ceremony ['sɛrɪmənɪ] n
cérémonie f

certain ['səːtən] adj certain
▷ a certain person une certaine
personne ▷ I'm absolutely certain it
was him. Je suis absolument certain
que c'était lui.; **I don't know for
certain.** Je n'en suis pas certain.;
to make certain s'assurer ▷ I
made certain the door was locked. Je
me suis assuré que la porte était
fermée à clé.

certainly ['səːtənlɪ] adv vraiment
▷ I certainly expected something
better. Je m'attendais vraiment
à quelque chose de mieux.;
Certainly not! Certainement
pas!; "**So it was a surprise?**" — "**It
certainly was!**" « Ç'était donc une
surprise? » — « Ça oui alors! »

certificate [sə'tɪfɪkɪt] n
certificat m

CFCs npl CFC mpl

chain [tʃeɪn] n chaîne f

chair [tʃɛəʳ] n ① chaise f ▷ a table
and 4 chairs une table et quatre
chaises ② (armchair) fauteuil m

chairlift ['tʃɛəlɪft] n télésiège m

chairperson ['tʃɛəpəːsn] n
président m, présidente f

chalet ['ʃæleɪ] n chalet m

chalk [tʃɔːk] n craie f

chalkboard ['tʃɔːkbɔːd] n
tableau m

challenge ['tʃælɪndʒ] n défi m
▶ vb ① défier ▷ to challenge
authority défier l'autorité; **She
challenged me to a race.** Elle m'a
proposé de faire la course avec
elle. ② contester ▷ to challenge
somebody's opinion contester l'avis
de quelqu'un

challenging ['tʃælɪndʒɪŋ] adj
stimulant ▷ a challenging job un
travail stimulant

champion ['tʃæmpɪən] n
champion m, championne f

championship ['tʃæmpɪənʃɪp] n
championnat m

chance [tʃɑːns] n ① chance f ▷ Do
you think I've got a chance? Tu crois
que j'ai une chance? ▷ Their chances
of winning are very good. Ils ont de
fortes chances de gagner.; **Not a
chance!** Pas question! ② occasion
f ▷ I'd like to have a chance to travel.
J'aimerais avoir l'occasion de
voyager.; **I'll write when I get the
chance.** J'écrirai quand j'aurai un
moment.; **by chance** par hasard
▷ We met by chance. Nous nous
sommes rencontrés par hasard.; **to
take a chance** prendre un risque
▷ I'm taking no chances! Je ne veux
prendre aucun risque!

change [tʃeɪndʒ] vb ① changer
▷ The town has changed a lot. La
ville a beaucoup changé. ▷ I'd like
to change $50. Je voudrais changer
cinquante dollars.

Use **changer de** when you
change one thing for another.

② changer de ▷ You have to change
planes in Edmonton. Il faut changer
d'avion à Edmonton. ▷ I'm going to
change my shoes. Je vais changer de
chaussures. ▷ He wants to change

his job. Il veut changer d'emploi.; **to change one's mind** changer d'avis ▷ *I've changed my mind.* J'ai changé d'avis.; **to change gears** changer de vitesse ❶ *se changer* ▷ *She's changing to go out.* Elle est en train de se changer pour sortir.; **to get changed** se changer ▷ *I'm going to get changed.* Je vais me changer. ❹ *(exchange)* échanger ▷ *Can I change this sweater? It's too small.* Est-ce que je peux échanger ce chandail? Il est trop petit.

▶ *n* ❶ changement *m* ▷ *There's been a change of plan.* Il y a eu un changement de programme. ❷ *(money)* monnaie *f* ▷ *I haven't got any change.* Je n'ai pas de monnaie.; **a change of clothes** des vêtements de rechange; **for a change** pour changer ▷ *Let's play tennis for a change.* Si on jouait au tennis pour changer?

changeable ['tʃeɪndʒəbl] *adj* variable

change room *n* ❶ *(in store)* salon d'essayage *m* ❷ *(for sport)* vestiaire *m*

channel ['tʃænl] *n (TV)* chaîne *f* ▷ *There's hockey on the other channel.* Il y a du hockey sur l'autre chaîne.

chaos ['keɪɒs] *n* chaos *m*

chapel ['tʃæpl] *n (part of church)* chapelle *f*

chapped [tʃæpt] *adj* gercé ▷ *I have chapped lips.* J'ai les lèvres gercées.

chapter ['tʃæptər] *n* chapitre *m*

character ['kærɪktər] *n*
❶ caractère *m* ▷ *Give me some idea of his character.* Décris-moi un peu son caractère.; **She's quite a character.** C'est un drôle de numéro. ❷ *(in play, film)* personnage *m* ▷ *The character played by Donald Sutherland...* Le personnage joué par Donald

Sutherland...

characteristic ['kærɪktə'rɪstɪk] *n* caractéristique *f*

charcoal ['tʃɑːkəʊl] *n* charbon de bois *m*

charge [tʃɑːdʒ] *n* frais *mpl* ▷ *Is there a charge for delivery?* Est-ce qu'il y a des frais de livraison?; **an extra charge** un supplément; **free of charge** gratuit; **to reverse the charges** appeler à frais virés ▷ *I'd like to reverse the charges.* Je voudrais appeler à frais virés.; **to be in charge** être responsable ▷ *She was in charge of the group.* Elle était responsable du groupe.

▶ *vb* ❶ *(money)* prendre ▷ *How much did she charge you?* Combien est-ce qu'elle vous a demandé? ▷ *They charge $10 an hour.* Ils demandent dix dollars de l'heure. ❷ *(with crime)* inculper ▷ *The police have charged him with fraud.* La police l'a inculpé de fraude.

charity ['tʃærɪti] *n* association *f* caritative ▷ *They gave the money to charity.* Ils ont donné l'argent à une association caritative.

charm [tʃɑːm] *n* charme *m* ▷ *He's got a lot of charm.* Il a beaucoup de charme.

charming ['tʃɑːmɪŋ] *adj* charmant

chart [tʃɑːt] *n* tableau *m (pl* tableaux) ▷ *The chart shows the increase in unemployment.* Le tableau montre la progression du chômage.; **the charts** le palmarès ▷ *This album is number one in the charts.* Cet album est numéro un au palmarès.

chase [tʃeɪs] *vb* pourchasser
▶ *n* poursuite *f* ▷ *a car chase* une poursuite en voiture

chat [tʃæt] *n* ❶ bavardage *m* ▷ *Enough chat; let's get to work.* Assez de bavardage; mettons-nous au

travail. ❷ (online) clavardage m; **to have a chat** bavarder
▶ vb ❶ bavarder ❷ (online) clavarder

chat room n clavardoir m

chauvinist ['ʃəʊvɪnɪst] n: **a male chauvinist** un machiste

cheap [tʃiːp] adj bon marché (f+pl bon marché) ▷ a cheap T-shirt un T-shirt bon marché

cheaper ['tʃiːpə'] adj moins cher (f moins chère) ▷ It's cheaper by bus. C'est moins cher en autobus.

cheat [tʃiːt] vb tricher ▷ You're cheating! Tu triches!

cheater ['tʃiːtə'] n tricheur m, tricheuse f

check [tʃɛk] n ❶ contrôle m ▷ a security check un contrôle de sécurité ❷ (mark) coche f ❸ (square in pattern) carreau m ▶ vb vérifier ▷ I'll check the time of the flight. Je vais vérifier l'heure du vol. ▷ Could you check the oil, please? Pourriez-vous vérifier le niveau d'huile, s'il vous plaît?; **to check in** (at airport) se présenter à l'enregistrement ▷ What time do I have to check in? À quelle heure est-ce que je dois me présenter à l'enregistrement? (2) (in hotel) se présenter à la réception; **to check on** jeter un coup d'œil sur ▷ Check on the baby. Jette un coup d'œil sur le bébé.; **to check out** (from hotel) régler sa note

checked [tʃɛkt] adj (fabric) à carreaux

checkers ['tʃɛkəz] plural noun dames fpl ▷ to play checkers jouer aux dames

check-in ['tʃɛkɪn] n enregistrement m

checkout ['tʃɛkaʊt] n caisse f

checkup ['tʃɛkʌp] n examen m de santé

cheek [tʃiːk] n joue f ▷ He kissed her on the cheek. Il l'a embrassée sur la joue.

cheer [tʃɪə'] n hourras mpl; **to give a cheer** pousser des hourras; **Cheers! (1)** (good health) À la vôtre! **(2)** (goodbye) Salut
▶ vb applaudir; **to cheer somebody up** remonter le moral à quelqu'un ▷ I was trying to cheer them up. J'essayais de leur remonter le moral.; **Cheer up!** Ne te laisse pas abattre!

cheerful ['tʃɪəful] adj gai

cheese [tʃiːz] n fromage m; **cheese curds** du fromage en grains

chef [ʃɛf] n chef m

chemical ['kɛmɪkl] adj chimique ▷ a chemical reaction une réaction chimique ▷ chemical weapons les armes chimiques f
▶ n produit chimique m

chemist ['kɛmɪst] n chimiste

chemistry ['kɛmɪstrɪ] n chimie f ▷ the chemistry lab le laboratoire de chimie

cheque [tʃɛk] n chèque m ▷ to write a cheque faire un chèque ▷ to pay by cheque payer par chèque

cherry ['tʃɛrɪ] n cerise f; **a cherry tree** un cerisier

chess [tʃɛs] n échecs mpl ▷ to play chess jouer aux échecs

chessboard ['tʃɛsbɔːd] n échiquier m

chest [tʃɛst] n (of person) poitrine f ▷ his chest measurement son tour de poitrine; **a chest of drawers** une commode

chestnut ['tʃɛsnʌt] n marron m ▷ roasted chestnuts les marrons grillés

chew [tʃuː] vb mâcher

chewing gum ['tʃuː-ɪŋ-] n gomme à mâcher f

chick [tʃɪk] n poussin m ▷ a hen and her chicks une poule et ses poussins

chicken ['tʃɪkɪn] n ❶ (meat) poulet m ❷ (live bird) poule f ▷ **to raise chickens** élever des poules

chicken pox [-pɒks] n varicelle f

chick peas npl pois mpl chiches

chief [tʃiːf] n chef m ▷ **the chief of** **security** le chef de la sécurité; **band chief** un chef de bande
▶ adj principal ▷ **Canada's chief exports** les articles d'exportation principaux du Canada

child [tʃaɪld] n enfant mf ▷ **all the children** tous les enfants

childish ['tʃaɪldɪʃ] adj puéril

children ['tʃɪldrən] npl see **child**

chili ['tʃɪlɪ] n ❶ (pepper) piment m ❷ (dish) chili m

chill [tʃɪl] vb mettre au frais ▷ **Put the wine in the fridge to chill.** Mets le vin au frais dans le réfrigérateur.

chilly ['tʃɪlɪ] adj froid m

chimney ['tʃɪmnɪ] n cheminée f

chin [tʃɪn] n menton m

china ['tʃaɪnə] n porcelaine f ▷ **a china plate** une assiette en porcelaine

chinook [tʃɪ'nuːk] n (wind) chinook m

chip [tʃɪp] n ❶ (potato chip) croustille f ▷ **a bag of chips** un sac de croustilles ❷ (fry) frite f ▷ **fish and chips** poisson et frites ❸ (chocolate) brisure f ❹ (in computer) puce f; **This plate has a chip in it.** Cette assiette est ébréchée.

chipmunk ['tʃɪpmʌŋk] n suisse m

chives [tʃaɪvz] npl ciboulette f

chocolate ['tʃɒklɪt] n chocolat m ▷ **a chocolate cake** un gâteau au chocolat; **hot chocolate** le chocolat chaud

chocolate chip n brisure de chocolat f; **a chocolate chip cookie** un biscuit aux brisures de chocolat

choice [tʃɔɪs] n choix m ▷ **I had no**

choice. Je n'avais pas le choix.

choir ['kwaɪə'] n chorale f ▷ **I sing in the school choir.** Je chante dans la chorale de l'école.

choke [tʃəʊk] vb s'étrangler; **He choked on a fishbone.** Il s'est étranglé avec une arête de poisson.

choose [tʃuːz] vb choisir ▷ **It's difficult to choose.** C'est difficile de choisir. ▷ **I chose to stay home.** J'ai décidé de rester chez moi.

chop [tʃɒp] vb ❶ émincer ▷ **Chop the onions.** Émincez les oignons. ❷ (wood) couper; **to chop down a tree** abattre un arbre
▶ n côtelette f ▷ **a pork chop** une côtelette de porc

chopsticks ['tʃɒpstɪks] npl baguettes fpl

chose, chosen [tʃəʊz, 'tʃəʊzn] vb see **choose**

Christian ['krɪstɪən] n chrétien m, chrétienne f
▶ adj chrétien m (f chrétienne)

Christmas ['krɪsməs] n Noël m ▷ **Merry Christmas!** Joyeux Noël!; **Christmas Day** le jour de Noël; **Christmas Eve** la veille de Noël

chronic ['krɒnɪk] adj chronique f ▷ **a chronic cough** une toux chronique

chunk [tʃʌŋk] n gros morceau m (pl gros morceaux) ▷ **Cut the meat into chunks.** Coupez la viande en gros morceaux.

church [tʃɜːtʃ] n église f

cider ['saɪdə'] n cidre m

cigarette [sɪgə'ret] n cigarette f

cinema ['sɪnəmə] n cinéma m

cinnamon ['sɪnəmən] n cannelle f

circle ['sɜːkl] n cercle m ▷ **to stand in a circle** faire cercle ▷ **to draw a circle** tracer un cercle ▷ **to go around in circles** tourner en rond
▶ vb encercler ▷ **Circle the correct answer.** Encerclez la bonne réponse.

circular [ˈsəːkjʊləʳ] *adj* circulaire

circulation [səːkjuˈleɪʃən] *n* ❶ *(of blood)* circulation *f* ❷ *(of newspaper)* tirage *m*

circumflex [ˈsəːkəmflɛks] *n* accent *m* circonflexe

circumstances [ˈsəːkəmstənsɪz] *npl* circonstances *fpl*

circus [ˈsəːkəs] *n* cirque *m*

citizen [ˈsɪtɪzn] *n* citoyen *m*, citoyenne *f* ▷ *a Canadian citizen* un citoyen canadien

citizenship [ˈsɪtɪznʃɪp] *n* citoyenneté *f*

city [ˈsɪtɪ] *n* ville *f*; **the city centre** le centre-ville ▷ *It's in the city centre.* C'est au centre-ville.

city hall *n* hôtel *m* de ville

civilization [sɪvɪlaɪˈzeɪʃən] *n* civilisation *f*

civil servant *n* fonctionnaire

civil war *n* guerre civile *f*

claim [kleɪm] *vb* ❶ prétendre ▷ *He claims to have found the money.* Il prétend avoir trouvé l'argent. ❷ réclamer ▷ *No one has claimed this jacket.* Personne n'a réclamé cette veste.
▶ *n* *(on insurance policy)* demande d'indemnité *f* ▷ *to make a claim* faire une demande d'indemnité

clam [klæm] *n* palourde *f*

clap [klæp] *vb* *(applaud)* applaudir; **to clap one's hands** frapper dans ses mains ▷ *I've trained my dog to sit when I clap my hands.* J'ai dressé mon chien à s'asseoir quand je frappe dans mes mains.

clarinet [klærɪˈnɛt] *n* clarinette *f* ▷ *I play the clarinet.* Je joue de la clarinette.

clash [klæʃ] *vb* ❶ *(colours)* jurer ▷ *These two colours clash.* Ces deux couleurs jurent. ❷ *(events)* tomber en même temps ▷ *The concert clashes with my party.* Le concert

tombe en même temps que ma soirée.

clasp [klɑːsp] *n* *(of necklace)* fermoir *m*

class [klɑːs] *n* ❶ *(group)* classe *f* ▷ *We're in the same class.* Nous sommes dans la même classe. ❷ *(lesson)* cours *m* ▷ *I go to dancing classes.* Je vais à des cours de danse.

classic [ˈklæsɪk] *adj* classique *m* ▷ *a classic example* un cas classique
▶ *n* *(book, film)* classique *m*

classical [ˈklæsɪkl] *adj* classique ▷ *I like classical music.* J'aime la musique classique.

classmate [ˈklɑːsmeɪt] *n* camarade de classe

classroom [ˈklɑːsruːm] *n* classe *f*

claw [klɔː] *n* ❶ *(of cat, dog)* griffe *f* ❷ *(of bird)* serre *f* ❸ *(of crab, lobster)* pince *f*

clay [kleɪ] *n* argile *f*

clean [kliːn] *adj* propre ▷ *a clean shirt* une chemise propre
▶ *vb* nettoyer

cleaner [ˈkliːnəʳ] *n* *(of building)* préposé au ménage *m*, préposée au ménage *f*

cleaners [ˈkliːnəz] *n* teinturerie *f*

clear [klɪəʳ] *adj* ❶ clair ▷ *a clear explanation* une explication claire ▷ *It's clear you don't believe me.* Il est clair que tu ne me crois pas. ❷ transparent ▷ *clear plastic* du plastique transparent ❸ *(distinct)* net ▷ *clear handwriting* une écriture nette ❹ *(road, way)* libre ▷ *The road's clear now.* La route est libre maintenant.
▶ *vb* ❶ dégager ▷ *The police are clearing the road after the accident.* La police dégage la route après l'accident. ❷ *(fog, mist)* se dissiper ▷ *The mist cleared.* La brume s'est dissipée.; **to clear the table** débarrasser la table ▷ *I'll clear the*

table. Je vais débarrasser la table.;
to clear up résoudre ▷ We've cleared
up the problem. Nous avons résolu
le problème.; **I think it's going to
clear up.** (weather) Je pense que le
temps va se lever.

clearing ['klɪərɪŋ] n clairière f ▷ a
clearing in the forest une clairière
dans la forêt

clearly ['klɪəlɪ] adv ❶ clairement
▷ She explained it very clearly. Elle
l'a expliqué très clairement. ❷ nettement ▷ The Labrador coast
was clearly visible. On distinguait
nettement la côte du Labrador.
❸ distinctement ▷ to speak clearly
parler distinctement

clementine ['klɛməntaɪn] n
clémentine f

clever ['klɛvər] adj astucieux (f
astucieuse) ▷ a clever system un
système astucieux; **What a clever
idea!** Quelle bonne idée!

click [klɪk] n (of door, camera) petit
bruit sec m
▶ vb (with mouse) cliquer; **to click
on an icon** cliquer sur une icône;
The lid clicked shut. Le couvercle
s'est fermé avec un petit bruit sec.

client ['klaɪənt] n client m, cliente f

cliff [klɪf] n falaise f

climate ['klaɪmɪt] n climat m

climb [klaɪm] vb ❶ escalader
▷ We're going to climb the Niagara
Escarpment. Nous allons escalader
l'escarpement du Niagara.
❷ (stairs) monter ❸ (tree) grimper
dans

clinic ['klɪnɪk] n clinique f

clip [klɪp] n ❶ (for hair) barrette f
❷ (film) court extrait m ▷ some clips
from his latest film quelques courts
extraits de son dernier film
▶ vb ❶ attacher ▷ Clip these
pages together. Attache ces pages.
❷ couper ▷ She clipped my bangs.

Elle m'a coupé la frange.; **to clip
an article out of the newspaper**
découper un article dans le journal

clip-art ['klɪpɑːt] n clipart m

clippers ['klɪpəz] npl: **nail clippers**
le coupe-ongle m (pl les coupe-
ongles)

cloakroom ['kləʊkrʊm] n (for
coats) vestiaire m

clock [klɒk] n ❶ horloge f ▷ the
church clock l'horloge de l'église
❷ (smaller) pendule f; **an alarm
clock** un réveil; **a clock-radio** un
radio-réveil

clockwork ['klɒkwəːk] n:
Everything went like clockwork.
Tout a marché comme sur des
roulettes.

clog [klɒg] vb boucher ▷ The drain is
clogged. L'égout est bouché.

clone [kləʊn] n (animal, plant)
clone m
▶ vb cloner ▷ a cloned sheep un
mouton cloné

close [kləʊz] adj, adv ❶ (near)
près ▷ The mall is very close. Le
centre commercial est tout près.;
close to près de ▷ The youth hostel
is close to the station. L'auberge
de jeunesse est près de la gare.;
Come closer. Rapproche-toi.;
to look at something close up
regarder quelque chose de près
❷ (in relationship) proche ▷ We're
just inviting close relations. Nous
n'invitons que les parents proches.
▷ She's a close friend of mine. C'est
une amie proche. ▷ I'm very close
to my brother. Je suis très proche de
mon frère. ❸ (contest) très serré
▷ It's going to be very close. Ça va être
très serré.
▶ vb ❶ fermer ▷ What time does
the pool close? La piscine ferme à
quelle heure? ▷ The stores close at
5.30. Les magasins ferment à cinq

heures et demie. ▷ *Please close the door.* Fermez la porte, s'il vous plaît. ❷ se fermer ▷ *The doors close automatically.* Les portes se ferment automatiquement.

closed [kləʊzd] *adj* fermé ▷ *The bank's closed.* La banque est fermée.

closely ['kləʊslɪ] *adv* (look, examine) de près

closet ['klɒzɪt] *n* garde-robe *m* ▷ *She hung her coat in the closet.* Elle a pendu son manteau dans la garde-robe.

close-up ['kləʊsʌp] *n* gros plan *m* ▷ *Here's a close-up of my boyfriend.* Voici un gros plan de mon petit ami.

cloth [klɒθ] *n* (material) tissu *m*; **a cloth** un chiffon ▷ *Wipe it with a damp cloth.* Nettoyez-le avec un chiffon humide.

clothes [kləʊðz] *npl* vêtements *mpl* ▷ *new clothes* des vêtements neufs; **a clothes line** un fil à linge; **a clothes peg** une pince à linge

cloud [klaʊd] *n* nuage *m*

cloudy ['klaʊdɪ] *adj* nuageux (*f* nuageuse)

clove [kləʊv] *n*: **a clove of garlic** une gousse d'ail

clown [klaʊn] *n* clown *m*

club [klʌb] *n* club *m* ▷ *a golf club* (society and for playing golf) un club de golf; **the youth club** le club de jeunes; **clubs** (in cards) le trèfle ▷ *the ace of clubs* l'as de trèfle

clue [kluː] *n* indice *m* ▷ *an important clue* un indice important; **I haven't a clue.** Je n'en ai pas la moindre idée.

clumsy ['klʌmzɪ] *adj* maladroit

clutch [klʌtʃ] *n* (of car) pédale d'embrayage *f*

clutter ['klʌtə*r*] *n* désordre *m* ▷ *There's too much clutter in here.* Il y a trop de désordre ici.
▸ *vb* encombrer ▷ *Don't clutter up the hallway.* N'encombrez pas le couloir. ▷ *a desk cluttered with papers and books* un bureau encombré de papiers et de livres

coach [kəʊtʃ] *n* entraîneur *m*, entraîneuse *f* ▷ *the hockey coach* l'entraîneur de l'équipe de hockey

coal [kəʊl] *n* charbon *m*; **a coal mine** une mine de charbon; **a coal miner** un mineur

coarse [kɔːs] *adj* ❶ (surface, fabric) rugueux (*f* rugueuse) ▷ *The bag was made of coarse cloth.* Le sac était fait d'un tissu rugueux. ❷ (vulgar) grossier (*f* grossière) ▷ *coarse language* un langage grossier

coast [kəʊst] *n* côte *f* ▷ *It's on the west coast of Canada.* C'est sur la côte ouest du Canada.

coast guard *n* (boat) garde-côte *m* (*pl* garde-côtes)

coat [kəʊt] *n* manteau *m* (*pl* manteaux) ▷ *a warm coat* un manteau chaud; **a coat of paint** une couche de peinture

coat hanger *n* cintre *m*

cobweb ['kɒbwɛb] *n* toile d'araignée *f*

cocoa ['kəʊkəʊ] *n* cacao *m* ▷ *a cup of cocoa* une tasse de cacao

coconut ['kəʊkənʌt] *n* noix de coco *f*

cod [kɒd] *n* morue *f*

code [kəʊd] *n* code *m*

coffee ['kɒfɪ] *n* café *m*; **A cup of coffee, please.** Un café, s'il vous plaît.

coffeepot ['kɒfɪpɒt] *n* cafetière *f*

coffee table *n* table basse *f*

coffin ['kɒfɪn] *n* cercueil *m*

coin [kɔɪn] *n* pièce de monnaie *f*

coincidence [kəʊ'ɪnsɪdəns] *n* coïncidence *f*

colander ['kɒləndə*r*] *n* passoire *f*

cold [kəʊld] *adj* froid *m* ▷ *The water's cold.* L'eau est froide.; **cold**

cuts l'assiette anglaise; **It's cold today.** Il fait froid aujourd'hui.; **to be cold** (person) avoir froid ▷ *I'm cold.* J'ai froid. ▷ *Are you cold?* Est-ce que tu as froid?
▶ *n* ❶ froid ▷ *I can't stand the cold.* Je ne supporte pas le froid. ❷ rhume *m* ▷ *to catch a cold* attraper un rhume; **to have a cold** avoir un rhume ▷ *I've got a bad cold.* J'ai un gros rhume.; **a cold sore** un bouton de fièvre

coleslaw ['kəʊlslɔː] *n* salade de chou

collapse [kə'læps] *vb* s'effondrer ▷ *He collapsed.* Il s'est effondré.

collar ['kɒlə'] *n* ❶ (of coat, shirt) col *m* ❷ (for animal) collier *m*

collarbone ['kɒləbəʊn] *n* clavicule *f* ▷ *I broke my collarbone.* Je me suis cassé la clavicule.

colleague ['kɒliːg] *n* collègue

collect [kə'lɛkt] *vb* ❶ ramasser ▷ *The teacher collected the homework.* Le professeur a ramassé les travaux. ❷ faire collection de ▷ *I collect stamps.* Je fais collection de timbres. ❸ faire une collecte ▷ *They're collecting for charity.* Ils font une collecte pour une association caritative.
▶ *adv*: **to call collect** téléphoner à frais virés

collect call *n* appel *m* à frais virés

collection [kə'lɛkʃən] *n*
❶ collection *f* ▷ *my CD collection* ma collection de CD ❷ collecte *f* ▷ *a collection for charity* une collecte pour une association caritative

collector [kə'lɛktə'] *n* collectionneur *m*, collectionneuse *f*

college ['kɒlɪdʒ] *n* collège *m* ▷ *a technical college* un collège d'enseignement technique

collide [kə'laɪd] *vb* entrer en collision

collision [kə'lɪʒən] *n* collision *f*

colon ['kəʊlən] *n* (punctuation mark) deux-points *m* (pl les deux-points)

colony ['kɒlənɪ] *n* colonie *f* ▷ *the colony of New France* la colonie de la Nouvelle France

colour ['kʌlə'] *n* couleur *f* ▷ *What colour is it?* C'est de quelle couleur?; **a colour printer** une imprimante couleur; **a colour scheme** une combinaison de couleurs

colourful ['kʌləful] *adj* aux couleurs vives ▷ *a colourful skirt* une jupe aux couleurs vives

colouring ['kʌlərɪŋ] *n* (for food) colorant *m*

column ['kɒləm] *n* ❶ colonne *f* ▷ *to format text in columns* disposer un texte en colonnes ❷ chronique *f* ▷ *He writes a column for the school newspaper.* Il écrit une chronique pour le journal de l'école.

coma ['kəʊmə] *n* coma *m* ▷ *to be in a coma* être dans le coma

comb [kəʊm] *n* peigne *m*
▶ *vb*: **to comb one's hair** se peigner ▷ *You haven't combed your hair.* Tu ne t'es pas peigné.

combination [kɒmbɪ'neɪʃən] *n* combinaison *f*

combine [kəm'baɪn] *vb* ❶ allier ▷ *The film combines humour with suspense.* Le film allie l'humour au suspense. ❷ concilier ▷ *It's difficult to combine a career with family.* Il est difficile de concilier carrière et vie de famille.

come [kʌm] *vb* ❶ venir ▷ *Can I come too?* Est-ce que je peux venir aussi? ▷ *Some friends came to see us.* Quelques amis sont venus nous voir. ▷ *I'll come with you.* Je viens avec toi. ❷ (arrive) arriver ▷ *I'm coming!* J'arrive! ▷ *They came late.* Ils sont arrivés en retard. ▷ *The* *letter came this morning.* La lettre est arrivée ce matin.; **to come back** revenir ▷ *Come back!* Reviens!; **to come down (1)** *(person, elevator)* descendre **(2)** *(prices)* baisser; **to come from** venir de ▷ *Where do you come from?* Tu viens d'où?; **to come in** entrer ▷ *Come in!* Entrez!; **Come on!** Allez!; **to come out** sortir ▷ *when we came out of the movie theatre* quand nous sommes sortis du cinéma ▷ *It's just come out on video.* Ça vient de sortir en vidéo.; **None of my photos have come out.** Mes photos n'ont rien donné.; **to come around** *(after faint, operation)* reprendre connaissance; **to come up** monter ▷ *Come up here!* Monte!; **to come up to somebody (1)** s'approcher de quelqu'un ▷ *She came up to me and kissed me.* Elle s'est approchée de moi et m'a embrassé. **(2)** *(to speak to them)* aborder quelqu'un ▷ *A man came up to me and said...* Un homme m'a abordé et m'a dit...

comedian [kə'miːdɪən] *n* comique

comedy ['kɒmɪdɪ] *n* comédie *f*

comfort ['kʌmfət] *vb* consoler ▷ *He tried to comfort her.* Il a essayé de la consoler.

comfortable ['kʌmfətəbl] *adj* ❶ *(bed, chair)* confortable ❷ *(person)* à l'aise ▷ *I'm very comfortable, thanks.* Je suis parfaitement à l'aise, merci.

comic ['kɒmɪk] *n* *(magazine)* illustré *m*

comic strip *n* bande dessinée *f*

coming ['kʌmɪŋ] *adj* prochain ▷ *in the coming months* au cours des prochains mois ▷ *this coming Thursday* jeudi prochain

comma ['kɒmə] *n* virgule *f*

command [kə'mɑːnd] *n* ordre *m*; **a good command of English** ▷ *une*

bonne maîtrise de l'anglais ▶ *vb* ordonner ▷ *He commanded us to leave.* Il nous a ordonné de partir.; **She commands respect.** Elle commande le respect.

comment ['kɒmɛnt] *n* commentaire *m* ▷ *He made no comment.* Il n'a fait aucun commentaire.; **No comment!** Je n'ai rien à dire!
▶ *vb*: **to comment on something** faire des commentaires sur quelque chose

commentary ['kɒməntərɪ] *n* *(on TV, radio)* reportage en direct *m*

commentator ['kɒmənteɪtə'] *n* commentateur sportif *m*, commentatrice sportive *f*

commercial [kə'mɜːʃəl] *n* annonce *f* publicitaire

commission [kə'mɪʃən] *n* commission *f* ▷ *Salesmen work on commission.* Les représentants travaillent à la commission.

commit [kə'mɪt] *vb*: **to commit a crime** commettre un crime; **to commit oneself** s'engager ▷ *I don't want to commit myself.* Je ne veux pas m'engager.; **to commit suicide** se suicider ▷ *She committed suicide.* Elle s'est suicidée.

committee [kə'mɪtɪ] *n* comité *m*

common ['kɒmən] *adj* courant *m* ▷ *a common expression* une expression courante; **in common** en commun ▷ *We have a lot in common.* Nous avons beaucoup de choses en commun.

Commons ['kɒmənz] *npl*: **the House of Commons** la Chambre des communes

common sense *n* bon sens *m* ▷ *Use your common sense!* Sers-toi de ton bon sens!

communicate [kə'mjuːnɪkeɪt] *vb* communiquer

communication [kəmjuːnɪ-ˈkeɪʃən] n communication

communism [ˈkɒmjunɪzəm] n communisme m

communist [ˈkɒmjunɪst] n communiste
▶ adj communiste

community [kəˈmjuːnɪtɪ] n communauté f

community centre n centre communautaire m

community college n collège communautaire m

commute [kəˈmjuːt] vb faire la navette ▷ She commutes between Kitchener and Toronto. Elle fait la navette entre Kitchener et Toronto.

commuter [kəˈmjuːtəˈ] n navetteur m, navetteuse f; **a commuter train** un train de banlieue

compact disc n disque compact m; **a compact disc player** un lecteur de DC

companion [kəmˈpænjən] n compagnon m, compagne f

company [ˈkʌmpənɪ] n ❶ société f ▷ She works for a big company. Elle travaille pour une grosse société. ❷ compagnie f ▷ an insurance company une compagnie d'assurance ▷ a theatre company une compagnie théâtrale; **to keep somebody company** tenir compagnie à quelqu'un ▷ I'll keep you company. Je vais te tenir compagnie.

comparatively [kəmˈpærətɪvlɪ] adv relativement

compare [kəmˈpɛəˈ] vb comparer ▷ People always compare him with his brother. On le compare toujours à son frère.; **compared with** en comparaison de ▷ Victoria is small compared with Vancouver. Victoria est une petite ville en comparaison de Vancouver.

comparison [kəmˈpærɪsn] n comparaison f

compartment [kəmˈpɑːtmənt] n compartiment m

compass [ˈkʌmpəs] n ❶ (for directions) boussole f ❷ (math instrument) compas m

compatible [kəmˈpætɪbl] adj compatible

compelling [kəmˈpɛlɪŋ] adj (gripping) fascinant ▷ It's a compelling film. C'est un film fascinant.

compensation [kɒmpənˈseɪʃən] n indemnité f ▷ They got $2000 compensation. Ils ont reçu une indemnité de deux mille dollars.

compete [kəmˈpiːt] vb participer ▷ I'm competing in the marathon. Je participe au marathon.; **to compete with someone** (sports) concourir avec quelqu'un; **to compete with someone** (general) rivaliser avec quelqu'un; **to compete for something** se disputer quelque chose ▷ There are 50 students competing for 6 places. Ils sont cinquante élèves à se disputer six places.

competent [ˈkɒmpɪtənt] adj compétent

competition [kɒmpɪˈtɪʃən] n concours m ▷ a singing competition un concours de chant

competitive [kəmˈpɛtɪtɪv] adj compétitif (f compétitive) ▷ a very competitive price un prix très compétitif; **to be competitive** (person) avoir l'esprit de compétition ▷ He's a very competitive person. Il a vraiment l'esprit de compétition.

competitor [kəmˈpɛtɪtəˈ] n concurrent m, concurrente f

complain [kəm'pleɪn] *vb* se plaindre ▷ *I'm going to complain to the manager.* Je vais me plaindre à la directrice. ▷ *We complained about the noise.* Nous nous sommes plaints du bruit.

complaint [kəm'pleɪnt] *n* plainte *f* ▷ *There were lots of complaints about the food.* Il y a eu beaucoup de plaintes à propos de la nourriture.

complete [kəm'pli:t] *adj* complet (*f* complète)

completely [kəm'pli:tlɪ] *adv* complètement

complex ['kɔmpleks] *adj* complexe

complexion [kəm'plekʃən] *n* teint *m*

complicated ['kɔmplɪkeɪtɪd] *adj* compliqué

compliment ['kɔmplɪmənt] *n* compliment *m*
▶ *vb* complimenter ▷ *They complimented me on my French.* Ils m'ont complimenté sur mon français.

complimentary [kɔmplɪ'mentərɪ] *adj*
❶ (*flattering*) élogieux (*f* élogieuse) ▷ *He was very complimentary about my poem.* Il a été très élogieux à propos de mon poème.
❷ (*free*) gratuit; **I have two complimentary tickets for tonight.** J'ai deux places gratuites pour ce soir.

composer [kəm'pəuzə^r] *n* compositeur *m*, compositrice *f*

compost ['kɔmpɔst] *n* compost *m*; **a compost heap** un tas de compost

comprehension [kɔmprɪ'henʃən] *n* compréhension *f*

comprehensive [kɔmprɪ'hensɪv] *adj* complet (*f* complète) ▷ *a comprehensive guide* un guide

complet

▌ Be careful not to translate **comprehensive** by **compréhensif**.

compromise ['kɔmprəmaɪz] *n* compromis *m* ▷ *We reached a compromise.* Nous sommes parvenus à un compromis.
▶ *vb:* **Let's compromise.** Essayons de trouver un compromis.

compulsory [kəm'pʌlsərɪ] *adj* obligatoire

computer [kəm'pju:tə^r] *n* ordinateur *m*

computer game *n* jeu électronique (*pl* jeux électroniques)

computer programmer *n* programmeur *m*, programmeuse *f* ▷ *She's a computer programmer.* Elle est programmeuse.

computer room *n* salle d'informatique *f*

computer science *n* informatique *f*

computing [kəm'pju:tɪŋ] *n* informatique *f*

concentrate ['kɔnsəntreɪt] *vb* se concentrer ▷ *I couldn't concentrate.* Je n'arrivais pas à me concentrer.

concentration [kɔnsən'treɪʃən] *n* concentration *f*

concern [kən'sə:n] *n* (*worry*) inquiétude *f* ▷ *They expressed concern about the school's image.* Ils ont exprimé leur inquiétude concernant l'image de l'école.; **That's none of your concern.** Ce n'est pas ton affaire.

concerned [kən'sə:nd] *adj:* **to be concerned** s'inquiéter ▷ *His mother is concerned about him.* Sa mère s'inquiète à son sujet.; **as far as I'm concerned** en ce qui me concerne

concerning [kən'sə:nɪŋ] *prep* concernant

concert ['kɔnsət] *n* concert *m*

conclusion [kən'klu:ʒən] n
conclusion f ▷ Your essay should
have an introduction and a conclusion.
Votre dissertation devrait avoir une
introduction et une conclusion.; **I
came to the conclusion that...**
J'ai conclu que...; **in conclusion** en
conclusion

concrete ['kɒŋkri:t] n béton m

condemn [kən'dem] vb
condamner ▷ The government
has condemned the decision. Le
gouvernement a condamné cette
décision.

condition [kən'dɪʃən] n
❶ condition f ▷ I'll do it, on one
condition... Je veux bien le faire, à
une condition... ❷ état m ▷ in bad
condition en mauvais état ▷ in good
condition en bon état

conditional [kən'dɪʃənl] n
conditionnel m

conditioner [kən'dɪʃənəʳ] n (for
hair) revitalisant m

condom ['kɒndəm] n condom m

condominium [kɒndə'mɪnɪəm]
n copropriété f ▷ We live in a
condominium. Nous habitons dans
une copropriété.

conduct [kən'dʌkt] vb (orchestra)
diriger

conductor [kən'dʌktəʳ] n chef
d'orchestre m

cone [kəʊn] n ▷ an ice
cream cone un cornet de crème
glacée

Confederation [kɒnfedə'reɪʃn]
n Confédération f ▷ fifty years after
Confederation cinquante ans après
la Confédération

conference ['kɒnfərns] n
conférence f

confess [kən'fes] vb avouer ▷ He
finally confessed. Il a fini par avouer.
▷ He confessed to the crime. Il a avoué
avoir commis le crime.

confession [kən'feʃən] n
confession f

confetti [kən'fetɪ] n confettis mpl

confidence ['kɒnfɪdns]
n ❶ confiance f ▷ I have
confidence in you. J'ai confiance
en toi. ❷ assurance f ▷ She
lacks confidence. Elle manque
d'assurance.

confident ['kɒnfɪdənt] adj sûr
▷ I'm confident everything will be okay.
Je suis sûr que tout ira bien.; **She
seems quite confident.** Elle a l'air
sûre d'elle.

confidential [kɒnfɪ'denʃəl] adj
confidentiel (f confidentielle)

confirm [kən'fəːm] vb (booking)
confirmer

confirmation [kɒnfə'meɪʃən] n
confirmation f

conflict [kən'flɪkt] n conflit m

confuse [kən'fjuːz] vb: **to confuse
somebody** embrouiller les idées de
quelqu'un ▷ Don't confuse me! Ne
m'embrouille pas les idées!

confused [kən'fjuːzd] adj
désorienté

confusing [kən'fjuːzɪŋ] adj
déroutant ▷ It was confusing at first.
C'était déroutant au début.; **The
traffic signs are confusing.** Les
panneaux de signalisation ne sont
pas clairs.

confusion [kən'fjuːʒən] n
confusion f

congratulate [kən'grætjʊleɪt] vb
féliciter ▷ My friends congratulated
me on passing the test. Mes amis
m'ont félicité d'avoir réussi à
l'examen.

congratulations
[kəngrætjʊ'leɪʃənz] npl
félicitations fpl ▷ Congratulations
on your new job! Félicitations pour
votre nouveau poste!

conjunction [kən'dʒʌŋkʃən] n

conjunction f

connect [kə'nɛkt] vb ① (plug in) brancher ▷ You have to connect the printer. Tu dois brancher l'imprimante. ② connecter ▷ to be connected to the Internet être connecté à l'Internet ③ associer ▷ I connect summer with camping. J'associe l'été au camping.

connection [kə'nɛkʃən] n ① rapport m ▷ There's no connection between the two events. Il n'y a aucun rapport entre les deux événements. ② (electrical) contact m ▷ There's a loose connection. Il y a un mauvais contact. ③ (of trains, planes, buses) correspondance f ▷ We missed our connection. Nous avons raté la correspondance.

conquer ['kɒŋkər] vb conquérir

conscience ['kɒnʃəns] n conscience f

conscientious [kɒnʃɪ'ɛnʃəs] adj consciencieux (f consciencieuse)

conscious ['kɒnʃəs] adj conscient

consciousness ['kɒnʃəsnɪs] n connaissance f; **to lose consciousness** perdre connaissance ▷ I lost consciousness. J'ai perdu connaissance.

consequence ['kɒnsɪkwəns] n conséquence f ▷ What are the consequences for the environment? Quelles sont les conséquences pour l'environnement?; **as a consequence** en conséquence; **to suffer the consequences** accepter les conséquences

consequently ['kɒnsɪkwəntlɪ] adv par conséquent

conservation [kɒnsə'veɪʃən] n protection f

conservative [kən'sə:vətɪv] adj conservateur (f conservatrice)

consider [kən'sɪdər] vb ① considérer ▷ He considers it a waste of time. Il considère que c'est une perte de temps. ② envisager ▷ We considered cancelling our holiday. Nous avons envisagé d'annuler nos vacances.; **I'm considering the idea.** J'y songe.

considerate [kən'sɪdərɪt] adj délicat

considering [kən'sɪdərɪŋ] prep ① étant donné ▷ Considering we were there for a month... Étant donné que nous étions là pour un mois... ② tout compte fait ▷ I got a good mark, considering. J'ai eu une bonne note, tout compte fait.

consist [kən'sɪst] vb: **to consist of** être composé de ▷ The band consists of three guitarists and a drummer. Le groupe est composé de trois guitaristes et une batteuse.

consonant ['kɒnsənənt] n consonne f

constant ['kɒnstənt] adj constant

constantly ['kɒnstəntlɪ] adv constamment

constitution [kɒnstɪ'tju:ʃən] n constitution f ▷ the Canadian constitution la Constitution canadienne

construct [kən'strʌkt] vb construire

construction [kən'strʌkʃən] n construction f

consult [kən'sʌlt] vb consulter

consumer [kən'sju:mər] n consommateur m, consommatrice f

contact ['kɒntækt] n contact m ▷ I'm in contact with her. Je suis en contact avec elle.
▶ vb joindre ▷ Where can we contact you? Où pouvons-nous vous joindre?

contact lenses [-'lɛnzɪz] npl verres mpl de contact

contact number n numéro de téléphone m

contagious [kən'teɪdʒəs] adj

contagieux (f **contagieuse**) ▷ It's not contagious. Ce n'est pas contagieux.

contain [kən'teɪn] vb contenir

container [kən'teɪnə^r] n contenant m ▷ a plastic container un contenant en plastique

contaminated [kən'tæmɪneɪtɪd] adj contaminé ▷ contaminated water de l'eau contaminée

contempt [kən'tempt] n mépris m

contents ['kɒntents] npl ● (of container) contenu m ● (of book) table f des matières

contest [kən'test] n concours m

contestant [kən'testənt] n concurrent m, concurrente f

context ['kɒntekst] n contexte m

continent ['kɒntɪnənt] n continent m ▷ How many continents are there? Combien y a-t-il de continents?

continental breakfast [kɒntɪ'nentl-] n déjeuner continental m

continue [kən'tɪnjuː] vb ● continuer ▷ She continued talking. Elle a continué à parler. ● (after interruption) reprendre ▷ We continued working after lunch. Nous avons repris le travail après le déjeuner.

continuous [kən'tɪnjuəs] adj continu

contraceptive [kɒntrə'septɪv] n contraceptif m

contract [kən'trækt] n contrat m

contradict [kɒntrə'dɪkt] vb contredire

contrary [kən'treərɪ] n: **on the contrary** au contraire

contrast [kən'trɑːst] n contraste m

contribute [kən'trɪbjuːt] vb ● (to success, achievement) contribuer ▷ The treaty will contribute to world peace. Le traité va contribuer à la

paix dans le monde. ● (share in) participer ▷ They didn't contribute to the discussion. Ils n'ont pas participé à la discussion. ● (give) donner ▷ She contributed $10. Elle a donné dix dollars.

contribution [kɒntrɪ'bjuːʃən] n contribution f

control [kən'trəʊl] n contrôle m; **to lose control** (of vehicle) perdre le contrôle ▷ He lost control of the car. Il a perdu le contrôle de son véhicule.; **the controls** (of machine) les commandes; **to be in control** être maître de la situation; **to keep control** (of people) se faire obéir ▷ He can't keep control of the class. Il n'arrive pas à se faire obéir de sa classe.; **out of control** (child, class) déchaîné

▶ vb ● (country, organization) diriger ● se faire obéir de ▷ She can't control the class. Elle n'arrive pas à se faire obéir de sa classe. ● maîtriser ▷ I couldn't control the horse. Je ne suis pas arrivé à maîtriser le cheval. ● (temperature, speed) régler; **to control oneself** se contrôler

controversial [kɒntrə'vɜːʃl] adj controversé ▷ a controversial book un livre controversé

convenience store [kən'viːnɪəns-] n dépanneur m

convenient [kən'viːnɪənt] adj: **The hotel is in a convenient location.** L'hôtel est bien situé.; **It's not a convenient time for me.** C'est une heure qui ne m'arrange pas.; **Would Monday be convenient for you?** Est-ce que lundi vous conviendrait?

conventional [kən'venʃənl] adj conventionnel (f **conventionnelle**)

conversation [kɒnvə'seɪʃən] n conversation f ▷ a French

conversation class un cours de conversation française

convert ['konvɜːt] *vb* transformer ▷ *We've converted the loft into a spare room.* Nous avons transformé le grenier en chambre d'amis.

convict ['kɒnvɪkt] *vb* reconnaître coupable ▷ *She was convicted of the crime.* Elle a été reconnue coupable du crime.

convince [kən'vɪns] *vb* persuader ▷ *I'm not convinced.* Je n'en suis pas persuadé.

cook [kʊk] *vb* ① faire la cuisine ▷ *I can't cook.* Je ne sais pas faire la cuisine. ② préparer ▷ *He's cooking supper.* Il est en train de préparer le souper. ③ faire cuire ▷ *Cook the pasta for 10 minutes.* Faites cuire les pâtes pendant dix minutes.; **to be cooked** être cuit ▷ *When the potatoes are cooked...* Lorsque les pommes de terre sont cuites...
▶ *n* cuisinier *m*, cuisinière *f* ▷ *Matthew's an excellent cook.* Matthew est un excellent cuisinier.

cookbook ['kʊkbʊk] *n* livre de cuisine *m*

cookie ['kʊkɪ] *n* biscuit *m*

cooking ['kʊkɪŋ] *n* cuisine *f* ▷ *I like cooking.* J'aime bien faire la cuisine.

cool [kuːl] *adj* ① frais (fraîche) ▷ *a cool place* un endroit frais ② (trendy, OK) cool ▷ *Your website is super!* Ton site Web est super! ③ (excellent) génial ▷ *You're coming along? Cool!* Tu viens aussi? C'est génial!; **to stay cool** (keep calm) garder son calme ▷ *She stayed cool.* Elle a gardé son calme.; **keep cool!** du calme!

co-operation [kəʊɒpə'reɪʃn] *n* coopération *f*

co-operative [kəʊ'ɒprətɪv] *adj* coopératif (f coopérative) ▷ *She was very co-operative.* Elle s'est montrée très coopérative.

cop [kɒp] *n* (informal) flic *m*

cope [kəʊp] *vb* se débrouiller ▷ *It was hard, but we coped.* C'était dur, mais nous nous sommes débrouillés.; **to cope with** faire face à ▷ *She has a lot of problems to cope with.* Elle doit faire face à de nombreux problèmes.

copper ['kɒpə] *n* cuivre *m* ▷ *a copper bracelet* un bracelet en cuivre

copy ['kɒpɪ] *n* ① (of letter, document) copie *f* ② (of book) exemplaire *m*
▶ *vb* copier ▷ *The teacher accused him of copying.* Le professeur l'a accusé d'avoir copié.; **to copy and paste** copier-coller

cord [kɔːd] *n* fil *m* ▷ *The cord isn't long enough.* Le fil n'est pas assez long.

cordless ['kɔːdlɪs] *adj* sans fil ▷ *a cordless mouse* une souris sans fil

core [kɔː] *n* (of fruit) trognon *m* ▷ *an apple core* un trognon de pomme

cork [kɔːk] *n* (of bottle) bouchon *m*

corkscrew ['kɔːkskruː] *n* tire-bouchon *m*

corn [kɔːn] *n* maïs *m*; **corn on the cob** l'épi *m* de maïs

corner ['kɔːnə] *n* coin *m* ▷ *in a corner of the room* dans un coin de la pièce; **the shop on the corner** la boutique au coin de la rue; **He lives just around the corner.** Il habite tout près d'ici.

corn starch [-stɑːtʃ] *n* amidon *m* de maïs

corporal punishment ['kɔːpərəl-] *n* châtiment corporel *m*

corpse [kɔːps] *n* cadavre *m*

correct [kə'rɛkt] *adj* exact ▷ *That's correct.* C'est exact.; **the correct choice** le bon choix; **the correct answer** la bonne réponse
▶ *vb* corriger

correction [kə'rɛkʃən] *n*

correction f

correctly [kəˈrɛktlɪ] adv
correctement

correspond [kɒrɪsˈpɒnd] vb
(match, agree) correspondre ▷ Write
down the letter that corresponds to
the correct answer. Écris la lettre qui
correspond à la bonne réponse.;
**She corresponds with her aunt
in India.** Elle correspond avec sa
tante en Inde.

corridor [ˈkɒrɪdɔːʳ] n couloir m

corruption [kəˈrʌpʃən] n
corruption f

cosmetics [kɒzˈmɛtɪks] npl
produits mpl de beauté

cosmetic surgery [kɒzˈmɛtɪk-
səːˈdʒərɪ] n chirurgie esthétique f

cost [kɒst] vb coûter ▷ The meal
costs a hundred dollars. Le repas
coûte cent dollars. ▷ How much
does it cost? Combien est-ce que ça
coûte? ▷ It costs too much. Ça coûte
trop cher.
▶ n coût m; **the cost of living** le
coût de la vie; **at all costs** à tout
prix; **to cut costs** réduire les coûts

costume [ˈkɒstjuːm] n costume m

cot [kɒt] n lit de camp m

cottage [ˈkɒtɪdʒ] n chalet m

cottage cheese n fromage
cottage

cotton [ˈkɒtn] n coton m ▷ a cotton
shirt une chemise en coton; **a
cotton ball** une boule de coton;
cotton candy la barbe à papa

couch [kautʃ] n canapé m

cough [kɒf] vb tousser
▶ n toux f ▷ a bad cough une
mauvaise toux; **I've got a cough.**
Je tousse.; **a cough drop** une
pastille

could [kud] vb see **can**

coulee [ˈkuːlɪ] n ravine f ▷ The
coulee is usually dry in summer. La
ravine est normalement sans eau

en été.

council [ˈkaunsl] n conseil; **He's
on the city council.** Il fait partie du
conseil municipal.; **She's on the
student council.** Elle fait partie du
conseil étudiant.

councillor [ˈkaunslə^r] n
conseiller municipal m, conseillère
municipale f

counsellor [ˈkaunslə^r] n
❶ conseiller m, conseillère
f; **a guidance counsellor** une
conseillère en orientation
❷ (camp) animateur m,
animatrice f

count [kaunt] vb compter; **to
count on** compter sur ▷ You can
count on me. Tu peux compter
sur moi.

counter [ˈkauntər] n ❶ (in store)
comptoir m ❷ (in post office, bank)
guichet m ❸ (in game) jeton m

counterfeit [ˈkauntəfɪt] adj faux
(f fausse) ▷ a counterfeit bill un faux
billet ▷ counterfeit money la fausse
monnaie

country [ˈkʌntrɪ] n ❶ pays m ▷ the
border between the two countries
la frontière entre les deux pays
❷ campagne f ▷ I live in the country.
J'habite à la campagne.; **country
music** la musique country; **a
country road** une route de
campagne

countryside [ˈkʌntrɪsaɪd] n
campagne f

county [ˈkauntɪ] n comté m

couple [ˈkʌpl] n couple m ▷ the
couple who live next door le couple qui
habite à côté; **a couple** deux ▷ a
couple of hours deux heures; **Could
you wait a couple of minutes?**
Pourriez-vous attendre quelques
minutes?

coupon [ˈkuːpɒn] n bon de
réduction m ▷ I have a coupon for 10%

off. J'ai un bon de réduction de dix pour cent.

courage ['kʌrɪdʒ] n courage m

courageous [kə'reɪdʒəs] adj courageux (f courageuse)

courier ['kʊrɪə'] n messageries fpl ▷ They sent it by courier. Ils l'ont envoyé par messageries.

Be careful not to translate **courier** by the French word **courrier**.

course [kɔːs] n ❶ cours m ▷ a French course un cours de français ▷ to take a course suivre un cours ❷ plat m ▷ the main course le plat principal; **the first course** l'entrée f ❸ terrain m ▷ a golf course un terrain de golf; **of course** bien sûr ▷ "Do you understand?" — "Of course I do!" « Tu comprends? » — « Bien sûr que oui! »

court [kɔːt] n ❶ (of law) tribunal m (pl tribunaux) ▷ He was in court last week. Il est passé devant le tribunal la semaine dernière. ❷ (tennis) court m ▷ There are tennis and squash courts. Il y a des courts de tennis et de squash.

courtyard ['kɔːtjɑːd] n cour f

cousin ['kʌzn] n cousin m, cousine f

cover ['kʌvə'] n ❶ (book cover, blanket) couverture f ❷ (duvet, computer) housse f; **a cover page** une page couverture; **blow someone's cover** démasquer quelqu'un
▶ vb ❶ couvrir ▷ My face was covered with mosquito bites. J'avais le visage couvert de piqûres de moustique. ❷ prendre en charge ▷ Our insurance didn't cover it. Notre assurance ne l'a pas pris en charge.; **to cover up a scandal** étouffer un scandale

coverage ['kʌvərɪdʒ] n couverture f ▷ media coverage la couverture

médiatique

cow [kau] n vache f

coward ['kauəd] n lâche ▷ She's a coward. Elle est lâche.

cowardly ['kauədlɪ] adj lâche

cowhand ['kauhænd] n vacher m, vachère f

coyote [kɔɪ'əutɪ] n coyote m

cozy ['kəuzɪ] adj douillet (f douillette)

crab [kræb] n crabe m

crack [kræk] n ❶ (in wall) fissure f ❷ (in cup, window) fêlure f; **I'll have a crack at it.** Je vais tenter le coup.
▶ vb (nut, egg) casser; **to crack a joke** sortir une blague

crack down on vb être ferme avec ▷ The police are cracking down on motorists who drive too fast. La police va être ferme avec les automobilistes qui roulent trop vite.

cracked [krækt] adj (cup, window) fêlé

cracker ['krækə'] n (biscuit) craquelin m

cradle ['kreɪdl] n berceau m (pl berceaux)

crafter ['krɑːftə'] n artisan m, artisane f

crafts [krɑːfts] n artisanat m ▷ to do crafts faire de l'artisanat; **a craft shop** une boutique d'artisanat

cram [kræm] n ❶ entasser ▷ We crammed our stuff into the trunk. Nous avons entassé nos affaires dans le coffre. ❷ préparer un examen

crammed [kræmd] adj: **crammed with** bourré de ▷ Her pack was crammed with books. Son sac à dos était bourré de livres.

cranberry ['krænbərɪ] n canneberge f ▷ turkey with cranberry sauce la dinde aux canneberges

crane [kreɪn] n (machine) grue f

crash [kræʃ] vb ❶ entrer en collision ▷ *The two cars crashed.* Les deux autos sont entrées en collision.; **to crash into something** rentrer dans quelque chose; **The dishes crashed to the floor.** La vaisselle s'est fracassée sur le plancher.; **The plane crashed.** L'avion s'est écrasé. ❷ (*computer*) se planter ▷ *My computer crashed.* Mon ordinateur s'est planté.
▶ *n* ❶ (*of car*) collision *f* ❷ (*of plane*) accident *m* ❸ (*sound*) fracas *m*; **a computer crash** un plantage d'ordinateur; **a crash helmet** un casque; **a crash course** un cours intensif

crawl [krɔːl] vb (*baby*) marcher à quatre pattes; **A spider crawled across the floor.** Une araignée avançait le long du plancher.
▶ *n* crawl *m* ▷ *to do the crawl* nager le crawl

crazy ['kreɪzɪ] adj fou (*f* folle)

cream [kriːm] *n* crème *f* ▷ *strawberries and cream* les fraises à la crème; **cream cheese** le fromage à la crème; **a cream puff** un chou à la crème

crease [kriːs] *n* ❶ pli *m* ❷ (*hockey*) zone de but *f*

creased [kriːst] adj froissé

create [kriːˈeɪt] vb créer

creation [kriːˈeɪʃən] *n* création *f*

creative [kriːˈeɪtɪv] adj créatif (*f* créative)

creature ['kriːtʃəʳ] *n* créature *f*

credit ['krɛdɪt] *n* crédit *m* ▷ *on credit* à crédit

credit card *n* carte de crédit *f*

creek [kriːk] *n* ruisseau *m*

creeps [kriːps] npl: **It gives me the creeps.** Ça me donne la chair de poule.

creep up [kriːpˈʌp] vb s'approcher à pas de loup; **to creep up on**

somebody s'approcher de quelqu'un à pas de loup

crept [krɛpt] vb *see* **creep up**

crew [kruː] *n* ❶ (*of ship, plane*) équipage *m*, équipe *f* ▷ *a film crew* une équipe de tournage

crib [krɪb] *n* lit d'enfant *m*

cricket ['krɪkɪt] *n* grillon *m*

crime [kraɪm] *n* ❶ crime *m* ▷ *Murder is a crime.* Le meurtre est un crime. ❷ (*lawlessness*) criminalité *f*; **to reduce crime** réduire la criminalité

criminal ['krɪmɪnl] *n* criminel, criminelle *f*
▶ adj criminel (*f* criminelle) ▷ *It's criminal!* C'est criminel!; **It's a criminal offence.** C'est un crime puni par la loi.; **to have a criminal record** avoir un casier judiciaire

crisis ['kraɪsɪs] *n* crise *f*

crisp [krɪsp] adj (*food*) croustillant

criterion [kraɪˈtɪərɪən] *n* critère *m*

critic ['krɪtɪk] *n* critique

critical ['krɪtɪkl] adj critique; **a critical remark** une critique

criticism ['krɪtɪsɪzəm] *n* critique

criticize ['krɪtɪsaɪz] vb critiquer

crochet ['krəʊʃeɪ] vb faire du crochet

crocodile ['krɒkədaɪl] *n* crocodile *m*

crook [krʊk] *n* (*criminal*) escroc *m* ▷ *That woman is a crook.* Cette femme est un escroc.

crooked ['krʊkɪd] adj ❶ (*bent*) tordu ▷ *a crooked line* une ligne tordue ❷ (*on an angle*) de travers ▷ *Your tie's crooked.* La cravate est de travers.

crop [krɒp] *n* ❶ récolte *f* ▷ *a good crop of apples* une bonne récolte de pommes ❷ culture *f* ▷ *Wheat is one of Canada's main crops.* Le blé est l'une des cultures les plus importantes du Canada.

cross [krɒs] *n* croix *f*

▶ vb (street, bridge) traverser; **to cross out** barrer; **to cross over** traverser

cross-check ['krɒstʃek] vb faire double échec à ▷ He cross-checked his opponent. Il a fait double échec à son adversaire.

cross-checking ['krɒstʃekɪŋ] n double échec m ▷ a penalty for cross-checking une punition pour double-échec

cross-country ['krɒs'kʌntrɪ] n (race) cross m; **cross-country skiing** le ski de fond

crossroads ['krɒsrəudz] n carrefour m

crosswalk ['krɒswɔːk] n passage à piétons m

crossword ['krɒswɜːd] n mots mpl croisés ▷ I like doing crosswords. J'aime faire les mots croisés.

crouch down vb s'accroupir

crow [krəu] n corbeau m (pl corbeaux)

crowd [kraud] n foule f; **the crowd** (spectators) les spectateurs

crowded ['kraudɪd] adj bondé

crown [kraun] n couronne f

crude [kruːd] adj (vulgar) grossier (f grossière)

cruel ['kruəl] adj cruel (f cruelle)

cruise [kruːz] n croisière f ▷ to go on a cruise faire une croisière

crumb [krʌm] n miette f

crunchy ['krʌntʃɪ] adj ① (cookie) croustillant ② (carrot, apple) croquant

crush [krʌʃ] vb écraser

crust [krʌst] n croûte f

crutch [krʌtʃ] n béquille f

cry [kraɪ] n cri m ▷ He gave a cry of surprise. Il a poussé un cri de surprise.; **Go on, have a good cry!** Vas-y, pleure un bon coup!
▶ vb pleurer ▷ The baby's crying. Le bébé pleure.

crystal ['krɪstl] n cristal m (pl cristaux)

cub [kʌb] n ① (bear) ourson m ② (wolf) louveteau m (pl louveteaux) ③ (lion) lionceau m (pl lionceaux) ④ (fox) renardeau m (pl renardeaux)

cube [kjuːb] n cube m

cubic ['kjuːbɪk] adj: **a cubic metre** un mètre cube

cucumber ['kjuːkʌmbər] n concombre m

cuddly ['kʌdlɪ] adj câlin

cue [kjuː] n ① signal m ② (for snooker, pool) queue de billard f

culprit ['kʌlprɪt] n coupable m

culture ['kʌltʃər] n culture f

cup [kʌp] n ① tasse f ▷ a china cup une tasse en porcelaine; **a cup of coffee** un café ② (trophy) coupe f

cupboard ['kʌbəd] n placard m

cure [kjuər] vb guérir
▶ n remède m

curious ['kjuərɪəs] adj curieux (f curieuse)

curl [kɜːl] n (in hair) boucle f
▶ vb ① boucler ▷ to curl one's hair boucler ses cheveux ② (sport) jouer au curling

curling ['kɜːlɪŋ] n curling m ▷ a curling league une ligue de curling

curling iron n fer à friser m

curly ['kɜːlɪ] adj ① (loosely curled) bouclé ② (tightly curled) frisé

currency ['kʌrnsɪ] n devise f ▷ foreign currency les devises étrangères

current ['kʌrnt] n courant m ▷ The current is very strong. Le courant est très fort.
▶ adj actuel (f actuelle); **current events** l'actualité

curriculum [kə'rɪkjuləm] n programme d'études m

curry ['kʌrɪ] n curry m

curse [kɜːs] n (spell) malédiction f

cursor ['kɜːsəʳ] n curseur m
curtain ['kɜːtn] n rideau m (pl rideaux); **to draw the curtains** tirer les rideaux
curved [kɜːvd] adj courbe ▷ a curved surface une surface courbe; **a curved line** une courbe
cushion ['kʊʃən] n coussin m
custard ['kʌstəd] n crème anglaise f
custody ['kʌstədɪ] n (of child) garde f
custom ['kʌstəm] n coutume f ▷ It's an old custom. C'est une ancienne coutume.
customer ['kʌstəməʳ] n client m, cliente f
customs ['kʌstəmz] npl douane f
customs officer n douanier m, douanière f
cut [kʌt] n ❶ coupure f ▷ He's got a cut on his forehead. Il a une coupure au front. ❷ coupe f ▷ a cut and blow-dry une coupe et un séchage à la brosse ❸ (in price, spending) réduction f
▸ vb ❶ couper ▷ I'll cut some bread. Je vais couper du pain.; **to cut oneself** se couper ▷ I cut my foot on a piece of glass. Je me suis coupé au pied avec un morceau de verre.; **to cut and paste** couper-coller ❷ (price, spending) réduire; **to cut down** (tree) abattre; **to cut off** couper ▷ The power was cut off. L'électricité a été coupée.; **to cut up** (vegetables, meat) hacher
cutback ['kʌtbæk] n réduction f ▷ staff cutbacks des réductions de personnel
cute [kjuːt] adj mignon (f mignonne)
cutlery ['kʌtlərɪ] n couverts mpl
cyberbullying ['saɪbəbʊlɪɪŋ] n cyberintimidation f
cybercafé ['saɪbəkæfeɪ] n

cybercafé m
cycle ['saɪkl] n cycle m; **a vicious cycle** un cycle infernal
cycling ['saɪklɪŋ] n cyclisme m
cyclist ['saɪklɪst] n cycliste
cylinder ['sɪlɪndəʳ] n cylindre m
cynical ['sɪnɪkl] adj cynique

d

dad [dæd] n ❶ père m ▷ *my dad* mon père ▷ *his dad* son père ❷ papa m

> Use **papa** only when you are talking to your father or using it as his name; otherwise use **père**.

Dad! Papa! ▷ *I'll ask Dad.* Je vais demander à papa.

daffodil ['dæfədɪl] n jonquille f

daily ['deɪlɪ] adj, adv ❶ quotidien (f quotidienne) ▷ *It's part of my daily routine.* Ça fait partie de mes occupations quotidiennes. ❷ tous les jours ▷ *The pool is open daily from 9 a.m. to 6 p.m.* La piscine est ouverte tous les jours de neuf heures à dix-huit heures.

dairy products ['dɛərɪ-] npl produits mpl laitiers

daisy ['deɪzɪ] n pâquerette f

dam [dæm] n barrage m

damage ['dæmɪdʒ] n dégâts mpl

▷ *The storm did a lot of damage.* La tempête a fait beaucoup de dégâts.
▶ vb endommager

damp [dæmp] adj humide

dance [dɑːns] n ❶ danse f ▷ *The last dance was a waltz.* La dernière danse était une valse. ❷ bal m ▷ *Are you going to the dance tonight?* Tu vas au bal ce soir?

▶ vb danser; **to go dancing** aller danser ▷ *Let's go dancing!* Si on allait danser?

dancer ['dɑːnsər] n danseur m, danseuse f

dandruff ['dændrəf] n pellicules fpl

danger ['deɪndʒər] n danger m; **in danger** en danger ▷ *His life is in danger.* Sa vie est en danger.; **to be in danger of** risquer de ▷ *We were in danger of missing the plane.* Nous risquions de rater l'avion.

dangerous ['deɪndʒrəs] adj dangereux (f dangereuse)

danish ['deɪnɪʃ] n (pastry) danoise f

dare [dɛər] vb oser; **to dare to do something** oser faire quelque chose ▷ *I didn't dare tell my parents.* Je n'ai pas osé le dire à mes parents.; **to dare someone to do something** défier quelqu'un de faire quelque chose

daring ['dɛərɪŋ] adj audacieux (f audacieuse)

dark [dɑːk] adj ❶ (room) sombre ▷ *It's dark. (inside)* Il fait sombre.; **It's dark outside.** Il fait nuit dehors.; **It's getting dark.** La nuit tombe. ❷ (colour) foncé ▷ *She's got dark hair.* Elle a les cheveux foncés. ▷ *a dark green sweater* un chandail vert foncé

▶ n noir m ▷ *I'm afraid of the dark.* J'ai peur du noir.; **after dark** après la tombée de la nuit

darkness ['dɑːknɪs] n obscurité f ▷ *The room was in darkness.* La chambre était dans l'obscurité.

darling ['dɑːlɪŋ] n chéri m, chérie f ▷ Thank you, darling! Merci, chéri!

dart [dɑːt] n fléchette f ▷ to play darts jouer aux fléchettes

dash [dæʃ] vb se précipiter ▷ Everyone dashed to the window to look. Tout le monde s'est précipité vers la fenêtre pour regarder.
▶ n (punctuation mark) tiret m

data ['deɪtə] npl données fpl

database ['deɪtəbeɪs] n (on computer) base de données f

date [deɪt] n ❶ date f ▷ my date of birth ma date de naissance; **to have a date with somebody** sortir avec quelqu'un ▷ She's got a date with her boyfriend tonight. Elle sort avec son petit ami ce soir.; **out of date (1)** (passport) périmé **(2)** (technology) dépassé **(3)** (clothes) démodé ❷ (fruit) datte f
▶ vb sortir ensemble ▷ They're dating. Ils sortent ensemble. ▷ He's dating my sister. Il sort avec ma sœur.

daughter ['dɔːtə'] n fille f

daughter-in-law ['dɔːtərɪnlɔː] n belle-fille f (pl belles-filles)

dawn [dɔːn] n aube f ▷ at dawn à l'aube

day [deɪ] n

Use **jour** to refer to the whole 24-hour period. **journée** only refers to the time when you are awake.

❶ jour m ▷ We stayed in St. John's for three days. Nous sommes restés trois jours à St. John's. ❷ journée f ▷ during the day dans la journée ▷ I stayed at home all day. Je suis resté à la maison toute la journée.; **the day before** la veille ▷ the day before my birthday la veille de mon anniversaire; **the day after** le lendemain ▷ the day after

tomorrow après-demain ▷ We're leaving the day after tomorrow. Nous partons après-demain.; **the day before yesterday** avant-hier ▷ He arrived the day before yesterday. Il est arrivé avant-hier.

daycare ['deɪkeə'] n (place) garderie f

daylight-saving time [deɪlaɪt'seɪvɪŋ-] n heure f avancée

dead [ded] adj, adv ❶ mort f ▷ He was already dead when the doctor came. Il était déjà mort quand le docteur est arrivé.; **She was shot dead.** Elle a été abattue. ❷ (totally) absolument ▷ You're dead right! Tu as absolument raison!

dead end n impasse f

deadline ['dedlaɪn] n date limite f ▷ The deadline for entries is May 2nd. La date limite d'inscription est le deux mai.

deaf [def] adj sourd

deafening ['defnɪŋ] adj assourdissant

deal [diːl] n marché m; **It's a deal!** Marché conclu!; **to make a deal with someone** conclure un marché avec quelqu'un; **a great deal** beaucoup ▷ a great deal of money beaucoup d'argent
▶ vb (cards) donner ▷ It's your turn to deal. C'est à toi de donner.; **to deal with something** s'occuper de quelque chose ▷ She promised to deal with it immediately. Elle a promis de s'en occuper immédiatement.

dealer ['diːlə'] n marchand m, marchande f

dealt [delt] vb see **deal**

dear [dɪə'] adj cher (f chère) ▷ Dear Mrs Duval Chère Madame Duval; **Dear Sir/Madam** (in a circular) Madame, Monsieur

death [deθ] n mort f ▷ after his death après sa mort; **I was bored to**

death. Je me suis ennuyé à mourir.

debate [dɪ'beɪt] n débat m
▷ vb débattre

debt [dɛt] n dette f ▷ He's got a lot of debts. Il a beaucoup de dettes.; **to be in debt** avoir des dettes

decade ['dɛkeɪd] n décennie f

decaffeinated [dɪ'kæfɪneɪtɪd] adj décaféine

decay [dɪ'keɪ] vb ❶ (vegetation, wood) pourrir ❷ (teeth) se carier ❸ (building) se délabrer ▷ a decaying mansion un manoir qui se délabre
▷ n (tooth) carie f

deceive [dɪ'siːv] vb tromper

December [dɪ'sɛmbəʳ] n décembre m; **in December** en décembre

decent ['diːsənt] adj convenable ▷ a decent education une éducation convenable; **He's a decent person.** Il est bien honnête.

decide [dɪ'saɪd] vb ❶ décider ▷ I decided to write to her. J'ai décidé de lui écrire. ❷ I decided not to go. J'ai décidé de ne pas y aller. ❸ se décider ▷ I can't decide. Je n'arrive pas à me décider. ▷ Haven't you decided yet? Tu ne t'es pas encore décidé?; **to decide on something** (together) se mettre d'accord sur quelque chose ▷ They haven't decided on a name yet. Ils ne se sont pas encore mis d'accord sur un nom.

decimal ['dɛsɪməl] adj décimal ▷ the decimal system le système décimal

decipher [dɪ'saɪfəʳ] vb déchiffrer ▷ I can't decipher his handwriting. Je ne déchiffre pas son écriture.

decision [dɪ'sɪʒən] n décision f; **to make a decision** prendre une décision

decisive [dɪ'saɪsɪv] adj (person) décidé

deck [dɛk] n ❶ (on house) terrasse f ❷ (of ship) pont; **on deck** sur le pont ❸ (of cards) jeu m (pl jeux)

declare [dɪ'klɛəʳ] vb déclarer

decorate ['dɛkəreɪt] vb ❶ décorer ▷ I decorated the cake with chocolate sprinkles. J'ai décoré le gâteau avec du chocolat granulé. ❷ (paint) peindre ❸ (wallpaper) tapisser

decrease [diːˈkriːs] n diminution f ▷ a decrease in the number of unemployed people une diminution du nombre de chômeurs
▷ vb diminuer

decriminalize [diːˈkrɪmɪnəlaɪz] vb décriminaliser

dedicated ['dɛdɪkeɪtɪd] adj dévoué ▷ a very dedicated teacher un professeur très dévoué; **dedicated to (1)** consacré à ▷ a museum dedicated to First Nations history un musée consacré à l'histoire des autochtones **(2)** dédicacé à ▷ The book is dedicated "to Emma, with love from Mike". Le livre est dédicacé « à Emma, avec tout mon amour, Mike ».

dedication [dɛdɪ'keɪʃən] n ❶ (commitment) dévouement m ❷ (in book, on radio) dédicace f

deduct [dɪ'dʌkt] vb déduire

deep [diːp] adj ❶ (water, hole, cut) profond ▷ Is it deep? Est-ce que c'est profond?; **How deep is the lake?** Quelle est la profondeur du lac?; **a hole 4 metres deep** un trou de quatre mètres de profondeur ❷ (snow) épais (f épaisse) ▷ The snow was really deep. Il y avait une épaisse couche de neige.; **He's got a deep voice.** Il a la voix grave.; **to take a deep breath** respirer à fond

deeply ['diːplɪ] adv profondément

deer [dɪəʳ] n chevreuil m

defeat [dɪ'fiːt] n défaite f
▷ vb battre

defect [dɪ'fekt] n défaut m

defence [dɪ'fens] n défense f

defend [dɪ'fend] vb défendre

define [dɪ'faɪn] vb définir

definite ['defɪnɪt] adj ❶ précis ▷ I don't have any definite plans. Je n'ai pas de projets précis. ❷ net (f nette) ▷ It's a definite improvement. Cela constitue une nette amélioration. ❸ sûr ▷ Perhaps we'll go to the Northwest Territories, but it's not definite. Nous irons peut-être aux Territoires du Nord-Ouest, mais ce n'est pas sûr.; **She was definite about it.** Elle a été catégorique.

definitely ['defɪnɪtlɪ] adv vraiment ▷ He's definitely the best player. C'est vraiment lui le meilleur joueur.; **"She's the best player." — "Definitely!"** « C'est la meilleure joueuse. » — « Certainement! »; **I definitely think they'll come.** Je suis sûr qu'ils vont venir.

definition [defɪ'nɪʃən] n définition f

degree [dɪ'griː] n ❶ degré m ▷ a temperature of 30 degrees une température de trente degrés ❷ baccalauréat m ▷ a degree in music un baccalauréat en musique

dehydrated [diːhaɪ'dreɪtɪd] adj déshydraté

delay [dɪ'leɪ] vb ❶ retarder ▷ We decided to delay our departure. Nous avons décidé de retarder notre départ. ❷ tarder ▷ Don't delay! Ne tarde pas!; **to be delayed** être retardé ▷ Our flight was delayed. Notre vol a été retardé.
▶ n retard m ▷ There will be delays on most flights. Il y aura des retards sur la plupart des vols.

> Be careful not to translate **delay** by **délai**.

delete [dɪ'liːt] vb ❶ (on computer, tape) effacer ❷ (cross out) rayer

deli ['delɪ] n charcuterie f

deliberate [dɪ'lɪbərɪt] adj délibéré

deliberately [dɪ'lɪbərɪtlɪ] adv exprès ▷ She did it deliberately. Elle l'a fait exprès.

delicate ['delɪkɪt] adj délicat

delicious [dɪ'lɪʃəs] adj délicieux (f délicieuse)

delight [dɪ'laɪt] n: **to her delight** à sa plus grande joie

delighted [dɪ'laɪtɪd] adj ravi ▷ He'll be delighted to see you. Il sera ravi de vous voir.

delightful [dɪ'laɪtful] adj (meal, evening) délicieux (f délicieuse)

deliver [dɪ'lɪvə] vb ❶ livrer ▷ I deliver newspapers. Je livre les journaux. ❷ (mail) distribuer

delivery [dɪ'lɪvərɪ] n livraison f

demand [dɪ'mɑːnd] vb exiger

> Be careful not to translate **to demand** by **demander**.

▶ n (for product) demande f

demanding [dɪ'mɑːndɪŋ] adj exigeant ▷ She's a very demanding teacher. C'est un professeur très exigeant.; **It's a very demanding job.** C'est un travail très astreignant.

demo ['deməʊ] n ❶ (product) modèle de démonstration m ❷ (software) version démo f ❸ (recording) CD de démonstration m

democracy [dɪ'mɒkrəsɪ] n démocratie f

democratic [demə'krætɪk] adj démocratique

demolish [dɪ'mɒlɪʃ] vb démolir

demonstrate ['demənstreɪt] vb ❶ (show) faire une démonstration de ▷ She demonstrated the technique. Elle a fait une démonstration de la technique. ❷ (protest) manifester;

to demonstrate against something manifester contre quelque chose

demonstration [dɛmən'streɪʃən] n ❶ (of method, technique) démonstration f ❷ (protest) manifestation f

demonstrator ['dɛmənstreɪtə'] n (protester) manifestant m, manifestante f

denim ['dɛnɪm] n (fabric) denim m ▷ **a denim jacket** une veste en denim

dense [dɛns] adj ❶ (crowd, fog) dense ❷ (smoke) dense (f épaisse)

dent [dɛnt] n bosse f ▶ vb cabosser

dental ['dɛntl] adj dentaire; **dental floss** le fil dentaire

dentist ['dɛntɪst] n dentiste ▷ **He is a dentist.** Il est dentiste.

deny [dɪ'naɪ] vb nier ▷ **She denied everything.** Elle a tout nié.

deodorant [di:'əʊdərənt] n déodorant m

depart [dɪ'pɑ:t] vb partir

department [dɪ'pɑ:tmənt] n ❶ département m ▷ **the English department** le département d'anglais ▷ **the shoe department** le département des chaussures

department store n grand magasin m

departure [dɪ'pɑ:tʃə'] n départ m

departure lounge n salle d'embarquement f

depend [dɪ'pɛnd] vb: **to depend on** dépendre de ▷ **The price depends on the quality.** Le prix dépend de la qualité.; **depending on the weather** selon le temps; **It depends.** Ça dépend.

deport [dɪ'pɔ:t] vb expulser

Le Grand Dérangement, or Great Deportation, refers to the mass expulsion of Acadians by the British military between

1755 and 1762. The exiles were scattered throughout the Maritimes and several American colonies, including Louisiana.

deposit [dɪ'pɒzɪt] n ❶ (bank) dépôt m ▷ **a deposit of 30 dollars** un dépôt de trente dollars ❷ (when renting something) caution f ▷ **You get the deposit back when you return the bike.** On vous remboursera la caution quand vous ramènerez le vélo.; **to put down a deposit** (as prepayment) verser un acompte ❸ (on bottle) consigne f ▶ vb déposer ▷ **I deposited 100 dollars into my account.** J'ai déposé cent dollars dans mon compte.

depressed [dɪ'prɛst] adj déprimé ▷ **I'm feeling depressed.** Je suis déprimé.

depressing [dɪ'prɛsɪŋ] adj déprimant

depth [dɛpθ] n profondeur f

descend [dɪ'sɛnd] vb descendre

describe [dɪs'kraɪb] vb décrire

description [dɪs'krɪpʃən] n description f

desert [dɪ'zɜ:t] n désert m

desert island n île f déserte

deserve [dɪ'zɜ:v] vb mériter

design [dɪ'zaɪn] n ❶ conception f ▷ **It's a completely new design.** C'est une conception entièrement nouvelle. ❷ motif m ▷ **a geometric design** un motif géométrique; **fashion design** le stylisme ▶ vb (clothes, furniture) dessiner; **designed for young people** conçu pour les jeunes

designer [dɪ'zaɪnə'] n (of clothes) styliste; **designer clothes** les vêtements griffés

desire [dɪ'zaɪə'] n désir m ▶ vb désirer

desk [dɛsk] n ❶ (in office) bureau m (pl bureaux) ❷ (for student) pupitre *m* ➌ *(in hotel)* réception *f* ➍ *(at airport)* comptoir *m*

desktop ['dɛsktɒp] *n (on computer)* bureau *m* ▷ *Save the file to the desktop.* Enregistre le fichier sur le bureau.

despair [dɪs'pɛəʳ] *n* désespoir *m*; **I was in despair.** J'étais désespéré.

desperate ['dɛspərɪt] *adj* désespéré ▷ *a desperate situation* une situation désespérée; **to get desperate** désespérer ▷ *I was getting desperate.* Je commençais à désespérer.

desperately ['dɛspərɪtlɪ] *adv* ➊ terriblement ▷ *We're desperately worried.* Nous sommes terriblement inquiets. ➋ désespérément ▷ *He was desperately trying to persuade her.* Il essayait désespérément de la persuader.

despise [dɪs'paɪz] *vb* mépriser

despite [dɪs'paɪt] *prep* malgré

dessert [dɪ'zəːt] *n* dessert *m* ▷ *for dessert* comme dessert

destination [dɛstɪ'neɪʃən] *n* destination *f*

destitute ['dɛstɪtjuːt] *adj* dépourvu ▷ *a destitute family* une famille dépourvue

destroy [dɪs'trɔɪ] *vb* détruire

destruction [dɪs'trʌkʃən] *n* destruction *f*

detail ['diːteɪl] *n* détail *m* ▷ *in detail* en détail

detailed ['diːteɪld] *adj* détaillé

detective [dɪ'tɛktɪv] *n* enquêteur *m*, enquêteuse *f*; **a private detective** un détective privé; **a detective story** un roman policier

detention [dɪ'tɛnʃən] *n*: **to get a detention** être en retenue

detergent [dɪ'təːdʒənt] *n* détergent *m*

deteriorate [dɪ'tɪərɪəreɪt] *vb* se détériorer

determined [dɪ'təːmɪnd] *adj* déterminé; **to be determined to do something** être déterminé à faire quelque chose ▷ *She's determined to succeed.* Elle est déterminée à réussir.

detour ['diːtuəʳ] *n* détour *m*

devastated ['dɛvəsteɪtɪd] *adj* anéanti ▷ *I was devastated.* J'étais anéanti.

devastating ['dɛvəsteɪtɪŋ] *adj* ➊ *(upsetting)* accablant ➋ *(flood, storm)* dévastateur *(f* dévastatrice*)*

develop [dɪ'vɛləp] *vb* ➊ développer ▷ *to get a film developed* faire développer un film ➋ se développer ▷ *Girls develop faster than boys.* Les filles se développent plus vite que les garçons.; **to develop into** se transformer en ▷ *The argument developed into a fight.* La dispute s'est transformée en bagarre.; **a developing country** un pays en voie de développement

development [dɪ'vɛləpmənt] *n* développement *m* ▷ *the latest developments* les derniers développements

device [dɪ'vaɪs] *n* appareil *m*

devil ['dɛvl] *n* diable *m*; **Poor devil!** Pauvre diable!

devise [dɪ'vaɪz] *vb* concevoir ▷ *We devised a plan.* Nous avons conçu un plan.

devoted [dɪ'vəutɪd] *adj* dévoué ▷ *He's completely devoted to her.* Il lui est très dévoué.

diabetes [daɪə'biːtiːz] *n* diabète *m*

diabetic [daɪə'bɛtɪk] *n* diabétique ▷ *I'm a diabetic.* Je suis diabétique.

diagonal [daɪ'ægənl] *adj* diagonal *(mpl* diagonaux*)*

diagram ['daɪəgræm] *n* diagramme *m*

dial ['daɪəl] *vb (number)* composer

dialogue ['daɪəlɒg] n dialogue m

dial tone n tonalité f

diamond ['daɪəmənd] n diamant m ▷ a diamond ring une bague en diamant; **diamonds** (cards) le carreau m

diaper ['daɪəpə'] n couche f

diarrhea [daɪə'riːə] n diarrhée f

diary ['daɪərɪ] n journal m (pl journaux) ▷ I keep a diary. Je tiens un journal.

dice [daɪs] npl dés

dictation [dɪk'teɪʃən] n dictée f

dictator [dɪk'teɪtə'] n dictateur m, dictatrice f

dictionary ['dɪkʃənrɪ] n dictionnaire m

did [dɪd] vb see **do**

die [daɪ] vb mourir ▷ He died last year. Il est mort l'année dernière.; **to be dying to do something** mourir d'envie de faire quelque chose ▷ I'm dying to see you. Je meurs d'envie de te voir.

diesel ['diːzl] n ❶ (fuel) carburant diesel ▷ 30 litres of diesel trente litres de carburant diesel m ❷ (car) voiture diesel f ▷ Our car is a diesel. Nous avons une voiture diesel.

diet ['daɪət] n ❶ alimentation f ▷ a healthy diet une alimentation saine ❷ (weight loss) régime m ▷ I'm on a diet. Je suis au régime.
▶ vb faire un régime ▷ I've been dieting for two months. Je fais un régime depuis deux mois.

dietitian [daɪə'tɪʃn] n diététiste ▷ He's a dietitian. Il est diététiste.

difference ['dɪfrəns] n différence f ▷ There's not much difference in age between us. Il n'y a pas une grande différence d'âge entre nous.; **It makes no difference.** Ça revient au même.

different ['dɪfrənt] adj différent ▷ We are very different. Nous sommes

très différents. ▷ Victoria is different from Vancouver. Victoria est différent de Vancouver.

difficult ['dɪfɪkəlt] adj difficile ▷ It's difficult to choose. C'est difficile de choisir.

difficulty ['dɪfɪkəltɪ] n difficulté f ▷ without difficulty sans difficulté; **to have difficulty doing something** avoir du mal à faire quelque chose

dig [dɪg] vb ❶ (hole) creuser ❷ (garden) bêcher; **to dig something up** déterrer quelque chose

digestion [dɪ'dʒestʃən] n digestion f

digital ['dɪdʒɪtl] adj numérique ▷ a digital camera un appareil photo numérique ▷ a digital recording un enregistrement audionumérique; **a digital watch** une montre à affichage numérique

dim [dɪm] adj (light) faible

dime [daɪm] n pièce de dix cents f; **They're a dime a dozen.** Il y en a à la pelle.

dimension [daɪ'mɛnʃən] n dimension f

diminish [dɪ'mɪnɪʃ] vb diminuer

diner ['daɪnə'] n petit restaurant m

dinghy ['dɪŋɪ] n: **a rubber dinghy** un canot pneumatique

dining room ['daɪnɪŋ-] n salle à manger f

dinner ['dɪnə'] n ❶ (at midday) dîner m ❷ (evening) souper m
• In Canada, Belgium,
• Switzerland, and some areas
• of France, **le dîner** is the noon
• meal. In Canada, **le souper** is
• the evening meal. Elsewhere in
• the francophone world, **le dîner**
• refers to the evening meal and
• **le souper** happens late in the
• evening, usually after a show.

dinnertime ['dɪnətaɪm] n
❶ (midday) heure f du dîner
❷ (midday) heure f du déjeuner
❸ (evening) heure f du souper
❹ (evening) heure f du dîner

dinosaur ['daɪnəsɔːʳ] n
dinosaure m

dip [dɪp] n (decrease) baisse f ▷ a dip
in prices une baisse de prix; **to go
for a dip** aller se baigner
▶ vb tremper ▷ She dipped a cookie
into her coffee. Elle a trempé un
biscuit dans son café.

diploma [dɪ'pləʊmə] n diplôme m
▷ a high school diploma un diplôme
en études secondaires

diplomat ['dɪpləmæt] n diplomate m

diplomatic [dɪplə'mætɪk] adj
diplomatique

direct [daɪ'rɛkt] adj, adv direct
▷ the most direct route le chemin le
plus direct ▷ You can fly direct from
Hamilton to Ottawa. Il y a un vol
direct de Hamilton à Ottawa.
▶ vb ❶ (film, program) réaliser
❷ (play, show) mettre en scène

direction [dɪ'rɛkʃən] n direction f
▷ We're going in the wrong direction.
Nous allons dans la mauvaise
direction.; **to ask somebody for
directions** demander son chemin
à quelqu'un

directly [dɪ'rɛktlɪ] adv
directement; **directly across from**
juste en face de; **to be directly
related** avoir un rapport direct

director [dɪ'rɛktəʳ] n ❶ (of
company) directeur m, directrice
f ❷ (of play) metteur en scène m
(pl metteurs en scène), metteure
en scène f (pl metteures en scène)
❸ (of film, programme) réalisateur
m, réalisatrice f

directory [dɪ'rɛktərɪ] n ❶ (phone
book) annuaire m ❷ (computing)
répertoire m

dirt [dəːt] n saleté f

dirt bike n moto tout-terrain f (pl
les motos tout-terrains)

dirty ['dəːtɪ] adj sale; **to get dirty**
se salir; **to get something dirty**
salir quelque chose

disabled [dɪs'eɪbld] adj handicapé

disadvantage [dɪsəd'vɑːntɪdʒ] n
désavantage m

disagree [dɪsə'griː] vb: **We always
disagree.** Nous ne sommes jamais
d'accord.; **I disagree!** Je ne suis pas
d'accord!; **He disagrees with me.** Il
n'est pas d'accord avec moi.

disagreement [dɪsə'griːmənt] n
désaccord m

disappear [dɪsə'pɪəʳ] vb
disparaître

disappearance [dɪsə'pɪərəns] n
disparition f

disappointed [dɪsə'pɔɪntɪd]
adj déçu

disappointing [dɪsə'pɔɪntɪŋ] adj
décevant

disappointment
[dɪsə'pɔɪntmənt] n déception f

disaster [dɪ'zɑːstəʳ] n désastre m

disastrous [dɪ'zɑːstrəs] adj
désastreux f (désastreuse)

disc [dɪsk] n disque m

discipline ['dɪsɪplɪn] n discipline f

disc jockey [-dʒɒkɪ] n disc-
jockey m

disconnect [dɪskə'nɛkt] vb
❶ (unplug) débrancher ❷ (log off)
se déconnecter ❸ (telephone, water
supply) couper

discount [dɪs'kaʊnt] n réduction
f ▷ a discount for students une
réduction pour les étudiants

discourage [dɪs'kʌrɪdʒ] vb
décourager; **to get discouraged** se
décourager ▷ Don't get discouraged!
Ne te décourage pas!

discover [dɪs'kʌvəʳ] vb découvrir

discrimination [dɪskrɪmɪ'neɪʃən]

n discrimination *f* ▷ *racial discrimination* la discrimination raciale

discuss [dɪˈskʌs] *vb* ❶ discuter ▷ *This trip has been discussed at length with my parents.* Ce voyage a été longuement discuté avec mes parents. ❷ discuter de ▷ *We discussed the problem of pollution.* Nous avons discuté du problème de la pollution. ▷ *We discussed it.* Nous en avons discuté.

discussion [dɪˈskʌʃən] *n* discussion *f*

disease [dɪˈziːz] *n* maladie *f*

disgraceful [dɪsˈgreɪsful] *adj* scandaleux (*f* scandaleuse)

disguise [dɪsˈgaɪz] *vb* déguiser ▷ *He was disguised as a policeman.* Il était déguisé en policier.

disgusted [dɪsˈgʌstɪd] *adj* dégoûté ▷ *I was absolutely disgusted.* J'étais complètement dégoûté.

disgusting [dɪsˈgʌstɪŋ] *adj* ❶ (*food, smell*) dégoûtant ▷ *It looks disgusting.* Ça a l'air dégoûtant. ❷ (*disgraceful*) honteux ▷ *That's disgusting!* C'est honteux!

dish [dɪʃ] *n* plat *m* ▷ *a china dish* un plat en porcelaine ▷ *a vegetarian dish* un plat végétarien; **to do the dishes** faire la vaisselle ▷ *She never does the dishes.* Elle ne fait jamais la vaisselle.

dishcloth [ˈdɪʃklɒθ] *n* lavette *f*

dish detergent *n* savon à vaisselle *m*

dishonest [dɪsˈɒnɪst] *adj* malhonnête

dishtowel [ˈdɪʃtaʊəl] *n* linge à vaisselle *m*

dishwasher [ˈdɪʃwɒʃəʳ] *n* lave-vaisselle *m* (*pl* lave-vaisselle)

disinfectant [dɪsɪnˈfɛktənt] *n* désinfectant *m*

disk [dɪsk] *n* disque *m*; **a floppy**

disk une disquette; **the hard disk** le disque dur

diskette [dɪsˈkɛt] *n* disquette *f*

dislike [dɪsˈlaɪk] *vb* ne pas aimer ▷ *I really dislike cabbage.* Je n'aime vraiment pas le chou.

▶ *n*: **my likes and dislikes** ce que j'aime et ce que je n'aime pas

dismal [ˈdɪzml] *adj* lugubre

dismiss [dɪsˈmɪs] *vb* (*employee*) renvoyer

disobey [dɪsəˈbeɪ] *vb* désobéir ▷ *to disobey one's parents* désobéir à ses parents; **to disobey a rule** violer une règle

disorganized [dɪsˈɔːgənaɪzd] *adj* désorganisé

disoriented [dɪsˈɔːriəntɪd] *adj* dépaysé

display [dɪsˈpleɪ] *n* étalage *m* ▷ *There was a lovely display of fruit in the window.* Il y avait un superbe étalage de fruits en vitrine.; **to be on display** être exposé ▷ *Her best paintings were on display.* Ses meilleurs tableaux étaient exposés.

▶ *vb* ❶ montrer ▷ *She proudly displayed her medal.* Elle a montré sa médaille avec fierté. ❷ (*in store window*) exposer

disposable [dɪsˈpəʊzəbl] *adj* jetable

disqualify [dɪsˈkwɒlɪfaɪ] *vb* disqualifier; **to be disqualified** être disqualifié ▷ *He was disqualified.* Il a été disqualifié.

disrespectful [dɪsrɪˈspɛktful] *adj*: **to be disrespectful towards someone** manquer de respect envers quelqu'un

disrupt [dɪsˈrʌpt] *vb* perturber ▷ *Protesters disrupted the meeting.* Des manifestants ont perturbé la réunion. ▷ *Bus service is being disrupted by the strike.* Les horaires d'autobus sont perturbés par la grève.

dissatisfied [dɪsˈsætɪsfaɪd]
adj : **We were dissatisfied with
the service.** Nous n'étions pas
satisfaits du service.

dissolve [dɪˈzɔlv] *vb* dissoudre

distance [ˈdɪstns] *n* distance
f ▷ *a distance of 40 kilometres* une
distance de quarante kilomètres ;
It's within walking distance. On
peut y aller à pied.; **in the distance**
au loin

distant [ˈdɪstnt] *adj* lointain ▷ *in
the distant future* dans un avenir
lointain

distinction [dɪsˈtɪŋkʃən] *n*
distinction *f* ▷ *to make a distinction
between...* faire la distinction
entre...

distinctive [dɪsˈtɪŋktɪv] *adj*
distinctif (*f* distinctive)

distinct society [dɪsˈtɪŋkt-]
n société distincte *f* ▷ *Quebec
considers itself a distinct society within
Canada.* Le Québec se considère
comme une société distincte au
sein du Canada.

distract [dɪsˈtrækt] *vb* distraire

distribute [dɪsˈtrɪbjuːt] *vb*
distribuer

district [ˈdɪstrɪkt] *n* ❶ (*of town*)
quartier *m* ❷ (*of country*) région *f*

disturb [dɪsˈtɜːb] *vb* déranger ▷ *I'm
sorry to disturb you.* Je suis désolé de
vous déranger.

ditch [dɪtʃ] *n* fossé *m*
▶ *vb* (*informal*) plaquer ▷ *Let's
ditch that idea.* Laissons tomber
cette idée.

dive [daɪv] *n* plongeon *m*
▶ *vb* plonger

diver [ˈdaɪvə^r] *n* plongeur *m*,
plongeuse *f*

divide [dɪˈvaɪd] *vb* ❶ diviser
▷ *Divide the chocolate bar in half.*
Divisez la barre de chocolat en

deux. ▷ *12 divided by 3 is 4.* Douze
divisé par trois égalent quatre.
❷ se diviser ▷ *We divided into two
groups.* Nous nous sommes divisés
en deux groupes.

diving [ˈdaɪvɪŋ] *n* plongée *f*; **a
diving board** un tremplin

division [dɪˈvɪʒən] *n* division *f*

divorce [dɪˈvɔːs] *n* divorce *m*

divorced [dɪˈvɔːst] *adj* divorcé
▷ *My parents are divorced.* Mes
parents sont divorcés.

dizzy [ˈdɪzɪ] *adj* : **to feel dizzy** avoir
la tête qui tourne ▷ *I feel dizzy.* J'ai la
tête qui tourne.

DJ *n* disc-jockey *m*

do [duː] *vb* ❶ faire ▷ *What are you
doing this evening?* Qu'est-ce que tu
fais ce soir? ▷ *I do a lot of biking.* Je
fais beaucoup de vélo. ▷ *I haven't
done my homework.* Je n'ai pas fait
mes devoirs. ▷ *She did it by herself.*
Elle l'a fait toute seule. ▷ *I'll do my
best.* Je ferai de mon mieux.; **to do
well (1)** marcher bien ▷ *The firm
is doing well.* L'entreprise marche
bien. ▷ *She's doing well at school.* Ses
études marchent bien. **(2)** être sur
la bonne voie ▷ *The patient is doing
well.* La malade est sur la bonne
voie. ❷ (*be enough*) aller ▷ *It's not
very good, but it'll do.* Ce n'est pas
très bon, mais ça ira.; **That'll do,
thanks.** Ça ira, merci.

> In English **do** is used to make
> questions. In French questions
> are made either with **est-ce
> que** or by reversing the order of
> verb and subject.

▷ *Do you like French food?* Est-ce que
vous aimez la cuisine française?
▷ *Where does he live?* Où est-ce qu'il
habite? ▷ *Do you speak English?*
Parlez-vous anglais?

> Use **ne...pas** in negative
> sentences for **don't**.

▷ *I don't understand.* Je ne comprends pas. ▷ *Why didn't you come?* Pourquoi n'êtes-vous pas venus?

do is not translated when it is used in place of another verb. ▷ *"I hate math." — "So do I."* « Je déteste les maths. » — « Moi aussi. » ▷ *"I didn't like the film." — "Neither did I."* « Je n'ai pas aimé le film. » — « Moi non plus. » ▷ *"Do you like horses?" — "No I don't."* « Est-ce que tu aimes les chevaux? » — « Non. »

Use **n'est-ce pas** to check information.

▷ *You go swimming on Fridays, don't you?* Tu fais de la natation le vendredi, n'est-ce pas?; **to do away with (1)** (*law, practice*) abolir **(2)** (*kill*) tuer; **to do up (1)** (*shoes*) lacer ▷ *Do up your shoes!* Lace tes chaussures! **(2)** (*shirt, cardigan*) boutonner; **to do up one's fly** fermer sa braguette; **to do without** se passer de ▷ *I couldn't do without my computer.* Je ne pourrais pas me passer de mon ordinateur.; **That has nothing to do with it.** Cela n'a rien à voir.

dock [dɒk] n (*for ships*) dock m

doctor ['dɒktə'] n médecin m ▷ *She's a doctor.* Elle est médecin.

document ['dɒkjumənt] n document m

documentary [dɒkju'mentərɪ] n documentaire m

dodge [dɒdʒ] vb (*attacker*) échapper à

dodgeball ['dɒdʒbɔːl] n ballon chasseur m

does [dʌz] vb see **do**

doesn't ['dʌznt] = **does not**

dog [dɒg] n ❶ chien m ❷ (*female*) chienne f

dogsled ['dɒgsled] n traîneau à chiens m ▷ *by dogsled* en traîneau à chiens.

dole out [dəʊl-] vb distribuer

doll [dɒl] n poupée f

dollar ['dɒlə'] n dollar m

dolphin ['dɒlfɪn] n dauphin m

domestic [də'mestɪk] adj: **a domestic flight** un vol intérieur; **domestic violence** la violence familiale

dominoes ['dɒmɪnəʊz] npl. **to have a game of dominoes** jouer une partie de dominos

donate [də'neɪt] vb donner

done [dʌn] vb see **do**

donkey ['dɒŋkɪ] n âne m

donor ['dəʊnə'] n ❶ (*to charity*) donateur m, donatrice f ❷ (*of blood, organs for transplant*) donneur m, donneuse f

don't [dəʊnt] = **do not**

door [dɔːʳ] n ❶ porte f ▷ *the first door on the right* la première porte à droite ❷ (*of car, bus*) portière f

doorbell ['dɔːbel] n sonnette f; **to ring the doorbell** sonner; **Suddenly the doorbell rang.** Soudain, on a sonné.

doorman ['dɔːmən] n portier m

doorstep ['dɔːstep] n pas de la porte m

dormitory ['dɔːmɪtrɪ] n dortoir m

dose [dəʊs] n dose f

dot [dɒt] n (*on letter "i", in email address*) point m; **on the dot** à l'heure pile ▷ *He arrived at 9 o'clock on the dot.* Il est arrivé à neuf heures pile.

double ['dʌbl] vb doubler ▷ *The number of overweight children has doubled.* Le nombre d'enfants obèses a doublé.
▸ adj, adv double m ▷ *a double helping* une double portion; **to cost double** coûter le double ▷ *First-class tickets cost double.* Les billets de première classe coûtent le

double.; **a double bed** un grand lit; **a double room** une chambre pour deux personnes

double bass ['dʌbl'beɪs] n contrebasse f ▷ I play the double bass. Je joue de la contrebasse.

double-click ['dʌbl'klɪk] vb double-cliquer ▷ to double-click on an icon double-cliquer sur une icône

doubles ['dʌblz] npl (in tennis) double m ▷ to play mixed doubles jouer en double mixte

double-spaced [dʌbl'speɪst] adj à double interligne

doubt [daut] n doute m ▷ I have my doubts. J'ai des doutes.
▶ vb douter de; **I doubt it.** J'en doute.; **to doubt that** douter que
▷ **douter que** has to be followed by a verb in the subjunctive.
▷ I doubt he'll agree. Je doute qu'il soit d'accord.

doubtful ['dautful] adj: **to be doubtful about doing something** hésiter à faire quelque chose ▷ I'm doubtful about going by myself. J'hésite à y aller tout seul.; **It's doubtful.** Ce n'est pas sûr.; **You sound doubtful.** Tu n'as pas l'air sûr.

dough [dəu] n pâte f

doughnut ['dəunʌt] n beigne m ▷ a jam doughnut un beigne à la confiture

down [daun] adv, adj, prep
❶ (below) en bas ▷ Her office is down on the first floor. Son bureau est en bas, au premier étage. ▷ It's down there. C'est là-bas. ❷ (on the ground) à terre ▷ He threw his down his racquet. Il a jeté sa raquette à terre.; **They live just down the road.** Ils habitent tout à côté.; **to come down** descendre ▷ Come down here. Descends.; **to go down** descendre ▷ The rabbit went down the hole. Le

lapin est descendu dans le terrier.; **to sit down** s'asseoir ▷ Please sit down. Asseyez-vous, s'il vous plaît.; **to feel down** se sentir déprimé ▷ I'm feeling a bit down. Je me sens un peu déprimée.; **The computer's down.** L'ordinateur est en panne.

downhill skiing ['daunhɪl-] n ski alpin m

download ['daunləud] vb télécharger ▷ to download a file télécharger un fichier

downpour ['daunpɔː'] n pluie torrentielle f ▷ a sudden downpour une pluie soudaine et torrentielle

downstairs ['daun'steəz] adv, adj ❶ au rez-de-chaussée ▷ The bathroom's downstairs. La salle de bain est au rez-de-chaussée. ❷ du rez-de-chaussée ▷ the downstairs bathroom la salle de bain du rez-de-chaussée; **the people downstairs** les voisins du dessous

downtown ['daun'taun] adv dans le centre-ville

doze [dauz] vb sommeiller; **to doze off** s'assoupir

dozen ['dʌzn] n douzaine f ▷ two dozen deux douzaines ▷ a dozen eggs une douzaine d'œufs; **I've told you that dozens of times.** Je t'ai dit ça des dizaines de fois.

drab [dræb] adj ❶ morne ❷ (clothes) terne

draft [drɑːft] n courant d'air m

drag [dræg] vb (thing, person) traîner
▶ n: **It's a real drag!** (informal) Quelle corvée!

dragon ['drægn] n dragon m

dragonfly ['drægənflaɪ] n libellule f

drain [dreɪn] n égout m ▷ The drains are blocked. Les égouts sont bouchés.
▶ vb (vegetables, pasta) égoutter

drainboard ['dreɪnbɔːd] n
égouttoir m

drainpipe ['dreɪnpaɪp] n tuyau
d'écoulement m

drama ['drɑːmə] n art m
dramatique ▷ *Drama is my favourite
subject.* L'art dramatique est ma
matière préférée.; **drama school**
l'école d'art dramatique m ▷ *I'd like to
go to drama school.* J'aimerais entrer
dans une école d'art dramatique.;
Greek drama le théâtre grec

dramatic [drə'mætɪk] adj
❶ spectaculaire ▷ *It was really
dramatic!* C'était vraiment
spectaculaire! ▷ *a dramatic
improvement* une amélioration
spectaculaire ❷ théâtral ▷ *a
dramatic entrance* une entrée
théâtrale

drank [dræŋk] vb see **drink**

drapes [dreɪps] npl rideaux mpl

drastic ['dræstɪk] adj (change)
radical (mpl radicaux); **to take
drastic action** prendre des
mesures énergiques

draw [drɔː] vb ❶ dessiner ▷ *She's good
at drawing.* Elle dessine bien.; **to
draw a picture** faire un dessin; **to
draw a picture of somebody** faire
le portrait de quelqu'un; **to draw
a line** tirer un trait; **to draw the
curtains** tirer les rideaux; **to draw
lots** tirer au sort
▶ n ❶ (sport) match nul m ▷ *The
game ended in a draw.* La partie s'est
soldée par un match nul. ❷ (in
lottery) tirage au sort ▷ *The draw
takes place on Saturday.* Le tirage au
sort a lieu samedi.

drawback ['drɔːbæk] n
inconvénient m

drawer ['drɔːə] n tiroir m

drawing ['drɔːɪŋ] n dessin m

drawn [drɔːn] vb see **draw**

dreadful ['drɛdful] adj ❶ terrible

▷ *a dreadful mistake* une terrible
erreur ❷ affreux (f affreuse) ▷ *The
weather was dreadful.* Il a fait un
temps affreux.

dreadlocks ['drɛdlɒks] npl tresses
fpl rasta

dream [driːm] vb rêver ▷ *I dreamed
I was in Nunavut.* J'ai rêvé que j'étais
au Nunavut.
▶ n rêve m ▷ *It was just a dream.* Ce
n'était qu'un rêve.; **a bad dream** un
cauchemar

drench [drɛntʃ] vb: **to get
drenched** se faire tremper ▷ *We
got drenched.* Nous nous sommes
fait tremper.

dress [drɛs] n ❶ robe f ❷ tenue
f ▷ *in traditional dress* en tenue
traditionnelle; **a dress rehearsal**
une répétition générale
▶ vb s'habiller ▷ *I got up, dressed,
and went downstairs.* Je me suis
levé, je me suis habillé et je suis
descendu.; **to dress somebody**
habiller quelqu'un ▷ *She dressed the
children.* Elle a habillé les enfants.;
to get dressed s'habiller ▷ *I got
dressed quickly.* Je me suis habillé
rapidement.; **to dress up** se
déguiser ▷ *I dressed up as a ghost.* Je
me suis déguisé en fantôme.

dressed [drɛst] adj habillé ▷ *I'm
not dressed yet.* Je ne suis pas encore
habillé.; **He was dressed in a
green sweater and jeans.** Il portait
un chandail vert et un jean.

dresser ['drɛsə] n (furniture)
commode f

dressing gown ['drɛsɪŋgaun] n
robe de chambre f

drew [druː] vb see **draw**

dried [draɪd] vb see **dry**

drift [drɪft] n: **a snow drift** une
congère
▶ vb ❶ (boat) aller à la dérive
❷ (snow) s'amonceler

drill [drɪl] n perceuse f
▶ vb percer ▷ to drill a hole percer un trou

drink [drɪŋk] n boisson f ▷ a cold drink une boisson fraîche ▷ a hot drink une boisson chaude; **Would you like a drink?** Voulez-vous quelque chose à boire?
▶ vb boire ▷ What would you like to drink? Qu'est-ce que vous voulez boire? ▷ She drank three cups of tea. Elle a bu trois tasses de thé.; **Don't drink and drive.** Pas d'alcool au volant.; **I don't drink.** Je ne bois pas d'alcool.

drinking water ['drɪŋkɪŋ-] n eau f potable

drip [drɪp] vb (tap) goutter; **dripping wet** complètement trempé

drive [draɪv] n tour en voiture m; **to go for a drive** aller faire un tour en voiture ▷ We went for a drive in the country. Nous sommes allés faire un tour à la campagne.; **We've got a long drive tomorrow.** Nous avons une longue route à faire demain.
▶ vb ❶ (a car) conduire ▷ He's learning to drive. Il apprend à conduire. ▷ Can you drive? Tu sais conduire? ❷ (go by car) aller en voiture ▷ "Did you fly?" — "No, we drove." « Vous êtes partis en avion? » — « Non, nous y sommes allés en voiture. » ❸ emmener en voiture ▷ My mother drives me to school. Ma mère m'emmène à l'école en voiture.; **to drive somebody home** raccompagner quelqu'un ▷ He offered to drive me home. Il m'a proposé de me raccompagner.; **to drive somebody crazy** rendre quelqu'un fou ▷ He drives me crazy. Il me rend folle.

driven ['drɪvn]; see **drive**

driver ['draɪvə^r] n ❶ conducteur

m, conductrice f ▷ She's an excellent driver. C'est une excellente conductrice. ❷ (of taxi, bus) chauffeur m ▷ He's a bus driver. Il est chauffeur d'autobus.

driver's licence ['draɪvəz-] n permis de conduire m

driveway ['draɪvweɪ] n entrée f

driving lesson ['draɪvɪŋ-] n leçon de conduite f

driving school n auto-école f

driving test n: **to take one's driving test** passer son examen de conduite automobile ▷ He's taking his driving test tomorrow. Il passe son examen de conduite automobile demain.; **She's just passed her driving test.** Elle vient d'avoir son permis.

drizzle ['drɪzl] vb bruiner

drop [drɒp] n ❶ goutte f ▷ a drop of water une goutte d'eau ❷ (decrease) baisse f ▷ a drop in temperature une baisse de température
▶ vb ❶ laisser tomber ▷ I dropped the glass and it broke. J'ai laissé tomber le verre et il s'est cassé. ▷ I'm going to drop chemistry. Je vais laisser tomber la chimie.; **to drop out of school** décrocher ▷ He dropped out before finishing Grade 12. Il a décroché avant de terminer son secondaire cinq. ❷ déposer ▷ Could you drop me at the station? Pouvez-vous me déposer à la gare?

drop-in centre ['drɒpɪn-] n centre de jour m

dropout ['drɒpaut] décrocheur m, décrocheuse f

drought [draut] n sécheresse f

drove [drəuv] vb see **drive**

drown [draun] vb se noyer ▷ A boy drowned here yesterday. Un jeune garçon s'est noyé ici hier.

drug [drʌg] n ❶ (medicine)

médicament m ▷ They need food and drugs. Ils ont besoin de nourriture et de médicaments. ❷ (illegal) drogue f ▷ hard drugs les drogues dures ▷ soft drugs les drogues douces; **to take drugs** se droguer; **a drug addict** un drogué ▷ She's a drug addict. C'est une droguée.

drugstore ['drʌgstɔːʳ] n pharmacie f

drum [drʌm] n tambour m ▷ an African drum un tambour africain; **a set of drums** une batterie; **drums** la batterie f ▷ I play drums. Je joue de la batterie.

drummer ['drʌməʳ] n (in rock group) batteur m, batteuse f

drunk [drʌŋk] adj ivre ▷ He was drunk. Il était ivre.; **drunk driving** une conduite en état d'ivresse
▶ n ivrogne f

dry [draɪ] adj ❶ sec (f sèche) ▷ The paint isn't dry yet. La peinture n'est pas encore sèche. ❷ (weather) sans pluie ▷ a long dry period une longue période sans pluie
▶ vb ❶ sécher ▷ The wash will dry quickly in the sun. Le linge va sécher vite au soleil. ▷ some dried flowers des fleurs séchées; **to dry one's hair** se sécher les cheveux ▷ I haven't dried my hair yet. Je ne me suis pas encore séché les cheveux. ❷ (clothes) faire sécher ▷ There's nowhere to dry your clothes here. Il n'y a pas d'endroit où faire sécher les vêtements ici.; **to dry the dishes** essuyer la vaisselle

dry cleaners n nettoyeur m

dryer ['draɪəʳ] n ❶ (machine) sécheuse f ❷ (rack) séchoir; **a hair dryer** un sèche-cheveux

dubbed [dʌbd] adj doublé ▷ The film was dubbed in French. Le film était doublé en français.

dubious ['djuːbɪəs] adj ❶ réticent

▷ My parents were a bit dubious about it. Mes parents étaient un peu réticents à ce sujet. ❷ douteux ▷ a dubious reputation une réputation douteuse

duck [dʌk] n canard m

duckling ['dʌklɪŋ] n caneton m

due [djuː] adj, adv: **The essay is due on Friday.** La rédaction doit être rendue vendredi.; **The plane's due in half an hour.** L'avion doit arriver dans une demi-heure.; **When's the baby due?** Le bébé est prévu pour quand?; **due to (1)** à cause de ▷ The trip was cancelled due to bad weather. Le voyage a été annulé à cause du mauvais temps. **(2)** dû à ▷ The fire was due to an electrical problem. L'incendie est dû à un problème électrique.; **to be due to do something** devoir faire quelque chose ▷ He's due to arrive tomorrow. Il doit arriver demain.

dug [dʌg] vb see **dig**

dull [dʌl] adj ❶ ennuyeux (f ennuyeuse) ▷ He's nice, but a bit dull. Il est sympathique, mais un peu ennuyeux. ❷ (weather, day) maussade

dumb [dʌm] adj bête ▷ That was a really dumb thing I did! C'était vraiment bête de ma part!

dump [dʌmp] n dépotoir m; **It's a real dump!** C'est un endroit miteux!
▶ vb déposer ▷ "no dumping" « défense de déposer des ordures » ▷ Just dump your things on the sofa. Tu peux déposer tes affaires sur le sofa.

duplex ['djuːplɛks] n duplex m (pl les duplex)

duration [djuəˈreɪʃən] n durée f

during ['djuərɪŋ] prep pendant ▷ during the day pendant la journée

dusk [dʌsk] n crépuscule m ▷ at dusk au crépuscule

dust [dʌst] *n* poussière *f*
► *vb* épousseter ▷ *I dusted the shelves.* J'ai épousseté les étagères.

dusty ['dʌstɪ] *adj* poussiéreux (*f* poussiéreuse)

duty ['djuːtɪ] *n* devoir *m* ▷ *It was her duty to tell the police.* C'était son devoir de prévenir la police.; **to be on duty (1)** (*policeman*) être de service **(2)** (*doctor, nurse*) être de garde

duty-free ['djuːtɪ'friː] *adj* hors *f*+*pl* taxes; **the duty-free shop** la boutique hors taxes

duvet ['duːveɪ] *n* couette *f*

DVD *n* DVD *m* (*pl* DVD) ▷ *I've got that movie on DVD.* J'ai ce film en DVD.

DVD player *n* lecteur de DVD *m*

dwarf [dwɔːf] *n* nain *m*, naine *f*

dye [daɪ] *vb* teindre ▷ *to dye one's hair* se teindre les cheveux ▷ *I dyed my T-shirt green.* J'ai teint mon T-shirt en vert.

dying ['daɪɪŋ] *vb see* **die**

dynamic [daɪ'næmɪk] *adj* dynamique

dyslexia [dɪs'leksɪə] *n* dyslexie *f*

e

each [iːtʃ] *adj, pron* ❶ chaque ▷ *each day* chaque jour ▷ *Each house in our street has its own garden.* Chaque maison dans notre rue a son propre jardin. ❷ chacun (*f* chacune) ▷ *The girls each have their own bedroom.* Les filles ont chacune leur chambre. ▷ *They have 10 points each.* Ils ont dix points chacun. ▷ *The plates cost $5 each.* Les assiettes coûtent cinq dollars chacune. ▷ *He gave each of us $10.* Il nous a donné dix dollars à chacun.

▌ Use a reflexive verb to translate **each other**.

They hate each other. Ils se détestent.; **We wrote to each other.** Nous nous sommes écrit.; **They don't know each other.** Ils ne se connaissent pas.

eager ['iːgəʳ] *adj*: **to be eager to do something** être impatient de faire quelque chose

eagle ['i:gl] n aigle m

ear [ɪə] n oreille f; **to perk up one's ears** dresser les oreilles

earache ['ɪəreɪk] n: **to have earache** avoir mal aux oreilles

earlier ['ə:lɪə] adv ❶ tout à l'heure ▷ I saw him earlier. Je l'ai vu tout à l'heure. ❷ (in the day) plus tôt ▷ I ought to get up earlier. Je dois me lever plus tôt.; **earlier than** avant

early ['ə:lɪ] adv, adj ❶ (early in the day) tôt ▷ I have to get up early. Je dois me lever tôt.; **to have an early night** se coucher tôt ❷ (ahead of time) d'avance ▷ I came early to get a good seat. Je suis venu d'avance pour avoir une bonne place.

earn [ə:n] vb gagner ▷ She earns $4 an hour for babysitting. Elle gagne quatre dollars de l'heure quand elle garde des enfants.

earnings ['ə:nɪŋz] npl salaire m

earring ['ɪərɪŋ] n boucle d'oreille f

earth [ə:θ] n terre f

earthquake ['ə:θkweɪk] n tremblement de terre m

easily ['i:zɪlɪ] adv facilement

east [i:st] adj, adv ❶ est (f+pl est) ▷ the east coast la côte est; **an east wind** un vent d'est; **east of** à l'est de ▷ It's east of Red Deer. C'est à l'est de Red Deer. ❷ vers l'est ▷ We were travelling east. Nous allions vers l'est.
▶ n est m ▷ in the east dans l'est

eastbound ['i:stbaund] adj: **The car was eastbound on the highway.** La voiture se trouvait sur l'autoroute en direction de l'est.; **Eastbound traffic is moving very slowly.** La circulation vers l'est avance très lentement.

Easter ['i:stə] n Pâques f ▷ at Easter à Pâques ▷ We went to my grandparents' for Easter. Nous sommes allés chez mes grands-

parents à Pâques.

eastern ['i:stən] adj: **the eastern part of the island** la partie est de l'île; **Eastern Europe** l'Europe de l'Est

easy ['i:zɪ] adj facile

easy chair n fauteuil m

easy-going ['i:zɪ'gəuɪŋ] adj facile à vivre (pl faciles à vivre) ▷ She's very easy-going. Elle est très facile à vivre.

eat [i:t] vb manger; **Would you like something to eat?** Est-ce que tu veux manger quelque chose?

eaten ['i:tn] vb see **eat**

eccentric [ɪk'sentrɪk] adj excentrique

echo ['ekəu] n écho m
▶ vb retentir ▷ Their shouts echoed across the lake. Leurs cris ont retenti jusqu'au bout du lac.

eclipse [ɪ'klɪps] n éclipse f ▷ a partial eclipse une éclipse partielle

eco-friendly [i:kəu'frendlɪ] adj respectueux de l'environnement (f respectueuse de l'environnement)

ecological [i:kə'lɒdʒɪkəl] adj écologique

ecology [ɪ'kɒlədʒɪ] n écologie f

e-commerce [i:kɒmə:s] n commerce électronique m

economic [i:kə'nɒmɪk] adj économique ▷ economic conditions les conditions économiques

economical [i:kə'nɒmɪkl] adj ❶ (person) économe ❷ (purchase, car) économique

economics [i:kə'nɒmɪks] n économie f ▷ He's studying economics. Il étudie les sciences économiques.

economize [ɪ'kɒnəmaɪz] vb faire des économies ▷ to economize on something faire des économies sur quelque chose

economy [ɪ'kɒnəmɪ] n économie f

ecosystem ['i:kəusɪstəm] n

écosystème m

eczema ['ɛksɪmə] n eczéma m

edge [ɛdʒ] n ❶ bord m; **on edge** tendu ❷ (advantage) avantage m

edgy ['ɛdʒɪ] adj tendu

edible ['ɛdɪbl] adj comestible

edit ['ɛdɪt] vb (text) éditer ▷ I have to edit my web page. Je dois éditer ma page Web.

editor ['ɛdɪtə'] n (of newspaper) rédacteur en chef m, rédactrice en chef f

educated ['ɛdjukeɪtɪd] adj cultivé

education [ɛdju'keɪʃən] n ❶ éducation f ▷ There should be more investment in education. On devrait investir plus dans l'éducation. ❷ (teaching) enseignement m ▷ She works in education. Elle travaille dans l'enseignement.

educational [ɛdju'keɪʃənl] adj (experience, toy) éducatif (f éducative) ▷ It was very educational. C'était très éducatif.

effect [ɪ'fɛkt] n effet m ▷ special effects les effets spéciaux

effective [ɪ'fɛktɪv] adj efficace

effectively [ɪ'fɛktɪvlɪ] adv efficacement

Be careful not to translate **effectively** by **effectivement**.

efficient [ɪ'fɪʃənt] adj efficace

effort ['ɛfət] n effort m

e.g. abbr p. ex. (= par exemple)

egg [ɛg] n œuf m ▷ a hard-boiled egg un œuf dur ▷ a soft-boiled egg un œuf à la coque ▷ a fried egg un œuf sur le plat; **scrambled eggs** les œufs brouillés

eh [eɪ] interjection hein ▷ C'était tout un match, hein? That was quite a match, eh?

eight [eɪt] num huit ▷ She's eight. Elle a huit ans.

eighteen [eɪ'tiːn] num dix-huit

▷ He's eighteen. Il a dix-huit ans.

eighteenth [eɪ'tiːnθ] adj dix-huitième ▷ your eighteenth birthday ton dix-huitième anniversaire ▷ the eighteenth floor le dix-huitième étage; **the eighteenth of August** le dix-huit août

eighth [eɪtθ] adj huitième ▷ the eighth floor le huitième étage; **the eighth of August** le huit août

eighty ['eɪtɪ] num quatre-vingts

either ['aɪðə'] adv, conj, pron non plus ▷ I don't like milk, and I don't like eggs either. Je n'aime pas le lait, et je n'aime pas les œufs non plus. ▷ "I've never been to Spain." — "I haven't either." « Je ne suis jamais allé en Espagne. » — « Moi non plus. »; **either...or** soit...soit ▷ You can have either ice cream or yogurt. Tu peux prendre soit une crème glacée soit un yogourt.; **either of them** l'un ou l'autre ▷ Take either of them. Prends l'un ou l'autre.; **I don't like either of them.** Je n'aime ni l'un ni l'autre.

elastic [ɪ'læstɪk] n élastique m

elbow ['ɛlbəu] n coude m

elder ['ɛldə'] adj aîné ▷ my elder sister ma sœur aînée

elderly ['ɛldəlɪ] adj âgé; **the elderly** les personnes âgées

eldest ['ɛldɪst] adj aîné ▷ my eldest sister ma sœur aînée ▷ He's the eldest. C'est l'aîné.

elect [ɪ'lɛkt] vb élire

election [ɪ'lɛkʃən] n élection f

electric [ɪ'lɛktrɪk] adj électrique ▷ an electric guitar une guitare électrique; **an electric blanket** une couverture chauffante

electrical [ɪ'lɛktrɪkl] adj électrique; **an electrical engineer** un ingénieur électricien

electrician [ɪlɛk'trɪʃən] n électricien m, électricienne f ▷ He's an electrician. Il est électricien.

electricity [ɪlɛk'trɪsɪtɪ] n
électricité f

electronic [ɪlɛk'trɒnɪk] adj
électronique

electronics [ɪlɛk'trɒnɪks] n
électronique f ▷ My hobby is
electronics. Ma passion, c'est
l'électronique.

elegant ['ɛlɪɡənt] adj élégant

elementary school [ɛlɪ'mɛn-
tərɪ-] n école f primaire

elephant ['ɛlɪfənt] n éléphant m

elevator ['ɛlɪveɪtə'] n ascenseur m

eleven [ɪ'lɛvn] num onze ▷ She's
eleven. Elle a onze ans.

eleventh [ɪ'lɛvnθ] adj onzième
▷ the eleventh floor le onzième étage
▷ the eleventh of August le onze août

else [ɛls] adv d'autre ▷ somebody
else quelqu'un d'autre ▷ nobody
else personne d'autre ▷ nothing
else rien d'autre; **something else**
autre chose; **anything else** autre
chose ▷ Would you like anything else?
Désirez-vous autre chose?; **I don't
want anything else.** Je ne veux
rien d'autre.; **somewhere else**
ailleurs; **anywhere else** n'importe
où ailleurs; **or else (1)** (otherwise)
sinon ▷ Study well or else you'll fail.
Étudie bien, sinon tu vas échouer.
(2) (alternatively) ou bien ▷ You can
call me, or else I can drop by your place
after school. Tu peux me téléphoner,
ou bien je peux passer chez toi
après l'école.

email ['iːmeɪl] n courriel m; **email
address** l'adresse f de courriel ▷ My
email address is... Mon adresse de
courriel, c'est...
  ▶ vb: **to email somebody** envoyer
un courriel à quelqu'un

embarrassed [ɪm'bærəst] adj
gêné ▷ I was really embarrassed.
J'étais vraiment gêné.

embarrassing [ɪm'bærəsɪŋ] adj

gênant ▷ It was so embarrassing.
C'était tellement gênant.

emergency [ɪ'mɜːdʒənsɪ] n
urgence f ▷ This is an emergency!
C'est une urgence!; **in an
emergency** en cas d'urgence;
an emergency exit une sortie
de secours; **an emergency
landing** un atterrissage forcé; **the
emergency services** les services
d'urgence

emigrate ['ɛmɪɡreɪt] vb émigrer

emission control [ɪ'mɪʃn-] n lutte
contre les émissions f

emotion [ɪ'məʊʃən] n émotion f

emotional [ɪ'məʊʃənl] adj
① (person) émotif (f émotive)
② plein d'émotion ▷ an emotional
farewell un adieu plein d'émotion
③ émotionnel ▷ an emotional shock
un choc émotionnel; **an emotional
issue** une question qui soulève les
passions; **to be on an emotional
roller coaster** être pris dans un
tourbillon d'émotions; **to become
emotional** être ému

> Be careful not to confuse
> **émotif** (having or showing
> strong emotions) with
> **émotionnel** (to do with the
> emotions).

emphasize ['ɛmfəsaɪz] vb: **to
emphasize something** insister
sur quelque chose; **to emphasize
that...** souligner que...

empire ['ɛmpaɪə'] n empire m

employ [ɪm'plɔɪ] vb employer
▷ The factory employs 600 people.
L'usine emploie six cents
personnes.

employee [ɪmplɔɪ'iː] n employé m,
employée f

employer [ɪm'plɔɪə'] n employeur
m, employeuse f

employment [ɪm'plɔɪmənt] n
emploi m

empty ['emptɪ] adj vide
▶vb vider; **to empty something out** vider quelque chose

encourage [ɪn'kʌrɪdʒ] vb encourager; **to encourage somebody to do something** encourager quelqu'un à faire quelque chose

encouragement [ɪn'kʌrɪdʒmənt] n encouragement m

encouraging [ɪn'kʌrɪdʒɪŋ] adj encourageant

encyclopedia [ɪnsaɪklə'piːdɪə] n encyclopédie f

end [end] n ❶ fin f ▷ the end of the movie la fin du film ▷ the end of the holidays la fin des vacances; **in the end** en fin de compte ▷ In the end I decided to stay home. En fin de compte, j'ai décidé de rester à la maison.; **It turned out all right in the end.** Ça s'est bien terminé. ❷ bout m ▷ at the end of the street au bout de la rue ▷ at the other end of the table à l'autre bout de la table; **for hours on end** des heures entières
▶vb finir ▷ What time does the movie end? À quelle heure est-ce que le film finit?; **to end up doing something** finir par faire quelque chose ▷ I ended up walking home. J'ai fini par rentrer chez moi à pied.

ending ['endɪŋ] n fin f ▷ It was an exciting movie, especially the ending. C'était un film passionnant, surtout la fin.

endless ['endlɪs] adj interminable ▷ The journey seemed endless. Le voyage a paru interminable.

enemy ['enəmɪ] n ennemi m, ennemie f

energetic [enə'dʒetɪk] adj (person) énergique

energy ['enədʒɪ] n énergie f

energy-efficient ['enədʒɪ'fɪʃənt]
adj éconergétique

enforce [ɪn'fɔːs] vb faire respecter ▷ to enforce a rule faire respecter un règlement

engaged [ɪn'geɪdʒd] adj fiancé ▷ She's engaged to my cousin. Elle est fiancée à mon cousin.; **to get engaged** se fiancer

engagement [ɪn'geɪdʒmənt] n fiançailles fpl ▷ an engagement ring une bague de fiançailles ▷ to break off one's engagement rompre ses fiançailles

engine ['endʒɪn] n moteur m

> Be careful not to translate **engine** by the French word **engin**.

engineer [endʒɪ'nɪə] n ingénieur m, ingénieure f ▷ She's an engineer. Elle est ingénieure.

engineering [endʒɪ'nɪərɪŋ] n ingénierie f

English ['ɪŋglɪʃ] adj anglais ▷ English grammar la grammaire anglaise
▶n anglais m ▷ Do you speak English? Est-ce que vous parlez anglais?

English-Canadian
['ɪŋglɪʃkə'neɪdɪən] adj canadien-anglais (f canadienne-anglaise) ▷ an English-Canadian family une famille canadienne-anglaise
▶n Canadien anglais m, Canadienne anglaise f ▷ She married an English-Canadian. Elle a épousé un Canadien anglais.

engrossed [ɪn'grəʊst] adj absorbé ▷ She was so engrossed by her book that she didn't hear me. Elle était si absorbée par son livre qu'elle ne m'a pas entendu.

enjoy [ɪn'dʒɔɪ] vb ❶ aimer ▷ Did you enjoy the film? Est-ce que vous avez aimé le film? ❷ **to enjoy oneself** s'amuser ▷ I really enjoyed myself. Je me suis vraiment bien amusé. ▷ Did

you enjoy yourselves at the party?
Est-ce que vous vous êtes bien
amusés à la fête? ❷ (benefit from)
jouir de ▷ My grandfather still enjoys
good health. Mon grand-père jouit
encore d'une bonne santé.

enjoyable [ɪnˈdʒɔɪəbl] adj
agréable

enlarge [ɪnˈlɑːdʒ] vb agrandir ▷ to
enlarge an image agrandir une image

enormous [ɪˈnɔːməs] adj énorme

enough [ɪˈnʌf] pron, adj assez de
▷ enough time assez de temps ▷ I
didn't have enough money. Je n'avais
pas assez d'argent. ▷ Do you have
enough? Tu en as assez? ▷ I've had
enough! J'en ai assez!; **big enough**
suffisamment grand; **warm
enough** suffisamment chaud;
That's enough. Ça suffit.

enter [ˈentəʳ] vb entrer ▷ She
entered the room. Elle est entrée
dans la salle. ▷ to enter text in a file
entrer du texte dans un fichier; **to
enter a competition** s'inscrire à
une compétition; **the Enter key** la
touche Entrée

entertain [entəˈteɪn] vb (guests)
recevoir

entertainer [entəˈteɪnəʳ] n artiste
mf de variétés

entertaining [entəˈteɪnɪŋ] adj
divertissant

entertainment [entəˈteɪnmənt]
n divertissement m ▷ The resort
offers outdoor sports, video nights, and
other entertainment. Le centre de
villégiature offre des sports de plein
air, des soirées vidéo et d'autres
divertissements.

enthusiasm [ɪnˈθuːziæzəm] n
enthousiasme m

enthusiastic [ɪnθuːzɪˈæstɪk] adj
enthousiaste

entire [ɪnˈtaɪəʳ] adj entier (f
entière) ▷ the entire world le monde

entier

entirely [ɪnˈtaɪəlɪ] adv
entièrement

entrance [ɪnˈtrɑːns] n entrée
f; **an entrance exam** un examen
d'admission; **entrance fee** le prix
d'entrée

entry [ˈentrɪ] n entrée f; **"no entry"**
(1) (on door) « défense d'entrer »
(2) (on road sign) « sens interdit », an
entry form une feuille d'inscription

envelope [ˈenvələup] n
enveloppe f

envious [ˈenvɪəs] adj envieux (f
envieuse)

environment [ɪnˈvaɪərnmənt] n
environnement m

environmental [ɪnvaɪərnˈmentl]
adj écologique

environmentalist
[ɪnvaɪərnˈmentlɪst] n
environnementaliste mf

environment-friendly
[ɪnˈvaɪərənmənтˈfrendlɪ] adj
écologique

envy [ˈenvɪ] n envie f
▶ vb envier ▷ I don't envy you! Je ne
t'envie pas!

epidemic [epɪˈdemɪk] n épidémie
f ▷ a flu epidemic une épidémie
de grippe

epilepsy [ˈepɪlepsɪ] n épilepsie f

episode [ˈepɪsəud] n (of TV series,
story) épisode m

equal [ˈiːkwl] adj égal (mpl égaux)
▶ vb égaler

equality [iːˈkwɔlɪtɪ] n égalité f

equator [ɪˈkweɪtəʳ] n équateur m

equipment [ɪˈkwɪpmənt] n
équipement m ▷ fishing equipment
l'équipement de pêche ▷ skiing
equipment l'équipement de ski

equipped [ɪˈkwɪpt] adj: **equipped
with** équipé de; **to be well
equipped** être bien équipé

equivalent [ɪˈkwɪvələnt] n

équivalent *m*; **equivalent to** équivalent à

erase [ɪ'reɪz] *vb* effacer

eraser [ɪ'reɪzə*] *n* gomme *f*

errand ['ɛrnd] *n* course *f* ▷ *I have to run a few errands for my mother.* J'ai quelques courses à faire pour ma mère.

error ['ɛrə*] *n* erreur *f*

escalator ['ɛskəleɪtə*] *n* escalier *m* roulant

escape [ɪ'skeɪp] *n* (*from prison*) évasion *f*
▷ *vb* s'échapper ▷ *A lion has escaped.* Un lion s'est échappé.; **to escape from prison** s'évader de prison

escarpment [ɪs'kɑːpmənt] *n* escarpement *m* ▷ *The Niagara escarpment* l'escarpement de Niagara

especially [ɪ'spɛʃlɪ] *adv* surtout ▷ *It's very hot there, especially in the summer.* Il fait très chaud là-bas, surtout en été.

essay ['ɛseɪ] *n* dissertation *f* ▷ *a history essay* une dissertation d'histoire

essential [ɪ'sɛnʃl] *adj* essentiel (*f* essentielle) ▷ *It's essential to bring warm clothes.* Il est essentiel d'apporter des vêtements chauds.

estate [ɪ'steɪt] *n* propriété *f*

estimate ['ɛstɪmeɪt] *vb* estimer ▷ *They estimated it would take three weeks.* Ils ont estimé que cela prendrait trois semaines.
▷ *n* estimation *f* ▷ *We asked for an estimate before getting the car repaired.* Nous avons demandé une estimation avant de faire réparer la voiture.

etc. *abbr* (= *et cetera*) etc.

ethnic ['ɛθnɪk] *adj* ethnique ▷ *an ethnic minority* une minorité ethnique

euro ['juərəu] *n* euro *m* ▷ *50 euros* 50 euros

evacuate [ɪ'vækjueɪt] *vb* évacuer

evaporate [ɪ'væpəreɪt] *vb* s'évaporer; **evaporated milk** le lait condensé

eve [iːv] *n*: **Christmas Eve** la veille de Noël; **New Year's Eve** la veille du Jour de l'An

even ['iːvn] *adv* même ▷ *I like all animals, even snakes.* J'aime tous les animaux, même les serpents.; **even if** même si ▷ *I'd never do that, even if you asked me to.* Je ne ferais jamais ça, même si tu me le demandais.; **not even** même pas ▷ *He never stops working, not even on the weekend.* Il n'arrête jamais de travailler, même pas la fin de semaine.; **even though** bien que

▮ **bien que** has to be followed by a verb in the subjunctive.

▷ *She never has any money, even though her parents are quite rich.* Elle n'a jamais d'argent, bien que ses parents soient assez riches.; **even more** encore plus ▷ *I liked the book even more than the movie.* J'ai encore plus aimé le livre que le film.
▷ *adj* ❶ régulier (*f* régulière) ▷ *an even layer of snow* une couche régulière de neige ❷ plat ▷ *an even surface* une surface toute plate; **an even number** un nombre pair; **to get even with somebody** prendre sa revanche sur quelqu'un ▷ *He wanted to get even with her.* Il voulait prendre sa revanche sur elle.; **The score is even.** On est à égalité.

evening ['iːvnɪŋ] *n* soir *m* ▷ *in the evening* le soir ▷ *yesterday evening* hier soir ▷ *tomorrow evening* demain soir; **all evening** toute la soirée; **Good evening!** Bonsoir!

event [ɪ'vɛnt] *n* événement *m*; **a sporting event** une épreuve sportive

eventful [ɪˈvɛntful] adj
mouvementé

eventually [ɪˈvɛntʃʊəlɪ] adv
finalement

> Be careful not to
> translate **eventually** by
> **éventuellement**.

ever [ˈɛvəʳ] adv: **Have you ever
been to Prince Edward Island?**
Est-ce que tu es déjà allé à l'Île-du-
Prince-Édouard?; **more than ever**
plus que jamais ▷ **happier than ever**
plus heureux que jamais; **Have
you ever seen her?** Vous l'avez
déjà vue?; **I haven't ever done
that.** Je ne l'ai jamais fait.; **the best
I've ever seen** le meilleur que j'aie
jamais vu; **for the first time ever**
pour la première fois; **ever since**
depuis que ▷ *Ever since I met him*
depuis que je l'ai rencontré; **ever
since then** depuis ce moment-là

every [ˈɛvrɪ] adj chaque ▷ *every
student* chaque élève; **every time**
chaque fois ▷ *Every time I see him
he's depressed.* Chaque fois que je
le vois, il est déprimé.; **every day**
tous les jours; **every week** toutes
les semaines; **every now and then**
de temps en temps; **every other
Friday** un vendredi sur deux; **every
three days** tous les trois jours

everybody [ˈɛvrɪbɒdɪ] pron tout le
monde ▷ *Everybody had a good time.*
Tout le monde s'est bien amusé.
▷ *Everybody makes mistakes.* Tout le
monde peut se tromper.

everyday [ˈɛvrɪdeɪ] adj
❶ (ordinary) de tous les jours
▷ *everyday clothes* les vêtements de
tous les jours ❷ (daily) quotidien
(f quotidienne) ▷ *everyday activities*
les activités quotidiennes; **an
everyday situation** une situation
courante

everyone [ˈɛvrɪwʌn] pron tout

le monde ▷ *Everyone opened their
presents.* Tout le monde a ouvert ses
cadeaux. ▷ *Everyone should have a
hobby.* Tout le monde devrait avoir
un passe-temps.

everything [ˈɛvrɪθɪŋ] pron tout
▷ *You've thought of everything!*
Tu as pensé à tout!; **Have you
remembered everything?** Est-ce
que tu n'as rien oublié?; **Money
isn't everything.** L'argent ne fait
pas le bonheur.

everywhere [ˈɛvrɪwɛəʳ] adv
partout ▷ *I looked everywhere, but I
couldn't find it.* J'ai regardé partout,
mais je n'ai pas pu le trouver.
▷ *There were policemen everywhere.* Il
y avait des policiers partout.

evil [ˈiːvl] adj mauvais
▶ n mal m (pl les maux)

ex- [ɛks] prefix ex- ▷ *his ex-wife* son
ex-femme

exact [ɪgˈzækt] adj exact

exactly [ɪgˈzæktlɪ] adv
exactement ▷ *exactly the same*
exactement le même ▷ *not exactly.*
pas exactement.; **It's exactly 10
o'clock.** Il est dix heures précises.

exaggerate [ɪgˈzædʒəreɪt] vb
exagérer

exaggeration [ɪgzædʒəˈreɪʃən] n
exagération f

exam [ɪgˈzæm] n examen m ▷ *a
French exam* un examen de français
▷ *the exam results* les résultats des
examens m

examination [ɪgzæmɪˈneɪʃən] n
examen m

examine [ɪgˈzæmɪn] vb examiner
▷ *He examined her passport.* Il a
examiné son passeport. ▷ *The
doctor examined him.* Le docteur l'a
examiné.

example [ɪgˈzɑːmpl] n exemple m;
for example par exemple

excellent [ˈɛksələnt] adj excellent

▷ *Her results were excellent.* Elle a eu d'excellents résultats.; **You can come? Excellent!** Tu peux venir? C'est super!

except [ɪkˈsɛpt] *prep* sauf ▷ *everyone except me* tout le monde sauf moi; **except for** sauf; **except that** sauf que ▷ *The weather was great, except that it was a bit cold.* Il a fait un temps superbe, sauf qu'il a fait un peu froid.

exception [ɪkˈsɛpʃən] *n* exception *f*; **to make an exception** faire une exception

exceptional [ɪkˈsɛpʃənl] *adj* exceptionnel (*f* exceptionnelle)

exchange [ɪksˈtʃeɪndʒ] *vb* échanger ▷ *I exchanged the book for a video.* J'ai échangé le livre contre une vidéo.

exchange rate *n* taux de change *m*

excited [ɪkˈsaɪtəd] *adj* excité

exciting [ɪkˈsaɪtɪŋ] *adj* passionnant

exclamation mark [ɛksklə'meɪʃən-] *n* point d'exclamation *m*

excuse [*n* ɪksˈkjuːs, *vb* ɪkˈskjuːz] *n* excuse *f*
▶ *vb* **①** excuser ▷ *Your lateness is excused.* Ton retard a été excusé. ▷ *She excused him from class.* Elle lui a permis de s'absenter de la classe. **②** dispenser ▷ *He was excused from writing the exam.* On l'a dispensé de passer l'examen.; **Excuse me!** Pardon!; **to excuse oneself** s'excuser

execute [ˈɛksɪkjuːt] *vb* exécuter

execution [ɛksɪˈkjuːʃən] *n* exécution *f*

executive [ɪɡˈzɛkjʊtɪv] *n* (*in business*) cadre *m* ▷ *He's an executive.* Il est cadre.

exercise [ˈɛksəsaɪz] *n* exercice

m; **an exercise bike** un vélo d'appartement; **an exercise book** un cahier

exhausted [ɪɡˈzɔːstɪd] *adj* épuisé

exhaust fumes [ɪɡˈzɔːst-] *npl* gaz *mpl* d'échappement

exhaust pipe [ɪɡˈzɔːst-] *n* tuyau d'échappement *m*

exhibition [ɛksɪˈbɪʃən] *n* exposition *f*

exist [ɪɡˈzɪst] *vb* exister

exit [ˈɛksɪt] *n* sortie *f*
▶ *vb* **①** sortir ▷ *Exit via the rear door.* Sortez par la porte arrière. **②** (*from vehicle*) descendre

exotic [ɪɡˈzɔtɪk] *adj* exotique

expand [ɪkˈspænd] *vb* **①** (*increase*) élargir ▷ *to expand one's knowledge* élargir ses connaissances **②** (*develop*) développer ▷ *to expand an idea* développer une idée

expect [ɪkˈspɛkt] *vb* **①** attendre ▷ *I'm expecting her for dinner.* Je l'attends pour dîner. ▷ *She's expecting a baby.* Elle attend un enfant. **②** s'attendre à ▷ *I was expecting the worst.* Je m'attendais au pire. **③** supposer ▷ *I expect it's a mistake.* Je suppose qu'il s'agit d'une erreur.

expedition [ɛkspəˈdɪʃən] *n* expédition *f*

expel [ɪkˈspɛl] *vb*: **to get expelled** (*from school*) se faire renvoyer

expenses [ɪkˈspɛnsɪz] *npl* frais *mpl*

expensive [ɪkˈspɛnsɪv] *adj* **①** cher (*f* chère) **②** dispendieux (*f* dispendieuse)

experience [ɪkˈspɪərɪəns] *n* expérience *f*

experienced [ɪkˈspɪərɪənst] *adj* expérimenté

experiment [ɪkˈspɛrɪmənt] *n* expérience *f*

expert [ˈɛkspɜːt] *n* spécialiste *m*, spécialiste *f* ▷ *She's a computer* *expert*. C'est une spécialiste en informatique.; **He's an expert cook.** Il cuisine très bien.

expire [ɪk'spaɪəʳ] *vb* expirer

explain [ɪk'spleɪn] *vb* expliquer

explanation [ɛksplə'neɪʃən] *n* explication *f*

explode [ɪk'spləʊd] *vb* exploser

exploit [ɪk'splɔɪt] *vb* exploiter

exploitation [ɛksplɔɪ'teɪʃən] *n* exploitation *f*

explore [ɪk'splɔːʳ] *vb* ❶ (*place*) explorer ❷ (*issue, possibilities*) étudier

explorer [ɪk'splɔːrəʳ] *n* explorateur *m*, exploratrice *f*

explosion [ɪk'spləʊʒən] *n* explosion *f*

explosive [ɪk'spləʊsɪv] *adj* explosif (*f* explosive)
▶ *n* explosif *m*

expose [ɪk'spəʊz] *vb* ❶ découvrir ❷ (*to sun, radiation*) exposer

express [ɪk'sprɛs] *vb* exprimer; **to express oneself** s'exprimer ▷ *It's not easy to express oneself in a foreign language.* Ce n'est pas facile de s'exprimer dans une langue étrangère.

expression [ɪk'sprɛʃən] *n* expression *f* ▷ *It's an English expression.* C'est une expression anglaise.

expressway [ɪk'sprɛsweɪ] *n* autoroute *f* urbaine

extension [ɪk'stɛnʃən] *n* ❶ (*of building*) annexe *f* ❷ (*telephone*) poste *m*; **Extension 3137, please.** Poste trente et un trente-sept, s'il vous plaît.

extensive [ɪk'stɛnsɪv] *adj* ❶ (*knowledge, range*) vaste ▷ *an extensive property* une vaste propriété ▷ *extensive knowledge of Canadian history* une vaste connaissance de l'histoire

canadienne ❷ (*damage, alterations*) considérable ▷ *The earthquake caused extensive damage.* Le tremblement de terre a causé des dommages considérables. ❸ approfondi ▷ *extensive research* des recherches approfondies; **extensive surgery** plusieurs interventions chirurgicales

extensively [ɪk'stɛnsɪvlɪ] *adv*: **He has travelled extensively in Europe.** Il a beaucoup voyagé en Europe.; **The building was extensively renovated last year.** Le bâtiment a été extensivement rénové l'année dernière.

extent [ɪk'stɛnt] *n*: **to some extent** dans une certaine mesure; **to the extent that** au point que

exterior [ɛk'stɪərɪəʳ] *adj* extérieur

extinct [ɪk'stɪŋkt] *adj*: **to become extinct** disparaître; **to be extinct** avoir disparu ▷ *The species is almost extinct.* Cette espèce a presque disparu.

extinguisher [ɪk'stɪŋgwɪʃəʳ] *n* (*fire extinguisher*) extincteur *m*

extra ['ɛkstrə] *adj, adv* supplémentaire ▷ *an extra blanket* une couverture supplémentaire; **to pay extra** payer un supplément; **Breakfast is extra.** Il y a un supplément pour le petit déjeuner.; **Do you have an extra pen?** As-tu un stylo à me passer?; **It costs extra.** Il y a un supplément.

extracurricular ['ɛkstrəkə'rɪkjʊləʳ] *adj* parascolaire

extraordinary [ɪk'strɔːdnrɪ] *adj* extraordinaire

extravagant [ɪk'strævəgənt] *adj* ❶ (*person*) dépensier (*f* dépensière) ❷ (*gift, wedding*) somptueux (*f* somptueuse)

extreme [ɪk'striːm] *adj* extrême

extremist [ɪk'striːmɪst] n
extrémiste mf
eye [aɪ] n œil m (pl yeux) ▷ I have
green eyes. J'ai les yeux verts.;
to keep an eye on something
surveiller quelque chose
eyebrow ['aɪbraʊ] n sourcil m
eyelash ['aɪlæʃ] n cil m
eyelid ['aɪlɪd] n paupière f
eyeliner ['aɪlaɪnəʳ] n ligneur m
eye shadow ['aɪʃædəʊ] n fard à
paupières m
eyesight ['aɪsaɪt] n vue f ▷ poor
eyesight une vue faible

fabric ['fæbrɪk] n tissu m
fabulous ['fæbjʊləs] adj
formidable ▷ The show was fabulous.
Le spectacle était formidable.
face [feɪs] n ❶ (of person) visage
m ❷ (of clock) cadran m ❸ (of
cliff) paroi f; **on the face of it** à
première vue; **in the face of these
difficulties** face à ces difficultés;
face to face face à face; **to
someone's face** sans détour ▷ She
said it right to my face. Elle me l'a dit
sans détour.
▶ vb (place, problem) faire face à; **to
face up to something** faire face à
quelque chose ▷ You must face up to
your responsibilities. Vous devez faire
face à vos responsabilités.
facecloth ['feɪsklɒθ] n
débarbouillette f
face-off ['feɪsɒf] n mise au jeu f
facilities [fə'sɪlɪtɪz] npl
équipement m ▷ This school has

excellent facilities. Cette école dispose d'excellents équipements.; **toilet facilities** les toilettes

fact [fækt] *n* fait *m*; **in fact** en fait

factory [ˈfæktərɪ] *n* usine *f*

fad [fæd] *n* engouement *m*

fade [feɪd] *vb* ① (*colour*) passer ▷ *The colour has faded in the sun.* La couleur a passé au soleil.; **My jeans have faded.** Mon jean est délavé. ② baisser ▷ *The light was fading fast.* La lumière baissait rapidement. ③ diminuer ▷ *The noise gradually faded.* Le bruit a diminué peu à peu.

fail [feɪl] *vb* ① rater ▷ *I failed the history exam.* J'ai raté l'examen d'histoire. ② échouer ▷ *In our class, no one failed.* Dans notre classe, personne n'a échoué. ▷ *Our efforts failed.* Nos efforts ont échoué. ③ lâcher ▷ *My brakes failed.* Mes freins ont lâché. ④ tomber en panne ▷ *The engine failed.* Le moteur est tombé en panne. ⑤ faiblir ▷ *His eyesight is failing.* Sa vue faiblit.; **to fail to do something** ne pas faire quelque chose ▷ *She failed to return her library books.* Elle n'a pas rendu ses livres à la bibliothèque.
▸ *n*: **without fail** sans faute

failure [ˈfeɪljər] *n* ① échec *m* ② *feelings of failure* un sentiment d'échec ② raté *m*, ratée *f* ▷ *You are not a failure.* Tu n'es pas un raté. ③ défaillance *f* ▷ *a mechanical failure* une défaillance mécanique

faint [feɪnt] *adj* faible ▷ *His voice was very faint.* Sa voix était très faible.; **to feel faint** se trouver mal
▸ *vb* s'évanouir ▷ *All of a sudden she fainted.* Tout à coup elle s'est évanouie.

fair [fɛər] *adj* ① juste ▷ *That's not fair.* Ce n'est pas juste. ② (*skin*) clair ▷ *people with fair skin* les gens

qui ont la peau claire ③ (*weather*) beau (*f* belle) ▷ *The weather was fair.* Il faisait beau. ④ (*good enough*) assez bon (*f* assez bonne) ▷ *I have a fair chance of winning.* J'ai d'assez bonnes chances de gagner. ⑤ (*sizeable*) considérable ▷ *That's a fair distance.* Ça représente une distance considérable.
▸ *n* foire *f* ▷ *They went to the fair.* Ils sont allés à la foire.; **a trade fair** une foire commerciale; **a book fair** une foire du livre

fairground [ˈfɛəɡraʊnd] *n* champ de foire *m*

fairly [ˈfɛəlɪ] *adv* ① équitablement ▷ *The cake was divided fairly.* Le gâteau a été partagé équitablement. ② (*quite*) assez ▷ *That's fairly good.* C'est assez bien.

fairness [ˈfɛənɪs] *n* justice *f*

fairy [ˈfɛərɪ] *n* fée *f*

fairy tale *n* conte de fées *m* (*pl* contes de fées)

faith [feɪθ] *n* ① foi *f* ▷ *the Catholic faith* la foi catholique ② confiance *f* ▷ *People have lost faith in the government.* Les gens ont perdu confiance dans le gouvernement.

faithful [ˈfeɪθful] *adj* fidèle

faithfully [ˈfeɪθfəlɪ] *adv*: **Yours faithfully…** (*in letter*) Veuillez agréer mes salutations distinguées…

fake [feɪk] *n* faux *m* ▷ *The painting was a fake.* Le tableau était un faux.
▸ *adj* faux *m* (*f* fausse) ▷ *She wore fake fur.* Elle portait une fausse fourrure.
▸ *vb* ① (*signature*) imiter ② (*photo, event*) truquer; **He faked a headache.** Il a fait semblant d'avoir mal à la tête.; **She's faking it.** Elle fait semblant.

fall [fɔːl] *n* ① chute *f* ▷ *a fall of snow* une chute de neige ▷ *She had a nasty*

fall. Elle a fait une mauvaise chute.; **the Niagara Falls** les chutes du Niagara ❷ automne *m*; **fall fair** la foire d'automne
▷ *vb* ❶ tomber ▷ *He tripped and fell.* Il a trébuché et il est tombé. ❷ baisser ▷ *Prices are falling.* Les prix baissent.; **to fall apart** tomber en morceaux; **Their marriage is falling apart.** Leur mariage s'effond.; **to fall behind** rester en arrière; **to fall down (1)** (*person*) tomber ▷ *She's fallen down.* Elle est tombée. **(2)** (*building*) s'écrouler ▷ *The house is slowly falling down.* La maison est en train de s'écrouler.; **to fall for (1)** se laisser prendre à ▷ *They fell for it.* Ils s'y sont laissé prendre. **(2)** tomber amoureux de ▷ *She's falling for him.* Elle est en train de tomber amoureuse de lui.; **to fall off** tomber de ▷ *The book fell off the shelf.* Le livre est tombé de l'étagère.; **to fall through** tomber à l'eau ▷ *Our plans have fallen through.* Nos projets sont tombés à l'eau.

fallen ['fɔ:lən] *vb see* **fall**

false [fɔ:ls] *adj* faux (*f* fausse); **a false alarm** une fausse alerte; **false teeth** le dentier

fame [feɪm] *n* renommée *f*

familiar [fə'mɪljə'] *adj* familier (*f* familière) ▷ *a familiar face* un visage familier; **to be familiar with something** bien connaître quelque chose ▷ *I'm familiar with his work.* Je connais bien ses œuvres.

family ['fæmɪlɪ] *n* famille *f*; **the Cooke family** la famille Cooke

famine ['fæmɪn] *n* famine *f*

famous ['feɪməs] *adj* célèbre

fan [fæn] *n* ❶ (*handheld*) éventail *m* ❷ (*electric*) ventilateur *m* ❸ fan ▷ *I'm a fan of Jann Arden.* Je suis un fan de Jann Arden.; **hockey fans** les fans de hockey

fanatic [fə'nætɪk] *n* fanatique

fancy ['fænsɪ] *adj* élaboré

fantastic [fæn'tæstɪk] *adj* fantastique

far [fɑ:'] *adj, adv* loin ▷ *Is it far?* Est-ce que c'est loin?; **far from** loin de ▷ *It's not far from London.* Ce n'est pas loin de London. ▷ *It's far from easy.* C'est loin d'être facile.; **How far is it?** C'est à quelle distance?; **How far is it to Hull?** Combien y a-t-il jusqu'à Hull?; **How far are you?** (*with a task*) Où en êtes-vous?; **at the far end** à l'autre bout ▷ *at the far end of the room* à l'autre bout de la pièce; **far better** beaucoup mieux; **as far as I know** pour autant que je sache

fare [fɛə'] *n* ❶ (*trains, buses*) prix du billet *m* ❷ (*taxi*) prix de la course *m*; **half fare** le demi-tarif; **full fare** le plein tarif

Far East *n* Extrême-Orient *m*; **in the Far East** en Extrême-Orient

far-fetched ['fɑ:'fetʃt] *adj* tiré par les cheveux

farm [fɑ:m] *n* ferme *f*

farmer ['fɑ:mə'] *n* ❶ agriculteur *m*, agricultrice *f* ▷ *He's a farmer.* Il est agriculteur. ❷ fermier *m*, fermière *f*

farmhouse ['fɑ:mhaus] *n* ferme *f*

farming ['fɑ:mɪŋ] *n* agriculture *f*; **dairy farming** l'industrie laitière

fascinating ['fæsɪneɪtɪŋ] *adj* fascinant

fashion ['fæʃən] *n* mode *f* ▷ *a fashion show* un défilé de mode; **in fashion** à la mode

fashionable ['fæʃnəbl] *adj* à la mode ▷ *She wears very fashionable clothes.* Elle porte des vêtements très à la mode. ▷ *a fashionable restaurant* un restaurant à la mode

fast [fɑ:st] *adj, adv* ❶ vite ▷ *He can run fast.* Il sait courir vite.

❷ rapide ▷ *a fast car* une voiture rapide; **fast food** la bouffe-minute; **fast forward** l'avance f rapide; **That clock's fast.** Cette pendule avance.; **She's fast asleep.** Elle est profondément endormie.

fat [fæt] *adj* gros (f grosse)
▶ n ❶ (on meat, in food) gras m ▷ *It's very high in fat.* C'est très gras ▷ *to cut down on fat* couper le gras ▷ (for cooking) matière grasse f; **body fat** le tissu adipeux

fatal ['feɪtl] *adj* ❶ (causing death) mortel (f mortelle) ▷ *a fatal accident* un accident mortel ❷ (disastrous) fatal ▷ *He made a fatal mistake.* Il a fait une erreur fatale.

father ['fɑːðə'] *n* père m ▷ *my father* mon père

father-in-law ['fɑːðərɪnlɔː] *n* beau-père m (*pl* beaux-pères)

fault [fɔːlt] *n* ❶ (mistake) faute f ▷ *It's my fault.* C'est de ma faute. ❷ (defect) défaut m ▷ *in spite of all her faults* malgré tous ses défauts; **a mechanical fault** une défaillance mécanique

faulty ['fɔːltɪ] *adj* défectueux (f défectueuse) ▷ *This machine is faulty.* Cette machine est défectueuse.

favour ['feɪvə'] *n* service m; **to do somebody a favour** rendre service à quelqu'un ▷ *Could you do me a favour?* Tu peux me rendre service?; **to be in favour of something** être pour quelque chose ▷ *I'm in favour of nuclear disarmament.* Je suis pour le désarmement nucléaire.

favourite ['feɪvrɪt] *adj* favori (f favorite) ▷ *Blue is my favourite colour.* Le bleu est ma couleur favorite.
▶ n favori m, favorite f ▷ *The Canadian is the favourite to win gold in speed skating.* La Canadienne est la favorite pour gagner l'or en

patinage de vitesse. ▷ *The next song is my favourite.* La prochaine chanson est ma favorite.

fawn [fɔːn] *n* faon m

fax [fæks] *n* ❶ (document) télécopie f; **to send somebody a fax** envoyer une télécopie à quelqu'un ❷ (machine) télécopieur m
▶ vb télécopier ▷ *Can you fax me your document?* Peux-tu me télécopier ton document?

fear [fɪə'] *n* peur f
▶ vb craindre ▷ *You have nothing to fear.* Vous n'avez rien à craindre.

feather ['fɛðə'] *n* plume f

feature ['fiːtʃə'] *n* (of person, object) caractéristique f ▷ *an important feature* une caractéristique essentielle; **a feature film** un long métrage

February ['fɛbruərɪ] *n* février m; **in February** en février

fed [fɛd] *vb see* **feed**

federal ['fɛdərəl] *adj* fédéral ▷ *the federal government* le gouvernement fédéral

fed up [fɛd'ʌp] *adj*: **to be fed up with something** en avoir marre de quelque chose ▷ *I'm fed up with waiting for him.* J'en ai marre de l'attendre.

feed [fiːd] *vb* donner à manger à ▷ *Have you fed the cat?* Est-ce que tu as donné à manger au chat?; **She worked hard to feed her family.** Elle travaillait dur pour nourrir sa famille.

feedback ['fiːdbæk] *n* rétroaction f ▷ *I need your feedback on my story.* J'ai besoin de ta rétroaction sur ma composition.

feel [fiːl] *vb* ❶ se sentir ▷ *I don't feel well.* Je ne me sens pas bien. ▷ *I feel a bit lonely.* Je me sens un peu seul. ❷ sentir ▷ *I didn't feel much pain.* Je n'ai presque rien senti. ❸ toucher

▷ *The doctor felt my forehead.* Le docteur m'a touché le front.; **I was feeling hungry.** J'avais faim.; **I was feeling cold, so I went inside.** J'avais froid, alors je suis rentré.; **I feel like... (want)** J'ai envie de... ▷ *Do you feel like an ice cream?* Tu as envie d'une crème glacée?

feeling ['fi:lɪŋ] n ❶ (physical) sensation *f* ▷ *a burning feeling* une sensation de brûlure ❷ (emotional) sentiment *m* ▷ *a feeling of satisfaction* un sentiment de satisfaction

feet [fi:t] *npl see* **foot**

fell [fel] *vb see* **fall**

felt [felt] *vb see* **feel**

felt pen *n* stylo-feutre *m*

female ['fi:meɪl] *adj* ❶ femelle *f* ▷ *a female animal* un animal femelle ❷ féminin ▷ *the female sex* le sexe féminin
▶ *n* (animal) femelle *f*

feminine ['femɪnɪn] *adj* féminin

feminist ['femɪnɪst] *n* féministe

fence [fens] *n* barrière *f*

fern [fɜ:n] *n* fougère *f*

ferret ['ferɪt] *n* furet *m*

ferry ['ferɪ] *n* traversier *m*

fertile ['fɜ:taɪl] *adj* fertile

fertilizer ['fɜ:tɪlaɪzə] *n* engrais *m*

festival ['festɪvəl] *n* festival *m* ▷ *a jazz festival* un festival de jazz

fetch [fetʃ] *vb* ❶ aller chercher ▷ *Fetch the bucket.* Va chercher le seau. ❷ (*sell for*) se vendre ▷ *His painting fetched $5000.* Son tableau s'est vendu cinq mille dollars.

fever ['fi:və] *n* (temperature) fièvre *f*

few [fju:] *adj, pron* (*not many*) peu de ▷ *few books* peu de livres; **a few (1)** quelques ▷ *a few hours* quelques heures **(2)** quelques-uns ▷ *"How many apples do you want?" — "A few."* « Tu veux combien de pommes? » — « Quelques-unes. »; **quite a few**

people pas mal de monde

fewer ['fju:ə] *adj* moins de ▷ *There are fewer people than there were yesterday.* Il y a moins de monde qu'hier. ▷ *There are fewer students in this class.* Il y a moins d'élèves dans cette classe.

fiancé [fɪ'ɑ̃:nseɪ] *n* fiancé *m*

fiancée [fɪ'ɑ̃:nseɪ] *n* fiancée *f*

fiction ['fɪkʃən] *n* (*novels*) romans *mpl*

field [fi:ld] *n* ❶ (*in countryside*) champ *m* ▷ *a field of wheat* un champ de blé ❷ (*for sport*) terrain *m* ▷ *a soccer field* un terrain de soccer ❸ (*subject*) domaine *m* ▷ *He's an expert in his field.* C'est un expert dans son domaine.; **a field trip** une sortie éducative

fierce [fɪəs] *adj* ❶ féroce ▷ *The dog looked very fierce.* Le chien avait l'air très féroce. ❷ violent ▷ *The wind was very fierce.* Le vent était très violent. ▷ *a fierce attack* une attaque violente

fifteen [fɪf'ti:n] *num* quinze ▷ *I'm fifteen.* J'ai quinze ans.

fifteenth [fɪf'ti:nθ] *adj* quinzième ▷ *the fifteenth floor* le quinzième étage; **the fifteenth of August** le quinze août

fifth [fɪfθ] *adj* cinquième ▷ *the fifth floor* le cinquième étage; **the fifth of August** le cinq août

fifty ['fɪftɪ] *num* cinquante ▷ *She's fifty.* Elle a cinquante ans.

fifty-fifty ['fɪftɪ'fɪftɪ] *adj, adv* moitié-moitié ▷ *They split the prize money fifty-fifty.* Ils ont partagé l'argent du prix moitié-moitié.; **a fifty-fifty chance** une chance sur deux

fight [faɪt] *n* ❶ bagarre *f* ▷ *There was a fight in the hallway.* Il y a eu une bagarre dans le couloir. ❷ lutte *f* ▷ *the fight against cancer* la lutte

contre le cancer
▶ vb ❶ se battre ▷ *They were fighting.* Ils se battaient. ❷ lutter contre ▷ *The doctors tried to fight the disease.* Les médecins ont essayé de lutter contre la maladie. ▷ *He fought against the urge to smoke.* Il a lutté contre son envie de fumer.

fighting ['faɪtɪŋ] *n* bagarres *fpl*
▷ *Fighting broke out in the schoolyard.* Des bagarres ont éclaté dans la cour de l'école.

figure ['fɪɡəʳ] *n* ❶ (number) chiffre *m* ▷ *Can you give me the exact figures?* Pouvez-vous me donner les chiffres exacts? ❷ (outline of person) silhouette *f* ▷ *I saw the figure of a man on the bridge.* J'ai vu la silhouette d'un homme sur le pont.; **I have to watch my figure.** Je dois faire attention à ma ligne. ❸ (personality) personnage *m* ▷ *She's an important political figure.* C'est un personnage politique important.

figure out *vb* ❶ calculer ▷ *I'll try to figure out how much it'll cost.* Je vais essayer de calculer combien ça va coûter. ❷ voir ▷ *I couldn't figure out what it meant.* Je n'arrivais pas à voir ce que ça voulait dire. ❸ cerner ▷ *I can't figure him out at all.* Je n'arrive pas du tout à le cerner.

figure skating *n* patinage artistique *m*

file [faɪl] *n* ❶ (document) dossier *m* ▷ *Have we got a file on the suspect?* Est-ce que nous avons un dossier sur le suspect? ❷ (on computer) fichier *m* ❸ (for nails, metal) lime *f*; **a file folder** une chemise
▶ *vb* ❶ (papers) classer ❷ (nails, metal) limer ▷ *to file one's nails* se limer les ongles

fill [fɪl] *vb* remplir ▷ *She filled the glass with water.* Elle a rempli le verre

d'eau.; **to fill in** boucher ▷ *He filled the hole in with soil.* Il a bouché le trou avec de la terre.; **to fill in for somebody** remplacer quelqu'un; **to fill out** remplir ▷ *Can you fill out this form, please?* Est-ce que vous pouvez remplir ce formulaire, s'il vous plaît?; **to fill up** remplir ▷ *She filled the cup up to the brim.* Elle a rempli la tasse à ras bords ; **Fill it up, please.** (at gas station) Le plein, s'il vous plaît.

film [fɪlm] *n* film *m*

filmmaker ['fɪlmmeɪkəʳ] *n* cinéaste

filthy ['fɪlθɪ] *adj* crasseux (f crasseuse)

final ['faɪnl] *adj* ❶ (last) dernier (f dernière) ▷ *our final farewells* nos derniers adieux ❷ (definite) définitif (f définitive) ▷ *a final decision* une décision définitive; **I'm not going and that's final.** Je n'y vais pas, un point c'est tout.
▶ *n* finale *f* ▷ *She's playing in the final.* Elle va disputer la finale.

finally ['faɪnəlɪ] *adv* ❶ (lastly) enfin ▷ *Finally, I would like to say...* Enfin, je voudrais dire... ❷ (eventually) finalement ▷ *They finally decided to leave on Saturday instead of Friday.* Ils ont finalement décidé de partir samedi au lieu de vendredi.

find [faɪnd] *vb* ❶ trouver ▷ *I can't find the exit.* Je ne trouve pas la sortie. ❷ (something lost) retrouver ▷ *Did you find your pen?* Est-ce que tu as retrouvé ton crayon?; **to find something out** découvrir quelque chose ▷ *I'm determined to find out the truth.* Je suis décidé à découvrir la vérité.; **to find out about (1)** (make enquiries) se renseigner ▷ *Try to find out about the price.* Essaye de te renseigner sur le prix. **(2)** (by chance) apprendre ▷ I found out about their secret plan. J'ai appris leur projet secret.

fine [faɪn] adj, adv ❶ (very good) excellent ▷ He's a fine musician. C'est un excellent musicien.; **to be fine** aller bien ▷ "How are you?" — "I'm fine." « Comment ça va? » — « Ça va bien. »; **I feel fine.** Je me sens bien.; **The weather is fine today.** Il fait beau aujourd'hui. ❷ (not coarse) fin ▷ She has very fine hair. Elle a les cheveux très fins.
▶ n ❶ amende f ▷ She got a $50 fine. Elle a eu une amende de cinquante dollars. ❷ (for traffic offence) contravention f ▷ I got a fine for driving through a red light. J'ai eu une contravention pour avoir grillé un feu rouge.

finger ['fɪŋgə] n doigt m; **my little finger** mon petit doigt

fingernail ['fɪŋgəneɪl] n ongle m

fingerprint ['fɪŋgəprɪnt] n empreinte f digitale

finish ['fɪnɪʃ] n (of race) arrivée f ▷ We saw the finish of the marathon. Nous avons vu l'arrivée du marathon.; **the finish line** la ligne d'arrivée; **a fight to the finish** un combat sans merci; **from start to finish** du début à la fin
▶ vb ❶ finir ▷ I've finished! J'ai fini!; **to finish doing something** finir de faire quelque chose ❷ terminer ▷ I've finished the book. J'ai terminé ce livre. ▷ The film has finished. Le film est terminé.

fir [fəːʳ] n sapin m; **Douglas fir** le douglas vert

fire ['faɪəʳ] n ❶ feu m (pl feux) ▷ He made a fire to warm himself. Il a fait du feu pour se réchauffer.; **to be on fire** être en feu ❷ (accidental) incendie m ▷ The house was destroyed by fire. La maison a été détruite par

un incendie.; **the fire department** les m pompiers; **a fire alarm** un avertisseur d'incendie; **a fire drill** un exercice d'incendie; **a fire engine** un camion d'incendie; **a fire escape** un escalier de secours; **a fire extinguisher** un extincteur; **a fire hydrant** une borne-fontaine (pl les bornes-fontaines); **a fire station** un poste de pompiers
▶ vb (shoot) tirer ▷ She fired twice. Elle a tiré deux fois.; **to fire at somebody** tirer sur quelqu'un ▷ The terrorist fired at the crowd. Le terroriste a tiré sur la foule.; **to fire a gun** tirer un coup de feu; **to fire somebody** mettre quelqu'un à la porte ▷ He was fired from his job. Il a été mis à la porte.

firefighter ['faɪəfaɪtəʳ] n pompier m, pompière f ▷ She's a firefighter. Elle est pompière.

fireplace ['faɪəpleɪs] n cheminée f

fireworks ['faɪəwəːks] npl feu m d'artifice ▷ Are you going to see the fireworks? Est-ce que tu vas voir le feu d'artifice?

firm [fəːm] adj ferme ▷ to be firm with somebody se montrer ferme avec quelqu'un
▶ n entreprise f ▷ She works for a large firm in Kitchener. Elle travaille pour une grande entreprise à Kitchener.

first [fəːst] adj, adv ❶ premier m (f première) ▷ the first of September le premier septembre ▷ the first time la première fois; **to come first** (in exam, race) arriver premier ▷ Who came first? Qui est arrivé premier? ❷ d'abord ▷ I want to get a job, but first I have to finish high school. Je veux trouver du travail, mais d'abord je dois finir mes études.; **first of all** tout d'abord
▶ n premier m, première f ▷ She was

the first to arrive. Elle est arrivée la première.; **at first** au début

first aid *n* premiers *mpl* soins; **a first aid kit** une trousse de premiers soins

first-class ['fɜːst'klɑːs] *adj* ❶ de première classe ▷ *He has booked a first-class ticket.* Il a réservé un billet de première classe. ❷ excellent ▷ *a first-class meal* un excellent repas

firstly ['fɜːstlɪ] *adv* premièrement ▷ *Firstly, let's see what the book is about.* Premièrement, voyons de quoi parle ce livre.

First Ministers *npl* premiers *mpl* ministres ▷ *a First Ministers' conference* une conférence des premiers ministres

First Nations *npl* Premières *fpl* Nations ▷ *the Assembly of First Nations* l'Assemblée des Premières Nations

fish [fɪʃ] *n* poisson *m* ▷ *I caught three fish.* J'ai pêché trois poissons. ▷ *I don't like fish.* Je n'aime pas le poisson.; **fish bone** l'arête *f*; **fish sticks** les *m* bâtonnets de poisson ▶ *vb* pêcher ▷ *to fish for trout* pêcher la truite; **to go fishing** aller à la pêche ▷ *We went fishing in the Miramichi River.* Nous sommes allés à la pêche sur la rivière Miramichi.

fisherman ['fɪʃəmən] *n* pêcheur *m*, pêcheuse *f* ▷ *She's a fisherman.* Elle est pêcheuse.

fishing ['fɪʃɪŋ] *n* pêche *f* ▷ *My hobby is fishing.* La pêche est mon passe-temps favori.

fishing boat ['fɪʃɪŋ-] *n* bateau de pêche *m*

fishing rod ['fɪʃɪŋ-] *n* canne à pêche *f*

fishing tackle ['fɪʃɪŋ-] *n* matériel de pêche

fist [fɪst] *n* poing *m*

fit [fɪt] *vb* ❶ (*be the right size*) être la

bonne taille ▷ *Does it fit?* Est-ce que c'est la bonne taille?

> In French you usually specify whether something is too big, small, tight etc.

These pants don't fit me.
(1) (*too big*) Ce pantalon est trop grand pour moi. (2) (*too small*) Ce pantalon est trop petit pour moi. ❷ (*match*) correspondre ▷ *That story doesn't fit with what he told us.* Cette histoire ne correspond pas à ce qu'il nous a dit. ❸ adapter ▷ *She fitted a plug to the hair dryer.* Elle a adapté une prise au sèche-cheveux.; **to fit in** s'adapter ▷ *She fits in well at her new school.* Elle s'est bien adaptée à sa nouvelle école.
▶ *adj* (*in condition*) en forme ▷ *He felt relaxed and fit after his holiday.* Il se sentait détendu et en forme après ses vacances.
▶ *n*: **to have a fit** (*be upset*) piquer une crise de nerfs ▷ *My mom will have a fit when she sees the carpet!* Ma mère va piquer une crise de nerfs quand elle va voir la moquette!; **a fit of coughing** une quinte de toux; **to be in fits of laughter** se tordre de rire

fitting room ['fɪtɪŋ-] *n* cabine d'essayage *f*

five [faɪv] *num* cinq ▷ *He's five.* Il a cinq ans.

fix [fɪks] *vb* ❶ (*mend*) réparer ▷ *Can you fix my bike?* Est-ce que tu peux réparer mon vélo? ❷ préparer ▷ *He fixed us a snack.* Il nous a préparé une collation.

fixed [fɪkst] *adj* fixe ▷ *at a fixed time* à une heure fixe ▷ *at a fixed price* à un prix fixe ▷ *a fixed-price menu* un menu à prix fixe; **My parents have very fixed ideas.** Mes parents ont des idées très arrêtées.

flabby ['flæbɪ] *adj* flasque

flag [flæg] n drapeau m (pl drapeaux)

flame [fleɪm] n flamme f

flap [flæp] vb ❶ (wings) battre de ▷ The bird flapped its wings. L'oiseau battait des ailes. ❷ (noisily) claquer ▷ The flags were flapping in the wind. Les drapeaux claquaient dans le vent.

flash [flæʃ] n flash m (pl flashes) ▷ Has your camera got a flash? Est-ce que ton appareil photo a un flash?; **a flash of lightning** un éclair; **in a flash** en un clin d'œil
▶ vb ❶ clignoter ▷ The police car's blue light was flashing. Le gyrophare de la voiture de police clignotait. ❷ projeter ▷ They flashed a light in his face. Ils lui ont projeté la lumière d'une lampe de poche en plein visage.; **She flashed her headlights.** Elle a fait un appel de phares.

flashlight ['flæʃlaɪt] n lampe de poche f

flat [flæt] adj, adv ❶ plat ▷ a flat roof un toit plat ❷ flat shoes des chaussures plates ❷ (tire) crevé ▷ I've got a flat tire. J'ai un pneu crevé. ❶ (music) faux ▷ We went flat in that last song. Nous avons chanté faux dans cette dernière chanson.; **B flat** si bémol

flatter ['flætər] vb flatter

flavour ['fleɪvər] n ❶ (taste) goût m ▷ It has a very strong flavour. Ça a un goût très fort. ❷ (variety) saveur f ▷ Which flavour of ice cream would you like? Quelle saveur de crème glacée est-ce que tu veux?

flavouring ['fleɪvərɪŋ] n arôme m

flea [fliː] n puce f; **a flea market** un marché aux puces

flew [fluː] vb see **fly**

flexible ['flɛksəbl] adj flexible ▷ flexible working hours les horaires

flexibles

flicker ['flɪkər] vb trembloter ▷ The light flickered. La lumière a trembloté.

flight [flaɪt] n vol m ▷ What time is the flight to Sault Ste. Marie? À quelle heure est le vol pour Sault Ste. Marie?; **a flight of stairs** un escalier

flight attendant [-ə'tɛndənt] n agent m de bord, agente f de bord

flip [flɪp] vb: **to flip a coin** tirer à pile ou face; **to flip through a book** feuilleter un livre; **Flip the card over.** Retourne la carte.

flippers ['flɪpəz] n ❶ (for people) palmes fpl ❷ (on animals) nageoires fpl

float [fləʊt] vb flotter ▷ A leaf was floating on the water. Une feuille flottait sur l'eau.

flock [flɒk] n: **a flock of sheep** un troupeau de moutons; **a flock of birds** un vol d'oiseaux

flood [flʌd] n ❶ inondation f ▷ The rain has caused many floods. La pluie a provoqué de nombreuses inondations. ❷ flot m ▷ He received a flood of letters. Il a reçu un flot de lettres.
▶ vb ❶ déborder ▷ The river has flooded. La rivière a débordé. ❷ inonder ▷ The river has flooded the village. La rivière a inondé le village.

flooding ['flʌdɪŋ] n inondations fpl

floor [flɔːr] n ❶ plancher m ▷ a hardwood floor un plancher de bois franc; **on the floor** par terre ❷ (storey) étage m ▷ the fourth floor le quatrième étage; **the ground floor** le premier étage; **on the third floor** au troisième étage

flop [flɒp] n fiasco m ▷ The movie was a flop. Le film a été un fiasco.

floppy disk ['flɒpɪ-] n disquette f

florist ['flɒrɪst] n fleuriste m

flour ['flaʊər] n farine f

flow [fləʊ] *vb* **❶** (*river*) couler **❷** (*flow out*) s'écouler ▷ *Water was flowing from the pipe.* De l'eau s'écoulait du tuyau.

flower ['flaʊə^r] *n* fleur *f*

flown [fləʊn] *vb see* **fly**

flu [fluː] *n* grippe *f* ▷ *She has the flu.* Elle a la grippe.; H1N1 flu grippe H1N1 *f*

fluent ['fluːənt] *adj*: **She speaks fluent French.** Elle parle couramment le français.

flung [flʌŋ] *vb see* **fling**

flush [flʌʃ] *vb*: **to flush the toilet** tirer la chasse

flute [fluːt] *n* flûte *f* ▷ *I play the flute.* Je joue de la flûte.

fly [flaɪ] *n* **❶** (*insect*) mouche *f* **❷** (*on pants*) braguette *f* **❸** (*on tent*) double toit *m*
  ▶ *vb* **❶** voler ▷ *The plane flies at a speed of 400 km per hour.* L'avion vole à quatre cents kilomètres à l'heure. **❷** (*passenger*) aller en avion ▷ *He flew from Goose Bay to Charlottetown.* Il est allé de Goose Bay à Charlottetown en avion.; **to fly away** s'envoler ▷ *The bird flew away.* L'oiseau s'est envolé.

foal [fəʊl] *n* poulain *m*

focus ['fəʊkəs] *n*: **to be out of focus** être flou ▷ *The house is out of focus in this photo.* La maison est floue sur cette photo.
  ▶ *vb* mettre au point ▷ *Try to focus the binoculars.* Essaye de mettre les jumelles au point.; **to focus on something (1)** (*with lens*) régler la mise au point sur quelque chose ▷ *The photographer focused on the bird.* La photographe a réglé la mise au point sur l'oiseau. **(2)** (*concentrate*) se concentrer sur quelque chose ▷ *Let's focus on the plot of the play.* Concentrons-nous sur l'intrigue de la pièce.

fog [fɔɡ] *n* brouillard *m*

foggy ['fɔɡɪ] *adj*: **It's foggy.** Il y a du brouillard.; **a foggy day** un jour de brouillard

foil [fɔɪl] *n* (*kitchen foil*) papier d'aluminium *m* ▷ *She wrapped the meat in foil.* Elle a enveloppé la viande dans du papier d'aluminium.

fold [fəʊld] *n* pli *m*
  ▶ *vb* plier ▷ *He folded the newspaper in half.* Il a plié le journal en deux.; **to fold something up** plier quelque chose; **to fold one's arms** croiser ses bras ▷ *She folded her arms.* Elle a croisé les bras.

folder ['fəʊldə^r] *n* **❶** chemise *f* ▷ *She kept all her letters in a folder.* Elle gardait toutes ses lettres dans une chemise. **❷** (*computer*) dossier *m*

folding ['fəʊldɪŋ] *adj*: **a folding chair** une chaise pliante; **a folding bed** un lit pliant

follow ['fɒləʊ] *vb* suivre ▷ *She followed him.* Elle l'a suivi. ▷ *You go first and I'll follow.* Va devant, je te suis.

following ['fɒləʊɪŋ] *adj* suivant ▷ *the following day* le jour suivant

fond [fɒnd] *adj*: **to be fond of somebody** aimer beaucoup quelqu'un ▷ *I'm very fond of him.* Je l'aime beaucoup.

font [fɒnt] *n* police de caractères *f*

food [fuːd] *n* nourriture *f*; **We need to buy some food.** Nous devons acheter à manger.; **cat food** la nourriture pour chat; **dog food** la nourriture pour chien; **a food bank** une banque alimentaire; **the food chain** la chaîne alimentaire; **food poisoning** l'intoxication *f* alimentaire

food processor [-'prəʊsɛsə^r] *n* robot *m*

fool [fuːl] *n* idiot *m*, idiote *f*
  ▶ *vb* **❶** (*tease*) plaisanter ▷ *I'm only fooling.* Je ne fais que plaisanter.

❷ (trick) duper ▷ You can't fool me.
Tu ne me duperas pas.; **to fool
around (1)** (waste time) perdre son
temps ▷ Stop fooling around and get
to work. Arrêtez de perdre votre
temps et mettez-vous au travail.
(2) (do silly things) faire des bêtises
(3) (with something) toucher à
▷ Don't fool around with drugs. Ne
touche pas à la drogue.

foolproof ['fuːlpruːf] adj infaillible

foosball ['fuːzbɔːl] n baby-foot m

foot [fut] n ❶ (of person) pied m
▷ My feet are aching. J'ai mal aux
pieds. ❷ (of animal) patte f ▷ The
dog's foot was injured. Le chien était
blessé à la patte.; **on foot** à pied
❸ (12 inches) pied m; **My dad is
6 feet tall.** Mon père mesure un
mètre quatre-vingt.

A **foot** is a nonmetric unit of
length equal to about 30 cm.

football ['futbɔːl] n ❶ (game)
football m ▷ I like playing football.
J'aime jouer au football. ❷ (ball)
ballon m ▷ I threw the football over
the fence. J'ai envoyé le ballon par
dessus la clôture.

footer ['futə'] n (word processing)
pied de page m

footprint ['futprɪnt] n trace de
pas f ▷ He saw some footprints in the
snow. Il a vu des traces de pas sur
la neige.

footstep ['futstɛp] n pas m ▷ I can
hear footsteps on the stairs. J'entends
des pas dans l'escalier.

for [fɔː'] prep

There are several ways of
translating **for**. Scan the
examples to find one that
is similar to what you want
to say.

❶ pour ▷ a present for me un cadeau
pour moi ▷ the bus for Sherbrooke
l'autobus pour Sherbrooke ▷ He

works for the government. Il travaille
pour le gouvernement. ▷ I'll do it for
you. Je vais le faire pour toi. ▷ Can
you do it for tomorrow? Est-ce que
vous pouvez le faire pour demain?
▷ Are you for or against the idea?
Êtes-vous pour ou contre cette
idée? ▷ The Bay of Fundy is famous
for its high tides. La baie de Fundy
est célèbre pour la hauteur de ses
marées.

When referring to periods of
time, use **pendant** for the
future and completed actions
in the past, and **depuis** (with
the French verb in the present
tense) for something that
started in the past and is still
going on.

❷ pendant ▷ He worked in France
for two years. Il a travaillé en France
pendant deux ans. ▷ She will be
away for a month. Elle sera absente
pendant un mois. ❸ depuis ▷ I've
been learning French for two years.
J'apprends le français depuis deux
ans. ▷ She's been away for a month.
Elle est absente depuis un mois.

You do not translate **for** after
sell or **buy**.

▷ I sold it for 50 dollars. Je l'ai vendu
cinquante dollars. ▷ He paid five
dollars for his ticket. Il a payé son
billet cinq dollars.; **What's the
French for "lion"?** Comment dit-on
"lion" en français?; **It's time for
lunch.** C'est l'heure du déjeuner.;
What for? Pour quoi faire? ▷ "Give
me some money!" — "What for?"
« Donne-moi de l'argent! » — « Pour
quoi faire? »; **What's it for?** Ça sert
à quoi?; **for sale** à vendre ▷ Their
house is for sale. Leur maison est
à vendre.

forbid [fə'bɪd] vb défendre;
to forbid somebody to do

something défendre à quelqu'un de faire quelque chose ▷ *I forbid you to go out tonight!* Je te défends de sortir ce soir.

forbidden [fəˈbɪdn] *adj* défendu ▷ *Smoking is strictly forbidden.* Il est strictement défendu de fumer.

force [fɔːs] *n* force f ▷ *the force of the explosion* la force de l'explosion; **in force** en vigueur ▷ *No-smoking rules are now in force.* Un règlement qui interdit de fumer est maintenant en vigueur.
▶ *vb* forcer ▷ *They forced her to open the safe.* Ils l'ont obligée à ouvrir le coffre-fort.

forecast [ˈfɔːkɑːst] *n*: **the weather forecast** la météo

foreground [ˈfɔːɡraʊnd] *n* premier plan *m* ▷ *in the foreground* au premier plan

forehead [ˈfɒrɪd] *n* front *m*

foreign [ˈfɒrɪn] *adj* étranger (f étrangère)

foresee [fɔːˈsiː] *vb* prévoir ▷ *She had foreseen the problem.* Elle avait prévu ce problème.

forest [ˈfɒrɪst] *n* forêt f

forestry [ˈfɒrɪstrɪ] *n* foresterie f ▷ *He wants to study forestry.* Il veut étudier en foresterie.

forever [fəˈrɛvəʳ] *adv* ❶ pour toujours ▷ *He's gone forever.* Il est parti pour toujours. ❷ (*always*) toujours ▷ *You're forever complaining.* Tu es toujours en train de te plaindre.

forgave, forgiven [fəˈɡeɪv, fəˈɡɪvn] *vb see* **forgive**

forge [fɔːdʒ] *vb* contrefaire ▷ *She tried to forge his signature.* Elle a essayé de contrefaire sa signature.

forged [fɔːdʒd] *adj* faux (f fausse) ▷ *forged banknotes* des faux billets

forget [fəˈɡɛt] *vb* oublier ▷ *I've forgotten his name.* J'ai oublié son

nom. ▷ *I'm sorry, I completely forgot!* Je suis désolé, j'ai complètement oublié!

forgive [fəˈɡɪv] *vb*: **to forgive somebody** pardonner à quelqu'un ▷ *I forgive you.* Je te pardonne.; **to forgive somebody for doing something** pardonner à quelqu'un d'avoir fait quelque chose ▷ *He forgave her for forgetting his birthday.* Il lui a pardonné d'avoir oublié son anniversaire.

forgot, forgotten [fəˈɡɒt, fəˈɡɒtn] *vb see* **forget**

fork [fɔːk] *n* ❶ (*for eating*) fourchette f ❷ (*for gardening*) fourche f ❸ (*in road*) bifurcation f

form [fɔːm] *n* ❶ (*paper*) formulaire *m* ▷ *to fill in a form* remplir un formulaire ❷ (*type*) forme f ▷ *I'm against hunting in any form.* Je suis contre la chasse sous toutes ses formes.; **in top form** en pleine forme

formal [ˈfɔːməl] *adj* ❶ (*occasion*) officiel (f officielle) ▷ *a formal dinner* un dîner officiel ❷ (*person*) guindé ❸ (*language*) soutenu ▷ *In English, "residence" is a formal term.* En anglais, "residence" est un terme soutenu.; **formal clothes** une tenue habillée; **She has no formal education.** Elle n'a pas fait beaucoup d'études.

format [ˈfɔːmæt] *vb* formater ▷ *to format a document* formater un document

formatting [ˈfɔːmætɪŋ] *n* formatage m

former [ˈfɔːməʳ] *adj* ancien (f ancienne) ▷ *a former student* un ancien élève ▷ *the former Prime Minister* l'ancien Premier ministre

formerly [ˈfɔːməlɪ] *adv* autrefois

fort [fɔːt] *n* fort *m*

forth [fɔːθ] *adv*: **to go back and**

forth aller et venir; **and so forth** et ainsi de suite

fortunate ['fɔːtʃənɪt] *adj*: **to be fortunate** avoir de la chance ▷ *He was extremely fortunate to survive.* Il a eu énormément de chance de survivre.; **It's fortunate that I remembered the map.** C'est une chance que j'aie pris la carte.

fortunately ['fɔːtʃənɪtlɪ] *adv* heureusement ▷ *Fortunately, it didn't rain.* Heureusement, il n'a pas plu.

fortune ['fɔːtʃən] *n* fortune *f* ▷ *She earns a fortune!* Elle gagne une fortune!; **to tell somebody's fortune** dire la bonne aventure à quelqu'un

forty ['fɔːtɪ] *num* quarante ▷ *He's forty.* Il a quarante ans.

forward ['fɔːwəd] *adv*: **to move forward** avancer
▶ *vb* faire suivre ▷ *He forwarded all my letters.* Il a fait suivre toutes mes lettres.

forward slash [-slæʃ] *n* barre oblique *f*

foster ['fɒstə] *vb*: **She has fostered more than fifteen children.** Elle a placé quinze enfants chez elle.

foster child *n* enfant *m* placé en foyer nourricier, enfant *f* placée en foyer nourricier

fought [fɔːt] *vb see* **fight**

foul [faul] *adj* infect ▷ *The weather was foul.* Le temps était infect. ▷ *What a foul smell!* Quelle odeur infecte!
▶ *n* faute *f* ▷ *Their goalie committed a foul.* Leur gardienne de but a fait une faute.

found [faund] *vb see* **find**
▶ *vb* fonder ▷ *John Graves Simcoe founded the town of York.* John Graves Simcoe a fondé la ville de York.

foundations [faun'deɪʃəns] *npl* fondations *fpl*

fountain ['fauntɪn] *n* fontaine *f*

four [fɔː] *num* quatre ▷ *She's four.* Elle a quatre ans.

fourteen ['fɔː'tiːn] *num* quatorze ▷ *I'm fourteen.* J'ai quatorze ans.

fourteenth ['fɔː'tiːnθ] *adj* quatorzième ▷ *the fourteenth floor* le quatorzième étage; **the fourteenth of August** le quatorze août

fourth ['fɔːθ] *adj* quatrième ▷ *the fourth floor* le quatrième étage

fox [fɒks] *n* renard *m*; **a fox cub** un renardeau

fragile ['frædʒaɪl] *adj* fragile

frame [freɪm] *n* (*for picture*) cadre *m*; **glasses frames** la monture de lunettes

Francophone ['frænkəfəun] *adj* francophone ▷ *a Francophone community* une communauté francophone
▶ *n* francophone ▷ *She's a Francophone.* C'est une francophone.

frankly ['frænklɪ] *adv* franchement ▷ *He spoke to me frankly.* Il m'a parlé franchement.

frantic ['fræntɪk] *adj*: **I was going frantic.** J'étais dans tous mes états.; **to be frantic with worry** être folle d'inquiétude; **a frantic attempt** un essai désespéré

fraud [frɔːd] *n* ❶ (*crime*) fraude *f* ▷ *He was jailed for fraud.* On l'a mis en prison pour fraude. ❷ (*person*) imposteur *m* ▷ *He's not a real doctor, he's a fraud.* Ce n'est pas un vrai médecin, c'est un imposteur.

freckles ['freklz] *npl* taches *fpl* de rousseur

free [friː] *adj* ❶ (*free of charge*) gratuit ▷ *a free brochure* une brochure gratuite ❷ (*not busy, not*

taken) libre ▷ Is this seat free? Est-ce que cette place est libre? ▷ Are you free after school? Tu es libre après l'école?
▷ vb libérer

freedom ['fri:dəm] n liberté f

free trade n libre-échange m

freeware ['fri:wɛə'] n gratuiciel m

freeze [fɪːɪ] vb ① geler ▷ The water had frozen. L'eau avait gelé. ② (food) congeler ▷ We froze the rest of the raspberries. Nous avons congelé le reste des framboises. ③ (stop moving) se figer; **Freeze!** Pas un geste!

freezer ['fri:zə'] n congélateur m

freeze-up ['fri:zʌp] n saison du gel f ▷ We have to close the cottage before freeze-up. Nous devons fermer le chalet avant la saison du gel.

freezing ['fri:zɪŋ] adj: **It's freezing!** Il fait un froid de canard! (informal); **I'm freezing!** (informal) Je suis gelé!; **3 degrees below freezing** moins trois

freight [freɪt] n (goods) cargaison f; **a freight train** un train de marchandises

French [frɛntʃ] adj français m ▷ a French song une chanson en français ▶ n (language) français m ▷ Do you speak French? Est-ce que tu parles français?; **the French** (people) les Français

French-Canadian ['frɛntʃkə'neɪdɪən] adj canadien-français (f canadienne-française) ▷ a French-Canadian family une famille canadienne-française ▶ n Canadien français m, Canadienne française f ▷ She married a French-Canadian. Elle a épousé un Canadien français.

French fries npl frites fpl

French horn n cor (d'harmonie) m ▷ I play the French horn. Je joue

du cor.

French stick n baguette f

French toast n pain doré m

French windows npl porte-fenêtre f (pl portes-fenêtres)

frequent [frɪ'kwɛnt] adj fréquent ▷ frequent showers des averses fréquentes; **There are frequent buses to the town centre.** Il y a beaucoup d'autobus pour le centre-ville.; **He's a frequent visitor here.** C'est un habitué ici.

fresh [frɛʃ] adj frais (f fraîche) ▷ I need some fresh air. J'ai besoin de prendre l'air.

fret [frɛt] vb se tracasser ▷ He was fretting about his exams. Il se tracassait au sujet de ses examens.

Friday ['fraɪdɪ] n vendredi m ▷ on Friday vendredi ▷ on Fridays le vendredi ▷ every Friday tous les vendredis ▷ last Friday vendredi dernier ▷ next Friday vendredi prochain

fridge [frɪdʒ] n frigo m

fried [fraɪd] adj frit ▷ fried mushrooms des champignons frits; **a fried egg** un œuf sur le plat

friend [frɛnd] n ami m, amie f ▶ vb (on Internet) ajouter comme ami(e)

friendly ['frɛndlɪ] adj ① gentil (f gentille) ▷ She's really friendly. Elle est vraiment gentille. ② accueillant ▷ Kitchener is a very friendly city. Kitchener est une ville très accueillante.

friendship ['frɛndʃɪp] n amitié f

fries [fraɪz] npl frites f

fright [fraɪt] n peur f ▷ I got a terrible fright! Ça m'a fait une peur terrible!

frighten ['fraɪtn] vb faire peur à ▷ Horror films frighten him. Les films d'horreur lui font peur.

frightening ['fraɪtnɪŋ] adj effrayant

fringe [frɪndʒ] n (on rug, clothing)
frange f
Frisbee® ['frɪzbɪ] n Frisbee® m
▷ to play Frisbee jouer au Frisbee
fro [frəʊ] adv: **to go to and fro**
aller et venir
frog [frɒg] n grenouille f
from [frɒm] prep de ▷ Where do
you come from? D'où venez-vous?
▷ I come from Cape Breton Island. Je
viens de l'île du Cap-Breton. ▷ a
letter from my sister une lettre de ma
sœur ▷ The hotel is one kilometre from
the beach. L'hôtel est à un kilomètre
de la plage.; **from ... to ... de ... à ...**
▷ He drove from Lethbridge to Swift
Current. Il a conduit de Lethbridge
à Swift Current. ▷ from 1 o'clock to
2 d'une heure à deux heures ▷ The
price was reduced from $10 to $5. Ils
ont réduit le prix de dix dollars à
cinq.; **from ... onwards** à partir
de... ▷ We'll be at home from 7 o'clock
onwards. Nous serons chez nous à
partir de sept heures.
front [frʌnt] n ❶ devant m ▷ the
front of the house le devant de la
maison; **in front** devant m ▷ a
house with a car in front une maison
avec une voiture devant ▷ the car in
front la voiture de devant; **in front
of** devant m ▷ in front of the house
devant la maison ▷ the car in front
of us la voiture devant nous; **in the
front** (of car) à l'avant ▷ I was sitting
in the front. J'étais assis à l'avant.;
at the front of the class à l'avant
de la classe ❸ (of body) ventre m
▷ to lie on one's front se coucher sur
le ventre
▶ adj ❶ de devant ❷ the front row
la rangée de devant ❷ avant ▷ the
front seats of the car les sièges avant
de la voiture; **the front door** la
porte d'entrée
frontier ['frʌntɪə*] n frontière f

frost [frɒst] n gel m
frosting ['frɒstɪŋ] n glaçage m
frosty ['frɒstɪ] adj: **It's frosty
today.** Il gèle aujourd'hui.
frown [fraʊn] vb froncer les
sourcils ▷ He frowned. Il a froncé
les sourcils.
froze [frəʊz] vb see **freeze**
frozen ['frəʊzn] adj ❶ gelé ▷ the
frozen pond l'étang gelé ❷ (food)
congelé ▷ frozen vegetables des
légumes congelés
fruit [fruːt] n fruit m; **fruit juice**
le jus de fruits; **a fruit salad** une
salade de fruits
frustrated [frʌs'treɪtɪd] adj frustré
fry [fraɪ] vb faire frire ▷ Fry the
onions for 5 minutes. Faites frire les
oignons pendant cinq minutes.
frying pan ['fraɪɪŋ-] n poêle f
fudge [fʌdʒ] n fudge m
fuel [fjʊəl] n (for car, plane)
carburant m ▷ to run out of fuel avoir
une panne de carburant
fuel-efficient [fjʊəl'fɪʃənt] adj
économique
fulfill [fʊl'fɪl] vb réaliser ▷ He
fulfilled his dream to visit China. Il a
réalisé son rêve de visiter la Chine.
full [fʊl] adj, adv ❶ plein ▷ The
tank's full. Le réservoir est plein.
❷ complet (f complète) ▷ She asked
for full information on the job. Elle
a demandé des renseignements
complets sur le poste.; **your
full name** vos nom et prénoms
▷ My full name is Ian John Marr. Je
m'appelle Ian John Marr.; **I'm full.**
(after meal) J'ai bien mangé.; **at full
speed** à toute vitesse ▷ She drove
at full speed. Elle conduisait à toute
vitesse.; **There was a full moon.**
C'était la pleine lune.; **a full house**
(for performance) une salle comble
full-time ['fʊltaɪm] adj, adv à plein
temps ▷ She has a full-time job. Elle a

un travail à plein temps. ▷ *She works full-time.* Elle travaille à plein temps.

fully ['fʊlɪ] *adv* complètement ▷ *He hasn't fully recovered from his illness.* Il n'est pas complètement remis de sa maladie.

fumes [fjuːmz] *npl* fumées *fpl* ▷ *The factory gave out dangerous fumes.* L'usine rejetait des fumées dangereuses.; **exhaust fumes** les gaz d'échappement

fun [fʌn] *adj* amusant ▷ *This is a fun book.* Ce livre est très amusant.; **She's a fun person.** On s'amuse bien avec elle.
▶ *n*: **to have fun** s'amuser ▷ *We had a lot of fun playing in the snow.* Nous nous sommes bien amusés à jouer dans la neige.; **for fun** pour rire ▷ *He entered the competition just for fun.* Il a participé à la compétition juste pour rire.; **to make fun of somebody** se moquer de quelqu'un ▷ *They made fun of her.* Ils se sont moqués d'elle.; **It's fun!** C'est amusant!; **Have fun!** Amuse-toi bien!

funds [fʌndz] *npl* fonds *mpl* ▷ *to raise funds* collecter des fonds

funeral ['fjuːnərəl] *n* funérailles *fpl*; **funeral home** le salon funéraire

funny ['fʌnɪ] *adj* ❶ (*amusing*) drôle ▷ *It was really funny.* C'était vraiment drôle. ❷ (*strange*) bizarre ▷ *There's something funny about him.* Il est un peu bizarre.; **to taste funny** avoir un drôle de goût

fur [fəː] *n* ❶ fourrure *f* ▷ *a fur coat* un manteau de fourrure ❷ poil *m* ▷ *the dog's fur* le poil du chien

furious ['fjʊərɪəs] *adj* furieux (*f* furieuse) ▷ *Dad was furious with me.* Papa était furieux contre moi.

furniture ['fəːnɪtʃə] *n* meubles *mpl* ▷ *a piece of furniture* un meuble; **to be part of the furniture** faire parti

du décor

further ['fəːðə] *adv, adj* plus loin ▷ *Moncton is further from Halifax than Truro is.* Moncton est plus loin de Halifax que Truro.; **How much further is it?** C'est encore loin?

fuse [fjuːz] *n* fusible *m* ▷ *The fuse has blown.* Le fusible a sauté.

fuss [fʌs] *n* agitation *f* ▷ *What's all the fuss about?* Qu'est ce que c'est que toute cette agitation?; **to make a fuss** faire des histoires ▷ *He's always making a fuss about nothing.* Il fait toujours des histoires pour rien.

fussy ['fʌsɪ] *adj* difficile ▷ *She is very fussy about her food.* Elle est très difficile sur la nourriture.

future ['fjuːtʃə] *n* ❶ avenir *m* ▷ *What are your plans for the future?* Quels sont vos projets pour l'avenir?; **in future** à l'avenir ▷ *Be more careful in future.* Sois plus prudent à l'avenir. ❷ (*in grammar*) futur *m* ▷ *Put this sentence into the future.* Mettez cette phrase au futur.

futuristic [fjuːtʃə'rɪstɪk] *adj* futuriste

g

gadget ['gædʒɪt] n gadget m
▷ *electronic gadgets* les gadgets
électroniques

gain [geɪn] vb gagner; **to gain
weight** prendre du poids; **to gain
speed** prendre de la vitesse

gallery ['gælərɪ] n musée m ▷ *an
art gallery* un musée d'art

gallop ['gæləp] vb galoper

gamble ['gæmbl] vb jouer ▷ *He
gambled $100 at the casino.* Il a joué
cent dollars au casino.

gambler ['gæmblə'] n joueur m,
joueuse f

game [geɪm] n ❶ jeu m (pl jeux)
▷ *The children were playing a game.*
Les enfants jouaient à un jeu.
❷ match m ▷ *a game of football* un
match de football; **a game of cards**
une partie de cartes

gang [gæŋ] n bande f

gangster ['gæŋstə'] n gangster m

gap [gæp] n ❶ trou m ▷ *There's a
gap in the hedge.* Il y a un trou dans la
haie. ❷ intervalle m ▷ *a gap of four
years* un intervalle de quatre ans

garage ['gærɑːʒ] n garage m; **a
garage sale** une vente-débarras

garbage ['gɑːbɪdʒ] n ordures fpl;
garbage can la poubelle

garden ['gɑːdn] n jardin m

gardener ['gɑːdnə'] n jardinier m,
jardinière f ▷ *He's a gardener.* Il est
jardinier.

gardening ['gɑːdnɪŋ] n jardinage
m ▷ *She loves gardening.* Elle aime le
jardinage.

garlic ['gɑːlɪk] n ail m

garment ['gɑːmənt] n vêtement m

gas [gæs] n ❶ gaz m; **a gas stove**
une cuisinière à gaz; **a gas leak** une
fuite de gaz ❷ (*gasoline*) essence
f; **to be out of gas** avoir une panne
d'essence

gasoline ['gæsəliːn] n essence f

gas station n station-service f

gate [geɪt] n ❶ (*of garden*) grille f
❷ (*of field*) barrière f ❸ (*at airport*)
porte f

gather ['gæðə'] vb ❶ (*assemble*)
se rassembler ▷ *People gathered
on Parliament Hill.* Les gens se
sont rassemblés sur la Colline du
Parlement. ❷ (*things*) ramasser
▷ *to gather wood for a fire* ramasser
du bois à brûler ▷ *He gathered up
his things and left.* Il a ramassé ses
affaires et est parti.; **I gather she
isn't coming.** Je crois comprendre
qu'elle ne viendra pas.; **to gather
dust** prendre la poussière; **to
gather speed** prendre de la vitesse
▷ *The train gathered speed.* Le train a
pris de la vitesse.

gave [geɪv] vb see **give**

gay [geɪ] adj homosexuel (f
homosexuelle)

gaze [geɪz] vb: **to gaze at
something** fixer quelque chose du

regard ▷ He gazed at her. Il l'a fixée du regard.

gear [gɪə^r] n **1** (car, bike) vitesse f ▷ in first gear en première vitesse ▷ to change gear changer de vitesse **2** matériel m ▷ camping gear le matériel de camping

gearshift ['gɪəʃɪft] n levier de vitesse m

geese [giːs] npl see **goose**

gel [dʒɛl] n gel m; **hair gel** le gel pour les cheveux

gem [dʒɛm] n pierre précieuse f

Gemini ['dʒɛmɪnaɪ] n Gémeaux mpl ▷ I'm a Gemini. Je suis Gémeaux.

gender ['dʒɛndə^r] n **1** (of person) sexe m **2** (of noun) genre m

gene [dʒiːn] n gène m

general ['dʒɛnərl] adj général (mpl généraux); **in general** en général

general election n élection f générale

general knowledge n connaissances fpl générales

generally ['dʒɛnrəlɪ] adv généralement ▷ I generally go shopping on Saturday. Généralement, je fais mon magasinage le samedi.

generation [dʒɛnə'reɪʃən] n génération f ▷ the younger generation la nouvelle génération

generator ['dʒɛnəreɪtə^r] n générateur m

generous ['dʒɛnərəs] adj généreux (f généreuse) ▷ That's very generous of you. C'est très généreux de votre part.

genetic [dʒɪ'nɛtɪk] adj génétique f

genetically-modified [dʒɪ'nɛtɪklɪ'mɔdɪfaɪd] adj génétiquement modifié

genetics [dʒɪ'nɛtɪks] n génétique f

genius ['dʒiːnɪəs] n génie m ▷ She's a genius! C'est un génie!

gentle ['dʒɛntl] adj doux (f douce)

gentleman ['dʒɛntlmən] n monsieur m (pl messieurs) ▷ Good morning, gentlemen. Bonjour messieurs.

gently ['dʒɛntlɪ] adv doucement

genuine ['dʒɛnjuɪn] adj **1** (real) véritable ▷ These are genuine diamonds. Ce sont de véritables diamants. **2** (sincere) sincère ▷ She's a very genuine person. C'est quelqu'un de très sincère.

geography [dʒɪ'ɔgrəfɪ] n géographie f

gerbil ['dʒəːbɪl] n gerbille f

germ [dʒəːm] n microbe m

gesture ['dʒɛstjə^r] n geste m
▶ vb: **She gestured towards the door.** Elle a désigné la porte d'un geste.; **He gestured to us to stand up.** Il nous a fait signe de nous lever.

get [gɛt] vb

> There are several ways of translating **get**. Scan the examples to find one that is similar to what you want to say.

1 (have, receive) avoir ▷ I got lots of presents. J'ai eu beaucoup de cadeaux. ▷ He got first prize. Il a eu le premier prix. ▷ She got good exam results. Elle a eu de bons résultats aux examens. ▷ How many have you got? Combien en avez-vous? **2** (fetch) aller chercher ▷ Quick, get help! Allez vite chercher de l'aide! **3** (catch) attraper ▷ They've got the thief. Ils ont attrapé le voleur. **4** (train, bus) prendre ▷ I'm getting the bus into town. Je prends l'autobus pour aller en ville. **5** (understand) comprendre ▷ I don't get it. Je ne comprends pas. **6** (go) aller ▷ How do you get to the library? Comment est-ce qu'on va à la bibliothèque? **7** (arrive) arriver ▷ He should get here soon. Il devrait arriver bientôt. ❽ (become) devenir ▷ to get old devenir vieux; **to get along with somebody** s'entendre avec quelqu'un ▷ He doesn't get along with his parents. Il ne s'entend pas avec ses parents. ▷ We got along really well. Nous nous sommes très bien entendus.; **to get at (1)** (reach) atteindre **(2)** (touch) toucher à; **to get away with something** faire quelque chose impunément ▷ He got away with skipping class. Il a fait l'école buissonnière impunément.; **to get something done** faire faire quelque chose ▷ to get one's hair cut se faire couper les cheveux; **to get something for somebody** trouver quelque chose pour quelqu'un ▷ The librarian got the book for me. Le bibliothécaire m'a trouvé le livre.; **to have got to do something** devoir faire quelque chose ▷ I've got to tell him. Je dois le lui dire.; **to get away** s'échapper ▷ One of the burglars got away. L'un des cambrioleurs s'est échappé.; **to get back (1)** rentrer ▷ What time did you get back? Tu es rentrée à quelle heure? **(2)** récupérer ▷ He got his money back. Il a récupéré son argent.; **to get in** rentrer ▷ What time did you get in last night? Tu es rentré à quelle heure hier soir?; **to get into** monter dans ▷ She got into the car. Elle est montée dans la voiture.; **to get off** (vehicle, bike) descendre de ▷ I got off the train. Je suis descendue du train.; **to get on** (vehicle) monter dans ▷ She got on the bus. Elle est montée dans l'autobus. **(2)** (bike) enfourcher ▷ He got on his bike. Il a enfourché son vélo.; **to get out** sortir ▷ She got out of the car. Elle est sortie de la voiture. ▷ Get out! Sortez!; **to get something out** sortir quelque

chose ▷ She got the map out. Elle a sorti la carte.; **to get over (1)** se remettre ▷ It took her a long time to get over the illness. Il lui a fallu longtemps pour se remettre de sa maladie. **(2)** surmonter ▷ He managed to get over the problem. Il a réussi à résoudre le problème.; **to get through to someone** réussir à communiquer avec quelqu'un ▷ I tried to phone her but couldn't get through. J'ai essayé de lui téléphoner, mais je n'ai pas réussi à la joindre.; **to get together** se retrouver ▷ Could we get together this evening? Pourrait-on se retrouver ce soir?; **to get up** se lever ▷ What time do you get up? Tu te lèves à quelle heure?

ghost [gəʊst] n fantôme m

giant ['dʒaɪənt] adj énorme ▷ They ate a giant meal. Ils ont mangé un énorme repas.
▶ n géant m, géante f

gift [gɪft] n ❶ (present) cadeau m (pl cadeaux); **a gift certificate** un chèque-cadeau ❷ (talent) don m; **to have a gift for something** être doué pour quelque chose ▷ My brother has a gift for painting. Mon frère est doué pour la peinture.

gifted ['gɪftɪd] adj doué ▷ She is a gifted dancer. Elle est douée pour la danse.

gift shop n boutique de cadeaux

gigabyte ['dʒɪɡəbaɪt] n gigaoctet m

gigantic [dʒaɪˈɡæntɪk] adj gigantesque

giggle ['ɡɪɡl] vb avoir le fou rire ▷ Every time I look at her, she giggles. Chaque fois que je la regarde, elle a le fou rire.

ginger ['dʒɪndʒə°] n gingembre m ▷ Add a teaspoon of ginger. Ajoutez une cuillère à café de gingembre.

giraffe [dʒɪˈrɑːf] n girafe f
girl [gɜːl] n ❶ fille f ▷ They have a girl and two boys. Ils ont une fille et deux garçons. ❷ (young) petite fille f ▷ a five-year-old girl une petite fille de cinq ans ❸ (older) jeune fille f ▷ a sixteen-year-old girl une jeune fille de seize ans ▷ a Canadian girl une jeune Canadienne
girlfriend [ˈɡɜːlfrɛnd] n ❶ (romantic) copine f ▷ His girlfriend's name is Justine. Sa copine s'appelle Justine. ❷ (friend) amie f ▷ She often went out with her girlfriends. Elle sortait souvent avec ses amies.
give [ɡɪv] vb donner; **to give something to somebody** donner quelque chose à quelqu'un ▷ He gave me $10. Il m'a donné dix dollars.; **to give something back to somebody** rendre quelque chose à quelqu'un ▷ I gave the book back to her. Je lui ai rendu le livre.; **to give something out** distribuer quelque chose ▷ The teacher gave out the books. Le professeur a distribué les livres.; **to give in** céder ▷ Her Mom gave in and let her go out. Sa mère a cédé et l'a laissée sortir.; **to give out** distribuer ▷ He gave out the exam papers. Il a distribué les feuilles d'examen.; **to give up** laisser tomber ▷ I couldn't do it, so I gave up. Je n'arrivais pas à le faire, alors j'ai laissé tomber.; **to give up doing something** arrêter de faire quelque chose ▷ She gave up smoking. Elle a arrêté de fumer.; **to give oneself up** se rendre ▷ The thief gave himself up. Le voleur s'est rendu.; **to give way** s'effondrer ▷ The floor gave way under our feet. Le plancher s'est effondré sous nos pieds.
glacier [ˈɡleɪsɪə] n glacier m
glad [ɡlæd] adj content ▷ She's

glad she did it. Elle est contente de l'avoir fait.
glamorous [ˈɡlæmərəs] adj ❶ (person) glamour ▷ She's very glamorous. Elle est très glamour. ❷ (job) prestigieux (f prestigieuse); **to have a glamorous lifestyle** vivre comme une star
glance [ɡlɑːns] vb; **to glance at something** jeter un coup d'œil à quelque chose ▷ She glanced at her watch. Elle a jeté un coup d'œil à sa montre.
▶ n coup d'œil m ▷ at first glance au premier coup d'œil
glare [ɡlɛə] vb; **to glare at somebody** lancer un regard furieux à quelqu'un ▷ He glared at me. Il m'a lancé un regard furieux.
glaring [ˈɡlɛərɪŋ] adj: **a glaring mistake** une erreur qui saute aux yeux
glass [ɡlɑːs] n verre m ▷ a glass of milk un verre de lait
glasses [ˈɡlɑːsɪz] npl lunettes fpl ▷ My dad wears glasses. Mon père porte des lunettes.
glide [ɡlaɪd] vb ❶ glisser ▷ The sled glided across the snow. Le traîneau glissait sur la neige. ❷ planer ▷ A bird glided through the air. Un oiseau planait dans l'air.
glider [ˈɡlaɪdə] n planeur m
gliding [ˈɡlaɪdɪŋ] n vol à voile m ▷ My hobby is gliding. Je fais du vol à voile.
global [ˈɡləʊbl] adj mondial (mpl mondiaux); **on a global scale** à l'échelle mondiale
global warming [-ˈwɔːmɪŋ] n réchauffement de la planète m
globe [ɡləʊb] n globe m
gloomy [ˈɡluːmɪ] adj ❶ morose ▷ She's been feeling very gloomy recently. Elle se sent très morose ces derniers temps. ❷ lugubre ▷ They

live in a small gloomy apartment. Ils habitent un petit appartement lugubre.

glorious ['glɔːrɪəs] *adj* magnifique

glove [glʌv] *n* gant *m*

glove compartment *n* boîte à gants *f*

glue [gluː] *n* colle *f*
▷ *vb* coller

GM *adj* (= *genetically modified*) génétiquement modifié ▷ *GM foods* les aliments génétiquement modifiés *m*

GMO *abbr* (= *genetically-modified organism*) OGM *m* (= *l'organisme génétiquement modifié*)

go [gəʊ] *vb* ❶ aller ▷ *I'm going to the movies tonight.* Je vais au cinéma ce soir. ▷ *"Where's your friend?" —"He's gone."* « Où est ton ami? » — « Il est parti. » ❷ (*go away*) s'en aller ▷ *I'm going now.* Je m'en vais. ❸ (*vehicle*) marcher ▷ *My car won't go.* Ma voiture ne marche pas.; **a hamburger to go** un hamburger à emporter; **how to go about something** comment s'y prendre pour faire quelque chose ▷ *I don't know how to go about it.* Je ne sais pas m'y prendre.; **to go home** rentrer à la maison ▷ *I go home at about 4 o'clock.* Je rentre à la maison vers quatre heures.; **to go for a walk** aller se promener ▷ *Shall we go for a walk?* Si on allait se promener?; **to go through with something** mettre quelque chose à exécution; **to let go of something** lâcher quelque chose; **How did it go?** Comment est-ce que ça s'est passé?; **I'm going to do it tomorrow.** Je vais le faire demain.; **It's going to be difficult.** Ça va être difficile.

go after *vb* suivre ▷ *Quick, go after them!* Vite, suivez-les!

go ahead *vb*: **The play will go ahead as planned.** La pièce aura bien lieu comme prévu.; **Let's go ahead with your plan.** Mettons votre projet à exécution.; **Go ahead!** Vas-y!

go around *vb* ❶ (*turn*) tourner ▷ *Do the wheels really go around?* Est-ce que les roues tournent vraiment? ❷ tourner autour de ▷ *The earth goes around the sun.* La terre tourne autour du soleil.; **to go around a corner** prendre un tournant; **to go around the shops** faire les boutiques; **There's a bug going around.** Il y a un microbe qui circule.

go away *vb* s'en aller ▷ *Go away!* Allez-vous-en!

go back *vb*

Use **rentrer** only when you are entering a building, usually your home; otherwise use **retourner**.

❶ retourner ▷ *We went back to the same place.* Nous sommes retournés au même endroit. ❷ rentrer ▷ *"Is she still here?" —"No, she's gone back home."* « Est-ce qu'elle est encore là? » — « Non, elle est rentrée chez elle. »

go by *vb* passer ▷ *Two police officers went by.* Deux policiers sont passés.

go down *vb* ❶ (*person*) descendre ▷ *to go down the stairs* descendre l'escalier ❷ (*decrease*) baisser ▷ *The price of computers has gone down.* Le prix des ordinateurs a baissé. ❸ (*deflate*) se dégonfler ▷ *My airbed kept going down.* Mon matelas gonflant se dégonflait constamment.

go for *vb* (*attack*) attaquer ▷ *Suddenly the dog went for me.* Soudain, le chien m'a attaqué.; **Go for it!** (*go on!*) Vas-y, fonce!

go in *vb* entrer ▷ *She knocked on the door and went in.* Elle a frappé à la porte et elle est entrée.

go off *vb* ❶ *(bomb)* exploser ▷ *The bomb went off.* La bombe a explosé. ❷ *(alarm, gun)* se déclencher ▷ *The fire alarm went off.* L'avertisseur d'incendie s'est déclenché. ❸ *(alarm clock)* sonner ▷ *My alarm clock goes off at seven every morning.* Mon réveil sonne à sept heures tous les matins. ❹ *(food)* tourner ▷ *The milk's gone off.* Le lait a tourné. ❺ *(go away)* partir ▷ *He went off in a huff.* Il est parti de mauvaise humeur.

go on *vb* ❶ *(happen)* se passer ▷ *What's going on?* Qu'est-ce qui se passe? ❷ *(carry on)* continuer ▷ *The concert went on until 11 o'clock at night.* Le concert a continué jusqu'à onze heures du soir. ❸ passer ▷ *Go on to the next question.* Passe à la prochaine question.; **to go on doing something** continuer à faire quelque chose ▷ *She went on reading.* Elle a continué à lire.; **Go on!** Allez! ▷ *Go on, tell me what the problem is!* Allez, dis-moi quel est le problème!

go out *vb* ❶ *(person)* sortir ▷ *Are you going out tonight?* Tu sors ce soir?; **to go out with somebody** sortir avec quelqu'un ▷ *Are you going out with him?* Est-ce que tu sors avec lui? ❷ *(light, fire, candle)* s'éteindre ▷ *Suddenly the lights went out.* Soudain, les lumières se sont éteintes.

go past *vb*: **to go past something** passer devant quelque chose ▷ *He went past the store.* Il est passé devant le magasin.

go through *vb* traverser ▷ *We went through Manitoba to get to Saskatchewan.* Nous avons traversé Manitoba pour aller à Saskatchewan.

go up *vb* ❶ *(person)* monter ▷ *to go up the stairs* monter l'escalier ❷ *(increase)* augmenter ▷ *The price has gone up.* Le prix a augmenté.; **to go up in flames** s'embraser ▷ *The whole factory went up in flames.* L'usine toute entière s'est embrasée.

go with *vb* aller avec ▷ *Does this blouse go with that skirt?* Est-ce que ce chemisier va avec cette jupe?

goal [gəʊl] *n* but *m* ▷ *to score a goal* marquer un but ▷ *His goal is to become the world champion.* Son but est de devenir champion du monde.

goalkeeper ['gəʊlkiːpəʳ] *n* gardien de but *m*, gardienne de but *f*

goat [gəʊt] *n* chèvre *f*; **goat cheese** le fromage de chèvre

god [gɒd] *n* dieu *m* *(pl dieux)* ▷ *I believe in God.* Je crois en Dieu.

goddess ['gɒdɪs] *n* déesse *f*

goggles ['gɒglz] *npl* ❶ *(of welder, mechanic etc)* lunettes *fpl* de protection ❷ *(of swimmer)* lunettes *fpl* de natation

gold [gəʊld] *n* or *m* ▷ *They found some gold.* Ils ont trouvé de l'or. ▷ *A gold necklace* un collier en or

goldfish ['gəʊldfɪʃ] *n* poisson rouge *m* ▷ *I've got five goldfish.* J'ai cinq poissons rouges.

gold-plated ['gəʊld'pleɪtɪd] *adj* plaqué or *(f* plaquée or)

golf [gɒlf] *n* golf *m* ▷ *My mom plays golf.* Ma mère joue au golf.; **a golf club** un club de golf; **a golf course** un terrain de golf

gone [gɒn] *vb see* **go**

good [gʊd] *adj* ❶ bon *(f* bonne) ▷ *It's a very good film.* C'est un très bon film. ▷ *Vegetables are good for you.* Les légumes sont bons pour la santé.; **to be good at something** être bon en quelque chose ▷ *Jane's* very good at soccer. Jane est très bonne en soccer. ❷ (*kind*) gentil (*f* gentille) ▷ *They were very good to me.* Ils ont été très gentils avec moi. ❸ (*not naughty*) sage ▷ *Be good!* Sois sage!; **for good** pour de bon; **Good morning!** Bonjour!; **Good afternoon!** Bonjour!; **Good evening!** Bonsoir!; **Good night!** Bonne nuit!; **It's no good complaining.** Cela ne sert à rien de se plaindre.

goodbye [gʊd'baɪ] *excl* au revoir!

Good Friday *n* Vendredi saint *m*

good-looking [gʊd'lʊkɪŋ] *adj* beau (*also* bel, *f* belle, *mpl* beaux) ▷ *He's good-looking.* Il est beau.

> The form **beau** changes to **bel** before a vowel and most words beginning with h.

▷ *Who's your good-looking friend?* Qui est ton bel ami?

good-natured [gʊd'neɪtʃəd] *adj* (*person*) facile à vivre

goods [gʊdz] *npl* (*in store*) marchandises *fpl*

Google® [ˈguːgl] *n* Google® *m*
  ▶ *vb* **google®** faire une recherche Google®

goose [guːs] *n* oie *f*

gooseberry [ˈgʊzbərɪ] *n* groseille à maquereau *f*

gopher [ˈgəʊfəʳ] *n* spermophile *m*

gorgeous [ˈgɔːdʒəs] *adj*
  ❶ superbe ▷ *She's gorgeous!* Elle est superbe! ❷ splendide ▷ *The weather was gorgeous.* Il a fait un temps splendide.

gorilla [gəˈrɪlə] *n* gorille *m*

gospel [ˈgɒspl] *n* (*music*) gospel *m*

gossip [ˈgɒsɪp] *n* ❶ (*rumours*) cancans *mpl* ▷ *Tell me the gossip!* Raconte-moi les cancans! ❷ (*woman*) commère *f* ▷ *She's such a gossip!* C'est une vraie commère! ❸ (*man*) bavard *m* ▷ *What a gossip!* Quel bavard!

  ▶ *vb* ❶ (*chat*) bavarder ▷ *They were always gossiping.* Ils étaient tout le temps en train de bavarder. ❷ (*about somebody*) faire des commérages ▷ *They gossiped about him.* Elles faisaient des commérages à son sujet.

got [gɒt] *vb* see **get**

gotten [ˈgɒtn] *vb* see **get**

government [ˈgʌvnmənt] *n* gouvernement *m*

Governor General [ˈgʌvənəʳ-] *n* gouverneur général *m*, gouverneure générale *f*

GP *n* (= *General Practitioner*) omnipraticien *m*, omnipraticienne *f*

GPS *abbr* (= *global positioning system*) GPS *m*

grab [græb] *vb* saisir

graceful [ˈgreɪsful] *adj* élégant

grade [greɪd] *n* (*at school*) note *f* ▷ *I got good grades this year.* J'ai eu de bonnes notes cette année.

grade school *n* école *f* élémentaire

gradual [ˈgrædjʊəl] *adj* progressif (*f* progressive)

gradually [ˈgrædjʊəlɪ] *adv* peu à peu ▷ *We gradually got used to it.* Nous nous y sommes habitués peu à peu.

graduate [ˈgrædjʊeɪt] *n* ❶ (*from university*) diplômé *m*, diplômée *f* ❷ (*from high school*) finissant *m*, finissante *f*
  ▶ *vb* ❶ (*from high school*) obtenir son diplôme ❷ (*from university*) obtenir son baccalauréat

graduation party [grædjuˈeɪʃən-] *n* bal des finissants *m*

graffiti [grəˈfiːtɪ] *npl* graffiti *mpl*

grain [greɪn] *n* ❶ (*of salt, sand*) grain *m* ❷ céréales *fpl* ▷ *wheat and other grains* le blé et d'autres céréales ▷ *Grains are essential to a healthy diet.* Les céréales sont essentielles pour une alimentation saine.

gram [græm] n gramme m

grammar ['græmə^r] n grammaire f

grammatical [grə'mætɪkl] adj
grammatical (mpl grammaticaux)

grand [grænd] adj somptueux (f
somptueuse) ▷ She lives in a very
grand house. Elle habite une maison
somptueuse.; **a grand piano** un
piano à queue

grandchild ['græntʃaɪld] n
petit-fils m, petite-fille f; **my
grandchildren** mes m petits-
enfants

granddaughter ['grændɔ:tə^r] n
petite-fille f (pl petites-filles)

grandfather ['grændfɑ:ðə^r] n
grand-père m (pl grands-pères)
▷ my grandfather mon grand-père

grandmother ['grænmʌðə^r] n
grand-mère f (pl grands-mères)
▷ my grandmother ma grand-mère

grandparents ['grændpeərənts]
npl grands-parents mpl ▷ my
grandparents mes grands-parents

grandson ['grænsʌn] n petit-fils m
(pl petits-fils)

grant [grɑ:nt] vb ❶ (give) accorder
▷ to grant political asylum accorder
l'asile politique ❷ (say yes to)
accepter ▷ They granted our request.
Ils ont accepté notre requête.

grape [greɪp] n (single grape) grain
de raisin m; **grapes** le raisin ▷ a
bunch of grapes une grappe de raisin
▷ I ate some grapes. J'ai mangé du
raisin.; **grape-flavoured** à saveur
de raisin

grapefruit ['greɪpfru:t] n
pamplemousse m

graph [grɑ:f] n graphique m

graphic organizer ['græfɪk'ɔ:
gənaɪzə^r] n organisateur m
graphique

graphics ['græfɪks] npl images fpl
de synthèse ▷ I designed the graphics

and she wrote the text. J'ai conçu les
images de synthèse et elle a écrit
le texte.; **He works in computer
graphics.** Il fait de l'infographie.

grasp [grɑ:sp] vb saisir

grass [grɑ:s] n herbe f ▷ The grass is
long. L'herbe est haute.; **to cut the
grass** tondre le gazon

grasshopper ['grɑ:shɒpə^r] n
sauterelle f

grate [greɪt] vb râper ▷ to grate
some cheese râper du fromage

grateful ['greɪtful] adj
reconnaissant ▷ We are grateful
for your help. Nous sommes
reconnaissants de votre aide.

grater ['greɪtə^r] n râpe f ▷ a cheese
grater une râpe à fromage

grave [greɪv] n tombe f

gravel ['grævl] n gravier m

graveyard ['greɪvjɑ:d] n
cimetière m

gravy ['greɪvi] n sauce f

grease [gri:s] n ❶ (cooking) graisse
f ❷ (engine) lubrifiant m

greasy ['gri:si] adj gras (f grasse)
▷ I have greasy hair. J'ai les cheveux
gras. ▷ The food was very greasy. La
nourriture était très grasse.

great [greɪt] adj ❶ génial (mpl
géniaux) ▷ That's great! C'est génial!
❷ grand ▷ a great event un grand
événement; **Greater Vancouver**
l'agglomération f de Vancouver

great-grandfather
[greɪt'grænfɑ:ðə^r] n arrière-grand-
père m (pl arrière-grands-pères)

great-grandmother
[greɪt'grænmʌðə^r] n arrière-
grand-mère f (pl arrière-grands-
mères)

Great Lakes n Grands mpl Lacs

greedy ['gri:di] adj ❶ (for food)
gourmand ▷ "I want some more
cake." — "Don't be so greedy!" « Je veux
encore du gâteau. » — « Ne sois pas

si gourmand! » ❷ *(for money)* avide

green [griːn] *adj* ❶ vert m ▷ *a green car* une voiture verte ▷ *a green light* un feu vert ▷ *a green salad* une salade verte ❷ *(movement, candidate)* écologiste ▷ *the Green Party* le parti écologiste
▶ *n* vert m ▷ *a dark green* un vert foncé; (**greens** *(vegetables)*) les légumes verts

greenhouse ['griːnhaʊs] *n* serre f; **the greenhouse effect** l'effet m de serre

greet [griːt] *vb* accueillir ▷ *He greeted me with a kiss.* Il m'a accueilli en me donnant un baiser.

greeting ['griːtɪŋ] *n*: **Greetings from Bangor!** Bonjour de Bangor!; **"Season's greetings"** "Meilleurs vœux pour les fêtes de fin d'année"

greeting card *n* carte de vœux f

grew [gruː] *vb see* **grow**

grey [greɪ] *adj* gris ▷ *She has grey hair.* Elle a les cheveux gris.; **He's going grey.** Il grisonne.

grey-haired [greɪ'hɛəd] *adj* grisonnant

grief [griːf] *n* chagrin m

grill [grɪl] *n (for food)* gril m; **a mixed grill** les f grillades
▶ *vb*: **to grill something** faire griller quelque chose; **grilled chicken** du poulet grillé

grim [grɪm] *adj* sinistre

grin [grɪn] *vb* sourire ▷ *He grinned at me.* Il m'a souri.
▶ *n* large sourire m

grind [graɪnd] *vb (coffee, pepper)* moudre

grip [grɪp] *vb* saisir

gripping ['grɪpɪŋ] *adj (exciting)* palpitant

grizzly bear ['grɪzlɪ-] *n* grizzly m

groan [grəʊn] *vb* gémir ▷ *She groaned with pain.* Elle a gémi sous l'effet de la douleur.

▶ *n (of pain)* gémissement m

groceries ['grəʊsərɪz] *npl* épicerie f ▷ *Would you put the groceries in the cupboard, please?* Pourrais-tu ranger l'épicerie dans l'armoire, s'il te plaît?

grocery store ['grəʊsɛrɪ-] *n* épicerie f

groom [gruːm] *n (bridegroom)* marié m ▷ *the groom and his best man* le marié et son témoin

grope [grəʊp] *vb*: **to grope for something** chercher quelque chose à tâtons ▷ *She groped for the light switch.* Elle a cherché à tâtons l'interrupteur.

gross [grəʊs] *adj (revolting)* dégoûtant ▷ *It was really gross!* C'était vraiment dégoûtant!

grossly ['grəʊslɪ] *adv* largement ▷ *They're grossly underpaid.* Ils sont largement sous-payés.

ground [graʊnd] *n* ❶ *(earth)* sol m ▷ *The ground's wet.* Le sol est mouillé. ❷ *(reason)* raison f ▷ *We have grounds for complaint.* Nous avons des raisons de nous plaindre.; **on the ground** par terre ▷ *We sat on the ground.* Nous nous sommes assis par terre.
▶ *vb see* **grind**; **ground coffee** le café moulu

ground floor *n* premier étage m; **on the ground floor** au rez-de-chaussée

groundhog ['graʊndhɒg] *n* marmotte commune f ▷ *Groundhog Day* le jour de la marmotte

group [gruːp] *n* groupe m; **a group home** un foyer de groupe

grow [grəʊ] *vb* ❶ *(plant)* pousser ▷ *Grass grows quickly.* L'herbe pousse vite. ❷ *(person, animal)* grandir ▷ *How you've grown!* Comme tu as grandi! ❸ *(increase)* augmenter ▷ *The number of unemployed people has grown.* Le nombre de chômeurs a augmenté. ❹ (*cultivate*) faire pousser ▷ *My mom grows tomatoes.* Ma mère fait pousser des tomates.; **to grow a beard** se laisser pousser la barbe; **to grow up** grandir ▷ *Oh, grow up!* Ne fais pas l'enfant!; **She's grown out of her jacket.** Sa veste est devenue trop petite pour elle.

growl [graʊl] *vb* grogner

grown [grəʊn] *vb see* **grow**

growth [grəʊθ] *n* croissance *f* ▷ *economic growth* la croissance économique

grudge [grʌdʒ] *n* rancune *f*; **to bear a grudge against somebody** garder rancune à quelqu'un à

gruesome ['gruːsəm] *adj* horrible

grumpy ['grʌmpi] *adj*
❶ marabout *m*, *f* ▷ *They're grumpy this morning.* Elles sont marabouts ce matin. ❷ grognon (*f* grognonne)

GST *n* TPS *f* (= *taxe sur les produits et services*)

guarantee [gærən'tiː] *n* garantie *f*; **a five-year guarantee** une garantie de cinq ans
▶ *vb* garantir ▷ *I can't guarantee he'll come.* Je ne peux pas garantir qu'il viendra.

guard [gɑːd] *vb* garder ▷ *They guarded the prisoner.* Ils gardaient le prisonnier.; **to guard against something** protéger contre quelque chose
▶ *n* (*person*) garde *m*; **to catch somebody off guard** prendre quelqu'un au dépourvu; **a guard dog** un chien de garde

guardian ['gɑːdiən] *n* (*legal*) tuteur *m*, tuteur *f* ▷ *The form must be signed by your parent or guardian.* La feuille doit être signée par ton parent ou tuteur.; **the guardians of freedom** les gardiens de la liberté

guess [gɛs] *vb* deviner ▷ *Can you*

guess what it is? Devine ce que c'est!; **to guess wrong** se tromper ▷ *She guessed wrong.* Elle s'est trompée.
▶ *n* supposition *f* ▷ *It's just a guess.* C'est une simple supposition.; **Take a guess!** Devine!

guest [gɛst] *n* ❶ invité *m*, invitée *f* ▷ *We have guests staying with us.* Nous avons des invités. ❷ (*of hotel*) client *m*, cliente *f*

guide [gaɪd] *n* (*book, person*) guide *m* ▷ *We bought a guide to Paris.* Nous avons acheté un guide sur Paris. ▷ *The guide showed us around the museum.* Le guide nous a fait visiter le musée.
▶ *vb* guider ▷ *She guided us through the caves.* Elle nous a guidés à travers les cavernes. ▷ *The guide showed us round the museum.* Le guide nous a fait visiter le musée.

guidebook ['gaɪdbʊk] *n* guide *m*

guide dog *n* chien d'aveugle *m*

guideline ['gaɪdlaɪn] *n* directive *f* ▷ *Here are some guidelines for your research projects.* Voici quelques directives générales pour vos projets de recherche.; **a rough guideline** une indication générale

guilty ['gɪlti] *adj* coupable ▷ *to feel guilty* se sentir coupable ▷ *She was found guilty.* Elle a été reconnue coupable.

guinea pig ['gɪnɪ-] *n* cobaye *m*

guitar [gɪ'tɑː] *n* guitare *f* ▷ *I play the guitar.* Je joue de la guitare.

gullible ['gʌlɪbl] *adj* crédule

gum [gʌm] *n* gomme à mâcher *f*; **gums** (*in mouth*) les gencives

gun [gʌn] *n* ❶ (*small*) pistolet *m* ❷ (*rifle*) fusil *m*

guru ['gʊruː] *n* gourou *m*

gust [gʌst] *n*: **a gust of wind** une rafale de vent

guy [gaɪ] *n* type *m* ▷ *Who's that guy?* C'est qui ce type? ▷ *He's a nice guy.*

C'est un type sympa.

gym [dʒɪm] n ❶ gymnase m ▷ *She goes to the gym every day.* Elle va tous les jours au gymnase. ❷ éducation f physique

gymnast ['dʒɪmnæst] n gymnaste ▷ *She's a gymnast.* Elle est gymnaste.

gymnastics [dʒɪm'næstɪks] n gymnastique f ▷ *to do gymnastics* faire de la gymnastique

h

habit ['hæbɪt] n habitude f ▷ *a bad habit* une mauvaise habitude

hack [hæk] vb: **to hack into a system** s'introduire dans un système

hacker ['hækəʳ] n pirate informatique

had [hæd] vb *see* **have**

hadn't ['hædnt]; = **had not**

hail [heɪl] n grêle f
▶ vb grêler ▷ *It's hailing.* Il grêle.

hair [hɛəʳ] n ❶ cheveux mpl ▷ *She has long hair.* Elle a les cheveux longs. ▷ *He has black hair.* Il a les cheveux noirs. ▷ *He's losing his hair.* Il perd ses cheveux.; **to brush one's hair** se brosser les cheveux ▷ *I'm brushing my hair.* Je me brosse les cheveux.; **to wash one's hair** se laver les cheveux ▷ *I need to wash my hair.* Il faut que je me lave les cheveux.; **to have one's hair cut** se faire couper les cheveux ▷ *I've just* had my hair cut. Je viens de me faire couper les cheveux.; **a hair (1)** *(from head)* un cheveu **(2)** *(from body)* un poil **❷** *(fur of animal)* pelage *m*

hairbrush ['heəbrʌʃ] *n* brosse à cheveux *f*

hair clip *n* la pince à cheveux

haircut ['heəkʌt] *n* coupe de cheveux *f*; **to have a haircut** se faire couper les cheveux ▷ *I've just had a haircut.* Je viens de me faire couper les cheveux.

hairdresser ['heədresə'] *n* coiffeur *m*, coiffeuse *f* ▷ *She's a hairdresser.* Elle est coiffeuse. ▷ *at the hairdresser's* chez le coiffeur

hair gel *n* gel pour les cheveux *m*

hair spray *n* laque *f*

hairstyle ['heəstail] *n* coiffure *f*

hairy ['heərɪ] *adj* poilu ▷ *hairy legs* les jambes poilues

half [hɑːf] *n* moitié *f* ▷ *half of the cake* la moitié du gâteau; **two and a half** deux et demi; **half an hour** une demi-heure; **half past ten** dix heures et demie; **half a kilo** cinq cents grammes; **to cut something in half** couper quelque chose en deux
▶ *adj, adv* **❶** demi ▷ *a half chicken* un demi-poulet **❷** à moitié ▷ *He was half asleep.* Il était à moitié endormi.

half-brother ['hɑːfbrʌðə'] *n* demi-frère *m*

half-hour ['hɑːf'auə'] *n* demi-heure *f*

half-price ['hɑːf'prais] *adj, adv*: **at half-price** à moitié prix

half-sister ['hɑːf'sistə'] *n* demi-sœur *f*

half-time [hɑːf'taim] *n* mi-temps *f* ▷ *The score at half-time was 6-4.* Le pointage à la mi-temps était 6-4.

halfway ['hɑːf'wei] *adv* **❶** à mi-chemin ▷ *halfway between Sudbury*

and Kenora à mi-chemin entre Sudbury et Kenora; **a halfway house** une maison de transition **❷** à la moitié ▷ *halfway through the chapter* à la moitié du chapitre

hall [hɔːl] *n* **❶** *(hallway)* couloir *m* **❷** *(large room)* salle *f* ▷ *the community hall* la salle communautaire

Halloween [hæləu'iːn] *n* Halloween *f*

hallway ['hɔːlwei] *n* vestibule *m*

ham [hæm] *n* jambon *m*; **a ham sandwich** un sandwich au jambon

hamburger ['hæmbə:gə'] *n* **❶** hamburger *m* **❷** *(meat)* le bœuf haché

hammer ['hæmə'] *n* marteau *m* (pl marteaux)

hamster ['hæmstə'] *n* hamster *m*

hand [hænd] *n* **❶** *(of person)* main *f*; **by hand** à la main; **to give somebody a hand** *(help)* donner un coup de main à quelqu'un ▷ *Can you give me a hand?* Tu peux me donner un coup de main? **(2)** *(applaud)* applaudir quelqu'un; **on the one hand…, on the other hand…** d'une part…, d'autre part… **❷** *(of clock)* aiguille *f*
▶ *vb* passer *p* ▷ *He handed me the book.* Il m'a passé le livre.; **to hand something in** rendre quelque chose ▷ *She handed her exam paper in.* Sa nous a copie d'examen.; **to hand something out** distribuer quelque chose ▷ *The teacher handed out the books.* Le professeur a distribué les livres.; **to hand something over** remettre quelque chose ▷ *She handed the keys over to me.* Elle m'a remis les clés.

handball ['hændbɔːl] *n* *(game)* handball *m*; **to play handball** jouer au handball

handbook ['hændbuk] *n*

manuel *m*

handcuffs ['hændkʌfs] *npl* menottes *f*

handful ['hændful] *n* la poignée ▷ *a handful of popcorn* une poignée de maïs soufflé

handheld ['hændheld] *adj* de poche ▷ *a handheld computer* un ordinateur de poche

handkerchief ['hæŋkətʃɪf] *n* mouchoir *m*

handle ['hændl] *n* **❶** (*of door*) poignée *f* **❷** (*of cup*) anse *f* **❸** (*of knife*) manche *m* **❹** (*of saucepan*) queue *f*
▶ *vb* **❶** (*use, control*) manœuvrer ▷ *to handle a canoe* manœuvrer un canot **❷** (*touch*) toucher ▷ *Don't handle the fruit.* Ne touchez pas aux fruits.; **He handled it well.** Il s'en est bien tiré.; **The teacher handled the travel arrangements.** La professeure s'est occupée de l'organisation du voyage.; **She knows how to handle children.** Elle sait bien s'y prendre avec les enfants.

handlebars ['hændlbɑːz] *npl* guidon *m*

handmade ['hændmeɪd] *adj* fait à la main

hands-free [hændz'friː] *adj* mains libres (*f+pl* mains libres) ▷ *a hands-free phone* un téléphone mains libres

handsome ['hænsəm] *adj* beau (*f* belle) ▷ *He's handsome.* Il est beau.

▍ The form **beau** changes to **bel** before a vowel and most words beginning with h. ▷ *a handsome man* un bel homme

handwriting ['hændraɪtɪŋ] *n* écriture *f*

handy ['hændɪ] *adj* **❶** pratique ▷ *This knife's very handy.* Ce couteau est très pratique. **❷** sous la main ▷ *Have you got a pen handy?* Est-ce

que tu as un stylo sous la main?

hang [hæŋ] *vb* **❶** accrocher ▷ *I hung the painting on the wall.* J'ai accroché le tableau au mur. **❷** pendre ▷ *They hanged the criminal.* Ils ont pendu le criminel.; **to hang around** traîner ▷ *Let's go hang around in the park for a while.* Si on allait traîner dans le parc quelque temps?; **to hang in** ne pas lâcher ▷ *Hang in there, you're almost done!* Ne lâche pas, tu as presque fini!; **to hang on** patienter ▷ *Hang on a minute please.* Patientez une minute s'il vous plaît.; **to hang up** **(1)** (*clothes*) accrocher ▷ *Hang your jacket up on the hook.* Accrochez votre manteau au portemanteau. **(2)** (*phone*) raccrocher ▷ *I tried to phone her but she hung up on me.* J'ai essayé de l'appeler, mais elle m'a raccroché au nez.

hanger ['hæŋəʳ] *n* (*coat hanger*) cintre *m*

hang-gliding ['hæŋglaɪdɪŋ] *n* deltaplane *m*; **to go hang-gliding** faire du deltaplane

happen ['hæpən] *vb* se passer ▷ *What happened?* Qu'est-ce qui s'est passé?; **as it happens** justement ▷ *As it happens, I don't want to go.* Justement, je ne veux pas y aller.; **I happened to find 5 dollars lying in the street.** Il m'est arrivé de trouver cinq dollars dans la rue.; **Do you happen to know this neighbour?** Connaîtrais-tu ce voisin, par hasard?

happily ['hæpɪlɪ] *adv* **❶** joyeusement ▷ *"Don't worry!" he said happily.* « Ne te fais pas de souci! » dit-il joyeusement. **❷** (*fortunately*) heureusement ▷ *Happily, everything went well.* Heureusement, tout s'est bien passé.

happiness ['hæpɪnɪs] n
bonheur m

happy ['hæpɪ] adj heureux (f
heureuse) *She looks happy.* Elle
a l'air heureuse.; **I'm very happy
with your work.** Je suis très
satisfait de ton travail.; **Happy
birthday!** Bonne fête!

harassment ['hærəsmənt] n
harcèlement m ▷ **sexual harassment**
le harcèlement sexuel

harbour ['hɑːbə^r] n port m

hard [hɑːd] adj, adv ❶ dur ▷ *This
cheese is very hard.* Ce fromage est
très dur. ▷ *He worked very hard.* Il a
travaillé très dur. ❷ difficile ▷ *This
question is too hard for me.* Cette
question est trop difficile pour
moi.; **hard copy** la copie papier; **to
be hard of hearing** être dur d'oreille

hard-boiled [hɑːd'bɔɪld] adj dur

hard disk n (of computer) disque
dur m

hardly ['hɑːdlɪ] adv: **I've hardly
got any money.** Je n'ai presque pas
d'argent.; **I hardly know you.** Je
te connais à peine.; **hardly ever**
presque jamais

hardware ['hɑːdwɛə^r] n
❶ (computing) matériel m ❷ (bolts,
hinges) quincaillerie f; **a hardware
store** une quincaillerie

hare [hɛə^r] n lièvre m

harm [hɑːm] vb: **to harm
somebody** faire du mal à quelqu'un
▷ *I didn't mean to harm you.* Je ne
voulais pas te faire de mal.; **to
harm something** nuire à quelque
chose ▷ *Chemicals harm the
environment.* Les produits chimiques
nuisent à l'environnement.

harmful ['hɑːmful] adj nuisible
▷ *harmful chemicals* des produits
chimiques nuisibles

harmless ['hɑːmlɪs] adj inoffensif
(f inoffensive) ▷ *Most spiders are*

harmless. La plupart des araignées
sont inoffensives.

harpoon [hɑː'puːn] n harpon m

harsh [hɑːʃ] adj dur

has [hæz] vb see **have**

hasn't ['hæznt]: = **has not**

hassle ['hæsl] n: **It's such a hassle.**
C'est toute une affaire.; **It isn't
worth the hassle.** Ça n'en vaut
pas la peine.

hat [hæt] n chapeau m (pl
chapeaux)

hate [heɪt] vb détester ▷ *I hate
math.* Je déteste les maths.

hatred ['heɪtrɪd] n haine f

hat trick n tour de chapeau m

haunted ['hɔːntɪd] adj hanté;
a haunted house une maison
hantée

have [hæv] vb ❶ avoir ▷ *Do you
have a sister?* Tu as une sœur? ▷ *He
has blue eyes.* Il a les yeux bleus. ▷ *I
have a cold.* J'ai un rhume. ▷ *He's
done it, hasn't he?* Il l'a fait, non?
▷ *"Have you got any money?"* — *"No,
I haven't!"* « Est-ce que tu as de
l'argent? » — « Non, je n'en ai pas! »

▌ The perfect tense of some
verbs is formed with **être**.

❷ être ▷ *They have arrived.* Ils sont
arrivés. ▷ *Has she gone?* Est-ce
qu'elle est partie? ❸ prendre
▷ *He had his breakfast.* Il a pris son
petit déjeuner. ▷ *to have a shower*
prendre une douche; **to have to
do something** devoir faire quelque
chose ▷ *She has to do it.* Elle doit le
faire.; **to have a party** faire une
fête; **to have one's hair cut** se faire
couper les cheveux; **I've had it!**
J'en ai assez!

haven't ['hævnt]: = **have not**

hawk [hɔːk] n faucon m

hay [heɪ] n foin m

hay fever n rhume des foins m ▷ *Do
you get hay fever?* Est-ce que vous

êtes sujet au rhume des foins?

hazardous waste ['hæzədəs-] n déchets mpl dangereux

hazelnut ['heɪzlnʌt] n noisette f

he [hi:] pron il ▷ He loves dogs. Il aime les chiens.

head [hed] n **❶** (of person) tête f ▷ All the praise went to her head. Tous les compliments lui sont montés à la tête. ▷ I bumped my head. Je me suis cogné la tête. **❷** (leader) chef m ▷ a head of state un chef d'État ▷ She's the head of the organization. Elle est la chef de l'organisation.; **from head to toe** de la tête aux pieds; **head first** la tête la première; **Get it into your head that...** Mets-toi dans la tête que...; **to be head over heels in love with someone** être follement amoureux de quelqu'un; **to have a head for figures** être doué pour les chiffres; **"Heads or tails?" — "Heads."** « Pile ou face? » — « Face. »
▷ vb: **to head for something** se diriger vers quelque chose ▷ They headed for the church. Ils se sont dirigés vers l'église.; **Who's heading up the project?** Qui est à la tête du projet?

headache ['hedeɪk] n: **I've got a headache.** J'ai mal à la tête.

headlight ['hedlaɪt] n phare m

headline ['hedlaɪn] n titre m

headphones ['hedfəʊnz] npl écouteurs mpl

headquarters ['hedkwɔːtəz] npl (of organization) siège m

heal [hiːl] vb **❶** (person) guérir ▷ He was healed. Il a été guéri. **❷** cicatriser ▷ The wound soon healed. La blessure a vite cicatrisé.

health [helθ] n santé f; **health care** les m soins de santé ▷ the Canadian health care system le système de soins canadien

healthy ['helθɪ] adj **❶** (person) en bonne santé ▷ She's a healthy person. Elle est en bonne santé. **❷** (climate, food) sain ▷ a healthy diet une alimentation saine

heap [hiːp] n tas m ▷ a heap of snow un tas de neige

hear [hɪə] vb **❶** entendre ▷ He heard the dog bark. Il a entendu le chien aboyer. ▷ She can't hear very well. Elle entend mal. ▷ I heard that she was ill. J'ai entendu dire qu'elle était malade.; **to hear about something** entendre parler de quelque chose **❷** (news) apprendre ▷ Did you hear the good news? Est-ce que tu as appris la bonne nouvelle?; **to hear from somebody** avoir des nouvelles de quelqu'un ▷ I haven't heard from him recently. Je n'ai pas eu de ses nouvelles récemment.

heart [hɑːt] n cœur m; **in his heart of hearts** au fond de lui-même; **to break someone's heart** briser le cœur de quelqu'un; **to learn something by heart** apprendre quelque chose par cœur; **the ace of hearts** l'as de cœur; **with all my heart** de tout mon cœur

heart attack n crise cardiaque f

heartbroken ['hɑːtbrəʊkən] adj: **to be heartbroken** avoir le cœur brisé

heat [hiːt] n chaleur f
▷ vb faire chauffer ▷ Heat gently for 5 minutes. Faire chauffer à feu doux pendant cinq minutes.; **to heat up (1)** (cooked food) faire réchauffer ▷ He heated the soup up. Il a fait réchauffer la soupe. **(2)** (water, oven) chauffer ▷ The water is heating up. L'eau chauffe.

heater ['hiːtə'] n (car, office) chaufferette f

heating ['hiːtɪŋ] n chauffage m

heaven ['hevn] n paradis m

heavily ['hɛvɪlɪ] *adv* lourdement ▷ *The car was heavily loaded.* La voiture était lourdement chargée.; **heavily armed** fortement armé; **heavily made up** très maquillé; **She's heavily into jazz.** Elle est mordue de jazz.

heavy ['hɛvɪ] *adj* ❶ lourd ▷ *This bag is very heavy.* Ce sac est très lourd.; **heavy rain** une grosse averse ❷ (*busy*) chargé ▷ *I've got a very heavy week ahead.* Je vais avoir une semaine très chargée. ❸ dense ▷ *heavy traffic* une circulation dense ❹ gros ▷ *a heavy sigh* un gros soupir ▷ *to do the heavy work* faire le gros travail

he'd [hiːd] = **he would**; **he had**

hedge [hɛdʒ] *n* haie *f*

heel [hiːl] *n* talon *m*

height [haɪt] *n* ❶ (*of person*) taille *f* ❷ (*of object*) hauteur *f* ❸ (*of mountain*) altitude *f*; **fear of heights** le vertige

held [hɛld] *vb see* **hold**

helicopter ['hɛlɪkɒptə] *n* hélicoptère *m*

hell [hɛl] *n* enfer *m*

he'll [hiːl] = **he will**; **he shall**

hello [hə'ləʊ] *excl* ❶ bonjour! ❷ (*on phone*) allô

helmet ['hɛlmɪt] *n* casque *m*

help [hɛlp] *vb* aider ▷ *Can you help me?* Est-ce que vous pouvez m'aider?; **Help!** Au secours!; **Help yourself!** Servez-vous!; **He can't help it.** Il n'y peut rien.
▶ *n* aide *f* ▷ *Do you need any help?* Vous avez besoin d'aide?

helpful ['hɛlpful] *adj* serviable ▷ *She was very helpful.* Elle a été très serviable.

helpline ['hɛlplaɪn] *n* ligne d'écoute téléphonique *f*

hen [hɛn] *n* poule *f*

her [həː] *adj* son *m*, sa *f*, ses *pl* ▷ *her*

father son père ▷ *her mother* sa mère ▷ *her parents* ses parents

sa becomes **son** before a vowel sound.

▷ *She's going to wash her hair.* Elle va se laver les cheveux. ▷ *She's brushing her teeth.* Elle se brosse les dents. ▷ *She hurt her foot.* Elle s'est fait mal au pied.
▶ *pron*

la becomes **l'** before a vowel sound.

❶ la ▷ *I can see her.* Je la vois. ▷ *Look at her!* Regarde-la! ▷ *I saw her.* Je l'ai vue.

Use **lui** when **her** means **to her**.

❷ lui ▷ *I gave her a book.* Je lui ai donné un livre. ▷ *I told her the truth.* Je lui ai dit la vérité.

Use **elle** after prepositions.

❸ elle ▷ *I'm going with her.* Je vais avec elle. ▷ *He sat next to her.* Il s'est assis à côté d'elle.

elle is also used in comparisons.

▷ *I'm older than her.* Je suis plus âgé qu'elle.

herb [həːb] *n* herbe *f*; **herbs** les *f* fines herbes ▷ *What herbs do you use in this sauce?* Quelles fines herbes utilise-t-on pour cette sauce?

here [hɪə] *adv* ici ▷ *I live here.* J'habite ici.; **here is...** voici... ▷ *Here's Mom.* Voici maman. ▷ *Here he is!* Le voici!; **here are...** voici... ▷ *Here are the books.* Voici les livres.

heritage ['hɛrɪtɪdʒ] *n* patrimoine *m*; **Heritage Day** la fête du Patrimoine

hero ['hɪərəʊ] *n* héros *m* ▷ *He's a real hero!* C'est un véritable héros!

heroine ['herəʊɪn] n héroïne f ▷ *the heroine of the novel* l'héroïne du roman

hers [hɜːz] pron le + m sien, la + f sienne, les + m siens, les + f siennes ▷ *"Is this her coat?" — "No, hers is black."* « C'est son manteau ? » — « Non, le sien est noir. » ▷ *"Is this her car?" — "No, hers is white."* « C'est sa voiture ? » — « Non, la sienne est blanche. » ▷ *my parents and hers* mes parents et les siens ▷ *my reasons and hers* mes raisons et les siennes; **Is this hers?** C'est à elle ? ▷ *This book is hers.* Ce livre est à elle. ▷ *"Whose is this?" — "It's hers."* « C'est à qui ? » — « À elle. »

herself [hɜːˈsɛlf] pron ❶ ▷ *She's hurt herself.* Elle s'est blessée. ❷ *(after preposition)* elle ▷ *She talked mainly about herself.* Elle a surtout parlé d'elle. ❸ elle-même ▷ *She did it herself.* Elle l'a fait elle-même.; **by herself** toute seule ▷ *She doesn't like travelling by herself.* Elle n'aime pas voyager toute seule.

he's [hiːz] : = **he is**; **he has**

hesitate ['hɛzɪteɪt] vb hésiter

heterosexual ['hɛtərəʊ'sɛksjʊəl] adj hétérosexuel (f hétérosexuelle)

hi [haɪ] excl salut !

hibernate ['haɪbəneɪt] vb hiberner

hiccups ['hɪkʌps] npl: **to have hiccups** avoir le hoquet

hide [haɪd] vb se cacher ▷ *He hid behind a bush.* Il s'est caché derrière un buisson.; **to hide something** cacher quelque chose ▷ *We hid the present.* Nous avons caché le cadeau.

hide-and-seek ['haɪdən'siːk] n: **to play hide-and-seek** jouer à la cachette

hideous ['hɪdɪəs] adj hideux (f hideuse)

high [haɪ] adj, adv ❶ haut ▷ *It's too high.* C'est trop haut.; **How high is the wall?** Quelle est la hauteur du mur ?; **The wall is 2 metres high.** Le mur fait deux mètres de haut. ❷ élevé ▷ *a high price* un prix élevé ▷ *a high temperature* une température élevée; **at high speed** à grande vitesse; **It's very high in fat.** C'est très gras.; **She's got a very high voice.** Elle a la voix très aiguë.

higher education ['haɪə-] n enseignement m supérieur

high heels npl chaussures fpl à talons hauts

high jump n (Sport) saut en hauteur m

highlight ['haɪlaɪt] n clou m ▷ *the highlight of the evening* le clou de la soirée
▷ vb ❶ *(emphasize)* souligner ❷ *(with highlighter pen)* surligner

highlighter ['haɪlaɪtə] n surligneur m

high-rise ['haɪraɪz] n tour f ▷ *I live in a high-rise.* Je demeure dans une tour d'habitation.

high school n école f secondaire

highsticking ['haɪstɪkɪŋ] n bâton m élevé ▷ *to get a penalty for highsticking* recevoir une punition pour bâton élevé

highway ['haɪweɪ] n autoroute f

hijack ['haɪdʒæk] vb détourner

hijacker ['haɪdʒækə] n pirate de l'air

hike [haɪk] n randonnée pédestre f

hiking ['haɪkɪŋ] n: **to go hiking** faire une randonnée pédestre; **hiking boots** les f chaussures de randonnée pédestre

hilarious [hɪ'lɛərɪəs] adj hilarant ▷ *It was hilarious!* C'était hilarant !

hill [hɪl] n colline f ▷ *She walked up the hill.* Elle a gravi la colline.

him [hɪm] *pron*
▪ **le** becomes **l'** before a vowel sound.
❶ le, l' ▷ *I can see him.* Je le vois. ▷ *Look at him!* Regarde-le! ▷ *I saw him.* Je l'ai vu.
▪ Use **lui** when **him** means **to him**, and after prepositions.
❷ lui ▷ *I gave him a book.* Je lui ai donné un livre. ▷ *I told him the truth.* Je lui ai dit la vérité. ▷ *I'm going with him.* Je vais avec lui. ▷ *She sat next to him.* Elle s'est assise à côté de lui.
▪ **lui** is also used in comparisons. ▷ *I'm older than him.* Je suis plus âgé que lui.

himself [hɪm'sɛlf] *pron* ❶ se ▷ *He hurt himself.* Il s'est blessé. ❷ lui ▷ *He talked mainly about himself.* Il a surtout parlé de lui. ❸ lui-même ▷ *He did it himself.* Il l'a fait lui-même.; **by himself** tout seul ▷ *He was travelling by himself.* Il voyageait tout seul.

Hindu ['hɪnduː] *adj* hindou ▷ *a Hindu temple* un temple hindou
▶ *n* hindou *m*, hindoue *f*

hint [hɪnt] *n* allusion *f*
▶ *vb* laisser entendre ▷ *He hinted that he was getting me a present.* Il m'a laissé entendre qu'il allait me donner un cadeau.; **What are you hinting at?** Qu'est-ce que vous voulez dire par là?

hip [hɪp] *n* hanche *f*

hippie ['hɪpɪ] *n* hippie

hippo ['hɪpəʊ] *n* hippopotame *m*

hire ['haɪə'] *vb* engager ▷ *They hired a receptionist.* Ils ont engagé une réceptionniste.

his [hɪz] *adj* son *m*, sa *f*, ses *pl* ▷ *his father* son père ▷ *his mother* sa mère ▷ *his parents* ses parents
▪ **sa** becomes **son** before a vowel sound.

his friend (1) (*male*) son ami

(2) (*female*) son amie
▪ Do not use **son/sa/ses** with parts of the body.
▷ *He's going to wash his hair.* Il va se laver les cheveux. ▷ *He's brushing his teeth.* Il se brosse les dents. ▷ *He hurt his foot.* Il s'est fait mal au pied.
▶ *pron* le + *m* sien, la + *f* sienne, les + *m* siens, les + *f* siennes ▷ *"Is this coat?"* — *"No, his is black."* « C'est son manteau? » — « Non, le sien est noir. » ▷ *"Is this his car?"* — *"No, his is white."* « C'est sa voiture? » — « Non, la sienne est blanche. » ▷ *my parents and his* mes parents et les siens ▷ *my reasons and his* mes raisons et les siennes; **Is this his?** C'est à lui? ▷ *This book is his.* Ce livre est à lui. ▷ *"Whose is this?"* — *"It's his."* « C'est à qui? » — « À lui. »

history ['hɪstərɪ] *n* histoire *f*

hit [hɪt] *vb* ❶ frapper ▷ *She hit the ball on the first try.* Elle a frappé la balle du premier coup. ❷ renverser ▷ *He was hit by a car.* Il a été renversé par une voiture. ❸ toucher ▷ *The arrow hit the target.* La flèche a touché la cible.; **I hit my head on the table.** Je me suis cogné la tête contre la table.; **It suddenly hit me that…** Je me suis soudain rendu compte que…; **to hit it off with somebody** bien s'entendre avec quelqu'un ▷ *She hit it off with his parents.* Elle s'est bien entendue avec ses parents.
▶ *n* ❶ (*song*) tube *m* ▷ *the band's latest hit* le dernier tube de la bande ❷ (*success*) succès *m* ▷ *The film was a huge hit.* Le film a eu un immense succès.

hitch [hɪtʃ] *n* contretemps *m* ▷ *There's been a slight hitch.* Il y a eu un léger contretemps.

hitchhike ['hɪtʃhaɪk] *vb* ❶ faire du pouce ▷ *She hitchhiked into* town Elle a fait du pouce jusqu'en ville. ❷ faire de l'auto-stop ▷ They hitchhiked to Summerside. Ils ont fait de l'auto-stop jusqu'à Summerside.

hitchhiker ['hɪtʃhaɪkə] n auto-stoppeur m, auto-stoppeuse f

hitchhiking ['hɪtʃhaɪkɪŋ] n auto-stop m ▷ Hitchhiking can be dangerous. Il peut être dangereux de faire de l'auto-stop.

HIV-negative ['eɪtʃaɪvi:'negətɪv] adj séronégatif (f séronégative)

HIV-positive ['eɪtʃaɪvi:'pɒzɪtɪv] adj séropositif (f séropositive)

hobby ['hɒbɪ] n passe-temps favori m ▷ What are your hobbies? Quels sont tes passe-temps favoris?

hockey ['hɒkɪ] n hockey m ▷ I play hockey. Je joue au hockey.; **a hockey stick** un bâton de hockey

hold [həʊld] n: **on hold** (on phone) en attente; **to get hold of someone** (reach) contacter quelqu'un; **to get hold of something** (obtain) trouver quelque chose ▷ Where did you get hold of that book? Où as-tu trouvé ce livre?
▶ vb ❶ (hold on to) tenir ▷ He held the baby. Il tenait le bébé. ❷ (contain) contenir ▷ This bottle holds one litre. cette bouteille contient un litre.; **to hold a meeting** avoir une réunion; **Hold the line!** (on telephone) Ne quittez pas!; **Hold it!** (wait) Attends!; **to hold one's breath** retenir son souffle.

hold back vb ❶ (tears) retenir ❷ se retenir ▷ I wanted to say something but I held back. J'ai voulu dire quelque chose, mais je me suis retenu.

hold on vb ❶ (keep hold) tenir bon ▷ The cliff was slippery but she managed to hold on. La falaise

était glissante, mais elle est parvenue à tenir bon.; **to hold on to something** se cramponner à quelque chose ▷ He held on to the chair. Il se cramponnait à la chaise. ❷ (wait) attendre ▷ Hold on, I'm coming! Attends, je viens!; **Hold on!** (on telephone) Ne quittez pas!

hold up vb: **to hold somebody up** (delay) retenir quelqu'un ▷ I was held up at the office. J'ai été retenu au bureau.; **to hold up a bank** (rob) cambrioler une banque (informal)

holdup ['həʊldʌp] n ❶ (at bank) vol à main armée m ❷ (delay) retard m ❸ (traffic jam) bouchon m

hole [həʊl] n trou m

holiday ['hɒlədɪ] n ❶ vacances fpl ▷ Did you have a good holiday? Tu as passé de bonnes vacances? ▷ our holidays in Newfoundland nos vacances à Terre-Neuve; **on holiday** en vacances ▷ to go on holiday partir en vacances ▷ We are on holiday. Nous sommes en vacances.; **the school holidays** les vacances scolaires ❷ (public holiday) jour férié m ▷ Next Wednesday is a holiday. Mercredi prochain est un jour férié. ❸ (day off) jour de congé m ▷ He took a day's holiday. Il a pris un jour de congé.; **a holiday resort** un centre villégiature

hollow ['hɒləʊ] adj creux (f creuse)

holly ['hɒlɪ] n houx m ▷ A sprig of holly un brin de houx

holy ['həʊlɪ] adj saint

home [həʊm] n maison f; **at home** à la maison; **Make yourself at home.** Faites comme chez vous.
▶ adv ❶ à la maison ▷ I'll be home at 5 o'clock. Je serai à la maison à cinq heures.; **to get home** rentrer ▷ What time did she get home? Elle est rentrée à quelle heure?

home game n match à domicile m

homeland ['hǝʊmlænd] n patrie f

homeless ['hǝʊmlɪs] adj itinérant ▷ a shelter for homeless youth un refuge pour les jeunes itinérants; **a homeless man** un itinérant; **a homeless woman** une itinérante

homelessness ['hǝʊmlɪsnɪs] n itinérance f

home page n page d'accueil f

homesick ['hǝʊmsɪk] adj: **to be homesick** avoir le mal du pays

homework ['hǝʊmwǝːk] n devoirs mpl ▷ Have you done your homework? Est-ce que tu as fait tes devoirs? ▷ my geography homework mes devoirs de géographie

homosexual [hɒmǝʊ'seksjʊǝl] adj homosexuel (f homosexuelle)
▶ n homosexuel m, homosexuelle f

honest ['ɒnɪst] adj ① (trustworthy) honnête ▷ She's a very honest person. Elle est très honnête. ② (sincere) franc (f franche) ▷ He was very honest with her. Il a été très franc avec elle.

honestly ['ɒnɪstlɪ] adv franchement ▷ I honestly don't know. Franchement, je n'en sais rien.

honesty ['ɒnɪstɪ] n honnêteté f

honey ['hʌnɪ] n miel m

honeymoon ['hʌnɪmuːn] n lune de miel f

honour ['ɒnǝ] n honneur m ▷ in honour of our grandparents en l'honneur de nos grands-parents; **the honour roll** le tableau d'honneur

hood [hʊd] n ① (on coat) capuchon m ② (of car) capot m

hook [hʊk] n crochet m ▷ He hung the painting on the hook. Il a suspendu le tableau au crochet.; **to take the phone off the hook** décrocher le téléphone; **a fish-hook** un hameçon

hope [hǝʊp] vb espérer ▷ I hope he comes. J'espère qu'il va venir. ▷ I'm hoping for good results. J'espère avoir de bons résultats.; **I hope so.** Je l'espère.; **I hope not.** J'espère que non.
▶ n espoir m; **to give up hope** perdre espoir ▷ Don't give up hope! Ne perds pas espoir!

hopeful ['hǝʊpfʊl] adj ① plein d'espoir ▷ I'm hopeful. Je suis plein d'espoir.; **She's hopeful of winning.** Elle a bon espoir de gagner. ② (situation) prometteur (f prometteuse) ▷ The prospects look hopeful. Les perspectives semblent prometteuses.

hopefully ['hǝʊpfʊlɪ] adv avec un peu de chance ▷ Hopefully he'll make it in time. Avec un peu de chance, il arrivera à temps.

hopeless ['hǝʊplɪs] adj ① désespéré ▷ The situation is hopeless. La situation est désespérée. ② nul (f nulle) ▷ I'm hopeless at math. Je suis nul en maths.; **It's hopeless, I can't do it!** C'est désespérant, je n'arrive pas à le faire!

horizon [hǝ'raɪzn] n horizon m

horizontal [hɒrɪ'zɒntl] adj horizontal (mpl horizontaux)

horn [hɔːn] n ① (of car) klaxon m ▷ He blew his horn. Il a klaxonné. ② corn m ▷ I play the horn. Je joue du cor. ③ (of animal) corne f

horoscope ['hɒrǝskǝʊp] n horoscope m

horrible ['hɒrɪbl] adj horrible ▷ What a horrible dress! Quelle robe horrible!

horrifying ['hɒrɪfaɪɪŋ] adj effrayant

horror ['hɒrǝ] n horreur f ▷ a horror movie un film d'horreur

horse [hɔːs] n cheval m (pl chevaux)

horse-racing ['hɔːsreɪsɪŋ] n

courses fpl de chevaux
horseshoe ['hɔ:ʃu:] n fer à cheval m

hose [həuz] n tuyau m (pl tuyaux)
▷ a garden hose un tuyau d'arrosage

hospital ['hɒspɪtl] n hôpital m (pl hôpitaux) ▷ Take me to the hospital! Emmenez-moi à l'hôpital! ▷ in the hospital à l'hôpital

hospitality [hɒspɪ'tælɪtɪ] n hospitalité f

host [həust] n hôte m, hôtesse f

hostage ['hɒstɪdʒ] n otage m; **to take somebody hostage** prendre quelqu'un en otage

hostel ['hɒstl] n (for refugees, homeless people) refuge m; **a youth hostel** une auberge de jeunesse

hostile ['hɒstaɪl] adj hostile

hot [hɒt] adj ❶ (warm) chaud ▷ a hot bath un bain chaud ▷ a hot country un pays chaud

⏐ When you are talking about a person being hot, you use **avoir chaud**.

▷ I'm hot. J'ai chaud. ▷ I'm too hot. J'ai trop chaud.

⏐ When you mean that the weather is hot, you use **faire chaud**.

▷ It's hot. Il fait chaud. ▷ It's very hot today. Il fait très chaud aujourd'hui.
❷ (spicy) épicé ▷ a very hot curry un curry très épicé

hot dog n hot-dog m

hotel [həu'tɛl] n hôtel m ▷ We stayed in a hotel. Nous avons logé à l'hôtel.

hotline ['hɒtlaɪn] n ❶ (for info, advice) service m d'assistance téléphonique ❷ (for help in crisis) ligne f d'écoute téléphonique ❸ (for phone-in show) ligne f ouverte

hour ['auə'] n heure f ▷ He always takes hours to get ready. Il passe toujours des heures à se préparer.;

a quarter of an hour un quart d'heure; **half an hour** une demi-heure; **two and a half hours** deux heures et demie

hourly ['auəlɪ] adj, adv toutes les heures ▷ There are hourly buses. Il y a des autobus toutes les heures.; **to be paid hourly** être payé à l'heure

house [hauz] n maison f; at his house chez lui; **We stayed at their house.** Nous sommes restés chez eux.; **House of Assembly** (Nfld) la Chambre d'assemblée; **House of Commons** la Chambre des communes

housework ['hauswз:k] n ménage m; **to do the housework** faire le ménage

how [hau] adv comment ▷ How are you? Comment allez-vous?; **How many?** Combien?; **How many...?** Combien de...? ▷ How many students are there in the class? Combien d'élèves y a-t-il dans la classe?; **How much?** Combien?; **How much...?** Combien de...? ▷ How much sugar do you want? Combien de sucre voulez-vous?; **How old are you?** Quel âge as-tu?; **How far is it to Rimouski?** Combien y a-t-il de kilomètres d'ici à Rimouski?; **How long have you been here?** Depuis combien de temps êtes-vous là?; **How do you say "apple" in French?** Comment dit-on « apple » en français?

however [hau'ɛvə'] conj pourtant ▷ This, however, isn't true. Pourtant, ce n'est pas vrai.

howl [haul] vb hurler

HTML n langage HTML m ▷ an HTML document un document en langage HTML

Hudson Bay ['hʌdsən-] n baie d'Hudson f

hug [hʌg] vb serrer dans ses bras ▷ He hugged her. Il l'a serrée dans

ses bras.
▶ n: **to give somebody a hug**
serrer quelqu'un dans ses bras ▷ *She gave them a hug.* Elle les a serrés dans ses bras.

huge [hju:dʒ] *adj* immense

hum [hʌm] *vb* fredonner

human ['hju:mən] *adj* humain
▷ *the human body* le corps humain;
human rights les droits de la personne ▷ *a human rights issue* une question relative aux droits de la personne; **human resources** (*available people*) les ressources humaines ▷ *We have both the human resources and the funds to carry out this project.* Nous avons les ressources humaines et financières pour réaliser ce projet.

human being [-'bi:ɪŋ] *n* être *m* humain

humankind [hju:mən'kaɪnd] *n* humanité *f*

humble ['hʌmbl] *adj* humble

humidex ['hju:mɪdeks] *n* humidex *m*

humour ['hju:mə*] *n* humour *m*;
to have a sense of humour avoir le sens de l'humour

hundred ['hʌndrəd] *num*: **a hundred** cent ▷ *a hundred dollars* cent dollars; **five hundred** cinq cents; **five hundred and one** cinq cent un; **hundreds of people** des centaines de personnes

hung [hʌŋ] *vb see* **hang**

hunger ['hʌŋgə*] *n* faim *f*

hungry ['hʌŋgrɪ] *adj*: **to be hungry** avoir faim ▷ *I'm hungry.* J'ai faim.

hunt [hʌnt] *vb* ❶ (*animal*) chasser;
to go hunting aller à la chasse ❷ (*criminal*) pourchasser ▷ *The police are hunting the criminal.* La police pourchasse le criminel.;
to hunt for something (*search*) chercher quelque chose partout ▷ *I*

hunted everywhere for that book. J'ai cherché ce livre partout.

hunting ['hʌntɪŋ] *n* chasse *f*

hurdle ['hə:dl] *n* obstacle *m*

hurricane ['hʌrɪkən] *n* ouragan *m*

hurry ['hʌrɪ] *vb* se dépêcher
▷ *She hurried back home.* Elle s'est dépêchée de rentrer chez elle.;
Hurry up! Dépêche-toi!
▶ n: **to be in a hurry** être pressé;
to do something in a hurry faire quelque chose en vitesse; **There's no hurry.** Rien ne presse.

hurt [hə:t] *vb*: **to hurt somebody**
(1) (*physically*) faire mal à quelqu'un ▷ *You're hurting me!* Tu me fais mal!
(2) (*emotionally*) blesser quelqu'un ▷ *His remarks really hurt me.* Ses remarques m'ont vraiment blessé.;
to hurt oneself se faire mal ▷ *I fell and hurt myself.* Je me suis fait mal en tombant.; **That hurts.** Ça fait mal. ▷ *It hurts to have a tooth out.* Ça fait mal de se faire arracher une dent.; **My leg hurts.** J'ai mal à la jambe.
▶ *adj* blessé ▷ *Were you badly hurt?* Est-ce que tu as été grièvement blessé? ▷ *He was hurt in the leg.* Il a été blessé à la jambe. ▷ *I was hurt by what she said.* J'ai été blessé par ce qu'elle a dit.; **Luckily, nobody got hurt.** Heureusement, il n'y a pas eu de blessés.

husband ['hʌzbənd] *n* mari *m*

hut [hʌt] *n* hutte *f*

hydro ['haɪdrəʊ] *n* électricité *f* ▷ *Hydro costs a lot.* L'électricité coûte cher.

hyperlink ['haɪpəlɪŋk] *n* hyperlien *m*

hyphen ['haɪfn] *n* trait d'union *m*

hypothesis [haɪ'pɒθɪsɪs] *n* hypothèse *f*

I [aɪ] *pron* ❶ je ▷ *I speak French.* Je parle français.

je changes to **j'** before a vowel and most words beginning with "h".

▷ *I love cats.* J'aime les chats. ❷ moi ▷ *my sister and I* ma sœur et moi

ice [aɪs] *n* ❶ glace *f* ▷ *There was ice on the lake.* Il y avait de la glace sur le lac. ❷ (*on road*) verglas *m*; **to break the ice** rompre la glace

iceberg ['aɪsbə:g] *n* iceberg *m*; **the tip of the iceberg** la pointe de l'iceberg

icebreaker ['aɪsbreɪkə'] *n* brise-glace *m* (*pl* les brise-glaces) ▷ *Icebreakers are used to navigate the Arctic.* On utilise des brise-glaces pour naviguer dans l'Arctique.

ice cream *n* crème glacée *f* ▷ *vanilla ice cream* la crème glacée à la vanille

ice cube *n* glaçon *m*

ice fishing *n* pêche sous la glace

f ▷ *to go ice fishing* faire de la pêche sous la glace

ice hockey *n* hockey sur glace *m*

ice rink *n* patinoire *f*

ice skating ['aɪsskeɪtɪŋ] *n* patinage sur glace *m*; **to go ice skating** faire du patin à glace

ice slide *n* glissade *f* ▷ *In winter the city builds an ice slide in the park.* L'hiver, la ville construit une glissade dans le parc.

ice storm *n* tempête de verglas *f*

icicle ['aɪsɪkl] *n* glaçon *m*

icing ['aɪsɪŋ] *n* (*on cake*) glaçage *m*; **icing sugar** le sucre glace

icon ['aɪkɔn] *n* icône *f*

icy ['aɪsɪ] *adj* glacial (*mpl* glaciaux) ▷ *There was an icy wind.* Il y avait un vent glacial.; **The roads are icy.** Il y a du verglas sur les routes.

I'd [aɪd] = **I had**; **I would**

ID card *n* carte d'identité *f*

idea [aɪ'dɪə] *n* idée *f* ▷ *Good idea!* Bonne idée!

ideal [aɪ'dɪəl] *adj* idéal (*mpl* idéaux)

identical [aɪ'dɛntɪkl] *adj* identique

identification [aɪdɛntɪfɪ'keɪʃən] *n* identification *f*

identify [aɪ'dɛntɪfaɪ] *vb* identifier

i.e. *abbr* c.-à-d. (= *c'est-à-dire*)

if [ɪf] *conj* si ▷ *You can have it if you like.* Tu peux le prendre si tu veux. ▷ *Do you know if he's there?* Savez-vous s'il est là?; **if only** si seulement ▷ *If only I had more money!* Si seulement j'avais plus d'argent!; **if not** sinon ▷ *Are you coming? If not, I'll go with my brother.* Est-ce que tu viens? Sinon, j'irai avec mon frère.

si changes to **s'** before **il** and **ils**.

igloo ['ɪglu:] *n* iglou *m*

ignorant ['ɪgnərənt] *adj* ignorant

ignore [ɪg'nɔ:'] *vb*: **to ignore something** ne tenir aucun compte de quelque chose ▷ *She ignored my advice.* Elle n'a tenu aucun compte de mes conseils.; **to ignore somebody** ignorer quelqu'un ▷ *She saw me, but she ignored me.* Elle m'a vu, mais elle m'a ignoré.; **Just ignore him!** Ne fais pas attention à lui!

ill [ɪl] *adj* (sick) malade

I'll [aɪl]: = **I will**

illegal [ɪ'liːɡl] *adj* illégal (mpl illégaux)

illegible [ɪ'lɛdʒɪbl] *adj* illisible

illness ['ɪlnɪs] *n* maladie f

illusion [ɪ'luːʒən] *n* illusion f

illustration [ɪlə'streɪʃən] *n* illustration f

image ['ɪmɪdʒ] *n* image f ▷ *The company has changed its image.* La société a changé d'image.

imagination [ɪmædʒɪ'neɪʃən] *n* imagination f

imagine [ɪ'mædʒɪn] *vb* imaginer ▷ *You can imagine how I felt!* Tu peux imaginer ce que j'ai ressenti! ▷ *"Is he angry?" — "I imagine so."* « Est-ce qu'il est en colère? » — « J'imagine que oui. »

imam [ɪ'mɑːm] *n* imam m

imitate ['ɪmɪteɪt] *vb* imiter

imitation [ɪmɪ'teɪʃən] *n* imitation f

immediate [ɪ'miːdɪət] *adj* immédiat ▷ *her immediate family* sa famille immédiate

immediately [ɪ'miːdɪətlɪ] *adv* immédiatement ▷ *I'll do it immediately.* Je vais le faire immédiatement.

immigrant ['ɪmɪɡrənt] *n* immigré m, immigrée f

immigration [ɪmɪ'ɡreɪʃən] *n* immigration f

immoral [ɪ'mɒrl] *adj* immoral (mpl immoraux)

impartial [ɪm'pɑːʃl] *adj* impartial (mpl impartiaux)

impatience [ɪm'peɪʃəns] *n* impatience f

impatient [ɪm'peɪʃənt] *adj* impatient; **to get impatient** s'impatienter ▷ *People are getting impatient.* Les gens commencent à s'impatienter.

impatiently [ɪm'peɪʃəntlɪ] *adv* avec impatience ▷ *We waited impatiently.* Nous avons attendu avec impatience.

impersonal [ɪm'pɜːsənl] *adj* impersonnel (f impersonnelle)

imply [ɪm'plaɪ] *vb* laisser entendre ▷ *She implied that she wasn't coming.* Elle a laissé entendre qu'elle ne venait pas.

importance [ɪm'pɔːtns] *n* importance f

important [ɪm'pɔːtnt] *adj* important

impossible [ɪm'pɒsɪbl] *adj* impossible

impress [ɪm'prɛs] *vb* impressionner ▷ *She's trying to impress you.* Elle essaie de t'impressionner.

impressed [ɪm'prɛst] *adj* impressionné ▷ *I'm very impressed!* Je suis très impressionné!

impression [ɪm'prɛʃən] *n* impression f ▷ *I was under the impression that...* J'avais l'impression que...

impressive [ɪm'prɛsɪv] *adj* impressionnant

improv ['ɪmprɒv] *n* improvisation f ▷ *We started an improv club in our school.* Nous avons fondé une ligue d'improvisation à l'école.

improve [ɪm'pruːv] *vb* ❶ (make better) améliorer ▷ *They have improved the service.* Ils ont amélioré le service. ❷ (get better) s'améliorer ▷ *The weather is improving.* Le temps s'améliore. ▷ *My French has improved.* Mon français s'est amélioré.

improvement [ɪm'pruːvmənt]
n ❶ (of condition) amélioration
f ▷ It's a great improvement. C'est
une nette amélioration. ❷ (of
learner) progrès m ▷ There's been an
improvement in your French. Tu as fait
des progrès en français.

improvise ['ɪmprəvaɪz] vb
improviser

in [ɪn] prep, adv

There are several ways of
translating **in**. Scan the
examples to find one that is
similar to what you want to
say. For other expressions with
in, see the verbs **go**, **come**, **get**,
give etc.

❶ dans ▷ in the house dans la
maison ▷ in my backpack dans mon
sac à dos ▷ I'll see you in three weeks.
Je te verrai dans trois semaines.
❷ à ▷ in the country à la campagne
▷ in school à l'école ▷ in hospital à
l'hôpital ▷ in Steinbach à Steinbach
▷ in spring au printemps ▷ in the sun
au soleil ▷ in the shade à l'ombre ▷ in
a loud voice à voix haute ▷ the boy in
the blue shirt le garçon à la chemise
bleue ▷ It was written in pencil.
C'était écrit au crayon. ❸ en
▷ in the month of May au mois de mai ❸ en
▷ in French en français ▷ in summer
en été ▷ in May en mai ▷ in 1996 en
dix-neuf cent quatre-vingt seize
▷ I did it in 3 hours. Je l'ai fait en trois
heures. ▷ in town en ville ▷ in prison
en prison ▷ in tears en larmes ▷ in
good condition en bon état

When **in** refers to a country
which is feminine, use **en**;
when the country is masculine,
use **au**; when the country is
plural, use **aux**.

▷ in France en France ▷ in Portugal
au Portugal ▷ in the United States
aux États-Unis ❹ de ▷ the best

team in the world la meilleure équipe
du monde ▷ The tallest person in the
family le plus grand de la famille
▷ at 4 o'clock in the afternoon à quatre
heures de l'après-midi ▷ at 6 in
the morning à six heures du matin;
In the afternoon I work at the
store. L'après-midi, je travaille au
magasin.; You look good in that
dress. Tu es jolie avec cette robe.;
in time à temps ▷ We arrived in time
for dinner. Nous sommes arrivés
à temps pour le dîner.; in here ici
▷ It's hot in here. Il fait chaud ici.;
in the rain sous la pluie; in the sixties
durant les années soixante; one
person in ten une personne sur
dix; to be in (at home, work) être là
▷ She wasn't in. Elle n'était pas là.; to
ask somebody in inviter quelqu'un
à entrer

inaccurate [ɪn'ækjurət] adj
inexact

inadequate [ɪn'ædɪkwət] adj
(measures, resources) inadéquat; I
felt completely inadequate. Je
ne me sentais absolument pas à
la hauteur.

incentive [ɪn'sɛntɪv] n: There is
no incentive to work. Il n'y a rien
qui incite à travailler.

inch [ɪntʃ] n pouce m
● An inch is a nonmetric unit equal
to about 2.5 cm.
6 inches quinze centimètres

incident ['ɪnsɪdnt] n incident m

inclined [ɪn'klaɪnd] adj: to be
inclined to do something avoir
tendance à faire quelque chose
▷ He's inclined to arrive late. Il a
tendance à arriver en retard.

include [ɪn'kluːd] vb comprendre
▷ Service is not included. Le service
n'est pas compris.

including [ɪn'kluːdɪŋ] prep
compris ▷ It will be 200 dollars,

including tax. Ça coûtera deux cents dollars, taxes comprises.

inclusive [ɪnˈkluːsɪv] *adj* compris
▷ *The inclusive price is 200 dollars.* Ça coûte deux cents dollars tout compris.; **pages 9 to 12 inclusive** de la page neuf à la page douze inclusivement; **inclusive language** la langue non sexiste

income [ˈɪnkʌm] *n* revenu *m*

income tax *n* impôt *m* sur le revenu

incompetent [ɪnˈkɒmpɪtnt] *adj* incompétent

incomplete [ɪnkəmˈpliːt] *adj* incomplet (*f* incomplète)

inconsistent [ɪnkənˈsɪstnt] *adj* ❶ (*behaviour*) changeant ❷ (*work, quality*) inégal ❸ (*statements*) contradictoire; **Her actions are inconsistent with what she says.** Ses actes ne concordent pas avec ce qu'elle dit.

inconvenience [ɪnkənˈviːnjəns] *n*: **I don't want to cause any inconvenience.** Je ne veux pas vous déranger.

inconvenient [ɪnkənˈviːnjənt] *adj* inopportun ▷ *at an inconvenient time* à un moment inopportun; **That's very inconvenient for me.** Ça ne m'arrange pas du tout.

incorrect [ɪnkəˈrɛkt] *adj* incorrect

increase [ˈɪnkriːs] *n* augmentation *f* ▷ *an increase in traffic accidents* une augmentation des accidents de la route
▶ *vb* augmenter

incredible [ɪnˈkrɛdɪbl] *adj* incroyable

indecisive [ɪndɪˈsaɪsɪv] *adj* (*person*) indécis

independence [ɪndɪˈpɛndns] *n* indépendance *f*

independent [ɪndɪˈpɛndnt] *adj* indépendant; **an independent**

school une école privée

index [ˈɪndɛks] *n* (*in book*) index *m*

index finger *n* index *m*

Indian summer [ˈɪndɪən-] *n* été *m* indien

indicate [ˈɪndɪkeɪt] *vb* indiquer

indigestion [ɪndɪˈdʒɛstʃən] *n* indigestion *f*; **I have indigestion.** J'ai une indigestion.

individual [ɪndɪˈvɪdjʊəl] *adj* individuel (*f* individuelle)
▶ *n* ❶ individu *m* ▷ *the rights of the individual* les droits de l'individu ❷ personne *f* ▷ *a rather strange individual* une personne un peu étrange; **She's a real individual.** Elle est vraiment unique.

indoor [ˈɪndɔː] *adj* d'intérieur ▷ *indoor activities* les activités d'intérieur ▷ *indoor shoes* les chaussures d'intérieur ▷ *indoor sports* les sports d'intérieur; **an indoor swimming pool** une piscine intérieure

indoors [ɪnˈdɔːz] *adv* à l'intérieur ▷ *They're indoors.* Ils sont à l'intérieur.; **to go indoors** rentrer ▷ *We'd better go indoors.* Nous ferions mieux de rentrer.

industrial [ɪnˈdʌstrɪəl] *adj* industriel (*f* industrielle)

industry [ˈɪndəstrɪ] *n* industrie *f* ▷ *the tourist industry* l'industrie du tourisme ▷ *the oil industry* l'industrie pétrolière ▷ *I'd like to work in industry.* J'aimerais travailler dans l'industrie.

inefficient [ɪnɪˈfɪʃənt] *adj* inefficace

inevitable [ɪnˈɛvɪtəbl] *adj* inévitable

inexpensive [ɪnɪkˈspɛnsɪv] *adj* bon marché (*f* + *pl* bon marché) ▷ *an inexpensive hotel* un hôtel bon marché ▷ *inexpensive holidays* des vacances bon marché

inexperienced [ɪnɪkˈspɪərɪənst] *adj* inexpérimenté

infection [ɪnˈfɛkʃən] *n* infection *f* ▷ *an ear infection* une infection de l'oreille; **a throat infection** un mal de gorge

infectious [ɪnˈfɛkʃəs] *adj* contagieux (*f* contagieuse) ▷ *It's not infectious.* Ce n'est pas contagieux.

infinite [ˈɪnfɪnɪt] *adj* ❶ infini ▷ *an infinite variety* une variété infinie ❷ illimité ▷ *The possibilities are infinite.* Les possibilités sont illimitées.

infinitive [ɪnˈfɪnɪtɪv] *n* infinitif *m*

inflatable [ɪnˈfleɪtəbl] *adj* (*mattress, dinghy*) gonflable

inflation [ɪnˈfleɪʃən] *n* inflation *f*

influence [ˈɪnfluəns] *n* influence *f* ▷ *He's a bad influence on her.* Il a mauvaise influence sur elle.
▶ *vb* influencer

infomercial [ˈɪnfəʊməˌʃl] *n* infopublicité *f*

inform [ɪnˈfɔːm] *vb* informer; **to inform somebody of something** informer quelqu'un de quelque chose ▷ *Nobody informed me of the new plan.* Personne ne m'a informé de ce nouveau projet.

informal [ɪnˈfɔːml] *adj* ❶ (*person, party*) décontracté ▷ "*informal dress*" « tenue décontractée » ❷ (*language*) familier (*f* familière) ▷ *informal language* le langage familier; **an informal visit from the principal** une visite non officielle du directeur

information [ɪnfəˈmeɪʃən] *n* ❶ renseignements *mpl* ▷ *important information* les renseignements importants; **a piece of information** un renseignement; **Could you give me some information about the Quebec Carnival?** Pourriez-vous

me renseigner sur le Carnaval de Québec?; **for your information** à titre de renseignement ❷ information *f* ▷ *I found some information for my project on pollution.* J'ai trouvé de l'information pour mon projet sur la pollution.

information desk *n* bureau de renseignements *m*

infuriating [ɪnˈfjuərɪeɪtɪŋ] *adj* exaspérant

ingenious [ɪnˈdʒiːnjəs] *adj* ingénieux (*f* ingénieuse)

ingredient [ɪnˈɡriːdɪənt] *n* ingrédient *m*

inhabitant [ɪnˈhæbɪtnt] *n* habitant *m*, habitante *f*

inherit [ɪnˈhɛrɪt] *vb* hériter de ▷ *She inherited her father's house.* Elle a hérité de la maison de son père.

initials [ɪˈnɪʃəlz] *npl* initiales *fpl* ▷ *My initials are CDT.* Mes initiales sont CDT.

initiative [ɪˈnɪʃətɪv] *n* initiative *f*

inject [ɪnˈdʒɛkt] *vb* (*drug*) injecter

injection [ɪnˈdʒɛkʃən] *n* piqûre *f*

injure [ˈɪndʒəˈ] *vb* blesser

injury [ˈɪndʒərɪ] *n* blessure *f*

injustice [ɪnˈdʒʌstɪs] *n* injustice *f*

ink [ɪŋk] *n* encre *f*

in-laws [ˈɪnlɔːz] *npl* beaux-parents *mpl*

inn [ɪn] *n* auberge *f*

inner [ˈɪnəˈ] *adj* intérieur; **the inner city** les quartiers déshérités du centre ville

inner tube *n* chambre à air *f*

innocent [ˈɪnəsnt] *adj* innocent

inquest [ˈɪnkwɛst] *n* enquête *f*

inquire [ɪnˈkwaɪəˈ] *vb*: **to inquire about something** se renseigner sur quelque chose ▷ *I'm going to inquire about show times.* Je vais me renseigner sur les horaires de cinéma.

inquiry [ɪnˈkwaɪərɪ] *n*: **to make**

inquiries about something faire des demandes de renseignement ▷ *"inquiries"* « renseignements »

inquisitive [ɪnˈkwɪzɪtɪv] *adj* curieux (*f* curieuse)

insane [ɪnˈseɪn] *adj* fou (*f* folle)

inscription [ɪnˈskrɪpʃən] *n* inscription *f*

insect [ˈɪnsɛkt] *n* insecte *m*

insect repellent *n* antimoustiques *m*

insensitive [ɪnˈsɛnsɪtɪv] *adj* indélicat ▷ *That was a bit insensitive of you.* C'était un peu indélicat de ta part.

insert [ɪnˈsɜːt] *n* insérer ▷ *Insert the CD in the drive.* Insère le CD dans le lecteur. ▷ *You should insert a paragraph here, explaining your point.* Tu devrais insérer un paragraphe ici pour expliquer.

inside [ˈɪnˈsaɪd] *n* intérieur *m*
▶ *adv, prep* à l'intérieur ▷ *They're inside.* Ils sont à l'intérieur. ▷ *inside the house* à l'intérieur de la maison; **to go inside** rentrer; **Come inside!** Rentrez!

insincere [ɪnsɪnˈsɪəʳ] *adj* peu sincère

insist [ɪnˈsɪst] *vb* insister ▷ *I didn't want to, but he insisted.* Je ne voulais pas, mais il a insisté.; **to insist on doing something** insister pour faire quelque chose ▷ *She insisted on paying.* Elle a insisté pour payer.; **He insisted he was innocent.** Il affirmait qu'il était innocent.

inspect [ɪnˈspɛkt] *vb* inspecter

inspector [ɪnˈspɛktəʳ] *n* inspecteur *m*, inspectrice *f*

install [ɪnˈstɔːl] *vb* installer ▷ *to install a piece of software* installer un logiciel ▷ *We've just installed new kitchen cupboards.* Nous venons d'installer de nouvelles armoires de cuisine.

instalment [ɪnˈstɔːlmənt] *n*
❶ (*payment*) versement *m* ▷ *to pay in instalments* payer en plusieurs versements ❷ (*episode*) épisode *m*

instance [ˈɪnstəns] *n*: **for instance** par exemple

instant [ˈɪnstənt] *adj* ❶ immédiat ▷ *It was an instant success.* Ça a été un succès immédiat. ❷ (*coffee, foods*) instantané ▷ *instant pudding* le pouding instantané; **instant messaging** la messagerie instantanée

instantly [ˈɪnstəntlɪ] *adv* tout de suite

instead [ɪnˈstɛd] *adv*: **instead of (1)** (*followed by noun*) à la place de ▷ *He went instead of his brother.* Il y est allé à la place de son frère. **(2)** (*followed by verb*) au lieu de ▷ *We played tennis instead of going swimming.* Nous avons joué au tennis au lieu d'aller nager.; **The pool was closed, so we played tennis instead.** La piscine était fermée, alors nous avons joué au tennis.

instinct [ˈɪnstɪŋkt] *n* instinct *m*

institute [ˈɪnstɪtjuːt] *n* institut *m*

institution [ɪnstɪˈtjuːʃən] *n* institution *f*

instruct [ɪnˈstrʌkt] *vb*: **to instruct somebody to do something** donner l'ordre à quelqu'un de faire quelque chose ▷ *She instructed us to wait outside.* Elle nous a donné l'ordre d'attendre dehors.

instructions [ɪnˈstrʌkʃənz] *npl* ❶ instructions *fpl* ▷ *Follow the instructions carefully.* Suivez soigneusement les instructions. ❷ (*for product*) mode *m* d'emploi ▷ *Where are the instructions?* Où est le mode d'emploi?

instructor [ɪnˈstrʌktəʳ] *n* moniteur *m*, monitrice *f* ▷ *a ski* *instructor* un moniteur de ski ▷ *a driving instructor* un moniteur d'auto-école

instrument ['ɪnstrəmənt] *n* instrument *m* ▷ *Do you play an instrument?* Est-ce que tu joues d'un instrument?

insufficient [ɪnsə'fɪʃənt] *adj* insuffisant

insulin ['ɪnsjulɪn] *n* insuline *f*

insult [ɪn'sʌlt] *n* insulte *f*
▶ *vb* insulter

insurance [ɪn'ʃuərəns] *n* assurance *f* ▷ *her car insurance* son assurance automobile; **an insurance policy** une police d'assurance

intelligent [ɪn'tɛlɪdʒənt] *adj* intelligent

intend [ɪn'tɛnd] *vb*: **to intend to do something** avoir l'intention de faire quelque chose ▷ *I intend to do French at university.* J'ai l'intention d'étudier le français à l'université.

intense [ɪn'tɛns] *adj* intense

intensive [ɪn'tɛnsɪv] *adj* intensif (f intensive)

intention [ɪn'tɛnʃən] *n* intention *f*

intercom ['ɪntəkɔm] *n* interphone *m*

interest ['ɪntrɪst] *n* intérêt *m* ▷ *to show an interest in something* manifester de l'intérêt pour quelque chose; **What interests do you have?** Quels sont tes centres d'intérêt?; **My main interest is music.** Ce qui m'intéresse le plus c'est la musique.; **an interest group** un groupe d'intérêt; **interest rate** (*bank account*) le taux d'intérêt
▶ *vb* intéresser ▷ *It doesn't interest me.* Ça ne m'intéresse pas.; **to be interested in something** s'intéresser à quelque chose ▷ *I'm not interested in politics.* Je ne

m'intéresse pas à la politique.

interesting ['ɪntrɪstɪŋ] *adj* intéressant

interfere [ɪntə'fɪə*ʳ*] *vb*: **Stop interfering in my social life.** Arrête de te mêler dans ma vie sociale.; **The weather interfered with our plans.** Le mauvais temps a contrarié nos projets.

interior [ɪn'tɪərɪə*ʳ*] *n* intérieur *m*

interior designer *n* décorateur d'intérieur *m*, décoratrice d'intérieur *f*

intermediate [ɪntə'miːdɪət] *adj* (*course, level*) moyen (f moyenne)

intermission [ɪntə'mɪʃən] *n* entracte *m*

internal [ɪn'təːnl] *adj* interne

international [ɪntə'næʃənl] *adj* international (mpl internationaux)

Internet ['ɪntənɛt] *n* Internet *m* ▷ *on the Internet* sur Internet

Internet café *n* cybercafé

Internet user *n* internaute *mf*

interpret [ɪn'təːprɪt] *vb* ❶ servir d'interprète ▷ *He couldn't speak French, so his friend interpreted.* Comme il ne savait pas le français, son ami a servi d'interprète. ❷ *I don't know how to interpret her response.* Je ne sais pas comment interpréter sa réaction.

interpreter [ɪn'təːprɪtə*ʳ*] *n* interprète *mf*

interrupt [ɪntə'rʌpt] *vb* interrompre

interruption [ɪntə'rʌpʃən] *n* interruption *f*

intersection [ɪntə'sɛkʃən] *n* intersection *f* ▷ *What's the nearest intersection?* Quelle est l'intersection la plus proche? ▷ *Turn left at the next intersection.* Tourne à gauche à la prochaine intersection.

interview ['ɪntəvjuː] *n* ❶ (*on TV, radio*) interview *f* ❷ (*for job*) entretien m

▶ vb (on TV, radio) interviewer

interviewer ['ɪntəvjuːə'] n
(on TV, radio) interviewer m,
intervieweuse f

intimate ['ɪntɪmeɪt] adj intime

into ['ɪntu] prep ❶ dans ▷ He
got into the car. Il est monté dans
la voiture. ❷ en ▷ I'm going into
town. Je vais en ville. ▷ Translate
it into French. Traduisez ça en
français. ▷ Divide into two groups.
Répartissez-vous en deux groupes.

intolerant [ɪn'tɒlərnt] adj
intolérant; **She's lactose-
intolerant.** Elle est intolérante
au lactose.

intramurals [ɪntrə'mjuərəlz] npl
les f activités intramurales ▷ Did
you sign up for intramurals? Tu t'es
inscrit aux activités intramurales?

introduce [ɪntrə'djuːs] vb
présenter ▷ I'd like to introduce my
grandmother. Je vous présente ma
grand-mère. ❷ en ▷ He introduced me to
his parents. Il m'a présentée à ses
parents.

introduction [ɪntrə'dʌkʃən] n (in
book) introduction f

intruder [ɪn'truːdə'] n intrus m,
intruse f

intuition [ɪntjuː'ɪʃən] n intuition f

Inuit ['ɪnuɪt] npl Inuits mpl
▶ adj Inuit ▷ traditional Inuit culture
la culture inuite traditionnelle

Inuk [ɪ'nuk] n Inuit m, Inuite f

invade [ɪn'veɪd] vb envahir;
to invade someone's privacy
s'ingérer dans la vie privée de
quelqu'un

invasion [ɪn'veɪʒən] n
envahissement m

invent [ɪn'vent] vb inventer

invention [ɪn'venʃən] n invention f

inventor [ɪn'ventə'] n inventeur m,
inventrice f

investigation [ɪnvestɪ'geɪʃən] n
(police) enquête f

investment [ɪn'vestmənt] n
investissement m ▷ Education
is an investment in your
future. L'éducation, c'est un
investissement dans ton avenir.

invincible [ɪn'vɪnsɪbl] adj
invincible ▷ He thinks he's invincible.
Il se croit invincible.

invisible [ɪn'vɪzɪbl] adj invisible

invitation [ɪnvɪ'teɪʃən] n
invitation f

invite [ɪn'vaɪt] vb inviter ▷ You're all
invited. Vous êtes tous invités.; **to
invite somebody to a party** inviter
quelqu'un à une fête

involve [ɪn'vɒlv] vb nécessiter
▷ This job involves a lot of travelling.
Ce travail nécessite de nombreux
déplacements.; **to be involved
in something** (crime, drugs) être
impliqué dans quelque chose; **to
be involved with somebody** (in
relationship) avoir une relation avec
quelqu'un

iPad® ['aɪpæd] n iPad® m

iPhone® ['aɪfəʊn] n iPhone® m

IQ n (= intelligence quotient) Q.I. m
(= quotient intellectuel)

iron ['aɪən] n ❶ (metal) fer m ❷ (for
clothes) fer à repasser m
▶ vb repasser

ironic [aɪ'rɒnɪk] adj ironique

ironing ['aɪənɪŋ] n repassage m
▷ to do the ironing faire le repassage

ironing board n planche à
repasser f

irregular [ɪ'regjulə'] adj irrégulier
(f irrégulière) ▷ an irregular verb un
verbe irrégulier

irrelevant [ɪ'reləvənt] adj hors de
propos ▷ That's irrelevant. C'est hors
de propos.

irresistible [ɪrɪ'zɪstɪbl] adj
irrésistible ▷ irresistible desserts des

desserts irrésistibles ▷ *an irresistible
urge* une envie irrésistible
irresponsible [ɪrɪˈspɒnsɪbl] *adj*
(person) irresponsable ▷ *That
was irresponsible of them.* C'était
irresponsable de leur part.
irritating [ˈɪrɪteɪtɪŋ] *adj* irritant
is [ɪz] *vb see* **be**
Islamic [ɪzˈlɑːmɪk] *adj* islamique
▷ *Islamic law* la loi islamique
island [ˈaɪlənd] *n* île *f*
isolated [ˈaɪsəleɪtɪd] *adj* isolé
ISP *n* (= *Internet service provider*)
fournisseur de services Internet *m*
issue [ˈɪʃuː] *n* ❶ (matter) question
f ▷ *a controversial issue* une question
controversée ❷ (of magazine)
numéro *m*
▶ *vb* (equipment, supplies) distribuer
it [ɪt] *pron*

> Remember to check if **it** stands
> for a masculine or feminine
> noun.

❶ il, elle ▷ *"Where's my book?" — "It's
on the table."* « Où est mon livre? »
— « Il est sur la table. » ▷ *"When does
the pool close?" — "It closes at 8."* « La
piscine ferme à quelle heure? » —
« Elle ferme à vingt heures. »

> Use **le** or **la** when **it** is the
> object of the sentence. **le** and
> **la** change to **l'** before a vowel
> and most words beginning
> with "h".

❷ le, l', la, l' ▷ *There's a croissant left.
Do you want it?* Il reste un croissant.
Tu le veux? ▷ *It's a good film. Did you
see it?* C'est un bon film. L'as-tu vu?
▷ *I don't want this apple. Take it.* Je ne
veux pas de cette pomme. Prends-
la. ▷ *"He's got a new car." — "Yes, I saw
it."* « Il a une nouvelle voiture. »
— « Oui, je l'ai vue. »; **It's raining.**
Il pleut.; **It's 6 o'clock.** Il est six
heures.; **It's Friday tomorrow.**
Demain, c'est vendredi.; **"Who**

is it?" — "It's me."** « Qui est-ce? »
— « C'est moi. »; **It's expensive.**
C'est cher.
italics [ɪˈtælɪks] *n* italique *f* ▷ *to
put a word in italics* mettre un mot
en italique
itch [ɪtʃ] *vb*: **It itches.** Ça me
démange.; **My head's itching.** J'ai
des démangeaisons à la tête.
itchy [ˈɪtʃɪ] *adj*: **My arm is itchy.** J'ai
le bras qui démange.
it'd [ˈɪtd]: = **it had**; **it would**
item [ˈaɪtəm] *n* (object) article *m*
itinerary [aɪˈtɪnərərɪ] *n*
itinéraire *m*
it'll [ˈɪtl]: = **it will**
its [ɪts] *adj*

> Remember to check if **its** refers
> to a masculine, feminine or
> plural noun.

son *m*, sa *f*, ses *pl* ▷ *What's its name?*
Quel est son nom? ▷ *Everything in
its place.* Chaque chose à sa place.
▷ *The dog is losing its hair.* Le chien
perd ses poils.
it's [ɪts]: = **it is**; **it has**
itself [ɪtˈsɛlf] *pron se*

> **se** changes to **s'** before a vowel
> and most words beginning
> with "h".

▷ *The bear was trying to defend itself.*
L'ours essayait de se défendre.
I've [aɪv]: = **I have**

j

jab [dʒæb] vb planter ▷ He jabbed his fork into the potato. Il a planté sa fourchette dans la pomme de terre.; **She jabbed me with her elbow.** Elle m'a donné un coup de coude.

jack [dʒæk] n ❶ (for car) cric m ❷ (playing card) valet m

jacket ['dʒækɪt] n veston m

jackknife ['dʒæknaɪf] n canif m

jackpot ['dʒækpɒt] n gros lot m; **to win the jackpot** gagner le gros lot

jail [dʒeɪl] n prison f; **to go to jail** aller en prison; **to put someone in jail** emprisonner quelqu'un

jam [dʒæm] n confiture f ▷ strawberry jam la confiture de fraises; **a traffic jam** un embouteillage; **to be in a jam** être dans le pétrin; **to get somebody out of a jam** sortir quelqu'un du pétrin

jam jar n pot à confiture m

jammed [dʒæmd] adj coincé ▷ The window's jammed. La fenêtre est coincée.

jam-packed [dʒæm'pækt] adj bondé ▷ The room was jam-packed. La salle était bondée.

janitor ['dʒænɪtə'] n concierge ▷ He's a janitor. Il est concierge.

January ['dʒænjuərɪ] n janvier m; **in January** en janvier

jar [dʒɑː'] n bocal m (pl bocaux) ▷ an empty jar un bocal vide; **a jar of honey** un pot de miel

javelin ['dʒævlɪn] n javelot m

jaw [dʒɔː] n mâchoire f

jazz [dʒæz] n jazz m

jealous ['dʒɛləs] adj jaloux (f jalouse)

jeans [dʒiːnz] npl jeans mpl

Jehovah's Witness [dʒɪ'həʊvəz-] n témoin de Jéhovah m ▷ She's a Jehovah's Witness. Elle est témoin de Jéhovah.

Jello® ['dʒɛləʊ] n gelée f

jelly ['dʒɛlɪ] n gelée f

jelly bean n bonbon haricot m

jellyfish ['dʒɛlɪfɪʃ] n méduse f

jersey ['dʒɜːzɪ] n ❶ (pullover) maillot m

jet [dʒɛt] n ❶ (plane) avion m à réaction ❷ jet m ▷ a jet of water un jet d'eau

jetlag ['dʒɛtlæg] n: **to be suffering from jetlag** subir les effets du décalage horaire

Jew [dʒuː] n juif m, juive f

jewel ['dʒuːəl] n bijou m (pl bijoux)

jeweller ['dʒuːələ'] n bijoutier m, bijoutière f ▷ He's a jeweller. Il est bijoutier.

jewellery ['dʒuːəlrɪ] n bijoux mpl

jewellery store n bijouterie f

Jewish ['dʒuːɪʃ] adj juif m (f juive)

jigsaw ['dʒɪgsɔː] n puzzle m

jingle ['dʒɪŋgl] vb ❶ (bells) tinter ❷ (coins) cliqueter

jinx [dʒɪŋks] n sort m ▷ *to put a jinx on something* jeter un sort à quelque chose

job [dʒɒb] n ❶ emploi m ▷ *He lost his job.* Il a perdu son emploi.; **I have a Saturday job.** Je travaille le samedi. ❷ (chore, task) travail m (pl travaux) ▷ *That was a difficult job.* C'était un travail difficile.

job centre ['dʒɒbsentəʳ] n centre d'emploi m

jobless ['dʒɒblɪs] adj sans emploi

jog [dʒɒg] vb faire du jogging

jogging ['dʒɒgɪŋ] n jogging m; **to go jogging** faire du jogging

join [dʒɔɪn] vb ❶ (become member of) s'inscrire à ▷ *I'm going to join the ski club.* Je vais m'inscrire au club de ski. ❷ se joindre à ▷ *Do you mind if I join you?* Puis-je me joindre à vous?

joint [dʒɔɪnt] n ❶ (in body) articulation f ❷ (of meat) rôti m

joke [dʒəuk] n plaisanterie f; **to tell a joke** raconter une plaisanterie; **He can't take a joke.** Il prend mal la plaisanterie.; **It's a joke.** (waste of time) C'est de la blague. ▷ *to play a joke on somebody* jouer un tour à quelqu'un
▷ vb plaisanter ▷ *I'm only joking.* Je plaisante.

jolly ['dʒɒlɪ] adj jovial (mpl joviaux)

jot down vb noter

journal ['dʒɜːnl] n journal m ▷ *She keeps a journal of her experiences.* Elle note ses expériences dans un journal.

journalism ['dʒɜːnəlɪzəm] n journalisme m

journalist ['dʒɜːnəlɪst] n journaliste ▷ *She's a journalist.* Elle est journaliste.

journey ['dʒɜːnɪ] n ❶ voyage m ▷ *I don't like long journeys.* Je n'aime pas les longs voyages.; **to go on a journey** faire un voyage ❷ (to school, work) trajet m ▷ *The journey to school takes about half an hour.* Il y a une demi-heure de trajet pour aller à l'école.; **a bus journey** un trajet en autobus

joy [dʒɔɪ] n joie f

joystick ['dʒɔɪstɪk] n (for computer game) manette de jeu f

judge [dʒʌdʒ] n juge ▷ *She's a judge.* Elle est juge.
▷ vb juger

judo ['dʒuːdəu] n judo m ▷ *My hobby is judo.* Je fais du judo.

jug [dʒʌg] n cruche f

juggler ['dʒʌgləʳ] n jongleur m, jongleuse f

juice [dʒuːs] n jus m ▷ *orange juice* le jus d'orange

July [dʒuːˈlaɪ] n juillet m; **in July** en juillet

jumble ['dʒʌmbl] n fouillis m ▷ *a jumble of information* un fouillis de renseignements; **a jumble of ideas** des pensées confuses; **a jumble of papers** des papiers en vrac; **Her thoughts were all in a jumble.** Ses pensées étaient toutes confuses.

jump [dʒʌmp] vb sauter; **to jump over something** sauter par-dessus quelque chose; **to jump out of the window** sauter par la fenêtre; **to jump off the roof** sauter du toit; **to jump to conclusions** sauter aux conclusions

jumper ['dʒʌmpəʳ] n robe chasuble f

June [dʒuːn] n juin m; **in June** en juin

jungle ['dʒʌŋgl] n jungle f

junior ['dʒuːnɪəʳ] adj ❶ (sports) junior (f+pl junior) ▷ *the junior leagues* les ligues junior ❷ (work) subalterne ▷ *a junior employee* un employé subalterne ❸ (in names) fils ▷ *Bill Smith, Jr.* Bill Smith, fils; **in junior high school** à l'école secondaire de premier cycle; **junior kindergarten** la prématernelle; **She's three years my junior.** Elle a trois ans de moins que moi.

junk [dʒʌŋk] n ❶ (old things) bric-à-brac no pl ▷ The attic's full of junk. Le grenier est rempli de bric-à-brac. ❷ (worthless stuff) camelote f ▷ Don't read that, it's junk. Ne lis pas ça, c'est de la camelote.; **a junk shop** un magasin d'objets usagés; **junk mail** la publicité-rebut; **junk email** le pourriel

junk food n ❶ (in general) malbouffe f ▷ My parents are against junk food. Mes parents sont contre la malbouffe. ▷ Junk food is becoming a problem in our society. La malbouffe est devenue un problème dans notre société. ❷ (specific food) aliment m vide ▷ Potato chips are junk food. Les croustilles sont un aliment vide. ▷ I ate junk food for lunch. J'ai mangé des aliments vides pour le dîner.

jury ['dʒʊərɪ] n jury m

just [dʒʌst] adv, adj juste ▷ just after Christmas juste après Noël ▷ We had just enough money. Nous avions juste assez d'argent. ▷ just in time juste à temps ▷ a just policy une politique juste; **They're just jealous.** Ils sont simplement jaloux.; **I'm rather busy just now.** Je suis assez occupé en ce moment.; **I did it just now.** Je viens de le faire.; **He's just arrived.** Il vient d'arriver.; **I'm just coming!** J'arrive!; **It's just a suggestion.** Ce n'est qu'une suggestion.; **just for you** spécialement pour toi; **to be just about to do something** être sur le point de faire quelque chose

justice ['dʒʌstɪs] n justice f

justify ['dʒʌstɪfaɪ] vb justifier

k

kangaroo [kæŋɡə'ruː] n kangourou m

karaoke [kɑːrə'əʊkɪ] n karaoké m

karate [kə'rɑːtɪ] n karaté m

kayak ['kaɪæk] n kayak m

kebab [kə'bæb] n brochette f

keen [kiːn] adj enthousiaste ▷ He doesn't seem very keen. Il n'a pas l'air très enthousiaste.; **She's a keen student.** C'est une étudiante assidue.; **to be keen on something** aimer quelque chose ▷ I'm not very keen on that band. Je n'aime pas trop cette bande.; **to be keen on doing something** avoir très envie de faire quelque chose ▷ I'm not very keen on going. Je n'ai pas très envie d'y aller.

keep [kiːp] vb ❶ (retain) garder ▷ You can keep it. Tu peux le garder. ❷ (remain) rester ▷ Keep still! Reste tranquille!; **Keep quiet!** Tais-toi!; **I keep forgetting my keys.** J'oublie tout le temps mes clés.; **to keep on doing something (1)** (continue) continuer à faire quelque chose ▷ He kept on reading. Il a continué à lire. **(2)** (repeatedly) ne pas arrêter de faire quelque chose ▷ The car keeps on breaking down. La voiture n'arrête pas de tomber en panne.; **"keep out"** « défense d'entrer »

keep up vb (someone) suivre ▷ She walks so fast I can't keep up. Elle marche tellement vite que je n'arrive pas à la suivre. ▷ I can't keep up with the rest of the class. Je n'arrive pas à suivre le reste de la classe.; **You should keep up your guitar lessons.** Tu devrais continuer tes cours de guitare.; **Keep it up!** Continue!

kennel ['kɛnl] n niche f

kept [kɛpt] vb see **keep**

kerosene ['kɛrəsiːn] n pétrole m

ketchup ['kɛtʃəp] n ketchup m

kettle ['kɛtl] n bouilloire f

key [kiː] n **①** clé f; **key word** le mot clé; **key card** la carte magnétique **②** (on keyboard) touche f **③** (music) ton m ▷ to change key changer de ton; **in the key of C** en do; **to sing off key** chanter faux; **key signature** l'armature f

keyboard ['kiːbɔːd] n clavier m ▷ The musician on keyboards is... Le musicien aux claviers est... ▷ a computer keyboard un clavier d'ordinateur

keychain ['kiːtʃeɪn] n porte-clés m

key in vb entrer ▷ to key in data entrer des données ▷ Key in your password. Entre ton mot de passe.

keypad ['kiːpæd] n pavé numérique m

kick [kɪk] n coup de pied m ▶ vb: **to kick somebody** donner un coup de pied à quelqu'un ▷ He kicked me. Il m'a donné un coup de

pied. ▷ She kicked the ball hard. Elle a donné un bon coup de pied dans le ballon.; **to kick off** (football, soccer) donner le coup d'envoi

kick-off ['kɪkɔf] n coup d'envoi m ▷ The kick-off is at 10 o'clock. Le coup d'envoi sera donné à dix heures.

kid [kɪd] n (child) jeune ▶ vb plaisanter ▷ I'm just kidding. Je plaisante.; **You're kidding!** Sans blague!

kidnap ['kɪdnæp] vb kidnapper

kidnapper ['kɪdnæpə¹] n kidnappeur m, kidnappeuse f

kidnapping ['kɪdnæpɪŋ] n enlèvement m

kidney ['kɪdnɪ] n **①** (human) rein m ▷ He's got kidney trouble. Il a des problèmes de reins. **②** (to eat) rognon m ▷ I don't like kidneys. Je n'aime pas les rognons.

kill [kɪl] vb tuer ▷ She was killed in a car accident. Elle a été tuée dans un accident de voiture.; **Luckily, nobody was killed.** Il n'y a heureusement pas eu de victimes.; **Six people were killed in the accident.** L'accident a fait six morts.; **to kill oneself** se suicider

killer ['kɪlə¹] n (murderer) meurtrier m, meurtrière f; **Meningitis can be a killer.** La méningite peut être mortelle.; **That math test was a killer.** Ce test de maths était tuant.; **killer whale** l'épaulard m

kiln [kɪln] n four à céramique m

kilo ['kiːləu] n kilo m ▷ 2 dollars a kilo deux dollars le kilo

kilometre ['kɪləmiːtə¹] n kilomètre m

kilt [kɪlt] n kilt m

kind [kaɪnd] adj gentil (f gentille); **to be kind to somebody** être gentil avec quelqu'un; **Thank you for being so kind.** Merci pour votre gentillesse.

▶ n sorte ▷ *It's a kind of sausage.*
C'est une sorte de saucisse.

kindergarten ['kɪndəgɑːtn] n
maternelle f

kindly ['kaɪndlɪ] adv gentiment
▷ *"Don't worry," she said kindly.*
« Ne t'en fais pas », m'a-t-elle dit
gentiment.; **Kindly refrain from
smoking.** Veuillez vous abstenir
de fumer.

kindness ['kaɪndnɪs] n
gentillesse f

king [kɪŋ] n roi m

kingdom ['kɪŋdəm] n royaume m

kiosk ['kiːɒsk] n kiosque m

kipper ['kɪpə] n hareng fumé m

kiss [kɪs] n baiser m ▷ *a passionate
kiss* un baiser passionné
▶ vb ❶ embrasser ▷ *He kissed
her passionately.* Il l'a embrassée
passionnément. ❷ s'embrasser
▷ *They kissed.* Ils se sont embrassés.

kit [kɪt] n trousse f ▷ *a tool kit* une
trousse à outils ▷ *a first aid kit* une
trousse de secours ▷ *a tire repair
kit* une trousse de réparations; **a
sewing kit** un nécessaire à couture

kitchen ['kɪtʃɪn] n cuisine f; **a
kitchen knife** un couteau de
cuisine

kite [kaɪt] n cerf-volant m (pl
cerfs-volants)

kitten ['kɪtn] n chaton m

knapsack ['næpsæk] n sac à dos m

knee [niː] n genou m (pl genoux);
He was on his knees. Il était à
genoux.

kneel (down) [niːl-] vb
s'agenouiller

knew [njuː] vb see **know**

knife [naɪf] n couteau m (pl
couteaux); **a kitchen knife** un
couteau de cuisine; **a hunting
knife** un couteau de chasse

knit [nɪt] vb tricoter

knitting ['nɪtɪŋ] n tricot m ▷ *I like*

knitting. J'aime faire du tricot.

knives [naɪvz] npl see **knife**

knob [nɒb] n (on door, radio, TV,
radiator) bouton m

knock [nɒk] vb frapper ▷ *Someone's
knocking at the door.* Quelqu'un
frappe à la porte.; **to knock
somebody down** renverser
quelqu'un; **to knock something
over** renverser quelque chose ▷ *She
knocked over a glass.* Elle a renversé
un verre.; **to knock somebody out
(stun)** assommer ▷ *They knocked
out the watchman.* Ils ont assommé
le gardien.
▶ n coup m

knot [nɒt] n nœud m; **to tie a knot
in something** faire un nœud à
quelque chose

know [nəu] vb

> Use **savoir** for knowing facts,
> **connaître** for knowing people
> and places.

❶ savoir ▷ *"It's a long way." — "Yes,
I know."* « C'est loin. » — « Oui, je
sais. » ▷ *I don't know.* Je ne sais pas.
▷ *I don't know what to do.* Je ne sais
pas quoi faire. ▷ *I don't know how
to do it.* Je ne sais pas comment
faire. ❷ connaître ▷ *I know her.* Je
la connais. ▷ *I know Halifax well.* Je
connais bien Halifax.; **I don't know
any German.** Je ne parle pas du
tout allemand.; **to know that...**
savoir que... ▷ *I know that you like
chocolate.* Je sais que tu aimes le
chocolat. ▷ *I didn't know that your
dad was a policeman.* Je ne savais
pas que ton père était policier.;
**to know about something
(1)** (be aware of) être au courant de
quelque chose ▷ *Do you know about
the meeting this afternoon?* Tu es au
courant de la réunion de cet après-
midi? **(2)** (be knowledgeable about)
s'y connaître en quelque chose

▷ *She knows a lot about cars.* Elle s'y
connaît en voitures. ▷ *I don't know
much about computers.* Je ne m'y
connais pas bien en informatique.;
to know how to do something
savoir faire quelque chose ▷ *He
knows how to swim.* Il sait nager.; **to
get to know somebody** apprendre
à connaître quelqu'un; **I'll let you
know tomorrow.** Je te le ferai
savoir demain.; **Let me know if
you need any help.** Si tu as besoin
d'aide, dis-le moi.; **How should
I know?** (*I don't know!*) Comment
veux-tu que je le sache?; **You never
know!** On ne sait jamais!

know-how ['nəuhau] *n* savoir-
faire *m*

know-it-all ['nəuɪtɔːl] *n* je-sais-
tout ▷ *He's such a know-it-all!* C'est
Monsieur je-sais-tout!

knowledge ['nɒlɪdʒ] *n*
connaissance *f*

knowledgeable ['nɒlɪdʒəbl]
adj: **to be knowledgeable
about something** s'y connaître
en quelque chose ▷ *She's very
knowledgeable about computers.* Elle
s'y connaît bien en informatique.

known [nəun] *vb see* **know**

lab [læb] *n* (= *laboratory*) labo *m*; **a
lab technician** un laborantin

label ['leɪbl] *n* étiquette *f*

laboratory [ləˈbɒrətərɪ] *n*
laboratoire *m*

labour ['leɪbə'] *n*: **to be in labour**
être en train d'accoucher; **the
labour market** le marché du
travail; **a labour union** un syndicat

Labour Day *n* fête du Travail *f*

labourer ['leɪbərə'] *n* ouvrier *m*;
a farm labourer un ouvrier agricole

Labrador ['læbrədɔː'] *n*
Labrador *m*

lace [leɪs] *n* ❶ (*of shoe*) lacet *m*
❷ dentelle *f* ▷ *a lace collar* un col
en dentelle

lack [læk] *n* manque *m* ▷ *He got
the job despite his lack of experience.*
Il a obtenu le poste en dépit de
son manque d'expérience.; **There
was no lack of volunteers.** Les
volontaires ne manquaient pas.

lacquer ['lækə'] n laque f

lacrosse [lə'krɒs] n crosse f ▷ a lacrosse stick une crosse

ladder ['lædə'] n échelle f

lady ['leɪdɪ] n dame f; **a young lady** une jeune fille; **Ladies and gentlemen...** Mesdames, Messieurs...; **the ladies' room** les toilettes fpl pour dames

ladybug ['leɪdɪbʌg] n coccinelle f

lag behind [læg-] vb rester en arrière

laid [leɪd] vb see **lay**

laid-back [leɪd'bæk] adj relax ▷ My mom is very laid-back. Ma mère est très relax.

lain [leɪn] vb see **lie**

lake [leɪk] n lac m; **Lake Erie** le lac Érié

lamb [læm] n agneau m (pl agneaux); **a lamb chop** une côtelette d'agneau

lame [leɪm] adj: **to be lame** boîter ▷ My pony is lame. Mon poney boîte.; **a lame excuse** une piètre excuse

lamp [læmp] n lampe f

lampshade ['læmpʃeɪd] n abat-jour m (pl abat-jour)

land [lænd] n ❶ terre f; **a piece of land** un terrain ❷ (country) pays m ▶ vb (plane, passenger) atterrir

landfill site ['lændfɪl-] n site d'enfouissement m

landing ['lændɪŋ] n ❶ (of plane) atterrissage m ❷ (of staircase) palier m

landlady ['lændleɪdɪ] n propriétaire

landline ['lændlaɪn] n ligne fixe f

landlord ['lændlɔːd] n propriétaire

landmark ['lændmɑːk] n (for finding your way) point de repère m; **The CN Tower is one of Toronto's most famous landmarks.** La tour CN est l'un des sites les plus célèbres du paysage torontois.

landowner ['lændəʊnə'] n propriétaire terrien m

landscape ['lændskeɪp] n paysage m

landslide ['lændslaɪd] n glissement de terrain m

lane [leɪn] n ❶ (leading to country house) entrée f ❷ (on highway) voie f ❸ (small road in city) ruelle f

language ['læŋgwɪdʒ] n ❶ langue f ▷ French isn't a difficult language. Le français n'est pas une langue difficile. ❷ langage m ▷ the origin of language l'origine du langage ▷ Watch your language! Surveille ton langage! ▷ body language le langage corporel; **to use bad language** dire des grossièretés

lantern ['læntn] n lanterne f

lap [læp] n ❶ (sport) tour de piste m ▷ I ran 10 laps. J'ai fait dix tours de piste en courant. ❷ (pool) longueur f ▷ I swam 30 laps. J'ai fait trente longueurs.; **on my lap** sur mes genoux

laptop ['læptɒp] n (computer) portable m

large [lɑːdʒ] adj ❶ grand ▷ a large house une grande maison ❷ (person, animal) gros (f grosse) ▷ a large dog un gros chien

largely ['lɑːdʒlɪ] adv en grande partie ▷ It's largely the fault of the government. C'est en grande partie la faute du gouvernement.

laryngitis [lærɪn'dʒaɪtɪs] n laryngite f

lasagna [lə'zænjə] n lasagne f

laser ['leɪzə'] n laser m; **a laser printer** une imprimante laser

last [lɑːst] adj, adv ❶ dernier (f dernière) ▷ last Friday vendredi dernier ▷ last week la semaine dernière ▷ last summer l'été dernier ❷ en dernier ▷ She arrived last. Elle est arrivée en dernier.; **"I lost my wallet." — "When did you see it**

last? « J'ai perdu mon portefeuille. » — « Quand est-ce que tu l'as vu pour la dernière fois? »; **When I last saw him, he was wearing a blue shirt.** La dernière fois que je l'ai vu, il portait une chemise bleue.; **the last time** la dernière fois ▷ *the last time I saw her* la dernière fois que je l'ai vue ▷ *That's the last time I take your advice!* C'est la dernière fois que je suis tes conseils!; **last night (1)** (*evening*) hier soir ▷ *I got home at midnight last night.* Je suis rentré à minuit hier soir. **(2)** (*sleeping hours*) la nuit dernière ▷ *I couldn't sleep last night.* J'ai du mal à dormir la nuit dernière.; **at last** enfin
▶ vb durer ▷ *The concert lasts two hours.* Le concert dure deux heures.

lastly [ˈlɑːstlɪ] *adv* finalement ▷ *Lastly, what time do you arrive?* Finalement, à quelle heure arrives-tu?

late [leɪt] *adj, adv* ❶ en retard ▷ *Hurry up or you'll be late!* Dépêche-toi, sinon tu vas être en retard! ▷ *I'm often late for school.* J'arrive souvent en retard à l'école.; **to arrive late** arriver en retard ▷ *She arrived late.* Elle est arrivée en retard. ❷ tard ▷ *I went to bed late.* Je me suis couché tard.; **in the late afternoon** en fin d'après-midi; **in late May** fin mai

lately [ˈleɪtlɪ] *adv* ces derniers temps ▷ *I haven't seen him lately.* Je ne l'ai pas vu ces derniers temps.

later [ˈleɪtəʳ] *adv* plus tard ▷ *I'll do it later.* Je ferai ça plus tard.; **See you later!** À tout à l'heure!

latest [ˈleɪtɪst] *adj* dernier (*f* dernière) ▷ *their latest album* leur dernier album; **at the latest** au plus tard ▷ *by 10 o'clock at the latest* à dix heures au plus tard

latter [ˈlætəʳ] *n* second *m*, seconde *f*; **the former…, the latter…** le

premier…, le second… ▷ *The former lives in Saskatchewan, the latter in New Brunswick.* Le premier habite en Saskatchewan, le second au Nouveau-Brunswick.; **The latter is the more expensive of the two systems.** Ce dernier système est le plus coûteux des deux.

laugh [lɑːf] *n* rire *m*; **It was a good laugh.** (*it was funny*) C'était bien amusant.
▶ vb rire *m*; **to laugh at something** (*make fun of*) se moquer de quelque chose ▷ *They laughed at her.* Ils se sont moqués d'elle.

launch [lɔːntʃ] *vb* (*product, rocket, boat*) lancer ▷ *They're going to launch a new model.* Ils vont lancer un nouveau modèle.

laundromat® [ˈlɔːndrəmæt] *n* lavoir *m*

laundry [ˈlɔːndrɪ] *n* ❶ (*clothes*) linge *m* ❷ (*task*) lavage *m* ▷ *to do the laundry* faire le lavage ▷ (*public, with machines*) lavoir *m* ▷ *Does this campground have a laundry?* Ce terrain de camping a-t-il un lavoir?; **laundry room** la salle de lavage; **coin laundry** le lavoir

Laurentians [lɔːˈrenʃənz] *npl* Laurentides *fpl* ▷ *We went camping in the Laurentians.* Nous avons fait du camping dans les Laurentides.

law [lɔː] *n* ❶ loi *f* ▷ *The laws are very strict.* Les lois sont très sévères.; **It's against the law.** C'est illégal. ❷ (*subject*) droit *m* ▷ *My brother is studying law.* Mon frère fait des études de droit.; **law and order** l'ordre *m* public; **law school** la faculté de droit

lawn [lɔːn] *n* pelouse *f*

lawnmower [ˈlɔːnməʊəʳ] *n* tondeuse à gazon *f*

lawyer [ˈlɔːjəʳ] *n* avocat *m*, avocate *f* ▷ *My mother's a lawyer.* Ma mère est avocate.

lay [leɪ] *vb*
 lay is also a form of **lie** VERB.
mettre ▷ *He laid the baby in her crib.* Il
a mis le bébé dans son lit.

lay off *vb* mettre à pied ▷ *My father
has been laid off.* Mon père a été
mis à pied.

layer ['leɪə] *n* **❶** couche f ▷ *the ozone
layer* la couche d'ozone

layout ['leɪaʊt] *n* **❶** (*publishing*)
mise en page f **❷** (*of house,
buildings*) disposition f ▷ *It took
me some time to get familiar with
the layout of the school.* J'ai mis un
certain temps à me familiariser
avec la disposition de l'école.

lazy ['leɪzɪ] *adj* paresseux (f
paresseuse)

lead [*n* lɛd, *vb* liːd] *n*
 This word has two
 pronunciations. Make sure you
 choose the right translation.
(*metal*) plomb m; **to be in the lead**
être en tête ▷ *Our team is in the
lead.* Notre équipe est en tête.; **to
have a two-point lead** avoir deux
points d'avance; **to take the lead
(1)** (*sports*) prendre la tête **(2)** (*act
first*) prendre l'initiative
 ▶ *vb* mener ▷ *the street that leads
to the arena* la rue qui mène à
l'aréna; **to lead the way** montrer le
chemin; **to lead somebody away**
emmener quelqu'un ▷ *The police led
the man away.* La police a emmené
l'homme.

leader ['liːdə'] *n* **❶** (*of expedition,
gang, political party*) chef m ▷ *She's
the party leader.* C'est le chef du
parti politique. **❷** (*of organization,
company*) dirigeant m, dirigeante f

lead singer [liːd-] *n* chanteur
principal m, chanteuse principale f

leaf [liːf] *n* feuille f

leaflet ['liːflɪt] *n* brochure f

league [liːg] *n* ligue f ▷ *They are at
the top of the league.* Ils sont en tête
de la ligue.; **a minor league** une
ligue mineure; **a major league** une
ligue majeure

leak [liːk] *n* fuite f ▷ *a gas leak* une
fuite de gaz
 ▶ *vb* (*pipe, water, gas*) fuir

lean [liːn] *adj* maigre ▷ *lean meat* la
viande maigre
 ▶ *vb* **❶** (*support oneself*) s'appuyer
▷ *He leaned against the wall.* Il s'est
appuyé contre le mur. **❷** (*support
an object*) appuyer ▷ *She leaned her
bike against the railing.* Elle a appuyé
son vélo contre la rampe.; **The
ladder was leaning against the
wall.** L'échelle était appuyée contre
le mur. **❸** (*bend*) se pencher ▷ *Don't
lean over too far.* Ne te penche pas
trop. ▷ *She leaned out of the window.*
Elle s'est penchée par la fenêtre.
 ▷ *to lean forward* se pencher en
avant

leap [liːp] *vb* sauter ▷ *They leapt
over the stream.* Ils ont sauté pour
traverser la rivière.; **He leapt out of
his chair when his team scored.**
Il s'est levé d'un bond lorsque son
équipe a marqué.

leap year *n* année f bissextile

learn [lɜːn] *vb* apprendre ▷ *I'm
learning to ski.* J'apprends à skier.

learner ['lɜːnə'] *n* **❶** She's **a quick
learner.** Elle apprend vite.; **second
language learners** ceux qui
apprennent une langue seconde

learnt [lɜːnt] *vb* see **learn**

leash [liːʃ] *n* laisse f ▷ *Keep your
dog on a leash.* Tenez votre chien
en laisse.

least [liːst] *adv, adj, pron*: **the least
(1)** (*followed by noun*) le moins de
▷ *It takes the least time.* C'est ce qui
prend le moins de temps. **(2)** (*after a
verb*) le moins ▷ *Music is the subject*

I like the least. La musique est la
matière que j'aime le moins.

When **least** is followed by
an adjective, the translation
depends on whether the
noun referred to is masculine,
feminine or plural.

the least... (1) le moins... ▷ *the least
expensive hotel* l'hôtel le moins cher
(2) la moins... ▷ *the least expensive
seat* la place la moins chère (3) les
moins... ▷ *the least expensive hotels*
les hôtels les moins chers ▷ *the least
expensive seats* les places les moins
chères; **It's the least I can do.** C'est
le moins que je puisse faire.; **at
least** (1) au moins ▷ *It'll cost at least
$200.* Ça va coûter au moins deux
cents dollars. (2) du moins ▷ ...
but at least nobody was hurt. ...mais
du moins personne n'a été blessé.
▷ *"It's totally unfair" — "at least,
that's my opinion."* « C'est vraiment
injuste » — « du moins c'est ce que
je pense. »

leather ['lɛðə'] n cuir m ▷ *a black
leather jacket* un manteau de
cuir noir

leave [li:v] n ① (from job)
congé m ▷ *sick leave* le congé de
maladie ▷ *maternity leave* le congé
de maternité ② (from army)
permission f ▷ *My brother is on
leave for a week.* Mon frère est en
permission pendant une semaine.
▶ vb ① (deliberately) laisser ▷ *Don't
leave your camera in the car.* Ne laisse
pas ton appareil-photo dans la
voiture. ② (by mistake) oublier ▷ *I
left my book at home.* J'ai oublié mon
livre à la maison. ▷ *Make sure you
haven't left anything behind.* Vérifiez
bien que vous n'avez rien oublié.
③ (go) partir ▷ *The bus leaves at 8.*
L'autobus part à huit heures. ▷ *She
just left.* Elle vient de partir. ④ (go

away from) quitter ▷ *We leave London
at six o'clock.* Nous quittons London
à six heures. ▷ *My sister left home last
year.* Ma sœur a quitté la maison
l'an dernier.; **to leave somebody
alone** laisser quelqu'un tranquille
▷ *Leave me alone!* Laisse-moi
tranquille!

leave out vb ① (person) mettre à
l'écart ▷ *Not knowing the language,
I felt really left out.* Comme je ne
connaissais pas la langue, je
me suis vraiment senti à l'écart.
② (word, sentence) omettre ▷ *You
left out a word there.* Tu as omis un
mot là.

leaves [li:vz] npl see **leaf**

lecture ['lɛktʃə'] n ① (public)
conférence f ② (at university) cours
magistral m (pl cours magistraux)
③ (scolding) sermon m ▷ *a lecture
on table manners* un sermon sur les
bonnes manières à table

Be careful not to translate
lecture by the French word
lecture.

▶ vb ① enseigner ▷ *He lectures
at the technical college.* Il enseigne
au collège technique. ② faire la
morale ▷ *He's always lecturing us.* Il
n'arrête pas de nous faire la morale.

led [lɛd] vb see **lead**

leek [li:k] n poireau m (pl poireaux)

left [lɛft] vb see **leave**
▶ adj, adv ① gauche f ▷ *my left hand*
ma main gauche ▷ *on the left side
of the road* sur le côté gauche de la
route ② à gauche ▷ *Turn left at the
traffic lights.* Tournez à gauche aux
prochains feux.; **I have no money
left.** Il ne me reste plus d'argent.
▶ n gauche f; **on the left** à gauche
▷ *Our house is on the left.* Notre
maison est à gauche.

left-hand ['lɛfthænd] adj: **the
left-hand side** la gauche ▷ *It's on

the left-hand side. C'est à gauche.
left-handed [ˌleftˈhændɪd] *adj*
gaucher (f gauchère)
leg [lɛg] *n* jambe f ▷ *She's broken
her leg.* Elle s'est cassé la jambe.; **a
chicken leg** une cuisse de poulet; **a
leg of lamb** un gigot d'agneau
legal [ˈliːgl] *adj* ❶ légal (mpl
légaux) ▷ *the legal driving age* l'âge
légal pour conduire ▷ *Is it legal to
copy this CD?* Est-il légal de faire une
copie de ce CD? ❷ juridique ▷ *the
legal system* le système juridique
▷ *legal aid* l'aide juridique f ▷ *legal
action* une poursuite juridique
legend [ˈlɛdʒənd] *n* légende f
leggings [ˈlɛgɪnz] *n* collant m
legible [ˈlɛdʒəbl] *adj* lisible
Legislative Assembly
[ˈlɛdʒɪslətɪv-] *n* Assemblée f
législative
leisure [ˈlɛʒəʳ] *n* loisirs mpl ▷ *What
do you do in your leisure time?* Qu'est-
ce que tu fais pendant tes loisirs?
leisure centre *n* centre de loisirs m
lemon [ˈlɛmən] *n* citron m
lemonade [ˌlɛməˈneɪd] *n*
limonade f
lend [lɛnd] *vb* prêter ▷ *I can lend
you some money.* Je peux te prêter
de l'argent.
length [lɛŋθ] *n* longueur f; **It's
about a metre in length.** Ça fait
environ un mètre de long.
lengthwise [ˈlɛŋθwaɪz] *adv* dans
le sens de la longueur
lens [lɛnz] *n* ❶ (contact lens) lentille
cornéenne f ❷ (of spectacles) verre
m ❸ (of camera) objectif m
lent [lɛnt] *vb see* **lend**
lentil [ˈlɛntl] *n* lentille f
Leo [ˈliːəʊ] *n* Lion m ▷ *I'm a Leo.* Je
suis Lion.
leotard [ˈliːətɑːd] *n* léotard m
lesbian [ˈlɛzbɪən] *n* lesbienne f
less [lɛs] *pron, adv, adj* ❶ moins

▷ *He's less athletic than her.* Il est
moins athlétique qu'elle. ▷ *A bit
less, please.* Un peu moins, s'il vous
plaît. ❷ moins de ▷ *I've got less time
for hobbies now.* J'ai moins de temps
pour les loisirs maintenant.; **less
than (1)** (with amounts) moins de
▷ *It's less than a kilometre from here.*
C'est à moins d'un kilomètre d'ici.
▷ *It costs less than 100 dollars.* Ça
coûte moins de cent dollars. ▷ *less
than half* moins de la moitié **(2)** (in
comparisons) moins que ▷ *He spent
less than me.* Il a dépensé moins que
moi. ▷ *I've got less than you.* J'en ai
moins que toi. ▷ *It cost less than we
thought.* Ça a coûté moins cher que
nous ne le pensions.
lesson [ˈlɛsn] *n* ❶ leçon f ▷ *a
French lesson* une leçon de français
▷ *"Lesson Sixteen" (in textbook)* "Leçon
seize" ❷ cours m ▷ *dancing lessons*
des cours de danse ▷ *Each lesson
lasts 40 minutes.* Chaque cours dure
quarante minutes.
let [lɛt] *vb* (allow) laisser; **to let
somebody do something** laisser
quelqu'un faire quelque chose
▷ *Let me have a look.* Laisse-moi
voir. ▷ *My parents won't let me stay
out that late.* Mes parents ne me
laissent pas sortir aussi tard.; **to
let somebody know** faire savoir à
quelqu'un ▷ *I'll let you know as soon
as possible.* Je vous le ferai savoir
dès que possible.; **to let down**
décevoir ▷ *I won't let you down.* Je ne
vous décevrai pas.; **to let go** lâcher
▷ *Let me go!* Lâche-moi! ▷ *Let go of
the rope.* Lâche la corde. ▷ *Let go!*
Lâche prise!; **to let in** laisser entrer
▷ *They wouldn't let me in because I
was under 18.* Ils ne m'ont pas laissé
entrer parce que j'avais moins de
dix-huit ans.; **to let out** laisser
sortir ▷ *Don't let the cat out.* Ne

laisse pas sortir le chat.; **to let up** (rain) diminuer

To make suggestions using **let's**, you can ask questions beginning with **si on**.

▷ *Let's go to a movie!* Si on allait au cinéma?; **Let's go!** Allons-y!

letter ['letər] n lettre f
lettuce ['letɪs] n salade f
leukemia [luˈkiːmɪə] n leucémie f
level ['levl] adj plan ▷ *A pool table must be perfectly level.* Une table de billard doit être parfaitement plane.

▶ n niveau m (pl niveaux) ▷ *The water level is rising.* Le niveau d'eau monte.
lever ['liːvər] n levier m
liable ['laɪəbl] adj: **He's liable to lose his temper.** Il se met facilement en colère.; **It's liable to snow tonight.** Il risque de neiger ce soir.
liar ['laɪər] n menteur m, menteuse f
liberal ['lɪbərl] adj (opinions) libéral (mpl libéraux)
liberation [lɪbəˈreɪʃən] n libération f
liberty ['lɪbətɪ] n liberté f
Libra ['liːbrə] n Balance f ▷ *I'm a Libra.* Je suis Balance.
librarian [laɪˈbrɛərɪən] n bibliothécaire ▷ *She's a librarian.* Elle est bibliothécaire.
library ['laɪbrərɪ] n bibliothèque f

Be careful not to translate **library** by **librairie**.

licence ['laɪsns] n permis m; **a driver's licence** un permis de conduire; **fishing licence** le permis de pêche; **licence plate** la plaque d'immatriculation; **licence number** le numéro d'immatriculation
lick [lɪk] vb lécher
licorice ['lɪkərɪs] n réglisse f

lid [lɪd] n couvercle m
lie [laɪ] vb (not tell the truth) mentir
▷ *I know she's lying.* Je sais qu'elle ment.; **to lie down** s'allonger; **to be lying down** être allongé; **He was lying on the sofa.** Il était allongé sur le sofa. ▷ *When I'm on holiday I lie on the beach all day.* Quand je suis en vacances, je reste allongé sur la plage toute la journée.

▶ n mensonge m; **to tell a lie** mentir; **That's a lie!** Ce n'est pas vrai!

lieutenant-governor
[lefˈtɛnənt-] n lieutenant-gouverneur m, lieutenante-gouverneure f
life [laɪf] n vie f
lifeboat ['laɪfbəʊt] n canot de sauvetage m
lifeguard ['laɪfgɑːd] n sauveteur m, sauveteure f
life jacket n gilet de sauvetage m
lifesaving ['laɪfseɪvɪŋ] n sauvetage m ▷ *I've done a course in lifesaving.* J'ai pris des cours de sauvetage.
lifestyle ['laɪfstaɪl] n style de vie m
lift [lɪft] vb soulever ▷ *It's too heavy. I can't lift it.* C'est trop lourd. Je ne peux pas le soulever.

▶ n: **He gave me a lift to the movie theatre.** Il m'a emmené au cinéma en voiture.; **Would you like a lift?** Est-ce que je peux vous déposer quelque part?

light [laɪt] adj ● (not heavy) léger (f légère) ▷ *a light jacket* un veston léger ▷ *a light meal* un repas léger ● (colour) clair ▷ *a light blue sweater* un chandail bleu clair

▶ n ● lumière f ▷ *to switch on the light* allumer la lumière ▷ *to switch off the light* éteindre la lumière
● lampe f ▷ *There's a light by my bed.*

Il y a une lampe près de mon lit.; **the traffic lights** les *m* feux; **Have you got a light?** (match, lighter) Avez-vous du feu?
▸ *vb* (candle, fire) allumer
light bulb *n* ampoule *f*
lighter ['laɪtə'] *n* briquet *m*
lighthouse ['laɪthaus] *n* phare *m*
lightning ['laɪtnɪŋ] *n* éclairs *mpl*; **a flash of lightning** un éclair
like [laɪk] *vb* ❶ aimer ▷ *I don't like mustard.* Je n'aime pas la moutarde. ▷ *I like riding.* J'aime monter à cheval.

> Note that **aimer** also means to love, so make sure you use **aimer bien** for just liking somebody.

❷ aimer bien ▷ *I like him, but I don't want to go out with him.* Je l'aime bien, mais je ne veux pas sortir avec lui.; **I'd like...** Je voudrais... ▷ *I'd like an orange juice, please.* Je voudrais un jus d'orange, s'il vous plaît. ▷ *Would you like some coffee?* Voulez-vous du café?; **I'd like to...** J'aimerais... ▷ *I'd like to go to Russia one day.* J'aimerais aller en Russie un jour. ▷ *I'd like to wash my hands.* J'aimerais me laver les mains.; **Would you like to go for a walk?** Tu veux aller faire une promenade?; **...if you like** si tu veux
▸ *prep* comme ▷ *It's fine like that.* C'est bien comme ça. ▷ *Do it like this.* Fais-le comme ça. ▷ *a city like St. John's* une ville comme St. John's ▷ *It's a bit like salmon.* C'est un peu comme du saumon.; **What's the weather like?** Quel temps fait-il?; **to look like somebody** ressembler à quelqu'un ▷ *You look like my brother.* Tu ressembles à mon frère.
likely ['laɪklɪ] *adj* probable ▷ *That's not very likely.* C'est peu probable.; **She's likely to come.**

Elle viendra probablement.; **She's not likely to come.** Elle ne viendra probablement pas.
lime [laɪm] *n* (fruit) lime *f*
limit ['lɪmɪt] *n* limite *f* ▷ *The speed limit is 100 km/h.* La vitesse limite est de cent kilomètres à l'heure.
limousine ['lɪməzi:n] *n* limousine *f*
limp [lɪmp] *vb* boiter
line [laɪn] *n* ❶ ligne *f* ▷ *a straight line* une ligne droite ▷ *a bus line* une ligne d'autobus ▷ *There's static on the line.* Il y a de la friture sur la ligne. ❷ (to divide, cancel) trait *m* ▷ *Draw a line under each answer.* Tirez un trait sous chaque réponse. ❸ (lineup) queue *f* ▷ *We had to stand in line.* Nous avons dû faire la queue. ❹ rangée *f* ▷ *a line of trees* une rangée d'arbres; **Hold the line, please.** Ne quittez pas.; **online** (computing) en ligne
linen ['lɪnɪn] *n* lin *m* ▷ *a linen jacket* un veston en lin
linguist ['lɪŋgwɪst] *n*: **to be a good linguist** être doué pour les langues ▷ *She's a good linguist.* Elle est douée pour les langues.
lining ['laɪnɪŋ] *n* (of jacket, skirt etc) doublure *f*
link [lɪŋk] *n* ❶ rapport *m* ▷ *the link between smoking and cancer* le rapport entre le tabagisme et le cancer ❷ (computing) lien *m*
▸ *vb* relier
linoleum [lɪ'nəuliəm] *n* linoléum *m*
lion ['laɪən] *n* lion *m*
lioness ['laɪənɪs] *n* lionne *f*
lip [lɪp] *n* lèvre *f*
lip-read ['lɪpri:d] *vb* lire sur les lèvres
lip salve [-sælv] *n* pommade pour les lèvres *f*
lipstick ['lɪpstɪk] *n* rouge à lèvres *m*
liquid ['lɪkwɪd] *adj* liquide *m*

▶ *n* liquide *m*

list [lɪst] *n* liste *f*
▶ *vb* faire une liste de ▷ *List your hobbies.* Fais une liste de tes passe-temps.

listen ['lɪsn] *vb* écouter ▷ *Listen to this!* Écoutez ceci! ▷ *Listen to me!* Écoutez-moi!

listener ['lɪsnər] *n* auditeur *m*, auditrice *f*

lit [lɪt] *vb see* **light**

literally ['lɪtrəlɪ] *adv* (*completely*) vraiment ▷ *It was literally impossible to find a seat.* Il était vraiment impossible de trouver une place.; **to translate literally** faire une traduction littérale

literature ['lɪtrɪtʃər] *n* littérature *f* ▷ *Canadian literature* la littérature canadienne

litre ['liːtər] *n* litre *m*

litter ['lɪtər] *n* ordures *fpl*

little ['lɪtl] *adj* petit ▷ *a little boy* un petit garçon; **a little** un peu ▷ *"How much would you like?" — "Just a little."* « Combien en voulez-vous ? » — « Juste un peu. »; **very little** très peu ▷ *We have very little time.* Nous avons très peu de temps.; **little by little** petit à petit

live [*adj* laɪv, *vb* lɪv] *adj* ❶ (*animal*) vivant ❷ (*broadcast*) en direct; **There's live music on Fridays.** Il y a des musiciens qui jouent le vendredi.
▶ *vb* ❶ vivre ▷ *I live with my grandmother.* Je vis avec ma grand-mère.; **to live on something** vivre de quelque chose ▷ *He lives on a small salary.* Il vit d'un modeste salaire. ❷ (*reside*) habiter ▷ *Where do you live?* Où est-ce que tu habites? ▷ *I live in Moncton.* J'habite à Moncton.; **to live together (1)** (*as roommates*) partager un appartement ▷ *She's living with*

two other students. Elle partage un appartement avec deux autres étudiantes. **(2)** vivre ensemble ▷ *My parents aren't living together any more.* Mes parents ne vivent plus ensemble.; **They're not married, they're living together.** Ils ne sont pas mariés, ils vivent en union libre.

lively ['laɪvlɪ] *adj* animé ▷ *It was a lively party.* C'était une soirée animée.; **He has a lively personality.** Il est plein de vitalité.

liver ['lɪvər] *n* foie *m*

lives [laɪvz] *npl* vies *fpl*

livestock ['laɪvstɔk] *n* animaux *mpl* d'élevage

living ['lɪvɪŋ] *n*: **to make a living** gagner sa vie; **What does she do for a living?** Qu'est-ce qu'elle fait dans la vie?

living room *n* salle de séjour *f*

lizard ['lɪzəd] *n* lézard *m*

load [ləʊd] *n*: **loads of** un tas de ▷ *loads of money* un tas d'argent; **That's a load of rubbish!** Tu ne dis que des niaiseries!
▶ *vb* charger ▷ *a trolley loaded with luggage* un chariot chargé de bagages

loaf [ləʊf] *n* pain *m*; **a loaf of bread** un pain
▶ *vb* traîner ▷ *Are you going to loaf around all day?* Tu vas traîner toute la journée?

loan [ləʊn] *n* prêt *m* ▷ *a bank loan* un prêt bancaire ▷ *to pay back a loan* payer un prêt
▶ *vb* prêter

loathe [ləʊð] *vb* détester ▷ *I loathe country music.* Je déteste la musique country.

loaves [ləʊvz] *npl see* **loaf**

lobby ['lɔbɪ] *n* hall *m* ▷ *in the hotel lobby* dans le hall de l'hôtel

lobster ['lɔbstər] *n* homard *m*

local ['ləʊkl] *adj* local (*mpl* locaux)

▷ *the local paper* le journal local ▷ *a local call* un appel local

location [ləʊ'keɪʃən] *n* endroit *m* ▷ *a hotel set in a beautiful location* un hôtel situé dans un endroit magnifique

> Be careful not to translate **location** by the French word **location**.

lock [lɒk] *n* serrure *f* ▷ *The lock is broken.* La serrure est cassée.
▶ *vb* fermer à clé ▷ *Make sure you lock your door.* N'oubliez pas de fermer votre porte à clé.

lock out *vb*: **The door slammed and I was locked out.** La porte a claqué et je me suis retrouvé à la porte.

locker ['lɒkər] *n* casier *m*; **the locker room** le vestiaire; **storage lockers** (airport, mall) la consigne automatique

locket ['lɒkɪt] *n* médaillon *m*

loft [lɒft] *n* grenier *m*

log [lɒg] *n* (of wood) bûche *f*

log in *vb* se connecter

log off *vb* se déconnecter

log on *vb* se connecter

log out *vb* se déconnecter

logical ['lɒdʒɪkl] *adj* logique

login ['lɒgɪn] *n* ❶ (action) ouverture *f* de session ❷ (ID) nom d'utilisateur *m*

logo ['ləʊgəʊ] *n* logo *m*

lollipop ['lɒlɪpɒp] *n* suçon *m*

loneliness ['ləʊnlɪnɪs] *n* solitude *f*

lonely ['ləʊnlɪ] *adj* seul; **to feel lonely** se sentir seul ▷ *He feels a bit lonely.* Il se sent un peu seul.

lonesome ['ləʊnsəm] *adj*: **to feel lonesome** se sentir seul

long [lɒŋ] *adj, adv* long (f longue) ▷ *She has long hair.* Elle a les cheveux longs. ▷ *The room is 6 metres long.* La pièce fait six mètres de long.; **how long?** (time) combien de

temps? ▷ *How long did you stay there?* Combien de temps êtes-vous resté là-bas? ▷ *How long have you been here?* Depuis combien de temps êtes-vous ici? ▷ *How long is the flight?* Combien de temps dure le vol?; **I've been waiting a long time.** J'attends depuis longtemps.; **It takes a long time.** Ça prend du temps.; **as long as** si ▷ *I'll come as long as it's not too expensive.* Je viendrai si ce n'est pas trop cher.
▶ *vb*: **to long to do something** attendre avec impatience de faire quelque chose; **I'm longing to see my dad again.** J'attends avec impatience de revoir mon père.

long-distance [lɒŋ'dɪstəns] *adj*: **a long-distance call** un appel interurbain; **to call long distance** faire un appel interurbain

longer ['lɒŋgər] *adv*: **They're no longer going out together.** Ils ne sortent plus ensemble.; **I can't stand it any longer.** Je ne peux plus le supporter.

long jump *n* saut en longueur *m*

look [lʊk] *n*: **to take a look** regarder ▷ *Take a look at this!* Regardez ceci!; **I don't like the look of it.** Ça ne me dit rien qui vaille.
▶ *vb* ❶ regarder ▷ *Look!* Regardez!; **to look at something** regarder quelque chose ▷ *Look at this picture.* Regardez cette image. ❷ (seem) avoir l'air ▷ *She looks surprised.* Elle a l'air surprise. ▷ *That cake looks delicious.* Ce gâteau a l'air délicieux. ▷ *It looks fine.* Ça a l'air bien.; **to look like somebody** ressembler à quelqu'un ▷ *He looks like his brother.* Il ressemble à son frère.; **What does he look like?** Comment est-il physiquement?; **Look out!** Attention!; **to look after**

s'occuper de ▷ *I look after my little sister.* Je m'occupe de ma petite sœur.; **to look for** chercher ▷ *I'm looking for my passport.* Je cherche mon passeport.; **to look forward to something** attendre avec impatience quelque chose avec impatience ▷ *I'm looking forward to the holidays.* J'attends les vacances avec impatience.; **Looking forward to hearing from you...** J'espère avoir bientôt de tes nouvelles....; **to look around** **(1)** (*look behind*) se retourner ▷ *I shouted and he looked around.* J'ai crié et il s'est retourné. **(2)** (*have a look*) jeter un coup d'œil ▷ *I'm just looking around.* Je jette simplement un coup d'œil.; **I like looking around the stores.** J'aime faire les magasins.; **to look up** (*word, name*) chercher ▷ *If you don't know a word, look it up in the dictionary.* Si vous ne connaissez pas un mot, cherchez-le dans le dictionnaire.

lookout ['lukaut] n (*scenic*) belvédère m

loon [luːn] n huard m

loonie ['luːnɪ] n huard m

loop [luːp] n boucle f ▷ *Make a loop in the ribbon.* Fais une boucle au ruban.; **to be in the loop** être au courant ▷ *Keep me in the loop.* Tiens-moi au courant.

loose [luːs] adj (*clothes*) ample; **loose change** la petite monnaie; **a loose sheet of paper** une feuille volante; **A tiger got loose.** Un tigre s'est échappé.; **This screw is loose.** Cette vis s'est desserrée.

lopsided [lɔp'saɪdɪd] adj de travers ▷ *Your sculpture looks a bit lopsided.* Ta sculpture semble un peu de travers.

lose [luːz] vb perdre ▷ *I lost my purse.* J'ai perdu mon sac à main.; **to get lost** se perdre ▷ *I was afraid of getting lost.* J'avais peur de me

perdre.

loser ['luːzəʳ] n perdant m, perdante f; **to be a bad loser** être mauvais perdant

loss [lɔs] n perte f

lost [lɔst] vb *see* **lose**
▷ adj perdu

lost-and-found [lɔstənˈfaund] n objets mpl perdus

lot [lɔt] n: **a lot** beaucoup; **a lot of** beaucoup de ▷ *a lot of work* beaucoup de travail ▷ *We saw a lot of interesting things.* Nous avons vu beaucoup de choses intéressantes.; **lots of** (*informal*) un tas de ▷ *She has lots of money.* Elle a un tas d'argent. ▷ *He has lots of friends.* Il a un tas d'amis.; **"What did you do on the weekend?" — "Not a lot."** « Qu'as-tu fait en fin de semaine? » — « Pas grand-chose. »; **"Do you like baseball?" — "Not a lot."** « Tu aimes le baseball? » — « Pas tellement. »; **That's the lot.** C'est tout.

lottery ['lɔtərɪ] n loterie f; **to win the lottery** gagner à la loterie

loud [laud] adj fort ▷ *The television is too loud.* La télévision est trop forte.

loudly ['laudlɪ] adv fort

lounge [laundʒ] n salon m

lousy ['lauzɪ] adj infect ▷ *The food in the cafeteria is lousy.* La nourriture de la cafétéria est infecte.; **I feel lousy.** Je ne me sens pas bien.

love [lʌv] n amour m; **to be in love** être amoureux ▷ *She's in love with him.* Elle est amoureuse de lui.; **to make love** faire l'amour; **Give your sister my love.** Embrasse ta sœur pour moi.; **Love, Rosemary.** Amitiés, Rosemary.
▷ vb **①** (*be in love with*) aimer ▷ *I love you.* Je t'aime. **②** (*like a lot*) aimer beaucoup ▷ *Everybody loves her.* Tout le monde l'aime beaucoup.

▷ *I'd love to come.* J'aimerais beaucoup venir. ❸ *(things)* adorer ▷ *I love chocolate.* J'adore le chocolat. ▷ *I love skiing.* J'adore le ski.

lovely [ˈlʌvlɪ] *adj* charmant ▷ *What a lovely surprise!* Quelle charmante surprise! ▷ *She's a lovely person.* Elle est charmante.; **It's a lovely day.** Il fait très beau aujourd'hui.; **a lovely meal** un repas délicieux; **They've got a lovely house.** Ils ont une très belle maison.; **Have a lovely time!** Amusez-vous bien!

lover [ˈlʌvə] *n* ❶ *(in relationship)* amant *m*, maîtresse *f* ❷ *(of hobby, wine)* amateur *m* ▷ *an art lover* un amateur d'art ▷ *He's a lover of good food.* Il est amateur de bonne cuisine.

low [ləʊ] *adj, adv (price, level)* bas *(f* basse*)* ▷ *That plane is flying very low.* Cet avion vole très bas. ▷ *in the low season* en basse saison

low-carb [ˈləʊkɑːb] *adj* faible en glucides ▷ *a low-carb snack* une collation faible en glucides

lower [ˈləʊə] *adj* inférieur ▷ *on the lower floor* à l'étage inférieur; **Lower Canada** le Bas-Canada
▶ *vb* baisser

low-fat [ˈləʊˈfæt] *adj* allégé ▷ *a low-fat yogurt* un yogourt allégé

loyal [ˈlɔɪəl] *adj* loyal

Loyalist [ˈlɔɪəlɪst] *n* Loyaliste

loyalty [ˈlɔɪəltɪ] *n* fidélité *f*

lozenge [ˈlɒzɪndʒ] *n* pastille *f*

luck [lʌk] *n* chance *f* ▷ *She hasn't had much luck.* Elle n'a pas eu beaucoup de chance.; **Good luck!** Bonne chance!; **Bad luck!** Pas de chance!

luckily [ˈlʌkɪlɪ] *adv* heureusement

lucky [ˈlʌkɪ] *adj*: **to be lucky (1)** *(be fortunate)* avoir de la chance ▷ *He's lucky. He has a job.* Il a de la chance. Il a un emploi. ▷ *"He wasn't hurt." —"That was lucky!"* « Il n'a pas été

blessé. » — « C'est une chance! » **(2)** *(bring luck)* porter bonheur ▷ *Four-leaf clovers are lucky.* Les trèfles à quatre feuilles portent bonheur.; **a lucky charm** un porte-bonheur

luggage [ˈlʌgɪdʒ] *n* bagages *mpl*

lukewarm [ˈluːkwɔːm] *adj (water, food)* tiède; **Their response was lukewarm.** Leur réaction a été peu enthousiaste.

lump [lʌmp] *n* ❶ morceau *m* (*pl* morceaux*)* ▷ *a lump of butter* un morceau de beurre ❷ *(swelling)* bosse *f* ▷ *He's got a lump on his forehead.* Il a une bosse sur le front.

lunatic [ˈluːnətɪk] *n* cinglé *m*, cinglée *f* ▷ *He's an absolute lunatic.* Il est complètement cinglé.

lunch [lʌntʃ] *n* midi *m*; **to have lunch** dîner ▷ *We have lunch at 12:30.* Nous dînons à midi et demie.

  ● In Canada, **le lunch** is the noon
  ● meal. In France, it refers to a light
  ● meal consisting of a cold buffet.

lung [lʌŋ] *n* poumon *m*; **lung cancer** le cancer du poumon

lurk [lɜːk] *vb* ❶ rôder ▷ *The criminal is still lurking in the neighbourhood.* Le malfaiteur rôde encore dans le quartier. ❷ *(on Internet)* badauder ▷ *She just lurks on that discussion group.* Elle ne fait que badauder dans ce groupe de discussion.

luscious [ˈlʌʃəs] *adj* délicieux *(f* délicieuse*)*

lush [lʌʃ] *adj* luxuriant

luxurious [lʌgˈzjʊərɪəs] *adj* luxueux *(f* luxueuse*)*

luxury [ˈlʌkʃərɪ] *n* luxe *m* ▷ *It was luxury!* C'était un vrai luxe!; **a luxury hotel** un hôtel de luxe

lying [ˈlaɪɪŋ] *vb* see **lie**

lynx [lɪŋks] *n* lynx *m*

lyrics [ˈlɪrɪks] *npl (of song)* paroles *fpl*

m

macaroni [mækəˈrəʊnɪ] n
macaronis mpl

machine [məˈʃiːn] n machine f

machinery [məˈʃiːnərɪ] n
machines fpl

mackerel [ˈmækrl] n maquereau
m (pl maquereaux)

mad [mæd] adj ❶ (angry) furieux
(f furieuse) ▷ She'll be mad when she
finds out. Elle sera furieuse quand
elle va s'en apercevoir. ❷ (insane)
fou m (f folle) ▷ You're mad! Tu es
fou!; **to get mad at somebody**
se fâcher contre quelqu'un; **like
mad** comme un fou ▷ I worked like
mad. J'ai travaillé comme un fou.;
mad cow disease la maladie de la
vache folle

madam [ˈmædəm] n madame
f ▷ Would you like to order, Madam?
Désirez-vous commander,
Madame?

made [meɪd] vb see **make**

madly [ˈmædlɪ] adv: **They're
madly in love.** Ils sont éperdument
amoureux.

madness [ˈmædnɪs] n folie f
▷ It's absolute madness. C'est de la
pure folie.

magazine [mægəˈziːn] n
magazine

magic [ˈmædʒɪk] adj magique ▷ a
magic wand une baguette magique;
a magic trick un tour de magie
▶ n magie f; **My hobby is magic.** Je
fais des tours de magie.

magician [məˈdʒɪʃən] n
(conjurer) prestidigitateur m,
prestidigitatrice f

magnet [ˈmægnɪt] n aimant m

magnificent [mægˈnɪfɪsnt] adj
magnifique ▷ a magnificent view une
vue magnifique

magnifying glass [ˈmægnɪfaɪɪŋ-]
n loupe f

maiden name [ˈmeɪdən-] n nom
de jeune fille m

mail [meɪl] n courrier m ▷ Here's
your mail. Voici ton courrier.; **email**
(electronic mail) le courriel; **by mail**
par la poste
▶ vb poster

mailbox [ˈmeɪlbɒks] n boîte aux
lettres f

mailing list [ˈmeɪlɪŋ-] n liste
d'adresses f

main [meɪn] adj principal (mpl
principaux) ▷ the main problem le
principal problème; **main road**
la grande route ▷ I don't like biking
on main roads. Je n'aime pas faire
du vélo sur les grandes routes.;
the main thing is to... l'essentiel
est de...

mainland [ˈmeɪnlənd] n
continent m ▷ A ferry travels between
Newfoundland and the mainland.
Un traversier circule entre Terre-
Neuve et le continent.; **the Lower**

Mainland la vallée du Bas-Fraser

mainly ['meɪnlɪ] *adv*
principalement

maintain [meɪn'teɪn] *vb*
❶ (machine, building) entretenir
❷ (insist) maintenir ▷ He maintains that he told the truth. Il maintient qu'il a dit la vérité.

maintenance ['meɪntənəns] *n* (of machine, building) entretien m

majesty ['mædʒɪstɪ] *n* majesté f; **Your Majesty** Votre Majesté

major ['meɪdʒəʳ] *adj* majeur ▷ a major problem un problème majeur; **in C major** en do majeur

majority [mə'dʒɒrɪtɪ] *n* majorité f

make [meɪk] *n* marque f ▷ What make is that car? De quelle marque est cette voiture?
▷ *vb* ❶ faire ▷ I'm going to make a cake. Je vais faire un gâteau. ▷ He made it himself. Il l'a fait lui-même. ▷ I make my bed every morning. Je fais mon lit tous les matins. ▷ 2 and 2 make 4. Deux et deux font quatre.
❷ (manufacture) fabriquer ▷ made in Canada fabriqué au Canada
❸ (earn) gagner ▷ She makes a lot of money. Elle gagne beaucoup d'argent.; **to make somebody do something** obliger quelqu'un à faire quelque chose ▷ My parents make me do my homework. Mes parents m'obligent à faire mes devoirs.; **to make lunch** préparer le repas ▷ He's making supper. Il prépare le souper.; **to make a phone call** donner un coup de téléphone ▷ I'd like to make a phone call. J'aimerais donner un coup de téléphone.; **to make fun of somebody** se moquer de quelqu'un ▷ They made fun of me. Ils se sont moqués de moi.

make it *vb* ❶ arriver ▷ We finally made it to Calgary. Nous sommes

enfin arrivés à Calgary.; **We made it to the finals.** Nous sommes allés en finale. ❷ venir ▷ I'm sorry, I can't make it tonight. Désolé, je ne peux pas venir ce soir. ❸ réussir ▷ Way to go! You made it! Bravo! Tu as réussi!

make out *vb* ❶ (read) déchiffrer ▷ I can't make out the address on the label. Je n'arrive pas à déchiffrer l'adresse sur l'étiquette. ❷ (understand) comprendre ▷ I can't make out what she's trying to say. Je n'arrive pas du tout à comprendre ce qu'elle veut dire. ❸ (claim, pretend) prétendre ▷ They're making out it was my fault. Ils prétendent que c'était ma faute.; **to make a cheque out to somebody** libeller un chèque à l'ordre de quelqu'un

make up *vb* ❶ (invent) inventer ▷ He made up the whole story. Il a inventé cette histoire de toutes pièces. ❷ (after argument) se réconcilier ▷ They had a quarrel, but soon made up. Ils se sont disputés, mais se sont vite réconciliés.

maker ['meɪkəʳ] *n* fabriquant m ▷ Europe's biggest car maker le plus grand fabricant de voitures d'Europe

make-up ['meɪkʌp] *n* maquillage m

male [meɪl] *adj* ❶ (animals, plants) mâle ▷ a male ostrich une autruche mâle

> When there are separate French words to refer to the female and male of an animal, **male** is often not translated.

▷ a male kitten un chaton ❷ (person, on official forms) masculin ▷ Sex: male. Sexe: masculin.; **Most football players are male.** La plupart des joueurs de football sont des hommes.; **a male chauvinist** un macho; **a male nurse** un infirmier

malicious [məˈlɪʃəs] *adj*
malveillant ▷ *a malicious rumour*
une rumeur malveillante

> Be careful not to translate
> **malicious** by **malicieux**.

mall [mɔːl] *n* centre commercial
mammoth [ˈmæməθ] *n*
mammouth *m*
   ▶ *adj* monstre *m* ▷ *a mammoth task*
un travail monstre
man [mæn] *n* homme *m* ▷ *an old
man* un vieil homme
manage [ˈmænɪdʒ] *vb* ❶ *(be in
charge of)* diriger ▷ *She manages
a big store.* Elle dirige un grand
magasin. ▷ *Who manages your
soccer team?* Qui dirige votre
équipe de soccer? ❷ *(get by)*
se débrouiller ▷ *We haven't got
much money, but we manage.* Nous
n'avons pas beaucoup d'argent,
mais nous nous débrouillons.
▷ *It's okay, I can manage.* Ça va, je
me débrouille.; **Can you manage
okay?** Tu y arrives?; **to manage
to do something** réussir à faire
quelque chose ▷ *Luckily I managed
to pass the exam.* J'ai heureusement
réussi à avoir mon examen.; **I can't
manage all that.** *(food)* C'est trop
pour moi.
manageable [ˈmænɪdʒəbl] *adj*
(task) faisable
management [ˈmænɪdʒmənt]
n ❶ *(work of managing)* gestion *f*
▷ *He's responsible for the management
of the company.* Il est responsable de
la gestion de la société. ❷ *(people
in charge)* direction *f* ▷ *"under new
management"* « changement de
direction »
manager [ˈmænɪdʒəʳ] *n* ❶ *(of
company)* directeur *m*, directrice
f ❷ *(of store, restaurant)* gérant *m*,
gérante *f* ❸ *(of sports team)* gérant

d'équipe *m*, gérante d'équipe *f*
❹ *(of performer)* imprésario *m*
mandarin [ˈmændərɪn] *n (fruit)*
mandarine *f*
mango [ˈmæŋɡəʊ] *n* mangue *f*
mania [ˈmeɪnɪə] *n* manie *f*
maniac [ˈmeɪnɪæk] *n* fou *m*, folle
f ▷ *She drives like a maniac.* Elle
conduit comme une folle.
manipulate [məˈnɪpjʊleɪt] *vb*
manipuler
Manitoba [ˌmænɪˈtəʊbə] *n*
Manitoba *m*
manner [ˈmænəʳ] *n* façon *f*; **They
were behaving in an odd manner.**
Ils se comportaient de façon
étrange.; **He has a confident
manner.** Il a de l'assurance.
manners *npl* manières *fpl* ▷ *good
manners* les bonnes manières
▷ *Her manners are appalling.* Elle a
de très mauvaises manières.; **It's
bad manners to speak with your
mouth full.** Ce n'est pas poli de
parler la bouche pleine.
manoeuvre [məˈnuːvəʳ] *vb*
manœuvrer
mansion [ˈmænʃən] *n* manoir *m*
mantelpiece [ˈmæntlpiːs] *n*
cheminée *f*
manual [ˈmænjuəl] *n* manuel *m*
   ▶ *adj*: **manual labour** la main-
d'œuvre; **manual controls** les *f*
commandes manuelles
manufacture [ˌmænjuˈfæktʃəʳ]
vb fabriquer
manufacturer [ˌmænjuˈfæktʃərəʳ]
n fabricant *m*
manure [məˈnjʊəʳ] *n* fumier *m*
manuscript [ˈmænjuskrɪpt] *n*
manuscrit *m*
many [ˈmenɪ] *adj, pron* beaucoup
de ▷ *The film has many special
effects.* Le film a beaucoup d'effets
spéciaux. ▷ *He doesn't have
many friends.* Il n'a pas beaucoup

d'amis. ▷ *Were there many people at the concert?* Est-ce qu'il y avait beaucoup de gens au concert?; **very many** beaucoup de ▷ *I don't have very many CDs.* Je n'ai pas beaucoup de CD.; **Not many.** Pas beaucoup.; **How many?** Combien? ▷ *How many do you want?* Combien en veux-tu?; **how many...?** combien de...? ▷ *How many euros do you get for a dollar?* Combien d'euros a-t-on pour un dollar?; **too many** trop ▷ *That's too many.* C'est trop.; **too many...** trop de... ▷ *She makes too many mistakes.* Elle fait trop d'erreurs.; **so many** autant ▷ *I didn't know there would be so many.* Je ne pensais pas qu'il y en aurait autant.; **so many...** autant de... ▷ *I've never seen so many books.* Je n'ai jamais vu autant de livres.

map [mæp] n ❶ (of country, area) carte f ❷ (of town) plan m

maple ['meɪpl] n érable m ▷ *maple syrup* le sirop d'érable ▷ *a maple leaf* une feuille d'érable

marathon ['mærəθən] n marathon m ▷ *the Terry Fox Marathon of Hope* le marathon d'espoir de Terry Fox

marble ['mɑːbl] n marbre m ▷ *a marble statue* une statue en marbre; **to play marbles** jouer aux billes

March [mɑːtʃ] n mars m; **in March** en mars; **March Break** la semaine de relâche

march [mɑːtʃ] n (demonstration) manifestation f ▷ *a peace march* une manifestation pour la paix
  ▶ vb ❶ (soldiers) marcher au pas ❷ (protesters) défiler

mare [mɛər] n jument f

margarine [mɑːdʒəˈriːn] n margarine f

margin ['mɑːdʒɪn] n marge f ▷ *Write notes in the margin.* Écrivez vos notes dans la marge.

marijuana [mærɪˈwɑːnə] n marijuana f

marina [məˈriːnə] n marina f

maritime ['mærɪtaɪm] adj maritime ▷ *the Maritime provinces* les provinces maritimes f; **the Maritimes** les Maritimes

mark [mɑːk] n ❶ (in school) note f ▷ *I get good marks in French.* J'ai de bonnes notes en français. ❷ (stain) tache f ▷ *You've got a mark on your skirt.* Tu as une tache sur ta jupe.
  ▶ vb corriger ▷ *The teacher hasn't marked my homework yet.* Le professeur n'a pas encore corrigé mon devoir.; **to mark up the price of something** majorer le prix de quelque chose

marker ['mɑːkər] n (pen) marqueur m

market ['mɑːkɪt] n marché m

marketing ['mɑːkɪtɪŋ] n marketing m

marketplace ['mɑːkɪtpleɪs] n place du marché f

marmalade ['mɑːməleɪd] n confiture d'oranges f

maroon [məˈruːn] adj (colour) bourgogne

marriage ['mærɪdʒ] n mariage m

married ['mærɪd] adj marié ▷ *They are not married.* Ils ne sont pas mariés. ▷ *They have been married for 15 years.* Ils sont mariés depuis quinze ans. ▷ *a married couple* un couple marié

marrow ['mærəʊ] n: **bone marrow** la moelle

marry ['mærɪ] vb épouser ▷ *He wants to marry her.* Il veut l'épouser.; **to get married** se marier ▷ *My sister's getting married in June.* Ma sœur se marie en juin.

marsh [mɑːʃ] n marais m

marshmallow [mɑːʃˈmæləʊ] n

guimauve f ▷ to roast marshmallows
rôtir des guimauves

martial ['mɑ:ʃl] adj: **martial arts**
les arts martiaux; **martial law** la
loi martiale

marvellous ['mɑ:vləs] adj
❶ excellent ▷ He's a marvellous
cook. C'est un excellent cuisinier.
❷ superbe ▷ The weather was
marvellous. Il a fait un temps
superbe.

> Be careful not to translate
> **marvellous** as **merveilleux**.

marzipan ['mɑ:zɪpæn] n pâte
d'amandes f

mascara [mæs'kɑːrə] n mascara m

mascot ['mæskət] n mascotte f
▷ The team's mascot is a wolverine.
La mascotte de l'équipe est le
carcajou.

masculine ['mæskjulin] adj
masculin

mashed potatoes [mæʃt-]
npl purée de pommes de terre
f ▷ sausages and mashed potatoes
des saucisses avec de la purée de
pommes de terre

mask [mɑ:sk] n masque m

masking tape ['mɑ:skɪŋ-] ruban-
cache m

mass [mæs] n ❶ multitude
▷ a mass of books and papers une
multitude de livres et de papiers
❷ (scientific) masse f ❸ (in church)
messe f ▷ to go to mass aller à la
messe; **the mass media** les médias

massage ['mæsɑːʒ] n massage m

massive ['mæsɪv] adj énorme

mass-produce ['mæsprə'djuːs] vb
fabriquer en série

master ['mɑ:stə'] vb maîtriser

masterpiece ['mɑ:stəpiːs] n chef-
d'œuvre m (pl chefs-d'œuvre)

mat [mæt] n ❶ (small rug) tapis
m ❷ (doormat) paillasson m; **a
bath mat** un tapis de baignoire; **an

exercise mat** un tapis d'exercice

match [mætʃ] n ❶ allumette
f ▷ a box of matches une boîte
d'allumettes ❷ (sport) match m (pl
matchs) ▷ a tennis match un match
de tennis; **He's no match for you.**
Il n'est pas de taille à lutter contre
toi.; **They're a good match.** Ils
sont bien assortis.
▶ vb être assorti à ▷ The jacket
matches the pants. La veste est
assortie au pantalon.; **These
colours don't match.** Ces couleurs
ne vont pas ensemble.

matching ['mætʃɪŋ] adj assorti
▷ My bedroom has matching wallpaper
and curtains. Ma chambre a du
papier peint et des rideaux assortis.

material [mə'tɪərɪəl] n ❶ (cloth)
tissu m ❷ (information, data)
documentation f ▷ I'm collecting
material for my project. Je rassemble
une documentation pour mon
dossier.; **raw materials** les f
matières premières

math [mæθ] n maths fpl

mathematics [mæθə'mætɪks] n
mathématiques fpl

matter ['mætə'] n question f
▷ It's a matter of life and death. C'est
une question de vie ou de mort.;
What's the matter? Qu'est-ce qui
ne va pas?; **as a matter of fact** en
fait; **for that matter** d'ailleurs; **no
matter what** quelles que soient les
circonstances; **no matter what
they say** quoi qu'ils disent; **no
matter where** où que ce soit
▶ vb: **it doesn't matter** (1) (I don't
mind) ça ne fait rien ▷ "I can't give
you the money today." — "It doesn't
matter." « Je ne peux pas te donner
l'argent aujourd'hui. » — « Ça ne fait
rien. » **(2)** (it makes no difference) ça
n'a pas d'importance ▷ "Shall I phone
today or tomorrow?" — "Whenever, it

doesn't matter." « Est-ce que j'appelle aujourd'hui ou demain? » — « Quand tu veux, ça n'a pas d'importance. »; **It matters a lot to me.** C'est très important pour moi.

mattress ['mætrɪs] n matelas m

mature [mə'tjʊər] adj mûr ▷ She's quite mature for her age. Elle est très mûre pour son âge.

maximum ['mæksɪmə] n maximum m
  ▶ adj maximum m (f+pl maximum)
  ▷ The maximum speed is 100 km/h. La vitesse maximum autorisée est de cent kilomètres à l'heure.; **the maximum amount** le maximum

May [meɪ] n mai m; **in May** en mai

may [meɪ] vb: **He may come.** Il va peut-être venir. ▷ It may rain. Il va peut-être pleuvoir.; **"Are you going to the party?" — "I don't know. I may."** « Est-ce que tu vas à la soirée? » — « Je ne sais pas. Peut-être. »; **May I come along?** Est-ce que je peux vous accompagner?

maybe ['meɪbiː] adv peut-être
  ▷ maybe not peut-être pas ▷ a bit boring, maybe peut-être un peu ennuyeux ▷ Maybe she's at home. Elle est peut-être chez elle. ▷ Maybe he'll change his mind. Il va peut-être changer d'avis.

mayonnaise [meɪə'neɪz] n mayonnaise f

mayor [mɛər] n maire m

maze [meɪz] n labyrinthe m

me [miː] pron
  me becomes **m'** before a vowel sound.

  ❶ me, m' ▷ Could you lend me your pen? Est-ce que tu peux me prêter ton stylo? ▷ Can you tell me the way to the community centre? Est-ce que vous pouvez m'indiquer le chemin du centre communautaire? ▷ Can you help me? Est-ce que tu peux

m'aider? ▷ They heard me. Ils m'ont entendu.

  moi is used in some exclamations and commands.

  ❷ moi ▷ Me too! Moi aussi!
  ▷ Excuse me! Excusez-moi! ▷ Look at me! Regarde-moi! ▷ Wait for me! Attends-moi! ▷ Come with me! Suivez-moi!

  moi is also used after prepositions and in comparisons.

  ▷ You're after me. Tu es après moi.
  ▷ Is it for me? C'est pour moi? ▷ She's older than me. Elle est plus âgée que moi.

meal [miːl] n repas m

mealtime ['miːltaɪm] n: **at mealtimes** aux heures de repas

mean [miːn] vb vouloir dire ▷ What does "complet" mean? Qu'est-ce que « complet » veut dire? ▷ I don't know what it means. Je ne sais pas ce que ça veut dire. ▷ What do you mean? Qu'est-ce que vous voulez dire? ▷ That's not what I meant. Ce n'est pas ce que je voulais dire.; **Which one do you mean?** Duquel veux-tu parler?; **Do you really mean it?** Tu es sérieux?; **to mean to do something** avoir l'intention de faire quelque chose ▷ I didn't mean to offend you. Je n'avais pas l'intention de vous blesser.
  ▶ adj (unkind) méchant ▷ You're being mean to me. Tu es méchant avec moi.; **That's a really mean thing to say!** Ce n'est vraiment pas gentil de dire ça!

meaning ['miːnɪŋ] n sens m

means [miːnz] n moyen m ▷ She'll do it by any possible means. Elle le fera par tous les moyens. ▷ a means of transport un moyen de transport; **by means of** au moyen de ▷ He got in by means of a stolen key. Il est entré au moyen d'une clé volée.; **by all means** bien sûr ▷ *"Can I come?"* — *"By all means!"* « Est-ce que je peux venir? » — « Bien sûr! »

meant [ment] *vb see* **mean**

meanwhile ['miːnwaɪl] *adv* pendant ce temps

measles ['miːzlz] *n* rougeole

measure ['meʒə'] *vb* **❶** mesurer ▷ *I measured the desk.* J'ai mesuré le bureau. **❷** faire ▷ *The room measures 3 metres by 4.* La pièce fait trois mètres sur quatre.

measurements ['meʒəmənts] *npl* **❶** *(of object)* dimensions *fpl* ▷ *What are the measurements of the room?* Quelles sont les dimensions de la pièce? **❷** *(of body)* mensurations *fpl* ▷ *What are your measurements?* Quelles sont tes mensurations?; **my waist measurement** mon tour de taille; **What's your neck measurement?** Quel est votre tour de cou?

meat [miːt] *n* viande *f* ▷ *I don't eat meat.* Je ne mange pas de viande.

mechanic [mɪ'kænɪk] *n* mécanicien *m*, mécanicienne *f* ▷ *He's a mechanic.* Il est mécanicien.

mechanical [mɪ'kænɪkl] *adj* mécanique

medal ['medl] *n* médaille *f*; **the gold medal** la médaille d'or

medallion [mɪ'dælɪən] *n* médaillon *m*

media ['miːdɪə] *npl* médias *mpl*

median strip ['miːdɪən-] *n* terre-plein central *m*

medical ['medɪkl] *adj* médical *(mpl* médicaux*)* ▷ *medical treatment* les soins médicaux; **medical insurance** l'assurance maladie; **a medical centre** un centre médical; **to have medical problems** avoir des problèmes de santé; **She's a medical student.** Elle est

étudiante en médecine.
▶ *n*: **to have a medical** passer un examen médical

medicine ['medsɪn] *n* **❶** *(subject)* médecine *f* ▷ *I want to study medicine.* Je veux étudier la médecine.; **alternative medicine** la médecine douce **❷** *(medication)* médicament *m* ▷ *I need some medicine.* J'ai besoin d'un médicament.

medieval [medɪ'iːvl] *adj* **❶** médiéval *(mpl* médiévaux*)* ▷ *a medieval town* une ville médiévale ▷ *in medieval times* à l'époque médiévale **❷** *(person)* du Moyen Âge ▷ *a medieval knight* un chevalier du Moyen Âge

mediocre [miːdɪ'əʊkə'] *adj* médiocre ▷ *I think they're a mediocre band.* À mon avis, c'est un groupe musical médiocre.

medium ['miːdɪəm] *adj* moyen *m (f* moyenne*)* ▷ *a man of medium height* un homme de taille moyenne

medium-sized ['miːdɪəm'saɪzd] *adj* de taille moyenne ▷ *a medium-sized town* une ville de taille moyenne

meet [miːt] *vb* **❶** *(by chance)* rencontrer ▷ *I met your sister in the street.* J'ai rencontré ta sœur dans la rue. ▷ *Have you met her before?* Tu l'as déjà rencontrée? **❷** se rencontrer ▷ *We met by chance in the shopping centre.* Nous nous sommes rencontrés par hasard au centre commercial. **❸** *(by arrangement)* retrouver ▷ *I'm going to meet my friends.* Je vais retrouver mes amis. **❹** se retrouver ▷ *Let's meet in front of the tourist office.* Retrouvons-nous devant le bureau de tourisme.; **I like meeting new people.** J'aime faire de nouvelles connaissances. **❺** *(pick up)* aller

chercher ▷ *I'll meet you at the airport.*
J'irai te chercher à l'aéroport. ; **to
meet up** se retrouver ▷ *What time
shall we meet up?* On se retrouve à
quelle heure?

meeting ['miːtɪŋ] *n* ❶ (*gathering*)
réunion *f* ▷ *a business meeting* une
réunion d'affaires ❷ (*encounter*)
rencontre *f* ▷ *their first meeting* leur
première rencontre

mega ['meɡə] *adj*: **He's mega rich.**
(*informal*) Il est hyper riche.

megabyte ['meɡəbaɪt] *n*
mégaoctet *m*

melody ['melədɪ] *n* mélodie *f*

melon ['melən] *n* melon *m*

melt [melt] *vb* fondre ▷ *The snow
is melting.* La neige est en train de
fondre.

member ['membəʳ] *n* membre
m ▷ *Are you a member of the Student
Council?* Es-tu membre du Conseil
des élèves? ; **We're all members
of society.** Nous faisons tous
partie de la société. ; **a Member
of Parliament** un député; **a
Member of the Legislative
Assembly** un député à l'Assemblée
législative; **a Member of the
National Assembly** un député de
l'Assemblée nationale; **a Member
of Provincial Parliament** un
député provincial

membership ['membəʃɪp] *n* (*of
party, union*) adhésion *f* ▷ *to apply
for membership* faire une demande
d'adhésion

membership card *n* carte de
membre *f*

memento [mə'mentəʊ] *n*
souvenir *m*

memorial [mɪ'mɔːrɪəl] *n*
monument *m* ▷ *a war memorial* un
monument aux morts; **a memorial
service** un service commémoratif

memorize ['meməraɪz] *vb*

apprendre par cœur

memory ['memərɪ] *n* ❶ (*also
for computer*) mémoire *f* ▷ *I don't
have a good memory.* Je n'ai pas
bonne mémoire. ▷ *Your computer
needs more memory.* Ton ordinateur
a besoin de plus de mémoire.
❷ (*recollection*) souvenir *m* ▷ *to
bring back memories* rappeler des
souvenirs

men [men] *npl see* **man** hommes
mpl

mend [mend] *vb* réparer

meningitis [menɪn'dʒaɪtɪs] *n*
méningite *f*

mental ['mentl] *adj* mental
(*mpl* mentaux) ▷ *a mental illness*
une maladie mentale; **a mental
hospital** un hôpital psychiatrique

mentality [men'tælɪtɪ] *n*
mentalité *f*

mention ['menʃən] *vb*
mentionner; **"Thank you!"
— "Don't mention it!"** « Merci! » —
« Il n'y a pas de quoi! »

menu ['menjuː] *n* menu *m* ▷ *Could
I have the menu please?* Est-ce que
je pourrais avoir le menu s'il vous
plaît?

meow [mɪ'aʊ] *vb* miauler

mercy ['mɜːsɪ] *n* pitié *f*

mere [mɪəʳ] *adj*: **a mere 5 percent**
à peine cinq pour cent; **It's a
mere formality.** C'est une simple
formalité. ; **the merest hint of
criticism** la moindre petite critique

meringue [mə'ræŋ] *n* meringue *f*

merry ['merɪ] *adj*: **Merry
Christmas!** Joyeux Noël!

mess [mes] *n* ❶ fouillis *m* ▷ *My
bedroom's usually a mess.* Il y a
généralement du fouillis dans ma
chambre. ❷ gâchis *m* ▷ *We'd better
clean up this mess.* Nous devrions
nettoyer ce gâchis. ; **in a mess** en
désordre

mess around vb: **to mess around with something** (interfere with) tripoter quelque chose ▷ Stop messing around with my computer! Arrête de tripoter mon ordinateur!; **Don't mess around with my things!** Ne touche pas à mes affaires!

mess up vb: **to mess something up** mettre la pagaille dans quelque chose ▷ My little brother has messed up my CDs. Mon petit frère a mis la pagaille dans mes CD.; **I'm sorry, I really messed up.** Je regrette, j'ai tout gâché.

message ['mɛsɪdʒ] n message m

messenger ['mɛsɪndʒə'] n messager m, messagère f

messy ['mɛsɪ] adj ❶ (dirty) salissant ▷ a messy job un travail salissant ❷ (untidy) en désordre ▷ Your desk is really messy. Ton bureau est vraiment en désordre. ❸ (person) désordonnée ▷ She's so messy! Elle est tellement désordonnée!; **My writing is terribly messy.** J'ai une écriture de cochon.

met [mɛt] vb see **meet**

metal ['mɛtl] n métal m (pl métaux)

meter ['miːtə'] n ❶ (for gas, hydro, taxi) compteur m ❷ (parking meter) parcomètre m

method ['mɛθəd] n méthode f

Métis [me'tiːs] n Métis m, Métisse f ▶ adj métis (f métisse)

metre ['miːtə'] n mètre m

metric ['mɛtrɪk] adj métrique

mice [maɪs] npl see **mouse**

microchip ['maɪkrəʊtʃɪp] n puce f

microphone ['maɪkrəfəʊn] n microphone m

microscope ['maɪkrəskəʊp] n microscope m

microwave oven ['maɪkrəweɪv-] n four à micro-ondes m

mid [mɪd] adj: **in mid May** à la mi-mai

midday [mɪd'deɪ] n midi m; **at midday** à midi

middle ['mɪdl] n ❶ milieu m ▷ in the middle of the road au milieu de la route ▷ in the middle of the night au milieu de la nuit ▷ the middle seat la place du milieu; **the Middle Ages** le Moyen Âge; **the Middle East** le Moyen-Orient

middle-aged [mɪdl'eɪdʒd] adj d'âge moyen ▷ a middle-aged man un homme d'âge moyen; **to be middle-aged** avoir la cinquantaine; **She's middle-aged.** Elle a la cinquantaine.

middle-class [mɪdl'klɑːs] adj de la classe moyenne ▷ a middle-class family une famille de la classe moyenne

middle name n deuxième prénom m

midnight ['mɪdnaɪt] n minuit m; **at midnight** à minuit

midwife ['mɪdwaɪf] n sage-femme f (pl sages-femmes) ▷ She's a midwife. Elle est sage-femme.

might [maɪt] vb

Use **peut-être** to express possibility.

▷ He might come later. Il va peut-être venir plus tard. ▷ We might go to the Yukon next year. Nous irons peut-être au Yukon l'an prochain. ▷ She might not have understood. Elle n'a peut-être pas compris.

migraine ['miːgreɪn] n migraine f ▷ I have a migraine. J'ai la migraine.

mike [maɪk] n micro m

mild [maɪld] adj doux (f douce) ▷ The winters are quite mild. Les hivers sont assez doux.

mile [maɪl] n mile m

A **mile** is a nonmetric unit equal to about 1.6 km.

▷ *It's five miles from here.* C'est à huit kilomètres d'ici.; **We walked miles!** Nous avons marché plusieurs kilomètres!

military [ˈmɪlɪtərɪ] *adj* militaire

milk [mɪlk] *n* lait m ▷ *tea with milk* du thé au lait
► *vb* traire

milk chocolate *n* chocolat au lait m

milkshake [ˈmɪlkʃeɪk] *n* lait fouetté m

mill [mɪl] *n* moulin m ▷ *a pepper mill* un moulin à poivre

millennium [mɪˈlenɪəm] *n* millénaire m ▷ *the third millennium* le troisième millénaire; **the millennium** le millénium

millimetre [ˈmɪlɪmiːtəʳ] *n* millimètre m

million [ˈmɪljən] *n* million m

millionaire [mɪljəˈneəʳ] *n* millionnaire m

mimic [ˈmɪmɪk] *vb* imiter

mincemeat pie [ˈmɪnsmiːt-] *n* tarte au mincemeat f

mind [maɪnd] *vb*: **Do you mind if I open the window?** Est-ce que ça vous dérange si j'ouvre la fenêtre?; **I don't mind.** Ça ne me dérange pas. ▷ *I don't mind the noise.* Le bruit ne me dérange pas.; **Never mind!** Ça ne fait rien!; **Mind the step!** Attention à la marche!
► *n* esprit *m* ▷ *a logical mind* un esprit logique ▷ *Great minds think alike.* Les grands esprits se rencontrent. ▷ *to come to mind* venir à l'esprit; **to make up one's mind** se décider ▷ *I haven't made up my mind yet.* Je ne me suis pas encore décidé.; **to change one's mind** changer d'avis ▷ *He changed his mind.* Il a changé d'avis.; **Are you out of your mind?** Tu as perdu la tête?; **What's on your mind?** À quoi penses-tu?; **to read**

somebody's mind lire dans les pensées de quelqu'un; **Put it out of your mind.** N'y pense plus.

mine [maɪn] *pron* le + m mien, la + f mienne, les + m miens, les + f miennes ▷ *"Is this your coat?"* — *"No, mine's black."* « C'est ton manteau? » — « Non, le mien est noir. » ▷ *"Is this your car?"* — *"No, mine's green."* « C'est ta voiture? » — « Non, la mienne est verte. » ▷ *her parents and mine* ses parents et les miens ▷ *Your hands are dirty. Mine are clean.* Tes mains sont sales. Les miennes sont propres.; **It's mine.** C'est à moi. ▷ *This book is mine.* Ce livre est à moi. ▷ *"Whose is this?"* — *"It's mine."* « C'est à qui? » — « À moi. »
► *n* mine f ▷ *a diamond mine* une mine de diamants ▷ *a land mine* une mine terrestre

miner [ˈmaɪnəʳ] *n* mineur m, mineuse f

mineral [ˈmɪnərəl] *n* minéral m (pl les minéraux)

mineral water *n* eau f minérale

miniature [ˈmɪnətʃəʳ] *adj* miniature f ▷ *a miniature version* une version miniature
► *n* miniature f

Minidisc® [ˈmɪnɪdɪsk] *n* minidisque m

minimum [ˈmɪnɪmʌm] *n* minimum m
► *adj* minimum m (f+pl minimum) ▷ *the minimum wage* le salaire minimum ▷ *The minimum age for driving is 16.* L'âge minimum pour conduire est seize ans.; **the minimum amount** le minimum m

miniskirt [ˈmɪnɪskɜːt] *n* minijupe f

minister [ˈmɪnɪstəʳ] *n* ❶ (*in government*) ministre m ❷ (*of church*) pasteur m

ministry [ˈmɪnɪstrɪ] *n* (*in government*) ministère m ▷ *the*

Ministry of the Environment le ministère de l'Environnement

mink [mɪŋk] n vison m

minor ['maɪnə²] adj mineur m ▷ a minor problem un problème mineur; **in D minor** en ré mineur; **a minor operation** une opération bénigne

minority [maɪˈnɒrɪtɪ] n minorité f

mint [mɪnt] n ❶ (plant) menthe f ▷ mint ice cream la crème glacée à la menthe ❷ (candy) bonbon à la menthe m

minus ['maɪnəs] prep moins ▷ 16 minus 3 is 13. Seize moins trois égale treize. ▷ It's minus two outside. Il fait moins deux dehors. ▷ I got a B minus. J'ai eu un B moins.

minute [maɪˈnjuːt] n minute f ▷ Wait a minute! Attends une minute! ▷ I'll do it right this minute. Je le ferai tout de suite.
▶ adj minuscule ▷ minute details des détails minuscules

miracle ['mɪrəkl] n miracle m

mirror ['mɪrə²] n ❶ (on wall) miroir m ❷ (in car) rétroviseur m

misbehave [mɪsbɪˈheɪv] vb se conduire mal

miscellaneous [mɪsɪˈleɪnɪəs] adj divers

mischief ['mɪstʃɪf] n bêtises fpl ▷ My little sister's always up to mischief. Ma petite sœur fait constamment des bêtises.

mischievous ['mɪstʃɪvəs] adj espiègle

miser ['maɪzə²] n avare mf

miserable ['mɪzərəbl] adj
❶ (person) malheureux m (f malheureuse) ▷ You look miserable. Tu as l'air malheureux. ❷ (weather) épouvantable ▷ The weather was miserable. Il faisait un temps épouvantable.; **to feel miserable** ne pas avoir le moral ▷ I'm feeling miserable. Je n'ai pas le moral.

misery ['mɪzərɪ] n (unhappiness) tristesse f ▷ All that money brought nothing but misery. Tout cet argent n'a apporté que de la tristesse.

misfortune [mɪsˈfɔːtʃən] n malheur m

mishap ['mɪshæp] n mésaventure f

misjudge [mɪsˈdʒʌdʒ] vb (person) mal juger ▷ I've misjudged him. Je l'ai mal jugé.; **He misjudged the turn.** Il a mal pris le virage.

misleading [mɪsˈliːdɪŋ] adj trompeur m (f trompeuse)

misplace [mɪsˈpleɪs] vb égarer ▷ I've misplaced my passport. J'ai égaré mon passeport.

Miss [mɪs] n ❶ Mademoiselle f (pl Mesdemoiselles) ❷ (in address) Mlle (pl Mlles)

Mademoiselle and Mlle are rarely used for single women any more, except in reference to a girl. It is better to use Madame (or the abbreviation Mme), the French equivalent of Ms, in person or in a letter.

miss [mɪs] vb ❶ rater ▷ Hurry or you'll miss the bus. Dépêche-toi ou tu vas rater l'autobus. ❷ He missed the target. Il a raté la cible. ❸ manquer ▷ to miss an opportunity manquer une occasion; **I miss you.** Tu me manques. ▷ I'm missing my family. Ma famille me manque.

missing ['mɪsɪŋ] adj manquant ▷ the missing piece la pièce manquante; **to be missing** avoir disparu ▷ My backpack is missing. Mon sac à dos a disparu. ▷ Two members of the group are missing. Deux membres du groupe ont disparu.

missionary ['mɪʃənrɪ] n missionnaire

mist [mɪst] n brume f

mistake [mɪsˈteɪk] n ❶ (slip)
faute f ▷ a spelling mistake une
faute d'orthographe; **to make a
mistake (1)** (be wrong, speaking)
faire une faute (2) (be mistaken) se
tromper ▷ I'm sorry, I made a mistake.
Je suis désolé, je me suis trompé.
❷ (misjudgement) erreur f ▷ It was
a mistake to buy those yellow shoes.
J'ai fait une erreur en achetant ces
chaussures jaunes.; **by mistake**
par erreur ▷ I took her bag by mistake.
J'ai pris son sac par erreur.
▶ vb: **He mistook me for my sister.**
Il m'a prise pour ma sœur.

mistaken [mɪsˈteɪkən] adj: **to be
mistaken** se tromper ▷ If you think
I'm going to get up at six o'clock, you're
mistaken. Si tu penses que je vais me
lever à six heures, tu te trompes.

mistook [mɪsˈtuk] vb see **mistake**

mistrust [mɪsˈtrʌst] vb se
méfier de

misty [ˈmɪstɪ] adj brumeux (f
brumeuse) ▷ a misty morning in a
matin brumeux

misunderstand [ˌmɪsʌndəˈstænd]
vb mal comprendre ▷ Sorry, I
misunderstood you. Je suis désolé, je
t'avais mal compris.

misunderstanding
[ˌmɪsʌndəˈstændɪŋ] n
malentendu m

mitten [ˈmɪtn] n mitaine f

mix [mɪks] n mélange m ▷ It's a mix
of science fiction and comedy. C'est
un mélange de science-fiction
et de comédie.; **a cake mix** une
préparation pour gâteau
▶ vb ❶ mélanger ▷ Mix the flour
with the sugar. Mélangez la farine
au sucre. ❷ combiner ▷ He's
mixing business with pleasure. Il
combine les affaires et le plaisir.;
**He doesn't mix with other
people.** Il se tient à l'écart.; **to mix

up** (people) confondre ▷ She always
mixes me up with my brother. Elle me
confond toujours avec mon frère.;
**The travel agent mixed up the
bookings.** L'agente de voyage s'est
embrouillée dans les réservations.;
I'm getting mixed up. Je ne m'y
retrouve plus.

mixed [mɪkst] adj: **a mixed salad**
une salade composée; **a mixed
family** une famille mixte; **a mixed
grill** un assortiment de grillades

mixture [ˈmɪkstʃəʳ] n mélange
m ▷ a mixture of spices un mélange
d'épices

mix-up [ˈmɪksʌp] n confusion f

moan [məun] vb gémir ▷ He was
moaning with pain. Il gémissait de
douleur.

mobile home [ˈməubaɪl-] n
maison mobile

mobile phone [ˈməubaɪl-] n
téléphone cellulaire m

moccasin [ˈmɔkəsɪn] n
mocassin m

mock [mɔk] vb ridiculiser
▶ adj: **a mock trial** une simulation
de procès; **a mock parliamentary
debate** une simulation de débat
parlementaire

model [ˈmɔdl] n ❶ (type) modèle
m ▷ His car is the latest model. Sa
voiture est le tout dernier modèle.
❷ (mock-up) maquette f ▷ a model
of the castle une maquette du
château ❸ (fashion) mannequin
m ▷ She's a famous model. C'est un
mannequin célèbre.
▶ adj: **a model plane** un modèle
réduit d'avion; **a model railway** un
modèle réduit de voie ferrée; **He's
a model student.** C'est un élève
modèle.
▶ vb: **She was modelling an Alfred
Sung outfit.** Elle présentait une
tenue de la collection Alfred Sung.

modem ['məʊdem] n modem m

moderate ['mɒdəreɪt] adj modéré
▷ Her views are quite moderate. Ses opinions sont assez modérées.;
a moderate amount of un peu de; **a moderate price** un prix raisonnable

modern ['mɒdən] adj moderne

modernize ['mɒdənaɪz] vb moderniser

modest ['mɒdɪst] adj modeste

modify ['mɒdɪfaɪ] vb modifier

moist [mɔɪst] adj (skin, soil) humide
▷ Make sure the soil is moist. Assurez-vous que la terre est humide.

moisture ['mɔɪstʃər] n humidité f

moisturizer ['mɔɪstʃəraɪzər] n
① (cream) crème hydratante f
② (lotion) lait hydratant m

mom [mɒm] n
> You use **maman** only when you are talking to your mother or using it as her name; otherwise use **mère**.

① mère f ▷ my mom ma mère ▷ her mom sa mère ② maman f ▷ Mom! Maman! ▷ I'll ask Mom. Je vais demander à maman.

moment ['məʊmənt] n instant m ▷ Could you wait a moment? Pouvez-vous attendre un instant? ▷ in a moment dans un instant ▷ Just a moment! Un instant!; **at the moment** en ce moment; **any moment now** d'un moment à l'autre ▷ They'll be arriving any moment now. Ils vont arriver d'un moment à l'autre.

momentous [məʊ'mentəs] adj (event) capital

monarch ['mɒnək] n monarque m

monarchy ['mɒnəkɪ] n monarchie f

monastery ['mɒnəstəri] n monastère m

Monday ['mʌndɪ] n lundi m ▷ on Monday lundi ▷ on Mondays le lundi ▷ every Monday tous les lundis ▷ last Monday lundi dernier ▷ next Monday lundi prochain

money ['mʌnɪ] n argent m ▷ I need to change some money. J'ai besoin de changer de l'argent.; **to make money** gagner de l'argent

monitor ['mɒnɪtər] n (of computer) moniteur m

monk [mʌŋk] n moine m

monkey ['mʌŋkɪ] n singe m

monopolize [mə'nɒpəlaɪz] vb monopoliser ▷ to monopolize the conversation monopoliser la conversation ▷ You're monopolizing the phone! Tu monopolises le téléphone!

monotonous [mə'nɒtənəs] adj monotone

monster ['mɒnstər] n monstre m

month [mʌnθ] n mois m ▷ this month ce mois-ci ▷ next month le mois prochain ▷ last month le mois dernier ▷ every month tous les mois ▷ at the end of the month à la fin du mois

monthly ['mʌnθlɪ] adj mensuel (f mensuelle)

monument ['mɒnjumənt] n monument m

mood [muːd] n humeur f; **to be in a bad mood** être de mauvaise humeur; **to be in a good mood** être de bonne humeur

moody ['muːdɪ] adj
① (temperamental) lunatique ② (in a bad mood) maussade

moon [muːn] n lune f ▷ There's a full moon tonight. Il y a pleine lune ce soir.; **to be over the moon** (happy) être aux anges

moonlight ['muːnlaɪt] n clair de lune m ▷ in the moonlight au clair de lune

moor [mʊər] vb (boat) amarrer

moose [muːs] n original m

mop [mɔp] n (for floor) vadrouille f

moped ['məuped] n cyclomoteur m

moral ['mɔrl] adj moral m (mpl moraux)
▶ n morale f ▷ the moral of the story la morale de l'histoire; **morals** la moralité

morale [mɔ'rɑːl] n moral m ▷ Their morale is very low. Leur moral est très bas.

more [mɔːʳ] adj, pron, adv

> When comparing one amount with another, you usually use **plus**.

❶ plus ▷ Fruit is more expensive in Britain. Les fruits sont plus chers en Grande-Bretagne. ▷ Could you speak more slowly? Est-ce que vous pourriez parler plus lentement? ▷ a bit more un peu plus ▷ There isn't any more. Il n'y en a plus.; **more...than** plus...que ▷ He's more athletic than me. Il est plus sportif que moi. ▷ She practises more than I do. Elle s'entraîne plus que moi. ▷ More boys play hockey than girls. Il y a plus de garçons que de filles qui jouent au hockey. ❷ (followed by noun) plus de ▷ There are more girls in the class. Il y a plus de filles dans la classe. ▷ I get more homework than you do. J'ai plus de devoirs que toi. ▷ I spent more than 500 dollars. J'ai dépensé plus de cinq cents dollars.

> When referring to an additional amount, more than there is already, you usually use **encore**.

❸ encore ▷ Is there any more? Est-ce qu'il y en a encore? ▷ Would you like some more? Vous en voulez encore? ▷ It'll take a few more days. Ça prendra encore quelques jours. ❹ (followed by noun) encore de ▷ Could I have some more fries? Est-ce

que je pourrais avoir encore des frites? ▷ Do you want some more tea? Voulez-vous encore du thé?; **more or less** plus ou moins; **more than ever** plus que jamais

moreover [mɔː'rəuvəʳ] adv en outre

morning ['mɔːnɪŋ] n matin m ▷ this morning ce matin ▷ tomorrow morning demain matin ▷ every morning tous les matins; **in the morning** le matin ▷ at 7 o'clock in the morning à sept heures du matin; **a morning paper** un journal du matin

mosque [mɔsk] n mosquée f

mosquito [mɔs'kiːtəu] n moustique m; **a mosquito bite** une piqûre de moustique

most [məust] adv, adj, pron

> Use **la plupart** when **most (of)** is followed by a plural noun and **la majeure partie (de)** when **most (of)** is followed by a singular noun.

❶ la plupart de ▷ most of my friends la plupart de mes amis ▷ most people la plupart des gens ▷ Most cats are affectionate. La plupart des chats sont affectueux.; **most of them** la plupart d'entre eux; **most of the time** la plupart du temps ❷ la majeure partie de ▷ most of the work la majeure partie du travail ▷ most of the class la majeure partie de la classe ▷ most of the night la majeure partie de la nuit; **the most** le plus ▷ He's the one who talks the most. C'est lui qui parle le plus.

> When **most** is followed by adjective, the translation depends on whether the noun referred to is masculine, feminine or plural.

the most... (1) le plus... ▷ the most expensive restaurant le restaurant le plus cher **(2)** la plus… ▷ *the most expensive seat* la place la plus chère **(3)** les plus… ▷ *the most expensive restaurants* les restaurants les plus chers ▷ *the most expensive seats* les places les plus chères; **for the most part** pour la plupart ▷ *The students seem to like French, for the most part.* Les élèves semblent aimer le français, pour la plupart.; **to make the most of something** profiter au maximum de quelque chose; **at the most** au maximum ▷ *Two hours at the most.* Deux heures au maximum.

mostly ['məʊstlɪ] *adv* : **I went mostly because my friends were going.** (*mainly*) J'y suis allé surtout parce que mes amis y allaient.; **The teachers are mostly quite nice.** La plupart des professeurs sont assez gentils.; **We mostly do the shopping on Saturdays.** (*usually*) D'habitude, nous magasinons le samedi.

motel [məʊ'tɛl] *n* motel *m*

moth [mɒθ] *n* papillon de nuit *m*

mother ['mʌðə^r] *n* mère *f* ▷ *my mother* ma mère; **mother tongue** la langue maternelle

mother-in-law ['mʌðərɪnlɔː] *n* belle-mère *f* (*pl* belles-mères)

Mother's Day *n* fête des Mères *f*

motion ['məʊʃən] *n*
❶ mouvement *m* ▷ *the motion of the train* le mouvement du train
❷ geste *m* ▷ *He made a motion towards the door.* Il a fait un geste vers la porte.; **in motion** en marche; **motion sickness** le mal des transports; **We were just going through the motions.** Nous le faisions tout à fait machinalement.

motionless ['məʊʃənlɪs] *adj* immobile

motivated ['məʊtɪveɪtɪd] *adj* motivé ▷ *She is highly motivated.* Elle est très motivée.

motivation [məʊtɪ'veɪʃən] *n* motivation *f*

motive ['məʊtɪv] *n* mobile *m* ▷ *the motive for the crime* le mobile du crime

motor ['məʊtə^r] *n* moteur *m* ▷ *The boat has a motor.* Le bateau a un moteur.

motorbike ['məʊtəbaɪk] *n* moto *f*

motorboat ['məʊtəbəʊt] *n* bateau à moteur *m*

motorcycle ['məʊtəsaɪkl] *n* motocyclette *f*

motorcyclist ['məʊtəsaɪklɪst] *n* motard *m*, motarde *f*

motorist ['məʊtərɪst] *n* automobiliste *mf*

mouldy ['məʊldɪ] *adj* moisi

mount [maʊnt] *vb* ❶ monter ▷ *He mounted his horse and rode off.* Il est monté à son cheval et est parti. ▷ *to mount a bicycle* monter sur un vélo ▷ *They're mounting a publicity campaign.* Ils montent une campagne publicitaire.
❷ augmenter ▷ *Tension is mounting.* La tension augmente.

mount up *vb* ❶ s'accumuler ▷ *The mail had mounted up during our holidays.* Les lettres s'étaient accumulées pendant nos vacances. ❷ augmenter ▷ *My savings are mounting up gradually.* Mes économies augmentent progressivement.

mountain ['maʊntɪn] *n* montagne *f*; **a mountain bike** un vélo de montagne; **a mountain range** une chaîne de montagnes

mountainous ['maʊntɪnəs] *adj* montagneux (*f* montagneuse)

Mountie ['maʊntɪ] *n* agent *m* de la GRC, agente *f* de la GRC

mouse [maus] n (also for computer) souris f ▷ white mice des souris blanches

mouse pad n tapis de souris m

mousse [muːs] n ❶ (food) mousse f ▷ chocolate mousse la mousse au chocolat ❷ (for hair) mousse coiffante f

moustache [məsˈtɑːʃ] n moustache f ▷ He has a moustache. Il a une moustache.; **a man with a moustache** un moustachu

mouth [mauθ] n bouche f

mouthful [ˈmauθful] n bouchée f

mouth organ n musique à bouche f ▷ I play the mouth organ. Je joue de la musique à bouche.

mouthwash [ˈmauθwɒʃ] n bain de bouche m

move [muːv] n ❶ tour m ▷ It's your move. C'est ton tour. ❷ déménagement m ▷ Our move from Edmundston to Pugwash... Notre déménagement d'Edmundston à Pugwash...; **to get a move on** se remuer ▷ Get a move on! Remue-toi!
▶ vb ❶ bouger ▷ Don't move! Ne bouge pas! ▷ Could you move your stuff please? Est-ce que tu peux bouger tes affaires s'il te plaît? ❷ avancer ▷ The car was moving very slowly. La voiture avançait très lentement. ❸ émouvoir ▷ I was very moved by the film. J'ai été très émue par ce film. ❹ déménager ▷ We're moving in July. Nous allons déménager en juillet.; **to move forward** avancer; **to move in** emménager ▷ They're moving in next week. Ils emménagent la semaine prochaine.; **to move over** se pousser ▷ Could you move over a bit? Est-ce que vous pouvez vous pousser un peu?

movement [ˈmuːvmənt] n

mouvement m

movie [ˈmuːvɪ] n film m; **the movies** le cinéma ▷ Let's go to the movies! Si on allait au cinéma?; **a movie star** une vedette de cinéma

moving [ˈmuːvɪŋ] adj ❶ (not stationary) en marche ▷ a moving bus un bus en marche ❷ (touching) touchant ▷ a moving story une histoire touchante; **a moving van** un camion de déménagement

mow [mau] vb tondre; **to mow the lawn** tondre le gazon

mower [ˈmauər] n tondeuse à gazon f

mown [maun] vb see **mow**

MP n député m ▷ She's an MP. Elle est député.

MP3 adj MP3 ▷ an MP3 file un fichier MP3 ▷ an MP3 player un lecteur MP3

Mr [ˈmɪstər] n ❶ Monsieur (pl Messieurs) ❷ (in address) M. (pl MM.)

Mrs [ˈmɪsɪz] n ❶ Madame (pl Mesdames) ❷ (in address) Mme (pl Mmes)

MS n (= multiple sclerosis) sclérose en plaques f ▷ He has MS. Il a la sclérose en plaques.

Ms [mɪz] n ❶ Madame (pl Mesdames) ❷ (in address) Mme (pl Mmes)
  ○ There isn't a direct equivalent of
  ○ **Ms** in French. If you are writing
  ○ to somebody and don't know
  ○ whether she is married, use
  ○ **Madame**.

much [mʌtʃ] adj, adv, pron ❶ (with verb, adjective, adverb) beaucoup ▷ Do you go out much? Tu sors beaucoup? ▷ I don't like sports much. Je n'aime pas beaucoup le sport. ▷ I feel much better now. Je me sens beaucoup mieux maintenant. ❷ (followed by noun) beaucoup de ▷ I haven't got much money. Je n'ai pas beaucoup d'argent. ▷ *I don't want much rice.* Je ne veux pas beaucoup de riz.; **very much** beaucoup ▷ *I enjoyed the film very much.* J'ai beaucoup apprécié le film. ▷ *Thank you very much.* Merci beaucoup. ▷ *I don't have very much money.* Je n'ai pas beaucoup d'argent.; **not much (1)** pas beaucoup ▷ *Do you have a lot of luggage?* — "No, not much." « As-tu beaucoup de bagages ? » — « Non, pas beaucoup. » **(2)** pas grand-chose ▷ *"What's on TV?"* — *"Not much."* « Qu'est-ce qu'il y a à la télé ? » — « Pas grand-chose. » ▷ *"What did you think of it?"* — *"Not much."* « Qu'est-ce que tu en as pensé ? » — « Pas grand-chose. »; **How much?** Combien ? ▷ *How much do you want?* Tu en veux combien ? ▷ *How much time do you have?* Tu as combien de temps ? ▷ *How much is it? (cost)* Combien est-ce que ça coûte ?; **too much** trop ▷ *That's too much!* C'est trop! ▷ *It costs too much.* Ça coûte trop cher. ▷ *They give us too much homework.* Ils nous donnent trop de devoirs.; **so much** autant ▷ *I didn't think it would cost so much.* Je ne pensais pas que ça coûterait autant. ▷ *I've never seen so much traffic.* Je n'ai jamais vu autant de circulation.

mud [mʌd] *n* boue *f*

muddle up ['mʌdl-] *vb (people)* confondre ▷ *He muddles me up with my sister.* Il me confond avec ma sœur.; **to get muddled up** s'embrouiller ▷ *I'm getting muddled up.* Je m'embrouille.

muddy ['mʌdɪ] *adj* boueux (*f* boueuse)

muesli ['mjuːzlɪ] *n* muesli *m*

muffin ['mʌfɪn] *n* muffin *m*

muffle ['mʌfl] *vb* ❶ *(voice)* étouffer ▷ *a muffled cry* un cri étouffé ▷ *in a muffled voice* d'une voix étouffée ❷ *(other sounds)* assourdir ▷ *to muffle the noise of traffic* assourdir le bruit de la circulation

muffler ['mʌflə'] *n* silencieux *m*

mug [mʌg] *n* grande tasse *f* ▷ *Do you want a cup or a mug?* Est-ce que vous voulez une tasse normale ou une grande tasse?; **mug shot** la photo d'identité judiciaire
▶ *vb* agresser ▷ *He was mugged in the city centre.* Il s'est fait agresser au centre ville.

mugger ['mʌgə'] *n* agresseur *m* ▷ *The mugger was a woman.* L'agresseur était une femme.

mugging ['mʌgɪŋ] *n* agression *f*

muggy ['mʌgɪ] *adj* lourd ▷ *It's muggy out today.* Le temps est lourd aujourd'hui.

multicultural ['mʌltɪ'kʌltʃərəl] *adj* multiculturel (*f* multiculturelle)

multimedia ['mʌltɪ'miːdɪə] *adj* multimédia ▷ *a multimedia presentation* une présentation multimédia

multiple choice test ['mʌltɪpl-] *n* test à choix multiple *m*

multiple sclerosis [-sklɪ'rəusɪs] *n* sclérose en plaques *f* ▷ *She has multiple sclerosis.* Elle a la sclérose en plaques.

multiplication [mʌltɪplɪ'keɪʃən] *n* multiplication *f*

multiply ['mʌltɪplaɪ] *vb* multiplier ▷ *to multiply 6 by 3* multiplier six par trois

multi-storey ['mʌltɪ'stɔːrɪ] *adj* à plusieurs étages ▷ *a multi-storey parking garage* un stationnement à plusieurs étages

mummy ['mʌmɪ] *n (Egyptian)* momie *f*

mumps [mʌmps] *n* oreillons *mpl*

municipal [mjuː'nɪsɪpl] *adj* municipal (*mpl* municipaux)

▷ municipal government le gouvernement municipal

mural ['mjʊərl] n murale f ▷ The Grade 8s painted a mural in the gym. Les élèves de huitième année ont peint une murale dans le gymnase.

murder ['mɜːdə] n meurtre m
▸ vb assassiner

murderer ['mɜːdərə] n assassin m, assassine f

muscle ['mʌsl] n muscle m

muscular ['mʌskjʊlə] adj musclé

museum [mjuːˈzɪəm] n musée m

mushroom ['mʌʃrʊm] n champignon m ▷ mushroom omelette l'omelette aux champignons

music ['mjuːzɪk] n musique f

musical ['mjuːzɪkl] adj doué pour la musique ▷ I'm not musical. Je ne suis pas doué pour la musique.; **a musical instrument** un instrument de musique
▸ n comédie musicale f

musician [mjuːˈzɪʃən] n musicien m, musicienne f

muskeg ['mʌskeɡ] n muskeg m

Muslim ['mʌzlɪm] n musulman m, musulmane f ▷ He's a Muslim. Il est musulman.
▸ adj musulman m

mussel ['mʌsl] n moule f

must [mʌst] vb

When **must** means that you assume or suppose something is true, use **devoir**; when it means that someone has to do something, e.g., **I must buy some presents**, there are two choices. You can use **devoir**, or you can use **il faut que...**, which comes from the verb **falloir** and is followed by a verb in the subjunctive. The expression **il faut que** is more conversational.

❶ devoir ▷ You must be tired. Tu dois être fatigué. ▷ There must be some problem. Il doit y avoir un problème. ▷ I must clean up my room. Je dois nettoyer ma chambre. ▷ We must win this game. Nous devons gagner ce match. ❷ il faut que ▷ I must buy some presents. Il faut que j'achète des cadeaux. ▷ I really must go now. Il faut que j'y aille.

When translating **must not**, you cannot use **devoir**. You must not lie. Il ne faut pas mentir.; **Students must not operate this machine.** Les élèves n'ont pas le droit d'utiliser cet appareil.; **You mustn't forget to send her a card.** N'oublie surtout pas de lui envoyer une carte.; **You must come and see us.** (invitation) Venez donc nous voir.

mustard ['mʌstəd] n moutarde f

mustn't ['mʌsnt] vb = **must not**

mute [mjuːt] adj muet (f muette)

mutter ['mʌtə] vb marmonner

my [maɪ] adj mon m, ma f, mes pl ▷ my father mon père ▷ my aunt ma tante ▷ my parents mes parents

ma becomes **mon** before a vowel sound.

my friend (1) (male) mon ami **(2)** (female) mon amie

Do not use **mon/ma/mes** with parts of the body.

▷ I want to wash my hair. Je voudrais me laver les cheveux. ▷ I'm going to brush my teeth. Je vais me brosser les dents. ▷ I've hurt my foot. Je me suis fait mal au pied.

myself [maɪˈsɛlf] pron ❶ me ▷ I've hurt myself. Je me suis fait mal. ▷ I really enjoyed myself. Je me suis vraiment bien amusé. ▷ ...when I look at myself in the mirror. ...quand je me regarde dans le miroir. ❷ moi ▷ I don't like talking about myself. Je n'aime pas parler de moi. ❶ moi-même ▷ *I made it myself.* Je l'ai fait moi-même.; **by myself** tout seul ▷ *I don't like travelling by myself.* Je n'aime pas voyager tout seul.

mysterious [mɪsˈtɪərɪəs] *adj* mystérieux (*f* mystérieuse)

mystery [ˈmɪstərɪ] *n* mystère *m*; **a murder mystery** (*novel*) un roman policier

myth [mɪθ] *n* ❶ (*legend*) mythe *m* ▷ *a Greek myth* un mythe grec ❷ (*untrue idea*) idée f reçue ▷ *That's a myth.* C'est une idée reçue.

mythology [mɪˈθɒlədʒɪ] *n* mythologie *f*

n

nag [næg] *vb* (*scold*) harceler ▷ *They're always nagging me.* Ils me harcèlent constamment.

nail [neɪl] *n* ❶ (*on finger, toe*) ongle *m* ▷ *Don't bite your nails!* Ne te ronge pas les ongles! ❷ (*made of metal*) clou *m*

nail brush *n* brosse à ongles *f*

nail clippers *npl* coupe-ongles *m* (*pl* coupe-ongles)

nail file *n* lime à ongles *f*

nail polish *n* vernis à ongles *m*; **nail polish remover** le dissolvant

naked [ˈneɪkɪd] *adj* nu

name [neɪm] *n* nom *m*; **What's your name?** Comment vous appelez-vous?; **to call somebody names** traiter quelqu'un de tous les noms

▶ *vb* ❶ (*call*) appeler ▷ *They named the baby Petra.* Ils ont appelé le bébé Petra.; **I was named after my uncle.** J'ai reçu le nom de mon oncle. ❷ nommer ▷ *Name the provinces.* Nomme les provinces.

nanny ['nænɪ] *n* bonne d'enfants *f* ▷ *She's a nanny.* C'est une bonne d'enfants.

nap [næp] *n* petit somme *m*; **to have a nap** faire un petit somme

napkin ['næpkɪn] *n* serviette *f*

narrow ['nærəʊ] *adj* étroit

narrow-minded [nærəʊ'maɪndɪd] *adj* borné

nasty ['nɑːstɪ] *adj* ❶ (*bad*) mauvais ▷ *a nasty cold* un mauvais rhume ▷ *a nasty smell* une mauvaise odeur ❷ (*unfriendly*) méchant ▷ *He gave me a nasty look.* Il m'a regardé d'un air méchant.

nation ['neɪʃən] *n* nation *f*

national ['næʃənl] *adj* national (*mpl* nationaux) ▷ *He's the national champion.* C'est le champion national., **the National Assembly** l'Assemblée nationale

national anthem *n* hymne *m* national ▷ *Our national anthem is "O Canada".* Notre hymne national est « Ô Canada ».

nationalism ['næʃnəlɪzəm] *n* nationalisme *m* ▷ *Québec nationalism* le nationalisme québécois

nationalist ['næʃnəlɪst] *n* nationaliste

nationality [næʃə'nælɪtɪ] *n* nationalité *f*

national park *n* parc national *m* (*pl* parcs nationaux)

native ['neɪtɪv] *adj* natal ▷ *my native country* mon pays natal; **native language** la langue maternelle ▷ *English is not their native language.* L'anglais n'est pas leur langue maternelle.; **Native Peoples** les *m* peuples autochtones

natural ['nætʃrəl] *adj* naturel (*f* naturelle); **natural resources** les *f* ressources naturelles

naturalist ['nætʃrəlɪst] *n* naturaliste

naturally ['nætʃrəlɪ] *adv* naturellement ▷ *Naturally, we were very disappointed.* Nous avons naturellement été très déçus.

nature ['neɪtʃə'] *n* nature *f*

naughty ['nɔːtɪ] *adj*

🔲 vilain usually goes before the noun.

vilain ▷ *Naughty dog!* Vilain chien! ▷ *Don't be naughty!* Ne fais pas le vilain!

nauseous ['nɔːsɪəs] *adj*: **to feel nauseous** avoir la nausée; **It made me nauseous.** Cela m'a donné la nausée.; **a nauseous smell** une odeur écœurante

navel ['neɪvl] *n* nombril *m*

navy ['neɪvɪ] *n* marine *f* ▷ *He's in the navy.* Il est dans la marine.

navy blue *adj* bleu marine (*f+pl* bleu marine) ▷ *a navy blue skirt* une jupe bleu marine

Nazi ['nɑːtsɪ] *n* nazi *m*, nazie *f* ▷ *the Nazis* les nazis

near [nɪə'] *adj* proche ▷ *It's fairly near.* C'est assez proche.; **It's near enough to walk.** On peut facilement y aller à pied.; **the nearest** le plus proche ▷ *Where's the nearest service station?* Où est la station-service la plus proche? ▷ *The nearest stores were three kilometres away.* Les magasins les plus proches étaient à trois kilomètres.

▶ *prep, adv* près de ▷ *I live near Fredericton.* J'habite près de Fredericton.; *near my house* près de chez moi; **near here** près d'ici ▷ *Is there a bank near here?* Est-ce qu'il y a une banque près d'ici?

nearby [nɪəˈbaɪ] *adv* à proximité
▷ *There's a supermarket nearby.* Il y a un supermarché à proximité.
▶ *adj* ❶ *(close)* proche ▷ *a nearby convenience store* un dépanneur proche ❷ *(neighbouring)* voisin *m*
▷ *We went to the nearby village of St. Jacob's.* Nous sommes allés à St. Jacob's, le village voisin.

nearly [ˈnɪəlɪ] *adv* presque
▷ *Dinner's nearly ready.* Le dîner est presque prêt. ▷ *I'm nearly 15.* J'ai presque quinze ans.; **I nearly missed the bus.** J'ai failli rater l'autobus.

neat [niːt] *adj* soigné ▷ *She has very neat writing.* Elle a une écriture très soignée.

neatly [ˈniːtlɪ] *adv* soigneusement
▷ *neatly folded* soigneusement plié;
neatly dressed impeccable

necessarily [ˈnɛsɪsrɪlɪ] *adv*: **not necessarily** pas forcément

necessary [ˈnɛsɪsrɪ] *adj* nécessaire

necessity [nɪˈsɛsɪtɪ] *n* nécessité *f*
▷ *A car is a necessity, not a luxury.* Une voiture est une nécessité et non pas un luxe.

neck [nɛk] *n* ❶ *(of body)* cou *m*;
a stiff neck un torticolis ❷ *(of garment)* encolure *f* ▷ *a V-neck sweater* un chandail avec une encolure en V

necklace [ˈnɛklɪs] *n* collier *m*

nectarine [ˈnɛktərɪn] *n* nectarine *f*

need [niːd] *vb* avoir besoin de ▷ *I need a bigger size.* J'ai besoin d'une plus grande taille.; **to need to do something** avoir besoin de faire quelque chose ▷ *I need to use the phone.* J'ai besoin d'utiliser le téléphone.
▶ *n*: **There's no need to make reservations.** Il n'est pas nécessaire de réserver.

needle [ˈniːdl] *n* aiguille *f*

negative [ˈnɛɡətɪv] *n* *(photo)* négatif *m*
▶ *adj* négatif *m* (*f* négative) ▷ *He's got a very negative attitude.* Il a une attitude très négative.

neglected [nɪˈɡlɛktɪd] *adj* *(untidy)* mal tenu ▷ *The garden is neglected.* Le jardin est mal tenu.

negotiate [nɪˈɡəʊʃɪeɪt] *vb* négocier

negotiations [nɪɡəʊʃɪˈeɪʃənz] *npl* négociations *fpl*

neighbour [ˈneɪbəʳ] *n* voisin *m*, voisine *f* ▷ *the neighbours' garden* le jardin des voisins

neighbourhood [ˈneɪbəhud] *n* quartier *m*

neither [ˈnaɪðəʳ] *pron, conj, adj* aucun des deux, aucune des deux
▷ *"Carrots or peas?" — "Neither, thanks."* « Des carottes ou des petits pois? » — « Aucun des deux merci. »
▷ *Neither of them is coming.* Aucun des deux ne vient.; **neither…nor…** ni…ni… ▷ *Neither my mom nor my dad is coming to the school play.* Ni ma mère ni mon père ne viennent à la scène de l'école.; **Neither do I.** Moi non plus. ▷ *"I don't like him." — "Neither do I!"* « Je ne l'aime pas. » — « Moi non plus! »; **Neither have I.** Moi non plus. ▷ *"I've never been to the Northwest Territories." — "Neither have I."* « Je ne suis jamais allé aux Territoires du Nord-Ouest. » — « Moi non plus. »

neon [ˈniːɒn] *n* néon *m*; **a neon light** une lampe au néon

nephew [ˈnɛvjuː] *n* neveu *m* (*pl* neveux) ▷ *my nephew* mon neveu

nerve [nɜːv] *n* ❶ nerf *m* ▷ *She sometimes gets on my nerves.* Elle me tape quelquefois sur les nerfs.
❷ *(boldness)* toupet *m* ▷ *He's got some nerve!* Il a du toupet!; **It's only nerves.** C'est de la nervosité.; **to**

have an attack of nerves avoir le trac

nerve-racking ['nɜːrækɪŋ] adj angoissant

nervous ['nɜːvəs] adj (tense) nerveux (f nerveuse) ▷ I bite my nails when I'm nervous. Je me ronge les ongles quand je suis nerveux.; **to be nervous about something** craindre quelque chose ▷ I'm nervous about my piano exam. Je crains mon examen de piano.; **to be nervous about doing something** craindre de faire quelque chose ▷ I'm a bit nervous about flying to Newfoundland by myself. Je crains un peu d'aller toute seule en avion à Terre-Neuve.

nest [nɛst] n nid m

Net [nɛt] n Internet m ▷ to surf the Net naviguer sur Internet

net [nɛt] n filet m ▷ a volleyball net un filet de volleyball

network ['nɛtwɜːk] n réseau m (pl réseaux)

neurotic [njuəˈrɒtɪk] adj névrosé

neutral ['njuːtrəl] adj neutre ▷ neutral colours des couleurs neutres ▷ a neutral country un pays neutre ▷ I don't want to take sides; I'm staying neutral. Je ne veux pas prendre parti; je vais rester neutre.

never ['nɛvər] adv ❶ jamais ▷ "Have you ever been to the West Coast?" — "No, never." « Est-ce que tu es déjà allé jusqu'à la côte Ouest? » — « Non, jamais. » ▷ "When are you going to phone him?" — "Never!" « Quand est-ce que tu vas l'appeler? » — « Jamais! »

> Add **ne** if the sentence contains a verb.

❷ ne...jamais ▷ I never watch soap operas. Je ne regarde jamais les téléromans. ▷ I have never been camping. Je n'ai jamais fait de

camping. ▷ Never leave valuables in your car. Ne laissez jamais d'objets de valeur dans votre voiture.; **Never again!** Plus jamais!; **Never mind.** Ça ne fait rien.

new [njuː] adj ❶ nouveau (f nouvelle, mpl nouveaux) ▷ her new bike son nouveau vélo ▷ I need a new dress. J'ai besoin d'une nouvelle robe.

> **nouveau** changes to **nouvel** before a vowel and most words beginning with "h".

▷ his new friend son nouvel ami; **New Age** le nouvel âge ▷ New Age music la musique nouvel âge ❷ (brand new) neuf (f neuve) ▷ They've got a new car. Ils ont une voiture neuve.

newborn ['njuːbɔːn] n nouveau-né m (pl nouveau-nés), nouveau-née f (pl nouveau-nées); **a newborn baby** un nouveau-né

New Brunswick [-ˈbrʌnzwɪk] n Nouveau-Brunswick m

newcomer ['njuːkʌmər] n nouveau venu m (pl nouveaux venus), nouvelle venue f

Newfoundland ['njuːfənlənd] n Terre-Neuve

news [njuːz] n ❶ nouvelles fpl ▷ good news de bonnes nouvelles ▷ I've had some bad news. J'ai reçu de mauvaises nouvelles. ▷ It was nice to get your news. J'ai été content d'avoir de tes nouvelles. ❷ (single piece of news) nouvelle f ▷ That's wonderful news! Quelle bonne nouvelle! ❸ (on TV) journal télévisé m ▷ I watch the news every evening. Je regarde le journal télévisé tous les soirs. ❹ (on radio) informations fpl ▷ I listen to the news every morning. J'écoute les informations tous les matins.

newspaper ['njuːzpeɪpər] n

journal m (pl journaux) ▷ *I deliver newspapers.* Je distribue des journaux.

newsstand ['nju:zstænd] n kiosque à journaux m

New Year's n Nouvel An m ▷ *to celebrate New Year's* fêter le Nouvel An; **Happy New Year!** Bonne Année!; **New Year's Day** le jour de l'An; **New Year's Eve** la veille du jour de l'An ▷ *a New Year's Eve party* un réveillon du jour de l'An

next [nɛkst] adj, adv, prep ● (*in time*) prochain ▷ *next Saturday* samedi prochain ▷ *next year* l'année prochaine ▷ *next summer* l'été prochain ● (*in sequence*) suivant ▷ *the next train* le train suivant ▷ *Next please!* Au suivant! ● (*afterwards*) ensuite ▷ *What shall I do next?* Qu'est-ce que je fais ensuite? ▷ *What happened next?* Qu'est-ce qui s'est passé ensuite?; **next to** à côté de ▷ *next to the bank* à côté de la banque; **the next day** le lendemain ▷ *The next day we visited Windsor.* Le lendemain nous avons visité Windsor.; **the next time** la prochaine fois ▷ *the next time you see her* la prochaine fois que tu la verras; **next door** à côté ▷ *They live next door.* Ils habitent à côté. ▷ *the people next door* les gens d'à côté; **the next room** la pièce d'à côté

nibble ['nɪbl] vb ● (*food*) grignoter ▷ *to nibble on a cookie* grignoter un biscuit ● mordiller ▷ *Don't nibble on your pencil.* Ne mordille pas ton crayon.; **nibble food** les m amuse-gueules

nice [naɪs] adj ● (*kind*) gentil (f gentille) ▷ *Your parents are very nice.* Tes parents sont très gentils. ▷ *It was nice of you to remember my birthday.* C'était gentil de ta part de te souvenir de ma fête.; **to be**

nice to somebody être gentil avec quelqu'un ● (*pretty*) joli ▷ *That's a nice dress!* Qu'est-ce qu'elle est jolie, cette robe! ▷ *Banff is a nice town.* Banff est une jolie ville. ● (*general term of approval*) bon (f bonne) ▷ *a nice cup of coffee* une bonne tasse de café; **Have a nice time!** Amuse-toi bien!; **nice weather** le beau temps; **It's a nice day.** Il fait beau.

nickel ['nɪkl] n ● (*coin*) pièce de cinq cents f ● (*mineral*) nickel m

nickname ['nɪkneɪm] n surnom m

niece [niːs] n nièce f ▷ *my niece* ma nièce

night [naɪt] n ● nuit f ▷ *I want a single room for two nights.* Je veux une chambre individuelle pour deux nuits.; **My mother works nights.** Ma mère travaille de nuit.; **at night** la nuit; **Good night!** Bonne nuit!; **a night club** une boîte de nuit ● (*evening*) soir m ▷ *tomorrow night* demain soir; **last night (1)** hier soir ▷ *We watched a video last night.* Nous avons regardé un vidéo hier soir. **(2)** la nuit dernière ▷ *Last night I had a bad dream.* La nuit dernière, j'ai fait un mauvais rêve.

nightgown ['naɪtgaʊn] n chemise de nuit f

nightmare ['naɪtmɛəᵊ] n cauchemar m ▷ *It was a real nightmare!* Ça a été un vrai cauchemar!; **to have a nightmare** faire un cauchemar

nightshirt ['naɪtʃəːt] n chemise de nuit f

nine [naɪn] num neuf ▷ *He's nine.* Il a neuf ans.

nineteen [naɪn'tiːn] num dix-neuf ▷ *She's nineteen.* Elle a dix-neuf ans.

nineteenth [naɪn'tiːnθ] adj dix-neuvième ▷ *the nineteenth day of our holidays* la dix-neuvième journée de nos vacances ▷ *the nineteenth* floor le dix-neuvième étage; **the nineteenth of August** le dix-neuf août

ninety ['naɪntɪ] num quatre-vingt-dix

ninth [naɪnθ] adj neuvième ▷ *the ninth floor* le neuvième étage; **the ninth of August** le neuf août

no [nəʊ] adv, adj ① non ▷ *'Are you coming?' — 'No.'* « Est-ce que vous venez? » — « Non. » ▷ *'Would you like some more?' — 'No thank you.'* « Vous en voulez encore? » — « Non merci. » ② (not any) pas de ▷ *There's no hot water.* Il n'y a pas d'eau chaude. ▷ *There's no mail on Sundays.* Il n'y a pas de courrier le dimanche. ▷ *No problem.* Pas de problème.; **I have no idea.** Je n'en ai aucune idée.; **No way!** Pas question!; **"no smoking"** « Défense de fumer »; **No kidding!** Sans blague!

nobody ['nəʊbədɪ] pron ① personne ▷ *'Who's going with you?' — 'Nobody.'* « Qui t'accompagne? » — « Personne. »

Add **ne** if the sentence contains a verb.

② ne...personne ▷ *There was nobody in the office.* Il n'y avait personne au bureau.; **Nobody likes this new rule.** Personne n'aime ce nouveau règlement.

nod [nɒd] vb (in agreement) acquiescer d'un signe de tête; **to nod at somebody** (as greeting) saluer quelqu'un d'un signe de tête

noise [nɔɪz] n bruit m ▷ *Please make less noise.* Faites moins de bruit, s'il vous plaît.

noisy ['nɔɪzɪ] adj bruyant

nominate ['nɒmɪneɪt] vb (propose) proposer ▷ *I nominate Ian Alexander as president of the society.* Je propose Ian Alexander comme président de la société.; **He was nominated for a Governor General's Award.** Il a été nominé pour un Prix du Gouverneur général.

none [nʌn] pron ① aucun, aucune f ▷ *'How many sisters do you have?' — 'None.'* « Tu as combien de sœurs? » — « Aucune. » ▷ *'What sports do you play?' — 'None.'* « Qu'est-ce que tu fais comme sport? » — « Je n'en fais aucun. »

Add **ne** if the sentence contains a verb.

② aucun...ne ▷ *None of my friends wanted to come.* Aucun de mes amis n'a voulu venir.; **There's none left.** Il n'y en a plus.; **There are none left.** Il n'y en a plus.

non-renewable ['nɒnrɪ'nju:əbl] adj non renouvelable ▷ *non-renewable resources* les ressources non renouvelables

nonsense ['nɒnsəns] n niaiseries fpl ▷ *She talks a lot of nonsense.* Elle dit beaucoup de niaiseries. ▷ *Nonsense!* Arrête tes niaiseries!

non-smoker ['nɒn'sməʊkə*] n non-fumeur m, non-fumeuse f ▷ *I'm a non-smoker.* Je suis non-fumeur.

non-smoking ['nɒn'sməʊkɪŋ] adj non-fumeur m ▷ *a non-smoking section* une section non-fumeurs

non-stop ['nɒn'stɒp] adj, adv ① direct ▷ *a non-stop flight* un vol direct ▷ *We flew non-stop.* Nous avons pris un vol direct. ② sans arrêt ▷ *He talks non-stop.* Il parle sans arrêt.

noodles ['nu:dlz] npl nouilles fpl

noon [nu:n] n midi m ▷ *at noon* à midi ▷ *before noon* avant midi

no one pron ① personne ▷ *'Who's going with you?' — 'No one.'* « Qui t'accompagne? » — « Personne. »

Add **ne** if the sentence contains a verb.

② ne...personne ▷ *There was no one*

in the office. Il n'y avait personne au bureau.; **No one likes homework.** Personne n'aime les devoirs.

nor [nɔːʳ] *conj*: **neither…nor** ni… ni ▷ *neither the mall nor the pool* ni le centre commercial, ni la piscine; **Nor do I.** Moi non plus. ▷ *"I didn't like the movie." — "Nor did I."* « Je n'ai pas aimé le film. » — « Moi non plus. »; **Nor have I.** Moi non plus. ▷ *"I haven't seen her." — "Nor have I."* « Je ne l'ai pas vue. » — « Moi non plus. »

normal ['nɔːml] *adj* ❶ (*usual*) habituel (f habituelle) ▷ *at the normal time* à l'heure habituelle ❷ (*standard*) normal (*mpl* normaux) ▷ *a normal car* une voiture normale

normally ['nɔːməlɪ] *adv* ❶ (*usually*) généralement ▷ *I normally arrive at nine o'clock.* J'arrive généralement à neuf heures. ❷ (*as normal*) normalement ▷ *In spite of the strike, the airports are operating normally.* Malgré la grève, les aéroports fonctionnent normalement.

north [nɔːθ] *adj, adv* ❶ nord *m* (f+pl nord) ▷ *the north shore* la rive nord; **a north wind** un vent du nord ❷ vers le nord ▷ *We were travelling north.* Nous allions vers le nord.; **north of** au nord de ▷ *It's north of Cobourg.* C'est au nord de Cobourg. ▶ **n** nord *m* ▷ *in the north* dans le nord

North America *n* Amérique *f* du Nord

northbound ['nɔːθbaund] *adj*: ▷ *The truck was northbound on Hwy 400.* Le camion se trouvait sur l'autoroute 400 en direction du nord.; **Northbound traffic is moving very slowly.** La circulation vers le nord avance très lentement.

northeast [nɔːθˈiːst] *n* nord-est *m* ▷ *in the northeast* au nord-est

northern ['nɔːðən] *adj*: **the northern part of the province** la partie nord de la province; **Northern Québec** le Nord du Québec; **the northern lights** l'aurore *f* boréale

North Pole *n* pôle Nord *m*

northwest [nɔːθˈwest] *n* nord-ouest *m* ▷ *in the northwest* au nord-ouest

Northwest Territories *n* Territoires *mpl* du Nord-Ouest

nose [nəuz] *n* nez *m* (*pl* nez); **to look down one's nose at someone** prendre quelqu'un de haut; **to turn up one's nose at something** faire le dégoûté devant quelque chose; **It was right under my nose.** C'était là juste sous mon nez.

nosebleed ['nəuzbliːd] *n*: **to have a nosebleed** saigner du nez ▷ *I often get nosebleeds.* Je saigne souvent du nez.

nosy ['nəuzɪ] *adj* fouineur (f fouineuse)

not [nɒt] *adv* ❶ pas ▷ *Are you coming or not?* Est-ce que tu viens ou pas?; **not really** pas vraiment; **not at all** pas du tout; **not yet** pas encore ▷ *"Are you finished?" — "Not yet."* « As-tu fini? » — « Pas encore. » ⚠ Add **ne** before a verb. ❷ ne…pas ▷ *I'm not sure.* Je ne suis pas sûr. ▷ *It's not raining.* Il ne pleut pas. ▷ *You shouldn't do that.* Tu ne devrais pas faire ça. ▷ *They haven't arrived yet.* Ils ne sont pas encore arrivés. ❸ non ▷ *I hope not.* J'espère que non. ▷ *"Can you lend me $10?" — "I'm afraid not."* « Est-ce que tu peux me prêter dix dollars? » — « Non, désolé. »

note [nəut] *n* ❶ note *f* ▷ *to take notes* prendre des notes ❷ (*letter*) mot *m* ▷ *I'll write her a note.* Je vais lui écrire un mot.

notebook ['nəʊtbʊk] n ❶ carnet m ❷ ordinateur m bloc-notes

note down vb noter

notepad ['nəʊtpæd] n bloc-notes m (pl blocs-notes)

nothing ['nʌθɪŋ] n ❶ rien ▷ "What's wrong?" — "Nothing." « Qu'est-ce qui ne va pas? » — « Rien. » ▷ nothing special rien de particulier

Add **ne** if the sentence contains a verb.

❷ ne…rien ▷ He does nothing. Il ne fait rien. ▷ He ate nothing for breakfast. Il n'a rien mangé au déjeuner.; **Nothing is open on Christmas Day.** Rien n'est ouvert le jour de Noël.

notice ['nəʊtɪs] n (sign) panneau m (pl panneaux); **to put up a notice** mettre un panneau; **a warning notice** un avertissement; **Don't take any notice of her!** Ne fais pas attention à elle!
▸ vb remarquer

notorious [nəʊˈtɔːrɪəs] adj notoire ▷ a notorious criminal un criminel notoire ▷ His pranks are notorious. Ses mauvais tours sont notoires.

noun [naʊn] n nom m

Nova Scotia ['nəʊvəˈskəʊʃə] n Nouvelle-Écosse f

novel ['nɒvl] n roman m

novelist ['nɒvəlɪst] n romancier m, romancière f

November [nəʊˈvɛmbə'] n novembre m; **in November** en novembre

now [naʊ] adv, conj maintenant ▷ What are you doing now? Qu'est-ce que tu fais maintenant?; **just now** en ce moment ▷ I'm rather busy just now. Je suis très occupé en ce moment.; **I did it just now.** Je viens de le faire.; **He should be there by now.** Il doit être arrivé à l'heure qu'il est.; **It should be ready by now.**

Ça devrait être déjà prêt.; **now and then** de temps en temps; **now that you're here…** maintenant que tu es là.

nowadays ['naʊədeɪz] adv de nos jours ▷ Nowadays we have better medical care. De nos jours, on a de meilleurs soins de santé.

nowhere ['nəʊwɛə'] adv nulle part ▷ nowhere else nulle part ailleurs

nuclear ['njuːklɪə'] adj nucléaire ▷ nuclear power l'énergie nucléaire ▷ a nuclear power station une centrale nucléaire ▷ the nuclear family la famille nucléaire

nude [njuːd] adj nu; **to sunbathe nude** faire du bronzage intégral

nudge [nʌdʒ] vb: **He nudged me when he saw them.** Elle m'a donné un coup de coude quand elle l'a vu.

nudist ['njuːdɪst] n nudiste

nuisance ['njuːsns] n: **It's a nuisance.** C'est très embêtant.; **Sorry to be a nuisance.** Désolé de vous déranger.

numb [nʌm] adj engourdi ▷ My leg's gone numb. J'ai les jambes engourdies.; **numb with cold** engourdi par le froid

number ['nʌmbə'] n ❶ (total amount) nombre m ▷ a large number of people un grand nombre de gens ❷ (of house, telephone, bank account) numéro m ▷ They live at number 5. Ils habitent au numéro cinq. ▷ What's your phone number? Quel est votre numéro de téléphone? ▷ You've got the wrong number. Vous vous êtes trompé de numéro. ❸ (figure, digit) chiffre m ▷ I can't read the second number. Je n'arrive pas à lire le deuxième chiffre.

nun [nʌn] n religieuse f ▷ She's a nun. Elle est religieuse.

Nunavut ['nʌnəvʊt] n Nunavut m

nurse [nɜːs] n infirmier m,

infirmière f ▷ She's a nurse. Elle est infirmière.

nursery ['nɜːsərɪ] n (for plants) pépinière f

nursery school n jardin d'enfants m

nut [nʌt] n ❶ (edible) noix f (pl noix) ❷ (made of metal) écrou m; **You're a nut!** Tu es dingue!

nutmeg ['nʌtmeg] n noix de muscade f

nutrient ['njuːtrɪənt] n nutriment m

nutrition [njuːˈtrɪʃən] n nutrition f

nutritional [njuːˈtrɪʃənl] adj nutritif (f nutritive) ▷ Junk food has almost no nutritional value. La malbouffe n'a presque aucune valeur nutritive.

nutritionist [njuːˈtrɪʃənɪst] n nutritionniste

nutritious [njuːˈtrɪʃəs] adj nutritif (f nutritive) ▷ a nutritious snack une collation nutritive

nuts [nʌts] adj: **He's nuts.** Il est dingue.

nylon ['naɪlɒn] n nylon m

oak [əʊk] n chêne m ▷ an oak table une table en chêne

oar [ɔːʳ] n aviron m

oatmeal ['əʊtmiːl] n gruau m

obedient [əˈbiːdɪənt] adj obéissant

obey [əˈbeɪ] vb: **to obey the rules** respecter le règlement; **to obey one's parents** obéir à ses parents

object [əbˈdʒɛkt] n objet m ▷ a familiar object un objet familier

objection [əbˈdʒɛkʃən] n objection f

objective [əbˈdʒɛktɪv] n objectif m

oboe ['əʊbəʊ] n hautbois m ▷ I play the oboe. Je joue du hautbois.

obscene [əbˈsiːn] adj obscène

observant [əbˈzɜːvnt] adj observateur (f observatrice)

observe [əbˈzɜːv] vb observer

obsessed [əbˈsɛst] adj obsédé ▷ He's obsessed with trains. Il est obsédé par les trains.

obsession [əbˈsɛʃən] n obsession f ▷ *It's getting to be an obsession with you.* Ça devient une obsession chez toi.; **Hockey is an obsession of mine.** Le hockey est une de mes passions.

obsolete [ˈɔbsəliːt] adj dépassé

obstacle [ˈɔbstəkl] n obstacle m

obstruct [əbˈstrʌkt] vb bloquer ▷ *A truck was obstructing the traffic.* Un camion bloquait la circulation.

obtain [əbˈteɪn] vb obtenir

obvious [ˈɔbvɪəs] adj évident

obviously [ˈɔbvɪəslɪ] adv ① (of course) évidemment ▷ *"Do you want to pass the exam?" — "Obviously!"* « Tu veux réussir à l'examen ? » — « Évidemment ! »; **Obviously not!** Bien sûr que non! ② (visibly) manifestement ▷ *She was obviously exhausted.* Elle était manifestement épuisée.

occasion [əˈkeɪʒən] n occasion f ▷ *a special occasion* une occasion spéciale; **on several occasions** à plusieurs reprises

occasionally [əˈkeɪʒənəlɪ] adv de temps en temps

occupation [ɔkjuˈpeɪʃən] n profession f

occupy [ˈɔkjupaɪ] vb occuper ▷ *That seat is occupied.* Cette place est occupée.

occur [əˈkɜː] vb (happen) avoir lieu ▷ *The accident occurred yesterday.* L'accident a eu lieu hier.; **It suddenly occurred to me that...** Il m'est soudain venu à l'esprit que...

ocean [ˈəʊʃən] n océan m

o'clock [əˈklɔk] adv: **at four o'clock** à quatre heures; **It's five o'clock.** Il est cinq heures.

October [ɔkˈtəʊbə] n octobre m; **in October** en octobre

octopus [ˈɔktəpəs] n pieuvre f

odd [ɔd] adj ① bizarre ▷ *That's odd!*

C'est bizarre! ② impair ▷ *an odd number* un chiffre impair

of [ɔv, əv] prep ① de d, du, des ▷ *some photos of my holiday* des photos de mes vacances ② a boy of ten un garçon de dix ans

de changes to d' before a vowel and most words beginning with "h".

▷ *a kilo of oranges* un kilo d'oranges

de + le changes to du, and de + les changes to des.

▷ *the end of the movie* la fin du film ▷ *the end of the holidays* la fin des vacances ③ (with quantity, amount) en ▷ *He has four sisters. I've met two of them.* Il a quatre sœurs. J'en ai rencontré deux. **Can I have half of that?** Je peux en avoir la moitié?; **three of us** trois d'entre nous; **a friend of mine** un de mes amis; **the 14th of September** le quatorze septembre; **That's very kind of you.** C'est très gentil de votre part.; **It's made of wood.** C'est en bois.

off [ɔf] adv, prep, adj

For other expressions with **off**, see the verbs **get**, **take**, **turn**, etc.

① (heater, light, TV) éteint ▷ *All the lights are off.* Toutes les lumières sont éteintes. ② (tap, gas) fermé ▷ *Are you sure the tap is off?* Tu es sûr que le robinet est fermé? ③ (cancelled) annulé ▷ *The game is off.* Le match est annulé.; **to be off sick** être malade; **a day off** un jour de congé ▷ *to take a day off work* prendre un jour de congé; **She's off school today.** Elle n'est pas à l'école aujourd'hui.; **I must be off now.** Je dois m'en aller maintenant.; **I'm off.** Je m'en vais.

offence [əˈfɛns] n (crime) délit; **No offence, but...** Sans vouloir t'offenser,...; **to take offence at**

something s'offenser de quelque chose

offend [əˈfɛnd] vb offenser ▷ Did my joke offend you? Est-ce que ma plaisanterie t'a offensé?; **to be offended by something** s'offenser de quelque chose

offensive [əˈfɛnsɪv] adj choquant

offer [ˈɒfəʳ] n proposition f ▷ a good offer une proposition intéressante ▷ Make me an offer. Faites-moi une proposition.; **$30 or best offer** 30 dollars ou offre la plus intéressante ▶ vb ❶ offrir ▷ He offered me a cookie. Il m'a offert un biscuit. ❷ proposer ▷ He offered to help me. Il m'a proposé de m'aider. ▷ I offered to go with them. Je leur ai proposé de les accompagner.

office [ˈɒfɪs] n bureau m (pl bureaux) ▷ She works in an office. Elle travaille dans un bureau.

officer [ˈɒfɪsəʳ] n ❶ (police) agent m de police, agente f de police ❷ (other) officier m, officière f

official [əˈfɪʃl] adj officiel (f officielle)

off-season [ˈɒfsiːzn] n: **It's cheaper during the off-season.** C'est moins cher hors saison.

offside [ˈɒfsaɪd] adj (sports) hors jeu

often [ˈɒfn] adv souvent ▷ It often rains. Il pleut souvent. ▷ How often do you go to the movies? Tu vas souvent au cinéma? ▷ I'd like to go skiing more often. J'aimerais aller skier plus souvent.

oil [ɔɪl] n ❶ (for lubrication, cooking) huile f; **an oil painting** une peinture à l'huile ❷ (crude oil) pétrole m ▷ oil from the Alberta tar sands le pétrole des sables bitumineux de l'Alberta ▶ vb graisser

oil rig n plateforme pétrolière f

▷ She works on an oil rig. Elle travaille sur une plateforme pétrolière.

oil slick n marée noire

oil well n puits de pétrole m

ointment [ˈɔɪntmənt] n onguent m

okay [ˈəʊˈkeɪ] excl, adj (agreed) d'accord ▷ "Could you call back later?" — "Okay!" « Tu peux rappeler plus tard? » — « D'accord! » ▷ I'll meet you at six o'clock, okay? Je te retrouve à six heures, d'accord? ▷ Is that okay? C'est d'accord?; **I'll do it tomorrow, if that's okay with you.** Je le ferai demain, si tu es d'accord.; **Are you okay?** Ça va?; **"How was your holiday?" — "It was okay."** « C'était comment les vacances? » — « Pas mal. »; **"What's your teacher like?" — "He's okay."** « Il est comment ton prof? » — « Il est sympathique. (informal) »

old [əʊld] adj ❶ vieux (f vieille) ▷ an old dog un vieux chien ▷ an old house une vieille maison

> ▌ **vieux** changes to **vieil** before
> ▌ a vowel and most words
> ▌ beginning with "h".

▷ an old man un vieil homme

> ▌ When talking about people it is
> ▌ more polite to use **âgé** instead
> ▌ of **vieux**.

❷ âgé ▷ old people les personnes âgées ❸ (former) ancien (f ancienne) ▷ my old school mon ancienne école; **How old are you?** Quel âge as-tu?; **He's ten years old.** Il a dix ans.; **my older brother** mon frère aîné ▷ my older sister ma sœur aînée; **She's two years older than me.** Elle a deux ans de plus que moi.; **I'm the oldest in the family.** Je suis l'aîné de la famille.

old-fashioned [ˈəʊldˈfæʃnd] adj ❶ démodé ▷ She wears old-fashioned clothes. Elle porte des

vêtements démodés. ❷ *(person)*
vieux jeu *(f+pl vieux jeux)* ▷ *My
parents are rather old-fashioned.* Mes
parents sont plutôt vieux jeu.

olive ['ɔlɪv] *n* olive *f*; **olive oil** l'huile
d'olive

Olympic [əʊ'lɪmpɪk] *adj*
olympique; **the Olympics** les *m*
Jeux olympiques

omelette ['ɔmlɪt] *n* omelette *f*

on [ɔn] *prep, adv*

> There are several ways of
> translating **on**. Scan the
> examples to find one that is
> similar to what you want to
> say. For other expressions
> with **on**, see the verbs **go**, **put**,
> **turn**, etc.

❶ sur ▷ *on the table* sur la table
▷ *on an island* sur une île ❷ à ▷ *on
the left* à gauche ▷ *on the 2nd floor*
au deuxième étage ▷ *I go to school
on my bike.* Je vais à l'école à vélo.;
on **TV** à la télé ▷ *What's on TV?*
Qu'est-ce qu'il y a à la télé?; **on the
radio** à la radio ▷ *I heard it on the
radio.* Je l'ai entendu à la radio.; **on
the bus (1)** *(by bus)* en autobus ▷ *I
go into town on the bus.* Je vais en
ville en autobus. **(2)** *(inside)* dans
l'autobus ▷ *There were no empty
seats on the bus.* Il n'y avait pas de
places libres dans l'autobus.; **on
holiday** en vacances ▷ *They're on
holiday.* Ils sont en vacances.; **on
strike** en grève

> With days and dates **on** is not
> translated.

▷ *on Friday* vendredi ▷ *on Fridays*
le vendredi ▷ *on Christmas Day* le
jour de Noël ▷ *on June 20th* le vingt
juin ▷ *on my birthday* le jour de mon
anniversaire
▶ *adj* ❶ *(heater, light, TV)* allumé
▷ *I think I left the light on.* Je crois
que j'ai laissé la lumière allumée.

❷ *(tap, gas)* ouvert ▷ *You left the tap
on.* Tu as laissé le robinet ouvert.
❸ *(machine)* en marche ▷ *Is the
dishwasher on?* Est-ce que le lave-
vaisselle est en marche?; **What's
on at the movie theatre?** Qu'est-
ce qui passe au cinéma?

once [wʌns] *adv* une fois ▷ *once a
week* une fois par semaine ▷ *once
more* encore une fois ▷ *I've been to
Nunavut once before.* J'ai déjà été une
fois au Nunavut.; **Once upon a
time...** Il était une fois...; **at once**
tout de suite; **all at once** *(suddenly)*
tout à coup; **once in a while** de
temps en temps

one [wʌn] *num, pron*

> Use **un** for masculine nouns
> and **une** for feminine nouns.

❶ un ▷ *one day* un jour ▷ *"Do you
need a stamp?" — "No thanks, I've got
one."* « Est-ce que tu as besoin d'un
timbre? » — « Non merci, j'en ai un. »
❷ *(feminine)* une ▷ *one minute*
une minute ▷ *I have one brother
and one sister.* J'ai un frère et une
sœur. ❸ *(impersonal)* on ▷ *One
never knows.* On ne sait jamais.;
one by one un à un; **one after the
other** l'un après l'autre; **this one
(1)** *(masculine)* celui-ci ▷ *"Which
foot is hurting?" — "This one."* « Quel
pied te fait mal? » — « Celui-ci. »
(2) *(feminine)* celle-ci ▷ *"Which is the
best photo?" — "This one."* « Quelle est
la meilleure photo? » — « Celle-ci. »;
that one (1) *(masculine)* celui-là
▷ *"Which bag is yours?" — "That one."*
« Lequel est ton sac? » — « Celui-là. »
(2) *(feminine)* celle-là ▷ *"Which seat
do you want?" — "That one."* « Quelle
place voulez-vous? » — « Celle-là. »

oneself [wʌn'self] *pron* ❶ se
▷ *to hurt oneself* se faire mal
❷ soi-même ▷ *It's quicker to do it
oneself.* C'est plus rapide de le faire

soi-même.

one-way ['wʌnweɪ] adj: **a one-way street** une impasse

onion ['ʌnjən] n oignon m ▷ **onion soup** la soupe à l'oignon

online ['ɒnlaɪn] adj en ligne

only ['əʊnlɪ] adv, adj, conj **①** seul ▷ Monday is the only day I'm free. Le lundi est le seul jour où je suis libre. ▷ French is the only subject I like. Le français est la seule matière que j'aime. ▷ seulement ▷ "How much was it?" — "Only $10." « Combien c'était? » — « Seulement dix dollars. » ▶ Not only is she intelligent, she's also very nice. Elle est non seulement intelligente, mais aussi très gentille. **②** ne...que ▷ We only want to stay for one night. Nous ne voulons rester qu'une nuit. ▷ These cassettes are only $5. Ces cassettes ne coûtent que cinq dollars. **③** mais ▷ I'd like the same sweater, only in black. Je voudrais le même chandail, mais en noir.; **an only child** un enfant unique

Ontario [ɒn'tɛərɪəʊ] n l'Ontario m

onwards ['ɒnwədz] adv à partir de ▷ from July onwards à partir de juillet

open ['əʊpn] adj **①** ouvert ▷ The bakery is open on Sunday morning. La boulangerie est ouverte le dimanche matin. ▷ I'm open to suggestions. Je suis ouvert aux suggestions. ▷ She was very open with me. Elle a été tout à fait franche avec moi. **②** vacant ▷ Is the position still open? Est-ce que le poste est encore vacant?; **in the open air** en plein air; **to have an open mind** avoir l'esprit ouvert

▶ vb **①** ouvrir ▷ Can I open the window? Est-ce que je peux ouvrir la fenêtre? ▷ What time do the stores open? Les magasins ouvrent à quelle

heure? **②** s'ouvrir ▷ The door opens automatically. La porte s'ouvre automatiquement. ▷ The door opened and in came the teacher. La porte s'est ouverte et la professeure est entrée.

opening ['əʊpnɪŋ] n **①** ouverture f ▷ the opening of Parliament l'ouverture de la session parlementaire ▷ an opening in the wall une ouverture dans le mur **②** (to cave, tunnel) entrée f **③** (in clouds) éclaircie f **④** (for specific job) poste vacant m ▷ We have an opening for a receptionist. Nous avons un poste vacant de réceptionniste. **⑤** (potential job opportunity) débouché m ▷ There are a lot of openings in the computer industry. Il y a beaucoup de débouchés dans l'informatique.

opera ['ɒprə] n opéra m

operate ['ɒpəreɪt] vb **①** fonctionner ▷ I don't know how the legal system operates in Québec. Je ne sais pas comment fonctionne le système judiciaire au Québec. **②** faire fonctionner ▷ How do you operate the VCR? Comment fait-on fonctionner le magnétoscope? **③** (medically) opérer ▷ to operate on someone opérer quelqu'un

operation [ɒpə'reɪʃən] n opération f ▷ a major operation une grave opération; **to have an operation** ▷ I have never had an operation. Je ne me suis jamais fait opérer.

operator ['ɒpəreɪtə] n (on telephone) standardiste

opinion [ə'pɪnjən] n avis m ▷ in my opinion à mon avis ▷ He asked me my opinion. Il m'a demandé mon avis.; **What's your opinion?** Qu'est-ce que vous en pensez?

opinion poll n sondage m

opponent [ə'pəʊnənt] n
adversaire mf

opportunity [ɒpə'tjuːnɪtɪ]
n occasion f; **to have the
opportunity to do something**
avoir l'occasion de faire quelque
chose ▷ I've never had the opportunity
to go to the Northwest Territories. Je
n'ai jamais eu l'occasion d'aller aux
Territoires du Nord-Ouest.

opposed [ə'pəʊzd] adj: ▷ I've always
been opposed to violence. J'ai toujours
été contre la violence.; **as opposed
to** par opposition à

opposing [ə'pəʊzɪŋ] adj (team)
opposé

opposite ['ɒpəzɪt] adj, prep
❶ opposé ▷ It's in the opposite
direction. C'est dans la direction
opposée. ❷ en face de ▷ the girl
sitting opposite me la fille assise en
face de moi; **the opposite sex**
l'autre sexe

opposition [ɒpə'zɪʃən] n
opposition f ▷ the leader of the
Opposition le chef de l'opposition
▷ We ran into a lot of opposition.
Nous avons rencontré beaucoup
d'opposition.

optimist ['ɒptɪmɪst] n optimiste mf

optimistic [ɒptɪ'mɪstɪk] adj
optimiste

option ['ɒpʃən] n (choice) choix m
▷ Our only option is to take the bus.
Notre seul choix est de prendre
l'autobus.

optional ['ɒpʃənl] adj facultatif (f
facultative)

optometrist [ɒp'tɒmətrɪst] n
optométriste mf ▷ I picked up my
new glasses at the optometrist's.
J'ai passé prendre mes nouvelles
lunettes chez l'optométriste.

or [ɔːʳ] conj ❶ ou ▷ Would you like tea
or coffee? Est-ce que tu veux du thé
ou du café?

Use **ni...ni** in negative
sentences.

▷ I don't eat meat or fish. Je ne mange
ni viande ni poisson. ❷ (otherwise)
sinon ▷ Hurry up or you'll miss the
bus. Dépêche-toi, sinon tu vas rater
l'autobus.; **Give me the money, or
else!** Donne-moi l'argent, sinon tu
vas le regretter!

oral ['ɔːrəl] adj oral (mpl oraux);
an oral presentation une
présentation orale

orange ['ɒrɪndʒ] n orange f; **an
orange juice** un jus d'orange
▷ adj orange (f+pl orange)

orchard ['ɔːtʃəd] n verger m

orchestra ['ɔːkɪstrə] n orchestre m
▷ I play in the school orchestra. Je joue
dans l'orchestre de l'école.

order ['ɔːdəʳ] n ❶ (sequence) ordre
m ▷ in alphabetical order en ordre
alphabétique ❷ (instruction)
commande f ▷ The waiter took
our order. Le serveur a pris notre
commande.; **in order to** pour ▷ She
mows lawns in order to earn money.
Elle tond les gazons pour gagner
de l'argent.; **"out of order"** « en
panne »

▷ vb commander ▷ I ordered a
hamburger and fries. J'ai commandé
un hamburger et des frites. ▷ Are
you ready to order? Vous êtes prêt à
commander?; **to order somebody
around** donner des ordres à
quelqu'un ▷ She was fed up with
being ordered around. Elle en avait
assez de toujours se faire donner
des ordres.

ordinary ['ɔːdnrɪ] adj ❶ ordinaire
▷ an ordinary day une journée
ordinaire ❷ (people) comme les
autres ▷ an ordinary family une
famille comme les autres ▷ He's
just an ordinary guy. C'est un type
comme les autres.

organ ['ɔːɡən] n ❶ (instrument) orgue m ▷ I play the organ. Je joue de l'orgue. ❷ (in body) organe m

organic [ɔːˈɡænɪk] adj (vegetables, fruit) biologique

organization [ɔːɡənaɪˈzeɪʃən] n organisation f

organize ['ɔːɡənaɪz] vb organiser

origin ['ɒrɪdʒɪn] n origine f

original [əˈrɪdʒɪnl] adj original (mpl originaux) ▷ It's a very original idea. C'est une idée très originale.; **Our original plan was to go camping.** Au départ, nous avions l'intention de faire du camping.

originally [əˈrɪdʒɪnəlɪ] adv au départ

ornament ['ɔːnəmənt] n bibelot m

orphan ['ɔːfn] n orphelin m, orpheline f

orthodontist [ɔːθəˈdɒntɪst] n orthodontiste mf ▷ I have to go to the orthodontist this afternoon. Il faut que j'aille chez l'orthodontiste cet après-midi.

ostrich ['ɒstrɪtʃ] n autruche f

other ['ʌðəʳ] adj, pron autre ▷ Have you got these jeans in other colours? Est-ce que vous avez ces jeans dans d'autres couleurs? ▷ on the other side of the street de l'autre côté de la rue ▷ the other day l'autre jour; **the other one** l'autre ▷ "This one?" — "No, the other one." « Celui-ci? » — « Non, l'autre. »; **the others** les autres ▷ The others are going but I'm not. Les autres y vont mais pas moi.; **every other day** tous les deux jours; **other than that** à part ça

otherwise ['ʌðəwaɪz] adv, conj ❶ (if not) sinon ▷ Write down the number, otherwise you'll forget it. Note le numéro, sinon tu vas l'oublier. ▷ Put some sunscreen on; you'll get burned otherwise. Mets une crème solaire, sinon tu vas

attraper des coups de soleil. ❷ (in other ways) à part ça ▷ I'm tired, but otherwise I'm fine. Je suis fatigué, mais à part ça, ça va.

otter ['ɒtəʳ] n loutre f

ought [ɔːt] vb

To translate **ought to** use the conditional tense of **devoir**.

▷ I ought to phone my parents. Je devrais appeler mes parents. ▷ He ought to win. Il devrait gagner.

our ['auəʳ] adj ❶ notre ▷ Our house is quite big. Notre maison est plutôt grande. ❷ (with plural) nos ▷ Our neighbours are very nice. Nos voisins sont très gentils.

ours [auəz] pron ❶ le + m nôtre ▷ Your garden is very big. Ours is much smaller. Votre jardin est très grand. Le nôtre est beaucoup plus petit. ❷ (with feminine) la nôtre ▷ Your school is very different from ours. Votre école est très différente de la nôtre. ❸ (with plural) les nôtres ▷ "Our teachers are strict." — "Ours are too." « Nos professeurs sont sévères. » — « Les nôtres aussi. »; **Is this ours?** C'est à nous? ▷ This car is ours. Cette voiture est à nous. ▷ "Whose is this?" — "It's ours." « C'est à qui? » — « À nous. »

ourselves [auəˈsɛlvz] pron ❶ nous ▷ We really enjoyed ourselves. Nous nous sommes vraiment bien amusés. ❷ nous-mêmes ▷ We built our garage ourselves. Nous avons construit notre garage nous-mêmes.

out [aut] adv

There are several ways of translating **out**. Scan the examples to find one that is similar to what you want to say. For other expressions with **out**, see the verbs **go**, **put**, **turn**, etc.

❶ (*outside*) dehors ▷ *It's cold out.* Il fait froid dehors. ❷ (*light, fire*) éteint ▷ *All the lights are out.* Toutes les lumières sont éteintes.; **She's out.** Elle est sortie.; **He's out shopping.** Il est sorti faire des courses.; **She's out for the afternoon.** Elle ne sera pas là de tout l'après-midi.; **out there** dehors ▷ *It's cold out there.* Il fait froid dehors.; **to go out** sortir ▷ *I'm going out tonight.* Je sors ce soir.; **to go out with somebody** sortir avec quelqu'un ▷ *She's been going out with him for two months.* Elle sort avec lui depuis deux mois.; **out of (1)** dans ▷ *to drink out of a glass* boire dans un verre **(2)** sur ▷ *in 9 cases out of 10* dans neuf cas sur dix **(3)** en dehors de ▷ *He lives out of town.* Il habite en dehors de la ville.; **3 km out of town** à trois kilomètres de la ville; **out of curiosity** par curiosité; **out of date (1)** (*expired*) périmé **(2)** (*outmoded*) démodé; **out of work** sans emploi; **That's out of the question.** C'est hors de question.; **You're out!** (*in game*) Tu es éliminé!

outbreak ['autbreik] n ❶ (*of disease*) épidémie f ▷ *an outbreak of the flu* une épidémie de grippe ❷ début m ▷ *the outbreak of war* le début de la guerre

outcome ['autkʌm] n issue f ▷ *What was the outcome of the negotiations?* Quelle a été l'issue des négociations?

outdoor [aut'dɔːʳ] adj en plein air ▷ *an outdoor swimming pool* une piscine en plein air; **outdoor activities** les activités de plein air

outdoors [aut'dɔːz] adv au grand air

outer ['autəʳ] adj extérieur ▷ *the outer surface* la surface

extérieure ▷ *the outer door* la porte extérieure; **outer space** l'espace m; **outer clothing** les m vêtements d'extérieur

outfit ['autfit] n tenue f ▷ *She bought a new outfit for the wedding.* Elle a acheté une nouvelle tenue pour le mariage.; **a cowboy outfit** un costume de cowboy

outgoing ['autgəuɪŋ] adj extraverti ▷ *He's very outgoing.* Il est très extraverti.

outhouse ['authaus] n toilettes fpl extérieures

outing ['autɪŋ] n sortie f ▷ *to go on an outing* faire une sortie

outline ['autlaɪn] n ❶ (*summary*) grandes fpl lignes ▷ *This is an outline of the plan.* Voici les grandes lignes du projet. ❷ (*shape*) contours mpl ▷ *We could see the outline of the mountain in the mist.* Nous distinguions les contours de la montagne dans la brume.

outlook ['autluk] n ❶ (*attitude*) attitude f ▷ *my outlook on life* mon attitude face à la vie ❷ (*prospects*) perspectives fpl ▷ *the economic outlook* les perspectives économiques; **The outlook is poor.** Les choses s'annoncent mal.

outnumber [aut'nʌmbəʳ] vb: **We're outnumbered.** Ils sont plus nombreux que nous.; **Girls outnumber boys three to one here.** Les filles sont trois fois plus nombreuses que les garçons ici.

outrageous [aut'reɪdʒəs] adj ❶ (*behaviour*) scandaleux (f scandaleuse) ❷ (*price*) exorbitant

outside [aut'saɪd] n extérieur m ▶ adj, adv, prep ❶ extérieur ▷ *the outside walls* les murs extérieurs ❷ dehors ▷ *It's very cold outside.* Il fait très froid dehors. ❸ en dehors de ▷ *outside the school* en dehors

de l'école ▷ *outside school hours* en
dehors des heures de cours

outskirts ['autskə:ts] *npl* banlieue
f ▷ *on the outskirts of the town* dans
les banlieues de la ville

outstanding [aut'stændɪŋ] *adj*
remarquable

oval ['əuvl] *adj* ovale

oven ['ʌvn] *n* four m

over ['əuvə'] *prep, adv, adj*

> When there is movement over
> something, use **par-dessus**;
> when something is located
> above something, use **au-
> dessus de**.

❶ par-dessus ▷ *The ball went
over the wall.* Le ballon est passé
par-dessus le mur. ❷ au-dessus
de ▷ *There's a mirror over the
washbasin.* Il y a un miroir au-dessus
du lavabo. ❸ (*more than*) plus de
▷ *It's over twenty kilos.* Ça pèse plus
de vingt kilos. ▷ *The temperature
was over thirty degrees.* Il faisait une
température de plus de trente
degrés. ❹ (*during*) pendant ▷ *over
the holidays* pendant les vacances
▷ *over Christmas* pendant les fêtes
de Noël ▷ (*finished*) terminé ▷ *I'll
be happy when the exams are over.* Je
serai content quand les examens
seront terminés; **over here** ici;
over there là-bas; **all over the
province** dans toute la province; **I
spilled coffee over my shirt.** J'ai
renversé du café sur ma chemise.

overall [əuvər'ɔ:l] *adv* (*generally*)
dans l'ensemble ▷ *My marks were
pretty good overall.* Mes notes
étaient assez bonnes dans
l'ensemble.

overalls ['əuvərɔ:lz] *npl* vêtements
mpl de travail

overcast ['əuvəkɑ:st] *adj* couvert
▷ *The sky was overcast.* Le ciel était
couvert.

overcharge [əuvə'tʃɑ:dʒ] *vb*: **He
overcharged me.** Il m'a fait payer
trop cher.; **They overcharged us
for the meal.** Ils nous ont fait payer
trop cher pour le repas.

overcoat ['əuvəkəut] *n*
pardessus *m*

overdone [əuvə'dʌn] *adj* (*food*)
trop cuit

overdose ['əuvədəus] *n* (*of drugs*)
surdose f ▷ *He died of an overdose.* Il a
succombé à une surdose.

overdue [əuvə'dju:] *adj*: **This book
is overdue.** Je suis en retard pour
rendre ce livre.

overestimate [əuvər'estɪmeɪt] *vb*
surestimer

overflow ['əuvəfləu] *vb* déborder
▷ *to overflow with enthusiasm*
déborder d'enthousiasme ▷ *The
toilet is overflowing.* La toilette
déborde. ▷ *The river has overflowed
its banks.* La rivière a débordé de
son lit.

overhead projector ['əuvəhɛd-]
n rétroprojecteur *m*

overlap ['əuvəlæp] *vb* se
chevaucher ▷ *The boards overlap.* Les
planches se chevauchent. ▷ *Your job
overlaps with mine.* Ton travail et le
mien se chevauchent.

overlook [əuvə'luk] *vb* ❶ (*have
view of*) donner sur ▷ *The hotel
overlooks the beach.* L'hôtel donne
sur la plage. ❷ (*forget about*)
négliger ▷ *She had overlooked one
important problem.* Elle avait négligé
un problème important.

overreact [əuvəri:'ækt] *vb* réagir
de façon exagérée ▷ *I may have
overreacted.* J'ai peut-être réagi de
façon exagérée.; **You're always
overreacting.** Tu dramatises
toujours tout.

overseas [əuvə'si:z] *adv* à
l'étranger ▷ *I'd like to work overseas.*

J'aimerais travailler à l'étranger.

oversight ['əʊvəsaɪt] n oubli m

oversleep [əʊvə'sliːp] vb se réveiller en retard ▷ I overslept this morning. Je me suis réveillé en retard ce matin.

overtime ['əʊvətaɪm] n
❶ heures fpl supplémentaires ▷ to work overtime faire des heures supplémentaires ❷ (sports) prolongation f ▷ thirty minutes of overtime trente minutes de prolongation ▷ The game went into overtime. Le match est allé en prolongation.

overweight [əʊvə'weɪt] adj trop gros (f trop grosse)

overwhelm [əʊvə'welm] vb
❶ accabler ▷ overwhelmed with work accablé de travail ▷ overwhelmed with sadness accablé de tristesse ❷ inonder ▷ We've been overwhelmed with offers of help. Nous sommes inondés d'offres d'aide. ❸ bouleverser ▷ The experience overwhelmed me. L'expérience m'a bouleversée.; **overwhelming support** un soutien enthousiaste; **Her kindness has been overwhelming.** Sa gentillesse m'a comblé.

owe [əʊ] vb devoir; **to owe somebody something** devoir quelque chose à quelqu'un ▷ I owe you $50. Je te dois cinquante dollars.

owl [aʊl] n hibou m (pl hiboux)

own [əʊn] adj propre ▷ I have my own cell phone. J'ai mon propre téléphone cellulaire.; **I'd like a room of my own.** J'aimerais avoir une chambre à moi.; **on his own** tout seul ▷ on her own toute seule ▷ on our own tout seuls
▶ vb posséder

own up vb avouer; **to own up to something** admettre quelque

chose

owner ['əʊnəʳ] n propriétaire

oxygen ['ɒksɪdʒən] n oxygène m

oyster ['ɔɪstəʳ] n huître f

ozone ['əʊzəʊn] n ozone f; **the ozone layer** la couche d'ozone

P

PA n: **the PA system** (public address) les m haut-parleurs

pace [peɪs] n (speed) allure f ▷ He was walking at a brisk pace. Il marchait à vive allure.

pacifier ['pæsɪfaɪə'] n sucette f

pack [pæk] vb faire ses bagages ▷ I'll help you pack. Je vais t'aider à faire tes bagages.; **I've already packed my suitcase.** J'ai déjà fait ma valise.
▶ n ❶ (packet) paquet m ▷ a pack of gum un paquet de gomme à mâcher ❷ (backpack) sac à dos m ▷ Carry it home in your pack. Rapporte-le chez toi dans ton sac à dos.; **a pack of cards** un jeu de cartes

package ['pækɪdʒ] n paquet m; **a package holiday** un voyage organisé

packed [pækt] adj (crowded) plein ▷ The movie theatre was packed. Le cinéma était plein.

packet ['pækɪt] n paquet ▷ a packet of sunflower seeds un paquet de graines de tournesol

pad [pæd] n (notepad) bloc-notes m (pl blocs-notes)

paddle ['pædl] vb ❶ (canoe) pagayer ❷ (play in water) faire trempette
▶ n ❶ (canoe) aviron m ❷ (chiefly kayak) pagaie f

padlock ['pædlɔk] n cadenas m

page [peɪdʒ] n ❶ (of book) page f ❷ (in Parliament) page f ▷ In Grade 6 I was a parliamentary page in Ottawa. En sixième année, j'ai été page parlementaire à Ottawa.
▶ vb: **to page somebody** faire appeler quelqu'un

pager ['peɪdʒə'] n téléavertisseur m

paid [peɪd] vb see **pay**
▶ adj ❶ (work) rémunéré ❷ payé ▷ 3 weeks' paid holiday trois semaines de congés payés

pail [peɪl] n seau m (pl seaux)

pain [peɪn] n douleur f ▷ a terrible pain une douleur insupportable; **I have a pain in my stomach.** J'ai mal à l'estomac.; **to be in pain** souffrir ▷ She's in a lot of pain. Elle souffre beaucoup.; **He's a real pain.** Il est vraiment pénible.

painful ['peɪnful] adj douloureux (f douloureuse) ▷ a painful injury une blessure douloureuse; **a painful experience** une expérience pénible; **Is it painful?** Ça te fait mal?

painkiller ['peɪnkɪlə'] n analgésique m

paint [peɪnt] n peinture f
▶ vb peindre ▷ to paint something green peindre quelque chose en vert

paintbrush ['peɪntbrʌʃ] n pinceau m (pl pinceaux)

painter ['peɪntə'] n peintre

painting ['peɪntɪŋ] n ❶ peinture

f ▷ *My hobby is painting.* Je fais de la peinture. ❷ *(picture)* tableau *m* (*pl* tableaux) ▷ *a painting by Picasso* un tableau de Picasso

pair [peə^r] *n* paire *f* ▷ *a pair of shoes* une paire de chaussures ▷ *a pair of scissors* une paire de ciseaux; **a pair of pants** un pantalon; **a pair of jeans** une paire de jeans; **a pair of underpants (1)** *(briefs)* une culotte **(2)** *(boxer shorts)* un caleçon; **in pairs** deux par deux

pal [pæl] *n* copain *m*, copine *f*

palace [ˈpæləs] *n* palais *m*

pale [peɪl] *adj* pâle ▷ *a pale blue shirt* une chemise bleu pâle

palm [pɑːm] *n* (*of hand*) paume *f*; **a palm tree** un palmier

pamphlet [ˈpæmflət] *n* brochure *f*

pan [pæn] *n* ❶ *(saucepan)* casserole *f* ❷ *(frying pan)* poêle *f* ❸ *(baking)* moule *m* ▷ *a cake pan* un moule à gâteau

pancake [ˈpænkeɪk] *n* crêpe *f*

pandemic [pænˈdɛmɪk] *n* pandémie *f*

panic [ˈpænɪk] *n* panique *f*
▶ *vb* s'affoler; **Don't panic!** Pas de panique!

panther [ˈpænθə^r] *n* panthère *f*

panties [ˈpæntɪz] *npl* culotte *f*

pantomime [ˈpæntəmaɪm] *n* pantomime *f*

pants [pænts] *npl* pantalon *m* ▷ *a pair of pants* un pantalon

pantyhose [ˈpæntɪhəʊz] *npl* bas-culotte *m* (*pl* bas-culottes)

paper [ˈpeɪpə^r] *n* ❶ papier *m* ▷ *a piece of paper* un morceau de papier ▷ *a paper towel* une serviette en papier ❷ *(newspaper)* journal *m* (*pl* journaux) ▷ *I saw an ad in the paper.* J'ai vu une annonce dans le journal.; **an exam paper** un examen écrit

paperback [ˈpeɪpəbæk] *n* livre de poche *m*

paperboy [ˈpeɪpəbɔɪ] *n* livreur de journaux *m*

paper clip *n* trombone *m*

papergirl [ˈpeɪpəgəːl] *n* livreuse de journaux *f*

paper route *n* tournée de distribution de journaux *f*

paperwork [ˈpeɪpəwəːk] *n* paperasse *f* ▷ *She had a lot of paperwork to do.* Elle avait beaucoup de paperasse à faire.

parachute [ˈpærəʃuːt] *n* parachute *m*

parade [pəˈreɪd] *n* défilé *m*

paradise [ˈpærədaɪs] *n* paradis *m* ▷ *a skiers' paradise* un paradis pour les skieurs

paragraph [ˈpærəgrɑːf] *n* paragraphe *m*

parallel [ˈpærəlɛl] *adj* parallèle

paralysed [ˈpærəlaɪzd] *adj* paralysé

paramedic [pærəˈmɛdɪk] *n* ambulancier *m* paramédical, ambulancière *f* paramédicale

parcel [ˈpɑːsl] *n* colis *m*

pardon [ˈpɑːdn] *n*: **Pardon?** Pardon?

parent [ˈpɛərənt] *n* ❶ *(father)* père *m* ❷ *(mother)* mère *f*; **my parents** mes parents *mpl*

park [pɑːk] *n* parc *m*; **a national park** un parc national; **a theme park** un parc d'attractions
▶ *vb* ❶ stationner ▷ *Where can I park my car?* Où est-ce que je peux stationner ma voiture? ❷ se garer ▷ *We couldn't find anywhere to park.* Nous avons eu du mal à nous garer.

parking [ˈpɑːkɪŋ] *n* stationnement *m* ▷ *"no parking"* « stationnement interdit »

parking lot *n* stationnement *m*

parking meter *n* parcomètre *m*

parking ticket *n* contravention de stationnement *f*

parliament ['pɑːləmənt] *n*
parlement *m*

parole [pə'rəʊl] *n*: **on parole** en
liberté conditionnelle

parrot ['pærət] *n* perroquet *m*

parsley ['pɑːslɪ] *n* persil *m*

part [pɑːt] *n* ❶ (*section*) partie
f ▷ *The first part of the movie was
boring.* La première partie du film
était ennuyeuse. ❷ (*component*)
pièce *f* ▷ *spare parts* les pièces de
rechange ❸ (*in play, film*) rôle *m*;
for the most part pour la plupart
▷ *They were co-operative for the most
part.* Ils se sont montrés coopératifs
pour la plupart.; **to do one's part**
fournir sa part ▷ *We each have to
do our part.* Nous devons chacun
fournir notre part.; **to take part
in something** participer à quelque
chose ▷ *A lot of people took part in the
demonstration.* Beaucoup de gens
ont participé à la manifestation.

part with *vb*: **to part with
something** se défaire de quelque
chose

participate [pɑː'tɪsɪpeɪt] *vb*
participer ▷ *The whole class
participated in the discussion.* Toute
la classe a participé à la discussion.

particular [pə'tɪkjʊlər] *adj*
particulier (*f* particulière) ▷ *Are you
looking for anything particular?* Est-ce
que vous voulez quelque chose de
particulier?; **nothing in particular**
rien de particulier

particularly [pə'tɪkjʊlələɪ] *adv*
particulièrement

parting ['pɑːtɪŋ] *n* (*in hair*) raie *f*

partly ['pɑːtlɪ] *adv* en partie

partner ['pɑːtnə*r*] *n* ❶ (*in game*)
partenaire *m* ❷ (*in business*) associé
m, associée *f* ❸ (*in dance*) cavalier
m, cavalière *f* ❹ (*boyfriend,
girlfriend*) compagnon *m*,
compagne *f*

part-time ['pɑːt'taɪm] *adj, adv* à
temps partiel ▷ *a part-time job* un
travail à temps partiel ▷ *She works
part-time.* Elle travaille à temps
partiel.

party ['pɑːtɪ] *n* ❶ fête *f* ▷ *a birthday
party* une fête d'anniversaire ▷ *a
New Year's party* une fête du Nouvel
An ▷ *a Halloween party* un
party d'Halloween ❷ (*more
formal*) soirée *f* ▷ *I'm going to a
party on Saturday.* Je vais à une
soirée samedi. ❸ (*political*) parti
m ▷ *the Conservative Party* le Parti
conservateur ❹ (*group*) groupe
m ▷ *reservations for a party of four*
une réservation pour un groupe
de quatre

pass [pɑːs] *n* ❶ (*in mountains*) col
m ▷ *The pass was blocked with snow.*
Le col était enneigé. ❷ (*in football*)
passe *f* ❸ laissez-passer *m* ▷ *You
can't get in without a pass.* Tu ne peux
pas entrer sans laissez-passer.
▶ *vb* ❶ (*exam*) réussir ▷ *to pass
an exam* réussir à un examen ▷ *I
hope I pass the exam.* J'espère que je
réussirai à l'examen. ▷ *Did you pass?*
Tu as réussi? ❷ passer ▷ *Could
you pass me the salt, please?* Est-ce
que vous pourriez me passer le
sel, s'il vous plaît? ▷ *The time has
passed quickly.* Le temps a passé
rapidement. ▷ *I pass his house on my way to school.*
Je passe devant chez lui en allant
à l'école. ❸ (*legislation*) adopter
▷ *The bill was passed.* On a adopté le
projet de loi.

> Be careful not to translate **to
> pass an exam** by *passer un
> examen.*

to pass for se faire passer pour
▷ *You could easily pass for 16.* Tu
pourrais te faire passer pour un
jeune de seize ans.; **to pass up an**

opportunity laisser passer une occasion

pass out vb ❶ (faint) s'évanouir ❷ (hand out) distribuer ▷ Pass out the workbooks, please. Distribue les cahiers, s'il te plaît.

passage ['pæsɪdʒ] n ❶ (piece of writing) passage m ▷ Read the passage carefully. Lisez attentivement le passage. ❷ (corridor) couloir m

passenger ['pæsɪndʒə] n passager m, passagère f

passerby [pɑːsə'baɪ] n passant m, passante f ▷ We asked a passerby for the time. Nous avons demandé l'heure à un passant.

passion ['pæʃən] n passion f

passive ['pæsɪv] adj passif (f passive); **passive smoking** le tabagisme passif

passport ['pɑːspɔːt] n passeport m ▷ passport control le contrôle des passeports

password ['pɑːswɜːd] n mot de passe m

past [pɑːst] adv, prep (beyond) après ▷ It's on the right, just past the station. C'est sur la droite, juste après la gare.; **to go past (1)** passer ▷ The bus went past without stopping. Le bus est passé sans s'arrêter. **(2)** passer devant ▷ The bus goes past our house. Le bus passe devant notre maison.; **It's half past ten.** Il est dix heures et demie.; **It's quarter past nine.** Il est neuf heures et quart.; **It's ten past eight.** Il est huit heures dix.; **It's past midnight.** Il est minuit passé.
▶ n passé m ▷ She lives in the past. Elle vit dans le passé.; **He had a difficult past.** Il a eu un passé difficile.; **in the past** (previously) autrefois ▷ This was common in the past. C'était courant autrefois.

pasta ['pæstə] n pâtes fpl ▷ Pasta is easy to cook. Les pâtes sont faciles à préparer.

paste [peɪst] n (glue) colle f

pastel ['pæstl] n crayon pastel m; **pastel colours** des tons pastels mpl

pastime ['pɑːstaɪm] n passe-temps m (pl passe-temps) ▷ Her favourite pastime is biking. Son passe-temps favori est le cyclisme.

pastry ['peɪstrɪ] n ❶ (dough) pâte f ▷ pie pastry la pâte à tarte ❷ (baked dessert) pâtisserie f ▷ a plate of pastries une assiette de pâtisseries

pat [pæt] vb: **She patted my cheek.** Elle m'a tapoté la joue.; **to pat someone on the back (1)** (literally) donner une petite tape à quelqu'un dans le dos **(2)** (compliment) congratuler quelqu'un

patch [pætʃ] n ❶ pièce f ▷ a patch of material une pièce de tissu ❷ (for flat tire) rustine f ❸ (colour) tache f ▷ a patch of blue une tache de bleu; **a patch of ice** une plaque de glace; **He's got a bald patch.** Il a le crâne dégarni.

patched [pætʃt] adj rapiécé ▷ a pair of patched jeans des jeans rapiécés

pâté ['pæteɪ] n pâté

path [pɑːθ] n ❶ (footpath) chemin ❷ (paved) allée f

pathetic [pə'θetɪk] adj lamentable ▷ Our team was pathetic. Notre équipe a été lamentable.

patience ['peɪʃns] n patience f ▷ He doesn't have much patience. Il n'a pas beaucoup de patience.

patient ['peɪʃnt] n patient, patiente f
▶ adj patient

patio ['pætɪəʊ] n patio m

patriotic [pætrɪ'ɒtɪk] adj patriote

patrol [pə'trəʊl] n patrouille f; **patrol car** la voiture de police

pattern ['pætən] n motif m
▷ *a geometric pattern* un motif
géométrique; **a sewing pattern**
un patron

pause [pɔːz] n pause

pavement ['peɪvmənt]
n ❶ (*roadway*) chaussée f
❷ (*elsewhere*) asphalte m

paw [pɔː] n patte f

pay [peɪ] n salaire m
▶vb ❶ payer ▷ *They pay her more on
Sundays.* Elle est payée davantage
le dimanche. ❷ régler ▷ *to pay
by cheque* régler par chèque ▷ *to
pay by credit card* régler par carte
de crédit; **to pay for something**
payer quelque chose ▷ *I paid for
my ticket.* J'ai payé mon billet. ▷ *I
paid 50 dollars for it.* Je l'ai payé
cinquante dollars.; **to pay
extra for something** payer un
supplément pour quelque chose
▷ *You have to pay extra for parking.*
Il faut payer un supplément
pour le stationnement.; **to pay
attention** faire attention ▷ *Don't
pay any attention to him!* Ne fais
pas attention à lui!; **to pay
somebody a visit** rendre visite
à quelqu'un ▷ *They paid us a visit
last night.* Ils nous ont rendu visite
hier soir.; **to pay somebody back**
rembourser quelqu'un ▷ *I'll pay you
back tomorrow.* Je te rembourserai
demain.

payable ['peɪəbl] adj: **Make the
cheque payable to "ABC Ltd".**
Libellez le chèque à l'ordre de
« ABC Ltd ».

payment ['peɪmənt] n
paiement m

pay phone n téléphone public m

PC n (= *personal computer*) PC m ▷ *She
typed the report on her PC.* Elle a tapé
le rapport sur son PC.

PE n éducation f physique ▷ *We*
have PE twice a week.* Nous avons
l'éducation physique deux fois par
semaine.

pea [piː] n petit pois m

peace [piːs] n ❶ (*after war*) paix f
❷ (*quietness*) calme

peaceful ['piːsful] adj ❶ (*calm*)
paisible ▷ *a peaceful afternoon* un
après-midi paisible ❷ (*not violent*)
pacifique ▷ *a peaceful protest* une
manifestation pacifique

peacekeeper ['piːskiːpə'] n
gardien de la paix m, gardienne
de la paix f

peacekeeping ['piːskiːpɪŋ] n
maintien de la paix m

peach [piːtʃ] n pêche f

peacock ['piːkɔk] n paon m

peak [piːk] n (*of mountain*) cime f;
the peak rate le plein tarif ▷ *You pay
the peak rate for calls at this time of
day.* On paie le plein tarif quand on
appelle à cette heure-ci.; **in peak
season** en haute saison
▶vb: **The temperature peaked
at 34 degrees.** La température a
atteint trente-quatre degrés à son
plus haut niveau.

peanut ['piːnʌt] n arachide f
▷ *a packet of peanuts* un paquet
d'arachides

peanut butter n beurre d'arachide
m ▷ *a peanut-butter sandwich* un
sandwich au beurre d'arachide

pear [peə'] n poire f

pearl [pɜːl] n perle f

pebble ['pebl] n galet m ▷ *a pebble
beach* une plage de galets

pecan ['piːkæn] n pacane f ▷ *a
pecan pie* une tarte aux pacanes

peculiar [pɪ'kjuːlɪə'] adj bizarre
▷ *He's a bit peculiar.* Il est un peu
bizarre.

pedal ['pedl] n pédale f
▶vb pédaler

pedestrian [pɪ'dɛstrɪən] n piéton

m, piétonne *f*

pedestrian crossing [-'krɒsɪŋ] *n* passage à piétons *m*

peek [pi:k] *n*: **to have a peek at something** jeter un coup d'œil à quelque chose; **No peeking!** On ne regarde pas!

peel [pi:l] *n* ❶ (*orange*) écorce *f* ❷ (*banana*) peau *f* ❸ (*apple, potato*) épluchure *f*
▷ *vb* ❶ éplucher ▷ *Shall I peel the potatoes?* J'épluche les pommes de terre? ❷ peler ▷ *My nose is peeling.* Mon nez pèle.

peer pressure ['pɪə'-] *n* pression des pairs *f*

peg [pɛg] *n* ❶ (*for coats*) portemanteau *m* (*pl* portemanteaux) ❷ (*clothes peg*) pince à linge *f* ❸ (*tent peg*) piquet *m*

pellet ['pɛlɪt] *n* boulette *f*

pemmican ['pɛmɪkən] *n* pemmican *m*

pen [pɛn] *n* stylo *m*

penalize ['pi:nəlaɪz] *vb* pénaliser

penalty ['pɛnltɪ] *n* ❶ (*punishment*) peine *f*; **the death penalty** la peine de mort ❷ (*sports*) punition *f* ▷ *a penalty for body-checking* une punition pour mise en échec corporel; **a penalty shot** un lancer de pénalité; **penalty box** le banc de punition; **a penalty kick** un coup de pied de pénalité

pencil ['pɛnsl] *n* crayon *m*; **in pencil** au crayon; **pencil crayons** les crayons de couleur

pencil case *n* trousse *f*

pencil sharpener [-'ʃɑ:pnə'] *n* taille-crayon *m*

pendant ['pɛndənt] *n* pendentif *m*

penguin ['pɛŋgwɪn] *n* pingouin *m*

penicillin [pɛnɪ'sɪlɪn] *n* pénicilline *f*

peninsula [pə'nɪnsjulə] *n* presqu'île *f*

penis ['pi:nɪs] *n* pénis *m*

penknife ['pɛnnaɪf] *n* canif *m*

pennant ['pɛnənt] *n* fanion *m* ▷ *Our school won the soccer pennant last year.* Notre école a gagné le fanion en soccer l'année dernière.

penny ['pɛnɪ] *n* cent *m*

penpal ['pɛnpæl] *n* correspondant *m*, correspondante *f*

pension ['pɛnʃən] *n* retraite *f*

pensioner ['pɛnʃənə'] *n* retraité *m*, retraitée *f*

pentathlon [pɛn'tæθlən] *n* pentathlon *m*

people ['pi:pl] *npl* ❶ gens *mpl* ▷ *The people were nice.* Les gens étaient sympathiques. ❷ (*individuals*) personnes *fpl* ▷ *six people* six personnes ▷ *several people* plusieurs personnes ❸ (*nation*) peuple *m* ▷ *Canada's native peoples* les peuples autochtones du Canada ▷ *to give more power to the people* donner plus de pouvoir au peuple; **How many people are there in your family?** Vous êtes combien dans votre famille?; **French people** les Français; **black people** les Noirs; **People say that...** On dit que...

pepper ['pɛpə'] *n* ❶ (*spice*) poivre *m* ▷ *Pass the pepper, please.* Passez-moi le poivre, s'il vous plaît. ❷ (*vegetable*) poivron *m* ▷ *a green pepper* un poivron vert ❸ (*chili*) piment *m* ▷ *hot peppers* les piments piquants

peppermint ['pɛpəmɪnt] *n* ❶ (*candy*) pastille de menthe *f* ❷ (*flavour*) menthe *f* ▷ *I don't like chocolate and mint together.* Je n'aime pas le chocolat et la menthe ensemble.; **peppermint chewing gum** la gomme à mâcher à la menthe

pepperoni [pɛpə'rəʊnɪ] *n*

pepperoni n

per [pɜː] prep par ▷ *per day* par jour
▷ *per week* par semaine; **30 miles
per hour** trente miles à l'heure

percent [pə'sɛnt] adv pour cent
▷ *fifty percent* cinquante pour cent

percentage [pə'sɛntɪdʒ] n
pourcentage m

percussion [pə'kʌʃən] n
percussion f ▷ *I play percussion.* Je
joue des percussions.

perfect [pə'fɛkt] adj parfait ▷ *She
speaks perfect English.* Elle parle un
anglais parfait.

perfectly ['pɜːfɪktlɪ] adv
parfaitement

perform [pə'fɔːm] vb (act, play)
jouer

performance [pə'fɔːməns]
n ❶ (show) spectacle m ▷ *The
performance lasts two hours.* Le
spectacle dure deux heures.
❷ (acting) interprétation
f ▷ *his performance as Hamlet*
son interprétation d'Hamlet
❸ (results) performance f ▷ *the
team's poor performance* la médiocre
performance de l'équipe

performing arts [pə'fɔːmɪŋ] npl
arts mpl de la scène

perfume ['pɜːfjuːm] n parfum m

perhaps [pə'hæps] adv peut-être
▷ *a bit boring, perhaps* peut-être un
peu ennuyeux ▷ *Perhaps he's sick.*
Il est peut-être malade.; **perhaps
not** peut-être pas

period ['pɪərɪəd] n ❶ période
f ▷ *for a limited period* pour
une période limitée ❷ (in
history) époque f ▷ *the Victorian
period* l'époque victorienne
❸ (punctuation) point m ▷ *You need
a period at the end of a sentence.* Il
faut un point à la fin de la phrase.
❹ (menstruation) règles fpl ▷ *I'm
having my period.* J'ai mes règles.

❺ (lesson time) cours m ▷ *Each
period lasts forty minutes.* Chaque
cours dure quarante minutes.

perm [pɜːm] n permanente f ▷ *She
has a perm.* Elle a une permanente.;
to get a perm se faire faire une
permanente

permafrost ['pɜːməfrɒst] n
pergélisol m

permanent ['pɜːmənənt] adj
permanent

permission [pə'mɪʃən] n
permission f ▷ *Could I have
permission to leave early?* Pourrais-je
avoir la permission de partir
plus tôt?

permit [pə'mɪt] n permis m ▷ *a
fishing permit* un permis de pêche

persecute ['pɜːsɪkjuːt] vb
persécuter

persistent [pə'sɪstənt] adj (person)
tenace

person ['pɜːsn] n personne f
▷ *She's a very nice person.* C'est une
personne très sympathique.; **in
person** en personne

personal ['pɜːsnl] adj personnel m
(f personnelle); **personals column**
les annonces personnelles fpl

personality [pɜːsə'nælɪtɪ] n
personnalité

personally ['pɜːsnəlɪ] adv
personnellement ▷ *I don't know
him personally.* Je ne le connais pas
personnellement. ▷ *Personally I
don't agree.* Personnellement, je ne
suis pas d'accord.

personal stereo n baladeur m

personnel [pɜːsə'nɛl] n
personnel m

perspiration [pɜːspɪ'reɪʃən] n
transpiration f

persuade [pə'sweɪd] vb persuader;
**to persuade somebody to do
something** persuader quelqu'un de
faire quelque chose ▷ *She persuaded*

me to go with her. Elle m'a persuadé de l'accompagner.

pessimist ['pesɪmɪst] n pessimiste ▷ *I'm a pessimist.* Je suis pessimiste.

pessimistic [pesɪ'mɪstɪk] adj pessimiste

pest [pest] n enquinineur m, enquinineuse f

pester ['pestə'] vb importuner

pesticide ['pestɪsaɪd] n pesticide m

pet [pet] n animal m de compagnie ▷ *Have you got a pet?* Est-ce que tu as un animal de compagnie?; **a pet shop** une animalerie

petition [pə'tɪʃən] n pétition f

petrified ['petrɪfaɪd] adj pétrifié

petroleum [pə'trəʊlɪəm] n pétrole m

phantom ['fæntəm] n fantôme m

pharmacy ['fɑ:məsɪ] n pharmacie f

philosophy [fɪ'lɒsəfɪ] n philosophie f

phobia ['fəʊbɪə] n phobie f

phone [fəʊn] n téléphone m ▷ *Where's the phone?* Où est le téléphone? ▷ *Is there a phone here?* Est-ce qu'il y a un téléphone ici?; **by phone** par téléphone; **to be on the phone** être au téléphone ▷ *She's on the phone at the moment.* Elle est au téléphone en ce moment.; **Can I use the phone, please?** Est-ce que je peux téléphoner, s'il vous plaît?
▷ vb ❶ appeler ▷ *I'll phone the library.* Je vais appeler la bibliothèque. ❷ téléphoner ▷ *Are you going to phone him, or send an email?* Tu vas lui téléphoner, ou envoyer un courriel?

phone bill n compte de téléphone m

phone book n annuaire m

phone booth n cabine téléphonique f

phone call n appel m ▷ *There's a*

phone call for you. Il y a un appel pour vous.; **to make a phone call** téléphoner ▷ *Can I make a phone call?* Est-ce que je peux téléphoner?

phone card n carte téléphonique f

phone number n numéro de téléphone m

photo ['fəʊtəʊ] n photo f; **to take a photo** prendre une photo; **to take a photo of somebody** prendre quelqu'un en photo

photocopier ['fəʊtəʊkɒpɪə'] n photocopieuse f

photocopy ['fəʊtəʊkɒpɪ] n photocopie f
▷ vb photocopier

photograph ['fəʊtəgræf] n photo f; **to take a photograph** prendre une photo; **to take a photograph of somebody** prendre quelqu'un en photo
▷ vb photographier

photographer [fə'tɒgrəfə'] n photographe m ▷ *She's a photographer.* Elle est photographe.

photography [fə'tɒgrəfɪ] n photo f ▷ *My hobby is photography.* Je fais de la photo.

phrase [freɪz] n expression f

phrase book n guide de conversation m

phys ed ['fɪz'ed] n éducation f physique

physical ['fɪzɪkl] adj physique f
▷ n examen m médical

physicist ['fɪzɪsɪst] n physicien m, physicienne f ▷ *He's a physicist.* Il est physicien.

physics ['fɪzɪks] n physique f ▷ *She teaches physics.* Elle enseigne la physique.

physiotherapist [fɪzɪəʊ'θerəpɪst] n physiothérapeute

physiotherapy [fɪzɪəʊ'θerəpɪ] n physiothérapie f

pianist ['pi:ənɪst] n pianiste

piano [pɪˈænəʊ] n piano m ▷ I play the piano. Je joue du piano. ▷ I take piano lessons. Je prends des leçons de piano.

pick [pɪk] n (guitar) médiator m; **The youngest gets first pick.** Le plus jeune choisit en premier. ; **Take your pick!** Faites votre choix!
▶ vb **①** (choose) choisir ▷ I picked the biggest piece. J'ai choisi le plus gros morceau. **②** (for team) sélectionner ▷ I've been picked for the team. J'ai été sélectionné pour faire partie de l'équipe. **③** (fruit, flowers) cueillir; **to pick on somebody** harceler quelqu'un ▷ He's always picking on me. Il me harcèle constamment. ; **to pick out (1)** choisir ▷ I like them all – it's difficult to pick one out. Ils me plaisent tous – c'est difficile d'en choisir un. **(2)** (distinguish) repérer ▷ I can pick out her voice on the recording. Je peux repérer sa voix sur l'enregistrement. **(3)** (recognize) reconnaître ▷ Can you pick me out in this picture? Peux-tu me reconnaître sur cette photo? ; **to pick up (1)** (collect) venir chercher ▷ We'll come to the airport to pick you up. Nous irons vous chercher à l'aéroport. **(2)** (from floor) ramasser ▷ Could you help me pick up the toys? Tu peux m'aider à ramasser les jouets? **(3)** (learn) apprendre ▷ I picked up some Spanish during my holiday. J'ai appris quelque mots d'espagnol pendant mes vacances.

picket [ˈpɪkɪt] vb piqueter ▷ The workers picketed the factory. Les ouvriers ont piqueté l'usine.; **a picket line** une ligne de piquetage

pickle [ˈpɪkl] n cornichon m ▷ dill pickles les cornichons à l'aneth

pickpocket [ˈpɪkpɒkɪt] n voleur à la tire m, voleuse à la tire f

pickup truck [ˈpɪkʌp-] n camionnette f

picky [ˈpɪkɪ] adj pointilleux (f pointilleuse) ▷ Our teacher is picky about grammar. Notre prof est pointilleux sur la grammaire.

picnic [ˈpɪknɪk] n pique-nique m; **to have a picnic** pique-niquer ▷ We had a picnic on the beach. Nous avons pique-niqué sur la plage.

picture [ˈpɪktʃə] n **①** illustration f ▷ Children's books have lots of pictures. Il y a beaucoup d'illustrations dans les livres pour enfants. **②** photo f ▷ My picture was in the paper. Ma photo était dans le journal. **③** (painting) tableau m (pl tableaux) ▷ a famous picture un tableau célèbre; **to paint a picture of something** peindre quelque chose **④** (drawing) dessin m; **to draw a picture of something** dessiner quelque chose

picturesque [pɪktʃəˈresk] adj pittoresque

pie [paɪ] n tarte f ▷ an apple pie une tarte aux pommes; **a pie chart** un graphique circulaire

piece [piːs] n morceau m (pl morceaux) ▷ A small piece, please. Un petit morceau, s'il vous plaît.; **a piece of furniture** un meuble; **a piece of advice** un conseil

pier [pɪə] n jetée f

pierce [pɪəs] vb percer ▷ She's going to get her ears pierced. Elle va se faire percer les oreilles. ▷ I have pierced ears. J'ai les oreilles percées.

piercing [ˈpɪəsɪŋ] adj perçant ▷ a piercing cry un cri perçant

pig [pɪg] n cochon m

pigeon [ˈpɪdʒən] n pigeon m

piggyback [ˈpɪgɪbæk] n: **to give somebody a piggyback** ▷ I can't give you a piggyback, you're too heavy. Je ne peux pas te porter sur mon dos, tu es trop lourd.

pigtail ['pɪgteɪl] n couette

pike [paɪk] n brochet m ▷ a northern pike un grand brochet

pile [paɪl] n ❶ (untidy heap) tas m ❷ (tidy stack) pile f
▶ vb ❶ (stack) empiler ▷ I piled the books on the table. J'ai empilé les livres sur la table. ❷ (heap) entasser ▷ She piles her dirty clothes on the floor. Elle entasse ses vêtements sales sur le plancher.; **to pile up** s'accumuler ▷ My homework is piling up. Mes devoirs s'accumulent.

pile-up ['paɪlʌp] n carambolage m

pill [pɪl] n pilule f; **to be on the Pill** prendre la pilule

pillar ['pɪlə'] n pilier m

pillow ['pɪləʊ] n oreiller m

pilot ['paɪlət] n pilote ▷ She's a pilot. Elle est pilote.

pimple ['pɪmpl] n bouton m

pin [pɪn] n épingle f; **I have pins and needles in my foot.** J'ai des fourmis dans le pied.; **to be on pins and needles** être sur des charbons ardents

PIN [pɪn] n (= personal identification number) NIP m

pinball ['pɪnbɔːl] n machine à boules f ▷ to play pinball jouer à la machine à boules

pinch [pɪntʃ] vb pincer ▷ He pinched me! Il m'a pincé!

pine [paɪn] n pin m ▷ a pine table une table en pin; **a pine cone** un cône de pin

pineapple ['paɪnæpl] n ananas m

pink [pɪŋk] adj rose

pioneer [paɪə'nɪə'] n pionnier m, pionnière f

pipe [paɪp] n ❶ (for water, gas) tuyau m (pl tuyaux) ▷ The pipes froze. Les tuyaux d'eau ont gelé. ❷ (for smoking) pipe f; **the pipes** (bagpipes) la cornemuse ▷ He plays the pipes. Il

joue de la cornemuse.

pirate ['paɪərət] n pirate

pirated ['paɪərətɪd] adj pirate ▷ a pirated video une vidéo pirate

Pisces ['paɪsiːz] n Poissons mpl ▷ I'm a Pisces. Je suis Poissons.

pistol ['pɪstl] n pistolet m

pit [pɪt] n ❶ (deep hole) fosse f ❷ (in fruit) noyau m ▷ a peach pit un noyau de pêche

pitch [pɪtʃ] n ❶ (baseball) lancer m ▷ That was a fast pitch. C'était un lancer rapide. ❷ (musical note) hauteur f; **Excitement was at fever pitch.** L'excitation était à son comble.
▶ vb ❶ (tent) planter ▷ We pitched our tent near the beach. Nous avons planté notre tente près de la plage. ❷ (baseball) lancer m ▷ Who's pitching? Qui est-ce qui lance?

pitcher ['pɪtʃə'] n ❶ (baseball) lanceur m, lanceuse f ❷ (jug) cruche f ▷ a pitcher of lemonade une cruche de limonade

pity ['pɪtɪ] n pitié f; **What a pity!** Quel dommage!
▶ vb plaindre

pizza ['piːtsə] n pizza f

place [pleɪs] n ❶ (location) endroit m ▷ It's a quiet place. C'est un endroit tranquille. ▷ There are a lot of interesting places to visit. Il y a beaucoup d'endroits intéressants à visiter. ❷ (space) place ▷ a parking place une place de stationnement ▷ She was not in her usual place. Elle n'était pas à sa place habituelle. ▷ There were six places at the table. Il y avait six places à la table.; **to take someone's place** prendre la place de quelqu'un; **to change places** changer de place ▷ I'll change places with you. Je changerai de place avec toi.; **to take place** avoir lieu; **at your place** chez toi ▷ Shall we

meet at your place? On se retrouve chez toi?; **to my place** chez moi ▷ *Do you want to come to my place?* Tu veux venir chez moi?; **I feel out of place here.** Je ne me sens pas à ma place ici.
  ▶vb ❶ poser ▷ *He placed his hand on the keyboard.* Il a posé la main sur le clavier. ❷ (*in competition, contest*) classer

placemat ['pleɪsmæt] n napperon m

plagiarism ['pleɪdʒərɪzəm] n plagiat m

plaid [plæd] adj écossais ▷ *a plaid shirt* une chemise écossaise

plain [pleɪn] n plaine f
  ▶adj, adv ❶ (*not patterned*) uni ▷ *a plain carpet* un tapis uni ❷ (*not fancy*) simple ▷ *a plain white blouse* un chemisier blanc simple

plan [plæn] n ❶ projet m ▷ *What are your plans for the holidays?* Quels sont tes projets pour les vacances? ▷ *to make plans* faire des projets; **Everything went according to plan.** Tout s'est passé comme prévu. ❷ (*map*) plan m ▷ *a floor plan of the new house* un plan à niveau de la nouvelle maison
  ▶vb ❶ (*make plans for*) préparer ▷ *We're planning a trip to Alberta.* Nous préparons un voyage en Alberta. ❷ (*make schedule for*) planifier ▷ *Plan your day carefully.* Planifiez votre journée avec soin.; **to plan to do something** avoir l'intention de faire quelque chose ▷ *I'm planning to go to university.* J'ai l'intention d'aller à l'université.

plane [pleɪn] n avion m ▷ *by plane* en avion

planet ['plænɪt] n planète f

planning ['plænɪŋ] n préparation f ▷ *The trip needs careful planning.* Le voyage nécessite une préparation

méticuleuse.; **family planning** la planification familiale

plant [plɑːnt] n ❶ plante f ▷ *to water the plants* arroser les plantes ❷ (*factory*) usine f
  ▶vb planter

plaque [plæk] n ❶ (*on wall*) plaque f ❷ (*on teeth*) plaque dentaire f

plaster ['plɑːstə'] n plâtre m; **a plaster cast** un plâtre

plastic ['plæstɪk] n plastique m ▷ *It's made of plastic.* C'est en plastique.
  ▶adj en plastique ▷ *a plastic bag* un sac en plastique ▷ *a plastic raincoat* un imperméable en plastique; **plastic surgery** la chirurgie esthétique; **plastic wrap** la pellicule de plastique

plate [pleɪt] n (*for food*) assiette f

platform ['plætfɔːm] n ❶ (*for performers*) estrade f ❷ (*at station*) quai m ▷ *on platform 7* sur le quai numéro sept

play [pleɪ] n ❶ pièce f ▷ *a play by Rick Salutin* une pièce de Rick Salutin; **to put on a play** monter une pièce
  ▶vb ❶ jouer ▷ *He's playing with his friends.* Il joue avec ses amis. ▷ *What sort of music do they play?* Quel genre de musique jouent-ils? ❷ (*against person, team*) jouer contre ▷ *Montreal will play Edmonton tomorrow night.* Montréal jouera contre Edmonton demain soir. ❸ (*sport, game*) jouer à ▷ *I play hockey.* Je joue au hockey. ▷ *Can you play chess?* Tu sais jouer aux échecs? ❹ (*instrument*) jouer de ▷ *I play the guitar.* Je joue de la guitare. ❺ (*record, cassette, music*) écouter ▷ *She's always playing that CD.* Elle écoute tout le temps ce CD.

play down vb dédramatiser ▷ *He tried to play down his illness.* Il a essayé de dédramatiser sa maladie.

player ['pleɪə'] n (of sport) joueur m, joueuse f ▷ a hockey player un joueur de hockey; **a piano player** un pianiste; **a bass player** un bassiste

playful ['pleɪful] adj espiègle

playground ['pleɪgraund] n ❶ (at school) cour de récréation f ❷ (in park) aire f de jeux

playing card ['pleɪŋ-] n carte à jouer f (pl cartes à jouer)

playing field ['pleɪŋ-] n terrain de sport m

playoffs ['pleɪɔfs] npl éliminatoires fpl

playtime ['pleɪtaɪm] n récréation f

playwright ['pleɪraɪt] n dramaturge

plead [pliːd] vb: **to plead guilty** plaider coupable; **I pleaded with them to stop.** Je les ai suppliés d'arrêter.

pleasant ['plɛznt] adj agréable

please [pliːz] excl ❶ (polite form) s'il vous plaît ▷ Two coffees, please. Deux cafés, s'il vous plaît. ❷ (familiar form) s'il te plaît ▷ Please write back soon. Réponds vite, s'il te plaît.

pleased [pliːzd] adj content ▷ My mother's not going to be very pleased. Ma mère ne va pas être contente du tout. ▷ It's beautiful: she'll be pleased with it. C'est beau : elle va être contente.; **Pleased to meet you!** Enchanté!

pleasure ['plɛʒə'] n plaisir m ▷ I read for pleasure. Je lis pour le plaisir.

plenty ['plɛntɪ] n largement assez ▷ I've got plenty. J'en ai largement assez. ▷ That's plenty, thanks. Ça suffit largement, merci.; **plenty of (1)** (a lot) beaucoup de ▷ I have plenty to do. J'ai beaucoup de choses à faire. **(2)** (enough) largement assez de ▷ I have plenty of money. J'ai largement assez d'argent. ▷ We've got plenty of time. Nous avons largement le temps.

pliers ['plaɪəz] npl pince f; **a pair of pliers** une pince

plot [plɒt] n ❶ (of story, play) intrigue f ❷ (against somebody) conspiration f ▷ a plot against the president une conspiration contre le président ❸ (of land) carré m ▷ a vegetable plot un carré de légumes ▶ vb comploter ▷ They were plotting to kill him. Ils complotaient de le tuer.

plough [plaʊ] n charrue f
▶ vb labourer

plow [plaʊ] n (snow) déneigeuse f
▶ vb déneiger ▷ Have they plowed the roads yet? Est-ce qu'on a déjà déneigé les rues?

plug [plʌg] n ❶ (electrical) prise de courant f ▷ The plug is faulty. La prise est défectueuse. ❷ (for sink) bouchon m

plug in vb brancher ▷ Is it plugged in? Est-ce que c'est branché?

plum [plʌm] n prune f ▷ **plum jam** la confiture de prunes

plumber ['plʌmə'] n plombier m, plombière f ▷ He's a plumber. Il est plombier.

plumbing ['plʌmɪŋ] n plomberie f ▷ Our cottage doesn't have indoor plumbing. Notre chalet n'a pas de plomberie intérieure.

plump [plʌmp] adj dodu

plunge [plʌndʒ] vb plonger

plural ['plʊərl] n pluriel m ▷ in the plural au pluriel

plus [plʌs] prep, adj plus ▷ 4 plus 3 equals 7. Quatre plus trois égalent sept. ▷ three children plus a dog trois enfants plus un chien; **I got a B plus.** J'ai eu un B plus.

p.m. abbr: **at 8 p.m.** à huit heures du soir
  ● In French, times are often given
  ● using the 24-hour clock.

at 2 p.m. à quatorze heures

pneumonia [njuːˈməʊnɪə] *n* pneumonie *f*

poached [pəʊtʃt] *adj* poché ⊳ *a poached egg* un œuf poché

pocket [ˈpɔkɪt] *n* poche *f*; **pocket money** l'argent *m* de poche ⊳ $10 *a week pocket money* dix dollars d'argent de poche par semaine

pocketknife [ˈpɔkɪtnaɪf] *n* canif *m*

poem [ˈpəʊɪm] *n* poème *m*

poet [ˈpəʊɪt] *n* poète *m*

poetry [ˈpəʊɪtrɪ] *n* poésie *f*

point [pɔɪnt] *n* ❶ (*spot, score*) point *m* ⊳ *a point on the horizon* un point à l'horizon ⊳ *They scored 5 points.* Ils ont marqué cinq points. ❷ (*comment*) remarque *f* ⊳ *He made some interesting points.* Il a fait quelques remarques intéressantes. ❸ (*tip*) pointe *f* ⊳ *a pencil with a sharp point* un crayon à la pointe aiguisée ❹ (*in time*) moment *m* ⊳ *At that point, we decided to leave.* À ce moment-là, nous avons décidé de partir.; **a point of view** un point de vue; **to get the point** comprendre ⊳ *Sorry, I don't get the point.* Désolé, je ne comprends pas.; **That's beside the point.** Cela n'a rien à voir.; **to the point** précis ⊳ *His answer was short and to the point.* Sa réponse était brève et précise.; **That's a good point!** C'est vrai; **There's no point.** Cela ne sert à rien.; **There's no point in waiting.** Cela ne sert à rien d'attendre.; **What's the point?** À quoi bon? ⊳ *What's the point of leaving so early?* À quoi bon partir si tôt?; **Punctuality isn't my strong point.** La ponctualité n'est pas mon fort.; **point five (2.5)** deux virgule cinq (2,5)

▶ *vb* montrer du doigt ⊳ *Don't point!* Ne montre pas du doigt!; **to point at somebody** montrer quelqu'un

du doigt ⊳ *She pointed at her friend.* Elle a montré son ami du doigt.; **to point a gun at somebody** braquer un revolver sur quelqu'un; **to point something out (1)** (*show*) montrer quelque chose ⊳ *The guide pointed out Sainte-Anne-de-Beaupré to us.* Le guide nous a montré Sainte-Anne-de-Beaupré. **(2)** (*mention*) signaler quelque chose ⊳ *I should point out that...* Je dois vous signaler que...

pointless [ˈpɔɪntlɪs] *adj* inutile ⊳ *It's pointless to argue.* Il est inutile de discuter.

poison [ˈpɔɪzn] *n* poison *m*
▶ *vb* empoisonner

poison ivy [-aɪvɪ] *n* herbe *f* à puce

poisonous [ˈpɔɪznəs] *adj* ❶ (*snake*) venimeux (*f* venimeuse) ❷ (*plant, mushroom*) vénéneux (*f* vénéneuse) ❸ (*gas*) toxique

poke [pəʊk] *vb*: **He poked the ground with his stick.** Il tapotait le sol avec sa canne.; **She poked me in the ribs.** Elle m'a enfoncé le doigt dans les côtes.

poker [ˈpəʊkə] *n* poker *m* ⊳ *I play poker.* Je joue au poker.

polar bear [pəʊlə-] *n* ours *m* blanc

pole [pəʊl] *n* poteau *m* (*pl* poteaux) ⊳ *a telephone pole* un poteau de téléphone; **a tent pole** un montant de tente; **a ski pole** un bâton de ski; **the North Pole** le pôle Nord; **the South Pole** le pôle Sud

pole vault [ˈpəʊlvɔːlt] *n* saut à la perche *m*

police [pəˈliːs] *npl* police *f* ⊳ *We called the police.* Nous avons appelé la police.; **a police car** une voiture de police; **a police dog** un chien policier; **a police station** un commissariat de police

police officer *n* policier *m*, policière *f* ⊳ *She's a police officer.* Elle est policière.

policy ['pɒlɪsɪ] n politique f ▷ the new immigration policy la nouvelle politique d'immigration

polish ['pɒlɪʃ] n ❶ (for shoes) cirage m ❷ (for furniture) cire f ▸ vb ❶ (shoes, furniture) cirer ❷ (glass) faire briller

polite [pə'laɪt] adj poli

politely [pə'laɪtlɪ] adv poliment

politeness [pə'laɪtnɪs] n politesse f

political [pə'lɪtɪkl] adj politique f; **political correctness** la rectitude politique

politically [pə'lɪtɪklɪ] adv: **politically correct** politiquement correct

politician [pɒlɪ'tɪʃən] n politicien m, politicienne f

politics ['pɒlɪtɪks] npl politique f ▷ I'm not interested in politics. La politique ne m'intéresse pas.

polka dots ['pɒlkə-] npl pois mpl ▷ a skirt with polka dots une jupe à pois

poll [pəʊl] n ❶ sondage m ▷ A recent poll revealed that... Un sondage récent a révélé que... ❷ (place to vote) bureau de vote m ▷ The polls close at 9 p.m. Les bureaux de vote ferment à neuf heures du soir.; **to go to the polls** aller voter ▸ vb: We polled all the students to find out which radio station was most popular. Nous avons sondé l'opinion de tous les élèves pour savoir quelle station de radio est la plus populaire.

pollen ['pɒlən] n pollen

pollute [pə'luːt] vb polluer ▷ We have polluted the rivers. Nous avons pollué les rivières.

pollution [pə'luːʃən] n pollution f

polo shirt ['pəʊləʊ-] n polo m

pond [pɒnd] n ❶ (big) étang m ❷ (smaller) mare f ❸ bassin m ▷ We've got a pond in our garden. Nous avons un bassin dans notre jardin.

pony ['pəʊnɪ] n poney m

ponytail ['pəʊnɪteɪl] n queue de cheval f ▷ He's got a ponytail. Il a une queue de cheval.

poodle ['puːdl] n caniche m

pool [puːl] n ❶ (for swimming) piscine f ❷ (pond) étang m ❸ (puddle) flaque f ❹ (game) billard américain m ▷ Let's have a game of pool. Jouons au billard américain.

poor [pʊə] adj ❶ pauvre ▷ a poor family une famille pauvre ▷ Your poor sister, she's very unlucky! Ta pauvre sœur, elle n'a vraiment pas de chance!; **the poor** les m pauvres ❷ (bad) médiocre ▷ a poor mark une note médiocre

poorly ['pʊəlɪ] adv mal ▷ poorly designed mal conçu

pop [pɒp] adj pop ▷ pop music la musique pop ▷ a pop star une vedette pop ▷ a pop group un groupe pop ▷ a pop song une chanson pop ▸ n boisson gazeuse f ▷ Do you want a can of pop? Tu veux une canette de boisson gazeuse?

popcorn ['pɒpkɔːn] n ❶ (popped) maïs soufflé m ❷ (unpopped) maïs à éclater m

pope [pəʊp] n pape m

poppy ['pɒpɪ] n coquelicot m

Popsicle® ['pɒpsɪkl] n sucette glacée f

popular ['pɒpjʊlə] adj populaire ▷ She's a very popular girl. C'est une fille très populaire. ▷ This is a very popular style. C'est un style très populaire.

population [pɒpjʊ'leɪʃən] n population f

pop-up ['pɒpʌp] adj contextuel (f contextuelle) ▷ a pop-up menu un menu contextuel

porch [pɔːtʃ] *n* porche *m*

porcupine [ˈpɔːkjupaɪn] *n* porc-épic *m* (pl porcs-épics) ▷ *a porcupine quill* un piquant de porc-épic

pork [pɔːk] *n* porc *m* ▷ *a pork chop* une côtelette de porc ▷ *I don't eat pork.* Je ne mange pas de porc.

pornographic [pɔːnəˈgræfik] *adj* pornographique ▷ *a pornographic magazine* un magazine pornographique

pornography [pɔːˈnɒgrəfi] *n* pornographie *f*

porridge [ˈpɒrɪdʒ] *n* gruau *m*

port [pɔːt] *n* (harbour) port *m*

portable [ˈpɔːtəbl] *adj* portable ▷ *a portable TV* un téléviseur portable

portion [ˈpɔːʃən] *n* portion *f* ▷ *a large portion of fries* une grosse portion de frites

portrait [ˈpɔːtreit] *n* portrait *m*

posh [pɒʃ] *adj* chic (*f+pl* chic) ▷ *a posh hotel* un hôtel chic

position [pəˈzɪʃən] *n* position *f* ▷ *an uncomfortable position* une position inconfortable

positive [ˈpɒzɪtɪv] *adj* ❶ (good) positif (*f* positive) ▷ *a positive attitude* une attitude positive ❷ (sure) certain ▷ *I'm positive.* J'en suis certain.

possess [pəˈzɛs] *vb* posséder

possession [pəˈzɛʃən] *n*: **Have you got all your possessions?** Est-ce tu as toutes tes affaires?

possibility [pɒsɪˈbɪlɪti] *n*: **It's a possibility.** C'est possible.

possible [ˈpɒsɪbl] *adj* possible ▷ *as soon as possible* aussitôt que possible

possibly [ˈpɒsɪblɪ] *adv* (perhaps) peut-être ▷ *"Are you coming to the party?" — "Possibly."* « Est-ce que tu viens à la soirée? » — « Peut-être. »; **...if you possibly can.** ...si cela vous est possible.; **I can't possibly**

come. Je ne peux vraiment pas venir.

post [pəʊst] *n* ❶ (on Internet) post *m* ▷ *Did you read that last post?* Tu as lu ce dernier post? ❷ (pole) poteau *m* (pl poteaux) ▷ *The ball hit the post.* Le ballon a heurté le poteau.
▶ *vb* poster ▷ *I just posted a comment on his blog.* Je viens de poster un commentaire sur son blogue.

postage [ˈpəʊstɪdʒ] *n* affranchissement *m*

postal code [ˈpəʊstəl-] *n* code postal *m*

postcard [ˈpəʊstkɑːd] *n* carte postale *f*

poster [ˈpəʊstəʳ] *n* affiche *f* ▷ *I have posters on my bedroom walls.* J'ai des affiches sur les murs de ma chambre. ▷ *There are posters all over town.* Il y a des affiches dans toute la ville.

postmark [ˈpəʊstmɑːk] *n* cachet de la poste *m*

post office *n* bureau de poste *m* ▷ *Where's the post office, please?* Où est le bureau de poste, s'il vous plaît? ▷ *She works for the post office.* Elle travaille au bureau de poste.

postpone [pəsˈpəʊn] *vb* remettre à plus tard ▷ *The match has been postponed.* Le match a été remis à plus tard.

postscript [ˈpəʊstskrɪpt] *n* post-scriptum *m*

posture [ˈpɒstʃəʳ] *n* posture *f* ▷ *Good posture is important when working at the computer.* La bonne posture est très importante quand on travaille à l'ordinateur.; **to have poor posture** se tenir mal

pot [pɒt] *n* ❶ (for cooking) casserole *f* ▷ *a pot of soup* une casserole de soupe ❷ (teapot) théière *f* ❸ (coffeepot) cafetière *f*; **the pots**

and pans les casseroles

potato [pəˈteɪtəʊ] n pomme de terre f ⊳ **potato salad** la salade de pommes de terre; **mashed potatoes** la purée de pommes de terre; **boiled potatoes** les pommes de terre bouillies; **a baked potato** une pomme de terre en robe des champs

potential [pəˈtɛnʃl] n: **He has great potential.** Il a de l'avenir.
▸ adj possible ⊳ **a potential problem** un problème possible

pothole [ˈpɒthəʊl] n (in road) nid de poule m

potlatch [ˈpɒtlætʃ] n potlatch m

potted plant [ˈpɒtɪd-] n plante en pot f

pottery [ˈpɒtərɪ] n poterie

pound [paʊnd] n livre f
• A pound is a nonmetric unit of mass equal to 454 g.
▸ vb battre ⊳ **My heart was pounding.** J'avais le cœur qui battait.

pour [pɔːʳ] vb ❶ (liquid) verser ⊳ **She poured some water into the pan.** Elle a versé de l'eau dans la casserole.; **He poured her a drink.** Il lui a servi à boire.; **Shall I pour you a cup of tea?** Je vous sers une tasse de thé? ❷ (rain) pleuvoir à verse ⊳ **It's pouring.** Il pleut à verse.; **in the pouring rain** sous une pluie torrentielle

pout [paʊt] vb faire la moue ⊳ **Don't pout.** Ne fais pas la moue.

poverty [ˈpɒvətɪ] n pauvreté f

powder [ˈpaʊdəʳ] n poudre

power [ˈpaʊəʳ] n ❶ (electricity) courant m ⊳ **The power's off.** Le courant est coupé.; **a power cut** une coupure de courant; **a power plant** une centrale électrique ❷ (energy) énergie f ⊳ **nuclear power** l'énergie nucléaire ⊳ **solar power** l'énergie solaire ❸ (authority)

pouvoir m ⊳ **to be in power** être au pouvoir ❹ (nation) puissance f ⊳ **the nuclear powers** les puissances nucléaires ⊳ **a world power** une puissance mondiale

powerful [ˈpaʊəfʊl] adj puissant

power play n attaque f à cinq

practical [ˈpræktɪkl] adj pratique ⊳ **a practical suggestion** un conseil pratique; **She's very practical.** Elle a l'esprit pratique.; **a practical joke** une farce; **a practical joker** un farceur ⊳ **She's a real practical joker!** Elle est une vraie farceuse!

practically [ˈpræktɪklɪ] adv pratiquement ⊳ **It's practically impossible.** C'est pratiquement impossible.

practice [ˈpræktɪs] n (for sport) entraînement m ⊳ **soccer practice** l'entraînement de soccer; **It's common practice in our school.** C'est ce qui se fait dans notre école.; **in practice** en pratique; **a medical practice** un cabinet médical; **out of practice** rouillé

practise [ˈpræktɪs] vb ❶ pratiquer ⊳ **I practised my French when we were in Quebec.** J'ai pratiqué mon français quand nous étions au Québec. ⊳ **I have to practise the piano.** Je dois pratiquer le piano.

┃ **pratiquer** can only be used
┃ with a following noun.

❷ s'exercer ⊳ **She loves basketball and practises dribbling every day.** Elle adore le basket-ball et s'exerce à dribbler tous les jours. ⊳ **I should practise more.** Je devrais m'exercer d'avantage. ❸ s'entraîner ⊳ **The team practises on Thursdays.** L'équipe s'entraîne le jeudi.

prairie [ˈprɛərɪ] n prairie f ⊳ **the Prairie provinces** les provinces des Prairies; **a prairie dog** un chien-de-prairie

praise [preɪz] vb faire l'éloge de ▷ *Everyone praises his cooking.* Tout le monde fait l'éloge de sa cuisine. ▷ *The teachers praised our work.* Les professeurs ont fait l'éloge de notre travail.

prank [præŋk] n farce f ▷ *to play a prank on somebody* faire une farce à quelqu'un

prawn [prɔːn] n crevette f

pray [preɪ] vb prier ▷ *to pray for something* prier pour quelque chose ▷ *to pray to God* prier Dieu

prayer [preər] n prière

precaution [prɪˈkɔːʃən] n précaution f; **to take precautions** prendre ses précautions

preceding [prɪˈsiːdɪŋ] adj précédent

precious [ˈprɛʃəs] adj précieux (f précieuse)

precise [prɪˈsaɪs] adj précis ▷ *at that precise moment* à cet instant précis

precisely [prɪˈsaɪslɪ] adv précisément ▷ *Precisely!* Précisément!; **at 10 a.m. precisely** à dix heures précises

predict [prɪˈdɪkt] vb prédire

predictable [prɪˈdɪktəbl] adj prévisible ▷ *The movie had a very predictable plot.* Le film avait une intrigue très prévisible.; **She's so predictable.** Ses réactions sont tellement prévisibles.

prefer [prɪˈfɜːʳ] vb préférer ▷ *Which would you prefer?* Lequel préfères-tu? ▷ *I prefer French to phys ed.* Je préfère le français à l'éducation physique.

preferably [ˈprɛfrəblɪ] adv de préférence ▷ *Save me a seat, preferably near the door.* Garde-moi une place, de préférence près de la porte.

preference [ˈprɛfrəns] n préférence f

pregnancy [ˈprɛgnənsɪ] n grossesse f

pregnant [ˈprɛgnənt] adj enceinte ▷ *She's six months pregnant.* Elle est enceinte de six mois.

prehistoric [ˈpriːhɪsˈtɔrɪk] adj préhistorique

prejudice [ˈprɛdʒʊdɪs] n
❶ préjugé m ▷ *That's just a prejudice.* C'est un préjugé.
❷ préjugés mpl ▷ *There's a lot of racial prejudice.* Il y a beaucoup de préjugés raciaux.

prejudiced [ˈprɛdʒʊdɪst] adj: **to be prejudiced against somebody** avoir des préjugés contre quelqu'un

premature [ˈprɛmətʃʊəʳ] adj prématuré; **a premature baby** un prématuré

premier [ˈprɛmɪəʳ] n premier ministre m, première ministre f ▷ *the premier of Manitoba* le premier ministre de Manitoba

premises [ˈprɛmɪsɪz] npl lieux mpl ▷ *to vacate the premises* vider les lieux ▷ *Smoking is not allowed on the premises.* Il est interdit de fumer sur les lieux.

preoccupied [priːˈɔkjʊpaɪd] adj préoccupé

preparation [ˈprɛpəˈreɪʃən] n préparation f

prepare [prɪˈpɛəʳ] vb préparer ▷ *to prepare a meal* préparer un repas ▷ *He has to prepare his valedictory address.* Il doit préparer son discours d'adieu.; **to prepare for something** se préparer pour quelque chose ▷ *We're preparing for our skiing holiday.* Nous nous préparons pour nos vacances de ski.

prepared [prɪˈpɛəd] adj: **to be prepared to do something** être prêt à faire quelque chose ▷ *I'm prepared to help you.* Je suis prêt à t'aider.

preschool ['priː'skuːl] *n* école *f* maternelle ▷ *My little brother goes to preschool.* Mon petit frère va à l'école maternelle.; **a preschool child** un enfant d'âge préscolaire

prescribe [prɪˈskraɪb] *vb* prescrire

prescription [prɪˈskrɪpʃən] *n* ordonnance *f* ▷ *You can't get it without a prescription.* On ne peut pas se le procurer sans ordonnance.; **a prescription drug** un médicament d'ordonnance

presence ['prɛzns] *n* présence *f*; **presence of mind** présence d'esprit

present [*adj, n* 'prɛznt, *vb* prɪ'zɛnt] *adj* ❶ (*in attendance*) présent *m* ▷ *He wasn't present at the meeting.* Il n'était pas présent à la réunion. ❷ (*current*) actuel (*f* actuelle) ▷ *the present situation* la situation actuelle; **the present tense** le présent
▶ *n* ❶ (*gift*) cadeau *m* (*pl* cadeaux) ▷ *I'm going to buy presents.* Je vais acheter des cadeaux.; **to give somebody a present** offrir un cadeau à quelqu'un ❷ (*time*) présent *m* ▷ *up to the present* jusqu'à présent; **for the present** pour l'instant; **at present** en ce moment
▶ *vb* ❶ (*play, concert*) donner ❷ (*information*) présenter; **to present somebody with something** (1) (*prize, medal*) remettre quelque chose à quelqu'un (2) (*gift*) offrir quelque chose à quelqu'un; **She presented herself very well.** Elle s'est très bien présentée.

presently ['prɛzntlɪ] *adv* (*at present*) actuellement ▷ *They're presently on tour.* Ils sont actuellement en tournée.

president ['prɛzɪdənt] *n* président *m*, présidente *f*

press [prɛs] *n* presse; **a press conference** une conférence de presse
▶ *vb* ❶ appuyer ▷ *Don't press too hard!* N'appuie pas trop fort! ❷ appuyer sur ▷ *He pressed the button.* Il a appuyé sur le bouton.

pressed [prɛst] *adj*: **We are pressed for time.** Le temps nous manqué.

pressure ['prɛʃə^r] *n* pression ▷ *She's under a lot of pressure at work.* Elle est sous pression au travail.; **a pressure group** un groupe de pression
▶ *vb* faire pression sur ▷ *My parents are pressuring me.* Mes parents font pression sur moi.

pressurize ['prɛʃəraɪz] *vb* pressuriser ▷ *a pressurized spacesuit* une combinaison spatiale pressurisée

prestige [prɛsˈtiːʒ] *n* prestige *m*

prestigious [prɛsˈtɪdʒəs] *adj* prestigieux (*f* prestigieuse)

presumably [prɪˈzjuːməblɪ] *adv* vraisemblablement

presume [prɪˈzjuːm] *vb* supposer ▷ *I presume so.* Je suppose que oui.

pretend [prɪˈtɛnd] *vb*: **to pretend to do something** faire semblant de faire quelque chose ▷ *He pretended to be asleep.* Il faisait semblant de dormir.

⏸ Be careful not to translate **to pretend** by **prétendre**.

pretty ['prɪtɪ] *adj, adv* ❶ joli ▷ *She's very pretty.* Elle est très jolie. ❷ (*rather*) plutôt ▷ *That film was pretty bad.* Ce film était plutôt mauvais.; **The weather was pretty awful.** Il faisait très mauvais temps.; **It's pretty much the same.** C'est pratiquement la même chose.

pretzel ['prɛtsəl] *n* bretzel *m*

prevent [prɪ'vɛnt] vb ❶ empêcher ▷ *They tried to prevent us from leaving.* Ils ont essayé de nous empêcher de partir. ❷ *(disease)* prévenir ▷ *in order to prevent AIDS* pour prévenir le sida ❸ *(accident, war, fire)* éviter

preventive [prɪ'vɛntɪv] *adj* préventif *(f* préventive*)* ▷ *preventive medicine* la médecine préventive; **preventive measures** des mesures de prévention

preview ['priːvjuː] *n (of movie)* bande-annonce *f*

previous ['priːvɪəs] *adj* précédent

previously ['priːvɪəslɪ] *adv* auparavant

prey [preɪ] *n* proie *f* ▷ *a bird of prey* un oiseau de proie

price [praɪs] *n* prix *m* ▷ *a high price* un prix élevé ▷ *the price list* la liste de prix

prick [prɪk] *vb* piquer ▷ *I pricked my finger.* Je me suis piqué le doigt.

prickly ['prɪklɪ] *adj* épineux *(f* épineuse*)* ▷ *a prickly plant* une plante épineuse

pride [praɪd] *n* ❶ *(positive)* fierté *f* ▷ *She's her parents' pride and joy.* Elle est la fierté de ses parents.; **to take pride in something** être fier de quelque chose ❷ *(arrogance)* orgueil *m* ▷ *Pride prevented him from apologizing.* L'orgueil l'a empêché de demander pardon.

priest [priːst] *n* prêtre *m* ▷ *He's a priest.* Il est prêtre.

primarily ['praɪmərɪlɪ] *adv* principalement

primary ['praɪmərɪ] *adj* ❶ *(main)* principal *(mpl* principaux*)* ▷ *our primary purpose* notre but principal ❷ *(first)* primaire ▷ *books for the primary grade level* des livres pour le niveau primaire

prime minister [praɪm-] *n* premier ministre *m*, première

ministre *f*

primitive ['prɪmɪtɪv] *adj* primitif *(f* primitive*)*

prince [prɪns] *n* prince *m* ▷ *the Prince of Wales* le prince de Galles

Prince Edward Island [-ɛdwəd-] *n* Île-du-Prince-Édouard *f*

princess [prɪn'sɛs] *n* princesse *f* ▷ *Princess Anne* la princesse Anne

principal ['prɪnsɪpl] *n* directeur *m*, directrice *f*

principle ['prɪnsɪpl] *n* principe *m*; **on principle** par principe

print [prɪnt] *n* ❶ *(photo)* tirage *m* ▷ *colour prints* des tirages en couleur ❷ *(letters)* caractères *mpl* ▷ *in small print* en petits caractères ❸ *(fingerprint)* empreinte *f* digitale ❹ *(picture)* gravure *f* ▷ *a framed print* une gravure encadrée
▶ *vb (print out, publish)* imprimer ▷ *Click on the icon to print the file.* Cliquez sur l'icône pour imprimer le fichier.

printer ['prɪntəʳ] *n (machine)* imprimante *f*

printout ['prɪntaut] *n* sortie d'imprimante *f*

priority [praɪ'ɒrɪtɪ] *n* priorité *f*

prison ['prɪzn] *n* prison *f*; **in prison** en prison

prisoner ['prɪznəʳ] *n* prisonnier *m*, prisonnière *f*

prison guard *n* gardien de prison *m*, gardienne de prison *f*

privacy ['prɪvəsɪ] *n* intimité *f*

private ['praɪvɪt] *adj* privé ▷ *a private school* une école privée; **private property** la propriété privée; **"private"** *(on envelope)* « personnel »; **a private bathroom** une salle de bain individuelle; **I take private lessons.** Je prends des cours particuliers.

privatize ['praɪvɪtaɪz] *vb* privatiser

privilege ['prɪvɪlɪdʒ] *n* privilège *m*

prize [praɪz] n prix m ▷ *to win a prize* gagner un prix

prizewinner ['praɪzwɪnər] n gagnant m, gagnante f

prize-winning ['praɪzwɪnɪŋ] adj primé ▷ *a prize-winning documentary* un film documentaire primé

pro [prəʊ] n (athlete) pro; **You're a real pro at making crêpes!** Tu es une vraie pro des crêpes!; **the pros and cons** le pour et le contre ▷ *We weighed the pros and cons.* Nous avons pesé le pour et le contre.

probability [prɒbə'bɪlɪtɪ] n probabilité f

probable ['prɒbəbl] adj probable

probably ['prɒbəblɪ] adv probablement ▷ *probably not* probablement pas

probation [prə'beɪʃən] n: **on probation** en liberté surveillée

problem ['prɒbləm] n problème m ▷ *No problem!* Pas de problème!

proceeds ['prəʊsiːdz] npl bénéfices mpl

process ['prəʊses] n processus m ▷ *the peace process* le processus de paix; **to be in the process of doing something** être en train de faire quelque chose ▷ *We're in the process of painting the kitchen.* Nous sommes en train de peindre la cuisine.

procession [prə'seʃən] n défilé m

procrastinate [prəʊ'kræstɪneɪt] vb: **I tend to procrastinate.** J'ai tendance à tout remettre au lendemain.

produce [prə'djuːs] vb ❶ (create, manufacture) produire ❷ (play, show) monter

producer [prə'djuːsər] n ❶ (of play, show) metteur en scène m, metteuse en scène f ❷ (business) producteur m, productrice f ▷ *Canada is the world's greatest producer of hydroelectric power.* Le Canada est le plus grand producteur d'hydro-électricité au monde.

product ['prɒdʌkt] n produit m

production [prə'dʌkʃən] n ❶ production f ▷ *world coffee production* la production mondiale de café ❷ (play, show) mise en scène f ▷ *a production of "Hamlet"* une mise en scène de « Hamlet »

profession [prə'feʃən] n profession f

professional [prə'feʃənl] n professionnel m, professionnelle f ▶ adj (player) professionnel m (f professionnelle) ▷ *a professional musician* un musicien professionnel; **a very professional piece of work** un vrai travail de professionnel

professor [prə'fesər] n professeur d'université m, professeure d'université f

profit ['prɒfɪt] n bénéfice m

profitable ['prɒfɪtəbl] adj rentable

program ['prəʊgræm] n ❶ programme m ▷ *a computer program* un programme informatique ❷ (on TV, radio) émission f ▷ *a TV program* une émission de télé ❸ (of events) programme m ▶ vb (computer) programmer

programmer ['prəʊgræmər] n programmeur m, programmeuse f ▷ *She's a programmer.* Elle est programmeuse.

programming ['prəʊgræmɪŋ] n programmation f

progress [prə'gres] n progrès m ▷ *You're making progress!* Vous faites des progrès!

prohibit [prə'hɪbɪt] vb interdire ▷ *Smoking is prohibited.* Il est interdit de fumer.

project [prə'dʒekt] n projet m ▷ *a*

development project un projet de développement ▷ *I'm doing a project on the rain forest.* Je travaille à un projet de recherche sur la forêt pluviale.

projector [prə'dʒɛktər] *n* projecteur *m*

promise ['prɒmɪs] *n* promesse *f* ▷ *He made me a promise.* Il m'a fait une promesse.; **That's a promise!** C'est promis!
▶ *vb* promettre ▷ *He promised to write.* Il a promis d'écrire. ▷ *I'll write, I promise!* J'écrirai, c'est promis!

promising ['prɒmɪsɪŋ] *adj* prometteur (*f* prometteuse) ▷ *a promising player* un joueur prometteur

promote [prə'məʊt] *vb* promouvoir ▷ *Our school tries to promote recycling.* Notre école essaie de promouvoir le recyclage. ▷ *We made posters to promote the school play.* Nous avons fait des affiches pour promouvoir la pièce de théâtre de l'école.; **to be promoted** être promu ▷ *She was promoted after six months.* Elle a été promue au bout de six mois.

promotion [prə'məʊʃən] *n* promotion *f*

prompt [prɒmpt] *adj, adv* ▷ *a prompt reply* une réponse rapide

promptly ['prɒmptlɪ] *adv*: **We left promptly at seven.** Nous sommes partis à sept heures précises.

pronoun ['prəʊnaʊn] *n* pronom *m*

pronounce [prə'naʊns] *vb* prononcer ▷ *How do you pronounce that word?* Comment est-ce qu'on prononce ce mot?

pronunciation [prənʌnsɪ'eɪʃən] *n* prononciation *f*

proof [pru:f] *n* preuve *f*

proofread ['pru:fri:d] *vb* relire et corriger ▷ *Don't forget to proofread*

your book report. N'oublie pas de relire et de corriger ton compte-rendu de livre.

prop [prɒp] *n* (*for play*) accessoire *m*

propaganda [prɒpə'gændə] *n* propagande *f*

propane ['prəʊpeɪn] *n* propane *m* ▷ *a propane cylinder* (*for camping*) une bonbonne de propane ▷ *a propane stove* un réchaud au propane

proper ['prɒpər] *adj* ❶ (*genuine*) vrai ▷ *proper French bread* du vrai pain français ▷ *We didn't have a proper lunch, just sandwiches.* Nous n'avons pas pris de vrai lunch, juste des sandwichs.; **It's difficult to get a proper job.** Il est difficile de trouver un travail correct.
❷ adéquat ▷ *You have to have the proper equipment.* Il faut avoir l'équipement adéquat. ▷ *We need proper training.* Il nous faut une formation adéquate.; **If you had come at the proper time...** Si tu étais venu à l'heure dite...

properly ['prɒpəlɪ] *adv* ❶ (*correctly*) comme il faut ▷ *You're not doing it properly.* Tu ne t'y prends pas comme il faut. ❷ (*appropriately*) convenablement ▷ *Dress properly for your interview.* Habille-toi convenablement pour ton entrevue.

property ['prɒpətɪ] *n* propriété *f*; **"private property"** « propriété privée »; **stolen property** les objets volés

proportional [prə'pɔ:ʃənɪt] *adj* proportionnel (*f* proportionnelle) ▷ *proportional representation* la représentation proportionnelle

proposal [prə'pəʊzl] *n* (*suggestion*) proposition *f*

propose [prə'pəʊz] *vb* proposer ▷ *I propose a new plan.* Je propose un changement de programme.;

to propose to do something
avoir l'intention de faire quelque
chose ▷ *What do you propose to do?*
Qu'est-ce que tu as l'intention de
faire?; **to propose to somebody**
(*for marriage*) demander quelqu'un
en mariage ▷ *He proposed to her at
the restaurant.* Il l'a demandée en
mariage au restaurant.

prosecute ['prɒsɪkjuːt] *vb*
poursuivre en justice ▷ *They were
prosecuted for murder.* Ils ont été
poursuivis en justice pour meutre.;
"Trespassers will be prosecuted"
« Défense d'entrer sous peine de
poursuites »

prospect [prə'spɛkt] *n* perspective
f ▷ *It'll improve my career prospects.*
Ça va améliorer mes perspectives
d'avenir.

protect [prə'tɛkt] *vb* protéger

protection [prə'tɛkʃən] *n*
protection *f*

protein ['prəʊtiːn] *n* protéine *f*

protest [*n* 'prəʊtɛst] *n* protestation *f*
▷ *He ignored their protests.* Il a ignoré
leurs protestations.; **a protest
march** une manifestation
▶ *vb* protester

Protestant ['prɒtɪstənt] *n*
protestant *m*, protestante *f*
▶ *adj* protestant *m* ▷ *a Protestant
church* une église protestante

protester [prə'tɛstər] *n*
manifestant *m*, manifestante *f*

proud [praud] *adj* fier (fière) ▷ *Her
parents are proud of her.* Ses parents
sont fiers d'elle.

prove [pruːv] *vb* prouver ▷ *The
police couldn't prove it.* La police n'a
pas pu le prouver.

proverb ['prɒvɜːb] *n* proverbe *m*

provide [prə'vaɪd] *vb* fournir;
**to provide somebody with
something** fournir quelque chose
à quelqu'un ▷ *They provided us with
maps.* Ils nous ont fourni des cartes.

provide for *vb* subvenir aux
besoins de ▷ *She can now provide
for her family.* Maintenant elle peut
subvenir aux besoins de sa famille.

provided [prə'vaɪdɪd] *conj* à
condition que

> **à condition que** has to be
> followed by the subjunctive.

▷ *He'll play in the next game provided
he comes to the practice.* Il jouera
dans le prochain match, à condition
qu'il vienne à l'entraînement.

province ['prɒvɪns] *n* province *f*

provincial [prə'vɪnʃəl] *adj*
provincial (*mpl* provinciaux)
▷ *the provincial capital* la capitale
provinciale

prowler ['praulər] *n* rôdeur *m*,
rôdeuse *f*

prune [pruːn] *n* pruneau *m* (*pl*
pruneaux)

pry [praɪ] *vb*: **to pry into other
people's affairs** mettre son nez
dans les affaires des autres

pseudonym ['sjuːdənɪm] *n*
pseudonyme *m*

psychiatrist [saɪ'kaɪətrɪst] *n*
psychiatre ▷ *She's a psychiatrist.* Elle
est psychiatre.

psychological [saɪkə'lɒdʒɪkl] *adj*
psychologique

psychologist [saɪ'kɒlədʒɪst] *n*
psychologue ▷ *He's a psychologist.* Il
est psychologue.

psychology [saɪ'kɒlədʒɪ] *n*
psychologie *f*

public ['pʌblɪk] *n* public *m* ▷ *open
to the public* ouvert au public; **in
public** en public
▶ *adj* public *m* (*f* publique); **a
public holiday** un jour férié; **public
opinion** l'opinion *f* publique; **the
public address system** les haut-
parleurs; **a public school** une école
publique; **public transport** les *m*

transports en commun; **public relations** les f relations publiques

publicity [pʌb'lɪsɪtɪ] n publicité f

publish ['pʌblɪʃ] vb publier

publisher ['pʌblɪʃər] n (company) maison d'édition f

puck [pʌk] n rondelle f

pudding ['pʊdɪŋ] n pouding m ▷ instant vanilla pudding du pouding instantané à la vanille; **rice pudding** le riz au lait

puddle ['pʌdl] n flaque f

puffin ['pʌfɪn] n macareux m

puff pastry [pʌf-] n pâte feuilletée f

pull [pʊl] vb **1** tirer ▷ Pull! Tirez! **2** (tooth, weed) arracher; **to pull the trigger** appuyer sur la gâchette; **to pull a muscle** se froisser un muscle ▷ I pulled a muscle when I was training. Je me suis froissé un muscle à l'entraînement.; **You're pulling my leg!** Tu me fais marcher!; **to pull off the road** arrêter la voiture sur le bord de la route; **to pull out (1)** (from driveway, parking space) sortir **(2)** (in traffic) sortir de la file ▷ The car pulled out to pass. La voiture est sortie de la file pour doubler. **(3)** (withdraw) se retirer ▷ He pulled out of the tournament. Il s'est retiré du tournoi.; **The police pulled us over.** La police nous a fait nous arrêter.; **to pull through** s'en sortir ▷ They think he'll pull through. Ils pensent qu'il va s'en sortir.; **to pull up** (car) s'arrêter ▷ A black car pulled up beside me. Une voiture noire s'est arrêtée à côté de moi.

pullover ['pʊləʊvər] n chandail m

pulse [pʌls] n pouls ▷ The nurse felt my pulse. L'infirmière a pris mon pouls.

pump [pʌmp] n pompe f ▷ a bicycle pump une pompe à vélo ▷ a gas pump une pompe à essence ▶ vb pomper; **to pump up** (tire) gonfler

pumpkin ['pʌmpkɪn] n citrouille f

punch [pʌntʃ] n **1** (blow) coup de poing m **2** (drink) punch m **3** (tool) perforateur m ▷ Use the three-hole punch on the teacher's desk. Utilise le perforateur à trois trous sur le bureau de la prof. ▶ vb **1** (hit) donner un coup de poing à ▷ She punched me! Elle m'a donné un coup de poing! **2** (papers) perforer ▷ The pages are already punched. Les feuilles sont déjà perforées. **3** (ticket) poinçonner ▷ He forgot to punch my ticket. Il a oublié de poinçonner mon billet.

punctual ['pʌŋktjʊəl] adj ponctuel (f ponctuelle)

punctuation [pʌŋktjʊ'eɪʃən] n ponctuation f

puncture ['pʌŋktʃər] vb (tire, balloon) crever

punish ['pʌnɪʃ] vb punir; **to punish somebody for something** punir quelqu'un de quelque chose; **to punish somebody for doing something** punir quelqu'un d'avoir fait quelque chose

punishment ['pʌnɪʃmənt] n punition f

punk [pʌŋk] n (person) punk; **a punk rock band** un groupe de punk rock

puppet ['pʌpɪt] n marionnette f

puppy ['pʌpɪ] n chiot m

purchase ['pɜːtʃɪs] vb acheter

pure [pjʊər] adj pur ▷ pure orange juice du pur jus d'orange ▷ the pure sciences les sciences pures

purple ['pɜːpl] adj violet (f violette)

purpose ['pɜːpəs] n but m ▷ What is the purpose of these changes? Quel est le but de ces changements? ▷ his *purpose in life* son but dans la vie; **on purpose** ▷ *She did it on purpose.* Elle l'a fait exprès.

purr [pɜː] *vb* ronronner

purse [pɜːs] *n* ① sac à main *m* (*pl* sacs à main) ② (*for coins*) porte-monnaie *m* (*pl* porte-monnaie)

pursue [pəˈsjuː] *vb* poursuivre

pursuit [pəˈsjuːt] *n*: **in pursuit of adventure** à la recherche de l'aventure; **She escaped with her brother in hot pursuit.** Elle s'est échappée avec son frère à ses trousses.

push [pʊʃ] *n*: **to give somebody a push** pousser quelqu'un ▷ *He gave me a push.* Il m'a poussé.; **a push for more affordable housing** une campagne pour des logements à loyer modéré
▷ *vb* ① pousser ▷ *Don't push!* Arrêtez de pousser! ② (*button*) appuyer sur; **to push somebody to do something** pousser quelqu'un à faire quelque chose ▷ *My parents are pushing me to take piano.* Mes parents me poussent à prendre des cours de piano.; **to push drugs** revendre de la drogue

push around *vb* bousculer ▷ *Stop pushing people around.* Arrête de bousculer les gens.

push through *vb* se frayer un passage ▷ *The paramedics pushed through the crowd.* Les ambulanciers se sont frayé un passage dans la foule.; **I pushed my way through.** Je me suis frayé un passage.

pusher [ˈpʊʃəʳ] *n* (*of drugs*) revendeur *m*, revendeuse *f*

push-up [ˈpʊʃʌp] *n* pompe *f*; **to do push-ups** faire des pompes

pussy willow [ˈpʊsɪˈwɪləʊ] *n* saule à chatons *m*

put [pʊt] *vb* ① (*place*) mettre ▷ *Where shall I put my things?* Où

est-ce que je peux mettre mes affaires? ▷ *He's putting the baby to bed.* Il met le bébé au lit. ② (*write*) écrire ▷ *Don't forget to put your name on the paper.* N'oubliez pas d'écrire votre nom sur la feuille.

put aside *vb* mettre de côté ▷ *Can you put this aside for me till tomorrow?* Est-ce que vous pouvez mettre ça de côté pour moi jusqu'à demain?

put away *vb* ranger ▷ *Can you put away the dishes, please?* Tu peux ranger la vaisselle, s'il te plaît?

put back *vb* (*replace*) remettre en place ▷ *Put it back when you've finished with it.* Remets-le en place une fois que tu auras fini.

put down *vb* ① poser ▷ *I'll put these bags down for a minute.* Je vais poser ces sacs une minute. ② (*in writing*) noter ▷ *I've put down a few ideas.* J'ai noté quelques idées. ③ (*belittle*) rabaisser ▷ *I don't like jokes that put other people down.* Je n'aime pas les plaisanteries qui rabaissent les autres. ▷ *Stop putting yourself down.* Arrête de te rabaisser.; **to have an animal put down** faire piquer un animal ▷ *We had to have our old dog put down.* Nous avons dû faire piquer notre vieux chien.

put forward *vb* ① (*clock*) avancer ▷ *Next week it'll be time to put the clocks forward an hour.* La semaine prochaine, il sera temps d'avancer les montres d'une heure. ② (*idea, argument*) ▷ *to put forward a suggestion* proposer une suggestion

put in *vb* (*install*) installer ▷ *We're going to get new cupboards put in.* Nous allons faire installer de nouvelles armoires.; **She has put in a lot of work on this project.** Elle a fourni beaucoup de travail pour ce projet.

put off vb ❶ (postpone) remettre à plus tard ▷ I keep putting it off. Je n'arrête pas de remettre ça à plus tard. ❷ (discourage) décourager ▷ He's not easily put off. Il ne se laisse pas facilement décourager.

put on vb ❶ (clothes, lipstick, record) mettre ▷ I'll put my coat on. Je vais mettre mon manteau. ❷ (play, show) monter ▷ We're putting on "Bon Voyage, Charlie Brown". Nous sommes en train de monter « Bon voyage, Charlie Brown ». ❸ mettre à cuire ▷ I'll put the potatoes on. Je vais mettre les pommes de terre à cuire.; **to put on weight** grossir ▷ He's put on a bit of weight. Il a un peu grossi. ▷ to put on two kilos gagner deux kilos

put out vb (light, cigarette, fire) éteindre ▷ It took them five hours to put out the fire. Ils ont mis cinq heures à éteindre l'incendie.

put through vb ❶ passer ▷ Can you put me through to the manager? Est-ce que vous pouvez me passer le directeur?; **I'm putting you through.** Je vous passe la communication. ❷ soumettre ▷ The new drug was put through a series of tests. On a soumis le nouveau médicament à une série d'épreuves.

put up vb ❶ (pin up) mettre ▷ The poster's great. I'll put it up on my wall. L'affiche est super. Je vais le mettre au mur. ❷ (tent) monter ▷ We put up our tent in a field. Nous avons monté la tente dans un champ. ❸ (price) augmenter ▷ They've put up the price. Ils ont augmenté le prix. ❹ (accommodate) héberger ▷ My friends will put me up for the night. Mes amis vont m'héberger pour la nuit.; **to put one's hand up** lever la main ▷ If you have any questions, put up your hand. Si vous avez une question, levez la main.; **to put up with something** supporter quelque chose ▷ I'm not going to put up with it any longer. Je ne vais pas supporter ça plus longtemps.

puzzle ['pʌzl] n (jigsaw) puzzle m

puzzled ['pʌzld] adj perplexe ▷ You look puzzled! Tu as l'air perplexe!

puzzling ['pʌzlɪŋ] adj déconcertant

pyjamas [pɪ'dʒɑːməz] npl pyjama m ▷ my pyjamas mon pyjama.; **a pair of pyjamas** un pyjama.; **a pyjama top** un haut de pyjama

pyramid ['pɪrəmɪd] n pyramide f

q

quaint [kweɪnt] *adj* (*house, village*) pittoresque

qualifications [kwɒlɪfɪˈkeɪʃənz] *npl* qualifications *fpl* ▷ *What are your qualifications?* Quelles sont vos qualifications professionnelles?

qualified [ˈkwɒlɪfaɪd] *adj* **①** (*trained*) qualifié ▷ *a qualified driving instructor* un moniteur d'auto-école qualifié **②** (*nurse, teacher*) diplômé ▷ *a qualified nurse* une infirmière diplômée

qualify [ˈkwɒlɪfaɪ] *vb* (*in competition*) se qualifier ▷ *Our team didn't qualify.* Notre équipe ne s'est pas qualifiée.; **to qualify for a job** avoir les compétences requises pour un poste; **to qualify for unemployment benefits** avoir droit aux allocations d'assurance-emploi; **That hardly qualifies as art.** Cela ne mérite guère le nom d'art.

quality [ˈkwɒlɪtɪ] *n* qualité *f* ▷ *good quality of life* une bonne qualité de vie ▷ *good quality ingredients* des ingrédients de bonne qualité ▷ *She has lots of good qualities.* Elle a beaucoup de qualités.

quantity [ˈkwɒntɪtɪ] *n* quantité *f*

quarantine [ˈkwɒrntiːn] *n* quarantaine *f* ▷ *in quarantine* en quarantaine

quarrel [ˈkwɒrl] *n* dispute *f*
▶ *vb* se disputer

quarry [ˈkwɒrɪ] *n* (*for stone*) carrière *f*

quarter [ˈkwɔːtə°] *n* quart *m*; **three quarters** trois quarts; **a quarter of an hour** un quart d'heure ▷ *three quarters of an hour* trois quarts d'heure; **a quarter after ten** dix heures et quart; **a quarter to eleven** onze heures moins le quart

quarterfinal [ˈkwɔːtəˈfaɪnl] *n* quart de finale *m*

quartet [kwɔːˈtɛt] *n* quatuor *m* ▷ *a string quartet* un quatuor à cordes

queasy [ˈkwiːzɪ] *adj*: **to feel queasy** avoir mal au cœur ▷ *I'm feeling queasy.* J'ai mal au cœur.

Québec [kwɪˈbɛk] *n* Québec *m*

queen [kwiːn] *n* **①** reine *f* ▷ *Queen Elizabeth* la reine Élisabeth **②** (*playing card*) dame *f* ▷ *the queen of hearts* la dame de cœur; **the Queen Mother** la reine mère; **beauty queen** la reine de beauté; **a queen-sized bed** un grand lit

query [ˈkwɪərɪ] *n* question *f*
▶ *vb* mettre en question ▷ *No one queried my decision.* Personne n'a mis en question ma décision.

question [ˈkwɛstʃən] *n* question *f* ▷ *Can I ask a question?* Est-ce que je peux poser une question? ▷ *That's a difficult question.* C'est une question difficile.; **It's out of the question.**

C'est hors de question.; **There's no question he's going to win.** Il est certain qu'il va gagner.; **There's no question of you paying!** Il n'est pas question que tu payes!
▶ vb interroger ▷ He was questioned by the police. Il a été interrogé par la police.

questionable ['kwɛstʃənəbl] adj douteux (f douteuse) ▷ questionable behaviour une conduite douteuse

question mark n point d'interrogation m

questionnaire [kwɛstʃə'nɛəʳ] n questionnaire m

quick [kwɪk] adj, adv rapide ▷ a quick lunch un déjeuner rapide ▷ It's quicker by train. C'est plus rapide en train.; **Be quick!** Dépêche-toi!; **She's a quick learner.** Elle apprend vite.; **Quick, phone the police!** Téléphonez vite à la police!

quickly ['kwɪklɪ] adv vite ▷ It was all over very quickly. Ça s'est passé très vite.

quicksand ['kwɪksænd] n sable mouvant m

quiet ['kwaɪət] adj ❶ (not talkative or noisy) silencieux (f silencieuse) ▷ You're very quiet today. Tu es bien silencieux aujourd'hui. ▷ The engine is very quiet. Le moteur est très silencieux. ❷ (peaceful) tranquille ▷ a quiet little town une petite ville tranquille ▷ a quiet weekend une fin de semaine tranquille; **Be quiet!** Tais-toi!; **Quiet!** Silence!

quietly ['kwaɪətlɪ] adv ❶ (speak) doucement ▷ "She's very sick," he said quietly. « Elle est très malade », déclara-t-il doucement. ❷ (move) silencieusement ▷ He quietly opened the door. Il a ouvert la porte sans faire de bruit.

quilt [kwɪlt] n ❶ (pieced, with special stitching) courtepointe f

❷ (comforter) douillette f

quit [kwɪt] vb (place, premises, job) quitter ▷ She's decided to quit her job. Elle a décidé de quitter son emploi.; **I quit!** J'abandonne!

quite [kwaɪt] adv ❶ (rather) assez ▷ It's quite warm today. Il fait assez chaud aujourd'hui. ❷ (entirely) tout à fait ▷ I'm not quite sure. Je n'en suis pas tout à fait sûr. ▷ It's not quite the same. Ce n'est pas tout à fait la même chose.; **quite good** pas mal; **I've been there quite a few times.** J'y suis allé pas mal de fois.; **quite a lot of money** pas mal d'argent; **It costs quite a lot to go to Europe.** Ça coûte assez cher d'aller en Europe.; **It's quite a long way.** C'est assez loin.; **It was quite a shock.** Ça a été tout un choc.; **There were quite a few people there.** Il y avait pas mal de gens.

quiz [kwɪz] n ❶ (in school) interrogation f ❷ (in magazine) questionnaire m; **a quiz show** un jeu-questionnaire

quota ['kwəʊtə] n quota m

quotation [kwəʊ'teɪʃən] n citation f ▷ a quotation from a book une citation d'un livre

quote [kwəʊt] n citation f ▷ a quote from Pierre Trudeau une citation de Pierre Trudeau; **quotes** (quotation marks) les m guillemets ▷ in quotes entre guillemets
▶ vb citer ▷ He's always quoting famous people. Il n'arrête pas de citer des gens célèbres.

r

rabbi ['ræbaɪ] *n* rabbin *m*
rabbit ['ræbɪt] *n* lapin *m*; **a rabbit hutch** un clapier
rabies ['reɪbiːz] *n* rage *f*; **a dog with rabies** un chien enragé
raccoon [rə'kuːn] *n* raton laveur *m*
race [reɪs] *n* ❶ (*sport*) course *f* ▷ *a bike race* une course cycliste ❷ (*species*) race *f* ▷ *the human race* la race humaine; **race relations** les relations interraciales
▶ *vb* ❶ (*have a race*) faire la course; **I'll race you!** On fait la course! ❷ courir ▷ *We raced to catch the bus.* Nous avons couru pour attraper l'autobus.
race car *n* voiture de course *f*
race car driver *n* pilote de course
racecourse ['reɪskɔːs] *n* champ de courses *m*
racehorse ['reɪshɔːs] *n* cheval de course *m* (*pl* chevaux de course)
racer ['reɪsəʳ] *n* (*bike*) vélo de course

racetrack ['reɪstræk] *n* piste *f*
racial ['reɪʃl] *adj* racial (*mpl* raciaux) ▷ *racial discrimination* la discrimination raciale
racism ['reɪsɪzəm] *n* racisme *m*
racist ['reɪsɪst] *adj* raciste
▶ *n* raciste
rack [ræk] *n* ❶ (*for luggage*) porte-bagages *m* (*pl* porte-bagages) ❷ (*for coats*) portemanteau *m* (*pl* portemanteaux) ❸ (*for dishes*) égouttoir *m*
racket ['rækɪt] *n* ❶ (*noise*) tapage *m* ▷ *They're making a terrible racket.* Ils font un tapage de tous les diables. ❷ (*informal*)
racquet ['rækɪt] *n* raquette *f*
radar ['reɪdɑː] *n* radar *m*
radiation [reɪdɪ'eɪʃən] *n* radiation *f*
radiator ['reɪdɪeɪtəʳ] *n* radiateur *m*
radio ['reɪdɪəʊ] *n* radio *f*; **on the radio** à la radio; **a radio station** une station de radio
radioactive ['reɪdɪəʊ'æktɪv] *adj* radioactif (*f* radioactive)
radio-controlled ['reɪdɪəʊkən'trəʊld] *adj* (*model plane, car*) téléguidé
radish ['rædɪʃ] *n* radis
raffle ['ræfl] *n* tombola *f* ▷ *a raffle ticket* un billet de tombola
raft [rɑːft] *n* radeau *m* (*pl* radeaux)
rag [ræg] *n* chiffon *m*; **dressed in rags** en haillons
rage [reɪdʒ] *n* rage *f*; **to be in a rage** être furieux ▷ *She was in a rage.* Elle était furieuse.; **It's all the rage.** Ça fait fureur.
raid [reɪd] *n* ❶ incursion *f* ▷ *a raid by enemy soldiers* une incursion de soldats ennemis ❷ descente *f* ▷ *a police raid* une descente de police
▶ *vb* ❶ (*military*) faire une incursion dans ❷ (*police*) faire une descente dans ▷ *The police raided the club.* La police a fait une descente dans

le club.

rail [reɪl] n (on railway line) rail m; **by rail** en train

railing ['reɪlɪŋ] n ❶ (on stairs) rampe f ❷ (on bridge, balcony) balustrade f ▷ Don't lean over the railing! Ne vous penchez pas sur la balustrade!

railway ['reɪlweɪ] n chemin de fer m ▷ the privatization of the railways la privatisation des chemins de fer; **a railway crossing** une traverse; **a railway line** une ligne de chemin de fer; **a railway station** une gare

rain [reɪn] n pluie f ▷ in the rain sous la pluie
  ▶ vb pleuvoir ▷ It rains a lot here. Il pleut beaucoup par ici.; **It's raining.** Il pleut.

rainbow ['reɪnbəʊ] n arc-en-ciel m (pl arcs-en-ciel)

raincoat ['reɪnkəʊt] n imperméable m

rainforest ['reɪnfɒrɪst] n forêt tropicale humide f

rainy ['reɪnɪ] adj pluvieux (f pluvieuse)

raise [reɪz] vb ❶ (lift) lever ▷ He raised his hand. Il a levé la main. ❷ (children, animals) élever ▷ We raise pigs. Nous élevons des porcs. ▷ They've raised three children. Ils ont élevé trois enfants. ❸ (improve) améliorer ▷ They want to raise standards in schools. Ils veulent améliorer le niveau dans les écoles.; **to raise money** collecter des fonds ▷ The school is raising money for a new gym. L'école collecte des fonds pour un nouveau gymnase.

raisin ['reɪzn] n raisin sec m

rake [reɪk] n râteau m (pl râteaux)

rally ['rælɪ] n ❶ (of people) rassemblement m ❷ (sport) rallye m ▷ a rally driver un pilote de rallye

ram [ræm] n (sheep) bélier m
  ▶ vb (vehicle) emboutir ▷ The thieves rammed a police car. Les voleurs ont embouti une voiture de police.

ramp [ræmp] n ❶ (for wheelchairs) rampe d'accès f ❷ (on highway) bretelle f

ran [ræn] vb see **run**

ranch [rɑːntʃ] n ranch m

random ['rændəm] adj: **a random selection** une sélection effectuée au hasard; **at random** au hasard ▷ We picked the number at random. Nous avons choisi le numéro au hasard.

rang [ræŋ] vb see **ring**

range [reɪndʒ] n ❶ choix m ▷ a wide range of colours un grand choix de coloris; **a range of subjects** diverses matières ▷ We study a range of subjects. Nous étudions diverses matières.; **a mountain range** une chaîne de montagnes
  ▶ vb: **to range from...to** se situer entre...et ▷ Temperatures in summer range from 18 to 33 degrees. Les températures estivales se situent entre dix-huit et trente-trois degrés.; **Tickets range from $5 to $40.** Les billets coûtent entre cinq et quarante dollars.

ranger ['reɪndʒəʳ] n garde forestier m, garde forestière f

rank [ræŋk] vb: **She ranks third in Canada in speed skating.** Elle est classée troisième au Canada pour le patinage de vitesse.

ransom ['rænsəm] n rançon f

rap [ræp] n (music) rap m ▷ a rap singer un chanteur de rap

rapids ['ræpɪdz] npl rapides mpl

rare [reəʳ] adj ❶ (unusual) rare ▷ a rare plant une plante rare ❷ (steak) saignant

rash [ræʃ] n éruption f de boutons ▷ I've got a rash on my chest. J'ai une éruption de boutons sur la poitrine.

raspberry [ˈrɑːzbərɪ] n framboise f ▷ *raspberry jam* la confiture de framboises

rat [ræt] n rat m

rate [reɪt] n ❶ *(price)* tarif m ▷ *There are reduced rates for students.* Il y a des tarifs réduits pour les étudiants. ❷ *(level)* taux m ▷ *the birth rate* le taux de naissances ▷ *a high rate of interest* un taux d'intérêt élevé
▶ vb: **He is rated the best.** Il est considéré comme le meilleur.; **How do you rate this film?** Qu'est-ce que vous pensez de ce film?; **This rates a 9 out of 10.** Cela mérite un 9 sur 10.

rather [ˈrɑːðəʳ] adv plutôt ▷ *I was rather disappointed.* J'étais plutôt déçu.; **rather than** plutôt que ▷ *We decided to camp rather than stay at a hotel.* Nous avons décidé de camper plutôt que d'aller à l'hôtel.; **I'd rather...** J'aimerais mieux... ▷ *I'd rather stay in tonight.* J'aimerais mieux rester à la maison ce soir. ▷ *"Would you like a candy?" — "I'd rather have an apple."* « Tu veux un bonbon? » — « J'aimerais mieux une pomme. »

rattle [ˈrætl] n *(for baby)* hochet m

rattlesnake [ˈrætlsneɪk] n serpent à sonnette m

rave [reɪv] vb s'extasier ▷ *They raved about the movie.* Ils se sont extasiés sur le film.
▶ n *(party)* rave m; **rave music** la musique rave

ravenous [ˈrævənəs] adj: **to be ravenous** avoir une faim de loup ▷ *I'm ravenous!* J'ai une faim de loup!

raw [rɔː] adj *(food)* cru; **raw materials** les matières premières

razor [ˈreɪzəʳ] n rasoir m ▷ *some disposable razors* des rasoirs jetables; **a razor blade** une lame de rasoir

RCMP n GRC f

reach [riːtʃ] n: **out of reach** hors de portée ▷ *The light switch was out of reach.* L'interrupteur était hors de portée.; **within easy reach of** à proximité de ▷ *The hotel is within easy reach of the town centre.* L'hôtel se trouve à proximité du centre-ville.
▶ vb ❶ arriver à ▷ *We reached the hotel at 7 p.m.* Nous sommes arrivés à l'hôtel à sept heures du soir. ▷ *Have you reached a decision?* Tu es arrivé à une décision? ❷ *(decision)* parvenir à ▷ *Eventually they reached a decision.* Ils sont finalement parvenus à une décision.; **He reached for his flashlight.** Il a tendu la main pour prendre sa lampe de poche.

react [riːˈækt] vb réagir

reaction [riːˈækʃən] n réaction f

reactor [riːˈæktəʳ] n réacteur m ▷ *a nuclear reactor* un réacteur nucléaire

read [riːd] vb lire ▷ *I don't read much.* Je ne lis pas beaucoup. ▷ *Have you read this book?* Est-ce que tu as lu ce livre? ▷ *Read the text out loud.* Lis le texte à haute voix.

reader [ˈriːdəʳ] n *(person)* lecteur m, lectrice f

readily [ˈrɛdɪlɪ] adv volontiers ▷ *She readily agreed.* Elle a accepté volontiers.

reading [ˈriːdɪŋ] n lecture f ▷ *Reading is one of my hobbies.* La lecture est l'une de mes activités favorites.

ready [ˈrɛdɪ] adj prêt ▷ *She's nearly ready.* Elle est presque prête. ▷ *He's always ready to help.* Il est toujours prêt à rendre service.; **to get ready** se préparer ▷ *She's getting ready to go out.* Elle est en train de se préparer pour sortir.; **to get something**

ready préparer quelque chose ▷ *He's getting dinner ready.* Il est en train de préparer le dîner.

ready-made ['rɛdɪ'meɪd] *adj* ❶ tout fait ▷ *ready-made curtains* des rideaux tous faits ▷ *a ready-made solution* une solution toute faite ❷ *(food)* cuisiné ▷ *a ready-made meal* un plat cuisiné

real [rɪəl] *adj* ❶ vrai ▷ *He wasn't a real policeman.* Ce n'était pas un vrai policier. ▷ *Her real name is Cordelia.* Son vrai nom est Cordelia. ❷ véritable ▷ *It's real leather.* C'est du cuir véritable. ▷ *It was a real nightmare.* C'était un véritable cauchemar.; **in real life** dans la réalité

real estate *n* immobilier *m* ▷ *He works in real estate.* Il travaille dans l'immobilier.; **a real estate agency** une agence immobilière; **a real estate agent** un agent immobilier

realistic [rɪə'lɪstɪk] *adj* réaliste

reality [rɪː'ælɪtɪ] *n* réalité *f*

realize ['rɪəlaɪz] *vb*: **to realize that...** se rendre compte que ... ▷ *We realized that something was wrong.* Nous nous sommes rendu compte que quelque chose n'allait pas.

really ['rɪəlɪ] *adv* vraiment ▷ *She's really nice.* Elle est vraiment sympathique. ▷ *"Do you want to go?" — "Not really."* « Tu veux y aller ? » — « Pas vraiment. »; **"I'm learning to ride." — "Really?"** « J'apprends à monter à cheval. » — « Ah bon ? »; **Do you really think so?** Tu es sûr?

rear [rɪə] *adj* arrière *(f+pl* arrière*)* ▷ *a rear wheel* une roue arrière ▶ *n* arrière *m* ▷ *at the rear of the train* à l'arrière du train

reason ['riːzn] *n* raison *f* ▷ *There's no reason to think that...* Il n'y a aucune raison de penser que...; **for**

security reasons pour des raisons de sécurité; **That was the main reason I went.** C'est surtout pour ça que j'y suis allé.

reasonable ['riːznəbl] *adj* ❶ *(sensible)* raisonnable ▷ *Be reasonable!* Sois raisonnable! ❷ *(not bad)* convenable ▷ *He wrote a reasonable essay.* Sa dissertation était convenable.

reasonably ['riːznəblɪ] *adv* raisonnablement ▷ *The team played reasonably well.* L'équipe a joué raisonnablement bien.; **reasonably priced accommodation** un logement à un prix raisonnable

reassure [riːə'ʃuə] *vb* rassurer

reassuring [riːə'ʃuərɪŋ] *adj* rassurant

rebellious [rɪ'bɛljəs] *adj* rebelle

reboot [riː'buːt] *vb* redémarrer ▷ *I rebooted the computer.* J'ai redémarré l'ordinateur.

receipt [rɪ'siːt] *n* reçu *m*

receive [rɪ'siːv] *vb* recevoir

receiver [rɪ'siːvə] *n (of phone)* combiné *m*; **to pick up the receiver** décrocher

recent ['riːsnt] *adj* récent

recently ['riːsntlɪ] *adv* ces derniers temps ▷ *I've been doing a lot of biking recently.* J'ai fait beaucoup de cyclisme ces derniers temps.

reception [rɪ'sɛpʃən] *n* réception ▷ *Please leave your key at reception.* Merci de laisser votre clé à la réception. ▷ *The reception will be at a big hotel.* La réception aura lieu dans un grand hôtel.

receptionist [rɪ'sɛpʃənɪst] *n* réceptionniste

recession [rɪ'sɛʃən] *n* récession *f*

recipe ['rɛsɪpɪ] *n* recette *f*

reclining [rɪ'klaɪnɪŋ] *adj*: **a reclining armchair** un fauteuil inclinable; **a reclining seat** (in plane, car) un siège inclinable

recognizable ['rekəgnaɪzəbl] adj reconnaissable

recognize ['rekəgnaɪz] vb reconnaître ▷ You'll recognize me by my red hair. Vous me reconnaîtrez à mes cheveux roux.

recommend [rekə'mend] vb recommander ▷ What do you recommend? Qu'est-ce que vous me recommandez?

reconsider [ri:kən'sɪdər] vb reconsidérer

record [n 'rekəd, vb rɪ'kɔːd] n
❶ (recording) disque m ▷ my favourite record mon disque préféré
❷ (sport) record m ▷ the world record le record du monde; **in record time** en un temps record ▷ She finished the job in record time. Elle a terminé le travail en un temps record.; **a criminal record** un casier judiciaire ▷ She's got a criminal record. Elle a un casier judiciaire.; **records** (of police, hospital) les archives ▷ I'll check the records. Je vais vérifier dans les archives.; **There is no record of your booking.** Il n'y a aucune trace de votre réservation.
▶ vb (on film, tape) enregistrer ▷ They've just recorded their new album. Ils viennent d'enregistrer leur nouveau disque.

recorder [rɪ'kɔːdər] n (instrument) flûte à bec f ▷ She plays the recorder. Elle joue de la flûte à bec.; **a cassette recorder** un magnétophone à cassettes; **a video recorder** un magnétoscope

recording [rɪ'kɔːdɪŋ] n enregistrement m

record player n tourne-disque m

recover [rɪ'kʌvər] vb se remettre ▷ He's recovering from a knee injury. Il se remet d'une blessure au genou.

recovery [rɪ'kʌvərɪ] n rétablissement; **Best wishes for a speedy recovery!** Meilleurs vœux de prompt rétablissement!

recreational vehicle [rekrɪ'eɪʃənl-] n caravane f

rec room ['rek-] n salle de jeux f

rectangle ['rektæŋgl] n rectangle m

rectangular [rek'tæŋgjulər] adj rectangulaire

recycle [ri:'saɪkl] vb recycler

recycling [ri:'saɪklɪŋ] n recyclage m

red [red] adj **❶** rouge ▷ a red rose une rose rouge ▷ red meat la viande rouge; **a red light** (traffic light) un feu rouge ▷ to go through a red light brûler un feu rouge **❷** (hair) roux m (f rousse) ▷ He's got red hair. Il a les cheveux roux.

Red Crescent [-'kresnt] n Croissant-Rouge

Red Cross n Croix-Rouge

redecorate [ri:'dekəreɪt] vb redécorer

red-haired [red'heəd] adj roux m (f rousse)

red-handed [red'hændɪd] adj: **to catch somebody red-handed** prendre quelqu'un la main dans le sac ▷ We were caught red-handed. Nous avons été pris la main dans le sac.

redhead ['redhed] n roux, rousse f

redo [ri:'du:] vb refaire

reduce [rɪ'dju:s] vb réduire ▷ at a reduced price à prix réduit; **Reduce, reuse, recycle.** Réduire, réutiliser, recycler.

reduction [rɪ'dʌkʃən] n réduction f ▷ a 5% reduction une réduction de cinq pour cent

redwood ['redwud] n séquoia m

reed [ri:d] n (plant) roseau m (pl roseaux)

reel [riːl] *n* (*on fishing rod*) moulinet *m*

reel in *vb* ramener ▷ *I reeled in a huge trout.* J'ai ramené une truite énorme.

refer [rɪˈfɜːʳ] *vb*: **to refer to** faire allusion à ▷ *What are you referring to?* À quoi faites-vous allusion?

referee [rɛfəˈriː] *n* arbitre *m*

reference [ˈrɛfrəns] *n* ❶ allusion *f* ▷ *He made no reference to the incident.* Il n'a fait aucune allusion à l'incident. ❷ (*for job application*) références *fpl* ▷ *Would you please give me a reference?* Pouvez-vous me fournir des références?; **a reference book** un ouvrage de référence

refill [ˈriːfɪl] *vb* remplir à nouveau ▷ *She refilled my glass.* Elle a rempli mon verre à nouveau.

refinery [rɪˈfaɪnərɪ] *n* raffinerie *f*

reflect [rɪˈflɛkt] *vb* (*light, image*) refléter

reflection [rɪˈflɛkʃən] *n* (*in mirror*) reflet *m*

reflex [ˈriːflɛks] *n* réflexe *m*

reflexive [rɪˈflɛksɪv] *adj* réfléchi ▷ *a reflexive verb* un verbe réfléchi

refresher course [rɪˈfrɛʃəˈ-] *n* cours de recyclage *m*

refreshing [rɪˈfrɛʃɪŋ] *adj* rafraîchissant

refreshments [rɪˈfrɛʃmənts] *npl* rafraîchissements *mpl*

refrigerator [rɪˈfrɪdʒəreɪtəʳ] *n* réfrigérateur *m*

refuel [riːˈfjuəl] *vb* se ravitailler en carburant ▷ *The plane stops in Montréal to refuel.* L'avion s'arrête à Montréal pour se ravitailler en carburant.

refuge [ˈrɛfjuːdʒ] *n* refuge *m*

refugee [rɛfjuˈdʒiː] *n* réfugié *m*, réfugiée *f*

refund [ˈriːfʌnd] *n* remboursement

m
   ▶ *vb* rembourser

refusal [rɪˈfjuːzəl] *n* refus *m*

refuse [rɪˈfjuːz] *vb* refuser

regain [rɪˈgeɪn] *vb*: **to regain consciousness** reprendre connaissance

regard [rɪˈgɑːd] *n*: **Give my regards to your mom.** Transmettez mon bon souvenir à ta mère.; **My parents send their regards.** Vous avez le bonjour de mes parents.; **with regard to** quant à ▷ *with regard to the new rule...* quant au nouveau règlement...
   ▶ *vb*: **to regard something as** considérer quelque chose comme; **as regards...** concernant...

regarding [rɪˈgɑːdɪŋ] *prep* relatif à (*f* relative à) ▷ *the laws regarding the export of animals* les lois relatives à l'exportation des animaux; **Regarding your oral presentations,...** Quant à vos présentations orales,...

regardless [rɪˈgɑːdlɪs] *adv* (*nevertheless*) quand même ▷ *We will go regardless.* Nous irons quand même.; **regardless of the weather** peu importe le temps; **regardless of the consequences** peu importent les conséquences

regiment [ˈrɛdʒɪmənt] *n* régiment *m*

region [ˈriːdʒən] *n* région *f*

regional [ˈriːdʒənl] *adj* régional (*pl* régionaux)

register [ˈrɛdʒɪstəʳ] *vb* (*sign up, enroll*) s'inscrire

registered [ˈrɛdʒɪstəd] *adj*: **a registered letter** une lettre recommandée

registration [rɛdʒɪsˈtreɪʃən] *n* inscription *f* ▷ *The deadline for registration is March 6.* La date limite pour l'inscription est le 6 mars.

regret [rɪ'grɛt] n regret m; **I have
no regrets.** Je ne regrette rien.
▶ vb regretter ▷ Give me the money or
you'll regret it! Donne-moi l'argent,
sinon tu vas le regretter!; **to regret
doing something** regretter d'avoir
fait quelque chose ▷ I regret saying
that. Je regrette d'avoir dit ça.

regular ['rɛgjulə'] adj ❶ régulier
(f régulière) ▷ at regular intervals
à intervalles réguliers ▷ a regular
verb un verbe régulier ❷ (standard)
normal (pl normaux) ▷ a regular
portion of fries une portion de frites
normale

regularly ['rɛgjuləlɪ] adv
régulièrement ▷ to exercise regularly
faire de l'exercice régulièrement

regulation [rɛgju'leɪʃən] n
règlement m

rehearsal [rɪ'hə:səl] n répétition f

rehearse [rɪ'hə:s] vb répéter

rein [reɪn] n rêne f ▷ the reins les
rênes

reindeer ['reɪndɪə'] n renne m

reject [rɪ'dʒɛkt] vb (idea, suggestion)
rejeter ▷ We rejected that idea right
away. Nous avons immédiatement
rejeté cette idée.; **I auditioned for
the part but they rejected me.**
J'ai auditionné pour le rôle, mais ils
m'ont rejeté.

relapse [rɪ'læps] n rechute f ▷ to
have a relapse faire une rechute

related [rɪ'leɪtɪd] adj (people)
apparenté ▷ We're related. Nous
sommes apparentés.; **The two
events were not related.** Il n'y
avait aucun rapport entre les deux
événements.

relation [rɪ'leɪʃən] n
❶ (connection) rapport m ▷ It has
no relation to reality. Cela n'a aucun
rapport avec la réalité.; **in relation
to** par rapport à ❷ (person) parent
m, parente f ▷ He's a distant relation.

C'est un parent éloigné.

relationship [rɪ'leɪʃənʃɪp] n
relations fpl ▷ We have a good
relationship. Nous avons de
bonnes relations.; **I'm not in a
relationship at the moment.** Je ne
sors avec personne en ce moment.

relative ['rɛlətɪv] n parent m,
parente f ▷ my close relatives mes
proches parents; **all her relatives**
toute sa famille

relatively ['rɛlətɪvlɪ] adv
relativement

relax [rɪ'læks] vb se détendre ▷ I
listen to music to relax. J'écoute de
la musique pour me détendre.;
Relax! Everything's fine. Ne t'en
fais pas! Tout va bien.

relaxation [ri:læk'seɪʃən] n
détente f ▷ I don't have much time for
relaxation. Je n'ai pas beaucoup de
moments de détente.

relaxed [rɪ'lækst] adj détendu

relaxing [rɪ'læksɪŋ] adj reposant;
I find cooking relaxing. Cela me
détend de faire la cuisine.

relay ['ri:leɪ] n: **a relay race** une
course de relais

release [rɪ'li:s] vb ❶ (prisoner)
libérer ❷ (report, news) divulguer
❸ (record, video) sortir
▶ n (from prison) libération f ▷ the
release of the hostages la libération
des otages; **the band's latest
release** le dernier disque du
groupe; **a press release** un
communiqué

relevant ['rɛləvənt] adj
(documents) approprié; **That's not
relevant.** Ça n'a aucun rapport.;
to be relevant to something être
en rapport avec quelque chose
▷ Education should be relevant to real
life. L'enseignement devrait être en
rapport avec la réalité.

reliable [rɪ'laɪəbl] adj fiable ▷ a

reliable car une voiture fiable ▷ *He's not very reliable.* Il n'est pas très fiable.

relief [rɪˈliːf] *n* soulagement *m* ▷ *That's a relief!* Quel soulagement!

relieve [rɪˈliːv] *vb* soulager ▷ *This injection will relieve the pain.* Cette piqûre va soulager la douleur. ▷ *I was relieved to hear...* J'ai été soulagé d'apprendre...

religion [rɪˈlɪdʒən] *n* religion *f*

religious [rɪˈlɪdʒəs] *adj* ❶ religieux (*f* religieuse) ▷ *my religious beliefs* mes croyances religieuses ❷ croyant ▷ *Are you religious?* Tu es croyant?

reluctant [rɪˈlʌktənt] *adj:* **to be reluctant to do something** être peu disposé à faire quelque chose ▷ *They were reluctant to help us.* Ils étaient peu disposés à nous aider.

reluctantly [rɪˈlʌktəntlɪ] *adv* à contrecœur ▷ *She reluctantly accepted.* Elle a accepté à contrecœur.

rely on [rɪˈlaɪ-] *vb* compter sur ▷ *I'm relying on you.* Je compte sur toi.

remain [rɪˈmeɪn] *vb* rester; **to remain silent** garder le silence

remaining [rɪˈmeɪnɪŋ] *adj:* **the remaining ingredients** le reste des ingrédients; **my one remaining friend** le seul ami qui me reste

remains [rɪˈmeɪnz] *npl* restes *mpl* ▷ *the remains of the picnic* les restes du pique-nique ▷ *human remains* des restes humains

remake [ˈriːmeɪk] *n* (*of film*) nouvelle version *f*

remark [rɪˈmɑːk] *n* remarque *f*

remarkable [rɪˈmɑːkəbl] *adj* remarquable

remarkably [rɪˈmɑːkəblɪ] *adv* remarquablement

remarry [riːˈmærɪ] *vb* se remarier

▷ *She remarried three years ago.* Elle s'est remariée il y a trois ans.

rematch [ˈriːmætʃ] *n:* **There will be a rematch on Friday.** Le match sera rejoué vendredi.

remedy [ˈrɛmədɪ] *n* remède *m* ▷ *a good remedy for sore throat* un bon remède contre le mal de gorge

remember [rɪˈmɛmbəˈ] *vb* se souvenir de ▷ *I can't remember his name.* Je ne me souviens pas de son nom. ▷ *I don't remember.* Je ne m'en souviens pas.

> In French you often say "don't forget" instead of **remember**.
> ▷ *Remember your passport!* N'oublie pas ton passeport! ▷ *Remember to write your name on the form.* N'oubliez pas d'écrire votre nom sur le formulaire.

Remembrance Day [rɪˈmɛmbrəns-] *n* jour *m* du Souvenir ▷ *on Remembrance Day* le jour du Souvenir

remind [rɪˈmaɪnd] *vb* rappeler ▷ *It reminds me of Newfoundland.* Cela me rappelle Terre-Neuve. ▷ *I'll remind you tomorrow.* Je te le rappellerai demain. ▷ *Remind me to speak to the principal.* Rappelle-moi de parler au directeur.

remorse [rɪˈmɔːs] *n* remords *m* ▷ *He showed no remorse.* Il n'a manifesté aucun remords.

remote [rɪˈməʊt] *adj* isolé ▷ *a remote village* un village isolé

remote control *n* télécommande *f*

remotely [rɪˈməʊtlɪ] *adv:* **I'm not remotely interested.** Je ne suis absolument pas intéressé.; **Do you think it would be remotely possible?** Pensez-vous que cela serait éventuellement possible?

removable [rɪˈmuːvəbl] *adj* amovible

remove [rɪˈmuːv] *vb* ❶ enlever

> *Please remove your bag from my seat.*
Est-ce que vous pouvez enlever
votre sac de mon siège? ▷ *She
removed her coat.* Elle a enlevé son
manteau. ❷ (*stain*) faire partir
▷ *Did you remove the stain?* Est-ce
que tu as fait partir la tache?

rendezvous ['rɒndɪvuː] n rendez-
vous m (pl rendez-vous)

renew [rɪ'njuː] vb (*passport, licence*)
renouveler

renewable [rɪ'njuːəbl] adj (*energy,
resource*) renouvelable

renovate ['renəveɪt] vb rénover
▷ *The building's been renovated.* Le
bâtiment a été rénové.

renowned [rɪ'naund] adj
renommé

rent [rent] n loyer m
▶ vb louer ▷ *We rented a car.* Nous
avons loué une voiture.

rental ['rentl] n location f ▷ *Car
rental is included in the price.* Le
prix comprend la location d'une voiture.

rental car n voiture de location

reorganize [riːˈɔːɡənaɪz] vb
réorganiser

rep [rep] n (= *representative*)
représentant m, représentante f

repaid [riːˈpeɪd] vb see **repay**

repair [rɪ'pɛəʳ] vb réparer ; **to get
something repaired** faire réparer
quelque chose ▷ *We got the washing
machine repaired.* Nous avons fait
réparer la laveuse.
▶ n réparation f

repay [riːˈpeɪ] vb (*money*)
rembourser

repayment [riːˈpeɪmənt] n
remboursement m

repeat [rɪ'piːt] vb répéter
▶ n répétition f ▷ *This lesson was
just a repeat of the last one.* Cette
leçon n'était qu'une répétition de la
précédente.

repeatedly [rɪ'piːtɪdlɪ] adv à

plusieurs reprises

repellent [rɪ'pɛlənt] n: **insect
repellent** l'insectifuge m;
mosquito repellent la lotion
antimoustiques

repetitive [rɪ'pɛtɪtɪv] adj
❶ (*movement, work*) répétitif (f
répétitive) ❷ (*writing, speech*) plein
de redites

replace [rɪ'pleɪs] vb remplacer

replay ['riːpleɪ] n reproduction f
▷ *an instant replay* une reproduction
instantanée

replica ['rɛplɪkə] n réplique f

reply [rɪ'plaɪ] n réponse f
▶ vb répondre

report [rɪ'pɔːt] n ❶ (*of event*)
compte rendu m (pl comptes
rendus) ❷ (*news report*) reportage
m ▷ *a report in the paper* un
reportage dans le journal ❸ (*at
school*) bulletin scolaire m ▷ *I got
a good report this term.* J'ai un bon
bulletin scolaire ce trimestre.;
report card le bulletin scolaire
▶ vb ❶ signaler ▷ *I reported the theft
to the police.* J'ai signalé le vol à la
police. ❷ se présenter ▷ *Report to
reception when you arrive.* Présentez-
vous à la réception à votre arrivée.;
to report on something rendre
compte de quelque chose

reporter [rɪ'pɔːtəʳ] n reporter
▷ *She is a reporter.* Elle est reporter.

represent [rɛprɪ'zɛnt] vb
représenter

representative [rɛprɪ'zɛntətɪv]
adj représentatif (f représentative)

reproduction [riːprəˈdʌkʃən] n
reproduction f

reptile ['rɛptaɪl] n reptile m

republic [rɪ'pʌblɪk] n république f

repulsive [rɪ'pʌlsɪv] adj
repoussant

reputable ['rɛpjutəbl] adj de
bonne réputation

reputation [rɛpjʊ'teɪʃən] *n*
réputation *f*

request [rɪ'kwɛst] *n* demande *f*
▶ *vb* demander

require [rɪ'kwaɪəʳ] *vb* exiger ▷ *The job requires a good knowledge of classical music.* Cet emploi exige une bonne connaissance de la musique classique.; **a required course** une matière obligatoire

requirement [rɪ'kwaɪəmənt] *n* condition requise *f* ▷ **to meet the requirements** remplir les conditions requises; **to meet somebody's requirements** (*please somebody*) satisfaire aux exigences de quelqu'un; **entry requirements** (*for university*) les critères d'admission

rerun ['riːrʌn] *n* rediffusion *f* ▷ *There's nothing but reruns on TV tonight.* Il n'y a que des rediffusions à la télé ce soir.

rescue ['rɛskjuː] *vb* sauver
▶ *n* ❶ sauvetage *m* ▷ *a rescue operation* une opération de sauvetage ▷ *a rescue team* une équipe de sauvetage ▷ *rescue services* les services de secours; **to come to somebody's rescue** venir au secours de quelqu'un ▷ *He came to my rescue.* Il est venu à mon secours.

research [rɪ'səːtʃ] *n*
❶ (*experimental*) recherche *f* ▷ *He's doing research.* Il fait de la recherche.
❷ (*theoretical*) recherches *fpl*
▷ *She's doing some research in the library.* Elle fait des recherches à la bibliothèque.

resemblance [rɪ'zɛmbləns] *n* ressemblance *f* ▷ *a strong family resemblance* une grande ressemblance de famille

resent [rɪ'zɛnt] *vb* être contrarié par ▷ *I really resented your criticism.* J'ai été vraiment contrarié par tes

critiques.

resentful [rɪ'zɛntful] *adj* plein de ressentiment; **to feel resentful towards somebody** en vouloir à quelqu'un

reservation [rɛzə'veɪʃən] *n* (*booking*) réservation *f* ▷ *I'd like to make a reservation for this evening.* J'aimerais faire une réservation pour ce soir.

reserve [rɪ'zəːv] *n* réserve *f* ▷ *a First Nations reserve* une réserve indienne ▷ *a nature reserve* une réserve naturelle; **oil reserves** des réserves de pétrole; **to hold something in reserve** tenir quelque chose en réserve
▶ *vb* réserver ▷ *I'd like to reserve a table for tomorrow evening.* J'aimerais réserver une table pour demain soir.

reserved [rɪ'zəːvd] *adj* réservé ▷ *a reserved seat* une place réservée

reservoir ['rɛzəvwɑː'] *n* réservoir *m*

resident ['rɛzɪdənt] *n* résident *m*, résidente *f*

residential [rɛzɪ'dɛnʃəl] *adj* résidentiel (*f* résidentielle) ▷ *a residential area* un quartier résidentiel

resign [rɪ'zaɪn] *vb* donner sa démission

resist [rɪ'zɪst] *vb* résister à ▷ *to resist authority* résister à l'autorité; **Sorry, I couldn't resist!** Pardon, je n'ai pas pu résister!; **I couldn't resist having another cookie.** Je n'ai pas pu m'empêcher de prendre encore un biscuit.

resolution [rɛzə'luːʃən] *n* résolution *f*; **Have you made any New Year's resolutions?** Tu as pris de bonnes résolutions pour l'année nouvelle?

resort [rɪ'zɔːt] *n* centre de

villégiature *m*; **a ski resort** une station de ski; **a seaside resort** une station balnéaire; **as a last resort** en dernier recours

resource [rɪ'sɔːs] *n* ressource *f*

resourceful [rɪ'sɔːsful] *adj* débrouillard

respect [rɪs'pɛkt] *n* respect *m* ▸ *vb* respecter

respectable [rɪs'pɛktəbl] *adj* ① respectable ② (standard, marks) correct

respectively [rɪs'pɛktɪvlɪ] *adv* respectivement

responsibility [rɪspɔnsɪ'bɪlɪtɪ] *n* responsabilité *f*

responsible [rɪs'pɔnsɪbl] *adj* ① responsable ▷ *He's responsible for booking the tickets.* Il est responsable de la réservation des billets. ▷ *Humans are responsible for the destruction of animal habitats.* Les humains sont responsables de la destruction des habitats des animaux.; **to hold somebody responsible for something** tenir quelqu'un responsable de quelque chose; **Who is responsible for this mess?** Qui a fait ce gâchis?; **She is responsible for our success.** Nous lui devons notre success.; **It's a responsible job.** C'est une poste à responsabilités. ② (mature) sérieux (*f* sérieuse) ▷ *You should be more responsible.* Tu devrais être un peu plus sérieux.

rest [rɛst] *n* ① (relaxation) repos *m* ▷ *five minutes' rest* cinq minutes de repos; **to have a rest** ▷ *We stopped to have a rest.* Nous nous sommes arrêtés pour nous reposer. ② (remainder) reste *m* ▷ *I'll do the rest.* Je ferai le reste. ▷ *the rest of the money* le reste de l'argent; **the rest of them** les autres ▷ *The rest of them went swimming.* Les autres

sont allés nager.
▸ *vb* ① (relax) se reposer ▷ *She's resting in her room.* Elle se repose dans sa chambre. ② (not overstrain) ménager ▷ *He has to rest his knee.* Il doit ménager son genou. ③ (lean) appuyer ▷ *I rested my bike against the wall.* J'ai appuyé mon vélo contre le mur.

restaurant [ˈrɔstərɔ̃ŋ] *n* restaurant *m* ▷ *We don't often go to restaurants.* Nous n'allons pas souvent au restaurant.; **a restaurant car** (on train) un wagon-restaurant

restful [ˈrɛstful] *adj* reposant

restless [ˈrɛstlɪs] *adj* agité

restoration [rɛstəˈreɪʃən] *n* restauration *f*

restore [rɪsˈtɔːʳ] *vb* (building, picture) restaurer

restrict [rɪsˈtrɪkt] *vb* limiter

rest stop *n* ① halte routière *f* ▷ *We ate our sandwiches at the rest stop.* Nous avons mangé nos sandwichs à la halte routière. ② (with restaurant, gas station) restauroute *m*

result [rɪ'zʌlt] *n* résultat *m* ▷ *my exam results* mes résultats d'examen ▷ *"What was the result?" — "One-nothing."* « Quel a été le résultat? » — « Un à zéro. »; **as a result of** à la suite de
▸ *vb*: **to result in** entraîner; **to result from** résulter de

resume [rɪ'zjuːm] *vb* reprendre ▷ *They've resumed work.* Ils ont repris le travail.

> Be careful not to translate **to resume** by *résumer*.

résumé [ˈreɪzjuːmeɪ] *n* curriculum vitae *m*

retire [rɪ'taɪəʳ] *vb* prendre sa retraite ▷ *He retired last year.* Il a pris sa retraite l'an dernier.

retired [rɪ'taɪəd] *adj* retraité ▷ *She's retired.* Elle est retraitée.; **a retired teacher** un professeur à la retraite

retirement [rɪ'taɪəmənt] *n* retraite *f*

retrace [riː'treɪs] *vb*: **to retrace one's steps** revenir sur ses pas ▷ *I retraced my steps.* Je suis revenu sur mes pas.

return [rɪ'tɜːn] *n* retour *m* ▷ *after our return* à notre retour; **the return trip** le voyage de retour; **a return match** un match retour; **a return ticket** un aller et retour ▷ *A return ticket to Winnipeg, please.* Un aller et retour pour Winnipeg, s'il vous plaît.; **It costs $500 return.** L'aller et retour coûte cinq cents dollars.; **in return** en échange ▷ *...and I help her in return ...et je l'aide en échange;* **in return for** en échange de; **Many happy returns!** Bonne fête!
▶ *vb* ❶ (*come back*) revenir ▷ *I've just returned from vacation.* Je viens de revenir de vacances.; **to return home** rentrer à la maison ❷ (*go back*) retourner ▷ *He returned to Inuvik the following year.* Il est retourné à Inuvik l'année suivante. ❸ (*give back*) rendre ▷ *She borrows my things and doesn't return them.* Elle m'emprunte mes affaires et ne me les rend pas.

reunion [riː'juːnɪən] *n* réunion *f*
reuse [riː'juːz] *vb* réutiliser
reveal [rɪ'viːl] *vb* révéler
revenge [rɪ'vɛndʒ] *n* vengeance *f* ▷ *in revenge* par vengeance; **to take revenge (1)** se venger ▷ *They planned to take revenge on him.* Ils voulaient se venger de lui. **(2)** (*sports*) prendre sa revanche ▷ *The player who was defeated yesterday will be able to take revenge at tomorrow's game.* La joueuse battue

hier pourra prendre sa revanche au match de demain.

reverse [rɪ'vɜːs] *vb* inverser ▷ *She reversed the two numbers by mistake.* Elle a inversé les deux chiffres par erreur.; **to reverse the charges** (*telephone*) virer les frais; **a call with charges reversed** un appel à frais virés
▶ *n*: **in reverse** dans l'ordre inverse ▷ *Now do the whole thing in reverse.* Maintenant fait tout dans l'ordre inverse.; **This is the reverse of what happened yesterday.** C'est le contraire de ce qui est arrivé hier.
▶ *adj* inverse ▷ *in reverse order* dans l'ordre inverse; **in reverse gear** en marche arrière

review [rɪ'vjuː] *n* ❶ révision *f* ▷ *We will have a thorough review before the test.* Nous ferons une révision complète avant l'épreuve. ❷ (*of book, film, programme*) critique *f* ▷ *The book had good reviews.* Ce livre a eu de bonnes critiques.
▶ *vb* ❶ réviser ▷ *The class reviewed the last chapter together.* La classe a révisé le dernier chapitre ensemble. ❷ faire la critique de ▷ *She reviewed the concert for the school newspaper.* Elle a fait la critique du concert pour le journal de l'école.

revise [rɪ'vaɪz] *vb* réviser ▷ *They revise the dictionary every five years.* On révise le dictionnaire tous les cinq ans. ▷ *the revised edition* l'édition révisée; **I've revised my opinion.** J'ai changé d'opinion.

revive [rɪ'vaɪv] *vb* ranimer ▷ *The nurses tried to revive him.* Les infirmières ont essayé de le ranimer.

revolting [rɪ'vəʊltɪŋ] *adj* dégoûtant

revolution [rɛvə'luːʃən] *n* révolution *f*; **the Quiet Revolution**

la révolution tranquille

revolutionary [rɛvəˈluːʃənrɪ] *adj*
révolutionnaire

revolve [rɪˈvɒlv] *vb* tourner ▷ *The
earth revolves around the sun.* La terre
tourne autour du soleil.

reward [rɪˈwɔːd] *n* récompense *f*;
a rewards card (*at store*) une carte
de fidélité

rewarding [rɪˈwɔːdɪŋ] *adj*
gratifiant ▷ *a rewarding job* un
travail gratifiant

rewind [riːˈwaɪnd] *vb* rembobiner
▷ *to rewind a cassette* rembobiner
une cassette

rheumatism [ˈruːmətɪzəm] *n*
rhumatisme *m*

rhinoceros [raɪˈnɒsərəs] *n*
rhinocéros *m*

rhubarb [ˈruːbɑːb] *n* rhubarbe *f* ▷ *a
rhubarb pie* une tarte à la rhubarbe

rhyme [raɪm] *vb* rimer

rhythm [ˈrɪðm] *n* rythme *m*

rib [rɪb] *n* côte *f*

ribbon [ˈrɪbən] *n* ruban *m*

rice [raɪs] *n* riz *m*; **rice pudding** le
pudding au riz

rich [rɪtʃ] *adj* riche; **the rich** les
m riches

rid [rɪd] *vb*: **to get rid of** se
débarrasser de ▷ *I want to get
rid of some old clothes.* Je veux me
débarrasser de vieux vêtements.

ridden [ˈrɪdn] *vb* see **ride**

ride [raɪd] *n*: **to go for a ride (1)** (*on
horse*) monter à cheval (*2*) (*on bike*)
faire un tour en vélo ▷ *We went for
a bike ride.* Nous sommes allés faire
un tour en vélo.; **Can you give
me a ride to the mall?** Tu peux
m'emmener au centre commercial
dans ta voiture?; **It's a short bus
ride to the town centre.** Ce n'est
pas loin du centre-ville en autobus.;
**I had three rides on the roller
coaster.** J'ai fait trois tours de

montagnes russes.
▶ *vb* (*on horse*) monter à cheval ▷ *I'm
learning to ride.* J'apprends à monter
à cheval.; **to ride a bike** faire du
vélo ▷ *Can you ride a bike?* Est-ce que
tu sais faire du vélo?; **We rode into
town on the bus.** Nous avons pris
l'autobus pour aller en ville.

rider [ˈraɪdə] *n* ❶ (*on horse*)
cavalier *m*, cavalière *f* ▷ *She's a good
rider.* C'est une bonne cavalière.
❷ (*on bike*) cycliste

ridiculous [rɪˈdɪkjʊləs] *adj* ridicule
▷ *Don't be ridiculous!* Ne sois pas
ridicule!

riding [ˈraɪdɪŋ] *n* ❶ (*for voting*)
circonscription électorale *f*
❷ équitation *f*; **to go riding** faire
de l'équitation; **a riding school** une
école d'équitation

rifle [ˈraɪfl] *n* fusil *m* ▷ *a hunting rifle*
un fusil de chasse

rig [rɪg] *vb* truquer. ▷ *The election
was rigged.* L'élection a été truquée.

right [raɪt] *adj, adv*

> There are several ways of
> translating **right**. Scan the
> examples to find one that
> is similar to what you want
> to say.

❶ (*factually correct, suitable*) bon (*f*
bonne) ▷ *the right answer* la bonne
réponse ▷ *It isn't the right size.* Ce
n'est pas la bonne taille. ▷ *We're
on the right train.* Nous sommes
dans le bon train.; **Is this the right
road for Peterborough?** Est-ce
que c'est bien la route pour aller
à Peterborough?; **to be right
(1)** (*person*) avoir raison ▷ *You were
right!* Tu avais raison! (*2*) (*statement,
opinion*) être vrai ▷ *That's right!* C'est
vrai! ❷ (*correctly*) correctement
▷ *Am I pronouncing it right?* Est-ce
que je prononce ça correctement?
❸ (*accurate*) juste ▷ *Do you have*

the right time? Est-ce que vous avez l'heure juste? ❹ (morally correct) bien ▷ It's not right to behave like that. Ce n'est pas bien d'agir comme ça.; **I think you did the right thing.** Je pense que tu as bien fait. ❺ (not left) droit m ▷ my right hand ma main droite ❻ (turn, look) à droite ▷ Turn right at the traffic lights. Tournez à droite aux prochains feux.; **Right! Let's get started.** Bon! On commence!; **right away** tout de suite ▷ I'll do it right away. Je vais le faire tout de suite.; **right side out** à l'endroit ▷ Put your T-shirt on again right side out. Remets ton T-shirt à l'endroit.; **right way up** à l'endroit ▷ This picture is sideways. It must be put the right way up. Ce tableau est de travers. Il faut le remettre à l'endroit.
▶ n ❶ droit m; **You have no right to do that.** Vous n'avez pas le droit de faire ça. ❷ (not left) droite f; **on the right** à droite ▷ Our house is on the right. Notre maison est à droite.; **right of way** la priorité ▷ It was our right of way. Nous avions la priorité.

right-hand [ˈraɪthænd] adj: **the right-hand side** la droite ▷ It's on the right-hand side. C'est à droite.; **the right-hand drawer** le tiroir de droite

right-handed [raɪtˈhændɪd] adj droitier (f droitière)

rightly [ˈraɪtlɪ] adv avec raison ▷ He rightly decided not to go. Il a décidé, avec raison, de ne pas y aller.; **if I remember rightly** si je me souviens bien

rim [rɪm] n ❶ (edge) bord m ❷ monture f ▷ glasses with wire rims des lunettes avec une monture métallique

ring [rɪŋ] n ❶ anneau m (pl anneaux) ▷ a gold ring un anneau

en or ❷ (with stones) bague f ▷ a diamond ring une bague de diamants; **a wedding ring** une alliance ❸ (circle) cercle m ▷ to stand in a ring se mettre en cercle ❹ (of bell) coup de sonnette m ▷ I was woken by a ring at the door. J'ai été réveillé par un coup de sonnette.
▶ vb sonner ▷ The phone's ringing. Le téléphone sonne.; **to ring the bell** (doorbell) sonner à la porte ▷ I rang the bell three times. J'ai sonné trois fois à la porte.

rink [rɪŋk] n ❶ (for ice-skating) patinoire f ❷ (for roller-skating) piste f

rinse [rɪns] vb rincer

riot [ˈraɪət] n émeute f
▶ vb faire une émeute

rip [rɪp] vb ❶ déchirer ▷ I've ripped my jeans. J'ai déchiré mes jeans. ❷ se déchirer ▷ My skirt ripped. Ma jupe s'est déchirée.

rip off vb ❶ (cheat) escroquer ▷ The hotel ripped us off. L'hôtel nous a escroqués. ❷ copier ▷ He ripped off that idea from a movie. Il a copié cette idée d'un film.

rip up vb déchirer ▷ He read the note and then ripped it up. Il a lu le mot, puis l'a déchiré.

ripe [raɪp] adj mûr

rip-off [ˈrɪpɒf] n: **It's a rip-off!** (informal) C'est du vol!; **Those shoes are just a rip-off of the other brand.** Ces souliers ne sont qu'une imitation de l'autre marque.

rise [raɪz] n (in prices, temperature) hausse f ▷ a sudden rise in temperature une hausse subite de température
▶ vb ❶ (increase) augmenter ▷ Prices are rising. Les prix augmentent. ❷ se lever ▷ The sun rises early in June. Le soleil se lève tôt en juin.

riser ['raɪzə^r] n: **to be an early riser** être matinal

risk [rɪsk] n risque m; **to take risks** prendre des risques; **It's at your own risk.** C'est à vos risques et périls.
▸ vb risquer ▷ *You risk getting a fine.* Vous risquez de recevoir une amende.; **I wouldn't risk it if I were you.** À votre place, je ne prendrais pas ce risque.

risky ['rɪskɪ] adj risqué

rival ['raɪvl] n rival m (pl rivaux), rivale f
▸ adj ❶ rival m ▷ *a rival gang* une bande rivale ❷ concurrent ▷ *a rival company* une société concurrente

rivalry ['raɪvlrɪ] n (between towns, schools) rivalité f

river ['rɪvə^r] n ❶ rivière f ▷ *The river runs alongside the canal.* La rivière longe le canal. ❷ (major) fleuve m ▷ *the Fraser River* le fleuve Fraser

road [rəud] n ❶ route f ▷ *There's a lot of traffic on the roads.* Il y a beaucoup de circulation sur les routes. ❷ (street) rue f ▷ *They live across the road.* Ils habitent de l'autre côté de la rue.

road map n carte routière f

road rage n rage au volant f

road sign ['rəudsaɪn] n panneau de signalisation m (pl panneaux de signalisation)

roast [rəust] adj rôti ▷ *roast chicken* le poulet rôti ▷ *roast potatoes* les pommes de terre rôties; **roast pork** le rôti de porc; **roast beef** le rôti de bœuf

rob [rɔb] vb: **to rob somebody** voler quelqu'un ▷ *I've been robbed.* On m'a volé.; **to rob somebody of something** voler quelque chose à quelqu'un ▷ *He was robbed of his wallet.* On lui a volé son portefeuille.; **to rob a bank**

dévaliser une banque

robber ['rɔbə^r] n voleur m; **a bank robber** un cambrioleur de banques

robbery ['rɔbərɪ] n vol m; **a bank robbery** un cambriolage de banque; **armed robbery** le vol à main armée

robin ['rɔbɪn] n rouge-gorge m

robot ['rəubɔt] n robot m

rock [rɔk] n ❶ (substance) roche f ▷ *They tunnelled through the rock.* Ils ont creusé un tunnel dans la roche. ❷ (boulder) rocher m ▷ *I sat on a rock.* Je me suis assis sur un rocher. ❸ (stone) pierre f ▷ *The crowd started to throw rocks.* La foule s'est mise à lancer des pierres. ❹ (music) rock m ▷ *a rock concert* un concert de rock ▷ *She's a rock star.* C'est une vedette de rock.; **rock and roll** le rock and roll
▸ vb ❶ bercer ▷ *He rocked the baby in his arms.* Il berçait le bébé dans les bras. ▷ *The little boat was gently rocked by the waves.* Le petit bateau était doucement bercé par les vagues. ❷ (shake) ébranler ▷ *The explosion rocked the building.* L'explosion a ébranlé le bâtiment.

rocket ['rɔkɪt] n (firework, spacecraft) fusée f

rock garden n rocaille f

rocking chair ['rɔkɪŋ-] n chaise berçante f

rocky ['rɔkɪ] adj rocheux (f rocheuse); **the Rocky Mountains** les montagnes Rocheuses

rod [rɔd] n (for fishing) canne à pêche f

rode [rəud] vb see **ride**

rodeo ['rəudɪəu] n rodéo m ▷ *The Calgary Stampede is a famous rodeo.* Le Stampede de Calgary est un rodéo célèbre.

role [rəul] n rôle m

role play n jeu de rôle m (pl jeux

de rôles) ▷ *to do a role play* faire un jeu de rôle

roll [rəʊl] n ❶ rouleau m (pl rouleaux) ▷ *a roll of tape* un rouleau de ruban adhésif ▷ *a roll of toilet paper* un rouleau de papier hygiénique; **to be on a roll** avoir le vent en poupe ❷ (bread) petit pain m

▸ vb rouler; **to roll out pastry** abaisser la pâte

roller ['rəʊlə'] n rouleau m (pl rouleaux)

Rollerblade® ['rəʊləbleɪd] n patin à roues alignées m ▷ *a pair of Rollerblades* une paire de patins à roues alignées

roller coaster [-kəʊstə'] n montagnes fpl russes

roller skates npl patins mpl à roulettes

roller skating n patinage à roulettes m; **to go roller skating** faire du patinage à roulettes

rolling pin ['rəʊlɪŋ-] n rouleau à pâtisserie m

romance [rə'mæns] n ❶ (novels) romans mpl d'amour ▷ *I read a lot of romance.* Je lis beaucoup de romans d'amour. ❷ (glamour) charme m ▷ *the romance of a walk in the moonlight* le charme d'une promenade au clair de la lune; **a holiday romance** une idylle de vacances

romantic [rə'mæntɪk] adj romantique

roof [ruːf] n toit m

roof rack n porte-bagages de toit m

room [ruːm] n ❶ pièce f ▷ *the biggest room in the house* la plus grande pièce de la maison ❷ (bedroom) chambre f ▷ *She's in her room.* Elle est dans sa chambre.; **a single room** une chambre pour

une personne; **a double room** une chambre pour deux personnes ❸ (in school) salle f ▷ *the music room* la salle de musique ❹ (space) place f ▷ *There's no room for that box.* Il n'y a pas de place pour cette boîte.

roommate ['ruːmmeɪt] n ❶ (in apartment) colocataire ▷ *My sister gets along very well with her roommates.* Ma sœur s'entend à merveille avec ses colocataires. ❷ (at boarding school) camarade de chambre

rooster ['ruːstə'] n coq m

root [ruːt] n racine f

root out vb traquer ▷ *They are determined to root out corruption.* Ils sont déterminés à traquer la corruption.

root beer n bière d'épinette f

rope [rəʊp] n corde f

rope in vb ❶ enrôler ▷ *I was roped in to help with the refreshments.* J'ai été enrôlé pour servir les rafraîchissements. ❷ se faire embarquer ▷ *She was roped into another insane project.* Elle s'est encore fait embarquer dans un projet de fous.

rose [rəʊz] vb see **rise**

▸ n (flower) rose f

rot [rɒt] vb pourrir

rotten ['rɒtn] adj (decayed) pourri ▷ *a rotten apple* une pomme pourrie; **rotten weather** un temps pourri; **That's a rotten thing to do.** Ce n'est vraiment pas gentil.; **to feel rotten** filer un mauvais coton (informal)

rough [rʌf] adj ❶ (surface) rugueux (f rugueuse) ▷ *My hands are rough.* J'ai les mains rugueuses. ❷ (game) violent ▷ *Hockey's a rough sport.* Le hockey est un sport violent. ❸ (area) difficile ▷ *It's a rough area.* C'est un quartier difficile. ❹ (water) houleux (f houleuse) ▷ *The sea was rough.* La mer était houleuse. ❽ approximatif (f approximative); **I've got a rough idea.** J'en ai une idée approximative.

roughly ['rʌflɪ] *adv* à peu près ▷ *It weighs roughly 20 kilos.* Ça pèse à peu près vingt kilos.

round [raʊnd] *adj* rond ▷ *a round table* une table ronde; **all year round** toute l'année
▶ *n* ❶ (*of tournament*) manche *f* ❷ (*of boxing match*) round *m*; **a round of golf** une partie de golf

round off *vb* ❶ (*figure*) arrondir ▷ *Round each figure off to the nearest hundred.* Arrondissez chaque chiffre à la centaine près. ❷ terminer ▷ *They rounded off the meal with lemon sherbet.* Ils ont terminé le repas par du sorbet au citron.

round up *vb* ❶ (*sheep, cattle, suspects*) rassembler ❷ (*figure*) arrondir

round trip *n* aller *m* et retour; **a round-trip ticket** un billet aller et retour

route [ruːt] *n* ❶ itinéraire *m* ▷ *We're planning our route.* Nous établissons notre itinéraire. ❷ (*of bus*) parcours *m*

routine ['ruːtiːn] *n*: **my daily routine** ma routine quotidienne

row [raʊ] *n* ❶ rangée *f* ▷ *a row of houses* une rangée de maisons ❷ (*of seats*) rang *m* ▷ *Our seats are in the front row.* Nos places se trouvent au premier rang.; **five times in a row** cinq fois d'affilée
▶ *vb* ❶ ramer ▷ *We took turns rowing.* Nous avons ramé à tour de rôle. ❷ (*as sport*) faire de l'aviron

rowboat ['rəʊbəʊt] *n* chaloupe *f*

rowing ['rəʊɪŋ] *n* (*sport*) aviron *m* ▷ *My hobby is rowing.* Je fais de l'aviron.

royal ['rɔɪəl] *adj* royal (*mpl* royaux); **the royal family** la famille royale

Royal Canadian Mounted Police *n* Gendarmerie royale du Canada *f*

rub [rʌb] *vb* ❶ (*stain*) frotter ❷ (*part of body*) se frotter ▷ *Don't rub your eyes!* Ne te frotte pas les yeux!; **to rub something out** effacer quelque chose

rubber ['rʌbə] *n* ❶ caoutchouc *m* ▷ *rubber soles* des semelles en caoutchouc ❷ (*eraser*) gomme à effacer *f* ▷ *Can I borrow your rubber?* Je peux emprunter ta gomme à effacer?; **a rubber band** un élastique

rubbish ['rʌbɪʃ] *n* ❶ (*refuse*) ordures *fpl* ▷ *When do they collect the rubbish?* Quand est-ce qu'ils ramassent les ordures? ❷ (*nonsense*) niaiserie *f* ▷ *Don't talk rubbish!* Ne dis pas de niaiseries!; **That's a load of rubbish!** (*informal*) C'est vraiment n'importe quoi!

rude [ruːd] *adj* ❶ (*impolite*) impoli ▷ *It's rude to interrupt.* C'est impoli de couper la parole aux gens. ❷ (*offensive*) grossier (*f* grossière) ▷ *a rude joke* une plaisanterie grossière ▷ *He was very rude to me.* Il a été très grossier avec moi.; **a rude word** un gros mot

rug [rʌg] *n* tapis *m* ▷ *a Persian rug* un tapis persan

ruin ['ruːɪn] *n* ruine *f* ▷ *the ruins of the castle* les ruines du château; **in ruins** en ruine
▶ *vb* ❶ abîmer ▷ *You'll ruin your shoes.* Tu vas abîmer tes chaussures. ❷ gâcher ▷ *It ruined our holiday.* Ça a gâché nos vacances. ❸ (*financially*) ruiner

rule [ruːl] *n* ❶ règle *f* ▷ *the rules of grammar* les règles de grammaire; **as a rule** en règle générale

❷ (regulation) règlement m ▷ It's
against the rules. C'est contre le
règlement.

rule out vb (possibility) écarter ▷ I'm
not ruling anything out. Je n'écarte
aucune possibilité.

ruler ['ruːləʳ] n règle f ▷ Can I borrow
your ruler? Je peux emprunter ta
règle?

rummage ['rʌmɪdʒ] vb fouiller
▷ She rummaged in her purse for some
change. Elle a fouillé dans son sac à
main pour trouver de la monnaie.

rummage sale n vente de charité f

rumour ['ruːməʳ] n rumeur f
▷ It's just a rumour. Ce n'est qu'une
rumeur.

run [rʌn] n ❶ (baseball) coup
de circuit m ▷ to hit a home run
frapper un coup de circuit ❷ (in
nylons) échelle f ▷ **to go for a run**
courir ▷ I go for a run every morning.
Je cours tous les matins. ▷ **I did a
ten-kilometre run.** J'ai couru dix
kilomètres. ▷ **on the run** en fuite
▷ The criminals are still on the run. Les
criminels sont toujours en fuite. ▷ **in
the long run** à long terme
▶ vb ❶ courir ▷ I ran five kilometres.
J'ai couru cinq kilomètres. ▷ **to
run a marathon** participer à un
marathon ❷ (manage) diriger
▷ She runs a large company. Elle dirige
une grosse société. ❸ (organize)
organiser ▷ They run music courses
in the holidays. Ils organisent des
cours de musique pendant les
vacances. ❹ (water) couler ▷ Don't
leave the tap running. Ne laisse
pas couler le robinet. ▷ **to run a
bath** faire couler un bain ❺ (by
car) conduire ▷ I can run you to the
station. Je peux te conduire à la
gare. ▷ **to run away** s'enfuir ▷ They
ran away before the police came. Ils
se sont enfuis avant l'arrivée de la

police. ; **Time is running out.** Il ne
reste plus beaucoup de temps. ; **to
run out of something** se trouver
à court de quelque chose ▷ We ran
out of money. Nous nous sommes
trouvés à court d'argent. ; **to
run somebody over** écraser quelqu'un ;
to get run over se faire écraser
▷ Be careful, or you'll get run over!
Fais attention, sinon tu vas te faire
écraser!

rung [rʌn] vb see **ring**

runner ['rʌnəʳ] n coureur m,
coureuse f

runner-up [rʌnəʳˈʌp] n second m,
seconde f

running ['rʌnɪŋ] n course f
▷ Running is my favourite sport. La
course est mon sport préféré.

running shoe n chaussure de
sport f

runway ['rʌnweɪ] n piste f

rural ['ruərəl] adj rural (mpl ruraux)

rush [rʌʃ] n hâte f; **in a rush** à
la hâte
▶ vb ❶ (run) se précipiter
▷ Everyone rushed outside. Tout
le monde s'est précipité dehors.
❷ (hurry) se dépêcher ▷ There's no
need to rush. Ce n'est pas la peine de
se dépêcher.

rush hour n heure f de pointe ▷ in
the rush hour à l'heure de pointe

rust [rʌst] n rouille f
▶ vb rouiller ▷ Your bike will rust if
you leave it out in the rain. Ton vélo va
rouiller si tu le laisses sous la pluie.

rusty ['rʌstɪ] adj rouillé ▷ a rusty
bike un vélo rouillé ▷ My French is
very rusty. Mon français est très
rouillé.

ruthless ['ruːθlɪs] adj sans pitié

RV n caravane f

rye [raɪ] n seigle m; **rye bread** le
pain de seigle

S

sack [sæk] *n* sac *m*; **to get the sack**
être mis à la porte
▶ *vb*: **to sack somebody** mettre
quelqu'un à la porte ▷ *She was
sacked.* On l'a mise à la porte.
sacred ['seɪkrɪd] *adj* sacré
sacrifice ['sækrɪfaɪs] *n* sacrifice *m*
sad [sæd] *adj* triste
saddle ['sædl] *n* selle *f*
saddlebag ['sædlbæg] *n* sacoche *f*
sadly ['sædlɪ] *adv* ❶ tristement
▷ *"She's gone," he said sadly.*
« Elle est partie, » a-t-il dit
tristement. ❷ (*unfortunately*)
malheureusement ▷ *Sadly, it was
too late.* Malheureusement, il était
trop tard.
safe [seɪf] *n* coffre-fort *m* (*pl*
coffres-forts) ▷ *He put the money
in the safe.* Il a mis l'argent dans le
coffre-fort.
▶ *adj* ❶ sans danger ▷ *Don't worry,
it's perfectly safe.* Ne vous inquiétez

pas, c'est absolument sans danger.;
Is it safe? Ça n'est pas dangereux?
❷ (*machine, ladder*) sécuritaire
▷ *This car isn't safe.* Cette voiture
n'est pas sécuritaire. ❸ (*out of
danger*) en sécurité ▷ *You're safe now.*
Vous êtes en sécurité maintenant.;
to feel safe se sentir en sécurité;
safe sex le sexe sans risques
safety ['seɪftɪ] *n* sécurité *f*; **a
safety belt** une ceinture de
sécurité; **a safety pin** une épingle
de sûreté
Sagittarius [sædʒɪ'tɛərɪəs] *n*
Sagittaire ▷ *I'm a Sagittarius.* Je suis
Sagittaire.
said [sɛd] *vb see* **say**
sail [seɪl] *n* voile *f*
▶ *vb* ❶ (*as skill, sport*) faire de la
voile ▷ *Do you know how to sail?*
Est-ce que tu sais faire de la voile?
❷ (*travel*) naviguer ❸ (*set off*)
prendre la mer ▷ *The boat sails at
eight o'clock.* Le bateau prend la mer
à huit heures.
sailboat ['seɪlbəʊt] *n* voilier *m*
sailing ['seɪlɪŋ] *n* voile *f* ▷ *Her hobby
is sailing.* Son passe-temps, c'est la
voile.; **to go sailing** faire de la voile;
a sailing ship un grand voilier
sailor ['seɪlə'] *n* matelot *m* ▷ *He's
a sailor.* Il est matelot.; **I'm not
much of a sailor.** Je n'ai pas le pied
très marin.
saint [seɪnt] *n* saint *m*, sainte *f*
sake [seɪk] *n*: **for the sake of** dans
l'intérêt de
salad ['sæləd] *n* salade *f* ▷ *a fruit
salad* une salade de fruits ▷ *a Caesar
salad* une salade César; **salad
dressing** la vinaigrette
salami [sə'lɑːmɪ] *n* salami *m*
salary ['sælərɪ] *n* salaire *m*
sale [seɪl] *n* (*reductions*) soldes
mpl ▷ *Spring sales will start
soon.* Les soldes du printemps

commenceront bientôt.; **on sale** en vente; The factory's for sale. L'usine est en vente.; **"for sale"** « à vendre »

sales assistant [seɪlz-] n vendeur m, vendeuse f ▷ She's a sales assistant. Elle est vendeuse.

sales rep [seɪlz-] n représentant m, représentante f

salmon ['sæmən] n saumon m

salon ['sælɒn] n salon m ▷ a hair salon un salon de coiffure ▷ a beauty salon un salon de beauté

salt [sɔːlt] n sel m

salty ['sɔːltɪ] adj salé

salute [sə'luːt] vb saluer

same [seɪm] adj même ▷ the same model le même modèle ▷ at the same time en même temps; **They're exactly the same.** Ils sont exactement pareils.; **It's not the same.** Ça n'est pas pareil.

sample ['sɑːmpl] n échantillon m

sand [sænd] n sable m

sandal ['sændl] n sandale f ▷ a pair of sandals une paire de sandales

sand castle ['sændkɑːsl] n château de sable m (pl châteaux de sable)

sandwich ['sændwɪtʃ] n sandwich m ▷ a cheese sandwich un sandwich au fromage

sang [sæŋ] vb see **sing**

sanitary napkin ['sænɪtrɪ] n serviette hygiénique f

sank [sæŋk] vb see **sink**

sarcastic [sɑː'kæstɪk] adj sarcastique

sardine [sɑː'diːn] n sardine f

SARS [sɑːz] abbr (= Severe Acute Respiratory Syndrome) SRAS m (= syndrome respiratoire aigu sévère)

Saskatchewan [sæ'skætʃəwən] n Saskatchewan f

sat [sæt] vb see **sit**

satellite ['sætəlaɪt] n satellite

m ▷ satellite television la télévision par satellite; **a satellite dish** une antenne parabolique

satisfactory [sætɪs'fæktərɪ] adj satisfaisant

satisfied ['sætɪsfaɪd] adj satisfait

Saturday ['sætədɪ] n samedi m ▷ on Saturday samedi ▷ on Saturdays le samedi ▷ every Saturday tous les samedis ▷ last Saturday samedi dernier ▷ next Saturday samedi prochain; **I've got a Saturday job.** Je travaille le samedi.

sauce [sɔːs] n sauce f

saucepan ['sɔːspən] n casserole f

saucer ['sɔːsə*] n soucoupe f

sauna ['sɔːnə] n sauna m

sausage ['sɒsɪdʒ] n ❶ saucisse f ❷ (sliced, served cold) saucisson m; **a sausage roll** un friand

save [seɪv] vb ❶ (save up money) mettre de côté ▷ I've saved 50 dollars already. J'ai déjà mis cinquante dollars de côté. ❷ (spend less) économiser ▷ I saved 20 dollars by waiting for the sale. J'ai économisé vingt dollars en attendant les soldes.; **to save time** gagner du temps ▷ We took a taxi to save time. Nous avons pris un taxi pour gagner du temps. ▷ It saved us time. Ça nous a fait gagner du temps. ❸ (rescue) sauver ▷ Luckily, all the passengers were saved. Heureusement, tous les passagers ont été sauvés. ❹ (on computer) sauvegarder ▷ I saved the file onto a diskette. J'ai sauvegardé le fichier sur disquette.; **to save up** mettre de l'argent de côté ▷ I'm saving up for a new bike. Je mets de l'argent de côté pour un nouveau vélo.

savings ['seɪvɪŋz] npl économies fpl ▷ She spent all her savings on a computer. Elle a dépensé toutes ses économies en achetant un ordinateur.

saw [sɔ:] vb see **see**
▷ n scie f

sax [sæks] n sax m (informal) ▷ I play the sax. Je joue du sax.

saxophone ['sæksəfəʊn] n saxophone m ▷ I play the saxophone. Je joue du saxophone.

say [seɪ] vb dire ▷ What did he say? Qu'est-ce qu'il a dit? ▷ Did you hear what she said? Tu as entendu ce qu'elle a dit?; **Could you say that again?** Pourriez-vous répéter, s'il vous plaît?; **That goes without saying.** Cela va sans dire.

saying ['seɪɪŋ] n dicton m ▷ It's just a saying. C'est juste un dicton.

scale [skeɪl] n ❶ (of map) échelle f ▷ a large-scale map une carte à grande échelle ❷ (size, extent) ampleur f ▷ a disaster on a massive scale un désastre d'une ampleur incroyable ❸ (in music) gamme f

scales [skeɪlz] npl balance f

scandal ['skændl] n ❶ (outrage) scandale m ▷ It caused a scandal. Ça a fait scandale. ❷ (gossip) commérages mpl ▷ It's just scandal. Ce ne sont que des commérages.

scar [skɑːʳ] n cicatrice f

scarce [skeəs] adj limité ▷ scarce resources des ressources limitées; **Jobs are scarce these days.** Il y a peu de travail ces temps-ci.

scarcely ['skeəslɪ] adv à peine ▷ I scarcely knew her. Je la connaissais à peine.

scare [skeəʳ] vb: **to scare somebody** faire peur à quelqu'un ▷ He scares me. Il me fait peur.

scarecrow ['skeəkrəʊ] n épouvantail m

scared [skeəd] adj: **to be scared** avoir peur ▷ I was scared stiff. J'avais terriblement peur.; **to be scared of** avoir peur de ▷ Are you scared of her?

Est-ce que tu as peur d'elle?

scarf [skɑːf] n foulard m

scary ['skeərɪ] adj effrayant ▷ It was really scary. C'était vraiment effrayant.

scene [siːn] n ❶ (place) lieux mpl ▷ The police were soon on the scene. La police est vite arrivée sur les lieux. ▷ the scene of the crime les lieux du crime ❷ (event, sight) spectacle m ▷ It was an amazing scene. C'était un spectacle étonnant.; **to make a scene** faire une scène

scenery ['siːnərɪ] n (landscape) paysage m

scent [sent] n (perfume) parfum m

schedule ['skɛdjuːl] n programme m ▷ a busy schedule un programme chargé; **on schedule** comme prévu; **to be behind schedule** avoir du retard

scheduled flight ['skɛdjuːld-] n vol régulier m

scheme [skiːm] n ❶ (idea) truc m ▷ a crazy scheme he dreamed up un truc farfelu qu'il a inventé ❷ (project) projet m ▷ the town's road-widening scheme le projet municipal d'élargissement des routes

scholarship ['skɔləʃɪp] n bourse f

school [skuːl] n école f; **to go to school** aller à l'école; **a school of fish** un banc de poissons

schoolbag ['skuːlbæg] n sac d'école m

schoolbook ['skuːlbʊk] n manuel scolaire m

school bus n autobus m scolaire

schoolyard ['skuːljɑːd] n cour d'école f

science ['saɪəns] n science f

science fiction n science-fiction f

scientific [saɪən'tɪfɪk] adj scientifique

scientist ['saɪəntɪst] n

❶ (academic) scientifique ❷ (doing research) chercheur m, chercheuse f

scissors ['sɪzəz] npl ciseaux mpl ▷ a pair of scissors une paire de ciseaux

scoff [skɒf] vb se moquer ▷ They scoffed at my idea. Ils se sont moqués de mon idée.

scooter ['sku:tə'] n trottinette f

scope [skəʊp] n dimension f ▷ the scope of the project la dimension du projet

score [skɔː'] n pointage m ▷ The score was three nothing. Le pointage était trois à zéro.
▶ vb (goal, point) marquer ▷ to score a goal marquer un but; **to score 6 out of 10** obtenir un pointage de six sur dix; **He shoots, he scores!** Il lance et compte!

Scorpio ['skɔ:piəʊ] n Scorpion m ▷ I'm a Scorpio. Je suis Scorpion.

scrambled eggs ['skræmbld-] npl œufs mpl brouillés

scrap [skræp] n ❶ bout m ▷ a scrap of paper un bout de papier; **They feed their dog scraps.** Ils nourrissent leur chien avec des restants. ❷ (fight) bagarre f; **scrap iron** la ferraille
▶ vb (plan) abandonner ▷ The idea was scrapped. L'idée a été abandonnée.

scrapbook ['skræpbuk] n album m

scratch [skrætʃ] vb ❶ gratter ▷ Can you scratch my back, please? Peux-tu me gratter le dos, s'il te plaît? ▷ Don't scratch your mosquito bites. Ne gratte pas tes piqûres de maringouin. ❷ (oneself) se gratter ▷ He scratched until it bled. Il s'est gratté jusqu'au sang. ▷ She scratched her head. Elle s'est gratté la tête.; **The cat scratched me.** Le chat m'a donné des coups de griffe.
▶ n (on skin) égratignure f; **to start from scratch** partir de zéro

scream [skri:m] n hurlement m
▶ vb hurler

screen [skri:n] n écran m

screen saver [-seɪvə'] n économiseur m d'écran

screw [skru:] n vis f

screwdriver ['skru:draɪvə'] n tournevis m

scribble ['skrɪbl] vb griffonner

scrub [skrʌb] vb récurer ▷ to scrub a pan récurer une casserole

sculpture ['skʌlptʃə'] n sculpture f

sea [siː] n mer f

seafood ['siːfuːd] n fruits mpl de mer ▷ I don't like seafood. Je n'aime pas les fruits de mer.

seagull ['siːgʌl] n mouette f

seal [siːl] n (animal) phoque m
▶ vb (letter) coller

search [sɜːtʃ] vb fouiller ▷ They searched the woods for her. Ils ont fouillé les bois pour la trouver.; **to search for something** chercher quelque chose ▷ He searched for evidence. Il cherchait des preuves.
▶ n fouille f

search engine n moteur de recherche

search party n expédition f de secours

seashore ['siːʃɔː'] n bord de la mer m ▷ on the seashore au bord de la mer

seasick ['siːsɪk] adj: **to be seasick** avoir le mal de mer

season ['siːzn] n saison f ▷ What's your favourite season? Quelle est ta saison préférée?; **in the off season** hors saison ▷ It's cheaper to go there in the off season. C'est moins cher d'y aller hors saison.; **during the holiday season** en période de vacances; **out of season** hors saison ▷ Cherries are out of season. Les cerises sont hors saison.; **a season ticket** un abonnement

seat [si:t] n siège m
seat belt n ceinture de sécurité f
seaweed ['si:wi:d] n algues fpl
second [sɪ'kɒnd] adj deuxième
▷ on the second page à la deuxième page; **to come second** (in race) arriver deuxième; **the second of March** le deux mars
▶ n seconde f ▷ It'll only take a second Ça va prendre juste une seconde.
secondary school ['sɛkəndərɪ-] n école f secondaire
second-class ['sɛkənd'klɑ:s] adj: **a second-class citizen** un citoyen de deuxième ordre
second-hand ['sɛkənd'hænd] adj usagé ▷ a secondhand car une voiture usagée
secondly ['sɛkəndlɪ] adv deuxièmement; **firstly...** **secondly...** premièrement... deuxièmement... ▷ Firstly, it's too expensive. Secondly, it wouldn't work anyway. Premièrement, c'est trop cher. Deuxièmement, ça ne marcherait quand même pas.
secret ['si:krɪt] adj secret m (f secrète) ▷ a secret mission une mission secrète
▶ n secret m ▷ It's a secret. C'est un secret. ▷ Can you keep a secret? Tu sais garder un secret?; **in secret** en secret
secretary ['sɛkrətrɪ] n secrétaire ▷ She's a secretary. Elle est secrétaire.
secretly ['si:krɪtlɪ] adv secrètement
section ['sɛkʃən] n section f
security [sɪ'kjuərɪtɪ] n ❶ sécurité f ▷ a feeling of security un sentiment de sécurité ▷ a campaign to improve airport security une campagne visant à améliorer la sécurité dans les aéroports; **job security** la sécurité de l'emploi; **a security guard** (on guard) un garde chargé de la sécurité ❷ (transporting money) un convoyeur de fonds
security guard n ❶ agent m de sécurité, agente f de sécurité ❷ (with armoured car) garde de voiture blindée
see [si:] vb voir ▷ I can't see. Je ne vois rien. ▷ I saw him yesterday. Je l'ai vu hier. ▷ Have you seen him? Est-ce que tu l'as vu?; **See you!** Salut!; **See you soon!** À bientôt!; **to see to something** s'occuper de quelque chose ▷ The window's stuck again. Can you see to it, please? La fenêtre est encore coincée. Peux-tu t'en occuper, s'il te plaît?
seed [si:d] n graine f ▷ sunflower seeds des graines de tournesol
seek [si:k] vb chercher; **to seek help** chercher de l'aide
seem [si:m] vb avoir l'air ▷ She seems tired. Elle a l'air fatiguée. ▷ The store seemed to be closed. Le magasin avait l'air d'être fermé.; **That seems like a good idea.** Ce n'est pas une mauvaise idée.; **It seems that...** Il paraît que... ▷ It seems they're getting married. Il paraît qu'ils vont se marier.; **There seems to be a problem.** Il semble y avoir un problème.
seen [si:n] vb see **see**
seesaw ['si:sɔ:] n balançoire à bascule f
see-through ['si:θru:] adj transparent
seldom ['sɛldəm] adv rarement
select [sɪ'lɛkt] vb sélectionner
selection [sɪ'lɛkʃən] n sélection f
self-assured [sɛlfə'ʃuəd] adj sûr de soi ▷ She's very self-assured. Elle est très sûre d'elle.
self-centred [sɛlf'sɛntəd] adj égocentrique
self-confidence [sɛlf'kɒnfɪdns] n confiance en soi f ▷ He hasn't got

much self-confidence. Il n'a pas très confiance en lui.

self-conscious [selfˈkɒnʃəs] adj: **to be self-conscious** (1) (embarrassed) être mal à l'aise ▷ She was really self-conscious at first. Elle était vraiment mal à l'aise au début. (2) (shy) manquer d'assurance ▷ He's always been rather self-conscious. Il a toujours manqué un peu d'assurance.

self-control [selfkənˈtrəʊl] n sang-froid m

self-defence [selfdɪˈfɛns] n autodéfense f ▷ self-defence classes les cours d'autodéfense; **She killed the dog in self-defence.** Elle a tué le chien en légitime défense.

self-discipline [selfˈdɪsɪplɪn] n autodiscipline f

self-disciplined [selfˈdɪsɪplɪnd] adj: **He is self-disciplined.** Il fait preuve d'autodiscipline.

self-employed [selfɪmˈplɔɪd] adj: **to be self-employed** travailler à son compte ▷ He's self-employed. Il travaille à son compte.; **the self-employed** les travailleurs autonomes

selfish [ˈselfɪʃ] adj égoïste ▷ Don't be so selfish. Ne sois pas si égoïste.

self-respect [selfrɪsˈpɛkt] n amour-propre m

self-serve [selfˈsɜːv] n libre-service m ▷ This gas station is a self-serve. Cette station-service est un libre-service.

sell [sɛl] vb vendre ▷ She sold it to me. Elle me l'a vendu.; **to sell off** liquider; **The tickets are all sold out.** Il ne reste plus de billets.; **The tickets sold out in three hours.** Tous les billets ont été vendus en trois heures.

sell out vb ❶ se vendre ▷ The tickets sold out in three hours. Les

billets se sont tous vendus en trois heures. ❷ (compromise one's standards) se prostituer ▷ The artist refused to sell out. L'artiste refuse de se prostituer.

selling price [ˈsɛlɪŋ-] n prix de vente m

semicircle [ˈsɛmɪsəːkl] n demi-cercle m

semicolon [semɪˈkəʊlən] n point-virgule m

semi-detached house [semɪdɪˈtætʃt-] n maison jumelée f ▷ We live in a semi-detached house. Nous habitons dans une maison jumelée.

semi-final [semɪˈfaɪnl] n demi-finale f

Senate [ˈsɛnɪt] n Sénat m

send [sɛnd] vb envoyer ▷ She sent me a birthday card. Elle m'a envoyé une carte de fête.; **to send back** renvoyer; **to send away for something** (free) se faire envoyer quelque chose ▷ I've sent away for a brochure. Je me suis fait envoyer une brochure.; **to send out** envoyer ▷ My mom sent me out to buy milk. Ma mère m'a envoyé acheter du lait.

sender [ˈsɛndəʳ] n expéditeur m, expéditrice f

senior [ˈsiːnɪəʳ] adj principal ▷ senior accountant la comptable principale ▷ senior architect l'architecte principal; **senior citizen** la personne âgée; **senior management** la haute direction; **senior manager** le cadre supérieur

sensational [sɛnˈseɪʃənl] adj sensationnel (f sensationnelle)

sense [sɛns] n ❶ (wisdom) bon sens m ▷ Use your common sense! Un peu de bon sens, voyons!; **It makes sense.** C'est logique.; **It doesn't make sense.** Ça n'a pas de sens. ❷ (faculty) sens m ▷ the five senses les cinq sens; **the sense of touch** le toucher; **the sense of smell** l'odorat m; **the sixth sense** le sixième sens; **sense of humour** le sens de l'humour ▷ *He has no sense of humour.* Il n'a aucun sens de l'humour.

▶ vb sentir ▷ *I sensed that she was afraid.* J'ai senti qu'elle avait peur.

senseless ['sɛnslɪs] adj insensé

sensible ['sɛnsɪbl] adj raisonnable
▷ *Be sensible!* Sois raisonnable!

Be careful not to translate **sensible** by the French word **sensible**.

sensitive ['sɛnsɪtɪv] adj sensible
▷ *She's very sensitive.* Elle est très sensible.

sensuous ['sɛnsjuəs] adj sensuel (f sensuelle)

sent [sɛnt] vb see **send**

sentence ['sɛntns] n ❶ phrase f ▷ *What does this sentence mean?* Que veut dire cette phrase? ❷ (judgment) condamnation f ❸ (punishment) peine f ▷ *the death sentence* la peine de mort; **He got a life sentence.** Il a été condamné à la réclusion à perpétuité.

▶ vb: **to sentence somebody to life imprisonment** condamner quelqu'un à la réclusion à perpétuité; **to sentence somebody to death** condamner quelqu'un à mort

sentimental [sɛntɪ'mɛntl] adj sentimental (mpl sentimentaux)

separate ['sɛpərɪt] adj séparé ▷ *I wrote it on a separate sheet.* Je l'ai écrit sur une feuille séparée.; **The children have separate rooms.** Les enfants ont chacun leur chambre.; **on separate occasions** à différentes reprises

▶ vb ❶ séparer ❷ (married couple) se séparer

separately ['sɛprɪtlɪ] adv séparément

separation [sɛpə'reɪʃən] n séparation f

separatism ['sɛprətɪzəm] n séparatisme m

separatist ['sɛprətɪst] n séparatiste

September [sɛp'tɛmbər] n septembre m; **in September** en septembre

sequel ['si:kwl] n (book, film) suite f

sequence ['si:kwəns] n ❶ ordre m; **in sequence** en ordre; **a sequence of events** une succession d'événements ❷ (in film) séquence f

series ['sɪərɪz] n ❶ série f ▷ *a TV series* une série télévisée ❷ (of numbers, events) suite f

serious ['sɪərɪəs] adj ❶ sérieux (f sérieuse) ▷ *You look very serious.* Tu as l'air sérieux.; **Are you serious?** Sérieusement? ❷ (illness, mistake) grave

seriously ['sɪərɪəslɪ] adv sérieusement ▷ *No, but seriously...* Non, mais sérieusement...; **to take somebody seriously** prendre quelqu'un au sérieux; **seriously injured** gravement blessé; **Seriously?** Vraiment?

sermon ['sə:mən] n sermon m

serve [sə:v] vb ❶ servir ▷ *Dinner is served.* Le souper est servi. ▷ *It's his turn to serve.* C'est à son tour de servir. ❷ (prison sentence) purger; **to serve time** être en prison; **It serves you right.** C'est bien fait pour toi.

▶ n (tennis) service m; **It's your serve.** C'est à toi de servir.

server ['sə:vər] n (computing) serveur m

service ['sə:vɪs] vb (car, washing machine) réviser

▶ *n* ❶ service *m* ▷ *Service is included.* Le service est compris. ❷ *(of car)* révision *f*; **a memorial service** un service commémoratif; **a funeral service** un service funèbre

service area *n* aire *f* de service

service charge *n* service *m* ▷ *There's no service charge.* Le service est compris.

service station *n* station-service *f* (*pl* stations-service)

serviette [sɜːvɪˈɛt] *n* serviette *f*

session [ˈsɛʃən] *n* séance *f*

set [sɛt] *n* ❶ jeu *m* (*pl* jeux) ▷ *a set of keys* un jeu de clés ▷ *a chess set* un jeu d'échecs; **a set of drums** une batterie; **a train set** un train électrique ❷ *(in tennis)* manche *f*
▶ *vb* ❶ mettre ▷ *I set the alarm for 7 o'clock.* J'ai mis le réveil à sept heures. ▷ *Set the plants on the floor.* Mets les plantes sur le plancher. ❷ *(record)* établir ▷ *The world record was set last year.* Le record du monde a été établi l'année dernière. ❸ *(sun)* se coucher ▷ *The sun was setting.* Le soleil se couchait.; **The film is set in Manitoba.** L'action du film se déroule au Manitoba.; **to set off** partir ▷ *We set off for Tadoussac at 9 o'clock.* Nous sommes partis pour Tadoussac à neuf heures.; **to set out** partir ▷ *We set out for Saint John at 9 o'clock.* Nous sommes partis pour Saint John à neuf heures.; **to set sail** prendre la mer; **to set the table** mettre la table

settle [ˈsɛtl] *vb* ❶ *(problem)* résoudre ❷ *(argument, account)* régler; **to settle down** *(calm down)* se calmer; **Settle down!** Du calme!; **to settle in** s'installer; **to settle on something** opter pour quelque chose

seven [ˈsɛvn] *num* sept ▷ *She's*

seven. Elle a sept ans.

seventeen [sɛvnˈtiːn] *num* dix-sept ▷ *He's seventeen.* Il a dix-sept ans.

seventeenth [sɛvnˈtiːnθ] *adj* dix-septième ▷ *his seventeenth birthday* son dix-septième anniversaire de naissance ▷ *the seventeenth floor* le dix-septième étage; **the seventeenth of August** le dix-sept août

seventh [ˈsɛvnθ] *adj* septième ▷ *the seventh floor* le septième étage; **the seventh of August** le sept août

seventy [ˈsɛvntɪ] *num* soixante-dix

several [ˈsɛvrəl] *adj, pron* plusieurs ▷ *several schools* plusieurs écoles; **several of them** plusieurs ▷ *I've seen several of them.* J'en ai vu plusieurs.

sew [səʊ] *vb* coudre; **to sew up** *(tear)* recoudre

sewing [ˈsəʊɪŋ] *n* couture *f* ▷ *I like sewing.* J'aime faire de la couture.; **a sewing machine** une machine à coudre

sewn [səʊn] *vb* see **sew**

sex [sɛks] *n* sexe *m*; **to have sex with somebody** coucher avec quelqu'un; **sex education** l'éducation *f* sexuelle

sexism [ˈsɛksɪzəm] *n* sexisme *m*

sexist [ˈsɛksɪst] *adj* sexiste

sexual [ˈsɛksjʊəl] *adj* sexuel (*f* sexuelle) ▷ *sexual discrimination* la discrimination sexuelle ▷ *sexual harassment* le harcèlement sexuel

sexuality [sɛksjʊˈælɪtɪ] *n* sexualité *f*

sexy [ˈsɛksɪ] *adj* sexy (*f+pl* sexy)

shabby [ˈʃæbɪ] *adj* miteux (*f* miteuse)

shade [ʃeɪd] *n* ❶ ombre *f*; **in the shade** à l'ombre ▷ *It was 35 degrees in the shade.* Il faisait trente-cinq à l'ombre. ❷ *(colour)* nuance *f* ▷ *a* *shade of blue* une nuance de bleu

shadow [ˈʃædəʊ] *n* ombre *f*

shake [ˈʃeɪk] *vb* ❶ secouer ▷ *She shook the rug.* Elle a secoué le tapis. ❷ (*tremble*) trembler ▷ *He was shaking with cold.* Il tremblait de froid.; **to shake one's head** (*in refusal*) faire non de la tête; **to shake hands with somebody** serrer la main à quelqu'un ▷ *They shook hands.* Ils se sont serré la main.

shaken [ˈʃeɪkən] *adj* secoué ▷ *I was feeling a bit shaken.* J'étais un peu secoué.

shaky [ˈʃeɪkɪ] *adj* (*hand, voice*) tremblant

shall [ʃæl] *vb*: **Shall I shut the window?** Vous voulez que je ferme la fenêtre?; **Shall we ask them to come with us?** Si on leur demandait de venir avec nous?

shallow [ˈʃæləʊ] *adj* (*water, pool*) peu profond

shambles [ˈʃæmblz] *n* pagaille *f* ▷ *It's a complete shambles.* C'est la pagaille complète.

shame [ʃeɪm] *n* honte *f* ▷ *The shame of it!* Quelle honte!; **What a shame!** Quel dommage!; **It's a shame that...** c'est dommage que...

> **c'est dommage que** has to be followed by a verb in the subjunctive.
> ▷ *It's a shame he isn't here.* C'est dommage qu'il ne soit pas ici.

shampoo [ʃæmˈpuː] *n* shampooing *m* ▷ *a bottle of shampoo* une bouteille de shampooing

shape [ʃeɪp] *n* forme *f*

share [ʃɛəʳ] *n* ❶ part *f* ▷ *Everybody pays their share.* Tout le monde paie sa part. ❷ (*in company*) action *f* ▷ *They have shares in several Canadian companies.* Ils ont des actions de plusieurs compagnies canadiennes.

▶ *vb* partager ▷ *to share a room with somebody* partager une chambre avec quelqu'un; **to share out** distribuer ▷ *They shared the sweets out among the children.* Ils ont distribué les bonbons aux enfants.

shark [ʃɑːk] *n* requin *m*

sharp [ʃɑːp] *adj* ❶ (*razor, knife*) tranchant ❷ (*spike, point*) pointu ❸ (*clever*) intelligent ▷ *She's very sharp.* Elle est très intelligente. ❹ (*elegant*) chic (*f* chic) ▷ *Those boots are really sharp!* Ces bottes sont vraiment chics!; **at two o'clock sharp** à deux heures pile

shave [ʃeɪv] *vb* (*oneself*) se raser; **to shave one's legs** se raser les jambes

shaver [ˈʃeɪvəʳ] *n*: **an electric shaver** un rasoir électrique

shaving cream [ˈʃeɪvɪŋ-] *n* crème à raser *f*

shaving foam [ˈʃeɪvɪŋfəʊm] *n* mousse à raser *f*

she [ʃiː] *pron* elle ▷ *She's very nice.* Elle est très gentille.

shed [ʃɛd] *n* remise *f*

she'd [ʃiːd] = **she had**; **she would**

sheep [ʃiːp] *n* mouton *m*

sheer [ʃɪəʳ] *adj* pur ▷ *It's sheer greed.* C'est de l'avidité pure.

sheet [ʃiːt] *n* (*on bed*) drap *m*; **a sheet of paper** une feuille de papier

shelf [ʃɛlf] *n* ❶ (*in house*) étagère *f* ❷ (*in store*) rayon *m*

shell [ʃɛl] *n* ❶ (*on beach*) coquillage *m* ❷ (*of egg, nut*) coquille *f* ❸ (*explosive*) obus *m*

she'll [ʃiːl] = **she will**

shellfish [ˈʃɛlfɪʃ] *n* fruits *m* de mer *pl*

shell suit *n* survêtement *m*

shelter [ˈʃɛltəʳ] *n*: **to take shelter** se mettre à l'abri; **a bus shelter** un arrêt d'autobus

shelves [ˈʃɛlvz] *npl see* **shelf**

shepherd [ˈʃɛpəd] n berger m

sheriff [ˈʃɛrɪf] n shérif m

she's [ʃiːz] = **she is**; **she has**

shield [ʃiːld] n bouclier m

shift [ʃɪft] n poste m ▷ Her shift starts at 8 o'clock. Son poste commence à huit heures. ▷ the night shift le poste de nuit
▶ vb ❶ changer ▷ His position on the issue continues to shift. Sa position sur cette question continue de changer. ▷ The meaning of this word has shifted. Le sens de ce mot a changé. ❷ (wind) tourner ▷ The wind has shifted a little. Le vent a tourné un peu. ❸ (eyes, gaze) détourner ▷ He shifted his gaze so as not to embarrass her. Il a détourné son regard pour ne pas l'embarrasser. ❹ (gears) passer ▷ She shifted into reverse. Elle a passé à la marche arrière. ▷ to shift into second gear passer en seconde; **to shift gears** changer de vitesse

shifty [ˈʃɪftɪ] adj ❶ (person) louche ▷ He looked shifty. Il avait l'air louche. ❷ (eyes) fuyant

shin [ʃɪn] n tibia m

shine [ʃaɪn] vb briller ▷ The sun was shining. Le soleil brillait.

shiny [ˈʃaɪnɪ] adj brillant

ship [ʃɪp] n ❶ bateau m (pl bateaux) ❷ (ocean-going) navire m

shipbuilding [ˈʃɪpbɪldɪŋ] n construction navale f

shipwreck [ˈʃɪprɛk] n naufrage m

shipwrecked [ˈʃɪprɛkt] adj: **to be shipwrecked** faire naufrage

shipyard [ˈʃɪpjɑːd] n chantier naval m

shirt [ʃəːt] n ❶ (man's) chemise f ❷ (woman's) chemisier m

shiver [ˈʃɪvə] vb frissonner

shock [ʃɒk] n choc m; **to get a shock (1)** (surprise) avoir un choc **(2)** (electric) recevoir un choc

électrique; **an electric shock** un choc électrique
▶ vb ❶ (upset) bouleverser ▷ They were shocked by the tragedy. Ils ont été bouleversés par la tragédie. ❷ (scandalize) choquer ▷ I was rather shocked by her attitude. J'ai été assez choqué par son attitude.

shocking [ˈʃɒkɪŋ] adj ❶ (scandalous) choquant ▷ It's shocking! C'est choquant! ❷ (upsetting) bouleversant ▷ That's a shocking piece of news. C'est une nouvelle bouleversante. ❸ (appalling) épouvantable ▷ a shocking waste un gaspillage épouvantable

shoe [ʃuː] n ❶ soulier m ❷ chaussure f

| In Canada, **le soulier** is used more frequently, while in other francophone countries **la chaussure** is most common.

shoelace [ˈʃuːleɪs] n lacet m

shoe polish n cirage m

shoe store n magasin de chaussures m

shone [ʃɒn] vb see **shine**

shook [ʃʊk] vb see **shake**

shoot [ʃuːt] vb ❶ (kill) abattre ▷ He was shot by a sniper. Il a été abattu par un tireur d'élite. ❷ (execute) fusiller ▷ He was shot at dawn. Il a été fusillé à l'aube. ❸ (gun) tirer ▷ Don't shoot! Ne tirez pas!; **to shoot at somebody** tirer sur quelqu'un; **She was shot in the leg.** (wounded) Elle a reçu une balle dans la jambe.; **to shoot an arrow** envoyer une flèche ❹ (film) tourner ▷ The film was shot in Toronto. Le film a été tourné à Toronto.

shooting [ˈʃuːtɪŋ] n ❶ coups mpl de feu ▷ They heard shooting. Ils ont entendu des coups de feu.; **a**

shooting une fusillade; **a drive-by shooting** un mitraillage à partir d'un véhicule

shop [ʃɒp] n ❶ (shop) boutique f ▷ *a gift shop* une boutique de cadeaux ▷ *a souvenir shop* une boutique de souvenirs

● In French, there are specific words for specific kinds of shop.

a doughnut shop une beignerie ❷ (workshop) atelier m ▷ *He has a shop in his basement.* Il a un atelier au sous-sol. ❸ (school subject) menuiserie f ▷ *I made a bookshelf in shop class.* J'ai fait une étagère en menuiserie.

shoplifting ['ʃɒplɪftɪŋ] n vol à l'étalage m

shopping ['ʃɒpɪŋ] n ❶ (purchases) achats mpl ▷ *Can you get the shopping from the car?* Tu peux aller chercher mes achats dans la voiture? ❷ magasinage m ▷ *I love shopping.* J'adore faire du magasinage ; **to go shopping** (1) (for food) faire l'épicerie (2) (for pleasure) faire du magasinage ; **a shopping bag** un sac à provisions ; **a shopping centre** un centre commercial

shore [ʃɔːʳ] n rivage m; **on shore** à terre

short [ʃɔːt] adj ❶ court ▷ *a short skirt* une jupe courte ▷ *short hair* les cheveux courts; **too short** trop court ▷ *It was a great holiday, but too short.* C'étaient des vacances super, mais trop courtes. ❷ (person, period of time) petit ▷ *She's quite short.* Elle est assez petite. ▷ *a short break* une petite pause ▷ *a short walk* une petite promenade; **to be short of something** être à court de quelque chose ▷ *I'm short of money.* Je suis à court d'argent.; **at short notice** au dernier moment;

In short, the answer's no. Bref, la réponse est non.

shortage ['ʃɔːtɪdʒ] n pénurie f ▷ *a water shortage* une pénurie d'eau

shortcut ['ʃɔːtkʌt] n raccourci m ▷ *I took a shortcut.* J'ai pris un raccourci.

shortly ['ʃɔːtlɪ] adv bientôt

shorts [ʃɔːts] npl short m; **a pair of shorts** un short

short-sighted [ʃɔːt'saɪtɪd] adj myope

short story n nouvelle f

shot [ʃɒt] vb see **shoot**
▶ n ❶ (gunshot) coup de feu m (pl coups de feu) ❷ (photo) photo f ▷ *a shot of the Château Frontenac* une photo du château Frontenac ❸ (vaccination) vaccin m ▷ *flu shot* le vaccin contre la grippe

should [ʃʊd] vb devoir ▷ *You should take more exercise.* Vous devriez faire plus d'exercice. ▷ *He should be there by now.* Il devrait être arrivé maintenant. ▷ *That shouldn't be too hard.* Ça ne devrait pas être trop difficile.; **should have** avoir dû ▷ *I should have told you before.* J'aurais dû te le dire avant.; **I should be so lucky!** Ça serait trop beau!

shoulder ['ʃəʊldəʳ] n épaule f; **a shoulder bag** un sac à bandoulière

shouldn't ['ʃʊdnt]; = **should not**

shout [ʃaʊt] vb crier ▷ *Don't shout!* Ne criez pas! ▷ *"Go away!" he shouted.* «Allez-vous-en!» a-t-il crié.
▶ n cri m

shovel ['ʃʌvl] n pelle f
▶ vb pelleter ▷ *After the snowstorm I shovelled the driveway.* Après la tempête de neige, j'ai pelleté l'entrée. ▷ *We shovelled the dirt into the hole.* Nous avons pelleté la terre dans le trou.

show [ʃəʊ] n ❶ (performance) spectacle m ❷ (TV) émission f

❸ (exhibition) salon m
▶ vb ❶ montrer; **to show somebody something** montrer quelque chose à quelqu'un ▷ *Have I shown you my new DVD?* Est-ce que je t'ai montré mon nouveau DVD? ▷ *She showed me how to set up a blog.* Elle m'a montré comment monter un blogue. ❸ faire preuve de ▷ *She showed great courage.* Elle a fait preuve de beaucoup de courage. ❸ (movie) projeter ▷ *What's showing at the movie theatre tonight?* Qu'est-ce qui est projeté au cinéma ce soir?; **It shows.** Ça se voit. ▷ *"I've never been riding before." — "It shows."* «Je n'ai jamais fait de cheval.» — «Ça se voit.»; **to show off** se vanter (informal); **to show up (1)** (arrive) se pointer ▷ *He showed up late as usual.* Il s'est pointé en retard comme d'habitude. **(2)** (be noticeable) ▷ *The yellow font doesn't show up well on the screen.* Les caractères jaunes ne se voient pas sur l'écran.; **to show somebody around** faire faire le tour à quelqu'un ▷ *She showed us around.* Elle nous a fait faire le tour.; **Your slip is showing.** On voit ton jupon.
shower ['ʃaʊə] n ❶ douche f; **to have a shower** prendre une douche ❷ (of rain) averse f
showing ['ʃəʊɪŋ] n (of film) projection f
shown [ʃəʊn] vb see **show**
show-off ['ʃəʊɒf] n vantard m, vantarde f
shrank [ʃræŋk] vb see **shrink**
shriek [ʃri:k] vb hurler
shrimp [ʃrɪmp] n crevette f ▷ *I like shrimp.* J'aime les crevettes.
shrink [ʃrɪŋk] vb (clothes, fabric) rétrécir
shrug [ʃrʌg] vb: **to shrug one's shoulders** hausser les épaules

shrunk [ʃrʌŋk] vb see **shrink**
shudder ['ʃʌdə] vb frissonner
shuffle ['ʃʌfl] vb: **to shuffle the cards** battre les cartes; **I put the CD on shuffle mode.** J'ai mis le CD en lecture aléatoire.
shut [ʃʌt] vb fermer ▷ *Shut the door.* Ferme la porte. ▷ *The door doesn't shut properly.* La porte ferme mal.; **The door slammed shut.** La porte a claqué.; **to shut down** fermer ▷ *The movie theatre shut down last year.* Le cinéma a fermé l'année dernière. ▷ *Did you shut down the computer?* As-tu fermé l'ordinateur?
shutters ['ʃʌtəz] n volets mpl
shuttle ['ʃʌtl] n navette f
shuttlecock ['ʃʌtlkɒk] n (badminton) volant m
shy [ʃaɪ] adj timide
sick [sɪk] adj ❶ (ill) malade ▷ *He was sick for four days.* Il a été malade pendant quatre jours. ❷ (joke, humour) de mauvais goût ▷ *That's really sick!* C'est vraiment de mauvais goût!; **to be sick** (vomit) vomir ▷ *I feel sick.* J'ai envie de vomir.; **to be sick of something** en avoir assez de quelque chose ▷ *I'm sick of your jokes.* J'en ai assez de tes plaisanteries.
sickening ['sɪknɪŋ] adj écœurant
sickness ['sɪknɪs] n maladie f
sick note n **①** (from parents) mot d'absence m **②** (from doctor) certificat médical m
side [saɪd] n **①** (of object, building, car) côté m ▷ *She was driving on the wrong side of the road.* Elle roulait du mauvais côté de la route. ▷ *She had the telephone by her side.* Le téléphone était à côté d'elle. **②** (of pool, river, road) bord m ▷ *by the side of the lake* au bord du lac **③** (of hill) flanc m; **He's on my side. (1)** (on my team) Il est dans mon équipe.

(2) (supporting me) Il est de mon côté.; **side by side** côte à côte; **the side entrance** l'entrée latérale; **to take sides** prendre parti ▷ She always takes his side. Elle prend toujours son parti.

side-effect ['saɪdɪfekt] n effet m secondaire

side street n petite rue transversale f

sidewalk ['saɪdwɔːk] n trottoir m

sideways ['saɪdweɪz] adv **①** (look, be facing) de côté **②** (move) de travers

sieve [sɪv] n passoire f

sigh [saɪ] n soupir m
▶ vb soupirer

sight [saɪt] n **①** vue f ▷ Stay within sight of the group. Restez à portée de vue du groupe. ▷ At the sight of the police, he took off. À la vue de la police, il s'est enfui.; **to know somebody by sight** connaître quelqu'un de vue **②** spectacle m ▷ It was an amazing sight. C'était un spectacle époustouflant.; **in sight** visible; **out of sight** hors de vue; **the sights** (tourist spots) les attractions touristiques; **to see the sights of London** visiter Londres

sightseeing ['saɪtsiːɪŋ] n tourisme m; **to go sightseeing** faire du tourisme

sign [saɪn] n **①** (notice) panneau m (pl panneaux) ▷ There was a big sign saying "private". Il y avait un grand panneau indiquant « privé ».; **a road sign** un panneau routier **②** (gesture, indication) signe m ▷ There's no sign of improvement. Il n'y a aucun signe d'amélioration.; **What sign are you?** (star sign) Tu es de quel signe?
▶ vb signer; **to sign up** s'inscrire ▷ She signed up for volleyball. Elle s'est

inscrite au volley-ball.

signal ['sɪgnl] n signal m (pl signaux)
▶ vb: **to signal to somebody** faire un signe à quelqu'un

signature ['sɪgnətʃə*] n signature f

significance [sɪg'nɪfɪkəns] n importance f

significant [sɪg'nɪfɪkənt] adj important

sign language n langage des signes m

signpost ['saɪnpəʊst] n poteau indicateur m

Sikh [siːk] n sikh m, sikhe f
▶ adj sikh m

silence ['saɪləns] n silence m

silent ['saɪlnt] adj silencieux (f silencieuse)

silk [sɪlk] n soie f
▶ adj en soie ▷ a silk scarf un foulard en soie

silky ['sɪlkɪ] adj soyeux (f soyeuse)

silly ['sɪlɪ] adj bête

silver ['sɪlvə*] n argent m ▷ a silver medal une médaille d'argent; **a silver van** une fourgonnette de couleur argent

similar ['sɪmɪlə*] adj semblable; **similar to** semblable à

simple ['sɪmpl] adj simple m ▷ It's very simple. C'est très simple.

simply ['sɪmplɪ] adv simplement ▷ It's simply not possible. Ça n'est tout simplement pas possible.

simultaneous [sɪməl'teɪnɪəs] adj simultané

sin [sɪn] n péché m
▶ vb pécher

since [sɪns] prep, adv, conj **①** depuis ▷ since yesterday depuis hier ▷ since then depuis ce moment-là ▷ I haven't seen him since. Je ne l'ai pas vu depuis.; **ever since** depuis ce moment-là **②** depuis que ▷ I haven't seen her since she left. Je ne

l'ai pas vue depuis qu'elle est partie.
❸ (because) puisque ▷ Since you're
tired, let's stay at home. Puisque tu es
fatigué, restons à la maison.

sincere [sɪnˈsɪəʳ] adj sincère

sincerely [sɪnˈsɪəlɪ] adv: **Yours
sincerely...** (1) (in business letter)
Veuillez agréer l'expression de mes
sentiments les meilleurs... (2) (in
personal letter) Cordialement...

sing [sɪŋ] vb chanter ▷ He sang out
of tune. Il chantait faux. ▷ Have you
ever sung this tune before? Vous avez
déjà chanté cet air-là?

singer [ˈsɪŋəʳ] n chanteur m,
chanteuse f

singing [ˈsɪŋɪŋ] n chant m ▷ singing
lessons des cours de chant

single [ˈsɪŋgl] adj (unmarried)
célibataire; **a single room** une
chambre pour une personne; **not a
single thing** rien du tout
▶ n: **a CD single** un CD simple

single parent n: **She's a single
parent.** Elle est parent unique.; **a
single-parent family** une famille
monoparentale

singles [ˈsɪŋglz] npl (in tennis)
simple m ▷ the women's singles le
simple dames

singular [ˈsɪŋgjuləʳ] n singulier m
▷ in the singular au singulier

sinister [ˈsɪnɪstəʳ] adj sinistre

sink [sɪŋk] n évier m
▶ vb couler

sir [səʳ] n monsieur m; **Yes, sir.** Oui,
Monsieur.

siren [ˈsaɪərn] n sirène f

sister [ˈsɪstəʳ] n sœur f ▷ my little
sister ma petite sœur

sister-in-law [ˈsɪstərɪnlɔ:] n belle-
sœur f (pl belles-sœurs)

sit [sɪt] vb s'asseoir ▷ She sat on the
chair. Elle s'est assise sur la chaise.;
to sit down s'asseoir ▷ Sit down,
please. Asseyez-vous, s'il vous plaît.;

to be sitting être assis

sitcom [ˈsɪtkɔm] n comédie
de situation f (pl comédies de
situation)

site [saɪt] n ❶ site m ▷ an
archaeological site un site
archéologique; **the site of the
accident** le lieu de l'accident
❷ (campsite) emplacement m
de camping; **a building site** un
chantier de construction

sitting room [ˈsɪtɪŋ-] n salon

situated [ˈsɪtjueɪtɪd] adj: **to be
situated** être situé ▷ The village is
situated on a hill. Le village est situé
sur une colline.

situation [sɪtjuˈeɪʃən] n situation f

six [sɪks] num six ▷ He's six. Il a
six ans.

sixteen [sɪksˈtiːn] num seize ▷ He's
sixteen. Il a seize ans.

sixteenth [sɪksˈtiːnθ] adj seizième
▷ the sixteenth floor le seizième
étage; **the sixteenth of August** le
seize août

sixth [sɪksθ] adj sixième ▷ the sixth
floor le sixième étage; **the sixth of
August** le six août

sixty [ˈsɪkstɪ] num soixante

size [saɪz] n ❶ (of object, clothing)
taille f ▷ What size do you take?
Quelle taille est-ce que vous
portez?; **I'm a size ten.** Je porte du
dix ans. ❷ (of shoes) pointure f; **I
take size six.** Je porte du six.

skate [skeɪt] vb ❶ (ice-skate) faire
du patin à glace ❷ (roller-skate)
faire du patin à roulettes

skateboard [ˈskeɪtbɔːd] n planche
à roulettes f

skateboarder [ˈskeɪtbɔːdəʳ] n
le/la planchiste

skateboarding [ˈskeɪtbɔːdɪŋ]
n planche à roulettes f ▷ to go
skateboarding faire de la planche
à roulettes ▷ She's a skateboarding

champ. C'est une vraie championne de la planche à roulettes. ▷ *My brother loves skateboarding.* Mon frère adore la planche à roulettes.

skater ['skeɪtə^r] *n* patineur *m*, patineuse *f*

skates [skeɪts] *npl* patins *mpl*

skating ['skeɪtɪŋ] *n* patin à glace *m* ▷ *to go skating* faire du patin à glace; **a skating rink** une patinoire

skeleton ['skɛlɪtn] *n* squelette *m*

sketch [skɛtʃ] *n* (*drawing*) croquis *m*
▶ *vb*: **to sketch something** faire un croquis de quelque chose

ski [skiː] *n* ski *m*; **ski boots** les *f* chaussures de ski; **a ski lift** un remonte-pente; **ski pants** le pantalon *m* de ski; **a ski pole** un bâton de ski; **a ski slope** une piste de ski; **a ski suit** une combinaison de ski
▶ *vb* skier ▷ *Can you ski?* Tu sais skier?

skid [skɪd] *vb* déraper

skier ['skiːə^r] *n* skieur *m*, skieuse *f*

skiing ['skiːɪŋ] *n* ski *m* ▷ *to go skiing* faire du ski; **to go on a skiing holiday** aller aux sports d'hiver

skilful ['skɪlfʊl] *adj* adroit

skill [skɪl] *n* talent *m* ▷ *He played with great skill.* Il a joué avec beaucoup de talent.

skilled [skɪld] *adj*: **a skilled worker** un ouvrier spécialisé

skim milk [skɪm-] *n* lait écrémé *m*

skimpy ['skɪmpɪ] *adj* ❶ (*clothes*) minuscule ❷ (*meal*) maigre

skin [skɪn] *n* peau *f* (*pl* peaux); **skin cancer** le cancer de la peau

skinhead ['skɪnhɛd] *n* skinhead

skinny ['skɪnɪ] *adj* maigre

skin-tight ['skɪntaɪt] *adj* collant

skip [skɪp] *vb* sauter ▷ *to skip a meal* sauter un repas; **to skip a class** sécher un cours

skirt [skəːt] *n* jupe *f*

skull [skʌl] *n* crâne *m*

sky [skaɪ] *n* ciel *m*

skyscraper ['skaɪskreɪpə^r] *n* gratte-ciel *m* (*pl* gratte-ciel)

slack [slæk] *adj* ❶ (*rope*) lâche ❷ (*person*) négligent

slam [slæm] *vb* claquer ▷ *The door slammed.* La porte a claqué. ▷ *She slammed the door.* Elle a claqué la porte.

slang [slæŋ] *n* argot *m*

slap [slæp] *n* claque *f*
▶ *vb*: **to slap somebody** donner une claque à quelqu'un

slapshot ['slæpʃɔt] *n* lancer frappé *m*

sled [slɛd] *n* traîneau *m*

sledding ['slɛdɪŋ] *n*: **to go sledding** faire du traîneau

sleep [sliːp] *n* sommeil *m*; **I need some sleep.** J'ai besoin de dormir.; **to go to sleep** s'endormir
▶ *vb* dormir ▷ *I couldn't sleep last night.* J'ai mal dormi la nuit dernière.; **to sleep with somebody** coucher avec quelqu'un; **to sleep together** coucher ensemble

sleep in *vb* ❶ (*accidentally*) ne pas se réveiller ▷ *I'm sorry I'm late, I slept in.* Désolé d'être en retard : je ne me suis pas réveillé. ❷ (*on purpose*) faire la grasse matinée

sleeping bag ['sliːpɪŋ-] *n* sac de couchage *m* (*pl* sacs de couchage)

sleeping pill ['sliːpɪŋ-] *n* somnifère *m*

sleepy ['sliːpɪ] *adj*: **to feel sleepy** avoir sommeil ▷ *I was feeling sleepy.* J'avais sommeil.; **a sleepy little village** un petit village tranquille

sleet [sliːt] *n* neige fondante *f*
▶ *vb*: **It's sleeting.** Il tombe de la neige fondante.

sleeve [sliːv] *n* ❶ manche *f* ▷ *long sleeves* les manches longues ▷ *short sleeves* les manches courtes ❷ (*record sleeve*) pochette *f*

sleigh [sleɪ] n traîneau m (pl traîneaux)

slept [slɛpt] vb see **sleep**

slice [slaɪs] n tranche f
▶ vb couper en tranches

slick [slɪk] n: **an oil slick** une marée noire

slide [slaɪd] n ❶ (in playground) glissoire f ❷ (photo) diapositive f
▶ vb glisser

slight [slaɪt] adj léger (f légère) ▷ a slight problem un léger problème ▷ a slight improvement une légère amélioration

slightly ['slaɪtlɪ] adv légèrement

slim [slɪm] adj mince

sling [slɪŋ] n écharpe f ▷ She had her arm in a sling. Elle avait le bras en écharpe.

slip [slɪp] n ❶ (mistake) erreur f ❷ (underskirt) jupon m; **a slip of paper** un bout de papier; **a slip of the tongue** un lapsus
▶ vb glisser ▷ I slipped on the ice. J'ai glissé sur le verglas.; **to slip up** (make a mistake) faire une erreur

slipper ['slɪpə'] n pantoufle f; **a pair of slippers** des pantoufles

slippery ['slɪpərɪ] adj glissant

slip-up ['slɪpʌp] n erreur f

slope [sləʊp] n pente f

sloppy ['slɒpɪ] adj ❶ (work) bâclé ❷ (person, appearance) négligé

slot [slɒt] n fente f

slot machine n (for gambling) machine à sous f

slough [slu:] n bourbier m

slow [sləʊ] adj, adv ❶ lent ▷ He's a bit slow. Il est un peu lent. ❷ lentement ▷ to go slow (person, car) aller lentement ▷ Drive slower! Conduisez plus lentement!; **My watch is slow.** Ma montre retarde.

slow down vb ralentir

slowly ['sləʊlɪ] adv lentement

slug [slʌg] n limace f

slum [slʌm] n (area) quartier insalubre m

slush [slʌʃ] n neige fondante f

sly [slaɪ] adj (person) rusé; **a sly smile** un sourire sournois

smack [smæk] n tape f
▶ vb: **to smack somebody** donner une tape à quelqu'un

small [smɔ:l] adj petit; **small change** la petite monnaie

smart [smɑ:t] adj ❶ (clever) intelligent; **a smart idea** une idée astucieuse ❷ (elegant) chic (f chic)

smash [smæʃ] vb ❶ (break) casser ▷ I've smashed my watch. J'ai cassé ma montre. ❷ (get broken) se briser ▷ The glass smashed into tiny pieces. Le verre s'est brisé en mille morceaux.

smell [smɛl] n odeur f; **the sense of smell** l'odorat m
▶ vb ❶ sentir mauvais ▷ That old dog really smells! Ce vieux chien sent vraiment mauvais!; **to smell like something** sentir quelque chose ▷ It smells like gas. Ça sent l'essence. ❷ (detect) sentir ▷ I can't smell anything. Je ne sens rien.

smelly ['smɛlɪ] adj qui sent mauvais ▷ He's got smelly feet. Il a les pieds qui sentent mauvais.

smile [smaɪl] n sourire m
▶ vb sourire m

smiley ['smaɪlɪ] n binette f

smoke [sməʊk] n fumée f
▶ vb fumer ▷ I don't smoke. Je ne fume pas.

smoked meat sandwich [sməʊkt-] n sandwich au smoked meat m

smoker ['sməʊkə'] n fumeur m, fumeuse f

smoking ['sməʊkɪŋ] n: **to give up smoking** arrêter de fumer; **Smoking is bad for you.** Le tabac, est mauvais pour la santé.; **"no**

smoking" « défense de fumer »

smooth [smuːð] adj ❶ (surface) lisse ❷ (person) mielleux (f mielleuse)

smudge [smʌdʒ] n bavure f

smug [smʌg] adj suffisant

smuggle [smʌgl] vb ❶ (goods) passer en fraude ▷ to smuggle cigarettes into a country faire passer des cigarettes en fraude dans un pays ❷ (people) faire passer clandestinement; **They managed to smuggle her out of prison.** Ils ont réussi à la faire sortir de prison clandestinement.

smuggler [smʌglə^r] n contrebandier m, contrebandière f

smuggling [smʌglɪŋ] n contrebande f

snack [snæk] n collation f; **to have a snack** manger une collation

snack bar n casse-croûte m (pl casse-croûte)

snail [sneɪl] n escargot m

snake [sneɪk] n serpent m

snap [snæp] vb (break) casser net ▷ The branch snapped. La branche a cassé net.; **to snap one's fingers** faire claquer ses doigts

snap fastener [-fɑːsnə^r] n bouton-pression m (pl boutons-pression)

snapshot [snæpʃɔt] n photo f

snarl [snɑːl] vb (animal) gronder

snatch [snætʃ] vb: **to snatch something from somebody** arracher quelque chose à quelqu'un ▷ He snatched the keys from my hand. Il m'a arraché les clés des mains.; **My purse was snatched.** On m'a arraché mon sac à main.

sneak [sniːk] vb: **to sneak in** entrer furtivement; **to sneak out** sortir furtivement; **to sneak up on somebody** s'approcher de quelqu'un sans faire de bruit

sneakers [sniːkəz] npl chaussures fpl de sport

sneeze [sniːz] vb éternuer

sniff [snɪf] vb ❶ renifler ▷ Stop sniffing! Arrête de renifler! ❷ flairer ▷ The dog sniffed my hand. Le chien m'a flairé la main.

snob [snɔb] n snob

snooker [snuːkə^r] n billard m ▷ to play snooker jouer au billard

snooze [snuːz] n petit somme m ▷ to have a snooze faire un petit somme

snore [snɔː^r] vb ronfler

snorkel [snɔːkl] n snorkel m
▶ vb faire du snorkel ▷ We went snorkelling. Nous sommes allés faire du snorkel.

snow [snəu] n neige f ▷ snow sports les sports d'hiver
▶ vb neiger ▷ It's snowing. Il neige.

snowball [snəubɔːl] n boule de neige f (pl boules de neige)

snowbank [snəubæŋk] n banc de neige (pl bancs de neige)

snow blindness [-blaɪndnɪs] n cécité des neiges f

snowblower [snəubləuə^r] n souffleuse f ▷ My father used the snowblower to clear the driveway. Mon père a passé la souffleuse pour déneiger l'entrée.

snowboard [snəubɔːd] n planche à neige f

snowboarder [snəubɔːdə^r] n planchiste

snowboarding [snəubɔː-dɪŋ] n planche à neige f ▷ to go snowboarding faire de la planche à neige

snowflake [snəufleɪk] n flocon de neige m (pl flocons de neige)

snowman [snəumæn] n bonhomme de neige m (pl bonshommes de neige) ▷ to build a snowman faire un bonhomme de neige

snowmobile ['snəuməubiːl] *n* motoneige *f*

snowmobiler ['snəuməubiːlə*r*] *n* motoneigiste *f*

snowplow ['snəuplau] *n* déneigeuse *f*

snowstorm ['snəustɔːm] *n* tempête de neige *f* (*pl* tempêtes de neige)

so [səu] *conj, adv* ❶ alors ▷ *The store was closed, so I went home.* Le magasin était fermé, alors je suis rentré chez moi. ▷ *So, have you always lived in Repentigny?* Alors, vous avez toujours vécu à Repentigny?; **So what?** Et alors? ❷ (*so that*) donc ▷ *It rained, so I got wet.* Il pleuvait, donc j'ai été mouillé. ❸ (*very*) tellement ▷ *It was so heavy!* C'était tellement lourd! ▷ *She was talking so fast I couldn't understand.* Elle parlait tellement vite que je ne comprenais pas.; **It's not so heavy!** Ça n'est pas si lourd que ça!; **"How's your father?" — "Not so good."** « Comment va ton père? » — « Pas très bien. »; **so much** (*a lot*) tellement ▷ *I love you so much.* Je t'aime tellement.; **so much…, so many…** tellement de… ▷ *I have so much work.* J'ai tellement de travail. ▷ *I have so many things to do today.* J'ai tellement de choses à faire aujourd'hui. ❹ (*in comparisons*) aussi ▷ *He's like his sister but not so outgoing.* Il est comme sa sœur mais pas aussi extraverti.; **so do I** moi aussi ▷ *"I love horses." — "So do I."* « J'aime les chevaux. » — « Moi aussi. »; **so have we** nous aussi ▷ *"I've been to Price Edward Island twice." — "So have we."* « Je suis allé à l'Île-du-Prince-Édouard deux fois. » — « Nous aussi. »; **I think so.** Je crois.; **I hope so.** J'espère bien.;

That's not so. Ça n'est pas le cas.; **so far** jusqu'à présent ▷ *It's been easy so far.* Ça a été facile jusqu'à présent.; **so far so good** jusqu'ici ça va; **ten or so people** environ dix personnes; **at five o'clock or so** à environ cinq heures

soak [səuk] *vb* tremper; **soaking wet** trempé

soaked *adj* trempé ▷ *By the time we got back we were soaked.* Nous sommes rentrés trempés.

soap [səup] *n* savon *m*

soap opera *n* téléroman *m*

sob [sɔb] *vb* sangloter ▷ *She was sobbing.* Elle sanglotait.

sober ['səubə*r*] *adj* sobre

sober up *vb* dessoûler

soccer ['sɔkə*r*] *n* soccer *m* ▷ *We play soccer twice a week.* Nous jouons au soccer deux fois par semaine.

social ['səuʃl] *adj* social (*mpl* sociaux) ▷ *a social class* une classe sociale; **I have a good social life.** Je vois beaucoup de monde.

social assistance *n* (*money*) aide *f* sociale; **to be on social assistance** recevoir de l'aide sociale

socialism ['səuʃəlɪzəm] *n* socialisme *m*

socialist ['səuʃəlɪst] *adj* socialiste ▶ *n* socialiste

social media *npl* médias sociaux *mpl*

social networking site *n* site de réseautage social *m*

social worker *n* travailleur social *m* (*pl* travailleurs sociaux), travailleuse sociale *f* ▷ *He's a social worker.* Il est travailleur social. ▷ *She's a social worker.* Elle est travailleuse sociale.

society [sə'saɪətɪ] *n* société *f* ▷ *We live in a multicultural society.* Nous vivons dans une société multiculturelle.

sociology [səusɪˈɒlədʒɪ] n sociologie f

sock [sɒk] n chaussette f

socket [ˈsɒkɪt] n prise de courant f (pl prises de courant)

soda [ˈsəudə] n (soda water) soda m

sofa [ˈsəufə] n divan m; **a sofa bed** un divan-lit

soft [sɒft] adj ❶ (fabric, texture) doux (f douce) ❷ (pillow, bed) mou (f molle); **soft cheeses** les fromages à pâte molle ❸ (hair) fin; **to be soft on somebody** (be kind to) être indulgent avec quelqu'un; **a soft drink** une boisson gazeuse

software [ˈsɒftwɛəʳ] n logiciels mpl ▷ *Have you installed all the software?* As-tu installé tous les logiciels?; **a piece of software** un logiciel ▷ *a piece of antivirus software* un logiciel antivirus

soggy [ˈsɒgɪ] adj ❶ (soaked) trempé ▷ *a soggy tissue* un mouchoir de papier trempé ❷ (not crisp) mou (f molle) ▷ *soggy fries* des frites molles

soil [sɔɪl] n terre f

solar [ˈsəuləʳ] adj solaire; **solar panel** le panneau solaire

solar power n énergie f solaire

sold [səuld] vb see **sell**

soldier [ˈsəuldʒəʳ] n soldat m, soldate f ▷ *She's a soldier.* Elle est soldate.

solid [ˈsɒlɪd] adj ❶ (not hollow) massif (f massive) ▷ *solid gold* l'or massif ❷ solide ▷ *a solid wall* un mur solide; **for three hours solid** pendant trois heures entières

solo [ˈsəuləu] n solo m ▷ *a guitar solo* un solo de guitare

solution [səˈluːʃən] n solution f

solve [sɒlv] vb résoudre

some [sʌm] adj, pron
> When **some** means "a certain amount of", use **du**, **de la** or **des** according to the gender of the French noun that follows it. **du** and **de la** become **de l'** when they are followed by a noun starting with a vowel.

❶ du ▷ *Would you like some bread?* Voulez-vous du pain? ▷ *Would you like some jam?* Voulez-vous de la confiture?, de l' ▷ *I would like some mineral water.* Je voudrais de l'eau minérale., des ❷ *I have some detective novels.* J'ai des romans policiers.; **Some people say that…** Il y a des gens qui disent que…; **some day** un de ces jours; **some day next week** un jour la semaine prochaine ❷ (some but not all) certains ▷ *"Are these mushrooms poisonous?" — "Only some."* « Est-ce que ces champignons sont vénéneux? » — « Certains le sont. »; **some of them** quelques-uns ▷ *I only sold some of them.* J'en ai seulement vendu quelques-uns.; **I only took some of it.** J'en ai seulement pris un peu.; **I'm going to buy some stamps. Do you want some too?** Je vais acheter des timbres. Est-ce que tu en veux aussi?; **"Would you like some coffee?" — "No thanks, I've got some."** « Tu veux du café? » — « Non merci, j'en ai déjà. »

somebody [ˈsʌmbədɪ] pron quelqu'un ▷ *Somebody stole my personal stereo.* Quelqu'un a volé mon baladeur.

somehow [ˈsʌmhau] adv: **I'll do it somehow.** Je trouverai le moyen de le faire.; **Somehow I don't think he believed me.** Quelque chose me dit qu'il ne m'a pas cru.

someone [ˈsʌmwʌn] pron quelqu'un ▷ *Someone stole my wallet.* Quelqu'un a volé mon porte-monnaie.

something [ˈsʌmθɪŋ] pron

quelque chose ▷ *something special* quelque chose de spécial ▷ *Wear something warm.* Mets quelque chose de chaud. ▷ *That's really something!* C'est vraiment quelque chose! ▷ *It cost 100 dollars, or something like that.* Ça a coûté cent dollars, ou quelque chose comme ça.

sometime ['sʌmtaɪm] *adv* un de ces jours ▷ *You must come and see us sometime.* Passez donc nous voir un de ces jours.; **sometime last month** dans le courant du mois dernier

sometimes ['sʌmtaɪmz] *adv* quelquefois ▷ *Sometimes I think she hates me.* Quelquefois j'ai l'impression qu'elle me déteste.

somewhere ['sʌmwεəʳ] *adv* quelque part ▷ *I left my keys somewhere.* J'ai laissé mes clés quelque part. ▷ *I'd like to go somewhere sunny.* J'aimerais aller quelque part où il fait du soleil.

son [sʌn] *n* fils *m*

song [sɔŋ] *n* chanson *f*

son-in-law ['sʌnɪnlɔː] *n* gendre *m*

soon [suːn] *adv* bientôt ▷ *very soon* très bientôt; **soon afterwards** peu après; **as soon as possible** aussitôt que possible

sooner ['suːnəʳ] *adv* plus tôt ▷ *Can't you come a bit sooner?* Tu ne peux pas venir un peu plus tôt?; **sooner or later** tôt ou tard

soot [sut] *n* suie *f*

sorcerer ['sɔːsərəʳ] *n* sorcier *m*

sore [sɔːʳ] *adj*: **My feet are sore.** J'ai mal aux pieds.; **It's sore.** Ça fait mal.; **That's a sore point.** C'est un point sensible.
▶ *n* plaie *f*

sorry ['sɔrɪ] *adj* désolé ▷ *I'm really sorry.* Je suis vraiment désolé. ▷ *I'm sorry, I don't have any change.* Je suis

désolé, je n'ai pas de monnaie. ▷ *I'm sorry I'm late.* Je suis désolée d'être en retard.; **sorry!** pardon!; **sorry? pardon?; I'm sorry about the noise.** Je m'excuse pour le bruit.; **You'll be sorry!** Tu le regretteras!; **to feel sorry for somebody** plaindre quelqu'un

sort [sɔːt] *n* sorte *f* ▷ *What sort of bike do you have?* Quelle sorte de vélo as-tu?

sort out *vb* ❶ *(objects)* ranger ❷ *(problems)* résoudre

so-so ['səʊsəʊ] *adv* comme ci comme ça ▷ *"How are you feeling?" — "So-so."* Comment est-ce que tu te sens? — «Comme ci comme ça.»

sought [sɔːt] *vb see* **to seek**

soul [səʊl] *n* ❶ *(spirit)* âme *f* ❷ musique soul *f*

sound [saʊnd] *n* ❶ *(noise)* bruit *m* ▷ *Don't make a sound!* Pas un bruit! ▷ *the sound of footsteps* des bruits de pas ▷ *son m* ▷ *Can I turn the sound down?* Je peux baisser le son?
▶ *vb*: **That sounds interesting.** Ça a l'air intéressant.; **It sounds as if she's doing well at school.** Elle a l'air de bien travailler à l'école.; **That sounds like a good idea.** C'est une bonne idée.
▶ *adj, adv* bon (f bonne) ▷ *That's sound advice.* C'est un bon conseil.; **sound asleep** profondément endormi

sound effects *npl* bruitage *m*; **sound effect specialist** le bruiteur ▷ *She's a sound effect specialist.* Elle est bruiteuse.

soundtrack ['saʊndtræk] *n* bande sonore *f*

soup [suːp] *n* soupe *f* ▷ *vegetable soup* la soupe aux légumes

sour ['saʊəʳ] *adj* aigre

south [saʊθ] *adj, adv* ❶ sud *m* (f+p

sud) ▷ *the south coast* la côte sud
❷ vers le sud ▷ *We were travelling
south.* Nous allions vers le sud.;
south of au sud de ▷ *It's south of
Hearst.* C'est au sud de Hearst.;
South America l'Amérique f du Sud
▶ n sud m ▷ *in the south* dans le
sud ▷ *the south of Ontario* le sud de
l'Ontario

southbound ['sauθbaund] *adj:*
**Southbound traffic is moving
very slowly.** La circulation
en direction du sud est très
ralentie.; **The suspect vehicle
was southbound on the 400.**
Le véhicule suspect se trouvait
sur l'autoroute 400 en direction
du sud.

southeast ['sauθ'i:st] *n* sud-est
m ▷ *southeast Alberta* le sud-est de
l'Alberta

southern ['sʌðən] *adj:* **the
southern part of the island** la
partie sud de l'île; **southern New
Brunswick** le sud du Nouveau-
Brunswick

South Pole *n* pôle Sud *m*

southwest ['sauθ'wɛst] *n*
sud-ouest *m* ▷ *southwest Yukon* le
sud-ouest du Yukon

souvenir [su:və'nɪər] *n* souvenir
m; **a souvenir shop** une boutique
de souvenirs

sovereigntist ['sɒvrɪntɪst] *n*
souverainiste

sovereignty ['sɒvrɪntɪ] *n*
souveraineté f ▷ *Are you in favour
of Quebec sovereignty?* Êtes-vous
en faveur de la souveraineté du
Québec?

soya [sɔɪ] *n* soya *m*

soy sauce [sɔɪ-] *n* sauce soya f

space [speɪs] *n* ❶ place f ▷ *There
isn't enough space.* Il n'y a pas
suffisamment de place.; **a parking
space** une place de stationnement

❷ (*universe, gap*) espace *m* ▷ *Leave
a space after your answer.* Laissez
un espace après votre réponse.; **a
space shuttle** une navette spatiale

spacecraft ['speɪskrɑːft] *n*
vaisseau spatial *m*

spade [speɪd] *n* pelle f; **spades** (*in
cards*) le pique *m* ▷ *the ace of spades*
l'as de pique

spam [spæm] *n* ❶ (*practice of
spamming*) pollupostage *m* ▷ *Spam
has become a real problem.* Le
pollupostage est devenu un vrai
problème. ❷ (*message*) polluriel *m*
▷ *I got some spam from that address.*
J'ai reçu des polluriels de cette
adresse.

spaniel ['spænjəl] *n* épagneul *m*

spank [spæŋk] *vb:* **to spank
somebody** donner une fessée à
quelqu'un

spare [spɛər] *adj* de rechange
▷ *spare batteries* des piles de
rechange ▷ *a spare part* une pièce
de rechange; **a spare room** une
chambre d'amis; **spare time** le
temps libre ▷ *What do you do in your
spare time?* Qu'est-ce que tu fais
pendant ton temps libre?; **spare
tire** un pneu de secours
▶ *vb:* **Can you spare a moment?**
Vous pouvez m'accorder un
instant?; **I can't spare the time.** Je
n'ai pas le temps.; **There's no room
to spare.** Il n'y a plus de place.; **We
arrived with time to spare.** Nous
sommes arrivés en avance.
▶ *n:* **a spare** un autre ▷ *"I've lost my
key." — "Have you got a spare?"* « J'ai
perdu ma clé. » — « En as-tu une
autre? »

sparkling ['spɑːklɪŋ] *adj* (*water*)
pétillant

sparrow ['spærəu] *n* moineau *m*
(*pl* moineaux)

speak [spiːk] *vb* parler ▷ *Do you*

speak English? Est-ce que vous parlez anglais?; **to speak to somebody** parler à quelqu'un ▷ *Have you spoken to him?* Tu lui as parlé? ▷ *She spoke to him about it.* Elle lui en a parlé.; **spoken French** le français parlé

speak up vb parler plus fort ▷ *Speak up, we can't hear you.* Parle plus fort, nous ne t'entendons pas.

speaker ['spiːkə^r] n ❶ (*loudspeaker*) haut-parleur m (pl haut-parleurs) ❷ (*in debate*) intervenant m, intervenante f ❸ (*at conference*) conférencier m, conférencière f

special ['spɛʃl] adj spécial (mpl spéciaux)

specialist ['spɛʃəlɪst] n spécialiste

specialize ['spɛʃəlaɪz] vb se spécialiser ▷ *We specialize in skiing equipment.* Nous nous spécialisons dans les articles de ski.

specially ['spɛʃlɪ] adv spécialement ▷ *It's specially designed for teenagers.* C'est spécialement conçu pour les adolescents.

specialty ['spɛʃəltɪ] n spécialité f

species ['spiːʃiːz] n espèce f

specific [spə'sɪfɪk] adj ❶ (*particular*) particulier (f particulière) ▷ *certain specific issues* certains problèmes particuliers ❷ (*precise*) précis ▷ *Could you be more specific?* Est-ce que vous pourriez être plus précise?

specifically [spə'sɪfɪklɪ] adv ❶ spécialement ▷ *It's specifically designed for teenagers.* C'est spécialement conçu pour les adolescents. ❷ particulièrement ▷ *on the subject of snow sports, or more specifically snowboarding* au sujet des sports d'hiver, ou plus particulièrement de la planche à neige; **I specifically said that...** J'ai

clairement dit que...

spectacular [spɛk'tækjələ^r] adj spectaculaire

spectator [spɛk'teɪtə^r] n spectateur m, spectatrice f

speech [spiːtʃ] n discours m ▷ *to make a speech* faire un discours

speechless ['spiːtʃlɪs] adj muet (f muette) ▷ *speechless with admiration* muet d'admiration; **I was speechless.** Je suis resté sans voix.

speed [spiːd] n vitesse f ▷ *a ten-speed bike* un vélo à dix vitesses ▷ *at top speed* à toute vitesse; **speed limit** la limite de vitesse ▷ *The speed limit is 50 km/h here.* La limite de vitesse ici est de 50 kilomètres par heure. ▷ *to break the speed limit* faire un excès de vitesse

speedboat ['spiːdbəʊt] n hors-bord m (pl hors-bord)

speeding ['spiːdɪŋ] n excès m de vitesse ▷ *He was fined for speeding.* Il a reçu une contravention pour excès de vitesse.

speedometer [spɪ'dɒmɪtə^r] n indicateur m de vitesse

speed up vb accélérer

spell [spɛl] vb ❶ (*in writing*) écrire ▷ *How do you spell that?* Comment est-ce que ça s'écrit? ❷ (*out loud*) épeler ▷ *Can you spell that please?* Est-ce que vous pouvez épeler, s'il vous plaît?; **I can't spell.** Je fais des fautes d'orthographe.

▶ n: **to cast a spell on somebody** jeter un sort à quelqu'un; **to be under somebody's spell** être sous le charme de quelqu'un

spelling ['spɛlɪŋ] n orthographe f ▷ *My spelling is terrible.* Je fais beaucoup de fautes d'orthographe.; **a spelling mistake** une faute d'orthographe

spend [spɛnd] vb ❶ (*money*)

dépenser ❷ (time) passer ▷ She spent a month in Quebec. Elle a passé un mois au Québec.

spice [spaɪs] n épice f

spicy ['spaɪsɪ] adj épicé

spider ['spaɪdə^r] n araignée f

spill [spɪl] vb ❶ (tip over) renverser ▷ He spilled his coffee on his pants. Il a renversé son café sur son pantalon. ❷ (get spilled) se répandre ▷ The soup spilled all over the table. La soupe s'est répandue sur la table.

spinach ['spɪnɪtʃ] n épinards mpl

spine [spaɪn] n colonne vertébrale f

spire ['spaɪə^r] n flèche f

spirit ['spɪrɪt] n ❶ esprit m ▷ the human spirit l'esprit humain ❷ (courage) courage m; **to be in good spirits** être de bonne humeur ❸ (energy) énergie f

spiritual ['spɪrɪtjuəl] adj spirituel (f spirituelle) ▷ the spiritual leader of Tibet le chef spirituel du Tibet ▷ spiritual development la croissance spirituelle

spit [spɪt] n salive f
▶ vb cracher; **to spit something out** cracher quelque chose

spite [spaɪt] n: **in spite of** malgré; **out of spite** par méchanceté
▶ vb contrarier ▷ She did it just to spite me. Elle a fait ça juste pour me contrarier.

spiteful ['spaɪtful] adj ❶ (action) méchant ❷ (person) rancunier (f rancunière)

splash [splæʃ] vb éclabousser ▷ Careful! Don't splash me! Attention! Ne m'éclabousse pas!
▶ n plouf m ▷ I heard a splash. J'ai entendu un plouf.; **a splash of colour** une touche de couleur

splendid ['splɛndɪd] adj splendide

splint [splɪnt] n attelle f

splinter ['splɪntə^r] n écharde f

split [splɪt] vb ❶ (break apart)

fendre ▷ He split the wood with an axe. Il a fendu le bois avec une hache. ❷ se fendre ▷ The ship hit a rock and split in two. Le bateau a percuté un rocher et s'est fendu en deux. ❸ (divide up) partager ▷ They decided to split the profits. Ils ont décidé de partager les bénéfices.; **to split up (1)** (couple) rompre **(2)** (group) se disperser

spoil [spɔɪl] vb ❶ (object) abîmer ❷ (occasion, experience) gâcher ❸ (child) gâter ❹ (food) se gâter ▷ The fruit is beginning to spoil. Les fruits commencent à se gâter.; **If you leave the milk on the counter it'll spoil.** Si tu laisses le lait sur le comptoir, il va tourner.

spoiled adj gâté ▷ a spoiled child une enfant gâtée

spoilsport ['spɔɪlspɔːt] n trouble-fête

spoke [spəuk] vb see **speak**
▶ n (of wheel) rayon m

spoken ['spəukn] vb see **speak**

spokesperson ['spəukspəːsn] n porte-parole (pl porte-parole)

sponge [spʌndʒ] n éponge f

sponsor ['spɒnsə^r] n commanditaire
▶ vb commanditer ▷ The festival was sponsored by... Le festival a été commandité par...

spontaneous [spɒn'teɪnɪəs] adj spontané

spooky ['spuːkɪ] adj ❶ (eerie) sinistre; **a spooky story** une histoire qui fait froid dans le dos ❷ (strange) étrange ▷ a spooky coincidence une étrange coïncidence

spoon [spuːn] n cuillère f; **a spoonful** une cuillerée

sport [spɔːt] n sport m ▷ What's your favourite sport? Quel est ton sport préféré?; **a sports bag** un sac de sport; **a sports car** une voiture de sport; **a sports jacket** une veste sport; **Come on, be a sport!** Allez, sois sympa!

sportswear ['spɔːtsweəʳ] n vêtements mpl de sport

sporty ['spɔːtɪ] adj sportif (f sportive) ▷ I'm not very sporty. Je ne suis pas très sportif.

spot [spɒt] n ❶ (mark) tache f ▷ There's a spot on your shirt. Il y a une tache sur ta chemise. ❷ (place) coin m ▷ It's a lovely spot for a picnic. C'est un coin agréable pour un pique-nique.; **on the spot** (immediately) sur-le-champ ▷ They gave her the job on the spot. Ils lui ont offert le poste sur-le-champ.
▶ vb repérer ❶ ▷ I spotted a mistake. J'ai repéré une faute.

spotless ['spɒtlɪs] adj immaculé

spotlight ['spɒtlaɪt] n projecteur m; **The universities have been in the spotlight recently.** Les universités ont été sous le feu des projecteurs ces derniers temps.

spouse [spauz] n époux m, épouse f

sprain [spreɪn] vb: **to sprain one's ankle** se faire une entorse à la cheville
▶ n entorse f ▷ It's just a sprain. C'est juste une entorse.

spray [spreɪ] n: **spray can** la bombe; **spray bottle** l'atomiseur m; **spray paint** la peinture en aérosol; **perfume spray** le parfum en atomiseur ▷ Do you have this perfume in spray form? Vous avez ce parfum en atomiseur?
▶ vb ❶ vaporiser ▷ to spray perfume on one's hand se vaporiser du parfum sur la main ❷ (crops) traiter ▷ They sprayed their crops with fertilizer. Ils ont traité leurs champs à l'engrais. ❸ (graffiti) peindre avec une bombe ▷ Somebody had sprayed

graffiti on the wall. Quelqu'un avait peint des graffitis avec une bombe sur le mur.

spread [spred] n: **cheese spread** le fromage à tartiner; **chocolate spread** le chocolat à tartiner
▶ vb ❶ étaler ▷ to spread butter on a slice of bread étaler du beurre sur une tranche de pain ❷ (disease, news) se propager ▷ The news spread rapidly. La nouvelle s'est propagée rapidement.; **to spread out** (people) se disperser ▷ The soldiers spread out across the field. Les soldats se sont dispersés dans le champ.

spreadsheet ['spredʃiːt] n (computer program) tableur m

spring [sprɪŋ] n ❶ (season) printemps m; **in spring** au printemps ▷ in spring au printemps ❷ (metal coil) ressort m ❸ (water hole) source f

spring cleaning [-kliːnɪŋ] n grand nettoyage du printemps m

sprinkler ['sprɪŋkləʳ] n (for lawn) arroseur m

sprint [sprɪnt] n sprint m
▶ vb courir à toute vitesse ▷ He sprinted for the bus. Il a couru à toute vitesse pour attraper le bus.

sprinter ['sprɪntəʳ] n sprinteur m, sprinteuse f

sprouts [sprauts] npl: **Brussels sprouts** les m choux de Bruxelles; **bean sprouts** les m germes de soya

spruce [spruːs] n épinette f

spy [spaɪ] n espion m, espionne f
▶ vb: **to spy on somebody** espionner quelqu'un

spying ['spaɪɪŋ] n espionnage m

squabble ['skwɒbl] vb se chamailler ▷ Stop squabbling! Arrêtez de vous chamailler!

square [skweəʳ] n ❶ carré m ▷ a square and a triangle un carré et un triangle ❷ place f ▷ the town square la place de l'hôtel de ville

▶ adj carré m ⊳ two square metres deux mètres carrés; **It's a metre square.** Ça fait deux mètres sur deux.

squash [skwɔʃ] n (sport) squash m ⊳ I play squash. Je joue au squash.; **a squash court** un court de squash; **a squash racquet** une raquette de squash

▶ vb écraser ⊳ You're squashing me. Tu m'écrases.

squeak [skwiːk] vb ① (mouse, child) pousser un petit cri ② (creak) grincer

squeeze [skwiːz] vb ① (fruit, toothpaste) presser ② (hand, arm) serrer; **to squeeze into some tight jeans** rentrer tout juste dans des jeans serrés

squeeze in vb ① trouver une petite place ⊳ It was a tiny car, but we managed to squeeze in. La voiture était toute petite, mais nous avons réussi à trouver une petite place. ② (for appointment) caser ⊳ I can squeeze you in at two o'clock. Je peux vous caser demain à deux heures.

squint [skwɪnt] vb loucher

squirrel ['skwɪrəl] n écureuil m

stab [stæb] vb poignarder

stable ['steɪbl] n écurie f

▶ adj stable ⊳ a stable relationship une relation stable

stack [stæk] n pile f ⊳ a stack of books une pile de livres

stadium ['steɪdɪəm] n stade m

staff [stɑːf] n ① (in company) personnel m ② (in school) professeurs mpl

staffroom ['stɑːfruːm] n salon des professeurs m

stage [steɪdʒ] n ① (in plays) scène f ② (for speeches, lectures) estrade f; **at this stage (1)** à ce stade ⊳ at this stage in the negotiations à ce stade des négociations **(2)** pour

l'instant ⊳ At this stage, it's too early to comment. Pour l'instant, il est trop tôt pour se prononcer.; **to do something in stages** faire quelque chose étape par étape

> Be careful not to translate stage by the French word stage.

stagger ['stægə'] vb chanceler

stain [steɪn] n tache f

▶ vb tacher

stainless steel ['steɪnlɪs-] n acier m inoxydable

stain remover [-rɪ'muːvə'] n détachant m

stair [stɛə'] n marche f

staircase ['stɛəkeɪs] n escalier m

stairs [stɛəz] npl escalier m

stale [steɪl] adj (bread) rassis

stalemate ['steɪlmeɪt] n ① (in chess) pat m ② impasse f ⊳ Negotiations have reached a stalemate. Les négociations sont dans l'impasse.

stall [stɔːl] n stand m ⊳ She has a stall at the market. Elle a un stand au marché.

▶ vb (car, engine) caler ⊳ The school bus stalled. L'autobus scolaire a calé.

stamina ['stæmɪnə] n endurance f

stammer ['stæmə'] vb bégayer ⊳ She stammered a reply. Elle a bégayé une réponse.

stamp [stæmp] vb ① (letter) affranchir ② tamponner ⊳ The customs agent stamped my passport. Le douanier a tamponné mon passeport.; **to stamp one's foot** taper du pied

▶ n ① timbre m ⊳ a 50-cent stamp un timbre de cinquante cents ⊳ My hobby is stamp collecting. Je collectionne les timbres.; **a stamp album** un album de timbres; **a stamp collection** une collection de timbres ② (rubber stamp) timbre en caoutchouc m

stamped [stæmpt] *adj* affranchi
▷ *The letter wasn't stamped.* La lettre
n'était pas affranchie.; **Enclose
a stamped self-addressed
envelope.** Joindre une enveloppe
affranchie à vos nom et adresse.

stand [stænd] *vb* ❶ (*be standing*)
être debout ▷ *He was standing by
the door.* Il était debout à la porte.
❷ (*stand up*) se lever ❸ (*tolerate,
withstand*) supporter ▷ *I can't stand
all this noise.* Je ne supporte pas
tout ce bruit.; **to stand for** (1) (*be
short for*) être l'abréviation de
▷ *"GST" stands for "Goods and Services
Tax".* « TPS » est l'abréviation de «
taxe sur les produits et services ».
(2) (*tolerate*) supporter ▷ *I won't
stand for it!* Je ne supporterai pas
ça!; **to stand in for somebody**
remplacer quelqu'un; **to stand
one's ground** tenir bon ▷ *If they try
to persuade you, stand your ground.* Si
elles essaient de te persuader, tiens
bon.; **to stand out** se distinguer
▷ *All the contestants were good, but
none of them stood out.* Tous les
concurrents étaient bons, mais
aucun ne se distinguait.; **She really
stands out in that orange coat.**
Tout le monde la remarque avec
ce manteau orange.; **to stand up**
(*get up*) se lever; **to stand up for**
défendre ▷ *Stand up for your rights!*
Défendez vos droits!

standard ['stændəd] *adj*
❶ courant ▷ *standard French* le
français courant ❷ (*equipment*)
ordinaire; **the standard procedure**
la procédure normale; **standard
time** l'heure normale ▷ *We're back
on standard time.* On est revenu à
l'heure normale.
▶ *n* niveau *m* (*pl* niveaux) ▷ *The
standard is very high.* Le niveau est

très haut.; **the standard of living**
le niveau de vie; **She has very high
standards.** Elle est très exigeante.

standby ticket ['stædbaɪ-] *n* billet
sans réservation *m*

standpoint ['stændpɔɪnt] *n* point
de vue *m*

stands [stændz] *npl* (*at sports
ground*) tribune *f*

stank [stæŋk] *vb see* **stink**

staple ['steɪpl] *n* ❶ agrafe *f*
❷ (*food*) aliment *m* de base ▷ *Rice
is an important staple.* Le riz est un
aliment de base important.
▶ *vb* agrafer

stapler ['steɪplə'] *n* brocheuse *f*

star [staː'] *n* ❶ (*in sky*) étoile *f*
❷ (*celebrity*) vedette *f* ▷ *He's a TV
star.* C'est une vedette de la télé.
▶ *vb* être la vedette ▷ *to star in a
film* être la vedette d'un film; **The
film stars Andrea Martin.** Le
film a pour vedette Andrea Martin.;
…starring Kiefer Sutherland
…avec Kiefer Sutherland

stare [stεə'] *vb*: **to stare at
something** fixer quelque chose

stark [staːk] *adv*: **stark naked**
complètement nu

start [staːt] *n* ❶ début *m* ▷ *It's not
much, but it's a start.* Ce n'est pas
grand chose, mais c'est un début.;
**Shall we make a start on the
dishes?** On commence à faire la
vaisselle? ❷ (*of race*) départ *m*
▶ *vb* ❶ commencer ▷ *What time
does it start?* À quelle heure est-ce
que ça commence?; **to start doing
something** commencer à faire
quelque chose ▷ *I started learning
French three years ago.* J'ai commencé
à apprendre le français il y a trois
ans. ❷ (*organization*) créer ▷ *He
wants to start his own business.* Il
veut créer sa propre entreprise.
❸ (*campaign*) organiser ▷ *She*

started a campaign against drugs. Elle a organisé une campagne contre la drogue. ❹ (car) démarrer ▷ He couldn't start the car. Il n'a pas réussi à démarrer la voiture. ▷ The car wouldn't start. La voiture ne voulait pas démarrer.; **to start off** (leave) partir ▷ We started off first thing in the morning. Nous sommes partis en début de matinée.

starve [stɑːv] vb mourir de faim ▷ People were literally starving. Les gens mouraient littéralement de faim.; **I'm starving!** Je meurs de faim!

state [steɪt] n état m; **he was in a real state** il était dans tous ses états; **the state** (government) l'État ▶ vb ❶ (say) déclarer ▷ She stated her intention to resign. Elle a déclaré son intention de démissionner. ❷ (give) donner ▷ Please state your name and address. Veuillez donner vos nom et adresse.

statement ['steɪtmənt] n déclaration f

station ['steɪʃən] n (railway) gare f; **the bus station** la gare d'autobus; **a police station** un poste de police; **a radio station** une station de radio

station wagon [-ˈwæɡən] n familiale f

statue ['stætjuː] n statue f

stay [steɪ] vb ❶ (remain) rester ▷ Stay here! Reste ici!; **to stay in** (not go out) rester à la maison; **to stay up** rester debout ▷ We stayed up till midnight. Nous sommes restés debout jusqu'à minuit. ❷ (spend the night) loger ▷ to stay with friends loger chez des amis ▷ Where are you staying? Où est-ce que vous logez?; **to stay the night** passer la nuit; **We stayed in Nova Scotia for a few days.** Nous avons passé

quelques jours en Nouvelle-Écosse. ▶ n séjour m ▷ my stay in the Gaspé mon séjour en Gaspésie

steady ['stedɪ] adj ❶ régulier (f régulière) ▷ steady progress des progrès réguliers ❷ stable ▷ a steady job un emploi stable ❸ (voice, hand) ferme ❹ (person) calme; **a steady boyfriend** un copain; **a steady girlfriend** une copine; **Steady!** Doucement!

steak [steɪk] n (beef) steak m ▷ "How would you like your steak?" — "Medium rare." « Quelle cuisson, votre steak? » — « À point. »

steal [stiːl] vb voler

steam [stiːm] n vapeur f ▷ a steam engine une locomotive à vapeur

steel [stiːl] n acier m ▷ a steel door une porte en acier

steep [stiːp] adj (slope) raide

steeple ['stiːpl] n clocher m

steering wheel ['stɪərɪŋ-] n volant m

step [step] n (pace) pas m ▷ He took a step forward. Il a fait un pas en avant. ❷ (stair) marche f ▷ She tripped over the step. Elle a trébuché sur la marche.
▶ vb: **to step aside** faire un pas de côté; **to step back** faire un pas en arrière

stepbrother ['stepbrʌðəʳ] n demi-frère m (pl demi-frères)

stepdaughter ['stepdɔːtəʳ] n belle-fille f (pl belles-filles)

stepfather ['stepfɑːðəʳ] n beau-père m (pl beaux-pères)

stepladder ['steplædəʳ] n escabeau m (pl escabeaux)

stepmother ['stepmʌðəʳ] n belle-mère f (pl belles-mères)

stepsister ['stepsɪstəʳ] n demi-sœur f (pl demi-sœurs)

stepson ['stepsʌn] n beau-fils m (pl beaux-fils)

stereo ['stɛrɪəʊ] n chaîne stéréo f (pl chaînes stéréo)

stew [stjuː] n ragoût m

stick [stɪk] n ❶ bâton m ❷ (walking stick) canne f ▷ vb (with adhesive) coller ▷ Stick the stamps on the envelope. Collez les timbres sur l'enveloppe.

stick out vb (project) sortir ▷ A pen was sticking out of his pocket. Un stylo sortait de sa poche.; **to stick out one's tongue** tirer la langue

sticker ['stɪkə] n autocollant m

sticky ['stɪkɪ] adj ❶ poisseux (f poisseuse) ▷ to have sticky hands avoir les mains poisseuses ❷ adhésif (f adhésive) ▷ a sticky label une étiquette adhésive

stiff [stɪf] adj, adv (rigid) rigide; **to have a stiff back** avoir mal au dos; **to feel stiff** avoir des courbatures; **to be bored stiff** s'ennuyer à mourir; **to be frozen stiff** être mort de froid; **to be scared stiff** être mort de peur

still [stɪl] adv ❶ encore ▷ I still haven't finished. Je n'ai pas encore fini. ▷ Are you still in bed? Tu es encore au lit?; **better still** encore mieux ❷ (even so) quand même ▷ She knows I don't like it, but she still does it. Elle sait que je n'aime pas ça, mais elle le fait quand même. ❸ (after all) enfin ▷ Still, it's the thought that counts. Enfin, c'est l'intention qui compte. ▷ adj: **Keep still!** Ne bouge pas!; **Sit still!** Reste tranquille!

sting [stɪŋ] n piqûre f ▷ a bee sting une piqûre d'abeille ▷ vb piquer ▷ I've been stung. J'ai été piqué.

stingy ['stɪndʒɪ] adj pingre

stink [stɪŋk] vb puer ▷ It stinks! Ça pue! ▷ n puanteur f

stir [stəː] vb remuer

stir-fry ['stəːfraɪ] n sauté m ▷ a vegetable stir-fry un sauté de légumes ▷ vb faire sauter ▷ I stir-fried the vegetables. J'ai fait sauter les légumes.

stitch [stɪtʃ] vb (cloth) coudre ▷ n ❶ (in sewing) point m ❷ (in wound) point de suture m ▷ I had five stitches. J'ai eu cinq points de suture.

stock [stɒk] n ❶ (supply) réserve f ❷ (in store) stock m ▷ in stock en stock; **out of stock** épuisé ❸ bouillon m ▷ chicken stock du bouillon de volaille ▷ vb (have in stock) avoir ▷ Do you stock camping stoves? Vous avez des réchauds de camping?; **to stock up** s'approvisionner ▷ to stock up on something s'approvisionner en quelque chose

stole, stolen vb see **steal**

stomach ['stʌmək] n estomac m

stomachache ['stʌməkeɪk] n: **to have a stomachache** avoir mal au ventre

stone [stəʊn] n ❶ (rock) pierre f ▷ a stone wall un mur en pierre ❷ (in fruit) noyau m (pl noyaux) ▷ a peach stone un noyau de pêche

stood [stʊd] vb see **stand**

stool [stuːl] n tabouret m

stop [stɒp] vb ❶ arrêter ▷ a campaign to stop whaling une campagne pour arrêter la chasse à la baleine ❷ s'arrêter ▷ The bus doesn't stop there. L'autobus ne s'arrête pas là. ▷ I think the rain's going to stop. Je pense qu'il va s'arrêter de pleuvoir.; **to stop doing something** arrêter de faire quelque chose ▷ to stop smoking arrêter de fumer; **to stop somebody from doing something**

empêcher quelqu'un de faire quelque chose; **Stop!** Stop!
▶ *n* arrêt *m* ▷ **a bus stop** un arrêt d'autobus; **This is my stop.** Je descends ici.

stopwatch ['stɒpwɒtʃ] *n* chronomètre *m*

store [stɔːʳ] *n* magasin *m* ▷ **a furniture store** un magasin de meubles
▶ *vb* ❶ garder ▷ **They store potatoes in the cellar.** Ils gardent des pommes de terre dans la cave. ❷ (*information*) enregistrer

storey ['stɔːrɪ] *n* étage *m* ▷ **a three-storey building** un immeuble à trois étages

storm [stɔːm] *n* ❶ tempête *f* ❷ (*thunderstorm*) orage *m*

stormy ['stɔːmɪ] *adj* orageux (*f* orageuse)

story ['stɔːrɪ] *n* ❶ histoire *f* ❷ (*oral, traditional*) conte *m* ▷ **stories from the Cree tradition** des contes cris ▷ **a book of classic children's stories** un livre de contes pour enfants

storyteller ['stɔːrɪtɛləʳ] *n* conteur *m*, conteuse *f*

stove [stəʊv] *n* ❶ (*in kitchen*) cuisinière *f* ❷ (*camping stove*) réchaud *m*

straight [streɪt] *adj, adv* ❶ droit ▷ **a straight line** une ligne droite ▷ **He looked straight ahead.** Il a regardé droit devant lui. ▷ **Go straight ahead.** Allez tout droit. ❷ raide ▷ **straight hair** les cheveux raides ❸ (*heterosexual*) hétéro ❹ directement ▷ **I went straight home.** Je suis rentré directement chez moi.

straightforward [streɪt'fɔːwəd] *adj* simple *m*

strain [streɪn] *n* stress *m*; **It was a strain.** C'était éprouvant.

▶ *vb* se faire mal à ▷ **I strained my back.** Je me suis fait mal au dos.; **to strain a muscle** se froisser un muscle

strained [streɪnd] *adj* (*muscle*) froissé

stranded ['strændɪd] *adj*: **We were stranded.** Nous étions coincés.

strange [streɪndʒ] *adj* bizarre ▷ **That's strange!** C'est bizarre!

stranger ['streɪndʒəʳ] *n* inconnu *m*, inconnue *f* ▷ **Don't talk to strangers.** Ne parle pas aux inconnus.; **I'm a stranger here.** Je ne suis pas d'ici.

strangle ['stræŋgl] *vb* étrangler

strap [stræp] *n* ❶ (*of purse, camera, suitcase*) courroie *f* ❷ (*of bra, dress*) bretelle *f* ❸ (*on shoe*) bride *f*

straw [strɔː] *n* paille *f*; **That's the last straw!** Ça, c'est le comble!

strawberry ['strɔːbərɪ] *n* fraise *f* ▷ **strawberry jam** la confiture de fraises ▷ **strawberry ice cream** la crème glacée à la fraise

stray [streɪ] *n*: **a stray cat** un chat errant

stream [striːm] *n* ruisseau *m* (*pl* ruisseaux)

street [striːt] *n* rue *f* ▷ **in the street** dans la rue

streetcar ['striːtkɑːʳ] *n* tramway *m*

streetlight ['striːtlaɪt] *n* réverbère *m*

street musician *n* musicien de rue *m*, musicienne de rue *f* ▷ **There are a lot of street musicians in Toronto.** Il y a beaucoup de musiciens de rue à Toronto.

street plan *n* plan de la ville *m*

streetwise ['striːtwaɪz] *adj* débrouillard

strength [strɛŋθ] *n* force *f*

stress [strɛs] *vb* souligner ▷ **I would like to stress that...** J'aimerais

souligner que...
▶ n stress m

stretch [strɛtʃ] vb ❶ (person, animal) s'étirer ▷ The dog woke up and stretched. Le chien s'est réveillé et s'est étiré. ❷ (get bigger) étirer ▷ My sweater stretched when I washed it. Mon chandail a étiré au lavage. ❸ (stretch out) tendre ▷ They stretched a rope between two trees. Ils ont tendu une corde entre deux arbres.; **to stretch out one's arms** tendre les bras

stretcher ['strɛtʃər] n civière f

stretchy ['strɛtʃɪ] adj élastique

strict [strɪkt] adj strict

strike [straɪk] n grève f; **to be on strike** être en grève; **to go on strike** se mettre en grève
▶ vb ❶ (hit) frapper ❷ (clock) sonner ▷ The clock struck three. L'horloge a sonné trois heures. ❸ (go on strike) se mettre en grève; **to strike a match** frotter une allumette

striker ['straɪkər] n (person on strike) gréviste

striking ['straɪkɪŋ] adj ❶ (noticeable) frappant ▷ a striking difference une différence frappante ❷ (on strike) en grève ▷ striking miners les mineurs en grève

string [strɪŋ] n ❶ ficelle f ▷ a piece of string un bout de ficelle ❷ (of violin, guitar) corde f

strip [strɪp] vb (get undressed) se déshabiller
▶ n bande f; **a comic strip** une bande dessinée

stripe [straɪp] n rayure f

striped ['straɪpt] adj à rayures ▷ a striped skirt une jupe à rayures

stroke [strəʊk] vb caresser
▶ n attaque f ▷ to have a stroke avoir une attaque

stroll [strəʊl] n: **to go for a stroll** aller faire une petite promenade

stroller ['strəʊlər] n landau m

strong [strɒŋ] adj ❶ fort ▷ She's very strong. Elle est très forte. ❷ (material) résistant

strongly ['strɒŋlɪ] adv fortement ▷ We recommend strongly that... Nous recommandons fortement que...; **He smelt strongly of tobacco.** Il sentait fort le tabac.; **strongly built** solidement bâti; **I don't feel strongly about it.** Ça m'est égal.

struck [strʌk] vb see **strike**

struggle ['strʌgl] vb (physically) se débattre ▷ She struggled, but she couldn't escape. Elle s'est débattue, mais elle n'a pas pu s'échapper.; **to struggle to do something** ❶ (fight) se battre pour faire quelque chose ▷ He struggled to get custody of his daughter. Il s'est battu pour obtenir la garde de sa fille. ❷ (have difficulty) avoir du mal à faire quelque chose
▶ n (for independence, equality) lutte f; **It was a struggle.** Ça a été laborieux.

stub [stʌb] n talon m ▷ Keep your ticket stub. Garde le talon de ton billet.

stub vb: **to stub one's toe** se cogner l'orteil ▷ I stubbed my toe on a stone. Je me suis cogné l'orteil contre une pierre.

stubborn ['stʌbən] adj têtu

stuck [stʌk] vb see **stick**
▶ adj (jammed) coincé ▷ It's stuck. C'est coincé.; **to get stuck** rester coincé ▷ We got stuck in a traffic jam. Nous sommes restés coincés dans un embouteillage.

stuck-up [stʌk'ʌp] adj coincé (informal)

stud [stʌd] n ❶ (earring) boucle d'oreille f ❷ (on football boots) clou m

student ['stju:dənt] *n* étudiant *m*, étudiante *f*

student driver *n* apprenti-conducteur *m*, apprentie-conductrice *f*; **"Student Driver"** (*on car*) « Étudiant au volant »

studio ['stju:dɪəʊ] *n* studio *m* ▷ *a TV studio* un studio de télévision; **studio apartment** un studio

study ['stʌdɪ] *vb* **❶** (*at university*) faire des études ▷ *I plan to study biology.* J'ai l'intention de faire des études en biologie. **❷** (*do homework*) travailler ▷ *I have to study tonight.* Je dois travailler ce soir.

stuff [stʌf] *n* **❶** (*substance*) chose *f* ▷ *I need some stuff for hay fever.* J'ai besoin de quelque chose contre le rhume des foins. **❷** (*things*) patentes *fpl* ▷ *There's some stuff on the table for you.* Il y a des patentes sur la table pour toi. ▷ *I have a ton of stuff to do this weekend.* J'ai plein de patentes à faire en fin de semaine. **❸** (*possessions*) affaires *fpl* ▷ *Have you got all your stuff?* Est-ce que tu as toutes tes affaires?
▶ *vb* **❶** (*cram*) fourrer ▷ *He stuffed the notebook into his pack.* Il a fourré le cahier dans son sac à dos. **❷** (*turkey*) farcir

stuffed [stʌft] *adj*: **stuffed animal** (1) (*toy*) l'animal en peluche (2) (*real*) l'animal empaillé; **No thanks, I'm stuffed!** Non, merci, j'ai l'estomac bien rempli!

stuffing ['stʌfɪŋ] *n* (*in turkey*) farce *f*

stuffy ['stʌfɪ] *adj* (*room*) mal aéré; **It's really stuffy in here.** On étouffe ici.

stumble ['stʌmbl] *vb* trébucher

stung [stʌŋ] *vb see* **sting**

stunk [stʌŋk] *vb see* **stink**

stunned [stʌnd] *adj* (*amazed*) sidéré ▷ *I was stunned.* J'étais sidérée.

stunning ['stʌnɪŋ] *adj* superbe

stunt [stʌnt] *n* (*in film*) cascade *f*

stunt actor *n* cascadeur *m*, cascadeuse *f*

stupid ['stju:pɪd] *adj* stupide ▷ *a stupid joke* une plaisanterie stupide; **Me, go jogging? Don't be stupid!** Moi, faire du jogging? Ne dis pas de niaiseries!

stutter ['stʌtə'] *vb* bégayer

style [staɪl] *n* style *m* ▷ *That's not his style.* Ça n'est pas son style.

subject [səb'dʒɛkt] *n* **❶** sujet *m* ▷ *The subject of my project was the Internet.* Le sujet de mon projet était Internet. **❷** (*at school*) matière *f* ▷ *What's your favourite subject?* Quelle est ta matière préférée?

subjunctive [səb'dʒʌŋktɪv] *n* subjonctif *m* ▷ *in the subjunctive* au subjonctif

submarine [sʌbmə'ri:n] *n* sous-marin *m*; **submarine sandwich** le sous-marin

subscription [səb'skrɪpʃən] *n* (*to paper, magazine*) abonnement *m*; **to take out a subscription to** s'abonner à

subsidize ['sʌbsɪdaɪz] *vb* subventionner

substance ['sʌbstəns] *n* substance *f*; **substance abuse** l'abus *m* de substances toxiques

substitute ['sʌbstɪtju:t] *n* (*person*) remplaçant *m*, remplaçante *f*
▶ *vb* substituer ▷ *to substitute A for B* substituer A à B

subtitled ['sʌbtaɪtld] *adj* sous-titré

subtitles ['sʌbtaɪtlz] *npl* sous-titres *mpl* ▷ *a French film with English subtitles* un film français avec des sous-titres en anglais

subtle ['sʌtl] *adj* subtil

subtract [səb'trækt] *vb* soustraire ▷ *to subtract 3 from 5* soustraire trois de cinq

suburb [ˈsʌbəːb] n banlieue f ▷ *a suburb of Vancouver* une banlieue de Vancouver ▷ *They live in the suburbs.* Ils habitent en banlieue.

suburban [səˈbəːbən] adj de banlieue ▷ *a suburban home* une maison de banlieue

subway [ˈsʌbweɪ] n métro m ▷ *a subway station* une station de métro

succeed [səkˈsiːd] vb réussir ▷ *to succeed in doing something* réussir à faire quelque chose

success [səkˈsɛs] n succès m ▷ *The play was a great success.* La pièce a eu beaucoup de succès.

successful [səkˈsɛsful] adj réussi ▷ *a successful attempt* une tentative réussie; **to be successful in doing something** réussir à faire quelque chose; **She's a successful entrepreneur.** Ses affaires marchent bien.

successfully [səkˈsɛsfəlɪ] adv avec succès

successor [səkˈsɛsəʳ] n successeur m, successeure f

such [sʌtʃ] adj, adv si ▷ *such nice people* des gens si gentils ▷ *such a long journey* un voyage si long; **such a lot of** tellement de ▷ *such a lot of work* tellement de travail; **such as** (like) comme ▷ *spicy dishes, such as Creole shrimp* les plats épicés, comme les crevettes à la créole; **not as such** pas exactement ▷ *He's not an expert as such, but...* Ce n'est pas exactement un expert, mais...; **There's no such thing.** Ça n'existe pas. ▷ *There's no such thing as the Sasquatch.* Le Sasquatch n'existe pas.

such-and-such [ˈsʌtʃənsʌtʃ] adj tel ou tel (f telle ou telle) ▷ *such-and-such a place* tel ou tel endroit

suck [sʌk] vb sucer ▷ *to suck one's thumb* sucer son pouce

sudden [ˈsʌdn] adj soudain ▷ *a sudden change* un changement soudain; **all of a sudden** tout à coup

suddenly [ˈsʌdnlɪ] adv ❶ (stop, leave, change) brusquement ❷ (die) subitement ❸ (at beginning of sentence) soudain ▷ *Suddenly, the door opened.* Soudain, la porte s'est ouverte.

suede [sweɪd] n suède m ▷ *a suede jacket* une veste en suède

suffer [ˈsʌfəʳ] vb souffrir ▷ *She was really suffering.* Elle souffrait beaucoup.; **to suffer from a disease** avoir une maladie ▷ *I suffer from hay fever.* J'ai le rhume des foins.

suffocate [ˈsʌfəkeɪt] vb suffoquer

sugar [ˈʃugəʳ] n sucre m ▷ *Do you take sugar?* Est-ce que vous prenez du sucre?; **a sugar bush** une érablière; **a sugar shack** une cabane à sucre

sugaring off [ˈʃugərɪŋ-] n temps des sucres m; **a sugaring-off party** une partie de sucre

suggest [səˈdʒɛst] vb suggérer ▷ *I suggested they set off early.* Je leur ai suggéré de partir de bonne heure.

suggestion [səˈdʒɛstʃən] n suggestion f ▷ *to make a suggestion* faire une suggestion

suicide [ˈsuːɪsaɪd] n suicide m; **to commit suicide** se suicider

suit [suːt] n ❶ (man's) costume m ❷ (woman's) tailleur m
▶ vb ❶ (be convenient for) convenir à ▷ *What time would suit you?* Quelle heure vous conviendrait? ▷ *That suits me fine.* Ça m'arrange.; **Suit yourself!** Comme tu veux! ❷ (look good on) aller bien à ▷ *That dress really suits you.* Cette robe te va vraiment bien.

suitable [ˈsuːtəbl] adj
❶ convenable ▷ *a suitable time*

une heure convenable ❷ (clothes) approprié ▷ suitable clothing des vêtements appropriés

suitcase ['suːtkeɪs] n valise f

suite [swiːt] n (of rooms) suite; **a bedroom suite** le mobilier de chambre à coucher

sulk [sʌlk] vb bouder

sulky ['sʌlkɪ] adj boudeur (f boudeuse)

sum [sʌm] n (amount) somme f ▷ a sum of money une somme d'argent

sum up vb résumer

summarize ['sʌməraɪz] vb résumer

summary ['sʌmərɪ] n résumé m

summer ['sʌmə⁰] n été m; **in summer** en été; **summer clothes** les vêtements d'été; **the summer holidays** les vacances d'été; **a summer camp** un camp de vacances

summit ['sʌmɪt] n sommet m

sun [sʌn] n soleil m ▷ in the sun au soleil

sunbathe ['sʌnbeɪð] vb se bronzer

sunblock ['sʌnblɒk] n écran m solaire

sunburn ['sʌnbəːn] n coup de soleil m

sunburned ['sʌnbəːnt] adj: **I got sunburned.** J'ai attrapé un coup de soleil.

Sunday ['sʌndɪ] n dimanche m ▷ on Sunday dimanche ▷ on Sundays le dimanche ▷ every Sunday tous les dimanches ▷ last Sunday dimanche dernier ▷ next Sunday dimanche prochain

sunflower ['sʌnflaʊə⁰] n tournesol m

sung [sʌŋ] vb see **sing**

sunglasses ['sʌnglɑːsɪz] npl lunettes fpl de soleil

sunk [sʌŋk] vb see **sink**

sunlight ['sʌnlaɪt] n soleil m;

Avoid exposure to sunlight. Évitez l'exposition au soleil.

sunny ['sʌnɪ] adj ensoleillé ▷ a sunny morning une matinée ensoleillée; **It's sunny.** Il fait du soleil.; **a sunny day** une belle journée

sunrise ['sʌnraɪz] n lever du soleil m

sunroof ['sʌnruːf] n toit ouvrant m

sunscreen ['sʌnskriːn] n écran m solaire

sunset ['sʌnsɛt] n coucher du soleil m

sunshine ['sʌnʃaɪn] n soleil m

sunstroke ['sʌnstrəʊk] n insolation f ▷ to get sunstroke attraper une insolation

suntan ['sʌntæn] n bronzage m; **suntan lotion** le lait solaire; **suntan oil** l'huile f solaire

super ['suːpə⁰] adj formidable

superb [suːˈpɜːb] adj superbe

supermarket ['suːpəmɑːkɪt] n supermarché m

supernatural [suːpə'nætʃərəl] adj surnaturel (f surnaturelle)

superstitious [suːpə'stɪʃəs] adj superstitieux (f superstitieuse)

supervise ['suːpəvaɪz] vb surveiller

supervisor ['suːpəvaɪzə⁰] n (in factory) superviseur m, superviseure f

supper ['sʌpə⁰] n souper m

supplement [sʌplɪ'mɛnt] n supplément m ▷ a vitamin supplement un supplément vitaminique

supplies [sə'plaɪz] npl ravitaillement m

supply [sə'plaɪ] vb (provide) fournir; **to supply somebody with something** fournir quelque chose à quelqu'un ▷ The centre supplied us with all the equipment. Le centre

nous a fourni tout l'équipement.
▶ n provision f ▷ a supply of
paper une provision de papier;
the water supply (to town)
l'approvisionnement m en eau

supply teacher n suppléant m,
suppléante f

support [sə'pɔːt] vb ❶ (encourage)
soutenir ▷ My mom has always
supported me. Ma mère m'a toujours
soutenu. ❷ (agree with) être
en faveur de ▷ I support the new
rule. Je suis en faveur du nouveau
règlement. ❸ (financially) subvenir
aux besoins de ▷ She had to support
five children on her own. Elle a dû
subvenir toute seule aux besoins de
cinq enfants.

Be careful not to translate **to
support** by **supporter**.

▶ n (backing) soutien m

supporter [sə'pɔːtə'] n
❶ sympathisant m, sympathisante
f ▷ a supporter of nuclear disarmament
un sympathisant du désarmement
nucléaire ❷ (donor) donateur m,
donatrice f

suppose [sə'pəuz] vb imaginer
▷ I suppose he's late. J'imagine qu'il
est en retard. ▷ Suppose you won
the lottery. Imaginez que vous
gagniez à la loterie.; **I suppose so.**
J'imagine.; **to be supposed to do
something** être censé faire quelque
chose ▷ You're supposed to show your
passport. On est censé montrer son
passeport.

supposing [sə'pəuzɪŋ] conj si
▷ Supposing you won the lottery... Si
tu gagnais à la loterie.

supreme [su'priːm] adj suprême
▷ the Supreme Court la Cour suprême

surcharge ['sɜːtʃɑːdʒ] n
surcharge f

sure [ʃuə'] adj sûr ▷ Are you sure? Tu
es sûr?; **Sure!** Bien sûr!; **to make**

sure that... vérifier que... ▷ I'm
going to make sure the door's locked.
Je vais vérifier que la porte est
fermée à clé.

surf [sɜːf] n ressac m
▶ vb surfer; **to go surfing** faire du
surf; **to surf the Net** surfer sur
Internet

surface ['sɜːfɪs] n surface f

surfboard ['sɜːfbɔːd] n planche de
surf f (pl planches de surf)

surfing ['sɜːfɪŋ] n surf m ▷ to go
surfing faire du surf

surgeon ['sɜːdʒən] n chirurgien m,
chirurgienne f ▷ She's a surgeon. Elle
est chirurgienne.

surgery ['sɜːdʒərɪ] n opération
f ▷ Surgery was required. Il a fallu
faire une opération. ▷ The surgery
is scheduled for Monday. L'opération
est prévue pour lundi.; **She
underwent extensive surgery.**
Elle a subi une grave intervention
chirurgicale.

surname ['sɜːneɪm] n nom de
famille m (pl noms de famille)

surprise [sə'praɪz] n surprise f

surprised [sə'praɪzd] adj surpris
▷ I was surprised to see him. J'ai été
surprise de le voir.

surprising [sə'praɪzɪŋ] adj
surprenant

surrender [sə'rɛndə'] vb capituler

surrogate mother ['sʌrəgɪt-] n
mère porteuse f

surround [sə'raund] vb encercler
▷ The police surrounded the house. La
police a encerclé la maison. ▷ You're
surrounded! Vous êtes encerclés!;
surrounded by entouré de ▷ The
house is surrounded by trees. La
maison est entourée d'arbres.

surroundings [sə'raundɪŋz]
npl cadre m ▷ a hotel in beautiful
surroundings un hôtel situé dans un
beau cadre

survey [sə:'veɪ] n (research) enquête f

survivor [sə'vaɪvə'] n survivant m, survivante f ▷ There were no survivors. Il n'y a pas eu de survivants.

suspect [səs'pekt] vb soupçonner
▶ n suspect m, suspecte f

suspend [səs'pend] vb ❶ (from school, team) exclure ▷ He's been suspended. Il s'est fait exclure. ❷ (from job) suspendre

suspenders [səs'pendəz] npl bretelles fpl

suspense [səs'pens] n ❶ (waiting) attente f ▷ The suspense was terrible. L'attente a été terrible. ❷ (in story) suspense m ▷ a film with lots of suspense un film avec beaucoup de suspense

suspension [səs'penʃən] n ❶ (from school, team) exclusion f ❷ (from job) suspension f

suspicious [səs'pɪʃəs] adj ❶ méfiant ▷ He was suspicious at first. Il était méfiant au début. ❷ (suspicious-looking) louche ▷ a suspicious person un individu louche

swallow ['swɒləʊ] vb avaler

swam [swæm] vb see **swim**

swan [swɒn] n cygne m

swap [swɒp] vb échanger ▷ Do you want to swap? Tu veux échanger? ▷ to swap A for B échanger A contre B

swat [swɒt] vb écraser

sway [sweɪ] vb osciller

swear [sweə'] vb (make an oath, curse) sacrer

swearword ['sweəwə:d] n sacre m

sweat [swet] n transpiration f
▶ vb transpirer

sweater ['swetə'] n chandail m

sweatshirt ['swetʃə:t] n chandail en molleton m

sweaty ['swetɪ] adj ❶ (person, face) en sueur ▷ I'm all sweaty. Je suis en sueur. ❷ (hands) moite

sweep [swi:p] vb balayer; **to sweep the floor** balayer

sweet [swi:t] adj ❶ (taste) sucré ❷ (kind) gentil (f gentille) ▷ That was really sweet of you. C'était vraiment gentil de ta part. ❸ (cute) mignon (f mignonne) ▷ Isn't she sweet? Comme elle est mignonne!; **sweet and sour pork** le porc à la sauce aigre-douce

sweets [swi:ts] npl sucreries fpl

sweltering ['sweltərɪŋ] adj: **It was sweltering.** Il faisait une chaleur étouffante.

swept [swept] vb see **sweep**

swerve [swə:v] vb faire une embardée ▷ He swerved to avoid the cyclist. Il a fait une embardée pour éviter la cycliste.

swim [swɪm] n: **to go for a swim** aller se baigner
▶ vb nager ▷ Can you swim? Tu sais nager?; **She swam across the river.** Elle a traversé la rivière à la nage.

swimmer ['swɪmə'] n nageur m, nageuse f ▷ She's a good swimmer. C'est une bonne nageuse.

swimming ['swɪmɪŋ] n natation f ▷ Do you like swimming? Tu aimes la natation?; **to go swimming** (in a pool) aller à la piscine; **a swimming pool** une piscine; **swimming trunks** le maillot de bain

swimsuit ['swɪmsu:t] n maillot de bain m

swing [swɪŋ] n (in playground, garden) balançoire f
▶ vb ❶ se balancer ▷ A bunch of keys swung from his belt. Un trousseau de clés se balançait à sa ceinture.; **Sam was swinging an umbrella as he walked.** Sam balançait son

parapluie en marchant. ❷ virer
▷ *The canoe swung round sharply. Le canot a viré brusquement.*

switch [swɪtʃ] n (for light, radio, etc.) interrupteur m
▶ vb changer de ▷ *We switched partners. Nous avons changé de partenaire.*

switch off vb ❶ (electrical appliance) éteindre ❷ (engine, machine) arrêter

switch on vb ❶ (electrical appliance) allumer ❷ (engine, machine) mettre en marche

swollen ['swəʊlən] adj (arm, leg) enflé

sword [sɔːd] n épée f

swore, sworn vb see **swear**

swum [swʌm] vb see **swim**

swung [swʌŋ] vb see **swing**

symbol ['sɪmbl] n symbole m

sympathetic [sɪmpəˈθetɪk] adj compréhensif (f compréhensive)
▷ *The teacher was very sympathetic and allowed me to leave before the end of the class. La professeure a été très compréhensive et m'a permis de partir avant la fin du cours.*

> Be careful not to translate **sympathetic** by **sympathique**.

sympathize ['sɪmpəθaɪz] vb:
to sympathize with somebody comprendre quelqu'un

sympathy ['sɪmpəθɪ] n compassion f

symptom ['sɪmptəm] n symptôme m

synagogue ['sɪnəgɒg] n synagogue f

syndrome ['sɪndrəum] n syndrome m; Down syndrome le syndrome de Down; Severe Acute Respiratory Syndrome le syndrome respiratoire aigu sévère; chronic fatigue

syndrome le syndrome de fatigue chronique

synthetic [sɪnˈθetɪk] adj synthétique ▷ *synthetic fibres des fibres synthétiques*

syringe [sɪˈrɪndʒ] n seringue f

system ['sɪstəm] n système m

t

table ['teɪbl] *n* table *f* ▷ *to set the table* mettre la table

tablecloth ['teɪblklɒθ] *n* nappe *f*

tablespoon ['teɪblspuːn] *n* cuillère à soupe *f*; **a tablespoon of sugar** une cuillerée à soupe de sucre

table tennis *n* ping-pong *m* ▷ *to play table tennis* jouer au ping-pong

tabloid ['tæblɔɪd] *n* tabloïd *m*

tackle ['tækl] *n* (*in football*) tacle *m*; **fishing tackle** le matériel de pêche ▶ *vb* **❶** (*in football*) tacler **❷** (*in rugby*) plaquer; **to tackle a problem** s'attaquer à un problème

tact [tækt] *n* tact *m*

tactful ['tæktful] *adj* plein(e) de tact

tactics ['tæktɪks] *npl* tactique *f*

tactless ['tæktlɪs] *adj*: **to be tactless** manquer de tact ▷ *a tactless remark* une remarque qui manque de tact

tadpole ['tædpəʊl] *n* têtard *m*

tag [tæg] *n* (*label*) étiquette *f*

tail [teɪl] *n* queue *f*; **Heads or tails?** Pile ou face?

tailor ['teɪləʳ] *n* tailleur *m*

take [teɪk] *vb* **❶** prendre ▷ *Are you taking your new camera?* Tu prends ton nouvel appareil photo? ▷ *He took a plate from the cupboard.* Il a pris une assiette dans l'armoire. ▷ *It takes about an hour.* Ça prend environ une heure. **❷** (*person*) emmener ▷ *She goes to Toronto every week, but she never takes me.* Elle va à Toronto toutes les semaines, mais elle ne m'emmène jamais.; **to take something somewhere** emporter quelque chose quelque part ▷ *Do you take your notebooks home?* Vous emportez vos cahiers chez vous? ▷ *Don't take anything valuable with you.* N'emportez pas d'objets de valeur.; **I'm going to take my coat to the cleaner's.** Je vais porter mon manteau chez le nettoyeur. **❸** (*effort, skill*) demander ▷ *that takes a lot of courage* cela demande beaucoup de courage; **It takes a lot of money to do that.** Il faut beaucoup d'argent pour faire ça. **❹** (*tolerate*) supporter ▷ *He can't take being criticized.* Il ne supporte pas d'être critiqué. **❺** (*test*) passer ▷ *She's taking her driving test next week.* Elle passe le test de conduire la semaine prochaine. **❻** (*subject*) faire ▷ *I decided to take French instead of music.* J'ai décidé de faire du français au lieu de la musique.

take after *vb* ressembler à ▷ *She takes after her mother.* Elle ressemble à sa mère.

take apart *vb*: **to take something apart** démonter quelque chose

take away *vb* **❶** (*object*) emporter **❷** (*person*) emmener; **to take something away** (*confiscate*) confisquer quelque chose

take back vb ➊ I took it back to the store. Je l'ai rapporté au magasin.; **I take it all back!** Je n'ai rien dit!

take down vb ➊ (poster, sign) enlever ➋ (painting, curtains) décrocher ➌ (tent, scaffolding) démonter ➍ (make a note of) prendre en note ▷ He took down the details in his notebook. Il a pris tous les détails en note dans son carnet.

take in vb (understand) comprendre ▷ I didn't really take it in. Je n'ai pas bien compris.

take off vb ➊ (plane) décoller ▷ The plane took off twenty minutes late. L'avion a décollé avec vingt minutes de retard. ➋ (clothes) enlever ▷ Take your coat off. Enlevez votre manteau.

take out vb (from container, pocket) sortir; **They took us out to the movies.** Il nous ont emmenés au cinéma.; **hot meals to take out** des plats chauds à emporter

take over vb prendre la relève ▷ I'll take over now. Je vais prendre la relève.; **to take over from somebody** remplacer quelqu'un

taken ['teɪkən] vb see **take**

takeoff ['teɪkɒf] n (of plane) décollage m

takeout ['teɪkaʊt] n ➊ (meal) plat à emporter m ➋ restaurant qui vend des plats à emporter m ▷ a Chinese takeout un restaurant chinois qui vend des plats à emporter

tale [teɪl] n (story) conte f

talent ['tælnt] n talent m ▷ He has lots of talent. Il a beaucoup de talent.; **to have a talent for something** être doué pour quelque chose ▷ He has a real talent for languages. Il est vraiment doué pour

les langues.

talented ['tæləntɪd] adj talentueux m (f talentueuse); **She's a talented pianist.** C'est une pianiste talentueuse.

talk [tɔːk] n ➊ (speech) exposé m ▷ She gave a talk on rock climbing. Elle a fait un exposé sur l'escalade. ➋ (conversation) conversation f ▷ I had a talk with my dad about it. J'ai eu une petite conversation avec mon père à ce sujet. ➌ (gossip) racontars mpl ▷ It's just talk. Ce sont des racontars.
▶ vb parler ▷ to talk about something parler de quelque chose; **to talk something over with somebody** discuter de quelque chose avec quelqu'un

talkative ['tɔːkətɪv] adj bavard

talk show n émission-débat f (pl émissions-débats)

tall [tɔːl] adj ➊ (person, tree) grand; **to be 2 metres tall** mesurer deux mètres ➋ (building) haut m

tame [teɪm] adj (animal) apprivoisé(e) ▷ They have a tame ferret. Ils ont un furet apprivoisé.

tampon ['tæmpən] n tampon m

tan [tæn] n bronzage m ▷ To have an amazing tan. avoir un bronzage superbe.

tangerine [tændʒəˈriːn] n mandarine f

tangle up ['tæŋgl-] vb emmêler ▷ My hair is all tangled up. Mes cheveux sont tout emmêlés.; **to get tangled up** s'emmêler ▷ His fishing line got tangled up with mine. Sa ligne de pêche s'est emmêlée dans la mienne.

tank [tæŋk] n ➊ (for water, gasoline) réservoir m ➋ (military) char d'assaut m; **a fish tank** un aquarium

tanker ['tæŋkə'] n ➊ (ship)

pétrolier m; **an oil tanker** un pétrolier ❷ (truck) camion-citerne m

tap [tæp] n ❶ (water tap) robinet m ❷ (gentle touch) petite tape f

tap-dancing ['tæpdɑːnsɪŋ] n claquette f ▷ I do tap-dancing. Je danse la claquette.

tape [teɪp] vb (record) enregistrer ▷ Did you tape that movie last night? As-tu enregistré le film hier soir?
▶ n ❶ cassette f ▷ a tape of Avril Lavigne une cassette de Avril Lavigne ❷ (adhesive tape) ruban adhésif m

tape measure n le galon à mesurer

target ['tɑːgɪt] n cible f

tart [tɑːt] n tartelette f ▷ a butter tart une tartelette aux raisins secs

tartan ['tɑːtn] adj écossais ▷ a tartan skirt une jupe écossaise

task [tɑːsk] n tâche f

taste [teɪst] n goût m ▷ It has a really strange taste. Ça a un goût vraiment bizarre. ▷ a joke in bad taste une plaisanterie de mauvais goût; **Would you like a taste?** Tu veux goûter?
▶ vb goûter ▷ Would you like to taste it? Vous voulez y goûter?; **to taste like something** avoir un goût de quelque chose ▷ It tastes like fish. Ça a un goût de poisson.; **You can taste the garlic in it.** Ça a bien le goût d'ail.

tasteful ['teɪstfʊl] adj de bon goût

tasteless ['teɪstlɪs] adj ❶ (food) fade ❷ (in bad taste) de mauvais goût ▷ a tasteless remark une remarque de mauvais goût

tasty ['teɪstɪ] adj savoureux (f savoureuse)

tattoo [tə'tuː] n tatouage m

taught [tɔːt] vb see **teach**

Taurus ['tɔːrəs] n Taureau m ▷ I'm a

Taurus. Je suis Taureau.

tax [tæks] n ❶ (on income) impôts mpl ❷ (on goods, alcohol) taxe f

taxi ['tæksɪ] n taxi m; **a taxi driver** un chauffeur de taxi; **a taxi stand** une station de taxi

TB n tuberculose f

tea [tiː] n thé m ▷ a cup of tea une tasse de thé; **a tea bag** un sachet de thé

teach [tiːtʃ] vb ❶ apprendre ▷ My sister taught me to swim. Ma sœur m'a appris à nager. ▷ That'll teach you! Ça t'apprendra! ❷ (in school) enseigner ▷ She teaches physics. Elle enseigne la physique.

teacher ['tiːtʃə'] n ❶ (in secondary school) professeur m, professeure f ▷ a math teacher un professeur de maths ▷ She's a teacher. Elle est professeure. ❷ (in primary school) enseignant m, enseignante f ▷ He's a primary school teacher. Il est enseignant.

teacher's pet ['tiːtʃəz-] n chouchou m, chouchoute f

teaching assistant ['tiːtʃɪŋ-] n aide-enseignant m, aide-enseignante f

team [tiːm] n équipe f ▷ a football team une équipe de football ▷ She was on my team. Elle était dans mon équipe.

teamwork ['tiːmwɜːk] n travail d'équipe m ▷ That's teamwork! C'est ça, le travail d'équipe! ▷ Teamwork makes all the difference. Travailler en équipe fait toute la différence.

teapot ['tiːpɒt] n théière f

tear [n tɪə', vb teə'] n larme f ▷ The child was in tears. L'enfant était en larmes.
▶ vb ❶ déchirer ▷ Be careful or you'll tear the page. Fais attention, tu vas déchirer la page. ❷ se déchirer ▷ It won't tear, it's very strong. Ça ne se

déchire pas, c'est très solide.; **to
tear up** déchirer ▷ *He tore up the
letter.* Il a déchiré la lettre.

tease [tiːz] *vb* ❶ *(unkindly)*
tourmenter ▷ *Stop teasing that
poor animal!* Arrête de tourmenter
ce pauvre animal! ❷ *(jokingly)*
taquiner ▷ *He's teasing you.* Il te
taquine. ▷ **I was only teasing.** Je
plaisantais.

teaspoon ['tiːspuːn] *n* petite
cuillère *f*; **a teaspoon of sugar** une
cuillerée à thé de sucre

tea towel *n* torchon *m*

technical ['tɛknɪkl] *adj* technique *f*

technician [tɛk'nɪʃən] *n*
technicien *m*, technicienne *f*

technique [tɛk'niːk] *n* technique *f*

technological [tɛknə'lɒdʒɪkl] *adj*
technologique

technology [tɛk'nɒlədʒɪ] *n*
technologie *f*

teddy bear ['tɛdɪ-] *n* nounours *m*

teenage ['tiːneɪdʒ] *adj* ❶ pour
les jeunes ▷ *a teenage magazine* un
magazine pour les jeunes ❷ *(boys,
girls)* adolescent ▷ *He has two
teenage daughters.* Il a deux filles
adolescentes.

teenager ['tiːneɪdʒə] *n*
adolescent *m*, adolescente *f*

teens [tiːnz] *npl*: **She's in her
teens.** C'est une adolescente.

teeth [tiːθ] *npl* dents *fpl*

teethe [tiːð] *vb* faire ses dents

teetotal ['tiː'təʊtl] *adj*: **I'm
teetotal.** Je ne bois jamais d'alcool.

telecommunications
['tɛlɪkəmjuːnɪ'keɪʃənz] *npl*
télécommunications *fpl*

telephone ['tɛlɪfəʊn] *n* téléphone
m ▷ *on the telephone* au téléphone;
a telephone booth une cabine
téléphonique; **a telephone
call** un coup de téléphone; **the
telephone directory** l'annuaire *m*;

a telephone number un numéro
de téléphone

telescope ['tɛlɪskəʊp] *n*
télescope *m*

television ['tɛlɪvɪʒən] *n* télévision
f; **on television** à la télévision; **a
television program** une émission
de télévision

television ad *n* publicité télévisée *f*

tell [tɛl] *vb* dire; **to tell somebody
something** dire quelque chose à
quelqu'un ▷ *Did you tell your mother?*
Tu l'as dit à ta mère? ▷ *I told him that
I was going on holiday.* Je lui ai dit
que je partais en vacances.; **to tell
somebody to do something** dire
à quelqu'un de faire quelque chose
▷ *He told me to wait a moment.* Il m'a
dit d'attendre un moment.; **to tell
lies** dire des mensonges; **to tell a
story** raconter une histoire; **I can't
tell the difference between them.**
Je n'arrive pas à les distinguer.

tell off *vb* gronder

temper ['tɛmpə] *n* caractère *m*
▷ *to have a bad temper.* avoir mauvais
caractère.; **to lose one's temper** se
mettre en colère ▷ *I lost my temper.*
Je me suis mis en colère.

temperature ['tɛmprətʃə] *n (of
oven, water, person)* température *f*;
The temperature was 30 degrees.
Il faisait trente degrés.; **to have a
temperature** avoir de la fièvre

temple ['tɛmpl] *n* temple *m*

temporary ['tɛmpərərɪ] *adj*
temporaire

tempt [tɛmpt] *vb* tenter ▷ *I'm
very tempted!* Je suis très tenté!;
**to tempt somebody to do
something** persuader quelqu'un de
faire quelque chose

temptation [tɛmp'teɪʃən] *n*
tentation *f*

tempting ['tɛmptɪŋ] *adj* tentant

ten [tɛn] *num* dix ▷ *She's ten.* Elle

a dix ans.

tenant ['tenənt] n locataire m, locataire f

tend [tend] vb: **to tend to do something** avoir tendance à faire quelque chose ▷ *He tends to arrive late.* Il a tendance à arriver en retard.

tender ['tendə'] adj ❶ *(food)* tendre ❷ *(part of body)* sensible ▷ *My feet are really tender.* J'ai les pieds très sensibles.

tennis ['tenɪs] n tennis m ▷ *Do you play tennis?* Vous jouez au tennis?; **a tennis ball** une balle de tennis; **a tennis court** un court de tennis; **a tennis racquet** une raquette de tennis

tense [tens] adj tendu
▶ n: **the present tense** le présent; **the future tense** le futur

tension ['tenʃən] n tension f

tent [tent] n tente f; **a tent peg** un piquet de tente; **a tent pole** un montant de tente

tenth [tenθ] adj dixième ▷ *the tenth floor* le dixième étage; **the tenth of August** le dix août

term [tɜːm] n ❶ *(at school)* trimestre m ❷ terme m ▷ *a short-term solution* une solution à court terme ▷ *a technical term* un terme technique; **to come to terms with something** accepter quelque chose

terminal ['tɜːmɪnl] adj *(illness, patient)* incurable
▶ n *(of computer)* un terminal; **an airport terminal** une aérogare

terminally ['tɜːmɪnlɪ] adv: **to be terminally ill** être condamné

terrace ['terəs] n *(patio)* terrasse f

terrible ['terəbl] adj épouvantable ▷ *He looks terrible.* Il a une mine épouvantable.

terribly ['terɪblɪ] adv
❶ terriblement ▷ *He suffered*

terribly. Il souffre terriblement.
❷ vraiment ▷ *I'm terribly sorry.* Je suis vraiment désolé.

terrier ['terɪə'] n terrier m

terrific [tə'rɪfɪk] adj *(wonderful)* super ▷ *That's terrific!* C'est super!; **You look terrific!** Tu es superbe!

terrified ['terɪfaɪd] adj terrifié ▷ *I was terrified!* J'étais terrifié!

Territorial Council [terɪ'tɔːrɪəl] n Conseil du territoire m

territory ['terɪtərɪ] n territoire m

terrorism ['terərɪzəm] n terrorisme m

terrorist ['terərɪst] n terroriste m; **a terrorist attack** un attentat terroriste

test [test] n ❶ *(at school: at school)* test m ▷ *I have a geography test today.* J'ai un test de géographie aujourd'hui. ❷ *(trial, check)* essai m ▷ *nuclear tests* les essais nucléaires ❸ *(medical)* analyse f ▷ *a blood test* une analyse de sang ▷ *They're going to do some more tests.* Ils vont faire d'autres analyses.; **driving test** l'examen du permis de conduire ▷ *She's taking her driving test tomorrow.* Elle subit son permis de conduire demain.
▶ vb ❶ essayer ▷ *to test something out* essayer quelque chose
❷ *(class)* interroger ▷ *My teacher tested us on the vocabulary.* Mon professeur nous a interrogés sur le vocabulaire.; **She was tested for drugs.** On lui a fait subir un contrôle antidopage.

test tube n éprouvette f

tetanus ['tetənəs] n tétanos m ▷ *a tetanus injection* un vaccin contre le tétanos

text [tekst] n ❶ texte m ❷ *(mobile phone)* minimessage m
▶ vb: **to text someone** envoyer un minimessage à quelqu'un

textbook ['tɛkstbʊk] n manuel m ▷ A French textbook un manuel de français

than [ðæn, ðən] conj que ▷ She's taller than me. Elle est plus grande que moi. ▷ I have more books than him. J'ai plus de livres que lui.; **more than ten years** plus de dix ans; **more than once** plus d'une fois

thank [θæŋk] vb remercier ▷ Don't forget to write and thank them. N'oublie pas de leur écrire pour les remercier.; **thank you** merci; **thank you very much** merci beaucoup

thanks [θæŋks] excl merci!; **thanks to** grâce à ▷ Thanks to her, everything went OK. Grâce à elle, tout s'est bien passé.

that [ðæt] adj, pron, conj

Use **ce** when **that** is followed by a masculine noun, and **cette** when **that** is followed by a feminine noun. **ce** changes to **cet** before a vowel and before most words beginning with "h".

❶ ce, cet, cette ▷ that book ce livre ▷ that man cet homme ▷ that woman cette femme; **that road** cette route; **that road** cette route-là; **that one (1)** (masculine) celui-là ▷ "This man?" — "No, that one." « Cet homme-ci? » — « Non, celui-là. » **(2)** (feminine) celle-là ▷ "Do you like this photo?" — "No, I prefer that one." « Tu aimes cette photo? » — « Non, je préfère celle-là. » ❷ ça ▷ You see that? Tu vois ça?; **What's that?** Qu'est-ce que c'est?; **Who's that?** Qui est-ce?; **Is that you?** C'est toi?; **That's...** C'est... ▷ That's my teacher. C'est mon prof. ▷ That's what she said. C'est ce qu'elle a dit.

In relative phrases use **qui** when **that** refers to the subject of the sentence, and **que** when it refers to the object.

❶ qui ▷ the man that saw us l'homme qui nous a vus ▷ the woman that spoke to us la femme qui nous a parlé ❹ que ▷ the man that we saw l'homme que nous avons vu

que changes to **qu'** before a vowel and before most words beginning with "h".

▷ the dog that she bought le chien qu'elle a acheté ▷ He thought that your brother was ill. Il pensait que ton frère était malade. ▷ I know that she likes chocolate. Je sais qu'elle aime le chocolat.; **the woman that we spoke to** la femme à qui nous avons parlé; **It was that big.** Il était grand comme ça.; **It's about that high.** C'est à peu près haut comme ça.; **It's not that difficult.** Ça n'est pas si difficile que ça.

thatched [θætʃt] adj: **a thatched cottage** une chaumière

the [ði:, ðə] art

Use **le** with a masculine noun, and **la** with a feminine noun. Use **l'** before a vowel and most words beginning with "h". For plural nouns always use **les**.

le, l', la ▷ the boy le garçon ▷ the man l'homme m ▷ the air l'air m ▷ the habit l'habitude f ▷ the girl la fille, les ▷ the children les enfants

theatre ['θɪətə'] n théâtre m

theft [θɛft] n vol m

their [ðɛə'] adj leur (pl leurs) ▷ their house leur maison ▷ their parents leurs parents

theirs [ðɛəz] pron le + m leur, la + fleur, les + pl leurs ▷ It's not our garage, it's theirs. Ce n'est pas notre garage, c'est le leur. ▷ It's not our car, it's theirs. Ce n'est pas notre voiture, c'est la leur. ▷ *They're not our ideas, they're theirs.* Ce ne sont pas nos idées, ce sont les leurs.; **Is this theirs?** **(1)** (*masculine owners*) C'est à eux? ▷ *This car is theirs.* Cette voiture est à eux. ▷ *"Whose is this?" — "It's theirs."* « C'est à qui? » — « À eux. » **(2)** (*feminine owners*) C'est à elles?

them [ðɛm, ðəm] *pron* **①** les ▷ *I didn't see them.* Je ne les ai pas vus.

  Use **leur** when **them** means **to them**.

② leur ▷ *I gave them some brochures.* Je leur ai donné des brochures. ▷ *I told them the truth.* Je leur ai dit la vérité.

  Use **eux** or **elles** after a preposition.

③ eux *m*, elles *f* ▷ *It's for them.* C'est pour eux. ▷ *My two sisters came, and my dad was with them.* Mes deux sœurs sont venues, et mon père était avec elles.

theme [θiːm] *n* thème *m*

theme park *n* parc d'attractions *m*

themselves [ðəm'sɛlvz] *pron* **①** se ▷ *Did they hurt themselves?* Est-ce qu'ils se sont fait mal? **②** eux-mêmes *m*, elles-mêmes *f* ▷ *They did it themselves.* Ils l'ont fait eux-mêmes.

then [ðɛn] *adv, conj* **①** (*next*) ensuite ▷ *I get dressed. Then I have breakfast.* Je m'habille. Ensuite je prends mon petit déjeuner. **②** (*in that case*) alors ▷ *"My pen's run out." — "Use a pencil then!"* « Il n'y a plus d'encre dans mon stylo. » — « Alors utilise un crayon! » **③** (*at that time*) à l'époque ▷ *There was no electricity then.* Il n'y avait pas d'électricité à l'époque.; **now and then** de temps en temps ▷ *"Do you play chess?" — "Now and then."* « Vous jouez aux échecs? » — « De temps en temps. »;

By then it was too late. Il était déjà trop tard.

therapy ['θɛrəpɪ] *n* thérapie *f*

there [ðɛəʳ] *adv* **①** là ▷ *Put it there, on the table.* Mets-le là, sur la table.; **over there** là-bas; **in there** là; **on there** là; **up there** là-haut; **down there** là-bas; **There he is!** Le voilà! **②** y ▷ *She went there on Friday.* Elle y est allée vendredi. ▷ *I've never been there.* Je n'y suis jamais allé.; **There is...** Il y a... ▷ *There's a factory near my house.* Il y a une usine près de chez moi.; **There are...** Il y a... ▷ *There are five people in my family.* Il y a cinq personnes dans ma famille.; **There has been an accident.** Il y a eu un accident.

therefore ['ðɛəfɔːʳ] *adv* donc

there's [ðɛəz] **= there is**; **there has**

thermometer [θə'mɒmɪtəʳ] *n* thermomètre *m*

Thermos® ['θəːmɒs] *n* thermos *m*

these [ðiːz] *adj, pron* **①** ces ▷ *these shoes* ces chaussures; **THESE shoes** ces chaussures-là **②** ceux-ci *m* ▷ *I want these!* Je veux ceux-ci!, celles-ci *f* ▷ *I'm looking for some sandals. Can I try these?* Je cherche des sandales. Je peux essayer celles-ci?

they [ðeɪ] *pron*

  Check if **they** stands for a masculine or feminine noun.

ils, elles ▷ *"Are there any tickets left?" — "No, they're all sold."* « Est-ce qu'il reste des billets? » — « Non, ils sont tous vendus. » ▷ *"Do you like those shoes?" — "No, they're horrible."* « Tu aimes ces chaussures? » — « Non, elles sont affreuses. »; **They say that...** On dit que...

thick [θɪk] *adj* (*not thin*) épais (*f* épaisse); **The walls are one metre thick.** Les murs font un mètre d'épaisseur.

thief [θiːf] *n* voleur *m*, voleuse *f*;

Stop thief! Au voleur!
thigh [θaɪ] n cuisse f
thin [θɪn] adj ❶ (person, slice)
mince f. ❷ (skinny) maigre
thing [θɪŋ] n ❶ chose f ▷ beautiful
things de belles choses ❷ (thingy)
patente f ▷ What's that thing
called? Comment s'appelle cette
patente? **my things** (belongings)
mes affaires; **You poor thing!**
Mon pauvre!
think [θɪŋk] vb ❶ (believe) penser
▷ I think you're wrong. Je pense que
vous avez tort. ❷ What do you think
about the war? Que pensez-vous de
la guerre? ❷ (spend time thinking)
réfléchir ▷ Think carefully before
you reply. Réfléchis bien avant de
répondre. ▷ I'll think about it. Je
vais y réfléchir.; **What are you
thinking about?** À quoi tu penses?
❸ (imagine) imaginer ▷ Think
what life would be like without cars.
Imaginez la vie sans voitures.; **I
think so.** Oui, je crois.; **I don't
think so.** Je ne crois pas.; **I'll think
it over.** Je vais y réfléchir.
third [θəːd] adj troisième ▷ the third
day le troisième jour ▷ the third time
la troisième fois ▷ I came third. Je
suis arrivé troisième.; **the third of
March** le trois mars
▶ n tiers m ▷ a third of the population
un tiers de la population
thirdly ['θəːdlɪ] adv troisièmement
thirst [θəːst] n soif f
thirsty ['θəːstɪ] adj: **to be thirsty**
avoir soif
thirteen [θəːˈtiːn] num treize ▷ I'm
thirteen. J'ai treize ans.
thirteenth [-ˈtiːnθ] adj treizième
▷ her thirteenth birthday son
treizième anniversaire ▷ the
thirteenth floor le treizième étage;
the thirteenth of August le
treize août

thirty ['θəːtɪ] num trente
this [ðɪs] adj, pron

Use ce when **this** is followed by
a masculine noun, and cette
when **this** is followed by a
feminine noun. ce changes to
cet before a vowel and before
most words beginning with "h".

❶ ce, cet, cette ▷ this book ce livre
▷ this man cet homme ▷ this woman
cette femme; **this road** cette
route; **THIS road** cette route-ci;
this one (1) (masculine) celui-ci ▷
"Pass me that pen." — "This one?"
« Passe-moi ce stylo. » — « Celui-ci? »
(2) (feminine) celle-ci ▷ Of the two
photos, I prefer this one. Des deux
photos, c'est celle-ci que je préfère.
❷ ça ▷ You see this? Tu vis ça?;
What's this? Qu'est-ce que c'est?;
This is my father. (introduction)
Je te présente mon père.; **This is
Gavin speaking.** (on the phone)
C'est Gavin à l'appareil.
thistle ['θɪsl] n chardon m
thorough ['θʌrə] adj minutieux (f
minutieuse) ▷ She's very thorough.
Elle est très minutieuse.
thoroughly ['θʌrəlɪ] adv (examine)
à fond
those [ðəuz] adj, pron ❶ ces
▷ those shoes ces chaussures;
THOSE shoes ces chaussures-là
❷ ceux-là m ▷ I want those! Je veux
ceux-là!, celles-là f ▷ I'm looking
for some sandals. Can I try those?
Je cherche des sandales. Je peux
essayer celles-là?
though [ðəu] conj, adv bien que

bien que has to be followed by
a verb in the subjunctive.

▷ Though it's raining... Bien qu'il
pleuve...; **He's a nice person,
though he's not very outgoing.**
Il est sympathique, mais pas très
extraverti.

thought [θɔːt] vb see **think**
▸ n (idea) idée f ▸ I've just had a
thought. Je viens d'avoir une idée.;
It was a nice thought, thank you.
C'est gentil de ta part, merci.

thoughtful ['θɔːtful] adj ❶ (deep
in thought) pensif (f pensive)
▸ You look thoughtful. Tu as l'air
pensif. ❷ (considerate) prévenant
▸ She's very thoughtful. Elle est très
prévenante.

thoughtless ['θɔːtlɪs] adj: **He's
completely thoughtless.** Il ne
pense absolument pas aux autres.

thousand ['θaʊzənd] num: **a
thousand** mille ▸ a thousand euros
mille euros; **$2000** deux mille
dollars; **thousands of people** des
milliers de personnes

thousandth ['θaʊzəntθ] adj, n
millième m

thread [θrɛd] n fil m

threat [θrɛt] n menace f

threaten ['θrɛtn] vb menacer ▸ to
threaten to do something menacer de
faire quelque chose

three [θriː] num trois ▸ She's three.
Elle a trois ans.

three-dimensional [ˌθriː
dɪ'mɛnʃənl] adj à trois dimensions

threw [θruː] vb see **throw**

thrifty ['θrɪfti] adj économe

thrill [θrɪl] n: **What a thrill!** Quelle
émotion

thrilled [θrɪld] adj: **I was thrilled.**
(pleased) J'étais absolument ravi.

thrilling ['θrɪlɪŋ] adj palpitant

throat [θrəʊt] n gorge f ▸ to have a
sore throat avoir mal à la gorge

throb [θrɒb] vb: **a throbbing
pain** un élancement; **My arm's
throbbing.** J'ai des élancements
dans le bras.

throne [θrəʊn] n trône m

through [θruː] prep, adj, adv
❶ par ▸ through the window par

la fenêtre ▸ I know her through my
sister. Je la connais par ma sœur.
▸ to go through Winnipeg passer par
Winnipeg; **to go through a tunnel**
traverser un tunnel ❷ à travers
▸ through the mist à travers la brume
▸ through the crowd à travers la foule
▸ The window was dirty and I couldn't
see through. La fenêtre était sale et
je n'arrivais pas à voir à travers.; **a
through train** un train direct; **"no
through road"** « impasse »

throughout [θruː'aʊt] prep:
throughout Nova Scotia
dans toute la Nouvelle-Écosse;
throughout the year pendant
toute l'année

throw [θrəʊ] vb lancer ▸ She threw
the ball to me. Elle m'a lancé le
ballon.; **to throw a party** organiser
une soirée; **That really threw him.**
Ça l'a décontenancé.; **to throw
away (1)** (garbage) jeter **(2)** (chance)
perdre; **to throw out (1)** (throw
away) jeter **(2)** (person) mettre à la
porte ▸ I threw him out. Je l'ai mis à
la porte.; **to throw up** vomir

thug [θʌɡ] n voyou

thumb [θʌm] n pouce m

thumbtack ['θʌmtæk] n punaise f

thunder ['θʌndər] n tonnerre m

thunderstorm ['θʌndəstɔːm] n
orage m

Thursday ['θɜːzdɪ] n jeudi m ▸ on
Thursday jeudi ▸ on Thursdays le
jeudi ▸ every Thursday tous les jeudis
▸ last Thursday jeudi dernier ▸ next
Thursday jeudi prochain

thyme [taɪm] n thym m

tick [tɪk] n (of clock) tic-tac m
▸ vb (clock) faire tic-tac

ticket ['tɪkɪt] n
    Be careful to choose correctly
    between **le ticket** and **le billet**.
❶ (for bus, subway, movie, museum)
ticket m ▸ a subway ticket un

ticket de métro ❷ (for plane, train, theatre, concert) billet m; **a parking ticket** une contravention (pour stationnement) une contravention pour excès de vitesse

ticket office n guichet m

tickle ['tɪkl] vb chatouiller

ticklish ['tɪklɪʃ] adj chatouilleux (f chatouilleuse) ▷ Are you ticklish? Tu es chatouilleux?

tick off vb: **to tick something off** cocher quelque chose; **to tick somebody off** enguirlander quelqu'un

tide [taɪd] n marée f; **high tide** la marée haute; **low tide** la marée basse

tidy ['taɪdɪ] adj ❶ (room) bien rangé ▷ Your room's very tidy. Ta chambre est bien rangée. ❷ (person) ordonné ▷ She's very tidy. Elle est très ordonnée.
▶ vb ranger ▷ Go and tidy your room. Va ranger ta chambre.; **to tidy up** ranger ▷ Don't forget to tidy up afterwards. N'oubliez pas de ranger après.

tie [taɪ] n (necktie) cravate f; **It was a tie.** (in sport) Ils ont fait match nul.
▶ vb ❶ (ribbon, shoelaces) nouer; **to tie a knot in something** faire un nœud à quelque chose ❷ (in sport) faire match nul ▷ They tied three all. Ils ont fait match nul, trois à trois.; **to tie up** ❶ (parcel) ficeler ❷ (dog, boat) attacher ❸ (prisoner) ligoter

tiger ['taɪɡəʳ] n tigre m

tight [taɪt] adj ❶ (tight-fitting) moulant(e) ▷ tight clothes les vêtements moulants ❷ (too tight) serré(e) ▷ These jeans are a bit tight. Ces jeans sont un peu serrés.

tighten ['taɪtn] vb ❶ (rope) tendre ❷ (screw) resserrer

tightly ['taɪtlɪ] adv (hold) fort

tights [taɪts] npl collant m

tile [taɪl] n (on wall, floor) carreau m (pl carreaux)

tiled [taɪld] adj (wall, floor, room) carrelé

till [tɪl] n caisse f
▶ prep, conj ❶ jusqu'à ▷ I waited till ten o'clock. J'ai attendu jusqu'à dix heures.; **till now** jusqu'à présent; **till then** jusque-là

> Use **avant** if the sentence you want to translate contains a negative, such as "not" or "never".

❷ avant ▷ It won't be ready till next week. Ça ne sera pas prêt avant la semaine prochaine. ▷ Till last year I'd never been to Gaspé. Avant l'année dernière, je n'étais jamais allé en Gaspésie.

time [taɪm] n ❶ (on clock) heure f ▷ What time is it? Quelle heure est-il? ▷ What time do you get up? À quelle heure tu te lèves? ▷ It was two o'clock, Vancouver time. Il était deux heures, heure de Vancouver.; **on time** ▷ She never arrives on time. Elle n'arrive jamais à l'heure. ❷ (amount of time) temps m ▷ I'm sorry, I don't have time. Je suis désolé, je n'ai pas le temps.; **from time to time** de temps en temps; **in time** à temps ▷ We arrived in time for lunch. Nous sommes arrivés à temps pour le dîner.; **just in time** juste à temps; **in no time** en un rien de temps ▷ It was ready in no time. Ce a été prêt en un rien de temps.; **It's time to go.** Il est temps de partir. ❸ (moment) moment m ▷ This isn't a good time to ask him. Ce n'est pas le bon moment pour lui demander.; **for the time being** pour le moment ❹ (occasion) fois f ▷ this time cette fois-ci ▷ next time la prochaine fois ▷ **two at a time** deux à la fois; **How many times?** Combien de fois?; **at times** parfois; **a long time** longtemps ▷ *Have you lived here for a long time?* Vous habitez ici depuis longtemps?; **in a week's time** dans une semaine ▷ *I'll come back in a month's time.* Je reviendrai dans un mois. ; **Come and see us any time.** Venez nous voir quand vous voulez.; **to have a good time** bien s'amuser ▷ *Did you have a good time?* Vous vous êtes bien amusés?; **2 times 2 is 4** deux fois deux égalent quatre

time off n temps libre m

timer ['taɪməʳ] n minuterie f

time-share ['taɪmʃeəʳ] n multipropriété f ▷ *We have a time-share ski chalet in Whistler.* Nous avons un chalet de ski en multipropriété à Whistler.

timetable ['taɪmteɪbl] n (for train, bus, school) horaire m

time zone n fuseau horaire m ▷ *Canada has six time zones.* Le Canada a six fuseaux horaires.

tin [tɪn] n (type of metal) étain m

tinsel ['tɪnsl] n guirlandes f

tinted ['tɪntɪd] adj (spectacles, glass) teinté

tiny ['taɪnɪ] adj minuscule

tip [tɪp] n ❶ (money) pourboire m ▷ *Shall I give him a tip?* Je lui donne un pourboire? ❷ (advice) conseil m ▷ *a useful tip* un bon conseil ❸ (informal: end) bout m ▷ *It's on the tip of my tongue.* Je l'ai sur le bout de la langue.
▸ vb donner un pourboire à ▷ *Don't forget to tip the taxi driver.* N'oubliez pas de donner un pourboire à la chauffeuse de taxi.; **to tip over** basculer ▷ *The vase tipped over.* Le vase a basculé.; **to tip something over** faire basculer quelque chose

▷ *She tipped over the vase.* Elle a fait basculer le vase.

tiptoe ['tɪptəʊ] n: **on tiptoe** sur la pointe des pieds

tire ['taɪəʳ] n pneu m; **tire pressure** la pression des pneus

tired ['taɪəd] adj fatigué ▷ *I'm tired.* Je suis fatigué.; **to be tired of something** en avoir assez de quelque chose

tiring ['taɪərɪŋ] adj fatigant

tissue ['tɪʃuː] n mouchoir de papier m ▷ *Have you got a tissue?* Tu as un mouchoir de papier?

title ['taɪtl] n titre m

title role n rôle principal m

to [tuː, tə] prep
à + le changes to **au**. à + les changes to **aux**.

❶ à, au, aux ▷ *to go to Toronto* aller à Toronto ▷ *to go to school* aller à l'école ▷ *a letter to his mother* une lettre à sa mère ▷ *the answer to the question* la réponse à la question ▷ *to go to the movies* aller au cinéma ▷ *We said goodbye to the neighbours.* Nous avons dit au revoir aux voisins.; **ready to go** prêt à partir; **ready to eat** prêt à manger; **It's easy to do.** C'est facile à faire.; **something to drink** quelque chose à boire; **I've got things to do.** J'ai des choses à faire.; **from…to…** de…à… ▷ *from nine o'clock to half past three* de neuf heures à trois heures et demie ❷ de ▷ *the train to London* le train de London ▷ *the road to Saskatoon* la route de Saskatoon ▷ *the key to the front door* la clé de la porte d'entrée; **It's difficult to say.** C'est difficile à dire.; **It's easy to criticize.** C'est facile de critiquer.
When referring to someone's house, store or office, use **chez**.
❸ chez ▷ *to go to the doctor's* aller chez le docteur ▷ *Let's go to her*

house. Si on allait chez elle? When **to** refers to a country which is feminine, use **en**; when the country is masculine, use **au**.

❹ en ▷ *to go to France* aller en France, au ▷ *to go to Portugal* aller au Portugal ❺ *(up to)* jusqu'à ▷ *to count to ten* compter jusqu'à dix ❻ *(in order to)* pour ▷ *I did it to help you.* Je l'ai fait pour vous aider. ▷ *He's too young to go to school.* Il est trop jeune pour aller à l'école.

toad [təud] *n* crapaud *m*

toadstool ['təudstuːl] *n* champignon vénéneux *m*

toast [təust] *n* toast *m* ▷ *a piece of toast with peanut butter* un toast avec du beurre d'arachide

toaster ['təustə'] *n* grille-pain *m* (*pl* grille-pain)

tobacco [tə'bækəu] *n* tabac *m*

toboggan [tə'bɒgən] *n* traîne sauvage *f*

tobogganing [tə'bɒgənɪŋ] *n*: **to go tobogganing** faire de la traîne sauvage

today [tə'deɪ] *adv* aujourd'hui ▷ *What did you do today?* Qu'est-ce tu as fait aujourd'hui?

toddler ['tɒdlə'] *n* bambin *m*, bambine *f*

toe [təu] *n* orteil *m*

toffee ['tɒfɪ] *n* caramel *m*

together [tə'geðə'] *adv* ❶ ensemble ▷ *Are they still together?* Ils sont toujours ensemble? ❷ *(at the same time)* en même temps ▷ *Don't all speak together!* Ne parlez pas tous en même temps!; **together with** (*with person*) avec

toilet ['tɔɪlət] *n* toilette *f*

toilet paper *n* papier hygiénique *m*

toiletries ['tɔɪlətrɪz] *npl* articles *mpl* de toilette

told [təuld] *vb* *see* **tell**

tolerant ['tɔlərnt] *adj* tolérant

toll booth ['təulbuːθ] *n* (*on bridge, highway*) poste de péage *m*

tomato [tə'mɑːtəu] *n* tomate *f* ▷ *tomato sauce* la sauce tomate ▷ *tomato soup* la soupe aux tomates

tomorrow [tə'mɒrəu] *adv* demain ▷ *tomorrow morning* demain matin ▷ *tomorrow night* demain soir; **the day after tomorrow** après-demain

ton [tʌn] *n* ▷ *a ton of homework* un tas de devoirs

tongue [tʌŋ] *n* langue *f*; **to say something tongue in cheek** dire quelque chose en plaisantant

tonic ['tɒnɪk] *n* (*tonic water*) soda tonique *m*

tonight [tə'naɪt] *adv* ❶ *(this evening)* ce soir ▷ *Are you going out tonight?* Tu sors ce soir? ❷ *(during the night)* cette nuit ▷ *I'll sleep well tonight.* Je dormirai bien cette nuit.

tonne [tʌn] *n* tonne *f*

tonsillitis [tɒnsɪ'laɪtɪs] *n* amygdalite *f*

tonsils ['tɒnslz] *npl* amygdales *fpl*

too [tuː] *adv, adj* ❶ *(as well)* aussi ▷ *My sister came too.* Ma sœur est venue aussi. ❷ *(excessively)* trop ▷ *The water's too hot.* L'eau est trop chaude. ▷ *We arrived too late.* Nous sommes arrivés trop tard.; **too much** (1) *(with noun)* trop de ▷ *too much noise* trop de bruit (2) *(with verb)* trop ▷ *He talks too much.* Il parle trop. (3) *(too expensive)* trop cher ▷ *Fifty dollars? That's too much.* Cinquante dollars? C'est trop cher.; **too many** trop de ▷ *too many hamburgers* trop de hamburgers; **too bad!** tant pis!

took [tuk] *vb* *see* **take**

tool [tuːl] *n* outil *m*; **a tool box** une boîte à outils

toolbar ['tuːlbɑː'] *n* barre d'outils *f*

toonie ['tuːnɪ] n deux dollars m

tooth [tuːθ] n dent f

toothache ['tuːθeɪk] n mal de dents m ▷ **to have a toothache** avoir mal aux dents

toothbrush ['tuːθbrʌʃ] n brosse à dents f

toothpaste ['tuːθpeɪst] n dentifrice m

top [tɒp] n ❶ (of page, ladder, garment) haut m ▷ **at the top of the page** en haut de la page; **a bikini top** un haut de bikini ❷ (of mountain) sommet m ❸ (of table) dessus m; **on top of** (on) sur ▷ **on top of the fridge** sur le frigo; **to be on top of things** avoir la situation bien en main; **There's tax on top of that.** Il y a de la taxe en plus.; **from top to bottom** de fond en comble ▷ **I searched the house from top to bottom.** J'ai fouillé la maison de fond en comble. ❹ (of box, jar) couvercle m ❺ (of bottle) bouchon m ▸ adj (first-class) grand ▷ **a top surgeon** une grande chirurgienne; **a top model** un mannequin vedette; **He always gets top marks in French.** Il a toujours d'excellentes notes en français.; **the top floor** le dernier étage ▷ **on the top floor** au dernier étage

topic ['tɒpɪk] n sujet m ▷ **The essay can be on any topic.** Cette dissertation peut être sur n'importe quel sujet.

topical ['tɒpɪkl] adj d'actualité ▷ **a topical issue** un sujet d'actualité

top-secret ['tɒp'siːkrɪt] adj très m secret, très f secrète ▷ **top-secret documents** des documents très secrets

tore, torn [tɔːr, tɔːn] vb see **tear**

tortoise ['tɔːtəs] n tortue f

torture ['tɔːtʃər] n torture f ▷ **It was pure torture.** C'était une vraie torture.
▸ vb torturer ▷ **Stop torturing that poor animal!** Arrête de torturer ce pauvre animal!

toss [tɒs] vb lancer; **to toss a salad** brasser une salade; **Shall we toss for it?** On joue à pile ou face?; **I tossed and turned all night.** Je n'ai pas arrêté de me tourner et de me retourner toute la nuit.

total ['təʊtl] adj total m (mpl totaux); **the total amount** le total ▸ n total m (pl totaux); **the grand total** le total

totally ['təʊtəlɪ] adv complètement ▷ **This thing is totally useless.** Cette chose est complètement inutile.

touch [tʌtʃ] n: **to get in touch with somebody** prendre contact avec quelqu'un; **to keep in touch with somebody** ne pas perdre contact avec quelqu'un; **Keep in touch!** Donne-moi de tes nouvelles!; **to lose touch** se perdre de vue; **to lose touch with somebody** perdre quelqu'un de vue
▸ vb toucher; **Don't touch that!** N'y touche pas!

touchdown ['tʌtʃdaʊn] n (football) essai m

touched [tʌtʃt] adj touché ▷ **I was really touched.** Ça m'a beaucoup touché.

touching ['tʌtʃɪŋ] adj touchant

touchpad ['tʌtʃpæd] n bloc à effleurement m

touchy ['tʌtʃɪ] adj susceptible ▷ **She's a bit touchy.** Elle est susceptible.

tough [tʌf] adj ❶ dur ▷ **It was tough, but I managed OK.** C'était dur, mais je m'en suis tiré. ▷ **It's a tough job.** C'est dur.; **The meat's tough.** La viande est coriace. ❷ (strong) solide ▷ **tough leather gloves** de solides gants en cuir ▷ *She's tough. She can take it.* Elle est solide. Elle tiendra le coup. ❸ *(rough, violent)* dangereux (f dangereuse); **He thinks he's a tough guy.** Il se prend pour un dur.; **Tough luck!** C'est comme ça!

toupee ['tu:peɪ] *n* postiche *m*

tour ['tʊə'] *n* ❶ *(of town, museum)* tour *m* ▷ *We went on a tour of the city.* Nous avons fait le tour de la ville.; **a guided tour** une visite guidée; **a package tour** un voyage organisé ❷ *(by singer, group)* tournée *f* ▷ *on tour* en tournée; **to go on tour** faire une tournée

▶ *vb:* **Ashley MacIsaac is touring Europe.** *(singer, artiste)* Ashley MacIsaac est en tournée en Europe.

tour guide *n* guide

tourism ['tʊərɪzm] *n* tourisme *m*

tourist ['tʊərɪst] *n* touriste; **tourist information office** le bureau d'information touristique

tournament ['tʊənəmənt] *n* tournoi *m*

towards [tə'wɔ:dz] *prep* ❶ *(in the direction of)* vers ▷ *She came towards me.* Elle est venue vers moi. ❷ *(of attitude)* envers ▷ *my feelings towards him* mes sentiments à son égard

towel ['taʊəl] *n* serviette *f*

tower ['taʊə'] *n* tour *f*

town [taʊn] *n* ville *f* ▷ *We went into town.* Nous sommes allés en ville.; **the town centre** le centre-ville; **the town hall** la mairie

tow truck ['təʊ-] *n* dépanneuse *f*

toy [tɔɪ] *n* jouet *m* ▷ *a toy store* un magasin de jouets; **a toy car** une petite voiture

trace [treɪs] *n* trace *f* ▷ *There was no trace of the robbers.* Il n'y avait pas de trace des voleurs.

▶ *vb* *(draw)* décalquer

tracing paper ['treɪsɪŋ-] *n* papier calque *m*

track [træk] *n* ❶ *(dirt road)* chemin *m* ❷ *(railway line)* voie ferrée *f* ❸ *(sports)* piste *f* ▷ *two laps of the track* deux tours de piste ❹ *(song)* chanson *f* ▷ *This is my favourite track on the CD.* C'est ma chanson préférée sur le CD. ❺ *(trail)* traces *fpl* ▷ *They followed the tracks for miles.* Ils ont suivi les traces pendant des kilomètres.

track down *vb:* **to track somebody down** retrouver quelqu'un ▷ *The police never tracked down the killer.* La police n'a jamais retrouvé l'assassin.

track and field *n* athlétisme *m*

tracksuit ['træksu:t] *n* survêtement *m*

tractor ['træktə'] *n* tracteur *m*

trade [treɪd] *n* ❶ commerce *m* ▷ *international trade* le commerce international ❷ *(skill, job)* métier *m* ▷ *to learn a trade* apprendre un métier

▶ *vb* ❶ échanger ▷ *Want to trade your apple for this orange?* Veux-tu échanger ta pomme contre cette orange? ❷ faire du commerce ▷ *Canada trades with many countries.* Le Canada fait du commerce avec de nombreux pays.

tradition [trə'dɪʃən] *n* tradition *f*

traditional [trə'dɪʃənl] *adj* traditionnel (f traditionnelle)

traffic ['træfɪk] *n* circulation *f* ▷ *The traffic was terrible.* Il y avait une circulation épouvantable.

traffic jam *n* embouteillage *m*

traffic lights *npl* feux *mpl*

tragedy ['trædʒədɪ] *n* tragédie *f*

tragic ['trædʒɪk] *adj* tragique

trailer ['treɪlə'] *n* ❶ *(vehicle)* remorque *f* ❷ *(for movie)* bande-annonce *f*

train [treɪn] n ❶ train m ❷ (on
subway) rame f
▶ vb (sports) s'entraîner ▷ to train for
a race s'entraîner pour une course;
to train as a teacher suivre une
formation d'enseignant; **to train
an animal to do something**
dresser un animal à faire quelque
chose

trained [treɪnd] adj: **She's a
trained nurse.** Elle est infirmière
diplômée.

trainee [treɪˈniː] n ❶ (in profession)
stagiaire ▷ He's a trainee. Il est
stagiaire. ❷ (apprentice) apprenti
m, apprentie f

trainer [ˈtreɪnəʳ] n ❶ (sports coach)
entraîneur m, entraîneure f ❷ (of
animals) dompteur m, dompteuse f

training [ˈtreɪnɪŋ] n ❶ formation
f ▷ a training course un stage
de formation ❷ (sports)
entraînement m

trampoline [ˈtræmpəliːn] n
trampoline m

tranquillizer [ˈtræŋkwɪlaɪzəʳ]
n tranquillisant m ▷ He's on
tranquillizers. Il prend des
tranquillisants.

Trans-Canada highway
[ˈtrænsˈkænədə-] n
Transcanadienne f

transfer [trænsˈfəːʳ] n ❶ (sticker)
décalque m ❷ transfert m ▷ a job
transfer un transfert d'emploi

transfusion [trænsˈfjuːʒən] n
transfusion f

transit [ˈtrænzɪt] n transit m ▷ in
transit en transit; **public transit**
les transports publics; **the transit
system** le système de transport

translate [trænzˈleɪt] vb traduire
▷ to translate something into English
traduire quelque chose en anglais

translation [trænzˈleɪʃən] n
traduction f

translator [trænzˈleɪtəʳ] n
traducteur m, traductrice f ▷ She's a
translator. Elle est traductrice.

transparency [trænsˈpærnsɪ]
n transparent m ▷ Put the
transparency on the overhead
projector. Mets le transparent dans
le rétroprojecteur.

transparent [trænsˈpærnt] adj
transparent m

transplant [ˈtrænsplɑːnt] n greffe
f ▷ a heart transplant une greffe du
cardiaque

transport [ˈtrænspɔːt] n transport
m ▷ public transport les transports
publics
▶ vb transporter

trap [træp] n piège m

trapeze [trəˈpiːz] n trapèze m;
trapeze artist le/la trapéziste

trash [træʃ] n ordures fpl; **the
trash can** la poubelle

traumatic [trɔːˈmætɪk] adj
traumatisant m ▷ It was a traumatic
experience. Ça a été une expérience
traumatisante.

traumatize [ˈtrɔːmətaɪz] vb
traumatiser

travel [ˈtrævl] n voyages mpl
▶ vb voyager ▷ I prefer to travel
by plane. Je préfère voyager en
avion.; **I'd like to travel around
the world.** J'aimerais faire le tour
du monde.; **We travelled over
800 kilometres.** Nous avons fait
plus de huit cents kilomètres.;
News travels fast! Les nouvelles
circulent vite!

travel agency n agence f de
voyages

travel agent n agent m de
voyages, agente f de voyages

traveller [ˈtrævləʳ] n voyageur m,
voyageuse f

traveller's cheque [ˈtrævləz-] n
chèque de voyage m

travelling ['trævlɪŋ] n: **I love travelling.** J'adore les voyages.

travel sickness n mal des transports m

tray [treɪ] n plateau m (pl plateaux)

treasure ['treʒə'] n trésor m

treat [triːt] n (food) gâterie f; **to give somebody a treat** (not food) faire plaisir à quelqu'un
▶ vb (well, badly) traiter; **to treat somebody to something** offrir quelque chose à quelqu'un ▷ He treated us to an ice cream. Il nous a offert une crème glacée.

treatment ['triːtmənt] n traitement m

treaty ['triːtɪ] n traité m

tree [triː] n arbre m

tremble ['trembl] vb trembler

tremendous [trɪ'mendəs] adj énorme ▷ a tremendous success un succès énorme

trend [trend] n (fashion) mode f

trendy ['trendɪ] adj branché

trial ['traɪəl] n (in court) procès m

triangle ['traɪæŋgl] n triangle m

trick [trɪk] n ❶ tour ▷ to play a trick on somebody jouer un tour à quelqu'un ❷ (knack) truc f ▷ It's not easy: there's a trick to it. Ce n'est pas facile: il y a un truc.
▶ vb: **to trick somebody** rouler quelqu'un

tricky ['trɪkɪ] adj délicat

trim [trɪm] vb ❶ (hair) égaliser ❷ (grass) tondre
▶ n (haircut) coupe d'entretien f ▷ to get a trim se faire faire une coupe d'entretien

trip [trɪp] n voyage m ▷ to go on a trip faire un voyage ▷ Have a good trip! Bon voyage!; **a day trip** une excursion d'une journée
▶ vb (stumble) trébucher

triple ['trɪpl] adj triple
▶ vb tripler

triplets ['trɪplɪts] npl ❶ (boys) triplés mpl ❷ (girls), triplées fpl

trivial ['trɪvɪəl] adj insignifiant

trombone [trɒm'bəʊn] n trombone m ▷ I play the trombone. Je joue du trombone.

troops [truːps] npl troupes fpl ▷ Canadian troops les troupes canadiennes

trophy ['trəʊfɪ] n trophée m ▷ to win a trophy gagner un trophée

tropical ['trɒpɪkl] adj tropical ▷ The weather was tropical. Il faisait une chaleur tropicale.

tropics ['trɒpɪks] npl tropiques mpl ▷ in the tropics sous les tropiques

trot [trɒt] vb trotter

trouble ['trʌbl] n problème m ▷ The trouble is, it's too expensive. Le problème, c'est que c'est trop cher.; **to be in trouble** avoir des ennuis; **What's the trouble?** Qu'est-ce qui ne va pas?; **stomach trouble** troubles gastriques; **to take a lot of trouble over something** se donner beaucoup de mal pour quelque chose; **Don't worry, it's no trouble.** Mais non, ça ne me dérange pas du tout.

troublemaker ['trʌblmeɪkə'] n perturbateur m, perturbatrice f

trout [traʊt] n truite f

truck [trʌk] n camion m

trucker ['trʌkə'] n camionneur m, camionneuse f

true [truː] adj vrai; **That's true.** C'est vrai.; **to come true** se réaliser ▷ I hope my dream will come true. J'espère que mon rêve se réalisera.; **true love** le grand amour

truly ['truːlɪ] adv vraiment ▷ It was a truly remarkable victory. C'était vraiment une victoire remarquable.; **Yours truly.** Je vous prie d'agréer mes salutations distinguées.

trumpet ['trʌmpɪt] n trompette f
▷ *She plays the trumpet.* Elle joue de
la trompette.

trunk [trʌŋk] n ❶ (of tree) tronc
m ❷ (of elephant) trompe f ❸ (of
car) coffre m

trust [trʌst] n confiance f ▷ *to have
trust in somebody* avoir confiance en
quelqu'un
▶ vb: **to trust somebody** faire
confiance à quelqu'un ▷ *Don't
you trust me?* Tu ne me fais pas
confiance? ▷ *Trust me!* Fais-moi
confiance!

trusting ['trʌstɪŋ] adj confiant

truth [truːθ] n vérité f

truthful ['truːθful] adj: **She's
a very truthful person.** Elle dit
toujours la vérité.

try [traɪ] n essai m ▷ *his third try*
son troisième essai; **to have a
try** essayer; **It's worth a try.** Ça
vaut la peine d'essayer.; **to give
something a try** essayer quelque
chose
▶ vb ❶ (attempt) essayer ▷ *to try
to do something* essayer de faire
quelque chose; **to try again** refaire
un essai ❷ (taste) goûter ▷ *Would
you like to try some?* Voulez-vous
goûter?; **to try on** (clothes) essayer;
to try something out essayer
quelque chose

T-shirt ['tiːʃəːt] n T-shirt m

tube [tjuːb] n tube m

tuberculosis [tjubəːkjuːˈləusɪs] n
tuberculose f

Tuesday ['tjuːzdɪ] n mardi m
▷ *on Tuesday* mardi ▷ *on Tuesdays*
le mardi ▷ *every Tuesday* tous les
mardis ▷ *last Tuesday* mardi dernier
▷ *next Tuesday* mardi prochain

tug-of-war [tʌgəvˈwɔːʳ] n lutte
à la corde f

tulip ['tjuːlɪp] n tulipe f

tuna ['tjuːnə] n thon m; **tuna
salad** la salade de thon

tundra ['tʌndrə] n toundra f

tune [tjuːn] n (melody) air m; **to
play in tune** jouer juste; **to sing
out of tune** chanter faux
▶ vb ❶ (instrument) accorder ▷ *You
need to tune your guitar.* Il faut que
tu accordes ta guitare. ❷ (radio)
syntoniser ▷ *I tuned the radio to CBC.*
J'ai syntonisé la radio sur Radio-
Canada.

tunnel ['tʌnl] n tunnel m

tuque [tuːk] n tuque f

turkey ['təːkɪ] n ❶ (meat) dinde f
❷ (live bird) dindon m

turn [təːn] n ❶ (bend in road)
tournant m; **"no left turn"**
« défense de tourner à gauche »
❷ (in game) tour ▷ *It's my turn!* C'est
à mon tour!
▶ vb ❶ tourner ▷ *Turn right at
the lights.* Tournez à droite aux
feux. ❷ (become) devenir ▷ *to
turn red* devenir rouge; **to turn
into something** se transformer
en quelque chose ▷ *The frog turned
into a prince.* La grenouille s'est
transformée en prince.

turn around vb ❶ (car) faire demi-
tour ❷ (person) se retourner

turn back vb faire demi-tour
▷ *We turned back.* Nous avons fait
demi-tour.

turn down vb ❶ (offer) refuser
❷ (radio, TV, heating) baisser ▷ *Shall
I turn the heating down?* Je baisse le
chauffage?

turn off vb ❶ (light, radio) éteindre
❷ (tap) fermer ❸ (engine) arrêter

turn on vb ❶ (light, radio) allumer
❷ (tap) ouvrir ❸ (engine) mettre
en marche

turn out vb: **It turned out to be
a mistake.** Il s'est avéré que c'était
une erreur.; **It turned out that
she was right.** Il s'est avéré qu'elle

avait raison.

turn up vb ❶ (arrive) arriver ❷ (increase) monter; **Could you turn up the radio?** Tu peux monter le son de la radio?

turnip ['tɜːnɪp] n navet m

turquoise ['tɜːkwɔɪz] adj (colour) turquoise (f+pl turquoise)

turtle ['tɜːtl] n tortue f

tutor ['tjuːtə*] n (private teacher) professeur particulier m, professeure particulière f

TV [tiːˈviː] n télé f

tweet [twiːt] n (on Twitter) tweet m ▶ vb (on Twitter) tweeter

tweezers ['twiːzəz] npl pince f à épiler

twelfth [twelfθ] adj douzième ▷ the twelfth floor le douzième étage; **the twelfth of August** le douze août

twelve [twelv] num douze ▷ He's twelve. Il a douze ans.; **twelve o'clock (1)** (midday) midi **(2)** (midnight) minuit

twentieth ['twentɪɪθ] adj vingtième ▷ the twentieth time la vingtième fois; **the twentieth of May** le vingt mai

twenty ['twentɪ] num vingt ▷ He's twenty. Il a vingt ans. ▷ **in twenty fourteen** en deux mille quatorze

twice [twaɪs] adv deux fois; **twice as much** deux fois plus ▷ He gets twice as much allowance as me. Il a deux fois plus d'argent de poche que moi.

twin [twɪn] n (boy, girl) jumeau m, jumelle f (f pl jumeaux, f pl jumelles); **my twin brother** mon frère jumeau; **her twin sister** sa sœur jumelle; **identical twins** les vrais jumeaux; **a twin room** une chambre à deux lits

twinned [twɪnd] adj jumelé ▷ Banff is twinned with Obama-cho.

Banff est jumelée avec Obama-cho.

twist [twɪst] vb ❶ (bend) tordre ❷ (distort) déformer ▷ You're twisting my words. Tu déformes ce que j'ai dit.

Twitter® ['twɪtə*] n Twitter® m

two [tuː] num deux ▷ She's two. Elle a deux ans.

type [taɪp] n type m ▷ What type of camera do you have? Quel type d'appareil photo as-tu? ▶ vb taper ▷ Type your password. Tape ton mot de passe.

typical ['tɪpɪkl] adj typique ▷ That's just typical! C'est typique!

tyrant ['taɪrənt] n tyran m ▷ He's a real tyrant. C'est un vrai tyran.

u

UFO ['juːfəʊ] n OVNI m (= objet volant non identifié)

ugh [əːh] excl yark!

ugly ['ʌglɪ] adj laid

ulcer ['ʌlsəʳ] n ulcère m

ultimate ['ʌltɪmət] adj suprême ▷ the ultimate challenge le défi suprême; **It was the ultimate adventure.** C'était la grande aventure.

ultimately ['ʌltɪmətlɪ] adv au bout du compte ▷ Ultimately, it's your decision. Au bout du compte, c'est votre décision.

umbrella [ʌm'brɛlə] n
❶ parapluie m **❷** (for sun) parasol m

umpire ['ʌmpaɪəʳ] n arbitre mf

UN n ONU f (= Organisation des Nations unies)

unable [ʌn'eɪbl] adj: **to be unable to do something** ne pas pouvoir faire quelque chose ▷ I was unable to come. Je n'ai pas pu venir.

unacceptable [ʌnək'sɛptəbl] adj inacceptable

unanimous [juː'nænɪməs] adj unanime ▷ a unanimous decision une décision unanime

unattended [ʌnə'tɛndɪd] adj: **to leave something unattended** laisser quelque chose sans surveillance ▷ Never leave pets unattended in your car. Ne laisser jamais d'animaux domestiques sans surveillance dans votre voiture.

unavoidable [ʌnə'vɔɪdəbl] adj inévitable

unaware [ʌnə'wɛəʳ] adj: **to be unaware (1)** (not know about) ignorer ▷ I was unaware of the rules. J'ignorais le règlement. **(2)** (not notice) ne pas se rendre compte ▷ She was unaware that she was being filmed. Elle ne s'était pas rendu compte qu'on la filmait.

unbearable [ʌn'bɛərəbl] adj insupportable

unbeatable [ʌn'biːtəbl] adj imbattable

unbelievable [ʌnbɪ'liːvəbl] adj incroyable

unborn [ʌn'bɔːn] adj: **the unborn child** le fœtus

unbreakable [ʌn'breɪkəbl] adj incassable

uncanny [ʌn'kænɪ] adj étrange ▷ That's uncanny! C'est étrange!; **an uncanny resemblance** une ressemblance troublante

uncertain [ʌn'sɜːtn] adj incertain ▷ The future is uncertain. L'avenir est incertain.; **to be uncertain about something** ne pas être sûr de quelque chose

uncivilized [ʌn'sɪvɪlaɪzd] adj barbare

uncle ['ʌŋkl] n oncle m ▷ my uncle

mon oncle

uncomfortable [ʌnˈkʌmfətəbl] adj ❶ (person) mal à l'aise ▷ I feel uncomfortable at their house. Je me sens mal à l'aise chez eux. ❷ pas confortable ▷ The seats are rather uncomfortable. Les sièges ne sont pas très confortables.

unconscious [ʌnˈkɒnʃəs] adj sans connaissance

uncontrollable [ʌnkənˈtrəʊləbl] adj incontrôlable

unconventional [ʌnkənˈvɛnʃənl] adj peu conventionnel (f peu conventionnelle)

under [ˈʌndəʳ] prep ❶ sous ▷ The cat's under the table. Le chat est sous la table. ▷ The tunnel goes under the Fraser River. Le tunnel passe sous le fleuve Fraser; **under there** là-dessous ▷ What's under there? Qu'est-ce qu'il y a là-dessous? ❷ (less than) moins de ▷ under 20 people moins de vingt personnes ▷ children under 10 les enfants de moins de dix ans

undercover [ʌndəˈkʌvəʳ] adj, adv secret (f secrète) ▷ an undercover agent un agent d'infiltration; **He was working undercover.** Il travaillait sous une fausse identité.

underestimate [ˈʌndərˈɛstɪmeɪt] vb sous-estimer ▷ I underestimated her. Je l'ai sous-estimée.

undergo [ʌndəˈɡəʊ] vb (operation, examination, change) subir; **to be undergoing repairs** être en réparation

underground [ˈʌndəɡraʊnd] adj, adv ❶ souterrain ▷ an underground parking garage un stationnement souterrain ❷ sous terre ▷ Moles live underground. Les taupes vivent sous terre.

underline [ʌndəˈlaɪn] vb souligner

underneath [ʌndəˈniːθ] prep, adv

❶ sous ▷ underneath the carpet sous le tapis ❷ dessous ▷ I got out of the car and looked underneath. Je suis descendu de la voiture et j'ai regardé dessous.

underpaid [ʌndəˈpeɪd] adj sous-payé ▷ I'm underpaid. Je suis sous-payé.

underpants [ˈʌndəpænts] npl ❶ (women's) culotte f ❷ (men's) caleçon m ❸ (all kinds, informal) bobettes

undershirt [ˈʌndəʃəːt] n camisole f

understand [ʌndəˈstænd] vb comprendre ▷ Do you understand? Vous comprenez? ▷ I don't understand this word. Je ne comprends pas ce mot. ▷ Is that understood? C'est compris?

understanding [ʌndəˈstændɪŋ] adj compréhensif (f compréhensive) ▷ She's very understanding. Elle est très compréhensive.

understood [ʌndəˈstʊd] vb see **understand**

undertaker [ˈʌndəteɪkəʳ] n ❶ (mortician) embaumeur m, embaumeuse f ❷ (funeral home director) directeur de salon funéraire m, directrice de salon funéraire f

underwater [ʌndəˈwɔːtəʳ] adj, adv sous l'eau ▷ This sequence was filmed underwater. Cette séquence a été filmée sous l'eau.; **an underwater camera** un appareil photographique sous-marin; **underwater photography** la photographie sous-marine

underwear [ˈʌndəweəʳ] n sous-vêtements mpl

underwent [ʌndəˈwɛnt] vb see **undergo**

undo [ʌnˈduː] vb (buttons, knot) défaire

undress [ʌn'dres] vb (get undressed) se déshabiller

unemployed [ʌnɪm'plɔɪd] adj au chômage ▷ He's unemployed. Il est au chômage. ▷ I've been unemployed for a year. Ça fait un an que je suis au chômage.; **the unemployed** les m chômeurs

unemployment [ʌnɪm'plɔɪmənt] n chômage m

unexpected [ʌnɪk'spektɪd] adj inattendu ▷ an unexpected visitor un visiteur inattendu

unexpectedly [ʌnɪk'spektɪdlɪ] adv à l'improviste ▷ They arrived unexpectedly. Ils sont arrivés à l'improviste.

unfair [ʌn'feəʳ] adj injuste ▷ It's unfair to everybody. C'est injuste pour tout le monde.

unfamiliar [ʌnfə'mɪliəʳ] adj: **I heard an unfamiliar voice.** J'ai entendu une voix que je ne connaissais pas.

unfold [ʌn'fəʊld] vb déplier ▷ She unfolded the map. Elle a déplié la carte.

unforgettable [ʌnfə'getəbl] adj inoubliable

unfortunately [ʌn'fɔːtʃnətlɪ] adv malheureusement ▷ Unfortunately, I arrived late. Malheureusement, je suis arrivé en retard.

unfriend [ʌn'frend] vb (on Internet) retirer de la liste d'amis

unfriendly [ʌn'frendlɪ] adj pas aimable ▷ The waiters are a bit unfriendly. Les serveurs ne sont pas très aimables.

ungrateful [ʌn'greɪtful] adj ingrat

unhappy [ʌn'hæpɪ] adj malheureux (f malheureuse) ▷ He was very unhappy as a child. Il était très malheureux quand il était petit.; **to look unhappy** avoir l'air triste

unhealthy [ʌn'helθɪ] adj
① (person) maladif (f maladive)
② (place, habit) malsain ③ (food) pas sain

uniform ['juːnɪfɔːm] n uniforme m ▷ the school uniform l'uniforme scolaire

unilingual ['juːnɪ'lɪŋgwəl] adj unilingue

uninhabited [ʌnɪn'hæbɪtɪd] adj inhabité

union ['juːnjən] n (trade union) syndicat m

unique [juː'niːk] adj unique

unit ['juːnɪt] n ① unité f ▷ a unit of measurement une unité de mesure ② (piece of furniture) élément m ▷ a kitchen unit un élément de cuisine

United Nations [juː'naɪtɪd-] n O.N.U. f (= Organisation des Nations Unies)

universe ['juːnɪvɜːs] n univers m

university [juːnɪ'vɜːsɪtɪ] n université f ▷ She's in university. Elle va à l'université. ▷ Do you want to go to university? Tu veux aller à l'université?

unleaded [ʌn'ledɪd] adj sans plomb

unless [ʌn'les] conj: **unless he leaves** à moins qu'il ne parte ▷ I won't come unless you phone me. Je ne viendrai pas à moins que tu ne me téléphones.

unlike [ʌn'laɪk] prep contrairement à ▷ Unlike him, I really enjoy flying. Contrairement à lui, j'adore prendre l'avion.

unlikely [ʌn'laɪklɪ] adj peu probable ▷ It's possible, but unlikely. C'est possible, mais peu probable.

unlisted [ʌn'lɪstɪd] adj: **an unlisted number** un numéro confidentiel

unload [ʌn'ləʊd] vb décharger ▷ We unloaded the car. Nous avons déchargé la voiture. ▷ *The trucks go there to unload.* Les camions y vont pour être déchargés.

unlock [ʌnˈlɒk] *vb* ouvrir ▷ *She unlocked the door of the car.* Elle a ouvert la portière de la voiture.

unlucky [ʌnˈlʌkɪ] *adj:* **to be unlucky (1)** (*number, object*) porter malheur ▷ *They say thirteen is an unlucky number.* On dit que le nombre treize porte malheur. **(2)** (*person*) ne pas avoir de chance ▷ *"Did you win?" — "No, I was unlucky."* « Vous avez gagné? » — « Non, je n'ai pas eu de chance. »

unmarried [ʌnˈmærɪd] *adj* (*person*) célibataire ▷ *an unmarried mother* une mère célibataire; **an unmarried couple** un couple non marié

unnatural [ʌnˈnætʃrəl] *adj* pas naturel (*f* pas naturelle)

unnecessary [ʌnˈnesəsərɪ] *adj* inutile

unofficial [ʌnəˈfɪʃl] *adj* (*meeting, leader*) non officiel (*f* non officielle)

unpack [ʌnˈpæk] *vb* ❶ défaire ▷ *I unpacked my suitcase.* J'ai défait ma valise. ❷ déballer ses affaires ▷ *I went to my room to unpack.* Je suis allé dans ma chambre pour déballer mes affaires. ▷ *I haven't unpacked my clothes yet.* Je n'ai pas encore déballé mes vêtements.

unpleasant [ʌnˈpleznt] *adj* désagréable

unplug [ʌnˈplʌɡ] *vb* débrancher

unpopular [ʌnˈpɒpjʊləʳ] *adj* impopulaire

unpredictable [ʌnprɪˈdɪktəbl] *adj* imprévisible

unreal [ʌnˈrɪəl] *adj* (*incredible*) incroyable ▷ *It was unreal!* C'était incroyable!

unrealistic [ˌʌnrɪəˈlɪstɪk] *adj* peu réaliste

unreasonable [ʌnˈriːznəbl] *adj* pas raisonnable ▷ *Her attitude was completely unreasonable.* Son attitude n'était pas du tout raisonnable.

unreliable [ˌʌnrɪˈlaɪəbl] *adj* (*car, machine*) pas fiable ▷ *It's a nice car, but a bit unreliable.* C'est une belle voiture, mais elle n'est pas très fiable.; **He's completely unreliable.** On ne peut pas du tout compter sur lui.

unroll [ʌnˈrəʊl] *vb* dérouler

unsatisfactory [ˈʌnsætɪsˈfæktərɪ] *adj* insatisfaisant

unscrew [ʌnˈskruː] *vb* dévisser ▷ *She unscrewed the top of the bottle.* Elle a dévissé le bouchon de la bouteille.

unshaven [ʌnˈʃeɪvn] *adj* mal rasé

unstable [ʌnˈsteɪbl] *adj* instable

unsteady [ʌnˈstedɪ] *adj* (*walk, voice*) mal assuré; **He was unsteady on his feet.** Il marchait d'un pas mal assuré.

unsuccessful [ˌʌnsəkˈsesfʊl] *adj* (*attempt*) vain; **to be unsuccessful in doing something** ne pas réussir à faire quelque chose ▷ *an unsuccessful artist* un artiste qui n'a pas réussi

unsuitable [ʌnˈsuːtəbl] *adj* (*clothes, equipment*) inapproprié

untidy [ʌnˈtaɪdɪ] *adj* ❶ en désordre ▷ *My bedroom's always untidy.* Ma chambre est toujours en désordre. ❷ (*appearance, person*) débraillé ▷ *He's always untidy.* Il est toujours débraillé. ❸ (*in character*) désordonné ▷ *She's a very untidy person.* Elle est très désordonnée.

untie [ʌnˈtaɪ] *vb* (*knot, parcel*) défaire ❷ (*animal*) détacher

until [ənˈtɪl] *prep, conj* ❶ jusqu'à ▷ *I waited until ten o'clock.* J'ai attendu jusqu'à dix heures.; **until now**

jusqu'à présent ▷ *It's never been a problem until now.* Ça n'a jamais été un problème jusqu'à présent. ; **until then** jusque-là ▷ *Until then I'd never been to Quebec.* Jusque-là je n'étais jamais allé au Québec.

> Use **avant** if the sentence you want to translate contains a negative, such as "not" or "never".

❷ avant ▷ *It won't be ready until next week.* Ça ne sera pas prêt avant la semaine prochaine. ▷ *Until last year I'd never been to New Brunswick.* Avant l'année dernière, je n'étais jamais allé au Nouveau-Brunswick.

unusual [ʌnˈjuːʒʊəl] *adj* ❶ insolite ▷ *an unusual shape* une forme insolite ❷ rare ▷ *It's unusual to get snow at this time of year.* Il est rare qu'il neige à cette époque de l'année.

unwilling [ʌnˈwɪlɪŋ] *adj*: **to be unwilling to do something** ne pas être disposé à faire quelque chose ▷ *He was unwilling to help me.* Il n'était pas disposé à m'aider.

unwind [ʌnˈwaɪnd] *vb* (*relax*) se détendre

unwise [ʌnˈwaɪz] *adj* (*person*) imprudent ▷ *That was rather unwise of you.* C'était plutôt imprudent de votre part.

unwound [ʌnˈwaʊnd] *vb see* **unwind**

unwrap [ʌnˈræp] *vb* déballer ▷ *After the meal we unwrapped the presents.* Après le repas, nous avons déballé les cadeaux.

up [ʌp] *prep, adv*

> For other expressions with **up**, see the verbs **go**, **come**, **put**, **turn** etc.

en haut ▷ *up on the hill* en haut de la colline; **up here** ici; **up there** là-haut; **up north** dans le nord; **to**

be up (*out of bed*) être debout ▷ *We were up at 6.* Nous étions debout à six heures. ▷ *He's not up yet.* Il n'est pas encore debout. ; **What's up?** Qu'est-ce qu'il y a? ▷ *What's up with him?* Qu'est-ce qu'il a? ; **to get up** (*in the morning*) se lever ▷ *What time do you get up?* À quelle heure est-ce que tu te lèves? ; **to go up** monter ▷ *The bus went up the hill.* L'autobus a monté la colline. ; **to go up to somebody** s'approcher de quelqu'un ▷ *She came up to me.* Elle s'est approchée de moi. ; **up to** (*as far as*) jusqu'à ▷ *to count up to fifty* compter jusqu'à cinquante ▷ *up to three hours* jusqu'à trois heures ▷ *up to now* jusqu'à présent ; **It's up to you.** C'est à vous de décider.

upbringing [ˈʌpbrɪŋɪŋ] *n* éducation f

update [ʌpˈdeɪt] *vb* mettre à jour ▷ *I've updated the file.* J'ai mis à jour le fichier.

uphill [ʌpˈhɪl] *adv*: **to go uphill** monter

upload [ˈʌpˈləʊd] *vb* télécharger vers le serveur ▷ *I uploaded the file without any trouble.* J'ai téléchargé le fichier vers le serveur sans difficulté.

▶ *n* téléchargement vers le serveur m ▷ *The upload isn't finished yet.* Le téléchargement vers le serveur n'est pas encore terminé.

upper [ˈʌpə²] *adj* supérieur ▷ *on the upper floor* à l'étage supérieur; **Upper Canada** le Haut-Canada

upright [ˈʌpraɪt] *adj*: **to stand upright** se tenir droit

upset [ˈʌpset] *n*: **a stomach upset** une indigestion

▶ *adj* contrarié ▷ *She's still a bit upset.* Elle est encore un peu contrariée. ; **I had an upset stomach.** J'avais l'estomac

dérangé.
▶ *vb*: **to upset somebody**
contrarier quelqu'un

upside down [ˈʌpsaɪd-] *adv* à
l'envers ▷ *That painting is upside
down.* Ce tableau est à l'envers.

upstairs [ʌpˈstɛəz] *adv* en haut
▷ "*Where's your coat?*" — "*It's upstairs.*"
« Où est ton manteau? » — « Il est en
haut. »; **to go upstairs** monter

uptight [ʌpˈtaɪt] *adj* tendu ▷ *She's
really uptight.* Elle est très tendue.

up-to-date [ˈʌptəˈdeɪt] *adj* ❶ (*car,
stereo*) moderne ❷ (*information*)
à jour ▷ *an up-to-date timetable* un
horaire à jour; **to bring something
up to date** moderniser quelque
chose

urgent [ˈəːdʒənt] *adj* urgent ▷ *Is it
urgent?* C'est urgent?

urine [ˈjuərɪn] *n* urine *f*

us [ʌs] *pron* nous ▷ *They helped us.*
Ils nous ont aidés. ▷ *They gave us a
map.* Ils nous ont donné une carte.

USB stick *n* clé USB *f*

use [*n* juːs, *vb* juːz] *n*: **It's no
use.** Ça ne sert à rien. ▷ *It's no use
shouting, she's deaf.* Ça ne sert à rien
de crier, elle est sourde.; **It's no
use, I can't do it.** Il n'y a rien à faire,
je n'y arrive pas.; **to make use of
something** utiliser quelque chose
▶ *vb* utiliser ▷ *Can we use a dictionary
on the exam?* Est-ce qu'on peut
utiliser un dictionnaire durant
l'examen?; **Can I use your phone?**
Je peux téléphoner?; **to use the
washroom** aller aux toilettes; **to
use up (1)** finir ▷ *We've used up all the
paint.* Nous avons fini la peinture.
(2) (*money*) dépenser; **I used to live
in Timmins.** J'habitais à Timmins
autrefois.; **I used to dislike math,
but now...** Avant, je n'aimais pas
les maths, mais maintenant...;
to be used to something avoir

l'habitude de quelque chose ▷ *He
wasn't used to driving on the left.* Il
n'avait pas l'habitude de conduire à
gauche. ▷ *Don't worry, I'm used to it.*
Ne t'inquiète pas, j'ai l'habitude.; **a
used car** une voiture usagée

useful [ˈjuːsful] *adj* utile

useless [ˈjuːslɪs] *adj* inutile ▷ *This
map is just useless.* Cette carte est
vraiment inutile.; **It's useless!** Ça
ne sert à rien!

user [ˈjuːzəʳ] *n* utilisateur *m*,
utilisatrice *f*

user-friendly [ˈjuːzəˈfrɛndlɪ] *adj*
facile à utiliser

usual [ˈjuːʒuəl] *adj* habituel (*f*
habituelle); **as usual** comme
d'habitude

usually [ˈjuːʒuəlɪ] *adv* ❶ (*generally*)
en général ▷ *I usually get to school
at about half past eight.* En général,
j'arrive à l'école vers huit heures
et demie. ❷ (*when making a
contrast*) d'habitude ▷ *Usually I
don't wear make-up, but today is a
special occasion.* D'habitude je ne
me maquille pas, mais aujourd'hui
c'est spécial.

utility room [juːˈtɪlɪtɪ-] *n* (*in
institution*) local d'entretien *m*

U-turn [ˈjuːˈtəːn] *n* demi-tour *m*
▷ *to do a U-turn* faire demi-tour

V

vacancy ['veɪkənsɪ] n **❶** (job) poste vacant m **❷** (room in hotel) chambre disponible f; **"no vacancies"** (on sign) « complet »

vacant ['veɪkənt] adj libre

vacation [və'keɪʃən] n vacances fpl ▷ to be on vacation être en vacances ▷ to take a vacation prendre des vacances

vaccinate ['væksɪneɪt] vb vacciner

vacuum ['vækjum] vb passer l'aspirateur ▷ to vacuum the hall passer l'aspirateur dans le couloir

vacuum cleaner n **❶** aspirateur m **❷** balayeuse f

vagina [və'dʒaɪnə] n vagin m

vague [veɪg] adj vague

vain [veɪn] adj vaniteux (f vaniteuse) ▷ He's so vain! Il est vraiment vaniteux!; **in vain** en vain

valentine ['væləntaɪn] n **❶** (person) valentin m, valentine f ▷ Will you be my valentine? Seras-tu ma valentine? **❷** (card) carte de la Saint-Valentin f ▷ I sent her a valentine. Je lui ai envoyé une carte de la Saint-Valentin.

Valentine's Day ['væləntaɪnz-] n Saint-Valentin f

valid ['vælɪd] adj valable ▷ This ticket is valid for three months. Ce billet est valable trois mois.

valley ['vælɪ] n vallée f

valuable ['væljuəbl] adj **❶** de valeur ▷ a valuable picture un tableau de valeur **❷** précieux (f précieuse) ▷ valuable help une aide précieuse

valuables ['væljuəblz] npl objets mpl de valeur ▷ Don't take any valuables with you. N'emportez pas d'objets de valeur.

value ['vælju:] n valeur f

van [væn] n camionnette f; **a moving van** un camion de déménagement

vandal ['vændl] n vandale m

vandalism ['vændəlɪzəm] n vandalisme m

vandalize ['vændəlaɪz] vb vandaliser

vanilla [və'nɪlə] n vanille f; **vanilla ice cream** la crème glacée à la vanille

vanish ['vænɪʃ] vb disparaître

variable ['veərɪəbl] adj variable

varied ['veərɪd] adj varié

variety [və'raɪətɪ] n variété f

various ['veərɪəs] adj plusieurs ▷ We visited various villages in the area. Nous avons visité plusieurs villages de la région.

vary ['veərɪ] vb varier

vase [vɑ:z] n vase m

VCR n (= video cassette recorder) magnétoscope m

veal [vi:l] n veau m

vegan ['vi:gən] n végétalien m, végétalienne f ▷ I'm a vegan. Je suis végétalien.

vegetable ['vɛdʒtəbl] n légume m ▷ vegetable soup la soupe aux légumes

vegetarian [vɛdʒɪ'tɛərɪən] adj végétarien m (f végétarienne) ▷ I'm vegetarian. Je suis végétarien. ▷ vegetarian lasagna une lasagne végétarienne
▶ n végétarien m, végétarienne f ▷ I'm a vegetarian. Je suis végétarien.

vegetation [vɛdʒɪ'teɪʃən] n végétation f

vehicle ['viːɪkl] n véhicule m

vein [veɪn] n veine f

velvet ['vɛlvɪt] n velours m

vending machine ['vɛndɪŋ-] n distributrice automatique f

Venetian blind [vɪ'niːʃən-] n store vénitien m

verb [vəːb] n verbe m

verdict ['vəːdɪkt] n verdict m

vertical ['vəːtɪkl] adj vertical (mpl verticaux)

very ['vɛrɪ] adv très ▷ very tall très grand ▷ not very interesting pas très intéressant; **very much** beaucoup

vest [vɛst] n veste f; **a fleece vest** une veste en polaire

vet [vɛt] n vétérinaire f ▷ She's a vet. Elle est vétérinaire.

via ['vaɪə] prep en passant par ▷ We went to Trois-Rivières via Québec City. Nous sommes allés à Trois-Rivières en passant par Québec.

vice-president [vaɪs'prɛzɪdənt] n vice-président m, vice-présidente f

vice-principal [vaɪs'prɪnsɪpl] n directeur-adjoint m, directrice-adjointe f

vice versa ['vaɪsɪ'vəːsə] adv vice versa

vicious ['vɪʃəs] adj ① brutal (mpl brutaux) ▷ a vicious attack une agression brutale ▷ (dog, person) méchant m; **a vicious circle** un

cercle vicieux

victim ['vɪktɪm] n victime f ▷ He was the victim of a mugging. Il a été victime d'une agression.

Victoria Day [vɪk'tɔːrɪə] n fête de la Reine f
- In Québec, **la fête de Dollard** is the same day as Victoria Day. It commemorates the death of Adam Dollard des Ormeaux and his 16 companions in 1660 in a hopeless battle to avert an Iroquois siege of Ville Marie (now Montréal). In 2002, this holiday was officially replaced by **la Journée nationale des patriotes.**

victory ['vɪktərɪ] n victoire f

video ['vɪdɪəʊ] vb ① (from TV) enregistrer ② (with video camera) filmer
▶ n ① (movie) vidéo f ▷ to watch a video regarder une vidéo ▷ a video of my family on holiday une vidéo de ma famille en vacances ▷ It's out on video. C'est sorti en vidéo. ② (videocassette) vidéocassette f ▷ She lent me a video. Elle m'a prêté une vidéocassette.; **a video camera** une caméra vidéo; **a videocassette** une vidéocassette; **a video game** un jeu vidéo ▷ She likes playing video games. Elle aime les jeux vidéo.; **a video recorder** un magnétoscope; **a video rental store** un vidéoclub

videoconference ['vɪdɪəʊ'kɒnfərns] n vidéoconférence f

view [vjuː] n ① vue f ▷ There's an amazing view when you get to the top. Il y a une vue extraordinaire quand on arrive au sommet. ② (opinion) avis m ▷ in my view à mon avis

viewer ['vjuːə'] n (television) téléspectateur m, téléspectatrice f

viewpoint ['vju:pɔɪnt] n point de vue m

vile [vaɪl] adj (smell, food) dégoûtant

village ['vɪlɪdʒ] n village m

villain ['vɪlən] n ❶ (criminal) malfaiteur m, malfaitrice f ❷ (in movie) méchant m, méchante f

vine [vaɪn] n vigne f

vinegar ['vɪnɪgə'] n vinaigre m

vineyard ['vɪnjɑːd] n vignoble m

viola [vɪ'əʊlə] n alto m ▷ I play the viola. Je joue de l'alto.

violence ['vaɪələns] n violence f

violent ['vaɪələnt] adj violent

violin [vaɪə'lɪn] n violon m ▷ I play the violin. Je joue du violon.

violinist [vaɪə'lɪnɪst] n violoniste

virgin ['vɜːdʒɪn] n vierge f ▷ to be a virgin être vierge

Virgo ['vɜːgəʊ] n Vierge f ▷ I'm a Virgo. Je suis Vierge.

virtual reality ['vɜːtjʊəl-] n réalité virtuelle f

virus ['vaɪərəs] n (also computing) virus m

visa ['viːzə] n visa m

visible ['vɪzəbl] adj visible

visit ['vɪzɪt] n ❶ (to museum) visite f ❷ (to country) séjour m ▷ Did you enjoy your visit to Nova Scotia? Ton séjour en Nouvelle-Écosse s'est bien passé?; **my last visit to my grandmother** la dernière fois que je suis allé voir ma grand-mère ▶ vb ❶ (person) rendre visite à ▷ to visit somebody rendre visite à quelqu'un ❷ (place) visiter ▷ We'd like to visit the zoo. Nous voudrions visiter le zoo.

visitor ['vɪzɪtə'] n ❶ (tourist) visiteur m, visiteuse f ❷ (guest) invité m, invitée f; **to have visitors** avoir de la visite

visual ['vɪzjʊəl] adj visuel (f visuelle)

visualize ['vɪzjʊəlaɪz] vb imaginer

vital ['vaɪtl] adj vital (mpl vitaux); **vital signs** les signes vitaux

vitamin ['vɪtəmɪn] n vitamine f

vivid ['vɪvɪd] adj (colour) vif (f vive); **to have a vivid imagination** avoir une imagination débordante

vocabulary [vəʊ'kæbjʊlərɪ] n vocabulaire m

vocational [vəʊ'keɪʃənl] adj professionnel (f professionnelle); **a vocational course** un stage de formation professionnelle

voice [vɔɪs] n voix f (pl voix)

voice mail n messagerie vocale f

volcano [vɔl'keɪnəʊ] n volcan m

volleyball ['vɔlɪbɔːl] n volley-ball m ▷ to play volleyball jouer au volley-ball

volt [vəʊlt] n volt m

voltage ['vəʊltɪdʒ] n voltage m

voluntary ['vɔləntərɪ] adj (contribution, statement) volontaire; **to do voluntary work** travailler bénévolement

volunteer [vɔlən'tɪə'] n volontaire ▶ vb: **to volunteer to do something** se porter volontaire pour faire quelque chose

vomit ['vɔmɪt] vb vomir

vote [vəʊt] vb voter

voter ['vəʊtə'] n électeur m, électrice f

voucher ['vaʊtʃə'] n bon m ▷ a gift voucher un bon d'achat

vowel ['vaʊəl] n voyelle f

vulgar ['vʌlgə'] adj vulgaire

W

wage [weɪdʒ] *n* salaire *m*
▷ *minimum wage* le salaire minimum

waist [weɪst] *n* taille *f*

wait [weɪt] *vb* attendre; **to wait for something** attendre quelque chose; **to wait for somebody** attendre quelqu'un ▷ *I'll wait for you.* Je t'attendrai.; **Wait for me!** Attends-moi!; **Wait a minute!** Attends!; **to keep somebody waiting** faire attendre quelqu'un ▷ *They kept us waiting for hours.* Ils nous ont fait attendre pendant des heures.; **I can't wait for the holidays.** J'ai hâte d'être en vacances.; **I can't wait to see him again.** J'ai hâte de le revoir.

wait up *vb* attendre pour se coucher ▷ *My mom always waits up till I get in.* Ma mère attend toujours que je rentre pour se coucher.

waiter ['weɪtə'] *n* serveur *m*

waiting list ['weɪtɪŋ-] *n* liste d'attente *f*

waiting room ['weɪtɪŋ-] *n* salle d'attente *f*

waitress ['weɪtrɪs] *n* serveuse *f*

wake up [weɪk-] *vb* se réveiller ▷ *I woke up at six o'clock.* Je me suis réveillé à six heures.; **to wake somebody up** réveiller quelqu'un ▷ *Please would you wake me up at seven o'clock?* Pourriez-vous me réveiller à sept heures?

walk [wɔːk] *vb* ❶ marcher ▷ *She walks fast.* Elle marche vite. ❷ (go on foot) aller à pied ▷ *Are you walking or going by bus?* Tu y vas à pied ou en autobus? ▷ *We walked 10 kilometres.* Nous avons fait dix kilomètres à pied.; **to walk the dog** promener le chien
▶ *n* promenade *f* ▷ *to go for a walk* faire une promenade; **It's 10 minutes' walk from here.** C'est à dix minutes d'ici à pied.

walkie-talkie ['wɔːkɪ'tɔːkɪ] *n* émetteur-récepteur *m* portatif

walking ['wɔːkɪŋ] *n* randonnée *f* ▷ *I did some walking in the Laurentians last summer.* J'ai fait de la randonnée dans les Laurentides l'été dernier.

walking stick *n* canne *f*

Walkman® ['wɔːkmən] *n* baladeur *m*

wall [wɔːl] *n* mur *m*

wallet ['wɔlɪt] *n* portefeuille *m*

walleye ['wɔːlaɪ] *n* doré *m*

wallpaper ['wɔːlpeɪpə'] *n* tapisserie *f*

walnut ['wɔːlnʌt] *n* noix *f* (*pl* noix)

wander ['wɔndə'] *vb*: **to wander around** flâner ▷ *I just wandered around for a while.* J'ai flâné un peu.

want [wɔnt] *vb* vouloir ▷ *Do you want some cake?* Tu veux du gâteau?; **to want to do something** vouloir faire quelque chose ▷ *I want to go to the movies.* Je veux aller au cinéma.

▷ *What do you want to do tomorrow?* Qu'est-ce que tu veux faire demain?

war [wɔː^r] n guerre f

ward [wɔːd] n (room in hospital) salle f

wardrobe ['wɔːdrəʊb] n
① (clothes) garde-robe f ▷ *She has an extensive wardrobe.* Elle a une garde-robe bien fournie. **②** (piece of furniture) armoire f

warehouse ['wɛəhaʊs] n entrepôt m

warm [wɔːm] adj **①** chaud ▷ *warm water* l'eau chaude; **It's warm in here.** Il fait chaud ici.; **to be warm** (person) avoir chaud ▷ *I'm too warm.* J'ai trop chaud. **③** chaleureux (f chaleureuse) ▷ *a warm welcome* un accueil chaleureux; **to warm up (1)** (for sports) s'échauffer **(2)** (food) réchauffer ▷ *I'll warm up some lasagna for you.* Je vais te réchauffer de la lasagne.

warn [wɔːn] vb prévenir ▷ *Well, I warned you!* Je t'avais prévenu!; **to warn somebody to do something** conseiller à quelqu'un de faire quelque chose

warning ['wɔːnɪŋ] n avertissement m

wart [wɔːt] n verrue f

was [wɒz] vb see **be**

wash [wɒʃ] vb **①** laver ▷ *to wash something* laver quelque chose **②** (get washed) se laver ▷ *Every morning I get up, wash and get dressed.* Tous les matins je me lève, je me lave et je m'habille.; **to wash one's hands** se laver les mains; **to wash one's hair** se laver les cheveux; **to wash the dishes** faire la vaisselle

washbasin ['wɒʃbeɪsn] n lavabo m

washcloth ['wɒʃklɒθ] n débarbouillette m

washing ['wɒʃɪŋ] n linge m ▷ *dirty washing* du linge sale; **Have you got any washing?** Tu as du linge à laver?; **to do the washing** faire le lavage

washing machine n laveuse f

wasn't ['wɒznt] = **was not**

wasp [wɒsp] n guêpe f

waste [weɪst] n **①** gaspillage m ▷ *It's such a waste!* C'est vraiment du gaspillage!; **It's a waste of time.** C'est une perte de temps. **②** (garbage) déchets mpl ▷ *nuclear waste* les déchets nucléaires
▶ vb gaspiller ▷ *I don't like wasting money.* Je n'aime pas gaspiller de l'argent.; **to waste time** perdre du temps ▷ *There's no time to waste.* Il n'y a pas de temps à perdre.

wastepaper basket ['weɪstpeɪpə-] n poubelle f

watch [wɒtʃ] n montre f
▶ vb **①** regarder ▷ *to watch television* regarder la télévision ▷ *Watch me!* Regarde-moi! **②** (keep a watch on) surveiller ▷ *The police were watching the house.* La police surveillait la maison.; **to watch out** faire attention; **Watch out!** Attention!

water ['wɔːtə^r] n eau f
▶ vb arroser ▷ *He was watering his tulips.* Il arrosait ses tulipes.

waterfall ['wɔːtəfɔːl] n cascade f

watering can ['wɔːtərɪŋ-] n arrosoir m

watermelon ['wɔːtəmɛlən] n melon d'eau m

waterproof ['wɔːtəpruːf] adj imperméable ▷ *Is this coat waterproof?* Ce manteau est-il imperméable?; **a waterproof watch** une montre étanche

water-skiing ['wɔːtəskiːɪŋ] n ski nautique m ▷ *to go water-skiing* faire du ski nautique

wave [weɪv] n **①** (in water) vague f **②** (of hand) signe m ▷ *We gave him a*

wave. Nous lui avons fait signe.
▶ vb faire un signe de la main ▶ to
wave at somebody faire un signe
de la main à quelqu'un; **to wave
goodbye** faire au revoir de la main
▷ I waved goodbye to her. Je lui ai fait
au revoir de la main.

wavy ['weɪvɪ] adj ondulé ▷ wavy
hair les cheveux ondulés ▷ a wavy
line une ligne ondulée

wax [wæks] n cire

way [weɪ] n ❶ (manner) façon
f ▷ She looked at me in a strange
way. Elle m'a regardé d'une façon
étrange.; **This book tells you the
right way to do it.** Ce livre explique
comment il faut faire.; **You're
doing it the wrong way.** Ce n'est
pas comme ça qu'il faut faire.; **in
a way...** dans un sens...; **a way
of life** un mode de vie ❷ (route)
chemin m ▷ I don't know the way. Je
ne connais pas le chemin.; **on the
way** en chemin ▷ We stopped on the
way. Nous nous sommes arrêtés
en chemin.; **It's a long way.** C'est
loin. ▷ Kenora is a long way from
Halifax. Kenora est loin de Halifax.;
Which way is it? C'est par où?;
The supermarket is this way. Le
supermarché est par ici.; **Do you
know the way to the mall?** Vous
savez comment aller au centre
commercial?; **He's on his way.** Il
arrive.; **the way in** l'entrée f; **the
way out** la sortie; **by the way...** en
passant...

we [wiː] pron nous ▷ We're staying
here for a week. Nous restons une
semaine ici.

weak [wiːk] adj faible

wealthy ['welθɪ] adj riche

weapon ['wepən] n arme f

wear [weəʳ] vb (clothes) porter
▷ He was wearing a hat. Il portait un
chapeau.; **She was wearing black.**

Elle était en noir.

weather ['weðəʳ] n temps m
▷ What was the weather like? Quel
temps a-t-il fait? ▷ The weather was
lovely. Il a fait un temps magnifique.

weather forecast n météo f

Web [web] n Web m

Web browser n navigateur Web m

webmaster ['webmɑːstəʳ] n
webmestre

webography [weˈbɒɡrəfɪ] n
webographie f

website ['websaɪt] n site Web m

webzine ['webziːn] n webzine m

we'd [wiːd] = we had; we would

wedding ['wedɪŋ] n mariage
m; **wedding anniversary**
l'anniversaire m de mariage;
wedding dress la robe de mariée

Wednesday ['wednzdɪ] n
mercredi m ▷ on Wednesday
mercredi ▷ on Wednesdays le
mercredi ▷ every Wednesday tous
les mercredis ▷ last Wednesday
mercredi dernier ▷ next Wednesday
mercredi prochain

weed [wiːd] n mauvaise herbe f
▷ The garden's full of weeds. Le jardin
est plein de mauvaises herbes.

week [wiːk] n semaine f ▷ last week
la semaine dernière ▷ every week
toutes les semaines ▷ next week la
semaine prochaine; **a week from
now** dans une semaine; **a week
from Friday** vendredi dans une
semaine

weekday ['wiːkdeɪ] n: **on
weekdays** en semaine

weekend [wiːkˈend] n fin de
semaine f ▷ on weekends la fin de
semaine ▷ last weekend la fin de
semaine dernière ▷ next weekend la
fin de semaine prochaine

weigh [weɪ] vb peser ▷ How much
do you weigh? Combien est-ce que tu
pèses? ▷ They weighed my suitcase.

On a pesé ma valise.; **to weigh oneself** se peser

weight [weɪt] n poids m; **to lose weight** maigrir; **to put on weight** grossir

weightlifter ['weɪtlɪftəʳ] n haltérophile mf

weightlifting ['weɪtlɪftɪŋ] n haltérophilie m

weird [wɪəd] adj bizarre

welcome ['welkəm] n accueil m ▷ They gave her a warm welcome. Ils lui ont fait un accueil chaleureux.; **Welcome!** Bienvenue! ▷ Welcome to Nunavut! Bienvenue au Nunavut!
▶ vb: **to welcome somebody** accueillir quelqu'un; **"Thank you!" — "You're welcome!"** « Merci! » — « De rien! »

well [wel] adj, adv ❶ bien ▷ You did that really well. Tu as très bien fait ça.; **to do well** réussir bien ▷ He's doing really well at school. Il réussit vraiment bien à l'école.; **to be well** (in good health) aller bien ▷ I'm not very well at the moment. Je ne vais pas très bien en ce moment.; **get well soon!** remets-toi vite!; **well done!** bravo! ❷ enfin ▷ It's enormous! Well, quite big anyway. C'est énorme! Enfin, c'est assez grand.; **as well** aussi ▷ We worked hard, but we had some fun as well. Nous avons travaillé dur, mais nous nous sommes bien amusés aussi. ▷ We went to Calgary as well as Edmonton. Nous sommes allés à Edmonton et à Calgary aussi.
▶ n puits m (pl puits)

we'll [wiːl] = **we will**

well-behaved ['welbɪ'heɪvd] adj sage

well-dressed ['wel'drest] adj bien habillé

well-known ['wel'nəʊn] adj célèbre ▷ a well-known movie star

une vedette de cinéma célèbre

well-off ['wel'ɒf] adj aisé

went [went] vb see **go**

were [wəːʳ] vb see **be**

we're [wɪəʳ]: = **we are**

weren't [wəːnt]: = **were not**

west [west] n ouest m ▷ in the west dans l'ouest; **the West** l'Occident m
▶ adj, adv ❶ ouest (f+pl ouest) ▷ the West Coast la côte Ouest; **west of** à l'ouest de ▷ Toronto is west of Ottawa. Toronto est à l'ouest d'Ottawa. ❷ vers l'ouest ▷ We were travelling west. Nous allions vers l'ouest.

westbound ['westbaʊnd] adj: **The truck was westbound on the highway.** Le camion roulait sur l'autoroute en direction de l'ouest.; **Westbound traffic is moving very slowly.** La circulation en direction de l'ouest est très ralentie.

western ['westən] n ❶ (movie) western m ❷ (sandwich) sandwich western m
▶ adj: **the western part of the island** la partie ouest de l'île; **Western Europe** l'Europe f de l'Ouest; **Western Canada** l'Ouest m du Canada

wet [wet] adj mouillé ▷ wet clothes les vêtements mouillés; **to get wet** se faire mouiller; **dripping wet** trempé; **wet weather** le temps pluvieux; **It was wet all week.** Il a plu toute la semaine.

wetsuit ['wetsuːt] n combinaison de plongée f (pl combinaisons de plongée)

we've [wiːv]: = **we have**

whale [weɪl] n baleine f

what [wɒt] adj, pron ❶ (which) quel (f quelle) ▷ What subjects are you taking? Quelles matières est-ce que tu fais? ▷ What colour is it? C'est de quelle couleur? ▷ What's the capital of Canada? Quelle est la capitale du Canada? ▷ *What a mess!* Quel fouillis! ❷ qu'est-ce que ▷ *What are you doing?* Qu'est-ce que vous faites? ▷ *What did you say?* Qu'est-ce que vous avez dit? ▷ *What is it?* Qu'est-ce que c'est? ▷ *What's the matter?* Qu'est-ce qu'il y a? ❸ qu'est-ce qui ▷ *What happened?* Qu'est-ce qui s'est passé? ▷ *What's bothering you?* Qu'est-ce qui te préoccupe?

> In relative phrases use **ce qui** or **ce que** depending on whether **what** refers to the subject or the object of the sentence.

❹ (subject) ce qui ▷ *I saw what happened.* J'ai vu ce qui est arrivé. ▷ *I know what's bothering me.* Je sais ce qui te préoccupe. ❺ (object) ce que ▷ *Tell me what you deal.* Dites-moi ce que vous avez fait. ▷ *I heard what he said.* J'ai entendu ce qu'il a dit.; **What!** (*what did you say*) Comment?; **What!** (*shocked*) Quoi!

wheat [wiːt] *n* blé *m*

wheel [wiːl] *n* roue *f*; **the steering wheel** le volant

wheelchair [ˈwiːltʃeəʳ] *n* fauteuil roulant *m*

when [wen] *adv, conj* quand ▷ *When did he leave?* Quand est-ce qu'il est parti? ▷ *She was reading when I came in.* Elle lisait quand je suis entré.

where [weəʳ] *adv, conj* où ▷ *Where's your sister today?* Où est ta sœur aujourd'hui? ▷ *Where do you live?* Où habites-tu? ▷ *Where are you going?* Où vas-tu? ▷ *a store where you can buy croissants* un magasin où l'on peut acheter des croissants

whether [ˈweðəʳ] *conj* si ▷ *I don't know whether to go or not.* Je ne sais pas si y aller ou non.

which [wɪtʃ] *adj, pron* ❶ quel (*f* quelle) ▷ *Which flavour do you want?*

Quel parfum est-ce que tu veux?

> When asking **which one** use **lequel** or **laquelle**, depending on whether the noun is masculine or feminine.

"I know her brother." — "Which one?" « Je connais son frère. » — « Lequel? »; **"I know his sister." — "Which one?"** « Je connais sa sœur. » — « Laquelle? »; **Which would you like?** Lequel est-ce que vous voulez?; **Which of these are yours?** Lesquels sont à vous?

> In relative phrases use **qui** or **que** depending on whether **which** refers to the subject or the object of the sentence.

❷ (subject) qui ▷ *the CD which is playing now* le CD qui passe maintenant ❸ (object) que ▷ *the CD which I bought today* le CD que j'ai acheté hier

while [waɪl] *conj* ❶ pendant que ▷ *You hold the flashlight while I look inside.* Tiens la lampe de poche pendant que je regarde à l'intérieur. ❷ alors que ▷ *She is very dynamic, while he is more laid-back.* Elle est très dynamique, alors qu'il est plus relax.
▶ *n* moment *m* ▷ *after a while* au bout d'un moment; **a while ago** il y a un moment ▷ *He was here a while ago.* Il était là il y a un moment.; **for a while** pendant quelque temps ▷ *I lived in Thunder Bay for a while.* J'ai vécu à Thunder Bay pendant quelque temps.; **quite a while** longtemps ▷ *quite a while ago* il y a longtemps ▷ *I haven't seen him for quite a while.* Ça fait longtemps que je ne l'ai pas vu.

whip [wɪp] *n* ❶ fouet *m* ❷ (*parliament*) whip
▶ *vb* ❶ (*person, animal*) fouetter ❷ (*eggs*) battre

whipped cream [wɪpt-] n crème fouettée f

whisk [wɪsk] n fouet m

whiskers ['wɪskəz] npl moustaches fpl

whisper ['wɪspə'] vb chuchoter

whistle ['wɪsl] n sifflet m; The referee blew her whistle. L'arbitre a sifflé.
▶ vb siffler

white [waɪt] adj blanc (f blanche)
▷ He has white hair. Il a les cheveux blancs.; **white bread** le pain blanc; **a white man** un Blanc; **a white woman** une Blanche; **white people** les Blancs

whiteout ['waɪtaʊt] n voile blanc m

whiz [wɪz] n virtuose

who [huː] pron ❶ qui ▷ Who said that? Qui a dit ça? ▷ Who is Adrienne Clarkson? Qui est Adrienne Clarkson?

> In relative phrases use **qui** or **que** depending on whether **who** refers to the subject or the object of the verb.

❷ (subject) qui ▷ the woman who saw us la femme qui nous a vus ▷ the woman who spoke to us la femme qui nous a parlé ❸ (object) que ▷ the man who saw us l'homme que nous avons vu ▷ the man who she married l'homme qu'elle a épousé

whole [haʊl] adj tout ▷ the whole class toute la classe ▷ the whole afternoon tout l'après-midi; **a whole box of chocolates** toute une boîte de chocolats; **the whole world** le monde entier; **whole wheat** le blé entier ▷ whole wheat pasta des pâtes au blé entier; **the whole works** le tout ▷ I had a ton of assignments, but I finished the whole works in one evening. J'avais un tas de devoirs, mais j'ai terminé le tout en une seule soirée.
▶ n: The whole of Toronto was snowbound. Toronto était complètement bloquée par la neige.; **The whole of Montréal was talking about it.** On en parlait dans tout Montréal.; **on the whole** dans l'ensemble

whom [huːm] pron qui ▷ Whom did you see? Qui avez-vous vu? ▷ the man to whom I spoke l'homme à qui j'ai parlé

whose [huːz] pron, adj ❶ à qui ▷ Whose is this? À qui est-ce? ▷ I know whose it is. Je sais à qui c'est. ▷ Whose book is this? À qui est ce livre? ❷ (after noun) dont ▷ the girl whose picture was in the paper la jeune fille dont la photo était dans le journal

why [waɪ] adv pourquoi ▷ Why did you do that? Pourquoi avez-vous fait ça? ▷ That's why he did it. Voilà pourquoi il a fait ça. ▷ Tell me why. Dis-moi pourquoi.; **"I've never been to Saskatchewan." — "Why not?"** « Je ne suis jamais allé en Saskatchewan. » — « Pourquoi? »; **All right, why not?** D'accord, pourquoi pas?

wicked ['wɪkɪd] adj ❶ (evil) méchant ❷ (really great) génial (mpl géniaux)

wide [waɪd] adj, adv large ▷ a wide road une route large; **wide open** grand ouvert ▷ The door was wide open. La porte était grande ouverte. ▷ The windows were wide open. Les fenêtres étaient grandes ouvertes.; **wide awake** complètement réveillé

widow ['wɪdəʊ] n veuve f ▷ She's a widow. Elle est veuve.

widower ['wɪdəʊə'] n veuf m ▷ He's a widower. Il est veuf.

width [wɪdθ] n largeur f

wife [waɪf] n femme f ▷ She's his wife. C'est sa femme.

wig [wɪg] n perruque f

wild [waɪld] adj ❶ (not tame) sauvage ❷ (crazy) fou (ffolle)

wilderness ['wɪldənɪs] n région sauvage f; **wilderness camping** le camping sauvage

wildlife ['waɪldlaɪf] n nature f ▷ I'm interested in wildlife. Je m'intéresse à la nature.

will [wɪl] n testament m ▷ She left me some money in her will. Elle m'a laissé de l'argent dans son testament.

▶ vb: **I'll show you your room.** Je vais te montrer ta chambre.; **I'll give you a hand.** Je vais t'aider.

> Use the French future tense when referring to the more distant future.

I will finish it tomorrow. Je le finirai demain.; **It won't take long.** Ça ne prendra pas longtemps.; **"Will you wash the dishes?" — "No, I won't."** « Est-ce que tu peux faire la vaisselle ? » — « Non. »; **Will you help me?** Est-ce que tu peux m'aider ?; **Will you be quiet!** Voulez-vous bien vous taire!; **That will be the paperboy.** Ça doit être le livreur de journaux.

willing ['wɪlɪŋ] adj: **to be willing to do something** être prêt à faire quelque chose

win [wɪn] vb gagner ▷ Did you win? Est-ce que tu as gagné?; **to win a prize** remporter un prix
▶ n victoire f

wind [waɪnd] vb ❶ (rope, wool, wire) enrouler ❷ (river, path) serpenter ▷ The road winds through the valley. La route serpente à travers la vallée.
▶ n [wɪnd] vent m ▷ There was a strong wind. Il y avait beaucoup

de vent.; **a wind instrument** un instrument à vent; **wind power** l'énergie f éolienne

wind chill ['wɪnd-] n refroidissement éolien m ▷ The wind chill factor is -10 today. Le facteur de refroidissement éolien est de moins dix degrés aujourd'hui.

windmill ['wɪndmɪl] n moulin à vent m (pl moulins à vent)

window ['wɪndəʊ] n ❶ fenêtre f ❷ (in car, train) vitre f; **a store window** une vitrine

windshield ['wɪndʃiːld] n pare-brise m (pl pare-brise)

windshield wiper [-'waɪpəʳ] n essuie-glace m (pl essuie-glace)

wind turbine [-'tɜːbɪn] éolienne f

windy ['wɪndɪ] adj (place) venteux (fventeuse); **It's windy.** Il y a du vent.

wing [wɪŋ] n aile f

wink [wɪŋk] n: **to wink at somebody** faire un clin d'œil à quelqu'un

winner ['wɪnəʳ] n gagnant m, gagnante f

winning ['wɪnɪŋ] adj: **the winning team** l'équipe gagnante; **the winning goal** le but décisif

winter ['wɪntəʳ] n hiver m; **in winter** en hiver

winterize ['wɪntəraɪz] vb hivériser ▷ We have to winterize our cottage. Nous devons hivériser le chalet.

winter sports npl sports mpl d'hiver

wipe [waɪp] vb essuyer; **to wipe one's feet** s'essuyer les pieds ▷ Wipe your feet! Essuie-toi les pieds!; **to wipe up** essuyer

wire ['waɪəʳ] n fil m

wireless ['waɪəlɪs] adj sans fil

wireless technology [-tek'nɒlədʒɪ] n technologie sans fil f

wisdom tooth ['wɪzdəm-] n dent de sagesse f (pl dents de sagesse)

wise [waɪz] *adj* sage

wish [wɪʃ] *vb*: **to wish for something** souhaiter quelque chose ▷ *What more could you wish for?* Que pourrais-tu souhaiter de plus?; **to wish to do something** désirer faire quelque chose ▷ *I wish to make a complaint.* Je désire porter plainte., **I wish you were here!** Si seulement tu étais ici!; **I wish you'd told me!** Si seulement tu m'en avais parlé!
▶ *n* vœu *m* (*pl* vœux) ▷ *to make a wish* faire un vœu; **"best wishes"** (*on greeting card*) « meilleurs vœux »; **"with best wishes, Kathy"** « bien amicalement, Kathy »

with [wɪð, wɪθ] *prep* ❶ avec ▷ *Come with me.* Venez avec moi. ▷ *He walks with a stick.* Il marche avec une canne.; **a woman with blue eyes** une femme aux yeux bleus ❷ (*at the home of*) chez ▷ *We stayed with friends.* Nous sommes restés chez des amis. ❸ (*with envy* vert de jalousie ▷ *to shake with fear* trembler de peur ▷ *Fill the jug with water.* Remplis la carafe d'eau.

within [wɪð'ɪn] *prep*: **The stores are within easy reach.** Les magasins sont à proximité.; **within a week** avant la fin d'une semaine

without [wɪð'aʊt] *prep* sans ▷ *without a coat* sans manteau ▷ *without speaking* sans parler

witness ['wɪtnɪs] *n* témoin ▷ *There were no witnesses.* Il n'y a pas de témoins.

witty ['wɪtɪ] *adj* spirituel (*f* spirituelle)

wives [waɪvz] *npl see* **wife**

wizard ['wɪzəd] *n* magicien *m*

wok [wɒk] *n* wok *m*

woke up, woken up [wəʊk-, 'wəʊkən-] *vb see* **wake up**

wolf [wʊlf] *n* loup *m*; **a wolf cub** un louveteau

wolverine ['wʊlvəriːn] *n* carcajou *m*

woman ['wʊmən] *n* femme *f* ▷ *a woman doctor* une femme médecin

won [wʌn] *vb see* **win**

wonder ['wʌndər] *vb* se demander ▷ *I wonder why he said that.* Je me demande pourquoi il a dit ça. ▷ *I wonder what that means.* Je me demande ce que ça veut dire. ▷ *I wonder where my sister is.* Je me demande où est ma sœur.

wonderful ['wʌndəful] *adj* formidable

won't [wəʊnt]: = **will not**

wood [wʊd] *n* bois *m* ▷ *It's made of wood.* C'est en bois.

wooden ['wʊdn] *adj* en bois ▷ *a wooden chair* une chaise en bois

woods [wʊdz] *npl* bois *m* ▷ *We went for a walk in the woods.* Nous sommes allés nous promener dans le bois.

woodworking ['wʊdwɜːkɪŋ] *n* menuiserie *f* ▷ *My hobby is woodworking.* Je fais de la menuiserie.

wool [wʊl] *n* laine *f* ▷ *a wool sweater* un chandail de laine

word [wɜːd] *n* mot *m* ▷ *a difficult word* un mot difficile; **What's the word for "store" in German?** Comment dit-on « magasin » en allemand?; **in other words** en d'autres termes; **to have a word with somebody** parler avec quelqu'un; **the words** (*lyrics*) les paroles ▷ *I really like the words of this song.* J'adore les paroles de cette chanson.

word processing [-'prəʊsesɪŋ] *n* traitement de texte *m*

wore [wɔːʳ] *vb see* **wear**

work [wɜːk] *n* travail *m* (*pl* travaux)

▷ *She's looking for work.* Elle cherche du travail. ▷ *He's at work at the moment.* Il est au travail en ce moment.; **It's hard work.** C'est dur.; **to be off work** (sick) être malade; **He's been off work for a week.** Il est malade depuis une semaine.; **He's out of work.** Il est sans emploi.
▶ vb ❶ (person) travailler ▷ *She works in a store.* Elle travaille dans un magasin. ▷ *to work hard* travailler dur ❷ (machine, plan) marcher ▷ *The heat isn't working.* Le chauffage ne marche pas. ▷ *My plan worked perfectly.* Mon plan a marché à merveille.; **to work out (1)** (exercise) faire de l'exercice ▷ *I work out twice a week.* Je fais de l'exercice deux fois par semaine. **(2)** (turn out) marcher ▷ *In the end it worked out really well.* Au bout du compte, ça a très bien marché. **(3)** (figure out) arriver à comprendre ▷ *I just couldn't work it out.* Je n'arrivais pas du tout à comprendre.; **It works out to $10 each.** Ça fait dix dollars chacun.

workaholic [wɜːkəˈhɒlɪk] n bourreau de travail

worker [ˈwɜːkəʳ] n ❶ (in factory) ouvrier m, ouvrière f; **He's a factory worker.** Il est ouvrier. ❷ (general) travailleur m, travailleuse f; **She's a good worker.** Elle travaille bien.

workforce [ˈwɜːkfɔːs] n population active f

workout [ˈwɜːkaut] n séance d'entraînement f

works [wɜːks] n: **the whole works** le tout ▷ *I had a ton of assignments, but I finished the whole works in one evening.* J'avais un tas de devoirs, mais j'ai terminé le tout en une seule soirée.; **a hamburger with the works** un hamburger tout garni

worksheet [ˈwɜːkʃiːt] n feuille d'exercices f

workshop [ˈwɜːkʃɒp] n atelier m ▷ *a drama workshop* un atelier de théâtre

workspace [ˈwɜːkspeɪs] n (computing) espace m de travail

workstation [ˈwɜːksteɪʃən] n poste de travail m (pl postes de travail)

world [wɜːld] n monde m; **He's the world champion.** Il est champion du monde.

worm [wɜːm] n ver m

worn [wɔːn] vb see **wear**
▶ adj usé ▷ *The carpet is a bit worn.* Le tapis est un peu usé.; **worn out** (tired) épuisé

worne [wɔːn] vb see **wear**

worried [ˈwʌrɪd] adj inquiet (f inquiète) ▷ *She's very worried.* Elle est très inquiète.; **to be worried about something** s'inquiéter pour quelque chose ▷ *I'm worried about the exams.* Je m'inquiète pour les examens.; **to look worried** avoir l'air inquiet ▷ *She looks a bit worried.* Elle a l'air un peu inquiète.

worry [ˈwʌrɪ] vb s'inquiéter; **Don't worry!** Ne t'inquiète pas!

worse [wɜːs] adj, adv ❶ pire m ▷ *It was even worse than that.* C'était encore pire que ça. ▷ *My marks were bad, but his were even worse.* Mes notes étaient mauvaises, mais les siennes étaient encore pires. ❷ plus mal ▷ *I'm feeling worse.* Je me sens plus mal.

worship [ˈwɜːʃɪp] vb (God) vénérer; **He really worships her.** Il est en adoration devant elle.

worst [wɜːst] adj: **the worst** le plus mauvais ▷ *the worst student in the class* le plus mauvais élève de la classe ▷ *She got the worst mark in the whole class.* Elle a eu la

plus mauvaise note de toute la classe.; **my worst enemy** mon pire ennemi.; **Math is my worst subject.** Les maths sont ma matière faible.
▶ *n* pire *m* ▷ *The worst of it is that...* Le pire c'est que...; **at worst** au pire; **if worst comes to worst** au pire

worth [wə:θ] *adj:* **to be worth** valoir ▷ *It's worth a lot of money.* Ça vaut très cher. ▷ *How much is it worth?* Ça vaut combien?; **It's worth it.** Ça vaut la peine. ▷ *Is it worth it?* Est-ce que ça vaut la peine? ▷ *It's not worth it.* Ça ne vaut pas la peine.

would [wud] *vb:* **Would you like a cookie?** Vous voulez un biscuit?; **Would you like to go see a movie?** Est-ce que tu veux aller voir un film?; **Would you close the door please?** Vous pouvez fermer la porte, s'il vous plaît?; **I'd like...** J'aimerais... ▷ *I'd like to go to Labrador.* J'aimerais aller au Labrador. ▷ *"Shall we go see a movie?" — "Yes, I'd like that."* « Si on allait voir un film? » — « Oui, j'aimerais bien. »; **I said I would do it.** J'ai dit que je le ferais.; **If you asked her, she'd do it.** Si vous le lui demandiez, elle le ferait.; **If you had asked him he would have done it.** Si vous le lui aviez demandé, il l'aurait fait.

wouldn't ['wudnt] = **would not**

wound [wu:nd] *n* blessure *f*
▶ *vb* blesser ▷ *He was wounded in the leg.* Il a été blessé à la jambe.

wound [waund] *vb see* **wind**

wrap [ræp] *vb* emballer ▷ *She's wrapping your birthday presents.* Elle est en train d'emballer tes cadeaux de fête.; **Can you wrap it for me please?** (*in store*) Vous pouvez me faire un emballage cadeau, s'il vous

plaît?; **to wrap up** emballer

wrapping paper ['ræpiŋ-] *n* papier emballage *m*

wreck [rɛk] *n* ❶ (*vehicle, machine*) tas de ferraille *m* ▷ *That car is a wreck!* Cette voiture est un tas de ferraille! ❷ (*person*) loque *f* ▷ *After the tournament I was a complete wreck.* Après le tournament, j'étais une véritable loque.
▶ *vb* ❶ (*building, vehicle*) démolir ▷ *The explosion wrecked the whole house.* L'explosion a démoli toute la maison. ❷ (*plan, holiday*) ruiner ▷ *The trip was wrecked by bad weather.* Le voyage a été ruiné par le mauvais temps.

wreckage ['rɛkidʒ] *n* ❶ (*of vehicle*) débris *mpl* ❷ (*of building*) décombres *mpl*

wrench [rɛntʃ] *n* clé anglaise *f*

wrestler ['rɛslə'] *n* lutteur *m*, lutteuse *f*

wrestling ['rɛslɪŋ] *n* lutte *f*

wrinkled ['rɪŋkld] *adj* ridé

wrist [rɪst] *n* poignet *m*

write [raɪt] *vb* écrire ▷ *to write a letter* écrire une lettre; **to write to somebody** écrire à quelqu'un ▷ *I'm going to write to him in French.* Je vais lui écrire en français.; **to write down** noter ▷ *I wrote down the address.* J'ai noté l'adresse.; **Can you write it down for me, please?** Vous pouvez me l'écrire, s'il vous plaît?

writer ['raɪtə'] *n* écrivain *m*, écrivaine *f* ▷ *She's a writer.* Elle est écrivaine.

writing ['raɪtɪŋ] *n* écriture *f* ▷ *I can't read your writing.* Je n'arrive pas à lire ton écriture.; **in writing** par écrit

written ['rɪtn] *vb see* **write**

wrong [rɒŋ] *adj, adv* ❶ (*incorrect*) faux (*fausse*) ▷ *The information they gave us was wrong.* Les renseignements qu'ils nous ont donnés étaient faux.; **the wrong answer** la mauvaise réponse; **You've got the wrong number.** Vous vous êtes trompé de numéro. ❷ (*morally bad*) mal ▷ *Some people think hunting is wrong.* Certains pensent que c'est mal de chasser.; **to be wrong** (*mistaken*) se tromper ▷ *You're wrong about that.* Tu te trompes.; **to do something wrong** se tromper ▷ *You've done it wrong.* Tu t'es trompé.; **to go wrong** (*plan*) mal tourner ▷ *The robbery went wrong and they got caught.* Le cambriolage a mal tourné et ils ont été pris.; **What's wrong?** Qu'est-ce qu'il y a?; **What's wrong with her?** Qu'est-ce qu'elle a?

wrote [rəʊt] *vb see* **write**

X-ray ['ɛksreɪ] *vb:* **to X-ray something** faire une radio de quelque chose ▷ *They X-rayed my arm.* Ils ont fait une radio de mon bras.
▶ *n* radio *f* ▷ *to have an X-ray* passer une radio

y

yacht [jɒt] n ❶ (sailing boat) voilier m ❷ (luxury motorboat) yacht m

yard [jɑːd] n ❶ (of building) cour f ▷ in the yard dans la cour ❷ (of house) jardin m

yawn [jɔːn] vb bâiller

year [jɪəʳ] n ❶ an m ▷ last year l'an dernier ▷ next year l'an prochain; **to be 15 years old** avoir quinze ans; **an eight-year-old child** un enfant de huit ans ❷ (duration) année f ▷ Mom has been sick for several years. Maman a été malade pendant plusieurs années. ▷ throughout the year à longueur d'année

yell [jɛl] vb hurler

yellow ['jɛləʊ] adj jaune

yes [jɛs] adv oui ▷ "Do you like it?" — "Yes." « Tu aimes ça? » — « Oui. » ▷ "You don't like it?" — "Yes I do!" « Tu n'aimes pas ça? » — « Mais oui, j'aime ça! »; **"Would you like a cup of tea?" — "Yes please."** « Voulez-vous une tasse de thé? » — « Je veux bien. »

yesterday ['jɛstədɪ] adv hier ▷ yesterday morning hier matin ▷ yesterday afternoon hier après-midi ▷ yesterday evening hier soir ▷ all day yesterday toute la journée d'hier

yet [jɛt] adv, conj ❶ encore; **not yet** pas encore ▷ It's not finished yet. Ce n'est pas encore fini.; **not as yet** pas encore ▷ There's no news as yet. Nous n'avons pas encore de nouvelles.; **Have you finished yet?** Vous avez fini? ❷ (nevertheless) pourtant ▷ It's nearly impossible, and yet it has to be done. C'est presque impossible, et pourtant il faut le faire.

yield [jiːld] vb (on road sign) céder le passage

yogurt n yogourt m

yolk [jəʊk] n jaune d'œuf m (pl jaunes d'œuf)

you [juː] pron

Only use **tu** when speaking to one person of your own age or younger. If in doubt use **vous**.

❶ (polite form or plural) vous ▷ Do you like basketball? Est-ce que vous aimez le basket-ball? ▷ Can I help you? Est-ce que je peux vous aider? ▷ It's for you. C'est pour vous. ❷ (familiar singular) tu ▷ Do you like basketball? Tu aimes le basket-ball?

vous never changes, but **tu** has different forms. When **you** is the object of the sentence use **te** not **tu**. **te** becomes **t'** before a vowel sound.

❸ te, t' ▷ I know you. Je te connais. ▷ I gave it to you. Je te l'ai donné. ▷ I saw you. Je t'ai vu. ▷ I'll help you. Je vais t'aider.

toi is used instead of **tu** after a preposition and in comparisons.

❹ toi ▷ *It's for you.* C'est pour toi. ▷ *I'll come with you.* Je viens avec toi. ▷ *She's younger than you.* Elle est plus jeune que toi.

young [jʌŋ] *adj* jeune; **young people** les jeunes

younger [ˈjʌŋɡəʳ] *adj* plus jeune ▷ *He's younger than me.* Il est plus jeune que moi.; **my younger brother** mon frère cadet; **my younger sister** ma sœur cadette

youngest [ˈjʌŋɡəst] *adj* le plus jeune, la plus jeune ▷ *my youngest brother* mon plus jeune frère ▷ *She's the youngest.* C'est la plus jeune.

your [jɔːʳ] *adj*

> Only use **ton/ta/tes** when speaking to one person of your own age or younger. If in doubt use **votre/vos**.

❶ *(polite form or plural)* votre, vos *pl* ▷ *your house* votre maison ▷ *your seats* vos places ❷ *(familiar singular)* ton *m*, ta *f*, tes *pl* ▷ *your brother* ton frère ▷ *your sister* ta sœur ▷ *your parents* tes parents

> **ta** becomes **ton** before a vowel sound

your friend (1) *(male)* ton ami **(2)** *(female)* ton amie

> Do not use **votre/vos** or **ton/ta/tes** with parts of the body.

▷ *Would you like to wash your hands?* Est-ce que vous voulez vous laver les mains? ▷ *Do you want to wash your hair?* Tu veux te laver les cheveux?

yours [jɔːz] *pron*

> Only use **le tien/la tienne/les tiens/les tiennes** when talking to one person of your own age or younger. If in doubt use **le vôtre/la vôtre/les vôtres**. The same applies to **à toi** and **à vous**.

❶ le + m vôtre, la + f vôtre, les + pl vôtres ▷ *I've lost my pen. Can I use yours?* J'ai perdu mon stylo. Je peux utiliser le vôtre? ▷ *I like that car. Is it yours?* J'aime cette voiture-là. C'est la vôtre? ▷ *my parents and yours* mes parents et les vôtres; **Is this yours?** C'est à vous? ▷ *This book is yours.* Ce livre est à vous. ▷ *"Whose is this?" — "It's yours."* « C'est à qui? » — « À vous. »; **Yours sincerely...** Veuillez agréer l'expression de mes sentiments les plus distingués... ❷ le + m tien, la + f tienne, les + m tiens, les + f tiennes ▷ *I've lost my pen. Can I use yours?* J'ai perdu mon stylo. Je peux utiliser le tien? ▷ *I like that car. Is it yours?* J'aime cette voiture-là. C'est la tienne? ▷ *my parents and yours* mes parents et les tiens ▷ *My hands are dirty, yours are clean.* Mes mains sont sales, les tiennes sont propres.; **Is this yours?** C'est à toi? ▷ *This book is yours.* Ce livre est à toi. ▷ *"Whose is this?" — "It's yours."* « C'est à qui? » — « À toi. »

yourself [jɔːˈsɛlf] *pron*

> Only use **te** when talking to one person of your own age or younger; use **vous** to everyone else. If in doubt use **vous**.

❶ *(polite form)* vous ▷ *Have you hurt yourself?* Est-ce que vous vous êtes fait mal? ▷ *Tell me about yourself!* Parlez-moi de vous! ❷ *(familiar form)* te ▷ *Have you hurt yourself?* Est-ce que tu t'es fait mal?

> After a preposition, use **toi** instead of **te**.

❸ *(familiar form)* toi ▷ *Tell me about yourself!* Parle-moi de toi! ❹ toi-même ▷ *Do it yourself!* Fais-le toi-même! ❺ vous-même ▷ *Do it yourself!* Faites-le vous-même!

yourselves [jɔːˈsɛlvz] *pron* ❶ vous ▷ *Did you enjoy yourselves?* Vous vous

êtes bien amusés? ❷ vous-mêmes
▷ *Did you make it yourselves?* Vous
l'avez fait vous-mêmes?
youth club *n* centre de jeunes *m*
youth hostel *n* auberge *f* de
jeunesse (*pl* auberges de jeunesse)
Yukon ['juːkɒn] *n* Yukon *m*

Z

Zamboni® [zæm'bəʊnɪ] *n*
surfaceuse *f*
zany ['zeɪnɪ] *adj* loufoque
zebra ['ziːbrə] *n* zèbre *m*
zero ['zɪərəʊ] *n* zéro *m*
zipper ['zɪpəʳ] *n* fermeture éclair® *f*
(*pl* fermetures éclair)
zip up [zɪp-] *vb* fermer ▷ *Zip up your
coat.* Ferme ton manteau.; **The
dress zips up the back.** La robe se
ferme avec une fermeture éclair
au dos.
zit [zɪt] *n* bouton *m*
zodiac ['zəʊdɪæk] *n* zodiaque *m*
▷ *the signs of the zodiac* les signes du
zodiaque
zone [zəʊn] *n* zone *f*
zoo [zuː] *n* zoo *m*
zoom lens ['zuːm-] *n* zoom *m*
zucchini [zuːˈkiːnɪ] *n* courgette *f*

FRENCH IN ACTION

FRENCH VERB TABLES

▶ aimer

to like or to love

IMPÉRATIF

aime
aimons
aimez

EXEMPLES

*Tu **aimes** le chocolat?* Do you like chocolate?
*Je t'**aime**.* I love you.
*J'**aimerais** aller en Grèce.* I'd like to go to Greece.

PARTICIPE PASSÉ

aimé

PRÉSENT

j'	aime
tu	aimes
il	aime
nous	aimons
vous	aimez
ils	aiment

PASSÉ COMPOSÉ

j'	ai aimé
tu	as aimé
il	a aimé
nous	avons aimé
vous	avez aimé
ils	ont aimé

FUTUR SIMPLE

j'	aimerai
tu	aimeras
il	aimera
nous	aimerons
vous	aimerez
ils	aimeront

FUTUR PROCHE

je	vais aimer
tu	vas aimer
il	va aimer
nous	allons aimer
vous	allez aimer
ils	vont aimer

IMPARFAIT

j'	aimais
tu	aimais
il	aimait
nous	aimions
vous	aimiez
ils	aimaient

CONDITIONNEL

j'	aimerais
tu	aimerais
il	aimerait
nous	aimerions
vous	aimeriez
ils	aimeraient

FRENCH VERB TABLES

▶ finir

to finish

EXEMPLES

Finis ta soupe! Finish your soup!
J'ai fini! I've finished!
Je **finirai** mes devoirs demain. I'll
finish my homework tomorrow.

IMPÉRATIF

finis
finissons
finissez

PARTICIPE PASSÉ

fini

PRÉSENT

je	finis
tu	finis
il	finit
nous	finissons
vous	finissent
ils	finissent

PASSÉ COMPOSÉ

j'	ai fini
tu	as fini
il	a fini
nous	avons fini
vous	avez fini
ils	ont fini

FUTUR SIMPLE

je	finirai
tu	finiras
il	finira
nous	finirons
vous	finirez
ils	finiront

FUTUR PROCHE

je	vais finir
tu	vas finir
il	va finir
nous	allons finir
vous	allez finir
ils	vont finir

IMPARFAIT

je	finissais
tu	finissais
il	finissait
nous	finissions
vous	finissiez
ils	finissaient

CONDITIONNEL

je	finirais
tu	finirais
il	finirait
nous	finirions
vous	finiriez
ils	finiraient

FRENCH VERB TABLES

▶ partir

*also **dormir, mentir, sentir serms, sentir servir, sortir**

to leave

IMPÉRATIF

pars
partons
partez

EXEMPLES

*Elle **part** pour Paris.* She's leaving for Paris.
*Nous **sommes partis** en vacances.* We left on vacation.
*Je **partirai** bientôt.* I'll leave soon.

PARTICIPE PASSÉ

attendu

PRÉSENT

je	**pars**
tu	**pars**
il	**part**
nous	par**tons**
vous	par**tez**
ils	par**tent**

FUTUR PROCHE

je	vais partir
tu	vas partir
il	va partir
nous	allons partir
vous	allez partir
ils	vont partir

PASSÉ COMPOSÉ

je	suis parti/partie
tu	es parti/partie
il	est parti/elle est partie
nous	sommes partis/parties
vous	êtes parti/partie/partis/parties
ils	sont partis/elles sont parties

IMPARFAIT

je	partais
tu	partais
il	partait
nous	partions
vous	partiez
ils	partaient

FUTUR SIMPLE

je	partirai
tu	partiras
il	partira
nous	partirons
vous	partirez
ils	partiront

CONDITIONNEL

je	partirais
tu	partirais
il	partirait
nous	partirions
vous	partiriez
ils	partiraient

FRENCH VERB TABLES

▶ attendre

to wait for

IMPÉRATIF

attends
attendons
attendez

PARTICIPE PASSÉ

attendu

EXEMPLES

Attends-moi! Wait for me!
Tu **attends** depuis longtemps? Have you been waiting long?
Je l'**ai attendu** à la poste. I waited for him at the post office.

PRÉSENT

j'	attend**s**
tu	attend**s**
il	attend
nous	attend**ons**
vous	attend**ez**
ils	attend**ent**

PASSÉ COMPOSÉ

j'	ai attendu
tu	as attendu
il	a attendu
nous	avons attendu
vous	avez attendu
ils	ont attendu

FUTUR SIMPLE

j'	attendrai
tu	attendras
il	attendra
nous	attendrons
vous	attendrez
ils	attendront

FUTUR PROCHE

je	vais attendre
tu	vas attendre
il	va attendre
nous	allons attendre
vous	allez attendre
ils	vont attendre

IMPARFAIT

j'	attendais
tu	attendais
il	attendait
nous	attendions
vous	attendiez
ils	attendaient

CONDITIONNEL

j'	attendrais
tu	attendrais
il	attendrait
nous	attendrions
vous	attendriez
ils	attendraient

FRENCH VERB TABLES

▶ se lever

to get up

EXEMPLES

*Je **me lève** chaque matin à sept heures.*
I get up at seven o'clock every morning.
*Il doit **se lever** tôt le matin.* He has
to get up early in the morning.
*Tu **t'es levée** de bonne heure, Corinne?*
You got up early, Corinne?

IMPÉRATIF

lève-toi
levons-nous
levez-vous

PARTICIPE PASSÉ

levé

PRÉSENT

je	me lève
tu	te lèves
il	se lève
nous	nous levons
vous	vous levez
ils	se lèvent

PASSÉ COMPOSÉ

je	me suis levé/levée
tu	t'es levé/levée
il	s'est levé/elle s'est levée
nous	nous sommes levés/levées
vous	vous êtes levé/levée/levés/levées
ils	se sont levés/elles se sont levées

FUTUR SIMPLE

je	me lèverai
tu	te lèveras
il	se lèvera
nous	nous lèverons
vous	vous lèverez
ils	se lèveront

FUTUR PROCHE

je	vais me lever
tu	vas te lever
il	va se lever
nous	allons nous lever
vous	allez vous lever
ils	vont se lever

IMPARFAIT

je	me levais
tu	te levais
il	se levait
nous	nous levions
vous	vous leviez
ils	se levaient

CONDITIONNEL

je	me lèverais
tu	te lèverais
il	se lèverait
nous	nous lèverions
vous	vous lèveriez
ils	se lèveraient

FRENCH VERB TABLES

▶ avoir

to have

IMPÉRATIF

aie
ayons
ayez

EXEMPLES

*Il **a** les yeux bleus.* He's got blue eyes.
*Quel âge **as**-tu?* How old are you?
*Il **a eu** un accident.* He's had an accident.
*J'**avais** faim.* I was hungry.

PARTICIPE PASSÉ

eu

PRÉSENT

j' ai
tu as
il a
nous avons
vous avez
ils ont

PASSÉ COMPOSÉ

j' ai eu
tu as eu
il a eu
nous avons eu
vous avez eu
ils ont eu

FUTUR SIMPLE

j' aurai
tu auras
il aura
nous aurons
vous aurez
ils auront

FUTUR PROCHE

je vais avoir
tu vas avoir
il va avoir
nous allons avoir
vous allez avoir
ils vont avoir

IMPARFAIT

j' avais
tu avais
il avait
nous avions
vous aviez
ils avaient

CONDITIONNEL

j' aurais
tu aurais
il aurait
nous aurions
vous auriez
ils auraient

FRENCH VERB TABLES

▶ être

to be

EXEMPLES

Mon père est professeur. My father's a teacher.
Quelle heure est-il? Il est 10 heures. What time is it? It's 10 o'clock.
Ils vont être à la maison ce soir. They'll be home tonight.

IMPÉRATIF

sois
soyons
soyez

PARTICIPE PASSÉ

été

PRÉSENT	FUTUR PROCHE
je suis	je vais être
tu es	tu vas être
il est	il va être
nous sommes	nous allons être
vous êtes	vous allez être
ils sont	ils vont être

PASSÉ COMPOSÉ	IMPARFAIT
j' ai été	j' étais
tu as été	tu étais
il a été	il était
nous avons été	nous étions
vous avez été	vous étiez
ils ont été	ils étaient

FUTUR SIMPLE	CONDITIONNEL
je serai	je serais
tu seras	tu serais
il sera	il serait
nous serons	nous serions
vous serez	vous seriez
ils seront	ils seraient

FRENCH VERB TABLES

▶ aller

to go

IMPÉRATIF

va
allons
allez

PARTICIPE PASSÉ

allé

EXEMPLES

*Vous **allez** au cinéma?* Are you going to the cinema?
*Je **suis allé** à Londres.* I went to London.
*Est-elle déjà **allée** chez elle?* Has she already gone home?

PRÉSENT

je	vais
tu	vas
il	va
nous	allons
vous	allez
ils	vont

PASSÉ COMPOSÉ

je	suis allé
tu	es allé
il	est allé
nous	sommes allés
vous	êtes allés
ils	sont allés

FUTUR SIMPLE

j'	irai
tu	iras
il	ira
nous	irons
vous	irez
ils	iront

FUTUR PROCHE

je	vais aller
tu	vas aller
il	va aller
nous	allons aller
vous	allez aller
ils	vont aller

IMPARFAIT

j'	allais
tu	allais
il	allait
nous	allions
vous	alliez
ils	allaient

CONDITIONNEL

j'	irais
tu	irais
il	irait
nous	irions
vous	iriez
ils	iraient

FRENCH VERB TABLES

▶ devoir

to have to

EXEMPLES

Je **dois** aller faire les courses ce matin.
I have to do the shopping this morning.
Il **a dû** faire ses devoirs hier soir. He had
to do his homework last night.
Il **devait** prendre le train pour aller
travailler. He had to go to work by train.

IMPÉRATIF

dois
devons
devez

PARTICIPE PASSÉ

dû

PRÉSENT

je	dois
tu	dois
il	doit
nous	devons
vous	devez
ils	doivent

PASSÉ COMPOSÉ

j'	ai dû
tu	as dû
il	a dû
nous	avons dû
vous	avez dû
ils	ont dû

FUTUR SIMPLE

je	devrai
tu	devras
il	devra
nous	devrons
vous	devrez
ils	devront

FUTUR PROCHE

je	vais devoir
tu	vas devoir
il	va devoir
nous	allons devoir
vous	allez devoir
ils	vont devoir

IMPARFAIT

je	devais
tu	devais
il	devait
nous	devions
vous	deviez
ils	devaient

CONDITIONNEL

je	devrais
tu	devrais
il	devrait
nous	devrions
vous	devriez
ils	devraient

FRENCH VERB TABLES

▶ dire

to say

IMPÉRATIF

dis
disons
dites

PARTICIPE PASSÉ

dit

EXEMPLES

Je **dis** toujours la vérité. I always tell the truth.
Elle nous **a dit** bonjour. She said good morning to us.
Dites bonjour, tout le monde! Say hello, everybody!

PRÉSENT

je	dis
tu	dis
il	dit
nous	disons
vous	dites
ils	disent

PASSÉ COMPOSÉ

j'	ai dit
tu	as dit
il	a dit
nous	avons dit
vous	avez dit
ils	ont dit

FUTUR SIMPLE

je	dirai
tu	diras
il	dira
nous	dirons
vous	direz
ils	diront

FUTUR PROCHE

je	vais dire
tu	vas dire
il	va dire
nous	allons dire
vous	allez dire
ils	vont dire

IMPARFAIT

je	disais
tu	disais
il	disait
nous	disions
vous	disiez
ils	disaient

CONDITIONNEL

je	dirais
tu	dirais
il	dirait
nous	dirions
vous	diriez
ils	diraient

FRENCH VERB TABLES

▶ faire

to do, to make

EXEMPLES

*Qu'est-ce que tu **fais**?* What are you doing?
*Qu'est-ce qu'il **a fait**?* What has he done? or What did he do?
*J'**ai fait** un gâteau.* I made a cake.

IMPÉRATIF

fais
faisons
faites

PARTICIPE PASSÉ

fait

PRÉSENT		FUTUR PROCHE	
je	fais	je	vais faire
tu	fais	tu	vas faire
il	fait	il	va faire
nous	faisons	nous	allons faire
vous	faites	vous	allez faire
ils	font	ils	vont faire

PASSÉ COMPOSÉ		IMPARFAIT	
j'	ai fait	je	faisais
tu	as fait	tu	faisais
il	a fait	il	faisait
nous	avons fait	nous	faisions
vous	avez fait	vous	faisiez
ils	ont fait	ils	faisaient

FUTUR SIMPLE		CONDITIONNEL	
je	ferai	je	ferais
tu	feras	tu	ferais
il	fera	il	ferait
nous	ferons	nous	ferions
vous	ferez	vous	feriez
ils	feront	ils	feraient

FRENCH VERB TABLES

▶ mettre

to put

IMPÉRATIF

mets
mettons
mettez

PARTICIPE PASSÉ

mis

EXEMPLES

Mets ton manteau! Put your coat on!
Où est-ce que tu **as mis** les clés?
  Where did you put the keys?
J'**ai mis** le livre sur la table. I put
  the book on the table.

PRÉSENT

je	mets
tu	mets
il	met
nous	mettons
vous	mettez
ils	mettent

PASSÉ COMPOSÉ

j'	ai mis
tu	as mis
il	a mis
nous	avons mis
vous	avez mis
ils	ont mis

FUTUR SIMPLE

je	mettrai
tu	mettras
il	mettra
nous	mettrons
vous	mettrez
ils	mettront

FUTUR PROCHE

je	vais mettre
tu	vas mettre
il	va mettre
nous	allons mettre
vous	allez mettre
ils	vont mettre

IMPARFAIT

je	mettais
tu	mettais
il	mettait
nous	mettions
vous	mettiez
ils	mettaient

CONDITIONNEL

je	mettrais
tu	mettrais
il	mettrait
nous	mettrions
vous	mettriez
ils	mettraient

FRENCH VERB TABLES

▶ pouvoir

can

EXEMPLES

Je **peux** *t'aider, si tu veux.* I can help
you if you like.
*J'ai fait tout ce que j'***ai pu***.* I did all I could.
Je ne **pourrai** *pas venir samedi.* I won't
be able to come on Saturday.

IMPÉRATIF

the imperative of **pouvoir**
is not used

PARTICIPE PASSÉ

pu

PRÉSENT

je	peux
tu	peux
il	peut
nous	pouvons
vous	pouvez
ils	peuvent

PASSÉ COMPOSÉ

j'	ai pu
tu	as pu
il	a pu
nous	avons pu
vous	avez pu
ils	ont pu

FUTUR SIMPLE

je	pourrai
tu	pourras
il	pourra
nous	pourrons
vous	pourrez
ils	pourront

FUTUR PROCHE

je	vais pouvoir
tu	vas pouvoir
il	va pouvoir
nous	allons pouvoir
vous	allez pouvoir
ils	vont pouvoir

IMPARFAIT

je	pouvais
tu	pouvais
il	pouvait
nous	pouvions
vous	pouviez
ils	pouvaient

CONDITIONNEL

je	pourrais
tu	pourrais
il	pourrait
nous	pourrions
vous	pourriez
ils	pourraient

FRENCH VERB TABLES

▶ prendre

*also **apprendre**, **comprendre***

to take

IMPÉRATIF

prends
prenons
prenez

EXEMPLES

Nous **prenons** le café après le souper.
We have coffee after supper.
Il **a pris** mon livre. He took my book.
Prends ces clés. Take these keys.

PARTICIPE PASSÉ

pris

PRÉSENT

je	prends
tu	prends
il	prend
nous	prenons
vous	prenez
ils	prennent

PASSÉ COMPOSÉ

j'	ai pris
tu	as pris
il	a pris
nous	avons pris
vous	avez pris
ils	ont pris

FUTUR SIMPLE

je	prendrai
tu	prendras
il	prendra
nous	prendrons
vous	prendrez
ils	prendront

FUTUR PROCHE

je	vais prendre
tu	vas prendre
il	va prendre
nous	allons prendre
vous	allez prendre
ils	vont prendre

IMPARFAIT

je	prenais
tu	prenais
il	prenait
nous	prenions
vous	preniez
ils	prenaient

CONDITIONNEL

je	prendrais
tu	prendrais
il	prendrait
nous	prendrions
vous	prendriez
ils	prendraient

FRENCH VERB TABLES

▶ venir

to come

IMPÉRATIF

viens
venons
venez

EXEMPLES

*Ils **viennent** nous voir ce soir.*
   They're coming to see us tonight.
***Viens** avec moi.* Come with me.
*Elles **est venue** toute seule.* She
   came alone.

PARTICIPE PASSÉ

venu

PRÉSENT

je	viens
tu	viens
il	vient
nous	venons
vous	venez
ils	viennent

PASSÉ COMPOSÉ

je	suis venu/venue
tu	es venu/venue
il	est venu/elle est venue
nous	sommes venus/venues
vous	êtes venu/venue/venus/ venues
ils	sont venus/elles sont venues

FUTUR SIMPLE

je	viendrai
tu	viendras
il	viendra
nous	viendrons
vous	viendrez
ils	viendront

FUTUR PROCHE

je	vais venir
tu	vas venir
il	va venir
nous	allons venir
vous	allez venir
ils	vont venir

IMPARFAIT

je	venais
tu	venais
il	venait
nous	venions
vous	veniez
ils	venaient

CONDITIONNEL

je	viendrais
tu	viendrais
il	viendrait
nous	viendrions
vous	viendriez
ils	viendraient

FRENCH VERB TABLES

▶ voir

to see

IMPÉRATIF

vois
voyons
voyez

EXEMPLES

*Venez me **voir** quand vous serez à Paris.*
Come and see me when you're in Paris.
*Je ne **vois** rien sans mes lunettes.*
I can't see anything without my glasses.
*Est-ce que tu l'**as vu**?* Did you see
him? or Have you seen him?

PARTICIPE PASSÉ

vu

PRÉSENT

je	vois
tu	vois
il	voit
nous	voyons
vous	voyez
ils	voient

PASSÉ COMPOSÉ

j'	ai vu
tu	as vu
il	a vu
nous	avons vu
vous	avez vu
ils	ont vu

FUTUR SIMPLE

je	verrai
tu	verras
il	verra
nous	verrons
vous	verrez
ils	verront

FUTUR PROCHE

je	vais voir
tu	vas voir
il	va voir
nous	allons voir
vous	allez voir
ils	vont voir

IMPARFAIT

je	voyais
tu	voyais
il	voyait
nous	voyions
vous	voyiez
ils	voyaient

CONDITIONNEL

je	verrais
tu	verrais
il	verrait
nous	verrions
vous	verriez
ils	verraient

FRENCH VERB TABLES

▶ vouloir

to want

EXEMPLES

*Elle **veut** un vélo pour Noël.*
  She wants a bike for Christmas.
*Ils **voulaient** aller au cinéma.*
  They wanted to go to the cinema.
*Tu **voudrais** une tasse de thé?*
  Would you like a cup of tea?

IMPÉRATIF

veuille
veuillons
veuillez

PARTICIPE PASSÉ

voulu

PRÉSENT

je	veux
tu	veux
il	veut
nous	voulons
vous	voulez
ils	veulent

PASSÉ COMPOSÉ

j'	ai voulu
tu	as voulu
il	a voulu
nous	avons voulu
vous	avez voulu
ils	ont voulu

FUTUR SIMPLE

je	voudrai
tu	voudras
il	voudra
nous	voudrons
vous	voudrez
ils	voudront

FUTUR PROCHE

je	vais vouloir
tu	vas vouloir
il	va vouloir
nous	allons vouloir
vous	allez vouloir
ils	vont vouloir

IMPARFAIT

je	voulais
tu	voulais
il	voulait
nous	voulions
vous	vouliez
ils	voulaient

CONDITIONNEL

je	voudrais
tu	voudrais
il	voudrait
nous	voudrions
vous	voudriez
ils	voudraient

IRREGULAR VERB FORMS

The following list is a summary of the main forms of other irregular verbs that you are likely to encounter. For **le présent**, all **je** and **nous** forms are shown. The **il**, **vous**, and **ils** forms are also included wherever the part of the verb that goes with them follows an unusual pattern. For all other tenses, only the **je** form is given.

INFINITIF	PRÉSENT	PASSÉ COMPOSÉ	IMPARFAIT	FUTUR	FUTUR PROCHE
acheter	j'achète nous achetons ils achètent	j'ai acheté	j'achetais	j'achèterai	je vais acheter
appeler	j'appelle il appelle nous appelons	j'ai appelé	j'appelais	j'appellerai	je vais appeler
apprendre	j'apprends nous apprenons vous apprenez ils apprennent	j'ai appris	j'apprenais	j'apprendrai	je vais apprendre
s'asseoir	je m'assieds nous nous asseyons vous vous asseyez ils s'asseyent	je me suis assis	je m'asseyais	je m'assiérai	je vais m'asseoir
battre	je bats il bat nous battons	j'ai battu	je battais	je battrai	je vais battre
boire	je bois nous buvons ils boivent	j'ai bu	je buvais	je boirai	je vais boire
bouillir	je bous nous bouillons	j'ai bouilli	je bouillais	je bouillirai	je vais bouillir
conclure	je conclus nous concluons	j'ai conclu	je concluais	je conclurai	je vais conclure
conduire	je conduis nous conduisons	j'ai conduit	je conduisais	je conduirai	je vais conduire
connaître	je connais il connaît nous connaissons	j'ai connu	je connaissais	je connaîtrai	je vais connaître
coudre	je couds nous cousons vous cousez ils cousent	j'ai cousu	je cousais	je coudrai	je vais coudre
courir	je cours nous courons	j'ai couru	je courais	je courrai	je vais courir
couvrir	je couvre nous couvrons	j'ai couvert	je couvrais	je couvrirai	je vais couvrir
craindre	je crains nous craignons	j'ai craint	je craignais	je craindrai	je vais craindre
créer	je crée nous créons	j'ai créé	je créais	je créerai	je vais créer
croire	je crois nous croyons ils croient	j'ai cru	je croyais	je croirai	je vais croire

INFINITIF	PRÉSENT	PASSÉ COMPOSÉ	IMPARFAIT	FUTUR	FUTUR PROCHE
croître	je croîs nous croissons	j'ai crû	je croissais	je croîtrai	je vais croître
cueillir	je cueille nous cueillons	j'ai cueilli	je cueillais	je cueillerai	je vais cueillir
cuire	je cuis nous cuisons ils cuisent	j'au cuit	je cuisais	je cuirai	je vais cuire
dormir	je dors nous dormons	j'ai dormi	je dormais	je dormirai	je vais dormir
écrire	j'écris nous écrivons	j'ai écrit	j'écrivais	j'écrirai	je vais écrire
falloir	il faut	il a fallu	il fallait	il faudra	il va falloir
fuir	je fuis nous fuyons ils fuient	j'ai fui	je fuyais	je fuirai	je vais fuir
haïr	je hais nous haïssons ils haïssent	j'ai haï	je haïssais	je haïrai	je vais haïr
jeter	je jette nous jetons ils jettent	j'ai jeté	je jetais	je jetterai	je vais jeter
joindre	je joins nous joignons	j'ai joint	je joignais	je joindrai	je vais joindre
lever	je lève nous levons ils lèvent	j'ai levé	je levais	je lèverai	je vais lever
lire	je lis nous lisons	j'ai lu	je lisais	je lirai	je vais lire
manger	je mange nous mangeons	j'ai mangé	je mangeais	je mangerai	je vais manger
mentir	je mens nous mentons	j'ai menti	je mentais	je mentirai	je vais mentir
mourir	je meurs nous mourons ils meurent	je suis mort je suis morte	je mourais	je mourrai	je vais mourir
naître	je nais il naît nous naissons	je suis né je suis née	je naissais	je naîtrai	je vais naître
offrir	j'offre nous offrons	j'ai offert	j'offrais	j'offrirai	je vais offrir
paraître	je parais il paraît nous paraissons	j'ai paru	je paraissais	je paraîtrai	je vais paraître
partir	je pars nous partons	je suis parti je suis partie	je partais	je partirai	je vais partir
plaire	je plais il plaît nous plaisons	j'ai plu	je plaisais	je plairai	je vais plaire
pleuvoir	il pleut	il a plu	il pleuvait	il pleuvra	il va pleuvoir
prendre	je prends nous prenons ils prennent	j'ai pris	je prenais	je prendrai	je vais prendre
recevoir	je reçois il reçoit ils reçoivent	j'ai reçu	je recevais	je recevrai	je vais recevoir

20

INFINITIF	PRÉSENT	PASSÉ COMPOSÉ	IMPARFAIT	FUTUR	FUTUR PROCHE
rire	je ris nous rions	j'ai ri	je riais	je rirai	je vais rire
savoir	je sais nous savons ils savent	j'ai su	je savais	je saurai	je vais savoir
servir	je sers nous servons	j'ai servi	je servais	je servirai	je vais servir
sortir	je sors nous sortons	je suis sorti je suis sortie	je sortais	je sortirai	je vais sortir
souffrir	je souffre nous souffrons	j'ai souffert	je souffrais	je souffrirai	je vais souffrir
suffire	je suffis nous suffisons	j'ai suffi	je suffisais	je suffirai	je vais suffire
suivre	je suis nous suivons	j'ai suivi	je suivais	je suivrai	je vais suivre
se taire	je me tais nous nous taisons	je me suis tu	je me taisais	je me tairai	je vais me taire
tenir	je tiens nous tenons ils tiennent	j'ai tenu	je tenais	je tiendrai	je vais tenir
vaincre	je vaincs il vainc nous vainquons	j'ai vaincu	je vainquais	je vaincrai	je vais vaincre
valoir	je vaux il vaut nous valons	j'ai valu	je valais	je vaudrai	je vais valoir
venir	je viens nous venons ils viennent	je suis venu je suis venue	je venais	je viendrai	je vais venir
vivre	je vis nous vivons	j'ai vécu	je vivais	je vivrai	je vais vivre

CORRESPONDENCE

▶ PERSONAL LETTER

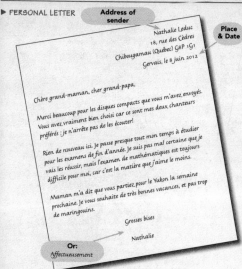

Address of sender

Place & Date

Nathalie Leduc
18, rue des Cèdres
Chibougamau (Québec) G8P 1G1

Gervais, le 8 juin 2012

Chère grand-maman, cher grand-papa,

Merci beaucoup pour les disques compacts que vous m'avez envoyés. Vous avez vraiment bien choisi car ce sont mes deux chanteurs préférés : je n'arrête pas de les écouter!

Rien de nouveau ici. Je passe presque tout mon temps à étudier pour les examens de fin d'année. Je suis pas mal certaine que je vais les réussir, mais l'examen de mathématiques est toujours difficile pour moi, car c'est la matière que j'aime le moins.

Maman m'a dit que vous partiez pour le Yukon la semaine prochaine. Je vous souhaite de très bonnes vacances, et pas trop de maringouins.

Grosses bises

Nathalie

Or:
Affectueusement

STARTING A PERSONAL LETTER

Merci pour ta lettre.	*Thank you for your letter.*
Ça m'a fait plaisir d'avoir de tes nouvelles.	*It was lovely to hear from you.*
Je suis désolé de ne pas t'avoir écrit plus tôt.	*I'm sorry I didn't write sooner.*

ENDING A PERSONAL LETTER

Donne de tes nouvelles!	*Keep in touch!*
Embrasse Sophie pour moi.	*Give my love to Sophie.*
Paul te fait ses amitiés.	*Paul sends his best wishes.*

CORRESPONDENCE

▶ BUSINESS LETTER

Place & Date

Mississauga, le 30 janvier 2012

Address of recipient

1 Madame Denise Beauchemin
Directrice du marketing
Envirocor
1279, avenue des Érables, bureau 27
Montréal (Québec) H7M 3R9

Salutation

2 Madame la directrice,

Je suis en septième année à l'école Burnham Road. Je fais des recherches sur des entreprises canadiennes qui fabriquent des produits qui respectent l'environnement.

J'ai lu que Envirocor fait des progrès remarquables dans ce domaine. Pourriez-vous s'il vous plaît m'envoyer des dépliants ou d'autres renseignements au sujet de vos produits? Ces renseignements m'aideront beaucoup dans mon travail.

Address of sender

3 Veuillez agréer, Madame, mes salutations distinguées.

Caroline Martin
3942, rue McCallion
Mississauga (Ontario) M4Z 2T6

Closing

1
- Start with the name of the individual.
- Follow with that person's position in the company.
- Do not use a comma at the end of each line.

2
- Do not use *cher* or *chère* in a business letter.
- Do not include the person's name after *Monsieur* or *Madame*.
- If you don't know the person's title, *Monsieur* or *Madame* is sufficient.

3
- Other possible closings include
  Veuillez recevoir, Madame, mes plus cordiales salutations.
  Veuillez agréer, Madame, mes sincères salutations.

23

CORRESPONDENCE

▶ E-MAIL

> To give your email address to someone in French, say:
> **Julie a commercial a b c point c a**

Nouveau message	
A :	julie@abc.ca
De :	patrick@onemo.net
Objet :	spectacle
Cc :	antoine@blt.com
Copie cachée :	

Fichier joint   **Envoyer**

Salut!

Je viens d'acheter le nouvel album de Rockstar. Il est génial!

J'ai trois billets gratuits pour leur spectacle à Montréal samedi prochain et j'espère que vous pourrez venir avec moi tous les deux!

À bientôt!

Nouveau message	New message
A	To
De	From
Objet	Subject
Cc	cc
Copie cachée	bcc
Fichier joint	Attachment
Envoyer	Send

TELEPHONE

▶ WHEN YOU DIAL A NUMBER

- **Bonjour! J'aimerais parler à Valérie.**
- Hello! Could I speak to Valérie, please?

- **Pourriez-vous lui demander de me rappeler, s'il vous plaît?**
- Would you ask him/her to call me back, please?

- **Je rappellerai dans une demi-heure.**
- I'll call back in half an hour.

▶ ANSWERING THE TELEPHONE

- **Bonjour! C'est Marc à l'appareil.**
- Hello! It's Marc speaking.

- **C'est moi.**
- Speaking.

- **Qui est à l'appareil?**
- Who's speaking?

▶ WHEN THE SWITCHBOARD ANSWERS

- **C'est de la part de qui?**
- Who shall I say is calling?

- **Je vous le/la passe.**
- I'm putting you through.

- **Ne quittez pas.**
- Please hold.

- **Voulez-vous laisser un message?**
- Would you like to leave a message?

▶ DIFFICULTIES

- **Je n'arrive pas à le/la/les rejoindre.**
- I can't get through.

- **La ligne est occupée.**
- The line is busy.

- **Je suis désolé, j'ai dû faire un faux numéro.**
- I'm sorry, I dialled the wrong number.

- **La ligne est très mauvaise.**
- This is a very bad line.

- **Leur téléphone est en dérangement.**
- Their phone is out of order.

NUMBERS

► CARDINAL NUMBERS

0 zéro	14 quatorze	71 soixante et onze
1 un, une	15 quinze	72 soixante-douze
2 deux	16 seize	80 quatre-vingts
3 trois	17 dix-sept	81 quatre-vingt-un(e)
4 quatre	18 dix-huit	90 quatre-vingt-dix
5 cinq	19 dix-neuf	91 quatre-vingt-onze
6 six	20 vingt	100 cent
7 sept	21 vingt et un(e)	
8 huit	22 vingt-deux	
9 neuf	30 trente	
10 dix	40 quarante	
11 onze	50 cinquante	
12 douze	60 soixante	
13 treize	70 soixante-dix	

101	cent un(e)	2,000	deux mille
300	trois cents	1,000,000	un million
301	trois cent un(e)		
1,000	mille		

► BIG NUMBERS

There are two systems for dealing with larger numbers: the Système international and the American system (used in the United States and in English Canada). The following chart shows the main differences.

Système international		American system
un million	1 000 000	one million
un milliard	1 000 000 000	one billion
un billion	1 000 000 000 000	one trillion
un trillion	1 000 000 000 000 000 000	one quintillion

NUMBERS

▶ FRACTIONS, DECIMALS, PERCENT

1/2	**un demi**
1/3	**un tiers**
2/3	**deux tiers**
1/4	**un quart**
1/5	**un cinquième**

0,5	**zéro virgule cinq (0,5)**
3,4	**trois virgule quatre (3,4)**

10%	**dix pour cent (10 %)**
100%	**cent pour cent (100 %)**

▶ ORDINAL NUMBERS

Use ordinal numbers for ranking people or things.

1st	**premier (1er), première (1re)**	14th	**quatorzième (14e)**
2nd	**deuxième (2e)**	15th	**quinzième (15e)**
3rd	**troisième (3e)**	16th	**seizième (16e)**
4th	**quatrième (4e)**	17th	**dix-septième (17e)**
5th	**cinquième (5e)**	18th	**dix-huitième (18e)**
6th	**sixième (6e)**	19th	**dix-neuvième (19e)**
7th	**septième (7e)**	20th	**vingtième (20e)**
8th	**huitième (8e)**	21st	**vingt et unième (21e)**
9th	**neuvième (9e)**	22nd	**vingt-deuxième (22e)**
10th	**dixième (10e)**	30th	**trentième (30e)**
11th	**onzième (11e)**	100th	**centième (100e)**
12th	**douzième (12e)**	101st	**cent unième (101e)**
13th	**treizième (13e)**	1000th	**millième (1000e)**

Use cardinal numbers for naming all days of the month except for the first day of the month. For the first, use the ordinal number.

Mon anniversaire est le dix-sept octobre.
C'est le premier mai.

DATE

▶ DAYS OF THE WEEK

Monday	lundi
Tuesday	mardi
Wednesday	mercredi
Thursday	jeudi
Friday	vendredi
Saturday	samedi
Sunday	dimanche

Next + day of week
Mardi prochain, nous allons au musée.
Next Tuesday we are going to the museum.

Last + day of week
Mercredi dernier, elle est allée au restaurant.
Last Wednesday she went to a restaurant.

▶ MONTHS OF THE YEAR

January	janvier
February	février
March	mars
April	avril
May	mai
June	juin
July	juillet
August	août
September	septembre
October	octobre
November	novembre
December	décembre

▶ RELIGIOUS FESTIVALS

Baisakhi	Vaisakhi
Christmas	Noël
Diwali	Diwali
Easter	Pâques
Eid	Eid
Good Friday	Vendredi saint
Hanukkah	Hanoukka
Holi	Holi
Passover	la Pâque juive
Ramadan	Ramadan
Wesak	Wesak
Yom Kippur	Yom Kippour

TIME

Quelle heure est-il? What time is it?
Il est...   It's...

une heure

une heure dix

une heure et quart

une heure et demie

deux heures moins vingt

deux heures moins le quart

À quelle heure?   At what time?

à minuit

à midi

à une heure (de l'après-midi)

à huit heures (du soir)

French times are often given using the twenty-four hour clock.

à 11 h 15
or
onze heures quinze

à 20 h 45
or
vingt heures quarante-cinq

29

COUNTRIES

In the table below, the first column is the English name of the country and the second column is the French name of the country. The last two columns are the French words for the nationality, as a noun. The corresponding adjective is the same, but is **not** capitalized:

Canadian (ADJECTIVE) = **canadien** MASC, **canadienne** FEM

Country names marked with an F have French as an official or administrative language.

Using prepositions with countries

- MASC country name: *in Canada, to Canada* = **au Canada**
  from Canada, of Canada = **du Canada**

- FEM country name: *in China, to China* = **en Chine**
  from China, of China = **de la Chine**

- PL country name: *in the Bahamas, to the Bahamas* = **aux Bahamas**
  from the Bahamas, of the Bahamas = **des Bahamas**

- remember that both **du** and **de la** become **de l'** before a vowel or silent *h*, and **au** becomes **à l'**: **à l'Afghanistan, de l'Angleterre**

Country	French name	Nationality – MASC.	Nationality – FEM
Afghanistan	l'Afghanistan MASC	Afghan	Afghane
Albania	l'Albanie FEM	Albanais	Albanaise
Algeria	F l'Algérie FEM	Algérien	Algérienne
Angola	l'Angola MASC	Angolais	Angolaise
Argentina	l'Argentine FEM	Argentin	Argentine
Armenia	l'Arménie FEM	Arménien	Arménienne
Australia	l'Australie FEM	Australien	Australienne
Austria	l'Autriche FEM	Autrichien	Autrichienne
Azerbaijan	l'Azerbaïdjan MASC	Azerbaïdjanais	Azerbaïdjanaise
Bahamas	les Bahamas FEM	Bahamien	Bahamienne
Bangladesh	le Bangladesh	Bangladais	Bangladaise
Barbados	la Barbade	Barbadien	Barbadienne
Belarus	la Biélorussie	Biélorusse	Biélorusse
Belgium	F la Belgique	Belge	Belge
Belize	le Bélize	Bélizien	Bélizienne
Benin	F le Bénin	Béninois	Béninoise
Burkina Faso	F le Burkina Faso	Burkinabé	Burkinabée
Bolivia	la Bolivie	Bolivien	Bolivienne
Bosnia-Herzegovina	la Bosnie-Herzégovnie	Bosniaque	Bosniaque
Brazil	le Brésil	Brésilien	Brésilienne

Country	French name	Nationality – MASC	Nationality – FEM
Bulgaria	la Bulgarie	Bulgare	Bulgare
Cambodia	le Cambodge	Cambodgien	Cambodgienne
Cameroon	F le Cameroun	Camerounais	Camerounaise
Canada	F le Canada	Canadien	Canadienne
Chile	le Chili	Chilien	Chilienne
China	la Chine	Chinois	Chinoise
Colombia	la Colombie	Colombien	Colombienne
Congo	F le Congo	Congolais	Congolaise
Costa Rica	le Costa Rica	Costaricain	Costaricaine
Croatia	la Croatie	Croate	Croate
Cuba	Cuba* FEM	Cubain	Cubaine
Czech Republic	la République tchèque	Tchèque	Tchèque
Denmark	le Danemark	Danois	Danoise
Ecuador	l'Équateur MASC	Équatorien	Équatorienne
Egypt	l'Égypte FEM	Égyptien	Égyptienne
El Salvador	le Salvador	Salvadorien	Salvadorienne
England	l'Angleterre FEM	Anglais	Anglaise
Estonia	l'Estonie FEM	Estonien	Estonienne
Ethiopia	l'Éthiopie FEM	Éthiopien	Éthiopienne
Finland	la Finlande	Finnois	Finnoise
France	F la France	Français	Française
Gabon	F le Gabon	Gabonais	Gabonaise
Gambia	la Gambie	Gambien	Gambienne
Germany	l'Allemagne FEM	Allemand	Allemande
Ghana	le Ghana	Ghanéen	Ghanéenne
Greece	la Grèce	Grec	Grecque
Guatemala	le Guatemala	Guatémaltèque	Guatémaltèque
Guinea	F la Guinée	Guinéen	Guinéenne
Guyana	F la Guyane	Guyanais	Guyanaise
Haiti	F Haïti* MASC	Haïtien	Haïtienne
Holland	la Hollande	Hollandais	Hollandaise
Honduras	le Honduras	Hondurien	Hondurienne
Hungary	la Hongrie	Hongrois	Hongroise
Iceland	l'Islande FEM	Islandais	Islandaise
India	l'Inde FEM	Indien	Indienne
Indonesia	l'Indonésie FEM	Indonésien	Indonésienne
Iran	l'Iran MASC	Iranien	Iranienne
Iraq	l'Iraq MASC	Iraquien	Iraquienne
Ireland	l'Irlande FEM	Irlandais	Irlandaise

Country	French name	Nationality – MASC	Nationality – FEM
Israel	Israël* MASC	Israélien	Israélienne
Italy	l'Italie FEM	italien	Italienne
Ivory Coast	F la Côte d'Ivoire	Ivoirien	Ivoirienne
Jamaica	la Jamaïque	Jamaïquain	Jamaïquaine
Japan	le Japon	Japonais	Japonaise
Kazakhstan	le Kazakhstan	Kazakh	Kazakhe
Kenya	le Kenya	Kényan	Kényane
Korea, North	la Corée du Nord	Nord-Coréen	Nord-Coréenne
Korea, South	la Corée du Sud	Sud-Coréen	Sud-Coréenne
Kuwait	le Koweït	Koweïtien	Koweïtienne
Laos	le Laos	Laotien	Laotienne
Latvia	la Lettonie	Letton	Lettone
Lebanon	le Liban	Libanais	Libanaise
Libya	la Libye	Libyen	Libyenne
Lithuania	la Lituanie	Lituanien	Lituanienne
Luxemburg	F le Luxembourg	Luxembourgeois	Luxembourgeoise
Madagascar	F Madagascar* MASC	Malgache	Malgache
Malaysia	la Malaisie	Malais	Malaise
Mali	F le Mali	Malien	Malienne
Mauritius	F Maurice* FEM	Mauricien	Mauricienne
Mauritania	F la Mauritanie	Mauritanien	Mauritanienne
Mexico	le Mexique	Mexicain	Mexicaine
Morocco	F le Maroc	Marocain	Marocaine
Mozambique	le Mozambique	Mozambicain	Mozambicaine
Namibia	la Namibie	Namibien	Namibienne
New Zealand	la Nouvelle-Zélande	Néo-Zélandais	Néo-Zélandaise
Nicaragua	le Nicaragua	Nicaraguayen	Nicaraguayenne
Niger	F le Niger	Nigérien	Nigérienne
Nigeria	le Nigeria	Nigérian	Nigériane
Norway	la Norvège	Norvégien	Norvégienne
Pakistan	le Pakistan	Pakistanais	Pakistanaise
Panama	le Panama	Panaméen	Panaméenne
Paraguay	le Paraguay	Paraguayen	Paraguayenne
Peru	le Pérou	Péruvien	Péruvienne
Philippines	les Philippines FEM	Philippin	Philippine
Poland	la Pologne	Polonais	Polonaise
Portugal	le Portugal	Portugais	Portugaise
Romania	la Roumanie	Roumain	Roumaine
Russia	la Russie	Russe	Russe

Country	French name	Nationality – MASC	Nationality – FEM
Rwanda	F le Rwanda	Rwandais	Rwandaise
Saudi Arabia	l'Arabie Saoudite FEM	Saoudien	Saoudienne
Scotland	l'Écosse FEM	Écossais	Écossaise
Senegal	F le Sénégal	Sénégalais	Sénégalaise
Serbia	la Serbie	Serbe	Serbe
Singapore	Singapour*	Singapourien	Singapourienne
Slovakia	la Slovaquie	Slovaque	Slovaque
Somalia	la Somalie	Somalien	Somalienne
South Africa	l'Afrique du Sud FEM	Sud-Africain	Sud-Africaine
Spain	l'Espagne FEM	Espagnol	Espagnole
Sri Lanka	le Sri Lanka	Sri-Lankais	Sri-Lankaise
Sudan	le Soudan	Soudanais	Soudanaise
Sweden	la Suède	Suédois	Suédoise
Switzerland	F la Suisse	Suisse	Suisse
Syria	la Syrie	Syrien	Syrienne
Taiwan	Taïwan*	Taïwanais	Taïwanaise
Tajikistan	le Tadjikistan	Tadjik	Tadjike
Tanzania	la Tanzanie	Tanzanien	Tanzanienne
Thailand	la Thaïlande	Thaïlandais	Thaïlandaise
Tunisia	F la Tunisie	Tunisien	Tunisienne
Turkey	la Turquie	Turc	Turque
Uganda	l'Ouganda MASC	Ougandais	Ougandaise
Ukraine	l'Ukraine FEM	Ukrainien	Ukrainienne
United Arab Emirates	les Émirats arabes unis MASC	Émirien	Émirienne
United Kingdom	le Royaume-Uni	Britannique	Britannique
United States	les États-Unis MASC	Américain	Américaine
Uruguay	l'Uruguay MASC	Uruguayen	Uruguayenne
Uzbekistan	l'Ouzbékistan MASC	Ouzbek	Ouzbek
Venezuela	le Venezuela	Vénézuélien	Vénézuélienne
Vietnam	le Vietnam	Vietnamien	Vietnamienne
Zaïre	F le Zaïre	Zaïrois	Zaïroise
Zambia	la Zambie	Zambien	Zambienne
Zimbabwe	le Zimbabwe	Zimbabwéen	Zimbabwéenne

*There is no article with **Cuba, Haïti, Israël, Maurice, Madagascar, Singapour** or **Taïwan.**
For **Cuba, Maurice, Madagascar, Singapour** or **Taïwan**, use **à** for *in* or *to*, and **de** for *of* or *from*.
For **Haïti** or **Israël**, use **en** for *in* or *to*, and **d'** for *of* or *from*.